LONDON, JULY, 1823.

MODERN PUBLICATIONS,

AND

Important Works on the Fine Arts,

PUBLISHED BY

HURST, ROBINSON, AND CO.

BOOK AND PRINT-SELLERS TO THE KING,

90, CHEAPSIDE, AND 8, PALL-MALL.

1

ENCYCLOPÆDIA BRITANNICA;

OR, DICTIONARY OF ARTS, SCIENCES, AND MISCELLANEOUS LITERATURE.

Sixth Edition. Revised, Corrected, and Improved.

In 20 Vols. 4to. With nearly 600 Engravings.

The Encyclopædia Britannica forms a Dictionary of Arts, Sciences, and Literature, on the most approved and comprehensive plan. It has been the leading object of its conductors to combine abstract with practical, and solid with pleasing, information, in such proportions as would be most useful and most acceptable to the public; on the whole, to render the Work at once a Dictionary of Science, a Book of Universal Reference, and a copious Abstract of the Literature and Philosophy of the Age.

The present Edition, now offered to the public, has received a variety of corrections and improvements. In the historical articles the narrative has been continued, so as to embrace all the most memorable events which have occurred down to the present time. The geographical and statistical articles have been adapted to the late political arrangements, and amended by incorporating the new information furnished by recent travellers, and references have been made to the new articles in the Supplement, now in course of publication.

2

THE EDINBURGH ANNUAL REGISTER,

From 1808 to 1820. In 18 Vols. 8vo. Closely printed in double columns.

The Edinburgh Annual Register has now been carried on for thirteen years, and the Publishers have received ample testimony as to the ability with which it has been conducted. A number of important features are now introduced, which have not, it is believed, found a place hitherto in any similar publication. Arrangements have been made, by which the delay that has occurred in bringing out the recent volumes will be completely obviated, and the work will be speedily brought up to the regular period.

A

3

QUENTIN DURWARD.

BY THE AUTHOR OF "WAVERLEY," "PEVERIL OF THE PEAK," &c. &c.

In 6 Vols. Post 8vo. Price 1*l.* 11*s.* 6d. Boards.

4

SUPPLEMENT
TO THE ENCYCLOPÆDIA BRITANNICA.

Edited by MACVEY NAPIER, F.R.S. Lond. and Edin.

Parts 1 to 11. Price 1*l.* 5*s.* each. With Engravings.

The plan of this Supplement is such as to render it not only a valuable companion to the various editions of the Encyclopædia Britannica, but of extensive utility as a separate work; being calculated, of itself, to furnish a view of the progress and present state of all the most important departments of human knowledge.

The First Volume is prefaced with the First Half of a Dissertation on the "History of the Moral and Political Sciences," by Mr. DUGALD STEWART. The Second, with the First Half of a similar Dissertation on the "History of the Mathematical and Physical Sciences," by Mr. PROFESSOR PLAYFAIR. And the Third, with a Dissertation on the "History of Chemical Science," from the earliest Ages to the present Time, by Mr. BRANDE, Professor of Chemistry in the Royal Institution of London. And the remaining Portions of the "Historical Dissertations," by Mr. STEWART and PROFESSOR PLAYFAIR, preface the Fourth and Fifth Vols.

5

THE EDINBURGH GAZETTEER,

OR, GEOGRAPHICAL DICTIONARY:

Containing a Description of the various Countries, Kingdoms, States, Cities, Towns, Mountains, &c. of the World;

An Account of the Government, Customs, and Religion of the Inhabitants, the Boundaries and Natural Productions of each Country, &c. &c.

Forming a complete Body of Geography, Physical, Political, Statistical, and Commercial.

Six large volumes, 8vo. double columns. Price 5*l.* 8*s.* Boards.

The great object of the present work has been to collect a complete body of Geographical knowledge, and to digest it into the most convenient form, namely, that of a Dictionary or Gazetteer. With a view to the more effectual execution of this task, it has been divided into distinct departments, which have been assigned to different contributors, all of them selected on a consideration of their being specially qualified, by their previous opportunities of information and habits of research, for collecting, on the subjects allotted them, whatever is either curious or important in Geographical Science.

Though it would be presumption in a work abounding in such multifarious details, to pretend to perfect accuracy, the publishers may confidently challenge a comparison for the EDINBURGH GAZETTEER, with any work of the kind ever laid before the public. They have only to add, that having purchased the copyright of Cruttwell's Gazetteer, that work is now superseded, all that was useful in it being embodied in the present publication.

6

ARROWSMITH'S NEW GENERAL ATLAS,

CONSTRUCTED FROM THE LATEST AUTHORITIES;

Exhibiting the Boundaries and Divisions;

Also, the Chains of Mountains, and other Geographical Features of all the known Countries in the World.

Comprehended in 53 Maps, from Original Drawings.

Large 4to. Price 1*l.* 16*s.* plain, or 2*l.* 12*s.* 6*d.* coloured.

*** *This work is intended as a companion to the above Gazetteer.*

7

BALLANTYNE'S NOVELISTS LIBRARY;

COMPRISING THE WORKS OF THE BEST ENGLISH NOVELISTS.

With Selections from the German, French, and Italian.
To which are prefixed,
The Lives of the Authors, and Critical Notices of their Writings.

BY A VERY CELEBRATED AUTHOR.

Volume the Fifth.—Containing the Novels of Sterne, Goldsmith, Dr. Johnson, Mackenzie, Horace Walpole, and Clara Reeve.
Beautifully printed in Royal 8vo. Price 1*l.* 8*s.* Boards.

Vol. I.—contains Fielding's Novels, complete. Price 1*l.* 8*s.* Boards.

Vols. II. & III.—contain Smollett's Novels and Translations. Price 2*l.* 16*s.* Boards.

Vol. IV.—contains Gil Blas—The Devil on Two Sticks—and Vanillo Gonzales, by Le Sage; and the Adventures of a Guinea, by Charles Johnstone.

This publication, of which five volumes are now before the public, is intended to comprise the works of the best of the English Novelists, together with selections from the German, French, and Italian, with Memoirs of the Authors' Lives, and Criticisms on their Writings prefixed. The works of each Author, as in the instance of those published, will be complete in a single volume, or in two or more, as the length of the compositions shall require, and so printed that any particular Author may be purchased separately. The high source, which will be at once recognised, from whence the Publishers have the honour of deriving their literary aid, and the importance of such powerful assistance, in presenting original and interesting Biographical Notices of the most celebrated Writers of Fiction, added to the introduction of many popular Novels which have not until now appeared in any collected publication of the Novelists, render this edition indisputably the most valuable and complete hitherto produced.

8

THE COOK'S ORACLE;

CONTAINING

RECEIPTS FOR PLAIN COOKERY ON THE MOST ECONOMICAL PLAN,

For private Families;

Also, the Art of composing the most simple and most highly-finished Broths, Gravies, Soups, Sauces, Store Sauces, and Flavouring Essences:

The Quantity of each Article is accurately stated by Weight and Measure;
The whole being the result of actual Experiments

INSTITUTED IN THE KITCHEN OF A PHYSICIAN.

The Fifth Edition. To which is added, One Hundred and Thirty New Receipts for Pastry, Preserves, Puddings;

And an easy, certain, and economical Process for preparing Pickles, by which they will be ready in a Fortnight, and remain good for Years.

Revised by the Author of "The Art of Invigorating Life."

12mo. Price 9*s.* Boards.

9

A VISIT TO SPAIN;

Detailing the Transactions which occurred during a Residence in that Country, in the latter Part of 1822, and the first Four Months of 1823; with an account of the removal of the court from Madrid to Seville; and general notices of the Manners, Customs, Costume, and Music of the Country.

By MICHAEL J. QUIN,

BARRISTER-AT-LAW, AND FELLOW OF THE ROYAL SOCIETY OF LITERATURE.

8vo. Price 12*s.* Boards.

10

THE HUT AND THE CASTLE;

A ROMANCE.

By the Author of "The Romance of the Pyrenees;" "Santo Sebastiano, or, the Young Protector," &c.

In 4 Vols. 12mo. Price 1*l.* 8*s.* Boards.

11

THE ART OF INVIGORATING AND PROLONGING LIFE,

BY FOOD, CLOTHES, AIR, EXERCISE, WINE, SLEEP, &c.

And Peptic Precepts,

Pointing out agreeable and effectual Methods to prevent and relieve Indigestion, and to regulate and strengthen the Action of the Stomach and Bowels:

To which is added—The Pleasure of making a Will.

BY THE AUTHOR OF "THE COOK'S ORACLE."

Fourth Edition. 12mo. Price 7*s.* Boards.

12

NOVELS AND TALES

OF THE AUTHOR OF "WAVERLEY."

Comprising Waverley—Guy Mannering—The Antiquary—Rob Roy—Tales of My Landlord, First, Second, and Third Series, with a copious Glossary.

A new Edition. In 12 Vols. 8vo.

With Vignette Title-pages of Scenes supposed to be described in these Works.

Price 7*l.* 4*s.* Boards.

13

HISTORICAL ROMANCES,

BY THE AUTHOR OF "WAVERLEY," &c.

Comprising Ivanhoe—The Monastery—The Abbot—and Kenilworth, With Vignette Title-pages of Scenes described in these Works.

In 6 Vols. 8vo. Price 3*l.* 12*s.* Boards,

To correspond with the Author's Novels and Tales.

14

PEVERIL OF THE PEAK;

A Romance. By the Author of "Waverley."

4 Vols. post 8vo. Price 2*l.* 2*s.* Boards.

15

THE LIFE OF WILLIAM HEY, Esq. F.R.S.

Member of the Royal College of Surgeons in London, &c. &c.; and late Senior Surgeon of the General Infirmary at Leeds.

By JOHN PEARSON, F.R.S. F.L.S. M.R.I. &c. &c.

In two Parts.—*Part I.*—The Professional Life, with Remarks on his Writings. *Part II.*—The Moral and Social Life, with Appendices.

Second Edition.—2 Vols. Post 8vo. Price 14*s.* Boards.

16

A CATALOGUE OF THE CELEBRATED COLLECTION OF PICTURES

OF THE LATE

JOHN JULIUS ANGERSTEIN, ESQ.

Containing a finished Etching of every Picture, and accompanied with Historical and Biographical Notices.

BY JOHN YOUNG.

ENGRAVER IN MEZZOTINTO TO HIS MAJESTY, AND KEEPER OF THE BRITISH INSTITUTION.

Royal 4to. Price 3*l.* 3*s.* Boards.
Imperial 4to. Proofs on India Paper, Price 6*l.* 6*s.* Boards.

17

THE HISTORY AND ANTIQUITIES OF THE ABBEY CHURCH OF ST. PETER, WESTMINSTER:

Including Notices and Biographical Memoirs of the Abbots and Deans of that Foundation, as well as a correct Copy of the Inscriptions on every Monument in this truly interesting and National Edifice.

Illustrated by J. P. NEALE.

The Literary Department by E. W. BRAYLEY.

The Plates consist of Ground Plans of the Building, comprehending, as far as is practicable, those shewing its ancient limits and state;—Views, exhibiting the general effects of the Edifice, both exterior and internal, and such of its parts as are marked by peculiarity of architecture, or beauty of feature;—enlarged Details of such detached portions as display, with the greatest force and interest, the variations of architectural style;—and Representations of such of the Monuments as demand particular notice, from connexion with history, or from excellence of execution.

In 2 Vols. with 61 Engravings.

		£	s.	d.
Royal quarto	price	10	10	0
Imperial quarto		15	15	0
Ditto, with Proofs on India paper, and Etchings, of which only twenty-five copies are printed		34	13	0
Crown folio, to correspond with the small paper of the new edition of Dugdale's Monasticon		21	0	0
Imperial folio, to correspond with the large paper of that work		34	13	0

*** Amongst the numerous fine Engravings in this Work are two finished in the first style of graphic excellence, shewing the ceremony of the Coronation of King George IV., and of the Installing of the Knights of the Bath, in 1812.

18

VEGETABLE MATERIA MEDICA OF THE UNITED STATES;

OR, MEDICAL BOTANY:

Containing a Botanical, General, and Medical History of Medicinal Plants, indigenous to the United States.

Illustrated by coloured Engravings, made after original Drawings from Nature.

BY WILLIAM P. C. BARTON, M. D.

Professor of Botany in the University of Pennsylvania.

In 2 Vols. 4to. Price 6*l.* 6*s.*

19

A FLORA OF NORTH AMERICA.

Illustrated by original coloured Figures, drawn from Nature,

BY WILLIAM P. C. BARTON, M. D.

Nos. 1 to 30. Price 6*s.* each.

20

ISABEL ST. ALBE; A NOVEL,

BY MISS CRUMPE.

In 3 Vols. 12mo. Price 18*s*. Boards.

21

THE GRAVE OF THE LAST SAXON;

OR, THE LEGEND OF THE CURFEW: A POEM.

By the Rev. WILLIAM LISLE BOWLES.

8vo. Price 6*s*. Boards.

22

LETTERS TO LORD BYRON,

ON A QUESTION OF POETICAL CRITICISM.

Third Edition. With Corrections.

To which are now first added, the Letter to Mr. CAMPBELL, and the Answer to the Writer in the "Quarterly Review," as far as they regard Poetical Criticism; together with an Answer to some Objections, and further Illustrations.

By the REV. WILLIAM LISLE BOWLES.

8vo. Price 7*s*. Boards.

23

CATILINE, A TRAGEDY,

IN FIVE ACTS: WITH OTHER POEMS.

By the REV. GEORGE CROLY, A.M.

Author of "PARIS IN 1815;"—"ANGEL OF THE WORLD," &c.

8vo. Price 8*s*. 6*d*. Boards.

24

GEMS, PRINCIPALLY FROM THE ANTIQUE,

Drawn and Etched by R. DAGLEY,

Author of "SELECT GEMS;"

With Verse Illustrations, by the REV. GEORGE CROLY, A.M.

Author of "THE ANGEL OF THE WORLD;"—"PARIS IN 1815," &c. &c.

Small 8vo. Price 8*s*. 6*d*. Boards.

25

CHRONOLOGICAL NOTES OF SCOTTISH AFFAIRS,

FROM 1630 TILL 1701;

Being chiefly taken from the Diary of LORD FOUNTAINHALL.

(ONLY 120 COPIES PRINTED.)

Quarto. Price 1*l*. 16*s*. Boards.

26

THE WORKS OF GARCILASSO DE LA VEGA,

SURNAMED THE PRINCE OF CASTILIAN POETS;

Translated into English Verse, with a Critical and Historical Essay on Spanish Poetry, and a Life of the Author.

BY J. H. WIFFEN.

One Volume, Post 8vo.

(Uniform with Lord Holland's Lives of Lope de Vega, and Guillen de Castro,)

Embellished with a Portrait and Engravings on Wood.

Price 12*s*. Boards.

27

NOVELS AND TALES

OF THE AUTHOR OF "WAVERLEY."

Containing Waverley—Guy Mannering—The Antiquary—Rob Roy—and Tales of My Landlord, First, Second, and Third Series.

In 16 Vols. Foolscap 8vo. With a Copious Glossary, and engraved Vignettes to each Volume. Price 6*l.* Boards.

The title-pages to this edition are embellished with Engravings from Drawings by Nasmyth, of real Scenes supposed to be described by the Author of these celebrated productions.

28

HISTORICAL ROMANCES.

BY THE AUTHOR OF "WAVERLEY," &c.

Comprising Ivanhoe—The Monastery—The Abbot—and Kenilworth.

With Vignette Title-pages of Scenes described in these Works.

In 8 Vols. Foolscap 8vo. Price 3*l.* Boards.

To correspond with the Author's Novels and Tales.

29

ILLUSTRATIONS OF THE NOVELS AND TALES

OF THE AUTHOR OF "WAVERLEY."

In 12 Prints. With Vignette Title.

Engraved by Heath, Warren, Engleheart, Romney, Lizars, &c.

From original Designs by William Allan.

8vo. Price 1*l.* 11*s.* 6*d.*

Proofs, on India Paper, Imperial 4to. 2*l.* 12*s.* 6*d.*

Proofs, before the Letters, Colombier 4to. 3*l.* 3*s.*

30

THE DUKE OF MERCIA; AN HISTORICAL DRAMA.

THE LAMENTATION OF IRELAND,

And other Poems,

BY SIR AUBREY DE VERE HUNT, BART.

8vo. Price 10*s.* 6*d.* Boards.

31

THE EDINBURGH PHILOSOPHICAL JOURNAL,

Conducted by Dr. BREWSTER and Professor JAMESON;

Exhibiting a View of the Progress of Discovery in Natural Philosophy, Chemistry, Natural History, Practical Mechanics, Geography, Statistics, Navigation, and the Fine and Useful Arts.

No. 1 to 16, (CONTINUED QUARTERLY) handsomely printed in 8 volumes, octavo, illustrated with numerous Engravings. Price 6*l.* Boards.

The object of this Journal (published in quarterly numbers) is to exhibit a condensed and popular view of the progress of every branch of useful knowledge, not only by the publication of original and valuable articles in the different departments of Science and the Arts, but by collecting notices from the great mass of materials in the Foreign Journals, and giving brief abstracts of the labours of eminent individuals in every part of the world.

32

HALIDON HILL:

A DRAMATIC SKETCH from SCOTTISH HISTORY.

By SIR WALTER SCOTT, Bart.

8vo. Price 6*s.* sewed.

33

DEDICATED, BY PERMISSION, TO THE KING.

THE

LOYAL AND NATIONAL SONGS OF ENGLAND,

FOR ONE, TWO, AND THREE VOICES;

Selected from original Manuscripts, and early-printed Copies in the Library of WILLIAM KITCHINER, M. D.

One Volume, Folio. Price 2*l.* 2*s.* Boards.

Among Fifty-seven other rare compositions, *Dr. John Bull's* "GOD SAVE THE KING" is now first printed in this number; also, the earliest-printed copy of "God save the King," and a complete score thereof for a full Band, for voices and instruments; and most of the Songs are so arranged that they may be sung as a Solo, a Duet, or a Trio.

*** The SECOND PORTION, comprising the SEA-SONGS OF ENGLAND, is in the Press, and will shortly be published.

34

OBSERVATIONS ON VOCAL MUSIC;

AND RULES FOR THE ACCENT AND EMPHASIS OF POETRY,

Which will ensure the proper Pronunciation and effective Expression of the Words.

By WILLIAM KITCHINER, M. D.

12mo. Price 4*s.* Boards.

35

THE PIRATE, A ROMANCE.

By the Author of "WAVERLEY."

In 3 Vols. Post octavo. Price 1*l.* 11*s.* 6*d.* Boards.

36

ILLUSTRATIONS OF BRITISH ORNITHOLOGY.

SERIES FIRST.—LAND BIRDS.

BY P. J. SELBY, ESQ.

Of Twizell-house, county of Northumberland, Member of the Wernerian Natural History Society of Edinburgh, &c.

Nos. 1 to 5. In elephant folio. Price 1*l.* 11*s.* 6*d.* each, plain; or 5*l.* 5*s.* finely coloured after Nature.

This work consists of Etchings, printed on drawing paper of 27½ inches by 23, after drawings taken by the Author, for the most part from living Specimens; and is accompanied by letter-press Description. The Figures are, for the greater part, of the natural size; the magnitude of the paper, in some instances, allowing, in the case of the smaller birds, of so many as ten being represented on the same plate.

37

THOMSON'S SELECT MELODIES OF SCOTLAND,

INTERSPERSED WITH THOSE OF IRELAND AND WALES,

United to the Songs of BURNS, SIR WALTER SCOTT, &c. with Symphonies and an Accompaniment for the Piano-Forte, Vols. 1 to 5, Royal 8vo. Boards. Price 12*s.* each.

38

MEMOIRS OF THE CELEBRATED

PERSONS COMPOSING THE KIT-CAT CLUB;

With a Prefatory Account of the ORIGIN of the ASSOCIATION; illustrated with 48 Portraits from the original Paintings by Sir GODFREY KNELLER.

One large Vol. super royal 4to. With 48 Plates. Price 4*l.* 4*s.* Boards.

39

THE HISTORY OF THE INGENIOUS GENTLEMAN,

DON QUIXOTTE OF LA MANCHA;

TRANSLATED FROM THE SPANISH BY MOTTEUX.—A NEW EDITION.

With copious Notes; and an Essay on the Life and Writings of Cervantes.

In 5 vols. post 8vo. Price 2*l.* 2*s.* Boards.

" We cannot omit the opportunity of calling attention to this new Edition of Don Quixotte—general attention, we are quite sure, it must, ere long, command; and general favor we think almost as certain. The English reader is now in possession of an Edition, not only infinitely superior to any that ever appeared in England; but, so far as we are able to judge, much more complete and satisfactory than any one which exists in the literature of Spain herself."—*Blackwood's Edinb. Mag. June,* 1822.

40

THE PHILOSOPHY OF ZOOLOGY;

Or, a general View of the Structure, Functions, and Classification of Animals.

BY JOHN FLEMING, D.D.

Minister of Flisk, Fifeshire; Fellow of the Royal Society of Edinburgh, of the Wernerian Natural History Society, &c.

In 2 Vols. 8vo. with Engravings. Price 1*l.* 10*s.* Boards.

41

THE WORKS OF JOHN DRYDEN,

Illustrated with Notes, Historical, Critical, and Explanatory;

AND A LIFE OF THE AUTHOR.

BY SIR WALTER SCOTT, BART.

In 18 vols. 8vo. Second Edition. Price 9*l.* 9*s.* Boards.

42

THE POETRY CONTAINED IN

THE NOVELS, TALES, AND ROMANCES,

OF THE AUTHOR OF "WAVERLEY:"

WITH SHORT INTRODUCTORY NOTICES FROM THE PROSE.

1 Vol. foolscap 8vo. with an engraved Title and Vignette View of Edinburgh. Price 9*s.* Boards.

43

THE FORTUNES OF NIGEL, A ROMANCE,

BY THE AUTHOR OF "WAVERLEY."

In 3 Vols. Post 8vo. Price 1*l.* 11*s.* 6*d.* Boards.

44

MEMOIRS OF GEORGE HERIOT,

Jeweller to King JAMES VI.

With an Historical Account of the Hospital, founded by him, at Edinburgh.

Foolscap 8vo. With Engravings. Price 7*s.* 6*d.* Boards.

The subject of the above Memoirs is a prominent character in the "Fortunes of Nigel," by the Author of "Waverley."

45

ESSAYS, DESCRIPTIVE AND MORAL;

ON SCENES IN ITALY, SWITZERLAND, AND FRANCE.

BY AN AMERICAN.

Post 8vo. Price 8*s.* Boards.

46

ILLUSTRATIONS OF GUY MANNERING;

A NOVEL.

BY THE AUTHOR OF "WAVERLEY."

In 7 Prints. Engraved by Charles Heath, from Drawings by R. Westall, R. A.

12mo. Price 9*s*. 6*d*.—8vo. 12*s*. 6*d*.—Proofs 4to. 1*l*. 4*s*.—Ditto, on India paper, 1*l*. 10*s*.—Ditto, before the letters, colombier 4to. 1*l*. 16*s*.

47

ILLUSTRATIONS OF THE MONASTERY;

A ROMANCE.

BY THE AUTHOR OF "WAVERLEY."

In 7 Prints; one of which is executed on Steel. Engraved by Charles Heath, from Drawings by R. Westall, R. A.

12mo. Price 9*s*. 6*d*.—8vo. 12*s*. 6*d*.—Proofs 4to. 1*l*. 4*s*.—Ditto, on India paper, 1*l*. 10*s*.—Ditto, before the letters, colombier 4to. 1*l*. 16*s*.

48

ILLUSTRATIONS OF IVANHOE;

A ROMANCE.

BY THE AUTHOR OF "WAVERLEY."

Engraved by Charles Heath, from Drawings by R. Westall, R. A.

Prints, medium 8vo. 16*s*.—Proofs, imperial 4to. 1*l*. 5*s*.—Ditto, on India paper, 1*l*. 10*s*.—A few Proofs, on India paper, before the letters, colombier 4to. 1*l*. 15*s*.

49

ILLUSTRATIONS OF KENILWORTH;

A ROMANCE.

By the Author of "WAVERLEY," "IVANHOE," &c.

In 7 Prints, after original Designs, by Charles Robert Leslie. Engraved by Heath, Scott, Engleheart, Romney, and Rolls.

Medium 8vo. 16*s*.—Proofs 4to. 1*l*. 4*s*.—on India paper, imperial 4to. 1*l*. 10*s*.—Ditto, before the letters, colombier 4to. 1*l*. 16*s*.

50

THE HOLY BIBLE,

Embellished with Thirty-one new Engravings, by Charles Heath, from Designs by Richard Westall, R. A.

Beautifully printed at the Oxford University Press, in 3 vols. small 4to.

Price 6*l*. Boards; and on a larger Paper, royal 4to., with Proof Plates, 10*l*. 10*s*. bds.

A few sets of proof impressions of the Plates are printed for separate sale upon India paper, on colombier 4to. The price of those before the writing is 8*l*. 8*s*., and with the writing 6*l*. 6*s*.—Proofs, colombier 4to., not on India, price 4*l*. 14*s*. 6*d*.

51

A GENERAL HISTORY OF THE COUNTY OF YORK:

BY THOMAS DUNHAM WHITAKER, LL.D. F.S.A. F.R.S.

Vicar of Whalley, and Rector of Heysham, in Lancashire.

Parts 1 to 12. In folio, on fine demy paper, 2*l*. 2*s*. each, and on super-royal drawing paper, with proof impressions of the plates, 4*l*. 4*s*.

52

THE POPULAR SUPERSTITIONS AND FESTIVE AMUSEMENTS OF THE HIGHLANDERS OF SCOTLAND.

BY W. GRANT STEWART.

One Volume, Foolscap 8vo. Price 6*s*. Boards.

53

HISTORY OF SULI AND PARGA,

Containing their Chronology and their Wars, particularly those with Ali Pasha, Prince of Greece.

Written originally in Modern Greek, and translated into English from the Italian of

C. GHERARDINI, OF MILAN,

CORRESPONDING MEMBER OF THE IONIAN ACADEMY.

Post 8vo. Price 7*s.* 6*d.* Boards.

54

BOYDELL'S ILLUSTRATIONS OF HOLY WRIT;

Being a Series of 100 Copper-plate Engravings,

From Designs by ISAAC TAYLOR, jun., of ONGAR,

Calculated to ornament all quarto and octavo Editions of the Bible.

Super-royal 4to. Price 6*l.* 6*s.* Boards.—Proof impressions, on India paper, 8*l.* 8*s.* Boards.

55

BOYDELL'S ILLUSTRATIONS

OF THE DRAMATIC WORKS OF SHAKESPEARE:

Consisting of 100 large Plates, in 2 vols. Atlas folio.

With Titles, Dedication, and explanatory Letter-press Description of each Plate.

A few Copies of Proof Impressions.

56

BOYDELL'S DRAMATIC WORKS OF SHAKESPEARE:

In 9 vols. folio; ornamented with 95 Plates, of a proper size to bind with the work.

57

LIBER VERITATIS;

OR, A COLLECTION OF 300 PRINTS AFTER THE ORIGINAL DESIGNS OF CLAUDE LE LORRAIN;

In the possession of his Grace the Duke of Devonshire, Earl Spencer, &c. &c.

Engraved by RICHARD EARLOM.

In 3 Vols. folio.

Each Volume may be had separate.

58

HOUGHTON GALLERY.

A Collection of 129 Prints after the most capital Pictures in the possession of the Emperor of Russia, formerly belonging to the Earl of Orford, at Houghton.

In 2 Vols. imperial folio.

59

LETTERS, LITERARY AND POLITICAL, ON POLAND,

Comprising Observations on Russia and other Sclavonian Nations and Tribes.

8vo. Price 12*s.* Boards.

60

BUNYAN's PILGRIM's PROGRESS.

Embellished with Six Engravings, from the Designs of RICHARD WESTALL, R.A.

Handsomely printed, in Foolscap 8vo. Price 10*s.* 6*d.* Boards.

61

THE POETICAL WORKS OF

SIR WALTER SCOTT, BART.

In 10 Vols. 18mo. beautifully printed by Ballantyne, price 3*l.* 13*s.* 6*d.*
With Ten Plates, after Designs by Smirke, and Vignette Titles;
Or, without Plates, 3*l.* 3*s.* Boards.

62

THE POETICAL WORKS OF

SIR WALTER SCOTT, BART.

Including The Minstrelsy, and Sir Tristrem.
Beautifully printed. In 10 Vols. 8vo. With a Vignette to each Volume,
And a Portrait of the Author.
Price 6*l.* Boards.

63

THE POETICAL WORKS OF

SIR WALTER SCOTT, BART.

In 8 Vols. Foolscap 8vo. With Portrait of the Author.
Price 3*l.* 12*s.* Boards.

64

A SERIES OF ILLUSTRATIONS
OF THE POETICAL WORKS OF SIR WALTER SCOTT, BART.

From Original Paintings, by R. Smirke, R. A.;
Beautifully Engraved by the most eminent Artists, to illustrate the
Foolscap, Octavo, and Quarto Editions.
Foolscap, price 12*s.*;—Octavo, 18*s.*;—Proofs, Quarto, 1*l.* 10*s.*
Proofs on India Paper, Imperial 4to. 1*l.* 18*s.*
Proofs on India Paper, before the Letters, Colombier 4to. 2*l.* 10*s.*

65

ADVENTURES OF GIL BLAS OF SANTILLANE.

Embellished with 24 Engravings, by the most eminent Artists,
From Paintings by ROBERT SMIRKE, R. A.
A new Edition. In 4 Vols. Foolscap 8vo. Price 1*l.* 16*s.* Boards.

A few Proof Impressions of the Plates, separate from the work, are printed on royal 4to. price 2*l.* 2*s.* Ditto on India paper, price 2*l.* 12*s.* 6*d.* and on India paper, before the description, price 3*l.* 3*s.*

66

DON QUIXOTTE DE LA MANCHA.

Embellished with 24 Engravings, by CHARLES HEATH,
From Drawings by RICHARD WESTALL, R. A.
A new Edition. In 4 Vols. Foolscap 8vo. Price 2*l.* 2*s.* Boards.

A few Proof Impressions of the Engravings, separate from the work, royal 4to. 2*l.* 2*s.* Ditto, before the letters, on India paper, 2*l.* 12*s.* 6*d.*

67

ADVENTURES OF HUNCHBACK.

From the "Arabian Nights Entertainments."
With 17 Prints, engraved by William Daniell, from Pictures painted by
Robert Smirke, R. A.
Imperial 4to.

68

THE THANE OF FIFE, A POEM.

BY WILLIAM TENNANT,

Author of "Anster Fair, and other Poems."

8vo. Price 9*s*. Boards.

69

THE WORKS OF JOHN HOME, ESQ.

NOW FIRST COLLECTED.

To which is prefixed, an Account of his Life and Writings.

BY HENRY MACKENZIE, ESQ. F. R. S. E.

In 3 Vols. 8vo. With a Portrait of Mr. Home, and other Plates and Maps, illustrative of the History of the Rebellion. Price 1*l*. 11*s*. 6*d*. Boards.

These volumes contain, besides the Life of Mr. Home, an Appendix of interesting Correspondence with Dr. Adam Ferguson, Dr. Carlyle, Mr. James M'Pherson, the Marquis of Bute, David Hume, &c. the Plays of Agis, Douglas, the Siege of Aquileia, the Fatal Discovery, Alonzo and Alfred, and his interesting Account of the Rebellion in 1745.

70

JOURNAL OF A

VOYAGE TO THE NORTHERN WHALE FISHERY,

Including Researches and Discoveries on the Eastern Coast of West Greenland, made in the Summer of the Year 1822, in the Ship Baffin, of Liverpool.

By WILLIAM SCORESBY, Junior, F. R. S. E. M. W. S. &c. &c. Commander.

In 8vo. with Maps and Plates, Price 16*s*. Boards.

71

AN ACCOUNT OF THE ARCTIC REGIONS,

WITH

A HISTORY AND DESCRIPTION OF THE NORTHERN WHALE-FISHERY.

BY WILLIAM SCORESBY, JUN. F. R. S. E.

In 2 Vols. 8vo. With 24 illustrative Engravings. Price 2*l*. 2*s*. Boards.

72

HISTORY OF THE INDIAN ARCHIPELAGO,

Containing an Account of the Manners, Arts, Languages, Religions, Institutions, and Commerce of its Inhabitants.

BY JOHN CRAWFURD, F. R. S.

Late British Resident at the Court of the Sultan of Java.

In 3 large Vols. 8vo. With 35 illustrative Maps and Engravings.

Price 2*l*. 12*s*. 6*d*. Boards.

73

A DESCRIPTION OF

THE WESTERN ISLANDS OF SCOTLAND,

INCLUDING THE ISLE OF MAN;

Comprising an Account of their Geological Structure, with Remarks on their Agriculture, Scenery, and Antiquities.

By JOHN M'CULLOCH, M. D. &c. &c.

In 2 Vols. 8vo. With a Volume of Plates 4to. Price 3*l*. 3*s*. Boards.

74

HISTORICAL ACCOUNT OF

DISCOVERIES AND TRAVELS IN AFRICA;

From the earliest Ages to the present Time; including the Substance of the late Dr. Leyden's Work on that Subject.

BY HUGH MURRAY, ESQ. F. R. S. E.

Second Edition. In 2 Vols. 8vo. With Maps. Price 1*l.* 7*s.* Boards.

75

A DESCRIPTION OF THE SHETLAND ISLANDS,

Comprising an Account of their Geology, Scenery, Antiquities, and Superstitions.

BY SAMUEL HIBBERT, M.D. M.F.S.E.

4to. With Maps and Plates. Price 3*l.* 3*s.* Boards.

This work will be found to contain many interesting particulars, illustrative of the Novel of "The Pirate."

76

A SYSTEM OF MINERALOGY:

BY ROBERT JAMESON,

Regius Professor of Natural History, Lecturer on Mineralogy, and Keeper of the Museum in the University of Edinburgh, &c. &c. &c.

Third Edition, greatly improved. With numerous Plates. In 3 Vols. 8vo.

Price 2*l.* 16*s.* 0*d.* Boards.

77

MANUAL OF MINERALOGY.

Containing an Account of Simple Minerals, and also, a Description and Arrangement of Mountain Rocks.

BY ROBERT JAMESON,

Professor of Natural History in the University of Edinburgh, &c. &c.

In 1 thick Vol. 8vo. Price 15*s.* Boards.

78

THE WORKS OF JOHN PLAYFAIR, Esq.

Late Professor of Natural Philosophy in the University of Edinburgh, &c. &c.

WITH A MEMOIR OF THE AUTHOR.

In 4 Vols. 8vo. Price 2*l.* 12*s.* 6*d.* Boards.

79

CONSCIENCE;

OR, THE BRIDAL NIGHT.

A Tragedy, in Five Acts.

BY JAMES HAYNES, ESQ.

As performed in the Theatre Royal, Drury-lane.

Second Edition. In 8vo. Price 4*s.* sewed.

80

DURAZZO; A TRAGEDY,

IN FIVE ACTS.

BY JAMES HAYNES, ESQ.

In 8vo. Price 4*s.* 6*d.* sewed.

81

HISTORY OF THE EUROPEAN LANGUAGES;

OR, RESEARCHES INTO THE AFFINITIES OF THE TEUTONIC, GREEK, CELTIC, SCLAVONIC, AND INDIAN NATIONS.

By the late ALEXANDER MURRAY, D. D.

Professor of Oriental Languages in the University of Edinburgh.

WITH A LIFE OF THE AUTHOR.

In 2 Vols. 8vo. Price 1*l.* 8*s.* Boards.

82

A GEOGRAPHICAL AND STATISTICAL

DESCRIPTION OF SCOTLAND.

BY JAMES PLAYFAIR, D. D.

Principal of the United College of St. Andrews.

In 2 vols. 8vo. with a large coloured Map. Price 1*l.* 4*s.* Boards.

83

FLORA SCOTICA;

OR, A DESCRIPTION OF SCOTTISH PLANTS,

Arranged both according to the Artificial and Natural Methods.

By WILLIAM JACKSON HOOKER, LL. D. F. R. A. and L. S.

In Two Parts. 8vo. Price 14*s.* Boards.

84

AN ABRIDGMENT OF ALL THE STATUTES

NOW IN FORCE RELATIVE TO THE REVENUE OF THE EXCISE IN GREAT BRITAIN;

Methodically arranged and Alphabetically digested.

By JAMES HUIE, Collector of Excise.

The Fourth Edition, revised and brought down to the end of the Year 1822.
One thick Vol. 8vo. Price 1*l.* 10*s.* Boards.

85

MILITARY MEMOIRS OF THE GREAT CIVIL WAR,

BEING THE MILITARY MEMOIRS OF JOHN GWYNNE;

And an Account of the Earl of Glencairn's Expedition, as General of his Majesty's Forces in the Highlands of Scotland:
In the Years 1653 and 1654.

BY A PERSON WHO WAS EYE AND EAR WITNESS TO EVERY TRANSACTION.

With an Appendix. In 4to. Price 1*l.* 16*s.* Boards.

86

A VIEW OF THE

ELEMENTARY PRINCIPLES OF EDUCATION,

Founded on the Study of the Nature of Man.

BY J. G. SPURZHEIM, M.D.

Of the Universities of Vienna and Paris, and Licentiate of the Royal College of Physicians of London.

1 Vol. 12mo. Price 7*s.* 6*d.* Boards.

87

A SEARCH OF TRUTH IN THE SCIENCE OF THE HUMAN MIND.

By the Rev. FREDERICK BEASLEY, D. D.
Provost of the University of Pennsylvania, &c. &c.
8vo. Price 14*s*. Boards.

88

HISTORICAL ACCOUNT OF DISCOVERIES AND TRAVELS IN ASIA,

From the earliest Ages to the present Time.
BY HUGH MURRAY, ESQ. F. R. S. E.
Author of "Historical Account of Discoveries in Africa."
In 3 Vols. 8vo. With 3 Maps. Price 2*l*. 2*s*. Boards.

89

POND'S FORTY-FOUR LANDSCAPES,

After Original Pictures, by Claude le Lorrain, Poussin, Rembrandt, &c.
Engraved by VIVARES, MASON, CHATELAINE, &c. &c.
Folio, sewed. Price 3*l*. 3*s*.

90

THE PLAYS OF SHAKESPEARE.

Printed from the Text of SAMUEL JOHNSON, GEORGE STEEVENS, and ISAAC REED.
Beautifully printed, in double Columns, by Ballantyne.
In 2 Vols. Royal 8vo. Price 1*l*. 16*s*. Boards.

91

HISTORICAL AND MISCELLANEOUS QUESTIONS,

FOR THE USE OF YOUNG PERSONS;
With a Selection of BRITISH and GENERAL BIOGRAPHY:
BY RICHMAL MANGNALL.
12mo. Price 5*s*. Bound.

92

BRITISH GALLERY OF ENGRAVINGS,

From Pictures of the Italian, Flemish, Dutch, and English Schools, in the possession of His Majesty, and several Noblemen and Gentlemen of the United Kingdom: with some Account of each Picture.

BY EDWARD FORSTER, A. M., F. R. S., AND S. A.

One Vol. folio. Containing 52 Engravings, executed in the line manner, by the most eminent Artists of this country.

93

TRACTS AND ESSAYS, MORAL AND THEOLOGICAL;

Including a Defence of the Doctrine of the Divinity of Christ, and of the Doctrine of the Atonement; with Obituaries, &c.
By the late WILLIAM HEY, Esq. F. R. S. &c. &c.
8vo. Price 16*s*. Boards.

L. Gesse Pinx.t Freeman Sculp.

J. S. C. F. FREY.

Author of a Hebrew Grammar & of a Hebrew, Latin & English Dictionary & Editor of Vander Hooght's Heb. Bible

Published Nov.r 1. 1815, for the Author by Gale & Fenner.

שַׁעַר הַשֵּׁנִי אֶל לְשׁוֹן הַקֹּדֶשׁ
סֵפֶר הַשָּׁרָשִׁים עִם תּוֹלְדוֹתֵיהֶם
בִּלְשׁוֹן עִבְרִי לַאטִין וּבְעֶנְגְּלִישׁ

A

HEBREW, LATIN, AND ENGLISH, Dictionary;

CONTAINING,

ALL THE HEBREW AND CHALDEE WORDS

USED IN THE

OLD TESTAMENT,

INCLUDING THE

PROPER NAMES,

ARRANGED UNDER ONE ALPHABET,

THE DERIVATIVES REFERRED TO THEIR RESPECTIVE ROOTS,

AND THE

SIGNIFICATION, IN *LATIN* AND ENGLISH,

ACCORDING TO THE BEST AUTHORITIES:

With copious Vocabularies,

LATIN AND HEBREW, AND ENGLISH AND HEBREW.

BY

JOSEPH SAMUEL C. F. FREY,

AUTHOR OF A HEBREW GRAMMAR, AND EDITOR OF A NEW EDITION OF VANDER HOOGHT'S HEBREW BIBLE.

IN TWO VOLUMES.

VOL. I.

London:

PUBLISHED FOR THE AUTHOR,
BY GALE AND FENNER, PATERNOSTER-ROW.

Printed by A. M'INTOSH,
LONDON SOCIETY'S OFFICE, SPITALFIELDS.

1815.

TO THE

HONOURABLE AND RIGHT REVEREND

HENRY,

LORD BISHOP OF GLOUCESTER.

My Lord,

I feel myself highly honoured by the permission to present the following Dictionary to the Public under the sanction of your Lordship's name.

Your Lordship's character as a Christian Prelate, for which I entertain the highest respect, needs not my commendation. But I cannot omit the present opportunity of publicly expressing my sincere gratitude for the zealous concern your Lordship has discovered for the welfare of my Jewish brethren, and for the success of the Society whose object is their conversion to the Christian Faith.

I am,

My Lord,

Your Lordship's much obliged,

and most obedient Servant,

J. S. C. F. FREY.

PREFACE.

IT would be easy to expatiate on the excellence of Hebrew learning, and the various advantages with which it is attended; but that is not the design of this preface. The increased and increasing cultivation of it by persons of all classes, indicates a general and growing sense of its utility, and supersedes the necessity of vindication or encomium.

Almost ever since the author has enjoyed the happiness of being a member of the Christian Church, and particularly since he has had the privilege of living in this highly favoured land; he has felt an ardent desire to call the attention of his fellow christians to this important study, and to assist them in the pursuit of it. With this view, he, more than two years ago, published a Grammar; which has obtained considerable approbation from some of the first Hebrew scholars,* and has been

* "After an attentive perusal of Mr. Frey's Grammar, and after comparing it with others, I have to remark—that, in general, it equals the best Hebrew Grammars that have appeared—that his plan is altogether of a different nature, and highly superior—that in his attempts to procure an accurate pronunciation of the Hebrew language, he excels all his predecessors—that his view of the Particles is a most superior and elaborate article—that, in

received by the public in a manner more than equal to his largest expectations.

---

fine, the Grammar possesses a rank high in Oriental Literature."—*Extract of a Letter from the Rev. James Kidd, Professor of Oriental Languages in the Marischal College and University of Aberdeen, to a friend in London.*

"His examples of nouns adjective, according to their variations in number and regimen, page 32 to 36, are a valuable addition; and the view of the pronouns is improved, page 39 to 44, particularly by adding the prefix ב, which occurs as often as any other form. He has also given a fuller Table of the Particles than any other grammarian, p. 85—92." *Bap. Mag.* 1813.

"One of Mr. Frey's objects in the composition of his Grammar, has been to render it *simple*, and yet *comprehensive.* The tables of accents and particles are very complete; and the reading lessons in Exercise IX. will shew how differently Hebrew is read by Jewish and by Christian scholars. The directions for the formation of Verbs through all their voices, moods, and tenses, are minutely given; and this part of the Grammar manifests the author's critical acquaintance with the language which he professes to teach. In short, we must remark that Mr. Frey's mode of teaching the Hebrew is very masterly; that it is singularly calculated to facilitate the student's intimate knowledge of that language; and that it makes us acquainted with the process adopted by the Rabbis in the education of Jewish youth."

Monthly Review, Sep. 1815.

"It is but just, indeed, to state, that some Grammars have been composed in English; but the number of these is small, and even these few are not free from considerable defects. The Grammar of Parkhurst is without points; and without the true vowels, all Hebrew becomes confusion: that by Newton labours under the same disadvantage: and Lyon's Hebrew Grammar, although it teaches the system of the points, is too short to lead to a perfect knowledge of the language.——From all these defects, that before us is completely free: Mr. Frey has given all the necessary rules, according to the best authorities; he has illustrated his rules with copious and apposite examples: he has given complete Tables of the Hebrew Particles: and at the end he has printed the whole Book of Psalms, from the excellent edition of the Hebrew Bible by Vander Hooght.——Upon the whole, therefore, we cannot but recommend this Grammar to general notice. It will be

Agreeably to the intention expressed in the preface to his Grammar, he now ventures to bring forward a Dictionary: for, notwithstanding the many Hebrew Lexicons and Dictionaries which have been already published, he has long been of opinion, that one was yet wanted for the use of *students* of that language.

Some Hebrew Lexicons contain only the Roots, with a few of the Derivatives; and in those which exhibit most or all of the derivative words, these are ranged under their respective Roots: so that persons who are not well acquainted with the rules for separating the Serviles from the Roots, are often at a loss where to find the word they want. The author feels no small satisfaction in being able to corroborate his opinion, of the impediment which this plan throws in the way of young students, by the authority of one of the first Hebraists of the last century. Dr. James Robertson, Professor of Oriental languages in the University of Edinburgh, in the preface to his *Clavis Pentateuchi*, has the following observation:* "It is well known to all who have the

---

found a complete introduction to the study of Hebrew; and the Lexicon to be published by the same author, will, if executed with the same ability, materially assist in the cultivation of Hebrew Literature. We hope, therefore, that Mr. F. will meet with encouragement in his endeavours to explain it. Of the price of this Work no one will complain, when the difficulty and expence of printing Hebrew are considered: it is within the reach of all; and the addition of the Psalms will render it peculiarly useful in schools.

* Notum est omnibus qui linguarum orientalium non plane prorsus ignari sunt, maximam difficultatem esse, etiam studiosis grammaticæ præceptis mediocriter imbutis, in radice investigandâ; ea enim est indoles non tantum Hebraicæ, sed etiam Chaldaicæ, Syriacæ, et Arabicæ, ut non tantum prono-

least acquaintance with the oriental tongues, that the principal difficulty they present, even to students tolerably familiar with their grammatical rules, lies in the investigation of the Roots: for it is the genius of the Hebrew, as well as of the Chaldee, Syriac, and Arabic, to unite possessive pronouns, and also inseparable particles, both with nouns and verbs; which proves a source of extreme perplexity to young scholars in those languages."

The learned professor complains,* as the result of his own experience in teaching, that in consequence of this difficulty, the progress of students in Hebrew was not at all proportioned to the labour employed, either by the tutor or the pupils. If there was cause for so serious a complaint, notwithstanding all the advantages enjoyed under such a tutor, it can excite no surprise, that many persons, not possessed of such advantages, have found the difficulty too great for their efforts to surmount, and have therefore abandoned the study in despair. The present Dictionary entirely removes this difficulty, by exhibiting the Roots and Derivatives all arranged under one alphabet; so that a person who is

---

mina possessiva, sed etiam particulæ inseparabiles, tum nominibus tum verbis conjungi ament; ita ut maxima difficultas tyronibus in hisce linguis ediscendis hinc oriretur. CLAVIS PENT. AUCTORE JACOBO ROBERTSON, S. T. D. &c. PRÆFAT. p. 2.

* Nos, per aliquot annos, profectum studiosorum in hâc linguâ ope Lexici, præcipuè ubi tantum radices extant, operæ a nobis et studiosis impensæ non omnino respondisse, persensimus.—Studium linguarum per se haud jucundum, et superioribus temporibus, ob defectum adminiculorum, tam difficile fuerat, ut ferè inaccessum, et inter doctos paucissimi linguam Hebræam callerent. IBID. p. 1, 2.

merely acquainted with the letters, may turn at once to any word used in the Old Testament.

The remark which has just been made, on the common method of placing the Derivatives under their respective Roots, is applicable to every Hebrew Lexicon or Dictionary the author has seen, except one, which he obtained from a friend, after his work was ready for press, and the prospectus was already before the public: *Lexicon Hebraico-Chaldaico-Latino-Biblicum, Auctore P*** Carmelita, &c. Sub auspiciis Dom. Passionei, Cardinalis, 2 Tom. Avenione,* 1765. The plan of this Lexicon, he had the pleasure of finding in many respects similar to his own; and he has not been backward to avail himself of all the assistance he could derive from it. It is a work of great merit, but being in Hebrew and Latin only, its use is consequently confined to those who have previously acquired a knowledge of Latin. The present Dictionary is adapted for all who understand either Latin or English.

Another difficulty, of less magnitude indeed than the former, but too considerable to be disregarded, arises from the proper names; which having no typographical mark of distinction, the young student often supposes them to be common Derivatives, and thus loses much time and labour in endeavouring to discover their Roots. The present work contains all the proper names found in the Old Testament, inserted in alphabetical order among the Derivatives. The Latin column gives the names, in most instances, as they have been written by the best authors in that language. The names in the English column are copied, without variation, from the authorised version.

Some Dictionaries contain so much superfluous criticism, that, in seeking for the meaning of a word, the student is frequently bewildered in a maze of extraneous matter: in this work, the significations are given in the most plain and concise manner, according to the best authorities. The author has no idea of superseding or depreciating the more elaborate productions of profound philologists for the use of the advanced Hebraist. He hopes it will be remembered that his design is to assist students in learning the language, and to facilitate the perusal of the Hebrew scriptures by persons who have made only a moderate proficiency, or who have received little or no instruction from a living tutor. With these humble pretensions, he conceived it would be unnecessary to accompany the various interpretations with particular references to the authorities by which they are supported. In cases where all respectable authorities are agreed, the insertion of their names would be ostentatious and useless: and in cases of real difficulty as to the true meaning, this Dictionary will be found to contain the different senses in which such words have been understood by the most eminent lexicographers and critics.

The Lexicons and Concordances which have been chiefly followed, beside that already mentioned, are those of Buxtorf, Robertson, and Taylor. Assistance has also been obtained from the Lexicons of Avenarius, Cocceius, Castell, and Pagninus; from the Concordance of Marius de Calasio, and from the Lyra Prophetica of Bythner. The interpretations of the Septuagint, or the Vulgate, have sometimes been preferred to those of succeeding writers. The work has been much indebted to the many valuable criticisms accumulated in Pool's Synopsis. Considerable aid has been derived from the ingenious and judicious labours of Albert Schultens and James Robertson. And in numerous instances, advantage has been taken of all the information furnished by historians, geographers, travellers, or any other writers, Jewish or christian, ancient or modern.

In the preface to his Grammar, the author proposed, after the example of several eminent lexicographers, to introduce into this work the pronunciation of every Hebrew word in Roman characters; but this was considered by many Hebraists, as rendered unnecessary by the ample directions and examples which he has given in his Grammar.* The omission of this part of

---

* The author apprehends there can be no impropriety in embracing the present occasion to correct a mistake in his Grammar, page 45. Having stated, in the chapter on verbs, that the Hebrew Language has but *one* conjugation, he proceeds, in a note, to assign "the reason why he differs from *all* the eminent grammarians that have gone before him, who numerate *seven* distinct conjugations." It will appear, from the following quotation, that, however unconsciously, he was then treading in the steps of some of the most eminent grammarians of modern times. Uti clarissimus Danzius et doctissimus Schultensius, Hebræos unam tantum conjugationem habuisse, *jure contendunt*, ob hanc perspicuam rationem, quod omnes verborum *diversæ species* seu modificationes, quæ *vulgo* æstimantur totidem *diversæ conjugationes*, quod ad terminationem et syllabam finalem, *reverà eodem modo conjugantur:* Nos itaque in hâcce Clavi, &c. ROBERTSON, *Ibid.* p. 7.

his original plan has enabled him to devote a column to the signification in Latin, which he has no doubt will be regarded as a valuable addition, especially by Hebrew Students on the Continent.

It will be universally admitted by the learned, that after a person has acquired a little knowledge of any language, no method is better adapted to perfect his acquaintance with it, than composing exercises or translating into it from his own or any other tongue. To enable the Hebrew student to avail himself of this mode of improvement, the author has, with much labour and care, compiled the latter part of this work, which contains the principal words in the Latin and English languages, with those words which correspond to them in Hebrew. With regard to the nouns and verbs, in this part, he has thought it sufficient to give the former in their simple forms, and merely the roots of the latter; and the whole without vowels: as before any successful attempts at composition can be made, the student must be well acquainted with all the inflexions of the verbs and the use of the various prefixes and suffixes; and by a reference to the first part, he will always be enabled to determine the accuracy or inaccuracy of his exercises in these respects, as well as to affix the proper vowels to any word he may want to employ. In these Vocabularies, the author has not used the roots of Latin or English verbs, but those tenses by which the Hebrew roots are generally translated.

The early sheets of this Dictionary, having been for

many months in the hands of the public, the author has had opportunities of hearing different opinions respecting the plan he has adopted; and it affords him great satisfaction to find the balance of opinions decidedly in its favour.*

---

* *From the* REV. THOMAS FRY, *A. M. Rector of Emberton, and Chaplain to the Right Hon. Lord Erskine; and* MR. D'ALLEMAND, *Teacher of Hebrew, Chaldee, &c. &c.*

"We have examined the specimen sent to us of your Hebrew Dictionary. There can be no doubt but that those who have little time, and no assistance from any Hebrew teacher, are greatly perplexed and retarded by the difficulty of finding the roots. The plan of your Dictionary will certainly remove this difficulty, and we therefore are happy to recommend it to the public patronage."

From the REV. *W. B.* COLLYER, *D.D. F.A.S. &c.*

"I have seen with the greatest satisfaction, and beg leave cordially to recommend your Hebrew, Latin, and English Dictionary, on a new and improved plan, which appears to me calculated for distinguished usefulness, particularly to facilitate the study of the sacred language."

From the REV. *J.* GILBERT, *Classical Tutor at Rotherham Academy.*

"You will accept my best acknowledgments for the numbers of your new work, and in complying with your request to look it over, and state my sentiments, I am happy to say, that your Dictionary appears to me to furnish what was before an important desideratum. The Student will be now in possession of the same facilities toward the attainment of Hebrew, with which SCHREVELIUS had before supplied him towards the acquisition of Greek; and though some may object to your work, as they have before to his, that it is too indulgent to indolence, yet the learner, and especially if he have not the assistance of a Tutor, will feel you to be entitled to his best thanks. Your labour will greatly lessen his; will save him much valuable time; and will, perhaps, in many instances, prevent him from relinquishing, in despair or disgust, a pursuit which he may now prosecute with ease and success. Besides the Derivatives, the addition of proper names is no unimportant advantage. On the whole the plan is calculated to be

Objections have, however, been raised; the principal ones he will just mention:

---

highly useful to those for whom it is designed, and it is so far executed with ability."

From the Rev. William Steadman, Tutor of the Academy at Bradford, Yorkshire.

"My Dear Sir,

I cannot but think that all the lovers of sacred literature must feel greatly indebted to you for the assistance you have rendered the English Student in the cultivation of the Hebrew tongue. Your edition of Van der Hooght furnishes a very seasonable supply of *Hebrew Bibles*, and does honour to the English press.—Your *Hebrew Grammar* is one of the most valuable I have met with. Had such an one fallen into my hands when I first began to study the Hebrew language, I should have made a much more speedy progress, and, in particular, should have acquired a far greater correctness in its pronunciation.—But your *Dictionary* I consider as a work of still greater importance, especially to such as apply themselves to the acquisition of the language without the assistance of a skilful tutor. To them, the finding of the roots, after all the direction the plainest grammar rules can give, remains an insuperable difficulty. That difficulty your Dictionary completely removes. I have wondered that nothing of the kind has been before undertaken; and felt greatly the want of such help myself, being destitute of a tutor in my application to the language: and I congratulate you on being the instrument in the hand of providence, of making the path to the acquisition of the language, in which the oracles of God were first delivered to mankind, so much more smooth and pleasant. Wishing you much success in all your endeavours for promoting the cause of learning and of christianity, both among gentiles and your own countrymen,

I remain, &c. &c."

From the Rev. W. Ballentine, Master of the South Crescent Academy, Bedford Square.

"It was with peculiar pleasure that I heard of your intention to publish a Hebrew Dictionary on the plan which you have adopted. And now that some of the parts lie before me, I assure you I am not disappointed. Your plan, which is to give every word found in the Old Testament in its Alpha-

Some persons have objected that he has done too much, by making the acquisition of the language so easy as to

---

betical order, together with its Root, is most excellent, and must, when completed, be an invaluable work to the young student. The same plan, pursued in some of the most approved Greek Lexicons, has, undoubtedly, tended to facilitate the acquisition of the Greek. May your work be no less generally useful in the study of the Hebrew scriptures. The execution, as well as its plan, is certainly calculated to give it general circulation."

"With great pleasure we notice the first part of another Hebrew Lexicon in English and Latin, by Mr. Frey. He proposes to arrange all the Roots and Derivatives under *one* Alphabet, so that any word in the Hebrew Bible may be found at once, without difficulty. In other Dictionaries, the Derivatives are to be found under their Roots *only*. When a learner, therefore, meets with a word he does not know, he must first ascertain the Root before he can find it. *To* a young student this is always a serious difficulty, often an insuperable *one; and even to* a veteran in the school, sometimes presents a wide scope for investigation and research. *In Mr. Frey's* plan he finds relief in a moment. This is the first and *distinguishing* excellence of the work. It contains further a complete catalogue of proper names. In the course of his reading, the young student meets with proper names which he does not know to be such, and in investigating the supposed or real Roots of which he spends much time and labour to little purpose. The catalogue here alphabetically arranged prevents this trouble. Each page of the Dictionary is divided into four columns. In the second, stand the Derivatives alphabetically arranged: in the first, the Roots, from which the Derivatives spring. In the same column are found the Roots, placed alphabetically, and with their meaning annexed. The third column contains a Latin, and the fourth, an English version. Such are the outlines of the plan pursued in this Dictionary. The typography is beautiful, and is much set off by the whiteness of the paper. It is a work of immense labour, and has not its merits affected by small spots and slight blemishes. May it go on and prosper."

Bap. Mag. Oct. 1814.

"This is a work intended for learners, who always, at first, find great difficulty in determining on the roots of Hebrew words, and are puzzled, hour encourage indolence in the student. To this he will reply with Dr. James Robertson, who replies to a similar objection against his *Clavis Pentateuchi*,* that the object of his labour has been to render the study of this language more and more easy, and that if it were in his power to make it ten times easier still, he would certainly do it.†

---

after hour, in searching after them. It is less a Dictionary, than a *companion* to the Dictionary; or rather, a preparative for the use of the Dictionary; and it follows the author's Grammar of the language with advantage.——It will certainly contribute to save the student's time, and thereby enable him to advance further in his general studies, if such be his disposition. His labour is shortened by this assistant; but, labour he must still expect to exert: if he will not dig in the mine, he shall find no gem to reward him.——Only those who have earnestly examined the subject, can conceive the labour of such a work, and the extensive stores of knowledge it requires. We must therefore pardon a few inaccuracies into which Mr. Frey has been betrayed by his learned guides.——The addition of the Latin renderings is judicious; it contributes essential assistance to the scholar; while it also promotes accuracy and correctness. We are glad to see that this gentleman's perseverance in the best of causes meets with support from the public, sufficient to induce him to continue his labours for the benefit of the religious world, as well as for his own nation in particular." *Literary Panorama, Nov.* 1814.

* Fatemur enim nos totos esse in hoc, ut studium hujus linguæ magis magisque facile redderemus, immo, si possemus, decuplo facilius reddere, nos non omissuros. *Ibid.* p. 2.

† As the excellent work just mentioned, and the Grammar, to which it constantly refers, are both in Latin, and can therefore afford no assistance to most Hebrew students in the present age, and as this remark is applicable to Bythner's *Lyra Prophetica*, and to most other useful works in this department of literature, the author has prepared and will shortly publish,—*Rudiments*

Others have objected that the author has *not done enough;* for, that with every derivative, he ought to have indicated the part of speech to which it belongs, and all the particulars necessary to a grammatical praxis. But to do this in a work containing *every* word in the Bible, perhaps, would have justly exposed him to the charge of encouraging idleness in the student, by leaving little or nothing for application to perform.

These objections cannot both be well founded; and the author is unable to discover any real foundation for either. They seem calculated to neutralize each other, and go far towards inducing him to hope that, with all the faults of his work, (and what human work is faultless?) he is at no very great distance from the proper medium between *doing too much* and doing *too little.*

For the use of the vowel points, the author thinks it unnecessary to offer either apology or defence. To persons who hold a different opinion, or entertain any doubts on the subject, he would recommend an attentive perusal of the following treatises: *A Dissertation on the Hebrew Vowel Points, shewing that they are an original and essential part of the Language,* by P. WHITFIELD, Liverpool, 1748. *A Dissertation concerning the Antiquity of the Hebrew Language, Letters, Vowel Points, and Accents,* by JOHN GILL, D.D. London,

---

of the *Hebrew Language,* with *Rules, Examples* and *Exercises,* for translating from English into Hebrew, as well as from Hebrew into English; together with a KEY to the *Book* of *Psalms,* containing the true *Pronunciation,* different *Significations,* and Grammatical *Analysis* of every word.

1767; and since reprinted among the doctor's sermons and tracts. *Dissertatio de Genuina Punctorum Vocalium Antiquitate, &c. præmissa Clavi Pentateuchi, Auctore* JACOBO ROBERTSON, S.T.D. *LING. ORIENTAL. PROFESS.* &c. Edinburgh, 1770. To the statements and arguments of these able and learned writers, nothing has yet been opposed that wears the appearance of plausibility. But till they shall have received a satisfactory answer, the system they maintain may justly be considered as having full possession of the field.

The author cannot conclude this preface without expressing those acknowledgments, which are so justly due, for the assistance and encouragement afforded him in his literary undertakings.

The labour, care, and patience, requisite in correcting and revising for the press Hebrew works, especially with points and accents, none can conceive but those who have actually been engaged in it. Yet having been blessed with a long continuance of uninterrupted health, and having been careful to redeem every moment of time, the Author has been enabled in the course of the last six years, notwithstanding numerous other and still more important engagements, to publish three editions of his Narrative;* his Hebrew Grammar; a new edition

* In the last Edition, Price, with the Portrait, 3s. without it, 2s. 6d. the Author has given an account of—his birth and education—his religious offices sustained amongst the Jews—the time and place of his embracing the Christian religion—some remarkable circumstances which led him to a further acquaintance with divine Truth—his entrance into the Missionary Seminary at Berlin—his design in coming to England—and his labours and

of Vander-Hooght's Hebrew Bible;* and the present work. He feels himself therefore under the strongest

success amongst his brethren the Jews; and has added—An Address to Christians, in which he has laid open the deplorable state of the Jews—enumerated the chief difficulties in the way of their conversion—enforced the obligations of Christians to promote this object—and directed to the means by which it may be assisted.——We are glad to see this interesting Narrative reprinted. The concluding chapter, added to this Edition, is especially worth the attention of Christians of all Denominations. The deplorable moral state of the Jews is little known; here we have it detailed by one of their own nation; and the contemplation of it cannot but excite in every bosom a very earnest desire that the veil may be rent from their eyes, that they may behold the repairer of the breach, the restorer of paths to dwell in." *Bapt. Mag.* 1813.

* "With a view to accommodate the students of Hebrew, the Rev. Mr. Frey, the resident *Preacher at the Chapel for* the conversion of the Jews, has undertaken to edite a *Hebrew Bible from the original of Van der Hooght*, which has always been considered as one of the most correct: fewer errors we *believe*, are to be *found* in it than in any other: a copy of it is rarely to be met with. Therefore a fac-simile of this most valuable Bible will be a great acquisition to Hebrew Scholars, because they will not only be supplied at a less expense but they will have no difficulty in being supplied.—The first three Numbers are printed on fine Paper superior to any thing we have seen of the kind, and the letter is as beautiful as the original.—Those who have seen the original Bible of Van der Hooght, which now sells for *six* Guineas, and are well acquainted with Hebrew, know the great difficulty which necessarily must attend printing with the vowel points, but when it is recollected that the accents also are to be added, the trouble and difficulty are greatly increased. Nothing so complete as this has ever been produced in England, it will do honour to the enterprizing spirit of the country.——We are sorry that Mr. Frey did not determine on taking off a larger quantity: the number is comparatively small and may not exceed the number of his Subscribers.—Hebrew Bibles have long been wanted; few are to be procured unless they are sent from the Continent: it is also proper to observe, that Bibles without vowel points cannot be of much use to the Hebrew

obligations, in the first place to offer up his unfeigned thanksgivings to Almighty God, "the Father of lights, from whom cometh every good and perfect gift." It is well known that the expense of printing in foreign or dead languages is very great. From some peculiar circumstances the expenses of the above publications have far exceeded the Author's original estimate, and he would most probably have been prevented from

---

critic, nor even in many instances can the accents be dispensed with, as a true translation of many passages cannot be had without them; which we hope to have an opportunity of proving in this Journal.—Both these, however, will be given in these elegant volumes."

Classical Journal, March, 1812.

"The work before us is intended to be an exact copy of Vander Hooght's celebrated edition. The type is at least equal in strength and distinctness to the Dutch edition, and the paper of the *common* copies is decidedly superior; the large paper copies are beautiful. Mr. Frey has wisely engaged Jewish compositors, who, from their childhood, were trained up to a familiarity with the punctuated and accentuated Hebrew. He himself carefully revises every word and mark, by the Bible of Salomon Proops, which the Jews consider the most accurate ever published; and he has engaged an accomplished Hebraist on the Masoretic plan, to assist him in the vast toil of correcting. By these means he has detected an unexpected number of errors in Vander Hooght's original edition." *Eclectic Review*, October, 1811.

"Every friend of Biblical knowledge, and especially the lovers of Hebrew Literature, will be gratified by the publication of the Hebrew Scriptures from the hands of a gentleman, whose ability cannot be doubted, and for whose integrity the Public (Jewish and Christian) possess no common guarantee. These, united to his well-known indefatigable industry, insure an attention to the work he is engaged in, rarely to be expected."

Bap. Mag. Sep. 1811.

completing them, had not the public acceptance of them also exceeded his expectations.

Of a large edition of his Hebrew Grammar a few only are left on hand. There was a considerable demand for his Hebrew Bible in the course of its publication in Parts, and the demand has been still greater since it has been completed. As a *Part only* of a Dictionary can be but of little use, the Author did not expect many copies of this work to be sold before the whole should be finished; he has however the gratification to state that the sale has greatly increased with the publication of each successive part; and now it is completed, he trusts it will meet with the general approbation of the Public. For these encouragements, as well as for the kind reception the Author has met with amongst Christians of all denominations while travelling more than thrice all over the United Kingdom to preach the everlasting gospel and to solicit contributions in aid of that cause which lieth nearest his heart, namely, the melioration of the temporal condition, and the promotion of the spiritual welfare, of his Jewish brethren, he finds himself utterly at a loss for words to express his feelings of thankfulness, and he will ever esteem it his duty to devote his time and talents to the service of the public.

As the acceptance of a work by the public often depends on the character it receives from respectable Critics, the Author feels himself much indebted to the Gentlemen connected with several of the literary journals, for their early and candid reviews of his different publications; and he indulges the hope that those who have not yet noticed his Dictionary will find it not altogether unworthy of their recommendation. The Author requests those Gentlemen who have so handsomely favoured him with testimonies in approbation of his works to accept this public tribute of thanks for their kindness.

It only remains, to subjoin a few particulars in explanation of the method pursued in the following work.

Every Derivative is inserted with all its prefixes and affixes, and its Root in the parallel column, as, from אֶאֱמִין | אמן.

If the word wanted be a Root, it must be sought in the alphabetical order of the *Derivatives*, and it will be found in the column of Roots; as, the root אָבַד page 1, stands in the column of Roots, next after the word אַבְנִתָּא in the column of Derivatives.

Where any Derivative is from the same Root as the word immediately preceding it, the Root is not repeated, but its place is supplied by a line, as, page 2,

אִבְדָה | אבד
אֲבֵדָה | —

There are many Hebrew Roots which are out of use, and the signification of which is uncertain; but they are retained in all Dictionaries on account of the words derived from them: such Roots are here printed in open letters, as אבב.

With a view to bring the work within as moderate limits as possible, the Author has frequently put into one line two words which are similar in sense, but which differ, either in the points, as אֲבֵדָה אֲבֵדָה; or in the gender, as אֲבַדְּתְּ אֲבַדְתְּ; or in one of the letters, as אוֹצְרוֹת אוֹצָרֹת, אֲבוֹשׁ אֲבוּשָׁה: and such words are, in many instances, abbreviated, either in the beginning, as אֲבִינָיִל--נַל; or at the end, as בְּנוֹיִם בְּנוֹ--; or in both, as וְהוֹתִירְךָ־תִךְ. Hence, if the Student seeks for a word which has וֹ, or וּ, or י, in the middle, and does not find it in its regular place let him seek for it without that letter, or vice versa, as אַבְשָׁלוֹם־לֹם; וַיְשַׁנּוּ־שַׁי; בְּמַלְאֹתָם־לֹד.

Proper Names, and words composed only of a preposition and an affix pronoun, as בִּי *in me*, have no root opposite.

Where there is a marginal reading different from the text, such difference is denoted by an open letter, as בְּכֹיִם.

May the blessing of God Almighty accompany this work, and make it the means of communicating a clearer knowledge of the Sacred Scriptures, and thereby exciting to a more useful and holy life, and to him shall be all the praise and glory. Amen.

Dec. 23, 1815.

INITIALS USED AT THE END OF THE PROPER NAMES.

N. M. Name *of a* Man
N. W. . . . . Woman
N. F. . . . . Family
N. N. . . . . Nation or People
N. P. . . . . Place, or *from* a Place
N. R. . . . . River
N. Mth. . . . . Month
N. S. . . . . Solemnity, or Feast
N. I. . . . . Idol

A

HEBREW, LATIN, & ENGLISH,

DICTIONARY.

A

Hebrew, Latin, and English

DICTIONARY.

ROOTS.	DERIVATIVES.	VERSIO.	SIGNIFICATION.
	אא		
אזר	אֲאַזֶּרְךָ	*Accingam te.*	I will gird thee.
אמן	אַאֲמִין	*Credam.*	I will believe.
אמץ	אַאַמִּצְכֶם	*Roborabo vos.*	I will strengthen you.
אסף	אֶאֱסֹף	*Congregabo.*	I will gather.
ארר	אָאֹר	*Maledicam.*	I will curse.
ארך	אַאֲרִיךְ	*Prolongabo.*	I will prolong.
	אב		
אבה	אָב אַב	*Pater, dux.*	A father, leader.
בוא	אָבֹא אָבֹאָה	*Veniam, ingrediar.*	I will go, will enter.
אבב			
	אֲבִגָיִל	*Abigail.*	Abigail, N. W.
	אֲבַגְתָא	*Abagtha.*	Abagtha, N. M.
אָבַד		*Periit, interiit.*	He perished, was lost.
—	אַבֵּד	*Perdere.*	To destroy.
—	אֹבֵד	*Periens.*	Perishing.
—	אָבֹד	*Perire.*	To perish.
—	אִבֵּד	*Destruxit.*	He destroyed.
—	אֹבֵד	*Perdens.*	Destroying.
—	אֲבֹד	*Perire.*	To perish.

ROOTS.	DERIVATIVES.	VERSIO.	SIGNIFICATION.
אבד	אָבְדָה אָבָדָה	*Periit.*	She perished.
—	אֲבֵדָה	*Res amissa.*	A thing lost.
—	אָבְדוּ אָבֵדוּ	*Perierunt.*	They are destroyed.
—	אֲבַדּוֹן	*Perditio.*	Destruction.
—	אֹבְדוֹת	*Res perditæ.*	Things lost.
—	אֲבָדְךָ אָבְדָךְ	*Perire te.*	That thou perish.
—	אֲבָדְכֶם	*Perire vos.*	That you perish.
—	אֲבָדָם	*Perire eos.*	That they perish.
—	אִבְּדָם	*Destruxit eos.*	He destroyed them.
—	אָבַדְנוּ אָבָדְנוּ	*Periimus.*	We perished.
—	אֲבֵדַת	*Res amissa.*	The thing lost.
—	אָבַדְתָּ אָבָדְתְּ	*Periisti.*	Thou art undone.
—	אִבַּדְתָּ	*Perdidisti.*	Thou hast destroyed.
—	אָבַדְתִּי	*Perii.*	I perished. [sented.
אָבָה		*Voluit, acquievit.*	He was willing, desired, con-
—	אֵבֶה	*Velox.*	Swift.
בהל	אֲבָהֵל	*Perturbor.*	I am troubled.
אבה	אֲבָהָתִי	*Patres mei.*	My fathers.
—	אֲבָהָתָךְ	*Patres tui.*	Thy fathers.
—	אֲבָהָתָנָא	*Patres nostri.* [runt.	Our fathers.
—	אָבוּ אָבוּא	*Voluerunt, acquieve-*	They were willing, consented.
בוא	אָבוֹא	*Veniam.*	I will come.
אבה	אֲבוּהִי	*Pater ejus.*	His father.
—	אֲבוֹי	*Luctus.*	Sorrow.
—	אֲבוּךְ	*Pater tuus.*	Thy father.
אבס	אָבוּס	*Saginatus.*	Fatted, crammed.
—	אֵבוּס	*Præsepe.*	A crib.
—	אֲבוּסִים	*Saginati.*	Fatted, Pl.
—	אֲבוּסֶךָ	*Præsepe tuum.*	Thy crib.
בוס	אֲבוּסֶנּוּ	*Conculcabo eum.*	I will tread him under foot.
בוש	אֵבוֹשׁ אֵבוֹשָׁה	*Pudore afficiar.*	I shall be ashamed.
אבה	אָבוֹת	*Patres, familiæ.*	The fathers, families.
—	אֲבוֹתַי	*Patres mei.* [rum.	My fathers.
—	אֲבוֹתֵיהֶם	*Patres, familiæ eo-*	Their fathers, families.
—	אֲבוֹתָיו	*Patres ejus.*	His fathers.
—	אֲבוֹתֶיךָ	*Patres tui.*	Thy fathers.
—	אֲבוֹתֵיכֶם	*Patres vestri.*	Your fathers.

ROOTS.	DERIVATIVES.	VERSIO.	SIGNIFICATION.
אבה	אֲבוֹתֵינוּ	*Patres nostri.*	Our fathers.
—	אֲבוֹתָם	*Patres eorum.*	Their fathers.
אבח			
בחן	אֶבְחָנְךָ	*Probabo te.*	I will prove thee.
בחר	אֶבְחַר אֶבְחֲרָה	*Eligam.*	I will choose.
—	אֶבְחָרֵהוּ	*Eligam eum.*	I will choose him.
אבח	אִבְחַת חָרֶב	*Gladii mucro.*	The point of a sword.
אבט			
בטח	אֶבְטַח	*Confidam.*	I will trust.
אבה	אָבִי	*Pater meus.*	My father.
—	אֲבִי	*Pater, dux.*	The father, leader.
	אֲבִי	*Abi.*	Abi, N. W.
בוא	אָבִי אָבִיא	*Adducam.*	I will bring.
	אֲבִי גִבְעוֹן	*Abi-gibon.*	Abi-gibon, N. M.
	אֲבִי עַלְבוֹן	*Abi-albon.*	Abi-albon, N. M.
בוא	אֲבִיאֲךָ	*Introducam te.*	I will introduce thee.
	אֲבִיאֵל	*Abiel.*	Abiel, N. M.
בוא	אֲבִיאֵם	*Adducam eos.*	I will bring them.
—	אֲבִיאֶנָּה	*Adducam eam.*	I will bring her.
—	אֲבִיאֶנּוּ	*Adducam eum.*	I will bring him.
אבב	אָבִיב	*Spica tenera.*	Green ears of corn.
	אֲבִיגַיִל־גַל	*Abigail.*	Abigail, N. W.
אבד	אֹבִידָה	*Perdam.*	I will destroy.
	אֲבִידָן	*Abidan.*	Abidan, N. M.
	אֲבִידָע	*Abida.*	Abida, N. M.
אבה	אָבִיהָ	*Pater ejus.*	Her father.
	אֲבִיָּה	*Abiiah*	Abijah, N. M. W.
אבה	אָבִיהוּ	*Pater ejus.*	His father.
	אֲבִיהוּד	*Abihud.*	Abihud, N. M.
	אֲבִיהוּא	*Abihu.*	Abihu, N. M.
	אֲבִיהַיִל	*Abihail.*	Abihail, N. W.
אבה	אֲבִיהֶם־ן	*Pater eorum.*	Their father.
—	אָבִיו	*Pater ejus.*	His father.
—	אֶבְיוֹן	*Pauper, egenus.*	A poor or needy person.
—	אֶבְיוֹנֶיהָ	*Pauperes sui.*	Her poor, Pl.
—	אֶבְיוֹנֵי	*Pauperes.*	The poor, Pl.
—	אֶבְיוֹנִים	*Egeni.*	Needy persons.

ROOTS.	DERIVATIVES.	VERSIO.	SIGNIFICATION.
אבה	אֶבְיוֹנְךָ	*Pauperes tui.*	Thy poor, Pl.
	אֲבִיחָיִל	*Abichail.*	Abihail, N. M. W.
נבט	אַבִּיט	*Aspiciam.*	I will behold.
	אֲבִיטוּב	*Abitub.*	Abitub, N. M.
	אֲבִיטָל	*Abital.*	Abital, N. W.
אבה	אָבִיךָ־ךְ	*Pater tuus.*	Thy father.
—	אֲבִיכֶם־ן	*Pater vester.*	Your father.
—	אֹבִים	*Volunt.*	They are willing.
	אֲבִיָּם	*Abiiam.*	Abijam, N. M.
	אֲבִימָאֵל	*Abimael.*	Abimael, N. M.
	אֲבִימֶלֶךְ	*Abimelech.*	Abimelech, N. M.
כון	אָבִין אָבִינָה	*Intelligam.*	I shall understand.
	אֲבִינָדָב	*Abinadab.*	Abinadab, N. M.
אבה	אָבִינוּ	*Pater noster.*	Our father.
—	אֶבְיוֹנִים	*Pauperes.*	The poor, Pl.
—	אֶבְיֹנְךָ	*Pauperes tui.*	Thy poor, Pl.
	אֲבִינֹעַם	*Abinoam.*	Abinoam, N. M.
	אֲבִינֵר	*Abiner.*	Abiner, N. M.
	אֶבְיָסָף	*Ebiasaph.*	Ebiasaph, N. M.
נבע	אַבִּיעָה	*Loquar.*	I will utter.
	אֲבִיעֶזֶר	*Abiezer.*	Abiezer, N. M.
אבר	אַבִּיר	*Potens, princeps.*	A mighty one, leader.
—	אַבִּירֵי	*Potentes.*	Mighty men.
—	אַבִּירַי	*Fortes mei.*	My valiant men.
—	אַבִּירָיו	*Fortes ejus.*	His valiant men.
—	אַבִּירֶיךָ	*Fortes tui.*	Thy valiant ones.
—	אַבִּירִים	*Potentes.*	Mighty men.
	אֲבִירָם	*Abiram.*	Abiram, N. M.
	אֲבִישָׁג	*Abisag.*	Abishag, N. W.
	אֲבִישׁוּעַ	*Abisua.*	Abishua, N. M.
	אֲבִישׁוּר	*Abisur.*	Abishur, N. M.
	אֲבִישַׁי	*Abisai.*	Abishai, N. M.
	אֲבִישָׁלוֹם	*Abisalom.*	Abishalom, N. M.
אבה	אָבִיתִי	*Volui.*	I would.
—	אֲבִיתֶם	*Voluistis.*	Ye would.
	אֶבְיָתָר	*Ebiatar.*	Abiathar, N. M.
אבך			

ROOTS.	DERIVATIVES.	VERSIO.	SIGNIFICATION.
בכה	אֶבְכֶּה	*Plorabo.*	I will bewail.
אָבַל		*Luxit.*	He mourned.
——	אֲבָל	*Sed, tamen, quia.*	But, yet, because.
——	אָבֵל	*Lugens.*	Weeping.
——	אֵבֶל	*Luctus.*	Mourning.
	אָבֵל	*Abel.*	Abel, N. P.
	אָבֵל בֵּית מַעֲכָה	*Abel-bet-mahacah.*	Abel-beth-maachah, N. P
	אָבֵל הַשִּׁטִּים	*Abel-sittim.*	Abel-shittim, N. P.
	אָבֵל כְּרָמִים	*Abel-cheramim.*	Abel-cheramin, N. P.
	אָבֵל מְחוֹלָה	*Abel-mecholah.*	Abel-meholah, N. P.
	אָבֵל מַיִם	*Abel-maim.*	Abel-maim, N. P.
	אָבֵל מִצְרַיִם	*Abel-mitsraim.*	Abel-mizraim, N. P.
אבל	אָבְלָה	*Luxit.*	She mourned.
——	אָבְלוּ	*Luxerunt.*	They mourned.
——	אֲבֵלוֹת אֲבֵלִים	*Lugentes.*	They that mourn.
——	אֶבְלֵךְ	*Luctus tuus.*	Thy mourning.
——	אֶבְלָם	*Luctus eorum.*	Their mourning.
בלע	אֲבַלַּע	*Subvertam.*	I will subvert.
——	אֲבַלֵּעַ	*Destruam.*	I will destroy.
אבן			
——	אֶבֶן אָבֶן	*Lapis.*	A stone.
	אֶבֶן בֹּהַן	*Eben-bohan.*	Eben-bohan, N. P.
	אֶבֶן הָעֵזֶר	*Aben-haezer.*	Eben-ezer, N. P.
	אֲבָנָה	*Abana.*	Abana, N. R.
בנה	אֶבְנֶה	*Ædificabo.*	I will build.
——	אִבָּנֶה	*Ædificabor.*	I shall be built.
אבן	אַבְנוֹ	*Lapis ejus.*	His stone.
אבנט	אַבְנֵט	*Balteus.*	A girdle.
——	אַבְנֵטִים	*Baltei.*	Girdles.
אבן	אַבְנֵי	*Lapides.*	Stones.
——	אֲבָנֶיהָ	*Lapides ejus.*	Her stones.
——	אַבְנֵיהֶם	*Lapides eorum.*	Their stones.
——	אֲבָנָיו	*Lapides ejus.*	His stones.
——	אֲבָנַיִךְ	*Lapides tui.*	Thy stones.
——	אֲבָנִים	*Lapides.*	Stones.
בנה	אֶבְנֵךְ	*Ædificabo te.*	I will build thee.
	אַבְנֵר	*Abner.*	Abner, N. M.

ROOTS.	DERIVATIVES.	VERSIO.	SIGNIFICATION.
בעה	אֶבְעֶא	*Quæram.*	I will ask.
—	אֲבַעְבֻּעֹת	*Pustulæ.*	Blains.
	אֶבֶץ	*Abetz.*	Abetz, N. M.
	אִבְצָן	*Jbsan.*	Jbzan, N. M.
אבק			
—	אָבָק אֲבַק	*Pulvis.*	Powder, dust.
—	אֲבָקָם	*Pulvis eorum.*	Their dust.
בקר	אֲבַקֵּר	*Requiram.*	I will seek out.
בקש	אֲבַקֵּשׁ־קֶּשׁ	*Quæram.*	I will seek.
	אֲבַקְשָׁה	*Quæram.*	I will seek.
	אֲבַקְשֶׁנּוּ	*Quæram eum.*	I will seek him.
אבק	אַבְקַת	*Pulvis.*	Powder.
אבר			
—	אֵבֶר אֶבְרָה	*Ala, penna.*	A wing, pen.
	אַבְרָהָם	*Abraham.*	Abraham, N. M.
ברח	אֶבְרַח	*Fugiam.*	I will flee.
ברך	אֲבָרֵךְ	*Benedicam.* [*pater.*	I will bless.
—	אַבְרֵךְ	*Flecte genua, tener*	Bow the knee, tender father.
—	אֲבָרְכָה	*Benedicam.*	I will bless.
—	אֲבָרֶכְךָ־רְכֶךָּ	*Benedicam tibi.*	I will bless theé.
—	אֲבָרְכֵם	*Benedicam eis.*	I will bless them.
	אַבְרָם	*Abram.*	Abram, N. M.
אבר	אֶבְרָתוֹ	*Ala ejus.*	His wing.
אוש	אֵבֹשָׁה	*Pudore afficiar.*	I shall be put to shame.
	אַבְשַׁי	*Abisai.*	Abishai, N. M.
	אַבְשָׁלוֹם־לֹם	*Absalom.*	Absalom, N. M.
	אֹבֹת	*Obot.*	Oboth, N. P.
אבה	אָבֹת	*Patres.*	Fathers.
—	אֲבֹתַי	*Patres mei.*	My fathers.
—	אֲבֹתֵיהֶם	*Patres eorum.*	Their fathers.
—	אֲבֹתָיו	*Patres ejus.*	His fathers.
—	אֲבֹתֶיךָ	*Patres tui.*	Thy fathers.
—	אֲבֹתֵיכֶם	*Patres vestri.*	Your fathers.
—	אֲבֹתֵינוּ	*Patres nostri.*	Our fathers.
—	אֲבֹתָם	*Patres eorum.*	Their fathers.

ROOTS	DERIVATIVES.	VERSIO.	SIGNIFICATION.
	אג		
	אָגֵא	*Age.*	Agee, N. M.
גאל	אֶגְאָל	*Redimam.*	I will redeem.
—	אֶגְאָלֵם	*Redimam eos.*	I will redeem them.
—	אֶגְאַלְתִּי	*Inquinavi.*	I stained.
	אֲגָג	*Agag.*	Agag, N. M.
	אֲגָגִי	*Agagites.*	Agagite, N. M.
אגר			
—	אֲגֻדּוֹת	*Fasciculi.*	Bunches, little bundles.
גדל	אַגְדִּיל	*Grandem faciam.*	I will make great.
—	אֶגְדַּל	*Magnus ero.*	I shall be great.
גדע	אֲגַדֵּעַ	*Succidam.*	I will cut down, asunder.
אגד	אֲגֻדַּת	*Fasciculus.*	A bunch, a little bundle.
אגז	אֱגוֹז	*Nux.*	A nut.
גוע	אֶגְוַע־וָעַ	*Expirabo.*	I shall expire.
נגף	אֶגּוֹף	*Percutiam.*	I will strike.
	אָגוּר	*Agur.*	Agur, N. M.
גור	אָגוּר	*Timebo.*	I shall fear.
	אָגוּרָה	*Habitabo.*	I will dwell.
אגז			
נגד	אַגִּיד אַגִּידָה	*Indicabo, annunciabo*	I will declare.
—	אַגִּידֶנּוּ	*Narrabo ei.*	I will tell him.
אגל			
גול	אָגִילָה	*Lætabor.*	I will rejoice.
גלה	אֲגַלֶּה אֶגְלָה	*Revelabo.*	I will shew, reveal.
אגל	אֶגְלֵי	*Stillæ.*	Drops.
	אֶגְלַיִם	*Eglaim.*	Eglaim, N. P.
אגם			
—	אֲגַם	*Stagnum.*	A pool of water.
—	אַגְמֵי	*Stagna.*	The ponds.
—	אַגְמֵיהֶם	*Stagna eorum.*	Their ponds.
—	אַגְמֹן	*Hamus.*	A hook.
אגן			
	אַגַּן	*Crater.*	A cup, bason.
אגף		[*ejus.*	
—	אֲגַפֶּיהָ	*Agmina, exercitus*	Her bands, troops, armies.

ROOTS.	DERIVATIVES.	VERSIO.	SIGNIFICATION.
אגף	אֲגַפָּיו	*Agmina ejus.*	His bands.
—	אֲגַפֶּיךָ	*Agmina tua.*	Thy bands.
אָגַר		*Collegit.*	He gathered.
—	אֹגֵר	*Congregans.*	Collecting together.
—	אִגְּרָא	*Epistola.*	A letter.
—	אָגְרָה	*Congregavit.*	She hath gathered.
—	אִגְּרוֹת	*Epistolæ.*	Letters.
—	אֲגַרְטְלֵי	*Pelves.*	Chargers.
גרע	אֶגְרַע	*Minuam.*	I will diminish.
גרש	אֲגָרֵשׁ	*Ejiciam.*	I will drive out.
—	אֲגָרְשֵׁם	*Ejiciam eos.*	I will drive them out.
—	אֲגָרְשֶׁנּוּ	*Ejiciam eum.*	I will drive him out.
אגר	אִגֶּרֶת אִגַּרְתָּא	*Epistola.*	A letter.
—	אִגְּרֹתֵיהֶם	*Epistolæ eorum.*	Their letters.
	אד		
דאג	אֶדְאַג	*Solicitus ero.*	I shall be sorry.
ארב			
דבק	אַדְבִּיק	*Adhærere faciam.*	I will cause to cleave to.
	אַדְבְּאֵל	*Adbeel.*	Adbeel, N. M.
דבר	אֲדַבֵּר אֲדַבְּרָה	*Loquar.*	I will speak.
	אֲדַד	*Adad.*	Adad, N. M.
דדה	אֶדַּדֶּה	*Incedam.*	I will go.
—	אֲדַדֵּם	*Incedam cum eis.*	I will go with them.
	אִדּוֹ	*Ido.* [*Idumæa.*	Iddo, N. M.
	אֱדוֹם	*Edom,* *Idumæus,*	Edom, N. M. P. N.
	אֲדוֹמִים	*Idumæi.*	Edomites, N. N.
אדן	אָדוֹן אֲדוֹן	*Dominus.*	Lord.
	אַדּוֹן	*Adon.*	Addon, N. M.
אדן	אֲדוֹנִי־נָי	*Dominus meus.*	My lord.
—	אֲדוֹנֶיהָ	*Dominus ejus.*	Her lord.
	אֲדוֹנִיָּה	*Adoniiah.*	Adonijah N. M.
אדן	אֲדוֹנֵיהֶם	*Domini eor um.*	Their lords.
—	אֲדוֹנִים	*Domini.*	Lords.
—	אֲדוֹנֵינוּ	*Domini nostri.*	Our lords.
	אֲדוֹרַיִם	*Adoraim.*	Adoraim, N. P.
דרש	אֱדוֹשׁ	*Triturando.*	Threshing.

ROOTS.	DERIVATIVES.	VERSIO.	SIGNIFICATION.
אוד	אֹדוֹת	*Causæ.*	The causes.
—	אֹדוֹתַי	*Causæ meæ.*	My causes.
—	אֹדוֹתֶיךָ	*Causæ tuæ.*	Thy causes.
נדח	אַדִּיחֵם	*Expellam eos.*	I will expel them.
אדן	אֱדַיִן	*Tunc, illicò.*	Then, there.
אדר	אַדִּיר	*Magnificus, grandis.*	Excellent, grand.
—	אַדִּירוֹ	*Magnificus ejus.*	His noble.
—	אַדִּירֵי	*Magnifici.*	The nobles.
—	אַדִּירֵיהֶם	*Magnifici eorum.*	Their nobles.
—	אַדִּירָיו	*Magnifici sui.*	His worthies.
—	אַדִּירֶיךָ	*Magnifici tui.*	Thy worthies.
—	אַדִּירִים	*Magnifici, potentes.*	Nobles, mighty ones.
דלג	אֲדַלֵּג	*Transiliam.*	I will leap.
	אֲדַלְיָא	*Adalia.*	Adalia, N. M.
אָדַם		*Rubuit.*	He was red.
—	אֹדֶם	*Sardius lapis.*	A sardius, a precious stone.
	אָדָם	*Adam.*	Adam, N. M.
אדם	אָדָם	*Homo.*	Man.
—	אָדֹם	*Ruber, rufus.*	Red.
—	אֲדַמְדָּם	*Subrufus.*	
—	אֲדַמְדָּמֹת	*Subrufæ.*	Reddish.
—	אֲדַמְדֶּמֶת	*Subrufa.*	
—	אֲדֻמָּה	*Rufa.*	Red.
—	אֲדָמָה	*Terra, humus.*	The earth, ground.
דמה	אֲדַמֶּה	*Comparabo.*	I will compare.
—	אֲדַמֶּה	*Assimilabo.*	I will liken.
	אַדְמָה אֲדָמָה	*Adma.*	Admah, N. P.
אדם	אָדְמוּ	*Rubebant.*	They were red.
—	אַדְמוֹנִי	*Ruber.*	Red.
—	אֲדָמוֹת	*Terræ.*	Lands.
	אֲדָמִי	*Adami.*	Adami, N. P.
	אֲדֹמִי	*Idumæus.*	Edomite, N. N.
	אֲדֻמִּים	*Adumim.*	Adummim, N. P.
אדם	אֲדֻמִּים	*Rubri.*	Red.
	אֲדֹמִיִּים	*Idumæi.*	Edomites, N. N.
	אֲדֹמִיּוֹת	*Idumææ.*	Edomites, N. N.
אדם	אַדְמַת	*Terra.*	The land.

ROOTS.	DERIVATIVES	VERSIO.	SIGNIFICATION.
	אַדְמָתָא	*Admata.*	Admatha, N. M.
אדם	אַדְמָתָהּ	*Terra ejus.*	Her land.
—	אַדְמָתוֹ	*Terra ejus.*	His land.
—	אַדְמָתִי	*Terra mea.*	My land.
—	אַדְמָתְךָ־מָתֶךָ	*Terra tua.*	Thy land.
—	אַדְמַתְכֶם	*Terra vestra.*	Your land.
—	אַדְמָתָם	*Terra ipsorum.*	Their land.
—	אַדְמָתֵנוּ	*Terra nostra.*	Our land.
אַדָּן			
	אַדָּן	*Addon.*	Addon, N M.
אדן	אֲדֹנוֹ	*Hæres ejus.*	His heir.
—	אֲדֹנִי	*Dominus meus.*	My Lord.
—	אֲדֹנֵי	*Domini.*	The Lords.
—	אַדְנֵי	*Bases.*	The Sockets.
—	אֲדֹנַי	*Domini mei.*	My Lords.
—	אֲדֹנָי	*Dominus.*	Lord.
	אֲדֹנִי בֶזֶק	*Adonibezek.*	Adoni-bezek, N. M.
	אֲדֹנִי צֶדֶק	*Adonizedec.*	Adoni-zedek, N. M.
אדן	אֲדֹנֶיהָ	*Dominus ejus.*	Her master.
—	אֲדָנֶיהָ	*Bases ejus.*	Her sockets.
—	אֲדֹנִיָּה־הוּ	*Adonijah.*	Adonijah, N. M.
—	אֲדֹנֵיהֶם	*Dominus eorum.*	Their lord.
—	אַדְנֵיהֶם	*Bases eorum.*	Their sockets.
—	אֲדָנָיו	*Bases ejus.*	His sockets.
—	אֲדֹנָיו	*Dominus ejus.*	His master.
—	אֲדֹנֶיךָ־נַיִךְ	*Dominus tuus.*	Thy master.
—	אֲדֹנֵיכֶם	*Dominus vester.*	Your master.
—	אֲדֹנִים	*Domini.*	Masters.
—	אֲדָנִים	*Bases.*	Sockets.
—	אֲדֹנֵינוּ	*Dominus noster.*	Our master.
	אֲדֹנִיקָם	*Adonicam.*	Adonikam, N. M.
	אֲדֹנִירָם	*Adoniram.*	Adoniram, N. M.
ידע	אֵדַע	*Cognoscam, sciam.*	I shall, or will know.
—	אֵדְעָה אֵדָעָה	*Cognoscam.*	I may know.
דקק	אֲדִקֵּם	*Comminuam eos.*	I will break them in pieces.
אדר			
	אֲדָר	*Addar.*	Addar. N. M.

ROOTS.	DERIVATIVES.	VERSIO.	SIGNIFICATION.
	אֲדָר	*Adar.*	Adar, N. Mth.
אדר	אֶדֶר	*Pallium, magnificen-* [*tia.*	A robe, magnificence.
—	אֲדַרְגָּזְרַיָּא	*Præsides.*	Judges.
	אַדָּרָה	*Addara.*	Adara, N. P.
דרש	אֶדְרוֹשׁ	*Requiram.*	I will require.
אדר	אַדְרַזְדָּא	*Festinanter.*	Diligently, quickly.
—	אִדְּרֵי	*Areæ.*	Threshing floors.
דרך,	אַדְרִיכֵם	*Deducam eos.*	I will lead them.
אדרכן	אֲדַרְכֹּנִים	*Drachmæ.*	Drams.
אדר	אַדִּרִם	*Fortes.*	Strong ones.
	אֲדֹרָם	*Adoram.*	Adoram, N. M.
	אַדְרַמֶּלֶךְ	*Adramelech.*	Adramelech, N. M. I.
	אֶדְרֶעִי	*Edrehi.*	Edrie, N. P.
דרש	אֶדְרשׁ	*Requiram.*	I will require, seek.
—	אִדָּרֵשׁ	*Requirar.*	I shall be required, sought.
—	אֶדְרְשֶׁנּוּ	*Requiram eum.*	I will seek him.
אדר	אַדֶּרֶת	*Pallium.*	A robe.
—	אַדַּרְתּוֹ	*Pallium ejus.*	His robe, garment.
—	אַדַּרְתָּם	*Magnificentia eorum*	Their glory.

אה

ROOTS.	DERIVATIVES.	VERSIO.	SIGNIFICATION.
אָהַב		*Dilexit.*	He loved.
—	אֵהָב	*Diligam.*	I will love.
—	אֱהַב	*Dilige.*	Love thou.
—	אֹהֵב	*Diligens.*	Loving.
—	אֲהֵבָהּ	*Amavit eam.*	He loved her.
—	אַהֲבָה	*Dilectio, amor.*	Love.
—	אֱהָבֶהָ	*Dilige eam.*	Love her.
—	אָהֲבוּ	*Dilexerunt.*	They loved.
—	אֲהֵבוֹ	*Dilixit eum.*	He loved him.
—	אֶהֱבוּ אֱהָבוּ	*Diligite.*	Love ye.
—	אֲהֵבוּךְ	*Dilexerunt te.*	They loved thee.
—	אֲהֵבוּם	*Dilexerunt eos.*	They loved them.
—	אֹהֲבֵי	*Amantes, amatores.*	The lovers.
—	אֹהֲבַי	*Amantes me.*	My lovers.
—	אֹהֲבִי	*Amicus meus.*	My friend.
—	[illegible]	*Amantes eam.*	Her lovers.

ROOTS.	DERIVATIVES.	VERSIO.	SIGNIFICATION.
אהב	אֹהֲבָיו	*Amantes eum.*	His lovers.
—	אֹהֲבֶיךָ־בָיִךְ	*Amantes te.*	Thy lovers.
—	אֹהֲבִים	*Amantes.*	Lovers.
—	אֳהָבִים	*Amòres, amatores.*	Loves, lovers.
—	אֲהֵבְךָ	*Dilexit te.*	He loved thee.
—	אֹהַבְךָ	*Amicus tuus.*	Thy friend.
—	אֹהֲבֵם	*Diligam eos.*	I will love them.
—	אֹהֶבֶת	*Amans.*	Loving.
—	אֲהֻבַת	*Dilecta.*	Beloved.
—	אַהֲבַת	*Amor.*	The love.
—	אָהַבְתָּ־תְּ	*Dilexisti.*	Thou didst love.
—	אֲהֵבַתְהוּ	*Dilexit eum.*	He loved him.
—	אַהֲבָתִי	*Amor meus.*	My love.
—	אָהַבְתִּי	*Dilexi.*	I loved.
—	אֹהַבְתִּי	*Amans.*	Loving.
—	אֲהַבְתִּיךָ־ךְ	*Dilexi te.*	I have loved thee.
—	אַהֲבָתְךָ	*Amor tuus.*	Thy love.
—	אֲהֵבָתֶךָ	*Amavit te.*	He loved thee.
—	אֲהַבְתֶּם	*Dilexistis.*	Ye have loved.
—	אַהֲבָתָם	*Amor eorum.*	Their love.
—	אֲהַבְתָּנוּ	*Dilexisti nos.*	Thou hast loved us.
—	אֲהַבְתָּנִי	*Dilexisti me.*	Thou hast loved me.
הגה	אֶהְגֶּה	*Meditabor.*	I will meditate.
	אֹהַד	*Ohad.*	Ohad, N. M.
	אֲהָהּ	*Ah! væ!*	Ah! alas!
אהה	אַהֲוָא	*Ahava.*	Ahava, N. R.
	אֲהוּבָה	*Dilecta.*	One beloved.
אהב	אֵהוּד	*Ehud.*	Ehud, N. M.
	אֲהוֹדֶנּוּ	*Celebrabo eum.*	I will praise him.
ידה	אֲהוֹדְעֶנָּה	*Indicabo ei.*	I will make known to him.
היה	אֱהִי אֶהְיֶה	*Ero.*	I will be.
אהל			
—	אֹהֶל	*Tentorium.*	A tabernacle, tent.
	אֹהֶל	*Ohel.*	Ohel, N. M.
	אָהֳלָה	*Aholah.*	Aholah, N. Fig.
אהל	אָהֳלֹה־לוֹ	*Tentorium ejus.*	His tent.
—	אָהֳלִי	*Tentorium meum.*	My tabernacle.

ROOTS.	DERIVATIVES.	VERSIO.	SIGNIFICATION.
אהל	אָהֳלִי	*Tentoria mea.*	**My tents.**
—	אָהֳלֵי	*Tentoria.*	**The tents.**
	אָהֳלִיאָב	*Aholiab.*	**Aholiab, N. M.**
	אָהֳלִיבָה	*Aholibah.*	**Aholibah, N. Fig.**
	אָהֳלִיבָמָה	*Aholibamah.*	**Aholibamah, N. W.**
אהל	אָהֳלֵיהֶם	*Tentoria eorum.*	**Their tents.**
—	אֹהָלֶיךָ	*Tentoria tua.*	**Thy tents.**
—	אָהֳלֵיכֶם	*Tentoria vestra.*	**Your tents.**
—	אֹהָלִים	*Tentoria.*	**Tents.**
—	אֲהָלִים	*Aloë.*	**Aloes.**
—	אָהָלְךָ-לֶךָ	*Tentorium tuum.*	**Thy tabernacle.**
הלך	אֶהֱלֹךְ אֲהַלֵּךְ	*Ibo.*	**I will go.**
הלל	אֲהַלֵּל-לְלָה	*Laudabo.*	**I will praise.**
—	אֲהַלְלֶךָּ	*Laudabo te.*	**I will praise thee.**
—	אֲהַלְלֶנּוּ	*Laudabo eum.*	**I will praise him.**
הפך	אֶהְפֹּךְ	*Convertam.*	**I will turn.**
הרג	אֶהֱרוֹג-רֹג	*Interficiam.*	**I will slay.**
	אַהֲרֹן	*Aharon.*	**Aaron, N. M.**
הרס	אֶהֱרֹס-רוֹס	*Diruam.*	**I will pull down.**
	או		
אוב			
אוה	אוֹ	*Vel, si, sed.*	**Or, if, but.**
	אוּאֵל	*Uel.*	**Uel, N. M.**
אוב	אוֹב	*Pytho.*	**A false prophet.**
אבד	אוֹבֵד	*Periens.*	**Perishing,**
	אוֹבִיל	*Obil.*	**Obil, N, M.**
יבל	אוֹבִילֵם	*Reducam eos.*	**I will lead them back.**
יבש	אוֹבִישׁ	*Arefaciam.*	**I will dry up.**
יבל	אוּבַל	*Flumen.*	**The river.**
—	אוּבָל	*Deferar.*	**I shall be brought back.**
אוד			
—	אוּד	*Torris.*	**A firebrand.**
ידה	אוֹדֶה	*Laudabo.*	**I will praise, celebrate.**
ידע	אוֹדִיעַ-ָה	*Scire faciam.*	**I will make to know.**
—	אוֹדִיעֲךָ	*Indicabo tibi.*	**I will make thee to know.**
—	אוֹדִיעֵם	*Ostendam eis.*	**I will cause them to know.**

ROOTS.	DERIVATIVES.	VERSIO.	SIGNIFICATION.
ידה	אוֹדְךָ־ךָ	*Celebrabo te.*	I will give thanks unto thee.
—	אוֹדֶנּוּ	*Celebrabo eum.*	I shall praise him.
אוד	אוֹדֹת	*Propter.*	Because of.
אוה			
—	אִוָּה	*Desideravit.*	He desired.
אהב	אוֹהֵב	*Diligens.*	Loving.
	אוּזַי	*Uzai.*	Uzai, N. M.
	אוּזָל	*Uzal.*	Uzal, N. M.
אוח			
יחל	אוֹחִיל־לָה	*Expectabo.*	I will hope.
חול	אוֹחִיל־לָה	*Dolebo.*	I shall grieve.
אטם	אוֹטֵם	*Occludens.*	He that shutteth.
אוי			
—	אוֹי	*Væ.*	Alas!
	אֱוִי	*Evi!*	Evi, N. M.
איב	אוֹיֵב	*Inimicus.*	An enemy.
—	אוֹיְבוֹ	*Inimicus ejus.*	His enemy.
	אוֹיְבַרַי	*Inimici mei.*	Mine enemies.
—	אוֹיְבִי	*Inimicus meus.*	Mine enemy.
—	אוֹיְבֵי	*Inimici.*	The enemies.
—	אוֹיְבֶיהָ	*Inimici ejus.*	Her enemies.
—	אוֹיְבֵיהֶם	*Inimici eorum.*	Their enemies.
—	אוֹיְבָיו	*Inimici ejus.*	His enemies.
—	אוֹיְבֶיךָ־בַיִךְ	*Inimici tui.*	Thine enemies.
—	אוֹיְבֵיכֶם	*Inimici vestri.*	Your enemies.
—	אוֹיְבִים	*Inimici.*	Enemies.
—	אוֹיְבֵינוּ	*Inimici nostri.*	Our enemies.
—	אוֹיִבְךָ אוֹיְבֶךָ	*Inimicus tuus.*	Thine enemy.
—	אוֹיְבֵנוּ	*Inimicus noster.*	Our enemy.
—	אוֹיַבְתִּי	*Inimica mea.*	O mine enemy.
אוי	אוֹיָה	*Heu! væ!*	Wo! alas!
אול			
—	אֱוִיל	*Stultus.*	fool.
	אֱוִיל מְרֹדַךְ	*Evil-merodach.*	Evil-merodach, N. M.
אול	אֱוִילִים	*Stulti.*	Fools.
אוה	אִוִּיתִיהָ	*Desideravi eam.*	I have desired her.
—	אִוִּיתִךְ	*Desideravi te.*	I have desired thee.

ROOTS.	DERIVATIVES.	VERSIO.	SIGNIFICATION.
יכח	אוֹכִיחַ	*Arguam.*	I will reprove, argue.
—	אוֹכִיחֲךָ	*Arguam te.*	I will reprove thee.
אכל	אוֹכִיל	*Cibus.*	Food, nourishment,
—	אוֹכֵל	*Comedens.*	Eating.
יכל	אוּכַל־כָּל	*Potero.*	I shall be able.
אכל	אוֹכֵלָה	*Consumens.*	Devouring.
—	אוֹכְלֶיהָ	*Comedentes eam.*	Those that consume her.
אול			
ילד	אִוָּלֵד	*Nascar.*	I shall be born.
אול	אֱוִלִי	*Stultus.*	Foolish.
—	אוּלַי	*Forte, si, nisi.*	Perhaps, if, unless.
	אוּלַי	*Ulai.*	Ulai, N. R.
ילד	אוֹלִיד	*Parere faciam.*	I will cause to bring forth.
ילך	אוֹלִיךְ	*Ire faciam.*	I will cause to go.
—	אוֹלִיכֵם	*Deducam eos.*	I will cause them to walk.
אול	אֱוִלִים	*Stulti.* [bulum.	Fools.
אלם	אוּלָם	*Sed, attamen, vesti-*	But, a porch.
	אוּלָם	*Ulam.*	Ulam, N. M.
איל	אוּלָם	*Robur eorum.*	Their strength.
אול	אִוֶּלֶת	*Stultitia.*	Foolishness.
	אִוַּלְתּוֹ	*Stultitia ejus.*	His foolishness.
—	אִוַּלְתִּי	*Stultitia mea.*	My foolishness.
	אוֹמָר	*Omar.*	Omar, N. M.
אמר	אוֹמֵר	*Dicens.*	Saying.
—	אוֹמְרָה	*Dicam.*	I will say.
—	אוֹמְרִים	*Dicentes.*	They that speak.
און			
—	אָוֶן	*Iniquitas.*	Iniquity,
	אָוֶן	*Aven.*	Aven, N. P.
	אוֹן	*On.*	On, N. M. P. or I.
און	אוֹן	*Substantia, robur.*	Substance, strength.
—	אוֹנוֹ	*Iniquitas, vanitas, potentia ejus.*	His iniquity, vanity, power.
—	אוֹנוֹ	*Robur ejus.*	His strength.
	אוֹנוֹ	*Ono.*	Ono, N. P.
און	אוֹנִי	*Robur meum.*	My strength.
—	אוֹנִים	*Vires, divitiæ.*	Strength, riches.

ROOTS.	DERIVATIVES.	VERSIO.	SIGNIFICATION.
אנה	אוֹנִים	*Lugentes.*	Mourners.
און	אוֹנְךָ	*Iniquitas tua.*	Thine iniquity.
—	אוֹנָם	*Robur, iniquitas eorum.*	Their strength, iniquity.
	אוֹנָם	*Onam.*	Onam, N. M.
	אוֹנָן	*Onan.*	Onan, N. M.
יסף	אוֹסִיף אוֹסַף	*Addam.*	I will add.
יעד	אִוָּעֵד	*Conveniam.*	I will meet.
	אוּפָז	*Uphaz.*	Uphaz, N. P.
	אוֹפִיר אוֹפִירָה	*Ophir.*	Ophir, N. M. P.
אפן	אוֹפָן־פַּן	*Rota.*	A wheel.
—	אוֹפַנֵּי אוֹפַנִּים	*Rotæ.*	Wheels.
—	אוֹפַנֵּיהֶם	*Rotæ eorum.*	Their wheels.
אוץ		*Urgit, festinavit.*	He urged, made haste.
יצא	אוֹצִיא אוֹצִיאָה	*Educam.*	I will bring forth.
אצר	אוֹצָר אוֹצַר	*Thesaurus.*	A treasure.
—	אוֹצָרוֹ	*Thesaurus ejus.*	His treasure.
—	אוֹצָרוֹת אוֹצָרֹת	*Thesauri.*	The treasures.
—	אוֹצְרוֹתֶיךָ	*Thesauri tui.*	Thy treasures.
—	אוֹצְרוֹתָם	*Thesauri eorum.*	Their treasures.
אצר	אוֹצְרֹתֶיהָ	*Thesauri ejus.*	Her treasures.
יקר	אוֹקִיר	*Pretiosum faciam.*	I will make precious.
אור		*Luxit.*	He shined.
—	אוֹר אוֹרָה	*Lux, lumen.*	Light.
	אוּר	*Ur.*	Ur, N. M. P.
ארב	אוֹרֵב	*Insidians.*	Lying in wait.
ארג	אוֹרְגִים	*Textores.*	Weavers.
אור	אוֹרָה	*Lux.*	Light.
ירה	אוֹרֶה	*Jaciam.*	I will shoot.
אור	אוֹרֵהוּ אוֹרוֹ	*Lux ejus.*	His light.
ארר	אוֹרוּ	*Maledicite.*	Curse ye,
	אוּרִי	*Uri.*	Uri. N. M.
אור	אוֹרִי	*Lux mea.*	My light.
	אוּרִיאֵל	*Uriel.*	Uriel, N. M.
ירד	אוֹרִידְךָ	*Dejiciam te.*	I will bring thee down.
—	אוֹרִידֵם	*Deducam eos.*	I will bring them down.
	אוּרִיָּה־יָהוּ	*Uriiah-hu.*	Urijah-hu, N. M.
אור	אוֹרִים	*Lumina.*	Lights.

ROOTS.	DERIVATIVES.	VERSIO.	SIGNIFICATION.
ירש	אוֹרִישׁ	*Ejiciam.*	I will cast out.
——	אוֹרִישֵׁם	*Expellam eos.*	I will drive them out.
אור	אוֹרְךָ אוֹרֶךָ	*Lux tua.*	Thy light.
——	אוֹרָם	*Lux eorum.*	Their light.
ירש	אִוָּרֵשׁ	*Pauper fiam.*	I shall be poor.
אור	אוֹרֹת אוֹרוֹת	*Olerā.*	Herbs.
ישב	אוֹשִׁיבְךָ	*Habitare faciam te.*	I will make thee to dwell.
ישע	אוֹשִׁיעַ	*Salvabo.*	I will save.
——	אוֹשִׁיעֶךָ	*Salvabo te.*	I shall save thee.
——	אוֹשִׁיעֵם	*Salvabo eos.*	I will save them.
——	אִוָּשֵׁעַ	*Salvabor.*	I shall be saved.
אות			
——	אוֹת	*Signum, tam nudum quam prodigiosum; aliam rem, præteritam præsentem aut futuram, indicans.*	A sign, mark, token monument, memorial, symbol, miracle.
אוה	אַוַּת	*Desiderium.*	The desire.
——	אִוְּתָה	*Expetit.*	She desireth.
את	אוֹתָהּ	*Eam, illam.*	Her.
——	אוֹתְהֶם אוֹתְהֶן	*Eos, illos.*	Them.
——	אוֹתוֹ	*Eum, illum, hunc.*	Him.
——	אוֹתִי	*Me.*	Me.
אוה	אִוִּתִיהָ	*Expetivi eam.*	I have desired her.
יתר	אוֹתִיר	*Relinquam.*	I will leave.
את	אוֹתְךָ־תָךְ	*Te.*	Thee.
——	אוֹתְכֶם	*Vos.* [*kos.*	You.
——	אוֹתָם־נָה	*Eos, illos, seipsos,*	Them, themselves, these.
——	אוֹתָנוּ	*Nos.*	We.
אות	אוֹתֹת	*Signa.*	Signs.
——	אוֹתֹתָם	*Signa eorum.*	Their signs.
	אז		
אז			
——	אָז	*Tunc, statim, insuper, nam, ideo, &c.*	Then, immediately, moreover, for, therefore, as, but, &c.

ROOTS.	DERIVATIVES.	VERSIO.	SIGNIFICATION.
זבח	אֶזְבְּחָה אֶזְבַּח	*Sacrificabo.*	I will sacrifice.
—	אֶזְבְּחָה	*Sacrificabo.*	I will sacrifice.
	אֶזְבָּי	*Ezbai.*	Ezbai, N. M.
אזד	אֲזָדָא	*Abiit, exiit.*	He is gone, gone away.
אזא	אֲזֵה	*Accensa.*	Hot.
אזב	אֵזוֹב	*Hyssopum.*	Hyssop.
אזר	אֵזוֹר	*Cingulum.*	A girdle.
—	אָזוּר	*Accinctus.*	Girded.
אז	אֱזַי	*Tunc.*	Then.
אזן	אָזִין	*Auscultavi.*	I gave ear.
זכר	אַזְכִּיר	*Memorabo.*	I will make mention.
—	אַזְכִּירָה	*Commemorabo.*	I will make to be remember- [ed.
—	אֶזְכֹּר־כֹּר	*Recordabor.*	I will remember.
—	אֶזְכְּרָה	*Recordabor.*	I will remember.
—	אֶזְכְּרֵךְ	*Recordabor tui.*	I will remember thee.
—	אֶזְכְּרֵכִי	*Recordabor tui.*	I will remember thee.
—	אֶזְכְּרֶנּוּ	*Recordabor illius.*	I shall remember him.
—	אַזְכָּרָתָהּ	*Suffimentum, odoramentum ejus.*	Its memorial, scent.
	אֶזֶל	*Ezel.*	Ezel, N. P.
אָזַל		*Profectus est, abiit, defecit, evanuit.*	He is gone, gone away, spent, failed.
—	אָזַל	*Abiit.*	He went away.
—	אֱזֶל	*Abi, perge.*	Go.
—	אָזְלוּ אָזְלוּ	*Abierunt, defecerunt*	They are gone, failed.
—	אֲזַלְנָא	*Ivimus.*	We went.
זמר	אָזְלַת	*Abiit.*	It is gone.
—	אֲזַמֵּר	*Psallam.*	I will sing praises.
—	אֲזַמְּרָה־מְּרָה	*Cantabo.*	I will sing praise.
—	אֲזַמֶּרְךָ־מֶּרְךָּ	*Canam te.*	I will praise thee.
אָזַן		*Auscultavit, aures præbuit, attendit, advertit.*	He hearkened, gave ear, attended, gave heed.
—	אֹזֶן	*Auris.*	An ear.
אזן	אֻזֵּן שֶׁאֱרָה	*Uzen-seerah.*	Uzzen-sherah, N. P.
	אָזְנוֹ	*Auris ejus.*	His ear.
	אַזְנוֹת תָּבוֹר	*Aznot-tabor.*	Aznoth-tabor, N. P.

ROOTS.	DERIVATIVES.	VERSIO.	SIGNIFICATION.
אזן	אָזְנֵי־נַי	*Aures meæ.*	My ears.
—	אָזְנִי	*Auris mea.*	My ear.
	אָזְנִי	*Ozni.*	Ozni, N. M. N.
	אֲזַנְיָה	*Azaniah.*	Azaniah, N. M.
אזן	אָזְנֵיהֶם	*Aures eorum.*	Their ears.
—	אָזְנָיו	*Aures ejus.*	His ears.
—	אָזְנֶיךָ אָזְנְךָ	*Aures tuæ.*	Thy ears.
—	אָזְנַיִם־נַיִם	*Aures.*	Ears.
—	אָזְנְךָ־נְךָ־נֶךָ	*Aures tuæ.*	Thy ears.
זין	אֲזֵנֶךָ	*Arma tua.*	Thy weapons.
אזן	אָזְנֵכֶם	*Aures vestræ.*	Your ears.
—	אָזְנָם	*Aures eorum.*	Their ears.
זעם	אֶזְעֹם	*Detestabor.*	I shall defy, abhor.
זעק	אֶזְעַק־עָק	*Clamabo.*	I will cry. [passed, boun
אָזַר		*Cinxit, accinxit.*	He girded, girded up, co
	אֱזָר	*Accinge.*	Gird up.
—			
זרה	אֱזָרֶה	*Dispergam.*	I will scatter.
אזר	אָזְרוּ	*Accincti sunt.*	They are girded.
	אֶזְרָחִי	*Ezrachites.*	Ezrahite, N. F.
זרע	אֶזְרָעָה	*Seram.*	I will sow.

אח

ROOTS.	DERIVATIVES.	VERSIO.	SIGNIFICATION.
אחה	אָח	*Heu.*	Alas!
—	אָח	*Frater, propinquus.*	A brother, a near relative.
	אַחְאָב	*Achab.*	Ahab.
חבר	אַחְבִּירָה	*Congeram.*	I will heap up.
חבל	אֶחְבֹּל	*Destruam, offendam.*	I will offend.
	אַחְבָּן	*Achban.*	Ahban, N. M.
חבש	אֶחֱבשׁ	*Alligabo.*	I will bind up.
—	אֶחְבְּשָׁה	*Sternam.*	I will saddle.
אחד			
—	אֶחָד אַחַד	*Unus a, um; alter, quidam, iidem, unusquisque, primus.*	A, one, another, any one certain, the same, ea every, first.
—	אֲחָדִים	*Iidem, aliquot, pauci*	The same, some, a few.
חדל	אֶחְדָּל	*Cessabo.*	I will cease.

ROOTS.	DERIVATIVES.	VERSIO.	SIGNIFICATION.
אחה			
—	אָחוּ	*Ulva, pratum.*	Water flag, a meadow.
חוה	אֲחַוְּא־־וֶּה	*Indicabo.*	I will shew.
	אֵחוּד	*Echud.*	Ehud, N. M.
חוד	אָחוּדָה	*Proponam.*	I will put forth.
אחז	אָחוּז	*Tentus.*	Taken.
—	אֲחוּזֵי־־זִים	*Infixi, comprehensi.*	Fastened, held.
	אֲחוֹחַ	*Achoach.*	Ahoah, N. M.
	אֲחוֹחִי	*Achochites.*	Ahohite, N. F.
חוה	אֲחַוְּךָ	*Indicabo tibi.*	I will shew thee.
	אֲחוּמַי	*Achumi.*	Ahumi, N. M.
חוס	אָחוּס	*Parcam.*	I will spare.
אחר	אָחוֹר	*Retro, a tergo.*	Backward, behind.
אחה	אָחוֹת אֲחוֹת	*Soror.*	A sister, the sister.
—	אֲחוֹתָהּ	*Soror ejus.*	Her sister.
—	אַחוֹתַי	*Sorores meæ.*	My sisters.
—	אֲחוֹתִי	*Soror mea.*	My sister.
—	אֲחוֹתַיִךְ	*Sorores tuæ.*	Thy sisters.
—	אֲחוֹתְךָ־תֵךְ	*Soror tua.*	Thy sister.
—	אֲחוֹתָם	*Soror eorum.*	Their sister.
—	אֲחֹתֵנוּ	*Soror nostra.*	Our Sister.
אָחָז		*Cepit, prehendit, invasit, apprehendit, tenuit, retinuit, possedit, adhæsit.*	He took, caught, seized, laid hold of, held, held fast, possessed, was fastened to.
	אָחָז	*Achaz.*	Ahaz, N. M.
חזה	אָחַז	*Videbo.*	I will behold.
אחז	אֱחֹז	*Apprehendere.*	To apprehend.
—	אָחֻז	*Captus.*	Taken.
—	אֹחֵז	*Tenens.*	Holding.
חזה	אֶחֱזֶה	*Videbo.*	I shall see.
אחז	אָחֲזָה	*Apprehendit.*	She laid hold.
—	אֲחֻזַּת	*Possessio.*	A possession.
—	אֹחֲזָה	*Apprehendam.*	I will take hold.
—	אָחֲזוּ	*Apprehenderunt.*	They laid hold of, seized.
—	אֶחֱזוּ	*Capite.*	Take ye.
—	אֲחָזוּנִי	*Apprehenderunt me.*	They have taken hold of me.

ROOTS.	DERIVATIVES.	VERSIO.	SIGNIFICATION.
	אַחְזַי	*Achzai.*	Ahasai, N. M.
	אֲחַזְיָה־הוּ	*Achaziah.*	Ahaziah, N. M.
	אֲחֻזָּם	*Achuzam.*	Ahuzam, N. M.
אחז	אֲחָזֻנִי	*Apprehendit me.*	He hath seized me.
חזק	אֲחַזֵּק	*Indurabo, roborabo.*	I will harden, strengthen.
—	אֲחַזְּקֶנּוּ	*Confirmabo eum.*	I will strengthen him.
	אֲחֻזַּת	*Possessio, hæreditas.*	The possession, inheritance.
אחז	אָחַזְתָּ	*Tenuisti.*	Thou holdedst.
—	אֹחֶזֶת	*Tenens.*	Holding.
	אֲחֻזַּת	*Achuzzath.*	Ahuzzath. N. M.
אחז	אֲחָזַתָּה	*Tenuit eam.*	It hath taken her.
—	אֲחֻזָּתוֹ	*Possessio ejus.*	His possession.
—	אֲחַזְתִּיו	*Apprehendi eum.*	I held him.
—	אֲחֻזַּתְכֶם	*Possessio vestra.*	Your possession.
—	אֲחֻזָּתָם	*Possessio eorum.*	Their possession.
—	אֲחָזָתַם	*Apprehendit eos.*	Took hold upon them.
—	אֲחָזַתְנִי	*Apprehendit me.*	Hath taken hold upon me.
חטא	אֶחֱטָא	*Peccabo.*	I will sin.
	אֲחִטוּב	*Achitub.*	Ahitub.
חטם	אֶחֱטָם	*Cohibebo.*	I will restrain.
חטא	אֲחַטֶּנָּה	*Expiabo illud.*	I will atone for it.
אחה	אֶחָי אַחַי אַחֵי אֲחֵי	*Fratres, fratres mei.*	The brethren, my brethren.
—	אָחִי	*Frater meus.*	My brother.
—	אֲחִי	*Frater : Achi.*	The brother : Ahi, N. M.
	אֵחִי	*Echi.*	Ehi, N. M.
	אֲחִיאָם	*Achiam.*	Ahiam, N. M.
חוד	אֲחִידָן	*Ænigmata.*	Hard sentences.
חיה	אֲחַיֶּה	*In vita conservabo.*	I shall keep alive.
	אֲחִיָּה־הוּ	*Achiiah.*	Ahijah, N. M.
חיה	אֶחְיֶה	*Vivam.*	I shall live, recover.
אחה	אַחֶיהָ	*Fratres ejus.*	Her brethren.
—	אָחִיהָ	*Frater ejus.*	Her brother.
—	אָחִיהוּ	*Frater ejus.*	His brother.
	אֲחִיהוּד	*Achihud.*	Ahihud, N. M.
אחה	אֲחִיהֶם	*Frater eorum.*	Their brother.
—	אֲחֵיהֶם	*Fratres eorum.*	Their brethren.
—	אֶחָיו	*Fratres ejus.*	His brethren.

ROOTS.	DERIVATIVES.	VERSIO.	SIGNIFICATION.
אחה	אָחִיו	*Frater ejus.*	His brother.
	אֲחִיוֹ	*Achio.*	Ahio, N. M.
אחה	אַחְיוֹתֵךְ	*Sorores tuæ.*	Thy sisters.
	אֲחִיהֻד	*Achichud.*	Ahihud, N. M.
	אֲחִיטוּב	*Achitub.*	Ahitub, N. M.
אחה	אַחֶיךָ אַחַיִךְ	*Fratres tui.*	Thy brethren.
—	אָחִיךָ אָחִיךְ	*Frater tuus.*	Thy brother.
—	אֲחֵיכֶם	*Fratres vestri.*	Your brethren.
—	אֲחִיכֶם	*Frater vester.*	Your brother.
יחל	אֲחִילָה	*Expectabo.*	I will wait.
	אֲחִילוּד	*Achilud.*	Ahilud, N. M.
אוח	אֹחִים	*Animalia terribilia.*	Terrible animals.
אחה	אַחִים	*Fratres.*	Brethren.
	אֲחִימוֹת	*Achimoth.*	Ahimoth, N. M.
	אֲחִימֶלֶךְ	*Achimelech,*	Ahimelech, N. M.
	אֲחִימָן־מַן	*Achiman.*	Ahiman, N. M.
	אֲחִימַעַץ־מַעַץ	*Achimaats.*	Ahimaaz, N. M.
	אַחְיָן	*Achian.*	Ahian, N. M.
	אֲחִינָדָב	*Achinadab.*	Ahinadab, N. M.
אחה	אַחֵינוּ	*Fratres nostri.*	Our brethren.
—	אָחִינוּ	*Frater noster.*	Our brother.
	אֲחִינֹעַם	*Achinoam.*	Ahinoam, N. M.
	אֲחִיסָמָךְ	*Achisamach.*	Ahisamach, N. M.
	אֲחִיעֶזֶר	*Achihezer.*	Ahiezer, N. M.
	אֲחִיקָם	*Achicam.*	Ahikam, N. M.
	אֲחִירָם	*Achiram.*	Ahiram, N. M.
	אֲחִירָמִי	*Achiramitæ.*	Ahiramites, N. F.
	אֲחִירַע	*Achira.*	Ahira, N. M.
חוש	אָחִישָׁה	*Accelerabo.*	I will hasten.
	אֲחִישָׁחַר	*Achisachar.*	Ahishahar, N. M.
חשו	אֲחִישֶׁנָּה	*Accelerabo illud.*	I will hasten it.
	אֲחִישָׁר	*Achisar.*	Ahishar, N. M.
אחה	אַחְיֹתֵיהֶם	*Sorores eorum.*	Their sisters.
—	אַחְיֹתָיו	*Sorores ejus.*	His sisters.
	אֲחִיתֹפֶל	*Achitophel.*	Ahitophel, N. M.
חכם	אֶחְכָּמָה	*Sapiens ero.*	I shall be wise.
חלל	אָחֵל	*Incipiam.*	I will begin.

ROOTS.	DERIVATIVES.	VERSIO.	SIGNIFICATION.
חלל	אַחֵל	*Profanabo.*	I will profane.
	אַחְלָב	*Achlab.*	Ahalab, N. P.
אחל	אַחֲלֵי־־לֵי	*Utinam.*	O that, I wish.
	אַחְלַי	*Achlai.*	Ahlai, N. M. W.
חלל	אֲחַלֵּל	*Violabo.*	I will break.
חלץ	אֲחַלְּצֵהוּ	*Eruam eum.*	I will deliver him.
—	אֲחַלֶּצְךָ	*Eripiam te.*	I will deliver thee.
חלק	אֲחַלֵּק־־לְּקָה	*Dividam.*	I will divide.
—	אֲחַלְּקֵם	*Dividam eos.*	I will divide them.
חמל	אֶחְמוֹל־־מֹל	*Clementia utar.*	I will pity.
	אַחְמְתָא	*Achmetha.*	Ahmetha, N. P.
חנן	אָחֹן	*Miserebor.*	I will be merciful.
	אֲחַסְבַּי	*Achashbai.*	Ahashbai, N. M.
חסה	אֶחֱסֶה	*Sperabo.*	I will trust.
חסר	אֶחְסָר	*Deficiam.*	I shall want.
חפץ	אֶחְפָּץ־־פֹּץ	*Volam.*	I will desire.
חפש	אֶחַפֵּשׂ	*Scrutabor.*	I will search.
חקר	אֶחְקֹר	*Explorabo.*	I will investigate.
—	אֶחְקְרֵהוּ	*Explorabo eum.*	I will investigate it.
	אַחֵר	*Acher.* [*quam.*	Aher, N. M.
אחר	אַחַר	*Post, postea, post-*	After, afterwards, after that.
—	אַחֵר	*Alius, alter, alienus.*	Another.
—	אֵחַר	*Tardavit.*	He delayed.
—	אֵחֲרוּ	*Tardaverunt.*	They delayed.
—	אַחֲרוֹן	*Posterior, postremus*	The last.
	אַחֲרוֹנִים	*Posteriores, postre-*	Last.
—	אֲחֵרוֹת	*Aliæ.* [*mi, ultimi.*	Others.
	אַחְרַח	*Achrach.*	Aharah, N. M.
	אֲחַרְחֵל	*Acharchel.*	Aharhel, N. M.
	אַחֲרָי־־רַי	*Post me.*	After me.
—	אַחֲרֵי	*Post, postea.*	After, afterwards.
—	אָחוֹר	*Pars posterior.*	The back part.
—	אֲחֹרָי	*Posteriora mea.*	My back parts.
—	אֲחֵרִי	*Alius.*	Another. [*waste.*
חרב	אַחֲרִיב	*Arefaciam, desolabo*	I will dry up, I will make
אחר	אַחֲרֶיהָ	*Post eam, extremum*	After her, her last end.
		ejus.	

ROOTS.	DERIVATIVES.	VERSIO.	SIGNIFICATION.
ארח	אַחֲרֵיהֶם	*Post eos.* [*terga.*	After them.
—	אָחֳרֵיהֶם	*Posteriora, eorum*	Their backs.
—	אַחֲרֵיהֶן־הֹן	*Post eas.*	After them.
—	אַחֲרָיו	*Post eum.*	After him.
—	אַחֲרֶיךָ־רַיִךְ	*Post te.*	After thee.
—	אַחֲרֵיכֶם	*Post vos.*	After you.
—	אֲחֵרִים־רִין	*Alii, alieni.*	Others.
—	אָחֳרֵין	*Demum.*	At the last.
—	אַחֲרֵינוּ	*Post nos.*	After us.
חרש	אַחֲרִישׁ	*Tacebo, reticebo.*	I will hold my peace.
אחר	אַחֲרִית	*Finis, extremum.*	The end, the last.
—	אַחֲרִיתָהּ	*Extremum ejus.*	Her last end.
—	אַחֲרִיתוֹ	*In postremo; finis, posteritas ejus.*	At the last, his latter end, his posterity.
אחר	אַחֲרִיתִי	*Finis meus.*	My last end.
—	אַחֲרִיתָם־תָן	*Finis eorum.*	Their end.
—	אַחֲרִיתֵנוּ	*Finis noster.*	Our end.
—	אָחֳרָן	*Alius, alter.*	Other.
—	אַחֲרֹנִים	*Ultimi, postremi, posteriores.*	The last, posterity.
—	אֲחֹרַנִּית	*Retrorsum.*	Backward.
חרש	אַחֲרִשׁ	*Tacebo.*	I shall be silent.
אחר	אַחֶרֶת	*Alter, alienus.*	Another, other, strange.
אחש			
—	אֲחַשְׁדַּרְפְּנֵי־נַיָּא	*Satrapæ, principes;* dignitas inter Persas.	The princes; *officers or nobles among the Persians.*
חשה	אֶחֱשֶׁה	*Tacebo.*	I will hold my peace.
	אֲחַשְׁוֵרוֹשׁ	*Achasueros.*	Ahasuerus, N. M.
חשך	אֶחֱשֹׂךְ	*Cohibebo.*	I will restrain.
	אֲחַשְׁתָּרִי	*Achastari.*	Haahastari, N. M.
אחד	אַחַת אֶחָת	*Una, alia, eadem, quædam, prima, singula, semel.*	A, an, one, another, the same, any, first, each, once.
נחת	אֲחַת	*Defer.*	Carry.
אחה	אֲחֹתָהּ	*Soror ejus.*	Her sister.
חתת	אֵחַתָּה	*Terrebor, pavebo.*	I shall be terrified, dismayed.

ROOTS.	DERIVATIVES.	VERSIO.	SIGNIFICATION.
אחה	אֲחֹתוֹ	*Soror ejus.*	His sister.
—	אֲחֹתִי	*Soror mea.*	My sister.
חתת	אֲחִתְּךָ	*Te consternabo, conteram.*	I will confound, consume thee.
אחה	אֲחֹתָם	*Soror eorum.*	Their sister.
—	אֲחֹתֵנוּ	*Soror nostra.*	Our sister.
	אט		
נטה	אָט	*Declinavit.*	He declined.
אטט	אַט	*Sensim.*	By degrees.
טבע	אֶטְבְּעָה	*Immergar.*	Let me sink.
אטד			
	אָטָד	*Rhamnus.*	A thorn, brier, bramble.
—	אָטָד	*Atad.*	Atad, N. M.
נטה	אַטֶּה	*Inclinabo, extendam.*	I will incline, extend.
טהר	אֲטַהֵר	*Mundabo.*	I will cleanse.
אטן	אֵטוּן	*Filum.*	Fine linen.
נטר	אֶטּוֹר	*Servabo.*	I will keep.
אטט			
טול	אֲטִילְךָ	*Projiciam te.*	I will cast thee forth.
אָטַם		*Obturavit, occlusit.*	He stopped up, closed.
—	אֹטֵם	*Obturans, occludens.*	Stopping, shutting.
—	אֲטֻמִים־מוֹת	*Clausi, clausæ, arctæ*	Closed, shut, narrow.
אטן			
טנף	אֲטַנְּפֵם	*Inquinabo eos.*	I will defile them.
טעם	אֶטְעַם	*Gustabo.*	I will taste.
נטף	אַטִּף	*Stillabo, vaticinabor.*	I will drop, prophesy.
	אָטֵר	*Ater.*	Ater, N. M.
אָטַר		*Obturavit, occlusit.*	He closed, shut up.
	אִטֵּר יַד יְמִינוֹ	*Impos manu dexterâ, ambidexter.*	One who has not the use of his right hand, or who uses both hands alike.
טרף	אֶטְרֹף	*Dilacerabo.*	I will tear in pieces.
	אי		
איה	אֵי	*Ubi, unde, quomodo?*	Where, whence, how?
—	אֵי זֶה	*Ubi, quænam, quo?*	Where, which, whither?
—	אֵי מִזֶּה	*Unde?*	Whence?

ROOTS.	DERIVATIVES.	VERSIO.	SIGNIFICATION.
איה	אִי	*Insula, væ!* secundum quosdam, *non.*	An island, wo! *some understand it to express a negation*, not.
	אִי כָבוֹד	*Ichabod.*	Ichabod, N. M.
אָיַב		*Inimicitias exercuit, inimicatus est, odio habuit, infestavit.*	He has hated, been at enmity with, been an adversary to.
——	אֹיֵב	*Inimicus.*	An enemy.
——	אֵיבָה	*Inimicitia.*	Enmity.
——	אֹיְבוֹ	*Inimicus ejus.*	His enemy.
——	אֹיְבַי־־בַי	*Inimici mei.*	My enemies.
——	אֹיְבֵי	*Inimici.*	The enemies.
——	אֹיְבִי	*Inimicus meus.*	My enemy.
——	אֹיְבֶיהָ	*Inimici ejus.*	Her enemies.
——	אֹיְבֵיהֶם	*Inimici eorum.*	Their enemies.
——	אֹיְבָיו	*Inimici ejus.*	His enemies.
——	אֹיְבֶיךָ־־בַיִךְ	*Inimici tui.*	Thy enemies.
——	אֹיְבֵיכֶם	*Inimici vestri.*	Your enemies.
——	אֹיְבֵינוּ	*Inimici nostri.*	Our enemies.
——	אֹיִבְךָ־־בֵךְ	*Inimicus tuus.*	Thy enemy.
——	אֹיִבְךָ	*Inimicus tuus.*	Thy enemy.
יבש	אִיבָשׁ	*Arescam.*	I shall be withered.
איב	אֵיבַת	*Inimicitia.*	The hatred.
——	אֵיבָתִי	*Inimicitia mea.*	My hatred.
יגע	אִיגָע	*Laborabo.*	I shall labour.
איד			
——	אֵיד	*Vapor, nubes, calamitas, pernicies, exitium, interitus.*	A vapour, cloud, calamity, distress, destruction.
——	אֵידוֹ	*Calamitas ejus.*	His calamity.
——	אֵידִי	*Calamitas mea.*	My calamity.
——	אֵידֶךָ	*Calamitas tua.*	Thy calamity.
——	אֵידָם	*Calamitas ipsorum.*	Their calamity.
איה			
——	אַיָּה	*Vultur.*	A vulture.
	אַיָּה	*Aiah.*	Ajah, N. M.

ROOTS.	DERIVATIVES.	VERSIO.	SIGNIFICATION.
איה	אַיֵּה	*Ubi?*	Where?
—	אַיּוֹ	*Ubi ille?*	Where is he?
	אִיּוֹב	*Job.*	Job, N. M.
אים	אָיֹם	*Terribilis.*	Terrible.
	אִיזֶבֶל	*Jezebel.*	Jezebel, N. W.
יחל	אֲיַחֵל	*Expectabo, sperabo.*	I will expect, will hope.
יטב	אֵיטִיב	*Beneficiam.*	I will do good.
איה	אִיֵּי	*Insulæ.*	The isles, islands.
—	אִיִּים	*Insulæ; bestiæ ululantes*, deserta aut insulas incolentes.	Islands; wild beasts that howl *inhabiting deserts or islands*
איך		[*ubi?*	
—	אֵיךְ	*Quomodo, qualiter,*	How, in what manner, where
איה	אַיֶּכָּה	*Ubi tu?*	Where art thou?
איך	אֵיכָה אֵיכָכָה	*Quomodo?*	How?
איל			
—	אַיָּל	*Cervus.*	A hart, stag.
—	אַיִל	*Aries.*	A ram. [of a building
—	אֵיל	*Postis, limen.*	A post, or any principal pa[rt]
—	אֱיָל	*Virtus, fortitudo.*	Strength, might, power.
—	אַיָּלָה	*Cerva.*	A hind.
—	אֵילָו אֵילָיו	*Postes ejus.*	Its posts.
	אַיָּלוֹן	*Ajalon.*	Ajalon, N. P.
	אֵילוֹן	*Elon.*	Elon, N. M.
איל	אַיָּלוֹת	*Cervæ.*	Hinds.
	אֵילוֹת.	*Eloth.*	Eloth, N. P.
איל	אֱיָלוּתִי	*Fortitudo mea.*	O my strength.
—	אֵילֵי	*Arietes.*	The rams.
ילל	אֲיֵלִיל	*Ejulabo.*	I will howl.
איל	אֵילִים	*Postes, columnæ.*	Posts, pillars.
ילד	אֵילְכָה	*Vadam.*	I will go.
	אֵילִם--לִמָה	*Elim, in Elim.*	Elim, in Elim, N. P.
	אֵילֹן	*Elon.*	Elon, N. M.
אלן	אֵילֹן--לֹנָא--נָה	*Arbor.*	A tree.
	אַיָּלֹנָה	*Ad Ajalon.*	To Ajalon, N. P.
	אֵילַת	*Elath.*	Elath, N. P.

ROOTS.	DERIVATIVES.	VERSIO.	SIGNIFICATION.
איל	אַיֶּלֶת	*Cerva.*	The hind.
איה	אַיָּם	*Ubi ipsi?*	Where are they?
אים		*[bilis.*	
—	אָיֹם	*Terribilis, formida-*	Terrible, formidable.
—	אֵימָה	*Terror.*	The fear.
—	אֲיֻמָּה.	*Terribilis.*	Terrible.
—	אֵימֶיךָ	*Terrores tui.*	Thy terrors.
	אֵימִים אֵימִם	*Emim.*	Emim, N. P.
אים	אֵימַת־־מָתָה	*Terror.*	Fear.
—	אֵימָתִי	*Terror meus.*	My fear.
אים	אֵימַתְכֶם	*Terror vester.*	Your fear.
אין		*[nemo.*	
—	אָיִן־אַיִן־אֵין	*Non, nihil, nullus,*	Not, nothing, none, no one.
אין	אֵינֵימוֹ	*Non ipsi.*	Not they.
—	אֵינְךָ	*Non tu.*	Not thou.
—	אֵינְכֶם	*Non vos.*	Not ye.
—	אֵינָם	*Non ipsi.*	Not they
—	אֵינֶנָּה	*Non ipsa.*	Not she.
—	אֵינֶנּוּ	*Non ipse.*	Not he.
—	אֵינֶנִּי	*Non ego.*	Not I.
ינק	אִינָק	*Sugam.*	I shall suck.
יסר	אַיְסִירֵם	*Eos corripiam.*	I will chastise them.
—	אֲיַסֵּר	*Castigabo.*	I will chastise.
	אִיעֶזֶר	*Iezer.*	Jeezer, N. M.
	אִיעֶזְרִי	*Iezeritæ.*	Jeezerites, N. F.
יעץ	אִיעֲצָה	*Consulam.*	I will counsel, guide.
—	אִיעָצְךָ־־צֵךְ	*Consulam tibi.*	I will give thee counsel.
איף			
—	אֵיפָה	*Epha*, modius.	An Ephah, *a measure*.
—	אֵיפֹה־פוֹא	*Ubinam, hic, nunc.*	Where, here, now.
—	אֵיפַת	*Epha*, modius.	The ephah.
ידא	אִירָא	*Timebo, metuam.*	I shall be afraid.
—	אִירָאֶנּוּ	*Timebo eum. [be eam*	I shall fear him.
ירש	אִירָשֶׁנָּה	*Possidebo, hæredita-*	I shall possess, inherit it.
איש			
	אִישׁ בֹּשֶׁת	*Isboset,*	Ishbosheth, N. M.
	אִישׁ טוֹב	*Istob.*	Ishtob, N. M.

ROOTS.	DERIVATIVES	VERSIO.	SIGNIFICATION.
איש	אִישׁ	*Vir, mas, maritus, homo, unusquisque, quidam, alter, quisquis.*	A man, a male, a husband, man, every one, any, each, another, whosoever.
	אִישָׁהּ	*Vir, maritus ejus.*	Her husband.
	אִישְׁהוֹד	*Ishod.*	Ishod, N. M.
איש	אִישׁוֹ	*Vir suus.*	His man.
——	אִישִׁי	*Vir, maritus meus.*	My husband.
——	אִישִׁים	*Viri.*	Men.
——	אִישֵׁךְ	*Vir tuus.*	Thy husband.
ישן	אִישַׁן	*Dormiam.*	I shall sleep.
ישר	אֲיַשֵּׁר	*Dirigam.*	I will direct.
אית			
——	אִיתוֹהִי	*Est ipsa.*	She, or it is.
——	אִיתַי	*Est, sunt.*	It is, they are.
	אִיתַי	*Ithai.*	Ithai, N. M.
	אִיתִיאֵל	*Ithiel.*	Ithiel, N. M.
אית	אִיתֵיכוֹן	*Vos estis.* [*ero.*	Ye are.
תמם	אֵיתָם	*Perfectus, integer*	I shall be perfect, upright.
	אִיתָמָר	*Ithamar.*	Ithamar, N. M.
	אֵיתָן	*Ethan.*	Ethan, N. M.
אית	אֵיתָן	*Fortis, durus, robustus, validus, asper, horridus, intractabilis, durabilis; vis, robur.*	Strong, rough, untractable, stubborn, hard, lasting; strength, force.
——	אִיתָנָא	*Sumus nos.*	We are.
אך			
——	אַךְ	*Tamen, sed, profecto, certe, saltem, tantum, quidem, etiam.*	Nevertheless, yet, but, surely, truly, at least, only, indeed, also.
כבד	אֲכַבֵּד	*Honorabo.* [*cabor.*	I will honour.
——	אִכָּבְדָה אִכָּבֵד	*Honorabor, glorifi-*	I will be honoured.
——	אֲכַבֶּדְךָ	*Honorabo te.*	I will honour thee.
	אַכַּד	*Achad.*	Accad, N. P.
נכה	אַכֶּה	*Percutiam.*	I will smite.

ROOTS.	DERIVATIVES.	VERSIO.	SIGNIFICATION.
אכל	אָכוֹל	*Comedere.*	To eat.
—	אֱכוֹל	*Comede.*	Eat thou.
כזב	אַכְזָב	*Mendax.*	Lying.
—	אֲכַזֵּב	*Mentiar.*	I shall lie.
—	אַכְזִיב־־בָה	*Achzib.* [*rox.*	Achzib, N. M.
כזר	אַכְזָר	*Crudelis, immitis, fe-*	Cruel, merciless, fierce.
—	אַכְזָרִי	*Crudelis.*	Cruel.
—	אַכְזְרִיּוּת	*Crudelitas.*	Cruelty.
כחד	אֲכַחֵד	*Celabo.*	I shall conceal.
כון	אָכִין־־נָה	*Parabo, stabiliam.*	I will prepare, establish.
נכר	אַכִּיר	*Cognoscam, agnoscam.*	I will discover, acknowledge.
	אָכִישׁ	*Achis.*	Achish, N. M.
נכה	אַכֶּכָּה	*Feriam, cædam te.*	I will smite, slay thee.
	אֻכָל	*Ucal.*	Ucal, N. M.
אָכַל		*Comedit, manducavit, devoravit, consumpsit, evertit, destruxit, cibavit, aluit.*	He ate, ate up, devoured, consumed, overturned, destroyed, fed, nourished.
—	אֱכָל אֱכֹל אָכֹל	*Comedere.*	To eat.
—	אֱכָל אֱכֹל	*Comede.*	Eat thou.
—	אֹכַל	*Comedam.*	I will eat.
—	אֹכֵל	*Comedens.*	Eating.
—	אֹכֶל	*Cibus, esca, præda.*	Food, meat, victuals, prey.
—	אֻכָּל	*Consumptus.*	Consumed.
—	אֶכְלָא	*Cohibebo.*	I will restrain.
—	אֲכֵלָה	*Comedam.*	I will eat.
—	אָכְלָה אָכָלָה	*Consumpsit, voravit.*	She hath consumed, devoured.
—	אֹכְלָה	*Comedam; comedens, consumens, devorans.* [*mere.*	I will eat; eating, consuming, devouring.
—	אֲכָלָה	*Comedere, consu-*	To eat, consume.
	אֲכָלָהוּ	*Comedit, voravit eum.*	He ate, devoured him.
	אֱכָלוּ	*Comedite.*	Eat ye.
—	אֲכָלוּ	*Proclamaverunt, instituerunt.*	They preferred, prosecuted.

ROOTS.	DERIVATIVES.	VERSIO.	SIGNIFICATION.
אכל	אָכְלוּ	*Comederunt, everte-*	They ate, destroyed.
—	אִכְלוּ	*Comedite. [runt.*	Eat ye.
—	אָכְלוּ	*Devoraverunt.*	They devoured.
—	אָכְלוֹ	*Comedere eum, devo-randum eum.*	To consume, devour him.
—	אֻכְּלוּ	*Consumpti sunt.*	They were consumed.
—	אֲכָלוּם	*Comederunt eos. [tes.*	They have devoured them.
—	אֹכְלֵי	*Comedentes, voran-*	Eating, devouring.
—	אִכְלִי	*Comede.*	Devour thou.
—	אֹכְלָיו	*Comedentes eum.*	Eating him.
—	אֹכְלַיִךְ	*Devorantes te. [tes.*	They that devour thee.
—	אֹכְלִים	*Comedentes, vastan-*	Eating, destroying.
—	אֲכָלְךָ	*Te comedere.*	That thou eat.
—	אֲכַלְךָ	*Consumam te.*	I will consume thee.
—	אָכְלְךָ	*Cibus tuus.*	Thy meat, food.
—	אֲכַלְכֵּל	*Alam, sustentabo.*	I will nourish, support.
—	אֲכָלְכֶם	*Comedere vos.*	That ye eat.
—	אָכְלָם	*Esca, cibus eorum.*	Their meat, food.
—	אָכַלְנוּ	*Comedimus. [me.*	We have eaten. [devoured me.
—	אֲכָלָנִי	*Comedit, consumpsit*	It hath eaten up, consumed,
—	אֹכְלַת אֹכֶלֶת	*Comedens.*	Eating.
—	אָכַלְתָּ	*Comedisti.*	Thou hast eaten.
—	אֲכָלַתְהוּ	*Devoravit eum.*	It has devoured him.
—	אָכַלְתִּי	*Comedi.*	I did eat.
—	אֲכָלַתְךְ	*Consumpsit te.*	It has devoured thee.
—	אֲכַלְתֶּם	*Comedistis.*	Ye have eaten.
—	אֲכָלַתְנִי	*Consumpsit me*	It hath eaten me up.
כון	אָכֵן	*Vere, profecto, sed.*	Truly, verily, certainly, but.
כנה	אֲכַנֶּה	*Cognominabo.*	I will give titles of honour.
נכה	אַכֶּנּוּ	*Percutiam eum.*	I will smite him.
כנע	אַכְנִיעַ	*Humiliabo.*	I will bring down.
כנה	אֲכַנְּךָ	*Cognominabo te.*	I will surname thee.
כסה	אֲכַסֶּה	*Operiam.*	I will cover.
—	אֲכַסֶּנּוּ	*Operiam ipsum.*	I will cover him.
כעס	אַכְעִיסֵם	*Irritabo eos.*	I will provoke them to anger.
—	אֶכְעַס	*Irascar.*	I will be angry.
אָכַף		*Incurvavit se.*	He bowed *himself*.

ROOTS.	DERIVATIVES.	VERSIO.	SIGNIFICATION.
כפף	אִכַּף	*Incurvabo* me.	I shall bow *myself*.
כפר	אֲכַפֵּר־־פָּרָה	*Expiabo, placabo.*	I will make an atonement.
אכר	אִכָּר	*Agricola.*	A husbandman.
כרת	אֶכְרוֹת	*Succidam, feriam; fœdus percutiam.*	I will cut down, will strike; will make a covenant.
אכר	אִכָּרֵיכֶם	*Agricolæ vestri.*	Your ploughmen.
—	אִכָּרִים	*Agricolæ.* [am.	Ploughmen.
כרת	אַכְרִית	*Excindam, destru-*	I will cut off, destroy.
—	אֶכְרֹת	*Pangam, paciscar.*	I will make, will covenant.
	אַכְשָׁף	*Achsaph*	Achshaph, N. P.
כתב	אֶכְתֹּב	*Scribam.*	I will write.
—	אֶכְתֲּבֶנָּה	*Scribam illud.*	I will write it.
	אל		
אל			
איל	אֵל	*Deus, fortis, summus*	God, the mighty, supreme.
אלה	אֶל	*A, ad, apud, contra, coram, cum, de, erga, in abl. in accus. inter, juxta, per, pro, prope, secundum, super, versus, usque ad.*	Of, to, at, against, before, with, concerning, toward, in, into, among, by, through, for, near, because of, according to, upon, unto.
אל	אַל	*Ne, nec, non, nihil-um, nequaquam, quo, quorsum.*	No, not, neither, nothing, not at all, whither.
	אֵלָא	*Ela.*	Elah, N. M.
לבן	אַלְבִּין	*Albescam.*	I shall be white.
לבש	אַלְבִּישׁ	*Induam.*	I will clothe.
—	אֶלְבָּשֶׁנָּה	*Induam eam.*	I shall put it on.
אלג			
—	אֶלְגָּבִישׁ	*Grando.*	Hail.
—	אַלְגּוּמִּים	*Algumim, lignum præstantissimum.*	Algum, *trees of a very durable nature.*
יָלַד		*Genuit, generavit, peperit, parturivit*	Begat, generated, brought forth.
ילד	אֵלֵד	*Pariam.*	I shall bear a child.

ROOTS.	DERIVATIVES.	VERSIO.	SIGNIFICATION.
	אֶלְדָּד	*Eldad.*	Eldad, N. M.
	אֶלְדָּעָה	*Eldaa.*	Eldaah, N. M.
אָלָה		*Juravit, adjuravit, maledixit, execratus est, juramento astrinxit sese vel alterum addita imprecatione, ejulavit.*	He has sworn, abjured, re- ed, cursed, bound him or another by an oath w an imprecation annex bewailed
—	אֵלֶּה	*Hi.*	These.
—	אָלֹה	*Jurare, pejerare.*	To swear, forswear.
—	אֵלָה	*Ela.*	Ela, N. M.
אלה	אֱלָה אֱלֹהַּ	*Deus.*	God.
—	אֵלָה	*Quercus.*	An oak.
—	אֱלָהָא	*Deus.*	God.
—	אֱלָהֵהּ	*Deus ejus.*	His God.
—	אֱלָהֲהוֹם אֱלָהֲהוֹן	*Deus eorum.*	Their God.
—	אֱלָהִי	*Deus meus.*	My God.
—	אֱלֹהֵי־־הֵי	*Deus, Dii.*	God, gods.
—	אֱלֹהֵי	*Deus, dii.*	The God, gods.
—	אֱלָהַיָּא	*Dii.*	Gods.
—	אֱלֹהֶיהָ	*Deus, dii ejus.*	Her God, gods.
—	אֱלֹהֵיהֶם־־הֶן	*Deus, dii eorum.*	Their God, gods.
—	אֱלֹהָיו	*Deus, dii ejus.*	His God, gods.
—	אֱלֹהֶיךָ־־הָיִךְ	*Deus tuus.*	Thy God.
—	אֱלֹהֵיכֶם	*Deus vester.*	Your God.
—	אֱלֹהִים	*Deus, dii.*	God, gods.
—	אֱלֹהֵימוֹ	*Deus eorum.*	Their God.
—	אֱלָהִין	*Dii.*	The gods.
—	אֱלֹהֵינוּ	*Deus noster.*	Our God.
—	אֱלָהָךְ	*Deus tuus.*	Thy God.
—	אֱלָהֲכֹם־־כוֹן	*Deus vester.*	Your God.
אל	אֲלֵהֶם־־הֶן	*Ad eos.*	Unto them.
אלה	אֱלָהָנָא אֱלֹהֵנוּ	*Deus noster.*	Our God.
—	אֱלוֹהַּ	*Deus.*	God.
—	אֱלוֹהַי־הַי	*Deus meus.*	My God.
	אֱלוּל	*Elul.*	Elul, N. Mth.

ROOTS.	DERIVATIVES.	VERSIO.	SIGNIFICATION.
	אֵלוֹן	*Allon.*	Allon, N. P.
	אַלּוֹן	*Allon.*	Allon, N. M.
אלה	אַלּוֹן אֵלוֹן	*Quercus.*	Oaks.
—	אַלּוֹנֵי אֵלוֹנֵי	*Quercus.*	The oaks.
—	אַלּוֹנִים	*Quercus.*	Oaks.
אלף	אַלּוּף	*Bos, dux.*	An ox, a leader.
—	אַלּוּפֵי	*Duces, principes.*	The leaders, princes.
—	אַלּוּפִי	*Dux meus.* [*eorum.*	My guide.
—	אַלּוּפֵיהֶם	*Duces, principes*	Their dukes, princes.
—	אַלּוּפֵינוּ	*Boves nostri.*	Our oxen.
	אָלוּשׁ	*Alus.* [*re.*	Alush, N. P.
אלה	אָלוֹת	*Maledictiones; jura-*	The curses; to swear.
	אֶלְזָבָד	*Elzabad.*	Elzabad, N. P.
אלח			
לחם	אֶלְחַם	*Comedam, vescar.*	I will eat, will feed.
	אֶלְחָנָן	*Elchanan.*	Elhanan, N. M.
אל	אֵלַי אֲלֵי	*Ad, erga, contra me.*	To, towards, against me.
איל	אֵלֵי	*Fortes.*	Strong.
אל	אֱלֵי	*Ad, in, juxta.*	To, into, by.
אלה	אֵלִי	*Deus meus.*	My God.
—	אֱלִי	*Ejula, plange.*	Lament, bewail thou.
אול	אֻלַי	*Fortasse.*	Peradventure, perhaps.
	אֱלִיאָב	*Eliab.*	Eliab, N. M.
	אֱלִיאֵל	*Eliel.*	Eliel, N. M.
	אֱלִיאָתָה	*Eliatha.*	Eliathah, N. M.
	אֱלִידָד	*Eliadad.*	Elidad, N. M.
	אֶלְיָדָע	*Eliada.* [*eam.*	Eliada, N. M.
אל	אֵלֶיהָ	*Ad, contra, super*	To, against, upon, her.
	אֵלִיָּה־־הוּ	*Elijah, Eliahu.*	Elijah, N. M.
	אֱלִיהוּ־־הוּא	*Elihu.*	Elihu, N. M.
	אֶלְיְהוֹעֵינַי	*Elihoenai.*	Elihoenai, N. M.
אל	אֲלֵיהֶם־־הֶן	*Ad, contra eos.*	Unto them.
אלה	אֵלֵיהֶם	*Quercus eorum.*	Their oaks.
איל	אֵלֵיהֶמָה	*Postes eorum.*	Their posts.
אל	אֵלָיו	*Ad, contra eum.*	To, against him.
	אֶלְיוֹעֵינַי	*Elioenai.*	Elioenai, N. M.
	אֶלְיַחְבָּא	*Eliachba.*	Eliachba, N. M.

ROOTS.	DERIVATIVES.	VERSIO.	SIGNIFICATION.
	אֱלִיחֹרֶף Elichoreph.		Elichoreph, N. M.
אֵל	אֵלֶיךָ אֵלַיִךְ A, contra, super te.		To, against, upon thee.
	אֲלֵיכֶם Ad vos.		Unto you.
אֱלִיל	אֱלִיל N'ihil, res nihili, nullius momenti, inutilis.		Nothing, a thing of nought, of no value, useless.
——	אֱלִילֵי Idola, simulachra.		Idols, images.
——	אֱלִילִים־לָם Idola.		Idols.
אֵלֵי	אֵלִים Potentes, dii.		The mighty, gods.
אַל	אֲלֵימוֹ Ad eos.		Unto them.
	אֱלִימֶלֶךְ Elimelech.		Elimelech, N. M.
אֵלֶן	אֵלֶּין Illi, illae; hi, hae.		Those, these.
לַן	אָלִין Morabor, pernoctabor.		I will remain, abide, lodge.
אֵל	אֵלֵינוּ Ad, erga nos.		Unto, toward us.
	אֶלְיָסָף Eliasaph.		Eliasaph, N. M.
	אֱלִיעֶזֶר Eliezer.		Eliezer, N, M.
	אֱלִיעָם Eliam.		Eliam, N. M.
	אֱלִיפַז Eliphaz.		Eliphaz, N. M.
	אֱלִיפָל Eliphal.		Eliphal, N. M.
	אֱלִיפְלֵהוּ Eliphehu.		Elipheleh, N. M.
	אֱלִיפֶלֶט Eliphelet.		Eliphalet, N. M.
	אֱלִיצוּר Elisor.		Elizur, N. M.
	אֱלִיצָפָן Elisaphan.		Elizaphan, N. M.
	אֱלִיקָא Elica.		Elika, N. M.
	אֶלְיָקִים Eliachim.		Eliakim, N. M.
	אֱלִישֶׁבַע Eliseba.		Elisheba, N. M.
	אֱלִישָׁה Elisha.		Elishah, N. M.
	אֱלִישׁוּעַ Elishua.		Elishua, N. M.
	אֶלְיָשִׁיב Eliasib.		Eliashib, N. M.
	אֱלִישָׁמָע Elisamah.		Elishama, N. M.
	אֱלִישָׁפָט Elisaphat.		Elishaphat, N. M.
אָלָה אָלֵךְ	אָלִית Jurasti, maledixisti.		Thou swearest, cursedst.
——	אֵלֶךְ Illi, isti.		Those.
יָלַךְ	אֵלֵךְ־לֵךְ Ibo, ambulabo, abibo		I will go, walk, depart.
לָכַד	אֶלְכֹּד Capiam.		I will take.

ROOTS.	DERIVATIVES.	VERSIO.	SIGNIFICATION.
ילך	אֵלְכָה אֵלְכָה	*Ibo, vadam.*	I will go.
אל	אֲלֵכֶם	*Ad vos.*	To you.
אלל			
ילל	אַלְלַי	*Væ.*	Wo.
אלם			
—	אֵלֶם	*Mutus, congregatio.*	Dumb, a congregation.
—	אֵלָם	*Porticus, vestibulum.*	A porch.
—	אִלֵּם	*Mutus.*	Dumb.
אלג	אַלְמֻגִּים	*Almugim,* lignum prætantissimum.	Almug, *trees of a very durable nature.*
למד	אֶלְמַד	*Discam.*	I will learn.
—	אֲלַמְּדָה	*Docebo.*	I will teach.
—	אֲלַמֶּדְכֶם	*Docebo vos.*	I will teach you.
—	אֲלַמְּדֵם	*Docebo illos.*	I shall teach them.
—	אֲלַמֶּדְתֶּם	*Docebo vos.*	I will teach you.
	אַלְמוֹדָד	*Almodad.*	Almodad, N. M.
אלם	אֲלֻמִּים	*Manipuli.*	Sheaves.
—	אִלְּמִים	*Muti.*	Dumb.
	אַלַמֶּלֶךְ	*Alammelech.*	Alammelech, N. P.
אלם	אַלְמָן	*Viduus, viduatus.*	Forsaken, *as a widow.*
—	אַלְמָנָה	*Vidua.*	A widow.
—	אַלְמָנוֹת	*Viduæ.*	Widows.
—	אַלְמְנוּת	*Viduitas.*	Widowhood.
—	אַלְמְנוּתָהּ	*Viduitas ejus.*	Her widowhood.
—	אַלְמְנוֹתֶיהָ	*Viduæ ejus.*	Her widows.
—	אַלְמְנוֹתָיו	*Viduæ ejus, ædes vel urbes desolatæ.*	Its, or their, widows, desolate palaces, or cities.
—	אַלְמְנוּתַיִךְ	*Viduitas tua.*	Thy widowhood.
—	אֲלֻמָּתִי	*Manipuli mei.*	My sheaves.
—	אֲלֻמֹּתָיו	*Manipuli ejus.*	His sheaves.
—	אֲלֻמֹּתֵיכֶם	*Manipuli vestri.*	Your sheaves.
אלן			
—	אֵלֶּן	*Illi, illæ, illa; hi, hæ, hæc.*	The, these, those.
	אֵלֹנִי	*Elonites.*	Elonites, N. F.
	אֶלְנַעַם	*Elnaam.*	Elnaam, N. M.
	אֶלְנָתָן	*Elnathan.*	Elnathan, N, M.

ROOTS.	DERIVATIVES.	VERSIO.	SIGNIFICATION.
	אֶלָּסָר	*Ellasar.*	Ellasar, N. M.
לעג	אֶלְעַג	*Subsannabo.*	I will mock, laugh to scorn.
	אֶלְעָד	*Elad.*	Elead, N. M.
	אֶלְעָדָה	*Eladah.*	Eladah, N. M.
	אֶלְעוּזַי	*Eluzai.*	Eluzai, N. M.
	אֶלְעָזָר	*Elhazar.*	Eleazar, N. M.
	אֶלְעָלֵא	*Eleale.*	Elealeh, N. P.
	אֶלְעָלֵה	*Eleale.*	Elealeh, N. M.
	אֶלְעָשָׂה	*Elhase.*	Eleasah, N. M.
	אֶלֶף	*Eleph.*	Eleph, N. M.
אָלַף		*Studuit, didicit, addidicit.*	He studied, learned, made a great proficiency in learning
—	אֶלֶף אָלֶף	*Mille.*	A thousand.
—	אֲלַף אַלְפָּא	*Mille.*	A thousand.
—	אַלְפֵי	*Millia, chiliades.*	Thousands.
—	אַלְפִּי	*Familia mea.* [*mini.*	My family.
—	אַלֻּפֵי	*Duces, principes, do-*	Chiefs, captains, princes, lords
—	אֲלָפֶיךָ	*Boves tui.*	Thy oxen, kine.
—	אֲלָפִים	*Millia, boves.*	Thousands, oxen.
—	אַלֻּפִים	*Duces, principes.*	Leaders, princes.
—	אַלְפַּיִם	*Duo millia.*	Two thousands.
—	אַלְפִים־־פִּן	*Millia.*	Thousands.
	אֱלִיפֶלֶט	*Eliphelet.*	Eliphelet, N. M.
	אֶלְפַּעַל	*Elphaal.*	Elphal, N. M.
אלץ			
	אֶלְצָפָן	*Elsaphan.*	Elzaphan, N. M.
לקח	אֶלָּקַח	*Tollar.*	I shall be taken away.
לקט	אֲלַקֳּטָה	*Colligam.*	I will gather, I will glean.
	אֶלְקָנָה	*Elcanah.*	Elkanah, N. M.
	אֶלְקֹשִׁי	*Elcosites.*	Elchoshite, N. P. or F.
אלה	אָלָתוֹ	*Juramentum, adjuratio ejus.*	His oath, adjuration.
	אֶלְתּוֹלַד	*Eltolad.*	Eltolad, N. R.
אלה	אָלָתִי	*Juramentum meum.*	My oath.
	אֶלְתְּקֵא־־ה	*Elteche.*	Eltekeh, N. P.
	אֶלְתְּקוֹן	*Eltecon.*	Eltekon, N. P.

ROOTS.	DERIVATIVES.	VERSIO.	SIGNIFICATION.
	אם		
אמם	אִם	*Si, num, sive, non, neque, nec, quod, quoniam, quia, quamvis, nisi, ne, ut non, cum, quoties, dum, verè, certe, O si.*	If, whether, or, not, neither, nor, whereas, since, because, though, unless, lest, that not, when, whenever, till, truly, surely, O that.
אמם	אֵם	*Mater.*	A mother.
מאס	אֶמְאַס	*Spernam, abominabor, rejiciam.*	I will despise, abhor, reject.
מגן	אֲמַגֶּנְךָ	*Tradam te.*	I will deliver thee.
מדד	אֲמֹדֵּד	*Metiar.*	I will measure.
	אַמָּה	*Amma.*	Ammah, N. P.
אמם	אִמָּהּ	*Mater ejus.*	Her mother.
—	אַמָּה	*Cubitus.*	A cubit.
	אֻמָּה	*Natio.*	A nation.
אמה	אָמָה	*Ancilla.*	A maid servant.
—	אַמְהוֹת	*Ancillæ.*	Handmaids.
אמם	אִמּוֹ	*Mater ejus.*	His mother.
מוט	אֶמּוֹט	*Dimovebor.*	I shall be moved.
	אָמוֹן אָמֹן	*Amon.*	Amon, N. M.
אמן	אָמוֹן	*Nutritus vel educatus.*	Educated, or brought up.
—	אֱמוּנָה	*Veritas, fides, stabilitas.*	Truth, faithfulness, firmness,
—	אֱמוּנוֹת	*Veritates, fidelitates.*	Truth, faithfulness.
—	אֱמוּנֵי	*Fideles.*	The faithful.
—	אֱמוּנִים	*Veritates.*	Truths.
—	אֱמוּנַת	*Veritas, firmitas.*	The truth, stability.
—	אֱמוּנָתוֹ	*Veritas, fides ejus.*	His truth, faithfulness.
—	אֱמוּנָתְךָ־־תְךָ	*Fides tua.*	Thy faithfulness.
	אָמוֹץ	*Amos.*	Amoz, N. M.
אמר	אֱמוֹר	*Dicere.*	To say.
אמם	אַמּוֹת	*Cubiti.*	Cubits.
מות	אָמוּת־־תָה	*Moriar.*	I shall die.
אמם	אֻמּוֹת	*Nationes.*	Nations.

ROOTS.	DERIVATIVES.	VERSIO	SIGNIFICATION.
מחה	אֶמְחֶה	*Delebo, perdam.*	I will blot out, destroy.
—	אֶמְחֶנּוּ	*Delebo eum.*	I will blot him out.
מחץ	אֶמְחָצֵם	*Transfigam, confringam eos.*	I will wound, bruise them.
מטר	אַמְטִיר	*Pluere faciam.*	I will cause to rain.
	אָמִי	*Ami.*	Ami, N. M.
אמם	אִמִּי	*Mater mea.*	My mother.
—	אֻמַּיָּא	*Nationes.*	Nations.
מול	אֲמִילָם	*Excindam eos.*	I will destroy them.
אים	אֵמִים	*Terrores, homines terrifici.*	Terrors, terrible men.
אמם	אַמִּין	*Cubiti.*	Cubits.
	אַמְנוֹן אֲמִינוֹן	*Aminon, Amnon.*	Amnon, N. M.
אמץ	אַמִּיץ	*Robustus, potens.*	Strong, mighty.
אמר	אָמִיר	*Ramus summus.*	The highest branch of a tree
מור	אָמִיר	*Commutabo.*	I will change.
מוש	אָמִישׁ	*Amovebo, recedam.*	I will remove, go back.
מות	אָמִית	*Interficiam.*	I will kill.
—	אֲמִיתֶךָ־תְךָ־תֵךְ	*Occidam te.*	I will kill thee.
אמם	אִמֶּךָ־־אִמֵּךְ	*Mater tua.*	Thy mother.
—	אִמְּכֶם־־כֶן	*Mater vestra.*	Your mother.
אמל			
מלא	אִמָּלֵא	*Replebo, complebo.*	I will fill, fulfil.
—	אִמָּלְאָה	*Replebor.*	I shall be replenished.
—	אֲמֻלָה	*Languida.*	Weak,
מלך	אֶמְלוֹךְ־־לֹךְ	*Regnabo.*	I will rule, will be king.
מלט	אֲמַלֵּט	*Liberabo, eripiam.*	I will deliver.
—	אִמָּלְטָה אִמָּלֵט	*Evadam.*	I shall escape.
—	אֲמַלֶּטְךָ	*Eripiam te.*	I will deliver thee.
אמל	אֻמְלַל־־לַל	*Elanguit, marcuit; infirmus, desolatus est.*	It languished, became weak, desolate.
—	אֻמְלְלָה־לָלָה		
—	אֻמְלְלוּ	*Languerunt, corruerunt.*	They languished, are fallen.
אמם			
—	אִמָּם	*Mater eorum.*	Their mother.
	אֲמָם	*Amam.*	Amam, N. P.

ROOTS.	DERIVATIVES.	VERSIO.	SIGNIFICATION.
אמן			
—	אָמָן	*Artifex.* [*tas.*	A skilful workman.
—	אָמֵן	*Amen, verus, veri-*	Amen, true, truth.
—	אֹמֶן	*Fides, veritas.*	Faith, fidelity, truth.
—	אֹמֵן	*Educator, nutritor.*	One who educates, a guardian
—	אֹמֶן	*Firmitas, fidelitas.*	Stability, faithfulness.
—	אֲמָנָה	*Constitutio firma, fœdus.*	A firm agreement, covenant.
—	אָמְנָה	*Verè.*	Indeed, truly.
	אֲמָנָה	*Amana.*	Amana, N. P.
	אַמְנוֹן־־נֹן	*Amnon.*	Amnon, N. P.
אמן	אֹמְנַיִךְ	*Nutritii tui.*	Thy nursing fathers.
—	אֱמֻנִים	*Veritates.*	Truths.
—	אָמְנָם אֻמְנָם	*Sanè, certè.*	Surely, certainly.
מנע	אֶמְנַע	*Cohibebo.*	I will keep back, withhold.
אמן	אֱמֻנָתוֹ	*Fides, veritas ejus.*	His faithfulness, truth.
—	אֹמַנְתּוֹ	*Nutrix ejus.*	His nurse.
מסה	אַמְסֶה	*Liquefaciam.*	I will water.
מעד	אֶמְעָד	*Vacillabo.*	I shall totter, slide.
אָמַץ		*Robustus, fortior, imperterritus fuit; contentis viribus egit, prævaluit.*	He was strong, more courageous; exerted the greatest strength, prevailed.
—	אֱמָץ	*Robora.*	Strengthen thou.
—	אֹמֶץ	*Robur.*	Strength.
—	אַמִּיץ	*Robustis, fortis.*	Strong, courageous.
מצא	אֶמְצָא	*Inveniam.*	I shall find.
—	אֶמְצָאֲךָ	*Inveniam te.*	I shall find thee.
אמץ	אַמְצָה	*Robur.*	Strength.
—	אָמְצוּ	*Fortiores sunt.*	They are stronger.
—	אַמְּצוּ	*Fortificate, roborate*	Confirm, strengthen ye.
	אַמְצִי	*Amsi.*	Amzi, N. M.
	אֲמַצְיָה־־יָהוּ	*Amasias.*	Amaziah, N. M.
—	אֲמֻצִּים	*Validi; subrufi.*	Strong; of a bright bay colour.
—	אִמַּצְתָּ־־תָּה	*Roborasti.*	Thou strengthenedst.
—	אִמַּצְתִּיךָ	*Roboravi te.*	I have strengthened thee.

ROOTS.	DERIVATIVES.	VERSIO.	SIGNIFICATION.
אָמַר		*Locutus est, dixit, edixit, narravit, jussit, ordinavit, cogitavit, constituit: loquens.*	He spoke, said, declared, related, commanded, appointed, thought, designed, resolved; saying.
—	אֱמֹר אָמֹר	*Dicere.*	To say.
—	אֱמַר	*Dixit.*	He said.
—	אֱמֹר	*Dic, dicite.*	Say, speak, tell thou.
	אִמֵּר	*Immer.*	Immer, N. M. P.
אמר	אֹמַר	*Dicam.*	I will say.
—	אֹמֵר	*Dicens, cogitans.*	Saying, thinking.
—	אֹמֶר	*Dictum, sermo.*	A speech, word.
—	אֹמְרָה	*Dicam.*	I will speak.
—	אָמְרָה	*Dixit.*	She said.
—	אָמְרוּ אֱמַרוּ	*Dixerunt.*	They said.
—	אִמְרוּ	*Dicite.*	Speak, say ye.
—	אִמְרוֹ	*Dictum ejus.*	His word.
—	אִמְרוּ	*Dicite, cogitate.*	Speak, think ye.
—	אֲמָרוֹת אִמְרוֹת	*Verba, sermones.*	The words.
—	אֲמָרַי־־רַי	*Verba mea.*	My words.
—	אִמְרִי	*Dic, dicite.*	Say thou.
—	אִמְרֵי	*Verba, sermones.*	The words.
—	אָמְרִי	*Dicere me.*	That I say.
	אֱמֹרִי	*Amorrhæus.*	Amorite, N. N.
	אִמְרִי	*Imri.*	Imri, N. M.
אמר	אֲמָרֶיהָ	*Sermones ejus.*	Her words.
	אֲמַרְיָה־־יָהוּ	*Amariae.*	Amariah, N. M.
אמר	אֲמָרָיו	*Verba ejus.*	His words.
—	אִמְרֵיכֶם	*Sermones vestri.*	Your words.
—	אֲמָרִים	*Dicta, sermones.*	Words.
—	אֹמְרִים אָמְרִין	*Dicentes.*	Saying.
—	אִמְּרִין	*Agni.*	Lambs.
—	אֲמָרְךָ אָמְרֵךְ	*Dicere te.*	That thou sayest.
—	אֲמָרְכֶם	*Dicere vos.*	That you say.
—	אֲמַרְנָא אָמַרְנוּ	*Diximus.*	We said.
	אַמְרָפֶל	*Amraphel.*	Amraphel, N. M.
מרר	אֲמַרֵּר	*Amaritudine afficiar*	I shall be in bitterness.

ROOTS.	DERIVATIVES.	VERSIO.	SIGNIFICATION.
אמר	אָמַרְתָּ אָמַרְתְּ	*Dixisti.*	Thou spakest.
—	אֹמֶרֶת	*Dicens.*	Saying.
—	אִמְרַת	*Sermo, verbum.*	The word.
—	אֹמְרֹת	*Dicentes.*	Saying.
—	אֲמַרְת	*Dixi.* [*ejus.*	I told.
—	אִמְרָתוֹ	*Verbum, edictum*	His word, commandment.
—	אִמְרָתִי	*Sermo meus.*	My speech.
—	אָמַרְתִּי	*Dixi.*	I said.
—	אִמְרָתְךָ־ֶךָ־ֵךְ	*Sermo tuus.*	Thy speech.
—	אֲמַרְתֶּם	*Dixistis.*	Ye spake.
אמש			
—	אָמֶשׁ אֶמֶשׁ	*Nocte præteritâ, heri, nuper.*	Last night, yesterday, lately.
משך	אֶמְשְׁכֵם	*Traham eos.*	I will draw them.
משל	אֶמְשֹׁל	*Dominabor.*	I will rule.
אמם	אַמַּת	*Cubitus, culmen.*	The cubit, summit, extent.
—	אַמּוֹת	*Cubiti.* [*tus.*	Cubits.
אמן	אֱמֶת	*Veritas, verus, rec-*	Truth, true, right.
אמה	אֲמָתָהּ	*Ancilla ejus.*	Her maid-servant.
—	אֲמָתוֹ	*Ancilla ejus.*	His maid-servant.
אמן	אֲמִתּוֹ	*Veritas ejus.*	His truth.
מתח	אַמְתְּחוֹת־־חֹת	*Sacci.*	Sacks.
—	אַמְתַּחַת	*Saccus.*	A sack.
—	אַמְתַּחְתּוֹ	*Saccus ejus.*	His sack.
—	אַמְתְּחֹתֵיכֶם	*Sacci vestri.*	Your sacks.
—	אַמְתְּחֹתֵינוּ	*Sacci nostri.*	Our sacks.
אמה	אֲמָתִי	*Ancilla mea.*	My maid-servant.
	אֲמִתַּי	*Amittai*	Amittai, N. M.
אמם	אַמָּתַיִם	*Cubiti duo.*	Two cubits.
—	אִמֹּתֵינוּ	*Matres nostræ.*	Our mothers.
אמה	אֲמָתֶךָ־־תְךָ	*Ancilla tua.*	Thy handmaid.
אמן	אֲמִתֶּךָ־־תְּךָ	*Veritas tua.*	Thy truth.
אמם	אִמָּתָם	*Matres eorum.*	Their mothers.
	אנ		
אן			
	אֹן	*On.*	On, N. P, or I.

ROOTS.	DERIVATIVES.	VERSIO.	SIGNIFICATION.
אן	אָן	*Quo, ubi, quousque.*	Whither, where, how long.
אנה	אֲנָא־־ה	*Ego. [fiteor.*	I.
אן	אָנָּא־ה	*Quæso, obsecro, con-*	I pray, beseech, confess.
אבב	אִנְבֵּהּ	*Fructus ejus.*	The fruit of it.
אָנָה		*Mœstus est, accidit, occurrere fecit, occasionem quæsivit*	He mourned, it befel, he caused to meet, sought an occasion.
אן	אָנָה	*Ubi, quo, quocumque.*	Where, whither, whithersoever
—	אָנֶה	*Quorsum, huc. [didit*	Whither, hither.
אנה	אִנָּה	*Occurrere fecit, tra-*	He caused to meet, delivered.
נהג	אֲנַהֶגְךָ	*Deducam te.*	I will lead thee.
און	אֹנוֹ	*Robur ejus.*	His strength.
אני	אָנוּ	*Nos.*	We.
נוח	אָנוּחַ	*Requiescam.*	I will rest.
אנה	אִנּוּן	*Ipsi.*	They, those.
נוס	אָנוּסָה	*Fugiam.*	I will flee.
אנש	אָנוּשׁ	*Desperatus, incurabilis, mortifer.*	Desperate, incurable, mortal.
	אֱנוֹשׁ	*Enos. [lis.*	Enos, N. M.
אנש	אֱנוֹשׁ אֱנָשׁ־שָׁא	*Homo, homo morta-*	A man, mortal man.
—	אֲנוּשָׁה	*Mortifera.*	Incurable, mortal.
נחם	אֶנָּחֵם	*Consolationem capiam, pœnitebit me.*	I will take comfort, I will repent.
—	אֲנַחֲמֵךְ	*Consolabor te.*	I will comfort thee.
—	אֲנַחֶמְכֶם	*Consolabor vos.*	I will comfort you.
אני	אֲנַחְנָא־־נָה	*Nos.*	We.
נחה	אַנְחֶנָּה	*Deducam eam.*	I will guide her.
אני	אֲנַחְנוּ אֲנֶחְנוּ	*Nos.*	We.
	אֲנָחֲרַת	*Anaharath. [ejus.*	Anaharath, N. P.
אנח	אַנְחָתָהּ	*Suspiria, gemitus*	Her sighing, groaning.
—	אַנְחָתִי	*Gemitus meus.*	My groaning.
	אַנְחֹתַי	*Suspiria mea.*	My sighs.
אני			
—	אֲנִי אָנִי	*Ego.*	I.
אנה	אֳנִי אֳנִיָּה	*Navis, classis.*	A ship, a navy.
—	אֳנִיּוֹת [illegible]	*Naves.*	Ships.
—	[illegible]	*Illæ.*	They, those.

ROOTS.	DERIVATIVES.	VERSIO.	SIGNIFICATION.
	אֲנִיעָם	*Aniam.*	Aniam, N. M.
אנך			
——	אֲנָךְ	*Perpendiculum.*	A plumb-line.
אני	אָנֹכִי	*Ego.*	I.
אָנַן		*Lamentatus est.*	He lamented.
אָנַס		*Coegit.*	He compelled, forced.
——	אֹנֵס	*Urgens, cogens.*	Pressing, compelling.
——	אָנֻס	*Absconditus.*	Concealed.
נסה	אֲנַסֶּה	*Tentabo.*	I will tempt, prove, try.
——	אֲנַסְּכָה	*Tentabo te.*	I will prove thee.
——	אֲנַסֶּנּוּ	*Tentabo eum.*	I will prove him.
אָנַף		*Succensuit, iratus est*	He was wroth, angry.
——	אַנְפּוֹהִי	*Vultus ejus.*	His visage.
——	אָנַפְתָּ	*Iratus es.*	Thou hast been displeased.
נצל	אִנָּצְלָה	*Eripiar, evadam.*	I shall be delivered, escape.
אנק			
נקה	אֲנַקֶּךָּ	*Te impunitum dimittam, absolvam.*	I will leave unpunished, will acquit thee.
אנק	אֲנָקַת	*Gemitus, clamor.*	The sighing, groaning, roaring
אנש			
נשא	אֶנָּשֵׂא	*Elevabo.*	I will lift up.
אנש	אַנְשֵׁי	*Homines.*	The men.
——	אֲנָשַׁי	*Homines mei.*	My men.
——	אֲנָשֶׁיהָ	*Homines ejus.*	Her men.
——	אַנְשֵׁיהֶן	*Viri earum.*	Their husbands.
——	אֲנָשָׁיו	*Homines ejus.*	His men.
——	אֲנָשֶׁיךָ	*Homines tui.*	Thy men.
——	אֲנָשִׁים	*Homines, viri.*	Men.
——	אֲנָשֵׁינוּ	*Homines nostri.*	Our men.
אני	אַנְתְּה	*Tu.*	Thou.
——	אַנְתּוּן	*Vos.*	Ye.
נתק	אֲנַתֵּק	*Divellam, rumpam.*	I will break, burst.
	אס		
	אָסָא	*Asa.*	Asa, N. M.
סבל	אֶסְבֹּל	*Portabo.*	I will carry.
סגד	אֶסְגּוֹד	*Procumbam.*	I shall fall down.

ROOTS.	DERIVATIVES	VERSIO.	SIGNIFICATION.
סוד	אָסוּךְ	*Lecythus.*	A cruise, vial, pot.
אסן			
—	אָסוֹן	*Mors, exitium.*	Death, or fatal mischief.
אסר	אָסוֹר	*Ligare, ligando.*	To bind, binding.
—	אָסוּר	*Vinctus, ligatus.*	Bound, tied.
סור	אָסוּר	*Declinabo, recedam.*	I will turn aside, depart.
אסר	אֲסוּרוֹת	*Vinctæ.*	Bound.
—	אֱסוּרָיו	*Vincula ejus.*	His bands.
—	אֲסוּרֶיךָ	*Vincti tui.*	Thy prisoners.
—	אֲסוּרִים	*Vincti, cincti.*	Bound, girded.
נסך	אַסִּיךְ	*Libabo.*	I will pour out, offer.
יסף	אֹסִיף	*Addam, pergam.*	I will add, proceed, continue.
סוף	אֲסִיפֵם	*Consumam eos.*	I will consume them.
סור	אָסִיר	*Amovebo, auferam.*	I will remove, take away.
אסר	אָסִיר אַסִּיר	*Vinctus.*	Bound.
	אַסִּיר	*Assir.*	Assir, N. M.
אסר	אֲסִירֵי	*Vincti.*	Bound, prisoners.
—	אֲסִירָיו	*Vincti, vincula ejus.*	His prisoners, his bands.
—	אֲסִירַיִךְ	*Vincti tui.*	Thy prisoners.
—	אֲסִירִים	*Vincti.*	Prisoners.
סלח	אֶסְלַח	*Condonabo.*	I will pardon.
אסם			
—	אֲסָמֶיךָ	*Horrea tua.*	Thy barns.
	אַסְנָה	*Asena.*	Aznah, N. M.
	אָסְנַפַּר	*Asnaphar.*	Asnapper, N. M.
	אָסְנַת	*Asenath.*	Asenath, N. M.
	אָסָף	*Asaph.*	Asaph, N. M.
אָסַף		*Collegit, congregavit, retraxit, revocavit, abstulit, removit, consumpsit.*	He gathered, assembled, withdrew, revoked, took away, removed, consumed, destroyed.
—	אָסֹף	*Consumere, congregare.*	To consume, assemble.
—	אֱסֹף	*Collige, retrahe, abstolle.*	Gather, withdraw, take away.
יסף	אֹסֵף אוֹסִף	*Addam, pergam.*	I will add, proceed, continue.
אסף	אֹסֶף	*Collectio, congregatio.*	The collection, gathering.
סוף	אָסֵף	*Consumam.*	I will consume.

ROOTS.	DERIVATIVES.	VERSIO.	SIGNIFICATION.
ספד	אֶסְפְּדָה	*Plangam.*	I will bewail.
אסף	אֲסֵפָה	*Congregatio.*	An assembly.
ספה	אֶסְפֶּה	*Addam, accumulabo.*	I will add, will heap up.
אסף	אֶסְפָה	*Collige, congrega.*	Gather, assemble thou.
—	אֹסְפָה	*Congregabo.*	I will assemble.
ספה	אֶסְפֶה	*Consumam.*	I will consume.
אסף	אִסְפוּ	*Congregate.* [*erunt.*	Gather, assemble ye.
—	אָסְפוּ	*Collegerunt, retrax-*	They gathered, withdrew.
—	אֲסֻפּוֹת	*Collectiones.*	Assemblies.
—	אִסְפִי	*Collige.*	Gather thou.
—	אָסְפֵי	*Consumpti.*	Consumed.
—	אֹסְפְךָ	*Colligam te.*	I will gather thee.
סוף	אָסֵפְךָ	*Disperdam te.* [*ea.*	I shall destroy thee. [them.
אסף	אֹסְפָם	*Colligens, collecturus*	Gathering, or about to gather
ספר	אֲסַפֵּר	*Numerabo.*	I will count.
—	אֲסַפְּרָה	*Enarrabo.*	I will declare.
—	אֲסַפְּרֵם	*Numerabo eos.*	I shall count them.
—	אָסְפַּרְנָא	*Cito, festinanter.*	Fast, forthwith, speedily.
—	אֲסַפְּרֶנָּה	*Enarrabo eam.*	I will declare it.
אסף	אָסַפְתָּ	*Abstulisti.*	Thou hast taken away.
	אַסְפָּתָא	*Aspata.*	Aspatha, N. M.
אסף	אָסַפְתִּי	*Congregavi.*	I have gathered.
—	אָסַפְתִּי	*Abstuli.*	I have taken away.
נסק	אֶסַּק	*Ascendam.*	I shall ascend.
	אַסִּר	*Assir.*	Assir, N. M.
אָסַר		*Ligavit, obligavit, vinxit, obstrinxit, accinxit, instruxit*	He tied, bound, girded, obliged, imprisoned, set in array.
—	אָסֹר	*Ligare.*	To bind.
	אֵסַר חַדּוֹן־־דֹּן	*Esar-chaddon.*	Esar-haddon, N. M.
אסר	אֱסָר	*Edictum.*	A decree.
—	אֱסֹר	*Liga*, scil. currum.	Prepare *a chariot.*
—	אִסָּר	*Obligatio.*	A bond, obligation.
—	אֱסָרָא	*Edictum.*	The decree.
סור	אָסֻרָה	*Divertam.*	I will turn aside.
אסר	אָסְרָה	*Obligavit se.*	She bound herself.
—	אִסְרוּ	*Ligate.*	Bind ye, harness.

ROOTS.	DERIVATIVES.	VERSIO.	SIGNIFICATION.
אסר	אָסְרוּ אִסְרוּ	*Vincti sunt.*	They are bound
—	אֲסֻרוֹת	*Ligatæ.*	Bound.
—	אֹסְרִי	*Ligans.*	Binding.
—	אֱסָרֶיהָ	*Obligationes ejus.*	Her bonds.
—	אֲסָרָם	*Vincivit eos.*	He bound them.
סתר	אַסְתִּיר־־רָה	*Abscondam.*	I will hide.
—	אֶסָּתֵר	*Abscondam me.*	I will hide myself.
	אֶסְתֵּר	*Esther.*	Esther, N. W.
	אע		
אע			
—	אֶע אֶעָא	*Lignum.*	Timber, wood.
עבד	אֶעֱבֹד	*Serviam.*	I shall serve.
—	אֶעֶבְדֶךָ	*Serviam tibi.* [*dier.*	I will serve thee.
עבר	אֶעֱבוֹר	*Transibo, transgre-*	I shall pass, transgress.
—	אַעֲבִיר	*Transire faciam, transferam.* [*ibo*	I will cause to pass.
—	אֶעֱבֹר	*Transibo, pertrans-*	I will pass over, pass through.
—	אֶעְבְּרָה אֶעֱבֹרָה	*Transibo.*	I will pass, go over.
עף	אֶעוּפָה	*Evolabo.*	I will fly away.
עזב	אֶעֱזֹב	*Derelinquam.* [*tam.*	I will forsake.
—	אֶעֶזְבָה	*Relinquam, dimit-*	I will leave off.
—	אֶעֶזְבְךָ אֶעֱזָבְךָ	*Derelinquam te.*	I will forsake thee
—	אֶעֶזְבֵם	*Derelinquam eos.*	I will forsake them.
עד	אֲעִידְךָ	*Testificabor tibi.*	I shall testify to thee.
יעל	אֹעִיל	*Utilitatem perspiciam, proficiam.*	I shall gain advantage, be profited.
עור	אֶעִירָה	*Evigilabo, exurgam.*	I will awake, arise.
עלה	אֶעֱלֶה אַעֲלֶה	*Ascendam, procedam, educam, reducam, ascendere faciam, offeram.*	I will go up, ascend, bring up, restore, make to ascend, offer.
עלז	אֶעֶלְזָה־־לֹזָה	*Exultabo, lætabor.*	I will rejoice.
עלם	אַעֲלִים	*Occultabo.*	I will hide.
עלה	אַעַלְךָ	*Ascendere faciam te.*	I will bring thee up.
עמד	אֶעֱמֹדָה	*Stabo.*	I will stand.
ענד	אֶעֶנְדֶנּוּ	*Alligabo eum.*	I will bind it.

ROOTS.	DERIVATIVES.	VERSIO.	SIGNIFICATION.
ענה	אֶעֱנֶה	Dicam, exaudiam,	I will speak, hear, answer, will
—	אֶעֱנֶה	respondebo ; ex-	be heard, afflicted.
—	אֵעָנֶה	audiar, affligar.	
—	אֲעַנֶּךָּ	Affligam te.	I will afflict thee.
—	אֶעֶנְךָּ אֶעֱנֶךָּ	Exaudiam te, respondebo tibi.	I will hear, will answer thee.
—	אֶעֱנֵם	Exaudiam eos.	I will hear them.
—	אֶעֱנֶנּוּ	Respondebo ei.	I will answer him.
עצר	אֶעֱצֹר	Claudam.	I will shut up.
ערב	אֶעֶרְבֶנּוּ	Spondebo pro eo.	I will be surety for him.
ערץ	אֶעֱרוֹץ	Timebo. [ordinabo.	I shall fear.
ערך	אֶעֱרֹךְ אֶעֶרְכָה	Parabo, disponam,	I will prepare, direct, order.
עשה	אֶעֱשֶׂה	Faciam.	I will make.
—	אֶעֶשְׂךָ	Præparabo te.	I will prepare thee
—	אֶעֱשֶׂנָּה	Faciam eam.	I will do it.
עשר	אֲעַשְּׂרֶנּוּ	Decimabo illud.	I will give the tenth of it.
עתר	אַעְתִּיר	Deprecabor.	I will intreat, intercede.
	אפ		
אנף	אַף אַף	Nasus, vultus ; ira.	A nose, a face ; anger.
—	אַף	Certe, profecto, imo, nam, etsi, quanto magis, sed, tamen.	Certainly, truly, moreover, also, yea, for, although, how much more, but, yet.
פאה	אַפְאֵיהֶם	Disjiciam in angulos exterminabo eos.	I will scatter them into corners, will exterminate them
פאר	אֲפָאֵר	Glorificabo.	I will glorify.
פגע	אֶפְגַּע	Occurram.	I will meet.
פגש	אֶפְגְּשֵׁם	Occurram iis.	I will meet them.
	אֵפֹד אֵפוֹד	Ephod, amiculum sacerdotale.	Ephod, *one of the sacerdotal vestments ; also* N. M.
אָפַד		Amicivit, accinxit.	He tied, girded.
פדה	אֶפְדֶּה	Redimam.	I will redeem.
—	אֶפְדֵּם	Redimam eos.	I will ransom them.
פדן	אַפַּדְנוֹ	Palatium ejus.	His palace.
אפד	אֲפֻדַּת	Amictus, pallium.	The attire, robe.
—	אֲפֻדָּתוֹ	Ephod ejus.	His ephod.
	אֵיפָה	Epha.	An ephah, *a measure.*

ROOTS.	DERIVATIVES.	VERSIO.	SIGNIFICATION.
אָפָה		*Coxit.*	He baked, *in an oven, or on* [*a hearth.*
אנף	אַפָּה	*Facies ejus.*	Her face.
אפה	אֹפֶה	*Coquus, pistor.*	The baker.
—	אֹפֵהֶם	*Pistor eorum.*	Their baker.
איף	אֵפוֹ אֵפוֹא	*Ubi, tunc, nunc.*	Where, then, now.
אפה	אֵפוּ	*Coquite.*	Bake ye.
אנף	אַפּוֹ	*Ira, vultus ejus.*	His wrath, his countenance.
פון	אָפוּנָה	*Hæsitabo, dubitabo.*	I shall hesitate, be in suspense.
פחד	אֶפְחָד	*Pavebo.*	I shall be afraid.
אנף	אַפִּי	*Furor meus.*	My wrath.
—	אַפֵּי	*Vultus, conspectus.*	The face, countenance, pre- [sence.
—	אַפֶּיהָ	*Facies ejus.*	Her face.
—	אַפָּיו	*Facies ejus.*	His face.
פוח	אָפִיחַ	*Afflabo.*	I will blow.
	אֲפִיחַ	*Aphia.*	Aphia, N. M.
אנף	אַפֶּיךָ	*Nares tuæ, vultus* [*tuus.*	Thy nostrils, thy face.
נפל	אַפִּיל	*Cadere faciam.*	I will cause to fall.
אפל	אֲפִילֹת	*Serotina, latentia.*	Late, not grown up.
אנף	אַפַּיִם	*Nares, iræ.*	Nostrils, anger.
	אַפַּיִם	*Aphaim.*	Appaim, N. M.
אנף	אַפֵּינוּ	*Nares nostræ.*	Our nostrils.
נפץ	אָפִיץ	*Dispergam.*	I will scatter.
—	אֲפִיצֵם	*Dispergam eos.*	I will scatter them.
	אֲפִיק	*Aphic.*	Aphick, N. P.
אפק	אֲפִיקֵי	*Flumina, alvei, torrentes, vires.*	The rivers, channels, brooks, strength.
—	אֲפִיקָיו	*Alvei ejus.*	His channels.
—	אֲפִיקֶיךָ	*Torrentes tui.*	Thy rivers.
—	אֲפִיקִים	*Fortes.*	Mighty ones.
פור	אָפִיר	*Frangam, irritum* [*faciam.*	I will break, make void.
אפה	אָפִיתִי	*Coxi.*	I have baked.
אנף	אַפְּךָ אַפְּךָ אַפֶּךָ	*Ira, indignatio tua.*	Thy wrath, anger.
אפל			
נפל	אֶפָּל־לָה	*Cadam.*	I shall fall.
אפל	אֹפֶל אֲפֵלָה	*Caligo.*	Darkness.
	אֶפְלָל	*Ephlal.*	Ephlal, N. M.
אנף	אַפָּם	*Nares, furor eorum*	Their nose, their anger.

ROOTS.	DERIVATIVES.	VERSIO.	SIGNIFICATION.
אפן	אֹפַן	*Rota.*	A wheel.
—	אֹפַנָּיו	*Rotæ ipsius.*	His wheels.
—	אֹפַנִּים	*Rotæ.* [*habuit.*	Wheels. [end.
אָפֵס		*Desiit, defecit, finem*	He failed, ceased, came to an
—	אֶפֶס	*Finis, extremum, defectus, nihil, nullus; non, præter, nisi, tantum.*	The end, extremity, failure, nothing, none; no, not, beside, except, only.
	אֶפֶס דַּמִּים	*Ephes-dammim.*	Ephes-dammim, N. M.
אפס	אַפְסֵי	*Fines, termini.*	The ends, extremities.
—	אָפְסָיִם	*Tali pedum.*	The ancle bones of the feet.
אפע			
—	אֶפְעֶה	*Vipera.*	A viper.
פעה	אֶפְעֶה	*Clamabo.*	I will cry.
פעל	אֶפְעַל	*Agam, operabor.*	I will do, will work.
אָפַף		*Circumdedit.*	He compassed about.
—	אָפְפוּ	*Circumdederunt.*	They have compassed.
—	אֲפָפוּנִי אֲפָפֻנִי	*Circumdederunt me.*	They compassed me.
אָפַק		*Sese coegit,* ad aliquid faciendum vel omittendum.	He constrained, or restrained himself, *to do or to omit any thing.*
	אֲפֵק	*Aphec.* [*puniam.*	Aphek, N. M.
פקד	אֶפְקֹד־קוֹד־קָד	*Visitabo, constituam,*	I will visit, punish, appoint.
פקח	אֶפְקַח	*Aperiam.* [*nam.*	I will open. [trust.
פקד	אַפְקִיד	*Commendabo, depo-*	I will commit, commend, en-
אפר			
—	אֵפֶר	*Pulvis, cinis.*	Dust, ashes.
פור	אָפֵר	*Frangam, irritum faciam.*	I will break, make void.
פרש	אֶפְרוֹשׂ־רֹשׂ	*Expandam.*	I will stretch out.
פרח	אֶפְרֹחָיו־חֶיהָ	*Pulli ejus.*	Her young ones.
—	אֶפְרֹחִים	*Pulli.*	Young ones.
פרה	אַפִּרְיוֹן	*Carruca seu lectica quâ vehi solebant sponsæ; vel thalamus nuptialis.*	A bridal chair or chariot; or a nuptial bed.
	אֶפְרָיִם	*Ephraim.*	Ephraim, N. M. T. P.

ROOTS.	DERIVATIVES.	VERSIO.	SIGNIFICATION.
	אֲפָרְסָיֵא אֲפָרְסַתְכָיֵא	Apharsæi, Apharsachæi.	Apharsites, Apharsachites.
פרע	אֶפְרַע	Retractabo.	I will go back.
	אֶפְרָת	Ephrata.	Ephratah, N. W. P.
	אֶפְרָתִי	Ephratæus.	An Ephrathite, N. F.
	אֶפְרָתִים	Ephratæi.	Ephrathites, N. F.
פשט	אַפְשִׁיטֶנָּה	Expoliabo eam.	I will strip her.
פשע	אֶפְשְׂעָה	Gradiar, incedam.	I will step, go.
אפת			
פתח	אֶפְתַּח אֶפְתְּחָה	Aperiam, dissolvam.	I will open, will loose.
—	אֲפַתֵּחַ	Solvam. [eum.	I will open.
פתה	אֲפַתֶּנּוּ	Pelliciam, decipiam	I will persuade, deceive him.
	אצ		
ארץ	אָץ	Festinavit, ursit; festinus, angustus.	He hastened, urged; hasty, narrow.
יצא	אֵצֵא	Exibo, egrediar.	I will go out, forth, away.
	אֶצְבּוֹן	Esbon.	Ezbon, N. M.
צבע	אֶצְבַּע	Digitus.	A finger.
—	אֶצְבָּעוֹ	Digitus ejus.	His finger.
—	אֶצְבָּעוֹת אֶצְבְּעָן	Digiti.	Fingers.
—	אֶצְבְּעוֹתַי	Digiti mei.	My fingers.
—	אֶצְבְּעוֹתָיו	Digiti ejus.	His fingers.
—	אֶצְבְּעוֹתֶיךָ	Digiti tui.	Thy fingers.
צדק	אַצְדִּיק אֶצְדַּק	Justificabo.	I will justify.
צוה	אֲצַוֶּה	Præcipiam, jubebo.	I will charge, command.
—	אֲצַוְּךָ אֲצַוְּךְ	Præcipiam tibi.	I will command thee.
צום	אָצוּם	Jejunabo.	I will fast.
צוה	אֲצַוֶּנּוּ	Præcipiam ei.	I will command him.
יצג	אַצִּיגָה	Ponam, relinquam.	I will place, leave.
נצל	אַצִּיל	Eripiam.	I will deliver.
אצל	אַצִּילָה	Ad axillam, ad alam ædificii.	To the arm-hole, to the wing *of a building*.
—	אַצִּילוֹת	Axillæ.	Arm-holes.
—	אַצִּילֵי	Axillæ.	The arm-holes.
—	אֲצִילֵי	Optimates.	Nobles.
נצל	אַצִּילֶךָּ	Eripiam te.	I will deliver thee.

ROOTS.	DERIVATIVES.	VERSIO.	SIGNIFICATION.
ארץ	אָצִים	*Urgentes, celerantes*	Urging, hastening.
צית	אֲצִיתֶנָּה	*Succendam eam.*	I will burn her.
	אֶצֶל	*Atsel.*	Azel, N. M.
אָצַל		*Reservavit, subtraxit, partitus est, seposuit.*	He reserved, withdrew, distributed, separated.
—	אֵצֶל	*Juxta, prope, apud, [ad, ab.*	Near, by, besides, from.
צלה	אֶצְלָהּ	*Apud eam.*	By her.
אצל	אֶצְלֶה	*Assabo.*	I will roast.
—	אֶצְלוֹ	*Apud eum.*	By him.
—	אֶצְלִי	*Apud me.*	By me.
	אֲצַלְיָהוּ	*Asalia.*	Azaliah, N. M.
אצל	אֶצְלָם	*Apud eos.*	By them.
—	אָצַלְתָּ	*Reservasti.*	Thou hast reserved.
—	אָצַלְתִּי	*Subtraxi.*	I kept from, withdrew.
	אֹצֶם	*Osem.*	Ozem, N. M.
צמח	אַצְמִיחַ	*Germinare faciam.*	I will cause to bud, grow up.
צמת	אַצְמִית	*Exscindam.*	I will cut off, destroy.
—	אַצְמִיתֵם	*Exscindam eos.*	I will destroy them.
צעד	אֶצְעָדָה	*Armilla, monile.*	A bracelet.
צעק	אֶצְעַק	*Clamabo. [bor.*	I will cry out.
צפה	אֲצַפֶּה	*Aspiciam, specula-*	I will look.
צפף	אֲצַפְצֵף	*Garriam.*	I shall chatter.
יצק	אֶצֹּק אֶצְּק	*Fundam, effundam.*	I will pour, pour out.
נצר	אֶצֹּר אֶצְּרָה	*Custodiam, servabo.*	I will keep.
	אֵצֶר	*Eser.*	Ezer, N. M.
אצר	אָצְרוּ	*Recondiderunt.*	They laid up in store.
—	אֹצָרוֹת אֹצְרוֹת	*Thesauri.*	Treasures.
יצר	אֶצָּרְךָ	*Formabo te.*	I will form thee.
נצר	אֶצֳּרֶנָּה	*Custodiam eam.*	I will keep her, or it.
ארץ	אַצְתִּי	*Acceleravi.*	I have hastened.

אק

ROOTS.	DERIVATIVES.	VERSIO.	SIGNIFICATION.
נקב	אֶקֹּב	*Maledicam.*	I shall curse.
קבץ	אֶקְבֹּץ	*Congregabo.*	I will gather.
—	אֲקַבֵּץ־־בְּצָה	*Congregabo.*	I will gather.
—	אֲקַבֶּצְךָ־־צֵךְ	*Congregabo te.*	I will gather thee.

ROOTS.	DERIVATIVES.	VERSIO.	SIGNIFICATION.
קבץ	אֲקַבְּצֵם	*Congregabo illos.*	I will gather them.
קבר	אֶקָּבֵר	*Sepeliar.*	I will be buried.
קדח	אֶקְדָּח	*Carbunculus.*	A carbuncle.
קדר	אַקְדִּירֵם	*Atrata reddam.*	I will make them dark.
קדם	אֲקַדֵּם	*Præveniam, occurram.*	I shall come before, shall meet
קדש	אֶקָּדֵשׁ	*Sanctificabor.*	I will be sanctified.
—	אֲקַדֵּשׁ	*Sanctificabo.*	I will sanctify.
קוה	אֲקַוֶּה	*Expectabo.* [*gabo.*	I will wait. [tend.
קוט	אָקוּט	*Fastidio habebo, liti-*	I shall be tired of, shall con-
קום	אָקוּם אָקוּמָה	*Surgam, assurgam.*	I will arise.
—	אֲקוֹמֵם	*Suscitabo.*	I will raise up.
לקח	אֶקַּח אֶקְחָה	*Capiam, accipiam.*	I will take, receive.
—	אֶקָּחֲךָ	*Capiam, ducam te.*	I will take, bring thee.
קטף	אֶקְטֹף	*Decerpam, excidam.*	I will crop off, cut off.
קום	אָקִים	*Erigam, stabiliam, præstabo.*	I will raise up, establish, perform.
— —	אֲקִימֶהָ	*Statuit, erexit eam.*	He set it up.
קוץ	אָקִיץ	*Evigilabo.*	I shall awake.
קנה	אֶקְנֶה	*Emam.* [*vebo eos.*	I will buy.
קנא	אַקְנִיאֵם	*Ad zelotypiam mo-*	I will move them to jealousy.
קצף	אֶקְצוֹף	*Irascar.*	I will be angry.
אקק			
קרא	אֶקְרָא	*Legam.* [*prædicabo*	I will read.
—	אֶקְרָא	*Invocabo, clamabo,*	I will call, cry, publish.
—	אֶקְרָאֶךָ	*Invocabo te.* [*eum.*	I will call upon thee.
קרב	אֲקָרְבֶנּוּ	*Appropinquabo*	I will approach him.
קרע	אֶקְרֶה	*Accedam, occurram.*	I will meet.
קרה	אֶקְרַע	*Findam, lacerabo.*	I will rend, tear.
—	אֶקְרָעֶנָּה	*Lacerabo illud.*	I will rend it.
קשה	אַקְשֶׁה	*Indurabo.*	I will harden.
	אר		
ארא	אֲרָא	*Ara.*	Ara, N. M.
ראה	אֶרְאֶה	*Videbo.* [*me.*	I shall see.
—	אֵרָאֶה	*Apparebo, ostendam*	I will appear, shew myself.

ROOTS.	DERIVATIVES.	VERSIO.	SIGNIFICATION.
ראה	אֶרְאֶךָּ	*Videbo te.*	I will see thee.
—	אַרְאֶךָּ	*Ostendam tibi.*	I will show to thee.
	אֲרִיאֵל אֲרִאֵל	*Ariel*, Hierosolyma.	Ariel, N. P, *Jerusalem.*
	אַרְאֵלִי	*Areli, Arelitæ.*	Arelites, N. M. F.
אראל	אֶרְאֶלָּם	*Fortes, feciales eorum.*	Their champions, heralds.
ראה	אֶרְאֵם	*Ostendam illis.*	I will shew to them.
—	אַרְאֶנּוּ	*Ostendam illi.*	I will shew to him.
—	אֶרְאֶנּוּ	*Videbo eum.*	I shall see him.
אָרַב		*Insidiatus est.*	He lay in wait.
—	אֱרֹב	*Insidiari.*	To lie in wait.
—	אֶרֶב	*Latibulum.*	A den.
—	אֹרֵב	*Insidians.*	Lying in wait.
	אֲרָב	*Arab.*	Arab, N. P.
	אַרְבֵּאל	*Arbel.*	Arbel, N. M.
רבה	אַרְבֶּה	*Multiplicabo; locusta*	I will multiply; a locust.
ארב	אָרְבוּ	*Insidiati sunt.*	They lay in wait.
—	אָרְבּוֹ	*Insidiæ ejus.*	His snares, treacheries.
—	אָרְבוֹת	*Cubiti, insidiæ.*	Elbows, snares.
—	אֲרֻבּוֹת	*Fenestræ,cataractæ.*	Windows, floodgates.
	אֲרֻבּוֹת	*Aruboth.*	Aruboth, N. P.
	אַרְבִּי	*Arbites.*	Arbite, N. F. or P.
ארב	אֹרְבִים	*Insidiantes.* [*eos.*	Liers in wait.
רבץ	אַרְבִּיצֵם	*Accubare faciam*	I will cause them to lie down.
רבע	אַרְבַּע אַרְבָּעָה	*Quatuor.*	Four.
—	אַרְבָּעָה	*Quatuor, quarta.*	Four, fourth.
—	אַרְבָּעִים	*Quadraginta, quadragesimus.*	Forty, fortieth.
—	אַרְבַּעַת	*Quatuor.*	The four.
רבע	אַרְבַּעְתָּיִם	*Quadruplum.*	Fourfold.
—	אַרְבַּעְתָּם	*Quatuor isti.*	Those four.
ארב	אָרַבְתִּי	*Insidiatus sum.*	I have laid wait.
—	אֲרֻבֹּתֵיהֶם	*Fenestræ eorum.*	Their windows.
ארג		*Texit.*	He weaved.
—	אֹרֵג	*Textor.*	A weaver.
—	אֶרֶג	*Radius.*	A shuttle.
	אַרְגֹּב	*Argob.*	Argob, N. M. P.

ROOTS.	DERIVATIVES.	VERSIO.	SIGNIFICATION.
ארג	אַרְגְּוָנָא	*Purpura.*	Purple or scarlet.
—	אֹרְגוֹת	*Texentes.*	Weaving.
רגז	אֶרְגָּז	*Tremam.*	I shall tremble.
—	אַרְגִּיז	*Commovebo.*	I will shake.
ארג	אֹרְגִים	*Texentes.*	Weaving, weavers.
רגע	אַרְגִּיעַ־־עָה	*Quiescere, erumpere faciam; succidam.*	I will cause to rest, to break forth; I will cut down.
ארג	אַרְגָּמָן	*Purpura.*	Purple or scarlet.
ירד	אֵרֵד אֵרְדָה	*Descendam.*	I will go down.
	אַרְדְּ	*Ard.*	Ard, N. M.
	אַרְדּוֹן	*Ardon.*	Ardon, N. M.
רדף	אֶרְדּוֹף אֶרְדֹּף אֶרְדְּפָה	*Persequar.*	I will pursue.
	אַרְדִּי	*Arditæ.*	Ardites, N. F.
	אֲרִדַי אֲרִידַי	*Aridai.*	Aridai, N. M.
אָרָה		*Collegit.*	He plucked, gathered.
ארר	אָרָה	*Maledic.*	Curse thou.
—	אֹרוּ	*Maledicite.*	Curse ye.
אור	אֹרוּ	*Illuminati sunt.*	They have been enlightened.
	אַרְוַד	*Arvad.*	Arvad, N. P.
	אֲרוֹדִי	*Arodi.*	Arodi, N. M.
	אַרְוָדִי	*Arvadites.*	Arvadite, N. F.
	אַרְוָדִי	*Arvadi.*	Arvadi, N. M.
ארך	אֲרוּכָה	*Curatio, reparatio.*	Healing, reparation.
רום	אָרוּם	*Exaltabor.*	I will be exalted.
—	אֲרוֹמָם	*Exaltabo me.*	I will exalt myself.
—	אֲרוֹמִמְךָ־־מִמְךְ	*Exaltabo te.*	I will exalt thee.
ארן	אֲרוֹן	*Arca.*	The ark.
	אֲרַוְנָה	*Arauna.*	Araunah, N. M.
רוץ	אָרוּץ אָרוּצָה	*Curram, percurram.*	I will run, run through.
—	אֲרוּצֵם אֲרִיצֵם	*Currere faciam, fugabo eos.*	I will make them run away.
ארר	אָרוֹר	*Maledicere.*	To curse.
—	אָרוּר	*Maledictus.*	Cursed.
—	אֲרוּרָה	*Maledicta.*	Cursed.
—	אֲרוּרִים	*Maledicti.*	Cursed.
ארה	אֻרוֹת אֻרְיוֹת	*Præsepia, stabula.*	Stalls, stables.

ROOTS.	DERIVATIVES.	VERSIO.	SIGNIFICATION.
ארר	אֲרוֹתִיהָ	*Maledixi ei.*	I have cursed him.
ארז			
—	אֶרֶז אַרְזָה	*Cedrus.*	A cedar tree.
—	אַרְזֵי	*Cedri.*	The cedars.
—	אֲרָזָיו	*Cedri ejus.*	His cedars.
—	אֲרָזֶיךָ	*Cedri tuæ.*	Thy cedars.
—	אֲרָזִים	*Cedri.*	Cedars.
	אָרַח	*Arach.*	Arah, N. M.
ארח		*Iter fecit, profectus est, ambulavit.*	He travelled, walked.
—	אֹרַח	*Via, semita, iter, consuetudo.*	A way, path, journey, custom.
—	אֲרֻחָה	*Commeatus, viaticum.*	Victuals, provisions for a journey.
—	אָרְחוֹ	*Via ejus.*	His way.
—	אָרְחוֹת אֳרָחוֹת	*Semitæ, viæ.*	The paths, ways.
—	אֹרְחוֹת	*Cœtus commeantes.*	Companies travelling together
—	אָרְחוֹתַי אָרְחֹתָי	*Semitæ meæ.*	My paths.
—	אָרְחוֹתָיו	*Viæ, itinera ejus.*	His ways.
—	אָרְחוֹתֶיךָ	*Semitæ, viæ tuæ.*	Thy paths, ways.
—	אָרְחוֹתָם	*Viæ eorum.*	Their ways.
—	אָרְחִי	*Via mea.*	My way.
—	אֹרְחִים	*Viatores.*	Wayfaring men.
רחק	אַרְחִיק	*Procul discedam vel amovebo.*	I will go, or remove far away.
ארח	אָרְחֶךָ	*Semita tua.*	Thy way.
רחם	אֲרַחֵם	*Miserebor.*	I will shew mercy.
—	אֶרְחָמְךָ	*Diligam te.*	I will love thee.
—	אֲרַחֲמֶנּוּ	*Miserebor ejus.*	I will have mercy upon him.
רחץ	אֶרְחַץ	*Lavabo.*	I will wash.
ארח	אֹרְחַת	*Turma, caterva,*	The troops, company.
—	אֲרֻחַת	*Cibarium, demensum cibi.*	Diet, an allowance of victuals
—	אָרְחֹתֵיהֶם	*Semitæ eorum.*	Their ways.
—	אָרְחֹתֶךָ	*Viæ tuæ.*	Thy ways.
ארה	אֲרִי אַרְיֵה	*Leo.*	A lion.
	אֻרִי	*Uri.*	Uri, N. M.
ארה	אֲרִיאֵל	*Fortes, leoni similes.*	Brave, lion-like.
ריב	אָרִיב	*Litigabo, contendam.*	I will plead, contend.

ROOTS.	DERIVATIVES.	VERSIO.	SIGNIFICATION.
רוד	אָרִיד	*Plangam, conquerar*	I shall mourn, complain.
	אֲרִידָתָא	*Aridatha.*	Aridatha, N. M.
	אֲרִיֵה	*Arie.*	Arieh, N. M.
ארה	אַרְיֵה	*Leo.*	A lion.
רוה	אֲרַיֶּוְךָ	*Irrigabo te.*	I will water thee.
	אַרְיוֹךְ	*Arioch.*	Arioch, N. M.
ארה	אֲרָיוֹת אַרְיָוָתָא	*Leones.*	Lions.
ריח	אָרִיחַ	*Odorabor.*	I will smell.
ארה	אֲרָיִים	*Leunculi.* [*diutius.*	Young lions.
ארך	אָרִיךְ	*Conveniens, decens;*	Meet, becoming; longer.
רום	אָרִים	*Exaltabo.*	I will exalt.
	אֲרִיסַי	*Arisai.* [*gabo eos.*	Arisai, N. M.
רוץ	אֲרִיצֵם	*Currere faciam, fu-*	I will cause them to run away.
—	אֲרִיצֶנּוּ	*Fugabo eum.*	I will make him run away.
ריק	אָרִיק	*Exseram, evaginabo*	I will draw out.
—	אֲרִיקֵם	*Evacuabo, ejiciam, delebo eos.*	I will empty, cast out, destroy them.
ארה	אָרִיתִי	*Collegi.*	I have gathered.
	אֶרֶךְ	*Erech.* [*protraxit.*	Erach, N. P. [ferred.
אָרַךְ		*Prolongavit, distulit,*	He prolonged, protracted, de-
—	אֶרֶךְ	*Longus, tardus.*	Long, slow.
—	אֹרֶךְ	*Longitudo.*	Length.
—	אָרְכָּהּ	*Longitudo ejus.*	Her length.
—	אֲרֻכָּה	*Longa, diutina.*	Long.
—	אֲרֻכָה אֲרוּכָה	*Curatio, reparatio.*	Healing, reparation.
—	אַרְכָה	*Prorogatio.*	A lengthening, continuance.
—	אָרְכוּ	*Prolongati fuerunt.*	They were prolonged.
—	אָרְכּוֹ	*Longitudo ejus.*	The length of it.
	אַרְכְּוָי	*Archevæi.*	Archevites, N. N.
	אַרְכִּי	*Archites.*	Archite, N. P. or F.
רכב	אַרְכִּיב	*Equitare faciam.*	I will make to ride.
ארך	אָרְכָּם	*Longitudo eorum.*	Their length.
—	אֲרֻכַת	*Sanitas.*	Health.
ארם			
	אֲרָם	*Aram.*	Aram, N. M. N. P.
	אֲרַם נַהֲרַיִם	*Aram-naharaim.*	Aram-naharaim, N. P.
ארם	אַרְמוֹן	*Palatium.*	A palace.

ROOTS.	DERIVATIVES.	VERSIO.	SIGNIFICATION.
	אֲרַמִּיָּה	*Aramia.*	A woman of Aram or Syria.
ארם	אֲרָמִית	*Syriacè.*	In the Syriac language.
—	אַרְמְנוֹת	*Palatia, ædes.*	Palaces.
—	אַרְמְנוֹתֶיהָ	*Palatia ejus.*	Her palaces.
—	אַרְמְנוֹתַיִךְ	*Palatia tua.*	Thy palaces.
	אַרְמֹנִי	*Armoni.*	Armoni, N. M.
ארה	אֲרֹן	*Arca.*	An ark, a chest, coffin.
	אֲרָן	*Aran.*	Aran, N. M.
	אֹרֶן	*Oren.*	Oren, N. M.
ארן			
—	אֹרֶן	*Pinus* vel *ornus.*	A pine or ash tree.
	אַרְנוֹן אַרְנֹן	*Arnon.*	Arnon, N. P. R.
רנן	אֲרַנֵּן	*Exultabo, cantabo.*	I will rejoice, or sing aloud.
	אָרְנָן	*Arnan.*	Arnan, N. M.
רנן	אַרְנִן	*Exultare faciam.*	I will cause to rejoice.
רוע	אָרַע	*Malefaciam.*	I will do hurt.
אריע	אַרְעָא	*Terra.*	The earth.
רע	אֲרַעא	*Inferius.*	Inferior.
רעב	אֶרְעַב	*Esuriam.*	I shall be hungry.
רעה	אֶרְעֶה	*Pascam.*	I will feed.
—	אֶרְעֶנָּה	*Pascam eam.*	I will feed her.
רפא	אֶרְפָּא־־פָּה	*Sanabo, curabo.*	I will heal, will cure.
—	אֶרְפָּאֵךְ	*Sanabo te.*	I will heal thee.
	אַרְפָּד	*Arphad.*	Arpad, N. P.
רפה	אַרְפֶּהָ	*Deseram, dimittam eam.*	I will leave her, let her go.
—	אַרְפְּךָ	*Derelinquam te.*	I will forsake thee.
	אַרְפַּכְשַׁד	*Arphaxad.*	Arphaxad, N. M.
רפה	אַרְפֶּנּוּ	*Dimittam eum.*	I will let him go.
ארץ			
—	אָרֶץ אֶרֶץ	*Terra, regio, patria.*	The earth, land, a country.
רוץ	אָרֻץ אָרֻצָה	*Curram, percurram.*	I will run, run through.
	אַרְצָא	*Arsa.*	Arza, N. M.
רצה	אֶרְצֶה	*Accipiam.*	I will accept.
ארץ	אַרְצָהּ	*Terra ejus.*	Her land.
—	אַרְצָה	*In, ad, super terram*	To, into, on, over the land, ground, country.
—	אַרְצוֹ	*Terra ejus.*	His land.
—	אֲרָצוֹת אַרְצוֹת	*Regiones, terræ.*	Countries, regions, lands.

ROOTS.	DERIVATIVES.	VERSIO.	SIGNIFICATION.
רצח	אֵרָצֵחַ	*Occidar.*	I shall be slain.
ארץ	אַרְצִי	*Terra mea.*	My land.
—	אַרְצְךָ אַרְצֶךָ	*Terra tua.*	Thy land.
—	אַרְצְכֶם	*Terra vestra.*	Your land.
—	אַרְצָם	*Terra eorum.*	Their land.
רצה	אֶרְצֵם	*Accipiam eos.*	I will accept them.
ארץ	אַרְצֵנוּ	*Terra nostra.*	Our country.
ארק			
רקע	אֶרְקָעֵם	*Obteram, dispergam eos.*	I will crush, disperse them.
אָרַר		*Maledixit.*	He cursed.
—	אֲרָרָהּ	*Maledixit ei.*	He hath cursed her.
	אֲרָרָט	*Ararat.*	Ararat, N. P.
	אֲרָרִי	*Ararites.*	Ararite, N. F,
ארר	אֹרְרֵי	*Maledicentes.*	They that curse.
—	אֹרְרֶיךָ	*Maledicentes tibi.*	They that curse thee.
ארשׂ			
ארשׁ			
—	אֵרַשׂ	*Desponsavit.*	He hath betrothed.
—	אֹרָשָׂה	*Desponsata est.*	She is betrothed.
רשע	אֶרְשָׁע	*Impius ero, impie agam.*	I shall be wicked, shall do wickedly.
ארש	אֵרַשְׂתִּי	*Desponsavi.*	I have espoused.
אור	אֹרֹת	*Olera.*	Herbs.
	אַרְתַּחְשַׁשְׁתָּא	*Artaxerxes.*	Artaxerxes, N. M.
	אַרְתַּחְשַׁסְתְּא	*Artaxerxes.*	Artaxerxes, N. M.
	אש		
אש			
—	אֵשׁ אֶשָּׁא	*Ignis.*	Fire.
נשא	אֶשָּׂא	*Attollam, feram, portabo, sumam, rapiam.*	I will lift up, bear, carry, take, take away.
שאב	אֶשְׁאַב	*Hauriam.*	I will draw.
שאר	אַשְׁאִיר	*Relinquam.*	I will leave.
שאל	אֶשְׁאַל־אֱלָה	*Petam.*	I will ask, desire.
—	אֶשְׁאָלְךָ	*Interrogabo te.*	I will ask of thee.

ROOTS.	DERIVATIVES.	VERSIO.	SIGNIFICATION.
נשׂא	אֶשָּׂאֶנּוּ	Portabo eum. [bitabo	I will bear it.
ישׁב	אֵשֵׁב	Sedebo, manebo, ha-	I will sit, remain, dwell.
שׁבר	אֶשְׁבּוֹר	Frangam, conteram	I will break, crush.
שׂבע	אַשְׂבִּיעַ	Saturabo.	I will satisfy.
—	אַשְׂבִּיעֵהוּ	Saturabo eum.	I will satisfy him.
—	אַשְׂבִּיעֵךְ	Saturabo te.	I will satisfy thee.
שׁבר	אַשְׁבִּיר	Matricem aperiam, adducam ad partum.	I shall bring to the birth.
שׁבת	אַשְׁבִּיתָה	Cessare faciam.	I will make to cease.
	אֶשְׁבָּל	Asbel.	Ashbal, N M.
	אֶשְׁבָּלִי	Asbelitæ.	Ashbelites, N. F.
	אֶשְׁבָּן	Esban.	Eshban, N. M.
שׁבע	אֶשָּׁבֵעַ	Jurabo.	I will swear.
—	אֶשְׂבַּע־בְּעָה	Satiabor	I shall be satisfied.
	אֶשְׁבָּעַל	Esbahal.	Esh-baal, N. M.
שׁבר	אֲשַׁבֵּר אֶשְׁבּׂר	Frangam, conteram.	I will break, crush.
שׂגב	אֲשַׂגְּבֵהוּ	Exaltabo eum.	I will set him on high.
אשׁד			
	אַשְׁדּוֹד־רָה	Asdod, Azotus.	Ashdod, N. P.
	אַשְׁדּוֹדִיּוֹת	Azotidæ.	Women of Ashdod, N. N.
	אַשְׁדּוֹדִים	Azotii.	Men of Ashdod, N. N.
	אַשְׁדּוֹדִית	Azoticè.	In the language of Ashdod.
אשׁד	אַשְׁדּוֹת אַשְׁדֹּת	Decursus, declivitates, radices.	The springs, declivities, bottoms.
אשׁ	אִשֶּׁה אִשֵּׁה	Oblatio ignita.	An offering made by fire.
אישׁ	אִשָּׁה	Mater, uxor; altera unaquæque.	A woman, a wife; another, any, every female.
אשׁ	אִשּׁוֹ	Ignis ejus.	His fire.
שׁוב	אָשׁוּב אָשׁוּבָה	Revertar.	I will return. [ed.
שׁוה	אֲשַׁוֶּה	Assimilabo, æquabor	I will liken, compare, be equal-
שׁוח	אֶשֹׂוֹחֵחַ	Meditabor.	I will meditate.
אשׁה	אֲשׁוּיֹתֶיהָ	Fundamenta ejus.	Her foundations.
שׁוע	אֲשַׁוֵּעַ אֲשַׁוַּע	Clamabo, vociferabo	I will cry, cry aloud.
שׁור	אָשׁוּר	Aspiciam, speculabor. [Assyria.	I will observe. [N. P.
	אַשּׁוּר־רָה	Assur, Assyrius,	Ashur, Assyrian, Assyria, N. M.

ROOTS.	DERIVATIVES.	VERSIO.	SIGNIFICATION.
	אַשּׁוּרִים	*Assurim.*	Ashurim, N. M.
רוש	אֲשׁוּרֶנּוּ	*Intuebor illum.*	I shall behold him.
שחה	אַשְׂחֶה	*Natare faciam.*	I will make to swim.
	אַשְׁחוּר	*Ashur.*	Ashur, N. M.
שחת	אַשְׁחִית	*Perdam.*	I will destroy.
—	אַשְׁחִיתֵם	*Perdam eos.*	I will destroy them.
שחק	אֶשְׂחָק	*Ridebo.* [*quæram.*	I will laugh. [gently.
שחר	אֲשַׁחֲרֶךָּ	*Diluculo, sedulo te.*	I will seek thee early, dili-
אש	אִשֵּׁי	Oblationes *ignitæ.*	Offerings made by fire.
אשש	אֻשְׁיָא	*Fundamenta.*	Foundations.
שוב	אָשִׁיב	*Reducam, redire faciam, restituam, reddam, respondebo.*	I will bring again, cause to return, restore, render, answer
שוב	אֲשִׁיבְךָ־־בְךָ	*Respondebo tibi.*	I will answer thee.
—	אֲשִׁיבֶנָּה	*Revocabo illud.*	I will reverse it.
—	אֲשִׁיבֶנּוּ	*Reducam eum, restituam illud, respondebo ei.* [*dam.*	I will bring him again, restore it, answer him.
נשג	אַשִּׂג	*Assequar, apprehen-*	I will overtake, seize.
אשה	אֻשְׁיוֹתֶיהָ	*Fundamenta ejus.*	Her foundations.
שוח	אָשִׂיחַ אָשִׂיחָה	*Meditabor, loquar.*	I will meditate, speak.
שום	אָשִׂים אָשִׂימָה	*Ponam, apponam.*	I will put, place, set, lay.
	אֲשִׁימָא	*Asima.*	Ashima, N. I.
שום	אֲשִׂימְךָ־־מֵךְ	*Ponam te.*	I will put thee.
—	אֲשִׂימֵם	*Ponam eos.*	I will put them.
—	אֲשִׂימֶנָּה	*Ponam eam.*	I will put her.
—	אֲשִׂימֶנּוּ	*Ponam eum.*	I will put him.
שור	אָשִׁיר אָשִׁירָה	*Cantabo.*	I will sing.
אשר	אֲשֵׁרָה	*Lucus.*	A grove.
—	אֲשֵׁירֶיךָ	*Luci tui.*	Thy groves.
שוש	אָשִׂישׂ	*Gaudebo.*	I will rejoice.
אשש	אֲשִׁישֵׁי	*Lagenæ.*	Flagons.
שות	אָשִׁית	*Ponam.*	I will put, place.
—	אֲשִׁיתְךָ־־תֵךְ	*Ponam te.*	I will put thee.
אשך			
—	אֶשֶׁךְ	*Testiculus.*	A testicle.

ROOTS.	DERIVATIVES.	VERSIO.	SIGNIFICATION.
שכב	אֶשְׁכָּב--כְּבָה	*Jacebo, recumbam.*	I will lie down.
	אֶשְׁכּוֹל	*Escol.*	Eshcol, N. P.
שכל	אֶשְׁכּוֹל--כֹּל	*Botrus, racemus.*	A cluster of grapes.
שכן	אֶשְׁכּוֹן-כָּן-כְּנָה	*Habitabo.*	I will dwell, inhabit.
שכח	אֶשְׁכַּח--כְּחָה	*Obliviscar.*	I will forget.
——	אֶשְׁכָּחֵךְ	*Obliviscar tui.*	I will forget thee.
שכל	אַשְׂכִּילָה	*Intelligam, prudenter agam.*	I will understand, behave myself wisely.
——	אַשְׂכִּילְךָ	*Erudiam te.*	I will instruct thee.
שכם	אַשְׁכֵּים	*Mane surgere.*	To rise early.
שכד	אַשְׁכִּיר	*Inebriabo.*	I will make drunk.
שכל	אֶשְׁכָּל	*Orbabor.*	I shall be deprived.
——	אַשְׁכְּלֹת	*Botri, racemi.*	Clusters.
——	אֶשְׁכְּלֹתֶיהָ	*Botri ejus.*	Her clusters.
אש	אֶשְׁכֶם	*Ignis vester.*	Your fire.
	אַשְׁכְּנַז	*Aschenaz.*	Ashkenaz, N. M.
שכר	אֶשְׁכָּר	*Munus, donum.*	A gift.
——	אֶשְׁכָּרֵךְ	*Munus tuum.*	Thy present, gift.
אשל			
——	אֵשֶׁל	*Nemus.*	A grove.
שלח	אֶשְׁלַח אֲשַׁלַּח	*Mittam.*	I will send.
——	אֶשְׁלָחֲךָ אֲשַׁלֵּחֲךָ	*Mittam te.*	I will send thee.
——	אֲשַׁלְּחֶנּוּ	*Mittam eum.*	I will send him.
שלך	אַשְׁלִיךְ	*Jaciam, projiciam.*	I will cast, cast out.
שלם	אֲשַׁלֵּם--לְמָה	*Reddam, retribuam.*	I will pay, recompence.
אָשַׁם		*Deliquit, reus fuit, desolavit.*	He transgressed, was guilty, destroyed.
——	אָשֹׁם	*Delinquere.*	To offend.
שמם	אָשֹׁם	*Desolabo.*	I will destroy.
אשם	אָשָׁם	*Delictum, reatus, victima pro delicto*	A tresspass, guiltiness, a trespass-offering.
——	אַשְׁמָה	*Delictum.*	A fault, delinquency.
——	אֲשָׁמוֹ	*Ejus reatus, sacrificium pro reatu.*	His tresspass, fault, trespass-offering.
——	אַשְׁמוֹת	*Delicta.*	Faults, sins.
שמח	אֶשְׂמַח--מְחָה	*Lætabor.*	I will rejoice, be glad.
שמד	אַשְׁמִיד	*Delebo, perdam.*	I will destroy.

ROOTS.	DERIVATIVES.	VERSIO.	SIGNIFICATION.
שמד	אַשְׁמִידְךָ	*Disperdam te.*	I will destroy thee.
אשם	אֲשֵׁמִים	*Rei, delinquentes.*	Guilty, faulty.
שמע	אַשְׁמִיעַ	*Audire faciam.*	I will cause to hear.
——	אַשְׁמִיעֲךָ	*Audire faciam te.*	I will cause thee to hear.
אשם	אֲשָׁמָם	*Eorum oblatio pro delicto.*	Their trespass offering.
שמם	אֲשִׁמֵּם	*Desolabo eos.*	I will make them desolate.
שמע	אֶשְׁמַע־־מְעָה	*Auscultabo, audiam.*	I will hearken, will hear.
שמר	אֶשְׁמֹר־־מְרָה	*Custodiam, observabo*	I will keep, observe.
——	אֶשְׁמְרָה	*Custodiam, observabo*	I will keep, observe
——	אַשְׁמֻרוֹת	*Vigiliæ.*	Night watches.
אשם	אַשְׁמַת	*Delictum.*	The trespass. [become guilty.
——	אָשַׁמְתְּ	*Deliquisti.* [*ejus.*	Thou hast transgressed or be-
——	אֲשָׁמוֹ	*Oblatio pro delicto*	His trespass offering.
——	אַשְׁמָתָם	*Delictum eorum.*	Their trespass.
——	אַשְׁמָתֵנוּ	*Delictum nostrum.*	Our trespass.
שנא	אֶשְׂנָא	*Odio habebo.*	I will hate.
שנב	אֶשְׁנַבִּי	*Fenestra mea.*	My casement.
	אַשְׁנָה	*Asna.*	Asna, N. P.
שנה	אֲשַׁנֶּה	*Mutabo.*	I will change.
——	אֶשְׁנֶה	*Iterabo.*	I will repeat.
	אֶשְׁעָן	*Eshen.*	Eshean, N. P.
אשף			
——	אַשְׁפָּה	*Pharetra.*	A quiver.
שפט	אֶשְׁפּוֹט־־פֹּט	*Judicabo.*	I will judge.
שפך	אֶשְׁפּוֹךְ־־פֹּךְ	*Effundam.*	I will pour out.
שפט	אִשָּׁפֵט	*Disceptabo.*	I will plead.
——	אֶשְׁפָּטְךָ	*Judicabo te.*	I will judge thee.
שפט	אֶשְׁפְּטֵם	*Judicabo eos.*	I will judge them.
אשף	אַשָּׁפַיָּא־פִין	*Astrologi.*	Astrologers.
שפל	אַשְׁפִּיל	*Humiliabo.*	I will lay low.
	אַשְׁפְּנַז	*Aspenaz.*	Ashpenaz, N. M.
אשף	אַשְׁפָּתוֹ	*Pharetra ejus.*	His quiver.
——	אַשְׁפַּתּוֹת	*Stercora.*	Dunghills.
שקד	אֶשְׁקֹד	*Vigilabo.*	I will watch.
שקה	אַשְׁקֶה	*Potum dabo.*	I will give drink.
נשק	אֶשָּׁקָה	*Osculabor*	I will kiss.

ROOTS.	DERIVATIVES	VERSIO.	SIGNIFICATION.
שקט	אֶשְׁקוֹט־קוֹטָה	*Quiescam.*	I will rest.
שקל	אֶשְׁקוֹל	*Appendam.*	I will pay, weigh out.
שקע	אַשְׁקִיעַ	*Profundum vel limpidum faciam.*	I will make deep or clear.
נשק	אֶשְׁקְךָ	*Osculabor te.*	I will kiss thee.
שקה	אַשְׁקְךָ	*Bibere faciam te.*	I will cause thee to drink.
	אַשְׁקְלוֹן	*Ascalon.*	Askelon, N. P.
	אַשְׁקְלוֹנִי	*Ascalonitæ.*	Askelonites, N. N.
שקה	אַשְׁקֶנָּה	*Irrigabo eam.*	I will water her.
שקר	אֶשְׁקֹר	*Mentiar, fallam.*	I will lie, deceive.
	אָשֵׁר	*Asher.*	Asher, N. M.
אָשַׁר		*Beatum dixit vel reddidit; incessit, direxit.*	He called or rendered happy; he walked, led, directed.
—	אֲשֶׁר	*Qui, quæ, quod, is qui, talis, qualis, quodcunque; quia quod, cum, ubi, quo, et, ideo, nam, postquam, prout, quamvis, quandoquidem, quomodo, si, ut, ita ut, vel.*	Who, which, he who, such, as, whatever: because, when, where, whither, and, therefore, for, after that, as, though, since, how, if, that, so that, or.
	אֲשַׂרְאֵל־לָה	*Asriel.*	Asriel, N. M.
אשר	אֲשֵׁרָה	*Lucus.*	A grove.
—	אַשְׁרֵהוּ	*Beatus ipse.*	Happy he.
—	אַשְּׁרוּ	*Dirigite, erigite.*	Direct, relieve ye.
—	אִשְׁרוּ	*Incipite.*	Walk ye.
—	אִשְּׁרוּנִי	*Beatam prædicabunt me.*	They shall call me blessed.
	אֲשֵׁרוֹת	*Asheroth.*	Asheroth, N. I.
אשר	אֲשֵׁרוֹת	*Luci.*	Groves.
—	אַשְׁרֵי	*Beati; beatitudines.*	Happy; blessedness.
—	אֲשֻׁרַי	*Gressus mei.*	My goings.
—	אֲשֻׁרִי	*Gressus meus.*	My step.
	אַשְׂרִיאֵל	*Asrael.*	Asrael, N. M.
אשר	אֲשֵׁרֵיהֶם	*Luci eorum.*	Their groves.
—	אֲשֵׁרָיו	*Luci ejus.*	His groves.

ROOTS.	DERIVATIVES.	VERSIO.	SIGNIFICATION.
אשר	אַשְׁרָיו	*Beatus ipse.*	Happy he.
—	אֲשֻׁרָיו	*Gressus ejus.*	His steps.
—	אַשְׁרֶיךָ־־רַיִךְ	*Beatus tu.*	Happy thou.
—	אַשְׁרֵיכֶם	*Beati vos.*	Happy ye.
	אֲשֻׁרִים	*Assyrii.*	Ashurites, N. N.
אשר	אֲשֵׁרִים	*Luci.*	Groves.
—	אֲשֻׁרֵנוּ אַשֻּׁרֵנוּ	*Gressus noster.*	Our steps.
שרק	אֶשְׁרְקָה	*Sibilabo.*	I will hiss.
אשש			
איש	אִשֹּׁת	*Mulieres.*	Women.
—	אֵשֶׁת	*Uxor.*	The wife.
	אֶשְׁתָּאוֹל־־אֹל	*Estaol*	Eshtaol, N. P.
שתה	אֶשְׁתֶּה	*Bibam.*	I will drink.
איש	אִשְׁתּוֹ	*Uxor ejus.*	His wife.
שלל	אֶשְׁתּוֹלְלוּ	*Spoliati sunt.*	They are spoiled.
שמם	אֶשְׁתּוֹמָם	*Obstupuit.*	He was astonished.
	אֶשְׁתּוֹן	*Eston.*	Eshton, N. M.
שנן	אֶשְׁתּוֹנָן	*Pungar.*	I shall be pricked.
שחה	אֶשְׁתַּחֲוֶה	*Incurvabo me.*	I will bow myself, will worship
איש	אִשְׁתִּי	*Uxor mea.*	My wife.
שתה	אִשְׁתִּיו	*Biberunt.*	They drank.
איש	אִשְׁתְּךָ־־תֵּךְ	*Uxor tua.*	Thy wife.
שתל	אֶשְׁתֳּלֶנּוּ	*Plantabo eum.*	I will plant it.
	אֶשְׁתְּמוֹעַ־־מֹעַ	*Estemoa.*	Eshtemoa, N. P.
שות	אֲשִׁתֵנוּ	*Ponam, constituam* [*eum.*	I will place, or make him.
שנא	אֶשְׁתַּנִּי	*Immutatus est.*	He was changed.
שעה	אֶשְׁתַּעֲשָׁע	*Oblectabo me.*	I will delight myself.
	את		
את			
—	אֶת אֵת	*Ab, ad, apud, contra, coram, cum, de, ex, erga, in, inter, per, præ, præter, prope, propter, secundum, super, versus.*	From, to, with, against, before, together, with, concerning, out of, towards, in, among, through, for, beside, by, because of, after, upon.

ROOTS.	DERIVATIVES.	VERSIO.	SIGNIFICATION.
את	אַתְּ אַתְ	*Tu.* [*nit.*	Thou. [fel.
אתה	אָתָא אֲתָא	*Venit, accessit, eve-*	He, or it, came, happened, be-
אפק	אֶתְאַפַּק	*Continebo me.* [*gam.*	I will restrain myself.
בון	אֶתְבּוֹנָן־נָן	*Considerabo, intelli-*	I will consider, understand.
	אֶתְבַּעַל	*Ethbaal.*	Ethbaal, N. M.
נזר	אִתְגְּזֶרֶת	*Abscissus est.*	He was cut out, or off.
אָתָה		*Venit, evenit.*	He or it came, befel.
—	אָתָה	*Venit.*	He came.
—	אָתֶה	*Veniens.*	Coming.
את	אַתָּה	*Tu.*	Thou.
—	אִתָּהּ	*Cum ea.*	With her.
—	אֹתָהּ	*Eam.*	Her.
הלך	אֶתְהַלֵּךְ	*Ambulabo.*	I will walk.
את	אֶתְהֶם	*Eos.*	Them.
—	אֶתְהֶן	*Eas.*	Them.
—	אִתּוֹ	*Cum eo.*	With him.
—	אֵתוֹ	*Ligo ejus.*	His coulter, ploughshare.
—	אֹתוֹ	*Eum.*	Him.
אתה	אָתוּ	*Venerunt.*	They came.
ידע	אֶתְוַדַּע	*Notum faciam me.*	I will make myself known.
אות	אָתוֹהִי	*Signa ejus.*	His signs.
אתן	אַתּוּן	*Fornax.*	The furnace.
—	אֲתוֹנוֹת	*Asinæ.*	Asses.
נתש	אֶתּוֹשׁ	*Evellam.*	I will pluck up.
אות	אֹתוֹת אֹתֹת	*Signa.*	Tokens.
—	אֹתוֹתָיו	*Signa ejus.*	His signs.
—	אוֹתֹתֵינוּ	*Signa nostra.*	Our signs.
—	אֹתוֹתָם	*Signa eorum.*	Their signs.
חבר	אֶתְחַבַּר	*Junxit se.*	He joined himself.
חנן	אֶתְחַנֶּן־נַּן	*Deprecabor.*	I will intreat.
	אִתַּי	*Itai.*	Ittai, N. M.
את	אִתִּי	*Mecum.*	With me.
—	אֹתִי	*Me.*	Me.
אות	אָתַיָּא	*Signa.*	Signs.
אתה	אֵתָיוּ	*Venite.*	Come ye.
את	אִתֵּיכֶם	*Ligones vestri.*	Your ploughshares.
אות	אָתִין	*Signa.*	Signs.

ROOTS.	DERIVATIVES.	VERSIO.	SIGNIFICATION.
יעט	אִתְיָעֲטוּ	*Consilium inierunt.*	They consulted together.
נתק	אַתִּיק	*Porticus.*	A gallery.
—	אַתִּיקִים	*Porticus.*	Galleries.
את	אִתָּךְ	*Tecum.*	With thee.
—	אִתְּכֶם	*Vobiscum.*	With you.
כרא	אֶתְכְּרִית	*Fracta est.*	She is broken.
	אֵתָם	*Etam.*	Etham, N. P.
את	אַתֶּם	*Vos.*	Ye.
—	אֹתָם	*Eos.*	Them.
—	אִתָּם	*Cum eis.*	With them.
תמל	אֶתְמוֹל	*Heri.*	Yesterday.
תמך	אֶתְמֹךְ	*Innitar, sustentabo.*	I will support, uphold.
אתן			
את	אֹתָן אֹתָנָה	*Eas.* [*nam.*	Them.
נתן	אֶתֵּן אֶתֶּן	*Dabo, tradam, po-*	I will give, deliver, set.
אית	אֵתָן	*Validus, fortis.*	Strong.
את	אַתֵּנָה	*Vos.*	Ye.
תנה	אֶתְנָה אֶתְנַן	*Merces.*	Reward, hire.
נתן	אֶתְּנָה	*Dabo.*	I will give.
—	אֶתְּנֵהוּ	*Dabo, tradam eum.*	I will give, or deliver him.
נהל	אֶתְנַהֲלָה	*Ducam me, incedam*	I will lead myself, walk on.
את	אִתָּנוּ	*Nobiscum.*	With us.
—	אֹתָנוּ	*Nos.*	Us.
אתה	אָתָנוּ	*Venimus.*	We come.
אתן	אֲתֹנוֹ	*Asina ejus.*	His ass.
—	אֲתֹנוֹת אֲתֹנֹת	*Asinæ.*	The asses.
	אֶתְנִי	*Ethni.*	Ethni, N. M.
	אֵתָנִים	*Ethanim.*	Ethanim, N. Mth.
אתן	אֲתֹנְךָ	*Asina tua.* [*nam te.*	Thy ass. [thee.
נתן	אֶתֶּנְךָ אֶתְּנֶךָּ	*Dabo, tradam, po-*	I will give up, deliver, make
	אֶתְנָן	*Ethnan.*	Ethnan, N. M.
נתן	אֶתְּנֶנָּה־־נֶּנּוּ	*Dabo eam, eum.*	I will give her, him.
תנה	אֶתְנַנֶּיהָ	*Dona, mercedes ejus*	Her gifts, wages.
עקר	אֶתְעַקְּרוּ	*Evulsa sunt.*	They were plucked up.
פאר	אֶתְפָּאַר	*Gloriabor.*	I will be glorified.
פלל	אֶתְפַּלָּל	*Orabo.*	I will pray.
נתץ	אֶתֹּץ	*Diruam, destruam.*	I will break down, destroy.

ROOTS.	DERIVATIVES.	VERSIO.	SIGNIFICATION.
קוט	אֶתְקוֹטָט	*Contendam, fastidiam, abominabor.*	I will contend with, loath, be weary of, abominate.
נתק	אֶתְּקֶנְךָּ	*Evellam te.*	I will pluck up thee.
אתר			
—	אֲתַר	*Locus.*	The place.
—	אַתְרֵהּ	*Locus ejus.*	His place.
רוע	אֶתְרוֹעָע	*Exultabo, jubilabo.*	I will triumph.
אות	אֹתֹתַי	*Signa mea.*	My signs.
—	אֹתֹתָיו	*Signa ejus.*	His signs.

בא

ROOTS.	DERIVATIVES.	VERSIO.	SIGNIFICATION.
בוא	בָּא	*Venit, ingressus est, occubuit ; veniens*	He came, went, entered, set ; coming.
—	בֹּא	*Venire, ingredi ; vade, veni, ingredere ; occasus.*	To come, enter ; go, come, enter thou ; the setting.
אבד	בָּאֲבַדּוֹן	*In interitu.*	In destruction.
—	בְּאָבְדַן	*In perditione.*	In the destruction.
אבב	בְּאִבּוֹ	*In virore ejus.*	In his greenness.
אבה	בַּאֲבוֹתֶיךָ	*In patribus tuis.*	In thy fathers.
—	בַּאֲבוֹתֵיכֶם	*In patres vestros.*	Unto your fathers.
אבב	בְּאִבֵּי	*In fructus.*	On the fruits.
אבן	בָּאֶבֶן בָּאָ־ בָּאֶ־	*Cum lapide, pondere.*	With a stone, a weight.
אבנט	בָּאַבְנֵט	*Balteo.*	With the girdle.
אבן	בְּאַבְנֵי	*Cum lapidibus.*	With the stones.
—	בָּאֲבָנִים	*Cum lapidibus.*	With stones.
אבר	בְּאֶבְרָתוֹ	*Alâ ejus.*	With his wing.
אגן	בָּאַגָּנוֹת	*In crateribus.*	In basons.
גרף	בְּאֶגְרוֹף־רֹף	*Pugno.*	With the fist.
אגר	בָּאִגְּרוֹת	*Cum epistolis.*	With the letters.
אדן	בֵּאדַיִן	*Tunc.*	Then.
אדר	בְּאַדִּיר	*Per potentem.*	By a mighty one.
אדם	בָּאָדָם בְּאָדָם	*In homine.*	Within man.
—	בָּאֲדָמָה	*In terra.*	In the land.
אדן	בַּאדֹנִי	*In dominum meum.*	Against my Lord.

ROOTS.	DERIVATIVES.	VERSIO.	SIGNIFICATION.
אדן	בַּאדֹנָי	*In Domino.*	In the Lord.
דרע	בְּאֶדְרָע	*Brachio, per vim.*	By force.
אדר	בְּאַדַּרְתּוֹ	*In pallio ejus.*	In his mantle.
בוא	בָּאָה	*Venit, ingressa est.*	She went, came, entered.
—	בֹּאָה	*Venire eam.*	She comes, her coming.
אהב	בְּאַהֲבָה	*Pro dilectione.*	For love.
—	בְּאֲהָבִים	*Amoribus.*	With loves.
—	בְּאַהֲבַת	*Pro dilectione.*	In the love.
—	בְּאַהֲבָתָהּ	*In amore ejus.* [*ejus*	With her love.
—	בְּאַהֲבָתוֹ	*Propter dilectionem*	In, or because of, his love.
אהל	בְּאֹהֶל בָּא־־	*In tentorio, in tentorium.*	In, into the tent, tabernacle.
—	בְּאָהֳלוֹ	*In tentorio ejus.*	In his tent.
—	בְּאָהֳלֵי	*In tentoriis.*	In his tents.
—	בְּאָהֳלֵיהֶם	*In tentoriis eorum.*	In their tents.
—	בְּאֹהָלֶיךָ	*In tentoriis tuis.*	In thy tents.
—	בְּאָהֳלֵיכֶם	*In tentoriis vestris.*	In your tents.
—	בְּאֹהָלִים	*In tentoriis.*	In tents.
—	בְּאָהָלֶךָ בְּאָהָלְךָ	*In tentorio tuo.* [*sunt*	In thy tent.
בוא	בָּאוּ	*Venerunt, ingressi*	They came, went in.
—	בֹּאוּ	*Venite, ingredimini.*	Come, enter ye.
—	בֹּאוֹ	*Venire se, introitus ejus.*	He came, his entrance.
אוב	בָּאוֹב	*Per pythonem.*	By the familiar spirit.
אלם	בָּאוּלָם	*In porticu.*	In the porch.
אול	בְּאִוַּלְתּוֹ	*In stultitia ejus.*	In his folly.
אפן	בָּאוֹפַנִּים	*In rotis.*	In wheels.
אצר	בְּאוֹצָרוֹת	*In thesauris.*	In storehouses.
—	בָּאוֹצָרוֹת	*In thesauris.*	In storehouses.
—	בְּאוֹצְרוֹתֶיךָ	*In thesauris tuis.*	In thy treasures.
—	בְּאוֹצְרֹתָי	*In thesauris meis.*	In my treasures.
—	בְּאוֹצְרֹתָיו	*In thesauris ejus.*	In his treasures.
אור	בָּאוֹר בְּאוֹר	*In luce, lumine.*	In the light.
—	בָּאוּר בְּאוּר	*In igne, flamma.*	In the fire, flame.
—	בָּאוּרִים	*Per urim.*	By the urim.
—	בְּאוֹרְךָ	*In luce tua.*	In thy light.
בוא	בָּאוֹת	*Venientes.*	Coming.

ROOTS.	DERIVATIVES.	VERSIO.	SIGNIFICATION.
אוה	בְּאַוַּת	*Pro desiderio.*	At pleasure, according to desire.
—	בְּאַוָּתִי	*Pro desiderio meo.*	In my desire.
אזב	בְּאֵזוֹב	*Cum hyssopo.*	With hyssop.
אזן	בְּאָזְנוֹ	*In aure ejus.*	In his ear.
—	בְּאָזְנַי־נַי	*In auribus meis.*	In my ears.
—	בְּאָזְנֵי	*In auribus.*	In the ears.
—	בְּאָזְנֵיהֶם	*In auribus eorum.*	In their ears.
—	בְּאָזְנָיו	*In auribus ejus.*	In his ears.
—	בְּאָזְנֶיךָ־נֶיךָ	*In auribus tuis.*	In thy ears.
—	בְּאָזְנֵיכֶם	*In auribus vestris.*	In your ears.
—	בְּאָזְנֵינוּ	*In auribus nostris.*	In our ears.
אזק	בְּאַזִּקִּים	*In catenis.*	In chains.
זרח	בְּאֶזְרָח	*Indigena.*	A native of the country.
אחד	בְּאֶחָד בְּאַחַד	*In uno, primo, quolibet.*	In one, the first, some.
אחה	בְּאָחוּ	*In prato.*	In a meadow.
אחר	בְּאָחוֹר	*In posterum.*	Till afterwards.
אחז	בֶּאֱחֹז	*In capiendo.*	In taking hold.
—	בַּאֲחֻזָּתוֹ	*In possessione ejus.*	In his possession.
—	בַּאֲחֻזָּתָם	*In possessione eorum*	In their possession.
אחה	בְּאָחִיהוּ	*Ad alterum.*	To another.
—	בְּאָחִיו	*In fratrem ejus.*	To, toward, against, his brother.
—	בְּאֶחָיו	*Inter fratres ejus.*	Among his brethren.
—	בְּאָחִיךָ	*In fratrem tuum.*	Toward thy brother.
דנה	בְּאַחַר דְּנָה	*Posthac, postea.*	After, afterwards.
אחר	בְּאַחֲרוֹנָה־־רֹנָה	*In fine.*	In the end.
—	בְּאַחֲרֵי	*Cum infima parte.*	With the hinder end.
—	בְּאַחֲרִית	*In postremo.*	In the last.
—	בְּאַחֲרִיתָהּ	*In extremo ejus.*	In her end.
—	בְּאַחֲרִיתֶךָ	*In extremo tuo.*	At thy end.
אחד	בְּאַחַת בְּאֶחָת	*In una.*	In one.
אחה	בַּאֲחֹתָהּ	*In sororem ejus.*	Toward, against her sister.
בוא	בֹּאִי	*Adventus, reditus meus; vade, ingredere.*	My coming, return; go, enter thou.
—	בָּאֵי	*Venientes.*	They that come.
איב	בְּאֵיבָה	*Per inimicitiam.*	In enmity.

ROOTS.	DERIVATIVES.	VERSIO.	SIGNIFICATION.
איב	בְּאֹיְבַי	*In inimicis.*	Amongst the enemies.
איד	בְּאֵידְכֶם	*In calamitate vestra.*	In, at your calamity.
בוא	בָּאֶיהָ	*Venientes ad eam.*	They that go unto her.
אי	בָּאִיִּי	*In insulis.*	In the isles.
—	בָּאִיִּים	*In insulis.*	In the islands.
איל	בְּאַיִל בְּאֵיל	*In ariete, per arietem.*	In, or with a ram.
—	בְּאַיָּלוֹת	*In cervis.*	By the hinds.
—	בָּאֵילִים	*Ad postes.* [*tes.*	By the posts.
בוא	בָּאִים	*Venientes, ingredientes.*	Coming, entering.
אים	בְּאֵימָה	*Cum timore.*	With fear.
אין	בְּאֵין	*Absque, ubi non, ita ut nemo.*	Without, where not, so that no one.
איש	בְּאִישׁ בָּאִישׁ	*In virum.*	Unto the man.
—	בְּאִישָׁהּ	*In virum ejus.*	To her husband.
—	בְּאִישׁוֹן	*In obscuritate.*	In the black, blackness.
אית	בְּאֵיתָן	*In robore.*	In strength.
בוא	בֹּאֶךָ	*Adventus tuus.*	Thy coming.
—	בֹּאֲךָ	*Venire, vadere te.*	Thou comest, goest.
—	בֹּאֲכָה	*Veniendo te.*	As thou comest.
אכל	בְּאָכְל	*In devorando.*	In devouring.
—	בֶּאֱכֹל	*Consumendo.*	In consuming.
—	בָּאֹכֶל	*Pro cibo.*	For food.
—	בְּאֹכְלֵי	*Inter comedentes.*	Among those that eat.
—	בַּאֲכָלְכֶם	*Comedendo vos.*	In your eating.
—	בְּאָכְלָם	*Comedendo ipsos.*	When they eat.
—	בְּאָכְלֵנוּ	*Comedendo nos.*	When we eat.
בוא	בֹּאֲכֶם	*Venire vos.*	That you come, your coming
אלה	בְּאֵל	*Per Deum.*	By God.
—	בְּאָלָה	*Cum execratione.*	With an oath, a curse.
—	בָּאֵלָה	*In quercu.*	In an oak.
אל	בְּאֵלֶּה בָּאֵלֶּה	*In illis, his.*	In them, these.
אלה	בֵּאלֹהָיו	*In Deo ejus.*	In his God.
—	בֵּאלֹהַי	*In Deo meo.*	In or by my God.
—	בֵּאלֹהֵי	*In Deo, in, per Deum*	In against, by the God.
—	בֵּאלֹהֶיהָ	*In, per Deum ejus.*	Against, by her God.
—	בֵּאלֹהָיו	*Per Deum ejus, in deo ejus.*	By, in his God.

ROOTS.	DERIVATIVES.	VERSIO.	SIGNIFICATION.
אלה	בֵּאלֹהֶיךָ	*Ad Deum tuum.*	To thy God.
—	בֵּאלֹהֵיכֶם	*In Deum vestrum.*	Toward, against your God.
—	בָּאֱלֹהִים	*Inter deos.*	Amongst the gods.
—	בֵּאלֹהִים	*In Deo; per, contra deum, deos.*	In, by, against God, gods.
—	בֵּאלֹהֵינוּ	*In Deum nostrum.*	Toward our God.
אלף	בְּאַלּוּף	*In duce.*	In a guide.
אלל	בָּאֱלִילִים	*In idolis.*	Amongst the idols.
איל	בָּאֵלִים	*Inter fortes*	Amongst the mighty.
אלה	בָּאֵלִים	*In diis.* [*suis.*	Amongst gods.
אלם	בְּאַלְמְנוֹתָיו	*In ædibus viduatis*	In their desolate houses.
אלן	בְּאֵלֹנֵי	*In planitie, querceto.*	In the plain, forest.
אלף	בְּאֶלֶף	*Cum mille.*	With a thousand.
—	בְּאַלְפָו־־פָּיו	*In millibus ejus.*	In his thousands.
—	בְּאַלְפֵי	*In millibus.*	Among the thousands.
בוא	בֹּאָם	*Venire eos, adventus eorum.*	They come, their coming.
אמם	בְּאִמָּהּ	*In matrem ejus.*	Against her mother.
—	בָּאַמָּה	*In cubito.* [*nere.*	In a cubit.
אמן	בֶּאֱמוּנָה־־מֻנָה	*In veritate, fide, mu-*	In truth, faithfulness, office.
—	בֶּאֱמוּנָתוֹ	*In fide ejus.*	In his faithfulness.
—	בֶּאֱמוּנָתִי	*In fide mea.*	In my faithfulness.
—	בֶּאֱמוּנָתֶךָ	*In veritate tua.*	In thy truth.
—	בֶּאֱמֻנָתְךָ	*In veritate tua.*	In thy truth.
—	בֶּאֱמוּנָתָם	*In veritate, munere eorum.*	In their truth, office.
אמם	בְּאִמְּכֶם	*Cum matre vestra.*	With your mother. [cation
אמן	בְּאָמְנָה	*In nutritione.*	When brought up, during edu-
אמץ	בְּאַמְּצוֹ	*Firmando eum.*	In establishing him.
אמר	בֶּאֱמֹר	*Dicendo.*	In speaking.
—	בְּאָמְרִי	*Dicendo me.*	In my speaking.
—	בְּאִמְרֵי	*In verbis.*	In words.
—	בְּאֹמְרִים	*Cum dicentibus.*	With those who say.
—	בֶּאֱמָרְכֶם	*Dicendo vos.*	In that ye say.
—	בְּאָמְרָם	*Dicendo eos.*	While they say.
—	בְּאִמְרָתֶךָ	*In verbo tuo.*	In thy word.
אמם	בְּאַמַּת	*In cubito.*	In a cubit.

ROOTS.	DERIVATIVES.	VERSIO.	SIGNIFICATION.
אמן	בֶּאֱמֶת	*In veritate; reverà fideliter.*	In truth; truly, faithfully.
מתח	בְּאַמְתַּחַת	*In sacco.*	In the sack.
—	בְּאַמְתַּחְתִּי	*In sacco meo.*	In my sack.
—	בְּאַמְתְּחֹתֵיכֶם	*In saccis vestris.*	In your sacks.
—	בְּאַמְתְּחֹתֵינוּ	*In saccis nostris.*	In our sacks.
אמן	בַּאֲמִתֶּךָ־־תְּךָ	*In veritate tua.*	In thy truth.
בוא	בֹּאָנָה	*Adventus eorum.*	Their coming.
—	בֹּאֵנוּ	*Reditus noster.*	Our returning.
—	בָּאנוּ	*Venimus.*	We came.
אנש	בֶּאֱנוֹשׁ	*In homine.*	In man.
אנח	בַּאֲנָחָה	*Cum gemitu.*	With sighing.
—	בְּאַנְחָתִי	*In gemitu meo.*	In or with my groaning.
און	בְּאוֹנִי	*In tristitia mea.*	In my sorrow.
אנה	בָּאֳנִי	*In classe.*	In the navy.
—	בָּאֳנִיָּה	*In navi.*	In the ship.
—	בָּאֳנִיּוֹת	*In navibus.*	In the ships.
אנק	בֶּאֱנֹק	*In clamando, gemendo.*	In crying, lamenting.
אנש	בְּאַנְשֵׁי	*Inter homines.*	Among the men.
—	בָּאֲנָשִׁים	*In, ex viris.*	In, among, from, of men.
אסם	בַּאֲסָמֶיךָ	*In horreis tuis.*	In thy barns, storehouses.
אסף	בָּאֲסֻפֵּי	*In cœtibus, vestibulis collegeris.*	In the assemblies, at the threshold.
—	בְּאָסְפְּךָ	*Colligendo te, cum*	When thou hast gathered.
—	בְּאָסְפְּכֶם	*Colligendo vos.*	When ye have gathered.
אסר	בְּאָסְרָם	*Vinciendo eos.*	When they bind.
אנף	בְּאַף בָּאַף	*In ira, in naso.*	With or in anger, in the nose.
—	בְּאַפּוֹ	*In ira ejus.*	In his anger.
—	בְּאַפִּי	*In ira mea. ejus.*	In my anger.
—	בְּאַפָּיו	*In nares, in naribus*	Into, in his nostrils.
—	בְּאַפַּיִם	*In ira.*	In anger.
אפק	בַּאֲפִיקִים	*Ad alveos.*	By the rivers.
אנף	בְּאַפְּךָ־־פֵּךְ	*In furore, naso, conspectu tuo.*	In thine anger, nose, presence.
אפל	בָּאֹפֶל בְּאֲפֵלָה	*In caligine.*	In darkness.
—	בַּאֲפֵלוֹת	*In summa caligine.*	In very great darkness.
אנף	בְּאַפָּם	*In ira eorum.*	In their anger.

ROOTS.	DERIVATIVES.	VERSIO.	SIGNIFICATION.
אפס	בְּאֶפֶס	*Absque.* [*mine.*	Without.
אפר	בָּאֵפֶר בְּאֵפֶר	*In cinere; cum vela-*	In, with ashes; with a veil.
צבע	בְּאֶצְבַּע	*Digito.*	With the finger.
—	בְּאֶצְבָּעוֹ	*Digito ejus.*	With his finger.
—	בְּאֶצְבָּעֲךָ	*Digito tuo.*	With thy finger.
—	בְּאֶצְבְּעֹתָיו	*Digitis ejus.*	With his fingers.
אצר	בְּאֹצְרוֹת	*In thesauris.*	In treasures.
—	בְּאֹצְרֹתָי	*In thesauris meis.*	In my treasures.
—	בְּאֹצְרֹתֶיהָ	*In thesauris ejus.*	In her treasures.
בָּאַר		*Declaravit, explanavit.* [*do; clare.*	He declared, explained.
—	בָּאֵר	*Declarare, declaran-*	To declare, declaring; clearly
—	בֵּאֵר	*Declaravit.*	He declared.
—	בְּאֵר	*Puteus.*	A well.
	בְּאֵר לַחַי רֹאִי	*Beer-lachai-roi.*	Beer-lahai-roi, N. P.
	בְּאֵר רָאמֹת	*Beer-ramath.*	Beer-ramath, N. P.
	בְּאֵר שֶׁבַע־שָׁבַע	*Beer-seba.*	Beer-sheba, N. P.
רבה	בָּאַרְבֶּה	*Pro locusta.*	For the locust.
ארב	בָּאֲרֻבּוֹת	*In fenestris.*	In the windows.
—	בְּאָרְבָּם	*In insidias eorum.*	While they lie in wait.
רבע	בְּאַרְבַּע	*In quatuor.*	In four.
—	בְּאַרְבָּעָה	*In quarta.*	In the fourth.
—	בְּאַרְבָּעִים	*In quadraginta, quadragesimo.*	In forty, in the fortieth.
—	בְּאַרְבַּעַת	*In quatuor.*	In the four.
ארג	בָּאַרְגָּז	*In capsa.*	In a coffer, box.
—	בָּאַרְגָּמָן	*In purpura.*	In purple.
	בְּאֵרָא	*Bera.*	Beera, N. M.
	בְּאֵרָה	*Bera.*	Beerah, N. M.
ארן	בָּאָרוֹן בָּאֲרוֹן	*In arcam, in arca.*	Into, in the ark.
	בְּאֵרוֹת	*Beroth.*	Beeroth, N. P.
באר	בֹּארוֹת	*Cisternæ.*	Cisterns.
—	בֶּאֱרוֹת בְּאֵרֹת	*Putei.*	Pits, wells.
ארז	בָּאֶרֶז	*In cedro.*	In cedar.
—	בָּאֲרָזַיִךְ	*In cedros tuas.*	On thy cedars.
—	בָּאֲרָזִים	*In cedris.*	In cedars.
ארח	בְּאֹרַח	*In semita.*	In a path.

ROOTS.	DERIVATIVES.	VERSIO.	SIGNIFICATION.
ארה	בְּאָרְחוֹתָיו	*In semitis ejus.*	In his paths.
	בְּאֵרִי	*Beeri.*	Beeri, N. M.
אור	בְּאֹרִים	*In vallibus.*	In the vallies.
ארך	בְּאֹרֶךְ בְּאֹרֶךְ	*In longitudine.*	In length.
באר	בְּאֵרֶךָ	*Puteus tuus.*	Thine own well.
ארם	בְּאַרְמוֹן	*In palatio.*	In the palace.
—	בְּאַרְמְנוֹתֶיהָ	*In palatiis ejus.*	In her palaces.
—	בְּאַרְמְנוֹתֵיהֶם	*In palatiis eorum.*	In their palaces.
—	בְּאַרְמְנוֹתָיִךְ	*In palatiis tuis.*	Within thy palaces.
—	בְּאַרְמְנוֹתֵינוּ	*In palatia nostra.*	Into our palaces.
ארע	בְּאַרְעָא	*In terra.* [ram.	In the earth.
ארץ	בְּאֶרֶץ בְּאָרֶץ	*In, per, super ter-*	On, to, through the earth.
—	בְּאַרְצוֹ	*In terra ejus.*	In his land.
—	בְּאַרְצוֹת בְּאַר"	*In terris, per terras.*	In, through, the lands.
—	בְּאַרְצִי	*In terra mea.*	In my land.
—	בְּאַרְצְךָ--צֵךְ	*In terra tua.*	In thy land.
—	בְּאַרְצְכֶם	*In terra vestra.*	In your land.
—	בְּאַרְצָם	*In terra eorum.*	In their land.
—	בְּאַרְצֵנוּ	*In terra nostra.*	In our land.
—	בְּאַרְצֹתָם	*In terris eorum.*	In their lands.
	בְּאֵרֹתִי־ ־תִים	*Beerothites.*	Beerothite, N. P. [some.
בָּאַשׁ		*Fœtuit.* [nem.	He or it stank, became loath-
אש	בָּאֵשׁ בְּאֵשׁ	*In igne; in, per ig-*	In, into, through, on fire.
באש	בְּאֹשׁ	*Fœtor.*	The stink.
—	בְּאַשׁ	*Displicuit ei.*	He was displeased.
—	בָּאְשָׁה	*Lolium.*	Cockle, or tares.
איש	בְּאִשָּׁה	*Propter uxorem.*	For a wife.
באש	בָּאְשׁוֹ	*Fœtor ejus.*	His stink.
—	בְּאֻשִׁים	*Labruscæ.*	Wild grapes.
אשש	בַּאֲשִׁישׁוֹת	*Lagenis.*	With flagons.
שכל	בְּאֶשְׁכּוֹל	*In botro.*	In the cluster.
באש	בְּאָשְׁם	*In fœtore eorum.*	In their stink.
אשם	בְּאַשְׁמָה	*In delicto.*	In a trespass.
—	בַּאֲשָׁמָיו	*In delictis ejus.*	In his trespasses.
שמן	בְּאַשְׁמַנִּים	*In locis pinguibus.*	In fat, or plentiful places.
שמר	בְּאַשְׁמֻרוֹת	*In vigiliis.*	In the night watches.
—	בְּאַשְׁמֹרֶת	*In vigilia.*	In the watch.

ROOTS.	DERIVATIVES.	VERSIO.	SIGNIFICATION.
אשם	בְּאַשְׁמַת	*Per delictum.*	By the sin.
—	בְּאַשְׁמָתֵינוּ	*In delictis nostris.*	In our trespasses.
—	בְּאַשְׁמָתָם	*In delictum eorum.*	For their trespass.
אשף	בְּאַשְׁפָּתוֹ	*In pharetra ejus.*	In his quiver.
אשר	בַּאֲשֶׁר	*In quo; quod, ubi.*	In which; because, where.
—	בַּאֲשֻׁרוֹ	*In gressu ejus.*	In his steps.
—	בְּאָשְׁרִי	*In felicitate mea.*	In my happiness.
איש	בְּאִשְׁתּוֹ	*Cum uxore ejus.*	With his wife.
בוא	בָּאתָ בָּאת	*Venisti.*	Thou art come.
—	בָּאתָה	*Ingressus es.*	Thou hast gone in.
אות	בְּאֹתוֹת--תֹת	*In, cum signis.*	In, with signs.
בוא	בָּאתִי	*Veni.*	I came.
—	בָּאתֶם	*Venistis.*	Ye came.
—	בָּאַתְנוּ	*Venit nobis.*	It is come upon us.
בתר	בָּאתַר	*Post.*	After.
	בב		
בוא	בְּבֹא בְּבוֹא	*Veniendo, ineundo.*	In coming, or entering.
—	בְּבֹאָה בְּבוֹאָהּ	*Ingrediendo eam.*	In her entering in.
—	בְּבִאָה	*In introitu.*	In the entry.
—	בְּבֹאוֹ בְּבוֹאוֹ	*Veniendo eum.*	In his coming.
—	בְּבֹאִי	*Veniendo me.*	When I come.
—	בְּבֹאֲךָ--אֵךְ	*Veniendo, ingrediendo te*	When thou comest in.
—	בְּבֹאֲכֶם	*Ingrediendo vos.*	When ye shall come in.
—	בְּבֹאָם בְּבֹאָן	*Ingrediendo eos, eas*	When they come in.
בבת	בְּבָבַת	*Pupillâ.*	In the apple *of an eye.*
בגד	בְּבֶגֶד בְּבָגֶד	*In veste.*	In the garment.
—	בְּבִגְדוֹ	*In perfidè agendo.*	In dealing deceitfully.
—	בְּבִגְדוֹ	*Per vestem ejus.*	By his garment.
—	בְּבִגְדֵי	*In vestibus.*	In the clothes.
—	בְּבִגְדֵיהֶם	*In vestibus ipsorum.*	With their garments.
—	בִּבְגָדָיו	*Vestibus suis.*	On his clothes.
—	בִּבְגָדִים	*Vestibus.*	With clothes.
בדד	בְּבַד	*Cum solo.*	By itself.
בבת			
בהל	בְּבְהִילוּ	*Festinanter.*	In haste.
—	בְּבֶהָלָה	*In anxietate.*	In trouble.

ROOTS.	DERIVATIVES.	VERSIO.	SIGNIFICATION.
בהם	בִּבְהֵמָה בַּבְּ־	*Cum, pro, de bestia; in, inter bestias.*	With, for, of a beast; on, over, among the beasts.
—	בַּבְּהֵמוֹת	*Inter belluas.*	Among the beasts.
—	בִּבְהֶמַת	*Inter animalia.*	Among the cattle.
בהר	בַּבַּהֶרֶת	*In papula.*	In the bright spot.
בור	בְּבוֹר בַּבּוֹר	*In fovea, carcere.*	In the pit, dungeon.
בטן	בַּבֶּטֶן בְּבֶטֶן	*In utero.*	In the belly, womb.
—	בְּבִטְנָהּ	*In utero suo.*	In her womb.
—	בְּבִטְנוֹ	*In ventre ejus.*	In his belly.
—	בְּבִטְנֵךְ	*In utero tuo.*	In thy womb.
—	בְּבִטְנֶךָ	*In ventre tuo.*	Within thy belly.
	בֵּבָי	*Bebai.*	Bebai, N. M.
בין	בְּבֵין	*Inter.*	Among.
בון	בְּבִינָה	*In intelligentia.*	In understanding.
ביר	בְּבִירְתָא	*In palatio.*	In the palace.
בית	בְּבֵית בְּבַיִת	*In domo, templo.*	In the house, temple.
—	בְּבֵיתָהּ	*In domo ejus.*	In her house.
—	בְּבֵיתוֹ	*In domo ejus.*	In his house.
—	בְּבֵיתִי	*In domo mea.*	In my house.
—	בְּבֵיתֶךָ־־תֵךְ	*In domo tua.*	In thy house.
בכר	בִּבְכוֹר בִּבְכֹר	*Primogenito.*	With the firstling.
—	בִּבְכוֹרוֹ	*In primogenito ejus.*	In his first-born.
—	בִּבְכוֹרֵיהֶם	*In primogenitis suis.*	In their first-born.
—	בִּבְכִי בִּבְכִי	*Cum fletu.*	With weeping.
	בָּבֶל	*Babel.*	Babel, N. P.
בל	בִּבְלִי	*Absque.*	Without.
בלע	בְּבַלַּע	*In absorbendo.*	In swallowing up, devouring.
במה	בַּבָּמָה	*In excelso.*	In the high place.
—	בַּבָּמוֹת	*In excelsis.*	In the high places.
—	בְּבָמוֹתָם	*In excelsis eorum.*	In their high places.
בנה	בְּבֵן	*In filio.*	In the son.
—	בִּבְנוֹ	*In filium ejus.*	Upon his son.
—	בִּבְנוֹת	*Inter filias.*	Among the daughters.
—	בִּבְנוֹתֵיִךְ	*In ædificare te.*	In that thou buildest.
—	בִּבְנוֹתֵכֶם	*Ædificando vos.*	In that ye have builded.
—	בִּבְנֵי	*Ex, in filiis; inter, contra filios.*	In, of, among, against the children.

ROOTS.	DERIVATIVES.	VERSIO.	SIGNIFICATION.
בנה	בְּבָנָיו	*Inter filios ejus.*	Among his sons.
—	בְּבָנֶיךָ	*Inter filios tuos.*	Amongst thy children.
—	בַּבָּנִים	*Inter filios.*	Among the children.
—	בְּבָנֵינוּ	*Cum filiis nostris.*	With our sons.
בעל	בִּבְעָלָיו	*In dominum ejus.*	To his owner.
בצץ	בַּבֹּץ	*In cœno.*	In the mire.
בצע	בְּבֶצַע	*In lucrum, avaritiam*	On the gain, covetousness.
בקע	בַּבִּקְעָה	*In vallem, in valle.*	Into, in a valley.
—	בְּבִקְעַת	*In campo.*	In the plain.
בקר	בַּבֹּקֶר	*In mane.*	In the morning.
—	בַּבָּקָר	*Pro bove, in bovem.*	For, upon an ox.
—	בַּבְּקָרִים	*Cum bobus.*	With oxen.
—	בִּבְקָרְךָ	*De armento tuo.*	Of thy herd.
בקש	בְּבַקָּשָׁתִי	*Pro petitione mea.*	At my request.
בור	בַּבֹּר	*In fovea.*	In the pit.
ברר	בְּבֹר	*In puritate.*	In purity.
בר	בַּבָּר	*Frumento.*	With corn.
ברד	בַּבָּרָד	*Cum grandine.*	With hail.
ברה	בְּבָרוּתִי	*In cibum meum.*	For my meat.
ברזל	בְּבַרְזֶל בַּבַּרְזֶל	*In, cum ferro.*	In, with iron.
ברח	בְּבֹרְחַ	*Fugiendo.*	In fleeing.
—	בְּבָרְחוֹ	*Fugiendo cum.*	When he fled.
—	בְּבָרְחִי	*Fugiendo me. [geres*	When I fled.
—	בְּבָרְחֲךָ	*Fugiendo te, dum fu-*	When thou fleddest.
ברת	בִּבְרִית בַּבְּרִית	*In, cum, fœdere.*	In, with the covenant.
—	בִּבְרִיתוֹ	*In fœdere ejus.*	In his covenant.
—	בִּבְרִיתִי	*In fœdere meo.*	In my covenant.
—	בִּבְרִיתֶךָ	*In fœdere tuo.*	In thy covenant.
ברך	בִּבְרָכָה	*In benedictione.*	In blessing.
—	בְּבָרְכוֹ	*In benedicendo ei.*	In blessing him.
—	בְּבִרְכַּת	*In benedictione.*	In the blessing.
בשם	בִּבְשָׂמִים	*Cum aromatibus.*	With sweet odours.
בשר	בִּבְשָׂר בַּבָּשָׂר	*Ex, in carne.*	From, in the flesh.
—	בִּבְשָׂרָהּ	*In carne ejus.*	In her flesh.
—	בִּבְשָׂרִי	*In carne mea.*	In my flesh.
—	בִּבְשַׂרְכֶם	*In carne vestra.*	In your flesh.
בוש	בְּבֹשֶׁת	*In pudore.*	In shame.

ROOTS.	DERIVATIVES.	VERSIO.	SIGNIFICATION.
בוש	בְּבָשְׁתֵּנוּ	*In pudore nostra.*	In our shame.
בנה	בְּבַת	*In filia.*	In the daughter.
בתל	בִּבְתוּלֶיהָ	*In virginitate ejus.*	In her virginity.
בית	בְּבָתֵּי	*In domibus.*	In the houses.
—	בְּבָתֵּיכֶם	*In domibus vestris.*	In your houses.
—	בְּבָתִּים	*In domibus.*	In houses.
בנה	בְּבִתְּכֶם	*In filia vestra.*	In your daughter.
	בג		
גאה	בְּגַאֲוָה	*In, cum superbia.*	In, with pride.
—	בִּגְאוֹן	*In superbia, elatione, sublimitate, gloria*	In, by, for the pride, swelling, height, glory.
—	בִּגְאוֹנָם	*In superbia eorum.*	In their pride.
—	בְּגַאֲוַת	*In, cum superbia.*	In, with the pride.
—	בְּגֵאוּת	*In, cum elatione.*	In, with the swelling.
—	בְּגַאֲוָתוֹ	*Propter elationem ejus.*	With the swelling thereof.
גבה	בְּגֹבַהּ	*Pro elatione.*	For the pride.
—	בְּגָבְהוֹ	*In altitudine ejus.*	In his height.
—	בְּגָבְהָם	*In altitudine eorum.*	In their height.
גבל	בִּגְבוּל	*In termino.*	In the border.
—	בִּגְבוּלֵיךְ	*In confiniis tuis.*	Within thy borders.
—	בִּגְבוּלָם בִּגְבֻלָם	*In termino eorum.*	In their border.
—	בִּגְבוּלֵנוּ	*In termino nostro.*	Within our border.
גבר	בְּגִבּוֹר	*Contra fortem.*	Against the mighty.
—	בִּגְבוּרָה	*In, cum potentia.*	In, with power.
—	בִּגְבוּרוֹת־בְּרֹת	*In robore.*	In the strength.
—	בַּגִּבּוֹרִים	*In, inter potentes.*	Against, among the mighty.
—	בִּגְבוּרַת	*In potentia.*	In the strength.
—	בִּגְבוּרָתוֹ	*In potentia ejus.*	In his might.
—	בִּגְבוּרֹתָיו	*Propter fortitudines ejus.*	For his mighty acts.
—	בִּגְבוּרָתָם	*Fortitudine eorum.*	By their might.
גבח	בְּגַבַּחַת	*In recalvatione.*	In bald forehead.
—	בְּגַבַּחְתּוֹ	*In recalvatione ejus.*	In his bald forehead.
גבל	בִּגְבֻלוֹ	*Per regionem ejus.*	Through his coast.

ROOTS.	DERIVATIVES.	VERSIO.	SIGNIFICATION.
גבל	בִּגְבֻלֶךָ	*In regionem tuam.*	Into thy coast.
—	בִּגְבֻלֹת	*In terminis.*	In the coasts.
—	בִּגְבֻלֹת	*In terminis eorum.*	In their coasts.
גבע	בְּגִבְעָה־עַת	*In colle.*	In the hill.
בָּגַד		*Prævaricatus est, perfide egit, fraudavit, fefellit.*	He prevaricated, acted treacherously or unfaithfully, cheated, deceived.
—	בֶּגֶד	*Vestis, perfidia.*	A garment, deceit.
—	בֶּגֶד בֶּגֶד	*Vestimentum, pannum.* [dus.	Raiment, a garment, a cloth.
—	בֹּגֵד בּוֹגֵד	*Prævaricans, perfi-*	A treacherous man.
—	בָּגְדָה	*Prævaricata est.*	She hath dealt treacherously.
—	בֹּגֵדָה	*Perfida.*	A treacherous woman.
—	בָּגְדוּ בָּגָדוּ	*Prævaricati sunt.*	They have dealt treacherously
—	בִּגְדוֹ	*Vestimentum ejus.*	His garment
גדד	בַּגְּדוּד	*In exercitu.*	In the army.
גדל	בַּגָּדוֹל	*A majore.*	At the eldest.
בגד	בֹּגְדוֹת	*Perfidæ.*	Treacherous women.
—	בְּגָדַי	*Vestimenta mea.*	My garments.
—	בִּגְדִי	*Vestimentum meum.*	My garment.
—	בִּגְדֵי	*Vestimenta.*	The garments.
גדה	בִּגְדִי	*Cum hædo.*	With a kid.
בגד	בֹּגְדִי	*Prævaricantes.*	Treacherous men.
—	בְּגָדֶיהָ	*Vestimenta ejus.*	Her garments.
—	בִּגְדֵיהֶם	*Vestimenta eorum.*	Their garments.
—	בְּגָדָיו	*Vestimenta ejus.*	His garments.
—	בְּגָדֶיךָ־דַיִךְ	*Vestimenta tua.*	Thy garments.
—	בִּגְדֵיכֶם	*Vestimenta vestra.*	Your garments.
—	בְּגָדִים	*Vestimenta.*	Garments.
—	בֹּגְדִים	*Prævaricatores.*	Treacherous men.
—	בְּגָדֵינוּ	*Vestimenta nostra.*	Our garments.
גדל	בְּגֹדֶל	*In magnitudine.*	In, by the greatness.
—	בְּגָדְלוֹ	*In magnitudine ejus.*	In his greatness.
—	בִּגְדֹלוֹת	*In magnis.*	In great things.
—	בְּגָדְלֶךָ	*In magnitudine tua.*	In thy greatness.
גדר	בַּגְּדֵרוֹת	*In sepibus.*	In the hedges.
בגד	בָּגַדְתָּה	*Perfide egisti.*	Thou hast dealt treacherously.

ROOTS.	DERIVATIVES.	VERSIO.	SIGNIFICATION.
בגד	בְּגַדְתִּי	*Prævaricatus sum.*	I have offended.
—	בְּגָדֶיךָ	*Vestimenta tua.*	Thy garments.
—	בְּגַדְתֶּם	*Prævaricati estis.*	Ye have transgressed.
גוא	בְּגוֹ בְּגוֹא	*In medio.*	In the midst.
בגד	בָּגוֹד	*Prævaricando.*	In dealing very treacherously.
—	בָּגוֹדָה	*Perfida.*	A treacherous woman.
גוא	בְּגֵוָהּ בְּגַוָּהּ	*In medio illius.*	In the midst of her.
גאה	בְּגֵוָה	*In superbia.*	In pride.
	בִּגְוַי	*Bigvai.*	Bigvai, N. M.
גוי	בְּגוֹי	*In gente, gentem.*	In, with, on a nation.
—	בְּגוֹיֵהֶם	*In gentibus eorum.*	In their nations.
—	בַּגּוֹיִם בְּגוֹ׳	*Inter gentes.*	Among the nations.
גוה	בִּגְוִיַּת	*In cadavere.*	In the carcase.
—	בִּגְוִיֹּתָם	*In corpora eorum.*	Upon their corpses.
גלה	בַּגּוֹלָה	*In captivitatem.*	Into captivity.
גוע	בִּגְוֹעַ	*Moriendo*	In, when dying.
גרל	בְּגוֹרָל בְּגוֹרָל	*Per sortem.*	By the lot.
—	בְּגוֹרָלוֹת	*Per sortes.*	By lots.
—	בְּגוֹרָלִי	*In sortem meam.*	Into my lot.
—	בְּגוֹרָלֶךָ	*In sorte tua.*	In thy lot.
גזז	בְּגִזַּת	*Cum vellere.*	With the fleece.
—	בְּגֹז	*Tondendo.*	In shearing.
—	בְּגָזִית	*Lapide exciso.*	With hewn stone.
גזל	בְּגָזֵל	*In rapina.*	In robbery.
גזר	בִּגְזֵרַת	*Ex decreto.*	By, from the decree.
גיא	בְּגֵי בְּגֵיא בַּגַּיְא	*In valle.*	In the valley.
גיד	בְּגִיד	*In nervo.*	In the sinew.
גוח	בְּגִיחוֹ	*Emergendo eum.*	When it brake forth.
גלל	בַּגַּלְגַּל	*In aëre, æthere.*	In the air, the heaven.
—	בְּגִלּוּלֵיהֶם	*Idolis eorum.*	With their idols.
—	בְּגִלּוּלָיו	*Idolis ejus.*	With his idols.
גלם	בִּגְלוֹמֵי	*In palliis.*	In clothes.
גלה	בְּגָלוֹתוֹ	*Deportando eum.*	When he carried away captive
גלל	בִּגְלַל	*Propter.*	For the sake, because of.
—	בְּגֶלְלֵי	*In stercoribus.*	With dung.
—	בִּגְלָלֵךְ בִּגְלָלֶךָ	*Propter te.*	Because of thee.
—	בִּגְלַלְכֶם	*Propter vos.*	For your sake.

ROOTS.	DERIVATIVES.	VERSIO.	SIGNIFICATION.
גמל	בִּגְמַלִּים	*In camelis.*	Among the camels.
גן	בְּגַן בַּגָּן	*In horto.*	In the garden.
גנב	בְּגַנָּבִים	*Inter fures.*	Among thieves.
—	בִּגְנֵבָתוֹ	*Pro furto ejus.*	For his theft.
גן	בַּגַּנּוֹת	*In hortis.*	In the gardens.
—	בַּגַּנִּים	*In hortis.*	In gardens.
געל	בְּגֹעַל	*Cum fastidio.*	To the loathing.
גער	בְּגַעֲרַת	*Per increpationem.*	At the rebuking.
—	בְּגַעֲרָתִי	*In increpatione mea.*	At my rebuke.
גפף	בְּגַפּוֹ	*Solus ipse.*	By himself alone.
גפן	בַּגֶּפֶן	*In vite.*	On the vine.
—	בַּגְּפָנִים	*In vitibus.*	In the vines.
גור	כַּגֵּר	*Tam peregrinus.*	Whether a stranger.
גרה	בְּגָרוֹן	*In gutture.*	In the throat.
—	בִּגְרוֹנָם	*In gutture eorum.*	In, through their throat.
גור	בִּגְרוּת	*In habitatione.*	In the habitation.
גרז	בַּגַּרְזֶן	*Cum securi.*	With the ax.
גרן	בַּגֹּרֶן	*In area.*	In the floor.
גשם	בְּגֶשְׁמְהוֹן	*In corpora eorum.*	Upon their bodies.
נגש	בְּגֶשֶׁת	*Accedendo.*	When come nigh.
—	בְּגִשְׁתָּם	*Accedendo eos.*	When they come near.
גתת	בְּגַת	*In torculari.*	In the wine-fat.
	בִּגְתָא־תָנָא	*Bigtha.*	Bigtha, N. M.
	בִּגְתָן	*Bigthan.*	Bigthan, N. M.

בד

ROOTS.	DERIVATIVES.	VERSIO.	SIGNIFICATION.
בד			
—	בַּד בָּד	*Linum; lineus.*	Linen; made of linen.
בדד	בַּד	*Solus.*	Alone.
בָּדָא		*Commentus est.*	He devised.
דאג	בִּדְאָגָה	*Cum solicitudine.*	With care, carefulness.
דבר	בַּדְּבִיר	*In oraculo.*	In the oracle.
—	בְּדָבָר	*In verbo, re.*	In a word or thing.
—	בִּדְבַר	*Consilio.*	By, through the counsel.
—	בַּדָּבָר	*In verbo, re.*	In the word, matter, thing.
—	בְּדֶבֶר בַּדֶּבֶר	*Cum peste.*	With pestilence.
—	בְּדַבֵּר	*In loquendo.*	In speaking.

ROOTS.	DERIVATIVES.	VERSIO.	SIGNIFICATION.
דבר	בִּדְבָרוֹ	*In verbo ejus.*	In his word.
—	בְּדַבְּרוֹ	*Loquendo eum.*	When he speaks.
—	בְּדַבְּרִי	*Loquendo me.*	When I speak.
—	בִּדְבָרַי	*In verbis meis.*	In, with my words.
—	בְּדִבְרֵי	*In verbis.*	With, in the words.
—	בִּדְבָרֶיהָ	*Verbis ejus.*	With her words.
—	בִּדְבָרָיו	*Verbis ejus.*	With his words.
—	בִּדְבָרֶיךָ	*In verbis tuis.*	With, in thy words.
—	בְּדִבְרֵיכֶם	*Verbis vestris.*	With your words.
—	בִּדְבָרִים בַּדְּ־	*In, de, cum verbis.*	In, by, with words.
—	בְּדַבֶּרְךָ	*Loquendo te.* [*tuum*	In thy speaking.
—	בִּדְבָרְךָ	*Juxta, in verbum*	According to, against thy word
—	בְּדַבֶּרְכֶם	*Loquendo vos.*	With your speaking.
—	בְּדַבְּרָם	*Loquendo eos.*	In their speaking.
דבשׁ	בִּדְבָשׁ	*Cum melle.*	With honey.
דוג	בִּדְגַת	*In piscem.* [*degit.*	Over the fish.
בָּדַד		*Solitarius fuit, solus*	He was solitary, lived alone.
—	בָּדָד	*Solus, solitarius.*	Alone, lonely.
	בְּדַד	*Bedad.*	Bedad, N. M.
דוד	בַּדּוּד	*In lebetem.*	Into a kettle.
—	בַּדּוּדָאִי	*Pro mandragoris.*	With the mandrakes.
—	בַּדּוּדִים	*In canistris.*	In baskets.
—	בַּדּוֹר בְּדֹר	*In generatione.*	In the generation.
די	בְּדֵי	*In, inter, sufficienter*	In, among, sufficiently.
בד	בַּדֵּי	*Vectes, rami.*	The staves, branches.
—	בַּדֶּיהָ	*Rami ejus.*	Her branches.
	בֵּדְיָה	*Badaias.* [*mendacia*	Bedeiah, N. M.
בד	בַּדָּיו	*Ejus vectes, membra,*	His staves, parts, lies.
דיה	בִּדְיוֹ	*Cum atramento.*	With ink.
בד	בַּדֶּיךָ	*Mendacia tua.*	Thy lies.
בדל	בְּדִיל	*Stannum.*	Tin.
—	בְּדִילָיִךְ	*Stannum tuum.*	Thy tin.
בד	בַּדִּים	*Linei; rami, vectes; mendaces.*	Made of linen; branches, staves; liars.
דושׁ	בְּדִישׁוֹ	*Triturando illum.*	When he treadeth out.
בָּדַל		*Separavit, divisit, selegit, discrevit.*	He separated, divided, selected made a distinction between.

ROOTS.	DERIVATIVES.	VERSIO.	SIGNIFICATION.
בדל	בְּדַל אֹזֶן	*Particula seu cartilago auris.*	A piece, or the cartilage *of an ear.*
דלת	בַּדֶּלֶת	*In ostio.*	At the door.
—	בְּדַלְתּוֹ	*In operculo ejus.*	In the lid or cover of it.
—	בְּדַלְתוֹת	*Fores.*	The doors.
—	בִּדְלָתַיִם	*Cum ostiis.*	With doors.
דם	בְּדָם בַּדָּם	*In sanguine.*	With, in blood.
דמה	בִּדְמוּת	*Ad similitudinem.*	In the likeness.
—	בִּדְמוּתוֹ	*Ad similitudinem sui*	In his own likeness.
—	בִּדְמִי	*In excisione.*	In the cutting off.
דם	בְּדָמִי	*In sanguine mea.*	In my blood.
—	בִּדְמֵי	*In sanguinibus.*	In the blood.
—	בְּדָמַיִךְ	*Sanguinibus tuis.*	In thy blood.
—	בְּדָמִים	*Sanguinibus [tuam.*	With blood.
—	בְּדָמֵךְ	*In sanguinibus tuis.*	In thy blood.
דמה	בְּדָמְךָ	*In similitudine*	In thy likeness.
דמע	בְּדִמְעָה	*In lachryma.*	In tears.
—	בִּדְמָעוֹת	*Cum lachrymis.*	With tears.
—	בְּדִמְעָתִי	*In lachryma mea.*	With my tears.
	בְּדָן	*Bedan.*	Bedan, N. M.
ידע	בְּדַעַת	*Cum scientia.*	With knowledge.
—	בְּדַעְתּוֹ	*Cognitione ejus.*	By his knowledge.
בָּדַק		*Rimatus est, restauravit, resarcivit.*	He examined in order to repair, restored, mended.
—	בֶּדֶק	*Ruptura, fissura.*	A breach.
—	בִּדְקֵךְ	*Ruina tua.*	Thy breach, ruin.
	בִּדְקַר	*Bidcar. [trum.*	Bidkar, N. M,
דרם	בַּדָּרוֹם	*Ad meridiem, aus-*	Toward the south.
דרך	בַּדֶּרֶךְ	*In via.*	In the way.
—	בִּדְרָכַי	*In viis meis.*	In my ways.
—	בְּדַרְכֵי	*In viis.*	In the ways.
—	בְּדַרְכֵיהֶם	*In viis eorum.*	In their ways.
—	בְּדַרְכֵיהֶן	*In viis earum.*	After their ways.
—	בִּדְרָכָיו	*In viis ejus.*	In his ways.
—	בִּדְרָכַיִךְ	*In viis tuis.*	In thy ways.
—	בְּדַרְכְּךָ־דַרְכֵּךְ	*In via tua.*	In thy way.
—	בְּדַרְכָּם	*Via sua.*	By their own way.

ROOTS.	DERIVATIVES.	VERSIO.	SIGNIFICATION.
דור	בְּדֹרֹתָיו	In generationibus ejus	In his generations.
דשן	בַּדֶּשֶׁן	In pinguedine. [gem	In fatness. [law.
דת	בְּדָת	De lege, secundum le-	Concerning, according to the
דתא	בְּדִתְאָא	In herba.	In the tender grass.
דת	בְּדָתֵי	Inter leges.	Among the laws.
	בה		
	בָּהּ	In, cum ea; super, per, propter, eam.	In, with, by, because of, above her.
	בֵּהּ	In illo.	In him.
אבק	בְּהֵאָבְקוֹ	Luctando illum.	While he wrestled.
ארך	בְּהַאֲרִיךְ	Morando. [me	In tarrying.
בוא	בַּהֲבִיאִי	Ducendo, inducendo	When I shall bring.
——	בַּהֲבִיאֲכֶם	Introducendo vos.	In that ye have brought.
נבט	בְּהַבִּיטִי	Respiciendo me.	When I have respect.
הבל	בַּהֶבֶל	In vanitate.	With vanity.
——	בְּהַבְלֵי	In vanitatibus.	Among the vanities.
——	בְּהַבְלֵיהֶם	Vanitatibus eorum.	With their vanities.
בנה	בְּהִבָּנֹתוֹ	Cum ædificaretur.	When it was in building.
ברא	בְּהִבָּרְאָם	Quando creati sunt.	When they were created.
הגה	בַּהֲגִיגִי	In meditatione mea.	During my meditation.
גלה	בְּהַגְלוֹת	Deportando.	In the carrying away.
——	בְּהִגָּלוֹת	Detegendo.	By discovering. [away.
——	בְּהַגְלוֹתִי	Transferendo me.	By my causing to be carried
נדף	בְּהִדֹּף	Expellendo, cum expulserit.	After he hath cast out.
הדר	בְּהָדָר	Cum gloria.	With majesty.
——	בַּהֲדָרִי	Ob decorem meum.	Through my comeliness.
——	בְּהַדְרֵי	In decoribus.	In the beauties.
דרך	בְּהַדֶּרֶךְ	In via.	In the way.
הדר	בְּהַדְרַת	In decore.	In the beauty.
בהה	בֹּהוּ	Inanitas.	Emptiness.
ילד	בְּהִוָּלֵד	Nascendo.	When born.
הלל	בְּהוֹלְלִים	In stultos.	At the foolish.
	בְּהוֹן	In illis.	In them.
יסד	בְּהִוָּסְדָם	Consultando eos.	While they took counsel.
יצא	בְּהוֹצִיאוֹ	Educendo eum.	When he brought forth.

ROOTS.	DERIVATIVES.	VERSIO.	SIGNIFICATION.
יצא	בְּהוֹצִיאִי	*Educendo me.*	When I brought forth.
—	בְּהוֹצִיאֲךָ	*Educendo te.*	When thou broughtest forth.
ירד	בְּהוֹרִדִי	*Demittendo me.*	When I cast down.
הוה	בְּהַוָּתוֹ	*In pravitate ejus.*	In his wickedness.
זרה	בְּהִזָּרוֹתֵיכֶם	*Cum dispersi eritis.*	When ye shall be scattered.
חבא	בְּהֵחָבֵא	*Abscondere se.*	To hide themselves.
בהט			
—	בָּהַט	*Porphyrites.*	A species of red marble.
היה	בִּהְיוֹת בִּהְיֹת	*Cum esset.*	When he was.
—	בִּהְיוֹתוֹ	*Dum esset ille.*	While he was.
—	בִּהְיוֹתֵךְ	*Quando esses.*	When thou wast.
—	בִּהְיוֹתְכֶם	*Cum essetis.*	When ye were.
—	בִּהְיוֹתָם	*Cum essent.*	When they were.
—	בִּהְיוֹתֵנוּ	*Cum essemus.*	When we were.
יטב	בְּהֵיטִיבוֹ	*Aptando eum.*	When he dresses.
הכל	בְּהֵיכָל	*In templo.*	In the temple.
—	בְּהֵיכְלָא	*In templum.*	Into the temple.
—	בְּהֵיכָלוֹ	*In templo ejus.*	In his temple.
—	בְּהֵיכְלֵי	*In palatiis.*	In the palaces.
—	בְּהֵיכָלִי	*In palatio meo.*	In my palace.
בהר	בָּהִיר	*Lucidus, splendens.*	Bright.
כבד	בְּהִכָּבְדִי	*Honorando me, cum honorandus ero.*	When I have gotten me honour.
נכה	בְּהַכּוֹתִי־־כֹּתִי	*Percutiendo me.*	When I smite.
כון	בְּהָכִין	*Parando, stabiliendo*	When prepared, established.
—	בַּהֲכִינוֹ	*Præparando eum.*	When he prepared.
כלם	בְּהַכְלִים	*Ignominia afficiendo.*	When put to shame
כרת	בְּהַכְרִית	*Exscindendo.*	In cutting off.
—	בְּהִכָּרֵת	*Succidendo.* [*tinavit.*	When cut off. [rified, hastened
בָּהַל		*Turbavit, terruit, fes-*	He troubled, confounded, ter-
—	בֶּהָלָה	*Terror, consternatio*	Terror, consternation.
הלל	בְּהִלּוֹ	*Splendere faciendo eum.*	When he caused to shine.
לחם	בְּהִלָּחֲמוֹ	*Pugnando eum.*	When he fought.
הלך	בַּהֲלִיכוֹתָם	*Eundo eos.*	In their walk.
הלל	בְּהַלֵּל	*Laudando.*	In praising.
בהם			

ROOTS.	DERIVATIVES.	VERSIO.	SIGNIFICATION.
	בָּהֶם בָּהֵן	*In, ex eis; inter, propter eos, eas.*	In, with, from, among, because of them.
בהם	בְּהֵמָה	*Bestia.*	A beast.
	בָּהֵמָּה	*Cum illis.*	By, with them.
מול	בְּהִמּוֹל	*Circumcidendo.*	In circumcising.
המן	בֶּהָמוֹן בַּהֲמוֹן	*In multitudine.*	In abundance.
בהם	בְּהֵמוֹת	*Bestiæ.*	The beasts.
—	בְּהֵמוֹת־־מֹת	*Bestiæ, jumenta*; secundum quosdam *elephas*, vel *hippotamus.*	Beasts, cattle; *according to some*, the elephant, or the hippopotamus or river-horse.
מיר	בְּהָמִיר	*Mutando.* [*eum.*	In removing, in the removal.
מול	בְּהִמֹּלוֹ	*In circumcidendo*	When he was circumcised.
מצא	בְּהִמָּצְאוֹ	*In inveniendo eum.*	While he may be found.
בהם	בֶּהֱמַת	*Bestia, pecus.*	The beasts, cattle.
—	בְּהֶמְתָּהּ	*Pecus ejus.*	Her cattle.
—	בְּהֶמְתּוֹ	*Pecus ejus.*	His beasts.
—	בְּהֶמְתְּךָ־־תֶּךָ	*Pecus tuum.*	Thy cattle.
—	בְּהֶמְתְּכֶם	*Pecus vestrum.*	Your cattle.
—	בְּהֶמְתָּם	*Pecus eorum.*	Their cattle.
—	בְּהֶמְתֵּנוּ	*Pecus nostrum.*	Our cattle.
בהן			
—	בֹּהֶן	*Pollex.*	The thumb, the great toe.
—	בְּהִנָּבְאוֹ	*Vaticinando eum.*	When he prophesied.
—	בְּהִנָּבְאִי	*Vaticinando me.*	When I prophesied.
נבא	בְּהִנָּבְאוֹתוֹ	*Vaticinando eum.*	When he hath prophesied.
נגף	בְּהִנָּגֵף	*Percutiendo.*	When smitten.
	בָּהֵנָּה	*In illis.*	In them.
בהן	בְּהֹנוֹת	*Pollices.* [*endo*	Thumbs.
נחל	בְּהַנְחִל	*In hæreditare faci-*	In dividing the inheritance.
נות	בְּהָנִיחַ	*Requiem dando.*	In giving rest. [over.
עבר	בְּהַעֲבִיר	*Transire faciendo.*	In causing to pass through, or
עוה	בְּהַעֲוֺתוֹ	*Inique agendo eum.*	If he acts iniquitously.
עלה	בְּהַעֲלוֹת	*Ascendere faciendo,*	In bringing up, offering.
—	בְּהֵעָלוֹת	*Ascendendo, abducendo.*	In going up, being withdrawn.
—	בְּהַעֲלֹתְךָ	*Accendendo te.*	When thou lightest.

ROOTS.	DERIVATIVES.	VERSIO.	SIGNIFICATION.
עצר	בְּהֵעָצֵר	*In claudendo.*	When shut up.
נפץ	בַּהֲפִיצִי	*Dispergendo me.*	When I shall scatter.
הפך	בַּהֲפֹךְ	*Subvertendo.*	In overthrowing.
פנה	בְּהַפְנוֹתוֹ	*Vertendo ipsum.*	When he turned.
פרד	בְּהַפְרִידוֹ	*Separando eum.*	When he separated.
נצה	בְּהַצּוֹתוֹ	*Certando ipsum.*	When he strove.
——	בְּהַצֹּתָם	*Rixando eos.*	When they strove.
בחק			
——	בֹּהַק	*Vitiligo, pustula alba*	Freckled spot.
קבץ	בְּהִקָּבֵץ	*Cum congregati sunt.*	When they are gathered.
קדש	בְּהִקָּדְשִׁי	*Sanctificundo me.*	When I shall be sanctified.
קהל	בְּהִקָּהֵל	*Congregando se.*	In gathering themselves.
קוץ	בְּהָקִיץ	*Evigilando.*	In awaking.
קצף	בְּהַקְצִיף	*Irasci faciendo.*	In provoking to wrath.
קרב	בְּהַקְרִבָם	*Offerendo eos.*	When they offer.
——	בְּהַקְרִיבְכֶם	*Offerendo vos.*	When ye bring.
——	בְּהַקְרִיבָם	*Offerendo eos*[*teretur*	When they offer.
קשה	בְּהַקְשֹׁתָהּ	*Cum difficultatem pa-*	When she was in difficulty.
בהר			
——	בְּהַר בָּהָר	*In monte.*	In the mount.
ראה	בְּהֵרָאוֹתוֹ	*Apparendo illum.*	When he appeareth.
ראה	בְּהַרְאֹתוֹ	*Ostendendo illum.*	When he shewed.
הרג	בַּהֲרֹג	*In occidendo.*	When slaying.
——	בְּהָרֵג	*In occidi.*	When slain.
——	בַּהֲרוּגִים	*In interfectos.*	Upon the slain.
בהר	בֶּהָרוֹת בֶּהָרֹת	*Vitiligines.*	Bright spots.
הרר	בְּהָרֵי	*In montibus.*	In the mountains.
ריח	בַּהֲרִיחוֹ	*Odorando eum.*	When it smelleth.
הרר	בֶּהָרִים	*In montibus.*	In the mountains.
רום	בַּהֲרִימְכֶם	*Elevando vos.*	When ye have heaved.
רוע	בְּהָרִיעַ	*In clangendo.*	During the shouting.
הרר	בְּהַרְרֵי	*In montibus.*	Upon the hills.
——	בְּהַרְרָם	*In monte eorum.*	On their mountain.
בהר	בַּהֶרֶת	*Vitiligo.*	A bright spot.
שבע	בְּהַשְׁבִּיעַ	*In adjurando.*	When charged with an oath.
שכל	בְּהַשְׂכִּיל	*Cum intellectu.*	With wisdom.
שמם	בְּהָשַּׁמָּה	*Quum desolata erit.*	When she or it shall be desolate.

ROOTS.	DERIVATIVES.	VERSIO.	SIGNIFICATION.
שמ	בְּהִשָּׁמַיִם	*In cœlis.*	In the heavens.
שמע	בְּהִשָּׁמַע	*Cum auditum est.*	When it was heard.
שע	בְּהִשָּׁעֶנְךָ	*Innitendo te.*	Because thou hast relied.
שפט	בְּהִשָּׁפֵט	*Judicando.*	When, or in judging.
—	בְּהִשָּׁפְטוֹ	*Cum judicatus erit.*	When he shall be judged.
שקט	בְּהַשְׁקֵט	*In quiete, quiescendo.*	In quietness.
שחה	בְּהִשְׁתַּחֲוָיָתִי	*In incurvando me.*	When I bow down myself.
שפך	בְּהִשְׁתַּפֵּךְ	*In effundendo te.*	In thy pouring out.
אסף	בְּהִתְאַסֵּף	*Congregando se.*	When they were gathered together.
בהל	בְּהִתְבַּהֲלָה	*Cum festinatione.*	In haste.
גלה	בְּהִתְגַּלּוֹת	*Manifestando se.*	In discovering itself.
הלך	בְּהִתְהַלֶּכְךָ	*Eundo te.*	When thou goest.
ידע	בְּהִתְוַדַּע	*Notum faciendo se*	While he made himself known
חבר	בְּהִתְחַבֶּרְךָ	*Jungendo te.*	For joining thyself.
חנן	בְּהִתְחַנְנוֹ	*Deprecando eum.*	When he besought.
יחש	בְּהִתְיַחֵשׂ	*In recensendo.*	When reckoned.
נדב	בְּהִתְנַדֵּב	*Offerendo spontè.*	When willingly offered.
נשא	בְּהִתְנַשֵּׂא	*Elevando se.*	In lifting up thyself.
עטף	בְּהִתְעַטֵּף	*Obruendo.*	When overwhelmed.
—	בְּהִתְעַטְּפָם	*Deficiendo eos.*	When they fainted, swooned.
פלל	בְּהִתְפַּלְלוֹ	*Orando illum.*	When he prayed.
	בו		
	בּוֹ בָּהּ	*In, ex eo; ad, per, propter eum.*	In, from, to, through, by, because of him.
בוא		*Venit, advenit, intravit, ingressus est, concubuit, occubuit, abivit, duxit, contigit, evenit, invasit.*	He or it came, came to, entered, went into, lay with, went down or set, went away, brought, happened, befel, came upon.
בוא	בּוֹא	*Veni, ingredere; venire; adventus; occasus.*	Come, enter thou; to come; the coming; the setting.
—	בּוֹאוֹ	*Veniendo eum.*	When he comes.
—	בּוֹאִי	*Veni; venire me.*	Come thou; I come.
—	בּוֹאֲךָ	*Venire te.*	Thou comest.

ROOTS.	DERIVATIVES.	VERSIO.	SIGNIFICATION.
בוא	בּוֹאֲךָ	*Adventus tuus.*	Thy coming.
—	בּוֹאֲנָה	*Veniendo eam.*	When she comes.
בוב			
בגד	בּוֹגֵד	*Perfidus, prævaricatio.*	A treacherous man, deceit, transgression.
—	בּוֹגְדִים	*Prævaricatores.*	The transgressors.
בדא	בּוֹדָאם	*Fingens ea*	Feigning them.
בדד	בּוֹדֵד	*Solitarius.*	Alone.
	בּוּז	*Buz.*	Buz, N. M. P.
בוז		*Contempsit, sprevit.*	He contemned, despised.
—	בּוּז	*Spernere.*	To despise.
—	בּוּז בּוּזָה	*Contemptus.*	Contempt.
בזה	בּוֹזֶה	*Spernens.*	Despising.
—	בּוֹזֵהוּ	*Spernens eum.*	Despising him.
—	בּוֹזַי	*Spernentes.*	Despising.
	בּוּזִי	*Buzi.*	Buzi, N. M.
בטא	בּוֹטֶה	*Effutiens.*	Prating, uttering foolishly.
בטח	בּוֹטֵחַ	*Confidens, securus.*	Trusting, confident.
—	בּוֹטְחִים	*Confidentes.*	Confiding, trusting.
	בַּוַּי	*Bavai.* [*confusus est.*	Bavai, N. M. [confounded.
בוך		*Implicitus, turbatus,*	He was entangled, perplexed,
בכה	בּוֹכִיָּה	*Flens.*	Weeping.
—	בּוֹכִים	*Flentes.*	Weeping.
בול			
—	בּוּל	*Proventus, pabulum.*	Produce, food.
	בּוּל	*Bul.*	Bul, N. Mth.
בון		*Sensit, animadvertit, perpendit, consideravit, discrevit, intellexit, docuit, instruxit.*	He perceived, observed, weighed, considered, distinguished, judged, understood, taught, instructed.
בנה	בּוֹנֶה בּוֹנֶה	*Ædificans.*	Building, building up.
	בּוּנָה	*Buna.*	Bunah, N. M.
	בּוּנִי	*Buni.*	Buni, N. M.
בנה	בּוֹנָיו	*Ædificatores ejus.*	The builders of it.
—	בּוֹנִים	*Ædificantes.*	Building. [destroyed.
בוס		*Calcavit, conculcavit*	He trod under foot, despised,

ROOTS.	DERIVATIVES.	VERSIO.	SIGNIFICATION.
בוס	בּוֹסִים	*Conculcantes.*	Treading down.
—	בּוֹסְסוּ	*Conculcarunt.*	They have trodden down.
בוץ			
—	בּוּץ	*Byssus.* [*cens.*	Fine linen, or cotton.
בצע	בּוֹצֵעַ	*Inhians, concupis-*	Coveting, greedy.
	בּוֹצֵץ	*Boses.*	Bozez, N. P.
בקק	בּוּקָה	*Evacuata.*	Empty.
בקע	בּוֹקֵעַ	*Findens, scindens.*	Dividing.
בקק	בּוֹקֵק	*Vacua, evacuans.*	Empty, making empty.
בקר	בּוֹקֵר	*Armentarius.*	A herdman.
בור			
—	בּוֹר	*Cisterna, fovea, carcer, sepulchrum.*	A pit, well, cistern, dungeon, grave.
ברא	בּוֹרֵא	*Creans, Creator.*	He that creates, the Creator.
—	בּוֹרְאֶךָ	*Creator tuus.*	Thy Creator.
בור	בּוֹרוֹ	*Cisterna ejus.*	His cistern.
בּוֹשׁ		*Pudore affecit, erubuit, pudefactus est*	He put to shame, was ashamed confounded.
בשש	בּוֹשׁ	*Diu.*	For a long time.
בוש	בּוֹשׁ	*Erubescere.*	To be ashamed.
—	בּוֹשָׁה	*Pudore affecta est.*	She was ashamed.
—	בּוּשָׁה	*Pudor.* [*vos.*	Shame. [shamed.
—	בּוֹשׁוּ	*Erubuerunt, pudeat*	They were ashamed, be ye a-
—	בּוֹשִׁי	*Erubesce.*	Be thou ashamed.
—	בּוֹשִׁים	*Erubescentes.*	Ashamed.
בשס	בּוֹשַׁסְכֶם	*Conculcare vos.*	That you trample upon.
	בז		
בח	בַּז	*Præda.*	Spoil, the prey.
—	בָּז	*Contemnens.*	Despising.
בָּזָא		*Prædatus est, spoliavit, diripuit, abstulit.*	He robbed, spoiled, took away, carried off.
בזז	בָּזְאוּ	*Diripuerunt.*	They spoiled.
זה	בְּזֹאת בָּזֹאת	*In, cum, per hoc.*	In, with, by this.
זבח	בְּזֶבַח בַּזֶּבַח	*Per, ad sacrificium*	By, with, to a sacrifice.
—	בְּזָבְחוֹ	*In sacrificare ipsum.*	While he offered.

ROOTS.	DERIVATIVES.	VERSIO.	SIGNIFICATION.
זבח	בְּזִבְחִי	*In sacrificium meum.*	At my sacrifice.
זוד	בְּזָדוֹן	*In, per superbiam.*	Presumptuously, by pride.
בָּזָה		*Contempsit, sprevit.*	He contemned, despised.
בזז	בִּזָּה	*Præda.*	Spoil.
—	בִּזָּהּ	*Præda ejus.*	His prey.
זה	בָּזֶה	*In hoc; hic.*	In, with this; here.
זהב	בְּזָהָב כַּזָּהָב	*In auro.*	In, with gold.
בוז	בָּזוּ	*Spreverunt.*	They despised.
—	בֹּזוּ	*Diripite.*	Spoil, plunder ye.
זוב	בְּזוֹבוֹ	*In semine ejus.*	In his issue.
בזז	בָּזוּז	*Direptus.*	Robbed.
בזה	בָּזוּי	*Contemptus.*	Despised.
—	בְּזוּיָה	*Contempta.*	Despised.
זנה	בְּזוֹנָה	*Pro meretrice.*	For a harlot.
בזז	בַּזּוֹנוּ	*Prædati sumus.*	We took for a prey.
בָּזַז		*Prædatus est, spoliavit, diripuit, abstulit.*	He robbed, spoiled, took away, carried off.
—	בָּזְזוּ בָּזְזוּ	*Prædati sunt.*	They took the spoil.
—	בֹּזְזֵיהֶם	*Spoliantes eos.*	Those that rob them.
—	בֹּזְזַיִךְ	*Spoliantes te.*	Plundering thee.
—	בֹּזְזִים	*Prædantes.*	Robbing.
—	בָּזַזְנוּ	*Prædati sumus.*	We took for a prey.
בזה	בִּזָּיוֹן	*Contemptus.*	Contempt.
	בִּזְיוֹתְיָה	*Biziothia*	Bisjothjah, N. P.
בזה	בָּזִינוּ	*Contempsimus.*	We have despised.
—	בָּזִית	*Contempsisti.*	Thou hast despised.
—	בָּזִיתָ	*Sprevisti.*	Thou hast despised.
זכר	בְּזָכְרֵנוּ	*Recordando nos.*	When we remembered.
זלל	בְּזֹלְלֵי	*Cum comessatoribus.*	With revellers.
זמם	בְּזִמָּה	*Malo animo.*	With a wicked mind.
זמן	בִּזְמַנֵּיהֶם	*Juxta tempora eorum.*	In their times *appointed.*
זמר	בְּזִמְרוֹת	*Psalmis.*	With psalms.
זנב	בִּזְנָבוֹ	*Per caudam ejus.*	By his tail.
זנה	בִּזְנוּנֶיהָ	*Scortationibus ejus.*	By her whoredoms.
—	בְּזְנוּתַיִךְ	*Scortationibus tuis.*	With thy whoredoms.
—	בִּזְנוֹתֵךְ	*In scortari te.*	Because thou hast gone a whoring.

ROOTS.	DERIVATIVES.	VERSIO.	SIGNIFICATION.
זנה	בִּזְנוּתָם	*Scortatione eorum.*	By their whoredom.
זעם	בְּזַעַם	*In indignatione.*	In the indignation.
זעף	בְּזַעַף	*In furore.*	In a rage.
זעק	בְּזַעֲקֵךְ	*Clamando te.*	When thou criest.
יזע	בְּזֵעַת	*In sudore.*	In the sweat.
בזק			
	בֶּזֶק	*Bezec.*	Bezek, N. P.
זקק	בַּזִּקִּים	*In compedibus.*	In, with chains, fetters.
זקן	בְּזָקֵן בַּזָּקֵן	*In senem.*	Against the ancient.
——	בְּזָקָן בַּזָּקָן	*In barba.*	On, by the beard.
——	בִּזְקָנוֹ	*Per barbam ejus.*	By his beard.
בָּזַר		*Dispersit, dissipavit.*	He dispersed, scattered.
——	בִּזַּר	*Dissipavit.*	He hath scattered.
זור	בְּזָרָה	*Cum aliena.*	With a strange woman.
זרע	בִּזְרוֹעַ	*Brachio.*	By, with an arm.
זור	בְּזָרִים	*Propter extraneos.*	With, on account of strange.
זרע	בְּזֶרַע	*Cum semine.*	With the seed.
——	בְּזַרְעוֹ	*In semine ejus.*	In his seed.
——	בִּזְרֹעוֹ	*Brachio ejus.*	With his arm.
——	בְּזַרְעֲךָ	*In semine tuo.*	In thy seed.
——	בְּזַרְעָם	*In semine eorum.*	In their seed.
זרת	בַּזֶּרֶת	*Cum palmo.*	With the span.
	בִּזְּתָא	*Bizta.*	Biztha, N. M.
בזה	בְּזִתָנִי	*Sprevisti me.*	Thou hast despised me.
	בח		
חבא	בְּחֻבִּי	*In sinu meo.*	In my bosom.
חבל	בְּחֶבֶל בְּחֶבֶל	*Fune, funiculo.*	By a line.
——	בְּחַבְלֵי	*In funibus.*	With, in cords.
——	בַּחֲבָלֶיהָ	*In doloribus ejus.*	In her pangs.
——	בַּחֲבָלִים	*In, cum funibus.*	In, by cords.
חבר	בַּחֲבָרַיִךְ	*Incantationibus tuis.*	With thine enchantments.
——	בַּחֹבָרֶת	*In conjunctione.*	In the coupling.
חגג	בְּחַג בֶּחָג	*In festo.*	In the feast.
חגה	בְּחַגְוֵי	*In scissuris.*	In the clefts.
חגג	בַּחַגִּים	*In festis.*	In the feasts.
——	בְּחַגֶּךָ	*In festo tuo.*	In thy feast.

ROOTS.	DERIVATIVES.	VERSIO.	SIGNIFICATION.
חגר	בַּחֲגֹרָתוֹ	*In balteo ejus.*	Upon his girdle.
חדה	בְּחֶדְוָה	*Cum gaudio.*	With joy.
חדר	בַּחֶדֶר בַּחֲדַר	*In cubiculo.*	In the chamber.
—	בְּחֶדֶר בְּחָדֶר	*In cubiculum.*	Into a chamber.
—	בְּחַדְרֵי	*In cubiculis.*	In the chambers.
—	בַּחֲדָרֶיךָ	*In cubicula tua.*	Into thy chambers.
חדש	בְּחֹדֶשׁ בַּחֹדֶשׁ	*In mense, novilunio.*	In the month, in the new moon.
—	בְּחָדְשָׁהּ	*In mense ejus.* [*ejus.*	In her month.
—	בְּחָדְשׁוֹ	*In mense, novilunio*	In his month, new moon.
חח	בַּחוֹחִים	*In vinculis, catenis.*	In bonds, chains.
חול	בַּחוֹל	*In arena.*	In the sand.
חמה	בַּחוֹמָה	*In muro.*	On a wall.
—	בְּחֹמַת	*In muro.*	In the wall.
—	בְּחוֹמֹת	*In muris.*	In the walls.
בחן	בָּחוֹן	*Turris speculatoria.*	A watch-tower.
חוץ	בַּחוּץ	*Foris, in vico.*	Without, in the street.
—	בַּחוּצוֹת	*In vicis.*	In the streets.
—	בְּחוּצוֹת	*In vicis.*	In the streets.
—	בְּחוּצוֹתֶיהָ	*In vicis ejus.*	In her streets.
—	בְּחוּצוֹתֵינוּ	*In vicis nostris.*	In our streets.
—	בְּחוּצֹתָיו	*In vicis eorum.*	In their streets.
חקק	בְּחוּקוֹ	*Constituendo eum.*	When he appointed.
—	בְּחוּקֵי	*In statutis.*	In the statutes.
בחר	בָּחוּר	*Electus, juvenis.*	Chosen, a young man.
—	בְּחוּרוֹתֶיךָ	*Juventutis tuæ.*	Of thy youth.
—	בַּחוּרֵי	*Juvenes.*	Young men.
—	בַּחוּרָי	*Juvenes mei.*	My young men,
—	בְּחוּרֵי	*Electi.*	The chosen.
—	בַּחוּרֶיהָ	*Juvenes ejus.*	Her young men.
—	בַּחוּרֵיהֶם	*Juvenes eorum.*	Their young men.
—	בַּחוּרָיו	*Juvenes ejus.*	His young men.
—	בַּחוּרֵיכֶם	*Juvenes vestri.*	Your young men.
—	בַּחוּרִים	*Juvenes.*	The young men.
—	בַּחֻרִים	*Bachurim.*	Bahurim, N. P.
חור	בַּחוּרִים	*In speluncis.*	In caves.
חזא	בְּחָזְוָא	*In visione.*	In a vision.
—	בְּחֶזְוֵי	*In visionibus.*	In the visions.

ROOTS.	DERIVATIVES.	VERSIO.	SIGNIFICATION.
חזא	בְּחֶזְוִי	*In visione mea.*	In my vision.
חזה	בְּחָזוֹן בַּחֲזוֹן	*In visione.*	In a vision.
—	בַּחֲזוֹת	*Videndo.*	While seeing.
חזק	בְּחָזָק בְּחֹזֶק	*Robore, potentia.*	By strength, power.
—	בְּחָזְקָה	*Fortiter, per vim.*	Mightily, by force.
—	בְּחָזְקֵנוּ	*Robore nostro.*	By our strength.
—	בְּחֶזְקַת	*Fortitudine, per vim*	By strength.
חח	בַּחַחִים	*Catenis.*	In chains.
חטא	בְּחֶטְאָהּ	*Pro peccatò ejus.*	For her sin.
—	בְּחֶטְאוֹ	*In peccato ejus.*	In his sin.
—	בְּחַטֹּאות־טֹּאת	*In, pro peccatis.* [*tra*	In, for the sins.
—	בְּחַטֹּאותֶיךָ	*Propter peccata ves-*	Because of thy sins.
—	בְּחַטֹּאותֵינוּ	*Ob peccata nostra.*	Because of our sins.
—	בַּחַטָּאִים	*In peccatores.* [*tra.*	Towards sinners.
—	בַּחֲטָאֵינוּ	*Propter peccata nos.*	For our sins.
—	בְּחַטָּאת	*Propter peccatum.*	For sin.
—	בְּחַטָּאתוֹ	*In peccato ejus.*	In his sin.
—	בְּחַטֹּאתֶיךָ	*Propter peccata tua.*	For thy sins.
—	בְּחַטֹּאתָם	*Peccatis suis.*	With their sins.
חנט	בְּחִטֵּי	*Cum triticis.*	With wheat.
חיה	בְּחֵי	*Per viventem.*	By him that liveth.
חוד	בְּחִידוֹת־דֹת	*Per ænigmata.*	By hard questions.
חיה	בְּחַיַּי	*In vita mea.*	In my life.
—	בְּחַיֶּיהָ	*In vita ejus.*	In her life time.
—	בְּחַיֵּיהֶם	*In vita eorum.*	In their life.
—	בְּחַיָּיו בְּחַיָּו	*In vita ejus.*	In his life.
—	בְּחַיֶּיךָ	*De vita tua.*	Of thy life.
—	בַּחַיִּים בַּחַיִּין	*In vita.*	In life.
חיל	בְּחַיִל בְּחַיִל	*In, cum exercitu.*	In, with an army.
—	בְּחָיִל	*Strenue, fortiter.*	Strongly.
—	בְּחֵילָהּ	*In copiis ejus.*	In his army.
חול	בְּחִילָה	*In dolore.*	In sorrow.
חיל	בְּחֵילוֹ	*In substantiam ejus.*	On his substance.
—	בְּחֵילֵךְ־לֵךְ־לָךְ	*Propter opes tuas, in virtute tua, in munitione tua.* [*ejus.*	Because of thy riches, by thy power, within thy walls.
בחן	בְּחִינָן	*Turres speculatoriæ*	His watch towers.

ROOTS.	DERIVATIVES.	VERSIO.	SIGNIFICATION.
חיק	בְּחֵיק בְּחֵיס	*In sinum, in sinu.*	Into, in the bosom.
—	בְּחֵיקָהּ	*In sinu ejus.*	In her bosom.
—	בְּחֵיקוֹ	*In sinu ejus.*	In his bosom.
—	בְּחֵיקִי	*In sinu meo.*	In my bosom.
—	בְּחֵיקֶךָ	*In sinu tuo.*	In thy bosom.
בחר	בְּחִיר	*Electus.*	Chosen.
—	בְּחִירוֹ	*Electus ejus.*	His chosen.
—	בְּחִירִי	*Electus meus.*	My chosen.
—	בְּחִירַי	*Electi mei.*	Mine elect.
—	בְּחִירָיו	*Electi ejus.*	His chosen,
—	בְּחִירֶיךָ	*Electi tui.*	Thy chosen.
חיה	בְּחַיַּת	*Cum bestiis.*	With the beasts.
חכה	בְּחַכָּה	*Hamo.*	With a hook.
חכך	בְּחִכִּי	*In palato meo.*	In the roof of my mouth.
חכם	בְּחָכְמָה	*In sapientia.*	In, by, with wisdom.
—	בְּחָכְמָתָהּ	*In sapientia ejus.*	In her wisdom.
—	בְּחָכְמָתוֹ	*In sapientia ejus.*	In his wisdom.
—	בְּחָכְמָתְךָ	*In sapientia tua.*	In, with thy wisdom.
בָּחַל		*Fastidivit.*	He loathed, abhorred.
חיל	בְּחֵל	*In fossa.*	In the trench.
—	בְּחֵל	*Juxta murum.*	By the wall.
חלב	בְּחָלָב בֶּחָלָב	*In lacte..*	With milk.
—	בַּחֲלֵב	*In lacte.*	In the milk.
—	בְּחֶלְבּוֹ	*Pinguedine ejus.*	With his fatness.
—	בְּחֶלְבֵי	*Cum adipibus.*	With the fat.
בחל	בָּחֲלָה	*Fastidivit.*	She abhorred.
חלם	בַּחֲלוֹם	*In somnio.*	In a dream.
—	בַּחֲלוֹמוֹת	*Per somnia.*	By dreams.
—	בַּחֲלוֹמִי־־לֹמִי	*In somnio meo.*	In my dream.
—	בַּחֲלוֹמֹתָם	*In somniis.*	In their dreams.
חלל	בְּחַלּוֹן בַּחַלּוֹן	*In fenestra.*	In the window.
—	בְּחַלּוֹנֵינוּ	*Per fenestras nostras*	Into, through our windows.
חלה	בַּחֲלוֹתָם	*Ægrotando eos.*	When they were sick.
—	בְּחָלְיוֹ	*In morbo ejus.*	In his sickness.
—	בָּחֳלָיִים	*Morbis.*	With sicknesses.
חלל	בֶּחָלִיל	*Cum tibia.*	With a pipe.
—	בֶּחָלָל בַּחֲלַל	*In occisum.*	On one slain.

ROOTS.	DERIVATIVES.	VERSIO.	SIGNIFICATION.
חלל	בַּחֲלִלִים	*Cum tibiis.*	With pipes.
חלם	בַּחֲלֹמוֹת	*Per somnia.*	By, with dreams.
חלמש	בַּחַלָּמִישׁ	*In petram, silicem, adamantem.*	Upon the rock, flint, adamant.
חלק	בְּחֵלֶק בְּחֶלְקָה	*In parte, agro.*	In the portion, the field.
—	בַּחֲלָקוֹת	*In lubricis* locis.	In slippery *places.*
—	בַּחֲלַקּוֹת	*Per blanditias.*	By flatteries.
—	בְּחַלְּקֵי	*In lævibus* lapidibus	Among the smooth *stones.*
—	בַּחֲלַקְלַקּוֹת	*Blanditiis.*	With flatteries.
—	בְּחַלְּקָם	*Dividendo eos.*	When they divide.
—	בְּחֶלְקַת	*In parte, possessione.*	In the portion, possession.
חלה	בַּחֲלֹתוֹ	*Cum ægrotasset.*	When he had been sick.
חמם	בְּחֹם	*In æstu.*	In the heat.
יחם	בְּחֵמָא	*Cum ira.*	With fury.
—	בְּחֵמָה	*In furore, ira.*	In a rage, in wrath.
חמא	בְּחֵמָה	*In butyro.*	In butter.
חמם	בְּחֻמּוֹ	*In æstu ejus.* [ejus.	In his heat.
חמד	בַּחֲמוּדוֹ	*Juxta desiderium*	According to his desire.
חמר	בַּחֲמוֹרִים	*In asinos.*	Upon asses.
חמה	בְּחֹמוֹתַיִךְ	*Contra muros tuos.*	Against thy walls.
חמל	בְּחֶמְלַת	*Pro clementia.*	In mercy.
חמם	בְּחֻמָּם	*In æstu eorum*	In their heat.
חמץ	בַּחֹמֶץ	*In aceto.*	In the vinegar.
חמר	בְּחֹמֶר בַּחֹמֶר	*In lutum, in luto.*	Into, in clay.
—	בַּחֵמָר	*Bitumine.*	With bitumen, or slimy clay.
—	בַּחֲמֹרִים	*In asinos.*	On asses.
חמש	בַּחֲמֵשׁ	*In quinque.* [quinta.	With five.
—	בַּחֲמִשָּׁה	*Propter quinque, in*	For five, in the fifth.
—	בַּחֲמִשִּׁי	*In quinto.*	In the fifth.
—	בַּחֲמִשִּׁים	*In quinquaginta.*	By fifty.
יחם	בַּחֲמַת	*In ira, furore.*	In the heat, wrath.
חמה	בַּחֲמֹתָהּ	*In socrum ejus.*	Against her mother-in-law.
יחם	בַּחֲמָתוֹ	*In furore ejus.*	In his wrath.
—	בַּחֲמָתִי	*In ira mea.*	In my fury.
—	בַּחֲמָתְךָ	*In ira tua.*	In thy fury.
בָּחַן		*Probavit, exploravit.*	He tried, proved.
—	בֹּחֵן	*Probans, explorans.*	Proving, trying.

ROOTS.	DERIVATIVES.	VERSIO.	SIGNIFICATION.
בחן	בֹּחַן	*Probatio.*	A trial.
—	בְּחָנוּ	*Probaverunt.*	They tempted.
—	בְּחָנוּנִי	*Probaverunt me.*	They proved me.
חנה	בַּחֲנִית	*Cum lancea, hasta.*	With the spear, javelin.
—	בַּחֲנִיתוֹ	*Cum lancea ejus.*	With his spear.
חנמל	בַּחֲנָמַל	*Cum glacie.*	With frost.
בחן	בְּחָנַנִי	*Probavit me.*	He hath tried me.
—	בְּחָנֵנִי	*Proba me. [pios.*	Try me. [fane.
חנף	בְּחַנְפֵי	*Inter hypocritas, im-*	Among hypocrites, with pro-
בחן	בְּחַנְתָּ	*Probasti.*	Thou hast proved.
—	בְּחַנְתָּנוּ	*Probasti nos.*	Thou hast proved us.
חסד	בְּחֶסֶד בְּ"	*In misericordia.*	In mercy.
—	בְּחַסְדְּךָ־דֶּךָ	*In misericordia tua.*	In thy mercy.
חסף	בַּחֲסַף	*Cum luto. [penuriam*	With clay.
חסר	בְּחֹסֶר בַּחֲסַר·	*In defectu, propter*	For want.
חפז	בְּחָפְזָהּ	*Festinando eam.*	As she made haste.
—	בְּחִפָּזוֹן	*Festinanter.*	In haste, speedily.
—	בְּחָפְזִי	*Festinando me.*	In my haste.
חפן	בְּחָפְנָיו	*In pugillis ejus.*	In his fists.
חפץ	בְּחֵפֶץ	*Juxta voluntatem.*	Willingly.
חצה	בַּחֲצִי בְּחֵצִי	*In medio, dimidio.*	In the midst, half.
חצץ	בַּחִצִּים	*Sagittis.*	With arrows.
חצן	בְּחֹצֶן	*In brachio, sinu.*	In arms, in the bosom.
חצץ	בֶּחָצָץ	*Lapillo, scrupo.*	With gravel, stone.
חצר	בַּחֲצֹצְרוֹת־רֹת	*Tubis.*	With trumpets.
—	בֶּחָצֵר בַּחֲצַר	*In atrio.*	In the court.
—	בַּחֲצֵרוֹ	*In atrio ejus.*	In his court.
—	בְּחַצְרוֹת	*In atriis.*	In the courts.
—	בְּחַצְרֵי	*In atriis. [rum.*	In the courts.
—	בְּחַצְרֵיהֶם	*In pagis, oppidis eo-*	In their villages, towns.
—	בַּחֲצֵרֶיךָ	*In atriis tuis.*	In thy courts.
חיק	בַּחֵק	*In sinu.*	In the bosom.
חקק	בְּחֻקוֹ	*Quum statueret.*	When he set.
—	בְּחֻקּוֹת־קֹּת	*In statutis.*	In the statutes.
—	בְּחֻקֹּתַי־קֹתַי	*In statutis meis.*	In my statutes.
	בְּחֻקַּי	*In statutis meis.*	In my statutes.
חיק	בְּחֵקִי	*In sinu meo.*	In my bosom.

ROOTS.	DERIVATIVES.	VERSIO.	SIGNIFICATION.
חקק	בְּחֻקָּיו	*In statutis ejus.*	In his statutes.
—	בְּחֻקֶּיךָ	*In statutis tuis.*	In thy statutes.
—	בְּחֻקֹּתֶיךָ	*In statutis tuis.*	In thy statutes,
בָּחַר		*Elegit, selegit.*	He chose, selected.
—	בֹּחֵר	*Eligens.*	Choosing.
—	בְּחַר	*Elige.*	Choose thou.
חרב	בְּחֶרֶב בֶּחָרֶב	*Gladio.*	By, with a sword.
—	בֶּחָרָבָה	*In sicco.*	In the dry land.
—	בְּחַרְבּוֹ	*Gladio ejus.*	With his sword.
—	בְּחַרְבוֹנֵי	*In siccitatates.*	Into the drought.
—	בֶּחֳרָבוֹת	*Per loca deserta.*	Through the deserts.
—	בֶּחֳרָבוֹת	*In desertis.*	In the deserts.
—	בַּחֲרָבוֹת	*Cultris.*	By, with knives.
—	בְּחַרְבוֹת	*Gladiis.*	By the swords.
—	בְּחַרְבוֹתֵיהֶם	*Cum gladiis eorum.*	With their swords.
—	בְּחַרְבוֹתָיו	*Gladiis, securibus ejus.*	With his axes.
—	בְּחַרְבוֹתָם	*Gladiis eorum.*	With their swords.
—	בְּחַרְבִּי	*Gladio meo.*	With my sword.
—	בְּחַרְבְּךָ	*Gladio tuo.*	With thy sword.
—	בְּחַרְבָּם	*Gladio eorum.*	By their sword.
בחר	בָּחֲרוּ	*Elegerunt.*	They chose.
—	בַּחֲרוּ	*Eligite.*	Choose ye.
חרז	בַּחֲרוּזִים	*Torquibus.*	With chains, rows, collars.
—	בַּחֲרוּמִי	*Buchuramites.*	Bahuramite, N. P.
חרה	בַּחֲרוֹן	*In æstu, furore.*	In the heat, fierceness.
חרץ	בֶּחָרוּץ	*Tribulâ.*	With a threshing instrument
חרה	בַּחֲרוֹת	*In ardescendo.*	When kindled.
כחר	בְּחֻרוֹתֶיךָ	*Juventutis tuæ.*	Of thy youth.
חרט	בְּחֶרֶט בְּחֶרֶט	*Stylo.*	With a graving tool.
חרטם	בַּחַרְטֻמִּים	*In magis, hariolis.*	Upon the magicians.
חרה	בָּחֳרִי	*Eligere me.*	When I chose.
—	בָּחֳרִי	*In furore.*	In great anger.
בחר	בַּחֻרֶיהָ	*Juvenes ejus.*	Her young men.
חור	בְּחֹרֵיהֶן	*In foraminibus earum.*	In their holes.
	בַּחֻרִים	*Bachurim.*	Bahurim, N. P.
חרש	בֶּחָרִישׁ	*In aratione.*	In ploughing.

ROOTS.	DERIVATIVES.	VERSIO.	SIGNIFICATION.
חרם	בְּחֵרֶם	*In anathemate.*	In, with the accursed thing.
—	בְּחֶרְמוֹ	*In sagena ejus.*	In his net.
—	בְּחֶרְמִי	*In reti meo.*	In my net.
חרף	בְּחֶרְפָּה	*Cum opprobrio.* [*eos.*	With reproach.
—	בְּחָרְפָם	*Probris lacessendo*	When they defied, reproached.
חרץ	בַּחֲרֻצוֹת	*Tribulis.*	With threshing instruments.
חרש	בַּחֹרְשָׁה	*In silva.*	In a wood.
בחר	בָּחַרְתָּ בָּחָרְתָּ	*Elegisti.*	Thou hast chosen.
—	בָּחָרְתִּי בָּחַרְתִּי	*Elegi.*	I chose.
—	בְּחַרְתִּיךָ	*Elegi te.*	I have chosen thee.
—	בְּחַרְתֶּם	*Elegistis.*	Ye have chosen.
חשב	בְּחֵשֶׁב	*Cingulo polymito.*	With the curious girdle.
חשך	בַּחֲשׁוֹכָא	*In tenebris.*	In the darkness.
—	בַּחֹשֶׁךְ בַּחֲשֵׁכָה	*In tenebris.*	In darkness.
חשן	בַּחֹשֶׁן	*Pectorali.*	With the breast plate.
חתת	בְּחִתִּיתָם	*Terrore eorum.*	With their terror.
חתם	בְּחֹתָמוֹ	*Sigillo ejus.*	With his seal.
	בט		
בָּטָא		*Effutivit.*	He spoke, or uttered rashly, [or unadvisedly.
טבע	בַּטַּבָּעֹת	*In annulos.*	Into the rings.
—	בְּטַבַּעַת	*Sigillo.*	With a seal.
—	בַּטַּבָּעֹת	*In annulis.*	In the rings.
טהר	בַּטָּהוֹר	*Super mundum.*	Upon him that is clean.
—	בְּטָהֳרָתוֹ	*In mundationem ejus*	To his cleansing.
טוב	בְּטוֹב בַּטּוֹב	*In, pro bono.*	In, for good.
—	בַּטּוֹב	*In bono.*	In the good.
—	בְּטוֹבָה	*In bono.*	In good, with pleasure
—	בְּטוּבְךָ	*In bonitate tua.*	In thy goodness.
—	בְּטוֹבַת	*In bono.*	In the good.
—	בְּטוֹבָתְךָ	*Pro bonitate tua.*	Of thy goodness.
בטח	בָּטוֹחַ בְּטוֹחַ	*Confidere.*	To trust.
—	בָּטוּחַ	*Confisus.*	Trusting.
בָּטַח		*Speravit, fidit, confidit, securus fuit.*	He hoped, trusted, relied upon, was secure.
	בֶּטַח	*Batach.*	Betah, N. P.
בטח	בֹּטֵחַ	*Fidens.*	Trusting.

ROOTS.	DERIVATIVES.	VERSIO.	SIGNIFICATION.
בטח	בֶּטַח	*Confidenter, tute.*	Confidently, safely.
—	בְּטַח	*Spera, confide.*	Hope, trust thou.
—	בֹּטֵחַ	*Confidens, securus.*	Trusting, confident.
—	בָּטְחָה	*Confidit.* [*derunt.*	She trusted.
—	בָּטְחוּ	*Speraverunt, confi-*	They hoped, trusted.
—	בִּטְחוּ	*Confidite.*	Trust ye.
—	בִּטָּחוֹן	*Spes, fiducia.*	Hope, confidence.
—	בַּטֻּחוֹת	*In renibus,securitas.*	In the inward parts, security.
—	בֹּטְחוֹת	*Confidentes, securæ.*	Trusting, secure.
—	בִּטְחֵךְ	*Fidere te.*	Thou hast trusted.
—	בָּטַחְנוּ	*Confidimus.*	We trusted.
—	בָּטַחְתָּ	*Confidisti.*	Thou trustedst.
—	בָּטַחְתִּי	*Confidi.*	I have trusted.
טיט	בַּטִּיט	*In lutum.*	Into the clay.
בָּטַל		*Cessavit.*	He ceased.
—	בְּטֵלָא	*Intermissa.*	Discontinued.
—	בַּטִּלוּ	*Cessare fecerunt.*	They caused to cease.
—	בָּטְלַת	*Cessavit.* [*dum.*	She ceased.
טמא	בְּטָמֵא	*In immundo, immun-*	In, to one that is unclean.
—	בְּטַמַּאֲכֶם	*Contaminando vos.*	When ye defile.
—	בְּטַמְּאָם	*Polluendo illos.*	When they defile.
—	בְּטֻמְאַת	*In immunditia.*	In the uncleanness.
—	בְּטֻמְאָתֵךְ	*In immunditia tua.*	In thy filthiness.
—	בְּטֻמְאָתָם	*In immunditia eorum*	In, with their uncleanness.
טמן	בַּטָּמוֹן	*In abscondito.*	In secret.
	בֶּטֶן	*Beten.*	Beten, N. P.
בטן			
—	בֶּטֶן	*Venter.*	A belly.
—	בָּטֶן	*Venter, uterus.*	The belly, the womb.
טנא	בַּטֶּנֶא	*In canistro.*	In a basket.
בטן	בִּטְנָהּ	*Venter, uterus ejus.*	Her belly, womb.
—	בִּטְנוֹ	*Venter ejus.* [*meum.*	His belly.
—	בִּטְנִי	*Venter, uterus: cor*	My belly, womb, heart.
	בְּטֹנִים	*Betonim.*	Betonim, N. P.
בטן	בָּטְנִים	*Avellanæ.*	Nuts.
—	בִּטְנְךָ בִּטְנֵךְ	*Venter tuus.* [*rum.*	Thy belly.
—	בִּטְנָם	*Venter, uterus eo-*	Their belly, womb.

ROOTS.	DERIVATIVES.	VERSIO.	SIGNIFICATION.
בטן	בִּטְנֵנוּ	*Venter noster.*	Our belly.
טעם	בְּטַעַם	*In sapore.*	In the taste.
טפף	בַּטַּף	*Usque ad parvulum*	Even to a little one.
טרם	בְּטֶרֶם	*Ante, antequam.*	Before.
	בי		
בי			
—	בִּי	*Obsecro, attende; in, contra, per me.*	O! I pray, attend; in, against, by me.
יאר	בִּיאוֹר בַּיְאֹר	*In flumine.*	In the river.
—	בַּיְאֹרִים	*Inter flumina.*	Among the rivers.
יבל	בַּיֹּבֵל	*In* anno *jubilæo.*	In the jubilee.
יבש	בִּיבֹשׁ	*Arescendo.*	When withered.
—	בַּיַּבָּשָׁה	*Per siccum.*	Over, on dry ground.
—	בַּיַּבֶּשֶׁת	*In sicco.*	Upon the dry land.
ינה	בְּיָגוֹן	*Cum dolore.*	With grief.
יד	בְּיַד בְּיָד	*Manu, per manum.*	By, through, with a hand.
—	בְּיָדָהּ	*In manu ejus.* [*ejus.*	In her hand.
—	בְּיָדָהּ	*In manum, in manu*	Into, in her hand.
—	בְּיָדָהֶם	*In manu sua.* [*ejus.*	In their hand.
—	בְּיָדוֹ	*In manum, manu*	Into, in, by his hand.
—	בְּיָדִי	*In manum meam.*	Into in my hand.
—	בַּיָּדִי	*In locis, in manus.*	In places, into hands.
—	בְּיָדֶיהָ	*In manibus ejus.*	In, with her hands.
—	בִּידֵיהֶם	*In manibus eorum.*	In their hands.
—	בִּידֵיהֶן	*In manibus earum.*	In their hands.
—	בְּיָדָיו	*In manibus ejus.*	In his hands.
—	בְּיָדֶיךָ	*In manu tua.*	In thy hand.
—	בְּיָדַיִם בְּיָדַיִן	*In manibus.* [*nu tua*	In, with hands.
—	בְּיָדְךָ בְּיָדֶךָ	*In manum tuam, ma-*	Into, in thy hand.
—	בְּיָדֵךְ בְּיָדְךָ	*In manu tua.*	In, with thy hand.
—	בְּיֶדְכֶם־כֶן	*In manu vestra.*	In your hand.
—	בְּיָדָם	*In, per manum eorum.* [*tram.*	Into, by their hand.
—	בְּיָדֵנוּ	*In, per manum nos-*	Into, by our hand.
היה	בְּיָהּ	*In Jah.* [*Jehovam.*	In Jah. [Jehovah.
—	בַּיהוָֹה	*In, a Jehova; in, per*	In, from, towards, by, against

ROOTS.	DERIVATIVES.	VERSIO.	SIGNIFICATION.
יוֹם	בְּיוֹם בַּיּוֹם	*In, a die.*	In, from the day.
—	בְּיוֹמָא	*In die.*	In a day.
—	בְּיוֹמוֹ	*In die ejus.*	Upon his day.
—	בְּיוֹמָם	*Per diem.*	By day.
יון	בְּיָוֵן	*In cæno.*	In mire.
ישב	בְּיוֹשְׁבֵי	*In habitatores.*	Against the inhabitants.
יזע	בַּיָּזַע	*In, cum sudore.*	In, with sweat.
יין	בְּיַיִן בַּיַּיִן בְּיֵין	*In vino, per vinum.*	In, with, through wine.
ילד	בַּיֶּלֶד	*In puerum.*	Against the child.
—	בְּיַלְדוּתֶךָ	*In juventute tua.*	In thy youth.
—	בְּיַלְדֵי בִּילָדֵי	*De filiis.*	Of the sons. [wife.
—	בְּיַלֶּדְכֶן	*Obstetricando vos.*	When ye do the office of a mid-
ים	בְּיָם בַּיָּם	*In, per mare, in mari*	Into, in, on, through the sea.
יום	בְּיָמַי	*In diebus meis.*	In my days.
—	בִּימֵי	*In diebus.*	In the days.
—	בִּימֵיהֶם	*In diebus eorum.*	In their days.
—	בְּיָמָיו	*In diebus ejus.*	In his days.
—	בְּיָמֶיךָ	*In diebus tuis.*	In thy days.
—	בִּימֵיכֶם	*In diebus vestris.*	In your days.
—	בַּיָּמִים	*In diebus.*	In the days.
ים	בַּיַּמִּים	*In maribus.* [am.	In the seas.
ימן	בִּימִין	*Dexterâ, ad dexter-*	With, at the right hand.
—	בִּימִינָהּ	*In dextera ejus.*	In her right hand.
—	בִּימִינוֹ	*Ad dexteram ejus.*	At his right hand.
—	בִּימִינִי	*In dextera mea.* [am	In my right hand.
—	בִּימִינְךָ־נֶךָ	*Per, ad dexteram tu-*	By, at thy right hand.
בין			
בין	בֵּין	*In, inter, sive.*	In, between, whether.
בון	בִּין	*Intelligere.* [tia.	To understand.
—	בִּינָה	*Considera; intelligen-*	Consider; understanding.
בין	בֵּינוֹ	*Inter eum.*	Between him.
—	בֵּינָיו	*Inter eos.* [ate.	Between them.
בון	בִּינוּ	*Intelligite, consider-*	Understand, consider ye.
בין	בֵּינוֹת	*Inter.*	Between.
בון	בִּינוֹת	*Intellige tia.*	Of understanding.
בין	בֵּינוֹתֵינוּ	*Inter nos*	Betwixt us.
—	בֵּינִי	*Inter me.*	Between me.

ROOTS.	DERIVATIVES.	VERSIO.	SIGNIFICATION.
בין	בֵּינֵיהֶם־הֶן ,	*Inter eos, eas.*	Between them.
—	בֵּינֵיכֶם	*Inter vos.*	Between you.
—	בֵּינֵינוּ	*Inter nos.*	Betwixt us.
—	בֵּינְךָ	*Inter te.*	Between thee.
—	בֵּינֵכֶם	*Inter vos.*	Between you.
בון	בִּינָה	*Intelligentia.*	Understanding.
—	בִּינֹתִי	*Intellexi.*	I understood.
בין	בֵּינֹתֵינוּ	*Inter nos.*	Between, among us.
בון	בִּינָתְךָ	*Intelligentia tua.*	Thy understanding.
בין	בֵּינֹתָם	*Inter eos.*	Between them.
יסד	בְּיָסְדוֹ	*Fundando ipsum.*	When he laid the foundation.
—	בְּיָסְדִי	*Fundando me.*	When I laid the foundation.
יער	בִּיעָרִים	*In sylvis.*	In the woods.
יען	בְּיַעַן	*Quia, propter.*	Because, because of.
יעף	בִּיעָף	*In sylvam, sylva.*	Into, in the wood.
יער	בְּיַעַר בַּיַּעַר	*Lassitudine.*	With weariness.
—	בְּיַעְרָהּ	*In sylva ejus.*	In her forest.
—	בְּיַעְרַת	*In favum.*	Into a honey-comb.
יפה	בְּיָפְיוֹ	*In decore ejus.*	In his beauty.
—	בְּיָפְיֶךָ בְּיָפְיֵךְ	*In pulchritudine tua.*	In thy beauty.
ביץ			
—	בֵּיצֵי	*Ova.*	Eggs.
—	בֵּיצֶיהָ	*Ova ejus.*	Her eggs.
—	בֵּיצִים	*Ova.*	Eggs.
יצק	בְּצָקְתּוֹ	*In fusione ejus.*	In its pouring out, or casting.
יקר	בִּיקָר	*In honore.*	In honour.
—	בִּיקָרוֹ	*In honore ejus.*	In his honour;
—	בִּיקְרוֹתֶיךָ	*Inter honoratas tuas*	Among thy honourable women
ביר			
ירא	בְּיִרְאָה	*In timore.*	In, with fear.
—	בְּיִרְאַת	*In timore.*	In the fear.
—	בְּיִרְאָתְךָ	*In timore tuo.*	In thy fear.
ירח	בְּיֶרַח	*In mense.*	In the month.
ירע	בִּירִיעָה	*In aulæo.*	In the curtain.
—	בִּירִיעֹת	*In aulæis.*	In the curtains.
ירד	בְּיַרְכְּתֵי	*In lateribus.*	On the sides.
—	בְּיַרְכָתַיִם	*In utroque latere.*	In the two sides.

ROOTS.	DERIVATIVES.	VERSIO.	SIGNIFICATION.
ביר	בִּירָנִיּוֹת	*Arces, palatia.*	Castles, palaces.
ירק	בִּירַקְרַק	*Flavo.*	With yellow.
ישב	בְּיֹשֵׁב	*In habitatore.*	In the inhabitant.
ישע	בִּישׁוּעָה	*In salute.*	With salvation.
—	בִּישׁוּעָתוֹ	*In salute ejus.*	In his salvation.
—	בִּישׁוּעָתִי	*In salute mea.*	In my salvation.
—	בִּישׁוּעָתֶךָ	*In salute tua.*	In thy salvation.
ישם	בִּישִׁימוֹן	*Per desertum.*	Through the wilderness.
ישש	בִּישִׁישִׁים	*In decrepitis.*	Among decrepid.
ישע	בְּיֵשַׁע	*In salute.*	In safety.
ישר	בְּיֹשֶׁר	*In rectitudine.*	With uprightness.
—	בְּיָשְׁרוֹ	*In rectitudine ejus.*	In his uprightness.
בית			
—	בַּיִת בָּיִת	*Domus, templum.*	A house, temple.
—	בֵּית	*Domus, templum, locus; intrinsecus.*	A, the house, temple, place; within.
—	בֵּית אָב	*Familia.*	A family, house of the father.
	בֵּית אָוֶן	*Beth-aven.*	Beth-aven, N. P.
	בֵּית אֵל	*Beth-el.*	Beth-el, N. P.
בית	בֵּית בָּמוֹת	*Fana, loca excelsa.*	Consecrated, high places.
	בֵּית בִּרְאִי	*Beth-birai.*	Beth-birei, N. P.
	בֵּית בָּרָה	*Beth-bara.*	Beth-barah, N. P.
	בֵּית גָּדֵר	*Beth-gader.*	Beth-gader, N. P.
	בֵּית גָּמוּל	*Beth-gamul.*	Beth-gamul, N. P.
	בֵּית דָּגוֹן דָּגֹן	*Beth-dagon.*	Beth-dagon, N.P.
בית	בֵּית הָאָבוֹת	*Familiæ.*	Houses of the fathers, families
—	בֵּית הַבּוֹר	*Domus foveæ, carcer*	The house of the pit, a prison.
	בֵּית הַיְשִׁימוֹת	*Beth-esimoth.*	Beth-jeshimoth, N. P.
	בֵּית הַכֶּרֶם	*Beth-acharem.*	Beth-haccerem, N, P.
	בֵּית הַלַּחְמִי	*Beth-leemites.*	Beth-lehemite, N. P.
בית	בֵּית הָעָם	*Domus populi, basilica.*	The house of the people, a public hall, or court.
	בֵּית הָעֲרָבָה	*Beth-araba.*	Beth-arabah, N. P.
	בֵּית הָרָם	*Beth-aram.*	Beth-aram, N. P.
	בֵּית הָרָן	*Beth-aran.*	Beth-haran, N. P.
	בֵּית הַשִּׁטָּה	*Beth-sitta.*	Beth-shittah, N. P.
	בֵּית הַשִּׁמְשִׁי	*Beth-semites.*	Beth-shemite, N. P.

ROOTS.	DERIVATIVES.	VERSIO.	SIGNIFICATION.
	בֵּית חָגְלָה	*Beth-chogla.*	Beth-hogla, N. P.
	בֵּית חָנָן	*Beth-hanan.*	Beth-hanan, N. P.
	בֵּית חֹרוֹן	*Beth-horon.*	Beth-horon, N. P.
	בֵּית כָּר	*Beth-car.*	Beth-car, N. P.
	בֵּית לְבָאוֹת	*Beth-lebaoth.*	Beth-lebaoth, N. P.
	בֵּית לֶחֶם	*Beth-lehem.*	Beth-lehem, N. P.
בית	בֵּית מִדּוֹת	*Domus mensurarum, vel amplissima.*	A house of measures, *that is,* very spacious.
—	בֵּית מִלְחַמְתִּי	*Domus belli mei, hostes mei.*	The house of my war, my enemies.
	בֵּית מְעוֹן	*Beth-meon.*	Beth-meon, N. P.
	בֵּית מַעֲכָה	*Beth-mahaca.*	Beth-maachah, N. P.
	בֵּית מַרְכָּבֹת	*Beth-marcaboth.*	Beth-marcaboth, N. P.
	בֵּית נִמְרָה	*Beth-nimra.*	Beth-nimrah, N. P.
	בֵּית עַזְמָוֶת	*Beth-azmaveth.*	Beth-azmaveth, N. P.
בית	בֵּית עֹלָמוֹ	*Domus æternitatis suæ; sepulchrum ejus, vel status animæ post mortem.*	The house of his eternity, or perpetuity; his sepulchre, or the state of departed spirits.
	בֵּית עֵמֶק	*Beth-emech.*	Beth-emek, N. P.
	בֵּית עֲנוֹת	*Beth-anoth, Beth-anath.*	Beth-anoth, Beth-anath, N.P.
	בֵּית פֶּלֶט	*Beth-phalet.*	Beth-palet, N P.
	בֵּית פְּעוֹר	*Beth-pheor.*	Beth-peor. N. P.
	בֵּית פַּצֵּץ	*Beth-pases.*	Beth-pazzez, N. P.
	בֵּית צוּר	*Beth-zur.*	Beth-zur, N. P.
	בֵּית רָפָא	*Beth-rapha.*	Beth-rapha, N. P.
	בֵּית שְׁאָן	*Beth-sean.*	Beth-shean, N. P.
	בֵּית שֶׁמֶשׁ	*Beth-semes.*	Beth-shemesh, N. P.
	בֵּית שָׁן	*Beth-san.*	Beth-shan, N. P.
	בֵּית תַּפּוּחַ	*Beth-tapua.*	Beth-tappuah, N. P.
בית	בֵּיתָא	*Templum.*	A temple.
יתד	בְּיָתֵד	*Clavo.*	With the pin, or nail.
בית	בֵּיתָה	*In domo; intrinsecus*	In the house; within.
—	בַּיְתָה	*Domus.*	The house.
—	בֵּיתָהּ בֵּיתֵהּ	*Domus ejus.*	Her house.
—	בֵּיתָה	*Ad, in domum.*	To, into the house.

ROOTS.	DERIVATIVES.	VERSIO.	SIGNIFICATION.
בית	בֵּיתוֹ	*Domus, familia ejus*	His house, family.
—	בֵּיתִי	*Domus mea.*	My house.
—	בֵּיתְךָ־־תֶךָ־־תֵךְ	*Domus, familia tua.*	Thy house, family.
—	בֵּיתָם	*Domus eorum.*	Their houses.
—	בִּיתַן	*Palatium.*	The palace.
יתר	בְּיֶתֶר	*In residuum.*	Unto the remnant,
	ככ		
		[te.	
	בְּךָ בָּךְ	*In, apud, per, contra*	In, to, with, by, against thee.
בכא			
—	בְּכָאִים	*Mori.*	The mulberry trees.
כבד	בַּכָּבֵד	*In jecur.*	Into the liver.
—	בִּכְבֹדִי־־בוֹדִי	*Per gloriam meam.*	By my glory.
—	בִּכְבֵדֻת	*Cum gravitate. [ria.*	Heavily, with difficulty.
—	בְּכָבוֹד	*Cum honore, in glo-*	With honour, in glory.
—	בִּכְבוֹדוֹ	*In gloria ejus.*	In his glory. [guished.
כבה	בְּכַבּוֹתְךָ	*In extinguendo te.*	When thou shalt be extin-
כבל	בְּכֶבֶל	*Cum compede.*	With a chain.
—	בְּכַבְלֵי	*Cum compedibus.*	With fetters.
כבר	בַּכְּבָרָה	*In cribro.*	In a sieve.
כבש	בַּכְּבָשִׂים	*In ovibus.*	Among the sheep.
כדד	בַּכַּד	*In hydria.*	In a pitcher.
בָּכָה		*Flevit, ploravit.*	He wept, lamented.
—	בֶּכֶה	*Fletus.*	A weeping, lamentation.
—	בֹּכֶה	*Flens.*	Weeping.
כה	בְּכֹה	*Sic.*	Thus, in that manner.
—	בְּכָה	*In te.*	In thee
כהן	בְּכֹהֲנֵי	*In sacerdotes.*	Upon the priests.
—	בְּכֹהֲנָיו	*Inter sacerdotes ejus*	Among his priests.
—	בַּכֹּהֲנִים	*In sacerdotibus.*	In the priests.
בכה	בְּכוֹ	*Flere.*	To weep.
—	בָּכוּ	*Fleverunt.*	They wept.
—	בְּכוּ	*Flete.*	Weep ye.
כבע	בְּכוֹבָעִים	*Cum galeis.*	With helmets.
ככב	בַּכּוֹכָבִים	*In stellas.*	At, on the stars.
בכר	בְּכוֹר בְּכֹר	*Primogenitus.*	First-born.

ROOTS.	DERIVATIVES.	VERSIO.	SIGNIFICATION.
כור	בְּכוּר	*In fornace.*	In the furnace.
בכר	בִּכּוּרָה	*Præcox fructus.*	The first ripe fruit.
—	בְּכוֹרוֹ בְּכֹרוֹ	*Primogenitus ejus.*	His first born.
—	בְּכוֹרִי בְּכֹרִי	*Primogenitus meus.*	My first born.
—	בִּכּוּרֵי	*Primitiæ.*	The first fruits.
—	בְּכוֹרֵי	*Primogeniti.*	The first born.
—	בִּכּוּרֶיךָ	*Primitiæ tuæ.*	Thy first fruits.
—	בִּכּוּרִים	*Primitiæ.*	The first fruits.
	בְּכוֹרַת	*Bechorath.*	Bechorath.
כשר	בַּכּוֹשָׁרוֹת	*Cum compedibus.*	With chains.
בכה	בָּכוּת	*Fletus, ploratus.*	Weeping, lamentation.
כזב	בְּכַזֶּבְכֶם	*Mentiendo vos.[bore*	By your lying.
כוח	בַּכֹּחַ בְּכֹחַ	*In, cum potentia, ro-*	In, with, by power, strength.
—	בְּכֹחוֹ	*Per potentiam ejus.*	By his power.
—	בְּכֹחִי	*Fortitudine mea.*	By my power.
—	בְּכֹחֲךָ	*Vi, virtute tua.*	By thy might, power.
—	בְּכֹחָם	*Secundum potestatem eorum.*	According to their power, ability.
כחש	בְּכַחַשׁ	*Mendacio.*	With falsehood.
בכה	בֶּכִי בְּכִי	*Fletus.*	Weeping.
כיד	בַּכִּידוֹן	*Cum hasta.*	With the spear.
כיר	בַּכִּיּוֹר	*In ahenum.*	Into the pan.
בכה	בִּכְיִי	*Fletus meus.*	My weeping.
—	בֹּכִים	*Fletus.*	Weeping, N. P.
—	בְּכֶינָה	*Flete.*	Weep ye.
—	בָּכִינוּ	*Flevimus.*	We wept.
כוס	בַּכּוֹס	*In calice.*	In the cup.
—	בְּכִיסְךָ	*In loculo tuo.*	In thy bag.
כשר	בַּכִּישׁוֹר	*Ad fusum.*	To the spindle.
בכה	בִּכְיתוֹ	*Luctus ejus.*	His mourning.
—	בָּכִיתִי	*Flevi.*	I wept.
—	בְּכִיתֶם	*Flevisti.*	Ye wept.
ככר	בַּכִּכָּר	*In planitie.*	In the plain.
—	בְּכִכָּרַיִם	*Pro duobus talentis.*	For two talents.
כלל	בְּכָל בְּכֹל	*Cum, in, ex omni, toto; omnibus, cunctis; quocunque.*	With, in, over all, the whole, every; wheresoever.

ROOTS.	DERIVATIVES.	VERSIO.	SIGNIFICATION.
כלל	בְּכֹל	*Contra omnes.*	Ag:inst every, all
—	בְּכָלְּהוֹן	*In omnibus ipsis.*	Over them all.
כלה	בִּכְלוֹת	*Consumendo.*	In consuming.
—	בְּכַלּוֹתִי	*Consummando me.*	When I accomplished.
—	בְּכַלּוֹתְךָ	*Absolvendo te.*	When thou hast made an end.
—	בְּכֶלַח	*In senectute.*	In a full age.
—	בִּכְלִי בַּכְּלִי	*In vàse.*	In a vessel.
—	בִּכְלֵי	*In, cum vasis, armis, instrumentis.*	In, with vessels, weapons, instruments.
—	בִּכְלִי	*In vase, sacculo, instrumento.*	In, with a vessel, bag, instrument.
—	בִּכְלֵיהֶם	*Inter vasa, supellectilia eorum.*	Amongst their vessels, goods,
—	בְּכִלְיוֹתַי	*In renes meos*	Into my reins.
—	בִּכְלֵיכֶם	*In vasis vestris.*	In your vessels.
—	בַּכֵּלִים	*Cum instrumentis.*	With the instruments.
כלל	בְּכֻלָּם	*In his omnibus.*	In all these.
כלם	בִּכְלִמָּה	*Cum pudore.*	With confusion.
	בָּכֶם	*In, ex nobis; in, inter contra nos.*	In, from, to, among, against us.
כנר	בְּכִנּוֹר	*Cum cithara.*	With a harp.
—	בַּכִּנּוֹר	*Cum cithara.*	With the harp.
כנף	בִּכְנַף	*In ora.*	Upon the skirt.
—	בִּכְנָפוֹ	*Cum ora ejus.*	With his skirt.
—	בִּכְנָפוֹת	*In extrema.*	At the ends, extremities.
—	בִּכְנָפֶיהָ	*In alis ejus.*	In her wings.
—	בְּכַנְפֵיהֶם	*In alis eorum.*	In their wings.
—	בִּכְנָפָיו	*Cum alis ejus.*	With his wings.
—	בִּכְנָפֶיךָ--פֵיךְ	*In oris tuis.*	In thy skirts.
כנר	בְּכִנֹּרוֹת	*Cum citharis*	With harps.
כסא	בַּכֵּסֶה	*In tempore statuto.*	In the time appointed.
כסל	בַּכְּסִילִים	*Inter stultos.*	Among fools.
—	בְּכִסְלֶךָ	*In fiducia tua.*	In thy confidence.
כסף	בְּכֶסֶף בַּכֶּסֶף	*In, cum, pro argento, pecunia.*	In, with, for silver, money.
—	בְּכַסְפָּא	*Cum pecunia.*	With money.

ROOTS.	DERIVATIVES.	VERSIO.	SIGNIFICATION.
כעס	בְּכַעַס	*Cum tristitia, indignatione.*	With grief, indignation.
—	בְּכַעְסוֹ	*Propter irritationem ejus.*	By his provocation.
כפף	בְּכַף בַּכַּף	*In manum, in manu*	Into, in the hand.
—	בְּכַפּוֹ	*In manu ejus.*	In his hand.
—	בְּכַפִּי	*In manu mea.*	In my hand.
—	בְּכַפַּי־פָּי	*In manibus meis.*	In my hands.
—	בְּכַפֵּיהֶם	*In manibus eorum.*	In their hands.
—	בְּכַפְּךָ	*Manu tua.*	With thy hand.
כפל	בְּכֶפֶל	*Cum duplice.*	With double.
כפר	בַּכֹּפֶר	*Cum bitumine, pice.*	With bitumen, pitch.
—	בְּכַפְּרִי	*Propitiando me.*	When I am pacified.
—	בַּכְּפָרִים	*In pagis.*	In the villages.
—	בְּכַפֶּרְךָ	*Expiando te.*	When thou hast made an atonement.
כפתר	בְּכַפְתֹּרֶיהָ	*In superliminaribus ejus.*	In the upper lintels of it.
בָּכַר		*Primogenitum constituit, maturavit*	He made, or constituted first born, brought to maturity.
כר	בְּכַר	*In clitellis.*	Among the panniers.
	בֶּכֶר	*Becher.*	Becker, N. P.
בכר	בְּכֹרָה	*Primogenitura.*	The birth-right.
—	בִּכְרָה	*Dromas.*	A dromedary.
	בֹּכְרוּ	*Bocheru.*	Bocheru, N. M.
בכר	בְּכֹרוֹת	*Primogenita.*	First born.
—	בִּכְרֵי	*Dromades.*	The dromedaries.
	בִּכְרִי	*Bichri.*	Bichri, N. M.
	בַּכְרִי	*Bachritæ.*	Bachrites, N. F.
בכר	בִּכָרִים	*Cum agnis.*	With the lambs.
—	בְּכֹרְךָ־רֶךָ	*Primogenitus tuus.*	Thy first-born.
כרם	בְּכֶרֶם	*In vineam, vinea.*	Into, in the vineyard.
—	בְּכַרְמֵי	*In vineis.*	In the vineyards.
—	בַּכְּרָמִים	*In vineis.*	In vineyards.
כרמל	בַּכַּרְמֶל	*In arvo.*	In the fruitful field.
כרת	בִּכְרֹת	*Fœdus ineundo.*	In making a league.
בכר	בְּכֹרָתוֹ	*Primogenitura ejus.*	His birth-right.
—	בְּכֹרָתִי	*Primogenitura mea.*	My birth-right.
כרת	בְּכָרְתִי	*In abscindere me.*	In that I cut off.
בכר	בְּכֹרָתְךָ	*Primogenitura tua.*	Thy birth-right.

ROOTS.	DERIVATIVES.	VERSIO.	SIGNIFICATION.
כשב	בְּכְּשָׂבִים	*Inter oves.*	Among the sheep.
כשל	בְּכַשִּׁיל	*Cum securi.*	With an ax.
כשף	בִּכְשָׁפֶיהָ	*Per maleficia ejus.*	Through her witchcrafts.
כתב	בִּכְתָב	*In scriptura, juxta scripturam.*	In the writing, the scripture.
—	בִּכְתֹבוֹ	*Scribendo eum.*	When he had written.
—	בַּכְּתֻבִים	*Inter conscriptos.*	Among the registered.
—	בִּכְתוֹב	*Describendo, inscribendo.*	In writing up, registering.
כתל	בְּכֻתְלַיָּא	*In muris.*	In the walls.
כתם	בְּכֶתֶם	*In, cum auro.*	In, with gold.
כתן	בְּכָתְנֹתָם	*In tunicis eorum.*	In their coats.
כתף	בַּכָּתֵף בְּכָתֵף	*In, super humerum.*	Upon the shoulder.
—	בִּכְתֵפָם	*In humeros eorum.*	Upon their shoulders.
כתר	בְּכֶתֶר	*Cum corona.*	With the crown.
	בל		
בל			
—	בַּל	*Non, ne, ut non, vix.*	Not, lest, that not, scarcely.
—	בָּל	*Cor, animus.*	The heart, mind,
	בֵּל	*Bel.*	Bel, N. l.
בָּלָא		*Contrivit, consumpsit*	He consumed, wore out.
לא	בְּלֹא בְּלוֹא	*Absque, ante, ita ut non, in illud quod non, extra, per ea quæ non, quia non*	Without, before, so that not, for that which not, by them which not, out of, because not.
	בְּלָאֲדָן	*Clam, sensim.*	Softly, gently.
לאט	בְּלָאט	*Baladan.*	Baladan, N. M.
לאם	בִּלְאֻמִּים	*In nationibus.*	Among the nations.
לבב	בְּלֵב בְּלֶב	*In corde, medio, medium.*	In, with the heart; in, into the [midst.
—	בְּלֵבָב	*In corde.*	In, with a heart.
—	בְּלָבָב	*In medium.*	Into the midst.
—	בִּלְבָבָהּ	*In corde ejus.*	In her heart.
—	בִּלְבָבוֹ	*In corde ejus.*	In his heart.
—	בִּלְבָבִי	*In corde meo.*	In my heart.
—	בִּלְבָבְךָ־בֶךְ	*In corde tuo.*	In thy heart.

ROOTS.	DERIVATIVES.	VERSIO.	SIGNIFICATION.
לבב	בִּלְבַבְכֶם	*In corde vestro.*	In, with your heart.
—	בִּלְבָבָם	*In corde eorum.*	In their heart.
—	בִּלְבָּהּ	*In corde ejus.*	In her heart.
—	בִּלְבּוֹ	*In corde ejus.*	In his heart.
לבן	בִּלְבוֹנָה	*Thure, suffimento.*	With incense.
לבש	בִּלְבוּשׁ	*In vestimento.*	In apparel.
—	בִּלְבוּשׁוֹ	*In veste ejus.*	In his apparel.
לבב	בִּלְבּוֹתָם	*In cordibus eorum.*	In their hearts.
—	בְּלִבִּי	*In corde meo.*	In my heart.
—	בְּלִבְּךָ בְּלִבֵּךְ	*In corde tuo.*	In thy heart.
—	בְּלִבָּם	*In corde eorum.*	In their heart.
לבש	בִּלְבֻשֵׁיהֶם	*In vestes eorum.*	On their garments.
להב	בְּלַבַּת	*In flamma.*	In the flame.
בָּלַג		*Confortavit, recreavit, roboravit.*	He strengthened, comforted, refreshed.
	בִּלְגָּה	*Bilgah.*	Bilgah, N. M.
	בִּלְגַּי	*Bilgai.*	Bilgai, N. M.
	בִּלְדַּד	*Bildad.*	Bildad, N. M.
ילד	בְּלֶדֶת	*Pariendo.*	In bearing.
—	בְּלִדְתָּהּ	*Pariendo eam.*	When she bare, travailed.
	בָּלָה	*Bala.*	Balah, N. P.
בָּלָה		*Veteravit, consumpsit, contrivit.*	He grew old, consumed, wasted.
—	בִּלָּה	*Vetustum fecit, consumpsit.*	He hath made old, consumed.
להב	בְּלַהַב	*In flamma.*	In the flame.
—	בְּלַהֲבֵי	*In flammis.*	With flames.
	בִּלְהָה	*Bilha.*	Bilhah, N. W.
בהל	בַּלָּהָה	*Turbatio.*	The trouble.
—	בַּלָּהוֹת בַּלָּהוֹת	*Terrores.*	The terrors.
להט	בְּלַהֲטֵיהֶם	*Per incantationes eorum.*	With their inchantments.
	בִּלְהָן	*Bilhan.*	Bilhan, N. M.
בלה	בָּלוּ	*Inveteraverunt.*	They waxed old.
—	בְּלוֹ	*Tributum.*	Tribute.
—	בְּלוֹאֵי בְּלוֹיֵי	*Veteres.*	Old.
בלל	בָּלוּל	*Mistus.*	Mingled.
—	בְּלוּלָה	*Mista.*	Mingled.

ROOTS.	DERIVATIVES.	VERSIO.	SIGNIFICATION.
בלל	בְּלוּלֹת	*Mistæ.*	Mingled.
בלה	בְּלוֹת	*Veteres, tritæ.*	Old, worn out.
—	בְּלוֹתִי	*Senescere me.*	I am grown old.
לחם	בִּלְחוּמוֹ	*In carnem, corpus vel cibum ejus.*	On his flesh, *that is,* his body, or food.
לחה	בִּלְחִי	*Cum maxilla.*	With a jaw bone.
—	בַּלְּחִי	*In maxilla.*	In the jaw bone.
—	בִּלְחָיֶיךָ	*In maxillis tuis.*	In thy jaw bones.
לחם	בַּלֶּחֶם בְּלֶחֶם	*In, cum, pro pane.*	With, in, for bread.
—	בְּלַחְמוֹ	*In, de pane ejus; cum fructu ejus.*	With, of his bread; with his fruit.
—	בְּלַחְמִי	*De pane meo.*	Of my bread.
—	בְּלַחְמֶךָ	*De pane tuo.* [nem.	Of thy bread.
לחץ	בְּלַחַץ בַּלַּחַץ	*Propter oppressio-*	Because of the oppression.
לוט	בַּלָּט	*Clam, abscondite.*	Softly, secretly.
להט	בְּלַהֲטֵיהֶם	*Per incantationes eorum.*	With their inchantments.
	בֵּלְטְשַׁאצַּר	*Beltasasar.* [quem.	Belteshazzar, N. M.
בל	בְּלִי	*Absque, non, nequa-*	Without, not, not at all.
ליל	בְּלֵיל	*In nocte.*	In the night.
בלל	בְּלִיל	*Pabulum.*	Provender.
ליל	בְּלַיְלָה בַּלַּיְלָה	*In, per noctem.*	In the night.
בלל	בְּלִילוֹ	*Pabulum ejus.*	His fodder.
ליל	בַּלֵּילוֹת	*Per noctes.*	In the nights.
—	בְּלֵילְיָא	*In nocte.*	In the night.
בלה	בָּלִים	*Veteres, triti.*	Old, worn out.
בל	בְּלִימָה	*Nihilum.*	Nothing.
יעל	בְּלִיַּעַל	*Pravus, impius, sceleratus; pravitas, impietas, scelus: Belial, nomen Diaboli.*	Wicked, impious, profligate; wickedness, impiety, profligacy: Belial, a name given to the devil.
ילך	בְּלֶכְתּוֹ	*Eundo eum.*	When he went.
—	בְּלֶכְתְּךָ	*Eundo, abeundo te.*	When thou goest, departest.
—	בְּלֶכְתָּם־תֶּן	*Eundo, eos, eas.*	As they went.
בָּלַל		*Confudit, miscuit, perfusus est, pabulum dedit.*	He confounded, mingled, was anointed, gave provender.

ROOTS.	DERIVATIVES.	VERSIO.	SIGNIFICATION.
לול	בַּלֻּלָאֹת	*In laqueolos.*	Into the loops.
בָּלַם		*Constrinxit.*	He bruised, curbed, restrained
למד	בְּלִמֻּדָי	*In discipulis meis.*	In, among my disciples.
—	בְּלָמְדִי	*Discendo me.*	When I learn.
בָּלַס		*Collegit.*	He gathered *fruit.*
	בָּלַע	*Bala.*	Balah, N. P.
	בֶּלַע	*Bela.*	Bela, N. M. P.
בָּלַע		*Absorbuit, deglutivit, texit, perdidit.*	He swallowed, devoured, covered, destroyed.
—	בַּלַּע	*Perde.*	Destroy thou. [ed.
—	בִּלַּע	*Absorbuit, destruxit.*	He has swallowed up, destroy-
לעג	בְּלַעֲגֵי	*Cum ridiculis, balbutientibus.*	With ridiculous, stammering.
בל	בִּלְעָדַי־דַי	*Præter me, non est penes me.*	Besides me, not in me.
—	בִּלְעֲדֵי	*Præter.*	Besides.
בלע	בִּלְּעוּ	*Perdiderunt.*	They have destroyed.
—	בִּלְעוֹ	*Deglutitionem, absorptum ejus.*	That which he has swallowed
—	בִּלְּעוּנוּ	*Absorbuerunt nos.*	They have swallowed us up.
—	בִּלְעִי	*Glutire me.*	I swallowed down.
	בַּלְעִי	*Belaitæ.*	Belaites, N. F.
בלע	בִּלְעֶךָ	*In guttur tuum.*	To thy throat.
	בִּלְעָם	*Bilham.*	Balaam, N. M. P.
בלע	בִּלְעָנוּ	*Deglutivit me.*	He has swallowed me up.
—	בִּלַּעֲנוּ	*Absorbuimus eum.*	We have swallowed him up.
—	בִּלַּעֲנוּהוּ	*Absorbuimus eum.*	We have swallowed him up.
לפד	בַּלַּפִּידִים	*In, cum lampadibus, facibus.*	In, with the lamps, torches.
	בָּלָק	*Balac.* [vit.	Balak, N. M.
בָּלַק		*Exinanivit, desola-*	He made waste, desolate.
	בֵּלְשַׁאצַּר	*Balsasar.*	Belshazzar, N. M.
לשן	בְּלָשׁוֹן בַּלָּשׁוֹן	*In lingua.*	In, with, by a tongue.
—	בִּלְשׁוֹנוֹ	*In lingua ejus.*	In, with his tongue.
—	בִּלְשׁוֹנִי	*In lingua mea.*	In, with my tongue.
לשך	בַּלְּשָׁכֹת	*In cubiculis.*	In the chambers.
—	בַּלִּשְׁכַּת	*In cubiculo.*	In the chamber.

ROOTS.	DERIVATIVES.	VERSIO.	SIGNIFICATION.
	בִּלְשָׁן	*Bilsan.*	Bilshan, N. M.
בלה	בָּלְתָה	*Veteravit, trita est.*	She is grown old, worn out.
—	בְּלֹתִי	*Senescere me.*	I am grown old.
בלל	בַּלֹּתִי	*Perfusus sum.*	I have been anointed.
בלת	בִּלְתִּי	*Præter, nisi, sine, ne, ut non, quia non, præter me.*	Except, besides, without, lest, that not, because not, beside me.
—	בִּלְתֶּךָ	*Præter te.*	Beside thee.
	בם		
	בָּם	*In, cum, de illis; inter, per eos.*	In, with, of, among, by, through them.
מאד	בִּמְאֹד	*Quamplurimum, copiose.*	Exceedingly, abundantly.
מאה	בִּמְאָה	*In, per centum.*	For, by a hundred.
אזן	בְּמֹאזְנֵי	*Cum bilancibus.*	With the balances.
—	בְּמֹאזְנַיָּא	*In bilancibus.*	In the balances.
—	בְּמֹאזְנַיִם	*In bilancibus.*	In the balances.
ארב	בְּמַאֲרָב	*In insidiis.*	In the lurking places.
ארר	בַּמְּאֵרָה	*Cum maledictione.*	With the curse.
בוא	בְּמָבוֹא	*Ad, per introitum.*	At, through the entry, entrance.
בחר	בְּמִבְחַר	*In delectu.*	In the choice.
בטח	בְּמִבְטַחַיִךְ	*In fiducias tuas.*	Towards, against thy confidences.
בון	בְּמֵבִין	*In intelligentem.*	Into a wise *man.*
בצר	בְּמִבְצָרֶיהָ	*In munitionibus ejus.*	In her fortresses.
—	בְּמִבְצָרִים	*In munitionibus.*	In strong holds.
בקש	בִּמְבַקְשֵׁי	*In quærentes.*	On persons seeking.
בוש	בִּמְבֻשָׁיו	*In pudendis ejus.*	In his privy parts.
גדל	בְּמִגְדְּלוֹתַיִךְ	*In turribus tuis.*	In thy towers.
גור	בַּמְּגוּרָה	*In horreo.*	In the barn.
—	בִּמְגוּרָיו	*In habitationibus ejus.*	In his dwellings.
—	בִּמְגוּרָם	*In habitatione eorum*	In their dwelling.
גלל	בִּמְגִלָּה	*In volumine.*	In the roll.
—	בִּמְגִלַּת	*In volumine.*	In the volume.
נגף	בַּמַּגֵּפָה	*In plaga, percussione*	In, by the plague, the stroke.
—	בְּמַגֵּפָה	*Per mortem repentinam.*	By sudden death.

ROOTS.	DERIVATIVES.	VERSIO.	SIGNIFICATION.
נדר	בַּמְּגֵרָה	*Serra.*	With a saw.
דבר	בַּמִּדְבָּר	*In, per desertum.*	Into, through the wilderness.
מדד	בַּמִּדָּה בְּמִדָּה	*In mensura.*	By measure.
מדן	בַּמְּדִינָה	*In provincia.*	In the province.
—	בַּמְּדִינוֹת בְּמְ׳׳	*In provinciis.*	In the provinces.
—	בִּמְדִינַת	*In provincia.*	In the province.
דוך	בַּמְּדֹכָה	*In mortario.*	In a mortar.
ידע	בְּמַדָּעֲךָ	*In cogitatione tua.*	In thy thought.
דרש	בְּמִדְרַשׁ	*In commentario.*	In the story, memorial, register.
	בָּמָה	*Bama.*	Bamah, N. P.
במה			
—	בָּמָה	*Fanum, locus altus.*	A consecrated, high place.
מה	בַּמֶּה בַּמָּה בְּמָה	*Quid; in quo; propter, in quod; in illum; quomodo.*	What, in, because of, to what; on, to that; how.
	בִּמְהָל	*Bimhal.*	Bimhal, N. M.
המר	בְּמַהֲמֹרוֹת	*In foveas.*	Into deep pits.
—	בְּמֹהַר	*In dote.*	In a dowry.
מהר	בִּמְהֵרָה	*Cito.*	Quickly.
	בְּמוֹ	*In, per.*	Into, through.
מוט	בְּמוֹט	*Mutando, vacillando*	In staggering, slipping.
—	בְּמוֹט	*Cum vecte, pertica.*	With a staff, a pole.
יסר	בְּמוּסָר	*In eruditionem.*	For instruction.
יעד	בְּמוֹעֲדוֹ בְּמֹעֲ׳׳	*In tempore ejus.*	In, at his appointed season.
—	בְּמוֹעֲדֶיהָ	*In solennitatibus ejus*	In her solemn feasts.
—	בְּמוֹעֲדָיו	*In temporibus ejus.*	In his appointed times.
—	בְּמוֹעֲדֵיכֶם	*In solennitatibus vestris.*	In your solemn feasts.
—	בְּמוֹעֲדִים	*In solennitatibus.*	In the solemn feasts.
—	בְּמוֹעֲדָם	*In tempore eorum.*	In their season.
יעץ	בְּמוֹעֲצוֹתֵיהֶם	*In consiliis eorum.*	In their counsels.
צוק	בְּמוּצָק	*In angusto* loco.	In a strait, narrow *place.*
יקש	בְּמוֹקְשִׁים	*In laqueis.*	Through snares.
ירד	בְּמוֹרָד בַּמּוֹרָד	*In descensu, præcipite*	In the going down, the declivity
ישב	בְּמוֹשְׁבֹתָם	*In habitationibus eorum.*	In their dwellings.
מות	בְּמוֹת	*In morte.*	In the death,

ROOTS.	DERIVATIVES.	VERSIO.	SIGNIFICATION.
מות	בְּמָוֶת	*In morte.*	In death.
במה	בָּמוֹת	*Excelsa.*	High places.
	בָּמוֹת	*Bamoth.*	Bamoth, N. P.
	בָּמוֹת בָּעַל	*Bamoth-baal.*	Bamoth-baal, N. P.
מות	בְּמוֹתוֹ בְּמֹתוֹ	*Moriendo eum; in morte ejus.*	At his death.
—	בְּמוֹתִי	*Moriendo me.*	When I am dead.
במה	בָּמוֹתַי בָּמֹתַי	*Excelsa mea.*	My high places.
—	בָּמוֹתֵי	*Excelsa.*	The high places.
—	בָּמוֹתָיו־מֹת״	*Excelsa ejus.*	His high places.
—	בָּמוֹתֶיךָ־מֹתֶ״	*Excelsa tua.*	Thy high places.
—	בָּמוֹתֵיכֶם־מֹתֵ״	*Excelsa vestra.*	Your high places.
—	בָּמוֹתֵימוֹ	*Excelsa eorum.*	Their high places.
—	בָּמוֹתָם	*Excelsa eorum.*	Their high places.
זבח	בַּמִּזְבֵּחַ	*In, super altare.*	Upon the altar.
זמם	בִּמְזִמּוֹת	*In cogitationibus.*	In the thoughts.
זמר	בַּמַּזְמֵרוֹת	*Cum falcibus.*	With pruning hooks.
זרה	בְּמִזְרֶה	*Cum ventilabro.*	With a fan.
זרק	בְּמִזְרְקֵי	*In crateribus.*	In bowls.
חבר	בַּמַּחְבֶּרֶת	*In junctura.*	In the coupling, joining.
חלל	בְּמָחוֹל בְּמָ״	*In choro.*	In the dance.
חזה	בַּמַּחֲזֶה	*In visione.*	In a vision.
מחר	בִּמְחִיר	*In, cum, pro pretio.*	At, with, for a price.
—	בִּמְחִירֵיהֶם	*Pretiis eorum.*	By their prices.
חלה	בְּמַחֲלֶה	*In morbo.*	By disease.
חלל	בִּמְחֹלוֹת	*In choreis.*	In dances.
חלה	בְּמַחֲלָיִים	*In morbis.*	In diseases.
חלק	בְּמַחְלְקוֹת	*Juxta divisiones.*	By courses, divisions.
—	בְּמַחְלְקוֹתֵיהֶם	*Juxta divisiones eorum.*	By their courses.
—	בְּמַחְלְקֹתָם	*Per divisiones eorum.*	By their courses.
—	בְּמַחְלְקָתְהוֹן	*In divisionibus eorum*	In their courses.
חנן	בְּמַחַן	*Miserendo.*	By shewing mercy.
חנה	בְּמַחֲנֶה	*In castra, turmam.*	Into the host, camp.
—	בַּמַּחֲנוֹת	*In castris.*	In the camp, tents.
חקק	בִּמְחֹקֵק	*Cum legislatore.*	By the lawgiver.
חשך	בְּמַחְשָׁךְ	*In tenebris.*	In the darkness.

ROOTS.	DERIVATIVES.	VERSIO.	SIGNIFICATION.
חשך	בְּמַחֲשַׁכִּים	*In tenebris.*	In darkness.
חתר	בַּמַּחְתֶּרֶת	*In suffossione.*	In digging up.
טאט	בְּמַטְאֲטֵא	*Cum scopa.*	With the besom.
נטה	בַּמִּטָּה	*In lecto.*	In the bed.
—	בַּמַּטֶּה	*Cum virga.*	With a, or the rod.
—	בְּמַטֵּהוּ	*Cum virga ejus.*[*cis*	With his rod.
מוט	בַּמֹּטוֹת	*Cum vectibus, perti-*	With the staves, poles.
נטה	בְּמַטָּיו	*Cum baculis ejus.*	With his staves, rods.
—	בְּמַטֶּךָ	*Cum baculo tuo.*	With thy rod.
מים	בְּמוֹ בְּמֵי	*In aquis; in aquas.*	In, to, by, at the waters.
	בְּמוֹ	*In.*	In, into.
מה	בְּמִי	*Per quem.*	By whom.
יטב	בְּמֵיטַב	*In optimo.* [*aquas.*	In the best. [ter, waters.
מים	בְּמַיִם בַּמָּיִם	*In aquis; in, ad, per*	Into, in, at, through the wa-
ישר	בַּמִּישׁוֹר	*In planitie.*	Upon the plain.
—	בְּמִישׁוֹר	*In planitie.*	On a plain place.
—	בְּמֵישָׁרִים	*In rectitudinibus.*	In uprightness.
יתר	בְּמֵיתָרֶיךָ	*In nervis tuis.*	Upon thy strings.
כאב	בְּמַכְאוֹב	*In dolore.*	With pain.
כוה	בְּמִכְוָה	*In adustione.*	In the burning.
כון	בַּמְּכוֹנָה	*Ad basin.*	At the base.
—	בִּמְכוֹנִי	*In loco me.*	In my place.
כלל	בְּמַכְלֻלִים	*In omnibus generibus*	In all kinds.
כמן	בְּמִכְמַנֵּי	*In thesauris.*	In the treasures.
כמר	בְּמַכְמֹרָיו	*In reticula ejus.*	Into his nets.
—	בְּמִכְמַרְתּוֹ	*In reti ejus.*	In his drag.
כסה	בְּמִכְסֵה	*Cum tegumento.*	With a covering.
כסס	בְּמִכְסַת	*Juxta numerum.*	According to the number.
כשף	בַּמְכַשְּׁפִים	*Contra maleficos, hariolos.*	Against the sorcerers.
כתב	בְּמִכְתָּב	*Juxta scripturam.*	According to the writing.
כתש	בַּמַּכְתֵּשׁ	*In mortario.*	In a mortar.
כתת	בִּמְכִתָּתוֹ	*In contusione vel frugmento ejus.*	In the bursting, or in the fragment of it.
מלא	בְּמְלֹאות	*Replendo.*	In filling, replenishing.
לאך	בַּמְּלָאכָה	*In opere.*	In the work.
—	בְּמַלְאֲכוּת	*In legatione.*	In the message.

ROOTS.	DERIVATIVES.	VERSIO.	SIGNIFICATION.
לאך	בְּמַלְאֲכֵי	*Contra nuncios.*	Against the messengers.
—	בִּמְלֶאכֶת בִּמְלֶ׳	*In opus, ministerium, substantiam.*	Upon the work, business, goods.
—	בִּמְלַאכְתּוֹ	*In opere ejus.*	In his work, business.
—	בְּמִלֻּאֹתָם-לוּ׳	*In impletionibus, patis eorum.*	In their fillings, inclosings.
לבן	בַּמַּלְבֵּן	*In lateraria* fornace	In the brick-kiln.
לון	בַּמָּלוֹן	*In diversorio.*	In the inn, the lodging place.
מלח	בַּמֶּלַח	*Cum sale.*	With salt.
לחם	בַּמִּלְחָמָה	*In prælio.*	In the battle.
מלט	בַּמֶּלֶט	*In, de sermonibus.*	In, by, from words.
מלל	בְּמִלִּים--ין	*In argilla, cæmento.*	In the clay, mortar.
לוץ	בִּמְלִיצֵי	*Propter legatos.*	On account of the ambassadors
מלך	בְּמֶלֶךְ בַּמֶּלֶךְ	*Cum rege; in, contra regem.*	With, on, by, on, against the king.
—	בִּמְלֹךְ	*Ad regnandum.*	To reigning.
—	בְּמַלְכָּה	*Erga reginam.*	Towards the queen.
—	בְּמַלְכּוֹ	*In regem ejus.*	To his king.
—	בְּמָלְכוֹ	*Regnando eum.*	In his reign.
—	בְּמַלְכוּת--תָא	*In regno.*	In the reign, the kingdom.
—	בַּמַּלְכוּת	*In regno.*	In the kingdom.
—	בְּמַלְכוּתוֹ	*In regno ejus.*	In his kingdom.
—	בְּמַלְכוּתִי	*In regno meo.*	In my kingdom.
—	בְּמַלְכוּתְךָ	*In regno tuo.*	In thy kingdom.
—	בְּמַלְכוּתָם	*In regno eorum.*	In their kingdom.
—	בַּמְּלָכִים	*Inter reges.*	Among the kings.
—	בְּמַלְכָּם	*In, per regem eorum*	To, by their king.
לבן	בַּמַּלְבֵּן	*Per* fornacem *lateratiam.*	Through the brick-kiln.
למד	בְּמַלְמַד	*Cum stimulo.*	With a goad.
לקח	בְּמֶלְקָחַיִם	*Cum forcipibus.*	With the tongs.
מלך	בְּמַמְלָכָה--בַּמַּ׳	*Contra regnum.*	Against the kingdom.
—	בְּמִנְחָה--בַּמִּ׳	*Cum munere, oblatione.*	With a gift, an offering.
מנן	בְּמִנִּים	*In chordis.*	On strings, stringed instruments.
נעם	בְּמַנְעַמֵּיהֶם	*In deliciis eorum.*	In their dainties.
סבב	בִּמְסִבּוֹ	*In accubitu ejus.*	At his table.

ROOTS.	DERIVATIVES	VERSIO.	SIGNIFICATION.
סכן	בְּמִסְכֵּנֻת	*In penuria.*	With scarcity.
סלל	בַּמְסִלָּה	*Per tritam viam.*	Along the high way.
—	בַּמְסִלּוֹת	*Per vias tutas.*	In the high ways.
—	בִּמְסִלּוֹתָם	*In semitis, cursibus eorum.*	In their paths, courses.
—	בִּמְסִלַּת	*In via trita.*	In the high way.
—	בִּמְסִלָּתוֹ	*In semita ejus.*	In his path.
סמר	בַּמַּסְמְרוֹת	*Cum clavis.*	With nails.
—	בְּמַסְמְרִים	*Cum clavis.*	With nails.
ספר	בְּמִסְפַּר־־פָּר	*Ad, juxta numerum.*	By number.
—	בְּמִסְפָּרָם	*Juxta numerum eorum.*	According to their number.
אסר	בְּמָסֹרֶת	*In vinculo.*	In the bond.
נסה	בְּמַסֹּת	*Per tentationes.*	By temptations.
סתר	בַּמִּסְתָּר	*Clam, in abscondito.*	In secret.
—	בְּמִסְתָּרִים	*In latibulis.*	In secret places.
עבה	בְּמַעֲבֵה	*In densitate.*	In the thickness, or clay ground
עגל	בַּמַּעְגָּל	*In vallo, ad plaustra*	In the trench, to the waggons.
—	בְּמַעְגְּלוֹתֶיךָ	*In orbitis tuis.*	In thy paths.
—	בְּמַעְגְּלוֹתָם	*In orbitis eorum.*	In their paths.
—	בְּמַעְגְּלֵי	*In, semitis, orbitis.*	In the paths, tracks. [ed time.
יעד	בְּמֹעֵד	*In tempore statuto.*	In the solemnity, the appoint-
עדר	בַּמַּעְדֵּר	*Cum sarculo.* [ne.	With the mattock, spade.
עזז	בְּמָעוֹז	*In robore, munitio-*	In the strength, in the fortress
ען	בְּמָעוֹן	*In habitaculo.*	In the habitation.
—	בִּמְעוֹנוֹת	*In cavernis.*	In dens.
—	בִּמְעוֹנוֹתֵינוּ	*In habitacula nostra.*	Into our habitations.
עזז	בְּמָעֻזִּי	*In robore meo.*	In my strength.
מעט	בִּמְעָט	*Cum paucis.*	By few.
מעה	בְּמֵעַי	*In visceribus meis.*	In my bowels.
—	בְּמֵעֵי	*In visceribus.*	In the bowels.
—	בְּמֵעָיו	*In visceribus ejus.*	In his bowels.
—	בְּמֵעֶיךָ	*In viscera tua.*	Into thy bowels.
מעל	בִּמְעִיל	*In pallio.*	With a robe.
—	בַּמַּעַל	*In prævaricatione.*	In the trespass.
—	בְּמַעַל	*In prævaricatione.*	In transgression.
עלה	בְּמַעַל	*Cum elevatione.*	With lifting up.

ROOTS.	DERIVATIVES.	VERSIO.	SIGNIFICATION.
עלה	בְּמַעֲלֵה	*In ascensu.*	By, at the ascent.
—	בְּמַעֲלֵה	*Per clivum.*	Over a hill.
מעל	בְּמַעֲלוֹ	*Propter prævaricationem ejus: prævaricando eum.*	For, because of his transgression; in that he transgresses.
עלה	בְּמַעֲלוֹת	*Per gradus.*	By steps.
—	בַּמַּעֲלוֹת	*Per gradus.*	By the degrees.
עלל	בְּמַעַלְלֵיהֶם	*Per opera eorum.*	With their actions.
—	בְּמַעֲלָלָיו	*In operibus ejus.*	In his doings.
מעל	בְּמַעֲלָם	*Propter prævaricationem eorum; prævaricando eos.*	On account of their trespass; in that they have transgressed.
עלה	בְּמַעֲלֹתָו׃	*Per gradus ejus.*	By his steps, stairs.
עמק	בְּמַעֲמַקֵּי	*In profundis.*	In the deeps.
ענה	בְּמַעֲנֵה	*In responso.*	By the answer.
עצד	בְּמַעֲצָד	*Cum securi.*	With an ax, or hatchet.
יעץ	בְּמֹעֲצוֹת	*In consiliis.*	In counsels.
—	בְּמֹעֲצוֹתָם	*In consiliis eorum.*	In their counsels.
ערב	בְּמַעֲרָבֵךְ	*In commercio, foro tuo.*	In thy commerce, market.
מער	בִּמְעָרָה	*In spelunca.*	In a cave.
—	בַּמְּעָרוֹת־־בִּמ"	*In speluncis. [acie.*	In the holes, caves. [army.
ערך	בַּמַּעֲרָכָה	*In loco ordinato, in*	In the ordered place, in the
ערץ	בְּמַעֲרָצָה	*Cum terrore, violenter.*	With terror, violently.
מער	בִּמְעָרַת	*In spelunca.*	In the cave.
עשה	בְּמַעֲשֵׂה	*In opere.*	On the work.
—	בְּמַעֲשֵׂי	*In operibus.*	With the works.
—	בְּמַעֲשֵׂיהֶם	*In operibus eorum.*	With their works.
—	בְּמַעֲשָׂיו	*In operibus ejus.*	In his works.
—	בְּמַעֲשֶׂיךָ	*In operibus tuis.*	In thy works.
—	בְּמַעֲשֵׂינוּ	*Propter opera nostra*	For our works.
פגע	בְּמַפְגִּיעַ	*Per intercedentem.*	By one who intercedes.
נפל	בְּמַפַּלְתָּם	*In ruinam eorum.*	On their fall.
פקד	בְּמִפְקַד	*Per mandatum, in loco constituto.*	At the commandment, in the appointed place.
מצא	בְּמֹצַאֲכֶם	*Inveniendo eos.*	When you find.

ROOTS.	DERIVATIVES.	VERSIO.	SIGNIFICATION.
מצד	בִּמְצַד־צָדָה	*In arce.*	In the castle.
—	בִּמְצָדוֹת־בִּמְצָ	*In munitionibus.*	In strong holds.
צוד	בִּמְצוֹדָה בִּמְצוֹ׳	*In reti.*	In a net.
—	בִּמְצוֹדָתִי	*In reti, laqueo meo.*	In my net, snare.
צול	בִּמְצוּלָה־בִּמְצָ׳	*In profundo.*	In the deep.
—	בִּמְצוֹלֹת־צוֹלוֹת	*In profunda.*	Into the deeps.
צור	בְּמָצוֹר בַּמָּצוֹר	*In obsidione.*	In the siege.
צוה	בְּמִצְוַת	*Juxta mandatum.*	At the commandment.
—	בְּמִצְוֹתָיו	*In præceptis ejus.*	In his commandments.
—	בְּמִצְוֹתֶיךָ	*In præceptis tuis.*	In thy commandments.
מצח	בְּמִצְחוֹ	*In fronte ejus.* [tem.	In his forehead. [eth.
צלח	בְּמַצְלִיחַ	*Propter prosperan-*	Because of him who prosper-
צלל	בִּמְצִלְתַּיִם־בִּמְ׳	*Cum cymbalis.*	With cymbals.
צעד	בְּמִצְעָדָיו	*In gressibus ejus.*	In his steps.
צער	בְּמִצְעָר	*Cum paucitate.*	With a small number.
יצק	בְּמֻצַקְתּוֹ	*In fusione ejus.*	In its casting, when it was cast
קדש	בְּמִקְדָּשׁ	*In sanctuario.*	In the sanctuary.
—	בְּמִקְדָּשׁוֹ	*In sanctuario ejus.*	In his sanctuary.
—	בְּמִקְדָּשִׁי	*In sanctuario meo.*	In my sanctuary.
קהל	בְּמַקְהֵלוֹת	*In congregationibus.*	In the congregations.
—	בְּמַקְהֵלִים	*In congregationibus.*	In the congregations.
קום	בְּמָקוֹם בַּמָּ׳ בְּמְ	*In loco.*	In a, the place.
—	בִּמְקוֹמוֹ־קֹמוֹ	*In loco ejus.*	In his place.
—	בִּמְקוֹמֵנוּ	*In loco nostro.*	In our place.
מקל	בַּמַּקֵּל	*Cum baculo.* [culis.	With a staff.
—	בַּמַּקְלוֹת	*Inter virgas, cum ba-*	Among the rods, with staves.
—	בְּמַקְלִי	*Cum baculo meo.*	With my staff.
קנה	בַּמִּקְנֶה	*Cum pecore.*	With cattle.
—	בְּמִקְנֵיכֶם	*Pro pecudibus vestris*	For your cattle.
—	בְּמִקְנְךָ	*In pecudibus tuis.*	Upon thy cattle.
קצע	בַּמִּקְצֹעַ	*In angulo.*	In the corner.
—	בַּמַּקְצֻעוֹת	*Cum asciis.*	With hatchets.
קרא	בַּמִּקְרָא	*In lectione.*	In the reading.
קשה	בְּמִקְשָׁה	*In cucumerario.*	In a garden of cucumbers.
יקש	בְּמֹקְשִׁים	*Per laqueos.*	Through snares.
מרר	בְּמַר	*Cum amaritudine.*	With bitterness.
ראה	בַּמַּרְאֶה־אָה	*In visione.*	In a vision.

ROOTS.	DERIVATIVES.	VERSIO.	SIGNIFICATION.
ראה	בְּמַרְאוֹת־אֹת	*In visionibus, in speculis.*	In the visions, in the mirrors.
רגם	בְּמַרְגֵּמָה	*In funda.*	In a sling.
מרד	בְּמֶרֶד	*In rebellione.*	In rebellion.
—	בְּמֹרְדֵי	*Inter rebellantes.*	Among those that rebel.
רום	בְּמָרוֹם בְּמָרוֹם	*In altum, excelso.*	On high.
—	בִּמְרוֹמָיו	*In excelsis suis.*	In his high places.
—	בַּמְּרוֹמִים	*In excelsis.*	In the heights.
מרר	בַּמְּרוֹרִים	*In amaritudinibus.*	With bitterness.
רחב	בַּמֶּרְחָב	*In latitudine.* [*gine.*	In a large place.
רחש	בַּמַּרְחֶשֶׁת	*In çacabo* vel *sarta-*	In the stew-pan *or* frying-pan.
רוב	בִּמְרִיבַת	*In contentione.*	In the strife.
רכב	בְּמֶרְכָּבָה	*In curru.*	In a chariot.
—	בְּמִרְכֶּבֶת	*In curru.*	In the chariot.
—	בְּמֶרְכַּבְתּוֹ	*In curru ejus.*	In his chariot.
רכל	בְּמַרְכֻלְתֵּךְ	*In mercatu tuo.*	Among thy merchandise.
רמה	בְּמִרְמָה	*In dolo.*	Through deceit.
רעה	בְּמִרְעֶה	*In pascuo.* [*entes.*	In a pasture. [doers.
רוע	בִּמְּרֵעִים	*Ob malos, malefaci-*	Because of wicked men, evil
רוץ	בִּמְרֻצוֹתָם	*In cursu eorum.*	In their course.
רצע	בַּמַּרְצֵעַ	*Cum subula.*	With an awl.
רקח	בְּמִרְקַחַת	*Per pigmentarium.*	By the perfumer.
נשא	בְּמַשָּׂא בְּמַשָּׂא	*In onere; in exaltatione* vocis, *in cantu.*	In the burden; in the lifting up *of the voice*, in music.
—	בְּמַשָּׁאוֹן	*Per deceptionem.*	By deceit.
שבר	בְּמִשְׁבַּר	*In ruptura.*	In the breaking through.
ישב	בְּמֹשְׁבֹתָם	*In habitaculis eorum.*	In their dwellings.
משך	בִּמְשׁוֹךְ בִּמְשֹׁךְ	*In trahendo, clangendo.*	In drawing out, making a long blast, sounding a trumpet.
שור	בַּמְּשׂוּרָה	*Per mensuram.*	By measure.
משח	בִּמְשִׁיחַ	*Contra unctum.*	Against the anointed.
—	בִּמְשִׁיחָי	*In unctos meos.*	To my anointed.
שכב	בַּמִּשְׁכָּב	*In lecto.*	In the bed.
—	בְּמִשְׁכָּבָהּ	*In cubile ejus.*	On her bed.
—	בְּמִשְׁכָּבוֹ	*In cubili ejus.*	In his bed.
משך	בְּמָשְׁכוֹ	*Trahendo eum.*	In drawing him.

ROOTS.	DERIVATIVES.	VERSIO.	SIGNIFICATION.
שכה	בְּמַשְׂכִּיּוֹת	*Inter figuras.*	In pictures, figured works.
—	בְּמַשְׂכִּתוֹ	*In imaginatione ejus*	In his own conceit.
משל	בְּמָשָׁל	*In parabola.*	In a parable.
שמן	בְּמִשְׁמַנֵּיהֶם	*E pinguibus eorum.*	Of the fat ones (the strongest or richest) of them.
—	בְּמִשְׁמַנָּיו	*Inter pingues ejus.*	Among his fat ones.
שמר	בְּמִשְׁמָר בַּמִ׳	*In custodia.*	In ward, custody.
—	בְּמִשְׁמָרוֹ	*In custodia ejus.*	In his watch.
—	בְּמִשְׁמְרוֹתֵיהֶם	*In ministeriis eorum*	In their charges, offices.
—	בְּמִשְׁמְרוֹתָם	*In functionibus eorum.*	In their charges.
—	בְּמִשְׁמֶרֶת	*In custodia.*	In charge.
—	בְּמִשְׁמַרְתָּם	*De ministerio suo.*	Respecting their charge.
שעל	בְּמִשְׁעוֹל	*In semita.*	In a path.
שען	בְּמִשְׁעֲנֹתָם	*Cum baculis eorum.*	With their staves.
שפח	בְּמִשְׁפְּחוֹתֵיהֶם	*Per familias eorum.*	Throughout their families.
—	בְּמִשְׁפְּחוֹתָם	*In familiis eorum.*	In their families.
שפט	בְּמִשְׁפָּט בַּמִ־	*In judicium, judicio.*	Into, in judgment.
—	בְּמִשְׁפָּטַי	*Juxta judicia mea.*	According to my judgments.
—	בְּמִשְׁפְּטֵיהֶם	*Secundum judicia eorum.*	According to their judgments
שקל	בְּמִשְׁקוֹל־־קָל	*In pondere.*	By weight.
—	בְּמִשְׁקָלוֹ	*In pondere ejus.*	In his full weight.
שתה	בְּמִשְׁתֵּה	*In convivio.*	At the banquet.
מות	בְּמֵת בַּמֵּת	*In mortuum, cadaver*	On a dead man, a corpse.
מתג	בְּמֶתֶג	*Cum lupato.*	With a bit.
מתה	בִּמְתֵי	*Cum paucis hominibus.*	With a few men
מות	בְּמֹתָיו	*In morte ejus.*	In his death.
—	בַּמֵּתִים	*Inter mortuos.*	Among the dead.
תכן	בְּמַתְכֻּנְתָּהּ	*Juxta compositionem ejus.*	According to the composition thereof.
מות	בְּמֻתָם	*Moriendo eos; post mortem eorum.*	When they die; after their death.
נתן	בְּמַתְּנוֹתֵיכֶם	*In muneribus vestris*	In, with your gifts.
—	בְּמַתְּנוֹתָם	*In donis eorum*	In their gifts.
מתן	בְּמָתְנֵיהֶם	*In, circa lumbos eorum.*	Upon, about their loins.
—	בְּמָתְנָיו	*In lumbis ejus.*	In his loins.

ROOTS.	DERIVATIVES.	VERSIO.	SIGNIFICATION.
מתן	בְּמָתְנֵינוּ	*In lumbos nostros.*	Upon our loins.
נתן	בְּמַתַּת	*De dono.*	Of a gift.
	בנ		
	בֶּן	*Ben.*	Ben, N. M.
בנה	בַּן	*Filia.*	A daughter.
——	בֵּן בֶּן בִּן	*Filius, ramus.*	A son, a branch.
	בֶּן אֲבִינָדָב	*Ben-abinadab.*	Ben-abinadab, N. M.
	בֶּן אוֹנִי	*Ben-oni.*	Ben-oni, N. M.
	בֶּן גֶּבֶר	*Ben-gheber.*	Ben-geber, N. M.
	בֶּן דֶּקֶר	*Ben-decar.*	Ben deker, N. M.
	בֶּן הֲדַד	*Ben-hadad.*	Ben-hadad, N. M.
	בֶּן הִנֹּם	*Ben-hinnom.*	Ben-hinnom, N. P.
	בֶּן זוֹחֵת	*Ben-zoheth.*	Ben-zoheth, N. M.
	בֶּן חוּר	*Ben-hur.*	Ben-hur, N. M.
	בֶּן חַיִל	*Ben-hiel.*	Ben-hiel, N. M.
	בֶּן חֶסֶד	*Ben-hased.*	Ben-hased, N. M.
	בֶּן עַמִּי	*Ben-ammi.*	Ben-ammi, N. M.
נאד	בְּנֹאדֶךָ	*In utrem tuum.*	Into thy bottle.
נוה	בִּנְאוֹת	*In pascuis.*	In pastures.
אמן	בְּנֶאֱמָנֵי	*In fideles.*	Upon the faithful.
נבא	בִּנְבוּאַת	*Juxta prophetiam.*	According to the prophecy.
——	בִּנְבִיאָיו	*Ad prophetas ejus.*	To his prophets.
——	בִּנְבִיאִים־־אִם	*Inter prophetas.*	Among the prophets.
נבל	בְּנֶבֶל	*Cum nablio, psalterio.*	With the psaltery.
——	בִּנְבָלִים	*Cum psalteriis.*	With psalteries.
——	בְּנִבְלַת	*In cadavere.*	In, with the carcase.
——	בְּנִבְלָתָהּ	*In cadaver ejus.*	On the carcase of it.
——	בְּנִבְלָתָם	*In cadaver eorum.*	On their carcase.
נגב	בְּנֶגֶב בַּנֶּגֶב	*In meridie.*	In the south.
——	בַּנֶּגְבָּה	*In, versus meridiem.*	Southward.
נגה	בְּנָגְהָא	*In diluculo.*	In the morning.
נגן	בִּנְגִינוֹת־נַת	*In instrumenta pulsatilia.*	On the stringed instruments.
——	בִּנְגִינוֹתָי	*In instrumenta pulsatilia mea.*	On my stringed instruments.
נגע	בְּנֶגַע בַּנֶּגַע	*In peste.*	In the plague.

ROOTS.	DERIVATIVES.	VERSIO.	SIGNIFICATION.
נגע	בְּנָגְעוֹ	*Attingendo eum.*	In touching it.
נגף	בְּנָגְפוֹ	*Percutiendo eum.*	When he smote.
נגש	בְּנֹגְשֵׂיהֶם	*In exactores eorum.*	Over their oppressors, exactors
נדב	בִּנְדָבָה	*In spontanea oblatione.*	In a free will offering.
—	בִּנְדִיבִים	*In principibus.*	In princes.
נדה	בְּנִדַּת	*In separatione; ob immunditiam.*	During the separation; on account of the uncleanness.
—	בְּנִדָּתָהּ	*In separatione ejus.*	In her separation.
בָּנָה		*Ædificavit, extruxit, restauravit.*	He built, raised, repaired.
—	בְּנֵה	*Ædifica; ædificata.*	Build thou; built.
—	בְּנֹה	*Ædificare.*	To build.
—	בֹּנֶה	*Ædificans.*	Building.
—	בְּנָהּ	*Filius ejus.*	Her son.
—	בְּנָהִי	*Ædificavit eam.*	He built her.
נהר	בַּנָּהָר	*Per flumen.*	Through the flood.
—	בִּנְהַר	*Ad, in fluvium.*	At, by the river.
—	בַּנְּהָרִים	*Per flumina tua.*	With thy rivers.
—	בִּנְהָרוֹתֶיךָ	*Contra flumina.*	Against the rivers.
בנה	בָּנָיו	*Filii ejus.*	His sons.
—	בָּנוּ	*Ædificaverunt.*	They built.
בוא	בָּנוּ	*Venimus.*	We came.
	בָּנוּ	*In, cum nobis.*	In, with us.
בנה	בְּנוּ	*Ædificate.*	Build ye.
—	בְּנֵי	*Filii.*	Sons.
—	בְּנוֹ בְּנוֹ	*Filius ejus.*	His son.
	בְּנוֹ	*Beno.*	Beno, N. M.
נוה	בִּנְוֵה בִּנְוֵה	*In pascuo, habitaculo*	In a pasture, in the dwelling.
בנה	בְּנוּהוּ	*Ædificaverunt eum.*	They built him.
—	בָּנוּי	*Ædificatus.*	Built.
	בִּנּוּי	*Binui.*	Binnui, N. M.
בנה	בְּנוּיִם	*Ædificati.*	Built.
נוס	בְּנוּסָם	*Fugiendo eos.*	As they fled.
בנה	בְּנוֹת	*Filiæ. [pagi.*	Daughters. [lages.
—	בְּנוֹת	*Ædificare; filiæ;*	To build; the daughters, vil-
	בְּנוֹת	*Benoth.*	Benoth, N. I.

ROOTS.	DERIVATIVES.	VERSIO.	SIGNIFICATION.
בנה	בְּנוֹתַי	*Filiæ meæ.*	My daughters.
—	בְּנוֹתֶיהָ בְּנֹתֶ־	*Pagi ejus.*	Her villages.
—	בְּנוֹתֵיהֶם בְּנֹ־	*Filiæ eorum.*	Their daughters.
—	בְּנוֹתַיִךְ	*Filiæ tuæ; pagi tui.*	Thy daughters; thy villages.
—	בְּנוֹתֶיךָ בְּנֹתֶ־	*Filiæ tuæ.*	Thy daughters.
—	בְּנוֹתֵיכֶם בְּנֹתֵ־	*Filiæ vestræ.*	Your daughters.
—	בְּנוֹתֵינוּ בְּנֹתֵ־	*Filiæ nostræ.*	Our daughters.
יתר	בַּנּוֹתָר	*De residuo.*	Of the rest, remainder.
נזק	בְּנֵזֶק	*In damnum.*	Against the damage.
נחל	בְּנַחַל בַּנַּחַל	*In valle, ad torrentem*	In the valley, by the brook.
—	בְּנַחֲלָה בַּנַּחֲלָה	*In hæreditatem.* [*bus*	For the, an inheritance.
—	בְּנַחֲלֵי	*In vallibus, torrenti-*	In valleys, in brooks.
—	בַּנְּחָלִים	*In vallibus; ad fluvios.*	In the valleys; by the rivers.
—	בְּנַחֲלַת	*In hæreditate.*	In the inheritance.
—	בְּנַחֲלָתוֹ	*In hæreditate ejus.*	In his inheritance.
—	בְּנַחֲלָתְךָ־־תְךָ	*In hæreditatem tuam*	Into thy inheritauce.
—	בְּנַחֲלַתְכֶם	*In hæreditatem vestram.*	For your inheritance.
—	בְּנַחֲלָתָם	*In hæreditate eorum*	In their inheritance.
נחם	בְּנַחֲמֵךְ	*In consolari te.*	In that thou art a comfort.
נחש	בַּנְּחֹשֶׁת	*In ære.*	In brass.
—	בַּנְחֻשְׁתַּיִם	*Cum catenis, compedibus æreis.*	With chains, fetters of brass.
נוח	בְּנַחַת	*In quiete.*	In quiet.
נטה	בִּנְטֹתִי	*Extendendo me.*	When I stretch forth.
	בָּנִי בְּנִי	*Bani.*	Bani, N. M.
בנה	בְּנִי	*Filius meus.*	My son.
—	בְּנוֹ	*Filius.*	A son.
—	בָּנַי בָּנָי	*Filii mei.*	My sons.
—	בְּנֵי	*Filii; pulli.*	Sons, children, young ones.
—	בֹּנֵי	*Ædificatores.*	Builders.
	בְּנֵי בְרַק	*Bene-berac.*	Bene-berak. N. P.
	בְּנֵי יַעֲקָן	*Bene-jaacan.*	Bene-jaakan, N. P.
	בְּנָיָה־־יָהוּ	*Benaias.*	Benaiah, N. M.
בנה	בָּנֶיהָ	*Filii ejus.* [*rum.*	Her sons.
נהה	בְּנִיהֶם	*In lamentatione eo-*	In their lamentation.

ROOTS	DERIVATIVES.	VERSIO.	SIGNIFICATION.
בנה	בְּנֵיהֶם בְּנֵיהוֹן	*Filii eorum, earum.*	Their children.
—	בָּנָיו	*Filii ejus.*	His sons.
—	בָּנֶיךָ בָּנַיִךְ	*Filii tui.*	Thy sons.
—	בֹּנַיִךְ	*Ædificatores tui.*	Thy builders.
—	בְּנֵיכֶם	*Filii vestri.*	Your children.
—	בֹּנִים	*Ædificantes.*	Builders.
—	בָּנִים	*Filii.*	Sons,
	בִּנְיָמִן	*Benjamin.*	Benjamin, N. M.
בנה	בִּנְיָן	*Ædificium.*	The building,
—	בָּנַיִן	*Ædificantes.*	Building.
—	בִּנְיָנָא	*Ædificium.*	A building.
—	בָּנֵינוּ	*Filii nostri.*	Our children.
	בֵּינֵנוּ	*Inter nos.*	Between us.
	בְּנִינוּ	*Beninu.*	Beninu, N. M.
בנה	בָּנִית בָּנִיתָ	*Ædificasti.*	Thou hast built.
—	בְּנִיתָהּ	*Ædificavi eam.*	I have built her, or it.
—	בָּנִיתִי בָּנִתִי	*Ædificavi.*	I have built.
—	בְּנִיתֶם	*Ædificastis.*	Ye have built.
—	בְּנֵךְ בִּנְךָ בְּנֶךָ	*Filius tuus.*	Thy son.
כבד	בְּנִכְבָּד	*In honoratum.* [*rum*	Against the honourable.
נכל	בְּנִכְלֵיהֶם	*In calliditatibus eo-*	In their wiles.
נכס	בִּנְכָסִים	*Cum opibus.*	With riches.
בנח	בְּנֵנוּ	*Filius noster.*	Our son.
בָּנַס		*Indignatus est.*	He was angry.
נסע	בִּנְסֹעַ	*Proficiscendo.*	In going forward.
—	בְּנָסְעָם	*Proficiscendo eos.*	As they journeyed.
נער	בִּנְעוּרֶיהָ	*In adolescentia, pue-*	In her youth, childhood.
		ritia ejus. [*earum*	
—	בִּנְעוּרֵיהֶם־הֶן	*In juventute eorum,*	In their youth.
—	בִּנְעוּרָיו	*In adolescentia ejus.*	In his youth.
נעם	בַּנְּעִימִים	*In delectationibus,*	In pleasures, pleasant places.
		jucundis.	
נעל	בַּנְּעָלִים	*Cum calceis.* [*scentem*	With shoes.
נער	בַּנַּעַר	*In puerum, adoles-*	On the boy, the young man.
—	בַּנֹּעַר	*In adolescentia.*	In youth.
—	בִּנְעָרוֹת	*Cum puellis.*	With the maidens.
—	בַּנְּעָרִי	*Rer pueros.*	By the young men.

ROOTS.	DERIVATIVES.	VERSIO.	SIGNIFICATION.
נער	בִּנְעֻרֶיהָ	*In pueritia ejus.*	In her youth.
—	בִּנְעָרֵינוּ	*Cum pueris nostris.*	With our children.
נפך	בְּנֹפֶךְ	*Cum smaragdo.*	With the emerald.
נפל	בִּנְפֹל	*Cadendo.*	In falling.
פלא	בְּנִפְלְאוֹתֶיךָ	*De mirabilibus tuis.*	Of thy wondrous works.
—	בְּנִפְלְאֹתָיו	*In mirabilia ejus.*	For his wondrous works.
נפל	בַּנֹּפְלִים	*Inter corruentes.*	Among them that fall.
נפש	בְּנֶפֶשׁ בְּנָפֶשׁ	*In anima, animam.*	In, for the soul, life.
—	בְּנַפְשׁוֹ	*In, cum anima ejus; in, contra animam ejus; juxta voluntatem ejus.*	In, with, for, against his life, at his pleasure.
—	בְּנַפְשׁוֹתֵיכֶם	*In animabus vestris.*	In your souls, hearts.
—	בְּנַפְשׁוֹתָם־שֹׁתָ׳	*Cum periculo vitæ eorum.*	At the peril of their lives.
—	בְּנַפְשִׁי־שִׁי	*In anima mea.*	For my life, in my soul.
—	בְּנַפְשְׁךָ	*In anima tua.*	In thy soul, with thyself.
—	בְּנַפְשָׁם	*In animam eorum.*	Into their soul.
—	בְּנַפְשֵׁנוּ	*Cum periculo vitæ nostræ.*	At the peril of our life.
נוף	בְּנָפַת	*In cribro.*	In, with the sieve.
נצה	בְּנֹצָתָהּ	*Cum pluma ejus.*	With his, *her* feathers.
נקב	בְּנָקְבוֹ	*Blasphemando eum.*	When he blasphemeth.
נקד	בַּנֹּקְדִים	*Inter armentarios.*	Among the herdmen.
נקר	בִּנְקוֹר	*Effodiendo.*	In digging, scooping out.
נקה	בְּנִקָּיוֹן	*In innocentia.*	In innocence.
נקק	בְּנִקִיק	*In fissura.*	In a hole.
נקם	בִּנְקֹם	*Ulciscendo.*	By revenging.
—	בִּנְקָמָה	*Per ultionem.*	By revenge.
נקר	בְּנִקְרוֹת	*In scissuras.*	Into the clefts.
—	בְּנִקְרַת	*In scissura.*	In the cleft.
ניר	בַּנֵּרוֹת	*Cum lucernis.*	With candles.
נשא	בְּנָשְׂאִי	*Elevando me.*	When I lift up.
איש	בַּנָּשִׁים	*Inter mulieres.*	Among the women.
נשך	בְּנֶשֶׁךְ בְּנֶ׳ בְּנֶ׳	*In, per usuram.*	On, by usury.
נשף	בְּנֶשֶׁף בְּנֶ׳	*In crepusculo.*	In the twilight.
נשק	בְּנֶשֶׁק בְּנֶ׳	*In arma.*	Upon the weapons.

ROOTS.	DERIVATIVES.	VERSIO.	SIGNIFICATION.
בון	בִּנְתָּה	*Intellixisti.*	Thou hast understood.
בנה	בָּנִתָה	*Ædificasti.*	Thou hast built.
—	בָּנְתָה	*Ædificavit.*	She has built.
נתב	בִּנְתִיב	*Per semitam.*	In the path.
—	בִּנְתִיבוֹת	*Per semitas.*	In paths.
—	בִּנְתִיבֹתֶיהָ	*In semitis ejus.*	In her paths.
—	בִּנְתִיבֹתָיו	*In semitis ejus.*	In his paths.
בנה	בְּנֹתָיו	*Filiæ ejus.*	His daughters.
—	בְּנֹתָם	*Filiæ eorum.*	Their daughters.
נתר	בַּנֶּתֶר	*Cum nitro.*	With nitre.
	בס		
סאה	בְּסַאסְאָה	*In mensura.*	In measure.
סבא	בְּסֹבְאֵי	*Inter ebriosos.*	Amongst drunkards.
סבך	בִּסְּבָךְ בִּסְבָךְ	*In dumo, in densum.*	In a bush, on the thick.
—	בְּסִבְכֵי	*In dumetis.*	In the thickets.
סבל	בַּסֵּבֶל	*Cum onere.*	With a burden.
—	בְּסִבְלֹתָם	*Cum oneribus eorum.*	With their burdens.
סד	בַּסַּד	*In cippum vel compedes.*	Into a fetter or shackles.
סוד	בְּסֹדָם	*In arcanum eorum.*	Into their secret.
סגר	בַּסּוּגַר	*In claustro.* [cætu.	In close confinement.
סוד	בְּסוֹד	*In arcano, consilio,*	In the secret, council, assembly
—	בְּסוֹדִי	*In consilio meo.*	In my counsel.
	בְּסוֹדְיָה	*Besodia.*	Besodeiah, N. M.
סוס	בְּסוּס	*Cum equo.*	With a horse.
—	בְּסוּסָו	*Cum equis ejus.*	With his horses.
—	בְּסוּסִים בַּסּוּ'	*In, pro equis.*	On, by, for horses.
סוף	בְּסוֹף	*In fine.*	At the end. [rushes.
—	בַּסּוּף	*In alga, junceto.*	In the flag, among the bul-
—	בְּסוּפָה'	*In turbine.*	In the whirlwind.
	בֵּסָי בֵּסַי	*Besai.*	Besai, N. M.
סיר	בַּסִּיר	*In olla.*	In the pot.
—	בַּסִּירוֹת בְּסִ'	*In ollis; cum hamis.*	In pots; with hooks.
—	בַּסִּירִים	*Cum spinis.* [ma.	With thorns.
סכך	בַּסָּךְ	*In numero, cum tur-*	With the multitude.
—	בְּסֻכָּה בַּסֻּכָּה	*In umbraculo.*	In a pavilion or shelter.

ROOTS.	DERIVATIVES.	VERSIO.	SIGNIFICATION.
סכך	בְּסֻכֹּה	*In tentorio ejus.*	In his tabernacle.
—	בַּסֻּכּוֹת בְּסֻכֹּת	*In tentoriis.*	In tents.
סכל	בְּסִכְלוּת	*In stultitiam.*	On folly.
סל	בַּסָּל בְּסַל	*In canistro.*	In a basket.
סלע	בַּסֶּלַע בְּסֶלַע	*In petra, rupe.*	In a rock, on the rock.
סמך	בְּסֹמְכֵי	*Inter sustentantes.*	Among them that uphold.
סנור	בַּסַּנְוֵרִים	*Cæcitate.*	With blindness.
סנסן	בְּסַנְסִנָּיו	*De ramis ejus.*	On his boughs.
בסס	בֹּסְסוּ	*Conculcaverunt.*	They have trodden under foot.
סעף	בִּסְעִף	*In cacumine.*	In the top.
—	בִּסְעִפֶּיהָ	*In ramis ejus.*	In her branches.
—	בִּסְעַפֹּתָיו	*In ramis ipsius.*	In his boughs.
סער	בְּסַעַר	*Per tempestatem.*	With a tempest.
—	בִּסְעָרָה בַּסְּ׳	*Per turbinem.*	By a whirlwind.
—	בִּסְעָרוֹת	*In turbinibus.*	With whirlwinds.
—	בְּסַעֲרֶךָ	*In tempestate tua.*	In, with thy tempest.
ספף	בַּסַּף בְּסַף	*In pelve, poste, limine.*	In the bason, gate, threshold.
—	בַּסִּפִּים	*Ad limina.*	In the gates.
ספר	בַּסַּפִּירִים	*In sapphiris.*	With sapphires.
ספל	בְּסֵפֶל	*In cratere.*	In a dish.
ספר	בְּסֵפֶר בַּסֵּפֶר	*In libro.*	In a book.
—	בַּסֵּפֶר	*In libro.*	In the book.
—	בַּסְּפָרִים	*Per libros, epistolas.*	By books, by letters.
—	בְּסִפְרָתֶךָ	*In libro tuo.*	In thy book.
בסר			
—	בֹּסֶר	*Omphax.*	An unripe, sour grape.
סרבל	בְּסַרְבָּלֵיהוֹן	*Cum palliis eorum.*	In their coats.
בסר	בִּסְרוֹ	*Omphax ejus.*	His unripe grape.
סרה	בְּסִרְיֹנוֹ	*In lorica ejus.*	In his brigandine, coat of mail.
סתר	בַּסֵּתֶר בְּ׳ בַּסְּ׳	*In occulto, in latibulo.*	In secret, in the covert.

בע

ROOTS.	DERIVATIVES.	VERSIO.	SIGNIFICATION.
בעה	בְּעָא	*Petiit.*	He requested.
—	בָּעֵא	*Petens.*	Requesting.
עבה	בְּעֳב	*In densitate.*	In the thickness.
עבד	בַּעֲבֹדָה	*In, pro servitute.*	In for the service.

ROOTS.	DERIVATIVES.	VERSIO.	SIGNIFICATION.
עבד	בְּעַבְדּוֹ	*Contra servum ejus.*	Against his servant.
—	בְּעַבְדִּי	*Contra servum meum.*	Against my servant.
—	בַּעֲבָדָיו	*In servis ejus.* [*um.*	In, with his servants.
—	בְּעַבְדְּךָ־־דֶּךָ	*In, super servum tu-*	Towards, upon thy servant.
—	בַּעֲבֹדַת	*In ministerio, pro opere.*	In the service, for the work.
—	בַּעֲבֹדָתָם	*In ministerio eorum.*	In their service.
—	בְּעַבְדֻתֵנוּ	*In servitute nostra.*	In our bondage. [of.
עבר	בַּעֲבוּר בַּעֲבֻר	*Quia, ut, pro, propter*	Because, that, for, on account
—	בַּעֲבוּרָהּ	*Propter eam.*	For her sake.
—	בַּעֲבוּרִי	*Propter me.*	For my sake.
—	בַּעֲבוּרְךָ־־רֵךְ	*Propter te.*	For thy sake.
—	בַּעֲבוּרָם	*Propter eos.*	For their sake.
עבט	בַּעֲבֹטוֹ	*Cum pignore ejus.*	With his pledge.
עבה	בַּעֲבִי	*In crassitiem.*	Upon the thickness.
—	בַּעֲבֵי	*In densitatibus*	In the thicknesses.
—	בְּעָבָיו	*In nubibus ejus.*	In his thick clouds.
—	בֶּעָבִים בְּ׳	*In nubes; in densas silvas.*	On the clouds; into the thick woods.
עבר	בַּעֲבֹר	*In transeundo.*	While passing by.
—	בְּעֵבֶר בֵּעֵבֶר	*Trans, ultra.*	Over, beyond.
—	בַּעֲבַר	*Trans.*	Beyond.
—	בְּעֶבְרָה	*In ira.*	In wrath.
—	בְּעָבְרוֹ	*Transeundo eum.*	As he passes over.
ערב	בְּעַבְרוֹת	*In campestribus, transitibus.* [*nes.*	In the plains, the passages.
עבר	בְּעַבְרוֹת	*Propter indignatio-*	Because of the rage.
—	בְּעֶבְרֵי	*Trans.*	Beyond.
—	בְּעָבְרְךָ	*Transeundo te.*	When thou art passed over.
—	בְּעָבְרְכֶם	*Transeundo, transgrediendo vos.*	When ye have gone over, have transgressed.
—	בְּעֶבְרַת	*In, per furorem.*	In the wrath.
—	בְּעֶבְרָתוֹ	*In furore ejus.*	In his wrath.
—	בְּעֶבְרָתִי	*In ira mea.*	In my wrath.
—	בְּעֶבְרָתְךָ	*Propter iram tuam.*	In thy wrath.
עבת	בַּעֲבֹתוֹת־־תִים	*Cum funibus.*	With ropes, bands.

ROOTS.	DERIVATIVES.	VERSIO.	SIGNIFICATION.
עגל	בְּעֶגְלָה בִּי	*Ad plaustrum.*	To the cart.
—	בַּעֲגָלוֹת	*In plaustris, curribus*	In the waggons, chariots.
—	בְּעֶגְלֵי	*Cum vitulis.*	With the calves.
—	בַּעֲגָלִים	*Cum vitulis.*	With calves.
—	בְּעֶגְלָתִי	*Cum vitula mea.*	With my heifer.
עד	בְּעַד	*Pro, propter, juxta, circum, in, per, super.*	For, on account of, near, about, upon, at, through, over.
—	בְּעֹד בְּעוֹד	*Cum adhuc.*	When yet.
יעד	בַּעֵדָה	*E cœtu.*	Of the congregation.
עד	בַּעֲדָהּ	*Super eam.*	Unto her.
—	בַּעֲדוֹ	*Circa, super eum.*	About, upon him.
עוד	בְּעֵדוֹתֶיךָ־דֹתֶ"	*In testimonia tua.*	Upon thy testimonies.
עד	בַּעֲדִי	*Pro, circa me.*	For, about me.
עדה	בַּעֲדִי	*Cum ornamento*	With an ornament.
עד	בַּעֲדֵינוּ־דֵנוּ	*Pro nobis.*	For us.
—	בַּעַדְךָ בַּעֲדֶךָ־דְךָ	*Pro te.*	For thee.
—	בַּעַדְכֶם	*Pro vobis.*	For you.
—	בַּעֲדָם	*Pro eis, super eos.*	For, upon them.
עדן	בְּעִדָּנָא	*In tempore.*	At the time.
עד	בַּעֲדֵנִי	*Circa me.*	About me.
עדף	בָּעֹדֵף	*In superfluo.*	In that which remaineth.
עדר	בְּעֵדֶר	*Cum grege.*	With a flock.
—	בְּעֶדְרוֹ	*In grege ejus.*	In his flock.
—	בְּעֶדְרֵי	*Inter greges.*	Among the flocks.
יעד	בַּעֲדַת	*In cœtu, congregatione*	Among the company, congregation.
—	בַּעֲדָתָם	*In cœtu eorum.*	In their company.
בָּעָה		*Petiit, quæsivit, perquisivit, tumuit, bullavit, fervefecit.*	He asked, enquired, made diligent search, swelled, boiled, caused to boil.
—	בָּעָה	*Orans.*	Praying.
—	בְּעוּ	*Petitio.*	A petition.
עד	בְּעוֹדָהּ	*Quum adhuc ipsa.*	While she yet.
עוד	בְּעוֹדִי	*Quamdiu ego.*	As long as I *exist.*
—	בְּעוֹדֶנּוּ	*Quum adhuc ille.*	While he yet.
—	בְּעוֹדֶנִּי	*Dum adhuc ego.*	While I yet.
עוה	בְּעָוֹן	*In iniquitate.*	In, with iniquity.

ROOTS.	DERIVATIVES.	VERSIO.	SIGNIFICATION.
עזז	בְּעֹז בְּעוֹז	*In robore.*	In strength, with the strength.
עלל	בְּעֹל	*Sub jugo.*	With, under the yoke.
עול	בְּעֶוֶל בְּעַוְלָה	*Per, propter iniquitatem.*	By, for the iniquity.
בעל	בְּעוּלָה	*Maritata.*	The married woman.
עלה	בְּעוֹלָה	*In holocaustum.*	For burnt offering.
עול	בְּעַוְלוֹ	*Propter iniquitatem ejus.*	For his iniquity.
עלה	בְּעוֹלוֹת בְּעֹל־	*Cum holocaustis.*	With burnt offerings.
עול	בְּעַוְלָתָה	*Ad iniquitatem.*	Unto iniquity.
עוה	בְּעָוֹן בְּעֲוֹן	*In, pro iniquitate.*	In, with, for the iniquity.
—	בַּעֲוֹנָהּ	*In iniquitate ejus.*	In her iniquity.
—	בַּעֲוֹנוֹ	*In iniquitate ejus.*	In his iniquity.
—	בַּעֲוֹנוֹת	*Propter iniquitates.*	In, for the iniquities.
—	בַּעֲוֹנִי בַּעֲוֹנִי	*Propter iniquitatem meam.*	Because of my iniquity.
—	בַּעֲוֹנֶךָ	*Iniquitate tua.*	By thy iniquity.
—	בַּעֲוֹנָם	*Ob iniquitatem eorum*	For their iniquity.
—	בַּעֲוֹנֹתַיִךְ	*In iniquitatibus tuis.*	In thy iniquities.
—	בַּעֲוֹנֹתֵיכֶם	*Propter iniquitates vestras.*	For your iniquities.
עוף	בְּעוֹף	*E volatili.*	Of fowl.
—	בְּעוֹפְפִי	*Vibrando me.*	When I brandish.
עור	בְּעוֹר בְּעוֹר	*In cute, pelle.*	In with a skin, the skin.
	בְּעוֹר	*Beor.*	Beor, N. M.
עור	בַּעִוָּרוֹן	*Cæcitate.*	With blindness.
—	בְּעוֹרִי	*In cute mea.*	In my skin.
בעה	בְּעוּתֶהָ	*Petitio ejus.*	His petition.
בעת	בִּעוּתֵי	*Terrores.*	The terrors.
—	בִּעוּתֶיךָ	*Terrores tui.*	Thy terrors.
	בֹּעַז	*Boaz.*	Boaz, N. M.
עזב	בְּעִזְבוֹנָיִךְ	*In nundinis tuis.*	In thy fairs.
—	בְּעָזְבְכֶם	*Derelinquendo vos.*	In that ye have forsaken.
—	בְּעָזְבָם	*Deserendo eos.*	Because they had forsaken.
עזז	בְּעֻזּוֹ	*Per potentiam ejus.*	By his power.
—	בַּעֲזוֹז	*In roborando.*	In strengthening.
עז	בָּעִזִּים	*Inter capras.*	Among the goats.
עזז	בְּעָזְּךָ בְּעֻזְּךָ	*Robore tuo.*	In thy strength.

ROOTS.	DERIVATIVES.	VERSIO.	SIGNIFICATION.
עזק	בְּעִזְקָתֵהּ	*Annulo suo.*	With his signet.
עזר	בַּעֲזֹר	*Adjuvando.*	In helping.
—	בְּעֶזְרוֹ	*In auxilio ejus.*	In his help.
—	בְּעֶזְרִי	*In auxilio meo*[*meos*	In my help.
—	בְּעֹזְרָי	*Inter auxiliatores*	Among my helpers.
—	בְּעֶזְרֶךָ	*In auxilio tuo.*	In thy help.
—	בְּעֶזְרָתִי	*In auxilium meum.*	For my help.
—	בְּעֶזְרָתֶךָ	*In auxilio tuo.*	In thy help.
בָּעַט		*Calcitravit.*	He kicked, spurned.
עט	בְּעֵט	*Cum stylo.*	With a pen, style, or graver.
עטף	בַּעֲטֹף בֵּעָטֵב	*In obruendo.* [*mate.*	When overwhelmed.
עטר	בָּעֲטָרָה	*Cum corona, diade-*	With the crown, or fillet.
עיה	בְּעִי	*In tumulum.*	To the tomb.
בעה	בְּעָיוּ	*Quærite.*	Enquire ye.
עים	בַּעְיָם	*Impetu, vehementia.*	With force, vehemence.
עין	בְּעַיִן בְּעֵין	*Prope fontem.* [*lum.*	By a fountain.
—	בָּעָיִן	*Pro oculo, ad ocu-*	For an eye, to eye.
בעה	בָּעַיִן	*Quærentes.*	Seeking.
—	בְּעֵינָא	*Quæsivimus.*	We sought.
עין	בְּעֵינוֹ בְּעֵינָו	*In oculo, oculis ejus.*	In his eye, eyes, sight.
—	בְּעֵינַי־נָי	*In oculis meis.*	In, before, with my eyes.
—	בְּעֵינֵי	*In oculis.*	In the eyes.
—	בְּעֵינֶיהָ	*In oculis ejus.*	In her eyes.
—	בְּעֵינֵיהֶם	*In oculis eorum.*	In their sight.
—	בְּעֵינֵיהֶן	*In oculis earum.*	In their eyes.
—	בְּעֵינָיו	*In oculis ejus.*	In his eyes, sight.
—	בְּעֵינֶיךָ־נַיִךְ	*In oculis tuis.*	In thy eyes.
—	בְּעֵינֵיכֶם	*In oculis vestris.*	In your eyes.
—	בְּעֵינֵינוּ	*In oculis nostris.*	In our eyes.
—	בְּעֵינֶךָ	*In oculo tuo.*	In, with thy eye.
ער	בָּעִיר	*In excitando.*	When rising.
עיר	בְּעִיר בָּעִיר	*In civitate.*	In the city.
בער	בְּעִירֹה	*Jumentum ejus.*	His beast.
עיר	בְּעִירוֹ	*In civitate ejus.*	In his city.
—	בְּעִירִי	*In civitate mea.*	In my city.
בער	בְּעִירְכֶם	*Jumenta vestra.*	Your beasts, cattle.
—	בְּעִירָם	*Pecudes eorum.*	Their beasts.

ROOTS.	DERIVATIVES.	VERSIO.	SIGNIFICATION.
עכר	בְּעֹכְרִי	*Inter turbantes me.*	Among them that trouble me.
בָּעַל		*Habuit, possedit, præditus est, deditus est* alicui rei, *imperavit, dominatus est, duxit uxorem, concubuit.*	He owned, had, possessed, was endued with, was given or addicted *to a thing*, had authority or dominion, married a wife, cohabited with her.
	בַּעַל	*Herus, dominus, maritus.*	The master, owner, husband.
	בַּעַל	*Baal.*	Baal, N. M. P. I.
	בַּעַל זְבוּב	*Baal-zebub.*	Baal-zebub, N. I.
	בַּעַל חָנָן	*Baal-chanan.*	Baal-hanan, N. M.
	בַּעַל חָצוֹר	*Baal-chazor.*	Baal-hazor, N. P.
	בַּעַל חֶרְמוֹן	*Baal-chermon.*	Baal-hermon, N. P.
בעל	בְּעֵל טְעֵם	*Consiliarius, vel cancellarius.*	A counsellor, or chancellor.
	בַּעַל מְעוֹן	*Baal-meon.*	Baal-meon, N. P.
	בַּעַל פְּעוֹר	*Baal-peor.*	Baal-peor, N. I.
	בַּעַל פְּרָצִים	*Baal-perazim.*	Baal-perazim, N. P.
	בַּעַל צְפוֹן	*Baal-zephon*	Baal-zephon, N. P.
	בַּעַל שָׁלִשָׁה	*Baal-salisa.*	Baal-shalisha, N. P.
	בַּעַל תָּמָר	*Baal-tamar.*	Baal-tamar, N. P.
עלל	בְּעֹל	*Sub jugo.*	With, under the yoke.
בעל	בַּעְלָהּ	*Maritus ejus.*	Her husband.
—	בַּעֲלוּ	*Dominati sunt.*	They had the dominion.
—	בְּעָלוּנוּ	*Dominati sunt nobis.*	They had dominion over us.
	בְּעָלוֹת	*Baaloth.*	Baaloth, N. P.
עלה	בַּעֲלוֹת	*Ascendendo, offerendo.*	In, while going up, offering.
—	בַּעֲלוֹתָהּ	*Ascendendo eam.*	When she came up.
—	בַּעֲלוֹתוֹ-לֹתוֹ	*Ascendendo eum.*	When he came up.
—	בְּעֹלֹתֵינוּ	*Holocaustis nostris*	With our burnt offerings.
—	בַּעֲלוֹתָם	*Ascendendo eos.*	When they came up.
עלט	בַּעֲלָטָה	*In caligine.*	In the dark.
עלל	בַּעֱלִי	*Cum pistillo.*	With a pestle.
בעל	בַּעְלִי	*Dominus meus.*	My lord.
	בְּעֶלְיָדָע	*Baaliada.*	Baaliada, N. M.
	בְּעַלְיָה	*Baalia.*	Bealiah, N. M.
בעל	בְּעָלֶיהָ	*Domini ejus.*	The owners of her, or it.

ROOTS.	DERIVATIVES.	VERSIO.	SIGNIFICATION.
בעל	בַּעֲלֵיהֶן	*Mariti earum.*	Their husbands.
—	בְּעָלָיו	*Dominus ejus ; prœditus eo.*	His owner ; a person endued with it.
עלה	בְּעֶלְיוֹן	*In excelso, supremo*	In the most high, the supreme
בעל	בַּעְלֵךְ	*Maritus tuus.* [*tino.*	Thy husband.
עלל	בַּעֲלִיל	*In fornace, vel ca-*	In a furnace, or crucible.
	בְּעָלִים	*Baalim.*	Baalim, N. I.
	בַּעֲלִיס	*Baalis.*	Baalis, N. M. [ber.
עלה	בַּעֲלִיַּת	*In cœnaculo.*	In the parlour, or upper cham-
—	בְּעֲלִיָּתֵהּ	*In cœnaculo ejus.*	In his chamber.
—	בַּעֲלִיָּתוֹ	*In cœnaculo ejus.*	In his upper chamber.
עלם	בְּעַלְמָה	*In, cum virgine.*	In, with a virgin.
עלץ	בַּעֲלֹץ	*Exultando.*	In rejoicing.
	בַּעֲלָת	*Baalath.*	Baalath, N. P.
בעל	בְּעֻלַת	*Maritata.*	A married woman.
—	בַּעֲלַת	*Domina.*	The mistress.
—	בָּעַלְתִּי	*Conjugio junctus sum*	I have been married.
עלה	בַּעֲלֹתִי	*Ascendendo me.*	When I go up.
—	בַּעֲלֹתְךָ	*Ascendendo te.*	When thou goest up. [people.
עמם	בָּעָם־בְּעַם	*In populo, populum.*	With, among, against, over, the
עמד	בְּעָמְדוֹ	*Stando eum.*	When he stood.
—	בְּעָמְדָם	*Stando eos.*	When they stood.
עמם	בְּעַמּוֹ	*In populo ejus.*	In, among his people.
עמד	בְּעַמּוּד	*In columna.*	In a, the pillar.
עמם	בְּעַמֵּי	*Cum populis.* [*meum*	With the people. [ple.
—	בְּעַמִּי	*In, inter populum*	Against, over, among my peo-
—	בְּעַמָּיו	*In populis ejus.*	Among his people.
—	בְּעַמֶּיךָ	*In populis tuis.*	Amongst thy people.
—	בָּעַמִּים	*Inter populos.*	Among the nations, people.
עמר	בְּעָמִיר	*In manipulo.*	In a sheaf.
עמת	בַּעֲמִיתוֹ	*Ad proximum ejus.*	Unto his neighbour.
עמם	בְּעַמֶּךָ־מְּךָ	*In, inter populum tuum.*	Against, among thy people.
עמל	בֶּעָמָל בַּעֲמַל	*Per laborem.*	By, with labour.
—	בַּעֲמָלוֹ	*Pro labore ejus.*	Of, for his labour.
—	בַּעֲמָלָם	*Pro labore eorum.*	For their labour.
עמם	בַּעֲמָמֶיךָ	*In populis tuis.*	Among thy people.

ROOTS.	DERIVATIVES.	VERSIO.	SIGNIFICATION.
עמק	בְּעֵמֶק בְּ׳	*In, inter, per vallem.*	Into, in, through the valley.
—	בְּעִמְקֵי	*In profundis.*	In the depths.
—	בַּעֲמָקִים	*In vallibus.*	In the valleys.
עמר	בָּעֹמֶר	*Homere*, medio.	With an omer, *a measure.*
—	בָּעֳמָרִים	*Inter manipulos.*	Amongst the sheaves.
	בְּעֹן	*Beon.*	Beon, N. P.
	בַּעֲנָא־נָה	*Baana.*	Baana, Baanah, N. M.
ענה	בָּעֳנִי	*In afflictionem.*	On the affliction.
—	בְּעָנְיוֹ	*In afflictione ejus.*	In his affliction.
—	בְּעָנְיִי	*In afflictione mea.*	In my affliction.
—	בְּעִנְיָן	*In negotio, occupatione.*	In business, occupation.
ענן	בֶּעָנָן	*In nube.*	In the cloud.
—	בְּעַנְנִי	*Obnubilando me.*	When I bring a cloud.
ענש	בַּעֲנֹשׁ	*Mulctando.*	In fining, or punishing by a fine
עפל	בַּעֲפֹלִים	*Cum mariscis.*	With emerods.
עוף	בְּעַפְעַפֵּי	*In palpebras, vel primos splendores.*	On the eyelids, or dawning light.
—	בְּעַפְעַפֶּיהָ	*Per palpebras ejus.*	By, with her eyelids.
עפר	בֶּעָפָר	*In pulvere.*	With, in the dust.
עץ	בְּעֵץ בְּ׳	*In arbore, ligno.*	In the tree, the wood.
עצב	בְּעֶצֶב בְּעֶ׳	*Cum dolore.*	With sorrow.
—	בְּעִצָּבוֹן	*In dolore.*	In sorrow.
יעץ	בְּעֵצָה	*Cum consilio.*	By counsel, with advice.
עץ	בְּעֵצוֹ	*Cum ligno ejus.*	With his wood.
עצם	בַּעֲצוּמָיו	*Per robustos ejus.*	By his strong ones.
עץ	בַּעֲצֵי	*Cum lignis; inter arbores.*	With the wood, among the trees.
—	בָּעֵצִים	*Inter ligna.*	Among the wood.
עצל	בַּעֲצַלְתַּיִם	*Propter pigritias, i.e. per pigritiam summam.*	By extreme slothfulness.
עצם	בְּעֶצֶם	*In os, osse.*	Upon, in a bone.
—	בְּעֶצֶם	*In osse, robore; ipsomet.*	In the bone, strength; in the same, the very same.
—	בְּעָצְם	*In robore.*	In, with thy strength.
—	בְּעַצְמוֹת	*In ossa.*	Upon the bones.

ROOTS.	DERIVATIVES.	VERSIO.	SIGNIFICATION.
עצם	בְּעַצְמוֹתַי־מֹתַי	*In ossibus meis.*	In my bones.
—	בְּעַצְמוֹתָיו־מֹת׳	*In ossibus ejus.*	In his bones.
—	בְּעָצְמִי	*In ossibus meis.* [*am.*	In my bones.
—	בְּעָצְמַת	*Propter robur, copi-*	For the strength, abundance.
עצר	בְּעַצְּרֹתֵיכֶם	*In solennitatibus vestris.*	In your solemn assemblies.
יעץ	בַּעֲצַת	*In consilio.*	In the counsel.
—	בַּעֲצָתְךָ	*Per consilium tuum.*	With thy counsel.
—	בַּעֲצָתָם	*Ad consilium eorum*	After, with their counsel.
עקב	בְּעָקֵב בַּעֲ׳	*Per calcaneum.*	By the heel.
—	בְּעָקְבָה	*In astutia.*	In subtilty.
—	בְּעִקְבֵי	*Per vestigia.*	By the footsteps.
עקרב	בְּעַקְרַבִּים	*Cum scorpionibus.*	With scorpions.
בָּעַר		*Succendit, arsit, combussit, iratus est, amovit, abstulit, depavit, desipuit,*	He kindled, burned, consumed, was angry, removed, took away, ate up, became foolish.
—	בַּעַר	*Insipiens, stupidus.*	Foolish, stupid.
—	בָּעֵר	*Accendere.*	To burn.
—	בִּעֵר	*Abstulit, removit.*	He took away, put away.
—	בֹּעֵר	*Ardens.*	Burning.
	בַּעֲרָא	*Baara.*	Baara, N. W.
	בְּעֹר	*Beor,*	Beor, N. M.
ערב	בְּעֶרֶב בְּ׳ בָּעֶ׳	*In vespera.* [*ne.*	In the evening.
—	בְּעֵרֶב בְּ׳	*In trama, subtegmi-*	In the woof. [sert.
—	בְּעֲרָבָה	*In planitie, solitudine*	In, through the plain, the de-
—	בְּעַרְבוֹת־בֹת	*In campis.*	In the plains.
—	בָּעֲרָבוֹת	*In supremis* cœlis.	In the highest *heavens.*
—	בַּעֹרְבִים	*Inter fidejubentes.*	Among them that are sureties.
בער	בָּעֲרָה	*Exarsit.*	She burned.
—	בֹּעֶרָה בֹּעֶ׳	*Ardens, succensa.*	Burning, heated.
—	בָּעֲרוּ	*Combusti sunt.*	They were burnt.
עור	בְּעוֹרוֹ	*In cute ejus.*	In his skin.
ערץ	בַּעֲרוּץ	*In fissura.*	In the cleft.
בער	בֹּעֲרוֹת	*Ardentes.*	Burning.
עיר	בְּעָרֵי	*In urbibus, in urbes.*	In, over the cities.
—	בְּעָרֶיהָ	*In urbibus ejus.*	In her cities.

ROOTS.	DERIVATIVES.	VERSIO.	SIGNIFICATION.
עיר	בְּעָרֵיהֶם	*In urbibus eorum.*	In their cities.
—	בְּעָרָיו	*In urbibus ejus.*	In his cities.
—	בְּעָרֵיכֶם	*In urbibus vestris.*	In your cities.
—	בֶּעָרִים	*In urbibus.*	In the cities.
בער	בֹּעֲרִים	*Insipientes, stupidi.*	Foolish, brutish.
עיר	בְּעָרֵינוּ	*In urbibus nostris.*	In our cities.
ערף	בַּעֲרִיפֶיהָ	*In cœlis, defluxionibus ejus.* [*tuam.*	In its heavens, in its defluxions.
ערך	בְּעֶרְכְּךָ־כְּךָ	*Juxta æstimationem*	By, according to thy estimation
ערל	בְּעָרְלָה	*Cum præputio.*	With the uncircumcision.
ערם	בְּעָרְמָה	*In dolo; callidè.*	With guile, craftily.
—	בְּעָרְמָם	*In astutia eorum.*	In their craftiness.
ערף	בְּעֹרֶף	*In cervice.*	In the neck.
—	בְּעָרְפִּי	*Per cervicem meam.*	In my neck.
ערפל	בַּעֲרָפֶל	*In nube, vel caligine densa.*	In the thick clouds, or darkness
בער	בֹּעֶרֶת	*Ardens.*	Burning.
—	בִּעַרְתָּ	*Abstulisti.*	Thou hast taken away.
—	בִּעַרְתִּי	*Abstuli.*	I have taken away.
—	בִּעַרְתִּיהָ	*Accendi illam.* [*tis.*	I have kindled it. [up.
—	בִּעַרְתֶּם	*Accendistis, depavis-*	Ye have kindled, have eaten
	בַּעְשָׁא	*Baasa.*	Baasha, N. M.
עשב	בְּעֵשֶׂב	*In herba.*	In the grass.
עשר	בֶּעָשׂוֹר־־שֹׂר	*In decima.*	In the tenth.
עשה	בַּעֲשׂוֹת	*Comprimendo.*	In bruising, pressing.
—	בַּעֲשׂוֹתִי	*Faciendo me.*	When I do.
—	בַּעֲשׂוֹתְךָ־־תֵךְ	*Faciendo te.* [*tes.*	When thou doest.
—	בְּעֹשֵׂי	*Inter, contra facien-*	Among them that do.
	בַּעֲשֵׂיָה	*Baaseia.*	Baaseiah, N. M.
עשה	בְּעֹשָׂיו	*In factoribus ejus.*	In his makers.
עשר	בַּעֲשִׂירִי	*In decima.*	In the tenth.
עשן	בֶּעָשָׁן בְּ׳	*In fumum, fumo.*	Into, in smoke.
עשק	בְּעֹשֶׁק בְּעֹשֶׁק	*In fraude, oppressione.*	In, by fraud, oppression, extortion. [tenth.
עשר	בְּעַשֵּׂר	*Decimando.*	In tithing, giving or taking the
—	בְּעָשְׁרוֹ	*In divitiis ejus.*	In his riches.
—	בַּעֲשִׂרִי	*In decima.*	In the tenth.

ROOTS.	DERIVATIVES.	VERSIO.	SIGNIFICATION.
עשר	בְּעֶשְׂרִים	*Pro viginti, in vicesimo.*	For twenty, in the twentieth.
—	בַּעֲשֹׂתָהּ	*Faciendo eam.* [*eum.*	While she does.
עשה	בַּעֲשֹׂתוֹ	*Faciendo, operando*	When he makes, works.
עשת	בְּעַשְׁתֵּי עֶשְׂרֵה	*In undecimo.*	In the eleventh.
	בְּעֶשְׁתְּרָה	*Beestera.*	Beeshterah, N. P.
בעת			
עתת	בָּעֵת בְּעֵת	*In tempore, juxta tempus.*	In time, at the time.
—	בְּעִתָּהּ	*In tempore ejus.*	In her time.
בעת	בְּעָתָה	*Terror, perturbatio.*	Terror, trouble.
—	בְּעָתֻהוּ	*Terruerunt eum.*	They made him afraid.
עתת	בְּעִתּוֹ	*In tempore ejus.*	In his season.
—	בְּעִתִּים בְּעִתִּים	*In temporibus.*	At, in times.
—	בְּעִתָּם	*In tempore eorum.*	In their season.
בעת	בְּעָתַתְנִי	*Terruit me.*	He affrighted me.
	בפ		
פאה	בִּפְאַת	*In latere, angulo.*	In the side, the corner.
פגע	בְּפִגְעוֹ	*Occurrendo eum.*	In meeting him.
פגר	בְּפִגְרֵי	*In cadavera.*	Upon the carcasses.
פה	בְּפֶה	*In ore.*	In, with the mouth.
פוך	בַּפּוּךְ	*In fuco, stibio, lapide pretioso nigricante.*	In, with pigment for the face; a black mineral, supposed to be black lead; a precious stone of the same colour.
פזז	בַּפָּז	*Auro puro.*	To fine gold.
פוח	בַּפָּח	*In laqueo.*	In the snare.
פחד	בְּפַחַד	*Per timorem.*	By the fear.
פחם	בְּפֶחָם	*In carbone.*	In the coal.
פה	בְּפִי	*In ore; in os meum.*	In the mouth; into my mouth
פיד	בְּפִיד	*Propter calamitatem.*	At the calamity.
—	בְּפִידוֹ	*In calamitate ejus.*	In his calamity.
פה	בְּפִיהָ	*In ore ejus.*	In her mouth.
—	בְּפִיהוּ	*In ore ejus.*	In his mouth.
—	בְּפִיהֶם	*In ore eorum.*	In their mouth.

ROOTS.	DERIVATIVES.	VERSIO.	SIGNIFICATION.
פה	בְּפִיו	*In ore ejus.*	In, with his mouth.
—	בְּפִיךָ־־ךְ	*In ore tuo.*	In, with thy mouth.
—	בְּפִיכֶם	*In ore vestro.*	In, with your mouth.
פלגש	בְּפִילַגְשׁוֹ	*In concubinam ejus.*	On his concubine.
—	בְּפִילַגְשִׁי	*In concubinam meam.*	On my concubine.
פה	בְּפִימוֹ	*In ore eorum.*	In their mouth.
פלג	בְּפְלַגּוֹת	*Propter divisiones, fluvios.*	For the divisions, the rivers.
—	בִּפְלֻגָּתְהוֹן	*In classibus eorum.*	In their divisions, classes.
פלך	בְּפֶלֶךְ	*In scipionem.*	On a staff.
פלל	בִּפְלִלִים	*Secundum judices.*	According to the judges.
פלס	בַּפֶּלֶס	*In statera.*	In scales.
פום	בְּפֻם	*In ore.*	In the mouth.
—	בְּפֻמָּהּ	*In ore ejus.*	In her mouth.
פנה	בִּפְנוֹתָם	*Respiciendo eos.*	When they look.
—	בִּפְנֵי	*Ad faciem, ante.*	To the face, before.
—	בְּפָנַי	*Ad faciem meam.*	To my face.
—	בְּפָנֶיהָ	*In faciem ejus.*	To her face.
—	בִּפְנֵיהֶם	*Ante facies eorum.*	Before their faces.
—	בְּפָנָיו	*In faciem ejus.*	To his face.
—	בְּפָנֶיךָ	*In faciem tuam.*	Before thy face.
—	בִּפְנֵיכֶם	*In facies vestras.*	Before your faces.
—	בְּפָנִים	*Ad faciem.*	To the face.
—	בִּפְנִימִי	*In interiore.*	Within.
פסל	בְּפֶסֶל	*In sculptili.*	In a graven image.
—	בִּפְסִלֵיהֶם	*Sculptilibus eorum.*	With their graven images.
פעל	בְּפֹעַל	*In opere.*	In the work.
—	בְּפָעָלְךָ	*In opere tuo.*	In thy work.
—	בְּפָעֳלָם	*Ad opus eorum.*	To their work.
פעם	בְּפַעַם בְּפ׳	*In vice.*	At the time, at this as at [other times.
פקד	בִּפְקֹד	*Numerando.*	In numbering.
—	בְּפִקָּדוֹן	*Depositum.*	A deposit, a trust.
—	בְּפִקּוּדֶיךָ־־קְדֶ׳	*In præceptis tuis.*	In thy precepts.
פר	בְּפַר בַּפַּר	*Cum juvenco.*	With a young bullock, or steer
פרר	בְּפָרוּר	*In olla.*	In a pot.
פרור	בַּפְּרְוָרִים	*In suburbiis.*	In the suburbs.

ROOTS.	DERIVATIVES.	VERSIO.	SIGNIFICATION.
פרח	בְּפְרֹחַ	*Florendo.*	In springing, flourishing.
פרה	בְּפְרִי	*In fructu.*	In the fruit.
—	בְּפִרְיוֹ	*Pro fructu ejus.*	For his fruit.
פר	בְּפָרִים	*Cum juvencis.*	With bullocks.
פרך	בְּפָרֶךְ בְּפֶרֶךְ	*Cum duritia, sævitia*	With rigour, cruelty.
פרס	בְּפַרְסוֹת	*Cum ungulis.*	With the hoofs.
פרע	בִּפְרֹעַ	*Ulciscendo.*	In avenging.
פרץ	בַּפֶּרֶץ	*In ruptura.*	In the breach.
—	בַּפְּרָצוֹת	*In rupturas.*	Into the gaps.
פרש	בְּפָרֵשׂ	*Dissipando.*	In scattering.
פוש	בְּפַשׁ	*In multitudine, prosperitate.*	In a multitude, in prosperity.
פשע	בְּפֶשַׁע בְּפֶ״	*In, pro prævaricatione.*	In, for the transgression.
פשת	בְּפִשְׁתֵּי	*In linis.*	In, with the flax.
—	בַּפִּשְׁתִּים	*Ex linis.*	Of linen.
פתה	בַּפְּתָאִים	*Inter simplices, imperitos.*	Among the simple, inexperienced.
—	בְּפִתְאֹם	*Repente.*	Suddenly.
פתת	בְּפַתְבַּג	*In portione cibi.*	With the portion of meat.
פתח	בְּפֶתַח בַּפֶּ״	*Ad ostium, in ostio.*	At, in the door.
—	בְּפִתְחֵי	*In ostiis.*	In the doors, gates.
—	בְּפִתְחִי	*Aperiendo me.*	When I have opened.
—	בִּפְתָחֶיהָ	*Intra portas ejus.*	Within her gates.
פתל	בְּפָתִיל	*Cum filo.*	With a thread.
פתע	בְּפֶתַע	*Subito.*	Suddenly.
	בצ		
צאן	בְּצֹאן בַּצֹּאן	*Cum, in grege, ovibus.*	With, among the flock, the sheep.
—	בְּצֹאנְךָ	*Pro pecudibus tuis.*	For thy cattle.
—	בְּצֹאנָם	*Cum gregibus eorum*	With their flocks.
—	בְּצֹאנֵנוּ	*Cum pecudibus nostris.*	With our flocks.
יצא	בְּצֵאת	*Exeundo; in fine.*	In going out; in the end.
בצץ	בִּצֹּאתָו	*Cœnosa ejus.*	His miry places.
יצא	בְּצֵאתוֹ	*Exeundo eum.*	When he goes out.
—	בְּצֵאתִי	*Exeundo me.*	When I go out.
—	בְּצֵאתְךָ־־תֵךְ	*Exeundo te.*	When thou goest out.
—	בְּצֵאתְכֶם	*Exeundo vos.*	When ye come out.

ROOTS.	DERIVATIVES.	VERSIO.	SIGNIFICATION.
יצא	בְּצֵאתָם	*Exeundo illos.*	When they come out.
צבא	בַּצָּבָא	*Ad bellum, exercitum*	To war, to the army.
—	בִּצְבָאוֹת	*Per capreas. [tris.*	By the roes.
—	בְּצִבְאוֹתֵינוּ	*Cum exercitibus nos-*	With our armies.
צדד	בְּצַד	*In latere.*	In the side.
—	בְּצִדָּהּ	*In latere ejus.*	In her side.
צדה	בִּצְדִיָּה	*Per insidias.*	By snares, lying in wait.
צדד	בְּצִדֵּיכֶם	*In lateribus vestris.*	In your sides.
צדק	בְּצֶדֶק בְּצֶ׳	*In, cum justitia.*	In, with righteousnes.
—	בִּצְדָקָה בִּצְדָ׳	*Per justitiam.*	By righteousness.
—	בְּצִדְקוֹ	*In justitia ejus.*	In his righteousness.
—	בְּצִדְקָתוֹ	*In justitia ejus.*	In his righteousness.
—	בְּצִדְקָתִי	*Propter justitiam meam.*	For my righteousness.
—	בְּצִדְקָתְךָ־תֶךָ	*In justitia tua.*	In thy righteousness.
—	בְּצַדְקָתֵךְ	*Justificando te.*	When thou justifiest.
—	בְּצִדְקָתָם	*Per justitiam eorum*	By their righteousness.
בצץ	בִּצָּה	*Cœnum.*	Mire.
צהר	בַּצָּהֳרָיִם	*In meridie.*	At noon.
צור	בְּצַוָּאר	*In collum.*	On the neck.
—	בְּצַוָּארוֹ	*In collo ejus.*	In his neck.
—	בְּצַוְּארֵי	*Circum colla.*	About the necks.
צום	בְּצוֹם בְּצ׳	*In jejunio.*	With fasting.
צור	בְּצוּר בַּצ׳	*In rupem, rupe.*	Upon, to, into, in a rock.
בצר	בְּצוּרָה	*Munita.*	Walled, fenced, fortified.
—	בְּצוּרוֹת־־רֹת	*Munitæ.*	Walled.
צור	בְּצוּרוֹת	*In rupibus.*	Among the rocks.
צוה	בְּצַוּוֹת	*Præcipiendo.*	In commanding.
—	בְּצַוּוֹתוֹ	*Præcipiendo eum.*	When he commands.
צחח	בִּצְחִחִיים	*In excelsis locis.*	On the high *places.*
—	בְּצַחְצָחוֹת	*In siccitatibus.*	In drought.
	בֵּצָי	*Besai.*	Bezai, N. M.
ציה	בַּצִּיָּה	*In deserto.*	In the wilderness.
—	בְּצָיוֹן	*In sicco.*	In a dry place.
—	בַּצִּיּוֹת	*Per arida.*	In the dry places.
—	בַּצִּים	*In navibus.*	In ships.
ציץ	בְּצִיצִת	*Per cincinnum.*	By a lock *of plaited hair.*

ROOTS.	DERIVATIVES.	VERSIO.	SIGNIFICATION.
בצר	בָּצִיר	*Vindemia.*	The vintage.
—	בְּצִירֶךָ	*Vindemia tua.*	Thy vintage.
בצל צלל	בְּצֵל בַּצֵּל	*In, sub umbra, tutela.*	In, under the shadow, defence
	בְּצַלְאֵל	*Bezaleel.*	Bezaleel, N. M.
צלל	בְּצִלָּהּ	*Sub umbra ejus.*	Under her shadow.
—	בְּצִלּוֹ	*In umbra ejus.*	In his shadow.
	בַּצְלוּת	*Bazluth.*	Bazluth. N. M.
צלח	בַּצַּלַּחַת	*In patina, sinu ejus.*	In his dish, bosom.
צלל	בְּצִלִּי	*In umbra mea.*	In my shadow.
צלם	בְּצֶלֶם	*In imagine.*	In the image.
—	בְּצַלְמוֹ	*In imagine ejus.*	In his image.
—	בְּצַלְמָוֶת	*In umbra mortis.*	In the shadow of death.
—	בְּצַלְמֵנוּ	*In imagine nostra.*	In our image.
צלע	בְּצֶלַע	*Ad latus.*	On the side.
—	בִּצְלָעוֹת	*Cum trabibus.*	With boards, planks.
צלל	בְּצִלְצְלֵי	*In cymbalis.*	Upon the cymbals.
צמא	בַּצָּמָא	*In siti.*	In thirst.
צמר	בְּצֶמֶר	*Ex lana.*	Of woollen.
צנן	בְּצִנָּה	*Cum clypeo.*	With a shield.
צנר	בַּצִּנּוֹר	*In fistulam, canalem*	To the pipe, canal, aqueduct.
צנן	בְּצִנּוֹת	*Cum spinis.*	With thorns.
בָּצַע		*Sauciavit, divisit, abscidit, abrupit, concupivit, lucratus est, perfecit.*	He wounded, divided, cut off, broke off, coveted, gained, finished.
—	בֶּצַע	*Avaritia, lucrum.*	Covetousness, gain.
—	בְּצֹעַ	*Quæstum facere.*	To gain.
—	בִּצַּע	*Complevit.*	He fulfilled.
—	בֹּצֵעַ	*Concupiscens.*	Coveting.
צעד	בְּצַעְדְּךָ	*Incedendo te.*	When thou marchest.
בצע	בִּצְעוֹ	*Cupiditas ejus.*	His covetousness.
צעף	בַּצָּעִיף	*Cum velamine.*	With a veil.
בצע	בִּצְעֵךְ בִּצְעֵךְ	*Avaritia tua.*	Thy covetousness.
—	בִּצְעָם	*Cupiditas eorum.*	Their covetousness.
צפן	בַּצָּפוֹן	*Ad aquilonem.*	Toward the north.
צפר	בְּצִפֹּרֶן	*Cum scalpro.*	With a graving tool.

ROOTS.	DERIVATIVES.	VERSIO.	SIGNIFICATION.
צפח	בְּצַפַּחַת	*In lecytho, ampulla.*	In a cruise, vial, jug.
צפה	בְּצִפִּיָּתֵנוּ	*In speculatione, expectatione nostra.*	In our watching, expectation.
צפרדע	בַּצְפַרְדְּעִים	*Cum ranis.*	With frogs.
בצץ			
בָּצֵק		*Intumuit, emollescebat maceratione.*	It swelled, softened by watering.
—	בָּצֵק	*Massa farinæ.* [*est.*	Dough.
—	בָּצֵקָה	*Intumuit, emollitus*	It swelled, was softened.
—	בָּצֵקוּ	*Intumuerunt, emolliti sunt.*	They swelled, were softened.
—	בְּצֵקוֹ	*Massa farinæ sua.*	His dough.
צקל	בְּצִקְלֹנוֹ	*In gluma ejus.*	In the husk of it.
	בָּצְקַת	*Boscath.*	Boscath, N. P.
יצק	בְּצֶקֶת	*Fundendo, conflando*	In pouring out, fusing, casting
בָּצַר		*Vindemiavit, eripuit, munivit, cohibuit.*	He gathered grapes, took away, fortified, restrained.
	בֶּצֶר	*Bezer.* [*tione.*	Bezer, N. M.
צור	בַּצָּר בְּצָר	*In angustia, tribula-*	In distress, tribulation.
בצר	בֶּצֶר בְּצֶר	*Aurum.*	Gold.
צור	בַּצָּרָה בְּצָ׳	*In angustia.*	In trouble
	בָּצְרָה	*Bozra.*	Bozrah, N. P.
צרר	בִּצְרוֹר	*In fasciculo, sacculo*	In the bundle, the bag.
צור	בְּצָרוֹת	*In angustiis.*	In troubles.
בצר	בְּצֻרוֹת--רֹת	*Munitæ.*	Walled, fenced.
צור	בְּצָרָיו	*In hostibus ejus.*	On his enemies.
בצר	בְּצָרֶיךָ	*Aurum tuum.*	Thy gold.
—	בֹּצְרִים	*Vindemiatores.*	Vintagers, grape-gatherers.
—	בַּצֹּרֶת	*Siccitas.*	Drought.
צור	בַּצָּרָתָה	*In angustia.*	In distress.
	בק		
	בַּקְבּוּק	*Bacbuc.*	Bakbuk, N. M.
קבר	בִּקְבוּרָה	*In sepultura.*	In burial.
קבץ	בְּקַבְּצִי	*Congregando me.*	When I gather.
בקבק	בַּקְבֻּק	*Lagena.*	A jug.
	בַּקְבֻּקְיָה	*Bacbuchia.*	Bakbukeiah, N. M.

ROOTS	DERIVATIVES.	VERSIO.	SIGNIFICATION.
	בַּקְבַּקַּר	*Bacbaccar.*	Bakbakkar, N. M.
קבר	בְּקֶבֶר בְּקָבֶר	*In sepulchro.*	In the sepulchre, the grave.
—	בְּקִבְרוֹ	*In sepulchro ejus.*	In his grave.
—	בְּקִבְרוֹת	*In sepulchris.*	In the sepulchres.
—	בְּקִבְרִי	*In sepulchro meo.*	In my grave.
—	בַּקְּבָרִים	*In sepulchris.*	Among the graves.
—	בְּקִבְרָתוֹ	*In sepulchro ejus.*	In his sepulchre.
—	בְּקִבְרֹתָיו	*In sepulchro ejus.*	In his sepulchre.
—	בְּקִבְרָתָם	*In sepulchro eorum.*	In their burying place.
קדש	בְּקָדוֹשׁ	*In sancto.*	In the holy one.
—	בַּקֹּדֶשׁ בְּקֹ׳	*In sanctitate, sanctuario.*	In holiness, in the san ctuary.
—	בְּקָדְשׁוֹ	*In sanctitate ejus.*	In his holiness.
—	בִּקְדֹשָׁיו	*In sanctis ejus.*	In his saints.
—	בְּקָדְשִׁי	*In sanctitate mea.*	In my holiness.
—	בַּקֳּדָשִׁים	*De rebus sacris.*	Of the holy things.
—	בַּקְּדֵשִׁים	*Inter impuros, impudicos.*	Among the unclean, unchaste
קהל	בְּקָהָל בִּקְהַל	*In cætu, congregatione.*	In the assembly, congregation
—	בִּקְהָלָם	*In cætum eorum.*	Into their assembly.
קוה	בַּקָּו	*Ad lineam.*	By line.
קול	בְּקוֹל בַּקּוֹל	*In, cum voce, ad vocem.*	In, with, to a voice.
—	בְּקוֹלָהּ בְּקֹלָהּ	*Ad vocem ejus.*	Unto her voice.
—	בְּקוֹלוֹ בְּקֹלוֹ	*Ad vocem ejus.*	To his voice.
—	בְּקוֹלִי בְּקֹלִי	*Ad vocem meam.*	Unto my voice.
—	בְּקוֹלֶךָ־־לֶךָ	*Ad vocem tuam.*	To thy voice.
—	בְּקוֹלָם	*Ad vocem eorum.*	Unto their voice.
—	בְּקוֹלֵנוּ בְּקֹלֵ׳	*Ad vocem nostram.*	To our voice.
קום	בְּקוּם	*Surgendo.*	In rising.
קום	בְּקוֹמָה	*In altitudine.*	In height.
	בְּקוּמוֹ	*Surgendo eum.*	When he ariseth.
	בְּקוֹמָתָם	*In altitudine eorum.*	In their height.
קצר	בַּקּוֹצֵר	*Ad messorem.*	To the reaper.
לקח	בְּקַחְתּוֹ	*Capiendo eum.*	When he takes.
	בְּקַחְתֵּךְ	*Accipiendo te.*	When thou receivest.
	בֻּקִּי	*Bucchi.*	Bukki, N. M.
קוא	בְּקִיאוֹ	*In vomitu ejus.*	In his vomit.
	בֻּקִּיָּהוּ	*Bucchiahu.*	Bukkiah, N. M.

ROOTS.	DERIVATIVES.	VERSIO.	SIGNIFICATION.
קטר	בְּקִיטוֹר	*In fumo.*	In the smoke.
קון	בְּקִינוֹתֵיהֶם	*In lamentationibus [eorum.*	In their lamentations.
בקע	בְּקִיעֵי	*Ruinæ.*	The breaches.
קיץ	בַּקַּיִץ	*In æstate.*	In the summer.
קיר	בַּקִּיר־בְּקִ־	*In, ad, contra pari- [etem.*	Into, to, against the wall.
—	בְּקִירוֹת־רֹת	*In parietibus.*	In the walls,
קול	בְּקֹל	*Cum voce.*	With a voice.
קלה	בְּקָלוֹן	*In ignominiam.*	Into shame.
קלח	בַּקַּלַּחַת	*In cacabo.*	In a caldron.
קול	בְּקֹלְכֶם	*Ad vocem vestram.*	To your voice.
קלל	בְּקַלְלוֹ	*Maledicendo eum.*	When he cursed.
קלע	בַּקֶּלַע	*Cum funda.*	With a sling.
קום	בַּקָּמָה	*In segetem.*	Into the standing corn.
—	בְּקָמוֹת	*In segetes.*	Into the standing corn.
—	בְּקָמֵיהֶם	*Apud insurgentes in eos.*	Among them who rise up against them
—	בְּקָמִים	*In insurgentes.*	On them that rise up.
קמץ	בְּקָמְצוֹ	*In pugillo ejus.*	In his handful.
קום	בְּקָמַת	*In segetes.*	Into the standing corn.
קנא	בְּקַנְאוֹ־־נְּאתוֹ	*Zelando eum.*	While he is zealous.
—	בְּקִנְאָתִי	*In zelotypia mea.*	In my jealousy.
קנה	בְּקָנֶה בְּקָ׳	*In scapo, calamo.*	In a stalk, reed.
קסם	בְּקָסֶם	*Divinando.*	In divining.
בָּקַע		*Perrupit, irrupit, erupit, fidit, divisit.*	He broke, broke through, broke into, broke forth, cleft, divided.
—	בֶּקַע	*Dimidium sicli.*	Half a shekel.
—	בִּקַּע	*Diffidit.*	He clave asunder.
—	בִּקְעָה	*Planities.*	A plain.
—	בִּקְּעוּ	*Ruperunt.*	They have broken.
—	בְּקָעוֹת	*Valles.*	The valleys.
—	בְּקָעִים	*Rupturæ*	The breaches.
—	בִּקְעָם	*Diffindere eos.*	They cleave asunder.
—	בָּקַעְתָּ	*Dividisti, diffidisti.*	Thou didst divide, cleave asun- [der.
—	בִּקְעַת	*Vallis.*	The valley.
קצה	בְּקָצָה	*In extremitate.*	At the end.
—	בְּקָצֵהוּ	*In extremitate ejus.*	In the extremity of it.

ROOTS.	DERIVATIVES.	VERSIO.	SIGNIFICATION.
קצר	בְּקָצִיר	*In messe.* [*mets.*	In the harvest.
—	בִּקְצִירִי	*In messe mea, ramis*	On my harvest, my branches.
קצף	בְּקִצְפִּי	*In indignatione mea.*	In my wrath.
—	בְּקֶצְפְּךָ	*In furore tuo.*	In thy wrath.
קצר	בְּקָצְרְךָ	*Metendo te.*	When thou reapest.
בָּקַק		*Exhausit, evacuavit, spoliavit, irritum fecit.*	He exhausted, emptied, spoiled, made void.
—	בְּקָקוּם	*Evacuarunt eos.*	They have emptied them out.
—	בֹּקְקִים	*Evacuantes.*	The emptiers.
בָּקַר		*Quæsivit, inquisivit, perquisivit.*	He sought, inquired, sought diligently.
—	בֹּקֶר	*Mane, matutinus.*	In the morning, early.
—	בָּקָר בְּקַר	*Bos, boves.*	A bullock, cattle, herds.
קרא	בִּקְרֹא	*Legendo.*	In reading. [upon.
—	בְּקֹרְאַי	*Inter invocantes.*	Among them that invoke, call
—	בְּקָרְאִי	*Invocando me.*	When I call.
קרב	בְּקָרֹב בִּקְרֹב	*Appropinquando.*	In approaching, coming near.
—	בְּקֶרֶב	*In medium, medio; intra, inter.*	Into, in the midst of; within, among.
—	בִּקְרָב	*Ad prælium.*	To battle. [herself.
—	בְּקִרְבָּהּ	*In medio ejus.*	In the midst of her, within
—	בְּקִרְבּוֹ	*In medio ejus.*	In the midst of him.
—	בְּקִרְבִּי	*In medio nostrûm.*	In the midst of us.
—	בִּקְרֹבַי	*In appropinquantibus ad me.*	In them that come nigh me.
—	בְּקִרְבֵּךְ־בְּךָ־בֵּךְ	*In medio tui.*	In the midst of thee.
—	בְּקִרְבְּכֶם	*In medio vestrûm.*	In the midst of you.
—	בְּקִרְבָּם	*In medio eorum.*	In the midst of them.
—	בְּקִרְבֵּנוּ	*In medio nostrûm.*	In the midst of us.
—	בְּקָרְבָתָם	*Accedendo eos.*	When they come near.
קרר	בְּקָרָה	*In frigore.*	In the cold.
קרב	בְּקָרוֹב	*In propinquo.*	Near.
קרח	בְּקָרַחַת	*In calvitio.*	In the bald-head.
—	בְּקָרַחְתּוֹ	*In calvitio ejus.*	In his bald-head.
קרה	בְּקֶרִי	*Ex adverso.*	On the contrary.
—	בְּקִרְיָה	*In urbe.*	In the city.

ROOTS.	DERIVATIVES.	VERSIO.	SIGNIFICATION.
בקר	בְּקָרִים	*Boves.*	Oxen.
——	בְּקָרֵינוּ	*Boves nostri.*	Our herds.
——	בְּקָרְךָ־רֶךָ	*Bos tuus.*	Thy cattle.
——	בְּקַרְכֶם	*Bos vester.*	Your beeves.
——	בְּקָרָם	*Bos eorum.*	Their cattle.
קרן	בְּקֶרֶן	*In cornu.*	In, with the horn.
——	בְּקַרְנָא	*In cornu.*	In the horn.
——	בְּקַרְנוֹת	*In cornua.*	On the horns.
——	בְּקַרְנַיָּא	*Ad cornua.*	To the horns.
——	בְּקַרְנָיו	*Per cornua ejus.*	By his horns.
קרס	בַּקְּרָסִים	*Cum ansulis, uncinis.*	With the taches, or little hooks.
קרקע	בְּקַרְקַע	*In solo, pavimento.*	In the floor, pavement.
בקר	בִּקֹּרֶת	*Flagellatio.*	A scourging.
בִּקֵּשׁ		*Quæsivit, inquisivit, requisivit, interrogavit, exegit, supplicavit, oravit.*	He sought, searched, inquired, required, asked, demanded, besought, supplicated, prayed.
——	בַּקֵּשׁ	*Quære.*	Seek thou.
בקש	בִּקְשָׁה	*Quæsivit, exegit.*	She sought, required.
——	בִּקְשֻׁהוּ	*Quæsiverunt eum.*	They sought him.
——	בִּקְשׁוּ	*Quæsiverunt.*	They sought.
——	בַּקְּשׁוּ	*Quærite.*	Seek ye.
——	בַּקְּשׁוּנִי	*Quærite me.*	Seek ye me.
——	בִּקְשֻׁנִי	*Quæsiverunt me.*	They sought me.
קשקש	בְּקַשְׂקְשֹׂתֶיךָ	*In squamis tuis.*	In thy scales.
קשר	בַּקֹּשְׁרִים	*Inter conspirantes, conjuratos.*	Among the conspirators.
קשת	בְּקֶשֶׁת בַּקָּ׳	*In, cum arcu.*	In, with the bow.
בקש	בַּקָּשָׁתוֹ	*Petitio ejus.*	His request.
——	בִּקַּשְׁתִּי	*Quævivi.*	I sought.
——	בַּקָּשָׁתִי	*Petitio mea.*	My request.
קשת	בְּקַשְׁתִּי	*In arcu meo.*	In my bow.
בקש	בִּקַּשְׁתִּיהוּ	*Quæsivi eum.*	I sought him.
——	בִּקַּשְׁתִּיו	*Quæsivi eum.*	I sought him.
——	בַּקָּשָׁתֵךְ	*Petitio tua.*	Thy request.
קשת	בְּקַשְׁתְּךָ	*Cum arcu tuo.*	With thy bow.
בקש	בִּקַּשְׁתֶּם	*Quæsivistis.*	Ye sought.

ROOTS.	DERIVATIVES.	VERSIO.	SIGNIFICATION.
	בר		
בר			
—	בַּר	*Filius.*	The son.
ברר	בָּר בַּר	*Frumentum.*	Corn, wheat.
בור.	בֹּר	*Fovea, cisterna.*	A, the pit, well, cistern.
בָּרָא		*Creavit.*	He created, brought into being
ברה	בְּרֵא	*Elige.*	Choose thou.
בר	בָּרָא	*Ager.*	The field.
ברא	בְּרֹא	*Creare.*	To create.
—	בְּרָא	*Crea.*	Create thou.
	בְּרֹאדַךְ בַּלְאֲדָן	*Berodac-baladan.*	Berodach-baladan, N. M.
ברא	בְּרָאָהּ	*Creavit eam.*	He created her.
—	בְּרִאָה	*Pinguis.*	Fat.
ראה	בָּרְאֹה	*In visione.*	In the vision.
—	בִּרְאוֹת	*Videndo, in visione.*	In seeing, in the vision.
—	בִּרְאוֹתָם־אֹתָם	*Videndo eos.*	When they see.
	בְּרָאיָה	*Beraia.*	Beraiah, N. M.
ברא	בְּרִאִים	*Pingues.* [*tuus.*	Fat. [tor
—	בֹּרַאֲךָ	*Creans te, Creator*	He who created thee, thy Crea-
—	בְּרָאָם	*Creavit eos.*	He created them.
—	בְּרָאָנוּ	*Creavit nos.*	He created us.
ראש	בְּרֹאשׁ	*In caput; pro duce.*	On the head; as captain.
—	בְּרֹאשׁ	*In vertice, capite.*	At, on, in the top, head.
—	בְּרֹאשָׁהּ	*In capite ejus.*	Upon her head.
—	בְּרֹאשָׁהּ	*In capite ejus.*	On her head.
—	בְּרָאשֵׁהֶם	*In capitibus eorum.*	On their heads.
—	בְּרֹאשׁוֹ	*In capite ejus.*	Upon his head.
—	בָּרִאשׁוֹן	*In primo.*	In the first.
—	בָּרִאשֹׁנָה	*In principio, prius.*	In the beginning, before.
—	בְּרָאשֵׁי	*In capitibus, cacuminibus.*	In the heads, the tops.
—	בְּרָאשֵׁיהֶם	*In capitibus eorum.*	On their heads, chiefs of them
—	בְּרָאשֵׁיכֶם	*In capita vestra.*	For your heads, or chiefs.
—	בְּרָאשֵׁינוּ	*Periculo capitum nostrorum.*	At the peril of our heads.
—	בְּרֵאשִׁית	*In principio.*	In the beginning.

ROOTS.	DERIVATIVES.	VERSIO.	SIGNIFICATION.
ראש	בְּרֵאשִׁיתָהּ	*In principio ejus.*	At her first time.
—	בְּרֹאשְׁךָ־־שֵׁךְ	*In caput tuum.*	Upon thy head.
—	בְּרֹאשְׁכֶם	*In caput vestrum.*	Upon your head.
—	בְּרֹאשָׁם	*In caput corum.*	Upon their head.
—	בָּרִאשׁוֹן	*In primo.*	In the first.
—	בָּרִאשֹׁנָה	*In principio; prius.*	In the first, the beginning; before.
—	בְּרֹאשֵׁנוּ	*In capite nostro.*	On our head.
—	בָּרִאשֹׁנִים	*In primis.*	In the first.
ברא	בָּרָאתָ	*Creavisti.*	Thou hast created.
ראה	בִּרְאֹתוֹ	*Videndo eum.*	When he sees.
—	בִּרְאֹתִי	*Videndo me.*	When I see.
ברא	בָּרָאתִי	*Creavi.*	I created.
—	בְּרָאתִיו	*Creavi eum.*	I created him.
—	בְּרָאתָם	*Creavisti eos.*	Thou hast created them.
רבב	בְּרַב	*In multo, per multos*	By many.
—	בְּרֹב בְּרֹב	*In, pro multitudine, magnitudine.*	By, in, for the multitude, the greatness.
—	בְּרִבְבוֹת	*Cum myriadibus.*	With ten thousands.
—	בְּרִבְבֹתָיו־־תָו	*Cum decem millia ejus.*	With his ten thousands.
רבה	בְּרְבּוֹת	*Multiplicando.*	In multiplying.
רבב	בִּרְבִיבִים	*In imbribus.*	With, in showers.
—	בָּרַבִּים בְּ׳	*In, cum multis.*	In, with many, multitudes.
רבע	בָּרְבִיעִי	*In quarto.*	In the fourth.
רוב	בְּרִבָם	*Litigando eos.*	When they contend.
רבע	בְּרִבְעִית	*Cum quarto.*	With the fourth part.
רגז	בְּרֹגֶז	*In furore. [ira.*	In rage.
—	בְּרֹגֶז	*Cum commotione, in*	With a noise, in wrath.
—	בְּרָגְזָה	*Cum tremore.*	With trembling.
רגל	בְּרֶגֶל בְּרַ׳	*Pro pede.*	For foot,
—	בְּרַגְלוֹ	*Ad pedem ejus.*	At his foot.
—	בְּרַגְלַי־־לַי	*Ad pedes meos.*	At my feet.
—	בְּרַגְלֵי	*Ad pedes.*	At the feet.
—	בְּרַגְלֶיהָ	*In pedibus ejus.*	In the feet of it.
—	בְּרַגְלֵיהֶם	*Ad pedes corum.*	At their feet.
—	בְּרַגְלָיו־־לָו	*In pedibus ejus; pedester.*	By, with, in his feet; on foot.

ROOTS.	DERIVATIVES.	VERSIO.	SIGNIFICATION.
רגל	בְּרַגְלֶיךָ	*Ad pedes tuos.*	At thy feet.
—	בְּרַגְלֵיכֶם	*Cum pedibus vestris.*	With your feet.
—	בְּרַגְלָיִם	*Sub pedibus.*	Under feet.
—	בְּרַגְלְךָ	*Cum pede tuo.*	With thy foot.
רגע	בְּרֶגַע	*In momento.*	For, in a moment.
רגש	בְּרֶגֶשׁ	*In cœtu.*	In company.
בָּרַד		*Grandinavit.*	It hailed.
—	בָּרָד	*Grando.*	Hail.
	בֶּרֶד	*Bered.*	Bered, N.M.P. [spots like hail
ברד	בְּרֻדִּים	*Grandinati, varii.*	Grisled, speckled with small
רדף	בְּרֹדְפַי	*In persequentes me.*	On them that persecute me.
—	בְּרָדְפָם	*Persequendo eos.*	As they pursued.
ירד	בְּרֶדֶת	*Descendendo.*	In descending, going down.
—	בְּרִדְתּוֹ	*Descendendo eum.*	When he goes down.
—	בְּרִדְתִּי	*Descendendo me.*	When I go down.
בָּרָה		*Edit, se refecit pastu, elegit, succidit.*	He ate, refreshed himself with food, chose, cut down.
ברר	בָּרָה	*Pura, electa.*	Pure, the chosen one.
בר	בְּרֵהּ	*Filius ejus.*	His son.
רהט	בָּרְהָטִים	*In canalibus.*	In the gutters, canals, troughs
בור	בֹּרוֹ	*Cisterna ejus.*	His cistern.
ברה	בְּרוּ	*Eligite.* [mente.	Choose ye. [mind.
רוח	בְּרוּחַ	*In vento, spiritu,*	In the wind, breath, spirit,
ברח	בָּרוֹחַ	*Fugiendo.* [tum.	In flying.
רוח	בְּרוּחַ בְּ״	*In vento; per spiri-*	In the mind, by the spirit.
—	בְּרוּחוֹ	*In vento, spiritu ejus*	By, in his wind, his spirit.
—	בְּרוּחִי	*In spiritu meo.*	In my spirit.
—	בְּרוּחֲךָ	*In vento, spiritu tuo.*	In, with thy wind, thy spirit.
—	בְּרוּחֲכֶם	*In spiritu vestro.*	In your spirit.
	בָּרוּךְ	*Baruc.*	Baruch, N.M.
ברך	בָּרוּךְ בְּ׳	*Benedictus.*	Blessed.
—	בָּרוֹךְ	*Benedicere.*	To bless.
—	בְּרוּכָה	*Benedicta.*	Blessed.
—	בְּרוּכֵי	*Benedicti.*	The blessed.
ברך	בְּרוּכִים ־רֻכֵ׳	*Benedicti.*	Blessed.
ברם	בְּרֹמִים	*Vestes pretiosæ.*	Rich, costly garments. [nings.
ברק	בְּרוֹק	*Fulgura.*	Lighten thou, send forth light-

ROOTS.	DERIVATIVES.	VERSIO.	SIGNIFICATION.
ברר	בָּרוּר	*Purus, politus.*	Pure, polished.
—	בְּרוּרָה	*Pura.*	Pure.
—	בְּרוּרִים	*Electi.*	Chosen.
ברש	בְּרוֹשׁ	*Abies.*	A fir-tree.
—	בְּרוֹשָׁיו	*Abietes ejus.*	His fir-trees.
—	בְּרוֹשִׁים	*Abietes; abiegni.*	Fir-trees; made of fir.
בור	בֹּרוֹת	*Foveæ, cisternæ.*	Wells, cisterns.
	בֵּרוֹתָה	*Berotha.*	Berothah, N. P.
ברת	בְּרוֹתִים	*Abietes; abiegni.*	Fir-trees; made of fir.
	בִּרְזָוִת	*Birzait.*	Birzavith, N. M.
ברזל	בַּרְזֶל	*Ferrum.*	Iron.
	בַּרְזִלַּי	*Barzillai.*	Barzillai, N. M.
בָּרַח		*Fugit, aufugit, transivit, percurrit.*	He fled, ran away, went over, ran through or across.
—	בֹּרֵחַ	*Fugiens.* [*tuosus.*	Fleeing. [crooked.
—	בָּרִחַ	*Fugax, allabens, tor-*	Swift in flight, sliding, slippery,
—	בְּרַח	*Fuge.*	Flee thou.
רחב	בְּרֹחַב בְּ׳	*In latitudine.*	In the breadth.
—	בִּרְחֹב	*In platea.*	In the street.
—	בְּרָחָבָה	*In latitudine; latè.*	At large.
—	בִּרְחֹבוֹת בָּ׳	*In plateis.*	In the streets.
—	בִּרְחֹבוֹתֶיהָ	*In plateis ejus.*	In her streets.
—	בִּרְחֹבוֹתֵינוּ	*In plateis nostris.*	In our streets.
ברח	בָּרְחוּ בָּרָ׳	*Fugerunt.*	They fled.
—	בִּרְחוּ	*Fugite.*	Flee ye.
רחב	בָּרְחוֹב בָּרְ׳	*In platea.*	In the street.
—	בִּרְחוֹבוֹתֶיהָ	*In plateis ejus.*	In her streets.
	בַּרְחוּמִי	*Barchumites.*	Barhumite, N. F. or P.
רחק	בְּרָחוֹק	*In longinquo.*	Afar off.
ברח	בְּרִחֶיהָ	*Vectes ejus.*	Her bars.
ריח	בָּרֵחַיִם	*In molis.*	In mills.
רחם	בְּרֶחֶם	*In utero.*	In the womb.
—	בְּרַחֲמֶיךָ	*In misericordiis tuis.*	In thy mercies.
רחם	בְּרַחֲמִים	*In misericordiis.*	In mercies.
רחץ	בְּרָחְץ	*Lavando.* [*pala.*	In washing.
רוח	בְּרַחַת	*Cum vento, vanno,*	With the wind, fan, shovel.
ברח	בֹּרַחַת	*Fugiens.*	Fleeing.

ROOTS.	DERIVATIVES.	VERSIO.	SIGNIFICATION.
בר	בְּרִי	*Filius meus. [renum*	My son.
ברר	בְּרִי	*Serenitas, cælum se-*	Fair weather, a clear sky.
	בְּרִי	*Beri.*	Beri, N. M.
ברא	בָּרִיא	*Pinguis.*	Fat.
—	בְּרִיאָה	*Creatio.*	A creation.
—	בְּרִיאוֹת	*Pingues.*	Fat.
רוב	בְּרִיב	*In litem.*	Into contention.
—	בְּרִיבוֹ	*In lite, causa ejus.*	In his cause.
ברא	בִּרְיָה	*Pinguis.*	Fat.
	בָּרִיחַ	*Bariach.*	Bariah, N. M.
ריח	בְּרֵיחַ	*In odore.*	The savour, smell.
ברח	בְּרִיחַ	*Vectis.*	The bar.
—	בְּרִיחֶהָ־־יהָ	*Vectes ejus.*	Her bars.
—	בְּרִיחֵי	*Vectes.*	Bars.
—	בְּרִיחָיו בְּרִחָו	*Vectes ejus.*	His bars.
—	בְּרִיחַיִךְ	*Vectes tui.*	Thy bars.
—	בְּרִיחִים	*Fugitivi.*	Fugitives.
—	בְּרִיחִם	*Vectes.*	Bars.
ברך	בָּרִיךְ	*Benedictus.*	Blessed.
	בְּרִיעָה	*Beria.*	Beriah, N. M.
	בְּרִיעִי	*Beriitæ.*	Beriites, N. F.
ריר	בְּרִיר	*In albumine, saliva.*	In the white, slaver, drivel.
	בְּרִית	*Berith.*	Berith, N. I. [soap.
ברר	בֹּרִית	*Radicula.*	An herb used for washing, like
ברת	בְּרִית	*Fœdus, pactum.*	The covenant.
—	בְּרִיתוֹ	*Fœdus ejus.*	His covenant.
—	בְּרִיתִי	*Fœdus meum.*	My covenant.
—	בְּרִיתֶךָ־תְךָ־תֵךְ	*Fœdus tuum.*	Thy covenant.
—	בְּרִיתְכֶם	*Fœdus vestrum.*	Your covenant.
בָּרַךְ		*Benedixit, salutavit, genua flexit.*	He blessed, saluted, bent his knees.
—	בָּרֵךְ	*Benedic, benedicere, benedicendo; genua flectens.*	Bless thou, to bless, in blessing; bending the knees.
ברך	בֵּרַךְ	*Benedixit.*	He blessed.
—	בָּרַךְ בֵּרֵךְ	*Benedixit.*	He blessed.
—	בֶּרֶךְ	*Genu.*	A knee.

ROOTS.	DERIVATIVES.	VERSIO.	SIGNIFICATION.
	בָּרַכְאֵל	*Barachel.*	Barachel, N. M.
רכב	בְּרֶכֶב	*In, cum curru.*	In, with a chariot.
—	בְּרִכְבּוֹ	*In curru ejus.*	In his chariot.
—	בְּרִכְבֵי	*In curribus.*	In chariots.
	בְּרָכָה	*Beracha.*	Berachah, N. M.
ברך	בְּרָכָה	*Benedictio.*	The blessing.
—	בֵּרְכוֹ בֵּרֲכוֹ	*Benedixit ei.*	He blessed him.
—	בָּרְכוּ בָּרֲכוּ	*Benedicite.*	Bless ye.
—	בֵּרְכוּ	*Benedixerunt.*	They blessed.
—	בִּרְכוֹהִי	*Genua ejus.*	His knees.
—	בֵּרְכוּנִי	*Benedixerunt mihi.*	They blessed me.
רכש	בִּרְכוּשׁ בִּרְכֻשׁ	*Cum facultatibus.*	With substance, riches.
ברך	בִּרְכוֹת	*Benedictiones.*	Blessings.
—	בְּרֵכוֹת	*Piscinæ.*	Pools, ponds, cisterns.
—	בִּרְכוֹת	*Benedictiones.*	The blessings.
—	בִּרְכוֹתֵיכֶם	*Benedictiones vestræ*	Your blessings.
—	בָּרְכִי	*Benedic.*	Bless thou.
—	בִּרְכַּי	*Genua mea.*	My knees.
—	בִּרְכַּיִ	*Genua.*	The knees.
—	בִּרְכֶּיהָ	*Genua ejus.*	Her knees.
	בֶּרֶכְיָה־־יָהוּ	*Barachias.*	Barachiah, N. M.
ברך	בִּרְכֵּיהֶם	*Genua eorum.*	Their knees.
—	בִּרְכָּיו־־כָּו	*Genua ejus.*	His knees.
—	בִּרְכַּיִם	*Genua.*	The knees.
—	בֵּרַכְךָ	*Benedixit tibi.*	He blessed thee.
רכל	בִּרְכֻלָּתֵךְ	*In mercatura tua.*	In thy traffick.
ברך	בֵּרַכְנוּ	*Benediximus.*	We blessed.
—	בֵּרַכְנוּכֶם	*Benediximus vobis.*	We blessed you.
—	בָּרֲכֵנִי	*Benedic mihi.*	Bless thou me.
—	בֵּרֲכָנִי	*Benedixit mihi.*	He blessed me.
—	בֵּרַכְתִּ	*Benedixi.*	I blessed.
—	בֵּרַכְתָּ	*Benedixisti.*	Thou blessedst.
—	בְּרֵכַת	*Piscina.*	A pool, pond, cistern.
—	בִּרְכַּת	*Benedictio.*	The blessing.
—	בִּרְכֹת	*Benedictiones.*	Blessings.
—	בֵּרַכְתִּי	*Benedixi.*	I blessed.
—	בִּרְכָתִי	*Benedictio mea.*	My blessing.

ROOTS.	DERIVATIVES.	VERSIO.	SIGNIFICATION.
ברך	בְּרְכָתֶךָ	*Benedictio tua.*	Thy blessing.
—	בֵּרַכְתָּנִי	*Benedixisti mihi.*	Thou blessedst me.
ברם			
—	בְּרַם	*Sed, veruntamen.*	But, nevertheless.
רמח	בָּרְמָחִים	*In lanceis.*	In, on the spears, javelins.
רנן	בְּרֹן	*Canendo.*	In singing.
—	בְּרִנָּה	*Cum cantu, exultatione*	With singing, rejoicing.
—	בִּרְנָנָה	*Cum cantu.*	With singing.
	בַּרְנֵעַ	*Barnea.*	Barnea, N. P.
רעה	בְּרֵעַ	*In amico.*	In a friend.
רוע	בְּרָע בָּ׳	*In malum, malo.*	Into, in evil, mischief, affliction.
—	בְּרֹעַ	*In tristitia.*	In the sorrow, sadness.
	בֶּרַע	*Bera.*	Bera, N. M.
רעב	בְּרָעָב	*In fame, per famem.*	In, by, for hunger, famine.
רעד	בִּרְעָדָה	*Cum tremore.*	With trembling.
רוע	בְּרָעָה	*In malum, malo.*	Into, in evil, mischief, affliction.
—	בְּרֵעֹה	*Vociferando eum.*	As he shouted.
רעה	בְּרֵעֵהוּ	*In, ad, contra proximum ejus.*	Towards, against his neighbour.
רוע	בְּרָעוֹת	*In malis.*	In calamities.
—	בְּרָעוֹתֵיהֶם	*In malis eorum.*	In their calamities.
רעה	בְּרֵעֲךָ־־עֶךָ	*In proximum tuum.*	Against thy neighbour.
רעם	בְּרַעַם	*Cum tonitru. [motu.*	With thunder. [earthquake.
רעש	בְּרַעַשׁ בָּ׳	*Cum tremore, terræ*	With the trembling, shaking,
רעה	בִּרְעֹתוֹ	*Pascendo eum.*	While he feeds.
רוע	בְּרָעָתוֹ	*In malitia ejus.*	In his wickedness.
—	בְּרָעָתִי	*In malo meo.*	In my calamity.
—	בְּרָעָתֶךָ־־תֵךְ	*In malo tuo.*	In thy mischief.
—	בְּרָעָתָם	*Per malitiam eorum.*	With their wickedness.
רפא	בָּרֹפְאִים	*In medicis.*	In the physicians.
רפת	בָּרְפָתִים	*In stabulis.*	In the stalls.
רצה	בִּרְצוֹן	*Pro benevolentia.*	With the favour.
—	בִּרְצוֹנוֹ	*In benevolentia ejus.*	In his favour.
—	בִּרְצוֹנְךָ	*In benevolentia tua.*	In, by thy favour.
—	בִּרְצוֹת	*Placendo.*	In pleasing.
—	בִּרְצוֹתִי	*Ob affectionem meam*	Because of my affection.
רצח	בְּרֶצַח	*In cæde.*	In the slaughter.

ROOTS.	DERIVATIVES.	VERSIO.	SIGNIFICATION.
רצץ	בְּרַצֵּי	*Cum fragmentis.*	With pieces, fragments.
רצה	בִּרְצֹתוֹ	*Complacendo eum.*	That he delights himself.
	בָּרָק	*Barac.*	Barak, N. M. [ning
בָּרַק		*Fulguravit.*	He lightened, sent forth light-
—	בְּרַק	*Fulgur, acies.*	Lightning. [*of a sword.*
—	בָּרָק	*Fulgur.*	Lightning, the glittering point
	בַּרְקוֹס	*Barcos.*	Barkos, N. M.
ברק	בְּרָקָיו	*Fulgura ejus.*	His lightnings.
—	בְּרָקִים	*Fulgura.* [*panso.*	Lightnings.
רקע	בִּרְקִיעַ	*In firmamento, ex-*	In the firmament, the expanse.
רקם	בְּרִקְמָה	*Cum opere phrygio.*	With broidered work.
רקק	בְּרַקָּתוֹ	*In tempora ejus.*	Into his temples.
בָּרַר		*Purgavit, exploravit, declaravit, elegit.*	He cleansed, purified, explored, declared, chose, selected
—	בְּרֻרוֹת	*Electæ.*	Chosen, select.
ברש			
—	בְּרֹשָׁיו	*Abietes ejus.*	His fir-trees.
רוש	בְּרָשִׁים	*In pauperes.*	Over the poor.
רשע	בְּרֶשַׁע	*In improbitate.*	In, by wickedness.
—	בִּרְשַׁע	*Birsa.* [*ejus.*	Birsha, N. M.
רשע	בְּרִשְׁעוֹ	*Propter impietatem*	For his wickedness.
—	בָּרְשָׁעִים	*In impio.*	Towards the wicked.
—	בְּרִשְׁעַת	*Propter impietatem.*	For the wickedness.
רשת	בְּרֶשֶׁת	*In rete, reti.*	Into, in a net.
—	בְּרִשְׁתּוֹ	*In rete ejus.*	In his net.
ברת			
	בֵּרֹתַי	*Berothai.*	Berotha, N. P.
	בֵּרֹתִי	*Berothitæ.*	Beerothites, N. P.
רתק	בָּרַתִּיקוֹת	*Per catenas.*	By the chains.
	בש		
בשש	בֹּשׁ	*Tarditas, mora.*	Slowness, delay.
שאג	בְּשַׁאֲגָתִי	*In rugitu meo.*	In my roaring.
שאל	בִּשְׁאוֹל	*In statu mortuorum, sive invisibili, sepulcro, inferno.*	In the state of the dead, or the invisible state, the grave, hell.
שאה	בְּשָׁאוֹן	*In tumultu.*	In a tumult.

ROOTS.	DERIVATIVES.	VERSIO.	SIGNIFICATION.
שאט	בִּשְׁאָט	*Cum contemptu.*	With contempt.
שאל	בִּשְׁאֵלָתִי	*Pro petitione mea.*	At my petition.
שאר	בִּשְׁאָר־אַר	*In reliquis.*	In the rest.
נשא	בִּשְׂאֵת	*In tumore.*	In the rising, swelling.
—	בַּשְׂאֵת	*Ferendo, afferendo.*	In bearing, bringing.
שוב	בְּשׁוּבוֹ	*Revertendo eum.*	When he returns.
שבט	בְּשֵׁבֶט בַּשֵּׁ־ בַּשָּׁ־	*Cum virga, baculo, stylo; in tribu.*	With a rod, staff, pen; in a tribe.
—	בְּשִׁבְטֵי	*In tribubus.*	Among the tribes.
—	בְּשִׁבְטָיו	*In tribubus eorum.*	Among their tribes.
—	בְּשִׁבְטֶךָ	*Per virgam tuam.*	By, with thy rod.
שבה	בִּשְׁבִי בַּשְּׁ׳	*In captivitate.*	In captivity.
—	בִּשְׁבִי	*In captivitate.*	In the captivity.
—	בַּשִּׁבְיָה	*In captivitate.*	Among the captives.
שבע	בַּשְּׁבִיעִ־ עִית	*In septimo, septima.*	In the seventh.
שבה	בַּשְּׁבִית	*In captivitatem.*	Into captivity.
שבל	בַּשִּׁבֳּלִים	*In spicis.*	In ears of corn.
שבע	בְּשֶׁבַע	*In septem. [tima.*	In seven.
—	בְּשִׁבְעָה	*Cum septem, in sep-*	With seven, in the seventh.
—	בִּשְׁבֻעָה	*Cum juramento.*	With an oath.
—	בְּשִׁבְעִים	*Cum septuaginta.*	With seventy.
—	בִּשְׁבֻעַת	*Cum juramento [tris*	With an oath.
—	בְּשָׁבֻעֹתֵיכֶם	*In hebdomadibus ves-*	In your weeks.
שבר	בַּשֶּׁבֶר	*Pro annona.*	For the food, the corn.
—	בְּשֶׁבֶר	*In contritione.*	In the bruising, crushing.
—	בְּשִׁבְרוֹן	*Cum fractione.*	With the breaking,
—	בְּשִׁבְרִי	*Confringendo me.*	When I break.
ישב	בְּשֶׁבֶת	*Manendo, habitando.*	In abiding, dwelling.
—	בַּשֶּׁבֶת	*In sede.*	In the seat.
שבת	בַּשַּׁבָּת	*In sabbato.*	On the sabbath.
—	בְּשַׁבַּתּוֹ	*In sabbato ejus.*	In his sabbath.
ישב	בְּשִׁבְתּוֹ	*Sedendo eum.*	While he sits.
שבת	בַּשַּׁבָּתוֹת	*In sabbatis.*	In the sabbaths.
ישב	בְּשִׁבְתִּי	*Residendo me.*	While I abide.
—	בְּשִׁבְתְּךָ	*Sedendo te.*	When thou sittest.
—	בְּשִׁבְתְּכֶם	*Habitando vos.*	When ye dwell.
—	בְּשִׁבְתָּם	*Habitando eos.*	When they dwell.

ROOTS.	DERIVATIVES.	VERSIO.	SIGNIFICATION.
ישב	בְּשִׁבְתֵּנוּ	*Sedendo nos.*	When we sit.
שבת	בְּשַׁבְּתֹתֵיכֶם	*In sabbatis vestris.*	In your sabbaths.
שגג	בִּשְׁגָגָה	*Per errorem.*	By, through error, mistake.
גם	בְּשַׁגָּם	*Eo quod etiam.*	For that also.
שגע	בְּשִׁגָּעוֹן בְּשׁ׳	*In amentia.*	In, with madness.
שדה	בַּשָּׂדֶה בָּ׳	*In, per agrum; in agro, regione.*	Into, through the field, in the field, country.
—	בִּשְׂדֵי	*In agris.*	In the field.
—	בְּשָׂדְךָ־דְךָ	*In agro tuo.*	In thy field.
שדם	בְּשַׁדְמוֹת	*In agris.*	In the fields.
שדף	בַּשִּׁדָּפוֹן	*Cum uredine.*	With blasting.
שדה	בִּשְׂדֹתָם	*In agris eorum.*	In their fields.
שה	בְּשֶׂה	*Per agnum.*	With a lamb.
שהם	בְּשֹׁהַם	*Cum oniche.*	With the onyx.
שוה	בַּשָּׁוְא	*In vanitate.*	In vanity.
בוש	בֹּשׁוּ	*Pudore affecti sunt.*	They were ashamed.
נשא	בְּשׂוֹא	*Elevando.*	In raising, lifting up.
שאה	בְּשׁוֹאָה	*In desolationem.* [do.	Into desolation.
שוב	בְּשׁוּב	*Redeundo, reverten-*	In turning back, returning.
—	בְּשׁוּבְבִי	*Reducendo me.*	When I bring them again.
—	בְּשׁוּבָה	*In conversione.*	In returning.
—	בְּשׁוּבוֹ	*Revertendo eum.*	When he returns.
—	בְּשׁוּבִי	*Redeundo me.*	When I return.
—	בְּשׁוּבְכֶם	*Revertendo vos.*	When ye turn again.
—	בְּשׁוּבֵנִי	*Revertendo me.*	When I returned.
שוט	בְּשׁוֹט	*In flagello.*	In, with the scourge.
—	בַּשֹּׁטִים	*Cum flagellis.*	With whips, scourges.
שול	בְּשׁוּלֶיהָ	*In fimbriis ejus.*	In her skirts.
שום	בְּשׂוּם	*Ponendo.*	In disposing, placing in order.
שום	בְּשׂוּמוֹ	*Ponendo eum.*	When he fixed, appointed.
—	בְּשׂוּמִי	*Ponendo me.*	When I fixed, placed.
שוע	בְּשַׁוְּעִי	*Clamando me.*	When I cry.
שפר	בְּשׁוֹפָר בַּשּׁ׳	*Cum tuba, buccina.*	With the trumpet.
—	בַּשּׁוֹפָרוֹת	*Cum tubis*	With the trumpets.
שוק	בַּשּׁוּק	*In, per vicum,*	In, through the street.
	בְּשׁוֹקָי	*In cruribus.*	In the legs.
—	בַּשְּׁוָקִים	*In vicis.*	In the streets.

ROOTS.	DERIVATIVES.	VERSIO.	SIGNIFICATION.
שור	בְּשׁוֹר	*Cum bove.*	With an ox.
	בְּשׂוֹר	*Besor.*	Besor, N. R.
בשר	בְּשׂוֹרָה	*Nuncius* bonus.	A *good* message.
שור	בְּשׁוּרָי	*In inimicos, invidos.*	Upon enemies.
סור	בְּשׂוּרִי	*Recedendo me.*	When I depart.
שרר	בְּשׁוֹרְרָי	*In hostes meos.*	On my enemies.
ששן	בַּשּׁוֹשַׁנִּים	*Inter lilia.*	Among the lilies.
שחד	בְּשֹׁחַד בְּשֹׁ׳	*In munere.*	In, with a present, bribe.
שחק	בִּשְׂחוֹק	*Ludendo.*	While making sport.
שחת	בִּשְׁחוּתוֹ	*In foveam ejus.*	Into his pit.
שחן	בִּשְׁחִין בַּשְׁ־	*In ulcere.*	In an ulcer.
שחת	בִּשְׁחִיתוֹתָם	*In foveis eorum.*	In their pits.
שחף	בַּשַּׁחֶפֶת	*Cum tabe.*	With a consumption.
שחק	בַּשַּׁחַק	*In cælo.*	In the heaven.
—	בַּשְּׁחָקִים	*In cælis.*	In the heavens.
שחר	בַּשַּׁחַר	*In aurora.*	In a morning.
שחת	בְּשַׁחֵת	*Perdendo.*	In destroying.
—	בְּשַׁחַת בַּ׳ בַּשָּׁ־	*In foveam.*	Into the pit, ditch.
—	בְּשַׁחְתָּם	*In fovea eorum.*	In their pit.
שטף	בְּשֶׁטֶף	*In inundatione.*	With a flood.
שוב	בְּשֵׂיבָה	*In canitie, senectute.*	In hoary hairs, old age.
ישב	בְּשִׁבְתּוֹ	*Manendo eum.*	While he abides.
שיד	בַּשִּׂיד	*Cum calce.*	With mortar, plaister.
שוח	בְּשִׂיחִי	*In sermone meo.*	In my speech.
שיר	בְּשִׁיר בַּשִּׁ־	*Cum cantico.*	With a song.
שכב	בְּשָׁכְבָהּ	*Accumbendo eam.*	When she lies down.
—	בְּשָׁכְבוֹ	*Cubando eum.*	When he lies down.
—	בְּשָׁכְבְּךָ	*Cubando te.*	When thou liest down.
כבר	בְּשֶׁכְּבָר	*In eo quod jam.*	Seeing that which now.
שוך	בְּשֻׂכּוֹת	*In cultris.*	In, with barbed irons.
שכל	בְּשֵׂכֶל	*Cum intellectu.*	With understanding, wisdom.
שכן	בִּשְׁכֹּן	*Habitando.*	While dwelling.
שכר	בַּשֵּׁכָר	*Propter siceram.*	With strong drink.
—	בִּשְׂכָרוֹ	*Pro mercede ejus.*	For his hire.
בָּשַׁל		*Coxit, aquâ coxit, torruit, maturavit.*	He baked, boiled, roasted, broiled, ripened.
	בְּשֶׁל	*Propter.*	Because of.

ROOTS.	DERIVATIVES.	VERSIO.	SIGNIFICATION.
בשל	בְּשֵׁלָה	*Coctus.*	Sodden.
—	בֻּשָּׁלָה	*Cocta est.*	It was sodden.
—	בִּשְּׁלוּ בִּשֽׁ-	*Coxerunt.*	They have sodden.
—	בַּשְּׁלוּ	*Coquite.*	Seethe ye.
שלה	בְּשַׁלְוָה	*In tranquillitate.*	Peaceably.
—	בְּשַׁלְוִי	*In quiete mea.*	In my tranquility.
שלם	בְּשָׁלוֹם בְּשָׁ-	*In pace.*	In peace.
—	בְּשִׁלּוּם	*Pro retributione.*	For a reward.
שלם	בִּשְׁלוֹמָהּ	*In pace ejus.*	In her peace.
שלש	בִּשְׁלוֹשָׁה	*Inter tres; in tertia.*	Among the three; in the third.
שלה	בְּשַׁלְוֹתַיִךְ	*In securitatibus tuis.*	In thy security.
שלח	בַּשֶּׁלַח בְּשֶׁ-	*Per gladium.*	By the sword.
—	בִּשְׁלֹחַ	*Mittendo.*	In sending.
—	בְּשַׁלַּח	*Dimittendo.*	In sending away.
—	בְּשַׁלְּחָהּ	*Emittendo eam.*	When she shoots forth.
—	בְּשַׁלְּחוֹ	*Emittendo eum.*	When he shoots forth.
—	בִּשְׁלֹחִי	*Mittendo me.*	When I send.
—	בְּשַׁלְּחִי	*Emittendo me.*	When I send forth.
—	בְּשַׁלֵּחֲךָ	*Dimittendo te.*	When thou sendest him away.
שלה	בַּשֶּׁלִי	*Secreto.*	Secretly.
	בְּשֶׁלִּי	*Propter me.*	For my sake.
שלש	בַּשְּׁלִישִׁי -שִׁית	*In tertio.*	In the third.
שלל	בַּשָּׁלָל	*In præda.*	Among the spoil.
	בִּשְׁלָם	*Bislam.*	Bishlam, N. M.
שלם	בְּשָׁלֹם בְּשָׁלֹם	*In pace; pacifice.*	In peace; peaceably.
בשל	בִּשְּׁלָם	*Coxit eos.*	He boiled them.
שלם	בַּשַּׂלְמָה בַּשַּׂ-	*Per vestem, cum veste*	By, with the garment.
	בְּשֶׁלְּמִי	*Propter quem.*	For whose sake. [with him.
שלם	בִּשְׁלֹמָיו	*In pacificos ejus.*	Against such as are at peace
—	בְּשַׂלְמָתוֹ	*In vestimento ejus.*	In his raiment.
שלש	בַּשָּׁלִשׁ	*In trientali, mensura*	In a measure.
—	בִּשְׁלֹשׁ	*In tribus.*	In the three.
—	בִּשְׁלֹשָׁה בִּשְׁ-	*Inter tres.*	Among the three.
—	בִּשְׁלֹשִׁים	*In tricesimo.*	In the thirtieth.
—	בַּשְּׁלִשִׁים	*In tertiis.*	In the third.
—	בִּשְׁלֹשִׁים	*In triginta.*	In thirty.
בשם			

ROOTS.	DERIVATIVES.	VERSIO.	SIGNIFICATION.
בשם	בֹּשֶׂם בֶּשֶׂם	*Aroma.* [*tim.*	Sweet spice.
שם	בְּשֵׁם בְּשֵׁ׳	*In nomine ; nomina-*	In, on the name; by name.
שמל	בִּשְׂמֹאולָהּ	*In sinistra ejus.*	In her left hand.
—	בִּשְׂמֹאלוֹ	*In sinistra ejus.*	In his left hand.
שם	בִּשְׁמוֹ	*In nomine ejus.*	In his name.
שמן	בִּשְׁמוֹנָה־־מֹנָה	*Cum octo ; in octavo.*	With eight; in the eighth.
—	בִּשְׁמוֹנִים־־מֹנִ׳	*In octogesimo.*	In the eightieth.
שמע	בִּשְׁמוּעָה	*Ob famam, rumorem*	For the rumour, report.
שמר	בִּשְׁמוֹר	*Observando.*	In observing.
שם	בִּשְׁמוֹת־־מֹת	*Per nomina.*	By names.
שמח	בְּשִׂמְחָה־־חַת	*In, cum lætitia.*	In, with mirth, gladness.
—	בִּשְׂמָחֹת	*In, cum lætitiis.*	In, with joys.
—	בְּשִׂמְחַתְכֶם	*In lætitia vestra.*	In your joy.
בשם	בְּשָׂמִי	*Aroma meum.*	My spice.
שם	בִּשְׁמִי	*In, per nomen meum.*	On, by my name.
—	בִּשְׁמֵי־־מַיִא	*In cœlis.*	In the heavens.
בשם	בְּשָׂמָיו	*Aromata ejus.*	His spices.
שמך	בִּשְׂמִיכָה	*Cum pallio, stragula.*	With a mantle, coverlet, rug.
בשם	בְּשָׂמִים	*Aromata.*	Spices. [heavens.
שם	בַּשָּׁמַיִם	*In cœlos, cœlis.*	Towards, against, into, in the
—	בְּשִׁמְךָ בִּשְׁמֶךָ	*In, per nomen tuum.*	By, through, in, on thy name.
—	בְּשִׁמְכָה	*In nomine tuo.*	In thy name.
שמל	בַּשִּׂמְלָה	*In panno, veste.*	In a cloth, garment.
—	בְּשִׂמְלֹתָם	*In vestibus eorum.*	In their clothes.
שם	בִּשְׁמָם	*Per nomen eorum.*	By their name.
שמם	בְּשִׁמָּמוֹן	*Cum desolatione.*	With desolation.
שמן	בַּשֶּׁמֶן בַּשֶּׁ׳ בְּשֶׁ׳	*In, cum oleo.*	In, with oil.
שמע	בִּשְׁמֹעַ	*Audiendo.*	In hearing.
—	בְּשָׁמְעוֹ	*Audiendo eum.*	When he heareth.
—	בְּשָׁמְעֲךָ	*Audiendo te.*	When thou hearest
—	בְּשָׁמְעֲכֶם	*Audiendo vos.*	When ye hear.
—	בְּשָׁמְעָם	*Audiendo eos.*	When they hear.
שמר	בְּשָׁמְרָם	*Observando eos.*	In keeping them.
שמש	בַּשֶּׁמֶשׁ	*Per sol.*	By the sun.
	בָּשְׂמַת	*Basemath.*	Bashemath, N. W.
שם	בִּשְׁמֹתָם	*Per nomina eorum.*	By their names.
	בָּשָׁן	*Basan.*	Bashan, N. P.

ROOTS.	DERIVATIVES.	VERSIO.	SIGNIFICATION.
שן	בְּשֵׁן	*Pro dente.*	For a tooth.
שנא	בְּשִׂנְאָה	*Per odium.*	Through hatred.
—	בְּשֹׂנְאַי	*In osores meos.*	Towards them who hate me.
—	בְּשֹׂנְאֵיהֶם	*In osores eorum.*	Towards those who hate them.
—	בְּשִׂנְאַת	*Propter odium.*	For hatred.
שנה	בְּשָׁנָה בַּשָּׁ׳	*In, per annum.*	In, by a year.
בוש	בָּשְׁנָה	*Pudor.*	Shame.
—	בֹּשְׁנוּ	*Pudore affecti sumus*	We were ashamed.
שנה	בְּשַׁנּוֹתוֹ	*Mutando eum.*	When he changes.
—	בַּשֵּׁנִי	*In secundo.*	In the second.
—	בִּשְׁנֵי	*In duobus.*	In the two.
שן	בְּשִׁנָּי	*Cum dentibus meis.*	With my teeth.
—	בְּשִׁנֵּיהֶם	*Cum dentibus eorum.*	With their teeth.
—	בְּשִׁנָּיו	*Cum dentibus ejus.*	With his teeth.
שנה	בִּשְׁנַיִם־־נֵים	*Cum duobus.*	With two.
—	בַּשָּׁנִים	*In annis.*	In years.
—	בִּשְׁנַת בַּשְּׁנַת	*In anno* [*conculcavit*	In the year. [upon.
בָּשַׁס		*Oneravit, fatigavit,*	He loaded, wearied, trampled
שעל	בְּשָׁעֳלוֹ	*In pugillo ejus.*	In the hollow of his hand.
—	בְּשַׁעֲלֵי	*Pro pugillis.*	For handfuls.
שעף	בִּשְׂעִפִּים	*In cogitationibus.*	In thoughts.
שער	בַּשַּׁעַר בְּשַׁ׳	*In, ad, per portam.*	To, into, in, through the gate.
—	בִּשְׂעָרָה	*In turbine.*	In a storm, tempest.
—	בְּשַׁעֲרֵי	*In portas.*	Into the gates.
—	בִּשְׁעָרֶיהָ	*In portis ejus.*	In her gates.
—	בִּשְׁעָרֶיךָ־־רַיִךְ	*In portis tuis.*	In thy gates.
—	בִּשְׁעָרֵיכֶם	*In portis vestris.*	In your gates.
—	בַּשְּׁעָרִים	*Per portas.*	Through the gates.
שפה	בְּשָׂפָה	*Per labium.*	With the lip.
שפח	בְּשִׁפְחָתֶךָ	*Ad ancillam tuam.*	To thy handmaid.
שפט	בִּשְׁפָטִים	*Per judicia.*	By judgments.
—	בְּשָׁפְטֶךָ	*Judicando te.*	When thou judgest.
שפך	בִּשְׁפֹּךְ	*Effundendo.*	In pouring out.
—	בְּשָׁפְכֵךְ	*Effundendo te.*	When thou pourest out.
שפל	בְּשֵׁפֶל	*In humilitate.*	In meanness, a low state.
—	בְּשֵׁפֶל	*In humilitate.*	In a low or feeble state.
—	בַּשְּׁפֵלָה	*In valle, planitie.*	In the valley, the plain.

ROOTS.	DERIVATIVES.	VERSIO.	SIGNIFICATION.
שפק	בְּשֶׂפֶק	*Cum plaga, ictu.*	With a stroke.
שפר	בִּשְׁפַרְפָּרָא	*Diluculo.*	In the morning.
שפה	בִּשְׂפַת	*In ora.*	In the edge, side.
—	בְּשִׂפְתוֹתֵיהֶם	*In labiis eorum.*	In their lips.
—	בְּשִׂפְתוֹתֶיךָ	*In labia tua.*	Into thy lips.
—	בְּשִׂפְתֵי	*In labiis.*	In the lips.
—	בִּשְׂפָתַי	*In labiis meis.*	In my lips.
—	בִּשְׂפָתָיו־־תָו	*Per labia ejus.*	With his lips.
—	בִּשְׂפָתֶיךָ	*In labiis tuis.*	In thy lips.
—	בִּשְׂפָתַיִם	*Per labia.*	With lips.
שצף	בְּשֶׁצֶף	*Cum modico.*	With a little.
שק	בַּשָּׂק	*Cum sacco, cilicio.*	With sackcloth.
—	בְּשַׂקּוֹ	*In sacco ejus.*	In his sack.
—	בַּשַּׂקִּים	*Cum saccis.*	With sackcloths.
שקל	בְּשֶׁקֶל	*Juxta siclum.*	After, according to the shekel.
שקר	בְּשֶׁקֶר בַּשֶּׁ׳	*In falsitate.*	In, with falsehood.
—	בְּשִׁקְרֵיהֶם	*Per mendacia eorum*	By their lies.
שקה	בְּשִׁקֲתוֹת	*In aquariis.* [*ciavit.*	In the watering troughs. [ings.
בִּשֵּׂר		*Nunciavit, annun-*	He brought tidings, good tid-
—	בִּשַּׂר	*Nunciavit.*	He brought tidings.
—	בָּשָׂר בְּשַׂר	*Caro.*	Flesh.
—	בִּשְׂרָא	*Caro.*	Flesh.
שרד	בַּשֶּׂרֶד	*Cum linea, amussi.*	With a line.
בשר	בְּשָׂרָהּ	*Caro ejus.* [*nuncii.*	Her flesh. [tidings.
—	בְּשֹׂרָה	*Nuncium, præmium*	A message, the reward of
—	בַּשְּׂרוּ	*Annunciate.*	Shew forth, declare ye.
—	בְּשָׂרוֹ	*Caro ejus.*	His flesh.
שור	בְּשָׁהוֹתֶיהָ	*In muros ejus.*	Upon her walls.
בשר	בְּשָׂרִי	*Caro mea.*	My flesh.
שור	בַּשִּׁרִים	*Cum canticis.*	With songs.
—	בְּשָׂרִים	*In principes.*	Over princes.
בשר	בְּשָׂרִים	*Carnes.*	Flesh.
שרר	בִּשְׁרִירוּת־־רִר׳	*In contemplations.*	In the imagination.
—	בְּשָׁרִירֵי	*In umbilicis.*	In the navels.
בשר	בְּשָׂרְךָ־־רֶךָ	*Caro tua.*	Thy flesh.
—	בְּשַׂרְכֶם	*Caro vestra.*	Your flesh.
—	בְּשָׂרָם	*Caro eorum.*	Their flesh.

ROOTS.	DERIVATIVES.	VERSIO.	SIGNIFICATION.
בשר	בְּשָׂרֵנוּ	*Caro nostra.*	Our flesh.
שרץ	בַּשֶּׁרֶץ	*Inter reptile.*	Among the creeping things.
שרש	בַּשַּׁרְשְׁרוֹת	*In catenas.*	On the chains.
בשר	בִּשַּׂרְתִּי	*Annunciavi.*	I have published.
שרת	בְּשָׁרְתָם	*Ministrando illos.*	While they minister.
בשש			
—	בֹּשֵׁשׁ	*Moratus est.*	He delayed.
שש	בַּשֵּׁשׁ	*In bysso.*	In, with fine linen.
ששה	בְּשֵׁשׁ	*In, cum, pro sex.*	In, with, for six.
שוש	בְּשָׂשׂוֹן	*In gaudio.*	In, with joy.
ששה	בַּשִּׁשִּׁי	*In sexto.*	In the sixth.
ששר	בַּשָּׁשַׁר	*Cum minio.*	With vermilion, or red paint.
בוש	בֹּשֶׁת	*Pudor.*	Shame.
—	בֹּשְׁתְּ	*Pudore affecta es.*	Thou wast ashamed.
שנה	בִּשְׁתֵּי	*In, pro duobus.*	In, for two. [warp.
שתה	בִּשְׁתִי בִּשְׁ׳׳	*In potatione, stamine*	In excessive drinking, in the
בוש	בֹּשְׁתִּי	*Erubui, confusus sum.*	I was ashamed.
שנה	בִּשְׁתַּיִם־־תֵּים	*In, cum, pro duobus.*	In, with, for two.
בוש	בָּשְׁתְּכֶם	*Pudor vester.*	Your shame.
—	בָּשְׁתָּם	*Pudor eorum.*	Their shame.

בת

ROOTS.	DERIVATIVES.	VERSIO.	SIGNIFICATION.
בת			
בבה	בָת	*Pupilla.* [quidorum	The pupil of the eye.
בת	בַת	*Bathus*, mensura li-	Bath, *a measure.*
בנה	בַּת	*Filia, cœtus.*	A daughter, the company.
—	בַּת אֵל נֵכָר	*Filia dei alieni, idololatrix.*	The daughter of a strange god, an idolatress.
—	בַּת הַיַּעֲנָה	*Struthiocamelus.*	An ostrich.
	בַּת רַבִּים	*Bath-rabbin.*	Bath-rabbin, N. P.
	בַּת שֶׁבַע	*Bath-seba.*	Bath-sheba, N. W.
	בַּת שׁוּעַ	*Bath-sua.*	Bath-shua, N. W.
בנה	בַּת שְׁנָתָהּ	*Annicula.*	In her first year.
תאן	בַּתְּאֵנָה בַּתְ׳	*In ficu.*	In the fig-tree.
תבה	בַּתֵּבָה	*In arca.*	In the ark.
בוא	בַּתְּבוּאֹת	*In proventibus.*	In the produce, the revenues.

ROOTS.	DERIVATIVES.	VERSIO.	SIGNIFICATION.
בון	בִּתְבוּנָה	*In intelligentia.*	In understanding.
—	בִּתְבוּנָם	*Pro intellectu eorum*	According to their understanding.
תבל	בְּתֵבֵל	*In orbe.*	In the habitable part.
בנה	בְּתַבְנִית	*In similitudinem.*	Into the similitude.
—	בְּתַבְנִיתָם	*In formam eorum.*	After their pattern, form.
תדר	בִּתְדִירָא	*Continuo.*	Continually.
בת	בָּתָה	*Desolatio.*	Desolation.
בנה	בִּתָּהּ	*Filia ejus.*	Her daughter.
תהה	בַּתֹּהוּ	*In nihilum.*	To nothing.
—	בְּתֹהוּ	*In deserto.*	In a wilderness.
הלל	בִּתְהִלָּה	*Cum laude.*	With praise.
—	בִּתְהִלָּתֶךָ	*In laude tua.*	In thy praise.
תהם	בַּתְּהֹמוֹת	*Per abyssos.*	Through the depths, abysses.
הפך	בְּתַהְפֻּכוֹת	*In perversitatibus.*	In the frowardness.
בנה	בִּתּוֹ	*Filia ejus.*	His daughter.
	בְּתוּאֵל	*Bethuel.*	Bethuel, N. M.
ידה	בְּתוֹדָה	*Cum laude, confessione.*	With praise, confession.
תוך	בְּתָוֶךְ	*In medio.*	In the midst.
—	בְּתוֹךְ	*In medium.*	Into the midst.
—	בְּתוֹכָהּ־־כה	*In medio ejus.*	In the midst of her.
—	בְּתוֹכְהֶנָה	*In medio earum.*	In the midst of them.
—	בְּתוֹכוֹ	*In medio ejus.*	In the midst of him.
יכח	בְּתוֹכָחוֹת־־כ׳	*Cum increpationibus.*	With rebukes.
—	בְּתוֹכַחְתּוֹ	*In castigatione ejus.*	In his correction.
תוך	בְּתוֹכִי	*In medio mei.*	Within me.
—	בְּתוֹכֵךְ	*In medio tui.*	In the midst of thee.
—	בְּתוֹכֵכִי	*In medium tui.*	Into the midst of thee.
—	בְּתוֹכְכֶם־־כְּכֶם	*In medio vestrûm.*	In the midst of you.
—	בְּתוֹכָם־־ת׳	*In medio eorum.*	In the midst of them.
—	בְּתוֹכֵנוּ	*In medio nostrûm.*	In the midst of us.
	בְּתוּל	*Bethul.*	Bethul, N. P.
בתל	בְּתוּלָה	*Virgo.*	A virgin.
—	בְּתוּלוֹת בְּתֻלֹת	*Virgines.*	Virgins.
—	בְּתוּלַי	*Virginitas mea.*	My virginity.
—	בְּתוּלַי	*Virginitas.*	The virginity.
—	בְּתוּלֶיהָ	*Virginitas ejus.*	Her virginity.
—	בְּתוּלֵיהֶן	*Virginitas earum.*	Their virginity.

ROOTS.	DERIVATIVES.	VERSIO.	SIGNIFICATION.
בתל	בְּתוּלִים	Virginitas. [no.	Virginity.
תלע	בְּתוֹלַעַת	In vermiculo, cocci-	In scarlet or crimson.
בתל	בְּתוּלַת	Virgo.	The virgin.
—	בְּתוּלֹתַי	Virgines meæ.	My virgins.
—	בְּתוּלֹתֶיהָ	Virgines ejus.	Her virgins.
תמם	בְּתֻמּוֹ	In integritate [suus.	In uprightness.
תעב	בְּתוֹעֲבוֹתָם	Per abominationes	By their abominations.
—	בְּתוֹעֵבֹת	Per abominationes.	With abominations.
—	בְּתוֹעֲבֹתֵיהֶם	Per abominationes eorum.	By their abominations.
ירה	בַּתּוֹרָה	In lege. [marum.	In the law.
תור	בַּתּוֹרִים	Inter ordines gem-	With rows *of jewels.*
ירה	בְּתוֹרַת	In lege.	In the law.
—	בְּתוֹרָתוֹ	In lege ejus.	In his law.
—	בְּתוֹרָתִי	In lege mea.	In my law.
—	בְּתוֹרֹתָיו	In legibus ejus	In his laws.
זנה	בְּתַזְנוּתַיִךְ	In scortationibus tuis	In thy whoredoms.
—	בְּתַזְנוּתָם	In scortatione eorum	In, with their whoredom.
חבל	בְּתַחְבּוּלֹתָו	Per consilia ejus. [tia	By his counsels.
—	בְּתַחְבֻּלוֹת	Per consilia pruden-	By wise counsels.
חלה	בְּתַחֲלֻאִים	In morbis.	In diseases.
חלל	בַּתְּחִלָּה	In principio, primo	In the beginning, at the first.
—	בִּתְחִלַּת	In principio.	At the beginning.
תחת	בְּתַחְתִּיּוֹת	In ima, imis.	Into, in the lowest parts.
—	בְּתַחְתִּית	In infimo.	In the lowest.
בנה	בִּתִּי	Filia mea.	My daughter.
בית	בָּתֵּי	Domus.	The houses.
	בִּתְיָה	Bithia.	Bithia, N. W.
בית	בָּתֵּיהֶם	Domus eorum.	Their houses.
—	בָּתָּיו	Domus ejus.	His houses.
—	בָּתֶּיךָ בָּתַּיִךְ	Domus tuæ.	Thy houses.
—	בָּתֵּיכֶם	Domus vestræ.	Your houses.
—	בָּתִּים	Domus, loca, cortinæ	Houses, places, hangings.
בת	בַּתִּים בַּתִּין	Bathi, mensur.	Baths, measr.
בית	בָּתֵּימוֹ	Domus eorum.	Their houses.
—	בָּתֵּינוּ	Domus nostræ.	Our houses.
בנה	בִּתֵּךְ	Filia tua.	Thy daughter.

ROOTS.	DERIVATIVES.	VERSIO.	SIGNIFICATION.
תוך	בְּתֹכְכֶם	*In medio vestrûm.*	In the midst of you.
תכל	בַּתְּכֵלֶת	*In hyacintho.*	In blue, or violet.
בתל			
—	בְּתוּלוֹת	*Virgines.*	Virgins.
תלם	בַּתֶּלֶם	*In sulco.*	In the furrows.
תמם	בְּתֹם בְּתָמִים	*In integritate.*	In uprightness.
תמה	בְּתִמָּהוֹן	*In stupore.*	In, with astonishment.
תמם	בְּתֻמּוֹ בְּתֻמָּתוֹ	*In integritate ejus.*	In his uprightness.
—	בְּתֻמִּי	*In integritate mea.*	In my integrity.
תמר	בְּתָמָר	*In palmam.*	To the palm tree.
תמם	בְּתֻמָּתֶךָ	*In integritate tua.*	In thine integrity.
בנה	בִּתֵּנוּ	*Filia nostra.*	Our daughter.
נום	בִּתְנוּמוֹת	*In dormitationibus.*	In slumberings.
תנר	בְּתַנּוּר בַּתַּ־	*In furno.*	In the oven.
תעה	בִּתְעוֹת	*Errando.*	In going astray.
עלה	בַּתְּעָלָה	*In fossa, aquæductu.*	In the trench, water-course.
עלל	בְּתַעֲלוּלֵיהֶם	*In illusionibus eorum*	In their delusions.
עלה	בִּתְעָלַת	*In aquæductu.*	In, by the conduit.
ענג	בְּתַעֲנוּגִים	*In deliciis.* [*pello.*	In delights.
תער	בְּתַעַר	*Cum novacula, scal-*	With a razor, knife.
—	בְּתַעְרָהּ	*In vagina ejus.*	In her sheath.
תפף	בְּתֹף	*In tympano.*	On the tabret, timbrel.
תפח	בַּתַּפּוּחִים	*Cum malis.*	With apples.
תפף	בְּתֻפִּים	*Cum tympanis.*	With timbrels.
פלל	בִּתְפִלָּה	*In oratione.*	In prayer.
—	בִּתְפִלַּת	*In orationem.*	Against the prayer.
תפש	בְּתָפְשָׂם	*Apprehendendo eos.*	When they take hold.
בָּתַק		*Confodit, transfixit.*	He stabbed, thrust through.
תקע	בִּתְקוֹעַ	*Cum tuba.*	With the trumpet.
—	בְּתֵקַע	*Cum clangore* tubæ.	With the sound *of a trumpet.*
—	בְּתֹקְעֵי	*Cum percutientibus.*	With them that strike.
תקף	בְּתֹקֶף	*In robore.*	In the strength.
—	בְּתֹקֶף	*Cum robore.*	With the strength.
בָּתַר		*Dissecuit, divisit.*	He cut in two, divided.
—	בָּתַר	*Divisit.*	He divided.
	בֶּתֶר	*Bether.*	Bether, N. P.
בתר	בִּתְרוֹ	*Pars ejus.*	His part, piece.

ROOTS.	DERIVATIVES.	VERSIO.	SIGNIFICATION.
	בִּתְרוֹן	*Bithron.*	Bithron, N. P.
רום	בִּתְרוּמַת	*De oblatione.*	Of an offering.
רוע	בִּתְרוּעָה	*Cum clangore.*	With shouting.
בתר	בְּתָרֵי	*Partes.*	The parts.
—	בְּתָרָיו	*Partes ejus.*	His parts.
רמה	בְּתַרְמִית	*In dolo.*	In deceit.
תרע	בְּתָרַע	*In porta.*	In the gate.
תרף	בַּתְּרָפִים	*Cum imaginibus.*	With images.
רשש	בַּתַּרְשִׁישׁ	*In beryllo.*	In, with the beryl.
שום	בִּתְשׂוּמֶת	*In positione.*	In the placing, putting.
תשע	בְּתִשְׁעָה	*In nona.*	On the ninth.
נתן	בְּתֵת	*Dando, tradendo.*	In giving, delivering.
—	בְּתִתּוֹ	*Dando eum.*	When he gives.
—	בְּתִתִּי	*Dando me.*	When I give.
—	בְּתִתְּךָ	*Dando te.*	When thou givest.
—	בְּתִתָּם	*Ponendo eos.*	In their setting, placing.
	גא		
גאה	גֵּא גֵּאֶה	*Superbus.*	Proud.
גָּאָה		*Extulit se, magnificentiam exercuit, ascendit, crevit.*	He lifted up himself, displayed magnificence, ascended, grew.
—	גֵּאָה גַּאֲוָה	*Superbia.*	Pride.
—	גָּאוּ	*Ascenderunt.*	They rose, ascended.
—	גְּאֹה	*Excellere.*	To excel.
	גְּאוּאֵל	*Gheuel.*	Geuel, N. M.
גאל	גְּאוּלַי.	*Redempti mei.*	My redeemed.
—	גְּאוּלֵי	*Redempti.*	The redeemed.
—	גְּאוּלִים	*Redempti.*	The redeemed.
גאה	גְּאוֹן גָּאוֹן	*Superbia, fastus, excellentia, gloria.*	Pride, pomp, excellency, majesty.
—	גְּאוֹנוֹ גְּאֹנוֹ	*Excellentia ejus.*	His excellency, majesty.
—	גְּאוֹנֶיךָ	*Gloriæ tuæ.*	Thy glories.
—	גְּאוֹנְךָ־נֶךָ	*Magnitudo tua.*	Thy greatness
—	גְּאוֹנָם	*Superbia eorum.*	Their pride.

ROOTS.	DERIVATIVES.	VERSIO.	SIGNIFICATION.
גאה	גֵּאוּת גַּאֲוָת	*Elatio, excellentia, gloria, superbia.*	A lifting up, excellency, majesty, glory, pride.
—	גַּאֲוָתוֹ	*Fastus, gloria ejus.*	His pride, glory.
—	גַּאֲוָתִי	*Gloria mea.*	My glory.
—	גַּאֲוָתְךָ־תֵךְ	*Excellentia tua.*	Thy excellency.
גיא	גֵּאָיוֹת	*Valles.*	The valleys.
גאה	גֵּאִים	*Superbi.*	The proud.
גָּאַל		*Asseruit, eripuit, liberavit, redemit, vindicavit, polluit, inquinavit.*	He claimed, challenged, rescued, delivered, redeemed, avenged, polluted, defiled.
—	גְּאֹל	*Redimere.*	To redeem.
—	גְּאַל	*Redime.* [*tor, vindex*	Redeem thou. [avenger.
—	גֹּאֵל גּוֹאֵל	*Redimens, redemp-*	Redeeming, a redeemer, an
—	גְּאָלָהּ	*Redime eam.*	Redeem thou her.
—	גְּאֻלָּה	*Redemptio.*	Redemption.
—	גֹּאֲלוֹ	*Redemptor ejus.*	His redeemer.
—	גֹּאֲלִי	*Redemptor meus.*	My redeemer.
—	גָּאֳלֵי	*Pollutiones.*	The pollutions.
—	גֹּאֲלֵךְ־לְךָ	*Redemptor tuus.*	Thy redeemer.
—	גֹּאַלְכֶם	*Redemptor vester.*	Your redeemer.
—	גְּאָלָם	*Redemit eos.*	He redeemed them.
—	גֹּאֲלָם	*Redemptor eorum.*	Their redeemer.
—	גֹּאֲלֵנוּ	*Redemptor noster.*	Our redeemer.
—	גֵּאַלְנוּךָ	*Polluimus te.*	We have polluted thee.
—	גְּאֻלַּת	*Redemptio.*	Redemption.
—	גָּאַלְתָּ	*Redemisti.*	Thou hast redeemed.
—	גְּאֻלָּתוֹ	*Redemptio ejus.*	His redemption.
—	גְּאֻלָּתִי	*Vindiciæ meæ.*	My claim.
—	גְּאַלְתִּיךָ	*Redemi te.*	I have redeemed thee.
—	גְּאֻלָּתְךָ	*Vindiciæ tuæ.*	Thy claim.
	גב		
גבב	גַּב	*Dorsum, altitudo.*	The back, height. [vault.
—	גֶּב	*Excelsum, fornix.*	A high place, arched room,
	גֹּב	*Gob.*	Gob, N. P.
נבא			

ROOTS.	DERIVATIVES.	VERSIO.	SIGNIFICATION.
גבא	גֶּבֶא	*Lacuna, palus, fossa*	A pit, pond, pool, ditch.
גבב			
גָּבַהּ		*Extulit, exaltavit, altus est, superbivit.*	He raised up, exalted, was high, tall, lofty, proud.
—	גֹּבַהּ	*Altitudo.* [*titudo.*	Height.
—	גָּבֹהַּ	*Altus, sublimis; al-*	High, lofty; height.
—	גֹּבַהּ	*Altitudo, fastus.*	Height, haughtiness.
—	גָּבְהָא	*Elevata est.*	She was exalted.
—	גְּבֹהָה	*Altus, elevatus.*	High, exalted.
—	גָּבְהוֹ	*Altitudo ejus.*	His height.
—	גָּבְהוּ	*Insuperbierunt, altiores fuerunt.*	They were haughty, were higher.
—	גְּבֹהוֹת	*Excelsa.*	High.
—	גַּבְהוּת	*Elatio.*	The loftiness.
—	גָּבְהֵי	*Altitudines.*	Highest.
—	גְּבֹהִים	*Elati.*	The high, lofty.
—	גָּבַהְתָּ	*Extulisti te.*	Thou hast lifted up thyself.
גבל	גְּבוּל	*Terminus.*	A border, coast, boundary.
—	גְּבוּלָהּ	*Terminus ejus.*	Her border.
—	גְּבוּלוֹ	*Terminus ejus.*	His border.
—	גְּבוּלוֹת גְּבֻלֹת	*Termini.*	The borders.
—	גְּבוּלִי	*Terminus meus.*	My border.
—	גְּבוּלֶיהָ	*Termini ejus.*	Her borders.
—	גְּבוּלֶיךָ	*Termini tui.*	Thy borders.
—	גְּבוּלְךָ — לְךָ — לֶךָ	*Terminus tuus.*	Thy border.
—	גְּבוּלְכֶם גְּבֻלְ־	*Terminus vester.*	Your border.
—	גְּבוּלָם	*Terminus eorum.*	Their border.
—	גְּבוּלָן	*Terminus earum.*	Their border.
גבר	גִּבּוֹר גִּבֹּר	*Fortis, potens; vir.*	Valiant, mighty; a man.
—	גְּבוּרָה	*Robur, potentia.*	Strength, might, power.
—	גְּבוּרוֹת	*Vires, potentiæ.*	Powers, strength.
—	גִּבּוֹרֵי גִּבֹּרֵי	*Fortes, potentes; viri*	Valiant, mighty men; men.
—	גִּבֹּרַי	*Potentes mei.*	My mighty men.
—	גִּבּוֹרֶיהָ	*Potentes ejus.*	Her mighty men.
—	גִּבּוֹרֵיהוּ	*Potentes ejus.*	His mighty men.
—	גִּבּוֹרָיו	*Potentes ejus.*	His mighty men.
—	גִּבּוֹרֶיךָ	*Potentes tui.*	Thy mighty men.

ROOTS.	DERIVATIVES.	VERSIO.	SIGNIFICATION.
גבר	גִּבּוֹרִים גִּבֹּרִים	*Fortes, potentes.*	Valiant, mighty men.
—	גִּבּוֹרָם	*Fortis eorum.*	Their champion.
—	גְּבוּרָתוֹ	*Robur, potentia ejus.*	His strength, might.
—	גְּבוּרֹתָיו־תָו	*Potentiæ ejus.*	His mighty acts.
—	גְּבוּרָתֶךָ	*Potentia tua.*	Thy power.
—	גְּבוּרַתְכֶם	*Robur vestrum.*	Your strength.
—	גְּבוּרָתָם	*Potentia eorum.*	Their power.
גבח			
—	גִּבֵּחַ	*Recalvaster.*	One whose forehead is bald.
	גַּבַּי	*Gabbai.*	Gabbai, N. M.
גבב	גַּבֵּי	*Umbones.*	Bosses.
—	גַּבִּי	*Dorsum meum.*	My back.
גוב	גֹּבַי	*Locustæ.*	Locusts.
גבב	גַּבֵּיהָ	*Dorsum ejus.*	Her back.
—	גַּבֵּיכֶם	*Eminentiæ vestræ.*	Your eminences.
גבא	גֵּבִים	*Fossæ, putei.*	Ditches, pits, wells.
גוב	גֵּבִים	*Locustæ.*	Locusts.
	גֵּבִים	*Ghebim.*	Gebim, N. P.
גבע	גְּבִיעַ	*Calix.*	A cup.
—	גְּבִיעִי	*Calix meus.*	My cup.
—	גְּבִיעֶיהָ	*Calices ejus.*	His bowls.
גבר	גְּבִיר	*Dominus.* [*nix tua.*	Lord. [room.
גבב	גַּבֵּךְ	*Excelsum tuum, for-*	Thy high place, thy arched
גָּבַל		*Limitem constituit, fines posuit, terminavit.*	He set up a boundary, set bounds to, terminated, limited.
—	גְּבֻל	*Terminus.*	A border.
	גְּבָל	*Ghebal.*	Gebal, N. P.
גבל	גְּבֻלוֹ	*Terminus ejus.*	His border.
—	גָּבְלוּ	*Constituerunt.*	They have set.
	גִּבְלִים	*Ghiblii.*	Giblites, N. P.
גבל	גְּבֻלְךָ־לֶךָ	*Terminus tuus.*	Thy border.
—	גְּבֻלַת	*Terminus.*	The border.
—	גְּבֻלָתוֹ	*Terminus ejus.*	His border.
גבן			
—	גִּבֵּן	*Gibbosus.*	Crook-backed.
—	גַּבְנֻנִּים	*Eminentes.*	High.

ROOTS.	DERIVATIVES.	VERSIO.	SIGNIFICATION.
גבע			
	גֶּבַע גָּבַע	*Gaba.*	Gaba, N. P.
	גֶּבַע בִּנְיָמִן	*Ghibea-benjamin.*	Gibeah-benjamin, N. P.
	גִּבְעָא גִּבְעָה	*Ghibea.*	Gibea, Gibeah, N. P.
גבע	גִּבְעָה	*Collis.*	The hill.
	גִּבְעוֹן	*Ghibeon.*	Gibeon, N. M. P.
	גִּבְעֹנִי־־נִים	*Ghibeonitæ.*	Gibeonites, N. P.
גבע	גִּבְעוֹת גְּבָעוֹת	*Colles.*	Hills, the hills.
—	גִּבְעוֹתֶיךָ	*Colles tui.*	Thy hills.
—	גְּבִעִים	*Calices.*	Cups.
גבעל	גִּבְעֹל	*In culmo.*	Bolled, risen in a stalk.
גבע	גִּבְעַת	*Collis.*	The hill.
	גִּבְעַת שָׁאוּל	*Ghibbath-saul.*	Gibeath-saul, N. P.
גבע	גִּבְעָתָהּ	*Collis ejus.*	Her hill.
—	גִּבְעָתִי	*Collis meus.*	My hill.
	גִּבְעָתִי	*Ghibbathita.*	Gibeathite, N. P.
גָּבַר		*Corroboravit, confirmavit, accrevit, prævaluit, superavit, excelluit.*	He strengthened, confirmed, established, increased, prevailed, excelled, surpassed.
גבר	גֶּבֶר גָּבֶר גְּבַר	*Vir.*	A man, the man.
	גֶּבֶר	*Gheber.*	Geber, N. M.
	גִּבָּר	*Ghibbar.*	Gibbar, N. P.
—	גָּבְרוּ	*Accreverunt, prævaluerunt.*	They increased, prevailed.
—	גָּבֵרוּ	*Fortiores fuerunt.*	They were stronger.
—	גִּבָּרֵי	*Fortes, potentes.*	Valiant, mighty men.
—	גֻּבְרַיָּא	*Viri.*	Men.
	גַּבְרִיאֵל	*Gabriel,* nomen angeli.	Gabriel, *the name of an angel.*
גבר	גְּבָרִים גֻּבְרִין	*Fortes, potentes; viri*	Valiant, mighty men; men.
—	גְּבֶרֶת גְּבָרֶת	*Domina.*	A lady, mistress.
—	גְּבִרְתָּהּ	*Domina ejus.*	Her mistress.
—	גְּבִרְתִּי	*Domina mea.*	My mistress.
—	גְּבֻרָתִי גְּבוּרָתִי	*Potentia mea.*	My power.
—	גְּבִרְתֵּךְ	*Domina tua.*	Thy mistress.
גבש			
גבב	גַּבֹּת	*Supercilia.*	Brows.
	גִּבְּתוֹן	*Ghibbethon.*	Gibbethon, N. P.

ROOTS.	DERIVATIVES.	VERSIO.	SIGNIFICATION.
	גג		
גג			
—	גַּג גָּג	*Tectum.*	The roof, top of the house.
—	גַּגּוֹ	*Tectum.*	His roof.
—	גַּגּוֹת	*Tecta.*	House-tops.
—	גַּגּוֹתֶיהָ	*Tecta ejus.*	Her roofs.
—	גַּגּוֹתֵיהֶם גַּגֹּתֵ׳	*Tecta eorum.*	Their roofs.
	גד		
	גָּד	*Gad.*	Gad, N. M. T.
גדד	גַּד	*Coriandrum.*	Coriander.
גדבר	גְּדָבְרַיָּא	*Quæstores.*	Treasurers.
	גִּדְגָּד	*Gadgad.*	Gidgad, N. P.
	גֻּדְגֹּדָה	*Gudgoda.*	Gudgodah, N. P.
גָּדַד		*Turmatim convenit, invasit; vastavit; seipsum incidit, laceravit.*	He gathered troops, invaded with troops; laid waste, depopulated; cut, mangled himself.
גדד	גְּדֻדֹת	*Incisiones.*	Incisions, cuttings.
גדה			
	גַּדָּה	*Gadda.*	Gaddah, N. P.
גדד	גֹּדּוּ	*Succidite.*	Hew down, cut ye down.
—	גְּדוּד	*Turma, exercitus.*	A, the troop, band, army.
—	גְּדוּדֶהָ	*Sulci ejus.*	Her furrows.
—	גְּדוּדֵי	*Turmæ, agmina.*	The bands, armies.
—	גְּדוּדָיו	*Exercitus ejus.*	His troops.
—	גְּדוּדִים	*Turmæ, latrones.*	Companies, troops of robbers.
גדל	גָּדוֹל גָּדֹל	*Magnus, grandis, multus, vehemens.*	Great, mighty, much, vehement.
—	גְּדוֹלָה גְּדֹלָה	*Magna.*	Great.
—	גְּדוֹלֵי	*Magnates.*	The great men.
—	גְּדוֹלֶיהָ	*Magnates ejus.*	Her great men.
—	גְּדוֹלִים גְּדֹ׳	*Magni.*	Great.
—	גְּדוֹלָם	*Maximus eorum.*	The greatest of them.
—	גְּדוֹלֹת גְּדֹלוֹת	*Magnæ.*	Great.
—	גְּדוּלָּתוֹ	*Magnificentia ejus.*	His majesty.

ROOTS.	DERIVATIVES.	VERSIO.	SIGNIFICATION.
גדע	גְּדוּעָה	*Abscissa est.*	She was cut off.
גדה	גְּדוֹתָיו	*Ripæ ejus.*	His banks.
	גָּדִי גַּדִּי	*Gaddi.*	Gaddi, N. M.
גדה	גְּדִי	*Hædus.*	A kid.
	גָּדִי	*Gaditæ.*	Gadites, N. T.
	גַּדִּיאֵל	*Gadiel.*	Gadiel, N. M.
גדה	גְּדָיֵי־־יִים	*Hædi.*	Kids.
גדש	גָּדִישׁ	*Meta frumenti; tumulus*	A shock of corn; the tomb.
גדה	גְּדִיֹתָיו	*Ripæ ejus.*	His banks.
—	גְּדִיֹּתַיִךְ	*Capellæ tuæ.*	Thy kids.
	גִּדֵּל	*Ghiddel.*	Giddel, N. M.
גָּדַל		*Magnus fuit, crevit, major evasit, ditatus est, enutrivit, educavit, magnifecit, grandem fecit, extulit se, superbivit, gloriatus est.*	He was great, grew, increased, became greater, was enriched, nourished, brought up, highly esteemed, made great, exalted himself, became proud, triumphed.
—	גַּדֵּל	*Crescere sinere.*	To let grow.
—	גָּדֹל	*Magnus.*	Great.
—	גִּדַּל	*Magnificavit.*	He magnified.
—	גִּדֵּל	*Educavit.*	He brought up, nourished.
—	גֹּדֶל	*Magnitudo.*	Greatness.
—	גָּדְלָה	*Crevit, magna fuit.*	She grew up, was great.
—	גִּדֵּלָה	*Enutrivit.*	She nourished, brought up.
—	גָּדְלוּ	*Adoleverunt, magni fuerunt.*	They grew up, were great.
—	גַּדְּלוּ	*Magnificate.*	Magnify ye.
—	גִּדְּלוֹ	*Magnificavit eum.*	He advanced, promoted him.
—	גָּדְלוֹ	*Magnitudo ejus*	His greatness.
—	גִּדְּלוּהוּ	*Crescere fecerunt eum*	They made him grow.
—	גְּדֹלוֹת	*Maximæ res.*	Very great things.
—	גְּדֹלֵי	*Magni, magnates.*	The great men.
—	גְּדַלְיָה־־יָהוּ	*Ghedalia.*	Gedaliah, N. M.
גדל	גְּדִלִים	*Institæ.*	Fringes, wreaths.
—	גַּדֶּלְךָ	*Magnificare te.*	To magnify thee.
—	גָּדְלֶךָ	*Magnitudo tua.*	Thy greatness.
—	גְּדֵלַנִי	*Crevit mecum.*	He was brought up with me.

ROOTS.	DERIVATIVES.	VERSIO.	SIGNIFICATION.
גדל	גָּדַלְתָּ	*Magnus fuisti.*	Thou wast, hast been great.
—	גְּדֻלַּת	*Magnitudo.*	The greatness.
—	גִּדַּלְתּוֹ	*Crescere fecistis eum*	Thou madest him grow.
—	גִּדַּלְתִּי	*Enutrivi.*	I have nourished.
—	גְּדֻלָּתִי	*Magnitudo mea.*	My greatness.
	גִּדַּלְתִּי	*Ghiddalti.*	Giddalti, N. M.
גָּדַע		*Abscidit, succidit, confregit, diruit.*	He cut off, cut down, broke in pieces, destroyed, demolished.
—	גִּדַּע	*Succidit.*	He cut down.
—	גִּדֵּעַ	*Succidit, confregit.*	He cut asunder, broke in pieces.
—	גֻּדְּעוּ	*Succisæ sunt.*	They are cut down.
	גִּדְעוֹן	*Ghideon.*	Gideon, N. M.
גדע	גְּדֻעִים	*Succisi.*	Hewn down.
	גִּדְעֹנִי	*Ghideoni.*	Gideoni, N. M.
גִּדֵּף		*Probris affecit, conviciatus est, blasphemavit.*	He reproached, reviled, blasphemed.
—	גִּדְּפוּ	*Blasphemarunt.*	They have blasphemed.
	גֶּדֶר	*Gheder.*	Geder, N. P.
גָּדַר		*Sepsit, circumsepsit, maceriam struxit.*	He hedged, fenced, inclosed, raised a mound or wall.
—	גָּדֵר	*Sepes, maceria.*	A mound, wall.
—	גֶּדֶר	*Sepes, maceria, paries*	The fence, hedge, wall.
	גֹּדֵר	*Sepiens.*	Inclosing, fencing.
—	גְּדֵרָה	*Sepes, maceria.*	A mound, wall.
	גְּדֵרָה	*Ghedera.*	Gederah, N. P.
גדר	גְּדֵרוֹ	*Maceria ejus.*	His wall.
—	גְּדֵרוֹת גְּדֵרֹת	*Septa.*	Inclosures, folds.
	גְּדֵרוֹת	*Ghederoth.*	Gederoth, N. P.
	גְּדֵרִי	*Ghederita.*	Gederite, N. P.
גדר	גְּדֵרֶיהָ	*Maceriæ ejus.*	Her walls.
—	גְּדֵרָיִךְ	*Maceriæ tuæ.*	Thy walls.
	גְּדֵרָתִי	*Ghederothita.*	Gederothite, N. P.
	גְּדֵרֹתַיִם	*Ghederothaim.*	Gederothaim, N. P.
גדר	גְּדֵרֹתָיו	*Maceriæ ejus.*	His walls.
גדש			

ROOTS.	DERIVATIVES.	VERSIO.	SIGNIFICATION.
	גה		
זה	גֵּה	*Hic, iste.*	This, that.
גָּהָה		*Sanavit, medetus est.*	He cured, healed.
—	גֵּהָה	*Medicina.*	A medicine. [downward.
גָּהַר		*Incurvavit se.*	He stooped, bent himself
	גו		
גוא			
—	גֵּו גּוֹא	*Medium [tor, vindex*	The midst. [avenger.
גאל	גּוֹאֵל	*Redimens, redemp-*	Redeeming, a redeemer, an
גוב			
—	גּוֹבָי	*Locustæ.*	Locusts.
	גּוֹג	*Gog.*	Gog, N. M.
גוה			
גאה	גֵּוָה	*Superbia. [traxit.*	Pride. [tracted.
גוז		*Abscidit, avulsit, ex-*	He cut off, plucked off, ex-
—	גּוֹזִי	*Avulsor meus.*	He who delivered me.
גזל	גּוֹזֵל	*Diripiens.*	Robbing, plundering.
—	גּוֹזָלָיו	*Pulli ejus.*	Her young ones.
	גּוֹזָן	*Gozan.*	Gozan, N. R.
גּוּחַ		*Eduxit, erupit, exiit; parturiit.*	He brought forth, broke out, burst forth, came forth, she was in labour.
גוי			
גוה	גֵּוִי	*Tergum meum.*	My back.
גוי	גּוֹי	*Gens.*	A nation.
—	גּוֹיִ	*Gens mea.*	My nation.
גוה	גְּוִיּוֹת	*Cadavera.*	The dead bodies.
גוי	גּוֹיֵי	*Gentes.*	The nations.
—	גּוֹיֶךָ גּוֹיַיִךְ	*Gens tua, gentes tuæ.*	Thy nation, nations.
—	גּוֹיִם גֹּיִם	*Gentes.*	The nations.
גוה	גְּוִיַּת	*Corpus.*	The body.
—	גְּוִיֹּת	*Corpora.*	The bodies.
—	גְּוִיָּתוֹ	*Corpus ejus.*	His body.
—	גְּוִיֹּתֵיהֶם	*Corpora eorum.*	Their bodies.
—	גְּוִיֹּתֵיהֶנָה	*Corpora earum.*	Their bodies.

ROOTS.	DERIVATIVES.	VERSIO.	SIGNIFICATION.
גוה	גְּוִיֹּתֵינוּ	*Corpora nostra.*	Our bodies.
—	גְּוִיָּתֵנוּ	*Corpora nostra.*	Our bodies.
—	גֵּוְךָ	*Corpus tuum.*	Thy body.
—	גֵּוְךָ גֵּוֶךָ גַּוֵּךְ	*Tergum tuum.*	Thy back.
גול		*Lætatus est, gaudio exultavit.*	He was glad, rejoiced, leaped for joy.
—	גִּיל	*Exultare.*	To exult, rejoice.
גלל	גּוֹל גֹּל	*Devolve.* [*tas.*	Roll, devolve, commit thou.
גלה	גּוֹלָה גֹּלָה	*Deportatio, captivi-*	Transportation, captivity.
—	גּוֹלֶה גֹּלֶה	*Revelans; captivus.*	Revealing, opening; a captive
—	גּוֹלִים	*Transmigrantes.*	They that go into captivity.
	גּוֹלָן	*Golan.*	Golan, N. P.
גוה	גֵּוָם	*Tergum eorum.*	Their back.
גמץ	גּוּמָּץ	*Fovea.*	A pit.
	גּוּנִי	*Guni.*	Guni, N. M. [died.
גָּוַע		*Expiravit, obiit.*	He expired, breathed his last,
—	גָּוְעוּ	*Expiraverunt.*	They expired.
—	גָּוַעְנוּ	*Obiimus.*	We died.
גער	גּוֹעֵר	*Objurgans.*	Chiding, rebuking.
גוף			
—	גּוּפֹת	*Corpora.*	The bodies.
—	גּוּפַת	*Corpus.*	The body.
גור		*Commoratus est, peregrinatus est, collegit, congregavit, timuit.*	He sojourned, dwelt for a time, lived as a stranger, collected, assembled, feared.
—	גּוּר	*Peregrinare; catulus*	Sojourn thou; a whelp.
	גּוּר	*Gur.*	Gur, N. P.
גור	גּוּרוּ	*Timete.*	Fear ye, be ye afraid.
—	גּוּרֶיהָ	*Catuli ejus.*	Her whelps.
—	גּוּרֵיהֶן	*Catuli earum.*	Their young ones.
גרל	גּוֹרָל גּוֹרַל	*Sors.*	The lot.
—	גּוֹרָלוֹ	*Sors ejus.*	His lot.
—	גּוֹרָלוֹת גּ״ר׳	*Sortes.*	Lots.
—	גּוֹרָלִי	*Sors mea.*	My lot.
—	גּוֹרָלְךָ--לֵךְ	*Sors tua.*	Thy lot.
—	גּוֹרָלָם	*Sors eorum.*	Their lot.

ROOTS.	DERIVATIVES.	VERSIO.	SIGNIFICATION.
גוש			
	גז		
גוז	גָּז	*Abscissus est.*	He was cut off.
—	גֵּז	*Vellus; herba tonsa vel depasta.*	The fleece; grass mown or eaten down.
—			
גזבר	גְּזַבְרַיָּא	*Thesaurarii.*	The treasurers.
גזל	גָּזוּל	*Raptus, direptus.*	Violently taken away, spoiled.
	גְּזוֹנִי	*Ghizonita.*	Gizonite, N. F. or P.
גָּזַז		*Abscidit, totondit, vulsit, abripuit.*	He cut off, sheared, mowed, hewed, plucked, took away.
—	גֹּזֵז	*Tondens.*	Shearing.
	גָּזֵז	*Gazez.*	Gazez, N. M.
גזז	גֹּזְזֵי גֹּזְזִים	*Tondentes, tonsores.*	Shearing, shearers.
—	גֹּזְזֶיהָ	*Tondentes eam.*	Shearing her.
—	גֹּזִּי	*Tonde.*	Shear thou, cut off.
—	גִּזֵּי	*Tonsiones.*	Mowings.
—	גָּזִית	*Lapis cæsus aut po- [litus.*	Hewn stone.
גָּזַל		*Rapuit, diripuit, eripuit, spoliavit.*	He took away by force, robbed, plundered, plucked, spoiled
—	גָּזֵל	*Diripiens; rapina.*	Robbery; robbing.
—	גֵּזֶל	*Rapina.*	Rapine, violence.
—	גְּזֵלָה	*Raptum.*	A thing taken away by vio- [lence.
—	גָּזְלוּ גָּזָלוּ	*Diripuerunt.*	They took away by violence.
—	גְּזֵלוֹת	*Rapinæ.*	Acts of violence, robberies.
—	גֹּזְלֵי	*Rapientes.*	Plucking off.
—	גְּזֵלַת	*Rapina.*	The spoil.
—	גָּזַלְתִּי	*Rapui.*	I took away.
	גַּזָּם	*Gazam.*	Gazzam, N. M.
גזע			
—	גִּזְעוֹ	*Stirps, truncus ejus.*	His stock, trunk, root.
—	גִּזְעָם	*Truncus eorum.*	Their stock.
	גָּזֶר גֶּזֶר	*Ghezer.*	Gezer, N. P.
גָּזַר		*Scidit, abscidit, excidit, decidit, decrevit. [lis.*	He cut asunder, divided, cut off; destroyed, decided, determined.
גזר	גְּזֵרָה	*Abscissa, inhabitabi-*	Cut off, uninhabitable.

ROOTS.	DERIVATIVES.	VERSIO.	SIGNIFICATION.
גזר	גִּזְרוּ גְּזֹרוּ	*Discindite.*	Divide ye, cut asunder.
—	גָּזְרִין	*Divini.*	The soothsayers, diviners.
—	גִּזְרָתָם	*Excisio eorum.*	Their cutting, polishing.
גזז	גִּזַּת	*Vellus.*	A fleece.
	גח		
גחן	גָּחוֹן	*Venter.*	The belly.
	גִּחוֹן גִּיחוֹן	*Ghihon.*	Gihon, N. P.
	גֵּחֲזִי גֵּיחֲזִי	*Ghehazi.*	Gehazi, N. M.
גוח	גֹּחִי	*Avulsor meus.*	He that took me out.
גחל			
—	גַּחֲלֵי	*Prunæ, carbones.*	Burning coals.
—	גֶּחָלֶיהָ	*Prunæ ejus*	Her coals.
—	גֶּחָלָיו	*Prunæ ejus.*	His coals.
—	גֶּחָלִים	*Carbones.*	Coals.
—	גַּחֶלֶת	*Pruna.*	A coal.
—	גַּחַלְתִּי	*Pruna mea.*	My coals.
	גַּחַם	*Gacham.*	Gaham, N. M.
גחן			
—	גְּחֹנְךָ	*Venter tuus.*	Thy belly.
	גָּחַר גַּחַר	*Gachar.*	Gahar, N. M.
	גי		
גיא	גַּי	*Vallis.*	The valley.
גיא			
—	גֵּיא גַּיְא גֵּיא	*Vallis.*	A valley.
גיד			
—	גִּיד	*Nervus.*	A sinew.
—	גִּידֵי	*Nervi.*	The sinews.
—	גִּידִים	*Nervi.*	Sinews.
	גִּיחַ	*Ghiach.*	Giah, N. P.
גיל			
גול	גִּיל גִּילָה	*Gaudium, exultatio.*	Exultation, joy, gladness.
—	גִּילוּ	*Exultate.* [*mea*	Be ye glad.
—	גִּילִי	*Exulta; exultatio*	Rejoice thou; my joy.
	גִּילֹנִי גִּלֹנִי	*Ghilonita.*	Gilonite, N. P.
גול	גִּילַת	*Exultatio.*	Joy.

ROOTS.	DERIVATIVES.	VERSIO.	SIGNIFICATION.
	גִּינַת	*Ghinath.*	Ginath, N. M.
גיר			
גור	גִּיר	*Calx.*	Chalk, lime, mortar.
—	גִּירָא	*Calx, tectorium.*	Chalk, lime, plaister.
	גִּישָׁן	*Ghesan.*	Geshan, N. M.
	גל		
גלל	גַּל גֶּל	*Acervus; scaturigo.*	A heap; a spring.
גלה	גַּל	*Aperi, detrahe.*	Open, remove thou.
—	גָּלֵא	*Revelans.*	Revealing.
גלב			
	גִּלְבֹּעַ	*Ghilboa.*	Gilboa, N. P.
	גִּלְגָּל	*Ghilgal.*	Gilgal, N. P.
גלל	גַּלְגַּל	*Rota.*	The wheel.
—	גַּלְגַּלּוֹהִי	*Rotæ ejus.*	His wheels.
—	גַּלְגַּלָּיו	*Rotæ ejus.*	His wheels.
—	גֻּלְגָּלְתּוֹ	*Cranium, caput ejus.*	His skull, head.
גלד			
גלד	גִּלְדִּי	*Cutis mea.*	My skin.
	גִּלֹה	*Ghilo.*	Giloh, N. P.
גָּלָה		*Migravit, demigravit, transtulit, deportavit, abductus est in captivitatem aperuit, detexit, revelavit.*	He removed, departed, carried away, transported, was led into captivity, opened, uncovered, revealed.
—	גֹּלֶה	*Revelans.*	Revealing.
—	גָּלֹה	*Migrare.*	To go away, depart.
—	גִּלָּה	*Revelavit, detexit.*	He revealed, disclosed.
גלל	גֹּלּוּ	*Volvite.*	Roll ye.
גלה	גָּלוּ	*Retexerunt; abducti sunt in captivitatem.*	They discovered; they were carried away into captivity.
—	גִּלּוּ	*Revelaverunt.*	They revealed, discovered.
—	גָּלוּי	*Apertus, revelatus.*	Opened, published, revealed.
גלל	גִּלּוּלֵי	*Idola.*	The idols.
—	גִּלּוּלֶיהָ	*Idola ejus.*	Her idols.

ROOTS.	DERIVATIVES.	VERSIO.	SIGNIFICATION.
גלל	גִּלּוּלֵיהֶם־־הֶן	*Idola eorum, earum.*	Their idols.
—	גִּלּוּלָיו	*Idola ejus.*	His idols.
—	גִּלּוּלֵיכֶם־־כֶן	*Idola vestra.*	Your idols.
—	גִּלּוּלִים	*Idola.*	Idols.
גלה	גָּלוּת	*Migratio, captivitas.*	Departure, captivity.
—	גָּלוֹת	*Migrare, abduci in captivitatem.*	To go away, to be carried into captivity.
גלל	גֻּלּוֹת גֻּלֹּת	*Scaturigines, fontes.*	Springs, fountains.
גלה	גָּלוּתָא	*Captivitas.*	Captivity.
גלל	גַּלּוֹתִי	*Devolvi.*	I rolled away.
גִּלַּח		*Rasit, abrasit, totondit.*	He shaved *the head.*
—	גֻּלַּח	*Rasus est.*	He was shaven.
—	גֻּלַּחְתִּי	*Rasus sum.*	I was shaven.
גלה	גַּלִּי	*Detege.*	Uncover thou.
—	גֻּלִּי גֻּלָּי	*Revelatus est.*	He was revealed.
גלל	גַּלֵּיהֶם	*Fluctus eorum.*	Their waves.
—	גַּלָּיו	*Fluctus ejus.*	His waves.
—	גִּלָּיוֹן	*Volumen.*	A roll, volume.
—	גַּלֶּיךָ	*Fluctus tui.*	Thy waves.
	גָּלִיל	*Galilæa.*	Galilee, N. P.
	גְּלִילוֹת	*Ghelilloth.*	Geliloth, N. P.
גלל	גְּלִילוֹת	*Confinia, limites.*	Confines, borders.
—	גְּלִילֵי	*Circuli, armillæ.*	Round chains, rings, bracelets
—	גְּלִילִים	*Volubilis.*	Folding, or turning both ways
	גַּלִּים	*Gallim.*	Gallim, N. P.
גלל	גַּלִּים	*Acervi; fluctus.*	Heaps; waves.
	גָּלְיָת	*Goliath.*	Goliath, N. M.
גלה	גִּלִּיתָ	*Revelasti.*	Thou hast revealed.
—	גִּלִּית	*Detexisti.*	Thou hast discovered.
—	גִּלִּיתִי גִּלֵּי	*Detexi.*	I uncovered.
	גָּלָל	*Galal.*	Galal, N. M.
גָּלַל		*Volvit, convolvit, devolvit, volutavit, polluit.*	He rolled, rolled together, rolled away, rolled along, polluted.
—	גָּלָל	*Rotatus, grandis* ut præ pondere rotetur, *marmoreus.*	Rolled, large *so as to be rolled on account of its weight,* marble.

ROOTS.	DERIVATIVES.	VERSIO.	SIGNIFICATION.
גלל	גְּלָלֵי	*Stercora.*	Dung, ordure.
	גִּלֲלַי	*Ghilalai.*	Gilalai, N. M.
גלל	גִּלּוּלֵיהֶם	*Idola eorum.*	Their idols.
גָּלַם		*Convolvit.*	He rolled up, wrapped together.
גלמד	גַּלְמוּד	*Solitarius.*	Solitary, desolate.
גלם	גָּלְמִי	*Embrio meus.*	My embryo.
גָּלַע		*Miscuit, immiscuit se*	He meddled, intermeddled.
	גַּלְעֵד	*Galed.*	Galeed, N. P.
	גִּלְעָד	*Ghilhad.*	Gilead, N. M. P.
	גִּלְעָדִי	*Ghilhadita.*	Gileadite, N. N.
	גִּלְעָדִים	*Ghilhaditæ.*	Gileadites, N. N.
גָּלַשׁ		*Splenduit, nituit, depavit.*	He shone, glistened, fed, grazed.
גלל	גֻּלַּת	*Lenticula.*	The bowl.
גלה	גָּלְתָה	*Migravit in captivitatem.*	She is gone away into captivity.
—	גִּלְּתָה	*Detexit.*	She hath uncovered.
—	גֻּלְּתָה	*In captivitatem abducta est.*	She has been led away captive

גמ

ROOTS.	DERIVATIVES.	VERSIO.	SIGNIFICATION.
גם			
—	גַּם	*Etiam, præterea, imo, quanquam, atque, sed, tamen, tam—quam.*	Also, moreover, yea, even and, although, but, yet, both—and.
גָּמָא		*Potavit, absorbuit.*	He drank, swallowed.
—	גַּמֶּא	*Absorbebit.*	He will swallow.
—	גֹּמֶא	*Juncus, papyrus.*	A bulrush, Egyptian reed, or rush.
גמד			
—	גֹּמֶד	*Cubitus.*	A cubit.
	גַּמָּדִים	*Gammadim.*	Gammadims, N. N.
גמל	גְּמוּל	*Ablactatus.*	The weaned child.
—	גְּמוּל	*Retributio, merces.*	A recompense, reward.
	גָּמוּל	*Gamul.*	Gamul, N. M.
גָּמַל	גְּמוּלֵי	*Ablactati.*	Weaned.
—	גְּמוּלָיו	*Beneficia ejus.*	His benefits.
—	גְּמוּלְךָ גְּמֻלְךָ	*Retributio tua.*	Thy recompense.
—	גְּמוּלְכֶם גְּמֻלְ׳	*Retributio vestra.*	Your recompense.
—	גְּמוּלָם	*Retributio eorum.*	Their recompense.

ROOTS.	DERIVATIVES.	VERSIO.	SIGNIFICATION.
	גִּמְזוֹ	*Ghimzo.* [*matus.*	Gimzo, N. P.
גמר	גָּמִיר	*Perfectus, consum-*	Perfect, consummate.
גָּמַל		*Retribuit, rependit, edidit, contulit bonum vel malum, ablactavit, educavit.* [*cens.*	He recompensed, rewarded, repaid, yielded, produced, conferred good, inflicted evil, weaned, brought up.
—	גֹּמֵל	*Retribuens, matures-*	Rewarding, ripening.
—	גָּמָל	*Camelus.* [*confer.*	A camel.
—	גְּמֹל	*Retribue, beneficium*	Reward thou, be bountiful.
—	גְּמָלָהּ	*Ablactare eam.*	She weans.
—	גָּמְלוּ	*Retribuerunt.*	They rewarded.
—	גְּמָלוּךְ	*Retribuerunt tibi.*	They rewarded thee.
—	גְּמֻלוֹת	*Retributiones.*	Recompenses.
	גְּמַלִּי	*Ghemali.*	Gemalli, N. M.
	גַּמְלִיאֵל	*Gamaliel.*	Gamaliel, N. M.
גמל	גְּמַלֵּיהֶם	*Cameli eorum.*	Their camels.
—	גְּמַלָּיו	*Cameli ejus.*	His camels.
—	גְּמַלֶּיךָ	*Cameli tui.*	Thy camels.
—	גְּמַלִּים	*Cameli.*	Camels.
—	גֹּמְלִים	*Retribuentes.*	Rewarding.
—	גְּמָלֵךְ	*Ablactare te.*	Thou weanest.
—	גְּמָלְךָ	*Retribuit tibi.*	He rewarded thee.
—	גְּמָלָם	*Contulit eis.*	He bestowed on them.
—	גָּמַלְנוּ	*Intulimus.*	We inflicted.
—	גְּמָלָנוּ	*Contulit nobis.*	He bestowed on us. [to him.
—	גְּמָלַתְהוּ	*Retribuit ei.*	She rewarded him, rendered
—	גְּמָלַתּוּ	*Ablactabit eum.*	She will wean him.
—	גָּמַלְתִּי	*Retribui.*	I have rewarded.
—	גְּמַלְתִּיךָ	*Retribui te.*	I have rewarded thee.
—	גְּמַלְתַּנִי	*Retribuisti mihi.*	Thou hast rewarded me.
גמץ			
גָּמַר		*Perfecit, defecit, desiit, consumptus est*	He completed, finished, failed, ceased, was consumed.
—	גֹּמֵר	*Perficiens.*	Performing, completing.
	גֹּמֶר	*Gomer.*	Gomer, N. M. W.
	גְּמַרְיָהוּ	*Gemaria.*	Gemariah, N. M.

ROOTS.	DERIVATIVES.	VERSIO.	SIGNIFICATION.
	גג		
גנן	גַּן	*Hortus.*	A garden.
גָּנַב		*Furatus est, surripuit, furtim abduxit.*	He stole, pilfered, withdrew or conveyed away privately.
—	גַּנָּב	*Fur.*	A, the thief.
—	גָּנֹב	*Furari, furando.*	To steal, by stealing.
—	גֹּנֵב	*Furans.*	Stealing.
—	גַּנֹּב	*Furtim abducere.*	To convey away by stealth.
—	גָּנְבוּ	*Furati sunt.*	They have stolen.
—	גְּנָבוּךְ	*Furati sunt te.*	They have stolen thee.
—	גַּנָּבִים	*Fures.*	Thieves.
—	גָּנַבְתָּ	*Furatus est.*	Thou hast stolen.
	גְּנֻבַת	*Ghenubath.*	Genubath, N. M.
גנב	גְּנָבַתּוּ	*Rapuit, surripuit eum.*	She carried him off, stole him away.
—	גְּנֻבְתִי	*Furtim ablatus.*	Stolen.
—	גֻּנַּבְתִּי	*Surreptus sum.*	I was stolen.
—	גְּנָבָתָם	*Furata est eos.*	She stole them.
—	גָּנוּב	*Furatus.*	Stolen.
—	גְּנוּבִים	*Furati.*	Stolen.
גנן	גָּנוֹן	*Protegere.*	To defend, protect.
—	גַּנּוֹת	*Horti.*	Gardens.
—	גַּנּוֹתֵיכֶם	*Horti vestri.*	Your gardens.
גנז			
—	גִּנְזֵי גִּנְזַיָּא	*Thesauri.*	Treasuries.
גנן	גַּנִּי	*Hortus meus.*	My garden.
—	גַּנִּים	*Horti.*	Gardens.
גָּנַן		*Obtexit, protexit.*	He covered, shielded, protected, defended.
—	גִּנַּת	*Hortus.*	The garden.
—	גַּנָּתוֹ	*Hortus ejus.*	His garden.
	גִּנְּתוֹן	*Ghinnethon.*	Ginnethon, N. M.
	גע		
נגע	גַּע	*Tange.*	Touch thou.
גָּעָה		*Mugivit.*	He lowed.
גָּעַל		*Fastidivit, abominatus est, respuit.*	He loathed, abhorred, rejected.

ROOTS.	DERIVATIVES.	VERSIO.	SIGNIFICATION.
	גַּעַל	*Gaal.*	Gaal, N. M.
געל	גָּעֲלָה	*Abominata est.*	She abhorred.
—	גָּעֲלוּ	*Fastidiverunt.*	They loathed.
—	גֹּעֶלֶת	*Fastidiens.*	Loathing.
—	גְּעַלְתִּים	*Abominatus sum eos*	I abhorred them.
גָּעַר		*Increpavit, objurgavit, compescuit, perdidit.*	He reproved, rebuked, checked, restrained, destroyed.
—	גְּעַר	*Increpa.*	Rebuke thou.
—	גֹּעֵר	*Increpans, perdens.*	Rebuking, destroying.
—	גְּעָרָה	*Increpatio.*	A rebuke.
—	גַּעֲרַת	*Objurgatio.*	The rebuke.
—	גָּעַרְתָּ	*Increpasti.*	Thou hast rebuked.
—	גַּעֲרָתְךָ	*Increpatio tua.*	Thy rebuke.
גָּעַשׁ		*Concussus est, commotus est, titubavit*	He was shaken, moved; agitated, staggered.
	גַּעַשׁ	*Gaas.*	Gaash, N. P.
	גֹּעָתָה	*Goatha.*	Goatha, N. P.
	גַּעְתָּם	*Gatam.*	Gatam, N. P.
	גפ		
גפף	גַּפֵּי	*Vertices, alæ, fastigia.*	The summits, wings, battlements.
—	גַּפֶּיהָ	*Alæ ejus.*	Her wings.
—	גַּפַּיִן	*Alæ.*	Wings.
גפן			
—	גֶּפֶן גָּפֶן	*Vitis.*	A, the vine.
—	גַּפְנָהּ	*Vitis ejus.*	Her vine.
—	גַּפְנוֹ	*Vitis ejus.*	His vine.
—	גַּפְנִי	*Vitis mea.*	My vine.
—	גַּפְנְךָ	*Vitis tua.*	Thy vine.
—	גַּפְנָם	*Vitis eorum.*	Their vine.
גפף			
גפר			
—	גֹּפֶר	*Gopher*, arbor, vel genus arborum resinosarum.	Gopher, *a tree, or a general name for trees abounding with resinous matter.*
—	גָּפְרִית	*Sulphur.*	Brimstone.

ROOTS.	DERIVATIVES.	VERSIO.	SIGNIFICATION.
	גר		
גיר	גִּר	*Calx.*	Calcined chalk, lime, mortar.
גור	גֵּר	*Peregrinus, advena.*	A stranger, foreigner, sojourner
—	גָּר	*Peregrinatus est; peregrinans; incola; congregans.*	He sojourned; sojourning; the inhabitant; gathering together.
	גֵּרָא	*Ghera.*	Gera, N. M.
גרב			
—	גָּרָב	*Psora, scabies.*	A scab, scurvy.
	גָּרֵב	*Gareb.*	Gareb, N. M. P.
גרגר	גַּרְגְּרִים	*Grana, baccæ.*	Grains, berries.
גרר	גַּרְגְּרֹתֶיךָ	*Guttur, collum tuum*	Thy throat, neck.
	גִּרְגָּשִׁי	*Ghirgasitæ.*	Girgashites, N. N.
גָּרַד		*Scabit, scalpsit se.*	He scraped himself.
גָּרָה		*Contendit, litem excitavit, bellum movit, miscuit se, ruminavit.*	He contended, stirred up strife, caused war, meddled, ruminated, chewed the cud.
גרר	גֵּרָה	*Rumen, ruminans, ruminatio; obolus sicli pars vicesima*	The cud, ruminating, rumination; a gerah, *a small piece of money*, the twentieth part of a shekel.
גור	גֵּרוֹ	*Peregrinus ejus.*	His stranger or sojourner.
—	גָּרוּ	*Peregrinati sunt.*	They were strangers.
גרר	גָּרוֹן	*Guttur.*	The throat.
—	גְּרוֹנִי	*Guttur meum.*	My throat.
—	גְּרוֹנֵךְ	*Guttur tuum.*	Thy throat.
גרש	גְּרוּשָׁה	*Repudiata.*	Put away, divorced.
גור	גֻּרוֹתָיו	*Catuli ejus.*	His whelps.
גרז			
	גִּרְזִי	*Ghezritæ.*	Gezrites, N. N.
	גְּרִזִּים	*Gherizim.*	Gerizim, N. P.
גרז	גַּרְזֶן	*Securis.*	An ax.
גור	גָּרֵי	*Habitantes, inquilini.*	They that dwell, inmates.
—	גֵּרִים גָּרִים	*Peregrini.*	Strangers.
גרל			

ROOTS.	DERIVATIVES.	VERSIO.	SIGNIFICATION.
גדל	גִּדֵּל	*Magnus.* [*fregit.*	Great. [broke bones in pieces.
גָּרַם		*Exossavit, ossa con-*	He picked or gnawed bones,
—	גֶּרֶם גָּרֶם	*Os; fortis.*	A, the bone; strong.
—	גָּרְמוּ	*Exossarunt.*	They gnawed the bones.
	גַּרְמִי	*Garmita.*	Garmite, N. F. or P.
—	גַּרְמֵהוֹן	*Ossa eorum.*	Their bones.
—	גְּרָמָיו	*Ossa ejus.*	His bones.
גרן			
—	גֹּרֶן	*Area.*	A threshing floor.
—	גָּרְנָה	*In aream.*	Into the floor.
—	גֳּרָנוֹת	*Areæ.*	Floors.
—	גָּרְנִי	*Areæ meæ.*	My floors.
גרר	גְּרֹנָם	*Guttur eorum.*	Their throat. [pieces.
גָּרַס		*Fregit, comminuit.*	He broke, crushed, broke in
—	גָּרְסָה	*Confracta est.*	She is broken.
גָּרַע		*Minuit, diminuit, ademit, subtraxit.*	He lessened, diminished, took from, abated, subtracted.
—	גְּרֻעָה	*Adempta, rasa.*	Taken away, cut off. [away.
גָּרַף		*Convolvit. devolvit.*	He rolled together, rolled
—	גְּרָפָם	*Devolvit eos.* [*secuit*	He rolled, carried them away.
גָּרַר		*Incidit, serravit, dis-*	He cut, sawed, cut in two.
	גְּרָר	*Gherar.*	Gerar, N. P.
גָּרַשׁ		*Expulit, ejecit, projecit, repudiavit.*	He expelled, cast out, cast forth, produced, divorced.
—	גֹּרֵשׁ	*Expellens.*	Driving out.
—	גָּרֵשׁ	*Ejice; expellere.*	Cast thou out; to expel.
—	גֶּרֶשׁ	*Proventus.*	The produce.
—	גֶּרֶשׂ	*Granum contusum.*	Corn beaten. [out.
—	גֹּרָשׁוּ	*Expulsi sunt.*	They were expelled, driven
	גֵּרְשׁוֹם--שם	*Ghersom.*	Gershom, N. M.
	גֵּרְשׁוֹן	*Gherson.*	Gershon, N. M.
—	גֵּרְשׁוּנִי	*Expulerunt me.*	They have driven me out.
	גֵּרְשֻׁנִּי	*Ghersonita.*	Gershonite, N. F.
גרש	גֵּרַשְׁתָּ	*Expulisti.*	Thou hast driven out.
—	גֵּרַשְׁתִּהוּ	*Ejeci eum.*	I have driven him out.
נור	גְּרֻשֹׁתֵיכֶם	*Exactiones, ejectiones vestras.*	Your exactions, expulsions.

ROOTS.	DERIVATIVES.	VERSIO.	SIGNIFICATION.
—	גַּרְתָּה	*Peregrinatus es.*	Thou hast sojourned.
—	גַּרְתִּי	*Peregrinatus sum.*	I have sojourned.
	גש		
נגש	גַּשׁ גֶּשׁ גְּשִׁי	*Accede.*	Go, come, draw thou near.
—	גְּשָׁה	*Accede, cede.*	Come thou near; give place.
—	גְּשׁוּ גֹּשׁוּ	*Accedite.*	Draw ye near.
	גְּשׁוּר	*Ghessur.*	Geshur, N. P.
	גְּשׁוּרִי	*Ghessuri.* [*cit.*	Geshuri, N. P.
גָּשַׁם		*Irrigavit, pluere fe-*	He watered, caused it to rain.
—	גֶּשֶׁם גָּשֶׁם	*Pluvia, imber.*	Rain, a shower.
	גֶּשֶׁם	*Ghessem.*	Geshem, N. M.
גשם	גִּשְׁמֵהּ--מֵהּ	*Corpus ejus.*	His body.
—	גֻּשְׁמָה	*Irrigata.*	Watered, rained upon.
—	גֶּשְׁמְהוֹן	*Corpora eorum.*	Their bodies.
—	גִּשְׁמֵי	*Pluviæ.*	Showers.
—	גִּשְׁמֵיהֶם	*Pluviæ eorum.*	Their rains.
—	גִּשְׁמֵיכֶם	*Pluviæ vestræ.*	Your rains.
—	גְּשָׁמִים	*Pluviæ.*	Rains, much rain.
	גֹּשֶׁן	*Gosen.*	Goshen, N. P.
	גִּשְׁפָּא	*Ghispa.*	Gispa, N. M.
גָּשַׁשׁ		*Palpavit, expalpavit.*	He felt, groped for.
נגש	גִּשְׁתּוֹ	*Accedere eum.*	He comes near.
	גת		
	גַּת	*Gath.*	Gath, N. P.
גתת	גַּת	*Torcular.*	A wine-press.
	גַּת רִמּוֹן	*Gath-rimmon.*	Gath-rimmon, N. P.
	גִּתָּה חֵפֶר	*Ghitta-chepher.*	Gittah-hepher, N. P.
גתת	גִּתּוֹת	*Torcularia.*	Wine-presses.
	גִּתִּי	*Gathæus.*	Gittite, N. P.
	גִּתִּים	*Gathæi.*	Gittites, N. P.
	גִּתַּיְמָה	*Ghitaim.*	Gittaim, N. P.
	גֶּתֶר	*Ghether.*	Gether, N. M.
גתת			

ROOTS.	DERIVATIVES.	VERSIO.	SIGNIFICATION.
	דא		
רא			
—	דָּא	*Istic, hæc, illa, altera*	That, this, one, another.
דָּאַב		*Languit præ fame vel siti, tabuit, mæstus fuit.*	He languished or fainted through hunger or thirst, pined away, was sorrowful.
—	דְּאָבָה	*Mæror.*	Sorrow.
—	דַּאֲבָה	*Doluit, mæsta est.*	She mourned, was sorrowful.
דָּאַג		*Solicitus, anxius fuit; timuit, formidavit.*	He was solicitous, anxious; he feared, dreaded.
	דֹּאֵג דּוֹאֵג	*Doëg.*	Doeg, N. M.
דוג	דָּאג	*Piscis.*	Fish.
דאג	דֹּאֵג	*Solicitus, metuens.*	Solicitous, afraid.
—	דְּאָגָה	*Solicitudo, anxietas.*	Solicitude, anxiety.
—	דֹּאֲגִים	*Soliciti, timentes.*	Solicitous, afraid.
—	דָּאַגְתְּ	*Timuisti.*	Thou hast been afraid.
דָּאָה		*Volavit.*	He flew.
דון	דָּאְנִין	*Judicantes.*	Judging.
	דֹּאר	*Dor.*	Dor, N. P.
דור	דָּאְרֵי דָּאְרִין	*Habitantes, habita-* [*tores.*	The inhabitants.
	דב		
דבב	דֹּב	*Ursus.*	A bear.
רבא			
—	דְּבָאֶךָ	*Robur tuum.*	Thy strength.
דָּבַב		*Mutivit, murmuravit, effutivit, infamavit.*	He muttered, murmured, grumbled, babbled, prated, slandered.
—	דִּבָּה	*Infamia.*	A slander.
	דְּבוֹרָה דְּבֹרָה	*Debora.*	Deborah, N. W.
דבח			
—	דָּבְחִין	*Immolantes.*	Offering, sacrificing.
—	דִּבְחִין	*Victimæ.*	Victims, sacrifices.
רבב	דֻּבִּים	*Ursi.*	Bears.
	דְּבִיר דְּבִר	*Debir.*	Debir, N. M. P.

ROOTS.	DERIVATIVES.	VERSIO.	SIGNIFICATION.
דבר דבך דבל	דְּבִיר	*Oraculum.*	The oracle.
—	דְּבֵלָה	*Palatha.*	A cake of figs.
—	דְּבֵלִים	*Palathæ.*	Cakes of figs.
—	דִּבְלַיִם	*Diblaim.*	Diblaim, N. M.
דבל	דְּבֶלֶת	*Massa, palatha.*	A lump, or cake of figs.
—	דִּבְלָתָה	*Diblata.*	Diblath, N. P.
—	דִּבְלָתַיִם	*Diblathaim.*	Diblathaim, N. P.
דָּבַק		*Conglutinatus est, adhæsit, cohæsit, persecutus est, assecutus est.*	He was glued, cemented, united, stuck, clave, adhered to, pursued, overtook.
—	דָּבֵק דְּבֵקָה	*Adhærens.*	Cleaving, joining to.
—	דָּבְקָה דָּבֵקָה	*Adhæsit, secuta est.*	She clave, followed.
—	דָּבְקוּ דָּבֵקוּ	*Adhæserunt, cohæserunt.*	They clave to, were joined together.
—	דָּבְקִין	*Adhærentes.*	Cleaving to.
—	דָּבַקְתִּי	*Adhæsi.*	I have adhered, stuck to.
דִּבֵּר		*Elocutus, allocutus, oblocutus est; dixit, pronunciavit, habuit sermonem, duxit, subjecit, perdidit.*	He spoke, spoke to, spoke against, said, pronounced, held conversation, led, subdued, overthrew, destroyed
—	דָּבָר	*Verbum, mandatum, consilium, res, factum, causa, modus, aliquid.*	A word, command, counsel, advice, matter, thing, deed, cause, manner, something, any thing.
—	דָּבֶר דֶּבֶר	*Pestis.*	A, the pestilence, plague.
—	דַּבֵּר דַּבֵּר	*Loquere; loqui.*	Speak thou; to speak.
—	דֻּבַּר	*Dictus.*	Spoken.
—	דְּבַר	*Verbum, res, causa.*	The word, thing, matter, cause.
—	דִּבֶּר דִּבֵּר	*Locutus est.*	He spake, has spoken.
—	דֹּבֵר	*Loquens.*	Speaking.
—	דִּבְּרָה	*Locuta est.*	She spoke.
—	דַּבְּרוֹ	*Loqui eum.*	He speaks.

ROOTS.	DERIVATIVES.	VERSIO.	SIGNIFICATION.
דבר	דַּבְּרוּ	*Loquimini.*	Speak ye.
—	דְּבָרוֹ־רִיו	*Verbum, dictum ejus*	His word, saying.
—	דִּבְּרוֹ	*Locutus est illud.*	He spoke it.
—	דִּבְּרוּ דִּבֵּרוּ	*Locuti sunt.*	They talked, spoke.
—	דֹּבְרוֹת	*Rates.*	Floats, rafts.
—	דְּבָרִי	*Verbum meum.*	My word.
—	דַּבְּרִי	*Loquere.*	Speak thou.
—	דַּבְּרִי	*Loquere; loqui me.*	Speak thou; I speak.
—	דְּבָרַי רַי	*Verba mea.*	My words. [deeds
—	דִּבְרֵי	*Verba, res, gesta.*	Words, things, matters, acts,
—	דֹּבְרֵי דּוֹבְ׳	*Loquentes.*	Speaking.
	דִּבְרִי	*Dibri.*	Dibri, N. M.
דבר	דְּבָרֶיהָ	*Verba ejus.*	Her words.
—	דִּבְרֵיהֶם	*Verba eorum.*	Their words.
—	דְּבָרָיו	*Verba ejus.*	His words.
—	דְּבָרָיךָ דְּבָרֶיךָ	*Verba tua.*	Thy words.
—	דִּבְרֵיכֶם	*Verba vestra.*	Your words.
—	דְּבָרִים	*Verba, res.*	Words, matters.
—	דְּבֹרִים	*Apes.*	Bees.
—	דֹּבְרִים	*Loquentes.*	Speaking.
—	דַּבֶּרְךָ	*Loqui te.*	Thou speakest.
—	דְּבָרְךָ־רֶךָ	*Verbum tuum.*	Thy word.
—	דַּבֶּרְכֶם	*Loqui vos.*	Ye speak.
—	דִּבַּרְנוּ	*Locuti sumus.*	We spoke.
—	דְּבָרֵנוּ	*Negotium nostrum.*	Our business.
	דָּבְרַת	*Daberat.*	Daberath, N. P.
דבר	דִּבַּרְתָּ	*Locutus es.*	Thou hast spoken.
—	דִּבְרַת	*Causa, ratio, finis.*	A cause, reason, end.
—	דֹּבֶרֶת	*Loquentes.*	Speaking.
—	דִּבַּרְתִּי	*Locutus sum.*	I have spoken.
—	דִּבְרָתִי	*Causa mea; ordo.*	My cause; the order.
—	דִּבַּרְתְּי	*Locuta es.*	Thou hast spoken.
—	דִּבַּרְתֶּם	*Locuti estis.*	Ye have said.
דבש			
—	דְּבַשׁ	*Mel.*	Honey.
—	דִּבְשִׁי	*Mel meus.*	My honey *comb.*
—	דַּבֶּשֶׁת	*Gibbum.*	The bunch.

ROOTS.	DERIVATIVES.	VERSIO.	SIGNIFICATION.
	דַּבֶּשֶׁת	*Dabaset.*	Dabbasheth, N. P.
דבב	דִּבַּת	*Infamia, calumnia.*	An evil report, slander.
—	דִּבָּתָם	*Calumnia eorum.*	Their slander, defamation.
	דג		
דוג	דָּג דָּגָה	*Piscis.* [star piscium.	A fish.
דָּגָה		*Multiplicatus est* in-	He was multiplied *like fishes.*
דגל	דָּגוּל	*Vexillarius, insignis*	A standard bearer, a distinguished person.
	דָּגוֹן דָּגֹן	*Dagon.*	Dagon, N. I.
דוג	דְּגֵי	*Pisces.*	The fishes.
—	דָּגִים	*Pisces.*	Fishes.
דגל			
—	דֶּגֶל	*Vexillum, insigne.*	The standard, ensign.
—	דִּגְלוֹ	*Vexillum ejus.*	His standard.
דגן			
—	דָּגָן	*Frumentum.*	Corn.
—	דְּגָנִי	*Frumentum meum.*	My corn.
—	דְּגָנְךָ דְּגָנֶךָ	*Frumentum tuum.*	Thy corn.
—	דְּגָנֵךְ	*Frumentum tuum.*	Thy corn.
—	דְּגָנָם	*Frumentum eorum.*	Their corn.
דָּגַר		*Collegit, incubuit; fovit.*	He gathered, hatched, cherished.
דוג	דְּגַת	*Piscis.*	The fish.
—	דְּגָתָם	*Piscis eorum.*	Their fish.
	דד		
דד			
דוד	דֹּד דּוֹד	*Patruus.*	An uncle, father's brother.
דָּדָה		*Incessit sensim.*	He walked softly, or slowly.
—	דֹּדוֹ דּוֹדוֹ	*Patruus ejus.*	His uncle.
	דֹּדָוָהוּ דּוֹדַי	*Dodavahu.*	Dodavah, N. M.
דוד	דֹּדִי דּוֹדִי	*Patruus meus.*	My uncle.
דד	דַּדֵּי	*Mammæ, ubera.*	The teats, paps, breasts.
—	דַּדֶּיהָ	*Ubera ejus.*	Her breasts.
—	דַּדַּיִךְ	*Ubera tua.*	Thy breasts.
דוד	דֹּדֶיךָ דֹּדַיִךְ	*Amores tui.*	Thy loves.

ROOTS.	DERIVATIVES.	VERSIO.	SIGNIFICATION.
דוד	דֹּדִים דּוֹדִים	*Amores.* [*tuus.*	Loves.
—	דֹּדְךָ דּוֹדֶךָ	*Patruus, patruelis*	Thy uncle, or paternal cousin
	דְּדָן	*Dedan.*	Dedan, N. M.
	דֹּדָנִים	*Dodanim.*	Dodanim, N. M.
	דְּדָנִים	*Dedanim.*	Dedanim, N N.
דוד	דֹּדָתוֹ	*Amita ejus.*	His aunt, father's sister.
—	דֹּדָתְךָ	*Amita ejus.*	Thy aunt.
	דה		
דהב			
—	דְּהַב דַּהֲבָא	*Aurum, aureus.*	Gold, golden.
	דֶּהָוֵא	*Dehavi.* [*est*	Dehavites, N. N.
דָּהַם		*Territus, attonitus*	He was terrified, astonished.
דָּהַר		*Calcitravit, cursitavit.*	He pranced, galloped.
—	דֹּהֵר	*Quadrupedans.*	Prancing, galloping.
—	דַּהֲרוֹת	*Calcitratus, cursitationes.*	The prancings, gallopings.
	דו		
דבב	דּוֹבֵב	*Loqui faciens.*	Causing to speak.
דוג		*Piscatus est.*	He fished.
—	דּוּגָה	*Piscatio.*	A fishing.
—	דַּוָּגִים	*Piscatores.*	The fishers, fishermen.
	דָּוִד דָּוִיד	*David.*	David, N. M.
דוד			
—	דּוּדָאֵי	*Canistra; mandragoræ.*	Baskets; mandrakes.
—	דּוּדָאִים	*Mandragoræ.*	Mandrakes.
—	דּוֹדָהּ	*Dilectus ejus.*	Her beloved.
	דּוֹדוֹ	*Dodo.*	Dodo, N. M.
	דּוֹדַי	*Dodai.*	Dodai, N. M.
דוד	דּוֹדַי	*Amores mei.*	My loves.
—	דּוֹדֶךָ	*Dilectus tuus.*	Thy beloved.
דוה			
—	דָּוָה	*Languida, menstrua*	Faint, menstruous.
—	דָּוֶה	*Languidus.*	Faint.

ROOTS.	DERIVATIVES.	VERSIO.	SIGNIFICATION.
דוח		*Expulit, eluvione abstulit, abluit.*	He cast out, carried away by a stream, washed, cleansed.
דוה	דְּוָי	*Languor.*	Faintness, sickness.
—	דְּוַי	*Languens.*	Languishing.
	דּוֹיֵג	*Doeg.*	Doeg, N. M.
דוך		*Tutudit.*	He beat, *as in a mortar.*
דום		*Siluit, quievit, substitit, expectavit.*	He was silent, was still, rested, stood still, waited, expected
דמם	דֹּם	*Tace, subsiste.*	Be silent, stand thou still.
דום	דּוּמָה	*Silentium, sepulcrum*	Silence, the grave.
דמה	דּוּמֶה	*Similis.*	Like.
	דּוּמָה	*Duma.*	Dumah, N. M. P.
דמם	דּוֹמִי	*Expecta.*	Wait thou.
דום	דּוּמִיָּה	*Silentium.*	Silence.
—	דּוּמָם	*Silens, tacens.*	Silent, dumb.
	דּוּמֶשֶׂק	*Damascus.*	Damascus, N. P.
דון		*Judicavit, judicium exercuit, disceptavit, causam egit.*	He judged, executed judgment, contended, pleaded a cause.
דנק	דּוֹנַג	*Cera.*	Wax.
דפק	דּוֹפֵק	*Pulsans.*	Knocking.
דוץ		*Exultavit, exsiliit [gaudio.*	He exulted, leaped for joy.
	דּוֹר	*Dor.*	Dor, N. P.
דור		*Habitavit, struit.*	He dwelt, lived, piled up.
—	דּוֹר דֹּר דָּר	*Generatio.*	A, the generation.
—	*דָּוֹר	*Generatio.*	A generation.
—	דּוּר	*Strue.*	Pile thou up.
	דּוּרָא	*Dura.*	Dura, N. P.
דור	דּוֹרוֹ	*Generatio ejus.*	His generation.
—	דּוֹרוֹת דֹּרוֹת	*Generationes.*	Generations.
—	דֹּרוֹתֵינוּ	*Generationes nostræ*	Our generations.
—	דּוֹרִי	*Ætas, vita mea.*	My age, life.
—	דּוֹרִים	*Generationes.*	Generations.
דרש	דּוֹרֵשׁ דֹּרֵשׁ	*Quærens, scrutans.*	Seeking, searching, examining
דוש		*Calcavit, trituravit, conculcavit, contrivit.*	He trod out, threshed, trampled on, broke, crushed.

ROOTS.	DERIVATIVES.	VERSIO.	SIGNIFICATION.
דוש	דוּשָׁם	*Triturare eos.*	They thresh.
דוה	דְּוֹתָהּ	*Menses ejus.*	Her periodical sickness.
	דח		
דָּחָה		*Depulit, expulit, impulit, detrusit.*	He drove away, cast off, pushed forward, cast down.
—	דְּחֹה	*Impellere.*	To push.
—	דֹּחֶה	*Depellens.*	Driving away.
—	דֹּחוּ	*Detrusi sunt.*	They have been cast down.
דחף	דְּחוּפִים	*Impulsi.*	Being hastened, urged forward
דחל	דְּחִיל-לָה	*Terribilis.*	Terrible, dreadful.
דחה	דְּחִיתַנִי	*Impulisti me.*	Thou hast thrust at me.
דְּחַל		*Metuit.*	He feared.
דחן			
דָּחַף		*Impulit, ursit.*	He hastened, urged, chased.
דָּחַק		*Pressit, vexavit.*	He pressed, oppressed, harassed.
	די		
די			
—	דַּי	*Sufficientia, sufficiens*	Sufficiency, enough, sufficient
—	דִּי	*Qui, quæ; ipse, ipsa; quisquis, quicquid; quocunque; quia, ut, sed.*	Who, which, what; he, she, that; whoever, whatever; wherever; because, that, but.
	דִּיבוֹן דִּיבֹן	*Dibon.*	Dibon, N. P.
דיה			
—	דַּיּוֹת	*Vultures.*	The vultures.
די	דַּיֶּךָ	*Sufficientia tua.*	Thy sufficiency, enough for thee.
—	דַּיָּם	*Sufficientia eorum.*	Enough for them.
	דִּימוֹן	*Dimon.*	Dimon, N. P.
	דִּימוֹנָה	*Dimona.*	Dimonah, N. P.
דון	דִּין דִּינָא	*Judica; judicium, causa, lis.*	Judge thou; the judgment, cause, strife
	דִּינָה	*Dina.*	Dinah, N. W.
דון	דִּינָה	*Judicium.*	Judgment.
—	דִּינוּ	*Judicate.*	Judge ye.
	דִּינָיֵא	*Dinæi.*	Dinaites, N. N.
דין	דִּינֵךְ	*Causa tua.*	Thy cause.

ROOTS.	DERIVATIVES.	VERSIO.	SIGNIFICATION.
דיק			
—	דָּיֵק	*Turris, propugnaculum, vallum, vel circummurale.*	A turret, fort, battery, or surrounding wall.
דוש	דִּיש	*Tritura.*	Threshing.
	דִּישׁוֹן דִּישָׁן	*Disan.*	Dishan, N. M.
	דכ		
דך			
—	דָּךְ דֵּךְ	*Hic, hæc; ille, illa.*	This, that.
דכה	דַּךְ	*Attritus, afflictus.*	The oppressed, afflicted.
דִּכָּא		*Fregit, confregit, contudit, attrivit, humiliavit, pressit.*	He broke, broke to pieces, beat down, bruised, crushed, humbled, oppressed.
—	דַּכָּא	*Attritus, contritus.*	Broken, crushed, contrite.
—	דַּכְּאוֹ	*Contererer illum.*	To bruise him.
—	דֻּכְּאוּ	*Humiliati sunt.*	They were humbled.
—	דַּכְּאֵי	*Contriti.*	The contrite.
—	דִּכִּאתָ	*Confregisti.*	Thou hast broken.
דָּכָה		*Fregit, contudit, depressit, afflixit.*	He broke, bruised, beat down depressed, afflicted.
דוך	דָּכוּ	*Tutuderunt.*	They beat, pounded.
דכה	דַּכְּיוֹ	*Attriti vel attritiones ejus.*	Persons afflicted by it, or its bruisings, *calumnies.*
—	דָּכְיָם	*Fluctus, rupturæ eorum.*	Their waves, breakers.
—	דִּכִּיתָ	*Contrivisti.*	Thou hast broken.
—	דִּכִּיתָנוּ	*Contrivisti nos.*	Thou hast broken us.
דכך			
דך	דִּכֵּן	*Hic, hæc; ille, illa.*	This, that.
דכף			
דכר			
—	דִּכְרוֹנָה	*Memoriale.*	A record
—	דִּכְרִין	*Arietes.*	Rams
—	דִּכְרָנַיָּא	*Commentarii.*	Registers.
	דל		
דלל	דַּל דָּל	*Pauper; ostium.*	Poor; the door.

ROOTS.	DERIVATIVES.	VERSIO.	SIGNIFICATION.
דָּלָה		*Hausit, extraxit, attenuavit, exhausit.*	He drew, drew out of, impaired, weakened, exhausted.
—	דְּלֹה	*Haurire.*	To draw.
דלל	דַּלּוּ	*Attenuati, exhausti sunt.*	They failed, were exhausted.
—	דַּלּוֹנוּ	*Attenuati sumus.*	We are brought low.
—	דַּלּוֹת	*Tenues.*	Thin, poor.
—	דַּלּוֹתִי	*Attenuatus sum.*	I am brought low.
דָּלַח		*Turbavit* aquam	He troubled, disturbed *water.*
	דְּלָיָה־־יָהוּ	*Dalaiah.*	Dalaiah, N. M.
—	דַּלְיוּ	*Attenuati sunt.*	They are wasted, impaired, enfeebled.
—	דָּלִיּוֹתָיו דָּלִי	*Rami ejus.*	His branches.
	דְּלִילָה	*Delila.*	Delilah, N. W.
דלל	דַּלִּים	*Pauperes, egeni.*	The poor, needy.
דלה	דִּלִּיתָנִי	*Extraxisti, suscepisti me.*	Thou hast drawn me out, taken me up, taken charge of me.
דָּלַל		*Minutus, attenuatus est.*	He was lessened, diminished, wasted, exhausted.
—	דָּלֲלוּ	*Attenuabuntur.*	They shall be dimished.
	דִּלְעָן	*Dilean.*	Dilean, N. P.
דָּלַף		*Stillavit, diffluxit, stillatim vel paulatim periit.*	He dropped, distilled, melted, dissolved, fell asunder, decayed by drops or gradually.
—	דֶּלֶף	*Stilla, stillicidium.*	A dropping.
—	דָּלְפָה	*Stillavit, diffluxit.*	She dropped, distilled, decayed.
	דַּלְפוֹן	*Dalphon.*	Dalphon, N. M.
דָּלַק		*Arsit, accensus est; insectatus, persecutus est.*	He burned, was inflamed; he closely pursued, persecuted.
—	דֹּלֵק	*Ardens.*	Burning.
—	דֹּלְקִים	*Ardentes.*	Burning.
—	דְּלָקֻנוּ	*Insectati sunt nos.*	They pursued us.
—	דָּלַקְתָּ	*Insectatus es.*	Thou hast hotly pursued.
דלת			
—	דֶּלֶת	*Janua.*	A door.
דלל	דַּלַּת	*Tenuitas, pauperes.*	Poverty, the poorest people.
דלת	דְּלָתוֹת	*Portæ, valvæ.*	Gates, folding doors.
—	דַּלְתוֹת	*Portæ, fores, pagellæ*	The gates, doors, leaves.

ROOTS.	DERIVATIVES.	VERSIO.	SIGNIFICATION.
דלת	דַּלְתוֹתָיו־תֹתָיו	*Fores ejus.*	His doors.
—	דַּלְתֵי	*Fores.*	The doors.
—	דַּלְתִי	*Fores meæ.*	My doors.
—	דְּלָתֶיהָ	*Portæ ejus.*	Her gates.
—	דְּלָתֶיךָ דַּלְתֹתֶיךָ	*Fores tuæ.*	Thy doors.
—	דְּלָתַיִם	*Januæ, valvæ.*	Gates, two-leaved gates.
—	דַּלְתֹתַי	*Ostia mea.*	My gates.
דם			
—	דָּם דַּם	*Sanguis; reatus sanguinis; cædes.*	Blood; the guilt of blood; murder.
דָּמָה		*Similis fuit, assimilavit, cogitavit, tacuit, desiit, excidit*	He resembled, likened, thought, was silent, failed, ceased, cut off, destroyed.
דם	דָּמָהּ	*Sanguis ejus.*	Her blood.
דמה	דָּמָה	*Similis.*	Like.
—	דְּמֵה	*Similis esto.*	Be thou like.
—	דִּמָּה	*Cogitavit.*	He thought.
דם	דָּמוֹ	*Sanguis ejus.*	His blood.
דמה	דָּמוּ	*Similes fuerunt.*	They were like.
דמם	דֹּם	*Tace, quiesce, abstine*	Be silent, be still, forbear [thou.
דמה	דִּמּוּ	*Cogitaverunt.*	They thought.
דום	דֹּמּוּ	*Silete; expectate.*	Be ye silent, still; wait ye.
דמה	דְּמוּת	*Similitudo.*	The likeness.
דם	דָּמִי	*Sanguis meus.*	My blood.
—	דְּמֵי	*Sanguines.*	Blood.
דום	דֳּמִי	*Silentium.*	Silence.
דמה	דָּמְיָה	*Similis.*	Like.
דום	דּוּמִיָּה	*Silentium.*	Silence.
דם	דָּמֶיהָ	*Sanguines ejus.*	Her blood.
—	דְּמֵיהֶם	*Sanguines eorum.*	Their blood.
—	דָּמָיו	*Sanguines ejus.*	His blood.
—	דָּמֵךְ	*Sanguis tuus.*	Thy blood.
—	דָּמִים	*Sanguines.*	Blood.
	דַּמִּים	*Dammim.*	Dammim, N. P.
דמה	דִּמִּינוּ	*Cogitavimus.*	We have thought.

ROOTS.	DERIVATIVES.	VERSIO.	SIGNIFICATION.
דמה	דָּמִינוּ	*Similes fuimus.*	We were like.
—	דִּמְיֹנוֹ	*Similitudo ejus.*	His likeness.
—	דִּמִּיתָ	*Cogitavisti.*	Thou thoughtest.
—	דָּמִיתָ	*Similis fuisti.*	Thou wast like.
—	דִּמִּיתִי	*Cogitavi.*	I thought.
—	דָּמִיתִי	*Assimilatus sum.*	I was likened.
—	דִּמִּיתִיךְ	*Assimilavi te.*	I have compared thee.
דם	דִּמְּךָ דָּמְךָ דָּמֵיךְ	*Sanguis tuus.*	Thy blood.
—	דִּמְכֶם	*Sanguis vester.*	Your blood.
דָּמַם		*Conticuit, siluit, quievit, destitit, abstinuit, expectavit.*	He held his peace, kept silence, rested, ceased, forbore, refrained, expected, waited.
דם	דָּמָם	*Sanguis eorum.*	Their blood.
דמם	דְּמָמָה	*Silentium.*	Silence.
דמן			
—	דֹּמֶן	*Fimus, stercus.*	Dung.
	דִּמְנָה	*Dimna.*	Dimnah, N. P.
דָּמַע		*Lachrymatus est.*	He wept, shed tears.
—	דִּמְעָה	*Lachryma.*	A tear.
—	דִּמְעַת	*Lachryma.*	The tear.
—	דִּמְעָתִי	*Lachryma mea.*	My tear.
—	דִּמְעָתֶךָ	*Lachryma tua.*	Thy tear.
	דַּמֶּשֶׂק	*Damascus.*	Damascus, N. P.
דמה	דָּמְתָה	*Similis fuit.*	She was like.
	דנ		
	דָּן	*Dan.*	Dan, N. M. T. P.
דן			
דון	דָּן	*Judicavit; judicans.*	He judged; judging.
	דָּנִאֵל דָּנִיֵּאל	*Daniel.*	Daniel, N. M.
דנג			
דן	דְּנָה	*Hic, hæc; ille, illa; alter, altera; hi, illi.*	This, that, one, another, these, those.
	דַּנָּה	*Danna.*	Dannah, N. P.
	דִּנְהָבָה	*Dinhaba.*	Dinhabah, N. P.

ROOTS.	DERIVATIVES.	VERSIO.	SIGNIFICATION.
דון	דָּנוּ	*Judicaverunt.*	They judged.
—	דָּנַנִי	*Judicavit me.*	He judged me.
	דע		
ידע	דַּע	*Scito, cognosce.*	Know, mark, observe thou.
—	דֵּעָה	*Scientia.*	Knowledge.
—	דְּעֵה	*Cognosce.*	Know thou.
—	דַּעֵהוּ	*Agnosce illum.*	Acknowledge thou him.
—	דְּעוּ	*Scitote, agnoscite.*	Know, mark, acknowledge ye.
	דְּעוּאֵל	*Dehuel.*	Deuel, N. M.
ידע	דֵּעוֹת	*Scientiæ.*	Knowledge.
—	דְּעִי	*Scito, agnosce.*	Know, acknowledge thou.
—	דֵּעִי	*Scientia, opinio mea.*	My knowledge, opinion.
—	דֵּעִים	*Scientiæ.* [*cit.*	Knowledge.
דָּעַךְ		*Extinctus est, defe-*	He was extinguished, he failed
—	דָּעֲכוּ דֹּעֲכוּ	*Extincti sunt.*	They were extinguished.
ידע	דַּעַת דָּעַת	*Scientia; cognoscere*	Knowledge; to know.
—	דַּעְתִּי	*Cognoscere me.*	I know.
—	דַּעְתְּךָ	*Scientia tua.*	Thy knowledge.
	דפ		
דפה			
דפה	דֳּפִי	*Convitium, calumnia*	Reproach, slander. [forward.
דָּפַק		*Pulsavit, propulit.*	He knocked, struck, drove
	דָּפְקָה	*Dophca.*	Dophkah, N. P.
	דק		[to pieces.
דקק	דַּק דָּק	*Comminutus est.*	He was beaten small, bruised
—	דַּקָּה	*Tenuis.*	Small.
—	דַּקּוּ	*Comminuti sunt.*	They were broken to pieces.
—	דַּקּוֹת	*Tenues.*	Thin.
	דִּקְלָה	*Dicla.*	Diklah, N. M.
דָּקַק		*Comminuit.*	He beat or stamped it into very small pieces. [through
דָּקַר		*Transfixit, perfodit.*	He stabbed, pierced, thrust
	דֶּקֶר	*Decar.*	Deker, N. M.
דקר	דָּקְרוּ	*Transfixerunt.*	They pierced.

ROOTS.	DERIVATIVES.	VERSIO.	SIGNIFICATION.
	דר		
דר			
דרא			
—	דֵּרָאוֹן	*Fastidium.*	Abhorrence.
דרב			
דרג			
	דַּרְדַּע	*Darda.*	Darda, N. M.
דרך	דְּרוּכָה	*Tensa, extenta.*	Bent, stretched, extended.
דרם	דָּרוֹם	*Auster.*	The south.
דרר	דְּרוֹר	*Libertas.*	Liberty.
דרש	דְּרוּשָׁה	*Quæsita.*	Sought.
—	דְּרוּשִׁים	*Quæsiti.*	Sought.
	דָּרְיָוֶשׁ	*Darius.*	Darius, N. M.
דָּרַךְ		*Incessit, calcavit, trituravit, tetendit, deduxit.*	He walked, trod, threshed, bent, stretched, extended, guided, led.
—	דֶּרֶךְ דָּֽרֶךְ	*Via, iter, mos, consuetudo.*	A, the way, road, journey, manner, custom.
—	דֹּרֵךְ	*Calcans.*	Treading.
—	דָּרְכָה	*Calcavit.*	She has trodden.
—	דַּרְכָּהּ	*Via ejus.*	Her way.
—	דַּרְכּוֹ	*Via ejus.*	His way.
—	דָּרְכוּ	*Calcarunt, tetenderunt.*	They have trodden, bent.
—	דְּרֻכוֹת	*Tensæ, extentæ.*	Bent, stretched, extended.
—	דֹּרְכֵי	*Tendentes.*	Bending, stretching.
—	דַּרְכֵי	*Viæ.*	Ways.
—	דַּרְכִּי דַּרְכּוֹ	*Via mea.*	My way.
—	דְּרָכַי־־כַי	*Viæ meæ.*	My ways.
—	דְּרָכֶיהָ	*Viæ ejus.*	Her ways.
—	דַּרְכֵיהֶם	*Viæ eorum.*	Their ways.
—	דְּרָכָיו דְּרָכָו	*Viæ ejus.*	His ways.
—	דְּרָכֶיךָ־־כֶיךָ	*Viæ tuæ.*	Thy ways.
—	דַּרְכֵיכֶם	*Viæ vestræ.*	Your ways.
—	דְּרָכִים דְּרָכִים	*Viæ.*	Ways.
—	דֹּרְכִים	*Calcantes.*	Treading.
—	דְּרָכֵינוּ	*Viæ nostræ.*	Our ways.

ROOTS.	DERIVATIVES.	VERSIO.	SIGNIFICATION.
דרך	דַּרְכְּךָ־כֵּךְ	*Via tua.*	Thy way.
—	דַּרְכְּכֶם	*Via vestra.*	Your way.
—	דַּרְכָּם	*Via eorum.*	Their way.
—	דַּרְכְּמוֹנִים	*Drachmæ,* numismata aurea.	Drams, *gold coins.*
—	דַּרְכֵּנוּ	*Via nostra.*	Our way.
—	דָּרַכְתָּ	*Calcasti.*	Thou didst tread.
—	דָּרַכְתִּי	*Calcavi.*	I have trodden.
דרם			
	דַּרְמֶשֶׂק	*Damascus.*	Damascus.
	דָּרַע	*Dara.*	Dara, N. M.
דרע			
	דַּרְקוֹן	*Darcon.*	Darkon, N. M.
דרר			
דָּרַשׁ		*Quæsivit, inquisivit. requisivit, interrogavit, consuluit*	He sought, searched, inquired, required, asked, consulted.
—	דָּרֹשׁ	*Quærere, requirere.*	To seek, require.
—	דְּרֹשׁ	*Interroga, consule.*	Inquire, consult thou.
—	דֹּרֵשׁ	*Quærens; quærere.*	To seek, seeking.
—	דָּרְשָׁה	*Quæsivi.*	She sought.
—	דְּרָשֻׁהוּ	*Inquisiverunt eum.*	They inquired for him.
—	דָּרָשׁוּ דָּרְשׁוּ	*Quæsiverunt.*	They sought.
—	דָּרְשׁוֹ	*Quærere eum.*	He seeks.
—	דִּרְשׁוּ	*Quærite, consulite.*	Seek, consult ye.
—	דְּרָשׁוּם	*Quæsiverunt eos.*	They have sought them.
	דִּישׁוֹן	*Dison.*	Dishon, N. M.
דרש	דְּרָשׁוּנִי	*Quæsiverunt me.*	They have sought me.
—	דִּרְשׁוּנִי	*Quærite me.*	Seek ye me.
—	דֹּרְשֵׁי	*Quærentes.*	Seeking.
—	דֹּרְשָׁיו דּוֹרְשָׁו	*Quærentes eum.*	Seeking him.
—	דֹּרְשֶׁיךָ	*Quærentes te.*	Seeking thee.
—	דְּרַשְׁנֻהוּ	*Quæsivimus eum.*	We sought him.
—	דָּרַשְׁנוּ	*Quæsivimus.*	We have sought.
—	דָּרַשְׁתָּ	*Quæsivisti.*	Thou hast sought.
—	דָּרַשְׁתִּי	*Quæsivi.*	I have sought.
—	דְּרַשְׁתִּיךָ	*Quæsivi te.*	I have sought thee.

ROOTS.	DERIVATIVES.	VERSIO.	SIGNIFICATION.
דור	דֹּרֹתֵיכֶם	*Generationes vestræ*	Your generations.
—	דֹּרֹתֵינוּ	*Generationes nostræ*	Our generations.
	דש		
דוש	דָּשׁ	*Trituravit.*	He threshed.
דָּשָׁא		*Germinavit.*	He sprang up, sprouted.
—	דֶּשֶׁא	*Herbilis.*	At grass, feeding on grass.
—	דֶּשֶׁא	*Germen, herba.*	The grass, herb.
—	דָּשְׁאוּ	*Germinarunt.*	They sprang.
דָּשֵׁן		*Impinguavit, pinguescit, in cinerem redegit, cineres amovit.*	He fattened or made fat, became fat, reduced to ashes, removed the ashes.
—	דָּשֵׁן	*Pinguis.*	Fat.
—	דֶּשֶׁן	*Pinguedo.*	Fatness.
—	דִּישֹׁן	*Dison.*	Dishon, N. M.
דשן	דִּשְׁנֵי	*Pingues.*	Fat.
—	דִּשְׁנִי	*Pinguedo mea.*	My fatness.
—	דְּשֵׁנִים	*Pingues.*	Fat.
—	דִּשַּׁנְתָּ	*Impinguasti, perunxisti.*	Thou hast fattened, anointed.
	דת		
דת			
—	דָּת דָּתָא	*Lex, decretum, mandatum.*	A law, decree, commandment.
—	דְּתָבְרַיָּא	*Consiliarii.*	Counsellors.
—	דָּתוֹ	*Lex ejus.*	His law.
—	דָּתֵי	*Leges.*	Laws.
	דֹּתָיְנָה	*Dothan.*	Dothan, N. P.
דת	דָּתְכוֹן	*Lex vestra.*	Your law.
	דָּתָן	*Dathan.*	Dathan, N. M.
	דֹּתָן	*Dathan.*	Dothan, N. M.

ROOTS.	DERIVATIVES.	VERSIO.	SIGNIFICATION.
	הא		
הא			
—	הָא הָא	*En, ecce, sicut.*	Lo, behold, even as.
אבה	הָאָב	*Pater.*	The father.
אבד	הָאֲבֵדָה	*Res amissa.*	The lost thing.
—	הָאֹבְדוֹת	*Pereuntes.*	Those who are perishing.
—	הָאֹבְדִים	*Pereuntes.*	Those who are perishing.
—	הָאֹבֶדֶת	*Periens.*	She who is perishing.
אבה	הָאָבוֹת	*Patres, familiæ.*	The fathers, families.
אוב	הָאֹבוֹת	*Pythones.*	Those who have familiar spirits.
בטח	הָאֲבַטִּחִים	*Pepones.*	The melons.
אבד	הַאֲבִיד	*Perdere.*	To destroy.
—	הַאֲבִידוֹ	*Perdere eum.*	He destroys.
אבה	הָאֶבְיוֹן	*Egenus.*	The poor *man.*
—	הָאֲבִיּוֹנָה	*Concupiscentia.*	Desire.
בכה	הַאֶבְכֶּה	*Num flebo?*	Shall I weep?
יבל	הָאֻבָל	*Fluvius.*	The river.
אבל	הָאֵבֶל	*Luctus.*	The mourning.
—	הֶאֱבַלְתִּי	*Lugere feci.*	I caused a mourning.
אבן	הָאֶבֶן	*Lapis; lapideus.*	The stone; stony.
אבנט	הָאַבְנֵט	*Balteus.*	The girdle.
אבן	הָאֲבָנִים	*Lapides; lapidei.*	The stones; of stone.
—	הָאָבְנָיִם	*Sellæ; rotæ.*	The stools, wheels.
אבר	הָאֵבֶר	*Ala.*	The wing.
אוב	הָאֹבֹת	*Pythones.*	Such as have familiar spirits.
אגם	הָאֲגַמִּים	*Stagna, paludes.*	The ponds, pools.
אגן	הָאַגָּנוֹת	*Crateres.*	The cups.
אגר	הָאִגֶּרֶת	*Epistola.*	The letter.
אדן	הָאָדוֹן הָאָדֹן	*Dominus.*	The lord.
אדר	הָאַדִּירִים	*Potentes.*	The mighty.
אדם	הָאָדָם	*Adam; homo; homines.*	Adam; the man; man; men.
—	הָאָדֹם	*Rufus.*	The red, that red.
—	הָאֲדָמָה	*Terra.*	The earth, land, ground.
אדן	הָאֲדֹנִים	*Domini.*	Lords, masters.
ידע	הַאֵדַע	*Num discernam?*	Shall I discern?

ROOTS.	DERIVATIVES.	VERSIO.	SIGNIFICATION.
דרש	הַאֶדְרשׁ	*Num ad inquirendum?*	Is it to inquire?
אדר	הָאַדֶּרֶת	*Pallium.*	The robe.
אהב	הָאַהֲבָה	*Amor.*	The love.
—	הָאֲהוּבָה	*Dilecta.*	The beloved.
אלה	הָאֵהֶל	*Hæc.*	This.
אהל	הָאֹהֶל	*Tentorium.*	The tent.
—	הָאֹהֱלָה	*In tentorium.*	Unto the tent.
—	הָאָהֳלִי	*Tentorium meum.*	My tent.
יבל	הָאוּבָל־־בַל	*Fluvius.*	The river.
אוד	הָאוּדִים	*Torres.*	The firebrands.
איב	הָאוֹיֵב הָאֹיֵב	*Inimicus.*	The enemy.
אול	הָאֱוִיל	*Stultus.*	The fool.
יכל	הַאוּכַל	*Num potero?*	Shall I be able?
אכל	הַאוֹכַל	*Num comedam?*	Shall I eat?
אלם	הָאוּלָם	*Porticus.*	The porch.
און	הָאָוֶן	*Iniquitas.*	The iniquity.
יסף	הַאוֹסִיף־־סִף	*Num addam, pergam?*	Shall I add, go on, proceed?
אפה	הָאוֹפִים	*Pistores.*	The bakers.
אפן	הָאוֹפַן־־פַן	*Rota.*	The wheel.
—	הָאוֹפַנִּים	*Rotæ.*	The wheels.
אצר	הָאוֹצָר	*Thesaurus.*	The treasure, treasury.
—	הָאֹצָרוֹת הָאֹצָ׳	*Thesauri.*	The treasures.
אור	הָאוֹר	*Lux.*	The light.
אות	הָאוֹת הָאֹת	*Signum.*	The sign, token.
את	הַאֹתִי הָאֹתִי	*An me?*	Me?
אזב	הָאֵזוֹב	*Hyssopum.*	The hyssop.
אזר	הָאֵזוֹר	*Cingulum.*	The girdle.
אזן	הֶאֱזִין	*Auscultavit.*	He attended, gave ear.
—	הַאֲזִינָה	*Ausculta.*	Attend thou, give ear.
—	הַאֲזִינוּ	*Auscultate.*	Attend ye, give ear.
—	הֶאֱזִינוּ	*Auscultaverunt.*	They attended, gave ear.
זכה	הַאֶזְכֶּה	*An purum habebo?*	Shall I count or esteem pure?
אזל	הָאֶזֶל	*Viatorius;* vel, secundum quosdam *nomen proprium.*	For the direction of travellers; *or, according to some,* a proper name.
אזן	הַאֲזִנָּה	*Auscultate.*	Hearken, attend ye.

ROOTS.	DERIVATIVES.	VERSIO.	SIGNIFICATION.
זקק	הָאזִקִּים	*Catenæ.*	The chains.
זרח	הָאֶזְרָח	*Indigena.*	A native of the country.
אח	הֶאָח הָאָח	*Heu! euge!* [*quidam*	Ah! aha! ha ha! [first.
אחד	הָאֶחָד הָאֶחָד	*Unus, alter, primus,*	One, the one, another, the
אחה	הָאַחֲוָה	*Fraternitas.*	The brotherhood.
אחז	הָאָחֻז	*Captus.*	Taken.
—	הָאֲחֻזוֹת	*Irretitæ, captæ.*	Entangled, caught.
חיה	הַאֶחְיֶה	*An revalescam?*	Shall I recover?
אחה	הַאֲחֵיכֶם	*An fratres vestri?*	*Shall* your brethren?
אחר	הָאַחֵר	*Alter.*	The other.
—	הָאַחֲרוֹן--רֹן	*Posterior, ultimus.*	The latter, last.
—	הָאַחֲרוֹנִים־רֹנִים	*Posteriores; novissimi.*	They who come after; the last.
—	הָאַחֶרֶת	*Alia, altera.*	The other.
אחש	הָאֲחַשְׁדַּרְפְּנִים	*Satrapæ, proreges.*	The lieutenants, viceroys.
אחשתר	הָאֲחַשְׁתְּרָנִים	*Muli.*	Mules.
אחד	הָאַחַת הָאֶחָת	*Una.*	The one.
אטד	הָאָטָד	*Rhamnus.*	The bramble.
אטט	הָאִטִּים	*Præstigiatores.*	The charmers.
אטם	הָאֲטֻמוֹת	*Clausæ.*	Closed.
אי	הָאִי	*Insula.*	The island.
איה	הָאַיָּה	*Vultur.*	The vulture.
אי	הָאִיִּים הָאִיִּן	*Insulæ.* [*nare.*	The isles.
איל	הָאַיִל הָאַיִל	*Aries; superlimi-*	The ram; the lintel.
—	הָאַיָּל	*Aries; cervus.*	The ram; the hart.
—	הָאֵילִים--לִם	*Arietes; postes.*	The rams; the posts.
—	הָאַיָּלִים	*Cervi.*	The harts.
אין	הַאֵין	*Nonne? an non?*	Not? no?
—	הַאֵינְךָ	*Nonne tu?*	Not thou?
אור	הֵאִירָה	*Splenduit.*	She shined.
—	הָאִירָה	*Illumina, lucere fac.*	Enlighten thou, make to shine
—	הֵאִירוּ	*Illuminaverunt.*	They enlightened.
איש	הָאִישׁ הַאִישׁ	*Vir. An vir?*	The man. A man?
אית	הַאִיתָךְ	*Nunquid es tu?*	Art thou?
נכה	הַאַכֶּה	*An percutiam?*	Shall I smite?
אכל	הֶאָכוֹל	*Num comedendo?*	In eating?
—	הָאֲכִילָה	*Cibus.*	The food.

ROOTS.	DERIVATIVES.	VERSIO.	SIGNIFICATION.
אכל	הַאֲכִילֻהוּ	*Ciba eum.*	Give him to eat.
—	הָאֹכֵל	*Comedens.*	Eating.
—	הָאֹכֶל	*Cibus.*	The food.
—	הָאֲכֹל	*Comedere.* [*tes.*	To eat.
—	הָאֹכְלִים	*Comedentes, vescen-*	Eating, feeding.
—	הָאֹכֶלֶת	*Comedens.*	Eating, she who eats.
—	הֶאֱכַלְתִּי	*Cibavi.*	I have fed.
—	הֶאֱכַלְתִּיךָ	*Cibavi te.*	I fed thee.
—	הֶאֱכַלְתָּם	*Comedere fecisti eos.*	Thou hast fed them.
אלה	הָאֵל	*Deus.*	God, the God.
—	הַאֵל	*Nunquid Deus?*	Is it God?
אל	הַאֶל	*An ad?*	*Is it* to?
—	הָאֵל	*Hi, illi.*	These, those.
אלג	הָאַלְגּוּמִּים	*Algumim*, arbor.	The algum *tree.*
אל	הָאֵלֶּה	*Hæc, ista.* [*catio.*	These, those things.
אלה	הָאָלָה	*Juramentum, impre-*	The oath, curse, imprecation.
—	הָאֵלָה הָאֵלָה	*Quercus.*	The oak.
—	הַאֱלֹהֵי	*An deus.*	A god.
—	הָאֱלֹהִים	*Deus, dii.*	God, the gods.
—	הָאַלּוֹן	*Quercus.*	An oak.
—	הָאָלוֹת	*Maledictiones.*	The curses.
—	הָאַלְיָה	*Cauda.*	The rump.
אלל	הָאֱלִיל	*Idolum.*	The idol.
—	הָאֱלִילִים—לִם	*Idola.*	The idols.
איל	הָאֵלִים	*Arietes.* [*dam?*	The rams.
ילך	הַאֵלֵךְ	*Vadam; num va-*	I will walk; shall I go?
אלם	הָאֻלָם	*Vestibulum.*	The porch.
אלג	הָאַלְמֻגִּים	*Almugim*, arbores.	The almug *trees.*
אלם	הָאַלְמָנָה	*Vidua.*	The widow.
אלף	הָאֶלֶף הָאָלֶף	*Mille.*	The thousand.
—	הָאֲלָפִים	*Millia.*	The thousands.
אם	הַאִם	*Nonne?*	*Is* not?
אמם	הָאֵם	*Mater.*	The mother.
—	הָאַמָּה	*Cubitus.*	The cubit.
אמה	הָאָמָה	*Ancilla.*	The bondwomen.
—	הָאֲמָהוֹת־הֹת	*Ancillæ.*	The maid servants.
אמן	הָאָמוֹן	*Multitudo.*	The multitude.

ROOTS.	DERIVATIVES.	VERSIO.	SIGNIFICATION.
אמן	הָאֱמוּנָה	*Veritas, fides.*	The truth, faithfulness.
אמר	הָאָמוּר	*Dictus.*	He who is called, named.
אמם	הָאֻמִּים	*O nationes.*	O ye people, nations.
אמן	הֶאֱמִין	*Credidit.*	He believed.
—	הֶאֱמִינוּ	*Crediderunt.*	They believed.
—	הַאֲמִינוּ	*Credite.*	Believe ye.
אמר	הֶאֱמִירְךָ	*Dicere fecit te.*	He hath avouched thee.
אמן	הָאֹמֵן	*Nutritus.*	The nursing father.
—	הָאֹמְנוֹת	*Columnæ.*	The pillars.
—	הָאֹמְנִים	*Educatores.*	Those who brought up.
—	הָאֱמֻנִים	*Nutriti.*	Those who are brought up.
—	הַאֻמְנָם	*An vere?*	Indeed? in very deed?
—	הֶאֱמַנְתִּי	*Credidi.*	I believed.
—	הֶאֱמַנְתֶּם	*Credidistis.*	Ye believed.
אמר	הֶאָמֹר	*An dicere, in dicendo*	*Is it* to say, in saying?
—	הָאָמַר	*Qui dixit.*	Who said.
—	הָאֹמֵר הָאֹמְרָה	*Dicens.*	He who says.
—	הָאֹמְרוֹת-־רִים	*Dicentes.*	Those who say.
—	הֶאֱמַרְתָּ	*Dicere fecisti.*	Thou hast avouched.
אמן	הָאֱמֶת הַאֱמֶת	*Veritas, fides.* [*talis*	The truth, faithfulness.
אנש	הַאֱנוֹשׁ	*An homo, homo mor-*	Shall man, mortal man?
אנח	הֵאָנַח	*Suspira, ingemisce.*	Sigh, groan thou.
אני	הַאֲנִי	*Num ego?*	*Shall* I?
—	הֶאָנֹכִי	*Num ego?*	*Have* I?
אנף	הָאֲנָפָה	*Avis irritabilis; fortasse ardea, vel falco montanus, vel species aquilæ.*	A bird remarkable for its furious disposition; *perhaps* the heron, or hawk, or a species of eagle.
אנק	הֵאָנֵק	*Clamare.*	To cry.
אנש	הָאֲנָשִׁים	*Viri.*	The men.
אסר	הָאֵסוּר	*Vinculum, carcer.*	The bond, binding, prison.
—	הָאֲסוּרִים-סִירִ׳	*Vincti.*	The prisoners.
אסף	הָאָסִיף	*Collectio.*	The collection, ingathering.
—	הָאֹסֵף	*Colligens.*	He that gathers.
—	הֵאָסֵף	*Congregando.*	In gathering.
—	הֵאָסֵף	*Congregari.*	To be gathered.
—	הֵאָסְפוּ	*Congregate vos.*	Assemble yourselves.

ROOTS.	DERIVATIVES.	VERSIO.	SIGNIFICATION.
אסף	הֵאָסְפִי	*Recipe te, reconde te*	Put up thyself, hide thyself.
—	הָאֲסֻפִּים	*Collecti, collectiones.*	Collected, the collections.
אסר	הֵאָסְרוּ	*Vinciemini.*	Ye shall be tied.
עלה	הַאֶעֱלֶה	*Num ascendam ?*	Shall I go up ?
אנף	הַאַף	*An etiam ?*	Is it also ?
—	הָאַף הָאָף	*Nasus, furor.*	The nose, the anger.
אפה	הָאֹפִים	*Pistores.*	The bakers.
אפס	הַאֶפֶס	*Nunquid non?*	Is there not ?
—	הֶאָפֵס	*An defecit?*	Has he utterly failed ?
אפר	הָאֵפֶר הָאֵפֶר	*Cinis.*	Ashes, the ashes.
פרח	הָאֶפְרֹחִים	*Pulli.*	The young ones.
אצר	הָאֹצְרִים	*Recondentes.*	Those who treasure up.
קדם	הַאֲקַדְּמֶנּוּ	*An præveniam eum, occurram ei?*	Shall I come before him, prevent, or meet him ?
אור	הָאֵר	*Lucere fac.*	Cause thou to shine.
ארב	הָאֹרֵב	*Insidians, insidiator.*	The ambush, the lier in wait.
רבה	הָאַרְבֶּה	*Locusta.*	The locust.
ארב	הָאֹרְבִים	*Insidiantes.*	Those who lie in wait.
רבע	הָאַרְבָּעִים	*Quadraginta; quadragesimus.*	Forty; the fortieth.
ארג	הָאֹרֶג	*Jugum.*	The beam, *weaver's beam.*
ארגז	הָאַרְגָּז	*Capsa.*	The box.
ארג	הָאַרְגָּמָן	*Purpura.*	The purple.
ירד	הַאֵרֵד	*Num descendam?*	Shall I go down ?
ארן	הָאָרוֹן־־רֹן	*Arca.*	The ark.
ארר	הָאֲרוּרָה	*Maledicta.*	The cursed.
ארז	הָאֶרֶז הָאָרֶז	*Cedrus.*	The cedar.
—	הָאֲרָזִים	*Cedri.*	The cedars.
ארח	הָאֹרֵחַ	*Iter faciens.*	The way-faring, travelling
—	הַאֹרַח	*An semita?*	The way ?
ארה	הָאֲרִי הָאַרְיֵה	*Leo.*	A lion.
—	הָאֲרָיוֹת	*Leones.*	The lions.
ארך	הֶאֱרִיךְ	*Distulit.*	He deferred.
—	הֶאֱרִיכוּ	*Prolongaverunt.*	They prolonged.
—	הַאֲרִיכִי	*Prolonga.*	Lengthen thou.
—	הָאֹרֶךְ	*Longitudo.*	The length.
רנב	הָאַרְנֶבֶת	*Lepus.*	The hare.

ROOTS.	DERIVATIVES.	VERSIO.	SIGNIFICATION.
ארץ	הָאָרֶץ	*Terra.*	The earth.
רצה	הַאֶרְצֶה	*Num accipiam?*	Shall I accept?
ארץ	הָאֲרָצוֹת--צֹת	*Terræ, regiones.*	The lands, countries.
ישה	הַאִשׁ	*Estne, suntne?*	Is there? are there?
אש	הָאֵשׁ	*Ignis.*	The fire.
——	הָאִשֶּׁה	Oblatio *ignita.*	An offering *made by fire.*
איש	הָאִשָּׁה	*Mulier.*	The woman.
נשג	הַאַשִּׂיגֶנּוּ	*An assequar eum?*	Shall I overtake him?
אשם	הַאֲשִׁימֵם	*Desola, perde eos.*	Destroy thou them.
שכל	הָאֶשְׁכּוֹל	*Botrus.*	The cluster of grapes.
אשל	הָאֵשֶׁל	*Arbor.* [*delicto.*	A tree. [fering.
אשם	הָאָשָׁם	*Delictum, oblatio pro*	The trespass, the trespass of-
שמר	הָאַשְׁמֹרֶת	*Vigilia.*	The watch.
שנב	הַאֶשְׁנָב	*Fenestra.* [*um.*	The window.
אשף	הָאַשְׁפּוֹת--פֹּת	*Stercus, sterquilini-*	Dung, a dunghill.
——	הָאַשָּׁפִים	*Astrologi.*	The astrologers.
אשר	הַאֲשֶׁר	*Nonne quod?*	Is not that which?
——	הָאֲשֵׁרָה	*Lucus.*	The grove.
——	הָאֲשֵׁרוֹת--רִים	*Luci.*	The groves.
את	הַאַתָּה	*Num tu?*	Whether thou?
אתן	הָאָתוֹן	*Asina.*	An ass, the ass.
אות	הָאֹתוֹת-תֹת	*Signa.*	The signs.
אתה	הָאֹתִיּוֹת	*Ventura.*	Things to come.
את	הָאַתֶּם	*Nunquid vos?*	Will ye?
נתן	הַאֶתֵּן	*An dabo?*	Shall I give?
אתן	הָאֲתֹנוֹת--נֹת	*Asinæ.*	The asses.
תור	הָאֲתָרִים	*Exploratores.*	The explorers, spies.
	הב		
יהב	הַב	*Da.*	Give thou.
בוא	הַבָּא	*Veniens.* [*set.*	He that comes.
——	הֲבָא	*Utrum venturus es-*	Whether he would come.
——	הָבֵא	*Adduc.*	Bring thou.
——	הַבָּאָה	*Veniens.*	She that comes.
——	הַבָּאוֹת--אֹת	*Venientes.*	They that come.
——	הַבָּאִים	*Venientes.*	They that come.
באש	הִבְאִישׁ	*Fœtuit, putruit.*	He stank, putrified.

ROOTS.	DERIVATIVES.	VERSIO.	SIGNIFICATION.
באש	הִבְאִישׁוּ	*Putruerunt.*	They stank.
בור	הַבֹּאר	*Fovea.*	A pit.
באר	הַבְּאֵר	*Puteus.*	The well.
—	הַבְּאֵרֹת	*Putei.*	The wells.
באש	הַבְאִשׁ	*Fætere facere.*	To cause to stink.
—	הִבְאַשְׁתֶּם	*Fætere fecistis.*	You have made to stink.
בוא	הֲבָאתָ	*An ingressus es?*	Hast thou entered?
—	הֵבֵאתָ הֵבֵיאתָ	*Adduxisti.*	Thou hast brought.
—	הֻבָאת	*Allata est.*	She was brought.
—	הֻבָאתָה	*Adductus es.*	Thou hast been brought.
—	הֵבֵאתִי	*Adduxi.*	I brought.
—	הֲבֵאתִיהָ הֲבִיא׳	*Adduxi eam.*	I have brought her.
—	הֲבֵאתִיו הֲבִי׳	*Adduxi eum.*	I have brought him.
—	הֲבֵאתֶם	*Adduxistis.*	Ye have brought.
—	הֲבֵאתָנוּ הֲבִיא׳	*Introduxisti nos.*	Thou broughtest us.
בגד	הַבֶּגֶד	*Vestimentum.*	The garment.
—	הַבְּגָדִים	*Vestimenta.*	The garments.
בד	הַבַּד	*Linum.*	The linen.
בדל	הַבְּדִיל	*Stannum.*	The tin.
—	הִבְדִּיל	*Separavit.*	He separated.
—	הִבְדִּילוּ	*Discreverunt.*	They divided, distinguished.
בד	הַבַּדִּים	*Linei; vectes.*	The linen; the stores.
בדא	הַבַּדִּים	*Mendaces.*	The liars.
בדל	הַבְדֵּל	*Separare, separando*	To separate, in separating.
—	הִבָּדְלוּ	*Separate vos.*	Separate yourselves.
בדלח	הַבְּדֹלַח	*Bdellium.*	Bdellium.
בדל	הִבְדַּלְתִּי	*Separavi.*	I have separated.
—	הִבְדַּלְתָּם	*Distinxisti eos.*	Thou didst separate them.
דרך	הַבְּדֶרֶךְ	*An juxta morem?*	Is it after the manner?
יהב	הָבָה	*Da; agedum.*	Give; come on, well.
—	הַבְהָבַי	*Dona mea.*	My gifts, offerings.
בהל	הִבְהִילָנִי	*Terruit me.*	He affrighted me.
בהם	הַבְּהֵמָה	*Jumentum, pecus.*	The beast, the cattle.
בהר	הַבַּהֶרֶת	*Vitiligo.*	The freckled spot.
יהב	הָבוּ הָבוּ	*Date, tribuite, ponite.*	Give, ascribe, set ye.
בוא	הֲבוֹא	*Num veniendo?*	Is it in coming?
בגד	הַבּוֹגֵד	*Perfide agens.*	He that acts unfaithfully.

ROOTS.	DERIVATIVES.	VERSIO.	SIGNIFICATION.
בגד	הַבּוֹגְדִים	*Perfide agentes.*	Those who deal treacherously.
בוז	הַבּוּז	*Contemptus.*	The contempt.
בטח	הַבּוֹטֵחַ	*Confidens.*	He that trusts.
בנה	הַבּוֹנֶה	*Ædificans.*	He that builds.
—	הַבּוֹנִים הַבֹּנִים	*Ædificantes.*	Those who build.
בקק	הִבּוֹק	*Evacuando.* [cer.	In emptying.
בור	הַבּוֹר	*Fovea, cisterna, car-*	The pit, cistern, dungeon.
בזז	הַבָּז הַבִּזָּה	*Præda.*	The prey.
בזק	הַבָּזָק	*Fulgor.*	The flash of lightning.
בחר	הַבַּחוּרִים	*Juvenes.*	The young men.
—	הַבֹּחֵר	*Eligens.*	He that chooses.
נבט	הַבֵּט הַבֶּט	*Intuere, respice.*	Look thou, have respect.
בטח	הַבֹּטְחָה	*Confidens.*	He that trusts.
—	הַבִּטָּחוֹן	*Fiducia.*	Confidence.
—	הַבֹּטְחִים	*Confidentes.*	They that trust.
—	הִבְטַחְתָּ	*Confidere fecisti.*	Thou madest to trust.
בטן	הַבֶּטֶן הַבָּטֶן	*Uterus.*	The womb.
נבט	הִבַּטְתֶּם	*Suspexistis.*	Ye have looked.
יהב	הָבִי	*Da, cedo.*	Bring.
בוא	הָבֵיא	*Referto.*	Carry thou.
—	הֵבִיא	*Adduxit.*	He brought.
—	הָבִיא	*Adducere, inferre.*	To bring, bring in.
—	הֵבִיאָה	*Attulit.*	She brought.
—	הָבִיאָה	*Affer.*	Bring thou.
—	הֵבִיאוּ	*Attulerunt.*	They brought.
—	הָבִיאוּ	*Afferte.*	Carry, bring ye.
—	הֱבִיאוֹ	*Adduxit eum.*	He brought him.
—	הֱבִיאוּהוּ	*Intulerunt eum.*	They brought him.
—	הֱבִיאוּךָ	*Adduxerunt te.*	They brought thee.
—	הֱבִיאוּם	*Adduxerunt eos.*	They brought them.
—	הָבִיאִי־אוּ	*Affer.*	Bring thou.
—	הֲבִיאֲךָ	*Adducere te.*	Thou bringest.
—	הֲבִיאֲכֶם	*Adducere vos.*	Ye bring.
—	הֱבִיאַנִי	*Adduxit me.*	He hath brought me.
—	הֲבִיאֹנֻם	*Introduximus eos.*	We have brought them.
—	הֲבִיאֹתַנִי	*Adduxisti me.*	Thou hast brought me.
נבט	הִבִּיט	*Aspexit.*	He beheld.

ROOTS.	DERIVATIVES.	VERSIO.	SIGNIFICATION.
נבט	הַבֵּט	*Respice.*	Look, see thou.
—	הַבִּיט	*Intueri.*	To look.
—	הַבִּיטָה־טָ	*Aspice.*	Behold thou.
—	הַבִּיטוּ	*Intuemini.*	Look ye.
—	הִבִּיטוּ	*Aspexerunt.*	They looked.
בון	הָבִין	*Intelligere.*	To understand.
—	הֵבִין	*Intellexit.*	He understood.
—	הֵבִינוּ	*Intellexerunt.*	They understood.
—	הָבִינוּ	*Intelligite, ostendite.*	Understand, shew ye.
—	הֲבִינוֹתֶם	*Intellexistis.*	Ye understood.
—	הֲבִינֵנִי	*Intelligere fac me.*	Make me to understand.
ביץ	הַבֵּיצִים	*Ova.*	The eggs.
ביר	הַבִּירָה	*Palatium.*	The palace.
בוש	הֹבִישׁ הוֹבִישׁ	*Pudore affectus est.*	He was made ashamed.
—	הֹבִישָׁה הוֹ׳	*Pudore affecta est.*	She was put to shame.
—	הֹבִישׁוּ הוֹ׳	*Pudore afficiemini.*	Be ye ashamed.
—	הֱבִישׁוֹת־־שֹׁתָה	*Pudore affecisti.*	Thou hast put to shame.
בית	הַבַּיִת הַבָּיִת	*Domus.*	The house.
—	הַבַּיְתָה הַבָּ׳	*In domum.*	Into the house.
—	הַבִּיתָן	*Palatium.*	The palace.
בכא	הַבְּכָא	*Morus, vel Baca, species arbusculæ*	The mulberry tree, or Baca, *a species of shrub.*
—	הַבְּכָאִים	*Mori, vel bacæ.*	The mulberry trees or bacas.
בכר	הַבְּכוֹר־־כֹר	*Primogenitus.*	The first born.
—	הַבִּכּוּרִים	*Primitiæ.*	The first fruits.
—	הַבְּכִירָה	*Primogenita.*	The first born.
—	הַבְּכֹרָה	*Primogenitura.*	The birth-right.
—	הַבִּכֻּרוֹת	*Primitiæ.*	The first fruits.
—	הַבִּכֻּרִים	*Primitiæ.*	The first fruits.
	הֶבֶל הָבֶל	*Abel.*	Abel, N. M.
הבל			
—	הֶבֶל הָבֶל הֲבֵל	*Inanis, vanus factus est; evanuit.*	He became empty, vain; vanished away.
—	הֶבְלוֹ	*Vanitas ejus.*	His vanity.
—	הַבְלֵי	*Vanitates.*	Vanities.
—	הֶבְלִי	*Vanitas mea.*	My vanity.
—	הֲבָלִים	*Vanitates.*	Vanities.

ROOTS.	DERIVATIVES.	VERSIO.	SIGNIFICATION.
הבל	הֶבְלֶךָ	*Vanitas tua.*	Thy vanity.
במה	הַבָּמָה	*Excelsum.*	The high place.
—	הַבָּמוֹת	*Excelsa*	High places.
חנה	הַבְּמַחֲנִים	*An in castris?*	Whether in camps, tents?
חבן			
בין	הָבֵן	*Intelligere.*	To understand.
בנה	הַבֵּן	*Filius.*	The son.
—	הֲבֵן	*An filius?*	A son?
נהר	הֲבַנְּהָרִים	*An contra flumina?*	Against the rivers?
בנה	הַבָּנוּי הַבְּנוּיָה	*Ædificatus.*	Built.
—	הַבָּנוֹת	*Filiæ.*	The daughters.
—	הַבָּנִים	*Filii; pulli.*	The children; the young ones
—	הֲבָנִים	*Nonne filii?*	No sons? [*tween two parties.*
בין	הַבֵּנַיִם	*Intermedius.*	A middle man, *interposing be-*
בנה	הַבִּנְיָן	*Ædificium.*	The building.
סוד	הַבְּסוֹד	*An arcanum?*	The secret?
בסר	הַבֹּסֶר	*Omphax.*	The sour grape.
עד	הֲבְעַד	*An per?*	*Is it* through?
בער	הַבְּעֵרָה	*Incendium.*	The fire.
בוץ	הַבּוּץ	*Byssus.*	Fine linen.
בצר	הַבָּצוֹר	*Vindemia; munita.*	The vintage; fenced.
בצל	הַבְּצָלִים	*Cepæ.*	The onions.
בצע	הַבָּצַע	*Lucrum.*	Gain.
בצק	הַבָּצֵק	*Massa farinæ.*	The dough.
בצר	הַבְּצֻרוֹת	*Munitæ.*	Defenced.
—	הַבַּצָּרוֹת	*Siccitates.*	Drought.
בקבק	הַבַּקְבֻּק	*Lagena.*	The bottle.
בקע	הֻבְקְעָה	*Perrupta est.*	She was broken up.
—	הַבִּקְעָה	*Vallis.*	The valley.
בקר	הַבֹּקֶר	*Diluculum, mane.*	The morning, in the morning.
—	הַבָּקָר	*Bos.* [*perlustravit.*	The herd. [ed.
הבר		*Contemplatus est,*	He viewed, observed, survey-
ברר	הַבָּר	*Triticum.*	The wheat.
ברא	הִבָּרְאֲךָ־רְאֶךָ	*Creari te.*	That thou wast created.
—	הִבָּרְאָם	*Creari eos.*	When they were created.
רבב	הֲבָרָב	*An multa?*	With great?
ברד	הַבָּרָד	*Grando.*	The hail.

ROOTS.	DERIVATIVES.	VERSIO.	SIGNIFICATION.
בור	הַבֹּ֫רָה	*In foveam.*	Into a pit.
ברר	הִבָּרוּ	*Purgamini.*	Be ye cleansed.
—	הָבֵרוּ	*Purgate.*	Cleanse ye.
—	הַבְּרוּרִים	*Electi.*	The chosen.
בור	הַבֹּרוֹת	*Foveæ.*	The pits.
ברזל	הַבַּרְזֶל	*Ferrum ; ferreus.*	The iron ; of iron.
הבר	הֹבְרֵי	*Contemplantes cœlos*	Observers *of the heavens*, astrologers.
ברא	הַבְּרִיאָה	*Pinguis.*	The fat.
—	הַבְּרִיאוֹת	*Pingues.*	The fat.
ברה	הַבִּרְיָה	*Cibus.*	The food.
ברח	הַבְּרִיחַ	*Vectis.*	The bar.
—	הִבְרִיחוּ	*Fugaverunt.*	They drove away.
—	הַבְּרִיחִם	*Vectes.*	The bars.
ברת	הַבְּרִית	*Fœdus.*	A, the covenant.
ברך	הַבְּרָכָה	*An benedictio ?*	A blessing ?
—	הַבְּרָכָה	*Benedictio.*	A, the blessing.
—	הַבְּרֵכָה	*Piscina.*	The pool, pond.
—	הַבְּרָכוֹת	*Benedictiones.*	Blessings.
—	הַבִּרְכַּיִם	*Genua.*	The knees.
ברק	הַבַּרְקָנִים	*Spinæ.*	Briers.
בוש	הֹבִשׁוּ	*Pudore affecti sunt.*	They were ashamed.
בשל	הִבְשִׁילוּ	*Maturaverunt.*	They brought forth ripe.
בשם	הַבֹּשֶׂם	*Aroma.*	Spice.
—	הַבְּשָׂמִים	*Aromata.*	The spices.
בשר	הַבָּשָׂר	*Caro.*	The flesh.
בנה	הַבַּת	*Filia.*	The daughter.
—	הֲבַת	*Num filia ?*	*Can* a daughter ?
בת	הַבַּת־־בַּת	*Bathus*, modius.	The bath, *measure.*
בתל	הַבְּתוּלָה	*Virgo.*	The virgin.
—	הַבְּתוּלוֹת־־לֹת	*Virgines.*	Virgins.
בת	הַבָּתּוֹת	*Deserta.*	The desolate places.
בנה	הַבָּתִּים	*Domus.*	The houses.
בת	הַבַּתִּים	*Bathi*, mod.	The baths, *measures.*

הג

ROOTS.	DERIVATIVES.	VERSIO.	SIGNIFICATION.
	הֵגֵא	*Heghe.*	Hege, N. M.
גיא	הַגֵּאָיוֹת	*Valles.*	The vallies.

ROOTS.	DERIVATIVES.	VERSIO.	SIGNIFICATION.
גאל	הַגֹּאֵל הַגּוֹ"	*Redimens.*	He that redeems.
—	הַגְּאֻלָּה	*Redemptio.*	The redemption.
גבה	הַגְבֵּהַּ	*Eleva, exalta.*	Raise, exalt thou.
—	הַגְּבֹהוֹת--הֹת	*Excelsa.*	The high.
—	הַגְּבֹהִים	*Excelsi.*	The high.
—	הִגְבַּהְתִּי	*Exaltavi.*	I have exalted.
גדל	הַגָּבוֹל	*Magnus.*	Great.
גבל	הַגְּבוּל--בֻל	*Terminus.*	The border.
גבר	הַגִּבּוֹר--בֹּר	*Potens.*	The mighty.
—	הַגִּבּוֹרִים--בֹּ"	*Potentes.*	Mighty men.
גבע	הַגָּבִיעַ	*Calix.*	The cup.
גבר	הַגְּבִירָה	*Regina.*	The queen.
גבל	הַגְבֵּל	*Terminum pone.*	Set thou bounds.
גבע	הַגִּבְעָה	*Collis.*	The hill.
—	הַגְּבָעוֹת	*Colles.*	The hills.
—	הַגִּבְעָתָה	*Ad collem.*	To the hill.
גבר	הַגֶּבֶר	*Vir.*	The man.
—	הַגְּבָרִים	*Viri.*	The men.
גג	הַגַּג הַגָּג	*Tectum.*	The roof.
—	הַגָּגָה	*Ad tectum.*	To the roof.
—	הַגַּגּוֹת	*Tecta.*	The house tops.
נגד	הַגֵּד--דָה"	*Nunciare; annuncia.*	To tell; declare thou.
—	הַגֵּד	*Annuncia.*	Tell, declare thou.
—	הֻגַּד	*Nunciatus est.*	He was declared.
גדד	הַגְּדוּד	*Turma, exercitus.*	The band, army.
גדל	הַגָּדוֹל--דֹל	*Magnus, major, natu major.*	The great, greater, elder.
—	הַגְּדוֹלָה--דֹ"	*Magna, major, natu major.*	The great, greater, elder.
—	הַגְּדוּלָּה--דֻ"	*Magnitudo.*	The greatness, magnificence.
—	הַגְּדוֹלִים--דֹ"	*Magni.*	The great.
גדה	הַגְּדִי	*Hædus.*	The kid.
גדל	הִגְדִּיל--דִּל	*Magnificavit; se extulit.*	He magnified; he exalted himself.
—	הִגְדִּילוּ	*Sese extulerunt.*	They magnified themselves.
—	הַגְּדֹלוֹת--לֹת	*Magnæ; magnæ res*	The great; great things.
—	הַגְּדֹלוֹת	*Maximæ res.*	Very great things.
—	הִגְדַּלְתָּ	*Magnificasti.*	Thou hast magnified.
—	הִגְדַּלְתִּי	*Magnificavi.*	I magnified, made great.

ROOTS.	DERIVATIVES.	VERSIO.	SIGNIFICATION.
גדר	הַגְּדֶרֶת	*Maceria.*	The wall.
—	הִגַּדְתָּ־־ה	*Indicasti.*	Thou hast told, shewed.
—	הִגַּדְתִּי	*Annunciavi.*	I have told.
הָגָה		*Meditatus, locutus est; mussitavit, gemuit, rugivit, sonum edidit, abstulit*	He meditated, spoke, muttered, groaned, mourned, roared, made any sound, took away.
—	הֶגֶה	*Sermo, cogitatio.*	A tale, a thought.
—	הֶגֶה	*Gemitus.*	Mourning.
—	הָגָה	*Abstulit.*	He took away.
—	הָגוֹ	*Auferre.*	To take away.
גוי	הַגּוֹי	*Gens.*	A, the nation.
—	הַגּוֹיִם	*Gentes.*	The nations.
גלה	הַגּוֹלָה הָגֹּלָה	*Captivitas.*	The captivity.
גרל	הַגּוֹרָל	*Sors.*	The lot.
גזבר	הַגִּזְבָּר	*Thesaurarius.*	The treasurer.
גזז	הַגִּזָּה	*Vellus.*	The fleece.
גזל	הַגְּזֵלָה	*Rapina, raptum.*	The robbery; the thing stolen
גזם	הַגָּזָם	*Eruca.*	The palmer-worm. [place
גזר	הַגִּזְרָה	*Structura separata.*	The separate structure, or
—	הַגְּזָרִים	*Divisiones.*	The pieces.
גחל	הַגֶּחָלִים	*Prunæ.*	The hot coals.
גיא	הַגַּיְא	*Vallis.*	The valley.
—	הַגֵּיאָוֹת	*Valles.*	The vallies.
הגה	הֲגִתִי	*Meditatio mea.*	My meditation.
נגד	הִגִּיד	*Nunciavit.*	He told.
—	הַגֵּיד	*Nunciare.*	To tell.
—	הִגִּידָה	*Nunciavit.*	She told.
—	הִגִּידָהּ	*Annunciavit eam.*	He declared her or it.
—	הַגִּידָה	*Nuncia.*	Tell thou.
—	הִגִּידוּ	*Nunciaverunt.*	They told.
—	הַגִּידוּ	*Annunciate.*	Tell, declare ye.
—	הַגִּידִי	*Indica.*	Tell thou.
הגה	הִגָּיוֹן	*Meditatio, cantus.*	A meditation, a song.
הגן	הֲגִינָה	*Recto; recta, elegans, separata.*	Directly; strait, elegant, separate.

ROOTS.	DERIVATIVES.	VERSIO.	SIGNIFICATION.
נגע	הִגִּיעַ	*Pervenit, advenit, dejecit, adjecit.*	He reached, came near, came to, brought down, brought to
—	הִגִּיעוּ	*Advenerunt.*	They came to.
—	הִגִּיעֵנוּ	*Pervenire nos.*	We come.
גור	הַגֵּרִים--גֵּר'	*Peregrini.*	The strangers.
נגש	הַגִּישָׁה	*Affer.*	Bring near.
—	הִגִּישׁוּ	*Attulerunt.*	They brought near.
—	הַגִּישׁוּ	*Afferte.*	Bring ye hither.
הגה	הָגִיתִי	*Meditatus sum.*	I meditated.
גלל	הַגַּל	*Cumulus.*	The heap.
גלב	הַגַּלָּבִים	*Tonsores.*	The barbers.
גלל	הַגַּלְגַּל	*Rota.*	The wheel.
—	הַגֻּלְגֹּלֶת	*Cranium.*	The skull.
גלה	הֶגְלָה	*Deportavit.*	He carried away.
—	הָגְלָה	*Deportatus est.*	He was carried away.
גלל	הַגֻּלָּה	*Lecythus.*	The bowl.
גלה	הֶגְלוּ	*Deportaverunt.*	They carried away.
—	הָגְלוּ	*Deportati sunt.*	They were carried away.
—	הִגָּלוּ	*Ostendite vos.*	Shew yourselves.
—	הַגָּלוּי	*Apertus.*	Opened, open.
גלל	הַגִּלּוּלִים--לל'	*Idola.*	The idols.
גלה	הַגְלוֹת	*Deportare.*	To carry away.
—	הַגְלוֹתָם	*Deportare eos.*	They carry away.
גלא	הֶגְלִי	*Deportavit.*	He carried away.
גלל	הַגְּלִילָה	*Regio.*	The country.
גלה	הַגִּלְיֹנִים	*Specula.*	The glasses, mirrors.
—	הִגְלִיתָ	*Deportasti.*	Thou hast removed.
—	הִגְלֵיתִי	*Deportavi.*	I have carried away.
—	הִגְלֵיתֶם	*Deportastis.*	Ye carried away.
גלל	הַגָּלָל	*Stercus.*	The dung.
גלה	הֶגְלָם	*Deportavit eos.*	He removed them.
—	הָגְלָת	*Deportata est.*	She was carried away.
—	הָגְלְתָה	*Deportata est.*	She was carried away.
גם	הֲגַם	*Num etiam?*	Is it also?
גמל	הַגְּמוּל	*Num retributio?*	*Is it* a recompense?
—	הַגְּמוּלָה	*Retributio.*	The reward.
גמא	הַגְמִיאִינִי	*Bibere fac me.*	Let me drink.

ROOTS.	DERIVATIVES.	VERSIO.	SIGNIFICATION.
גמל	הַגָּמָל	*Camelus.*	The camel.
—	הִגָּמֵל	*Ablactari.*	To be weaned.
—	הַגְּמַלִּים	*Cameli.*	The camels.
הגן			
—	הַגַּן	*Hortus.*	The garden.
גנב	הֲגָנֹב	*Num furandum?*	Is it to steal?
—	הַגַּנָּב	*Fur.*	The thief.
—	הַגֹּנֵב	*Furans.*	He that steals.
—	הַגְּנֵבָה	*Furtum.*	The theft.
גנן	הַגַּנּוֹת	*Horti.*	The gardens.
נגע	הִגַּעַתְּ	*Pervenisti.*	Thou art come.
גפן	הַגָּפֶן	*Vitis.*	The vine.
גור	הַגֵּר	*Peregrinus.*	The stranger.
—	הַגָּר	*Peregrinans.*	He that sojourns.
	הָגָר	*Hagar.*	Hagar, N. W.
	הַגְרִאִים	*Hagaritæ.*	Hagarites, N. F.
גרר	הַגֵּרָה	*Rumen.*	The cud.
גרז	הַגַּרְזֶן	*Securis.*	The ax.
	הַגְרִי	*Hagarita.*	Hagarite, N. F.
גור	הַגֵּרִים	*Peregrinantes.*	They that sojourn.
גרן	הַגֹּרֶן	*Area.*	The threshing floor.
—	הַגְּרָנוֹת	*Areæ.*	The threshing floors.
נגש	הַגִּשָׁה	*Affer.*	Bring thou hither.
—	הֻגָּשׁוּ	*Admoti sunt.*	They were put.
—	הַגִּשׁוּ	*Afferte.*	Bring ye hither.
גשם	הַגֶּשֶׁם־־גּ״	*Pluvia.*	The rain.
נגש	הִגַּשְׁתֶּם	*Obtulistis.*	Ye have offered.
	הד		
הדד	הֵד	*Clamor, celeusma.*	The shouting.
דאה	הַדָּאָה	*Vultur.*	The vulture.
דבב	הַדֹּב	*Ursus.*	The bear.
דבק	הִדְבִּיקֻהוּ	*Persecuti sunt eum.*	They followed hard after him.
—	הִדְבִּיקַתְהוּ	*Assecutus est eum.*	He overtook him.
דבר	הַדְּבִיר	*Oraculum.*	The oracle.
דבק	הַדְּבֵקִים	*Adhærentes.*	Those that cleave to.
—	הַדְּבָקִים	*Juncturæ.*	The joints.

ROOTS.	DERIVATIVES.	VERSIO.	SIGNIFICATION.
דבק	הִדְבַּקְתִּי	*Adhærere feci.*	I caused to cleave to.
דבר	הַדֹּבֵר	*Loquens.*	He that speaks.
—	הַדָּבָר	*Verbum, res, causa.*	The word, thing, cause.
—	הַדֶּבֶר־דֶּ״	*Pestis.*	The pestilence.
—	הֲדָבָר	*An verbum?*	A word?
—	הַדָּבְרוֹ	*Caula eorum.*	Their fold.
—	הַדֹּבְרוֹת	*Loquentes.*	They that speak.
—	הַדָּבָרַי	*Consiliarii mei.*	My counsellors.
—	הַדָּבָרַיָּא	*Consiliarii.*	The counsellors.
—	הַדְּבֹרִים	*Apes.*	The bees.
—	הַדְּבָרִים	*Verba, res.*	The words, things.
דבש	הַדְּבָשׁ	*Mel.*	The honey.
דוג	הַדָּג־גָה	*Piscis.*	The fish.
—	הַדָּגִים	*Pisces.*	The fishes.
דגן	הַדָּגָן	*Frumentum.*	The corn.
	הֲדַד	*Hadad.*	Hadad, N. M.
	הֲדַדְרִמּוֹן	*Hadadrimmon.*	Hadadrimmon, N. P.
הָדָה		*Emisit, porrexit, immisit.*	He thrust forth, stretched out, placed in or upon.
הוד	הוֹדוֹ	*Decor ejus.*	His glory.
ידה	הוֹדוּ	*Confitemini, celebrate.*	Confess, praise ye.
	הֹדּוּ	*Hodu, pars Indiæ.*	Hodu, part of India.
דבב	הַדּוֹב	*Ursus.*	The bear.
דוד	הַדּוּד	*Canistrum.*	The basket.
—	הַדּוּדָאִים	*Mandragoræ.*	The mandrakes.
דוך	הַדּוּכִיפַת	*Upupa, gallus sylvestris.*	The Upupa, or houp, a small bird.
דלג	הַדּוֹלֵג	*Insiliens.*	He that leaps upon.
הדם	הֲדוֹם־דֹם	*Scabellum.*	A, the footstool.
הדר	הָדוּר	*Decoratus.*	Adorned.
דור	הַדּוֹר	*Generatio.*	The generation.
	הֲדוֹרָם	*Hadoram.*	Hadoram, N. M.
נדח	הַדְּחוּיָה	*Impulsa, casura.*	Pushed, about to fall, tottering.
—	הִדַּחְתִּי	*Expuli.*	I have driven out.
—	הִדַּחְתִּיךָ	*Expuli te.*	I have driven thee out.
—	הִדַּחְתִּים	*Expuli eos.*	I have driven them out.
—	הִדַּחְתֶּם	*Expulistis.*	Ye have cast out.
—	הִדַּחְתָּם	*Expulisti eos.*	Thou hast driven them out.

ROOTS.	DERIVATIVES.	VERSIO.	SIGNIFICATION.
	הִדַּי	*Hidai.*	Hiddai, N. M.
דוג	הַדַּיָּגִים	*Piscatores.*	The fishers.
נדח	הִדִּיחוּ	*Depulerunt.*	They have driven away.
—	הַדִּיחִי	*Expellere me.*	That I drive out.
—	הִדִּיחֲךָ	*Expulit te.*	He hath driven out thee.
—	הִדִּיחָם	*Expulit eos.*	He drove them out.
—	הַדִּיחֵמוֹ	*Expelle eos.*	Do thou cast them out.
—	הֶדִּיחָנוּ	*Ejecit me.*	He hath cast me out.
הָדַךְ		*Contrivit.*	He trod down, crushed.
דלל	הַדַּל	*Tenuis.*	The poor, mean.
—	הַדַּלִּים	*Pauperes.*	The poor.
דלק	הַדְלֵק	*Succendere.*	To kindle.
דלת	הַדֶּלֶת־דָּ׳	*Ostium, janua.*	The door, gate.
—	הַדְּלָתוֹת	*Valvæ, januæ.*	The doors, gates.
הדם			
דם	הַדָּם	*Sanguis.*	The blood.
—	הֲדַם	*Num sanguis?*	The blood?
—	הַדָּמִים	*Sanguines.*	The blood.
הדם	הַדָּמִין	*Frusta.*	Pieces.
דמם	הֲדִמָּנוּ	*Silere fecit nos.*	He put us to silence.
הדס			
—	הֲדַס	*Myrtus.*	A, the myrtle, myrtle-tree.
	הֲדַסָּה	*Hadassa.*	Hadassah, N. W.
ידע	הַדָּעַת־־דַּ׳	*Scire; scientia.*	To know; the knowledge.
הָדַף		*Trusit, pepulit.*	He pushed, thrust, drove away
—	הֲדָפוֹ	*Depulit eum.*	He thrust him.
דקק	הָדֵק	*Comminuere.*	To beat very small. [pieces.
—	הֵדָק	*Contrivit, comminuit*	He crushed, stamped into small
—	הַדַּקּוּ	*Comminuit.*	He brake in pieces.
—	הַדַּקּוֹת־־קַּת	*Tenues.*	The thin.
הָדַר		*Decoravit, honoravit, reveritus est.*	He adorned, honoured, reverenced.
—	הֶדֶר	*Gloria, honor.*	The glory, honour.
—	הָדָר הֲדַר	*Decor.*	The beauty.
	הֲדַר	*Hadar.*	Hadar, N. M.
דרבן	הַדָּרְבָן	*Stimulus.*	The goad.
הדר	הֲדָרָהּ.	*Decor ejus.*	Her beauty.

ROOTS.	DERIVATIVES.	VERSIO.	SIGNIFICATION.
דרם	הַדָּרוֹם	*Auster.*	The south.
דרר	הַדְּרוֹר	*Libertas.*	The liberty.
דור	הַדֹּרוֹת	*Generationes.*	The generations.
הדר	הֲדָרִי	*Gloria mea.*	My glory.
—	הַדְרִי	*Decor meus.*	My comeliness.
דרך	הִדְרִיכָהּ	*Calcare eam.*	To tread upon, or thresh her.
—	הִדְרִיכֻהוּ	*Conculcarunt eum.*	They trod him down.
—	הַדְרִיכֵנִי	*Deduc me.*	Lead thou me.
הדר	הֲדָרֵךְ	*Decor tuus.*	Thy comeliness.
דרך	הַדֹּרֵךְ	*Calcans, tendens.*	He that treads, stretches.
—	הַדֶּרֶךְ־־דָּ׳	*Via.*	The way.
—	הֲדַרְכִּי	*Num via mea?*	My way?
—	הַדְּרָכַי	*Num viæ meæ?*	My ways?
—	הַדְּרָכִים	*Viæ.*	The ways.
—	הִדְרַכְתִּיךָ	*Deduxi te.*	I have led thee.
	הֲדֹרָם	*Hadoram.* [zer.	Hadoram, N. M.
	הֲדַדְעֶזֶר־־עֶ׳	*Hadadezer, Hadare-*	Hadadezer, Hadarezer.
דרש	הַדֹּרֵשׁ	*Quærens.*	He that seeks.
הדר	הַדַּרְתָּ	*Glorificasti.*	Thou hast glorified.
—	הַדְרַת	*Honor, gloria.*	The honour, glory.
דשן	הַדֶּשֶׁן־־דָּ׳	*Cinis.*	The ashes.
—	הַדַּשְּׁנָה	*Impinguata est.*	She or it is made fat.
דת	הַדָּת	*Decretum.*	The decree.

הה

ROOTS.	DERIVATIVES.	VERSIO.	SIGNIFICATION.
הה			
—	הָהּ	*Væ!*	Wo!
הבל	הַהֶבֶל	*Vanitas.*	The vanity.
הדס	הַהֲדַסִּים	*Myrti.*	Myrtle-trees.
הוא	הַהוּא	*Ille, ipse.*	He, that.
—	הַהִוא	*Illa, ipsa.*	She, that.
הלך	הַהוֹלֵךְ־־הֹלֵ׳	*Iens, abiens.*	He that goes, goes away.
—	הַהוֹלְכִים־־הֹלְ׳	*Euntes.*	They that go, walk.
היא	הַהִיא	*Illa, ipsa.*	She, that.
יטב	הַהֵיטֵב	*Num benefacere?*	*Is it* to do well?
הכל	הַהֵיכָל	*Templum.*	The temple.
מור	הַהֵימִיר	*An mutavit?*	Has he changed?

ROOTS.	DERIVATIVES.	VERSIO.	SIGNIFICATION.
היה	הֶהָיְתָה	*Num fuit?*	Has she been?
כון	הַהֵכִין	*Quod præparavit.*	That he prepared.
הלך	הֶהָלְכוּא	*Qui iverunt.*	Who went.
—	הַהֹלֶכֶת	*Iens.*	She that goes.
—	הַהֹלְכֹת	*Euntes.*	Those that go.
הלל	הַהֻלָּלָה	*Laudata est.*	She was celebrated, renowned.
הוא	הָהֵם הַהֵמָּה	*Illi, ipsi.* [*copia.*	They, those. [dance.
המן	הֶהָמוֹן הֲהָ״	*Multitudo, tumultus;*	The multitude, tumult; abun-
מות	הֶהָמֵת	*An interficiendo?*	In putting to death?
הוא	הָהֵנָּה	*Illæ, ipsæ.*	These, those.
סכן	הַהַסְכֵּן	*An assuescendo?*	In being accustomed, wont?
חפך	הַהֲפוּכָה	*Subversa.*	She that was overthrown.
—	הָהְפַּךְ	*Conversus est.*	He has been turned.
—	הַהֲפֵכָה	*Subversio.*	The overthrow.
—	הַהֹפְכִי	*Convertens.*	He that turns.
—	הַהֹפְכִים	*Vertentes.*	They that turn.
נצל	הַהִצִּילוּ	*Liberaverunt.*	They have delivered.
—	הַהַצֵּל	*Num liberando?*	In delivering?
צלח	הַהִצְלִיחַ	*An secundavit?*	Has he prospered?
קדש	הַהִקְדִּישׁ	*Quod consecravit.*	That he dedicated.
הרר	הָהָר	*Mons.*	The mountain.
הרג	הַהֲרֵגָה	*Cædes.*	Slaughter.
חרר	הָהָרָה	*Versus, in montem.*	Towards, into the mountain.
הרג	הַהֲרוּגִים	*Occisi.*	Those that were slain.
הרס	הֶהָרוּס	*Dirutus.*	Broken down.
הרה	הֶהָרוֹתֶיהָ	*Prægnantes ejus.*	Her pregnant women.
הרר	הֶהָרִים	*Montes.*	The mountains.
רום	הַהֵרִימוּ	*Obtulerunt.*	They offered.
ארם	הַהַרְמוֹנָה	*In palatium.*	Into the palace.
שוב	הֶהָשֵׁב	*An reducendo?*	In bringing again?
ישב	הַהֹשִׁיב	*Qui duxit.*	Who has taken, married.
—	הַהֹשִׁיבוּ	*Qui duxerunt.*	Who have taken.
	הו		
הוא			
—	הוּא	*Ille, ipse.*	He, that.
—	הָוָא	*Fuit.*	He was.

ROOTS.	DERIVATIVES.	VERSIO.	SIGNIFICATION.
הוא	הֱוָא	*Esto.*	Be thou.
—	הִוא	*Ipsa.*	She.
—	הוּא	*Ille.*	He.
יאל	הוֹאִיל	*Voluit; incepit.*	He was willing; he began.
—	הוֹאִילוּ	*Velitis.*	Be ye willing, content.
—	הוֹאֶל הוֹאֵל	*Velis.*	Be thou willing, content.
—	הוֹאַלְנוּ	*Voluimus.*	We were willing.
—	הוֹאַלְתָּ	*Voluisti.* [*volui.*	Thou wast willing. [ed.
—	הוֹאַלְתִּי	*Induxi in animum,*	I have taken upon me, resolv-
בוא	הוּבָא	*Illatus est.*	He was brought in.
—	הוּבְאוּ	*Adducti sunt.*	They were brought.
יבש	הוֹבִישׁ	*Arefecit, aruit.*	He dried up, was dried up.
בוש	הוֹבִישׁ הֹבְאִישׁ	*Pudore affectus est.*	He was ashamed.
יבש	הוֹבִישָׁה	*Aruit.*	She is dried up.
—	הוֹבַשְׁתָּ	*Arefecisti.*	Thou driedst up.
בוש	הוֹבַשְׁתָּ	*Pudore affecisti.*	Thou hast put to shame.
יבש	הוֹבַשְׁתִּי	*Arefeci.*	I dried up.
יגה	הוֹגָה	*Mœrore affecit.*	He has afflicted, caused grief.
—	הוֹגָהּ	*Mœrore affecit eam.*	He has afflicted her.
יגע	הוֹגַעְנוּ	*Fatigavimus.*	We have wearied.
—	הוֹגַעְתִּיךָ	*Fatigavi te.*	I have wearied thee.
—	הוֹגַעְתֶּם	*Fatigastis.*	Ye have wearied.
—	הוֹגַעְתָּנִי	*Fatigasti me.*	Thou hast wearied me.
	הוֹד	*Hod.*	Hod, N. M.
הוד			
—	הוֹד	*Decus, gloria, majestas.*	Beauty, honour, glory, majesty.
ידה	הוֹדוּ	*Celebrate, laudate.*	Celebrate, praise ye.
הוד	הוֹדוֹ	*Gloria ejus.*	His glory.
	הוֹדַוְיָה	*Hodavia.*	Hodaviah, N. M.
ידה	הוֹדוֹת	*Gratias agere.*	To give thanks.
	הוֹדִיָּה	*Hodia.*	Hodiah, N. W.
	הוֹדַיְוָהוּ	*Hodaia.*	Hodaiah, N. M.
ידה	הוֹדִינוּ	*Gratias egimus.*	We gave thanks. [known.
ידע	הוֹדִיעַ	*Notum fecit, facere.*	He made known, to make
—	הוֹדִיעוּ	*Notum fecerunt; notum facite.*	They made known; make ye known.

ROOTS.	DERIVATIVES.	VERSIO.	SIGNIFICATION.
ידע	הוֹדִיעֲךָ	*Notum facere tibi.*	To make known to thee.
—	הוֹדִיעֵם	*Ostende eis.*	Shew, discover thou to them.
—	הוֹדִיעֻנוּ	*Instruite nos.*	Inform, tell ye us.
—	הוֹדִיעֵנִי	*Notum fac mihi.*	Make me know.
—	הוֹדִיעָנִי	*Indicavit mihi.*	He has discovered to me.
הוד	הוֹדְךָ הוֹדֶךָ	*Gloria tua.*	Thy glory.
ידע	הוֹדַע	*Ostende, doce.*	Shew, teach thou.
—	הוֹדַע	*Notum fecit.*	He made known.
—	הוּדַע	*Notum fieri mihi.*	To be made known to me.
—	הוֹדִעֲךָ	*Ostendit tibi.*	He shewed, discovered to me.
—	הוֹדִעֵנִי	*Ostende mihi.*	Shew, declare thou to me.
—	הוֹדַעְתָּ	*Ostendisti.*	Thou hast shewed.
—	הוֹדַעְתִּי	*Ostendi.*	I have shewed.
—	הוֹדַעְתִּיךָ	*Notum feci tibi.*	I have made known to thee.
—	הוֹדַעְתָּנָא	*Ostendisti nobis.*	Thou madest known to us.
—	הוֹדַעְתָּנִי	*Indicasti.*	Thou hast told me.
הָוָה		*Fuit.*	He was.
—	הָוָה	*Fuit.*	He was.
—	הֱוֵה	*Esto.*	Be thou.
—	הֹוָה	*Calamitas.*	Calamity.
—	הֹוֶה	*Existens.*	Existing, being.
	הוֹהָם	*Hoham.*	Hoham, N. M.
הוא	הֲווֹ	*Fuerunt.*	They were, have been.
הוה	הֱווֹ	*Estote.* [*tates.*	Be ye. [nesses.
—	הַוּוֹת	*Calamitates, pravi-*	Mischiefs, calamities, wicked-
חדד	הוּחַדָּה	*Exacuta est.*	She was sharpened.
יחל	הוֹחִילִי־חִלִי	*Expecta, spera.*	Expect, hope thou.
חלל	הוּחַל	*Inceptus est.*	He or it was begun.
יחל	הוֹחַלְתִּי	*Expectavi.*	I waited.
טול	הוּטְלוּ	*Ejecti sunt.*	They were cast out.
הוי			
הוה	הֱוִי	*Esto.*	Be thou.
הוי	הוֹי	*Væ, heu!*	Wo, ah, alas!
ידע	הַיּוֹדֵעַ	*Sciens, cognoscens.*	He that knows.
היה	הוֹיָה	*Est.*	She is.
הוה	הֲוֵית	*Fui.*	I was, have been.
—	הֲוֵיתָ	*Fuisti.*	Thou wast, hast been.

ROOTS.	DERIVATIVES.	VERSIO.	SIGNIFICATION.
הוך		*Ivit, pervenit.*	He went, came.
נכה	הוּכָּה	*Percussus, cæsus est.*	He was smitten, slain.
יכח	הוכח	*Increpa.* [re-	Rebuke thou.
—	הוֹכֵחַ	*Increpare, discepta-*	To reprove, argue, reason.
כון	הוּכַן	*Præparatus est.*	He is prepared.
ילד	הוֹלִד	*Genuit.*	He begat.
—	הִוָּלְדָהּ	*Nasci eam.*	That she was born.
—	הִוָּלְדוֹ	*Nasci eum.*	That he was born.
—	הוֹלַדְתָּ	*Genuisti.*	Thou hast begotten.
—	הוּלֶּדֶת הֻלֶּ׳	*Nasci.*	To be born.
—	הוֹלִיד הֹלִיד	*Genuit.*	He begat.
—	הוֹלִידוּ	*Genuerunt.*	They begat.
—	הוֹלִידוֹ	*Gignere eum.*	That he begat.
ילך	הוֹלִיךְ	*Abduxit.*	He carried away.
—	הוֹלִיכְךָ	*Deduxit te.*	He led thee.
—	הוֹלִיכָם	*Deduxit eos.*	He led them.
הלך	הָוֹלֵךְ	*Ire.*	To go.
—	הוֹלֵךְ	*Iens, veniens, vadens*	Going, coming, walking.
—	הוֹלְכוֹת הֹלְכוֹת	*Euntes.*	Going.
—	הוֹלְכִים הֹלְ׳	*Euntes.*	Going.
הלל	הוּלָּלוּ	*Laudatæ sunt* in nuptiis, epithalamio *celebratæsunt*	They were praised *in marriage*, they were celebrated *by a nuptial song.* [ness.
—	הוֹלֵלוֹת־־הֹלֵ׳	*Insaniæ.*	Extravagancies, acts of mad-
—	הוֹלֵלוּת	*Insania.*	Madness.
—	הוֹלְלִים	*Stulti.*	The foolish.
הלם	הוֹלֵם	*Percussio.*	The stroke.
הום		*Commovit, turbavit, perstrepuit, contrivit.*	He moved, shook, disturbed, made a great noise, crushed
המה	הוֹמָה	*Tumultuans.*	Being in an uproar.
—	הוֹמֶה הֹמֶה	*Strepens.*	Making a noise.
—	הוֹמִיָּה הֹמִ׳	*Strepens, tumultuans*	Clamorous, tumultuous.
	הוֹמָם	*Homam.*	Homam, N. M.
מות	הוּמַת	*Interfectus est.*	He was slain.
הון			[ficiency.
—	הון	*Opes, sufficientia.*	Wealth, riches, substance, suf-

ROOTS.	DERIVATIVES.	VERSIO.	SIGNIFICATION.
ינה	הוֹנָה	*Oppressit.*	He oppressed.
——	הוֹנוּ	*Oppresserunt.*	They oppressed.
הון	הוֹנוֹ	*Opes ejus.*	His substance.
נוח	הוֹנַת	*Quietem dedit.*	He gave rest.
הון	הוֹנְךָ. הוֹנֶךָ	*Divitiæ tuæ.*	Thy riches.
נוף	הוּנַף	*Agitatus est.*	He was waved, agitated.
יסד	הוּסַד	*Fundatus est.*	He was founded, the foundation was laid.
——	הִוָּסְדָהּ	*Fundari eam.*	That she was founded.
יסף	הוֹסַפְתָּ	*Addidisti.*	Thou hast added.
——	הוּסְפַת	*Addita est.*	She was added.
סור	הוּסַר	*Ablatus est.*	He was taken away.
יסר	הִוָּסְרוּ	*Erudimini.*	Be ye instructed.
——	הִוָּסְרִי	*Eruditor.*	Be thou instructed.
יעל	הוֹעִיל	*Profuit.*	He profited.
יפע	הוֹפִיעַ	*Illuxit, effulsit; illucesce, illustris appare.*	He shined, shined forth, shine thou forth, appear illustrious.
——	הוֹפִיעָה	*Illucesce*	Shine thou forth. [ed.
——	הוֹפַעְתָּ	*Illuminasti.*	Thou hast shined upon, adorn-
יצא	הוֹצֵא הַוְצֵא	*Produc, educito.*	Bring thou forth, bring out.
——	הוּצָא	*Produxit.*	He brought forth.
——	הוּצָאת	*Educta est.*	She was brought forth.
——	הוֹצֵאִי הוֹצִיאִי	*Educere me.*	I bring forth.
——	הוֹצִאֲךָ הוֹצִיאֲךָ	*Eduxit te.*	He brought thee out.
——	הוֹצֵאתָ	*Eduxisti.*	Thou hast brought forth.
——	הוֹצֵאתִי	*Eduxi, protuli.*	I brought out or forth.
——	הוֹצֵאתִיהָ	*Protuli eam.*	I brought her forth.
——	הוֹצֵאתִיךָ	*Eduxi te.*	I brought thee out.
——	הוֹצֵאתִים	*Eduxi eos.*	I brought them out.
——	הוֹצֵאתֶם	*Eduxistis.*	Ye have brought forth.
——	הוֹצֵאתָנוּ	*Eduxisti nos.*	Thou broughtest us out.
——	הוֹצֵאתָנִי	*Eduxisti me.*	Thou broughtest me forth.
——	הוֹצִיא	*Eduxit; educere.*	He brought forth; to bring out.
——	הוֹצִיאֶהָ	*Educ eam.*	Bring thou her out.
——	הוֹצִיאָה	*Educ.*	Bring thou out. [forth.
——	הוֹצִיאוּ	*Eduxerunt; educite*	They brought forth; bring ye

ROOTS.	DERIVATIVES.	VERSIO.	SIGNIFICATION.
יצא	הוֹצִיאוּהָ	*Educite eam.*	Bring ye her forth.
—	הוֹצִיאָם	*Eduxit eos.*	He brought them out.
—	הוֹצִיאֵם	*Educ eos.*	Bring thou them out.
—	הוֹצִיאָנוּ	*Eduxit nos.*	He brought us out.
—	הוֹצִיאֵנִי	*Educ me.*	Bring thou me out.
יצק	הוּצַק	*Diffusus est.*	He, it was poured over.
קום	הוּקַם	*Erectus est.*	He was raised up.
הרג	הוֹרֵג	*Interficiens.*	Slaying, he that kills.
—	הוֹרַגְנוּ	*Occisi sumus.*	We have been killed.
ירד	הוֹרֵד	*Depone, dejice.*	Put thou off, cast down.
—	הוֹרִד הוֹרִיד	*Dejecit.*	He brought down.
—	הוּרַד	*Depressus est.*	He was put down.
—	הוֹרִדֻהוּ	*Deduxerunt eum; deducite eum.*	They brought him down; bring ye him down.
—	הוֹרַדְנוּ	*Deduximus.*	We have brought down.
—	הוֹרַדְתֵּנוּ	*Demisisti nos.*	Thou didst let us down.
ירה	הוֹרֵהוּ	*Docuit eum.*	He instructed him.
—	הוֹרוּנִי	*Docete me.*	Teach ye me.
הרה	הוֹרַי	*Genitores mei.*	My progenitors.
—	הוֹרִידוּ	*Deducite; detulerunt.*	Carry ye down; they took down.
—	הוֹרִידִי	*Demitte.*	Send thou down.
ירש	הוֹרִישׁ הֹרִישׁ	*Expulit, ejecit.*	He drove out; dispossessed.
—	הוֹרִישׁוֹ	*Expellere eum.*	He drives out.
—	הוֹרִישׁוּ	*Expulerunt.*	They expelled.
—	הוֹרִישָׁם	*Expellere eos.*	To drive them out.
	הוֹרָם	*Horam.*	Horam, N. M.
רום	הוּרַם הֻרַם	*Elevatus, oblatus, ablatus est*	He was raised, heaved, offered, taken away.
ירה	הוֹרֵנִי הֹרֵי	*Doce me.*	Teach thou me.
ריק	הוּרַק	*Evacuatus est.*	He was emptied.
ירש	הוֹרַשְׁתָּ	*Expulisti.*	Thou didst drive out.
—	הוֹרַשְׁתָּנוּ	*Possidere fecisti nos.*	Thou hast given us to inherit.
הרה	הוֹרָתִי	*Genetrix mea.*	She that conceived me.
—	הוֹרָתָם	*Genetrix eorum.*	She that conceived them.
ירה	הוֹרֵתָנִי	*Docuisti me.*	Thou hast taught me.
ישב	הוֹשֵׁב	*Habitare fac.*	Make thou to dwell.
שוב	הוּשַׁב	*Redditus est.*	He has been restored.
ישב	הוֹשַׁבְתִּי	*Habitare feci.*	I made to dwell.

ROOTS.	DERIVATIVES.	VERSIO.	SIGNIFICATION.
ישב	הוֹשִׁיבַנִי	*Habitare fecit me.*	He has made me to dwell.
ישע	הוֹשִׁיעַ	*Servavit; servare.*	He saved; to save.
—	הוֹשִׁיעָה	*Servavit; serva.*	She saved; save thou.
—	הוֹשִׁיעוֹ	*Servavit eum.*	He saved him.
—	הוֹשִׁיעָם	*Servavit eos.*	He saved them.
—	הוֹשִׁיעֵנוּ	*Serva nos.*	Save thou us.
—	הוֹשִׁיעֵנִי	*Serva me.*	Save thou me.
	הוֹשָׁמָע	*Hosama.*	Hoshama, N. M.
ישע	הוֹשַׁע	*Serva.*	Save thou.
	הוֹשֵׁעַ	*Hosea.*	Hoshea, Hosea, N. M.
	הוֹשַׁעְיָה	*Hosaia.*	Hoshaiah, N. M.
ישע	הוֹשַׁעְתָּ	*Servasti.*	Thou savedst.
—	הוֹשַׁעְתֶּם	*Servastis.*	Ye delivered.
—	הוֹשַׁעְתָּנוּ	*Servasti nos.*	Thou hast saved us.
ישר	הַוְשַׁר	*Dirige.*	Make thou straight.
הוה	הָוַת הָוַת	*Fuit, facta est.*	She was, became.
—	הַוּת	*Mala, calamitates.*	Mischiefs, calamities.
	הוֹתִיר	*Hothir.*	Hothir, N. M.
יתר	הוֹתִיר	*Reliquit; relinquere*	He left; to leave.
התל	הוּתַל	*Illusus.*	Deceived.
יתר	הוֹתֵר	*Relinque, serva.*	Leave, preserve thou.
—	הוֹתִרָה	*Reliquit, servavit.*	She left, reserved.
	הז		
זה	הַזֹּאת־־ה	*Hæc, ista.*	This, that.
—	הֲזֹאת	*Num hæc?* [*rans.*	Is this?
זוב	הַזָּב	*Fluens, fluxu, labo-*	Flowing, he that has an issue.
זבח	הַזֶּבַח־־ן	*Sacrificium, victima.*	The sacrifice, victim.
—	הַזֹּבֵחַ	*Immolans.*	He that offers sacrifice.
—	הַזְּבָחִים	*Sacrificia.*	The sacrifices.
—	הַזֹּבְחִים	*Immolantes.*	They that sacrifice.
זוד	הַזָּדוֹן	*Superbia.*	The pride.
—	הַזֵּדִים	*Superbi*	The proud.
זה	הַזֶּה	*Hic, ipse.*	This, that.
הז	הֲזֶה	*Num hic?*	Is this?
זהב	הַזָּהָב	*Aurum; aureus.*	The gold; golden.
זהר	הִזָּהֵר	*Monitus esto.*	Be thou admonished.

ROOTS.	DERIVATIVES.	VERSIO.	SIGNIFICATION.
זהר	הִזְהַרְתָּ	*Admonuisti.*	Thou warnedst.
—	הִזְהַרְתּוֹ	*Admonuisti eum.*	Thou warnedst him.
זנה	הַזּוֹנָה	*Meretrix:*	The harlot.
—	הַזּוֹנָה	*Scortans.*	She who commits whoredom.
—	הַזּוֹנֹת הַזֹּנוֹת	*Scortantes.*	They that go a whoring.
זוד	הֵזִידוּ	*Superbe egerunt.*	They acted proudly.
—	הַזֵּידוֹנִים	*Superbi, tumidi.*	The proud, swelling.
נזל	הִזִּיל	*Fluere fecit.*	He caused to flow.
זול	הִזִּילוּהָ	*Spreverunt eam* [*tes*	They despised her. [ing.
הזה	הֹזִים	*Stertentes, somnian-*	Those who are snoring, dream-
נזר	הַזִּירוֹ	*Separare se.*	To separate himself.
זית	הַזַּיִת	*Oliva.*	The olive tree.
—	הַזֵּיתִים	*Olivæ; olivetа*	The olives; olive yards.
זכך	הִזַּכּוּ	*Purificate vos.*	Purify yourselves.
זכר	הִזְכִּיר	*Memoravit.*	He made mention.
—	הַזְכִּיר	*Memoriam statuere.*	To keep in remembrance.
—	הַזְכִּירוּ	*Commemorate.*	Make mention.
—	הַזְכִּירֵנִי	*Fac me recordari.*	Put me in remembrance.
—	הַזָּכָר	*Mas.* [*tum.*	The male.
—	הַזִּכָּרוֹן	*Memoria, monimen-*	The memory, memorial.
—	הַזְּכָרִים	*Mares, masculi.*	The males. [memory.
—	הַזְכִּרְכֶם	*Memorare vos.*	That ye mention or keep in
—	הִזָּכֶרְכֶם	*Recordari vos.*	That ye remember.
—	הַזִּכְרֹנוֹת	*Monumenta.*	The records.
זלזל	הַזַּלְזַלִּים	*Palmites.*	The sprigs or shoots of a vine.
זול	הַזָּלִים	*Prodigentes.*	They that lavish, squander.
זמם	הַזִּמָּה	*Scelus.*	The wickedness.
זמר	הַזְּמוֹרָה	*Palmes.*	The branch.
—	הַזָּמִיר	*Cantus, cantio.*	The singing.
זנב	הַזָּנָב	*Cauda.*	The tail.
—	הַזְּנָבוֹת	*Caudæ.*	The tails.
זנה	הַזְנֹת	*Scortari.*	To commit whoredom. [dom.
—	הִזְנוּ	*Scortati sunt.*	They have committed whore-
זנח	הִזְנִיחַ	*Abjecit.*	He cast away.
—	הִזְנִיחָם	*Rejecit eos.*	He cast them off.
זנה	הַזֹּנִים	*Scortantes.*	They that go a whoring [dom
—	הִזְנִית	*Scortatus es.*	Thou hast committed whore-

ROOTS.	DERIVATIVES.	VERSIO.	SIGNIFICATION.
זעם	הַזַּעַם	*Ira, indignatio.*	The wrath, indignation.
זעק	הַזְעַק	*Convoca.*	Call thou together, assemble.
—	הַזְּעָקָה	*Clamor.*	The cry.
זקן	הַזָּקֵן	*Senex.*	The old man.
—	הַזָּקָן	*Barba.*	The beard.
—	הַזְּקֵנִים	*Senes, seniores.*	The old men, the elders.
זרע	הַזְּרוֹעַ־רֹעַ	*Brachium.*	The arm.
זור	הַזָּרִים	*Alieni, extranei.*	The strangers, foreigners.
זרע	הַזֶּרַע־רַ	*Semen.*	The seed.
—	הַזֵּרֹעִים	*Legumina.*	The pulse.
—	הַזֹּרְעִים	*Seminantes.*	They that sow.
זרק	הַזֹּרֵק	*Spargens.*	He that sprinkles.
	הח		
חבא	הֶחְבָּאוּ	*Latitarunt.*	They lay hid.
—	הֶחְבְּאָתָה	*Abscondit.*	She hid.
—	הֶחְבִּיאָה	*Abscondit.*	She hid.
—	הֶחְבִּיאָנִי	*Abscondit me.*	He hid me.
חבל	הַחֶבֶל	*Funiculus.*	The line.
—	הַחֹבֵל	*Nauclerus, navarchus.*	The pilot, captain.
—	הַחֹבְלִים	*Funiculi.*	The bands.
חבר	הַחֹבֶרֶת	*Junctura.*	The coupling, joining.
חבה	הַחֲבִתִּים	*Sartagines.*	The pans.
חגג	הֶחָג	*Festum, solemnitas.*	The feast, festival.
חגב	הֶחָגָב	*Locusta.*	The locust.
חגר	הֶחָגוּר	*Accinctus.*	He that is girded.
חדל	הֶחֳדַלְתִּי	*Num deseram?*	Shall I leave, forsake?
חדר	הֶחָדֶר	*In cubiculum; auster*	Into the chamber; the south.
—	הַחַדְרָה הֶחָ׳	*In cubiculum.*	Into the chamber.
—	הַחֹדֶרֶת	*Penetralia penetrans*	Entering into the secret chambers.
חדש	הֶחָדָשׁ	*Novus.*	The new.
—	הַחֹדֶשׁ	*Mensis, novilunium.*	The month, new moon.
—	הַחֲדָשָׁה	*Nova.*	The new.
—	הַחֲדָשִׁים	*Novi.*	The new.
—	הֶחֳדָשִׁים	*Menses, novilunia.*	The months, new moons.
חוח	הַחוֹחַ	*Carduus.*	The thistle.
—	הַחוֹחִים	*Spinae.*	The thorns.

ROOTS.	DERIVATIVES.	VERSIO.	SIGNIFICATION.
חול	הַחוֹל	*Arena.*	The sand.
—	הַחוֹלֶה	*Ægrotans.*	He that is sick.
—	הַחוֹלָה	*Ægrota.*	She that is sick.
חמה	הַחוֹמָה--חֹמָה	*Murus.*	The wall.
חוה	הַחֲוֻנִי	*Indicate.*	Shew ye to me.
חנה	הַחוֹנִים	*Castrametantes, considentes.*	Those that encamp, light, pitch.
חסה	הַחוֹסִים--חֹסִים	*Sperantes.*	They that trust.
חוץ	הַחוּץ--צָה	*Foras, extra.*	From abroad, without.
חור	הַחוֹר	*Foramen.*	The hole.
חזה	הַחֹזֶה	*Videns.*	He that sees, the seer.
—	הֶחָזֶה	*Pectus.*	The breast.
—	הֶחָזוֹן הַחִזָּיוֹן	*Visio.*	The vision.
—	הֶחָזוֹת	*Pectora.*	The breasts.
—	הַחֹזִים	*Videntes.*	They that see, the seers.
חזק	הֶחֱזִיק	*Prehendit, retinuit, confirmavit, instauravit.*	He took, retained, strengthened, repaired.
—	הֶחֱזִיקָה	*Prehendit, firmavit.*	She seized, strengthened.
—	הֶחֱזִיקוּ	*Retinuerunt, instaurarunt.*	They held fast, repaired.
—	הַחֲזִיקוּ	*Confirmate.*	Make ye strong.
—	הַחֲזִיקִי	*Confirma.*	Make thou strong.
—	הֶחֱזִיקִי	*Prehendere me.*	I take.
—	הֶחֱזִיקֵךְ	*Apprehendit te.*	She has taken thee.
—	הֶחֱזִיקַתְהוּ	*Apprehendit eum.*	She took hold of him.
חזר	הַחֲזִיר	*Sus.*	The swine.
חזק	הַחֲזֵק	*Prehende, robora.*	Take hold, strengthen thou.
—	הֶחָזָק	*Num robustus?*	Whether strong?
—	הַחֲזָקָה	*Potens, valida.*	The mighty, strong.
—	הֶחֱזַקְתִּי	*Tenui, apprehendi.*	I held fast.
—	הֶחֱזַקְתִּיךָ	*Prehendi te.*	I have taken thee.
—	הֶחֱזִקַתְנוּ	*Apprehendit nos.*	He has taken hold of us.
—	הֶחֱזִקַתְנִי	*Apprehendit me.*	He has taken hold of me.
חטא	הַחַטָּאָה	*Peccans.*	He that sins, sinful.
—	הַחַטָּאִים	*Peccantes.*	They that sin, sinners.
—	הַחַטָּאת	*Peccans; peccatum, victima pro peccato*	She that sins; the sin, the sin-offering.

ROOTS.	DERIVATIVES.	VERSIO.	SIGNIFICATION.
חטא	הַחֹטֵאת	*Peccans.*	She that sins.
—	הַחֲטִי	*Peccare facere.*	To cause to sin.
—	הֶחֱטִיא	*Peccare fecit.*	He made to sin.
—	הֶחֱטִיאוּ	*Peccare fecerunt.*	They made to sin.
חנט	הַחִטִּים	*Tritica.*	The wheats.
חיה	הֶחָי	*Vivens.*	The living, he that lives.
—	הֶחָי הַחַי	*Vivus.*	Living, alive.
חוד	הַחִידָה	*Ænigma.*	The riddle.
חיה	הַחַיָּה	*Vivens, viva; vita, animal, bestia, cœtus, caterva.*	The living, alive; the life, animal, beast, company, troop, multitude.
—	הֶחֱיָה	*In vita conservavit; vitam restituit.*	He preserved in life; he restored life.
—	הַחֲיוּ	*In vita servate.*	Keep ye alive.
—	הַחַיּוֹת	*Animalia.*	Animals, living creatures.
—	הַחַיִּים	*Vitæ; vivi.*	The lives; the living.
—	הֶחֱיֵיתִי	*Vivum servavi.*	I saved alive.
—	הַחֲיִיתֶם	*In vita servastis.*	Ye have saved alive.
חיל	הַחַיִל	*Facultas, robur, fortitudo, exercitus.*	The wealth, strength, valour, host, army.
—	הֶחָיִל	*Robur, exercitus.*	The strength, army.
—	הַחֲיָלִים	*Exercitus.*	The hosts, armies.
חוץ	הַחִיצוֹן	*Exterior.*	The outward.
—	הַחִיצוֹנָה--צֹנָה	*Exterior; extrinsecus.*	The outward; without.
חוש	הֵחִישׁוּ	*Festinaverunt.*	They hastened.
חיה	הַחֲיִיתֶם	*In vita servastis.*	Ye have saved alive.
—	הֶחֱיִיתָנוּ	*Vivos servasti nos.*	Thou hast saved our lives.
חכם	הֶחָכָם	*Sapiens. An sapiens?*	The wise man. A wise man?
—	הַחָכְמָה	*Sapientia.*	The wisdom.
—	הַחֲכָמוֹת	*Sapientes.*	The wise women.
—	הַחֲכָמִים	*Sapientes.*	The wise men.
חלל	הָחֵל הָחֵ׳	*Incipe; incipere.*	Begin thou; to begin.
—	הַחֹל	*Profanus; profanare; incepit.*	The unholy, profane; to profane, defile; he began.
חלב	הֶחָלָב	*Lac.*	The milk.
—	הַחֵלֶב	*Adeps.*	The fat.
—	הַחֲלָבִים	*Adipes.*	The fat.

ROOTS.	DERIVATIVES.	VERSIO.	SIGNIFICATION.
חלר	הַחֹלֶד	*Mustela.*	The weasel.
חלל	הֵחֵלָּה	*Cœpit.*	She began.
—	הַחַלָּה	*Placenta.*	The cake.
—	הֵחֵלּוּ	*Cœperunt.*	They began.
חלה	הֶחֱלוּ	*Ægrotare fecerunt.*	They have made sick.
חלם	הַחֲלוֹם	*Somnium.*	The dream.
חלן	הַחַלּוֹן	*Fenestra.*	The window.
חלץ	הֶחָלוּץ	*Expeditus, armatus.*	Ready, armed.
חלל	הַחִלּוֹתָ	*Cœpisti.*	Thou hast begun.
חלה	הֶחֱלִי	*Dolore affecit.*	He hath put to grief.
—	הַחֹלִי	*Morbus.*	The sickness.
חלף	הַחֲלִיפוֹת	*Mutationes, vices.*	Changes, courses.
חלק	הֶחֱלִיק	*Blanditus.*	He flattered.
—	הֶחֱלִיקָה	*Blandita est.*	She flattered.
חלה	הֶחֱלֵיתִי	*Morbo affeci.*	I made sick.
—	הָחֳלֵיתִי	*Vulneratus sum.*	I have been wounded.
חלל	הֶחָלָל	*Occisus.*	He that is slain.
—	הַחֲלָלִים	*Vulnerati, occisi.*	The wounded, slain.
—	הַחִלָּם	*Incipere eos.*	They begin.
חלם	הַחֲלֹמוֹת	*Somnia.*	The dreams.
חלמיש	הַחַלָּמִישׁ	*Silex.*	The flint.
חלל	הַחַלֹּנוֹת--נִים	*Fenestræ.*	The windows.
חלץ	הֵחָלְצוּ	*Accingite.*	Gird ye on, arm.
חלק	הַחֵלֶק	*Pars.*	A part.
—	הֶחָלָק	*Glaber, nudus.*	Bare, barren.
—	הַחֶלְקָה	*Ager, pars.*	The field, ground, piece.
—	הַחֲלָקִים	*Partes.*	The portions.
חלש	הַחַלָּשׁ	*Debilis.*	The weak.
חלל	הַחִלֹּתִי	*Cœpi.*	I have begun.
חמד	הַחֶמְדָּה	*Desiderium.*	The desire, desirable.
—	הַחֲמֻדוֹת	*Pulcherrimi.*	The most beautiful.
חמם	הַחַמָּה	*Sol.*	The sun.
יחם	הַחֵמָה	*Furor.*	The fury.
חמר	הַחֲמוֹר--מֹר	*Asinus.*	The ass.
—	הַחֲמוֹרִים--מֹרִי	*Asini.*	The asses.
חמה	הַחֹמוֹת	*Muri.*	The walls.
חמש	הַחֲמִישִׁי--מִשִּׁי	*Quintus.*	The fifth.

ROOTS.	DERIVATIVES.	VERSIO.	SIGNIFICATION.
חמש	הַחֲמִישִׁת־מִשׁ"	*Quinta.*	The fifth.
חמם	הַחַמָּנִים	*Simulachra solaria.*	Images dedicated to the sun.
חמס	הֶחָמָס	*Iniquitas.*	The iniquity.
חמר	הַחֹמֶר	*Lutum.*	The clay.
חמש	הַחֹמֶשׁ	*Quinta* costa.	The fifth *rib.*
—	הַחֲמִשָּׁה	*Quinque.*	Five.
—	הַחֲמִשִּׁים	*Quinquaginta, quinquagesimus.*	The fifty, the fiftieth.
—	הַחֲמֻשִׁים	*Armati.*	The armed men.
חמת	הַחֵמֶת	*Uter, lagena.*	The bottle, *a bag made of goat's skin.*
חמה	הַחֹמֹתַיִם־־תַיִם	*Muri duo.*	The two walls.
חנן	הַחֵן	*Gratia.*	Favour.
חנט	הַחֲנֻטִים	*Conditi.*	Those which are embalmed.
חנה	הַחֲנֻיוֹת	*Cellulæ.*	The cabins.
—	הַחֹנִים	*Considentes, castrametantes.*	Those that lie, are encamped.
—	הַחֲנִית	*Lancea, hasta.*	The javelin, spear.
—	הַחֲנִיתִים	*Hastæ.*	The spears.
חנן	הַחִנָּם	*An gratis?*	For nought?
חסד	הַחֶסֶד	*Misericordia.*	The mercy.
—	הַחֲסָדִים	*Misericordiæ.*	The mercies.
—	הַחֲסִידָה	*Ciconia.*	The stork.
חסל	הֶחָסִיל	*Bruchus.*	A kind of locust or caterpillar.
חסר	הֶחְסִיר	*Indiguit, caruit.*	He wanted.
חסן	הֶחָסֹן	*Fortis, robustus.*	The strong.
—	הֶחֱסִנוּ	*Possiderunt.*	They possessed.
חפר	הֶחְפִּיר	*Pudore affectus est.*	He was ashamed.
חפץ	הַחֵפֶץ	*Num voluntas?*	Any pleasure?
—	הֶחָפֵץ	*Qui voluit.*	Who would, desired.
—	הֶחָפֹץ	*Num volendo?*	In desiring?
—	הַחֲפֵצִים	*Volentes.*	Those who desire.
חפש	הַחָפְשִׁית־־וֹת	*Separata.*	The separate, detached.
חצב	הַחֹצֵב	*Cædens.*	He that hews, cuts out.
חוץ	הַחִיצוֹנָה־־צֹנָה	*Exterior.*	The outer, outward.
חצה	הַחֲצִי־־חֵ'	*Dimidium.*	The half.
חצץ	הַחֵצִי	*Sagitta.*	The arrow.
—	הַחִצִּים־־י	*Sagittæ.*	The arrows.
חצר	הֶחָצִיר	*Porrum.*	The leek.

ROOTS.	DERIVATIVES.	VERSIO.	SIGNIFICATION.
חצר	הֶחָצֵר	*Atrium.*	The court.
—	הַחֲצֵרוֹת־רִים	*Atria, villæ.*	The courts, villages.
חקק	הַחֻקָּה	*Statutum.*	The ordinance, statute.
—	הַחֻקִּים	*Statuta.*	The ordinances.
—	הַחֹקְקִים	*Statuentes.*	They that decree.
חקר	הַחֵקֶר	*An investigatione?*	By searching?
חרב	הֵחָרֵב	*Occidi.*	To be slain.
—	הַחֶרֶב־הֶחָ׳	*Gladius.*	The sword.
—	הֶחָרֵב	*Vastatus.*	The desolate, laid waste.
—	הֶחָרָבָה	*Siccum.*	The dry land.
—	הֶחָרֵבָה	*Vastata est.*	She is laid waste.
—	הֶחָרֵבוֹת	*Vastatæ.*	The waste.
—	הֶחֳרָבוֹת	*Vastitates.*	The wastes.
—	הֶחָרֵבֶת	*Vastata est.*	She was destroyed.
—	הֶחֱרַבְתִּי	*Vastavi.* [*es locustæ.*	I made waste. [cust.
חרגל	הַחַרְגֹּל	*Cantharus, vel speci-*	The beetle, or a species of lo-
חרד	הַחֲרָדָה	*Tremor, solicitudo.*	The trembling, solicitude.
—	הַחֲרֵדִים	*Trementes.*	They that tremble. [flamed.
חרה	הֶחֱרָה	*Accendit se.*	He kindled himself, was in-
חרץ	הֶחָרוּץ	*Decisio.*	The decision.
חרטם	הַחַרְטֻמִּים־מִּם	*Magi.*	The magicians.
חרב	הֶחֱרִיב	*Vastavit.*	He laid waste.
—	הֶחֱרִיבוּ	*Vastaverunt.*	They laid waste.
חרד	הֶחֱרִיד	*Perterruit.* [*didit.*	He discomfited. [stroyed.
חרם	הֶחֱרִים־רִם	*Exterminavit, per-*	He exterminated, utterly de-
חרר	הַחֹרִים	*Nobiles, magnates.*	The nobles, grandees.
חור	הַחֹרִים	*Foramina.*	The holes.
חרם	הֶחֱרִימוּ	*Exterminarunt.*	They destroyed utterly.
—	הַחֲרִימוּ	*Exterminate.*	Destroy ye utterly.
—	הֶחֱרִימָם	*Exterminavit eos.*	He destroyed them utterly.
—	הַחֲרִימָם	*Exterminare eos.*	To exterminate, root out them
חרש	הַחֲרִישׁוּ	*Tacete.*	Keep ye silence.
—	הַחֲרִישִׁי	*Tace.*	Hold thy peace. [*or iron.*
חרך	הַחֲרַכִּים	*Cancelli.*	The lattices, *cross bars of wood*
חרם	הַחֲרֵם	*Exterminare, de-struere.* [*ma.*	To exterminate, destroy.
—	הַחֵרֶם	*Res devota, anathe-*	The devoted thing, the curse.

ROOTS.	DERIVATIVES.	VERSIO.	SIGNIFICATION.
חרם	הֶחֱרַמְנוּ	*Funditus excidimus.*	We have utterly destroyed.
—	הֶחֱרַמְתִּי	*Funditus excidi.*	I have utterly destroyed.
—	הֶחֱרַמְתֶּם	*Funditus excidistis.*	Ye utterly destroyed.
חרס	הֶחָרֶס הַחַרְסָה	*Sol.*	The sun.
חרף	הַחֹרֶף	*Hyems, hyemalis.*	The winter, winterly.
חרש	הֶחֱרִשׁ	*Tacuit.*	He held his peace, was silent.
—	הַחֲרֵשׁ	*Tace; tacere.*	Be silent; to be silent. [man.
—	הַחֹרֵשׁ	*Arans, arator.*	He that ploughs, the plough-
—	הַחֹרֶשׁ	*Virgultum.*	The bough or twig.
—	הֶחָרָשׁ	*Faber, artifex.*	The workman, artificer.
—	הַחֵרְשִׁים	*Surdi.*	The deaf.
—	הַחָרָשִׁים	*Artifices, fabri.*	The workmen, artificers.
—	הֶחֱרַשְׁתִּי	*Tacui.*	I kept silence.
חשב	הַחֹשְׁבִים	*Cogitantes.*	They that think.
חשה	הֶחֱשׁוּ	*Tacete.*	Be ye silent.
חשך	הֶחְשִׁיךְ	*Tenebrescere fecit.*	He made dark.
חשה	הֶחֱשֵׁיתִי	*Tacui.*	I held my peace.
חשך	הַחֹשֶׁךְ	*Obscuritas, tenebræ*	The darkness.
חשמל	הַחַשְׁמַל־־מַלָה	*Electrum*, metallum ex auro et argento vel ære conflatum	Electrum, *a metal composed of gold and silver or brass.*
חתם	הֶחָתוּם	*Obsignatus.*	He that is sealed.
—	הַחֲתוּמִים	*Obsignati.*	Those that are sealed.
—	הֶחְתִּים	*Obstruxit, clausit.*	He stopped, shut.
—	הַחוֹתֶמֶת	*Sigillum.*	The signet.
חתת	הַחִתֹּתָ	*Confregisti.*	Thou hast broken.
	הט		
נטה	הַט	*Inclina.*	Incline thou, bow down.
טוב	הַטֹּבָה הַטּוֹבָה	*Bona, bonitas.*	The good, goodness.
—	הַטֹּבוֹת־־בִים	*Boni, optimi.*	The good, these good, the best
טבח	הַטַּבָּח	*Coquus.* [*lites.*	The cook. [soldiers, guards.
—	הַטַּבָּחִים	*Lanii, milites, satel-*	The butchers, slaughtermen,
טבע	הָטְבְּעוּ	*Demersi sunt.*	They were sunk.
—	הָטְבָּעוּ	*Infixi, fundati sunt.*	They were fastened, settled.
—	הַטַּבַּעַת	*Annulus.*	The ring.

ROOTS.	DERIVATIVES.	VERSIO.	SIGNIFICATION.
טבע	הַטַּבָּעֹת־־עוֹת	*Annuli.*	The rings.
נטה	הַטֵּה	*Inclina.*	Incline thou, bow down.
—	הִטָּה	*Inclinavit, extendit.*	He inclined, extended.
—	הִטָּהוּ	*Declinare fecit eum.*	He turned him aside.
טהר	הַטָּהוֹר־הֹר	*Mundus, purus.*	The clean, pure.
—	הַטְּהוֹרָה־־הֹרָה,	*Munda, pura.*	The clean, pure.
—	הַטָּהֳרָה	*Munditics.*	The purification.
—	הִטֶּהָרוּ	*Mundaverunt se.*	They cleansed themselves.
—	הִטָּהֲרוּ	*Mundati sunt.*	They were purified.
—	הִטָּהַרְנוּ	*Mundati sumus.*	We are cleansed.
נטה	הִטּוּ	*Inclinarunt, declinarunt.*	They inclined, turned away.
—	הַטּוּ	*Inclinate, declinate.*	Incline ye, turn ye aside.
טוב	הֲטוֹב־־בָה	*Num bonum, melius?*	Whether it be good, better?
—	הַטּוֹב	*Bonus, melior, optimus.*	The good, better, best.
—	הֲטוֹבִים	*An boni?*	Whether *they be* good?
טוח	הִטּוֹחַ־־טַּח	*Oblini, obduci.*	To be plaistered.
טור	הַטּוּר	*Ordo.*	The row.
טוח	הַטָּחִים	*Oblinentes.*	They that daub.
טחן	הַטַּחֲנָה	*Molitura.*	The grinding.
—	הַטֹּחֲנוֹת	*Molentes.*	They that grind, the grinders.
נטה	הַטִּי	*Inclina.*	Let down, incline thou.
יטב	הֵטִיבָה הֵיטִ׳	*Benefac.* [cinnarunt.	Do thou good. [well made.
—	הֵטִיבוּ	*Benefecerunt, con-*	They have done well, have
טוב	הֱטִיבוֹתָ־־בֹתָ	*Benefecisti.* [cane.	Thou didst well. [moniously.
—	הֵטִיבִי	*Benefac, numerosè*	Perform thou well, sing har-
טוח	הַטִּיחַ	*Litura.*	The daubing.
טיל	הֵטִיל	*Emisit, excitavit.*	He sent out, raised.
טור	הַטִּירוֹת	*Ordines.*	The rows.
נטה	הִטִּיתִי	*Inclinavi.*	I have inclined.
—	הִטִּיתֶם	*Inclinavistis.*	Ye have inclined.
טלל	הַטַּל־־טָּ׳	*Ros.*	The dew.
טמא	הַטָּמֵא	*Immundus, pollutus.*	The unclean, polluted.
—	הִטַּמָּאָה	*Polluta est.*	She is defiled.
—	הַטְּמֵאָה	*Immunda.*	The unclean.
—	הַטֻּמְאָה	*Immunditics.*	The uncleanness.

ROOTS.	DERIVATIVES.	VERSIO.	SIGNIFICATION.
טמא	הַטְּמֵאִים	*Immundi.*	The unclean, defiled.
טנא	הַטֶּנֶא	*Canistrum.*	The basket. [duced.
טעה	הִטְעוּ	*Errare fecerunt.*	They have caused to err, se-
טפף	הַטַּף־־טַף	*Parvuli.*	Children, families.
טפח	הַטְּפָחוֹת	*Subgrundia.*	The eaves, the coping.
טרף	הַטְרִיפֵנִי	*Ale me.*	Feed thou me.
טרם	הֲטֶרֶם	*An nondum?*	Not yet?
טרף	הַטְּרֵפָה	*Discerptus.*	He that is torn.
נטה	הִטַּתּוּ	*Declinare fecit eum.*	She caused him to turn aside.
	הי		
הוא	הִיא	*Ipse, ipsa.*	He, she, that.
אבה	הֲיֹאבֶה	*Num volet?*	Will he be willing?
אכל	הֲיֵאָכֵל	*An comedetur?*	Will it be eaten?
אמר	הֲיֹאמַר	*Num dicet?*	Shall or will he say?
יאר	הַיְאֹר	*Flumen.*	The river.
—	הַיְאֹרָה	*In flumen.*	Into the river.
—	הַיְאֹרִים	*Flumina.*	The rivers.
אתה	הַיְאִתוֹן	*Introitus.* [etinum.	The entrance. [ram's horn.
יבל	הַיֹּבֵל־־יוֹ׳	*Jubilæus; cornu ari-*	The jubilee; the trumpet of
—	הַיֹּבְלִים־־יוֹ׳	*Arietini.*	Of ram's horns.
יבש	הַיַּבָּשָׁה	*Arida.*	The dry.
—	הַיַּבֵּשׁוֹת	*Aridæ.* [crescet?	The dry.
נאה	הֲיִנְאָה	*Num se extollet,*	Will it raise itself, grow up?
נגד	הֲיַגִּיד	*An annunciabit?*	Will he declare?
יד	הַיָּד	*Manus.*	The hand.
—	הֲיַד	*Num manus?*	The hand?
הדד	הֵידָד	*Clamor, celeusma.*	The shouting.
ידע	הֲיָדוֹעַ־־דֹעַ	*Num scire?*	Is it to know?
ידה	הַיְדוֹת	*Gratiarum actiones.*	The thanksgivings.
—	הַיְדוֹת	*Gratiarum actio.*	The thanksgiving.
יד	הַיָּדוֹת־־דֹת	*Partes, fulcra.*	The parts, stays.
—	הַיָּדַיִם־־דַיִם	*Manus.*	The hands.
ידע	הַיֹּדְעִים	*Scientes.*	Those who know.
—	הַיִּדְּעֹנִי	*Ariolus.*	The wizard.
—	הַיִּדְּעֹנִים	*Arioli.*	The wizards.
—	הֲיָדַעְתָּ	*Nostine?*	Hast thou known?

ROOTS.	DERIVATIVES.	VERSIO.	SIGNIFICATION.
ידע	הֲיְדַעְתֶּם	*An scivistis?*	Have ye known?
הָיָה		*Fuit, factus est, languit, defecit.*	He was, became, fainted, sunk, was exhausted.
—	הֱיֵא הָיֹה	*Esse.*	To be.
—	הָיָה	*Fuerunt.*	They were.
הוה	הֲיְהֹוָה	*Num dominus?*	The Lord?
היה	הֲיִהְיֶה	*Num erit?*	Will he be?
הפך	הֲיַהֲפֹךְ	*An mutabit?*	Will he change?
היה	הָיוּ	*Fuerunt.*	They were.
—	הָיוֹ	*Esse.*	To be.
—	הֱיוּ	*Estote.*	Be ye.
ידה	הֲיוֹדְךָ	*Num celebrabit te?*	Shall he praise thee?
ידע	הֲיִוָּדַע	*Num cognoscetur?*	Will he be known?
חול	הֲיוּחַל	*Num fiet ut pariat?*	Will it be made to bring forth?
יכל	הֲיוּכַל	*Num poterit?*	Will he be able?
ילד	הַיּוּלָּד	*Qui conceptus est.*	That has been conceived.
יום	הַיּוֹם	*Dies.*	The day.
יון	הַיָּוֵן	*Cœnum.*	The clay.
ינה	הַיּוֹנָה	*Columba; opprimens*	The dove; he that oppresses.
יצא	הַיּוֹצֵא הַיֹּצֵא	*Egrediens.*	He that comes out.
—	הַיּוֹצְאִים הַיֹּצְ׳	*Egredientes.*	They who come out, go forth.
—	הַיּוֹצֵאת הַיֹּצֵ׳	*Egrediens.*	She that goes forth.
יצר	הַיּוֹצֵר הַיֹּצֵר	*Figulus.*	The potter.
—	הַיּוֹצְרִים	*Figuli.*	The potters.
יצא	הַיּוֹצֵאת	*Exeuns.*	She that comes out.
ירד	הַיּוֹרְדוֹת	*Descendentes.*	They that go down.
ירה	הַיּוֹרִים	*Jaculantes.*	They that shoot, the archers.
ירש	הַיּוֹרֵשׁ הַיֹּרֵשׁ	*Hæres.*	The heir.
ישב	הַיּוֹשֵׁב הַיֹּשֵׁב	*Habitans.*	He that dwells.
—	הַיּוֹשְׁבִים הַיֹּשְׁ׳	*Habitantes.*	They that dwell.
—	הַיּוֹשֶׁבֶת הַיֹּשֶׁ״	*Habitans.*	She that dwells.
היה	הֱיוֹת	*Esse, fieri.*	To be, to become.
—	הֱיוֹתָהּ	*Esse eam.*	That she is.
—	הֱיוֹתוֹ	*Esse eum.*	That he is.
—	הֱיוֹתִי	*Esse me.*	That I am.
—	הֱיוֹתְךָ־־תֵךְ	*Esse te.*	That thou art.
—	הֱיוֹתְכֶם	*Esse vos.*	That ye are.

ROOTS.	DERIVATIVES.	VERSIO.	SIGNIFICATION.
היה	הֱיוֹתָם	*Esse eos.*	That they are.
—	הֱיוֹתֵנוּ	*Esse nos.*	That we are.
יתר	הַיּוֹתֵר	*Residuum.*	The rest, remainder.
זבח	הֲיִזְבְּחוּ	*Num sacrificabunt?*	Will they sacrifice? [thee?
חבר	הַיְחָבְרְךָ	*Num jungetur tibi?*	Shall it be connected with
יחד	הַיָּחִיד	*Unicus.* [cet?	Only.
חיה	הֲיִחְיֶה	*Num vivet, revivis-*	Shall he live, live again?
—	הַיְחַיּוּ	*An restituent, excitabunt?*	Will they revive, raise up?
יחש	הַיַּחַשׂ	*Genealogia.*	The genealogy.
חתה	הֲיַחְתֶּה	*Num capiet?* [dulo.	Shall he take?
יטב	הֵיטֵב־־טֵיב	*Benefacere; bene, se-*	To do good; well, diligently.
—	הֵיטַבְתָּ־־תְ	*Benefecisti, meliorem fecisti.*	Thou hast done well, performed better.
—	הֵיטִיב	*Benefecit.* [canite.	He hath done good.
—	הֵיטִיבוּ	*Emendate; numerose*	Amend ye; sing melodiously.
טמא	הֲיִטְמָא	*Num polluetur?*	Shall it be defiled?
היה	הֱיִי	*Esto.*	Be thou.
יטב	הֲיִיטַב	*Num bonum erit?*	Will it be acceptable?
יין	הַיַּיִן־־יָּ	*Vinum.*	The wine.
היה	הָיִינוּ	*Fuimus, eramus.*	We have been, were.
—	הָיִיתָ־־יִתְ־־ית	*Fuisti.*	Thou wast.
—	הָיִיתִי	*Fui.*	I was.
—	הֱיִיתֶם	*Fuistis.*	Ye have been.
היך			
—	הֵיךְ	*Quomodo?*	How?
יכל	הֲיָכוֹל־־כֹל	*Num valendo?*	In being able?
הכל	הֵיכַל־־כָל	*Palatium.*	The palace.
יכל	הֲיָכֹל	*Num potuit?*	Was he able?
הכל	הֵיכְלָא	*Templum.*	The temple.
כלה	הַיְכַלּוּ	*An consummabunt?*	Will they finish?
הכל	הֵיכָלוֹ	*Templum ejus.*	His temple.
—	הֵיכָלוֹת	*Templa.*	Temples.
—	הֵיכְלֵי	*Palatia.*	Palaces.
—	הֵיכָלֶךָ	*Templum tuum.*	Thy temple. [nant?
כרת	הֲיִכְרֹת	*Num feriet, panget?*	Will he strike, make *a* cove-
ילד	הַיֶּלֶד־־יָּ	*Puer.*	The child, boy.

ROOTS.	DERIVATIVES.	VERSIO.	SIGNIFICATION.
ילד	הַיַּלְדָּה	Puella.	The damsel.
—	הַיַּלְדוּת	Pueritia, juventus.	Childhood, youth.
—	הַיֹּלְדוֹת	Quæ pepererunt.	Who bare.
—	הַיְלָדִים	Pueri, juvenes.	The children, young men.
—	הַיְלָדִים	Nati.	Born, the children.
—	הַיֹּלֶדֶת	Pariens.	She that bears.
—	הַיָּלוּד	Natus.	Born, the child, boy.
—	הַיִּלּוֹד	Natus.	He that is born.
—	הַיִּלּוֹדִים	Nati.	They that are born.
יָלַךְ	הֵילִיכִי	Abduc.	Take thou away.
יָלַל	הֵילִילוּ	Ejulate.	Howl ye.
—	הֵילִילִי	Ejula.	Howl thou.
יָלַךְ	הֲיֵלֵךְ	Num ambulabit?	Will he walk?
—	הֲיֵלְכוּ	Num ambulabunt?	Will they walk?
יָלַל	הֵילֵל	Ejula.	Howl thou.
הָלַל	הֵילֵל	Lucifer. [custæ.	Lucifer. [of locust.
יָלַק	הַיֶּלֶק־יְ	Bruchus, species lo-	The canker worm, a species
ים	הַיָּם	Mare; occidens.	The sea; the west.
—	הֲיָם	Num mare?	A sea?
—	הַיָּמָּה	Ad, in mare.	To, into the sea.
—	הַיַּמִּים	Maria.	The seas.
יום	הַיָּמִים־מִין	Dies.	The days
ימן	הַיָּמִין	Dexter; dextera.	The right; the right-hand.
—	הַיְמִינִי־מָנִי	Dexter.	The right, on the right-hand.
—	הֵימִינִי	Ito ad dexteram.	Go thou to the right.
מלט	הֲיִמָּלֵט	Num evadet?	Shall he escape?
יום	הַיָּמִם	Dies.	The days.
—	הֵימָם	Hemam.	Hemam, N. M.
—	הֵימָן	Heman.	Heman, N. M.
אמן	הֶאֱמִן	Credidit.	He believed.
ימן	הַיְמָנִית	Dextera. [dorum.	The right ear, hand, foot.
הין	הִין	Hin, mensura liqui-	A hin, the sixth of an ephah.
	הֵין	Voluit, paratus est.	He was willing, prepared.
נהק	הֲיִנְהַק	Num rudet?	Will he bray?
נטר	הֲיִנְטוֹר	Num reservabit?	Will he reserve?
ינק	הֵינִיקָה	Lactavit.	She suckled.
—	הַיֹּנֵק	Sugens.	The sucking child.

ROOTS.	DERIVATIVES.	VERSIO.	SIGNIFICATION.
ינשף	הַיַּנְשׁוּף	*Ibis, ulula, vel bubo.*	The ibis, *a kind of stork*, the owl, or the bittern.
סגר	הֲיַסְגִּירוּ	*Num tradent ?*	Will they deliver ?
—	הֲיַסְגִּרֻנִי	*Num tradent me ?*	Will they deliver me up ?
יסד	הַיְסוֹד	*Fundamentum.*	The foundation.
ספר	הַיְסֻפַּר	*Num enarrabitur ?*	Shall it be told, declared ?
יסר	הַיֹּסֵר	*Nonne castigans ?*	Not he that chastiseth ?
יעץ	הַיְּעוּצָה	*Quod consultum est.*	That is purposed.
עזב	הֲיַעֲזֹב	*Num relinquet ?*	Will he leave ?
—	הֲיַעַזְבוּ	*Num relinquent, permittent ?*	Will they leave, expose, abandon ?
יעה	הַיָּעִים	*Palæ, scopæ.*	The spades, shovels.
עלה	הֲיַעֲלֶה	*Num ascendet ?*	Shall he go up ?
יעל	הַיְּעֵלִים	*Rupicapræ.*	The wild goats.
עמד	הֲיַעֲמֹד	*Num sustinebit ?*	Will he endure ?
—	הֲיַעַמְדוּ	*Num constabunt ?*	Will they stand ?
עיף	הַיָּעֵף	*Fessus.*	He that is weary, faint.
—	הַיְּעֵפִים	*Fessi.*	They that are weary, faint.
יער	הַיַּעַר־־ִי	*Sylva.*	The wood, forest.
—	הַיַּעְרָה	*In sylvam, sylva.*	Into, in the wood.
—	הַיְּעָרִים	*Sylvæ.*	The woods, forests.
ערך	הֲיַעֲרֹךְ	*An æstimabit ?*	Will he esteem ?
עשה	הֲיַעֲשֶׂה	*Num faciet ?* [*ma.*	Will he make ?
יפה	הַיָּפָה	*Pulchra, pulcherri-*	The fair, fairest.
—	הַיָּפוֹת	*Pulchræ.*	The fair.
—	הַיֹּפִי	*Pulchritudo.*	The beauty.
פלא	הֲיִפָּלֵא	*Num difficile erit ?*	Shall it be hard, difficult ?
נפל	הֲיִפְּלוּ	*Num cadent ?*	Shall they fall ?
יצא	הַיֹּצְאִים	*Egredientes.*	Those who go forth.
—	הַיֹּצֵאת	*Egrediens.*	She that comes forth.
צהר	הַיִּצְהָר	*Oleum.*	The oil.
יצע	הַיָּצוּעַ	*Stratum.*	The bed, couch.
צלח	הֲיִצְלַח	*An prosperabitur ?*	Shall he prosper ?
—	הֲיִצְלָח	*An proderit ?*	Will it be advantageous ?
יקב	הַיֶּקֶב־־ִי	*Torcular.*	The press *for wine or oil.*
—	הַיְקָבִים	*Torcularia.*	The presses.
קבע	הֲיִקְבַּע	*An spoliabit ?*	Will he rob ?

ROOTS.	DERIVATIVES.	VERSIO.	SIGNIFICATION.
קדש	הֲיִקְדַּשׁ	*An sanctificabitur ?*	Shall it be holy ?
קום	הַיְקוּם	*Substantia.*	The substance.
לקח	הֲיֻקַּח	*Num tolletur ?*	Shall he be taken ?
יקר	הַיְקָר	*Pretium.*	The price.
——	הַיְקָרִים	*Pretiosi, incluti.*	The precious, excellent. [thee
קרה	הֲיִקְרֵךְ	*Utrum eveniet tibi ?*	Whether it shall happen to
ירא	הַיָּרֵא	*Timens, timidus.*	He that fears, fearful.
רבה	הֲיַרְבֶּה	*An multiplicabit ?*	Will he multiply, make many?
ירד	הֲיֵרֵד	*Num descendet ?*	Will he go down ?
——	הַיֹּרֵד	*Descendens.*	He that goes down.
——	הַיֹּרְדִים	*Descendentes.*	They that go or come down.
——	הַיֹּרֶדֶת	*Descendens.*	She that goes down.
ירה	הַיֹּרֶה	*Jaciens, jaculans.*	He who casts, hurls, shoots.
ירח	הַיָּרֵחַ	*Luna.* [*tores.*	The moon.
ירה	הַיֹּרִים	*Jaculantes, jacula-*	They that shoot, the archers.
ירע	הַיְרִיעָה	*Cortina.*	The curtain.
——	הַיְרִיעֹת	*Cortinæ.*	The curtains.
ירך	הַיָּרֵךְ	*Femur.*	The thigh.
רעע	הֲיָרֹעַ	*Num franget? [piet?*	Shall he break ? [with, accept ?
רצה	הֲיִרְצֶה	*Num probabit, acci-*	Will he approve, be pleased
רוץ	הֲיְרֻצוּן	*Num current ?*	Shall they run ?
רצה	הֲיִרְצְךָ	*An gratum habebit, accipiet te ?*	Will he be pleased with thee, accept thee ?
ירק	הַיָּרָק	*Olus.*	The herbs.
ירש	הַיְרֻשָּׁה	*Hæreditas.*	The inheritance
ישה	הֲיֵשׁ	*Num est ; estne ?*	Is there ?
נשא	הֲיִשָּׂא	*Num suscipiet ?*	Will he take, receive, bear?
שאג	הֲיִשְׁאַג	*An rugiet ?*	Will he roar ?
ישב	הַיֹּשְׁבָה	*Sita.*	She that is situate.
——	הַיֹּשְׁבִי	*Habitans.*	He that dwells.
שוב	הֲיָשׁוּב	*An revertetur ?*	Shall he return ?
ישע	הַיְשׁוּעָה	*Salus.*	The salvation.
ישם	הַיְשִׁימֹן	*Solitudo.*	The wilderness.
ישה	הֲיֶשְׁכֶם	*An vos estis ?*	Whether you are ?
שלם	הֲיְשֻׁלַּם	*Num rependetur ?*	Shall he be recompensed ? [en?
שמע	הֲיִשְׁמְעוּ	*Utrum audient ?*	Whether they will hear, heark-
ישן	הַיְשָׁנָה	*Vetus.*	The old.

ROOTS.	DERIVATIVES.	VERSIO.	SIGNIFICATION.
ישר	הַיָּשָׁר	*Rectum.*	The right.
—	הַיְשָׁרָה	*Rectitudo.*	Uprightness.
יתד	הַיָּתֵד־יָתֵד	*Clavus.*	The nail, pin.
—	הַיְתֵדֹת	*Clavi.*	The pins, nails.
היה	הָיְתָה־יָ	*Fuit.*	She was.
אתה	הֵיתִי	*Adduxit.*	He brought.
—	הֵיתָיו	*Attulerunt.*	They brought.
—	הֵיתָיוּ	*Adducti sunt.*	They were brought.
היה	הֱיִתֶם	*Fuistis.*	Ye were, have been.
נתן	הֲיִתֵּן	*Num dabit?*	Will he give?
פאר	הֲיִתְפָּאֵר	*Num gloriabitur?*	Shall he boast?
יתר	הַיְתָרִים	*Vimina, nervi, lora.*	The withs, strings, thongs.
—	הַיֹּתֶרֶת	*Reticulum.*	The caul.
	הכ		
נכה	הַךְ	*Percute.*	Smite thou.
כאב	הַכְּאֵב	*Dolor.*	The grief.
—	הִכְאַבְתִּיו	*Dolore affeci eum.*	I have made him sad.
—	הַכְאוֹב	*Conturbare, atterere*	To disquiet, trouble, afflict.
כבד	הַכְבֵּד	*Aggrava.* [vis.	Make thou heavy.
—	הַכָּבֵד	*Jecur; magnus, gra-*	The liver; great, heavy.
—	הַכָּבֹד־כְּבוּדָּה	*Substantia, gloria.*	The substance, the glory.
—	הִכָּבֵד	*Gloriare.*	Glory thou.
—	הִכָּבְדִי	*Honorari me.*	That I am honoured, glorified.
—	הִכְבַּדְתָּ	*Aggravasti.*	Thou hast heavily laid.
—	הִכְבַּדְתִּי	*Aggravavi, induravi*	I have aggravated, hardened.
—	הַכָּבוֹד	*Gloria; gloriosus.*	The glory; glorious.
—	הִכְבִּיד	*Aggravavit* [varunt	He made heavy, aggravated.
—	הִכְבִּידוּ	*Gravarunt, aggra-*	They burdened, made heavy.
כבס	הֻכַּבֵּס	*Lavari.*	To be washed.
כבש	הַכֶּבֶשׂ	*Agnus.*	The lamb.
—	הַכִּבְשָׂה	*Agna.*	The lamb.
—	הַכְּבָשִׂים	*Agni, oves.*	The lambs, sheep.
—	הַכִּבְשָׁן	*Fornax.*	The furnace.
כדד	הַכַּדִּים	*Hydriæ.*	The pitchers.
נכה	הִכָּה	*Percussit.*	He smote.
—	הַכֵּה	*Percutere; percute.*	To smite; smite thou.

ROOTS.	DERIVATIVES.	VERSIO.	SIGNIFICATION.
נכה	הֻכָּה	*Percussus est.*	He was smitten.
—	הִכָּהוּ	*Percussit eum.*	He smote him.
—	הַכֻּהוּ	*Percutite eum.*	Smite ye him.
—	הִכֻּהוּ	*Percusserunt eum.*	They smote him.
כהן	הַכֹּהֵן	*Sacerdos.*	The priest.
—	הַכְּהֻנָּה	*Sacerdotium.*	The priesthood.
—	הַכְּהֻנּוֹת	*Partes sacerdotales.*	The priestly functions.
—	הַכֹּהֲנִים	*Sacerdotes.*	The priests.
נכה	הִכּוּ	*Percusserunt.*	They smote.
—	הַכּוּ	*Percutite.*	Smite ye.
—	הֻכּוּ	*Percussi sunt.*	They were smitten.
ככב	הַכּוֹכָבִים	*Stellæ.*	The stars.
נכה	הִכּוּם	*Percusserunt eos.*	They smote them.
—	הַכּוּם	*Percutite eos.*	Smite ye them.
כון	הִכּוֹן־־כֹּן	*Paratus esto.*	Be thou prepared.
נכה	הִכּוּנִי	*Percusserunt me.*	They smote me.
כוס	הַכּוֹס	*Bubo; vel onocrotalus.*	The little owl; or the onocrotalus, *a species of water-fowl*
נכה	הַכּוֹת	*Percutere.*	To smite.
—	הַכּוֹתְךָ	*Percutere te.*	To smite thee.
כתר	הַכּוֹתֶרֶת	*Capitulum.*	The chapiter.
זה	הֲכָזֶה	*Num sicut hic?*	Is he like this?
זנה	הַכְזוֹנָה	*Num ut meretrix?*	As a harlot?
יכח	הֹכַחְתָּ	*Destinasti.*	Thou hast appointed.
כי	הֲכִי	*An recte; num quia?*	Rightly, because?
יצר	הֲכַיּוֹצֵר	*Num sicut figulus?*	As the potter?
כיר	הַכִּיּוֹר־־יֹּר	*Concha, labrum.*	The laver.
יכח	הֹכִיחַ	*Destinavit.*	He has appointed.
כול	הָכִיל	*Continere.*	To restrain, hold in.
יום	הֲכִימֵי	*An sicut dies?*	As the days?
כון	הֵכִין	*Paravit, stabilivit.*	He prepared, established.
—	הָכִין	*Parabis.*	Thou shalt prepare.
—	הֱכִינָהּ	*Paravit eam.*	He prepared her.
—	הָכִינוֹ	*Preparare eum.*	That he prepares.
—	הֱכִינוֹ	*Confirmavit eum.*	He confirmed, established him
—	הֵכִינוּ	*Præpararunt.*	They prepared.
—	הָכִינוּ	*Præparate.*	Prepare ye.

ROOTS.	DERIVATIVES.	VERSIO.	SIGNIFICATION.
כון	הֲכִינוֹנְנוּ	*Paravimus.*	We have prepared.
—	הֲכִינוֹתָ	*Præparasti.*	Thou hast prepared.
—	הֲכִינוֹתִי	*Præparavi.*	I have prepared.
נכה	הַכֵּינִי	*Percute me.*	Smite thou me.
כון	הֲכִינָנִי	*Stabilivit me.*	He has established me.
נכר	הִכִּיר	*Agnovit.*	He acknowledged.
—	הִכִּירֻהוּ הִכִּרֻ־	*Cognoverunt eum.*	They knew him.
—	הִכִּירוֹ	*Agnovit eum.*	He discerned him.
—	הִכִּירוּ	*Cognoverunt.*	They knew.
כיר	הַכִּיּרוֹת־־רֹת	*Conchæ, labra.*	The lavers.
נכה	הִכִּיתָ־־ה	*Percussisti.*	Thou smotest.
—	הִכִּיתוֹ	*Percussisti eum.*	Thou hast smitten him.
—	הִכֵּיתִי	*Percussi.*	I have smitten, slain.
—	הֻכֵּיתִי	*Percussus sum.*	I have been smitten, wounded.
—	הִכִּיתִיךָ־־ךְ	*Percussi te.*	I smote thee.
—	הִכִּיתֶם	*Percussistis.*	Ye have smitten.
—	הִכִּיתָנוּ	*Percussisti nos.*	Thou hast smitten us.
—	הִכִּיתַנִי	*Percussisti me.*	Thou hast smitten me.
ככר	הַכִּכָּר	*Planities; talentum.*	The plain; the talent.
הכל			
כלל	הַכֹּל	*Omnis, omnes, totus.*	All, the whole.
—	הֲכֹל	*An totus?*	The whole?
כלא	הַכֶּלֶא הַכְּלִיא	*Carcer.*	The prison.
כלב	הַכֶּלֶב	*Canis.*	The dog.
—	הֲכֶלֶב	*Num canis?*	A dog?
—	הַכְּלָבִים	*Canes.*	The dogs.
כלה	הַכְּלִי	*Vas.*	The vessel.
—	הַכְּלָיוֹת־־יֹת	*Renes.*	The kidneys.
—	הַכֵּלִים	*Vasa, instrumenta.*	The vessels, instruments.
כלם	הַכְלִים הִכָּלֵם	*Erubescere.* [eum.	To blush, be ashamed.
—	הִכְלִמוֹ	*Ignominia affecit*	He put him to shame.
—	הָכְלַמְנוּ	*Pudore affecti sumus*	We were made ashamed.
—	הֶכְלַמְנוּם	*Pudore affecimus eos*	We made them ashamed.
נכה	הִכָּם	*Percussit eos.*	He smote them.
מות	הַכְּמוֹת	*Num sicut moritur?*	As dieth?
נכה	הַכְּמַכַּת	*Num sicut plaga?*	As the stroke?
כמר	הַכְּמָרִים	*Sacrificuli.*	The *idolatrous* priests.

ROOTS.	DERIVATIVES.	VERSIO.	SIGNIFICATION.
כון	הָכֵן	*Parando, firmando.*	In preparing, fixing firmly.
—	הֲכִנּוּ	*Præparavimus.*	We have prepared.
כנר	הַכִּנּוֹר	*Cithara.*	The harp.
כנן	הַכִּנִּים	*Pediculi.*	The lice.
כנע	הִכְנִיעַ	*Depressit.*	He humbled, brought low.
—	הַכְנִיעֵהוּ	*Deprime eum.*	Bring thou him low.
כנן	הַכִּנָּם	*Pediculorum copia, vel morbus pediculosus.*	The swarm of lice, or the disease of lice in the human body.
כנע	הִכָּנְעוֹ	*Humiliare se.*	That he humbled himself.
כנף	הַכָּנָף	*Ora.*	The borders.
—	הַכְּנָפַיִם	*Alæ.*	The wings.
כון	הֲכִנֹתִי	*Paravi.*	I prepared.
כסא	הַכִּסֵּא	*Solium.*	The throne.
—	הַכֶּסֶא	*Tempus statum.*	The time appointed.
כסה	הִכָּסוֹת	*Tegi.*	To be covered.
כסל	הַכְּסִיל	*Stultus.*	The fool.
—	הַכְּסִילִים	*Stulti.*	The fools.
—	הַכְּסָלִים	*Ilia.*	The flanks.
כסף	הַכֶּסֶף־־כָּ׳	*Argentum, argenteus; nummus.*	The silver, made of silver; the money
כעס	הִכְעִיס	*Irritavit.*	He provoked to anger.
—	הִכְעִיסוּ	*Irritaverunt.*	They provoked to anger.
—	הִכְעִיסוֹ	*Irritavit eum.*	He provoked him.
—	הִכְעִסֻנִי־־עָס׳	*Irritaverunt me.*	They provoked me.
—	הַכַּעַס	*Irritamentum.*	The provocation.
—	הַכְעִסוּנִי	*Irritare me.*	That they provoked me to anger.
—	הַכְּעָסִים	*Irritamenta.*	The provocations.
—	הִכְעַסְתָּ	*Irritasti.*	Thou hast provoked to anger.
כפף	הַכַּף	*Cochleare, acerra.*	The spoon, censer.
—	הֲכַף	*Num manus?*	The hands?
—	הַכְּפוּפִים	*Incurvati.*	Those who are bowed down.
—	הַכַּפּוֹת־־פֹּת	*Acerræ, cochlearia.*	The censers, the spoons.
כפר	הַכְּפִירִים	*Leones juvenes.*	The young lions.
כפש	הִכְפִּישַׁנִי	*Depressit, involvit, operuit me;* secundum quosdam, *cibavit me.*	He hath plunged, involved, covered me; *according to some,* he hath fed me.

ROOTS.	DERIVATIVES.	VERSIO.	SIGNIFICATION.
כפר	הַכֹּפֶר	*Cyprus.*	The cyprus, or camphor shrub
—	הַכִּפֻּרִים	*Expiationes.*	The atonements. [seat.
—	הַכַּפֹּרֶת	*Propitiatorium.*	The propitiatory or mercy
כפתר	הַכַּפְתּוֹר	*Superliminare.* [*ejus*	The lintel.
צעק	הַכְּצַעֲקָתָהּ	*An juxta clamorem*	Whether according to his cry.
הָכַר		*Obfirmavit se, incubuit, oppressit.*	He hardened himself, became inflexible, oppressed.
נכר	הַכֵּר	*Cognoscere.*	To know. [to have respect.
—	הַכֶּר	*Cognosce; agnoscere*	Know thou; to acknowledge,
כרב	הַכְּרֻבִים־־רוּ׳	*Cherubim.*	The cherubim.
—	הַכְּרוּב	*Cherub.*	The cherub.
כר	הַכָּרִי	*Duces.*	The captains.
—	הַכָּרִים ׳	*Agni.*	The lambs.
כרע	הִכְרִיעַ	*Prostravit.*	He smote down.
—	הַכְרִיעֵהוּ	*Prosterne eum.*	Cast thou him down.
כרת	הַכְרִית	*Exscindere.*	To cut off.
—	הִכְרִית	*Excidit.*	He hath cut off.
—	הִכְרִיתוּ	*Exciderunt.*	They cut off, destroyed.
—	הַכְרִיתְךָ	*Exscindere te.*	To cut thee off.
כרם	הַכֶּרֶם־־כָּ׳	*Vinea.*	The vineyard.
—	הַכְּרָמִים	*Vineæ.*	The vineyards.
כרע	הַכְרֵעַ	*Deprimere.*	To bring low, cast down.
—	הַכְּרָעַיִם־־עַ׳	*Crura.*	The legs.
—	הִכְרַעְתַּנִי	*Depressisti me.*	Thou hast brought me low.
כרת	הַכֹּרֵת	*Succidens.*	He that cuts down, the feller.
נכר	הַכָּרַת	*Agnitio.*	The acknowledgment.
כרת	הִכָּרֵת	*Exscindi.*	To be cut off.
—	הִכְרַת	*Excisus est.*	He is cut off.
—	הִכְרַתִּי	*Excidi.*	I have cut off.
כשב	הַכֶּשֶׂב	*Agnus.*	The lamb.
—	הַכְּשָׂבִים	*Oves.*	The sheep.
כשל	הִכְשִׁיל	*Ruere fecit.*	He hath made to fall.
כשר	הַכְשֵׁיר	*Dirigere.*	To direct.
כשל	הִכְשַׁלְתֶּם	*Impingere fecistis.*	Ye have caused to stumble.
כתב	הַכְּתָב	*Scriptura.*	The writing.
—	הַכְּתֻבִים	*Scripti.*	They that are, were written.
—	הַכֹּתְבִים	*Subscribentes.*	They that subscribe.

ROOTS.	DERIVATIVES.	VERSIO.	SIGNIFICATION.
נכה	הֻכָּתָה	*Percussa est.*	She was smitten.
—	הַכֹּתוֹ	*Percutere eum.*	That he smites.
כתב	הַכָּתוּב	*Scriptus.*	He or that which is written.
—	הַכְּתוּבָה	*Scripta.*	She or that which is written.
—	הַכְּתוּבוֹת	*Scriptæ.*	They that are written.
—	הַכְּתוּבִים	*Scripti.*	They that are written.
נכה	הַכֹּתִי	*Percutere me.*	That I smite.
כתם	הַכֶּתֶם	*Aurum.*	Gold.
כתן	הַכְּתֹנֶת הַכֻּתֹּנֶת	*Tunica: an tunica?*	The coat: whether the coat?
—	הַכָּתְנֹת	*Tunicæ.*	The coats.
כתף	הַכָּתֵף	*Latus.*	The side.
—	הַכְּתֵפוֹת	*Humeralia.*	The shoulder-pieces.
כתר	הַכֹּתָרוֹת־־רֹת	*Capitula.*	The chapiters.
—	הַכֹּתֶרֶת	*Capitulum.*	The chapiter.
	הל		
חלא			
לא	הֲלֹא־־לֹא־־לוֹא	*Annon? nonne?*	*Is* not? *are* not?
הלא	הָלְאָה	*Ultra, postea.*	Yonder, beyond, afterwards.
לאה	הַלְאוֹת	*Fatigare.*	To weary.
אלה	הַלְאֵל	*Num pro Deo?*	For God?
לאה	הֶלְאָנִי	*Fatigavit me.*	He made me weary.
—	הֶלְאָת	*Fatigavit se.*	She wearied herself.
—	הֶלְאֵתִיךָ	*Fatigavi te.*	I have wearied thee.
לבב	הַלֵּב־־בָב	*Cor.*	The heart.
—	הַלְּבִבוֹת	*Placentæ.*	The cakes.
לבן	הַלְּבוֹנָה־־בֹנָה	*Thus.*	The frankincense.
לבש	הַלְּבוּשׁ	*Vestimentum* [*dum?*	The apparel.
בזז	הֲלָבֹז	*Num ad diripien-*	To plunder, rob, spoil.
לבן	הִלְבִּינוּ	*Albuerunt.*	They became white.
לבש	הִלְבִּישָׁה	*Induit.*	She put on.
—	הִלְבִּישׁוּ	*Induerunt.*	They clothed.
—	הִלְבִּישַׁנִי	*Induit me.*	He hath clothed me.
בנה	הַלָּבֶן	*Num vir?*	A man?
לבן	הַלָּבָן	*Albus; albor.*	The white; the whiteness.
—	הַלְּבֵנָה	*Later.*	The brick
—	הַלְּבָנָה	*Luna.*	The moon.

ROOTS.	DERIVATIVES.	VERSIO.	SIGNIFICATION.
לבן	הַלְּבֵנִים	*Lateres.*	The bricks.
לבש	הַלָּבֻשׁ	*Indutus.*	Clothed.
——	הַלֹּבְשִׁים	*Induentes.* [*dum ?*	They that clothe.
דרש	הֲלִדְרֹשׁ	*Num ad quæren-*	To inquire ?
לא	הֲלֹה	*Annon ? nonne ?*	*Is* not ? *are* not ?
להב	הַלַּהַב	*Flamma.* [*dum ?*	The flame.
יכח	הַלְהוֹכֵחַ	*Num ad increpan-*	To reprove ?
הוא	הֲלָהֶן	*Nunquid eis ?* [*me ?*	For them ?
הרג	הַלְהָרְגֵנִי	*Num ad occidendum*	To kill me ?
לוט	הַלּוֹט	*Obductus; operimen- tum*	He or that which is spread ; the covering.
הלך	הָלוֹךְ־לֵךְ	*Ire, ambulare; vade.*	To go, walk ; go thou.
הלל	הִלּוּלִים	*Laudes.*	Praises.
הלם	הֲלוּמֵי	*Oppressi, contusi.*	Oppressed, overcome.
לז	הַלָּז	*Hic, hæc, ille, illa.*	This, that.
——	הַלָּזֶה	*Hic, ille.*	This, that.
——	הֲלָזֶה	*Nunquid istud ?*	That ?
——	הַלֵּזוּ	*Hæc ipsa.*	This, that.
לוח	הַלֻּחוֹת־־חֹת	*Tabulæ.*	The tables.
לחה	הַלְּחִי־־לְּ	*Maxilla.*	The cheek.
לחם	הַלֶּחֶם־־לָּ	*Panis.*	The bread.
——	הִלָּחֵם	*Pugna.*	Fight thou.
——	הִלָּחֲמוֹ	*Pugnare eum.*	That he fights.
לחץ	הַלַּחַץ	*Oppressio.*	The oppression.
——	הַלֹּחֲצִים	*Opprimentes.* [*um ?*	They that oppress.
יעץ	הַלְיוֹעֵץ	*Num in consiliari-*	For a counsellor ?
ילד	הֹלִיכוּ	*Ducite.*	Carry ye.
הלך	הֲלִיכוֹת־כֹת	*Gressus, incessus.*	The steps, goings.
——	הֲלִיכוֹתֶיךָ	*Incessus tui.*	Thy goings.
——	הֲלִיכִי	*Gressus mei.*	My steps.
ליל	הַלַּיְלָה־לַּי	*Nox.*	The night.
ילל	הֵילִילוּ	*Ejulate.*	Howl ye.
ליל	הַלֵּילוֹת	*Noctes.*	The nights.
ילל	הֵילִילִי	*Ejula.*	Howl thou.
לון	הֲלִינֹתֶם	*Murmurastis.*	Ye have murmured.
לוץ	הֱלִיצֻנִי	*Illuserunt me.* [*nos ?*	They have mocked me.
ירש	הַלְיָרְשֵׁנוּ	*Num ad possidendum*	Is it to take possession of us ?

ROOTS.	DERIVATIVES.	VERSIO.	SIGNIFICATION.
הָלַךְ		*Ambulavit, ivit, venit, adiit, abiit, exiit, rediit, profectus est.*	He walked, went, came, went to, departed, went away, went out of, returned, travelled.
—	הֲלֹךְ	*Venire.*	To come.
—	הֵלֶךְ	*Decursus; viator.*	A running down; a traveller.
—	הוֹלֵךְ	*Iens, veniens, ambulans, procedens, pergens.*	Going, coming, walking, proceeding, advancing.
—	הוֹלְכָה	*Vadens.*	Going.
—	הָלְכָה־־לִי	*Abiit.*	She went away, is gone.
—	הָלְכוּ־־לִי	*Iverunt.*	They went. [go.
—	הֹלְכוּ	*Abite; ire fecerunt.*	Go ye away; they caused to
—	הֹלְכֵי	*Ambulantes.*	Walking.
—	הָלַכְנוּ	*Venimus.*	We came.
כפף	הֲלָכֹף	*Num incurvare?*	To bow down?
הלך	הָלַכְתָּ־־תְּ״	*Ivisti, ambulasti.*	Thou wentest, walkedst.
—	הָלַכְתִּי הִלַּ״ הִלַּ׳	*Ivi, ambulavi.*	I went, walked.
—	הֲלַכְתֶּם	*Ivistis.*	Ye went.
הָלַל		*Laudavit, gloriatus est, splenduit, insanivit.*	He praised, boasted, shined, raged, was mad.
—	הִלֵּל	*Laudavit, jactavit.*	He praised, boasted.
—	הִלֵּל	*Hillel.*	Hillel, N. M.
לול	הַלֻּלָאוֹת	*Laqueoli.*	The loops.
הלל	הַלְלוּ	*Laudate.*	Praise ye.
—	הַלְלוּהוּ	*Laudate eum.*	Praise ye him.
—	הַלְלוּיָהּ ·	*Laudate Dominum.*	Praise ye the Lord.
—	הִלְלוּךָ	*Laudaverunt te.*	They praised thee.
—	הַלְלִי	*Lauda.* [vimus.	Praise thou.
—	הִלַּלְנוּ	*Laudavimus, jacta-*	We have praised, boasted.
—	הִלַּלְתִּיךָ	*Laudavi.*	I praised thee.
—	הֵלֶם	*Helem.*	Helem, N. M.
הָלַם		*Contudit, confregit, percussit, quassavit.*	He knocked, beat, broke to pieces, smote.
—	הֲלֹם	*Hic, huc, illuc.*	There, hither, thither.

ROOTS.	DERIVATIVES.	VERSIO.	SIGNIFICATION.
הלם	הָלְמוּ	*Contuderunt, quassati sunt.*	They have broken down, were shattered.
—	הֲלָמוּנִי	*Contuderunt me.*	They have beaten me.
מען	הַלְמַעַנְךָ	*Num propter te?*	For thee? on thy account?
מות	הַלַּמֵּתִים	*Num mortuis?*	To the dead?
	הֲלָנוּ	*An ex nostris?*	From our?
נצח	הֲלָנֶצַח	*Num in perpetuum?*	For ever?
לעג	הַלַּעַג	*Sanna.*	The scorning.
עלם	הַלְעוֹלָם	*Num in æternum?*	For ever?
—	הַלְעוֹלָמִים	*Num in sæcula?*	For ever?
לעט	הַלְעִיטֵנִי	*Fac me gustare.*	Feed me, let me taste.
לפד	הַלַּפִּידִים־־דִם	*Lampades, faces.*	The lamps, torches.
לקח	הִלָּקַח	*Capi.*	To be taken.
—	הִלָּקְחוֹ	*Capi eum.*	That he is, was taken.
—	הַלֹּקְחִים	*Capientes, sumentes.*	They that take.
לקש	הַלָּקֶשׁ	*Herba serotina.*	The latter grass.
רשע	הֲלָרָשָׁע	*Num improbo?*	To the wicked?
לשן	הַלָּשׁוֹן־־שֹׁן	*Lingua, sinus.*	The tongue, bay.
לשך	הַלִּשְׁכָּה	*Cubiculum.*	The chamber.
—	הַלְּשָׁכוֹת־לְשָׁכ״	*Cubicula.*	The chambers.
שלל	הֲלִשְׁלֹל	*Num ad prædandum?*	To take a spoil?

המ

ROOTS.	DERIVATIVES.	VERSIO.	SIGNIFICATION.
	הֵם	*Ii, illi, ipsi.*	They, those.
אדם	הַמְאָדָּמִים	*Rubefacti.*	Dyed red.
מאה	הַמֵּאָה	*Centum.*	An hundred.
אור	הַמָּאוֹר	*Lumen.*	The light.
מאה	הַמֵּאוֹת	*Centum, centuriæ.*	Hundred, hundreds.
אזר	הַמְאַזְּרֵנִי	*Accingens me.*	He that girdeth me.
מאה	הַמֵּאיוֹת	*Centuriæ.*	Hundreds.
אכל	הַמַּאֲכִלְךָ	*Cibans te.*	He who feeds thee.
—	הַמַּאֲכֶלֶת	*Culter, gladius.*	The knife, sword.
אמן	הַמַּאֲמִין	*Credens.*	He that believes.
מאן	הַמֵּאֲנִים	*Renuentes.*	They that refuse.
מאס	הַמָּאֹס	*Num reprobando?*	In rejecting?
ארב	הַמַּאֲרָב־־אֹ״	*Insidiæ.*	The ambushment.
ארר	הַמְּאֵרָה	*Maledictio.*	The curse.

ROOTS.	DERIVATIVES.	VERSIO.	SIGNIFICATION.
ארר	הַמְאָרְרִים	*Maledicentes.*	Cursing.
ארש	הַמְאֹרָשָׂה	*Desponsata.*	She that is betrothed.
אור	הַמְּאֹרֹת	*Luminaria.*	The lights.
מאה	הַמָּאתַיִם	*Ducenti.*	The two hundred.
בדל	הַמֻּבְדָּלוֹת	*Separatæ.*	Those who are separated.
בוא	הַמָּבוֹא	*Introitus.*	The entry, entrance.
——	הַמֵּבִוֹא	*Adducens.*	He that brings.
נבל	הַמַּבּוּל	*Diluvium.*	The flood.
נבע	הַמַּבּוּעַ	*Fons.*	The fountain.
בוא	הַמְּבִיאִים	*Afferentes.*	They that bring.
נבט	הַמַּבִּיט	*Intuens.*	He that looketh.
בין	הַמֵּבִין	*Intelligens, considerans, peritus.*	He that understands, considers, is skilful.
בון	הַמְּבִינִים־־ןּ	*Erudientes.*	They that teach.
——	הֲמִבִּינָתְךָ	*Num per intelligentiam tuam?*	By thy understanding, wisdom?
בל	הֲמִבְּלִי	*Nonne, quia?*	Not, because?
בלג	הַמַּבְלִיג	*Recreans.*	He that strengthens, recruits.
בל	הֲמִבַּלְעֲדֵי	*Num absque?*	Without?
בער	הַמַּבְעִר	*Succendens.*	He that kindles.
בצר	הַמִּבְצָר	*Munitio.*	The fortress.
בקש	הַמְבַקְשִׁים	*Quærentes.*	They that seek.
בשל	הַמְבַשְּׁלִים	*Coquentes.*	They that cook.
בשר	הַמְבַשֵּׂר	*Nuncius.*	The messenger.
——	הַמְבַשְּׂרוֹת	*Nunciantes.*	Those that publish.
גבה	הַמַּגְבִּיהִי	*Exaltans.*	He that exalteth.
גבע	הַמִּגְבָּעֹת	*Tiaræ, galeri.*	The caps, bonnets, turbans.
גדל	הַמַּגְדִּילִים	*Efferentes, attollentes.*	That magnify, exalt.
——	הַמִּגְדָּל	*Turris.*	The tower.
——	הַמִּגְדָּלוֹת־־לִים	*Turres.*	The towers.
נגד	הַמַּגִּיד	*Annuncians; nuncius*	He that tells; a messenger.
גלל	הַמְּגִלָּה	*Volumen.*	The roll.
גלה	הַמֻּגְלִים	*Deportati.*	They that are carried away captive.
גנן	הַמָּגֵן	*Clypeus.*	The shield.
——	הַמָּגִנּוֹת־־נִּים	*Clypei.*	The shields.
גער	הַמִּגְעֶרֶת	*Increpatio.*	The rebuke.
נגף	הַמַּגֵּפָה	*Plaga.*	The stroke, plague.

ROOTS.	DERIVATIVES.	VERSIO.	SIGNIFICATION.
דבר	הַמְדַבֵּר	*Loquens.*	He that speaks.
—	הַמִּדְבָּר	*Desertum.*	The wilderness.
—	הֲמִדְבָּר	*Num desertum?*	A wilderness?
—	הַמִּדְבָּרָה	*Ad, in desertum.*	To, into the wilderness.
—	הַמְדַבְּרִים	*Loquentes.*	They that speak.
מדד	הַמִּדָּה	*Mensura.*	The measure.
דור	הַמְּדוּרָה	*Pyra.*	The pyre, pile for fire.
מדן	הַמְּדִינָה	*Provincia.*	The province.
—	הַמְּדִינוֹת	*Provinciæ.*	The provinces.
דרג	הַמַּדְרֵגָה	*Gradus.* [*cipitia.*	The steps, stairs. [precipices.
—	הַמַּדְרֵגוֹת	*Gradus, turres, præ-*	The steps, towers, steep places,
	הַמְּדָתָא	*Hammedatha.*	Hammedatha, N. M.
הָמָה		*Fremuit, personuit, commovit, turbavit.*	He raged, roared, made a great noise, moved, disturbed, agitated.
—	הֹמֶה	*Strepens.*	Raging, making a great noise.
הוא	הֵמָּה	*Illi, ipsi.*	They, those.
המם	הַמְּהוּמָה	*Commotio, tumultus.*	The commotion, tumult.
הלך	הַמְהַלֵּךְ	*Incedens.*	Walking.
—	הַמְהַלְּכִים	*Ambulantes.*	They that walk.
הפך	הַמַּהְפֶּכֶת־פָּכֶ׳	*Cippus, carcer.*	The stocks, prison.
הוא	הֵמּוֹ	*Illi.* [*barunt.*	They, those.
המה	הָמוּ	*Fremuerunt, contur-*	They raged, disturbed.
בוא	הַמּוּבָא	*Delatus.*	He that was brought.
מוט	הַמּוֹט	*Vectis.*	A bar.
—	הַמּוֹטָה	*Jugum.*	The yoke.
מכר	הַמּוֹכֵר	*Vendens.*	He that sells.
מול	הִמּוֹל	*Circumcidi.*	To be circumcised.
ילד	הַמּוֹלְדִים	*Gignentes.*	They that beget.
המל	הֲמוּלָה	*Tumultus, clamor.*	A tumult, clamour.
ילד	הַמּוֹלִיד	*Parere faciens.*	Causing to bring forth.
ילך	הַמּוֹלִיךְ	*Deducens.*	He that leads, conducts.
—	הַמּוֹלִיכְךָ	*Deducens te.*	He who leads thee.
מות	הַמּוּמָתִים־מֻמָ׳	*Interfecti.*	Those who are, or were, slain.
הוא	הֵמּוֹן	*Illi.* [*pia.*	They, those. [dance.
המן	הֲמוֹן הֲ׳	*Tumultus, turba, co-*	The tumult, multitude, abun-
—	הֲמוֹנָה	*Hamona.*	Hamonah, N. P.

ROOTS.	DERIVATIVES.	VERSIO.	SIGNIFICATION.
המן	הֲמוֹנֹה־־נוֹ	*Multitudo ejus.*	His multitude.
—	הֲמוֹנָהּ	*Multitudo ejus.*	Her multitude.
—	הֲמוֹנֶיהָ	*Copiæ ejus.*	Her multitudes.
—	הֲמוֹנֵךְ	*Multitudo tua.*	Thy multitude.
סור	הַמּוּסָרִים	*Amoti.*	Those that are removed.
יעד	הַמּוֹעֵד	*Tempus statutum, conventus, festum.*	The time appointed, assembly, feast, festival.
—	הַמּוּעָדָה	*Constitutio.*	The appointment.
יפת	הַמּוֹפֵת	*Portentum.*	The wonder, prodigy.
יצא	הַמּוֹצָאִים	*Exeuntes, egredientes.*	They that go out, come forth
—	הַמּוֹצִיא	*Educens.*	He that brings out.
—	הַמּוֹצִיאֲךָ	*Educens te.*	He that brings thee out.
יקע	הַמּוּקָעִים	*Suspensi.*	The persons hanged.
מור	הַמּוֹר הַמֹּר	*Myrrha.*	Myrrh.
ירא	הַמּוֹרָא	*Terror.*	The terror.
מרד	הַמּוֹרְדִים־־מֹּרְ׳	*Rebellantes.*	Those that rebel.
ירה	הַמּוֹרֶה	*Pluvia autumnalis.*	The former or autumnal rain.
—	הַמּוֹרִים־־רָאִם	*Jaculantes.*	Those who shoot, the archers.
שוב	הַמּוּשָׁב	*Restitutus, repositus.*	He that is restored, replaced.
ישע	הַמּוֹשִׁיעַ	*Servans.*	He who saves.
משל	הַמּוֹשֵׁל	*Dominans, dominator.*	He that rules, the governor.
—	הַמּוֹשְׁלִים	*Præsidentes.*	The governors.
המה	הֹמוֹת	*Frementes.*	Roaring, mourning.
מות	הַמָּוֶת־־וְתָה	*Mors.*	The death.
זבח	הַמִּזְבֵּחַ־־בָּח	*Ara, altare.*	The altar.
—	הַמִּזְבֵּחָה	*Super altare.*	On the altar.
—	הַמִּזְבְּחוֹת־־חֹת	*Aræ.*	The altars.
מזג	הַמָּזֶג	*Mistura.*	The liquor, mixture.
זוז	הַמְּזוּזָה	*Postis.*	The door-post.
—	הַמְּזוּזוֹת־־זֹת	*Postes.*	The posts.
זון	הַמָּזוֹן	*Alimentum.*	Victual, food.
זכר	הַמַּזְכִּיר	*Memorator, monitor*	The recorder, remembrancer.
—	הַמַּזְכִּירִים	*Memorantes.*	They that make mention.
זלג	הַמַּזְלֵג	*Fuscina.*	The flesh hook.
—	הַמִּזְלָגוֹת־־גֹת	*Fuscinæ.*	The flesh hooks.
זמר	הַמְזַמְּרוֹת	*Emunctoria.*	The snuffers.
זמם	הַמְּזִמָּתָה	*Scelus gravissimum.*	The very great wickedness.

ROOTS.	DERIVATIVES.	VERSIO.	SIGNIFICATION.
זרח	הַמִּזְרָח	*Oriens.*	The east.
זרק	הַמִּזְרָק	*Crater.*	The bowl.
—	הַמִּזְרְקוֹת--קֹת	*Pelves.*	The basons.
חבא	הַמַּחֲבֹאִים	*Latibula.*	The lurking places.
חבת	הַמַּחֲבַת	*Sartago.*	A pan.
חזק	הַמַּחֲזִיק	*Tenens.*	He that holds.
חטא	הַמְחַטֵּא	*Expians.*	He that expiates, atones for sin.
חכה	הַמְחַכֶּה	*Expectans.*	He that expects.
—	הַמְחַכִּים	*Expectantes.*	They that wait.
חלה	הַמַּחֲלָה	*Morbus, infirmitas.*	The disease, infirmity.
חלל	הַמְחֻלָּל	*Profanatus.*	He that is profaned.
—	הַמְּחֹלְלוֹת	*Saltantes.* [*festivæ.*	They that dance. [garments.
חלץ	הַמַּחֲלָצוֹת	*Vestes mutatoriæ vel*	Changeable suits or festive
חלק	הַמַּחְלְקוֹת	*Divisiones.*	The courses.
—	הַמַּחֲלֹקֶת	*Divisio, turma* [*citus*	The course, division, company.
חנה	הַמַּחֲנֶה	*Castra, turma, exer-*	The camp, host, army.
—	הַמַּחֲנוֹת--נֹת	*Castra.*	The camp, camps.
חצב	הַמְחַצֶּבֶת	*Excidens.*	She that cuts off.
חצה	הַמֶּחֱצָה	*Dimidium.*	The half. [the carved work.
חקק	הַמְחֻקֶּה	*Sculptus, sculptura.*	He or that which is carved,
חרב	הַמַּחֲרֶבֶת	*Exsiccans.*	She that drieth.
מחר	הַמָּחֳרָת	*Crastinum.*	The next day.
חשב	הַמַּחֲשָׁבֹת	*Cogitationes.*	The thoughts.
חתה	הַמַּחְתָּה	*Thuribulum.*	The censer.
—	הַמַּחְתּוֹת--תֹּת	*Acerræ, trullæ.*	The censers, fire pans.
נטה	הַמִּטָּה	*Lectus, feretrum.*	The bed, bier.
—	הַמַּטֶּה	*Virga, tribus.*	The staff, tribe.
טהר	הַמְטַהֵר	*Purgans, mundans.*	He that purifies, cleanses.
—	הַמִּטַּהֵר	*Mundandus.*	He that is to be cleansed.
נטה	הַמִּטּוֹת	*Lecti.*	The beds.
—	הַמַּטּוֹת--טֹּת	*Tribus.*	The tribes.
מטר	הִמְטִיר	*Pluere fecit.*	He caused it to rain.
טעם	הַמַּטְעַמִּים	*Cupediæ.*	The savoury meat, dainties.
טפח	הַמִּטְפַּחַת	*Peplum.*	The veil or mantle.
מטר	הַמָּטָר	*Pluvia.*	The rain.
נטר	הַמַּטָּרָה	*Custodia, carcer.*	The prison. [crowds.
המה	הֹמִיּוֹת	*Tumultuantes, turbæ*	Tumultuous assemblies,

ROOTS.	DERIVATIVES.	VERSIO.	SIGNIFICATION.
יחל	הַמְיַחֲלִים	*Sperantes.*	They that hope.
ילד	הַמְיַלֶּדֶת	*Obstetrix.*	The midwife.
—	הַמְיַלְּדֹת	*Obstetrices.*	The midwives.
מים	הַמַּיִם--מָּי׳	*Aqua, aquæ.*	The water, waters.
—	הַמַּיְמָה	*Ad aquam.*	Unto the water.
יום	הֲמִיָּמֶיךָ	*A vel in diebus tuis?*	Since or in thy days?
מור	הֵמִיר	*Mutavit.*	He changed.
ירא	הֲמִיִּרְאָתְךָ	*Num timore tui?*	For fear of thee?
ישר	הַמִּישֹׁר	*Planities.*	The plain.
—	הַמְיַשְּׁרִים	*Recte euntes.*	Those who go straight forward
מות	הָמִית	*Interficere.*	To kill
המם	הֶמְיַת	*Sonitus.*	The noise.
מות	הֵמִית	*Interfecit.*	He slew.
—	הֲמִיתוֹ	*Interficere illum.*	To kill him.
—	הֵמִיתוּ	*Interfecerunt.*	They slew.
—	הֱמִיתָם	*Interfecit eos.*	He slew them.
—	הֲמִיתֵנִי	*Interfice me.*	Slay thou me.
—	הֱמִיתַתְהוּ	*Interfecit eum.*	She slew him.
כבד	הַמְכַבֵּד	*Num honorans?*	He that honours?
כבר	הַמַּכְבֵּר	*Stragula.*	A coverlet.
נכה	הַמַּכֶּה	*Percutiens, cædens.*	He who smites, kills.
—	הַמַּכָּה	*Plaga, vulnus.*	The stroke, wound.
—	הַמֻּכֶּה	*Occisus.*	He that was slain.
—	הַמֻּכָּה	*Occisa*	She that was slain.
—	הַמַּכֵּהוּ	*Percutiens eum.*	He that smites him.
כוה	הַמִּכְוָה	*Adustio.*	The burning.
כון	הַמְּכוֹנָה--כֹנָה	*Basis.*	The base, pedestal, or foot.
—	הַמְּכוֹנוֹת--כֹנ״	*Bases.*	The bases.
נכה	הַמַּכּוֹת	*Vulnera.* [tes.	The wounds.
—	הַמַּכִּים	*Percutientes, cæden-*	They that smite, kill.
כון	הַמֵּכִין	*Præparans.*	He who prepareth.
כסס	הַמֶּכֶס	*Tributum.* [opcriens.	The tribute.
כסה	הַמְכַסֶּה	*An celaturus sum?*	Shall I hide? he that covers.
כעס	הַמַּכְעִסִים	*Irritantes.*	They that provoke to anger.
מכר	הִמָּכְרוֹ	*Vendi eum.*	That he was sold.
—	הַמֹּכֶרֶת	*Vendens.*	He that sells.
כשל	הַמִּכְשֹׁלִים	*Offendicula, ruinæ.*	The stumbling-blocks, ruins.

ROOTS.	DERIVATIVES.	VERSIO.	SIGNIFICATION.
כתש	הַמַּכְתֵּשׁ	*Cavitas.*	A hollow place.
המל			
מלא	הַמְּלֵאָה־־מְ׳	*Plena, gravida.*	She that is full, pregnant.
—	הַמְּלֵאִים	*Pleni.*	They that are full.
—	הַמִּלֻּאִים	*Impletiones, consecrationes.*	The fillings, consecrations.
לאך	הַמַּלְאָךְ	*Nuncius, angelus.*	The messenger, angel.
—	הַמְּלָאכָה	*Opus.*	The work.
—	הַמַּלְאָכִים	*Nuncii, angeli.*	The messengers, angels.
מלך	הַמְּלָאכִים	*Reges.*	The kings.
לבש	הַמַּלְבּוּשׁ	*Vestis.*	The vestment, apparel.
—	הַמַּלְבִּשְׁכֶם	*Vestiens vos.*	He who clothes you.
מול	הִמֹּלוּ	*Circumcidite vos.*	Circumcise yourselves.
מלך	הַמְּלוּכָה־־לְ׳	*Regnum.*	The kingdom, reign.
לון	הַמָּלוֹן	*Hospitium.*	The lodging, inn.
מלח	הַמֶּלַח הַמֶּלַח	*Sal.*	The salt.
—	הַמַּלָּחִים	*Nautæ.*	The mariners.
לחם	הַמִּלְחָמָה	*Bellum, prælium.*	The war, battle.
—	הַמִּלְחָמוֹת	*Bella, prælia.*	The wars, battles.
מלח	הָמְלַחַתְּ	*Salita es.*	Thou hast been salted.
מל ט	הִמָּלֵט	*Eripe te; confugere*	Escape thou; to escape.
—	הִמָּלְטִי	*Libera te.*	Deliver thyself.
מלך	הִמְלִיךְ	*Regnare fecit, regem constituit.*	He caused to reign, he constituted king.
—	הִמְלִיכוּ	*Reges constituerunt*	They have set up kings.
לוץ	הַמֵּלִיץ	*Interpres.*	An interpreter.
מלך	הֲמָלֹךְ	*An regnando?*	In reigning?
—	הָמְלַךְ	*Rex factus est.*	He was made king.
—	הַמֹּלֵךְ	*Regnans.*	He that reigns.
	הַמֶּלֶךְ	*Hammelec.*	Hammelech, N. M.
מלך	הַמֶּלֶךְ	*Rex.*	The king.
—	הַמַּלְכָּה	*Regina.*	The queen.
—	הַמַּלְכוּת	*Regnum.*	The kingdom.
מלך	הַמְּלָכִים	*Reges.*	The kings.
—	הִמְלַכְתָּ	*Regem constituisti.*	Thou hast made king.
—	הִמְלַכְתִּי	*Regem constitui.*	I have constituted king.
—	הִמְלַכְתִּיךָ	*Regem constitui te.*	I have made thee king.
—	הִמְלַכְתַּנִי	*Regem fecisti me.*	Thou hast made me king.

ROOTS.	DERIVATIVES.	VERSIO.	SIGNIFICATION.
למד	הַמְלַמֵּד	*Docens.*	He that teacheth.
לצר	הַמֶּלְצַר	*Præfectus;* vel nom. propr. *Hamelzar.*	The steward; *or a proper name,* Hamelzar.
לקח	הַמַּלְקוֹחַ	*Præda.*	The booty, prey.
לקק	הַמְלַקְקִים	*Lambentes.*	They that lap or lick.
לתח	הַמֶּלְתָּחָה	*Vestiarium.*	The vestry, wardrobe.
הָמַם		*Turbavit, quassavit, concidit, contrivit.*	He threw into disorder, agitated, harassed, discomfited, crushed.
מכר	הַמִּמְכָּר	*Venditio.*	The selling.
מלא	הַמְמַלְאִים	*Implentes.*	Those who fill.
מלט	הַמְמַלְּטִים	*Liberantes.*	They that deliver.
מלך	הַמַּמְלִיךְ	*Regnare faciens.*	He that makes king.
——	הַמַּמְלָכָה	*Regnum.*	The kingdom.
——	הַמַּמְלָכוֹת־־לֹ׳	*Regna.*	The kingdoms.
המם	הֲמָמָם	*Contrivit eos.*	He harassed, crushed them.
מן	הֲמִמֶּנּוּ	*An ex eo?*	From him?
המם	הֲמָמַנִי	*Contrivit me.*	He crushed me.
מן	הֲמִמֶּנִּי	*An a me?*[*colligens.*	From me?
מעט	הַמַּמְעִיט	*Minuens, minimum*	He that gathereth least.
משל	הַמֶּמְשָׁלָה	*Dominium.*	The dominion.
——	הַמֹּשְׁלִים	*Dominantes.*	They that rule.
	הָמָן	*Haman.*	Haman, N. M.
הָמַן		*Auxit, multiplicavit.*	He increased, multiplied.
מן	הֲמִן	*An de? Nonne ex?*	Of? Not from?
מנה	הַמָּן	*Manna.*	The manna. [an adulteress.
נאף	הַמְנָאֶפֶת	*Mœchans, adultera.*	She that commits adultery,
נגן	הַמְנַגֵּן	*Pulsator, fidicen.*	The minstrel, player on a stringed instrument.
נדה	הַמְנַדִּים	*Amoventes.*	They that put away.
מנה	הַמָּנָה	*Pars, portio.*	The part, portion.
נהר	הַמִּנְהָרוֹת	*Antra.*	The dens.
נוח	הַמְּנוּחָה	*Requies.*	The rest.
נור	הַמְּנוֹרָה־־נֹרָה	*Candelabrum.*	The candlestick.
ינח	הַמֻּנָּח	*Relictus.* [*tum.*	He that is left. [offering.
מנח	הַמִּנְחָה	*Munus, oblatio, fer-*	The present, oblation, meat-
המן	הֲמֹנִים	*Multitudines.*	Multitudes.

ROOTS.	DERIVATIVES.	VERSIO.	SIGNIFICATION.
המן	הֲמֹנְכֶם	*Multitudo vestra.*	Your multitude.
נעל	הַמַּנְעוּל	*Pessulus, sera.*	The lock, bolt, bar.
נקה	הַמְנַקִּיּוֹת	*Scopulæ, pateræ.*	The bowls, dishes.
נור	הַמְּנֹרוֹת	*Candelabra.*	The candlesticks.
המס			
מסס	הִמֵּס	*Liquefieri.*	To be melted.
——	הַמַּס הַמָּס	*Tributum.*	The tribute.
סגר	הַמַּסְגֵּר	*Faber.*	The smith.
——	הַמִּסְגְּרוֹת	*Claustra.*	The borders.
——	הַמִּסְגֶּרֶת	*Claustrum.*	The border, inclosure.
סדר	הַמִּסְדְּרוֹנָה	*Per vestibulum.*	Through the porch.
מסס	הֵמַסּוּ	*Liquefecerunt.*	They have melted.
סוה	הַמַּסְוֶה	*Velamen.*	The veil.
נסה	הַמַּסּוֹת	*Tentationes.*	The temptations.
מסה	הִמְסִיו	*Liquefecerunt, dissolverunt.*	They made to melt, dissolved
המס	הֲמָסִים	*Liquefactiones, fusuræ.*	The meltings, *as by founders.*
מסך	הַמָּסָךְ	*Operimentum.*	The veil, covering.
נסך	הַמַּסֵּכָה	*Idolum fusile.*	The molten image.
סכן	הַמְסֻכָּן	*Indigens.*	He that is poor.
——	הַמִּסְכֵּן	*Pauper.*	The poor.
——	הַמִּסְכְּנוֹת	*Horrea, thesauri.*	The storehouses, treasures.
נסך	הַמַּסֶּכֶת	*Tela.*	The web.
סלא	הַמְסֻלָּאִים	*Æquiparati.*	They who are comparable.
סלל	הַמְסִלָּה	*Via trita vel publica*	The highway.
——	הַמְסִלּוֹת	*Viæ, semitæ.*	The ways, highways.
ספד	הַמִּסְפֵּד	*Planctus.*	The mourning.
ספח	הַמִּסְפָּחוֹת	*Ricæ, cervicalia, pepla.*	The kerchiefs, vails, mantles.
——	הַמִּסְפַּחַת	*Scabies.*	The scab.
ספר	הַמִּסְפָּר	*Numerus.*	The number.
נסה	הַמַּסֹּת	*Tentationes, experientiæ.*	Temptations, trials.
סתר	הַמַּסְתִּיר	*Occultans.*	He that hideth.
עבר	הַמַּעְבְּרוֹת	*Vada, transitus* [*tus*	The fords, passages.
עגל	הַמַּעְגָּלָה	*Ad plaustrum; ambi-*	To the waggon; the circuit.
מעד	הַמְעַד	*Fac nutare.*	Make thou to shake.
עזז	הַמָּעוֹז	*Robur, arx.*	The strength, strong hold.
מעט	הַמְעַט	*An paucus, parum?*	Few, a little?

ROOTS.	DERIVATIVES.	VERSIO.	SIGNIFICATION.
עטר	הַמְעַטְּרָה	*Coronans.*	The crowning, she that crowneth.
——	הַמְעַטְּרֵכִי	*Coronans te.*	He that crowneth thee.
מעל	הַמְּעִיל	*Pallium.*	The robe.
עין	הַמַּעְיָנוֹת	*Fontes.*	The fountains.
עון	הַמְּעֹנִים	*Habitacula.*	The habitations.
מעל	הַמַּעַל	*Prævaricatio.*	The treachery.
עלה	הַמַּעֲלֶה	*Educens, inducens.*	He that brings up, puts on.
——	הַמַּעֲלָה	*Ascensus, dignitas.*	The ascent, dignity.
——	הַמַּעֲלוֹת	*Gradus.*	The steps.
——	הַמַּעַלְךָ	*Educens te.*	He that brings thee up.
——	הַמַּעֲלָם	*Educens eos.*	He that brings them up.
עמק	הַמַּעֲמִיקִים	*Latitantes, profunda consilia facientes.*	They that seek concealment, form deep designs.
עם	הֲמֵעִמְּךָ	*An a te?*	From thee? according to thy mind?
ערב	הַמַּעֲרָב	*Occidens.*	The west.
ערה	הַמְּעָרָה	*Spelunca.*	The cave.
——	הַמְּעָרוֹת	*Speluncæ.*	The caves.
ערך	הַמַּעֲרָכָה	*Ordinatio; acies; in exercitum.*	The setting in order; the army; into, towards the army.
——	הַמַּעֲרֶכֶת־רָכֶת	*Ordo.*	The row.
ערה	הַמְּעָרַת	*An spelunca?*	The den?
עשה	הַמַּעֲשֶׂה	*Factum, opus.*	The deed, work, business.
——	הַמַּעֲשִׂים	*Opera.*	The works.
עשק	הַמְעֻשָּׁקָה	*Oppressa.*	She that is oppressed, O thou oppressed.
עשר	הַמַּעֲשֵׂר	*Decimæ.*	The tithes.
——	הַמְעַשְּׂרִים	*Decimantes.*	Those who have tithes.
עתק	הַמַּעְתִּיק	*Transferens.*	He that removes.
פקד	הַמָּפְקָדִים	*Præfecti.*	They that are set over, officers
פשע	הַמִּפְשָׂעָה	*Nates.*	The buttocks.
פתח	הַמַּפְתֵּחַ	*Clavis.*	The key.
יפת	הַמֹּפְתִים	*Portenta.*	The wonders, prodigies.
פתן	הַמִּפְתָּן	*Limen.*	The threshold.
מיץ	הַמֵּץ	*Premens, expilator.*	He that presses, the extortioner.
מצא	הַמָּצָא	*Inveniri; invenietur*	To be found; he will be found.
——	הַמֹּצְאוֹת	*Invenientes, eventa.*	They that find, that befal.
——	הַמֹּצְאִים	*Invenientes.*	They that find.
——	הַמְצָאתַנִי	*Num invenisti me?*	Hast thou found me?

ROOTS.	DERIVATIVES.	VERSIO.	SIGNIFICATION.
יצב	הַמַּצָּב הַמַּצָּבָה	*Statio, præsidium.*	The station, garrison.
צבא	הַמַּצְבָּא	*Milites colligens, exercens, conscribens.*	He that enlists, musters, trains, soldiers.
יצב	הַמַּצֵּבָה	*Statua.*	The pillar, image.
—	הַמַּצֵּבוֹת--בֹת	*Statuæ.*	The images.
מצד	הַמְּצָדוֹת	*Munitiones.*	The strong holds.
—	הַמְּצוּדָה	*Munitio.*	The strong hold.
צוה	הַמִּצְוָה	*Præceptum, lex.*	The commandment, the law.
צור	הַמָּצוֹר	*Obsidio.*	The siege.
—	הַמְּצוּרוֹת	*Munitiones.*	The strong holds.
צרע	הַמְּצוֹרָע צָרָע	*Leprosus.*	The leper.
צוה	הַמִּצְוֹת	*Præcepta.*	The commandments.
מצץ	הַמַּצּוֹת	*Azyma.*	The unleavened *cakes.*
מצא	הִמְצִיאוּ	*Obtulerunt.*	They presented.
נצל	הַמַּצִּיל	*Eripiens.*	He that delivers.
צוק	הַמֵּצִיק	*Premens, oppressor.*	He that presses, the oppressor.
מצא	הִמְצִיתִךָ	*Tradidi te.*	I have delivered thee.
צמח	הַמַּצְמִיחַ	*Germinare faciens.*	He who maketh to grow.
צנף	הַמִּצְנֶפֶת--נֶפֶת	*Diadema, cidaris.*	The mitre, diadem, turban.
יצע	הַמַּצָּע	*Stratum.*	The bed.
צפה	הַמְצַפֶּה	*Speculator.*	The watchman.
—	הַמִּצְפָּה	*Specula.*	The watch-tower.
צפצף	הַמְצַפְצְפִים	*Pipientes, garrientes*	They that peep, chatter.
צור	הַמֵּצַר	*Angustia.*	The distress.
—	הַמְּצָרוֹת	*Munitæ.*	The fenced, fortified *places.*
—	הַמְּצָרִים	*Angustiæ.*	The straits.
צרע	הַמְּצֹרָעִים	*Leprosi.*	The lepers.
מקק	הָמַק	*Tabefieri.*	To consume away.
קבר	הַמְקַבְּרִים	*Sepelientes.*	They that bury.
נקב	הַמַּקֶּבֶת	*Malleus.*	A hammer.
קדש	הַמַּקְדִּישׁ	*Sanctificans, consecrans.*	He that sanctifies, dedicates.
—	הַמְקֻדָּשׁ	*Sanctificatus.*	He that is sanctified.
—	הַמִּקְדָּשׁ--דָּשׁ	*Sanctuarium.*	The sanctuary.
—	הַמְקֻדָּשִׁים	*Consecrati.*	They that are consecrated.
קום	הַמָּקוֹם	*Locus.*	The place.
—	הַמְּקוֹמוֹת--מֹת	*Loca.*	The places.
לקח	הַמַּקָּחוֹת	*Merces.*	The merchandize.

ROOTS.	DERIVATIVES.	VERSIO.	SIGNIFICATION.
קטר	הַמְּקַטְּרִים־טְּרִי	*Adolentes.*	They that burn incense.
——	הַמְקַטְּרוֹת	*Aræ thurariæ.*	The altars of incense.
מקל	הַמַּקְלוֹת	*Virgæ.*	The rods.
קלט	הַמִּקְלָט	*Refugium.*	The refuge.
קלל	הַמְקַלֵּל	*Maledicens.*	He that curseth.
קום	הַמְּקֹמוֹת	*Loca.* [*vocans.*	The places.
קנא	הַמַּקְנֶא	*Ad zelotypiam pro-*	He that provokes to jealousy.
——	הַמְקַנֵּא	*Num æmulans ?*	He that envieth ?
קנה	הַמִּקְנֶה	*Pecus.*	The cattle.
——	הַמִּקְנָה	*Emptio.*	The purchase.
קצע	הַמִּקְצוֹעַ־־צֹעַ	*Angulus.*	The turning, the corner.
——	הַמִּקְצֹעֹת	*Anguli.*	The corners. [apartment.
קרר	הַמְּקֵרָה	*Refrigerium.*	The summer parlour, or cool
קרה	הַמְקָרֶה	*Contignans.*	He who layeth the beams.
קרב	הַמַּקְרִיב	*Offerens.*	He that offers.
קשר	הַמְקֻשָּׁרוֹת	*Firmæ, compacto corpore præditæ.*	The strong, those of a compact or strong body.
המר			
מור	הָמֵר	*Mutare, mutando.*	To change, in changing.
מרר	הֵמַר	*Amaritudine affecit.*	He hath dealt bitterly.
——	הַמָּר	*Amarus.*	The bitter.
ראה	הַמַּרְאֶה־־אָה	*Visio, aspectus.*	The vision, appearance.
רבה	הַמַּרְבֶּה	*Augens.*	He that increases.
רגז	הַמַּרְגִּיז	*Commovens.*	He that shakes.
רגל	הַמְרַגְּלִים	*Explorantes.*	They that explore or spy out.
רגע	הַמַּרְגֵּעָה	*Requies.*	The rest, repose.
מרד	הַמְּרָדוֹת	*Rebellio.* [*barunt-*	The rebellion.
מרה	הִמְרוּ	*Rebellarunt, exacer*	They rebelled, provoked.
רום	הַמָּרוֹם	*Cœli.*	The heavens.
רוץ	הַמֵּרוֹץ	*Cursus.*	The race.
רצץ	הַמְּרוּצָה	*Concussio, extorsio.*	The violence, extortion.
רחק	הַמֶּרְחָק	*Longinquus.*	He that is far off.
מרה	הַמֶּרִי	*Rebellio.*	The rebellion.
——	הַמֹּרִים	*Rebelles.*	Ye rebels.
מרר	הַמְּרִים	*Amaritudines.*	Bitternesses.
ריק	הַמְּרִיקִים	*Evacuantes.*	They that empty.
רכב	הַמֶּרְכָּב	*Sella.*	The saddle.

ROOTS.	DERIVATIVES.	VERSIO.	SIGNIFICATION.
רכב	הַמֶּרְכָּבָה	*Currus.*	The chariot.
רעה	הַמִּרְעֶה	*Pascuum.*	The pasture.
רצח	הַמְרַצֵּחַ	*Homicida.*	The murderer.
רצע	הַמַּרְצֵעַ	*Subula.*	The awl.
מרק	הַמָּרָק	*Jus.* [*tura.*	The broth.
רקח	הַמִּרְקָחָה	*Compositio, condi-*	The composition, seasoning.
—	הַמִּרְקַחַת	*Unguentum.*	The ointment.
רשע	הַמִּרְשַׁעַת	*Impia.*	That wicked *woman.*
נשא	הַמַּשָּׂא	*Onus, prophetia.*	The burden, prophecy.
שבע	הַמַּשְׂבִּיעַ	*Saturans.*	He who satisfieth.
שבר	הַמַּשְׁבִּיר	*Vendens.*	He that sells.
שבץ	הַמִּשְׁבְּצוֹת־צֹת	*Fundæ, palæ.*	The ouches, beazils, sockets.
שגב	הַמִּשְׂגָּב	*Locus excelsus.*	The high place.
שגע	הַמְשֻׁגָּע	*Insanus.*	The mad *man.*
נשר	הַמַּשּׂוֹר	*Serra.*	The saw.
שור	הַמְשׁוֹרֵר	*Cantor.*	The singer.
משח	הִמָּשַׁח	*Ungi.*	To be anointed.
—	הַמִּשְׁחָה	*Unctio.*	The anointing.
—	הַמְּשֻׁחִים	*Uncti.*	The anointed.
שחת	הֲמַשְׁחִית	*Num destrues?*	Wilt thou destroy? [er.
—	הַמַּשְׁחִית	*Vastans, vastator.*	He that destroys, the destroy-
—	הַמַּשְׁחִיתִים	*Vastantes.*	They that destroy.
שחק	הַמְשַׂחֲקוֹת	*Ludentes.*	Those who play. [siah.
משח	הַמָּשִׁיחַ	*Unctus, Messias.*	He that is anointed, the Mes-
שכב	הַמִּשְׁכָּב	*Stratum, lectus.*	The bed.
שכל	הַמַּשְׂכִּיל	*Intelligens, prudens.*	The wise, prudent.
—	הַמַּשְׂכִּילִים	*Intelligentes.*	The wise, understanding.
שכן	הַמִּשְׁכָּן	*Tentorium.*	The tabernacle.
משל	הַמֹּשֵׁל	*Dominans.*	He that rules, the ruler.
—	הֲמָשֹׁל	*An dominari?*	Whether to rule?
—	הַמֶּמְשָׁל	*Dominium.*	The dominion.
—	הַמָּשָׁל	*Parabola.*	The proverb, parable.
שלח	הַמְשַׁלֵּחַ	*Emittens.*	He that sendeth forth.
—	הַמְשֻׁלָּחִים	*Missi.*	They who were sent.
משל	הַמֹּשְׁלִים	*Parabolicè loquentes*	They that speak in proverbs.
שלש	הַמְשֻׁלָּשׁ	*Triplex.*	Threefold.
שמח	הַמְשַׂמֵּחַ	*Lætificans.*	He that cheers, gladdens.

ROOTS.	DERIVATIVES.	VERSIO.	SIGNIFICATION.
שמר	הַמִּשְׁמָר	*Custodia.*	The watch, guard.
שנה	הַמִּשְׁנֶה	*Secundus.*	The second.
—	הַמִּשְׁנִים	*Secundarii.*	Those of the second degree.
שען	הַמִּשְׁעֶנֶת	*Baculus.*	The staff.
שפח	הַמִּשְׁפָּחָה	*Familia.*	The family.
—	הַמִּשְׁפָּחוֹת	*Familiæ.*	The families.
שפט	הַמִּשְׁפָּט	*Judicium.*	The judgment.
—	הַמִּשְׁפָּטִים	*Judicia.*	The judgments.
שפל	הַמַּשְׁפִּילִי	*Humilians se.*	He who humbleth *himself.*
שפת	הַמִּשְׁפְּתַיִם־־תָ׳	*Repagula.*	The folds.
שקה	הַמַּשְׁקֶה	*Pincerna.*	The butler.
שקף	הַמַּשְׁקוֹף	*Superliminare.*	The lintel.
שקה	הַמַּשְׁקִים	*Pincernæ.*	The butlers.
שקל	הַמִּשְׁקָל	*Pondus.*	The weight.
שרה	הַמִּשְׂרָה	*Principatus.*	The government.
שור	הַמְשֹׁרְרִים	*Cantores.*	The singers.
שרת	הַמַּשְׂרֵת	*Sartago.*	The pan.
—	הַמְשָׁרְתִים	*Ministrantes.*	They that serve.
שתה	הַמִּשְׁתֶּה	*Convivium.*	The feast. [selves, worship.
שחה	הַמִּשְׁתַּחֲוִים	*Incurvantes se.*	They that bow down them-
מות	הֲמֵת	*Num mortuus?*	Dead?
—	הַמֵּת	*Mortuus.*	The dead.
—	הָמֵת	*Interficiendo.*	In killing.
אבל	הַמִּתְאַבְּלִים	*Lugentes.*	They that mourn.
אוה	הַמִּתְאַוִּים	*Concupiscentes.*	They that desire.
	הַמְּתֹאָר	*Hammathoar.*	Hammathoar, N. P.
ברך	הַמִּתְבָּרֵךְ	*Benedicens se.*	He that blesseth himself.
מות	הַמֵּתָה	*Moribunda.*	She that dieth.
—	הֱמִתֻהוּ	*Interfecerunt eum.*	They put him to death.
הלך	הַמִּתְהַלְּכִים	*Ambulantes.*	They that walk.
הלל	הַמִּתְהַלֵּל	*Jactans se.*	He that glorieth.
—	הַמִּתְהַלְלִים	*Jactantes se.*	They that boast themselves.
הפך	הַמִּתְהַפֶּכֶת	*Vertens se.*	Turning himself.
מות	הֻמָתוּ	*Interfecti sunt.*	They were put to death.
חבא	הַמִּתְחַבְּאִים	*Latentes.*	They that hide themselves.
חזק	הַמִּתְחַזְּקִים	*Roborantes se, viriliter agentes.*	They who strengthen themselves, act manfully.

ROOTS.	DERIVATIVES.	VERSIO.	SIGNIFICATION.
יחש	הַמִּתְיַחְשִׂים־־חְ׳	*Genealogias suas texentes.*	They that reckon their genealogies.
מות	הַמֵּתִים	*Mortui.*	The dead.
תכן	הַמְתֻכָּן	*Pensus.*	Being weighed.
מות	הֲמִתֶּם	*Interfecistis.*	Ye have killed.
נבא	הַמִּתְנַבֵּא	*Vaticinans.*	He that prophesies.
——	הַמִּתְנַבְּאוֹת	*Vaticinantes.*	They that prophesy.
נדב	הַמִּתְנַדֵּב	*Sponte offerens.*	He who willingly offers himself.
——	הַמִּתְנַדְּבִים	*Sponte offerentes.*	They that offer themselves willingly.
תעב	הַמְתַעֲבִים	*Abominantes.*	They that abhor.
תעה	הַמַּתְעִים	*Seducentes.*	They that draw aside.
פרץ	הַמִּתְפָּרְצִים	*Subducentes se, au fugientes.*	They that withdraw themselves, run away.
קדש	הַמִּתְקַדְּשִׁים	*Sanctificantes se.*	They that sanctify themselves
קשר	הַמִּתְקַשְּׁרִים	*Conjurantes.*	They that conspire.
	הנ		
הן			
——	הֵן הֶן הִן	*En, ecce; si, sive.*	Lo, behold; if, whether.
אהב	הַנֶּאֱהָבִים	*Dilecti, amabiles.*	The beloved, the lovely.
אכל	הַנֶּאֱכֶלֶת	*Quæ comeditur.*	That which is eaten.
אמן	הַנֶּאֱמָן	*Fidelis.*	The faithful.
——	הַנֶּאֱמָנִים	*Stabiles.*	The sure, steadfast.
אנח	הַנֶּאֱנָחִים	*Suspirantes.*	They that sigh.
נאף	הַנֹּאֵף	*Adulter.*	The adulterer.
נבא	הִנָּבֵא	*Vaticinari; vaticinare*	To prophesy; prophesy thou
——	הַנִּבָּא	*Vaticinans.*	He that prophesies.
——	הַנִּבְּאוּ	*Vaticinati sunt.*	They prophesied.
——	הַנִּבְּאִים־־בִּ׳	*Vaticinantes.*	They that prophesy.
——	הַנְּבִאִים־בִיא׳	*Prophetæ.*	The prophets.
בדל	הַנִּבְדָּל	*Separatus.*	He that is separated.
נבא	הַנְּבוּאָה	*Vaticinium.*	The prophecy.
——	הַנָּבִיא	*Propheta.*	The prophet.
——	הַנְּבִיאָה	*Prophetissa.*	The prophetess.
נבל	הַנֶּבֶל־־נֵּ׳	*Nablium, psalterium*	The lute, psaltery.
——	הַנְּבָלָה	*Stultitia, flagitium.*	The folly, villany.

ROOTS.	DERIVATIVES.	VERSIO.	SIGNIFICATION.
נבל	הַנְּבֵלָה	*Cadaver.*	The carcase.
—	הַנְּבָלוֹת	*Stultæ, perditæ.*	The foolish, abandoned [gons.
—	הַנְּבָלִים	*Stulti; utres, lagenæ.*	The foolish, fools; bottles, fla-
בנה	הַנִּבְנֶה	*Ædificatus.*	He that is built.
נגב	הַנֶּגֶב	*Auster.*	The south.
—	הַנֶּגְבָּה	*Ad meridiem.*	Toward the south.
נגה	הַנֹּגַהּ	*Splendor.*	The brightness.
נגד	הַנָּגִיד	*Dux.*	The leader.
גלה	הֲנִגְלֹה	*Num revelando?*	In discovering?
—	הֲנִגְלוּ	*Num detecti sunt?*	Have they been disclosed?
נגע	הַנֶּגַע־־גַּ	*Plaga.*	The plague.
—	הַנֹּגֵעַ־־גֹּ	*Tangens.*	He that toucheth.
—	הַנֹּגְעִים	*Tangentes.*	They that touch.
—	הַנֹּגַעַת	*Tangens.*	She that toucheth.
נגף	הַנֶּגֶף־־גֶּ	*Plaga.*	The plague.
נגר	הַנִּגָּרִים	*Effusi.*	Spilt.
נגש	הַנֹּגֵשׂ	*Exactor.*	The exactor, oppressor.
—	הַנֹּגְשִׂים	*Exactores.*	The task-masters.
—	הַנִּגָּשִׁים	*Accedentes.*	They that come near.
נדב	הַנְּדָבָה	*Oblatio spontanea.*	The free-will offering.
דבר	הַנִּדְבָּרִים	*Obloquentes.*	They that are talking against.
נדה	הַנִּדָּה	*Separatio, immundities; menstruala.*	The separation, uncleanness; menstruous.
נדח	הַנִּדַּחַת	*Expulsa.*	She that was driven away.
נדר	הַנֹּדֵר	*Vovens.*	He that vows.
הן	הִנֵּה־־נֶּה	*Ecce.*	Behold.
—	הֵנָּה	*Huc, illuc.*	Hither, thither.
הוא	הֵנָּה	*Hæ, ipsæ.*	These, they, those.
היה	הֲנִהְיְתָה	*Utrum factum sit.*	Whether there hath been.
נהל	הַנַּהֲלֹלִים	*Dumi, arbusta.*	Bushes, shrubs.
נהר	הַנָּהָר	*Flumen.*	The river.
—	הַנְּהָרוֹת־־רֹת	*Flumina.*	The rivers.
הרס	הַנֶּהֱרָסוֹת	*Destructæ.*	The ruined *places.*
הן	הִנּוֹ	*Ecce ille.*	Behold he.
נוה	הַנָּוֶה	*Caula.*	The sheep cote.
—	הַנָּוָה	*Decora, pulchra.*	The comely, beautiful.
נטה	הַנּוֹטֶה	*Extendens.*	He that stretches out, extends

ROOTS.	DERIVATIVES.	VERSIO.	SIGNIFICATION.
נטע	הַנּוֹטֵעַ	*Plantans.*	He that plants.
ילד	הַנּוֹלָד	*Natus.*	He that was born.
—	הַנּוֹלָדִים	*Nati.*	They that were born.
יעד	הַנּוֹעָדִים	*Convenientes.*	The persons assembled.
נצה	הַנּוֹצָה	*Pluma.*	The wing, feathers.
ירא	הַנּוֹרָא	*Formidabilis.*	The terrible.
—	הַנּוֹרָאֹת	*Terribiles.*	The terrible.
ישב	הַנּוֹשָׁבוֹת	*Habitatæ.*	The inhabited.
נתן	הַנּוֹתֵן־־נֹּתֵן	*Donans, ponens.*	He that gives, places.
יתר	הַנּוֹתָר	*Residuus.*	The remainder.
—	הַנּוֹתָרוֹת־־רֹת	*Residuæ.*	The rest.
—	הַנּוֹתָרִים	*Residui.*	The rest.
—	הַנּוֹתֶרֶת	*Quod relictum est.*	That which remaineth.
נזד	הַנָּזִיד	*Pulmentum.*	The pottage.
—	הַנָּזִיר	*Nazaræus.*	The Nazarite.
נזם	הַנֶּזֶם	*Inauris.*	The ear-ring.
—	הַנְּזָמִים	*Inaures.*	The ear-rings.
נזר	הִנָּזֵר	*Separando me.*	Separating myself.
—	הַנֵּזֶר	*Corona, diadema.*	The crown, diadem.
—	הַנְּזִרִים	*Nazaræi.*	The Nazarites.
ינח	הַנַּח	*Relinque, sine.*	Leave thou, let alone.
—	הִנִּחַ	*Reposuit.*	He laid up.
—	הַנִּחוּ	*Relinquite, deponite.*	Leave ye, lay up.
נחל	הַנְחִילוֹ	*Possidere facere eum*	That he makes to inherit.
נחה	הִנְחִיתָם	*Duxisti eos.*	Thou leddest them.
נחל	הַנַּחַל־־בְּ	*Flumen.*	The brook.
—	הַנַּחֲלָה	*Hæreditas.*	The inheritance.
—	הַנְּחָלוֹת	*Possessiones.*	The inheritances.
—	הַנְּחָלִים	*Flumina.*	The brooks.
—	הִנְחַלְתִּי	*Possidere feci.*	I have caused to inherit.
—	הָנְחַלְתִּי	*Possidere factus sum*	I am made to possess.
נחם	הִנָּחֵם	*Consolari; pœnitere*	To be comforted; to repent.
יחם	הַנֵּחָמִים	*Incalescentes.*	Becoming inflamed.
חמד	הַנֶּחֱמָדִים	*Desiderabiles.*	Desirable, to be desired.
נחה	הִנְחַנִי	*Duxit me.*	He has led me. [tending.
חרה	הַנֶּחֱרִים	*Irritati, contendentes*	They that are incensed, con-
נחש	הַנָּחָשׁ	*Serpens.*	The serpent.

ROOTS.	DERIVATIVES.	VERSIO.	SIGNIFICATION.
נחשׁ	הַנְּחָשִׁים	*Serpentes.*	The serpents.
חשל	הַנֶּחֱשָׁלִים	*Debiles.*	Feeble.
נחשׁ	הַנְּחֹשֶׁת	*Æs; æneus.*	The brass; brazen.
נחת	הָנְחַת	*Depositus est.*	He was deposed.
—	הַנְחַת	*Descendere fac.*	Cause thou to come down.
נטה	הַנְּטוּיָה	*Extenta.*	The stretched out.
נטשׁ	הַנְּטִישׁוֹת	*Propagines.*	The branches, plants, shoots.
נטע	הֲנֹטֵעַ	*Num plantans?*	He that plants?
נטף	הַנְּטִפוֹת	*Torques.*	The chains.
נוא	הֵנִיא	*Irritum fecit.*	He made of none effect.
נוח	הֵנִיחַ	*Quiescere fecit.*	He has given rest.
—	הָנִיחַ	*Requiem dare.*	To give rest.
ינח	הִנִּיחַ	*Reliquit, sivit, dejecit*	He left, suffered, cast down.
—	הַנִּיחָה	*Sine, dimitte.*	Suffer, let alone.
—	הִנִּיחוּ	*Posuerunt.*	They placed, set down.
—	הַנִּיחוּ	*Quietem concedite.*	Do ye give rest.
נוח	הָנִיחוּ	*Quiescere facite.*	Do ye cause to rest.
—	הֵנִיחוּ	*Quietem reddiderunt*	They have quieted.
—	הַנִּיחֹחַ	*Quies, res grata.*	Rest, complacency, acceptance
—	הֲנִיחֹתִי	*Quiescere facere me.*	That I have caused to rest.
נוס	הֵנִיס	*Fugavit.*	He made to flee.
נוע	הֵנִיעָה	*Movit, agitavit.*	She hath shaken.
—	הֲנִיעֵמוֹ	*Disperge eos.* [*tulit.*	Scatter thou them.
נוף	הֵנִיף	*Levavit, agitavit, ab-*	He lifted up, waved, offered.
—	הָנִיפוּ	*Agitate.*	Shake ye.
—	הֲנִיפוֹתִי	*Levavi.*	I have lifted up.
—	הֲנִיפְכֶם	*Agitare vos.*	When ye wave.
ינק	הֵנִיקוּ	*Lactarunt.*	They gave suck.
הן	הִנְּךָ־הִנָּךְ־הִנָּךְ	*Ecce tu.*	Behold thou.
כבד	הַנִּכְבָּד	*Gloriosus.*	Glorious.
הן	הִנְּכָה	*Ecce tu.*	Behold thou. [troyed.
כחד	הַנִּכְחָדוֹת	*Excisæ, perditæ.*	They that are cut off, des-
כלם	הַנִּכְלָמוֹת	*Confusæ.*	They that are confounded.
—	הַנִּכְלָמִים	*Pudore affecti.*	They that are ashamed.
נכר	הַנֵּכָר	*Alienus; alienigena.*	The strange; the stranger.
—	הַנָּכְרִי	*Alienigena.*	The stranger, foreigner.
—	הַנָּכְרִיּוֹת	*Alienigenæ.*	The strange, foreign *women*.

ROOTS.	DERIVATIVES.	VERSIO.	SIGNIFICATION.
כשל	הַנִּכְשָׁל	*Collapsus.*	He that has slipped, stumbled.
לוה	הַנִּלְוָה	*Adhæsus.*	He that is joined.
—	הַנִּלְוִים	*Adjuncti.*	They that are joined.
לחם	הַנִּלְחָם	*Pugnans.*	He that fights.
—	הַנִּלְחָמִים	*Pugnantes.*	They that fight.
ילך	הֲנֵלֵךְ	*Num ibimus?*	Shall we go?
לכד	הַנִּלְכָּד	*Deprehensus.*	He that is taken.
הן	הִנָּם־־נֹּם	*Ecce ipsi.*	Behold they.
	הִנֹּם	*Hinnom.*	Hinnom, N. M. P.
מכר	הַנִּמְכָּרִים	*Venundati.*	They that are sold.
מלט	הַנִּמְלָט	*Effugiens.*	He that escapeth.
נמל	הַנְּמָלִים	*Formicæ.*	The ants.
מצא	הֲנִמְצָא	*Num invenietur?*	Will he be found?
—	הַנִּמְצָא	*Inventus, repertus.*	He that is found.
—	הַנִּמְצָאָה	*Reperta.*	She that is found.
—	הַנִּמְצְאוּ	*Inventi, præsentes.*	They that are found, present.
—	הַנִּמְצָאוֹת־־אֹת	*Inventæ, præsentes.*	They that are found, present.
—	הַנִּמְצָאִים־־צִי	*Inventi, præsentes.*	They that are found, present
הן	הִנֵּנוּ־־נּ‍ּנ‍ּ־־נֵנוּ	*Ecce nos.*	Behold we.
—	הִנְנִי־־נִ־־נֶּנִּי	*Ecce ego.*	Behold I.
נוס	הַנָּס	*Fugiens.*	He that fleeth.
נסס	הַנֵּס	*Vexillum, signum.*	The standard, banner, sign.
נסה	הֲנִסָּה	*Num tentavit?*	Has he assayed, attempted?
סוג	הַנְּסוֹגִים	*Aversi.*	They that are turned back.
נסך	הַנְּסוּכָה	*Expansa, obducta.*	She that is spread abroad, over
—	הַנָּסֶךְ	*Tegumentum.*	A covering.
ספה	הַנִּסְפֶּה	*Adjunctus.*	He that is joined.
סתר	הַנִּסְתָּרוֹת־־רֹת	*Absconditæ.*	The hidden.
	הֵנַע	*Hena.*	Hena, N. P.
יעד	הַנֹּעָדִים	*Congregati.*	They who are assembled.
נער	הַנְּעוּרִים	*Juventus, juvenes.*	The youth, youths.
עזב	הַנֶּעֱזָבוֹת	*Derelictæ.*	They that are forsaken.
נעם	הַנְּעִימִים	*Jucundi.*	The sweet.
עלל	הַנֵּעֵל	*Introduxit.*	He brought in.
נעל	הַנָּעַל	*Calceamentum.*	The shoe.
נעץ	הַנַּעֲצוּץ	*Spina.*	The thorn.
—	הַנַּעֲצוּצִים	*Spinæ.*	The thorns.

ROOTS.	DERIVATIVES.	VERSIO.	SIGNIFICATION.
נער	הַנַּעַר־־נַ֫	*Puer, juvenis, adolescens.*	The boy, lad, youth, young man.
—	הַנַּעַר־־עֲרָה	*Puella.*	The damsel.
—	הַנְּעָרוֹת	*Puellæ.*	The maidens.
—	הַנְּעָרִים	*Pueri, juvenes.*	The boys, lads, young men.
—	הַנְּעֹרֶת	*Stupa.*	The tow.
עשה	הֲנַעֲשֶׂה	*Num faciemus?*	Shall we do?
—	הַנַּעֲשׂוֹת	*Quæ fiunt.*	Which are done.
נפל	הַנְּפִילִים־־פִלִ׳	*Gigantes.*	The giants.
נפק	הַנְפִיקוּ־־פִּקוּ	*Deportaverunt.*	They carried away, transported
נפל	הַנֵּפֶל	*Abortus.*	An untimely birth.
—	הַנֹּפֵל	*Cadens.*	He that falls.
—	הַנֹּפְלִים	*Cadentes; transfugæ*	They that fall; the fugitives.
—	הַנֹּפֶלֶת	*Corruens.*	She that falls.
נפק	הַנְפֵק	*Eduxit.*	He took out.
נפש	הַנֶּפֶשׁ־־נָ֫	*Anima.*	The soul.
—	הַנְּפָשׁוֹת	*Animæ.*	The souls.
נוף	הַנָּפֶת	*Tractus.*	The countries.
—	הֲנַפְתָּ	*Elevasti.*	Thou liftedst up.
נצה	הַנֵּץ	*Accipiter.*	The hawk.
יצב	הַנִּצָּב	*Præfectus.*	He that is set over.
—	הַנִּצָּבָה	*Subsistens.*	She that stands still.
—	הַנִּצָּבוֹת	*Astantes.*	They that stand.
	הַנִּצָּבִים	*Astantes; præfecti.*	They that stand; officers.
—	הַנִּצֶּבֶת	*Astans.*	She that stands.
נצץ	הֵנֵצוּ	*Germinarunt.*	They budded, blossomed.
נצל	הִנָּצֵל	*Erue te.*	Deliver thyself.
צמד	הַנִּצְמָדִים	*Adjungentes se.*	They that join themselves.
נצץ	הַנִּצָּנִים	*Flores.*	The flowers.
קבץ	הַנִּקְבָּצִים	*Congregati.*	The persons gathered, assembled.
נקד	הַנְּקֻדּוֹת	*Variegatæ.*	They that are speckled.
נקה	הִנָּקֵה	*Impunitum esse.*	To be unpunished.
קהל	הַנִּקְהָלִים	*Congregati.*	They that are assembled.
נקה	הִנָּקִי	*Immunis esto.*	Be thou free.
—	הַנָּקִי	*Innocens.*	Innocent.
קלל	הֲנָקֵל	*Nonne leve?*	Not a light thing?
—	הֲנָקְלָה	*Num leve?*	A light thing?

ROOTS.	DERIVATIVES.	VERSIO.	SIGNIFICATION.
נקם	הִנָּֽקְמוּ	*Ulciscimini.*	Take ye vengeance.
קרא	הַנִּקְרָא	*Vocatus.*	He that is called.
—	הַנִּקְרָאִים	*Vocati.*	They that are called.
ראה	הַנִּרְאָה	*Apparuit.*	He that appeared.
—	הַנִּרְאֶה	*Apparens.*	He that appears.
נור	הַנֵּרוֹת־־רֹת	*Lucernæ.*	The lamps.
רצח	הַנִּרְצָחָה	*Occisa.*	She that was slain.
נשא	הַנֹּשֵׂא	*Portans.*	He that beareth.
—	הִנָּשֵׂא	*Attolle te.*	Lift up thyself.
—	הַנִּשְׂאוֹת	*Elevatæ.*	They that are lifted up.
—	הַנֹּשְׂאִים	*Portantes.*	They that bear, carry.
—	הַנְּשֻׂאִים	*Portati.*	They that are carried.
—	הַנְּשִׂאִים־־שִׂי״	*Principes.*	The princes, rulers.
—	הַנְּשִׂאָם	*Principes.*	The princes, rulers.
שאר	הַנִּשְׁאָר	*Remanens, relictus.*	He that remains, is left.
—	הַנִּשְׁאָרָה	*Relicta.*	She that is left.
—	הַנִּשְׁאָרוֹת	*Relictæ.*	They that are left.
—	הַנִּשְׁאָרִים	*Relicti,*	They that remain.
—	הַנִּשְׁאֶרֶת־־אָ׳	*Relicta.*	She that remains.
שבע	הַנִּשְׁבָּע	*Jurans.*	He that sweareth.
—	הַנִּשְׁבָּעִים	*Jurantes.*	They that swear.
שבר	הַנִּשְׁבֶּרֶת	*Fracta.*	She that is broken. [state.
נשה	הַנָּשֶׁה	*Luxatus, relaxatus.*	He that is in a loose, relaxed
שוב	הֲנָשׁוּב	*Num revertemur?*	Shall we return?
נשך	הַנָּשׁוּךְ	*Morsus.*	He that is bitten.
שחת	הַנִּשְׁחָתוֹת	*Corruptæ.*	The corrupt.
נשא	הַנָּשִׂיא	*Princeps.*	The prince.
נשה	הַנָּשִׁים	*Mulieres.*	The women.
נשך	הַנֹּשֵׁךְ	*Mordens.*	He that biteth.
—	הַנְּשָׁכוֹת	*Cubicula.*	The chambers.
שכח	הַנִּשְׁכָּחִים	*Oblivioni traditi.*	Forgotten.
נשך	הַנֹּשְׁכִים	*Mordentes.*	They that bite.
שמם	הַנְּשַׁמָּה	*Desolata.*	The desolate.
נשם	הַנְּשָׁמָה	*Anima, spiritus.*	The breath, spirit.
שמם	הַנְּשַׁמּוֹת	*Desolatæ.*	The desolate.
שמע	הֲנִשְׁמַע	*Num auditus est?*	Has he been heard?
—	הַנִּשְׁמַעַת	*Audita.*	She that is heard.

ROOTS.	DERIVATIVES.	VERSIO.	SIGNIFICATION.
נשק	הַנֶּשֶׁק־־נֶּ׳	*Armamentarium.*	The armoury.
שקף	הַנִּשְׁקָף	*Respiciens.*	He that looketh.
—	הַנִּשְׁקָפָה	*Apparens.*	She that looks forth, appears.
נשר	הַנֶּשֶׁר־־נֶּ׳	*Aquila.*	The eagle.
נשת	הַנִּשְׁתְּוָן	*Epistola.*	The letter.
נתח	הַנְּתָחִים	*Membra, frusta.*	The parts, pieces.
נתן	הִנָּתֵן	*Traditus.*	He that is delivered.
—	הִנָּתֹן	*Tradendo, dando.*	In delivering, giving.
—	הַנֹּתְנִים	*Dantes, ponentes.*	They that give, set, place.
נתץ	הַנְּתֻצִים	*Diruti.*	They that are thrown down.
נתק	הַנֶּתֶק	*Porrigo.*	The scall, morbid baldness.
—	הָנְתְּקוּ	*Subducti sunt.*	They were drawn away.
	הס		
הסה	הַס הָס	*Sile.* [*vertit.*	Keep thou silence. [turned.
סבב	הֵסֵב	*Circuire fecit; con-*	He caused to come about; he
—	הָסֵב	*Circumda; diverte.*	Encompass thou; turn away.
—	הַסֹּבֵב	*Circumdans.*	He that compasseth.
—	הַסֹּבְבִים	*Circuientes.*	They that go about.
—	הֵסֵבּוּ	*Circumduxerunt.*	They have brought about.
—	הָסֵבִּי	*Averte.*	Turn thou away.
—	הַסָּבִיב	*Circuitus.*	The circuit.
—	הַסֹּבֵיב־־הַסּוֹ׳	*Circumdans.*	He that encompasseth.
סבל	הַסַּבָּל	*Bajulus.*	The bearer of burdens. [ters.
—	הַסַּבָּלִים	*Bajuli.*	The bearers of burdens, por-
סבב	הֲסִבֹּתָ	*Convertisti.*	Thou hast turned.
סגר	הִסְגִּיר	*Inclusit, conclusit.*	He shut up, concluded.
—	הַסְגִּירוֹ	*Tradere illum.*	To deliver him.
—	הִסְגִּירָם	*Inclusit eos.*	He shut them up.
—	הַסְגִּירָם	*Tradere eos.*	That they deliver up.
סגן	הַסְּגָנִים	*Principes.*	The rulers.
סגר	הִסָּגֵר	*Include te.*	Shut up thyself.
—	הִסְגַּרְתַּנִי	*Inclusisti me.*	Thou hast shut me up.
הִסָּה		*Siluit, conticuit.*	He was silent, held his peace.
סהר	הַסֹּהַר	*Carcer.*	The prison.
—	הַסָּהַר	*Rotundus.*	The round.
הסה	הַסּוּ	*Silete.*	Hold ye your peace.

ROOTS.	DERIVATIVES.	VERSIO.	SIGNIFICATION.
סכך	הַסּוֹכֵךְ	*Obtegens, protegens.*	He that covers, protects.
סוס	הַסּוּס	*Equus.*	The horse.
——	הַסּוּסִים	*Equi.*	The horses.
סוף	הַסּוּף	*Juncetum, alga.*	The flags, sea-weeds.
ספד	הַסּוֹפְדִים	*Plangentes.*	They that mourn.
ספר	הַסּוֹפֵר הַסֹּפֵר	*Scriba.*	The scribe.
אסר	הַסּוּרִים	*Vincti.* [detriti.	Those that are bound.
סחב	הַסְּחָבוֹת	*Panni veteres seu*	Old or worn out cloths, rags.
יסף	הוֹסִיף	*Addidit.*	He added.
סיר	הַסִּיר	*Olla* [tit.	The pot. [away.
סור	הֵסִיר	*Amovit, ejecit, aver-*	He removed, cast out, turned
——	הָסֵר	*Amove.*	Remove thou.
——	הֱסִירָהּ	*Amovit eam.*	He removed her.
——	הֵסִירוּ	*Amoverunt.*	They took away.
——	הָסִירוּ	*Amovete.*	Remove ye, put away.
סיר	הַסִּירוֹת־־רֹת	*Ollæ.*	The pots.
סור	הֲסִרוֹתִי־־רֹתִי	*Abstuli, removi.*	I have taken away, removed.
——	הָסִירִי	*Amove.*	Put thou away.
——	הַסִּירִים	*Spinæ.*	The thorns.
——	הֲסִירְךָ	*Removere te.*	That thou take away.
——	הֲסִירְכֶם	*Auferre vos.*	That ye take away.
סות	הֱסִיתוּךָ	*Incitarunt te.*	They have stirred up thee.
——	הֱסִיתְךָ	*Abduxit te.*	He has removed thee.
——	הֱסִיתְךָ	*Incitavit te.*	He has stirred thee up.
נסך	הַסֵּךְ	*Fac libari.*	Cause thou to be poured.
סכך	הַסֻּכּוֹת־־כֹּת	*Tentoria.*	The tabernacles.
——	הַסֹּכֵךְ	*Tegumentum.*	The covering.
סכל	הַסֶּכֶל	*Stultitia.*	The folly.
——	הַסִּכְלוּת	*Stultitia.*	The folly.
——	הִסְכַּלְתָּ	*Stulte egisti.*	Thou hast done foolishly.
——	הִסְכַּלְתִּי	*Stulte egi.*	I have acted foolishly.
סכן	הַסֹּכֵן	*Thesaurarius.*	The treasurer.
——	הַסְכֶּן	*Assuesce.*	Acquaint thyself.
סכן	הִסְכַּנְתָּ	*Assuevisti.*	Thou hast been acquainted
——	הִסְכַּנְתִּי	*Consuevi.*	I was wont, accustomed.
סכת	הַסְכֵּת	*Ausculta.*	Hearken thou.
סל	הַסַּל	*Canistrum.*	The basket.

ROOTS.	DERIVATIVES.	VERSIO.	SIGNIFICATION.
סלח	הַסֹּלֵחַ	*Condonans.*	He who forgiveth.
—	הַסְּלִיחָה	*Condonatio.*	The forgiveness.
סל	הַסַּלִּים	*Canistra.*	The baskets.
סלל	הַסֹּלְלוֹת	*Aggeres.*	The mounts.
סלע	הַסֶּלַע הַסָּ׳	*Rupes.*	The rock.
—	הַסְּלָעִים	*Saxa.* [*racissimæ.*	The rocks. [ingly voracious.
—	הַסָּלְעָם	*Species locustæ vo-*	A species of locust exceed-
סלת	הַסֹּלֶת	*Simila.*	The fine flour.
סמדר	הַסְּמָדַר	*Uva prima.*	The early or tender grape.
סם	הַסַּמִּים	*Aromata.*	Sweet aromatic spices.
סמל	הַסֶּמֶל	*Simulachrum.*	The image.
	הַסְּנָאָה	*Hasenaa.*	Hassenaah, N. M.
	הַסְּנָאָה־־נוּאָה	*Hasenua.*	Hasenuah, N. M.
סנה	הַסְּנֶה	*Rubus.*	The bush.
סעף	הַסְּעִפִּים	*Cogitationes.*	The opinions, thoughts.
סער	הַסַּעַר	*Procella.*	The tempest.
—	הַסְּעָרָה	*Turbo.*	The whirlwind. [post.
ספף	הַסַּף־הַסָּף	*Limen, postis.*	The threshold, door, door-
—	הַסִּפִּים	*Pelves; limina, postes, cardines.*	The basons; the thresholds, gates, doors, posts, hinges.
ספן	הַסְּפִינָה	*Navis.*	The ship.
ספר	הַסַּפִּיר	*Sapphirus.*	The sapphire.
ספל	הַסֵּפֶל	*Crater.*	The bowl.
ספן	הַסִּפֻּן	*Tabulatum.*	The cieling.
ספר	הַסֵּפֶר	*Liber, epistola.*	The book, letter.
—	הַסְּפָר	*Enumeratio.*	The numbering.
—	הַסְּפָרִים	*Epistolæ, scripturæ.*	The letters, writings.
נסק	הַסִּקוּ	*Sustulerunt, duxère.*	They took up, brought.
סור	הָסֵר	*Auferre* [*amovendo*	To take away. [in removing.
—	הָסֵר	*Amove; auferre;*	Remove thou; to take away;
סיר	הַסִּרוֹת	*Ollæ.*	The pots.
סרה	הַסִּרְיֹנוֹת	*Loricæ.* [*rius.*	The coats of mail.
סרס	הַסָּרִיס	*Eunuchus, cubicula-*	The eunuch, chamberlain.
—	הַסָּרִיסִים־־רִסִ׳	*Eunuchi, cubicularii*	The eunuchs, chamberlains.
סרן	הַסְּרָנִים	*Principes.*	The lords, chiefs, princes.
סרפד	הַסִּרְפָּד	*Urtica, paliurus.*	The brier.
סרר	הַסֹּרְרִים	*Rebelles.*	The rebellious.

ROOTS.	DERIVATIVES.	VERSIO.	SIGNIFICATION.
סור	הֲסִרֹתִי	*Removi.*	I removed.
סות	הֵסִתָּה	*Incitavit.*	She stirred up.
סתה	הַסְּתָו	*Hyems.*	The winter. [keeper.
ספף	הִסְתּוֹפֵף	*In limine esse.*	To be at the threshold, a door-
סתר	הִסְתִּיר	*Abscondit.*	He has hidden.
—	הִסְתִּירוּ	*Absconderunt.*	They have hidden.
—	הִסְתִּירָנִי	*Abscondit me.* [re.	He hath hidden me.
—	הַסְתֵּר	*Absconde; abscondere.*	Hide thou; to hide.
—	הִסָּתֵר	*Absconde te.*	Hide thyself.
—	הִסְתַּרְתָּ	*Abscondisti.*	Thou hast hidden.
—	הִסְתַּרְתִּי	*Abscondi.*	I hid.

הע

ROOTS.	DERIVATIVES.	VERSIO.	SIGNIFICATION.
עבד	הָעֹבֵד	*Ministrans, operans.*	He that serves, works.
—	הַעֶבֶד	*Num servus?*	A servant?
—	הָעֶבֶד	*Servus.* [terium.	The servant.
—	הָעֲבֹדָה־־בוֹ׳	*Servitus, opus, ministe-*	The bondage, work, service.
—	הָעֲבָדִים	*Servi.*	The men servants.
—	הָעֹבְדִים	*Servientes.*	They that serve.
—	הֶעֱבַדְתִּיךָ	*Colere feci te.*	I have caused thee to serve.
—	הֶעֱבַדְתַּנִי	*Servire fecisti me.*	Thou hast made me to serve.
עבט	הָעֲבוֹט	*Pignus.*	The pledge.
עבד	הֶעֱבִיד	*Servire fecit.*	He caused to serve.
עוב	הֶעָבִים	*Nubes.*	The clouds.
עבר	הַעֲבִיר	*Traducendo.* [tulit.	In bringing over. [moved.
—	הֶעֱבִיר	*Transire fecit, trans-*	He caused to pass over, re-
—	הֶעֱבִירוּ	*Traduxerunt.*	They caused to pass through.
—	הַעֲבִירוּנִי	*Transferte me.*	Carry me away.
עבר	הָעֹבֵר	*Transiens.*	He that passes through or over
—	הַעֲבֵר הַעֲבֵר	*Aufer, transfer.*	Take away, remove thou.
—	הָעֵבֶר	*In adversum.*	To the opposite side.
—	הָעֲבָרָה	*Scapha.* [gredientes.	A ferry-boat. [transgress.
—	הָעֹבְרִים	*Transeuntes, trans-*	They that go by, pass over,
—	הַעֲבִרֵנוּ	*Nos facere transire.*	To let us pass.
—	הֶעֱבַרְתָּ	*Transire fecisti.*	Thou hast caused to pass over
—	הֶעֱבַרְתִּי	*Transire feci.*	I have caused to pass over.
עבת	הָעֲבֹתִים	*Funes contorti.*	The twined ropes or cords.

ROOTS.	DERIVATIVES.	VERSIO.	SIGNIFICATION.
עבת	הָעֲבֹתֹת	*Catenæ contortæ.*	The wreathen chains.
ענל	הָעֵגֶל	*Vitulus.*	The calf.
—	הָעֲגָלָה	*Plaustrum.*	The cart, waggon.
—	הָעֶגְלָה	*Vitula.*	The heifer.
—	הָעֲגָלוֹת־־לֹת	*Plaustra.* [*tus est.*	The waggons.
עוד	הֵעִד	*Contestatus,testifica-*	He protested, testified.
	הָעֵד	*Contestare; contes-*	Charge, protest thou; in pro-
—		*tando; testis.*	testing; the witness.
יעד	הָעֵדָה	*Cœtus, conventus.*	The assembly, congregation.
עוד	הָעֵדוּת־־דֻת	*Testimonium* [*regia*	The testimony.
—	הֶעְדִּיו	*Abstulerunt.*	They took away.
עדה	הָעֲדוּת	*Ornamentum, vestis*	The ornament, the royal robe.
עד	הָעֵדִים	*Testes.*	The witnesses. [than enough.
עדף	הֶעְדִּיף	*Superabundavit.*	He superabounded, had more
—	הָעֹדֵף	*Superfluus.*	The overplus.
—	הָעֹדְפִים	*Superbundantes.*	They that are over and above
—	הָעֹדֶפֶת	*Redundans.*	That which remaineth.
עדר	הָעֵדֶר	*Grex.*	The flock.
—	הָעֲדָרִים	*Greges.*	The flocks.
עוד	הָעֵדֹת	*Testimonia.*	The testimonies.
—	הַעֵדֹתָ ה	*Contestatus es.*[*sum.*	Thou chargedst. [testified.
	הַעֵדֹתִי־־עִי	*Attestatus, testatus*	I called to witness, protested,
	הַעוֹד	*Adhuc?*	Still, yet?
—	הַעוֹדָם	*An adhuc illi?*	Whether they yet?
—	הַעוֹדֶנּוּ	*Num adhuc ille?*	He yet?
עוה	הֶעֱוָה	*Inique egit.*	He did perversely, wickedly.
—	הַעֲוֵה	*Inique agere.*	To commit iniquity.
—	הֶעֱוּוּ	*Perverterunt.*	They have perverted.
—	הֶעֱוִינוּ	*Inique egimus.*	We have committed iniquity.
—	הֶעֱוֵיתִי	*Inique egi; perverti*	I have donewickedly,perverted
עלה	הָעֹלָה	*Holocaustum.*	The burnt offering.
עלה	הָעֹלוֹת־־לִים	*Ascendentes.*	They that go up.
עלם	הָעוֹלָם־־עֹלָם	*Sæculum.*	An age, for ever, everlasting.
עוה	הֶעָוֹן	*Iniquitas.*	The iniquity.
עוף	הָעוֹף	*Volatile; avis.*	The fowl, bird.
עפר	הָעוֹפֶרֶת־־עֹפֶ׳	*Plumbum, plumbeus.*	The lead, leaden.
עור	הָעוֹר	*Pellis, cutis.*	The hide, skin.

ROOTS.	DERIVATIVES.	VERSIO.	SIGNIFICATION.
עור	הָעִוֵּר	*Cæcus.*	The blind.
—	הָעִוְרִים	*Cæci.*	The blind.
עוז	הָעֵז	*Congrega.*	Gather thou.
עזז	הֵעֵז	*Roboravit.*	He has hardened.
עזב	הַעֹזְבִים	*Relinquentes.*	They who leave.
—	הָעֹזֶבֶת	*Derelinquens.*	He that forsakes.
עזז	הֵעֵזָה	*Obfirmavit.*	She strengthened.
עוז	הָעִזוּ	*Congregate vos.*	Gather yourselves. [ing.
עזב	הָעֲזוּבָה	*Derelicta; derelictio.*	She that is forsaken, a forsak-
עז	הָעִזִּים	*Capræ.* [aquilæ.	The goats.
עזז	הָעָזְנִיָּה	*Haliæetus, species*	The sea-eagle.
עזר	הָעֲזָרָה	*Atrium.*	The court.
עטף	הָעֲטוּפִים	*Deficientes.*	They that fall or faint.
עטה	הֶעֱטִיתָ	*Operuisti.*	Thou hast covered.
עטלף	הָעֲטַלֵּף	*Vespertilio.*	The bat.
עטף	הָעֲטֻפִים	*Serotini, debiliores.*	The late, the feebler.
עטר	הָעֲטָרָה	*Corona.*	The crown.
	הָעָי	*Hai.*	Ai, N. P.
עוד	הֵעִיד	*Contestatus est.*	He protested.
—	הֵעִידוּ	*Testificati sunt.*	They testified.
—	הַעִידֹתָ	*Testificatus es.*	Thou didst testify.
עוז	הָעִיזוּ	*Congregate vos, con-fugite.* [*confugêre.*	Gather yourselves together, flee ye. [gether, they fled.
—	הֵעִיזוּ	*Congregarunt se,*	They gathered themselves to-
עיט	הָעַיִט־הָ	*Volucris, avis.*	The bird.
עין	הָעַיִן הָעָיִן	*Fons; oculus.*	The fountain; the eye.
—	הָעַיְנָה	*Ad fontem.*	To the well, fountain.
—	הָעֲיָנוֹת	*Fontes.*	The fountains.
—	הַעֵינֵי	*Num oculi?*	The eyes?
עור	הֵעִיר	*Excitavit, suscitavit*	He stirred up, raised up.
עיר	הָעִיר	*Civitas.*	The city.
—	הָעִירָה	*Ad civitatem.*	To the city.
עור	הָעִירָה	*Expergiscere.*	Stir up thyself.
—	הָעִירוּ	*Suscitate.*	Wake ye up.
—	הַעִירוֹתִי	*Excitavi.*	I have raised up.
—	הַעִירֹתִיהוּ	*Suscitavi eum.* [*tia.*	I have raised him up.
עכס	הָעֲכָסִים	*Ornamenta, tinnien-*	The tinkling ornaments.

ROOTS.	DERIVATIVES.	VERSIO.	SIGNIFICATION.
עלל	הָעֹל	*Jugum.* [*Educito.*	The yoke. [out, up.
עלה	הַעַל	*An ad? ad contra?*	To? Against? Bring thou
—	הֹעַל	*Introductus est.*	He was brought in.
עלה	הָעֹלָה	*Ascendens.*	He that goeth up.
—	הֶעָלֶה	*An folium?* [*tum.*	A leaf?
—	הָעֹלָה	*Ascensus; holocaus-*	The going up, burnt-offering.
—	הֶעֱלָה הֶעֱ׳ הֶעְ׳	*Ascendere fecit; eduxit, advexit, obtulit.*	He caused to ascend, brought, brought up, brought to, offered.
—	הַעֲלֵה	*Offer, deporta.*	Offer thou, carry up.
—	הֹעֲלָה	*Oblatus, relatus est.*	He was offered, mentioned.
—	הֹעֲלוּ	*Introducti sunt* [*runt*	They have been brought in.
—	הֶעֱלוּ	*Eduxerunt, obtule-*	They brought up, offered.
—	הַעֲלוּ	*Afferte, adducite.*	Carry, bring ye.
—	הֵעָלוּ	*Recedite.*	Depart ye.
—	הֶעֱלוּךָ	*Eduxerunt te.*	They brought thee up.
—	הַעֲלוֹת	*Offerre.*	To offer.
—	הָעֹלוֹת	*Holocausta.*	The burnt-offerings.
—	הֵעָלוֹת	*Attolli.*	To be taken up.
—	הַעֲלוֹתִי	*Educere me.*	That I brought up.
—	הַעֲלִי	*Ascendere fac.*	Bring thou up.
—	הָעֲלִיָּה	*Cœnaculum.*	The chamber, parlour.
—	הָעֶלְיוֹן	*Superior.*	The upper,
—	הָעֶלְיוֹנָה	*Superior.*	The upper.
—	הָעֶלְיוֹנֹת	*Superiores.*	The upper.
עלז	הָעַלִּיזָה	*Exultabunda.*	The joyous, rejoicing.
עלל	הָעֲלִילִיָּה	*Opus.* [*dentes.*	The work.
עלה	הָעֹלִים	*Ascendentes, rece-*	They that go up, depart.
עלם	הֶעְלִים	*Celavit.*	He hath hidden.
—	הֶעְלִימוּ	*Occultarunt.*	They have hidden.
עלה	הֶעֱלִית	*Obtulisti.*	Thou hast offered.
—	הֶעֱלִיתָ־לִיתָ	*Eduxisti.*	Thou hast brought up.
—	הֶעֱלִיתִי	*Eduxi.*	I brought up.
—	הֶעֱלִיתָנוּ־־תָנוּ	*Eduxisti nos.*	Thou hast brought us up.
—	הֶעֶלְךָ	*Eduxit te.*	He brought thee up.
עלם	הַעְלֵם	*Occultando.*	In hiding.
—	הָעֶלֶם	*Adolescens.*	The youth, stripling.

ROOTS.	DERIVATIVES.	VERSIO.	SIGNIFICATION.
עלם	הָעַלְמָה	*Virgo, puella.*	The virgin, maid.
עלה	הֶעֱלָנוּ	*Eduxit nos.*	He brought us up.
עלל	הַעֲלֵנִי	*Introduc me.*	Bring thou me in.
עלה	הָעֹלֹת	*Ascendentes.*	They that come up.
—	הַעֲלָתָה	*Deducta est.*	She was brought up.
—	הֵעָלֹתוֹ	*Attolli eum.*	That he was taken up.
—	הַעֲלֹתִי	*Educere me.*	That I bring up.
—	הֶעֱלִתִיךָ	*Eduxi te.*	I brought thee up.
—	הֶעֱלָתָם	*Eduxit nos.*	She brought them up.
עמם	הָעָם	*Populus.*	The people.
עמד	הָעֹמֵד	*Stans.*	He that stands.
—	הַעֲמֵד	*Constitue.*	Set, place thou.
—	הָעַמֻּד־־מּוּד	*Columna.*	The pillar.
—	הָעֹמְדוֹת	*Astantes.*	They that stand by.
—	הָעַמֻּדִים־־מּוּ׳	*Columnæ.*	The pillars.
—	הָעֹמְדִים	*Stantes, præsidentes.*	They that stand, preside over.
—	הֶעֱמַדְתָּ	*Constituisti.*	Thou hast appointed. [tled
—	הֶעֱמַדְתָּה	*Stare fecisti.*	Thou hast made to stand, set-
—	הֶעֱמַדְתִּי	*Constitui, posui.*	I have appointed, set.
—	הֶעֱמַדְתִּיךָ	*Constitui te.*	I have raised thee up.
—	הֶעֱמִיד	*Constituit, posuit.*	He set up, placed
עמם	הָעַמִּים	*Populi, gentes.*	The people, nations.
עמס	הֶעֱמִיס־־עְ׳	*Imposuit, oneravit.*	He laid upon, burdened.
עמק	הֶעֱמִיק	*Profundum fecit.*	He made deep.
—	הֶעֱמִיקוּ־־מִקוּ	*Profundum fecerunt*	They have made deep.
עמל	הֶעָמָל	*Labor.*	The labour.
עמס	הָעֲמֻסִים	*Gestati.*	Who are borne.
עמק	הַעֲמֵק	*Profundum fac.*	Deepen thou, make deep.
—	הָעֵמֶק	*Vallis.*	The valley.
—	הֶעֱמִקָה	*Profunda.*	Deep.
—	הָעֲמָקִים	*Valles.*	The vallies.
עמר	הָעֳמָרִים	*Manipuli.*	The sheaves.
ענב	הָעֲנָבִים	*Uvæ.*	The grapes.
ענה	הָעֹנֶה	*Exaudiens.*	He that hears.
—	הֶעָנִי	*Pauper.*	The poor.
—	הָעֲנִיִּים	*Pauperes.*	The poor.
—	הָעֹנִים	*Respondentes.*	They that answer.

ROOTS.	DERIVATIVES.	VERSIO.	SIGNIFICATION.
ענה	הָעִנְיָן	*Occupatio.*	The business.
ענק	הַעֲנֵיק	*Munerando.*	In rewarding.
ענה	הֶעָנָן	*Nubes.*	The cloud.
ענק	הָעֲנָקוֹת	*Torques.*	The chains.
עפר	הֶעָפָר	*Pulvis.*	The dust.
עץ	הָעֵץ	*Arbor, lignum.*	The tree, wood.
עצב	הָעֵצֶב	*Simulachrum.*	The idol.
—	הָעֲצַבִּים	*Simulachra.*	The idols.
—	הָעֲצָבִים	*Dolores.*	The sorrows.
יעץ	הָעֵצָה	*Consilium.*	The counsel.
עצה	הֶעָצֶה	*Spina dorsi.*	The back bone.
עצם	הָעֲצוּמִים	*Validæ.*	The strong.
עץ	הָעֵצִים	*Arbores, ligna.*	The trees, wood.
עצל	הֶעָצֵל	*Piger.*	The slothful, sluggard.
עצם	הָעֲצָמוֹת--מִים	*Ossa.*	The bones.
עקב	הֶעָקֹב	*Tortuosus, curvus.*	The crooked.
עקד	הָעֲקֻדִּים	*Variegati.* [nus.	The ring-streaked, speckled.
ערב	הָעֶרֶב--הָעָ'	*Vespera; vesperti-*	The evening; in the evening.
—	הָעֵרֶב	*Trama, subtegmen.*	The woof.
—	הֶעָרֹב	*Colluvies.*	The swarms.
—	הָעֹרֵב	*Corvus.*	The raven.
—	הָעֲרָבָה	*Planities.*	The plain.
—	הָעֵרָבוֹן	*Pignus.*	The pledge.
—	הָעֹרְבִים	*Corvi.*	The ravens.
—	הָעֲרָבִים	*Salices.*	The willows.
—	הָעַרְבַּיִם	*Duæ vesperæ.*	The two evenings. [vered.
ערה	הֶעֱרָה	*Effudit, nudavit.*	He hath poured out, unco-
ערף	הָעֲרוּפָה	*Decollata.*	She that is beheaded.
ערך	הֶעֱרִיךְ	*Taxavit.*	He taxed.
עיר	הֶעָרִים	*Civitates.*	The cities.
ערך	הָעֲרֻכוֹת	*Ordinatæ.*	Those that are laid in order.
—	הַעֹרְכִים	*Instruentes.*	They that set in order.
—	הַעֶרְכְּךָ	*Æstimatio tua.*	Thy estimation.
ערל	הֶעָרֵל	*Incircumcisus.*	The uncircumcised.
—	הָעֲרָלוֹת	*Præputia.*	The foreskins.
—	הָעֲרֵלִים	*Incircumcisi.*	The uncircumcised.
ערם	הָעֲרֵמָה	*Acervus.*	The heap.

ROOTS.	DERIVATIVES.	VERSIO.	SIGNIFICATION.
שרם	הָעֲרֵמוֹת	*Acervi.*	The heaps.
ערג	הָעַרְעָר	*Debilis.*	The weak.
ערפל	הָעֲרָפֶל	*Caligo.*	The thick darkness.
ערק	הַעֹרְקִים	*Fugientes.*	Fleeing.
עשה	הָעֹשֶׂה־־שָׂה	*Faciens.*	He that worketh.
—	הֶעָשׂוּ	*Factus.*	He who is made.
—	הָעֹשׂוֹ	*Qui fecit eum.*	He that made him. [done.
—	הֶעָשׂוּי	*Factus.*	He or that which is made or
—	הָעֲשׂוּיָה	*Facta.*	She that was made.
—	הָעֲשׂוּיִם	*Facti.*	They that were made.
—	הֵעָשׂוֹתוֹ	*Fieri illud.*	When it is made.
—	הָעֲשֻׂיָה	*Facta, parata.*	She that was made, prepared.
—	הָעֹשִׂים	*Facientes, operantes*	They that do, make, work.
עשר	הֶעָשִׁיר	*Dives.*	The rich.
—	הָעֲשִׂירִי	*Decimus.*	The tenth.
—	הָעֲשִׂירִית	*Decima.*	The tenth.
עשן	הֶעָשָׁן	*Fumus.*	The smoke.
—	הָעֲשֵׁנִים	*Fumantes.*	The smoking.
עשק	הָעֹשֶׁק	*Oppressio, extortio.*	The oppression, extortion.
—	הָעֹשְׁקוֹת	*Opprimentes.*	They that oppress.
—	הָעֲשׁוּקִים	*Oppressi.*	The oppressed.
עשר	הָעֹשֶׁר	*Opulentia, divitiæ.*	The wealth, riches.
—	הֶעָשֹׂר הָעֲשָׂרָה	*Decem.*	The ten.
—	הָעֲשִׂרִי	*Decimus.*	The tenth.
—	הָעֶשְׂרִים	*Viginti, vicesimus.*	The twenty, twentieth.
—	הָעֲשִׂרִית	*Decima.*	The tenth.
—	הֶעֱשַׁרְתָּ	*Ditasti.*	Thou hast enriched.
—	הֶעֱשַׁרְתִּי	*Ditavi.*	I have made rich.
עשה	הָעֹשֹׂת	*Facientes.*	They that do, commit.
עתת	הָעֵת	*Tempus.*	The time.
—	הַעֵת	*Num tempus?*	The time ?
עתד	הָעַתֻּדִים־תּוּדִים	*Hirci.*	The he-goats.
—	הָעֲתִידִים	*Parati.*	They who are ready.
עתת	הָעִתִּים	*Tempora.* [*tulerunt.*	The times. [copied out.
עתק	הֶעְתִּיקוּ	*Removerunt, trans-*	They removed, transcribed,
עתר	הַעְתִּירוּ	*Orate.*	Pray, intreat ye.

ROOTS.	DERIVATIVES.	VERSIO.	SIGNIFICATION.
	הפ		
פאר	הַפְּאֵרִים	*Tiaræ.*	The bonnets, turbans.
פאה	הַפְּאֹת	*Anguli.*	The corners.
פוג	הֲפֻגוֹת	*Intermissiones.*	The intermissions.
פגע	הִפְגִּיעַ	*Incurrere fecit.*	He hath made to meet.
—	הִפְגִּעוּ	*Intercesserunt.*	They made intercession.
—	הִפְגַּעְתִּי	*Occurrere feci.*	I caused to meet.
פגר	הַפֶּגֶר	*Cadaver.*	The dead body.
—	הַפְּגָרִים	*Cadavera.*	The carcases.
פדה	הַפִּדְיוֹם	*Redemptio.*	The redemption.
—	הַפְּדֻיִים	*Redempti.*	The redeemed.
פדר	הַפֶּדֶר	*Adeps.*	The fat.
פה	הַפֶּה	*Os.*	The mouth. [ing.
הפך	הָפוֹךְ	*Evertere, evertendo*	To overthrow, in overthrow-
—	הֲפוּכָה	*Versa.*	She that is turned.
פצה	הַפּוֹצֶה	*Aperiens, liberans.*	He that opens, delivers.
פור	הַפּוּר	*Sors.*	The lot.
פוח	הָפֵחַ	*Illaqueando.*	In ensnaring.
—	הַפָּח	*Laqueus.*	The snare.
פחד	הַפַּחַד	*Metus, formido.*	The fear, dread.
פחה	הַפֶּחָה	*Dux, princeps.*	The captain, governor.
—	הַפַּחוֹת	*Duces, principes.*	The captains, governors.
פחד	הִפְחִיד	*Expavefecit.*	He made to fear, shake.
פחת	הַפַּחַת	*Foveæ.*	The pit. [have exhausted.
נפח	הִפַּחְתִּי	*Efflare feci; exhausi*	I have caused to breathe out,
פחת	הַפְּחָתִים	*Foveæ.*	The pits.
פוח	הָפִיחִי	*Perfla.*	Blow thou.
נפל	הִפִּיל	*Cadere fecit; dejecit*	He let fall, cast down.
פלגש	הַפִּילַגְשִׁים	*Concubinæ.*	The concubines.
נפל	הִפִּילָה	*Dejecit.*	She hath cast down.
—	הַפִּילוּ	*Projicite* sortem.	Cast ye *lots.*
—	הִפִּילוּ	*Jecerunt, remiserunt*	They cast, remitted.
פוץ	הֲפִיצוֹתִיךְ--פִּצ׳	*Dispersi te.*	I have scattered thee.
—	הֲפִיצוֹתִים	*Dispersi eos.*	I have scattered them.
—	הֲפִיצוֹתֶם--פִּצ״	*Dispersistis.*	Ye have scattered.
—	הֱפִיצְךָ	*Dispersit te.*	He hath scattered thee.

ROOTS.	DERIVATIVES.	VERSIO.	SIGNIFICATION.
פוץ	הֱפִיצָם	*Dispersit eos.*	He hath scattered them.
פור	הֵפִיר	*Irritum fecit.*	He hath broken, made void.
הָפַךְ		*Vertit, avertit, convertit, evertit, pervertit, mutavit.*	He turned, turned away, converted, overturned, overthrew, perverted, changed.
—	הֲפֹךְ	*Verte.*	Turn thou.
—	הֶפֶךְ	*Contrarius.*	The contrary.
—	הָפְכָה	*Vertit, mutavit.*	She turned, changed.
—	הָפְכוּ	*Verterunt se.*	They turned back.
—	הָפְכִי	*Subvertere me.*	That I overthrow.
—	הָפְכְּכֶם	*Subvertere vos.*	That you subvert.
—	הָפְכָם	*Evertere eos.*	To overturn them.
—	הֲפַכְפַּךְ	*Perversus.*	Perverse, froward.
—	הָפַכְתָּ	*Vertisti.*	Thou hast turned.
—	הָפַכְתִּי	*Subverti.*	I have overthrown.
—	הֲפַכְתֶּם	*Vertistis.*	Ye have turned.
פלא	הַפְלֵא	*Mirifice agere.*	To do wonderfully.
—	הִפְלָא־־ליא	*Mirifice egit.*	He did wonderfully.
—	הַפְלָאוֹת	*Mirabilia.*	The wonderful things. [them.
פלה	הַפְלֵה	*Insignes fac* [sortem.	Distinguish, signalize thou
נפל	הַפִּלָהּ	*Cadere fac eam per*	Cause thou it to fall *by lot.*
פלה	הִפְלָה	*Selegit, distinxit.*	He selected, distinguished.
נפל	הִפִּלֻהוּ	*Corruere fecerunt.*	They made him fall.
פלט	הַפְּלֵטָה־־לֵיטָה	*Effugiens, profuga.*	She that is escaped.
—	הַפָּלִיט	*Profugus, effugiens.*	The fugitive, he that escapes.
נפל	הִפַּלְנוּ	*Jecimus.* [*distribui.*	We have cast. [by lot.
—	הִפַּלְתִּי	*Cadere feci, sorte*	I have caused to fall, divided
—	הִפַּלְתָּם	*Dejecisti eos.*	Thou castedst them down.
פנן	הַפִּנָּה	*Angulus.*	The corner.
פנה	הַפֹּנֶה	*Respiciens.*	He that looks.
—	הִפְנָה	*Obvertit.*	He hath turned about.
—	הָפְנוּ	*Aversi sunt.*	They are turned away.
—	הִפְנוּ	*Verterunt se.*	They turned themselves back.
—	הַפֹּנוֹת	*Respicientes.*	They that look.
פנן	הַפִּנּוֹת־־נִּים	*Anguli, turres.*	The corners, towers.
פנה	הֲפָנָיו	*Num facies ejus ?*	His face ?
—	הַפָּנִים	*Facies.*	Faces.

ROOTS.	DERIVATIVES.	VERSIO.	SIGNIFICATION.
פנה	הַפְּנִימִי־־מִית	*Interior.*	The inner.
—	הַפְּנִימִיּוֹת	*Interiores, intimæ.*	The inner, inmost.
—	הַפְּנִימִים	*Interiores, intimi.*	The inner, inmost.
—	הִפְנְתָה	*Vertit se.*	She turneth herself.
פסח	הַפִּסֵּחַ	*Claudus.*	The lame.
—	הַפִּסְחִים	*Claudi.*	The lame.
—	הַפְּסָחִים	*Victimæ paschales.*	The passover-victims.
פסל	הַפְּסִילִים	*Sculptilia.*	The carved images.
פסס	הַפַּסִּים	*Polymiti.*	Embroidered, of divers colours.
פסל	הַפֶּסֶל־־פֶּ״	*Sculptile.*	The graven image.
פעם	הַפַּעַם־־פָּ״	*Nunc, semel.*	This time, now, once.
—	הַפַּעֲמֹנִים	*Tintinnabula.*	The bells.
פוץ	הָפֵץ	*Disperge.*	Cast abroad, scatter thou.
פצר	הַפְּצִירָה	*Lima.*	The file.
	הַפִּצֵּץ	*Haphses.*	Aphses, N. M.
פצר	הַפְצַר	*Transgredi.*	To transgress.
פקד	הִפָּקֵד	*Desiderari.*	To be wanting, missing.
—	הַפְקֵד	*Præfice.*	Appoint thou. [entrusted.
—	הָפְקַד	*Depositus est.*	He was deposited, committed,
—	הַפְּקֻדָּה	*Visitatio.*	The visitation.
—	הִפְקִדוּ	*Deposuerunt.*	They laid up.
—	הַפִּקָּדוֹן	*Depositum.*	The deposit, trust. [numbered.
—	הַפְּקֻדִים	*Præfecti; numerati*	The officers; those who are
—	הַפְּקֻדֹּת	*Præfecturæ.*	The wards, charges, offices.
—	הִפְקַדְתּוֹ	*Præfecisti eum.*	Thou hast appointed him.
—	הִפְקַדְתִּי	*Præfeci.*	I have set in authority.
—	הִפְקַדְתִּיךָ	*Præfeci te.*	I have appointed thee.
—	הִפְקִיד	*Præfecit.*	He hath appointed.
—	הַפָּקִיד	*Præfectus.*	The overseer, superintendent.
פקע	הַפְּקָעִים	*Cucurbitæ.*	The knops, gourds.
פר	הַפָּר	*Juvencus.*	The bullock.
פור	הֵפֵר־־פִ׳	*Irritum fecit.*	He made void.
—	הָפֵר	*Irritum fac, faciendo*	Break thou; in making void.
פרד	הַפֶּרֶד	*Mulus.*	The mule. [rated.
—	הִפָּרֶד	*Separa te; separari.*	Separate thyself; to be sepa-
—	הַפִּרְדָּה	*Mula.*	The mule.
פרדס	הַפַּרְדֵּס	*Saltus, sylva.*	The forest.

ROOTS.	DERIVATIVES.	VERSIO.	SIGNIFICATION.
	הַפָּרָה	*Hapara.*	Parah, N. P.
פר	הַפָּרָה	*Juvenca.*	The heifer.
פור	הָפֵרָה	*Irritum fac.*	Break thou, make void.
—	הֵפֵרוּ	*Irritum fecerunt.*	They have made void.
פרז	הַפְּרָזִים	*Rusticani.*	Of the country.
פרץ	הַפְּרוּצָה	*Perrupta.*	The broken.
פר	הַפָּרוֹת	*Vaccæ.*	The kine, cows.
פרז	הַפְּרָזוֹת	*Pagi, non murati.*	The villages, unwalled *towns.*
—	הַפְּרָזִי	*Pagus, non muratus*	The village, unwalled *town.*
פרח	הֲפָרְחָה	*An floresceret?*	Whether she flourished?
פרט	הַפֹּרְטִים	*Modulantes.*	They that chant.
פרד	הִפְרִיד	*Segregavit.*	He separated.
פר	הַפָּרִים	*Juvenci.*	The bullocks.
פרס	הִפְרִיסָה	*Fidit, divisit.*	She clave, divided.
—	הִפְרִיסוּ	*Fiderunt.*	They divided.
פרע	הִפְרִיעַ	*Nudavit, pervertit.*	He made naked, perverted.
פרך	הַפָּרֹכֶת	*Velum.*	The veil.
פור	הֵפֵרָם	*Irrita fecit ea.*	He made them void.
פרה	הִפְרַנִי	*Fœcundavit me.*	He hath made me fruitful.
פרס	הַפֶּרֶס	*Ossifraga,* aquilæ species.	The ossifrage, a fowl of the eagle kind.
—	הַפַּרְסָה	*Ungula.*	The hoof.
פרץ	הַפֹּרֵץ	*Effractor.*	The breaker.
—	הַפְּרָצִים	*Rupturæ.*	The breaches.
פרק	הַפֶּרֶק	*Compitum.*	The cross-way.
פרשד	הַפַּרְשְׁדֹנָה	*Fimus, stercus.*	The dirt, dung.
פרש	הַפָּרָשִׁים	*Equites.*	The horsemen.
פרת	הַפַּרְתְּמִים	*Proceres, principes.*	The nobles, princes.
פשט	הִפְשִׁיט	*Detraxit, nudavit.*	He hath stripped.
—	הִפְשִׁיטוּ	*Detraxerunt.*	They stripped.
פשע	הַפֶּשַׁע	*Prævaricatio.*	The transgression.
—	הַפֹּשְׁעִים	*Prævaricatores.*	The transgressors.
פשת	הַפִּשְׁתִּים	*Lina.*	The linen.
פתח	הַפֶּתַח־־פִּי	*Ostium.*	The door.
—	הַפֶּתְחָה	*Ad ostium.*	At the door.
—	הַפְּתָחִים	*Ostia.*	The doors.

ROOTS.	DERIVATIVES.	VERSIO.	SIGNIFICATION.
	הצ		
יצא	הַצֹּאִים	*Sordidi.*	The filthy.
צאן	הַצֹּאן	*Grex, pecus.*	The flock, cattle.
—	הֲצֹאן	*Num greges?*	The flocks?
יצא	הַצֶּאֱצָאִים	*Prognati.*	The offspring.
צבא	הַצָּבָא	*Militia, exercitus.*	The warfare, host, army.
—	הַצְּבָאוֹת	*Agmina, exercitus.*	The hosts, armies.
—	הַצֹּבְאוֹת־־אֹת	*Convenientes.*	They that meet, assemble.
—	הַצֹּבְאִים	*Militantes.*	They that war, fight.
—	הַצְּבִי	*Caprea mas,* vel potius *antelaphus.*	The roe-buck, *or rather* the antelope.
צבה	הַצְּבִי־־צְ׳	*Decus, gloria.*	The beauty, glory.
צבא	הַצְּבָיִם	*Capræ, antelaphi.*	The roes, antelopes.
יצב	הִצַּבְתָּ	*Præfecisti.*	Thou hast set over.
צבת	הַצְּבָתִים	*Manipuli, fasciculi.*	Handfuls, bundles.
יצג	הַצֵּג	*Ponere.*	To set, place.
צוד	הַצָּד	*Venatus est.*	He hunted, took in hunting.
צדא	הַצְּדָא	*Num verum?*	Is it true?
צדק	הַצַּדִּיק	*Justus, innocens.*	The just, righteous, innocent.
—	הַצְדִּיקוּ	*Justificate.*	Justify ye, pronounce just.
—	הַצַּדִּיקִים־־קִם	*Justi.*	The righteous.
—	הַצֶּדֶק־־צְדָקָה	*Justitia.*	The righteousness.
צהב	הַצָּהֹב	*Flavus.*	The yellow.
צהר	הַצָּהֳרָיִם־־רַיִם	*Meridies.*	The noon-day.
נצה	הִצּוּ	*Rixas moverunt.*	They strove, contended.
צום	הֲצוֹם	*An jejunando?*	In fasting?
—	הַצּוֹמוֹת	*Jejunia.*	The fastings.
צור	הַצּוּר	*Rupes.*	The rock.
צוד	הִצְטַיַּדְנוּ	*In viaticum sumpsimus.*	We took for *our* provision.
יצב	הִצִּיב	*Statuit.*	He set up.
—	הִצִּיבוּ	*Posuerunt.*	They set.
—	הַצִּיבִי	*Statue.*	Set thou.
יצג	הִצִּיגַנִי	*Constituit me.*	He hath made me.
צין	הַצִּיּוּן	*Monumentum.*	The monument.
נצל	הַצִּיל	*Eruere.*	To rescue, deliver.
—	הִצִּיל	*Eripuit, liberavit.*	He delivered, rescued.

ROOTS.	DERIVATIVES.	VERSIO.	SIGNIFICATION.
נצל	הַצִּילָה	*Eripe.*	Deliver thou.
—	הִצִּילוֹ	*Eripuit eum.*	He delivered him.
—	הִצִּילוּ	*Eripuerunt.*	They delivered.
—	הַצִּילוּ	*Eripite.*	Deliver ye.
—	הִצִּילָם	*Eripuit eos.*	He delivered them.
—	הִצִּילָנוּ	*Eripuit nos.*	He delivered us.
—	הַצִּילֵנוּ	*Eripe nos.*	Deliver thou us.
—	הַצִּילֵנִי	*Eripe me.*	Deliver thou me.
—	הִצִּילַנִי־־לִי	*Eripuit me.*	He delivered me.
צנק	הַצִּינֹק	*Cippus.*	The stocks.
צוף	הֵצִיף	*Exundare fecit.*	He made to overflow.
צוק	הֵצִיקָה	*Pressit, ursit.*	She pressed, urged.
—	הֱצִיקַתְהוּ	*Pressit eum.* [*me.*	She pressed, urged him.
—	הֱצִיקַתְנִי	*Arctavit, oppressit*	He straitened, oppressed me.
יצת	הִצִּית	*Accendit.*	He hath kindled.
—	הִצִּיתוּ	*Succenderunt.*	They set on fire.
צלל	הַצֵּל	*Umbra.*	The shadow.
נצל	הַצֵּל	*Eripiendo, eripe.*	In delivering, deliver thou.
צלח	הִצְלִחַ	*Prosperavit.*	He prospered.
—	הַצְּלָחַת	*Scutella.*	The dish, pan.
—	הִצְלִיחַ	*Secundavit.*	He hath prospered.
—	הַצְלִיחָה	*Secunda.*	Prosper thou, send prosperity
—	הִצְלִיחוֹ	*Secundavit eum.*	He made him to prosper.
צלל	הַצְּלָלִים	*Umbræ.*	The shadows.
	הַצְלֶלְפּוֹנִי	*Hazelelponi.*	Hazelelponi, N. W.
נצל	הִצַּלְנוּ	*Eripuimus.*	We have recovered. [ber.
צלע	הַצֵּלָע	*Costa; ala, latus.*	The rib; the wing, side-cham-
—	הַצֹּלֵעָה	*Claudicans.*	She that halteth.
—	הַצְּלָעוֹת־־עֹת	*Tabulata.*	The boards, cielings.
צלל	הַצְלָצַל	*Locusta.*	The locust.
נצל	הִצַּלְתָּ	*Eripuisti.*	Thou hast delivered.
—	הִצַּלְתִּיךָ	*Eripui te.*	I delivered thee.
—	הִצַּלְתֶּם	*Eripuistis.*	Ye have delivered.
צמא	הַצָּמֵא הַצְּמֵאָה	*Sitiens.*	The thirsty.
צמד	הַצְּמִידִים	*Armillæ.*	The bracelets.
צמח	הַצֹּמֵחַ	*Germinans.*	He that grows, sprouts.
עמת	הַצְמִיתֵם	*Excide eos.*	Cut thou them off.

ROOTS.	DERIVATIVES.	VERSIO.	SIGNIFICATION.
צמר	הַצֶּמֶר	*Lana.*	The wool.
צמת	הִצְמַתָּה	*Excidisti.*	Thou hast cut off, destroyed.
הצן			
צנן	הַצִּנָּה	*Scutum.*	A shield.
צנף	הַצָּנִיף	*Cidaris, diadema.*	The turban, mitre, diadem.
צעד	הַצְּעָדָה	*Incessus.*	The walking, marching.
צעף	הַצָּעִיף	*Velamen* vel *peplum.*	A veil or mantle.
צער	הַצָּעִיר־צְעִירָה	*Natuminor, minimus*	The younger, youngest.
צעק	הַצְּעָקָה	*Clamor.*	The cry.
—	הֲצַעֲקָתוֹ	*Num clamor ejus?*	His cry ?
צער	הַצְּעָרִים	*Parvuli.*	The little ones.
צפה	הַצֹּפֶה	*Speculans, speculator*	He that watches, the watchman
צפן	הַצָּפוֹן	*Aquilo.*	The north.
—	הַצָּפוֹנָה	*Ad aquilonem.*	To, towards the north.
—	הַצְּפוֹנִי	*Aquilonaris.*	The northern.
צפר	הַצִּפּוֹר־־פֹּר	*Avis.*	The bird.
צפה	הַצֹּפִים	*Speculatores.*	The watchmen.
צפן	הַצְפִּינוֹ	*Absconde eum.*	Hide thou him.
צפר	הַצְּפִירָה־־פִרָה	*Mane, diluculum.*	The morning.
צפה	הַצְּפִית	*Specula.*	The watch tower.
צפרדע	הַצְּפַרְדֵּעַ	*Rana.*	The frog.
—	הַצְּפַרְדְּעִים	*Ranæ.*	The frogs.
צור	הַצַּר־־צָר	*Hostis.*	The enemy.
—	הָצֵר	*Angere, affligere.*	To straiten, afflict, distress.
—	הַצֹּר	*Rupes.*	The rock.
—	הַצָּרָה	*Angustia.*	Distress.
צרע	הַצָּרוּעַ	*Leprosus.*	The leper.
צור	הַצָּרוֹת	*Angustiæ.*	The troubles.
צרה	הֲצֳרִי	*Num balsamum?*	Balm?
צרח	הַצְּרִיחַ	*Arx, turris.*	The hold, fortress, tower.
צור	הַצֻּרִים	*Rupes.* [*dentes.*	The rocks.
—	הַצָּרִים	*Aggredientes, obsi-*	They that assault, besiege.
צרע	הַצִּרְעָה	*Crabro.*	The hornet.
—	הַצָּרַעַת־־רַ֫	*Lepra.*	The leprosy.
צרף	הַצֹּרְפִי	*Conflans, aurifaber.*	The founder, smith, goldsmith
—	הַצֹּרְפִים	*Aurifabri.* [*nans.*	The goldsmiths.
צרר	הַצֹּרֵר	*Opprimens, oppug-*	He that oppresseth, opposeth.

ROOTS.	DERIVATIVES.	VERSIO.	SIGNIFICATION.
	הכ		
קאה	הַקָּאַת	*Pelicanus.*	The pelican.
קבב	הַקֻּבָּה	*Tentorium, thalamus*	The tent, the bed-chamber.
קבר	הַקְּבוּרָה	*Sepultura.*	The burial.
קבץ	הִקָּבְצוּ	*Congregate vos.*	Gather yourselves together.
קבר	הַקֶּבֶר	*Sepulchrum.*	The sepulchre.
—	הַקְּבָרִים	*Sepulchra.*	The sepulchres.
קדש	הַקָּדוֹשׁ	*Sanctus.*	The holy.
—	הַקְּדוֹשִׁים	*Sancti.*	The holy.
קדח	הַקַּדַּחַת	*Febris ardens.*	The burning ague, fever.
קדם	הַקָּדִים	*Eurus; orientalis.*	The east wind; the eastern.
—	הַקָּדִימָה	*Versus orientem.*	Toward the east.
—	הִקְדִּימֻנִי	*Prævenit me.*	He hath prevented me.
קדש	הִקְדִּישׁ	*Paravit, dicavit, consecravit, sanctificavit.*	He prepared, devoted, dedicated, consecrated, hallowed, sanctified.
—	הִקְדִּישׁוּ	*Consecraverunt.*	They dedicated.
קדם	הַקַּדְמוֹנָה	*Orientalis.*	The eastern.
—	הַקַּדְמוֹנִי	*Antiquus.*	The ancient.
קדר	הַקְּדֹרִים	*Atri, tetri.*	The black, blackish.
קדש	הַקֹּדֶשׁ	*Sanctus, sanctum; sanctitas, sanctuarium.*	The holy *person*, holy *thing*, the holiness, the sanctuary.
—	הַקָּדֵשׁ	*Cinædus.*	The sodomite.
—	הַקְדִּשׁ	*Sanctificando.*	In dedicating, sanctifying.
—	הַקְּדֵשָׁה	*Meretrix.*	The harlot.
—	הַקְּדֵשׁוֹת	*Scorta.*	The harlots.
—	הַקְּדֵשִׁים	*Catamiti.*	The sodomites.
—	הַקֳּדָשִׁים	*Sancti, sanctum sanctorum, res consecratæ.*	The holy, the holy of holies, the dedicated things.
—	הִקְדַּשְׁתִּי	*Sanctificavi.*	I hallowed, sanctified.
—	הִקְדַּשְׁתִּיךָ	*Sanctificavi te.*	I sanctified thee.
קהל	הִקְהִילוּ	*Congregarunt.*	They assembled.
—	הַקְהִילוּ	*Congregate.*	Assemble, gather ye.
—	הַקְהֵל הַקְהֵל	*Congrega.*	Gather thou together.

ROOTS.	DERIVATIVES.	VERSIO.	SIGNIFICATION.
קהל	הַקָּהָל	*Cœtus, congregatio.*	The assembly, congregation.
—	הִקְהַלְתָּ	*Congregasti.*	Thou hast gathered.
—	הַקּוֹהֶלֶת	*Concionator.*	The preacher.
קול	הַקּוֹל הַקֹּל	*Vox.*	The voice.
—	הֲקוֹלְךָ הֲקֹלְךָ	*Num vox tua?*	Thy voice?
—	הַקּוֹלֹת	*Tonitrua.*	The thunders.
קום	הַקּוֹמָה	*Statura, altitudo.*	The stature, height.
—	הַקּוֹמִים הַקָּמִים	*Insurgentes.*	They that rise up *against.*
קנה	הַקּוֹנֶה הַקֹּנֶה	*Emptor.*	The buyer.
קסם	הַקּוֹסֵם	*Divinans, divinator.*	The diviner, sooth-sayer.
	הַקּוֹץ	*Haccoz.*	Hakkoz, N. M.
קצר	הַקּוֹצֵר	*Messor.*	The harvest-man, reaper.
—	הַקּוֹצְרִים הַקֹּצְ־	*Messores.*	The reapers.
קרא	הַקּוֹרֵא הַקֹּרֵא	*Clamans, invocans.*	He that cries, calls.
קרה	הַקּוֹרָה	*Tignum.*	A beam.
קטר	הִקְטִיר	*Adolevit.*	He burnt, burnt incense.
—	הִקְטִירוּ	*Adoleverunt.*	They burnt incense.
	הַקָּטָן	*Haccatan.* [*minimus*	Hakkatan, N. M. [youngest.
קטן	הַקָּטָן הַקָּטֹן	*Parvus; natu minor,*	The little one; the younger,
—	הַקְּטַנָּה	*Minor, natu minor.*	The less, younger.
—	הַקְּטַנּוֹת־־נִּים	*Parvæ, minores.*	The small, younger.
קטף	הַקְּטַפִּים	*Parvuli, minimi.*	The small, the least.
קטר	הַקְטֵר	*Suffitus.*	The incense.
—	הַקְטֵר	*Adole.*	Burn thou.
—	הַקְּטֹרֶת	*Suffimentum.*	The incense.
קום	הֵקִים	*Statuit, erexit, excitavit, stabilivit.*	He set up, lifted up, raised up confirmed, established.
—	הָקִים הָקֵים	*Erigere, præstare.*	To set up, accomplish.
—	הֵקִים	*Erexit.*	He set up.
—	הֱקִימֵהוּ	*Constituit eum*[*eum.*	He made him.
—	הֲקִימוֹ	*Stabilire se,præstare*	That he establishes, performs.
—	הָקִימוּ	*Confirmate.* [*runt.*	Confirm, establish ye.
—	הֵקִימוּ	*Statuerunt, erexe*	They have set up.
—	הֱקִימַת הֵ־ הָ־	*Stetit, se erexit.*	She stood, raised up herself.
—	הֲקִימֹתָ	*Erexisti.*	Thou hast set up.
—	הֲקִימֹת	*Erexi.*	I have set up.
—	הֲקִימֹתִי הֲקִמֹ־	*Stabilivi, præstavi.*	I have established, performed.

ROOTS.	DERIVATIVES.	VERSIO.	SIGNIFICATION.
	הַקַּיִן	*Haccain.*	Haccain, Cain, N. P.
קין	הַקִּינָה	*Lamentatio.*	The lamentation.
—	הַקִּינוֹת	*Lamentationes.*	The lamentations.
יקף	הַקֵּיף	*Circumeundo.*	In going round.
—	הִקִּיף	*Circumdedit.*	He hath compassed.
—	הִקִּיפָה	*Circumivit.*	She has gone round about.
—	הִקִּיפוּ	*Circumdederunt.*	They compassed about.
—	הִקִּיפוּנִי	*Circumdederunt me.*	They have surrounded me.
קיץ	הַקַּיִץ	*Æstas, æstivus.* [*est.*	The summer.
—	הֵקִיץ	*Evigilavit, excitatus*	He awoke, was aroused.
—	הָקִיצָה	*Evigila.*	Awake thou.
	הָקִיצוּ	*Evigilate.*	Awake ye.
קצה	הַקִּיצוֹנָה--צֹנָה	*Extrema.*	The uttermost.
קוץ	הֱקִיצוֹתִי--צֹתִי	*Evigilavi.*	I awaked.
קיק	הַקִּיקָיוֹן	*Cucurbita.*	The gourd.
קיר	הַקִּיר	*Paries.*	The wall.
—	הַקִּירוֹת	*Parietes.*	The walls.
קלל	הָקֵל	*Leva.* [*lem reddidit.*	Lighten thou [vile, or debased
—	הֵקַל	*Leviter afflixit; vi-*	He lightly afflicted; he made
—	הַקַּל	*Levis, velox.*	The light, swift.
—	הֲקַלּוּ	*Utrum decrevissent.*	If they were abated.
—	הֵקַלּוּ	*Vilipenderunt.*	They have set light by.
קול	הַקֹּלוֹת	*Tonitrua.*	The thunders.
קלה	הַקָּלִיא	*Polenta.*	The parched *corn.*
קלל	הַקְּלָלָה	*Maledictio.*	The curse.
—	הַקְּלָלוֹת	*Maledictiones.*	The curses.
קלע	הַקֶּלַע	*Funda.*	A sling.
—	הַקַּלָּעִים	*Funditores.* [*mus.*	The slingers.
קלל	הַקְּלֹקֵל	*Levissimus, vilissi-*	Very light, mean, vile.
—	הֲקִלֹּתַנִי	*Sprevisti me.*	Ye despised me.
קום	הֻקַּם	*Constitutus est.*	He was set up, appointed.
—	הָקֵם	*Erigendo; confirma.*	In raising up; establish thou.
קום	הַקָּמָה	*Seges.*	The standing corn.
קמח	הַקֶּמַח	*Farina.*	The meal. [established him.
קום	הֲקֵמֹתוֹ	*Stabilivisti eum.*	Thou hast made him to stand,
קנא	הַקִּנְאָה	*Zelus, invidia.*	The zeal, jealousy, envy.
—	הַקְּנָאֹת	*Zelotypiæ.*	The jealousies.

ROOTS.	DERIVATIVES.	VERSIO.	SIGNIFICATION.
קנה	הַקָּנֶה	*Arundo.*	The reed.
—	הַקָּנִים	*Rami.* [*me.*	The branches.
—	הִקְנַנִי	*Pecuariam docuit*	He taught me to keep cattle.
קסם	הַקֶּסֶם	*Divinatio.*	The divination.
—	הַקֹּסְמִים	*Divini.*	The diviners.
קסת	הַקֶּסֶת	*Atramentarium.*	The ink-horn.
קער	הַקְּעָרָה	*Scutella.*	The charger.
—	הַקְּעָרֹת	*Scutellæ.*	The dishes.
יקף	הַקֵּף	*Circumeundo.*	In going about.
קפא	הַקֹּפְאִים	*Concreti.*	They that are thickened.
קצץ	הֲקֵץ	*Num finis ?*	An end ?
—	הַקֵּץ	*Finis.*	The end.
קצה	הַקָּצֶה	*Finis, extremum.*	The end, extremity.
—	הִקְצוּ	*Abraserunt.*	They scraped off.
קצב	הַקְּצוּבוֹת	*Tonsæ.*	They that are shorn.
קצר	הֲקָצוֹר	*Num abbreviando ?*	In shortening ?
קצה	הִקְצוֹת	*Abradere.*	To scrape off.
—	הַקְּצָוֹת	*Extremitates.*	The ends.
קצר	הַקָּצִיר	*Messis.*	The harvest.
קצף	הַקֶּצֶף	*Fervens ira.*	The wrath.
—	הִקְצַפְתָּ	*Ad iram provocasti.*	Thou provokedst to wrath.
—	הִקְצַפְתֶּם	*Ad iram provocastis*	Ye provoked to wrath.
קצר	הֲקָצַר	*An angustatus est ?*	Is he straitened ?
—	הִקְצַרְתָּ	*Abbreviasti.*	Thou hast shortened.
יקר	הֹקַר	*Rarum fac; subtrahe*	Make scarce; withdraw thou.
קרא	הַקְּרֻאִים־רוּ׳	*Vocati, invitati.*	They that are bidden, called,
		[*se ; offerre.*	invited. [near; to offer.
קרב	הַקְרֵב	*Accedere fac, accer-*	Cause to approach, bring thou
—	הַקָּרֵב	*Accedens.* [*mus.*	He that cometh nigh.
—	הַקָּרֹב	*Propinquus, proxi-*	The near, the next.
—	הַקֶּרֶב	*Intestinum.*	The inwards.
—	הִקְרִב	*Obtulit, admovit.*	He offered, presented, brought
—	הַקְּרֹבָה	*Propinqua.* [*eum.*	She that is nigh.
—	הִקְרִבוּהִי	*Accedere fecerunt*	They brought him near.
—	הַקְּרֹבוֹת	*Propinquæ.*	Those that are near.
—	הַקְּרֹבִים־רוֹ׳	*Propinqui.*	They that are nigh.
—	הַקְּרֵבִים	*Appropinquantes.*	They that come near.

ROOTS.	DERIVATIVES.	VERSIO.	SIGNIFICATION.
קרב	הַקָּרְבָּן	*Oblatio.*	The offering.
קרדם	הַקַּרְדֻּמּוֹת	*Secures.*	The axes.
קור	הֵקֵרָה	*Scaturire fecit.*	She caused to spring up[speed
קרה	הַקְרֵה	*Occurrere fac.*	Cause thou to meet, send good
—	הִקְרָה	*Occurrere fecit.*	He brought.
קרב	הַקְּרוֹבָה	*Propinqua.*	She that is nigh.
קרה	הַקֹּרוֹת	*Trabes.*	The beams.
קרח	הַקֶּרַח הַקָּרַח	*Gelu, glacies.*	The frost, ice, crystal.
קרא	הַקְּרִיאָה	*Prædicatio.*	The preaching.
קרב	הִקְרִיב	*Accedere fecit, obtulit, admovit.*	He brought, offered, presented.
—	הַקְרִיב	*Offerre.*	To offer.
—	הִקְרִיבָה	*Admovit, obtulit.*	She brought forth, presented.
—	הַקְרִיבֵהוּ	*Offer illud.*	Offer thou it.
—	הַקְרִיבוֹ	*Offerre eum.*	That he offers.
—	הִקְרִיבוּ	*Obtulerunt.*	They offered.
—	הִקְרִיבָם	*Obtulerunt eos.*	They offered them.
קרה	הַקִּרְיָה	*Civitas.*	The city.
קרן	הַקֶּרֶן	*Cornu.*	The horn.
—	הַקְּרָנוֹת	*Cornua.*	The horns.
קרס	הַקְּרָסִים	*Ansulæ, uncini.*	The taches, hooks, or clasps.
קרקע	הַקַּרְקַע־קָע	*Solum.*	The floor.
קרש	הַקֶּרֶשׁ־הַקָּ׳	*Tabula.*	The board.
—	הַקְּרָשִׁים	*Tabulæ.*	The boards. [fel.
קרה	הַקֹּרֹת	*Contingentia, eventa*	The things that happen, be-
קשא	הַקִּשֻּׁאִים	*Cucumeres.*	The cucumbers.
קשב	הַקְשֵׁב הַקְשִׁיבִי	*Attende.*	Attend thou, mark well.
—	הִקְשַׁבְתָּ	*Attendisti.*	Thou hast hearkened.
—	הִקְשַׁבְתִּי	*Attendi.*	I hearkened.
קשה	הַקָּשֶׁה־שָׁה	*Dura, ardua.* [vit.	The hard, stubborn, rough.
קשה	הִקְשָׁה	*Induravit, aggrava-*	He hardened, made heavy.
—	הִקְשׁוּ	*Induraverunt.*	They hardened.
—	הַקְּשָׂוֹת	*Opercula.*	The covers.
קשב	הִקְשִׁיב	*Attendit.*	He hath attended.
—	הַקְשִׁיבָה	*Attende.*	Attend thou, give heed.
—	הִקְשִׁיבוּ	*Attenderunt.*	They hearkened.
—	הַקְשִׁיבוּ	*Attendite.*	Hearken ye.

ROOTS.	DERIVATIVES.	VERSIO.	SIGNIFICATION.
קשת	הַקְּשִׁיתַ	*Duriter tractavit* [*ti*	He used hardly. [a difficulty.
קשה	הִקְשִׁיתָ	*Difficultatem objecis-*	Thou hast done hard, started
קשר	הַקֶּשֶׁר	*Conjuratio.* [*rati.*	The conspiracy.
—	הַקֹּשְׁרִים	*Conjurantes, conju-*	They that conspire.
—	הַקְּשֻׁרִים	*Firmi, compacto cor-pore præditi.*	The strong, those of a compact or strong body.
קשת	הַקֶּשֶׁת	*Arcus.*	The bow.
	הר		
הרר	הַר	*Mons.*	A mount.
	הֹר	*Hor.*	Hor, N. P.
	הָרָא	*Hara.*	Hara, N. M. [phet.
ראה	הָרֹאֶה	*Videns; propheta.*	He that sees; the seer, pro-
—	הֲרֹאֶה	*An videns?*	Seeing?
—	הֵרָאֵה	*Ostende te.*	Shew thyself.
—	הֶרְאָה	*Ostendit.*	He shewed.
—	הָרֹאוֹת־־אֹת	*Videntes.*	Those that see.
—	הֵרָאוֹת	*Videri, apparere.*	To be seen, to appear.
—	הַרְאוֹתְכָה	*Ostendere tibi.*	To shew to thee.
—	הַרְאוֹתָם	*Ostendere illis.* [*se.*	To shew to them.
—	הָרְאֻיוֹת	*Convenientes, formo-*	The meet, suitable, agreeable.
—	הָרֹאִים	*Videntes.*	They that see.
—	הַרְאִינִי	*Ostende mihi.*	Shew to me, let me see.
ראש	הֲרִאישׁוֹן	*Num primus?*	The first?
ראה	הִרְאִיתָ	*Ostendisti.*	Thou hast shewed.
—	הֲרָאִיתָ	*An vidisti?*	Hast thou seen?
—	הָרְאֵיתָ	*Ostensus est.*	He was shewed.
—	הֶרְאִיתִיךָ	*Ostendi tibi.*	I have shewed to thee.
—	הֶרְאִיתִים־־תִם	*Ostendi ipsis.*	I have shewed to them.
—	הַרְאִיתֶם	*Num vidistis?*	Have ye seen?
—	הִרְאִיתַנִי־־נוּ	*Ostendisti mihi.*	Thou hast shewed to me.
—	הֶרְאֲךָ	*Ostendit tibi.*	He shewed to thee.
—	הֶרְאָם	*Ostendit eis.*	He shewed to them.
—	הֶרְאָנוּ	*Ostendit nobis.*	He shewed to us.
—	הַרְאֵנוּ	*Ostende nobis.*	Shew thou to us.
—	הֶרְאָנִי	*Ostendit mihi.*	He shewed to me.
—	הִרְאַנִי	*Ostendit mihi.*	He hath shewed to me.

ROOTS.	DERIVATIVES	VERSIO.	SIGNIFICATION.
ראה	הַרְאֵנִי	*Ostende mihi.*	Shew thou to me.
רוש	הָרָאשׁ	*Pauper.*	The poor.
ראש	הָרֹאשׁ	*Caput, vertex, dux, princeps, agmen; primus, summus.*	The head, top, leader, chief, company; the first, principal, highest.
—	הֲרֹאשׁ	*Num caput?*	The head?
—	הָרֹאשָׁה	*Capitalis vel summus.*	The head *or* highest.
—	הָרִאשׁוֹן־־שֹׁן	*Primus, prior.*	The first, former.
—	הָרִאשׁוֹנָה־־שֹׁ׳	*Prima.*	The first.
—	הָרִאשׁוֹנִים־־שֹׁ׳	*Primi, priores, antiqui.*	The first, former, chief, elder.
—	הָרָאשִׁים	*Capita, agmina.*	The heads, companies.
—	הָרִאשֹׁנוֹת	*Primæ, priores.*	The first, former.
—	הָרִאשֹׁנִית	*Prima.*	The first.
ראה	הָרְאֵתָ	*Ostensa est tibi.*	It was shewn thee.
—	הַרְאֹתוֹ	*Ostendere eum.*	To shew him.
—	הַרְאֹתְךָ	*Ostendere tibi*	To shew to thee.
רבה	הֶרֶב הַרְבֵּה	*Multiplica; plurimum*	Multiply thou; very much.
רבב	הָרַב הָרָב	*Magnus, multus.*	The great, much, many.
—	הֲרֹב	*An multitudo?*	A, the multitude?
רוב	הֲרֹב	*An contendere?*	To contend?
רבה	הִרְבָּה	*Multiplicavit.*	He hath multiplied.
—	הַרְבָּה	*Multiplicando.*	In multiplying.
—	הַרְבֵּה	*Multiplica, accumula.*	Multiply thou, heap on.
—	הִרְבּוּ	*Multiplicarunt.*	They had many, multiplied.
—	הַרְבּוּ	*Multiplicate.*	Multiply ye.
—	הַרְבּוֹת	*Multiplicare, augendo.*	To multiply, in increasing.
—	הַרְבִּי	*Multiplica.*	Multiply thou.
רבב	הָרַבִּים	*Multi.*	The many.
רבה	הִרְבִּינוּ	*Multiplicavimus.*	We have multiplied.
רבע	הָרְבִיעִי־־בִעִי	*Quartus.*	The fourth.
—	הָרְבִיעִית־־עִת	*Quarta.*	The fourth.
רבה	הִרְבֵּית הִרְבִּיתָ	*Multiplicasti.*	Thou hast multiplied.
—	הִרְבֵּיתִי	*Multiplicavi.*	I multiplied.
—	הִרְבִּיתֶם	*Multiplicastis.*	Ye have multiplied.
רבע	הָרְבִעִית	*Quarta.*	The fourth.
רבץ	הָרֹבֵץ	*Cubans.*	He that lieth, coucheth.
רבה	הִרְבְּתָה	*Multiplicavit.*	She multiplied.

ROOTS.	DERIVATIVES.	VERSIO.	SIGNIFICATION.
הָרַג		*Occidit, interfecit.*	He slew, killed.
—	הָרֹג	*Occidendo.*	In killing.
—	הֲרֹג	*Occide.*	Slay thou.
—	הֶרֶג	*Occisio, cædes.*	Slaughter.
—	הֹרַג	*Occisus est.*	He was slain.
—	הֹרֵג	*Interficiens.*	Slaying, the slayer.
—	הֲרֵגָה	*Occisio.*	Slaughter.
—	הֲרָגוֹ	*Occidit eum.*	He slew him.
—	הָרְגוּ הָרָגוּ	*Occiderunt.*	They slew.
—	הִרְגוּ הֲרֹגוּ	*Occidite.*	Slay ye.
—	הֲרָגוּם	*Interfecerunt eos.*	They slew them.
רגז	הִרְגִּזוּ	*Provocaverunt.*	They provoked, incensed.
—	הִרְגַּזְתַּנִי	*Commovisti me.*	Thou hast disquieted me.
הרג	הֲרֻגֵי	*Occisi.*	The slain.
—	הֲרֻגֶיהָ	*Interfecti ab ea.*	Slain by her.
—	הֲרֻגָיו	*Interfecti ab eo.*	They that are slain by him.
רגז	הִרְגִּיז	*Concussit.*	He shook.
הרג	הֲרֻגִים	*Occisi.*	Slain.
—	הֹרְגִים	*Occidentes.*	Slaying.
רגע	הַרְגִּיעַ	*Quietam reddere.*	To give rest to.
—	הִרְגִּיעָה	*Quievit.*	She rested.
הרג	הֹרְגֶךָ	*Occidens te.*	He that slayeth thee.
רגל	הָרַגְלָיִם	*Pedes.*	The feet.
הרג	הֲרָגָם	*Occidit eos.*	He slew them.
—	הָרְגֵנִי	*Occide me.*	Kill thou me.
רגע	הַרְגִּעִי	*Quiesce.*	Rest thou.
רגש	הִרְגִּשׁוּ	*Convenerunt.*	They assembled.
הרג	הָרַגְתָּ־־גְתְּ	*Occidisti.*	Thou hast slain.
—	הֲרָגַתְהוּ	*Interfecit eum.*	She slew him.
—	הָרַגְתִּי	*Occidi.*	I have slain.
—	הֲרַגְתִּיךָ־־תִּיךְ	*Occidi te.*	I killed thee.
—	הֲרַגְתִּים	*Interfeci illos.*	I slew them.
—	הֲרַגְתֶּם	*Occidistis.*	Ye slew.
—	הֲרַגְתָּנִי	*Occidisti me.*	Thou killedst me.
רדד	הָרֹדֵד	*Subjiciens.* [*nantes.*	He who subdueth.
רדה	הָרֹדִים	*Præsidentes, domi-*	They that preside, bear rule.
רדף	הִרְדִּיפֻהוּ	*Persecuti sunt eum.*	They chased, pursued him.

ROOTS.	DERIVATIVES.	VERSIO.	SIGNIFICATION.
רדף	הָרֹדְפִים	*Persequentes.*	They that pursue.
הָרָה		*Concepit.*	She conceived.
—	הָרָה	*Prægnans, gravida.*	Pregnant, with child.
—	הָרֹה הוֹרֹה	*Concipere.*	To conceive.
הרר	הָרָה	*In montem.*	To the mountain.
הרה	הֹרָה	*Conceptus est.*	He was conceived.
רהב	הִרְהִבֻנִי	*Superarunt me, prævaluerunt mihi, corroborarunt me*	They have overcome me, have prevailed over me, have confirmed me.
רהט	הָרְהָטִים	*Canales.*	The canals, troughs.
הרה	הָרוֹ הֹרוֹ	*Concipiendo.*	In conceiving.
ראה	הֲרוֹאֶה	*An videns ?*	A seer ?
הרג	הֲרוּגֶיהָ	*Interfecti ejus.*	Her slain.
—	הֲרוּגִים	*Occisi.*	The slain.
רדף	הָרוֹדֵף	*Persequens.*	The pursuer.
—	הָרוֹדְפִים	*Persequentes.*	They that pursue.
רוה	הָרָוָה	*Ebria ; ebrietas.*	The drunken ; drunkenness.
—	הִרְוָה	*Irrigavit, inebriavit*	He watered, made drunk.
רוח	הָרוּחַ	*Halitus, ventus, flatus, spiritus.*	The breath, wind, blast, spirit.
—	הָרְוָחָה	*Relaxatio, respiratio, dilatatio.*	The respite, enlargement, rest
—	הָרוּחוֹת־־רֹ׳	*Spiritus, venti.*	The spirits, winds.
רוה	הִרְוֵיתִי	*Satiavi.*	I have satiated.
—	הִרְוִיתָנִי	*Satiasti me.*	Thou hast filled me.
	הָרוּם	*Harum.*	Harum, N. M.
רוה	הִרְוַנִי	*Inebriavit me.*	He hath made me drunken.
רפא	הָרוֹפֵא הָרֹ׳	*Sanans.*	He that healeth.
רצח	הָרוֹצֵחַ־־רֹ׳	*Occidens, homicida.*	He that kills, the murderer.
הרה	הָרוֹת	*Gravidæ.*	Women with child.
רחב	הִרְחִיב־־חִיב	*Dilatavit.*	He hath enlarged.
—	הַרְחֶב	*Dilata.*	Open thou wide.
—	הָרְחָבָה	*Lata, latior.*	The broad, broader.
—	הָרְחֹבוֹת	*Plateæ.*	The streets.
—	הַרְחִבִי־־חִיבִי	*Dilata.*	Enlarge thou.
—	הִרְחַבְתָּ־־תָ	*Dilatasti.*	Thou hast enlarged.
—	הָרְחוֹב	*Platea.*	The street.

ROOTS.	DERIVATIVES.	VERSIO.	SIGNIFICATION.
רחק	הָרָחוֹק	*Longinquus.*	He that is far off.
—	הַרְחוֹקִים־־חֹקִ"	*Longinqui.*	They that are far.
רחב	הַרְחִיב	*Dilatare.*	To enlarge.
—	הִרְחִיבָה	*Dilatavit.*	She hath enlarged.
—	הִרְחִיבוּ	*Dilatarunt.*	They have enlarged.
ריח	הָרֵחָיִם	*Molæ.* [*amovit.*	The mills, millstones.
רחק	הִרְחִיק	*Ablegavit, procul*	He removed, put far away.
—	הַרְחִיקֵהוּ	*Procul amove eum.*	Put thou him far away.
—	הִרְחִיקוּ	*Procul abierunt.*	They went far away.
—	הַרְחִיקָם	*Ablegare eos.*	To remove them far away.
רחל	הָרְחֵלִים	*Oves.*	The sheep. [*ture-eagle.*
רחם	הָרָחָם־־מָה	Species vulturis.	*A species of vulture or vul-*
—	הָרַחֲמִים	*Misericordiæ.*	The mercies.
רחץ	הָרַחְצָה	*Lavacrum.* [*procul.*	The washing. [afar off.
רחק	הַרְחֵק	*Ablega; recedendo;*	Put thou away; in removing;
—	הַרְחַק	*Ablega.*	Put thou away.
—	הָרְחֹקוֹת־־קֹת	*Longinquæ.*	They that are far off.
—	הִרְחַקְתָּ	*Ablegasti.*	Thou hast put far away.
—	הִרְחַקְתִּים	*Ablegavi eos.*	I have cast them far off.
הרר	הָרֵי	*Montes.*	The mountains.
—	הָרֲי־־רָי	*Montes, montes mei.*	The mountains, my mountains
ריב	הָרִיב	*Lis, causa.*	The strife, controversy.
הרר	הָרָיו	*Montes ejus.*	His mountains.
הרה	הֵרָיוֹן	*Conceptus.*	The conception.
הרר	הָרִים	*Montes.*	The hills, mountains.
רום	הֵרִים	*Extulit, tradidit.*	He lifted up, delivered, gave.
—	הֻרַים	*Allatus, ablatus est.*	He was lifted up, taken away.
—	הָרִים	*Extollere.*	To lift up; promotion.
—	הָרִימָה	*Attolle.*	Lift thou up.
—	הָרִימוּ	*Attollite.*	Lift ye up.
—	הֵרִימוּ	*Obtulerunt.*	They offered up.
—	הֲרִימוֹתָ־־תָה	*Extulisti.*	Thou hast exalted, set up.
—	הֲרִימוֹתִי־־מֹתִי	*Extuli.*	I have lifted up, exalted.
—	הָרִימִי	*Extolle.*	Lift thou up.
—	הֲרִימֹתִיךָ־־מֹתִ'	*Extuli te.*	I exalted thee.
הרה	הֵרָיוֹן	*Conceptus.*	Conception.
—	הָרִינוּ	*Concepimus.*	We have conceived.

ROOTS.	DERIVATIVES.	VERSIO.	SIGNIFICATION.
הרס	הֲרִיסֻתֵךְ	*Destructio tua.*	Thy destruction.
רוע	הֵרִיעוּ	*Clamaverunt.*	They shouted.
—	הָרִיעוּ	*Clangite.*	Shout ye.
—	הָרִיעִי	*Clange.*	Shout thou.
רוף	הֲרִיפוֹת	*Grana, tritica con-* [*tusa.*	Ground corn, wheat.
הרה	הָרִיתִי	*Concepi.*	I have conceived.
רכך	הֵרַךְ	*Emollivit.*	He made soft.
—	הָרַךְ	*Mollis.*	The soft, tender.
רכב	הָרֶכֶב־־ךָ	*Currus.*	The chariot. [ride.
—	הַרְכֵּב	*Impone, equitare fac.*	Put thou, place on, cause to
—	הִרְכַּבְתָּ	*Equitare fecisti.*	Thou hast caused to ride.
רכך	הָרַכָּה	*Tenera, delicata.*	The tender, delicate.
רכש	הָרְכוּשׁ־־כֻשׁ	*Substantia, facultas.*	The substance, property.
רכל	הָרֹכְלִים	*Aromatarii.*	The spice merchants.
הרר	הַרְכֶם	*Mons vester.*	Your mountain.
רכש	הָרֶכֶשׁ	*Jumenta.*	The working cattle.
רום	הָרֵם־־רִֽי	*Attolle.*	Lift thou up.
—	הָרָמָה	*Excelsa.*	The high.
—	הֵרֹמּוּ	*Tollite vos.*	Lift up yourselves.
	הָרִמּוֹן	*Rimmon.*	Rimmon, N. I.
רמן	הָרִמּוֹן	*Malum punicum.*	The pomegranate.
—	הָרִמּוֹנִים־־מֹנֵי	*Mala punica.*	The pomegranates.
רמח	הָרְמָחִים	*Hastæ.*	The spears.
רום	הָרָמִים	*Excelsi.*	The high.
רמך	הָרַמָּכִים	*Muli.*	The mules.
רמש	הָרֶמֶשׂ	*Reptile.*	The creeping thing.
—	הָרֹמֵשׂ	*Repens.*	He that creeps.
—	הָרֹמֶשֶׂת	*Repens.*	She that creeps.
רום	הֲרִמֹתִי	*Extuli.*	I have lifted up.
	הָרָן	*Haran.*	Haran, N. M. P.
רנן	הָרִנָּה	*Clamor.*	The cry, shouting.
ירה	הֹרָנִי	*Projecit me.*	He hath cast me.
רנן	הַרְנִינוּ	*Cantate, exultate.*	Sing, exult ye.
הָרַס		*Irrupit, perrupit, evertit, diruit, destruxit, demolivit.*	He broke in, broke through, overturned, broke down, destroyed, demolished.
—	הָרֹס	*Evertendo.*	In overthrowing, destroying.

ROOTS.	DERIVATIVES.	VERSIO.	SIGNIFICATION.
הרס	הֹרֵס	*Destruens.*	Destroying.
—	הֲרֹס	*Destrue.*	Destroy thou.
—	הָרָסוּ	*Diruerunt.*	They have thrown down.
רוע	הֵרַע	*Male fecit.*	He hath done evil.
—	הָרֵעַ	*Male facere.*	To do evil.
—	הָרָע	*Malum.*	The evil.
רעה	הָרֵעַ	*Amicus.*	The friend.
רעב	הָרָעֵב	*Famelicus.*	The hungry.
—	הָרָעָב	*Fames.* [*litia.*	The famine.
רוע	הָרָעָה	*Malus, malum, ma-*	The evil, mischief, wickedness
רעה	הָרֹעֶה	*Pascens, pastor.*	He that feeds, the shepherd.
רוע	הֵרֵעוּ	*Male fecerunt.*	They did evil.
—	הֲרֵעוֹתָ	*Male fecisti*	Thou hast done evil, ill treated
—	הָרָשָׁע	*Malæ, mala.*	The wicked.
—	הֲרֵעוֹתִי	*Male feci.*	I have done evil, injured.
—	הָרָעִים	*Mali.*	The evil, wicked.
רעה	הָרֹעִים	*Pascentes, pastores.*	They that feed, the shepherds.
רעם	הִרְעִים	*Tonavit.*	He thundered.
רעף	הַרְעִיפוּ	*Stillate.*	Distil ye, drop down.
רעל	הָרְעָלוּ	*Conquassati sunt.*	They were terribly shaken.
רעם	הַרְעִמָהּ	*Fremere facere eam*	To make her fret.
רעש	הָרַעַשׁ־ךְ	*Motus, concussio.*	The shaking, earthquake.
—	הִרְעַשְׁתָּה	*Tremere fecisti.*	Thou hast made to tremble.
—	הִרְעַשְׁתִּי	*Tremere feci.*	I made to shake.
רוע	הֲרֵעֹתָ־תָה	*Male fecisti.*	Thou hast done evil, ill treated
—	הֲרֵעֹתִי	*Male feci.*	I have done evil.
—	הֲרֵעֹתֶם	*Male fecistis.*	Ye have done evil.
רפה	הֶרֶף	*Remitte, desine.*	Let thou alone, stay, desist.
רפא	הֵרָפֵא	*Curari.*	To be healed.
—	הָרֹפְאִים	*Sanantes, medici.*	They that heal, the physicians
—	הָרְפָאִים	*Mortui.*	The dead.
	הָרָפָה	*Harapha.*	Haraphah, N. M.
רפה	הַרְפֵּה	*Remitte.*	Let thou alone.
—	הֲרָפָה	*An debilis ?*	Weak ?
—	הַרְפּוּ	*Desistite.*	Be ye still, desist.
רוף	הָרִפוֹת	*Tritica contusa.*	The ground wheat.
רצץ	הָרָצוּץ	*Fractus, contritus.*	The broken, bruised.

ROOTS.	DERIVATIVES.	VERSIO.	SIGNIFICATION.
רצח	הֲרָצַחְתָּ	*An occidisti?*	Hast thou killed.
רוץ	הָרָצִים	*Currentes, cursores.*	They that run, the runners.
—	הָרָצִין	*Currentes.*	The runners.
רצף	הָרִצְפָּה	*Pavimentum.*	The pavement.
רצץ	הָרְצֻצוֹת	*Conterentes, opprimentes.*	They that crush, oppress.
רק	הֲרַק	*An duntaxat?*	Only?
	הָרַקּוֹן	*Harakon.*	Rakkon, N. P.
רקק	הָרַקּוֹת	*Tenues.*	The thin, lean.
ריק	הָרֵקוֹת	*Vacuæ, inanes.* [cus	The empty, vain.
רקח	הָרֶקַח	*Conditura, aromati-*	The spice, spiced.
—	הָרַקָּחִים	*Unguentarii.*	The apothecaries, perfumers.
ריק	הָרֵקִים	*Vacui, vani*[*mentum*	The empty, vain.
רקע	הָרָקִיעַ	*Expansum, firma-*	The expanse, firmament.
רקם	הָרִקְמָה	*Varii colores, opus phrygionicum.*	The various colours, embroidered work.
הרר			
—	הֲרָרֵי	*Montes.*	Mountains.
—	הֲרָרִי	*Mons meus.*	My mountain.
—	הָרָרִי	*Hararita.* [*tus.*	Hararite, N. F. or P.
רשם	הָרָשׁוּם	*Exaratus, designa-*	The marked, noted.
רשע	הִרְשִׁיעַ	*Inique fecit.*	He did wickedly.
—	הָרָשָׁע	*Improbus, impius.*	The wicked.
—	הָרֶשַׁע־־ךְ	*Iniquitas, impietas.*	The iniquity, wickedness
—	הָרְשָׁעָה	*Impia.*	The wicked.
—	הָרִשְׁעָה	*Improbitas.*	The wickedness.
—	הָרְשָׁעִים	*Impii.*	The wicked, ungodly.
—	הִרְשַׁעְנוּ	*Impie egimus.*	We have done wickedly
—	הָרֶשֶׁת־־ךְ	*Rete.*	The net.
הרה	הָרַת	*Gravida, prægnans.*	Great, pregnant,
—	הָרָתָה	*Concepit.*	She conceived.
רתק	הָרַתּוֹק	*Catena.*	The chain.
ירה	הֹרֵתִיךָ	*Docui te.*	I have taught thee.
	הש		
נשא	הַשֵּׁא	*Decipere, seducere*	To deceive, seduce.
שאב	הַשֹּׁאֲבֹת	*Haurientes*	They that draw.

ROOTS.	DERIVATIVES.	VERSIO.	SIGNIFICATION.
שאט	הַשְּׁאטוֹת־־טִים	*Spernentes.*	They that despise.
שאר	הִשְׁאִיר	*Reliquit, remansit.*	He left, remained.
—	הִשְׁאִרוּ	*Reliquerunt.*	They left.
שאל	הַשְּׁאֵלָה	*Petitio; precaria; consecratio, fœnus.*	The petition; obtained by intreaty; the consecration, loan
—	הַשֹּׁאֲלִים	*Petentes.*	They that ask.
—	הֲשָׁאַלְתִּי	*An petivi?*	Did I desire?
—	הִשְׁאִלְתִּיהוּ	*Petere feci eum, devovi, reddidi, commodavi.*	I have made him supplicate, have devoted, restored, lent him.
שאן	הַשַּׁאֲנַנִּם	*Tranquilli, securi.*	They that are at ease, secure.
שאף	הַשֹּׁאֲפִים	*Anhelantes, absorbentes.*	They that pant, swallow up.
שאר	הַשְּׁאֵרִית	*Residuum.*	The remnant, residue.
—	הִשְׁאַרְנוּ	*Reliquimus.*	We left.
שאה	הַשֵּׁאת	*Desolatio.*	The desolation.
נשא	הִשֵּׁאתָ	*Decepisti.*	Thou hast deceived.
שוב	הַשָּׁב	*Repositus.*	He that is returned, replaced.
—	הָשֵׁב־־שִׁי	*Restitue, reduc; reducendo, reddere.*	Restore thou, bring back; in bringing back, to return.
—	הַשָּׁבָה	*Quæ reversa est.*	She that came back.
—	הֲשִׁבֵהוּ	*Reduc eum.*	Bring thou him back.
—	הֵשִׁבוּ	*Reduxerunt.*	They brought back, returned.
שבע	הַשָּׁבוּעַ	*Hebdomada.*	The week.
—	הַשְּׁבוּעָה־בֻעָה	*Juramentum.*	The oath.
שבט	הַשֵּׁבֶט	*Tribus.*	The tribe.
—	הַשָּׁבֶט	*Virga.*	The rod.
—	הַשְּׁבָטִים	*Tribus.*	The tribes.
שבה	הַשְּׁבִי־־שֶׁי	*Captivitas.*	The captivity.
—	הַשִּׁבְיָה	*Captivitas.*	The captivity.
שוב	הַשָּׁבִים	*Revertentes.*	They that come again.
שבע	הִשְׁבִּיעַ	*Adjuravit.*	He charged with an oath
—	הִשְׂבִּיעַ	*Satiavit.*	He satisfied.
—	הִשְׁבִּיעוֹ	*Adjuravit eum.*	He made him swear.
—	הַשְּׁבִיעִי־־בְעִי	*Septimus.*	The seventh.
—	הַשְּׁבִיעִית־־בְעִי	*Septima.*	The seventh.
—	הִשְׁבִּיעֶךָ	*Adjuravit te.*	He made thee swear.

ROOTS.	DERIVATIVES.	VERSIO.	SIGNIFICATION.
שבע	הִשְׁבִּיעַנִי	*Adjuravit me.*	He made me swear.
—	הִשְׂבִּיעַנִי	*Saturavit me.*	He hath filled me.
שבת	הִשְׁבִּית	*Cessare fecit.*	He caused to cease.
—	הַשְׁבִּיתוּ	*Cessare facite.*	Cause ye to cease.
שבך	הַשְּׂבָכָה	*Reticulum, cancel-* [*lum.*	The net work, lattice.
—	הַשְּׂבָכוֹת	*Reticula.*	The net works.
שבל	הַשִּׁבֳּלִים	*Spicæ.*	The ears of corn.
שבע	הַשָּׂבָע	*Saturitas, abundan-* [*tia.*	The plenty, abundance.
—	הִשָּׁבֵעַ	*Adjurando.*	In swearing, adjuring.
—	הַשְּׁבִעִי	*Septimus.*	The seventh.
—	הִשָּׁבַע	*Jurando.*	In swearing.
—	הַשִּׁבְעָה	*Septem.*	The seven.
—	הִשָּׁבְעָה	*Jura.*	Swear thou.
—	הִשָּׁבְעוּ	*Jurate.*	Swear ye.
—	הַשָּׁבֻעוֹת־־עִים	*Hebdomadæ.*	The weeks.
—	הִשְׂבַּעְתָּ	*Satiasti.*	Thou filledst.
—	הִשְׁבַּעְתִּי	*Adjuravi.*	I charged, adjured
—	הִשְׁבַּעְתִּיךָ	*Adjuravi te.*	I made thee to swear.
—	הִשְׁבַּעְתָּנוּ	*Adjurasti nos.*	Thou madest us to swear.
שבץ	הַשָּׁבָץ	*Angustia; lorica.*	The anguish; the coat of mail
שבר	הַשֶּׁבֶר	*Annona.*	The corn.
—	הָשְׁבַּרְתִּי	*Confractus sum.*	I am bruised, broken, crushed
ישב	הַשֶּׁבֶת	*Sedere; sessio.*	To sit; the sitting.
שבת	הִשְׁבַּתָּ	*Cessare fecisti.*	Thou hast made to cease.
—	הַשַּׁבָּת	*Sabbatum.*	The sabbath.
—	הַשַּׁבָּתוֹת	*Sabbata,*	The sabbaths.
—	הִשְׁבַּתִּי	*Cessare feci.*	I have made to cease.
שוב	הֲשֵׁבֹתֶם	*Reddidistis.*	Ye returned, restored.
נשג	הַשֵּׂג	*Assequendo.*	In overtaking.
שגג	הַשֹּׁגֶגֶת	*Errans.*	He that errs, sins ignorantly.
שגה	הִשְׂגּוּ	*Auxerunt.*	They increased.
שגח	הִשְׁגִּיחַ	*Prospexit.*	He looked.
שגה	הַשֹּׁגִים	*Errantes.*	They that err.
שדד	הַשֹּׁד	*Vastitas.*	The desolation.
—	הַשֹּׁדֵד	*Vastans, vastator.*	He that spoils, the spoiler.
שדה	הַשָּׂדֶה	*Ager.*	The field.
שדד	הַשְּׁדוּדָה	*Vastata.*	She that is destroyed.

ROOTS.	DERIVATIVES.	VERSIO.	SIGNIFICATION.
שדר	הַשְּׂדֵרוֹת	*Ordines.*	The ranges, rows.
שדה	הַשָּׂדֹת	*Agri.*	The fields.
נשה	הִשָּׁהּ	*Privavit eam.*	He deprived her.
שה	הַשֶּׂה	*Agnus.*	The lamb.
שהם	הַשֹּׁהַם	*Onyx.*	The onyx.
שהר	הַשַּׂהֲרֹנִים	*Lunulæ*, ornamenta.	The little moons.
שוא	הַשָּׁוְא	*Vanitas, mendacium*	The vanity, falsehood.
שוב	הַשּׁוֹבֵבָה	*Aversa, rebellis.*	The backsliding, rebellious.
שדד	הַשּׁוֹדְדִים	*Vastatores.*	The spoilers.
שטף	הַשּׁוֹטֵף	*Inundans.*	The overflowing.
שטר	הַשּׁוֹטֵר	*Præfectus.*	The ruler, officer.
שום	הַשּׁוּמִים	*Allia.* [*des.*	The garlic.
שמר	הַשּׁוֹמְרִים־־שֹׁ׳	*Speculatores, custo-*	The spies, watchmen, keepers.
שער	הַשּׁוֹעֵר־־שֹׁ׳	*Janitor.*	The porter.
——	הַשּׁוֹעֲרִים־־שֹׁ׳	*Janitores.*	The porters.
שפט	הַשּׁוֹפֵט־־שֹׁ׳	*Judex.*	The judge.
שפר	הַשּׁוֹפָר	*Tuba.*	The trumpet.
——	הַשּׁוֹפָרוֹת	*Tubæ.*	The trumpets.
שוק	הַשּׁוֹק	*Armus.*	The shoulder.
שור	הַשּׁוֹר	*Bos.*	The ox.
שחח	הֵשַׁח	*Prostravit, dejecit.*	He brought down, cast down.
שחד	הַשֹּׁחַד	*Munus.*	The gift.
שחה	הַשֹּׂחֶה	*Natans.*	He that swimmeth.
שחט	הַשְּׁחוּטָה־חֻטָה	*Mactata.*	The slain.
שחן	הַשְּׁחִין	*Ulcus.*	The boil, ulcer.
שחת	הִשְׁחִית	*Corrupit.*	He corrupted.
——	הַשְׁחִית	*Perdere.* [*derunt.*	To destroy.
——	הִשְׁחִיתוּ	*Corruperunt, perdi*	They corrupted, destroyed.
——	הַשְׁחִיתֶךָ	*Perdere te.*	To destroy thee.
——	הַשְׁחִיתָם	*Disperdere eos.*	To destroy them.
שחף	הַשָּׁחַף	*Larus.*	The sea-mew or gull.
——	הַשַּׁחֶפֶת	*Tabes.*	The consumption.
שחק	הַשְּׂחֹק	*Risus.*	The laughter.
שחר	הַשַּׁחַר־־שָׁ׳	*Aurora.*	The morning.
——	הַשְּׁחֹרִים	*Nigri.* [*corruptio.*	The black.
שחת	הַשָּׁחַת	*Fovea, sepulchrum,*	The pit, grave, corruption.
——	הַשְׁחֵת	*Corrumpendo.*	In corrupting.

ROOTS.	DERIVATIVES.	VERSIO.	SIGNIFICATION.
שוט	הַשָּׁטִים	*Remiges.*	The rowers.
שטף	הַשֶּׁטֶף	*Inundatio.*	The flood, inundation.
שטר	הַשֹּׁטְרִים	*Præfecti.*	The officers.
נשא	הִשִּׁיא	*Decepit.*	He hath deceived.
—	הִשִּׁיאוּךָ	*Deceperunt te.*	They have deceived thee.
—	הִשִּׁיאֶךָ	*Decepit te.*	He hath deceived thee.
—	הִשִּׁיאַנִי	*Seduxit me.*	She beguiled, deceived me.
שוב	הָשִׁיב	*Restitue.*	Restore thou.
—	הָשִׁיב	*Reddere, revocare.*	To restore; to recal.
—	הֵשִׁיב	*Reddidit, restituit, reduxit, remisit, recuperavit.*	He rendered, restored, brought back, sent back, recovered.
—	הָשִׁיבָה	*Restitue, reduc.*	Restore thou, bring back.
—	הֱשִׁיבוֹ	*Reduxit eum.*	He brought him back.
—	הֵשִׁיבוּ	*Reddiderunt.*	They returned, restored.
—	הָשִׁיבוּ	*Restituite.*	Restore ye.
—	הֹשִׁיבוּ	*Duxerunt.*	They took, married.
—	הֱשִׁיבוֹתָ	*Avertisti.*	Thou hast turned.
—	הֲשִׁיבֵנוּ	*Reduc, converte nos.*	Turn thou us again.
—	הֱשִׁיבֹנוּ	*Retulimus.*	We brought again.
—	הֱשִׁיבַנִי	*Reduxit me,*	He hath turned me.
—	הֲשִׁיבֵנִי	*Responde mihi.*	Answer thou me.
נשג	הִשִּׂיגָה	*Adepta est.*	She attained, obtained.
—	הִשִּׂיגוּ	*Attigerunt, prehenderunt.*	They attained, took hold of.
—	הִשִּׂיגוּהָ	*Assecuti sunt eam.*	They overtook her.
—	הִשִּׂיגוּנִי	*Assecuti sunt me.*	They have taken hold upon me.
שיח	הַשִּׂיחִם	*Arbusta.*	The shrubs.
שום	הָשִׂימִי	*Pone me.*	Place thou me.
שוק	הֵשִׁיקוּ	*Redundarunt.*	They overflowed.
שור	הַשִּׁיר	*Canticum, musica.*	The song, musick,
—	הַשִּׁירָה	*Canticum.*	The song.
—	הֵשִׂירוּ	*Principes constituerunt.*	They have made princes.
—	הַשִּׁירִים	*Cantica.*	The songs.
שכב	הַשֹּׁכֵב	*Cubans.*	He that lies down.
—	הַשְׁכֵּב	*Cubare faciendo.*	In making to lie down.
—	הַשֹּׁכְבִים	*Cubantes, jacentes.*	They that lie down.
שכן	הַשֹּׁכוֹנֵי	*Habitantes.*	They that dwell.

ROOTS.	DERIVATIVES.	VERSIO.	SIGNIFICATION.
שכח	הֲשָׁכַח	*An oblitus est?*	Hath he forgotten?
—	הַשְּׁכֵחִים	*Obliviscentes.*	They that forget.
—	הַשְׁכַּחְנָא	*Invenimus.*	We have found.
—	הַשְׁכַּחַת	*Inveni.*	I have found.
—	הֲשְׁכַחְתֶּם	*Num obliti estis?*	Have ye forgotten?
שכב	הִשְׁכִּיבָה	*Collocavit.*	She laid, placed.
שכל	הִשְׂכִּיל	*Intelligere fecit.*	He made *me* understand.
—	הַשְׂכִּילוּ	*Intelligite.*	Understand ye, be wise.
—	הִשְׂכִּילוּ	*Intellexerunt.*	They understood, considered.
שכם	הַשְׁכֵּם־־כֵּם	*Mane surge, surgere*	Rise thou, to rise early.
—	הִשְׁכִּימוּ	*Mane surrexerunt.*	They rose early.
שכר	הַשְּׂכִירָה	*Mercenaria.*	She that is hired.
—	הַשְׁכִּירֻהוּ	*Inebriate illum.*	Make ye him drunken.
שכל	הַשְׂכֵּל	*Intelligere; intelligentia.*	To understand; the understanding.
—	הִשְׂכַּלְתִּי	*Intellexi.*	I have understood.
שכן	הַשֹּׁכֵן	*Habitans, commorans.*	He that dwells, abides.
—	הַשְּׁכֵנוֹת	*Vicinæ.*	The neighbours.
—	הַשֹּׁכְנִים	*Habitantes.*	They that dwell.
שכר	הַשֵּׁכָר	*Sicera.*	The strong drink.
שלה	הַשַּׁל	*Error, imprudentia.*	The error, imprudence.
שלב	הַשְּׁלַבִּים	*Projecturæ, scalæ.*	The ledges, stairs, steps.
שלג	הַשָּׁלֶג	*Nivis.*	The snow.
שלו	הַשְּׂלָו	*Coturnix.*	The quail.
שלם	הֲשָׁלוֹם	*Num pax?*	Is peace? is it well?
—	הַשָּׁלוֹם	*Pax.*	The peace, prosperity.
שלש	הַשְּׁלוֹשָׁה־לֹשָׁה	*Tres.*	The three.
—	הַשְּׁלוֹשִׁים־־לֹשִׁ׳	*Triginta.*	The thirty.
—	הַשָּׁלִושִׁים־לִשִׁ׳	*Tribuni, duces.*	The captains, leaders.
שלח	וְהַשֶּׁלַח הַשָּׁלַח	*Missile.*	The dart, javelin.
—	הַשֹּׁלֵחַ	*Mittens.*	He that sends.
—	הַשֻּׁלְחָן	*Mensa.*	The table.
—	הַשֻּׁלְחָנוֹת	*Mensæ.*	The tables.
שלט	הַשְּׁלָטִים	*Scuta.*	The shields.
—	הַשַּׁלִּיט	*Præfectus.*	The ruler, governor.
שלך	הִשְׁלִיךְ	*Jecit, dejecit, projecit.*	He cast, cast down, cast forth.
—	הִשְׁלִיכָה	*Conjecit.*	She cast.

ROOTS.	DERIVATIVES.	VERSIO.	SIGNIFICATION.
שלך	הִשְׁלִיכֻהוּ	*Projice eum.* [*runt.*	Cast thou him.
—	הִשְׁלִיכוּ	*Ejecerunt, abjece-*	They have cast out, cast away.
—	הַשְׁלִיכוּ	*Abjicite.*	Cast ye away.
—	הִשְׁלִיכָם	*Ejecit eos.*	He cast them out.
שלם	הִשְׁלִימָה	*Pacem fecit.*	She hath made peace.
—	הִשְׁלִימוּ	*Pacem fecerunt.*	They have made peace.
שלש	הַשָּׁלִישׁ	*Tribunus, dux.*	The captain, leader.
—	הַשְּׁלִישִׁי	*Tertius.*	The third.
—	הַשְּׁלִישִׁית--שִׁת	*Tertia* pars.	The third *part.*
שלך	הַשְׁלֵךְ	*Jace.*	Cast thou.
—	הַשָּׁלָךְ	*Mergus;* secund. alios *catarractes.*	The cormorant; *according to others,* the catarract, or plungeon.
—	הָשְׁלְכָה	*Dejecta est.*	She was cast down.
—	הַשְׁלִכֵהוּ	*Projice eum.*	Cast thou him.
—	הַשְׁלִכוֹ	*Ejicere eum.*	To cast him out.
—	הִשְׁלִכוֹ	*Ejecit eum.*	He cast him out.
—	הִשְׁלַכְתָּ	*Projecisti.*	Thou threwest.
—	הָשְׁלַכְתָּ	*Projectus es.*	Thou art cast.
—	הָשְׁלַכְתִּי	*Projectus sum.*	I was cast.
—	הִשְׁלַכְתִּי	*Projeci.*	I have cast out.
—	הִשְׁלַכְתִּיךָ	*Projeci te.*	I will cast thee.
שלל	הַשָּׁלָל	*Spolium, præda.*	The spoil, prey.
—	הַשֹּׁלְלִים	*Deprædantes.*	They that spoil.
שלם	הַשִּׁלֻּם	*Retributio.*	The recompence.
—	הַשְׁלֵם	*Repone.*	Replace thou.
—	הָשְׁלְמָה	*Pacata fuit.*	She was at peace.
—	הַשְּׁלָמִים	*Sacrificia salutaria vel pacifica.*	The peace-offerings.
שלש	הַשָּׁלֹשׁ הַשְּׁלֹשִׁי	*Tres.*	The three.
—	הַשְּׁלִשִׁי--שִׁים	*Tertius.*	The third.
—	הַשְּׁלֹשִׁים	*Triginta.*	The thirty.
—	הַשְּׁלִשִׁית	*Tertia.*	The third.
	הָשֵׁם	*Hasem.*	Hashem, N. M.
שום	הַשָּׂם	*Ponens.*	He that puts.
שם	הַשֵּׁם	*Nomen.*	The name.
שמל	הַשְּׂמֹאול--מאל	*Sinistra.*	The left.

ROOTS.	DERIVATIVES.	VERSIO.	SIGNIFICATION.
שמל	הַשְּׂמָאלִי	*Sinister.*	The left.
—	הַשְּׂמָאלִית	*Sinistra.*	The left.
שמד	הַשְׁמֵד	*Disperdendo.* [re.	In destroying.
—	הַשְׁמֵד	*Disperde; disperde-*	Destroy thou; to destroy.
—	הִשְׁמְדוֹ--מִדוֹ	*Disperdidit eum.*	He destroyed him.
—	הִשָּׁמְדְךָ--מֶדְךָ	*Disperdi te.*	That thou be destroyed.
—	הִשָּׁמֶדְךָ	*Disperdi te.*	That thou be destroyed.
—	הִשָּׁמְדָם	*Disperdi eos.*	That they be destroyed.
—	הַשְׁמִדָם	*Disperdere eos.*	To destroy them.
—	הִשְׁמַדְתִּי	*Disperdidi.*	I destroyed.
שום	הַשָּׂמָה	*Posuit, fecit.*	She hath placed, made.
שמם	הָשַּׁמָּה	*Desolari eam.*	That she is desolate.
—	הֵשַׁמּוּ	*Vastaverunt.*	They laid waste.
שמע	הַשְּׁמוּעָה	*Fama, rumor.*	The fame, rumour, tidings.
שמם	הֲשִׁמּוֹתָ	*Desolasti.*	Thou hast made desolate.
שמח	הַשִּׂמְחָה	*Lætitia.*	The joy.
—	הַשְּׂמֵחִים	*Lætantes.*	They that rejoice.
—	הִשְׂמַחְתָּ	*Lætificasti.*	Thou hast made to rejoice.
שמד	הִשְׁמִיד	*Disperdidit.*	He destroyed.
—	הַשְׁמִיד	*Disperdere eum.*	That he destroys.
—	הִשְׁמִידוּ	*Disperdiderunt.*	They did destroy.
—	הֶשְׁמִידוּם	*Deleverunt eos.*	They destroyed them.
—	הַשְׁמִידָם	*Disperdere eos.*	To destroy them.
—	הִשְׁמִידָם	*Disperdiderunt eos.*	They destroyed them.
שמל	הַשְׂמִילִי	*Sinistram pete.*	Take thou the left.
שם	הַשָּׁמַיִם--מָיִם	*Cælum, cæli.*	The heaven, heavens.
—	הַשָּׁמַיְמָה--מַי	*Ad cælum.*	Towards the heaven.
שמן	הַשְּׁמִינִי	*Octavus.*	The eighth.
—	הַשְּׁמִינִית--נִת	*Octava.*	The eighth. [claimed
שמע	הִשְׁמִיעַ	*Audire fecit.*	He made to be heard, pro-
—	הִשְׁמִיעוּ	*Audiri fecerunt.*	They caused to be heard.
—	הַשְׁמִיעוּ	*Audiri facite.*	Publish ye.
—	הִשְׁמִיעֲךָ	*Audire fecit te.*	He made thee to hear.
—	הִשְׁמִיעָנוּ	*Audire fecit nos.*	He made us to hear.
—	הַשְׁמִיעֻנוּ	*Audire facite nos.*	Declare ye to us.
—	הַשְׁמִיעֵנִי--עֵנִי	*Audire fac me.*	Cause thou me to hear.
שמל	הַשִּׂמְלָה	*Vestimentum.*	The garment.

ROOTS.	DERIVATIVES.	VERSIO.	SIGNIFICATION.
שמם	הַשְׁמֵם	*Desolando.*	In making desolate.
—	הַשֹּׁמֵם	*Desolatus.*	The desolate.
—	הַשֹּׁמֵמוֹת	*Desolatæ.*	The desolate.
שמן	הַשֶּׁמֶן הַשָּׁמֶן	*Oleum, unguentum.*	The oil, ointment·
—	הַשְׁמֵן	*Impingua.*	Make thou fat.
—	הַשְּׁמֵנָה	*Num pinguis?*	The fat?
שמע	הַשֹּׁמֵעַ	*Audiens.*	He that hears.
—	הֲשָׁמַע	*Num audivit?*	Has he heard?
—	הַשְּׁמֻעָה	*Fama, rumor.*	The report.
—	הַשֹּׁמְעִים	*Audientes.*	They that hear.
—	הִשְׁמַעְתָּ	*Audiri fecisti.*	Thou didst cause to be heard.
—	הִשְׁמַעְתִּיךָ	*Audire feci te.*	I have told thee.
שמר	הַשֹּׁמֵר	*Servans.*	He that keeps.
—	הֲשֹׁמֵר	*Num custos?*	The keeper?
—	הִשָּׁמֶר־־מֶר	*Cave.*	Beware thou.
—	הִשָּׁמְרוּ־־מְ׳	*Cavete.*	Beware ye.
—	הֲשֹׁמְרִים	*Num custodientes?*	Do they keep?
שמש	הַשֶּׁמֶשׁ־־שֶׁ׳	*Sol.*	The sun.
שום	הֲשַׂמְתָּ	*Num posuisti?*	Hast thou placed, set?
שן	הַשֵּׁן	*Dens, scopulus.*	The tooth, rock, crag.
שנא	הַשִּׂנְאָה	*Odium.*	The hatred.
שנה	הַשָּׁנָה	*Annus.*	The year.
שנא	הַשְּׂנוּאָה	*Exosa.*	The hated.
שנה	הִשָּׁנוֹת	*Iterari.* [*cineum.*	To be repeated, doubled.
—	הַשָּׁנִי	*Coccus, filum coc-*	The scarlet, scarlet thread.
—	הַשֵּׁנִי	*Secundus, alter.*	The second, other.
—	הַשָּׁנִים	*Anni.*	The years.
—	הַשְּׁנַיִם־־נַיִם	*Duo.*	The two.
שן	הַשִּׁנַּיִם	*Dentes.*	The teeth.
שנה	הַשֵּׁנִית	*Secunda, altera.*	The second, other.
שסע	הַשְּׁסוּעָה	*Fissa, divisa.*	The clov.n, divided.
שעה	הָשַׁע	*Claude, desiste.*	Shut, close, desist thou.
שער	הַשָּׂעִיר	*Hircus.*	The goat.
—	הַשְּׂעִרִם	*Hirci.*	The goats.
—	הַשַּׁעַר־הַשּׁ׳	*Porta, janua.*	The gate.
—	הַשַּׁעְרָה הַשֹּׁעֵר׳	*Ad portam.*	At the gate.
—	הַשַּׂעֲרָה.	*Ad pilum.*	At an hair.

ROOTS.	DERIVATIVES.	VERSIO.	SIGNIFICATION.
שער	הַשְּׂעֹרָה	*Hordeum.*	The barley.
—	הַשְּׁעָרִים	*Portæ.*	The gates.
—	הַשְּׂעֹרִים	*Hordea.* [*pes.*	The barley.
—	הַשֹּׁעָרִים	*Fœtidæ, acerbæ, tur-*	The filthy, nauseous, vile.
שפך	הַשָּׁפוּךְ	*Effusus.*	The shed, poured out.
שפח	הַשִּׁפְחָה	*Ancilla.*	The maid-servant.
—	הַשְּׁפָחוֹת	*Ancillæ.*	The handmaids.
שפט	הֲשֹׁפֵט	*Num judex?*	The judge?
—	הַשֹּׁפְטִים	*Judices.*	The judges.
שפל	הִשְׁפִּיל	*Depressit.*	He laid low.
—	הַשְׁפִּיל	*Deprimere.*	To abase.
—	הִשְׁפִּילוּ	*Depresserunt.*	They have cast down.
—	הַשְׁפִּילוּ	*Deprimite.*	Abase ye.
שפך	הִשָּׁפֵךְ	*Effundi.*	To be poured out.
—	הַשֹּׁפְכִים	*Effundentes.*	They that shed, pour out.
שפל	הַשָּׁפָלָה	*Depressus.*	He that is brought low.
—	הַשְּׁפֵלָה	*Vallis, planities.*	The valley, plain.
—	הִשְׁפַּלְתָּ	*Depressisti.*	Thou hast humbled.
—	הִשְׁפַּלְתִּי	*Dejeci.*	I have brought down.
שפן	הַשָּׁפָן	*Cuniculus.*	The cony.
שק	הַשַּׂק	*Saccus.*	The sackcloth.
שקד	הַשָּׁקֵד	*Amygdalus.*	The almond-tree.
שקה	הַשְׁקֵהוּ	*Bibere fac illum.*	Cause thou him to drink.
—	הַשְׁקוּ	*Adaquate.*	Water ye.
שקץ	הַשִּׁקּוּץ	*Abominatio.*	The abomination.
—	הַשִּׁקּוּצִים	*Abominationes.*	The abominations.
שקט	הַשְׁקֵט	*Quiescere; quies.*	To rest; the quietness.
—	הַשֹּׁקְטִים	*Quiescentes.*	They that are at rest.
שוק	הַשֹּׁקַיִם	*Crura.*	The legs.
שקה	הַשְׁקִינִי	*Bibendum da mihi.*	Do thou let me drink.
שקף	הִשְׁקִיף	*Prospexit.*	He looked down.
—	הַשְׁקִיפָה	*Prospice.*	Look thou down.
שקה	הִשְׁקִיתָנוּ	*Bibere fecisti nos.*	Thou hast made us to drink.
שקל	הַשֶּׁקֶל-הַשָּׁ'	*Siclus.*	The shekel.
שקץ	הַשִּׁקֻּצִים	*Abominationes.*	The abominations.
שקר	הַשֶּׁקֶר-הַשָּׁ'	*Mendacium.*	The lie, falsehood.
שקה	הַשֹּׁקֶת	*Canalis.*	The trough.

ROOTS.	DERIVATIVES.	VERSIO.	SIGNIFICATION.
שקה	הַשְׁקָתָה	*Bibere fecit.*	She made to drink.
שור	הַשָּׂר הַשַּׂר	*Princeps, dux.*	The chief, captain.
שרב	הַשָּׁרָב	*Locus torridus.*	The parched ground.
שרבט	הַשַּׁרְבִיט	*Sceptrum.*	The sceptre.
שרג	הַשָּׂרִגִים	*Palmites.*	The branches.
שרד	הַשְּׂרָד	*Ministerium.*	The service.
שרה	הַשִּׁרְיוֹן־־יָן	*Lorica.*	The coat of mail.
שור	הַשָּׁרִים	*Canentes.*	They that sing.
—	הַשָּׂרִים	*Duces, principes.*	The captains, chiefs.
שדם	הַשְּׁדֵמוֹת	*Agri.* [*um.*	The fields.
שרף	הַשְּׂרֵפָה	*Combustio, incendi-*	The burning, the fire.
—	הַשְּׂרֻפִים	*Combusti.*	They that were burnt.
—	הַשְּׂרָפִים	*Comburentes.*	The burning, fiery.
שרץ	הַשֹּׁרֵץ	*Reptans.*	He that creeps.
—	הַשֶּׁרֶץ הַשֶּׁ׳	*Reptile.*	The reptile, creeping thing.
—	הַשֹּׁרֶצֶת	*Repens.*	She that creepeth.
שרת	הַשָּׁרֵת	*Ministerium.*	The ministry, service.
שש	הַשֵּׁשׁ	*Byssus.*	The fine linen.
—	הַשִּׁשָּׁה	*Sex.*	The six.
—	הַשִּׁשִּׁי	*Sextus.*	The sixth.
—	הַשִּׁשִּׁית	*Sexta.*	The sixth.
שות	הַשָּׁתוֹת	*Fundamenta.*	The foundations.
שחה	הִשְׁתַּחֲווּ	*Incurvarunt se; incurvate vos.*	They have worshipped; worship ye, bow ye down.
—	הִשְׁתַּחֲוֵיתִי	*Incurvavi me.*	I have bowed myself down.
שתה	הַשְּׁתִי	*Stamen.*	The warp.
—	הַשֹּׁתִים	*Bibentes.*	They that drink.
שכח	הִשְׁתְּכַח	*Inventus est.*	He was found.
—	הִשְׁתְּכַחַת	*Inventa est.*	She was found.
שעה	הִשְׁתַּעַשְׁעוּ	*Respicite.* [*tando.*	Look ye about.
שרר	הִשְׂתָּרֵר	*Principatum affec-*	In making *thyself* a prince.

הת

ROOTS.	DERIVATIVES.	VERSIO.	SIGNIFICATION.
תא	הַתָּא	*Conclave.*	The chamber.
אבל	הִתְאַבֵּל	*Luxit.*	He mourned.
—	הִתְאַבְּלִי	*Luge.*	Mourn thou.
אוה	הִתְאַוָּה	*Concupivit.*	He coveted.

ROOTS.	DERIVATIVES.	VERSIO.	SIGNIFICATION.
אוה	הִתְאַוּוּ	*Concupiverunt.*	They lusted, desired.
—	הִתְאַוֵּיתִי	*Desideravi.*	I have desired.
תא	הַתָּאוֹת	*Conclavia.*	The chambers.
אזר	הִתְאַזָּר	*Accinxit se.*	He hath girded himself.
—	הִתְאַזְּרוּ	*Accingite vos.*	Gird yourselves.
אחד	הִתְאַחֲדִי	*Unito te.*	Unite thyself.
תא	הַתָּאִים	*Conclavia.*	The chambers.
אמן	הֲתַאֲמִין	*Num credes ?*	Wilt thou believe.
אמץ	הִתְאַמֵּץ	*Confirmavit se.*	He strengthened himself.
תאן	הַתְּאֵנָה	*Ficus.*	The fig-tree.
—	הַתְּאֵנִים	*Ficus.*	The figs.
אנף	הִתְאַנַּף	*Iratus est.*	He was angry. [selves ?
אפק	הֲתְאַפְּקוּ	*Continuerunt se ?*	Have they restrained them-
באש	הִתְבָּאֲשׁוּ	*Exosos se fecerunt.*	They made themselves odious
תבה	הַתֵּבָה	*Arca.*	The ark.
בוא	הֲתָבוֹא	*Num veniet ?*	Shall he come ?
—	הַתְּבוּאָה	*Proventus.*	The produce, fruit.
בון	הַתְּבוּנָה	*Intelligentia.*	The understanding.
—	הִתְבּוֹנָן	*Animadvertit.*	He considered.
—	הִתְבּוֹנְנוּ	*Animadverterunt.*	They considered.
—	הִתְבּוֹנְנוּ	*Animadvertite.*	Consider ye.
בטח	הֲתִבְטַח	*Num confides ?*	Wilt thou trust ?
תבן	הַתֶּבֶן	*Stramen, palea.*	The straw, stubble.
בנה	הַתַּבְנִית	*Forma, exemplar.*	The form, pattern. [ed.
בון	הִתְבּוֹנַנְתָּ	*Intellexisti.*	Thou hast understood, perceiv-
בקע	הִתְבַּקָּעוּ	*Scissi sunt.*	They are rent, divided.
גזר	הִתְגְּזֶרֶת	*Excisus est.*	He was cut out of.
גלל	הִתְגַּלְגְּלוּ	*Volverunt se.*	They rolled themselves.
גלח	הִתְגַּלְּחוֹ	*Radi eum.*	That he is shaven.
גלע	הִתְגַּלַּע	*Immisceri.*	To be meddled with.
גרה	הִתְגָּרִית	*Contendisti.*	Thou hast contended.
ידע	הֲתֵדַע	*Num cognosces ?*	Wilt thou know ?
תהה	הַתֹּהוּ	*Inanitas.*	The vanity, emptiness.
הלך	הִתְהַלֵּךְ	*Ambulavit.*	He walked.
—	הִתְהַלֵּךְ	*Ambula* [*bulate.*	Walk thou.
—	הִתְהַלְּכוּ	*Ambulaverunt : am-*	They walked, walk ye.
—	הִתְהַלַּכְנוּ	*Ambulavimus.*	We have walked.

ROOTS.	DERIVATIVES.	VERSIO.	SIGNIFICATION.
הלך	הִתְהַלַּכְתָּ	*Ambulavisti.*	Thou hast walked.
—	הִתְהַלַּכְתִּי־־לִ״	*Ambulavi.*	I have walked.
הלל	הִתְהַלְלוּ	*Gloriamini.*	Glory ye.
תוה	הַתָּו	*Signum.*	The mark, sign.
ידה	הַתּוֹדָה	*Laus.*	The praise.
—	הַתּוֹדֹת	*Chori.*	The choirs.
תוה	הִתְווּ	*Determinarunt.*	They limited, fixed bounds.
תוך	הַתָּוֶךְ	*Medium.*	The middle.
תלע	הַתּוֹלַעַת־־לַ׳	*Coccus.*	The scarlet.
תעב	הַתּוֹעֵבָה־־תּ״	*Abominatio.*	The abomination.
—	הַתּוֹעֵבוֹת־־תּ׳	*Abominationes.*	The abominations.
—	הַתּוֹעֲבֹת־־עֲ׳	*Abominationes.*	The abominations.
יצא	הֲתוֹצִיא־־תּ׳	*An educes?*	Wilt thou bring forth?
תור	הַתּוֹר	*Turtur.*	The turtle.
ירד	הֲתוֹרִדֵנִי	*Num deduces me?*	Wilt thou bring me down?
ירה	הַתּוֹרָה	*Lex.*	The law.
—	הַתּוֹרֹת	*Leges.*	The laws.
ישב	הַתּוֹשָׁבִים	*Advenæ.*	The strangers.
תזז	הֵתַז	*Succidit.*	He cut down.
חבא	הִתְחַבְּאוּ	*Latitarunt.*	They hid themselves.
חבר	הִתְחַבְּרוּת	*Consociatio.*	The association, league.
חזק	הִתְחַזֵּק	*Confirmavit se; confirma te.*	He strengthened himself; strengthen thyself.
—	הִתְחַזְּקוּ	*Confirmate vos.*	Strengthen yourselves.
—	הִתְחַזַּקְתִּי	*Confirmavi me.*	I strengthened myself.
חלל	הַתְּחִלָּה	*Initium.*	The beginning.
חיה	הֲתִתְחַיֶּינָה	*Num vivent?*	Shall they live?
חמס	הַתַּחְמָס	*Struthio mas*, vel *noctua*, species bubonis.	The male ostrich, *or* the night-hawk, *a species of owl.*
חנן	הִתְחַנַּנְתָּה	*Deprecatus es.*	Thou hast made supplication.
—	הִתְחַנַּנְתִּי	*Deprecatus sum.*	I have made supplication.
חפש	הִתְחַפֵּשׂ	*Vestes mutavit, exuit*	He changed, put off his garments, disguised himself.
חרד	הִתְחָרַךְ	*Adustus est.*	He was singed.
תחש	הַתַּחַשׁ	*Taxus*; vel. sec. al. *attritio, rasura.*	The badger; *or accord. to some*, the rubbing, scraping.

ROOTS.	DERIVATIVES.	VERSIO.	SIGNIFICATION.
תחש	הַתְּחָשִׁים	*Taxi; rasuræ.*	The badgers; the shavings.
תחת	הֲתַחַת	*An loco?*	Instead?
—	הַתַּחְתּוֹן־־תּוֹנָה	*Inferior, infimus.*	The lower, lowest.
חתן	הִתְחַתֵּן	*Affinitatem contrahe, contrahere.*	Contract thou—to contract—affinity, or relationship by marriage,
תוב	הֲתִיב	*Retulit.*	He returned *answer.*
—	הֲתִיבוּנָא	*Retulerunt.*	They returned *answer.*
אתה	הֵתָיוּ	*Venite.*	Come ye.
יחש	הִתְיַחֵשׂ	*Recenseri.*	To be reckoned by genealogy.
—	הִתְיַחְשׂוּ	*Recensiti sunt.*	That they were reckoned by genealogy. [genealogies.
—	הִתְיַחְשָׂם	*Recenseri eos.*	That they are reckoned by
יטב	הֲתֵיטְבִי	*An melior?*	Art thou better?
נתך	הִתִּיכוּ	*Fuderunt.*	They have poured.
תוך	הַתִּיכוֹנָה־־כֹנָה	*Media.*	The middle.
—	הַתִּיכֹן	*Medius.*	The middle.
ימן	הַתֵּימָן	*Australis.*	The southern.
יצב	הִתְיַצֵּב־־צְּבָה	*Consiste.* [*sistite.*	Stand thou fast. [still
—	הִתְיַצְּבוּ	*Steterunt; state, con-*	They stood; stand ye, stand
נתק	הַתִּיקֵנוּ	*Elicere, avellere nos*	That we draw, pluck out.
ירש	הַתִּירוֹשׁ	*Mustum, vinum novum.*	The wine, new wine.
תיש	הַתְּיָשִׁים	*Hirci.*	The goats.
	הֲתָךְ	*Hatac.*	Hatach, N. M.
כבד	הִתְכַּבֵּד	*Numerosum te effice*	Make thyself many.
—	הִתְכַּבְּדִי	*Numerosam te effice*	Make thyself many.
תכל	הַתְּכֵלֶת	*Hyacinthus.*	The blue or violet.
מכר	הִתְמַכֶּרְךָ	*Vendi te.* [*lit.*	That thou art sold. [ed upon.
הָתֵל		*Illusit, delusit, fefel-*	He mocked, deluded, impos-
—	הָתֵל	*Illudere.*	To mock, deceive.
—	הֵתֶל	*Illusit, fefellit.*	He deluded, deceived.
לאה	הַתְּלָאָה	*Labor, molestia.*	The labour, trouble.
לבש	הֲתַלְבִּישׁ	*An vesties, indues?*	Wilt thou clothe, put on?
התל	הַתֻּלִים	*Illusores.*	The mockers.
ילך	הֲתֵלֵךְ	*Num ibis?*	Wilt thou go?
—	הֲתֵלְכִי	*Num ibis?*	Wilt thou go?

ROOTS.	DERIVATIVES.	VERSIO.	SIGNIFICATION.
תלע	הַתֹּלַעַת	*Vermis.*	The worm.
התל	הֵתַלְתָּ	*Illusisti.*	Thou hast mocked.
תמם	הָתֵם	*Consumendo.*	In consuming.
מוג	הִתְמֹגְגוּ־־מֹ׳	*Colliquerunt.*	They melted.
מהמה	הִתְמַהְמְהוּ	*Immoremini.*	Stay, tarry ye.
—	הִתְמַהְמְהָם.	*Cunctari eos.*	That they tarry, linger.
—	הִתְמַהְמָהְנוּ	*Morati sumus.*	We have lingered.
—	הִתְמַהְמָהְתִּי	*Cunctatus sum.*	I delayed.
תמם	הֵתַמּוּ	*Perfecerunt.*	They ended, completed.
—	הֲתַמּוּ	*Num completi sunt?*	Are they complete, are all here?
מוט	הִתְמוֹטְטָה	*Commovit se.*	She hath shaken herself.
מור	הַתְּמוּרָה	*Mutatio.*	The change.
תמד	הַתָּמִיד	*Jugis.*	The continual, perpetual.
מכר	הִתְמַכֵּר	*Vendidit se.*	He sold himself.
—	הִתְמַכֶּרְךָ	*Vendere te.*	To sell thyself.
מלא	הֲתְמַלֵּא	*An implebis?*	Wilt thou fill?
—	הִתְמַלִּי	*Repletus est.*	He is full.
מלך	הֲתִמְלֹךְ	*Num regnabis?*	Shalt thou reign?
תמר	הַתְּמֹרָה	*Palma.*	The palm-tree.
—	הַתִּמֹּרוֹת	*Palmæ.*	The palm-trees.
—	הַתְּמָרִים	*Palmæ.*	The palm-trees.
נגש	הִתְנַגְּשׁוּ	*Accedite.*	Draw ye near.
נדב	הִתְנַדֵּב	*Sponte offerri.*	To be willingly offered.
—	הִתְנַדְּבוּ־־דָּבוּ	*Sponte obtulerunt.*	They offered willingly.
—	הִתְנַדְּבוּת	*Spontanea oblatio.*	The free-will offering.
—	הִתְנַדְּבָם	*Sponte offerre eos*	That they offered willingly.
—	הִתְנַדַּבְתִּי	*Sponte obtuli.* [*runt.*	I have willingly offered.
תנה	הִתְנוּ	*Mercede conduxe-*	They have hired.
נוף	הַתְּנוּפָה	*Agitatio; oblatio agitata.*	The waving, shaking; the wave offering.
תנר	הַתַּנּוּרִים	*Fornaces.*	The furnaces.
נחל	הִתְנַחֵל	*Possidere.*	To possess, inherit.
תנן	הַתַּנִּים	*Dracones.*	The dragons.
—	הַתַּנִּין	*Draco.*	The dragon.
—	הַתַּנִּינִים	*Ceti.*	The whales.
נער	הִתְנַעֲרִי	*Excute te.*	Shake thyself.
נפל	הִתְנַפַּלְתִּי	*Prostravi me.*	I fell down, prostrated myself

ROOTS.	DERIVATIVES.	VERSIO.	SIGNIFICATION.
נשא	הִתְנַשֵּׂא	*Efferre se.*	To lift up himself.
נשם	הַתִּנְשֶׁמֶת	*Noctua;* sec. al. *cygnus,* vel *anser.*	The owl; *according to others* the swan, *or* goose.
עבר	הִתְעַבָּר	*Iratus est.*	He was wroth.
—	הִתְעַבַּרְתָּ	*Iratus es.*	Thou hast been wroth.
תעב	הִתְעַבְתָּ	*Scelestius egisti.*	Thou hast acted more wickedly
תעה	הִתְעָה	*Seduxit.*	He seduced, caused to err.
—	הִתְעוּ	*Errare fecerunt.*	They caused me to wander.
עוד	הַתְּעוּדָה	*Testimonium.*	The testimony.
תעה	הִתְעוּם	*Errare fecerunt eos*	They have made them go [astray.
עוף	הֲתָעִיף	*An injicies, volare facies?*	Wilt thou set, place, cause to fly?
עור	הִתְעוֹרְרִי	*Expergiscere.*	Awake, awake thou.
תעב	הִתְעִיבוּ	*Abominabile fecêre.*	They have done abominably.
עלה	הַתְּעָלָה	*Aquæductus.*	The trench, water-course.
עלל	הִתְעַלֵּל	*Operatus est, effecit.*	He performed, effected.
—	הִתְעַלַּלְתְּ	*Illusisti.*	Thou hast mocked.
—	הִתְעַלַּלְתִּי	*Operatus sum.*	I have wrought, effected.
ענה	הִתְעַנָּה	*Afflictus est.*	He was afflicted.
—	הִתְעַנִּיתָ	*Afflictus es.*	Thou hast been afflicted.
ערב	הִתְעָרֵב	*Sponsionem fac.*	Give thou security, pledge.
—	הַתַּעֲרֻבוֹת	*Sponsiones, obsides.*	The pledges, hostages.
עשק	הִתְעַשְּׂקוּ	*Contenderunt.*	They strove, contended.
עתד	הִתְעַתְּדוּ	*Paratæ sunt.*	They were ready.
תעה	הִתְעֵתִים	*Seduxistis.*	Ye led astray.
תפף	הַתֹּף	*Tympanum.*	The timbrel.
פאר	הִתְפָּאֵר	*Gloriare.*	Glory thou.
נפח	הַתַּפּוּחַ	*Malus.*	The apple-tree.
נפל	הֲתִפּוֹל	*Num cadet?*	Will he fall?
פור	הִתְפּוֹרְרָה	*Disrupta est.*	She is broken down.
פלל	הַתְּפִלָּה	*Oratio, precatio.*	The prayer.
—	הִתְפַּלֵּל	*Oravit.*	He prayed.
—	הִתְפַּלֵּל	*Ora.*	Pray thou.
—	הִתְפַּלַּלְתָּ	*Oravisti.*	Thou hast prayed.
—	הִתְפַּלַּלְתִּי	*Oravi.*	I have prayed.
פלש	הִתְפַּלָּשִׁי	*Volve te.*	Roll thyself.
פקד	הִתְפָּקְדוּ־־הָ׳	*Numerati sunt.*	They were numbered.

ROOTS.	DERIVATIVES.	VERSIO.	SIGNIFICATION.
פרק	הִתְפָּרְקוּ	*Confracti sunt.*	They were broken.
—	הִתְפָּרְקוּ	*Abrumpite.*	Break ye off.
פתח	הִתְפַּתְּחִי	*Solve te.*	Loose thyself.
צוד	הֲתָצוּד	*Num venaberis?*	Wilt thou hunt?
צלח	הֲתִצְלָח	*Num prosperabitur?*	Shall he prosper?
—	הֲתִצְלָח	*Anne prosperabitur.*	Whether it shall prosper.
קבץ	הִתְקַבְּצוּ	*Congregati sunt; congregate vos.*	They were gathered together gather yourselves together.
קדר	הִתְקַדְּרוּ	*Obscurati sunt.*	They were made dark.
קדש	הִתְקַדֵּשׁ	*Sanctificatus est.*	He, it was kept holy.
—	הִתְקַדְּשׁוּ	*Sanctificarunt se; sanctificate vos.*	They sanctified themselves; sanctify yourselves.
—	הִתְקַדְּשׁוּ	*Sanctificati sunt.*	They were sanctified.
קוה	הַתִּקְוָה	*Spes.*	The hope.
תקע	הַתְּקוּעָה	*Fixa.*	The fixed, fastened.
קשש	הִתְקוֹשְׁשׁוּ	*Congregate vos.*	Gather yourselves together.
קלל	הִתְקַלְקְלוּ	*Moti, agitati sunt.*	They were moved, agitated.
נתק	הַתִּקֵם	*Avelle eos.*	Pluck thou them out.
תקן	הָתְקַנְתִּ	*Confirmatus sum.*	I was established.
קשר	הֲתְקַשֵּׁר	*Num ligabis?*	Wilt thou bind?
—	הֲתְקַשֵּׁר	*An colligabis?*	Wilt thou bind?
—	הִתְקַשְּׁרוּ	*Conjurarunt.*	They conspired.
נתר	הַתֵּר	*Solvere.*	To loose, undo.
רגז	הִתְרַגֶּזְךָ	*Commoveri, irasci te*	That thou art agitated, angry.
רום	הַתְּרוּמָה	*Oblatio elevata.*	The heave-offering.
—	הִתְרוֹמַמְתָּ	*Extulisti te.*	Thou hast lifted up thyself.
רוע	הַתְּרוּעָה	*Clangor.*	The shout.
רעע	הִתְרוֹעֲעִי	*Jubila.*	Triumph thou.
רחץ	הִתְרַחֲצוּ	*Confisi sunt.*	They trusted.
—	הִתְרַחַצְתִּי	*Lavabo me.*	I will wash myself.
רום	הֲתָרִים	*Num attolles?*	Wilt thou lift up?
תור	הַתָּרִים	*Exploranted.*	They that search.
—	הַתֹּרִים	*Turtures.* [eum?	The turtles, turtle-doves.
רעש	הֲתַרְעִישֶׁנּוּ	*An tremere facies*	Wilt thou make him afraid?
רעל	הַתַּרְעֵלָה	*Horror, trepidatio.*	The horror, trembling.
רעע	הִתְרֹעֲעָה	*Confracta est.*	She is broken. [grown remiss.
רפה	הִתְרַפִּיתָ	*Remisse te gessisti.*	Thou hast fainted, failed,

ROOTS.	DERIVATIVES.	VERSIO.	SIGNIFICATION.
רפס	הִתְרַפֵּס	*Prosterne te.*	Humble thyself.
ישע	הַתְּשׁוּעָה	*Salus.*	The safety, deliverance.
שחת	הֲתַשְׁחִית	*An perdes?*	Wilt thou destroy?
שחק	הַתְשַׂחֶק	*Num ludes?*	Wilt thou play?
שום	הֲתָשִׂים	*Num pones?*	Wilt thou put?
תשע	הַתְּשִׁיעִי־שְׁעִי	*Nonus.*	The ninth.
—	הַתְּשִׁיעִית	*Nona.*	The ninth.
—	הַתְּשִׁיעִת־שִׁעִית	*Nona.*	The ninth.
שכח	הֲתִשְׁכַּח	*Num obliviscetur?*	Will she forget?
שלח	הַתְשַׁלַּח	*Num mittes?*	Wilt thou send?
שמר	הֲתִשְׁמֹר	*Utrum observabis.*	Whether thou wilt keep.
ישע	הַתְּשֻׁעָה	*Salus.*	The salvation, victory.
שפט	הֲתִשְׁפּוֹט־־פֹּט	*Num judicabis?*	Wilt thou judge? [wait.
הָתַת		*Irruit, insidiatus est.*	He set upon, assaulted, lay in
נתן	הֲתִתֵּן	*Num dabis?*	Wilt thou give?
—	הֲתִתְּנֵם	*Num trades eos?*	Wilt thou deliver them?

וא

ROOTS.	DERIVATIVES.	VERSIO.	SIGNIFICATION.
אלף	וַאֲאַלֶּפְךָ	*Et docebo te.*	And I shall teach thee.
אבה	וְאָב	*Et pater.*	And a father.
בוא	וְאָבָא־־אָה	*Et adduxi.*	And I brought.
—	וָאֲבָאֵם־־בִיאֵם	*Et adduxi eos.*	And I brought them.
אבד	וְאָבַד	*Et peribit.*	And he shall perish.
—	וְאַבֵּד	*Et perdere.*	And to destroy.
—	וְאִבַּד	*Et disperdet.*	And he will destroy.
—	וְאָבְדָה	*Et peribit.*	And she shall perish.
—	וַאֲבֵדָה	*Et interitus.*	And destruction.
—	וְאָבְדוּ	*Et peribunt.*	And they shall perish.
—	וַאֲבַדּוֹן	*Et perditio.*	And destruction.
בדל	וָאַבְדִּילָה	*Et separavi.*	And I separated.
אבד	וָאַבֶּדְךָ	*Et perdidi te.*	And I have destroyed thee.
בדל	וָאַבְדִּל	*Et discrevi.*	And I have severed.
אבד	וַאֲבַדּוֹן	*Et perditio.*	And destruction.
—	וְאִבַּדְתִּי	*Et disperdam.*	And I will destroy. [stroy.
—	וַאֲבַדְתֶּם	*Et peribitis, perdetis*	And ye shall perish, shall de-

ROOTS.	DERIVATIVES.	VERSIO.	SIGNIFICATION.
אבד	וְאִבַּדְתֶּם	*Et perdetis.*	And ye shall destroy.
בוא	וְאָבוֹא	*Et veniam.* [*redii.*	And I will come.
—	וְאָבוֹא־־בֹּא	*Et veni, introivi,*	And I came, entered, returned
—	וְאָבוֹאָה	*Et veniam, ingrediar*	And I will come, enter.
בוס	וְאָבוּס	*Et conculcabo.*	And I will tread down.
אבה	וְאָבוֹת	*Et patres.*	And the fathers.
—	וְאֲבוֹתַי	*Et patres mei.*	And my fathers.
—	וְאֲבוֹתֵיהֶם־־ב"	*Et patres eorum.*	And their fathers.
—	וַאֲבוֹתֵיכֶם־בֹּת'	*Et patres vestri.*	And your fathers
—	וַאֲבוֹתֵינוּ־־בֹּת'	*Et patres nostri.*	And our fathers.
—	וַאֲבוֹתָם	*Et patres eorum.*	And their fathers.
בחר	וָאֶבְחַר	*Et elegi.*	And I have chosen.
אבה	וְאָבִי	*Et pater meus.*	And my father.
—	וַאֲבִי	*Et pater.*	And the father.
בוא	וְאָבִיא־־בָּאה	*Et adduxi, induxi.*	And I brought, brought in.
אבה	וְאָבִיהָ	*Et pater ejus.*	And her father.
—	וַאֲבִיהֶם	*Et pater eorum.*	And their father.
—	וְאָבִיו	*Et pater ejus.*	And his father.
—	וְאֶבְיוֹן	*Et egenus, pauper.*	And needy, poor.
—	וְאֶבְיוֹנֵי	*Et pauperes.*	And the poor.
—	וְאֶבְיוֹנִים	*Et egeni.*	And needy.
נבט	וָאַבִּיט	*Et aspexi, contemplatus sum.* [*abo.*	And I looked, observed.
—	וְאַבִּיטָה	*Et videbo, consider-*	And I will see, consider.
אבה	וְאָבִיךָ	*Et pater tuus.*	And thy father.
—	וַאֲבִיכֶן	*Et pater vester.*	And your father.
בון	וָאָבִינָה	*Et aspexi, intellexi.*	And I viewed, understood.
—	וְאָבִינָה	*Et intelligam.*	And I shall understand.
בכה	וָאֶבְכֶּה	*Et flevi.*	And I wept.
—	וְאֶבְכֶּה	*Et flebo.*	And I shall bewail.
אבל	וְאָבַל	*Et lugebit.*	And he will mourn.
—	וְאֵבֶל	*Et luctus.*	And mourning.
—	וְאָבְלוּ	*Et lugebunt.*	And they shall mourn. [myself
בלג	וְאַבְלִיגָה	*Et recreabo me.*	And I will comfort, recruit
אבן	וְאֶבֶן וָא"־־אָ"	*Et lapis.*	And stone.
—	וְאַבְנָא	*Et lapis.*	And the stone.
בנה	וָאֶבְנֶה	*Et ædificavi.*	And I have built.

ROOTS.	DERIVATIVES	VERSIO.	SIGNIFICATION.
בנה	וְאֶבְנֶה	*Et ædificabo.*	And I will build.
—	וְאִבָּנֶה	*Et ædificabor, filios suscipiam.*	And I shall be built, shall have children.
אבנט	וְאַבְנֵט	*Et cingulus.*	And a girdle.
—	וְאַבְנֵטְךָ	*Et cingulus tuus.*	And thy girdle.
אבן	וְאַבְנֵי	*Et lapides.*	And stones.
—	וְאַבְנֶיךָ	*Et lapides tui.*	And thy stones.
—	וַאֲבָנִים	*Et lapides.*	And stones.
בנה	וְאֶבְנֶנָּה	*Et ædificabo eam.*	And I shall build her.
בקש	וָאֲבַקֵּשׁ־־קְשָׁה	*Et quæsivi.*	And I sought.
—	וָאֲבַקְשֵׁהוּ	*Et quæsivi eum.*	And I sought him.
ברה	וְאֶבְרֶה	*Et comedam.*	And I shall eat.
ברח	וָאַבְרִיחֵהוּ	*Et fugavi eum.*	And I chased him.
ברך	וָאֲבָרֵךְ	*Et benedixi.*	And I blessed.
—	וַאֲבָרְכָה	*Et benedicam.*	And I will bless.
—	וָאֲבָרְכֵהוּ־רְ	*Et benedixi ei.*	And I blessed him.
—	וַאֲבָרֶכְךָ־־רְכֶךָּ	*Et benedicam tibi.*	And I will bless thee.
—	וַאֲבָרֶכְכָה	*Et benedicam tibi.*	And I will bless thee.
—	וַאֲבָרֲכֵם	*Et benedicam eis.*	And I will bless them.
אבר	וְאֶבְרוֹתֶיהָ	*Et alæ ejus.*	And her wings, feathers.
בשר	וַאֲבַשְּׂרָה	*Et nunciabo.*	And I will bear tidings.
אבה	וַאֲבֹתֶיךָ	*Et patres tui.*	And thy fathers.
נגד	וָאַגִּד	*Et annunciavi.*	And I have told, declared.
גדל	וַאֲגַדְּלָה	*Et magnificabo.*	And I will magnify.
—	וַאֲגַדְּלֶנּוּ	*Et magnificabo eum.*	And I will magnify him.
גדע	וָאֲגַדֵּעַ	*Et succidi.*	And I have cut asunder.
אגד	וַאֲגֻדָּתוֹ	*Et agmen ejus.*	And his troop.
גוע	וְאֶגְוַע	*Et expirabo.*	And I shall expire.
נגד	וָאַגִּיד	*Et indicavi*	And I have shewn, declared.
—	וְאַגִּידָה	*Et nunciabo.*	And I will tell.
אגם	וְאַגְמוֹן־־מֹן	*Et olla, lebes.*	And a pot, cauldron.
—	וְאַגְמֵי	*Et stagna.*	And the pools, ponds.
—	וַאֲגַמִּים	*Et stagna.*	And pools, ponds.
נגף	וָאֶגֹּף	*Et percussi.*	And I struck, smote.
גרע	וְאֶגְרַע	*Et minui.*	And I have diminished.
גרש	וָאֲגָרֵשׁ	*Et expuli.*	And I have cast out.
—	וַאֲגָרְשֶׁנּוּ	*Et expellam eum.*	And I will cast him out.

ROOTS.	DERIVATIVES.	VERSIO.	SIGNIFICATION.
אגר	וְאִגֶּרֶת	*Et epistola.*	And a letter.
איד	וְאֵד	*Et vapor.*	And a vapour, mist.
דבר	וַאֲדַבֵּר־־בְּרָה	*Et loquar.*	And I will speak.
—	וָאֲדַבֵּר־בְּרָה־בְּ"	*Et locutus sum.*	And I spake.
אדם	וְאָדוֹם	*Et rubicundus.*	And ruddy.
אדן	וֶאֱדַיִן	*Et tunc.*	And then.
אדר	וְאַדִּירֵי	*Et magnifici.*	And the excellent.
—	וְאַדִּירֵיהֶם־־דִּרֵ"	*Et magnifici eorum.*	And their nobles.
אדם	וְאָדָם	*Et homo.*	And the man.
—	וָאֶדֹּם	*Et tacui.*	And I kept silence.
—	וַאֲדָמָה	*Et terra.*	And the earth.
—	וְאַדְמֹנִי	*Et rubicundus.*	And ruddy.
—	וְאַדְמָתְךָ	*Et terra tua.*	And thy land.
—	וְאַדְמָתֵנוּ	*Et terra nostra.*	And our land.
אדן	וַאדֹנִי	*Et dominus.* [*meus.*	And the lord.
—	וַאֲדֹנִי־־נִי	*Et dominus, dominus*	And the lord, my lord.
—	וְאַדְנֵיהֶם	*Et bases eorum.*	And their sockets.
—	וַאֲדָנָיו	*Et bases ejus.*	And his sockets.
—	וַאדֹנֵינוּ	*Et dominus noster.*	And our lord.
ידע	וָאֵדַע	*Et cognovi.*	And I knew.
—	וְאֵדְעָה	*Et cognoscam.*	And I shall know.
—	וָאֵדְעָה־־דָ"	*Et novi, intellexi.*	And I knew, understood.
—	וָאֵדָעֲךָ	*Et cognovi te.*	And I knew thee.
—	וְאֵדָעֲךָ	*Et noscam te.*	And I shall know thee.
דרך	וְאֶדְרְכֵם	*Et calcabo eos.*	And I will tread on them.
דרש	וְאֶדְרְשָׁה	*Et inquiram.*	And I will enquire.
אהב	וְאֹהֵב	*Et amans.*	And loving.
—	וָאֹהַב	*Et dilexi.*	And I loved.
—	וְאַהֲבָה	*Et dilectio.*	And the love.
—	וָאֹהֲבֵהוּ	*Et dilexi eum.*	And I loved him.
—	וְאֹהֲבוֹ	*Et diligens eum*	And he that loveth him.
—	וֶאֱהָבוּ	*Et diligite.*	And love ye.
—	וְאֹהֲבֵי	*Et diligentes.*	And they that love.
—	וְאֹהֲבֶיהָ	*Et diligentes eam.*	And they that love her.
—	וְאֹהֲבָיו	*Et diligentes eum.*	And they that love him.
—	וַאֲהֵבְךָ	*Et dilexit te.*	And he hath loved thee.
—	וָאֹהֲבֵם	*Et dilexi eos.*	And I have loved them.

ROOTS.	DERIVATIVES.	VERSIO.	SIGNIFICATION.
אהב	וְאָהַבְתָּ	*Et diliges.*	And thou shalt love.
—	וְאַהֲבַת	*Et diligere, amor.*	A d to love, the love.
—	וַאֲהַבְתֶּם	*Et diligetis.*	And ye shall love.
—	וְאָהוּב	*Et dilectus.*	And the beloved
היה	וָאֱהִי וָאֶהְיֶה	*Et fui.*	And I have been.
—	וְאֶהְיֶה	*Et ero.*	And I will be.
המה	וְאָהִימָה	*Et perstrepam.*	And I will make a noise.
אהל	וְאֹהֶל	*Et tentorium.*	And the tent, tabernacle.
—	וַאֲהָלוֹת	*Et aloë.*	And aloes.
—	וְאָהֳלֵיהֶם	*Et tentoria eorum.*	And their tents.
—	וְאֹהָלִים	*Et tentoria.*	And the tents.
הלל	וַאֲהַלְלָה	*Et laudabo.*	And I will praise.
המה	וְאֶהֱמֶה	*Et perstrepam.*	And I will cry aloud.
—	וְאֶהֱמָיָה	*Et turbatus sum.*	And I was troubled.
הרג	וַאֲהַרְגָּה	*Et occidam.*	And I will slay.
—	וָאֶהֶרְגֵהוּ	*Et interfeci eum.*	And I slew him.
ידה	וְאוֹדֶה	*Et celebrabo.*	And I will praise.
—	וְאוֹדְךָ־דֶךָּ	*Et laudabo te.*	And I will praise thee.
ידע	וָאִוָּדַע	*Et notum feci me.*	And I made myself known.
איב	וְאוֹיֵב	*Et inimicus.*	And the enemy.
אול	וֶאֱוִיל	*Et stultus.*	And a fool.
—	וֶאֱוִילִים	*Et stulti.*	And the fools.
אכל	וְאוֹכְלָה וְאֹכַ׳־כְ׳	*Et comedam*	And I will eat.
ילך	וְאוֹלִיכָה	*Et deducam.*	And I will bring, lead.
—	וָאוֹלֵךְ	*Et deduxi, adduxi.*	And I led, brought.
אלם	וְאוּלָם וְאֻלָם	*Et porticus; et sed, tamen, certe.*	And the porch; and but, yet, howbeit, surely.
אול	וְאִוֶּלֶת	*Et stultitia.*	And the folly.
אמר	וָאוֹמַר וָאֹמַר	*Et dixi.*	And I said.
און	וְאָוֶן	*Et iniquitas.*	And iniquity.
—	וָאָוֶן	*Et iniquitas, vanitas*	And iniquity, vanity.
—	וְאוֹנוֹ	*Et vires, robur ejus.*	And his force, strength.
יסף	וְאוֹסְפָה	*Et addam.*	And I will add.
יסר	וָאִוָּסֵר	*Et castigatus sum.*	And I was chastised.
אפן	וְאוֹפָן	*Et rota.*	And a wheel.
יצא	וָאוֹצִא־צִיא	*Et produxi, eduxi.*	And I brought forth, out of.
צוה	וָאֲצַוֶּה	*Et præcepi.*	And I commanded.

ROOTS.	DERIVATIVES.	VERSIO.	SIGNIFICATION.
יצא	וְאוֹצִיאֵם	*Et eduxi eos.* [*stitui.*	And I brought them forth.
אצר	וְאוֹצָרָה	*Et thesaurarios con-*	And I made treasurers.
—	וְאוֹצְרוֹת־־צָ׳	*Et thesauri.*	And treasures.
—	וְאוֹצְרוֹתֶיךָ־רֹתָ׳	*Et thesauri tui.*	And thy treasures.
אור	וְאוֹר וָאוֹר	*Et illucet; et lux.*	And he shines; and light.
ארב	וְאוֹרֵב וְאֹרֵב	*Et insidiator.*	And the ambush, lier in wait.
אור	וְאוֹרוֹ	*Et lux ejus.*	And his light.
ירד	וְאוֹרִדְךָ	*Et deducam te.*	And I will bring thee down.
—	וְאוֹרִיד	*Et dejeci.*	And I have put down.
ירה	וְאוֹרְךָ	*Et docebo te.*	And I will teach thee. [him.
ירש	וְאוֹרִשֶׁנּוּ	*Et expellam eum.*	And I will expel, disinherit
ישע	וְאוֹשִׁיעָה	*Et servavi.*	And I delivered.
—	וְאִוָּשֵׁעָה	*Et servabor.*	And I shall be saved.
את	וְאוֹתָהּ וְאֹתָהּ	*Et ipsam, eam.*	And her.
—	וְאוֹתִי וְאֹתִי	*Et me.*	And me.
—	וְאוֹתָם וְאֹתָם	*Et ipsos, eos.*	And them.
—	וְאוֹתָנוּ	*Et nos.*	And us.
יתר	וָאִוָּתֵר	*Et relictus sum.*	And I am left.
אז	וְאָז	*Et tunc.*	And then.
אזב	וְאֵזֹב וְאֵזוֹב	*Et hyssopum.*	And hyssop.
זבח	וְאֶזְבְּחָה	*Et sacrificabo.*	And I will sacrifice.
אזר	וְאֵזוֹר	*Et cingulus.*	And a girdle.
זכר	וָאֶזְכֹּר	*Et recordatus sum.*	And I have remembered.
אזל	וְאֹזֵל	*Et abiens.*	And going away.
זמר	וַאֲזַמְּרָה־־מֵּ׳	*Et cantabo.*	And I will sing praise. [thee.
—	וַאֲזַמֶּרְךָ	*Et canam te*	And I will give praises unto
אזן	וְאֹזֶן	*Et auris*	And the ear.
—	וְאִזֵּן	*Et auscultavit.*	And he gave good heed.
—	וְאָזְנֵי	*Et aures.*	And the ears.
—	וְאָזְנַי	*Et aures mei.*	And mine ears.
—	וְאָזְנֵיהֶם	*Et aures eorum.*	And their ears.
—	וְאָזְנָיו	*Et aures ejus.*	And his ears.
—	וְאָזְנֶיךָ־־נֶיךָ	*Et aures tui.*	And thine ears.
—	וְאָזְנַיִם	*Et aures.*	And ears.
זעק	וָאֶזְעַק	*Et clamavi.* [*si eos.*	And I cried. [them.
זרה	וָאֶזְרֵם	*Et ventilavi, disper-*	And I have fanned, scattered
זרע	וְאֶזְרֹעִי	*Et brachium meum.*	And mine arm.

ROOTS.	DERIVATIVES.	VERSIO.	SIGNIFICATION.
זרע	וְאֶזְרָעֵם	*Et seminabo eos.*	And I will sow them.
אחה	וְאָח וְאָח	*Et frater.*	And a brother.
חבא	וָאֵחָבֵא	*Et abscondi me.*	And I hid myself.
—	וָאֶחְבָּא	*Et abscondi.*	And I hid.
חבש	וָאֶחְבְּשֵׁךְ	*Et accinxi te.* [*mus.*	And I girded thee.
אחד	וְאַחַד וְאֶחָד	*Et unus, alter, pri-*	And one, another, first.
חדל	וְאֶחְדְּלָה	*Et desinam.*	And I shall forbear.
חוה	וְאַחֲוָיַת	*Et declaratio.*	And the declaration.
—	וַאֲחַוֶּךָּ	*Et indicabo tibi.* [*ge.*	And I will shew to thee.[hind.
אחר	וְאָחוֹר	*Et postea, retro, a ter-*	And afterwards, backwards, be-
אחה	וְאָחוֹת	*Et soror.*	And the sister.
חוה	וְאַחֲוָתִי	*Et oratio mea.*	And my speech.
אחה	וְאַחוֹתַיִךְ	*Et sorores tuæ.*	And thy sisters.
—	וַאֲחוֹתֵךְ	*Et soror tua.*	And thy sister.
אחז	וָאֹחַז	*Et cepi.*	And I took.
—	וְאָחַז	*Et apprehendit.*	And he took hold.
—	וְאָחַז	*Et captus.*	And taken.
—	וֶאֱחֹז	*Et apprehende.*	And take hold thou.
—	וָאֹחֲזֵה	*Et apprehendi.*	And I took hold.
—	וַאֲחֻזָּה	*Et possessio.*	And a possession.
חזה	וָאֶחֱזֶה	*Et vidi.*	And I saw.
אחז	וֶאֱחֹזוּ	*Et tenete.*	And hold ye.
—	וֶאֱחֹזִי	*Et tene.* [*firmabo.*	And hold thou.
חזק	וְאַחְזִק	*Et prehendam, con-*	And I will hold, will strengthen
אחז	וַאֲחֻזַּת	*Et possessio.*	And the possession.
—	וַאֲחֻזָּתְךָ	*Et possessio tua.*	And thy possession.
—	וַאֲחֻזָּתָם	*Et possessio eorum.*	And their possession.
אחה	וְאַחַי	*Et fratres mei.*	And my brethren.
—	וְאָחִי	*Et frater.*	And a brother.
חיה	וְאֶחְיֶה	*Et vivam.*	And I shall live.
—	וַאֲחַיֶּה	*Et vivere faciam.*	And I will make alive.
אחה	וַאֲחֵיהֶם	*Et fratres eorum.*	And their brethren.
—	וְאֶחָיו	*Et fratres ejus.*	And his brethren.
—	וְאָחִיו	*Et frater ejus.*	And his brother.
—	וְאַחֶיךָ	*Et fratres tui.*	And thy brethren.
—	וַאֲחֵיכֶם	*Et fratres vestri.*	And your brethren.
—	וְאַחִים	*Et fratres.*	And brethren.

ROOTS.	DERIVATIVES.	VERSIO.	SIGNIFICATION.
אחה	וְאָחִינוּ	*Et frater noster.*	And our brother.
—	וְאַחְיֹתֵיהֶם	*Et sorores eorum.*	And their sisters.
חלל	וָאֵחַל	*Et profanatus sum.*	And I am profaned.
—	וָאֲחַלֵּל	*Et profanavi.*	And I have profaned.
—	וָאֲחַלֶּלְךָ	*Et profanabo te.*	And I will profane thee.
חלם	וְאַחְלָמָה	*Et amethystus.*	And an amethyst.
חלץ	וָאֲחַלְּצָה	*Et eripui.*	And I have delivered.
—	וָאֲחַלֶּצְךָ	*Et eripui te*	And I delivered thee.
חמד	וַאֶחְמְדֵם	*Et concupivi eos.*	And I coveted them.
חמל	וָאֶחְמֹל	*Et peperci.*	And I had pity, spared.
חפר	וָאֶחְפּוֹר־־פֹּר	*Et fodi.*	And I digged.
אחר	וְאַחַר	*Et postea.*	And afterwards.
—	וָאֵחַר	*Et moratus sum.*	And I stayed.
—	וְאַחֵר	*Et alius.*	And another.
חרב	וְאַחֲרִב־־רִי	*Et siccavi.*	And I have dried up.
אחר	וְאַחֲרוֹ	*Et alter.*	And the other.
—	וְאַחֲרוֹן	*Et posterior.*	And the latter.
—	וְאַחֲרַי	*Et post me.*	And after me.
—	וְאַחֲרֵי	*Et postea, postquam*	And afterwards, after that.
—	וְאָחֳרִי	*Et alter.*	And the other.
—	וְאַחֲרֶיהָ	*Et post eam.*	And after her.
—	וְאַחֲרֵיהֶם	*Et post eos, posteri [eorum*	And after them, their posterity
—	וְאַחֲרָיו	*Et post eum.*	And after him.
—	וְאַחֲרֶיךָ־־רַיִךְ	*Et post te.*	And after thee.
—	וְאַחֲרִית	*Et finis.*	And the end.
—	וְאַחֲרִיתָהּ	*Et finis ejus.*	And her end.
—	וְאַחֲרִיתוֹ	*Et finis ejus.*	And his end.
—	וְאַחֲרִיתְךָ־־תֵךְ	*Et postremum tuum*	And thy remnant.
—	וְאַחֲרִיתְכֶן	*Et posteritas vestra.*	And your posterity.
—	וְאַחֲרִיתָם	*Et postremum eorum*	And their last.
—	וְאָחֳרָן	*Et alius.*	And another.
חשב	וָאֲחַשְּׁבָה	*Et putavi.*	And I thought.
אחש	וַאֲחַשְׁדַּרְפְּנַיָּא	*Et principes.*	And princes.
חשך	וָאֶחְשׂךְ	*Et cohibui.*	And I withheld.
אחד	וְאַחַת	*Et una, prima.*	And one, first.
אחה	וַאֲחֹתוֹ	*Et soror ejus.*	And his sister.
—	וַאֲחוֹתִי	*Et soror mea.*	And my sister.

ROOTS.	DERIVATIVES.	VERSIO.	SIGNIFICATION.
חתם	וָאֶחְתֹּם	*Et obsignavi.*	And I sealed.
חתר	וָאֶחְתֹּר	*Et fodi.*	And I digged.
נטה	וָאַט	*Et extendi.*	And I stretched out.
——	וְאַט	*Et demisi, porrexi.*	And I sent down, extended.
טהר	וְאֶטְהָר	*Et mundabor.*	And I shall be cleansed.
יטב	וְאֵטִיבָה	*Et benefaciam.*	And I will deal well.
טמא	וָאֲטַמֵּא	*Et pollui.*	And I polluted.
טמן	וָאֶטְמְנֵהוּ	*Et abscondi eum.*	And I hid him, or it.
איה	וְאֵי	*Et ubi.*	And where.
אי	וְאִי	*Et væ.*	And woe.
איב	וְאֵיבָה	*Et inimicitia.*	And enmity,
——	וְאֹיְבַי	*Et inimici mei.*	And my enemies.
——	וְאֹיְבֵי	*Et inimici.*	And the enemies.
——	וְאֹיְבָיו	*Et inimici ejus.*	And his enemies.
——	וְאֹיְבֵינוּ	*Et inimicus nostri.*	And our enemies.
——	וְאָיַבְתִּי	*Et inimicus ero.*	And I will be an enemy.
איד	וְאֵיד	*Et exitium.*	And destruction.
——	וְאֵידְכֶם	*Et exitium vestrum.*	And your destruction.
איה	וְאַיֵּה וְאַיֵּו	*Et ubi.*	And where.
——	וְאַיּוֹ	*Et ubi ipse.*	And where he.
יחל	וַאֲיַחֵלָה	*Et expectavi.*	And I waited.
יטב	וְאֵיטִיבָה	*Et benefaciam.*	And I will deal well.
אי	וְאִיֵּי	*Et insulæ.*	And the isles.
——	וְאִיִּים	*Et insulæ.*	And the islands.
איך	וְאֵיךְ	*Et quomodo.*	And how.
——	וְאֵיכָכָה	*Et quomodo.*	And how
איל	וְאֵיל ךָ״	*Et aries.*	And a ram.
——	וְאֵילָו	*Et postes ejus.*	And his posts.
אי	וְאִילוֹ	*Et væ illi.*	And woe to him.
איל	וְאֵילֵי	*Et arietes.*	And the rams.
ילל	וְאֵילִילָה	*Et ejulabo.*	And I will howl.
איל	וְאֵילִים־־לִם	*Et arietes.*	And rams.
אלם	וְאֵילַמָּיו־־מָּו	*Et vestibula ejus.*	And his porches.
אים	וְאֵימוֹת	*Et terrores.*	And the terrors.
ימן	וְאֵימִנָה	*Et dexteram tenebo.*	And I will take the right.
אים	וְאֵימָתְךָ	*Et terror tuus.*	And thy dread.
אין	וְאַיִן וָאָיִן	*Et non.*	And not.

ROOTS.	DERIVATIVES.	VERSIO.	SIGNIFICATION.
אין	וְאֵין וְאַיִן	*Et not, neque.*	And not, nor.
—	וְאֵינְךָ־נֵךְ	*Et non tu.*	And not thou.
—	וְאֵינָם	*Et non, neque ipsi.*	And not, nor they.
—	וְאֵינֵמוֹ	*Et non ipsi.*	And they not.
—	וְאֵינֶנּוּ	*Et non ipse.*	And he not.
—	וְאֵינֶנִּי	*Et non ego.*	And I not.
איף	וְאֵיפֹה	*Et ubi.*	And where.
יקץ	וָאִיקָץ	*Et evigilavi.*	And I awoke.
ירא	וָאִירָה	*Et timui.* [quisque.	And I was afraid. [one.
איש	וְאִישׁ ךָ"	*Et homo, quisquam,*	And a man, some man, every
—	וְאִישָׁהּ	*Et vir, maritus ejus*	And her husband.
שום	וָאָישִׂמָה	*Et posui.*	And I placed.
ישן	וְאִישָׁן	*Et dormiam.*	And I will sleep.
—	וָאִישָׁנָה	*Et dormivi.*	And I slept.
אית	וְאֵיתָנִים	*Et fortes.* [tamen.	And the mighty. [ing.
אך	וְאַךְ	*Et profecto, quidem,*	And surely, yet, notwithstand-
נכה	וָאַךְ	*Et percussi.*	And I smote.
כבד	וְאֶכָּבֵד	*Et gloriosus ero.*	And I shall be glorious.
—	וְאֶכָּבֵד וְאֶכַבְּדָה	*Et honorabor.*	And I will be honoured.
—	וַאֲכַבְּדָה	*Et gloriam tribuam.*	And I will glorify.
—	וַאֲכַבְּדֵהוּ	*Et honorabo eum.*	And I will honour him.
נכה	וְאַכֶּה	*Et feriam, cædam.*	And I will smite, slay.
—	וָאַכֶּה	*Et percussi.*	And I smote.
—	וָאַכֵּהוּ	*Et percussi eum.*	And I smote him.
—	וֶאֱכוֹל	*Et comede.*	And eat thou.
אכל	וְאִכְלוּ	*Et comedite.*	And eat ye.
כחד	וָאַכְחִד	*Et excidi.*	And I cut off.
נכר	וָאַכִּירָה	*Et intellexi.*	And I understood, perceived.
אכל	וְאָכֹל	*Et comedendo.*	And in eating.
—	וְאָכַל־־כָּ"	*Et comedit.*	And he ate.
—	וָאֹכַל־־כַל	*Et comedi.*	And I ate.
—	וֶאֱכֹל־־כָל	*Et comede.* [dens.	And eat thou.
—	וְאֹכַל־כֹל	*Et comedam, come-*	And I will eat, eating.
—	וָאֲכַל	*Et consumpsi.*	And I have consumed.
—	וַאֲכָלָהּ	*Et comedet eam.*	And he shall eat her.
—	וָאֹכְלָה	*Et comedi.*	And I have eaten.
—	וֶאֱכֹלָה	*Et comede.*	And eat thou.

ROOTS.	DERIVATIVES.	VERSIO.	SIGNIFICATION.
אכל	וְאָכְלָה	*Et consumet.*	And she shall consume.
—	וְאָכְלָה	*Et devorabit.*	And she shall devour.
—	וַאֲכַלֶּה	*Et consumam.*	And I will consume.
כלה	וַאֲכָלֻהוּ	*Et comedent eum.*	And they shall eat him.
אכל	וַאֲכָלוֹ	*Et comedet eum.*	And he shall eat him.
—	וְאָכְלוּ	*Et edent, consument*	And they shall eat, consume.
—	וְאִכְלוּ וֶאֱכֹלוּ	*Et comedite.*	And eat ye.
—	וַאֲכַלוּ	*Et accusaverunt.*	And they accused.
—	וְאִכְלוּהָ	*Et comedite eum.*	And eat ye him.
—	וַאֲכָלוּם	*Et consument eos.*	And they shall devour them.
—	וְאֹכְלַי	*Et comedentes.*	And they that eat.
—	וְאֹכְלָיו	*Et comedentes eum.*	And they that eat him.
—	וְאֹכְלִים	*Et comedentes.*	And the eaters.
כול	וָאֲכַלְכְּלֵם	*Et pavi eos.*	And I fed them.
כלה	וָאֲכַלֵּם	*Et consumpsi eos.*	And I have consumed them.
—	וַאֲכַלֵּם	*Et consumam eos.*	And I will consume them.
אכל	וָאֹכְלֵם	*Et comedi eos.*	And I did eat them.
—	וְאֹכְלֵם	*Et devorabo eos.*	And I will devour them.
—	וַאֲכַלְנֻהוּ	*Et comedemus eum.*	And we will eat him.
—	וְאָכַלְתָּ־־תְּ	*Et comedes, destrues*	And thou shalt eat, destroy.
—	וְאָכַלְתִּי	*Et comedam.*	And I shall eat.
—	וַאֲכַלְתֶּם	*Et comedetis.*	And ye shall eat.
—	וַאֲכָלָתַם	*Et comedet eos.*	And he shall eat them.
—	וָאֲכַסֶּה	*Et operui.*	And I covered.
כסה	וַאֲכַסֵּךְ	*Et operui te.*	And I covered thee.
כפף	וְאַכְפִּי	*Et manus mea.*	And my hand.
כרה	וָאֶכְּרֶהָ	*Et coemi eam.*	And I bought, procured her.
כרת	וָאַכְרִית	*Et excidi.*	And I have cut off.
כרע	וָאֶכְרְעָה	*Et procubui.*	And I fell prostrate.
כרת	וְאֶכְרֹת	*Et succidam.*	And I will cut down.
—	וָאַכְרִתָה	*Et excidi.*	And I have cut off.
—	וְאֶכְרְתָה	*Et percutiam.*	And I will smite.
כתת	וָאֶכֹּת	*Et contrivi.*	And I have stamped.
כתב	וְאֶכְתֹּב	*Et scribam.*	And I will write.
—	וָאֶכְתֹּב	*Et subscripsi.*	And I subscribed.
אלה	וְאֵל	*Et Deus.*	And God.
אל	וְאַל	*Et non, neque.*	And not, neither, nor.

ROOTS.	DERIVATIVES.	VERSIO.	SIGNIFICATION.
אל	וְאֶל	*Et ad, ab, in.*	And to, from, in.
לבש	וָאַלְבִּשֵׁךְ	*Et vestivi te.*	And I clothed thee.
אלג	וְאַלְגוּמִּים	*Et algumim.*	And algum trees.
ילד	וָאֵלֵד	*Et pêperi.*	And I was delivered of a child
אלה	וְאֵלֶּה	*Et hi, illi, hæ, ipsæ.*	And these, those.
——	וְאֵלָה	*Et quercus.*	And oaks.
——	וֶאֱלָהָא	*Et Deus.*	And the God.
——	וֵאלֹהֵי	*Et Deus, dii.*	And the God, gods.
——	וֵאלֹהַי־־הָי	*Et Deus meus.*	And my God.
——	וֵאלֹהֵיהֶם	*Et dii eorum.*	And their gods.
——	וֵאלֹהָיו	*Et Deus ejus.*	And his God.
——	וֵאלֹהֶיךָ	*Et Deus tuus.*	And thy God.
——	וֵאלֹהִים	*Et Deus.*	And God.
——	וֵאלֹהֵינוּ	*Et Deus noster.*	And our God.
אל	וַאֲלֵהֶם	*Et ad eos.*	And to them.
אלו	וְאִלּוּ	*Et ecce.*	And behold.
——	וְאִלּוּ	*Et si.*	And if.
אלה	וֶאֱלוֹהַּ	*Et Deus.*	And God.
אלל	וֶאֱלִיל	*Et nihil.*	And nothing.
אלה	וְאַלּוֹן	*Et quercus.*	And the oak.
אל	וְאֵלַי	*Et ad, contra me.*	And to, against me.
——	וַאֲלֵיהֶם	*Et ad eos.*	And to them.
——	וְאֵלֶיךָ־־לַיִךְ	*Et ad te*	And to thee.
אלל	וֶאֱלִילֵי	*Et idola.*	And idols.
ילד	וְאֵלֵךְ	*Et ibo, abibo.*	And I will go, depart.
——	וָאֵלֵךְ	*Et abivi.*	And I departed.
——	וָאֵלֵךְ	*Et ivi, profectus sum*	And I went, have gone.
——	וְאֵלְכָה	*Et ibo, abibo.*	And I will go, depart.
——	וְאֵלְכָה	*Et ibo.*	And I will go.
למד	וְאֶלְמְדָה	*Et discam.*	And I shall learn.
אלם	וְאֵלַמָּו	*Et vestibula ejus.*	And his porches.
——	וְאַלְמוֹן	*Et viduitas.*	And widowhood.
——	וְאֵלַמּוֹת	*Et vestibula.*	And the porches.
——	וְאֵלַמֵּי	*Et vestibula.*	And the porches.
——	וְאַלְמָנָה	*Et vidua.*	And the widow.
——	וְאַלְמָנוֹת	*Et viduæ.*	And the widows.
——	וְאַלְמְנוֹתָיו־נֹתָ"	*Et viduæ ejus.*	And his widows.

ROOTS.	DERIVATIVES.	VERSIO.	SIGNIFICATION.
אלם	וְאַלְמְנוֹתֶיךָ	*Et viduæ tuæ.*	And thy widows.
אלף	וְאֶלֶף ךְ־־אָ	*Et mille.*	And a thousand.
—	וְאַלְפַּיִם	*Et duo millia.*	And two thousand.
—	וַאֲלָפִים	*Et boves.*	And oxen.
לקט	וַאֲלַקֳטָה	*Et colligam.*	And I will gather, glean.
אם	וְאִם	*Et si, aut, utrum.*	And if, or, whether.
אמם	וְאֵם ךְ	*Et mater.* [*am te.*	And a mother.
מאס	וְאֶמְאָסְאךָ	*Et spernam, respu-*	And I will despise, reject thee
אמם	וְאִמָּהּ	*Et mater ejus.*	And her mother.
—	וְאַמָּה	*Et cubitus.*	And a cubit.
אמה	וְאָמָה	*Et ancillæ.*	And handmaids.
—	וְאַמְהוֹתַי־הֹתַי	*Et ancillæ meæ.*	And my maids.
—	וְאַמְהֹתֶיהָ	*Et ancillæ ejus.*	And her maids.
—	וְאַמְהֹתֵהֶם	*Et ancillæ eorum.*	And their maids.
—	וַאֲמָהֹתָיו	*Et ancilla ejus.*	And his maid-servant.
—	וְאַמְהֹתֵיכֶם	*Et ancillæ vestræ.*	And your maid-servants.
אמם	וְאִמּוֹ	*Et mater ejus.*	And his mother.
אמן	וֶאֱמוּנָה	*Et veritas, fides.*	And truth, faithfulness.
—	וֶאֱמוּנָתוֹ	*Et veritas ejus.*	And his truth.
—	וֶאֱמוּנָתִי	*Et fides mea.*	And my faithfulness.
—	וֶאֱמוּנָתְךָ	*Et fides tua.*	And thy faithfulness.
אמם	וְאַמּוֹת	*Et cubiti.*	And the cubits.
מחה	וְאֶמְחֶה	*Et delebo.*	And I will blot out.
מחץ	וָאֶמְחָצֵם	*Et transfixi eos.*	And I have wounded them.
אמם	וְאִמִּי	*Et mater mea.*	And my mother.
אמץ	וְאַמִּיץ	*Et robustus, potens.*	And the strong, mighty.
אמם	וְאִמְּךָ־־מֵּךְ־־מֶּךָ	*Et mater tua.*	And thy mother.
מלא	וָאֲמַלֵּא	*Et replevi.*	And I have filled.
—	וַאֲמַלְאֵהוּ	*Et implebo eum.*	And I will fill him.
מלט	וַאֲמַלֵּט	*Et eripiam.*	And I will deliver.
—	וְאִמָּלְטָה	*Et evasi.*	And I have escaped.
מלך	וָאַמְלִיךְ	*Et regnare feci.*	And I have made king.
אמל	וְאֻמְלַל	*Et languebit.*	And he shall languish.
אמן	וְאָמֵן	*Et amen.* [*tio.*	And amen. [distribution.
—	וַאֲמָנָה	*Et constans distribu-*	And a certain portion, regular
מנע	וָאֶמְנַע	*Et cohibui.*	And I restrained.
אמץ	וֶאֱמַץ־מָץ	*Et esto fortis.*	And be thou of good courage.

ROOTS.	DERIVATIVES.	VERSIO.	SIGNIFICATION.
אמץ	וְאִמֵּץ	*Et obfirmavit.*	And he made obstinate.
—	וְאַמִּץ	*Et validus, potens.*	And strong, mighty.
מצא	וָאֶמְצָא	*Et inveni.*	And I found.
—	וְאֶמְצָאֵהוּ	*Et inveniam eum.*	And I shall find him.
—	וָאֶמְצָאֶךָּ	*Et inveni te.*	And I have found thee.
אמץ	וְאַמְּצֵהוּ	*Et robora eum.*	And strengthen thou him.
—	וְאִמְצוּ	*Et fortes estote.*	And be ye courageous.
אמר	וְאָמַר	*Et dicat.*	And he will say.
—	וֶאֱמָר	*Et dic.*	And tell, say thou.
—	וַאֲמַר	*Et dixit.*	And he said.
—	וְאֹמַר	*Et dicam.*	And I will say.
—	וְאֹמֵר	*Et dicens.*	And saying.
—	וְאֹמְרָה	*Et dicam.*	And I will say.
—	וָאֹמְרָה	*Et dixi.*	And I said.
—	וְאָמְרָה	*Et dixit, dicet.*	And she said, will say.
—	וְאָמְרוּ	*Et dixerunt, dicent.*	And they said, will say.
—	וְאִמְרוּ	*Et dicite.*	And say ye.
מרט	וָאֶמְרְטָה	*Et evulsi.*	And I plucked off.
—	וָאֶמְרְטֵם	*Et depilavi eos.*	And I plucked off their hair.
אמר	וְאֹמְרִים־־ין	*Et dicentes.*	And saying.
—	וְאִמְּרִין	*Et agni.*	And lambs.
—	וְאֹמַרְנוּ	*Et dicemus.*	And we will say.
—	וַאֲמֶרֶת	*Et dixit.*	And she said.
—	וְאָמַרְתָּ־־תִּ׳	*Et dices.*	And thou shalt say.
—	וְאָמַרְתִּי	*Et dicam.*	And I will say.
—	וַאֲמַרְתֶּם	*Et dicetis.*	And ye will say.
משש	וַאֲמֻשְּׁךָ	*Et palpabo te.*	And I shall feel thee.
מות	וְאָמֻת	*Et moriar.* [*vere.*	And I shall die.
אמן	וֶאֱמֶת	*Et veritas, verus,*	And truth, true, right, truly.
—	וַאֲמִתּוֹ	*Et veritas ejus.*	And his truth.
אמה	וַאֲמָתוֹ	*Et ancilla ejus.*	And his maid-servant.
אים	וְאֵמָתוֹ	*Et terror ejus.*	And his dread, fear.
אמה	וַאֲמָתִי	*Et ancilla mea.*	And my maid-servant.
אמם	וְאַמָּתַיִם	*Et duo cubiti.*	And two cubits.
אמן	וַאֲמִתְּךָ	*Et veritas tua.*	And thy truth.
אמה	וַאֲמָתְךָ־־תֶךָ	*Et ancilla tua.*	And thy maid.
אים	וְאֵמְתָנִי	*Et terribilis.*	And terrible.

ROOTS.	DERIVATIVES.	VERSIO.	SIGNIFICATION.
מות	וָאֲמֹתְתֵהוּ	*Et interfeci eum.*	And I slew him.
אבב	וְאִנְבֵּהּ	*Et fructus ejus.*	And his fruit.
ידע	וְאֵנְדַּע	*Et cognoscam.*	And I shall know.
אנא	וַאֲנָה	*Et ego.*	And I.
אן	וְאָנָה	*Et quo, ubi.*	And whither, where.
—	וָאָנָה	*Et illuc.*	And thither.
אנה	וְאָנוּ	*Et mærebunt.*	And they shall lament.
נוה	וְאַנְוֵהוּ	*Et faciam eum mihi centrum omnis laudis et gloriæ.*	And I will make him the centre or object of all my praise and glory.
אנש	וָאֲנוּשָׁה	*Et anxius, tristis fui.*	And I have been anxious, sad.
אנח	וַאֲנָחָה	*Et gemitus, luctus.*	And sighing, groaning, grief.
נחה	וְאַנְחֵהוּ	*Et ducam eum.*	And I will lead him.
נחם	וַאֲנַחֶמְךָ	*Et solabor te.*	And I will comfort thee.
אני	וַאֲנַחְנוּ	*Et nos.*	And we.
אנח	וְאַנְחָתִי	*Et gemitus meus.*	And my groaning.
אני	וַאֲנִי	*Et ego.*	And I.
אנה	וָאֳנִי	*Et classis.*	And a navy *of ships*.
—	וַאֲנִיָּה	*Et tristitia.*	And sorrow.
—	וָאֳנִיּוֹת	*Et naves.*	And the ships.
נוע	וְאָנִיעָה	*Et commovebo.*	And I will move, shake.
אני	וְאָנֹכִי	*Et ego.*	And I.
נעל	וָאֶנְעָלֵךְ	*Et calceavi te.*	And I have shod thee.
נער	וְאִנָּעֵר	*Et excutiam me.*	And I will shake myself.
אנף	וְאָנַפְתָּ	*Et iratus eris.*	And thou wilt be angry.
אנק	וַאֲנָקָה	*Et vociferatio.*	And crying out.
נקם	וְאִנָּקְמָה	*Et ulciscar.*	And I will avenge.
אנש	וְאָנֻשׁ	*Et desperate impius, mortifer.*	And desperately wicked, mortally diseased.
—	וֶאֱנוֹשׁ	*Et homo.*	And man.
—	וְאַנְשֵׁי	*Et viri.*	And men.
—	וְאַנְשֵׁיהֶם	*Et viri eorum.*	And their men.
—	וַאֲנָשָׁיו	*Et viri ejus.*	And his men.
—	וַאֲנָשֶׁיךָ	*Et viri tui.*	And thy men.
—	וַאֲנָשִׁים	*Et homines, viri.*	And man.
אנת	וְאַנְתְּ־־תָּה	*Et tu.*	And thou.
נתח	וַאֲנַתְּחֶהָ	*Et concidi eam.*	And I have cut her in pieces.

ROOTS.	DERIVATIVES.	VERSIO.	SIGNIFICATION.
סבב	וָאֲסוֹבְבָה	*Et circumibo.*	And I will go about.
סור	וָאָסִיר	*Et amovi.*	And I have removed.
—	וְאָסִיר	*Et amovebo.*	And I will remove.
—	וְאָסִירָה	*Et auferam.*	And I will take away.
סוך	וָאָסֻכֵךְ	*Et unxi te.*	And I anointed thee.
סלד	וַאֲסַלְּדָה	*Et exiliam.*	And I will leap for joy.
סלח	וְאֶסְלַח	*Et condonabo.*	And I will pardon.
סער	וָאֲסָעֲרֵם	*Et dispersi eos.*	And I scattered them.
אסף	וְאָסַף	*Et colligetur.* [*rabit.*	And he shall be gathered.
—	וְאָסַף	*Et colliget, recupe-*	And he will gather, recover.
יסף	וְאֹסְפָה	*Et addam.*	And I will add.
אסף	וְאָסְפוּ	*Et colligerunt.*	And they shall assemble.
—	וְאָסְפוּ	*Et colligentur.*	And they shall be gathered.
ספר	וַאֲסַפֵּר־־פְּרָה	*Et enarrabo.*	And I will tell, declare.
אסף	וְאָסַפְתָּ	*Et colliges.*	And thou shalt gather.
—	וְאָסַפְתָּה	*Et amittes.*	And thou wilt lose.
—	וַאֲסַפְתּוֹ	*Et recipies eum.*	And thou shalt recover him.
—	וְאָסַפְתִּי	*Et colligam.*	And I will gather.
אסר	וֶאֱסָרָא	*Et lex, decretum.*	And the law, decree.
—	וְאָסְרָה	*Et astringet se.*	And she will bind herself.
—	וֶאֱסָרָהּ	*Et oblatio ejus.*	And her bond.
—	וֶאֱסָרֶהָ־־רֶיהָ	*Et oblationes ejus.*	And her bonds.
—	וַאֲסָרוּךָ	*Et vinxerunt te.*	And they have bound thee.
יסר	וְאֶסֳּרֵם	*Et castigabo eos.*	And I will chastise them.
אסר	וַאֲסַרְנוּהוּ	*Et vinciemus eum.*	And we will bind him.
—	וַאֲסַרְתֶּם	*Et ligabitis, jungetis*	And ye shall tie, harness.
סתר	וָאַסְתִּיר	*Et abscondi.*	And I have hid.
—	וְאֶסָּתֵר	*Et abscondam.*	And I will hide.
אע	וָאָע	*Et lignum.*	And timber.
עבר	וָאֶעֱבֹר	*Et transivi.*	And I passed.
—	וָאֶעְבְּרָה	*Et transivi.* [*tus sum*	And I passed over.
עוד	וָאָעֵד	*Et contestatus, testa-*	And I protested, testified.
עדה	וָאֶעְדֵּךְ	*Et ornavi te.*	And I decked thee.
עזב	וְאֶעֶזְבָה	*Et derelinquam.*	And I will leave.
עוד	וָאָעִיד	*Et testificatus sum.*	And I testified.
—	וָאָעִידָה	*Et attestatus sum.*	And I testified.
—	וְאָעִידָה	*Et attestabor.*	And I will testify.

ROOTS.	DERIVATIVES.	VERSIO.	SIGNIFICATION.
עלה	וָאַעַל	*Et ascendi, obtuli.*	And I went up, offered.
—	וָאַעֲלֶה--לֶה	*Et ascendere feci.*	And I have made to come up.
עלז	וָאֶעֱלֹז	*Et exultavi.*	And I rejoiced.
עלם	ואַעְלִים	*Et occultabo.*	And I will hide.
עלץ	וְאֶעֶלְצָה	*Et exultabo.*	And I will rejoice.
עמד	וָאֶעֱמֹד	*Et steti.*	And I stood.
—	וָאַעֲמִדֵם	*Et statui eos.*	And I set them.
—	וָאַעֲמִיד	*Et statui, collocavi.*	And I set, placed.
—	וָאַעֲמִידָה	*Et constitui.*	And I appointed.
ענה	וָאַעַן	*Et respondi.*	And I answered.
—	וְאֶעֱנֶה--עְ	*Et respondebo.*	And I will answer.
—	וַאֲעַנֶּה	*Et affligam.*	And I will afflict.
—	וְאֶעֱנֵהוּ	*Et respondebo illi.*	And I will answer him.
—	וְאֶעֱנֵךְ	*Et respondebo tibi.*	And I will answer thee.
—	וְאֶעֱנֵם	*Et exaudiam eos.*	And I will hear them.
ערך	וְאֶעֶרְכָה	*Et ordinabo.*	And I will set in order.
עשה	וָאַעַשׂ	*Et feci.*	And I made.
—	וָאֶעֱשֶׂה	*Et feci.*	And I did.
—	וְאֶעֱשֶׂה	*Et faciam.*	And I will do.
עשר	וָאַעְשִׁיר--שֶׁר	*Et ditatus sum.*	And I am rich.
עשה	וְאֶעֶשְׂךָ	*Et faciam te.* [*ira.*	And I will make thee.
אף	וְאַף	*Et etiam, quanquam*	And also, however, the wrath.
אפד	וְאָפַדְתָּ	*Et accinges.*	And thou shalt gird.
אפה	וְאָפָה	*Et coquet.*	And he will bake.
—	וְאָפוּ	*Et coquent.*	And they shall bake.
אף	וְאַפּוֹ	*Et ira ejus.*	And his wrath.
אפד	וְאֵפוֹד	*Et ephod.*	And an ephod.
פחד	וְאֶפְחַד	*Et timebo.*	And I shall fear.
אף	וְאַפִּי	*Et ira mea.*	And mine anger.
פוץ	וָאָפִיץ	*Et dispersi.*	And I have scattered.
—	וַאֲפִיצֵם	*Et dispergam eos.*	And I will scatter them.
אפה	וְאָפִית	*Et coques.*	And thou shalt bake.
אפל	וְאֹפֶל	*Et caligo.*	And darkness.
נפל	וָאֶפֹּל	*Et cecidi.*	And I fell.
—	וָאֶפְּלָה	*Et corrui.*	And I fell.
אפל	וַאֲפֵלָה	*Et caligo.*	And darkness.
פלט	וַאֲפַלְּטָה	*Et evadam.*	And I shall escape, be delivered

ROOTS.	DERIVATIVES.	VERSIO.	SIGNIFICATION.
פלט.	וָאֲפַלְּטֵהוּ	*Et liberabo eum.*	And I will deliver him.
אפל	וַאֲפֵלָתְךָ	*Et caligo tua.*	And thy darkness.
פנה	וָאֵפֶן	*Et verti me.*	And I turned myself.
—	וְאֶפְנֶה	*Et vertam me.*	And I will turn myself.
אפס	וְאֶפֶס	*Et tantum, non, nihil*	And only, not, nothing.
—	וְאַפְסִי	*Et præter me.*	And beside me.
פסל	וָאֶפְסֹל	*Et dolavi, sculpsi.*	And I have hewed, engraven.
פקד	וָאֶפְקֹד	*Et visitavi.*	And I have visited.
אפק	וַאֲפִקִים	*Et torrentes.*	And the rapid rivers.
אפר	וָאֵפֶר	*Et pulvis, cinis.*	And dust, ashes.
פרח	וְאֶפְרֹחָיו	*Et pulli ejus.*	And his young ones.
פרש	וָאֶפְרֹשׂ	*Et expandi.*	And I spread.
—	וָאֶפְרְשָׂה	*Et extendi.*	And I spread out.
פתה	וָאֶפָּת	*Et deceptus sum.*	And I was deceived.
פתח	וָאֶפְתַּח	*Et aperui.*	And I opened.
אפת	וְאַפְּתֹם	*Et reditus.*	And the revenue.
ארץ	וְאָץ	*Et festinans, festinus*	And he that hasteth.
יצא	וָאֵצֵא־־צְאָה	*Et exivi.*	And I went forth.
—	וְאֵצְאָה	*Et egrediar.*	And I will go forth.
צבע	וְאֶצְבְּעוֹת־־עֹת	*Et digiti.*	And fingers.
—	וְאֶצְבְּעֹתֵיכֶם	*Et digiti vestri.*	And your fingers.
—	וְאֶצְבְּעָת	*Et digiti.*	And the toes.
—	וְאֶצְבְּעָתָא	*Et digiti.*	And toes.
—	וְאֶצְבְּעֹתַי	*Et digiti mei.*	And my fingers
—	וְאֶצְבְּעֹתָיו	*Et digiti ejus.*	And his fingers.
צוה	וָאֲצַו	*Et jussi.*	And I commanded.
—	וָאֲצַוֶּה	*Et præcepi.*	And I charged.
—	וַאֲצַוֶּנּוּ	*Et præcipiam ei.*	And I shall command him.
יצע	וְאַצִּיעָה	*Et substernam.*	And I shall make my bed.
נצל	וָאַצִּיל־־צִל	*Et eripui.*	And I delivered.
אצל	וְאֵצֶל	*Et prope, apud.*	And near, at.
—	וְאָצַלְתִּי	*Et seposui.*	And I kept, withheld.
צמת	וְאַצְמִיתֵם	*Et excindam eos.*	And I will destroy them.
צעד	וְאֶצְעָדָה	*Et armilla, monile.*	And the bracelet.
צעק	וָאֶצְעָקָה	*Et clamavi.*	And I cried.
צפה	וַאֲצַפֶּה	*Et aspiciam.*	And I will look.
נצר	וְאֶצְּרָה	*Et custodiam.*	And I shall keep.

ROOTS.	DERIVATIVES.	VERSIO.	SIGNIFICATION.
אצר	וְאֹצָרוֹת	*Et thesauri.*	And treasuries.
נצר	וְאֶצָּרְךָ	*Et servabo te.*	And I will keep thee.
—	וְאֶצְּרֶנָּה־־צֶּ׳	*Et custodiam eam.*	And I shall keep her, or it.
צרף	וְאֶצְרֹף	*Et purgabo.* [*eum.*	And I will purify, refine.
—	וְאֶצְרְפֵנוּ	*Et probabo, purgabo*	And I will try, purify him.
אצר	וְאֹצְרֹתֵיהֶם	*Et thesauri eorum.*	And their treasures.
קבץ	וְאֲקַבְּצָה	*Et congregabo.*	And I will gather.
—	וָאֶקְבְּצָה	*Et congregavi.*	And I gathered together.
—	וָאֶקְבְּצֵם־־אֲ‍ַק׳	*Et congregavi eos.*	And I gathered them together
—	וְאִקַבְּצֵם	*Et congregabo eos.*	And I will gather them.
קבר	וְאֶקְבְּרָה	*Et sepeliam.*	And I will bury.
—	וָאֶקְבְּרֶהָ	*Et sepelivi eam.*	And I buried her.
קדד	וָאֶקֹּד	*Et inclinavi me.*	And I bowed down my head.
קדר	וָאַקְדִּר	*Et atrum reddidi, lugere feci.*	And I made dark, caused to mourn.
אקק	וְאַקּוֹ	*Et hircus sylvestris.*	And the wild goat.
קבב	וָאֶקּוֹב	*Et maledixi.*	And I have cursed.
קוה	וַאֲקַוֶּה	*Et expectabo.*	And I will wait.
—	וָאֲקַוֶּה	*Et expectavi.*	And I have waited.
קום	וָאָקוּם	*Et surrexi.*	And I rose
—	וְאָקוּמָה	*Et surgam.*	And I will arise.
לקח	וָאֶקַּח	*Et cepi, abstuli.*	And I took, took away.
—	וְאֶקַּח	*Et auferam.*	And I will take away.
—	וְאֶקְחָה	*Et capiam.*	And I will fetch.
—	וָאֶקְחָה	*Et cepi.*	And I took.
—	וְאֶקָּחֵהוּ	*Et tollam eum.*	And I will fetch him.
—	וָאֶקָּחֵם	*Et cepi eos.*	And I took them.
קום	וָאָקִים	*Et erexi.*	And I raised up.
—	וְאָקִימָה	*Et surgam.*	And I will arise.
—	וַאֲקַיְּמָה	*Et præstabo.*	And I will perform.
קלל	וָאֵקַל	*Et vilis habita sum.*	And I was despised.
—	וָאֲקַלְלֵם	*Et maledixi eis.*	And I cursed them.
קום	וָאָקֻם	*Et surrexi.*	And I arose.
קנה	וָאֶקְנֶה	*Et emi.*	And I bought.
קוץ	וָאָקֻץ	*Et abominatus sum.*	And I abhorred.
קצף	וְאֶקְצֹף	*Et irascar.*	And I shall be angry.
קרא	וָאֶקְרָא	*Et vocavi, clamavi.*	And I called, cried, published

ROOTS.	DERIVATI VES.	VERSIO.	SIGNIFICATION.
קרא	וָאֶקְרָאֶה	*Et vocavi.*	And I have called.
קרב	וָאֶקְרַב	*Et accessi.*	And I approached, came near.
קרע	וָאֶקְרַע	*Et scidi, laceravi.*	And I have rent, torn.
—	וְאֶקְרַע	*Et lacerabo.*	And I will tear, rend.
ראה	וָאֵרֶא־־אה	*Et vidi.*	And I saw, beheld.
—	וְאֵרֶא	*Et videbo.*	And I shall see.
—	וָאֵרָא	*Et apparui.*	And I appeared.
—	וְאֶרְאֶה	*Et videbo.*	And I will see.
—	וָאֶרְאֶה	*Et vidi.*	And I saw.
—	וְאֵרָאֶה	*Et apparebo.*	And I shall appear.
—	וְאַרְאֵהוּ	*Et ostendam illi.*	And I will shew to him.
—	וְאַרְאֶךָּ	*Et ostendam tibi.*	And I will shew to thee.
—	וָאֶרְאֶךָּ	*Et vidi te.*	And I saw thee.
—	וְאֶרְאֶנּוּ	*Et videbo eum.*	And I shall see him.
ארב	וְאָרַב	*Et insidiabitur.*	And he will lie in wait.
—	וֶאֱרֹב	*Et insidiare.*	And lie thou in wait.
רבה	וְאַרְבֶּה	*Et multiplicabo.*	And I will multiply.
—	וָאַרְבֶּה	*Et multiplicavi.*	And I have multiplied.
—	וְאַרְבֵּהוּ	*Et augebo eum.*	And I will increase him.
רבע	וְאַרְבַּע	*Et quatuor.*	And four.
—	וְאַרְבָּעָה־־בָּ׳	*Et quatuor.*	And four.
—	וְאַרְבָּעִים	*Et quadraginta.*	And forty.
—	וְאַרְבַּעַת	*Et quatuor.*	And the four.
ארב	וַאֲרֻבֹּת	*Et fenestræ.*	And the windows, lattices.
—	וַאֲרַבְתֶּם	*Et insidiabimini.*	And ye shall lie in wait.
ארג	וְאֹרֵג	*Et textor.*	And the weaver.
—	וְאֹרְגִים	*Et textores.*	And the weavers.
ארג	וְאַרְגָּמָן	*Et purpura.*	And purple or scarlet.
ירד	וָאֵרֵד	*Et descendi.*	And I have come down.
רדף	וְאֶרְדְּפָה	*Et persequar.*	And I will pursue.
ארו	וַאֲרוּ	*Et ecce.*	And behold.
ארה	וְאָרוּהָ	*Et carpserunt.*	And they have plucked her.
ארן	וַאֲרוֹן	*Et arca.*	And the ark.
רוץ	וְאָרוּצָה	*Et curram.*	And I will run.
ארר	וְאָרוּר	*Et maledictus.*	And cursed.
ארה	וְאֻרְוֹת	*Et præsepia, stabula*	And stalls, stables.
ארר	וְאָרוֹתִי	*Et maledicam.*	And I will curse.

ROOTS.	DERIVATIVES.	VERSIO.	SIGNIFICATION.
ארז	וְאֶרֶז וָאָ־	*Et cedrus.*	And the cedar.
—	וַאֲרָזִים־־רִ־	*Et cedri.*	And cedars.
ארח	וְאָרַח	*Et incedet.*	And he will go.
—	וְאֹרַח	*Et via.*	And the way.
—	וְאָרְחוֹת	*Et semitæ.*	And the paths.
רחץ	וָאֶרְחַץ	*Et lavavi.*	And I have washed.
—	וָאֶרְחָצֵךְ	*Et lavavi te.*	And I have washed thee.
ארח	וְאֹרְחֹתֶהָ	*Et viæ ejus.*	And his ways.
—	וַאֲרֻחָתוֹ	*Et cibarium.*	And the diet, victuals.
רוב	וָאָרִיב־־בָה	*Et contendi.*	And I contended.
ארה	וְאַרְיֵה	*Et leo.*	And the lion.
ארך	וְאֹרֶךְ	*Et longitudo.*	And the length.
—	וְאֶרֶךְ	*Et longus, tardus.*	And long, slow.
רכב	וְאֶרְכַּב	*Et equitabo.*	And I will ride.
—	וְאַרְכֻּבָתֵהּ	*Et genua ejus.*	And his knees.
ארך	וְאָרְכָּה	*Et longitudo.*	And the length.
—	וְאָרְכּוֹ	*Et longitudo ejus.*	And his length.
—	וַאֲרֻכָתְךָ	*Et sanitas tua.*	And thy health.
ארם	וְאַרְמוֹן	*Et palatium.*	And the palace.
רום	וַאֲרֹמְמֶנְהוּ	*Et exaltabo eum.*	And I will exalt him.
ארם	וְאַרְמְנֹתָיו	*Et palatia ejus.*	And his palaces.
רמס	וָאֶרְמְסֵם	*Et calcabo eos.* [*cabo*	And I will trample them.
רנן	וַאֲרַנֵּן	*Et cantabo, prædi-*	And I will sing aloud, proclaim
ארע	וְאַרְעָא	*Et terra.*	And earth.
רעה	וָאֶרְעֶה	*Et pascam, pavi.*	And I will feed, have fed.
רפא	וְאֶרְפָּא	*Et sanabo.*	And I will heal.
—	וְאֵרָפֵא	*Et sanabor.*	And I shall be healed.
—	וְאֶרְפָּאֵהוּ	*Et sanabo eum.*	And I will heal him.
ארץ	וְאֶרֶץ־־נָאָ־	*Et terra.*	And the land.
—	וְאַרְצָה	*Et terra.*	And the land.
רצה	וְאֶרְצֶה	*Et accipiam eam.*	And I will accept her.
ארץ	וְאַרְצֵךְ	*Et terra tua.*	And thy land.
—	וְאַרְצֵנוּ	*Et terra nostra.*	And our land.
ארק	וְאַרְקָא	*Et terra.*	And the earth.
ארר	וְאֹרְרֶיךָ	*Et maledicentes tibi.*	And they that curse thee.
ארש	וַאֲרֶשֶׁת	*Et petitio.*	And the request.
—	וְאֵרַשְׂתִּיךְ	*Et desponsabo te.*	And I will betroth thee.

ROOTS.	DERIVATIVES.	VERSIO.	SIGNIFICATION.
אש	וְאֵשׁ וָאֵשׁ	*Et ignis.*	And fire.
נשא	וְאֶשָּׂא	*Et feram.*	And I will bear.
—	וָאֶשָּׂא	*Et sumpsi, tuli.*	And I took, lifted.
שאל	וָאֶשְׁאַל	*Et interrogavi.*	And I asked.
—	וְאֶשְׁאָלְךָ	*Et interrogabo te.*	And I will demand of thee.
—	וְאֶשְׁאָלֵם	*Et interrogabo eos.*	And I will ask them.
—	וָאֶשְׁאָלֵם	*Et interrogavi eos.*	And I asked them.
נשא	וְאֶשָּׂאֶנּוּ	*Et feram eum.*	And I shall bear him or it.
שאף	וְאֶשְׁאַף	*Et deglutiam.*	And I will swallow up, devour.
—	וָאֶשְׁאָפָה	*Et anhelavi.*	And I have panted.
ישב	וָאֵשֵׁב	*Et sedi, mansi.*	And I sat, remained, abode.
שוב	וָאָשֻׁב--שֵׁב	*Et retuli.*	And I returned.
ישב	וְאֵשֵׁב	*Et sedebo, habitabo.*	And I will sit, remain, dwell.
—	וְאֵשְׁבָה	*Et habitabo.*	And I will dwell.
—	וַאֲשֵׁבָה	*Et incolam.*	And I will dwell.
—	וָאֵשְׁבָה	*Et sedi.*	And I sat down.
שבע	וְאַשְׁבִּיעֲךָ	*Et adjurabo te.*	And I will make thee swear.
—	וָאַשְׁבִּיעֵם	*Et adjuravi eos.*	And I took an oath of them.
—	וָאֶשָּׁבַע	*Et juravi.*	And I sware. [the full.
—	וָאַשְׁבִּעַ--שׂ	*Et adjuravi, satiavi*	And I made to swear, fed to
שבר	וָאֶשְׁבֹּר	*Et fregi.*	And I brake.
—	וָאֲשַׁבְּרָה	*Et confregi.*	And I brake in pieces.
—	וָאֲשַׁבְּרֵם	*Et confregi eos.*	And I brake them.
שגה	וָאֶשְׁגֶּה	*Et erravi.*	And I have erred.
אשד	וְאֶשֶׁד	*Et fluxus, rivus.*	And the stream or rill.
איש	וְאִשָּׁה	*Et mulier, uxor.*	And a woman, wife.
אש	וְאִשֶּׁה	*Et* oblatio *ignita.*	And an offering made by fire.
שוב	וְאָשׁוּב	*Et revertar.*	And I will turn, return.
—	וָאָשׁוּב	*Et reversus sum.*	And I turned back, returned.
—	וְאָשׁוּבָה	*Et revertar.*	And I will come again.
שוה	וְאֶשְׁוֶה	*Et æquabor.*	And I shall be equal, compared
אשש	וְאָשׁוֹהִי	*Et fundamentà ejus.*	And his foundation.
שוע	וַאֲשַׁוַּע	*Et clamabo.*	And I will shout.
—	וָאֲשַׁוֵּעָה	*Et clamavi.*	And I cried, shouted. [him.
שור	וַאֲשׁוּרֶנּוּ	*Et intuebor illum.*	And I shall observe, behold
שחט	וָאֶשְׂחַט	*Et expressi.*	And I pressed, squeezed.
שחת	וָאַשְׁחִיתֵךְ	*Et disperdidi te.*	And I destroyed thee.

ROOTS.	DERIVATIVES.	VERSIO.	SIGNIFICATION.
שחק	וְאֶשְׁחָקֵם	*Et contundam eos.*	And I will beat them.
שטף	וָאֶשְׁטֹף	*Et immersione ablui*	And I thoroughly washed away.
אשש	וְאֻשַּׁיָּא	*Et fundamenta.*	And the foundations.
שוב	וָאָשִׁיב	*Et respondi.*	And I answered.
—	וְאָשִׁיב	*Et restituam.* [*debo.*	And I will restore. [answer.
—	וְאָשִׁיבָה	*Et reducam, respon-*	And I will bring back, will
—	וָאָשִׁיבָה	*Et reduxi, retuli.*	And I brought again, returned
—	וַאֲשִׁיבֵךְ	*Et reducam te.*	And I will bring thee again.
נשג	וְאַשִּׂיגֵם	*Et assequar eos.*	And I will overtake them.
שוח	וְאָשִׂיחָה	*Et meditabor.*	And I will meditate.
שום	וָאָשִׂים־שָׂם	*Et posui.*	And I have put, set.
—	וְאָשִׂים	*Et ponam.*	And I will set, place.
—	וָאָשִׂימָה	*Et posui.*	And I put.
—	וְאָשִׂימָה־שָּׁמָּה	*Et ponam.*	And I will put.
אשר	וַאֲשֵׁרֵיהֶם	*Et luci eorum.*	And their groves.
אשש	וַאֲשִׁישָׁה	*Et lagena.*	And a flagon.
שות	וַאֲשִׁיתֵהוּ	*Et ponam eum.*	And I will place, lay him.
שכל	וְאֶשְׁכּוֹל	*Et botrus, racemus.*	And the cluster.
שכן	וְאֶשְׁכּוֹן	*Et habitabo.*	And I will dwell.
—	וְאֶשְׁכֹּנָה	*Et habitabo, sedebo.*	And I will be at rest, dwell.
—	וְאַשְׁכִּנָה	*Et habitare faciam.*	And I will cause to dwell.
שכר	וַאֲשַׁכְּרֵם	*Et inebriabo eos.*	And I will make them drunk.
שלח	וְאֶשְׁלַח	*Et mittam.*	And I will send.
—	וָאֶשְׁלַח	*Et misi.*	And I sent.
—	וָאֶשְׁלַח	*Et misi.*	And I have sent.
—	וְאֶשְׁלְחָה	*Et mittam.*	And I will send.
—	וָאֶשְׁלְחָה	*Et misi.*	And I have sent.
—	וַאֲשַׁלְּחָה	*Et dimittam.*	And I will dismiss, let go.
—	וַאֲשַׁלְּחֶהָ	*Et misi eam.*	And I sent her.
—	וַאֲשַׁלְּחֵהוּ	*Et dimisi eum.*	And I sent him away.
—	וְאֶשְׁלָחֲךָ	*Et mittam te.*	And I will send thee.
—	וָאֲשַׁלֵּחֲךָ	*Et dimisi te.*	And I sent thee away.
—	וַאֲשַׁלֵּחֲךָ	*Et dimittam te.*	And I will send thee away.
—	וְאֶשְׁלָחֵם	*Et mittam eos.*	And I will send them.
שלך	וָאַשְׁלִךְ־לָךְ	*Et abjeci.*	And I cast away.
—	וָאַשְׁלִכָה	*Et projeci.*	And I cast forth.
—	וָאַשְׁלִכֵהוּ	*Et conjeci illum.*	And I cast him.

ROOTS.	DERIVATIVES.	VERSIO.	SIGNIFICATION.
שלך	וָאַשְׁלִכֵם	*Et abjeci illos.*	And I have cast them off.
שלם	וַאֲשַׁלֵּם	*Et rependam.*	And I will repay.
—	וַאֲשַׁלְּמָה	*Et rependam.*	And I will requite.
אשם	וְאָשֵׁם	*Et reus erit.*	And he shall be guilty.
אש	וְאִשָּׁם	*Et ignis eorum.*	And their fire.
שמל	וְאַשְׂמְאִילָה	*Et sinistram tenebo.*	And I will keep the left.
אשם	וְאָשְׁמָה	*Et rea erit.*	And she shall be guilty.
—	וְאָשֵׁמוּ	*Et rei erunt.*	And they shall be guilty.
שמר	וְאַשְׁמוּרָה	*Et vigilia.*	And a watch.
אשם	וְאַשְׁמוֹתַי	*Et delicta mea.*	And my sins.
שמח	וְאֶשְׂמְחָה	*Et lætabor.*	And I will rejoice.
שמד	וָאַשְׁמִיד	*Et perdidi.*	And I have destroyed.
—	וְאַשְׁמִידֵם	*Et disperdam eos.*	And I will destroy them.
—	וָאַשְׁמִדֵם	*Et disperdidi eos.*	And I destroyed them.
אשם	וַאֲשֵׁמִים	*Et rei, delinquentes.*	And guilty.
שמע	וְאַשְׁמִיעֲךָ	*Et indicabo tibi.*	And I will shew to thee.
—	וְאַשְׁמִעֵם-מִעֵם	*Et audire faciam eos*	And I will make them hear.
שום	וַאֲשִׂמֵם	*Et constituam eos.*	And I will make, appoint them
שמע	וָאֶשְׁמַע--מַע	*Et audivi.*	And I heard.
—	וְאֶשְׁמְעָה	*Et audiam.*	And I will hear.
—	וָאֶשְׁמְעָה	*Et audivi.*	And I heard.
שמר	וְאֶשְׁמְרָה	*Et custodiam.*	And I will keep.
—	וָאֶשְׁמְרָה	*Et observavi.*	And I have observed.
—	וְאֶשְׁמְרֶנָּה	*Et observabo eam.*	And I shall observe her.
אשם	וְאָשַׁמְתְּ	*Et reus fies.*	And thou wilt be found guilty.
—	וְאַשְׁמָתֵנוּ	*Et delictum nostrum*	And our trespass.
שעה	וְאֶשְׁעָה	*Et respiciam.*	And I will have respect.
שען	וְאֶשָּׁעֵן	*Et innitar.*	And I shall lean.
אשף	וְאַשָּׁף	*Et astrologus.*	And an astrologer.
שפט	וְאִשָּׁפְטָה	*Et disceptabo.*	And I will plead, reason.
שפך	וָאֶשְׁפֹּךְ	*Et effudi.*	And I have poured out.
—	וְאֶשְׁפְּכָה	*Et effundam.*	And I will pour out.
שפר	וְאֶשְׁפָּר	*Et frustum carnis.*	And a piece of flesh.
שקה	וָאַשְׁקֶה	*Et bibere feci.*	And I made to drink.
שקט	וְאֶשְׁקוֹט	*Et quiescam.*	And I shall be quiet.
שקל	וָאֶשְׁקוֹלָה	*Et appendi.*	And I weighed.
—	וָאֶשְׁקֹל	*Et appendi.*	And I weighed.

ROOTS.	DERIVATIVES.	VERSIO.	SIGNIFICATION.
שקל	וָאֶשְׁקְלָה־־קֲלָה	*Et appendi.*	And I weighed.
אשר	וַאֲשֶׁר	*Et qui, quæ, quòd.*	And who, which, that, because
—	וְאַשֵּׁר	*Et dirige.*	And guide, direct thou.
ישב	וָאֵשֵׁב	*Et remansi.*	And I abode, remained.
אשר	וְאִשְׁרוּ	*Et incedite.*	And go ye.
—	וְאִשְּׁרוּ	*Et beatos prædica-* [*bunt.*	And they shall call them blessed
—	וְאַשְׁרֵי	*Et felices.*	And happy.
—	וַאֲשֵׁרֵיהֶם	*Et luci eorum.*	And their groves.
—	וַאֲשֵׁרִים	*Et luci.*	And groves.
—	וְאֻשַּׁרְנָא	*Et muri.*	And the walls.
שרף	וָאֶשְׂרֹף	*Et combussi.*	And I have burnt.
איש	וְאֵשֶׁת	*Et uxor.*	And the wife.
שתה	וָאֵשְׁתְּ	*Et bibi.*	And I drank.
שדר	וְאֶשְׁתַּדּוּר	*Et conspiratio.*	And sedition, conspiracy.
שתה	וְאֶשְׁתֶּה	*Et bibam.*	And I shall drink.
איש	וְאִשְׁתּוֹ	*Et uxor ejus.*	And his wife.
שמם	וָאֶשְׁתּוֹמֵם	*Et obstupui.*	And I wondered.
—	וָאֶשְׁתּוֹמֵם	*Et obstupui.*	And I was astonished.
שחה	וָאֶשְׁתַּחֲוֶה	*Et incurvavi me.*	And I worshipped.
—	וְאֶשְׁתַּחֲוֶה	*Et prosternam me.*	And I will prostrate myself.
שתה	וָאֶשְׁתְּיוּ	*Et biberunt.*	And they drank.
איש	וְאִשְׁתְּךָ	*Et uxor tua.*	And thy wife.
שמר	וָאֶשְׁתַּמֵּר	*Et cavi mihi.*	And I kept myself.
—	וָאֶשְׁתַּמְּרָה	*Et custodivi me.*	And I have kept myself.
שעה	וְאֶשְׁתַּעֲשַׁע	*Et oblectabo me.*	And I will delight myself.
את	וְאַתְּ וְאַתְּ	*Et tu.*	And thou.
—	וְאֵת וְאֶת	*Et ad, cum.*	And to, with.
אבל	וָאֶתְאַבְּלָה	*Et luxi.*	And I mourned.
אפק	וָאֶתְאַפַּק	*Et mihi vim feci.*	And I forced myself.
בון	וָאֶתְבּוֹנֵן	*Et animadverti.*	And I have considered.
את	וְאַתָּה וְא־ וְא־	*Et tu.*	And thou.
אתה	וְאָתָה	*Et venit.*	And he came.
הלך	וְאֶתְהַלְּכָה	*Et incedam.*	And I will walk.
את	וְאֶתְהֶן	*Et eas.*	And them, those.
אתה	וְאֵתוּ	*Et venite.*	And come ye.
את	וְאִתּוֹ	*Et cum ipso.*	And with him.
—	וְאֹתוֹ	*Et ipsum.*	And him.

ROOTS.	DERIVATIVES.	VERSIO.	SIGNIFICATION.
ידה	וָאֶתְוַדֶּה	*Et confessus sum.*	And I made my confession.
אתן	וְאַתּוּנָא	*Et fornax.*	And the furnace.
נתק	וְאַתּוּקֵיהָא	*Et porticus ejus.*	And his porch.
חנן	וָאֶתְחַנַּן	*Et oravi.*	And I besought.
את	וְאַתְּי	*Et tu.*	And thou.
אתה	וְאֹתִיּוֹת	*Et ventura.*	And things that are coming.
יצב	וְאֶתְיַצְּבָה	*Et sistam me.*	And I will set myself.
את	וְאֹתָךְ־תְךְ	*Et te.*	And thee.
—	וְאֶתְכֶם	*Et vos.*	And you.
—	וְאִתְּכֶם	*Et vobiscum.*	And with you.
—	וְאַתֶּם	*Et vos.*	And you.
תמל	וְאֶתְמוֹל	*Et nuper.*	And of late.
מלט	וָאֶתְמַלְּטָה	*Et evasi.*	And I have escaped.
משל	וָאֶתְמַשֵּׁל	*Et assimilatus sum.*	And I have become like.
נתן	וָאֶתֵּן־־תֶּן	*Et dedi, tradidi, posui*	And I gave, delivered, put.
—	וְאֶתֵּן־־תֵּן	*Et dabo.*	And I will give.
את	וְאַתֵּן	*Et vos.*	And ye.
נתן	וְאֶתְּנָה־־תֵּנָה	*Et dabo, dedi.*	And I will give, have given.
את	וְאַתֵּנָה	*Et vos.*	And ye.
נתן	וָאֶתְּנָה	*Et dedi, posui.*	And I have given, put.
—	וָאֶתְּנֶהָ	*Et dedi eam.*	And I gave her.
—	וָאֶתְּנֵהוּ	*Et tradidi eum.*	And I have delivered him.
את	וְאִתָּנוּ	*Et nobiscum.*	And with us.
נחם	וְאֶתְנֶחָם	*Et consolatus sum.*	And I have comforted myself.
נתן	וָאֶתְּנֵךְ	*Et tradidi te. [tui.*	And I delivered thee. [thee.
—	וְאֶתֶּנְךָ	*Et te ducam, consti-*	And I will bring, have made
—	וּנְתַתִּיךָ וְאֶתְּנֵךְ	*Et dabo, statuam te.*	And I will give, make thee.
—	וָאֶתְּנֵם	*Et dedi eos.*	And I have given them.
תנה	וְאֶתְנַן	*Et merces.*	And reward.
נתן	וָאֶתְּנֶנָּה	*Et dedi eam.*	And I gave her.
תנה	וְאֶתְנַנָּה	*Et merces ejus.*	And her hire.
נתן	וְאֶתְּנֶנּוּ	*Et dabo eum.*	And I will give him.
נפל	וָאֶתְנַפַּל	*Et prostravi me.*	And I fell down.
אתן	וַאֲתֹנֹת	*Et asinæ.*	And she-asses.
תעב	וָאֶתְעֲבָה	*Et abominatus sum.*	And I have abhorred.
פלל	וְאֶתְפַּלֵּל	*Et orabo.*	And I will pray.
—	וָאֶתְפַּלֵּל	*Et oravi.*	And I prayed.

ROOTS.	DERIVATIVES.	VERSIO.	SIGNIFICATION.
פלל	וָאֶתְפַּלְלָה	*Et oravi.*	And I prayed.
תפש	וָאֶתְפֹּשׂ	*Et prehendi.*	And I took.
קוט	וָאֶתְקוֹטָטָה	*Et contendi, fastidivi abominatus sum.*	And I contended with, loathed, was weary of, abominated.
אות	וְאֹתֹתָם	*Et signa eorum.*	And their signs.
	וב		
בוא	וָבֹא	*Et venire, ingredi.*	And to come, enter thou.
—	וָבָא	*Et iens, veniens.*	And going, coming.
—	וּבָא	*Et veniet, ibit, ingredietur, occidet.*	And he will come, go, enter, set.
—	וּבֹא	*Et ito, veni.*	And go, come thou.
אבד	וּבַאֲבוֹד	*Et pereundo.*	And in perishing.
—	וּבְאָבְדָם	*Et pereundo ipsos.*	And when they perish.
אבן	וּבָאֶבֶן וּבְ־	*Et cum, in lapide.*	And with, in a stone.
אבנט	וּבְאַבְנֵט	*Et cum balteo.*	And with a girdle.
אבן	וּבָאֲבָנִים	*Et cum lapidibus.*	And with stones. [thers.
אבה	וּבַאֲבֹתֵיכֶם	*Et in patres vestros.*	And toward, against your fa-
אדם	וּבָאָדָם	*Et in homine.*	And in man, mankind.
—	וּבְאָדָם	*Et per hominem.*	And by a man.
בוא	וּבָאָה וּבָאת	*Et veniet*	And she shall come.
—	וָבֹאָה	*Et veni.*	And come thou.
אהל	וּבְאֹהֶל	*Et in tentorium.*	And into the tent.
בוא	וָבָאוּ	*Et venerunt.*	And they came.
—	וּבָאוּ	*Et venite.* [venit.	And come ye.
—	וּבֹאוּ וָבֹאוּ	*Et ite, ingredimini,*	And go, enter ye, he came.
און	וּבְאוֹנוֹ	*Et in robore ejus.*	And in, by his strength.
אצר	וּבְאוֹצְרוֹת אֹצְ׳	*Et in thesauris.*	And in the treasuries.
—	וּבְאוֹצְרוֹתַיִךְ	*Et in thesauris tuis.*	And in thy treasures.
באש	וּבְאוּשְׁתָא	*Et mala.*	And bad.
בוא	וּבָאוֹת	*Et ingredientes.*	And they entering.
אזב	וּבָאֵזוֹב	*Et cum hyssopo.*	And with the hyssop.
אזן	וּבְאָזְנֵי	*Et in auribus.*	And in, with the ears.
—	וּבְאָזְנָיו	*Et in auribus ejus.*	And in, with their ears.
—	וּבְאָזְנֶיךָ	*Et in auribus tuis.*	And in, with thine ears.
זרע	וּבְאֶזְרוֹעַ	*Et cum brachio.*	And with an arm. [country.
זרח	וּבְאֶזְרַח	*Et sive indigena.*	And whether a native of the

ROOTS.	DERIVATIVES.	VERSIO.	SIGNIFICATION.
אחד	וּבְאֶחָד	*Et in prima.*	And in the first.
אחה	וּבְאָחִיו	*Et in fratrem ejus.*	And towards his brother.
—	וּבְאַחֵיכֶם	*Et in fratres vestros*	And over your brethren.
אחר	וּבְאַחֲרִית	*Et in fine.*	And at the end, the latter time
—	וּבְאַחֲרִיתוֹ	*Et in extremo ejus.*	And at his latter end.
אחד	וּבְאַחַת	*Et simul.*	And together, together with.
בוא	וּבֹאִי	*Et ingredere.*	And enter thou, go in.
איב	וּבְאֹיְבַי	*Et in inimicos meos.*	And upon mine enemies.
בוא	וּבָאִים	*Et venientes.*	And coming.
אים	וּבָאֵימִים	*Et in terriculamenta*	And upon idols, frightful or terrible to their worshippers
אין	וּבְאֵין	*Et in non, absque.*	And where not, without.
בוא	וּבֹאֲךָ	*Et veniendo te.*	And when thou comest.
—	וּבֹאֶךָ־־וּבוֹ״	*Et ingressus tuus.*	And thy entrance.
—	וְּבִאֲךָ	*Et introducet te.*	And he shall bring thee in.
אלה	וּבָאֵלֶּה	*Et inter ipsos.*	And among them.
—	וּבֵאלֹהֵי	*Et de Deo.*	And of the God.
—	וּבֵאלֹהַי	*Et per Deum meum.*	And by my God.
—	וּבֵאלֹהֵיהֶם	*Et in deos eorum.*	And upon their gods.
—	וּבֵאלֹהָיו	*Et in Deum ejus.*	And towards his God.
אלם	וּבָאֵלָם	*Et in vestibulo.*	And in the porch
אלה	וּבְאָלָתוֹ	*Et in juramento ejus*	And in his oath.
אמר	וּבְאָמְרִי	*Et dicendo me.*	And when I say.
—	וּבְאִמְרֵיכֶם	*Et dictis vestris.*	And with your speeches.
אמן	וּבֶאֱמֶת	*Et in veritate.*	And in truth.
בוא	וּבָאנוּ	*Et veniemus.*	And we shall come.
אנה	וּבָאֳנִיּוֹת	*Et cum navibus.*	And with ships.
אנש	וּבְאַנְשֵׁי	*Et de viris.*	And of men.
אסר	וּבֶאֱסוּר	*Et cum vinculo.*	And with a bond.
אנף	וּבְאַף	*Et in ira.*	And in wrath.
—	וּבְאַפְּכֶם	*Et ad nares vestras.*	And to your nostrils.
אפס	וּבְאֶפֶס	*Et ubi non, sine.*	And where not, without, in want of.
באר	וּבָאֵר	*Et explana.*	And make thou it plain.
—	וּבְאֵר	*Et fovea.*	And a pit.
רבע	וּבְאַרְבַּע	*Et in quarto.*	And in the fourth.
—	וּבְאַרְבָּעָה	*Et in quarta.*	And in the fourth.
ארג	וּבְאַרְגָּוָן־־גָּמָן	*Et in purpura.*	And in purple or scarlet.

ROOTS.	DERIVATIVES.	VERSIO.	SIGNIFICATION.
ארע	ובְאַרְעָא	*Et in terra.*	And in earth.
ארץ	ובְאֶרֶץ־ובָאָ״	*Et in terra.*	And in the land.
—	ובְאַרְצְכֶם	*Et in terra vestra.*	And in your land.
באש	ובָאַשׁ	*Et fœtebit.*	And he shall stink.
אש	ובָאֵשׁ ובָאֵשׁ	*Et in igne.* [*radices.*	And by the fire. [toms.
אשד	ובְאַשְׁדוֹת	*Et in decursibus, ad*	And in the springs, at the bot-
איש	ובְאִשָּׁה	*Et pro uxore.*	And for a wife.
אשם	ובְאַשְׁמָתֵנוּ	*Et pro delicto nostro*	And for our trespass.
אשר	ובַאֲשֶׁר	*Et ubi.*	And where.
איש	ובְאֵשֶׁת	*Et in uxorem.*	And toward the wife.
—	ובְאִשְׁתּוֹ	*Et in uxorem ejus.*	And toward his wife.
בוא	ובָאתָ־תָ־־ת	*Et venies, ibis.*	And thou shalt come, go.
אות	ובְאֹתוֹת	*Et cum signis.*	And with signs.
בוא	ובָאתִי	*Et veni, veniam.*	And I came, will come.
—	ובָאתֶם	*Et ibitis, venito.*	And ye will go, come thou.
—	ובְבֹא־־בֹא	*Et veniendo.*	And in coming.
—	ובְבֹאָהּ	*Et veniendo eam.*	And when she comes.
—	ובְבֹאוֹ	*Et veniendo eum.*	And as he cometh.
בהם	ובַבְּהֵמָה	*Et in pecudes.*	And upon the cattle.
—	ובִבְהֶמְתְּךָ	*Et inter pecus tuum*	And among thy cattle.
—	ובִבְהֶמְתֵּנוּ	*Et in pecus nostrum*	And over our cattle.
בוץ	ובַבּוּץ	*Et in bysso.*	And in fine linen.
בור	ובַבּוֹר	*Et in fovea,carcere.*	And in the pit, dungeon.
בזז	ובַבִּזָּה ובַ״	*Et in prædam.*	And on the spoil.
בטח	ובְבִטְחָה	*Et in fiducia.*	And in confidence.
בית	ובְבַיִת	*Et in domum, domo.*	And to, into, in the house.
—	ובְבֵיתוֹ	*Et in domo sua.*	And in his own house.
—	ובְבֵיתִי	*Et in domo mea.*	And in my house.
בכה	ובִבְכִי	*Et in fletu.*	And with weeping.
בנה	ובִבְנָהּ	*Et in filium ejus.*	And towards her son.
—	ובִבְנוֹת	*Et ædificando.*	And in building.
—	ובִבְנוֹתֶיהָ־־נֹתֶ׳	*Et in pagis ejus*[*tris*	And in her towns.
—	ובִבְנוֹתֵנוּ	*Et cum filiabus nos-*	And with our daughters.
—	ובִבְנֵי	*Et inter filios.*	And among the children.
—	ובְבָנֶיהָ	*Et in filios ejus.*	And towards her children.
—	ובְבָנֶיךָ	*Et in filios tuos.*	And towards thy children.
בקר	ובַבֹּקֶר	*Et in diluculo, mane*	And in the morning.

ROOTS.	DERIVATIVES.	VERSIO.	SIGNIFICATION.
בקר	וּבְבָקָר	Et in bobus. [rum.	And in oxen.
—	וּבִבְקָרָם	Et cum armento eo-	And with their herd.
—	וּבִבְקָרֵנוּ	Et cum bobus nostris	And with our herd.
ברד	וּבְבָרָד	Et cum grandine.	And with hail.
בור	וּבַבֹּרוֹת	Et in foveis.	And in pits.
ברזל	וּבְבַרְזֶל	Et cum ferro.	And with iron.
בשר	וּבִבְשָׂרִי	Et in carnemea.	And in my flesh.
—	וּבִבְשָׂרָם	Et in carne eorum.	And in their flesh.
בוש	וּבְבֹשֶׁת	Et in pudorem.	And to shame, confusion.
בנה	וּבְבִתָּהּ	Et in filiam ejus.	And towards her daughter.
בית	וּבְבָתֵּי	Et in domibus.	And in houses.
—	וּבְבָתֵּיהֶם	Et in domibus eorum	And in their houses.
—	וּבְבָתֶּיךָ	Et in domus tuas.	And into thy houses.
גאה	וּבְגַאֲוָתוֹ	Et in excellentia ejus	And in his excellency.
גבר	וּבִגְבוּרָתְךָ	Et per robur tuum.	And by thy strength.
בגד	וּבֶגֶד	Et vestis, perfidia.	And a garment, deceit.
—	וּבִגְדֵי	Et vestes.	And the garments.
—	וּבְגָדָיו	Et vestes ejus.	And his garments.
—	וּבְגָדֶיךָ	Et vestes tuæ.	And thy garments.
—	וּבִגְדֵיכֶם	Et vestes vestræ.	And your clothes.
—	וּבְגָדִים	Et vestes.	And garments.
גדל	וּבְגֹדֶל	Et in magnitudine.	And in greatness.
גוי	וּבַגּוֹיִם	Et inter gentes.	And among the nations.
גלה	וּבַגּוֹלָה	Et in captivitatem.	And into captivity.
גזל	וּבְגָזֵל	Et in rapina.	And in robbery.
גיא	וּבְגֵי	Et in valle.	And in the valley.
גלל	וּבְגִלּוּלֵי	Et in idolis.	And in, with the idols.
—	וּבְגִלּוּלֵיהֶם	Et cum idolis eorum	And with their idols.
—	וּבְגִלּוּלַיִךְ	Et in idolis tuis.	And in thine idols.
—	וּבְגִלּוּלֵיכֶם	Et cum idolis vestris	And with your idols.
גלח	וּבְגַלְּחוֹ	Et tondendo eum.	And when he shaves.
גלל	וּבִגְלַל	Et propter.	And for, because of.
גמל	וּבַגְּמַלִּים	Et in camelis.	And on camels.
גנז	וּבְגִנְזֵי	Et in thesauris.	And in treasuries.
גפן	וּבַגֶּפֶן	Et in vite.	And in the vine.
גור	וּבַגֵּר	Et in peregrino.	And in a stranger.
גרב	וּבְגָרָב	Et cum psora, scabie	And with the scab, scurvy.

ROOTS.	DERIVATIVES.	VERSIO.	SIGNIFICATION.
דאג	וּבִדְאָגָה	*Et cum solicitudine.*	And with care, anxiety.
דבר	וּבְדַבֵּר	*Et loquendo.*	And in speaking.
—	וּבַדָּבָר־וּבִדְבָר	*Et per rem.*	And through the thing.
—	וּבַדָּבֶר־־דֶ׳	*Et peste.*	And by, with the pestilence.
—	וּבְדַבְּרוֹ	*Et loquendo eum.*	And when he speaks.
—	וּבְדַבְּרִי	*Et loquendo me.*	And when I speak.
—	וּבִדְבָרֶיךָ	*Et in verbo tuo.*	And in thy word.
דוד	וּבַדְּוָדִים	*Et in lebetibus.*	And in caldrons.
בדל	וּבְדִיל	*Et stannum.*	And tin.
דלק	וּבַדַּלֶּקֶת	*Et in febri.*	And in a fever.
דלת	וּבַדֶּלֶת	*Et ad ostium.*	And to the door.
דם	וּבְדָם־־דָ״	*Et in sanguine.*	And in blood.
—	וּבִדְמֵי	*Et in sanguinibus.*	And in the blood.
דמשק	וּבִדְמֶשֶׁק	*Et in angulo.*	And in a corner.
ידע	וּבְדַעַת	*Et in scientia.*	And in knowledge.
בדר	וּבַדֵּרוּ	*Et dispergite.*	And scatter ye.
דרך	וּבְדֶרֶךְ	*Et in via.*	And in the way.
—	וּבַדֶּרֶךְ	*Et per viam.*	And by the way.
—	וּבְדַרְכּוֹ	*Et per viam ejus.*	And by his way.
—	וּבְדַרְכֵי	*Et in viis.*	And in the ways.
	וּבָהּ	*Et in ea.*	And in her.
ארך	וּבְהַאֲרִיךְ	*Et morando.*	And in tarrying.
נגע	וּבְהַגִּיעַ	*Et veniendo.*	And in coming.
בהה	וָבֹהוּ	*Et inanitas.*	And emptiness.
ידה	וּבְהוֹדוֹת	*Et confitendo.*	And in acknowledging, giving thanks.
יצא	וּבְהוֹצִיאָם	*Et educendo eos.*	And when they bring out.
הוה	וּבְהַוּוֹת	*Et in pravitate.*	And in naughtiness.
הכל	וּבְהֵיכָלוֹ	*Et in templo ejus.*	And in his temple.
כנע	וּבְהִכָּנְעוֹ	*Et humiliando se.*	And when he humbles himself.
כשל	וּבְהִכָּשְׁלָם	*Et corruendo eos.*	And when they fall.
בהל	וּבֶהָלוֹת	*Et terrores.*	And terrors.
הלל	וּבְהַלֵּל	*Et laudando.*	And in praising.
	וּבָהֶם	*Et in illis.*	And in them.
בהם	וּבְהֵמָה	*Et bestia, pecus.*	And beast, cattle.
מרה	וּבְהַמְרוֹתָם	*Et irritando eos.*	And in their provocation.
בהם	וּבְהֶמְתָּהּ	*Et pecus ejus.*	And her cattle.
—	וּבְהֶמְתֶּךָ	*Et pecus tuum.*	And thy cattle.

ROOTS.	DERIVATIVES.	VERSIO.	SIGNIFICATION.
בהם	וּבְהֶמְתְּכֶם	*Et pecus vestrum.*	And your cattle.
—	וּבְהֶמְתָּם	*Et pecus eorum.*	And their cattle.
—	וּבְהֶמְתֵּנוּ	*Et pecus nostrum.*	And our cattle.
נשא	וּבְהִנָּשֵׂא	*Et attollendo se.*	And in lifting themselves up.
—	וּבְהִנָּשְׂאָם	*Et evehendo eos.*	And when those are lifted up.
עטף	וּבְהֵעָטֵף	*Et elanguendo.*	And when grown languid, weak
עלה.	וּבְהֵעָלוֹת	*Et attollendo.*	And when taken up.
—	וּבְהַעֲלוֹתִי	*Et educendo me.*	And when I bring up.
—	וּבְהַעֲלֹת	*Et accendendo.*	And in lighting, kindling.
—	וּבְהֵעָלֹתוֹ	*Et attollendo eum.*	But when he was taken up.
נפל	וּבְהַפִּילְכֶם	*Et sorte dividendo eos*	And in dividing them by lot.
קבץ	וּבְהִקָּבֵץ	*Et congregando se.*	And when they were assembled
קהל	וּבְהַקְהִיל	*Et congregando.*	And in gathering together.
הרר	וּבָהָר וּבְהַר	*Et in monte.*	And in the mount.
—	וּבְהָרֵי	*Et in montibus.*	And upon the mountains.
שכל	וּבְהַשְׂכִּיל	*Et erudiendo.*	And in instructing.
שען	וּבְהִשָּׁעֶנְךָ	*Et innitendo te.*	And in thy relying.
—	וּבְהִשָּׁעֲנָם	*Et innitendo eos.*	And when they lean.
בהל	וּבְהִתְבַּהֲלָה	*Et cum festinatione.*	And in haste.
	וּבוֹ	*Et ad eum, in ipso.*	And to him, in him.
בוא	וָבוֹא	*Et venire, inire.*	And to come, enter.
—	וּבוֹאִי	*Et veni.*	And I came.
בגד	וּבוֹגֵד	*Et prævaricans.*	And dealing treacherously.
—	וּבוֹגְדִים	*Et perfidi.*	And the perfidious, treacherous
בוז	וָבוּז וּבוּז	*Et contemptus.*	And contempt.
בזה	וּבוֹזָיו	*Et spernentes.*	And despising.
בטח	וּבוֹטֵחַ וּבֹטֵחַ	*Et confidens.*	And he that trusteth.
בכה	וּבוֹכֶה וּבֹכֶה	*Et flens.*	And weeping.
בלס	וּבוֹלֵס	*Et collector.*	And a gatherer.
בלק	וּבוֹלְקָהּ	*Et vastans eam.*	And making her waste.
בנה	וּבוֹנִים	*Et ædificantes.*	And building.
ברץ	וּבוּץ	*Et byssus.*	And fine linen.
בור	וּבוֹר	*Et fovea.*	And the pit.
ברא	וּבוֹרֵא וּבֹרֵא	*Et creans.*	And he that created.
בוש	וּבוֹשָׁה	*Et pudore afficietur.*	And she shall be ashamed.
זה	וּבְזֹאת	*Et propter hoc.*	And for, on account of this.
זפח	וּבְזִבְחֵינוּ	*Et sacrificiis nostris*	And with our sacrifices.

ROOTS.	DERIVATIVES.	VERSIO.	SIGNIFICATION.
זה	וּבָזֶה	*Et in hoc.*	And in this.
בזה	וּבָזָה	*Et sprevit.*	And he despised.
זהב	וּבְזָהָב וּבַ׳	*Et in auro.*	And in, with gold.
בזה	וּבְזוּי	*Et contemptus.*	And despised.
בזז	וּבָזַז	*Et spoliabit*	And he shall spoil.
——	וּבָזְזוּ	*Et prædabuntur.*	And they shall rob.
——	וּבֹזְזוּ	*Et diripientur.*	And they shall be robbed.
——	וּבְזָזוּם	*Et diripient eos.*	And they shall spoil them.
בזה	וּבֹזַי	*Et spernentes me.*	And they that despise me.
זיק	וּבְזִיקוֹת	*Et in scintillis.*	And in the sparks.
זעף	וּבְזַעְפּוֹ	*Et in indignari eum*	And while he is wroth.
זפת	וּבַזָּפֶת	*Et cum pice. [tris.*	And with pitch.
זקן	וּבִזְקֵנֵנוּ	*Et cum senibus nos-*	And with our elders.
זרע	וּבִזְרוֹעַ־־רֹעַ	*Et cum brachio [um*	And with an arm.
——	וּבִזְרוֹעִי	*Et per brachium me-*	And by my arm.
——	וּבִזְרֹעֲךָ־־רֹעֲךָ	*Et brachio tuo.*	And by thy arm.
——	וּבְזַרְעֲךָ־־עֲךָ	*Et in semine tuo.*	And in thy seed.
חבל	וּבְחֶבֶל	*Et in func.*	And in, with a cord.
——	וּבְחַבְלֵי	*Et cum funibus.*	And with the cords.
חבר	וּבַחֲבֻרָתוֹ	*Et per livorem ejus.*	And with his stripes.
חגג	וּבְחַג	*Et in festo.*	And in the feast.
——	וּבַחַגִּים	*Et in festis.*	And in the feasts.
חדר	וּבַחֲדַר	*Et in cubiculum.*	And into the chamber.
——	וּבְחַדְרֵי	*Et in cubiculis.*	And in chambers.
חדש	וּבַחֹדֶשׁ	*Et in mense.*	And in the month.
——	וּבֶחֳדָשִׁים	*Et in noviluniis.*	And in the new moons.
חוח	וּבְחוֹחַ	*Et cum hamo.*	And with a hook, barb.
——	וּבַחֲוָחִים	*Et in spinis.*	And in thorns.
חמה	וּבַחוֹמָה	*Et in muro.*	And upon wall.
——	וּבְחוֹמַת	*Et in muro.*	And on the wall.
——	וּבְחוֹמֹתַי	*Et intra muros meos*	And within my walls.
חפף	וּבְחוֹף	*Et in littore.*	And on the shore.
חוץ	וּבְחוּצוֹת־־חֻ׳	*Et in plateis.*	And in the streets.
בחר	וּבָחוֹר	*Et eligere.*	And to choose.
——	וּבַחוּרֵי	*Et electi, juvenes.*	And the chosen, young men.
——	וּבַחוּרַי	*Et juvenes mei.*	And my young men.
——	וּבַחוּרָיו	*Et juvenes ejus.*	And his young men.

ROOTS.	DERIVATIVES.	VERSIO.	SIGNIFICATION.
בחר	וּבַחוּרִים	*Et juvenes.*	And the young men.
חזה	וּבְחֶזְוֹת	*Et in visionibus.*	And in the visions.
חזק	וּבְחָזְקָה	*Et per vim.*	And with force.
חטא	וּבְחֵטְא	*Et in peccato.*	And in sin.
—	וּבְחַטֹּאות	*Et in peccatis.*	And in sins.
—	וּבְחַטֹּאתוֹ־־תָיו	*Et in peccatis ejus.*	And in his sins.
חיה	וּבַחַיָּה	*Et in bestia.*	And in beast.
חוץ	וּבַחִיצוֹן	*Et extrinsecus.*	And without.
חיק	וּבְחֵיקוֹ	*Et in sinu ejus* [*meam*	And in his bosom.
חכם	וּבְחָכְמָתִי	*Et per sapientiam*	And by my wisdom.
חלל	וּבְחַלְלוֹ	*Et profanando eum.*	And as he defileth.
חמד	וּבַחֲמֻדוֹת	*Et cum rebus desiderabilibus.*	And with the pleasant things.
יחם	וּבְחֵמָה	*Et in ira.* [*ejus.*	And in wrath.
חמל	וּבְחֶמְלָתוֹ	*Et pro clementia*	And in his pity.
חמר	וּבַחֲמֹר	*Et cum asino.*	And with an ass.
—	וּבַחֲמֹרִים	*Et pro asinis.*	And for the asses.
חמש	וּבַחֲמִשָּׁה	*Et in quinta.*	And in the fifth.
יחם	וּבַחֲמָתוֹ	*Et in ira ejus.*	And in his wrath.
—	וּבַחֲמָתִי	*Et in furore meo.*	And in my fury.
—	וּבַחֲמָתְךָ	*Et in ira tua.* [*rans.*	And in thy wrath.
בחן	וּבֹחֵן	*Et probans, explo-*	And proving, trying.
—	וָבַחַן	*Et turris.*	And a tower.
—	וּבְחָנוּנִי	*Et probate me.*	And prove ye me.
חנה	וּבַחֲנִית	*Et cum hasta.*	And with a spear.
חנך	וּבַחֲנֻכַּת	*Et in dedicatione.*	And at the dedication.
בחן	וּבָחַנְתָּ	*Et probabis, probasti*	And thou wilt try, hast tried.
חנה	וּבַחֲנֹת	*Et castra ponendo.*	And in pitching a camp.
בחן	וּבְחַנְתִּים	*Et probabo eos.*	And I will try them.
חסד	וּבְחֶסֶד	*Et in misericordia.*	And through mercy.
—	וּבְחַסְדְּךָ	*Et begniguitate tua.*	And by, of thy mercy, kindness
חסר	וּבְחֹסֶר	*Et in defectu.*	And in want.
חצץ	וּבַחִצִּים וּבַ׳	*Et cum sagittis.*	And with arrows.
חצר	וּבַחֲצֹצְרוֹת	*Et cum tubis.*	And with trumpets.
—	וּבַחֲצֵרוֹת	*Et in atriis.*	And in the courts.
—	וּבְחַצְרֹתֵיהֶם	*Et in atriis eorum.*	And in their courts.
חקר	וּבַחֵקֶר	*Et in investigatione*	And in the search.

ROOTS.	DERIVATIVES.	VERSIO.	SIGNIFICATION.
חקק	וּבְחֻקֹּתַי	*Et in statutis meis.*	And in my statutes.
—	וּבְחֻקֹּתֵיהֶם	*Et in statutis eorum*	And in their ordinances.
—	וּבְחֻקֹּתָיו	*Et in statutis ejus.*	And in his statutes.
בחר	וּבָחַר	*Et eliget.*	And he shall choose.
—	וּבָחֹר	*Et eligendo.*	And in choosing.
חרב	וּבְחֶרֶב וּבְ׳	*Et cum gladio.*	And with the sword.
—	וּבְחַרְבּוֹ	*Et per gladium ejus.*	And by his sword.
בחר	וּבָחַרוּ	*Et elegerunt.*	And they have chosen.
חרה	וּבַחֲרוֹנוֹ	*Et in ira ejus.*	And in his anger.
חרר	וּבַחַרְחֻר	*Et cum æstu.*	And with a burning.
בחר	וּבַחֻרֵיהֶם	*Et juvenes eorum.*	And their young men.
—	וּבַחֻרִים	*Et juvenes.*	And the young men. [ments.
חרץ	וּבַחֲרִיצֵי	*Et cum tribulis.*	And with the threshing instru-
חרס	וּבֶחָרֶס	*Et scabie aspera.*	And with a rough itch.
חרף	וּבַחֹרֶף	*Et in hyeme.*	And in winter.
—	וּבְחֶרְפָּה	*Et in opprobrio.*	And in reproach. [struments.
חרץ	וּבַחֲרִצֵי	*Et sub tribulis.*	And under the threshing in-
חרש	וּבֶחֳרָשִׁים	*Et in saltibus.*	And in forests.
—	וּבַחֲרֹשֶׁת	*Et in sculptura.*	And in carving, engraving.
בחר	וּבָחַרְתָּ	*Et eliges.*	And thou shalt choose.
—	וּבָחַרְתִּי	*Et elegi.*	And I have chosen.
חשך	וּבַחֹשֶׁךְ	*Et in tenebris.*	And in darkness.
טוב	וּבְטוּב	*Et in bonitate.*	And in goodness.
—	וּבְטוּבְךָ	*Et in bonitate tua.*	And in thy goodness.
בטח	וָבֶטַח	*Et fiducia.*	And confidence.
—	וּבְטַח	*Et confide.*	And trust, confide thou.
—	וּבֹטֵחַ	*Et confidens.*	And trusting.
—	וּבִטְחוּ	*Et confidite.*	And trust ye.
—	וּבְטֻחוֹת	*Et securitas.*	And security.
טוח	וּבְטָחִים	*Et in oblinentibus.*	And upon them that daub.
בטח	וּבָטַחְתָּ	*Et confides.* [*eorum.*	And thou shalt be secure.
טיר	וּבְטִירֹתָם	*Et arcibus, palatiis*	And by their castles, palaces.
טלל	וּבְטַל	*Et in rore.*	And in dew.
בטל	וּבָטְלוּ	*Et cessare fecerunt.*	And they have made to cease.
—	וּבָטְלוּ	*Et cessabunt.*	And they shall cease.
בטן	וּבֶטֶן	*Et venter, uterus.*	And the belly, womb.
—	וּבִטְנִי	*Et venter meus.*	And my belly.

ROOTS.	DERIVATIVES.	VERSIO.	SIGNIFICATION.
בטן	וּבִטְנָם	*Et venter eorum.*	And their belly.
טרם	וּבְטֶרֶם	*Et antequam.*	And before.
יבל	וּבַיֹּבֵל	*Et in jubilæo.*	And in the jubilee.
יד	וּבְיַד־־יַ־	*Et cum manu.*	And with the hand.
—	וּבְיָדוֹ	*Et in manu ejus*	And in his hand.
—	וּבְיָדָיו	*Et per manus ejus.*	And with his hands.
—	וּבִידֵיכֶם	*Et manibus vestris.*	And by, with your hands.
—	וּבְיָדְךָ	*Et per manum tuam*	And by, with thy hand. [Lord.
היה	וּבַיהוָֹה	*Et in Dominum.*	And towards, against the
יום	וּבְיוֹם וּבַיּוֹם	*Et in die.*	And on the day.
—	וּבְיוֹמֵי	*Et in diebus.*	And in the days.
—	וּבְיוֹמֵיהוֹן	*Et in diebus eorum.*	And in their days.
יין	וּבַיַּיִן וּבְיַיִן	*Et in, cum vino.*	And in, with wine.
ילד	וּבַיְלָדִי	*Et in natis.*	And in the children.
לקט	וּבַיַּלְקוּט	*Et in pera.*	And in a bag, satchel.
יום	וּבִימֵי	*Et in diebus.*	And in the days.
—	וּבְיָמַי	*Et in diebus meis*	And in my days.
—	וּבִימֵיכֶם	*Et in diebus vestris.*	And in your days.
—	וּבְיָמִים־־בַי־	*Et in diebus.*	And in days.
בין	וּבֵין	*Et inter.*	And between.
בון	וּבִין	*Et intellige.*	And understand thou.
—	וּבִינָה	*Et intelligentia.*	And understanding.
בין	וּבֵינוֹ	*Et inter eum.*	And between him.
—	וּבֵינֵיהֶם	*Et inter eos.*	And between them.
—	וּבֵינֶיךָ־־נְךָ	*Et inter te.*	And between thee.
—	וּבֵינֵיכֶם	*Et inter vos.*	And between you.
—	וּבֵינְךָ־־נֶךָ	*Et inter te.*	And between thee.
בון	וּבִינַת	*Et intelligentia.* [tra	And the understanding.
—	וּבִינַתְכֶם	*Et intelligentia ves-*	And your understanding.
יען	וּבְיַעַן	*Et in eo quod.*	And in that, forasmuch as.
ירא	וּבְיִרְאַת	*Et per timorem.*	And by the fear.
ירק	וּבַיֵּרָקוֹן	*Et cum rubigine.*	And with mildew.
ישב	וּבְיֹשְׁבֵי	*Et inter habitantes.*	And among the inhabitants.
ישע	וּבִישׁוּעָתְךָ	*Et in salute tua.*	And in thy salvation.
ישר	וּבְיֹשֶׁר	*Et in rectitudine.*	And in uprightness.
—	וּבְיִשְׁרַת	*Et in rectitudine.*	And in the uprightness.
בית	וּבַיִת	*Et domus.*	And the house.

ROOTS.	DERIVATIVES.	VERSIO.	SIGNIFICATION.
בית	ובית	*Et domus.*	And a house.
—	וָבַיְתָה	*Et intrinsecus.*	And within.
—	וּבַיְתָה	*Et in domo.*	And in the house.
—	וּבֵיתֵה	*Et domus ejus.*	And his house.
—	וּבֵיתָהּ	*Et domus ejus.*	And her house.
—	וּבֵיתוֹ	*Et domus ejus.*	And his house.
—	וּבֵיתִי	*Et domus mea.*	And my house.
—	וּבֵיתְךָ־־ךְ־ת	*Et domus tua.* [tua.	And thy house.
—	וּבֵיתֶךָ	*Et domus, familia*	And thy houshold.
—	וּבֵיתְכֶם	*Et domus vestræ.*	And your houses, household.
יתר	וּבְיֶתֶר	*Et in residuum.*	And towards the remnant.
	וָבָךְ	*Et contra te.*	And against thee.
	וּבָךְ	*Et in te.*	And towards thee.
כבד	וּבִכְבוֹדָם	*Et in gloria eorum.*	And in their glory.
בכה	וּבָכֹה וּבָכוֹ	*Et flere.*	And to weep.
	וּבְכָה	*Et in te.*	And to thee.
כהן	וּבְכֹּהֲנִים	*Et in sacerdotibus.*	And in the priests.
בכה	וּבָכוּ	*Et fleverunt.*	And they have wept.
—	וּבְכוּ	*Et flete.*	And weep ye.
בכר	וּבִכּוּרֵי	*Et primitiæ.* [eorum	And the first fruits.
כחש	וּבְכַחֲשֵׁיהֶם	*Et cum mendaciis*	And with their lies.
בכה	וּבְכִי	*Et fletus.*	And weeping, lamentation.
כיד	וּבְכִידוֹן	*Et cum clypeo.*	And with a shield.
כיס	וּבְכִיס	*Et cum sacculo.* [ta.	And with the bag.
כלל	וּבְכָל וּבְכֹל	*Et in, cum omni, to-*	And with all, the whole.
כלה	וּבִכְלֵי	*Et in, cum vasis, ar-mis, instrumentis.*	And in, with the vessels, wea-pons, instruments.
—	וּבִכְלִי	*Et cum instrumento.*	And with the instrument.
—	וּבְכֵלָיו	*Et in vasis ejus.*	And in his vessels.
כון	וּבְכֵן	*Et tunc.*	And then.
כנר	וּבְכִנּוֹר	*Et cum cithara.*	And with a harp.
—	וּבְכִנֹּרוֹת	*Et cum citharis.*	And with harps.
כסף	וּבְכֶסֶף וּבַכֶּסֶף	*Et cum argento.*	And with silver.
כפף	וּבְכַפַּי	*Et in manibus meis.*	And in my hands.
כיף	וּבַכֵּפִים	*Et in rupes.*	And upon the rocks.
כפן	וּבְכָפָן	*Et propter famem.*	And for hunger.
כפר	וּבַכְּפָרִים	*Et in pagis.*	And in the villages.

ROOTS.	DERIVATIVES.	VERSIO.	SIGNIFICATION.
כור	וּבְכִּרְכָּרוֹת	*Et in carrucis.*	And upon the cars.
כרם	וּבְכֶרֶם	*Et in vineam.*	And into the vineyard.
—	וּבִכְרָמִים	*Et in vineis.*	And in the vineyards.
בכר	וּבְכֹרֹת	*Et primogenita.*	And the first-born.
כשל	וּבְכָשְׁלוֹ	*Et impingendo.*	And in stumbling.
כשר	וּבְכִשְׁרוֹן	*Et in rectitudine.*	And in uprightness.
כתב	וּבִכְתָב	*Et in scriptura.*	And in the writing.
בכה	וּבָכְתָה	*Et flebit.*	And she shall bewail.
כתף	וּבְכָתֵף	*Et cum humero.*	And with the shoulder.
בל	וּבַל	*Et non, nec.*	And not, nor.
לבב	וּבְלֵב וּבְלֵבָב	*Et in corde.*	And in the heart.
—	וּבִלְבָבוֹ	*Et in corde ejus.*	And in his heart.
—	וּבִלְבָבְךָ	*Et in corde tuo*	And in thy heart.
לבן	וּבִלְבֵנִים	*Et ex lateribus.*	And of bricks.
להב	וּבְלֶהָבָה	*Et per flammam.*	And by flame.
לא	וּבְלוֹא	*Et absque.*	And without.
בלה	וּבְלוֹיֵ	*Et veteres.*	And old.
לול	וּבְלוּלִים	*Et per cochleas.*	And by winding stairs.
לחם	וּבְלֶחֶם	*Et de pane.*	And of the bread.
ליל	וּבְלַיְלָה־־לָ	*Et in nocte.*	And in the night.
בל	וּבְלִיַּעַל	*Et impius, scelestus.*	And wicked, profligate.
ילך	וּבְלֶכֶת	*Et eundo.*	And in going.
—	וּבְלֶכְתְּךָ	*Et eundo te.*	And when thou goest.
—	וּבְלֶכְתָּם	*Et abeundo eos.*	And when they depart.
בלע	וּבִלַּע	*Et absorbebit.*	And he will swallow up, destroy.
בל	וּבִלְעָדֶיךָ	*Et sine te.*	And without thee.
בלע	וּבְלָעָה	*Et deglutiet.*	And she will swallow.
לשן	וּבְלָשׁוֹן	*Et in lingua.*	And in the language.
—	וּבִלְשׁוֹנָם	*Et cum lingua eorum*	And with their tongue.
	וּבָם	*Et propter ipsos.*	And on account of them.
אמר	וּבְמַאֲמַר	*Et per verbum.*	And by the word.
גדל	וּבְמִגְדָּלוֹת	*Et in turribus.*	And in the towers.
מגד	וּבְמִגְדָּנוֹת	*Et rebus pretiosis*	And with precious things.
גזר	וּבְמַגְזְרֹת	*Et sub securibus.*	And under axes.
גרר	וּבִמְגֵרוֹת	*Et cum serris.*	And with saws.
דבר	וּבְמִדְבָּר	*Et in deserto.*	And in the wilderness.
מה	וּבַמֶּה־־מָּה	*Et per quod.*	And by what.

ROOTS.	DERIVATIVES.	VERSIO.	SIGNIFICATION.
מוט	וּבְמוֹט	*Et amovendo.* [*tris.*	And in removing.
יעד	וּבְמוֹעֲדֵיכֶם	*Et solennitatibus ves-*	And in your solemn days.
—	וּבְמוֹעֲדִים	*Et in solennitatibus.*	And in the solemnities.
יפת	וּבְמוֹפְתִים-מֹפְ׳	*Et cum prodigiis.*	And with wonders, prodigies.
ירא	וּבְמוֹרָא--מֹרָא	*Et in terrore.*	And in terror, fear.
—	וּבְמוֹרָאִים	*Et per terrores.*	And by terrors.
ישב	וּבְמוֹשָׁב	*Et in sede.*	And in the seat.
מות	וּבְמוֹת	*Et moriendo.*	And in dying, being dead.
במה	וּבָמוֹת	*Et excelsa loca.*	And the high places.
מות	וּבְמוֹתוֹ	*Et moriendo eum.*	And when he dieth.
—	וּבְמוֹתָם	*Et in morte eorum.*	And in their death.
זרה	וּבַמִּזְרֶה	*Et cum ventilabro.*	And with the fan.
חוג	וּבַמְּחוּגָה	*Et cum circino.*	And with the compass.
חלל	וּבִמְחֹלוֹת--לֹת	*Et in choris.*	And in, with dances.
—	וּבִמְחִלּוֹת	*Et in speluncas.*	And into the caves.
מים	וּבַמַּיִם וּבְמַיִם	*Et in aqua, aquis.*	And in the water, waters.
—	וּבַמַּיִם	*Et per aquas.*	And through the waters.
ישר	וּבַמִּישׁוֹר	*Et in planitie.*	And in the plain.
—	וּבְמִישׁוֹר	*Et in rectitudine.*	And in uprightness.
כתב	וּבְמִכְתָּב	*Et ex scripto.*	And according to the writing.
לאך	וּבְמַלְאָכָיו	*Et in angelis ejus.*	And in his angels. [fulfilled.
מלא	וּבִמְלֹאת	*Et in complendo.*	And when they shall have been
—	וּבִמְלוֹאת	*Et ad complendum.*	And at the completion.
לחם	וּבְמִלְחָמָה	*Et in bello.*	And in war.
—	וּבְמִלְחֲמוֹת	*Et in bellis.*	And in battles.
מלך	וּבְמַלְכוּת	*Et in regno.*	And in the reign.
—	וּבְמַלְכוּתִי	*Et in regno meo.*	And in my kingdom.
—	וּבְמַלְכֵי	*Et contra reges.*	And against the kings.
נאף	וּבִמְנָאֲפִים	*Et in adulteros.*	And against the adulterers.
נוח	וּבִמְנוּחֹת	*Et in locis quietis.*	And in resting places.
נוס	וּבִמְנוּסָה	*Et in fuga.*	And in flight.
מנח	וּבְמִנְחָה	*Et in oblatione.*	And with offering.
—	וּבְמִנְחַת	*Et in sacrificio.*	And at the sacrifice.
—	וּבְמִנְחָתִי	*Et in oblatione mea.*	And in my offering.
נוע	וּבִמְנַעַנְעִים	*Et in sistris.*	And on cornets.
נור	וּבַמְּנֹרָה	*Et in candelabro.*	And in the candlestick.
ספד	וּבְמִסְפֵּד	*Et in luctu.*	And with mourning.

ROOTS.	DERIVATIVES.	VERSIO.	SIGNIFICATION.
ספר	וּבְמִסְפָּר	*Et secundum numerum.* [*eorum.*	And according to the number.
יסר	וּבְמֹסְרָם	*Et in eruditionem*	And for their instruction.
ען	וּבִמְעוֹנוֹתֶיהָ	*Et habitaculis eorum*	And in their places.
עלה	וּבַמַּעֲלוֹת וּבְמַ׳	*Et per gradus.*	And by steps.
מער	וּבַמְּעָרוֹת	*Et in speluncis.*	And in the caves.
צוה	וּבַמִּצְוָה	*Et in mandato.*	And in the commandment.
צוק	וּבְמָצוֹק	*Et in angustia.*	And in the straitness.
מצץ	וּבַמַּצּוֹת	*Et in azymis.*	And with unleavened cakes.
צוה	וּבְמִצְוֹתָיו	*Et in præceptis ejus*	And in his commandments.
צלל	וּבִמְצִלְתַּיִם־תָּ֫יִם	*Et cum cymbalis.*	And with cymbals.
צנף	וּבְמִצְנֶפֶת	*Et cum cidari.*	And with the mitre, turban.
נקב	וּבַמַּקָּבוֹת וּבְמַ׳	*Et cum malleis.*	And with hammers.
קום	וּבַמָּקוֹם וּבְמָ׳	*Et in loco.*	And in the place.
קלל	וּבְמַקֵּל	*Et in baculo.*	And in, with the staff.
קנה	וּבְמִקְנֶה־־נֵה	*Et pro, cum pecude.*	And for, with the cattle.
ראה	וּבְמַרְאֵה	*Et in aspectu.*	And in the sight.
רבה	וּבְמַרְבִּית	*Et in augmen.*	And for increase. [*tries.*
רחק	וּבַמֶּרְחַקִּים	*Et in remotis* terris.	And in remote, distant *coun-*
מרר	וּבִמְרִירוּת	*Et cum amaritudine*	And with bitterness.
רכב	וּבַמֶּרְכָּבָה	*Et in curru.*	And in the chariot.
רמה	וּבְמִרְמָה	*Et cum fraude.*	And with deceit.
שאר	וּבְמִשְׁאֲרוֹתֶיךָ	*Et in mactris tuis.*	And in thy kneading troughs.
שור	וּבַמְּשׂוּרָה	*Et in mensura.*	And in measure.
שכן	וּבְמִשְׁכָּן	*Et in tentorio.*	And in a tabernacle.
—	וּבְמִשְׁכְּנוֹת	*Et in tabernaculis.*	And in dwellings.
משל	וּבְמְשֹׁל	*Et dominando.*	And in ruling.
שמן	וּבְמִשְׁמַנֵּי	*Et in pinguia.* [*ejus.*	And upon the fat.
שמר	וּבְמִשְׁמְרָיו	*Et in observationes*	And for his offices.
שפח	וּבְמִשְׁפַּחְתּוֹ	*Et in familiam ejus.*	And against his family.
שפט	וּבְמִשְׁפָּט	*Et in judicio.*	And in judgment.
—	וּבְמִשְׁפָּטַי	*Et in judiciis meis.*	And in my judgments. [ments
—	וּבְמִשְׁפְּטֵיהֶם	*Et in judiciis eorum*	And according to their judg-
—	וּבְמִשְׁפָּטֶיךָ	*Et in judicia tua.*	And against thy judgments.
שרף	וּבְמִשְׂרְפוֹת	*Et ob combustiones.*	And with the burnings.
תכן	וּבְמַתְכֻּנְתּוֹ	*Et secundum summam ejus.*	And according to his sum, weight.

ROOTS.	DERIVATIVES.	VERSIO.	SIGNIFICATION.
בנה	וּבֵן וּבֶן וּבֵן	*Et filius.*	And a son.
נבא	וּבִנְבִאֵי־־בִיאֵי	*Et in prophetis.*	And in the prophets.
—	וּבְנָבִיא	*Et prophetam.*	And by a prophet.
—	וּבִנְבִיאַי	*Et in prophetas meos*	And towards my prophets.
נבל	וּבִנְבָלִים	*Et cum psalteriis.*	And with psalteries.
—	וּבְנִבְלָתָם	*Et in cadaver eorum*	And towards their carcase.
נגב	וּבַנֶּגֶב	*Et in austro.*	And in the south.
נגע	וּבְנִגְעֵי	*Et cum ictibus.*	And with the stripes.
—	וּבִנְגָעִים	*Et cum plagis.* [*vit.*	And with stripes.
בנה	וּבָנָה	*Et extruet, ædifica-*	And he will build, hath built.
נהר	וּבַנְּהָרוֹת	*Et in fluviis.* [*truent*	And in the rivers. [build.
פנה	וּבָנוּ	*Et ædificarunt, ex-*	And they have built, shall
—	וּבְנוּ	*Et ædificate.*	And build ye.
—	וּבְנוֹ וּבְנוֹהִי	*Et filii ejus.*	And his sons.
—	וּבְנוּ	*Et ædificaverunt.*	And they builded.
—	וּבְנוֹת וּבָנוֹת	*Et filiæ.*	And the daughters. [owl.
—	וּבְנוֹת יַעֲנָה	*Et ululæ filiæ.*	And owls, daughters of the
—	וּבְנוֹתַי	*Et filiæ meæ.* [*ejus.*	And my daughters. [lages
—	וּבְנוֹתֶיהָ־־נ״	*Et filiæ, oppida, pagi*	And her daughters, towns, vil-
—	וּבְנוֹתֵיהֶם־־נ״	*Et filiæ eorum.*	And their daughters.
—	וּבְנוֹתָיו־־נ״	*Et filiæ ejus.*	And his daughters.
—	וּבְנוֹתֶיךָ־תַיִךְ	*Et filiæ tuæ.*	And thy daughters.
—	וּבְנוֹתֵיכֶם־־נ״	*Et filiæ vestræ.*	And your daughters.
—	וּבְנוֹתֵינוּ־־נ״	*Et filiæ nostræ.*	And our daughters.
נוח	וּבְנֻחֹה	*Et quiescendo ipsam*	And when she or it resteth.
נחל	וּבַנְּחָלִים	*Et in fluviis.* [*ejus.*	And in the rivers.
—	וּבְנַחֲלָתוֹ	*Et in hæreditatem*	And with his inheritance.
נחש	וּבַנְּחֹשֶׁת וּבִנְ״	*Et in, cum ære.*	And in, with brass.
בנה	וּבְנִי	*Et filius meus.*	And my son. [ones.
—	וּבְנֵי	*Et filii, pulli.*	And the sons, children, young
—	וּבָנַי	*Et filii mei.*	And my sons.
—	וּבֹנֵי	*Et ædificantes.*	And the builders.
—	וּבָנֶיהָ	*Et filii ejus.*	And her children.
—	וּבְנֵיהֶם	*Et filii eorum.*	And their sons.
—	וּבְנֵיהֶן	*Et filii earum.*	And their children.
—	וּבָנָיו	*Et filii ejus.*	And his sons.
—	וּבָנֶיךָ	*Et filii tui.*	And thy sons.

ROOTS.	DERIVATIVES.	VERSIO.	SIGNIFICATION.
בנה	וּבְנֵיכֶם	*Et filii vestri.*	And your children.
—	וּבָנִים	*Et filii.*	And children.
—	וּבֹנַיִן	*Et ædificantes.*	And building.
—	וּבָנֵינוּ	*Et filii nostri.*	And our sons.
—	וּבָנִינוּ	*Et ædificabimus.*	And we will build.
—	וּבָנִיתָ	*Et ædificabis.*	And thou shalt build.
—	וּבָנִיתִי	*Et ædificabo.*	And I will build.
—	וּבְנִיתִיהָ	*Et ædificabo eam.*	And I will build her.
—	וּבְנִיתִים	*Et ædificabo eos.*	And I will build them.
—	וּבִנְךָ וּבִנֵךְ	*Et filius tuus.*	And thy son.
נסך	וּבְנִסְכֵּיהֶם	*Et cum libaminibus.*	And with the drink-offerings.
נסע	וּבִנְסֹעַ	*Et proficiscendo.*	And when setting forward.
נעל	וּבְנַעֲלוֹ	*Et in calceo ejus.*	And in his shoe.
נער	וּבַנְּעָרִים	*Et in pueros.*	And towards the young men.
נוף	וּבְנָפוֹת	*Et in tractibus.*	And in the coasts, borders.
פלא	וּבְנִפְלָאוֹת	*Et cum mirabilibus.*	And with wonderful things.
נפש	וּבְנֶפֶשׁ	*Et in animo.*	And in, with a mind.
—	וּבְנַפְשִׁי	*Et in animo meo.*	And in my mind.
נצר	וּבַנְּצוּרִים	*Et in monumentis, locis desertis.*	And in the monuments, desert places.
נקה	וּבְנִקְיֹן	*Et in innocentia.*	And in the innocency.
נקק	וּבִנְקִיקֵי	*Et in fissuris.*	And in the holes.
שבע	וּבַנִּשְׁבָּעִים	*Et in jurantes.*	And against swearers.
אנש	וּבְנָשֶׁיךָ	*Et in uxores tuas.*	And towards thy wives.
סבב	וּבִסְבִיבֵי	*Et in circuitibus.*	And in the places about.
סוס	וּבַסּוּסִים	*Et in equis.*	And on horses.
סוף	וּבְסוּפָתְךָ	*Et turbine tuo.*	And with thy storm.
סל	וּבַסַּל	*Et in canistro.*	And in the basket.
סלע	וּבַסְּלָעִים	*Et in rupibus.*	And in rocks.
סעף	וּבִסְעִפֵי	*Et in cacumina.*	And unto the tops.
בסר	וּבֹסֶר	*Et omphax.*	And the sour grape.
סתם	וּבִסְתָם	*Et in occulto.*	And in the hidden.
בעה	וּבְעָא־־ה	*Et petiit.*	And he requested, desired.
עבד	וּבַעֲבָדֶיךָ	*Et in servos tuos.*	And upon thy servants.
—	וּבְעַבְדֻתֵנוּ	*Et in servitio nostro.*	And in our bondage.
עבר	וּבַעֲבוּר	*Et ut, propter.*	And that, on account of.
עד	וּבְעַד	*Et pro, circa, super.*	And for, about, upon.

ROOTS.	DERIVATIVES.	VERSIO.	SIGNIFICATION.
עד	וּבְעֵדוֹתָיו	*Et in testimoniis ejus*	And in his testimonies.
בעה	וּבְעוּ	*Et petierunt.*	And they sought.
עוד	וּבְעוֹד	*Et adhuc, post.*	And yet, after.
עול	וּבַעֲוֺלוֹ	*Et pro iniquitate ejus*	And for his iniquity.
עוה	וּבַעֲוֺנוֹת	*Et propter iniquitates. [tes nostras.*	And for the iniquities.
——	וּבַעֲוֺנֹתֵינוּ	*Et propter iniquita-*	And for our iniquities.
עוף	וּבְעוֹף וּבְ׳	*Et e volatili.*	And of fowl.
עור	וּבְעִוָּרוֹן	*Et cum cæcitate.*	And with blindness.
עז	וּבְעִזִּים	*Et in capris.*	And among the goats.
עזק	וּבְעִזְקַת	*Et cum annulo.*	And with the signet.
עין	וּבְעֵינֵי	*Et in oculis.*	And in the eyes.
עיר	וּבְעִירוֹ	*Et in civitate ejus.*	And in his city.
ערם	וּבְעֵירֹם	*Et in nuditate.*	And in nakedness.
בער	וּבְעִירָם	*Et pecudes eorum.*	And their beasts.
——	וּבְעִירֵנוּ	*Et jumenta nostra.*	And our cattle.
בעל	וּבָעַל	*Et uxorem duxit.*	And he hath married a wife.
——	וּבַעַל	*Et herus, dominus.*	And a master, lord.
——	וּבְעָלָהּ	*Et duxit eam.*	And he married her.
——	וּבַעֲלֵי	*Et domini.*	And the masters.
עלל	וּבַעֲלִילוֹתֶיךָ	*Et de factis tuis.*	And of, at thy doings.
——	וּבַעֲלִילוֹתָם	*Et factis eorum.*	And by their doings.
בעל	וּבְעַלְתָּהּ	*Et eris maritus ejus*	And thou shalt be her husband
עמם	וּבְעָם	*Et cum populo.*	And with people.
עמד	וּבְעַמֻּד־־מוּד	*Et in columna.*	And in the pillar.
——	וּבְעָמְדָם	*Et stando eos.*	And when they stand.
עמם	וּבְעַמֶּךָ־מְּךָ	*Et in populum tuum*	And upon thy people.
עמל	וּבֶעָמָל	*Et in laborem.*	And in the labour.
——	וּבַעֲמָלְךָ	*Et in labore tuo.*	And in thy labour.
עמק	וּבָעֵמֶק	*Et in valle.*	And in the valley.
ענן	וּבֶעָנָן	*Et in nube.*	And in a cloud.
ענף	וּבְעַנְפּוֹהִי	*Et in ramis ejus.*	And upon his branches.
עפל	וּבַעְפָלִים	*Et cum mariscis.*	And with the emerods.
עפר	וּבֶעָפָר	*Et in pulvere.*	And in the dust.
עץ	וּבְעֵץ	*Et in ligno.*	And in the wood.
עצב	וּבְעַצְּבַת	*Et in dolore.*	And in sorrow.
עץ	וּבַעֲצֵי	*Et cum lignis.*	And with timber.

ROOTS.	DERIVATIVES.	VERSIO.	SIGNIFICATION.
עץ	וּבָעֵצִים	*Et cum lignis.*	And with wood.
עצם	וּבַעֲצָמוֹת	*Et cum ossibus.*	And with bones.
בער	וּבִעֵר	*Et accendet, pascet.*	And he shall burn, shall feed.
—	וָבַעַר	*Et insipiens, stupidus*	And the foolish, stupid, brutish
ערב	וּבָעֶרֶב	*Et in vespera.*	And in the evening.
—	וּבָעֲרָבָה	*Et in planitie.*	And in the plain.
בער	וּבָעֲרָה	*Et exardebit.*	And she shall burn.
—	וּבָעֲרוּ	*Et accendentur.*	And they shall burn, be burnt.
—	וּבִעֲרוּ	*Et accendent.*	And they shall set on fire.
עיר	וּבְעָרֵי	*Et in urbibus.*	And in the cities.
—	וּבְעָרָיו	*Et in urbibus ejus.*	And in his cities.
בער	וּבִעַרְתָּ	*Et auferes.*	And thou shalt put away.
—	וּבִעַרְתִּי	*Et auferam.*	And I will take away.
עשב	וּבְעֵשֶׂב	*Et in herba.*	And in the herb.
עשר	וּבֶעָשׂוֹר	*Et in decima.*	And on the tenth.
עשק	וּבְעֹשְׁקֵי	*Et in opprimentes.*	And against those that oppress
עתת	וּבְעֵת וּבָעֵת	*Et in tempore.*	And at the time, when.
—	וּבָעִתִּים	*Et in temporibus.*	And in times.
בעת	וּבִעֲתַתּוּ	*Et perturbavit eum.*	And he troubled him.
פגר	וּבְפִגְרֵי	*Et in cadavera.*	And on the carcases.
פחז	וּבְפַחֲזוּתָם	*Et levitate eorum.*	And by their lightness.
פה	וּבְפִי	*Et in ore.* [*rum.*	And in, with, by the mouth.
פסל	וּבְפְסִילֵיהֶם	*Et in sculptilibus eo-*	And with their graven images
פרד	וּבַפְּרָדִים	*Et in mulis.*	And upon mules.
פרה	וּבִפְרִי	*Et in fructu.* [*vitia.*	And in the fruit.
פרך	וּבְפָרֶךְ	*Et cum duritia, sæ-*	And with rigour, cruelty.
פרש	וּבְפָרָשָׁיו	*Et cum equitibus ejus*	And with his horsemen.
—	וּבְפָרָשִׁים	*Et cum equitibus.*	And with horsemen.
—	וּבְפָרִשְׂכֶם	*Et tendendo vos.*	And when ye stretch forth.
פשע	וּבְפִשְׁעֵיכֶם	*Et propter prævari-cationes vestras.*	And for your transgressions.
פתת	וּבִפְתוֹתֵי	*Et propter frustula.*	And for pieces *of meat.*
פתח	וּבְפִתְחֵי	*Et in ostiis.*	And in the doors.
צון	וּבַצֹּאן	*Et in ovibus.*	And upon the sheep.
—	וּבְצֹאנְךָ	*Et e grege tuo.*	And of thy flock.
יצא	וּבְצֵאתוֹ	*Et exeundo eum.*	And when he goeth out.
—	וּבְצֵאתָם	*Et exeundo illos.*	And as they go forth.

ROOTS.	DERIVATIVES.	VERSIO.	SIGNIFICATION.
צבה	וּבַצַּבִּים	*Et in lecticis.*	And in litters.
צדק	וּבִצְדָקָה	*Et in justitia.*	And in righteousness.
—	וּבְצִדְקָתְךָ	*Et in justitia tua.*	And in thy righteousness.
בצץ	וּבִצָּה	*Et cœnum.*	And mire.
צום	וּבְצוֹם	*Et in jejunio.*	And with fasting.
צוק	וּבְצוֹק	*Et in angustia.*	And in distress, trouble.
צור	וּבְצוּר	*Et in, pro rupe.*	And in, for, the rock.
בצר	וּבְצוּרֹת	*Et munitæ.*	And the walled, fenced.
—	וּבָצִיר	*Et vindemia.*	And the vintage.
צלל	וּבְצֵל	*Et in, sub umbra.*	And in, under the shadow.
—	וּבְצִלּוֹ	*Et sub umbra ejus.*	And under his shadow.
צלח	וּבְצֶלָחוֹת	*Et in patinis.*	And in dishes.
צלע	וּבְצַלְעִי	*Et in claudicatione mea.*	And in my halting, adversity.
צלל	וּבְצִלְצַל	*Et fuscina, harpagone.*	And with a spear, harpoon.
—	וּבְצֶלְצְלִים	*Et cum cymbalis.*	And with cymbals.
צמא	וּבְצָמָא	*Et in siti.*	And in thirst.
בצע	וּבֹצֵעַ	*Et avarus.*	And the covetous.
צער	וּבִצְעִירוֹ	*Et in natu minimo ejus.*	And in his youngest.
בצע	וּבְצָעֵם	*Et divide eos.*	And cut, divide thou them.
צפר	וּבַצִּפֹּר	*Et cum ave.*	And with the bird.
צור	וּבְצָרָה	*Et in angustia*	And in distress.
בצר	וּבְצֻרוֹת--רֹת	*Et munitæ.*	And walled, fenced.
צרח	וּבַצְּרִחִים	*Et in turribus, arcibus.*	And in towers, high places.
בקק	וּבַקְבֻּק	*Et lagena.*	And a cruse, jug.
קדח	וּבַקַּדַּחַת	*Et febri ardente.*	And with a burning fever.
קהל	וּבִקְהַל	*Et in cœtu.*	And in the company.
—	וּבְקָהָל	*Et cum cœtu.*	And with an assembly.
קול	וּבְקוֹל	*Et cum voce.*	And with a voice.
—	וּבְקוֹלוֹ--קֹלוֹ	*Et ad vocem ejus.*	And at his voice.
—	וּבְקוֹלִי	*Et cum voce mea.*	And with my voice.
קום	וּבְקוּם	*Et surgendo.*	And in, when rising.
—	וּבְקוּמָהּ--קָמָה	*Et surgendo eam.*	And when she arises.
קום	וּבְקוּמֶךָ	*Et surgendo te.*	And when thou risest up.
קטן	וּבַקָּטֹן	*Et cum parvulo.*	And with the little one.
קיר	וּבַקִּיר	*Et cum pariete.*	And with the wall.
קנא	וּבְקִנְאָתִי	*Et in zelotypia mea.*	And in my jealousy.

ROOTS.	DERIVATIVES.	VERSIO.	SIGNIFICATION.
בקע	וּבֹקֵעַ	*Et diffindens.*	And cleaving.
—	וּבָקְעָה	*Et rumpet.*	And she shall break, hatch.
—	וּבַקְּעֵהוּ	*Et divide eum.*	And divide thou him.
—	וּבָקַעְתָּ	*Et fidisti, findes.*	And thou didst rend, wilt rend
—	וּבְקָעֹת	*Et valles.*	And the vallies.
—	וּבִקַּעְתִּי	*Et diffindam.*	And I will rend.
קצה	וּבְקָצֵה	*Et ad extremum.*	And to the end.
קצר	וּבְקָצִיר	*Et in messe.*	And in harvest.
קצף	וּבְקֶצֶף	*Et in indignatione.*	And in indignation.
קצר	וּבְקֻצְרְכֶם	*Et metendo vos.*	And when ye reap.
בקר	וָבֹקֶר	*Et mane.*	And morning.
—	וּבָקָר	*Et bos, boves.*	And oxen.
קרב	וּבְקֶרֶב	*Et in medio. [illo.*	And in the midst.
—	וּבְקִרְבּוֹ	*Et in medio ejus, in*	And in his midst, within him.
—	וּבְקִרְבָּם	*Et in medio eorum.*	And among them.
—	וּבְקָרְבָתָם	*Et accedendo eos.*	And when they come near.
קרדם	וּבְקַרְדֻּמּוֹת	*Et cum securibus.*	And with axes.
בקר	וּבִקְּרוּ־־ךָ	*Et quæsiverunt.*	And they made search.
—	וּבְקָרֶךָ	*Et boves tui.*	And thy herds.
—	וּבְקָרְךָ	*Et bos tuus.*	And thy cattle.
—	וּבְקַרְכֶם	*Et bos vester.*	And your herds.
—	וּבְקָרָם	*Et boves eorum.*	And their herds.
קרן	וּבְקַרְנֵיכֶם	*Et cornibus vestris.*	And with your horns.
קרע	וּבְקָרְעִי	*Et lacerando.*	And in rending, tearing.
בקר	וּבִקַּרְתִּים	*Et quæram eos.*	And I will seek them.
בקש	וּבִקֵּשׁ	*Et requiret.*	And he will enquire.
—	וּבַקֵּשׁ	*Et quære.*	And seek thou.
—	וּבִקְשׁוּ	*Et quæsiverunt.*	And they have sought.
—	וּבַקְשׁוּ	*Et quærite.*	And seek ye.
קשת	וּבְקֶשֶׁת	*Et cum arcu.*	And with the bow.
בקש	וּבַקָּשָׁתִי	*Et petitio mea.*	And my request.
קשת	וּבְקַשְׁתִּי	*Et cum arcu meo.*	And with my bow.
—	וּבְקַשְׁתְּךָ	*Et cum arcu tuo.*	And with thy bow.
בקש	וּבִקְשָׁתַם	*Et quæret eos [retis.*	And she shall seek them.
—	וּבִקַּשְׁתֶּם	*Et quæsivistis, quæ-*	And ye have sought, shall seek
בקק	וּבַקֹּתִי	*Et evacuabo.*	And I will make void.
ברר	וּבַר	*Et purus, mundus.*	And pure, clean.

ROOTS.	DERIVATIVES.	VERSIO.	SIGNIFICATION.
ברא	וּבָרָא	*Et creavit, creabit.*	And he has created, will create
—	וּבָרֵא	*Et succidendo.*	And in dispatching, cutting [down.
ראה	וּבִרְאוֹת	*Et videndo.*	And in seeing.
ראש	וּבְרֹאשׁ	*Et in vertice, capite*	And on the top, head.
—	וּבְרָאשֵׁי	*Et in principio.*	And in the beginning.
ברא	וּבֵרֵאתָ	*Et succides.*	And thou shalt cut down.
—	וּבֵרֵאתוֹ	*Et succides eum.*	And thou shalt cut him down.
רבב	וּבְרֹב	*Et in magnitudine.*	And in the greatness.
ברה	וּבַרְבֻּרִים	*Et gallinacei capones.*	And fatted fowls.
רגל	וּבְרַגְלֵיהֶם	*Et cum pedibus eorum.*	And with their feet.
רגע	וּבְרֶגַע	*Et in momento.*	And in a moment.
ברד	וּבָרַד	*Et grandinabit.*	And it shall hail.
—	וּבָרָד	*Et grando.*	And hail.
—	וּבְרֻדִּים	*Et grandinati, varii.*	And grisled, with small spots [like hail.
ירד	וּבְרֶדֶת	*Et descendendo.*	And in descending, falling.
רוח	וּבְרוּחַ	*Et per ventum, spiritum.*	And with, by the wind, spirit.
ברך	וּבָרוּךְ וּבְרוּכָה	*Et benedictus.*	And blessed.
רום	וּבְרוֹמָם	*Et attollendo illos.*	And when they were lifted up
ברר	וּבָרוֹתִי	*Et expurgabo.*	And I will purge out.
ברזל	וּבַרְזֶל	*Et ferrum, ferreus.*	And iron, of iron.
רחב	וּבָרְחֹבוֹת	*Et in plateis.*	And in the broad ways, streets
—	וּבִרְחֹבֹתֶיהָ	*Et in plateis ejus.*	And in her streets.
—	וּבָרְחוֹב	*Et in platea.*	And in the street.
רחם	וּבְרַחֲמֶיךָ	*Et pro misericordiis tuis.*	And for thy mercies.
—	וּבְרַחֲמִים	*Et in misericordiis.*	And in mercies.
ברא	וּבָרִיא	*Et pinguis, integer.*	And fat, firm.
—	וּבְרִיאֵי	*Et pingues.*	And the fat.
—	וּבְרִיאֹת	*Et pinguiores.*	And fatter.
ברח	וּבְרִיחַ	*Et vectis.*	And a, the bar.
—	וּבְרִיחֵי	*Et vectes.*	And the bars.
—	וּבְרִיחָיו	*Et vectes ejus.*	And his bars.
—	וּבְרִיחִים	*Et vectes.*	And bars.
ברת	וּבְרִית	*Et fœdus, pactum.*	And the covenant.
—	וּבְרִיתוֹ	*Et fœdus ejus.*	And his covenant.
—	וּבְרִיתִי	*Et fœdus meum.*	And my covenant.
—	וּבְרִיתְךָ	*Et fœdus tuum.*	And thy covenant.

ROOTS.	DERIVATIVES.	VERSIO.	SIGNIFICATION.
ברך	וּבֵרַךְ	*Et benedixit.*	And he hath blessed.
—	וּבֵרַךְ	*Et benedixit, benedi-[cet.*	And he hath blessed, will bless.
—	וּבָרֵךְ	*Et benedic.*	And bless thou.
רכב	וּבְרֶכֶב־־בְ׳	*Et in, cum curru.*	And in, with a chariot.
—	וּבְרִכְבּוֹ	*Et cum curru ejus.*	And with his chariot.
ברך	וּבְרָכָה	*Et benedictio.*	And a blessing.
—	וּבְרַכוּ	*Et benedicetis.*	And ye shall bless.
—	וּבָרְכוּ	*Et benedicite.*	And bless ye.
—	וּבֵרְכוּ	*Et benedixerunt.*	And they have blessed.
רכש	וּבִרְכוּשׁ	*Et cum facultatibus*	And with goods.
ברך	וּבִרְכַּיִם	*Et genua.*	And the knees.
—	וּבֵרַכְךָ־־רְכֶךָ	*Et benedicet tibi.*	And he shall bless thee.
—	וּבֵרַכְתָּ	*Et benedices.*	And thou shalt bless.
—	וּבֵרַכְתִּי	*Et benedicam.*	And I will bless.
—	וּבִרְכָתִי	*Et benedictio mea.*	And my blessing.
—	וּבֵרַכְתִּיהָ	*Et benedicam ei.*	And I will bless her.
—	וּבֵרַכְתִּיךָ	*Et benedicam tibi.*	And I will bless thee.
—	וּבֵרַכְתֶּם	*Et benedicetis.*	And ye shall bless.
רמח	וּבְרֹמַח	*Et cum lancea.*	And with the spear.
—	וּבְרְמָחִים	*Et cum lanceolis.*	And with lancets.
רעב	וּבְרָעָב	*Et per famem.*	And by famine.
רעה	וּבְרַעְיוֹן	*Et de molestia.*	And of, from the trouble, vex-[ation.
רעש	וּבְרַעַשׁ	*Et cum terræ motu.*	And with earthquake.
רעה	וּבְרָעָתֵךְ	*Et in malitia tua.*	And in thy wickedness.
—	וּבְרָעָתָם	*Et in malitia eorum.*	And in their wickedness.
רצה	וּבִרְצוֹנִי	*Et in favore meo.*	And in my favour.
—	וּבִרְצוֹנְךָ	*Et in favore tuo.*	And in thy favour.
—	וּבִרְצֹנָם	*Et in voluntate sua.*	And in their self-will.
ברק	וּבָרָק	*Et fulgur.*	And lightning.
—	וּבָרָק	*Et fulgur, acies.*	And the lightning, bright point [*of a spear*
—	וּבְרָקִים	*Et fulgura.*	And lightnings.
—	וּבָרֶקֶת־־רְקַת	*Et carbunculus.*	And a carbuncle.
רשע	וּבְרִשְׁעַת	*Et pro impietate.*	And for the wickedness.
—	וּבְרִשְׁעָתוֹ	*Et impietate ejus.*	And by his wickedness.
בור	וּבֹרֹת	*Et foveæ, putei.*	And pits, wells.
בוש	וּבֹשׁ	*Et pudore afficietur.*	And he shall be made ashamed
נשא	וּבִשְׂאֵת	*Et tollendo, afferendo*	And in lifting up, offering.

ROOTS.	DERIVATIVES.	VERSIO.	SIGNIFICATION.
שבע	וּבִשְׁבוּעָה	*Et cum juramento.*	And with an oath.
שבט	וּבְשֵׁבֶט	*Et in tribum.*	And towards the tribe.
שבע	וּבַשְּׁבִיעִי	*Et cum septimo.*	And with the seventh.
—	וּבְשֶׁבַע	*Et in septem.*	And in seven.
—	וּבְשִׁבְעָה	*Et per septem.*	And in, by, through seven.
—	וּבְשִׁבְעַת	*Et in septimo.*	And in the seventh.
שבת	וּבַשַּׁבָּתוֹת	*Et in sabbatis.*	And in the sabbaths.
שדה	וּבַשָּׂדֶה	*Et in agro.*	And in the field.
—	וּבַשָּׂדָי	*Et in agros.*	And into the fields.
שרף	וּבַשִּׁדָּפוֹן	*Et cum uredine.*	And with blasting.
בוש	וָבֹשׁוּ	*Et pudore affectisunt*	And they were ashamed.
שוב	וּבְשׁוּב	*Et revertendo.*	And in returning.
שוע	וּבְשַׁוְּעוֹ	*Et clamando eum.*	And when he crieth.
שפר	וּבְשׁוֹפָרוֹת	*Et cum tubis.*	And with trumpets.
שחט	וּבְשַׁחֲטָם	*Et immolando eos.*	And when they slay, sacrifice
שטף	וּבְשֶׁטֶף	*Et in inundatione.*	And with a flood.
שור	וּבְשִׁיר	*Et cum cantico.*	And with a song, singing.
—	וּבְשִׁירִים	*Et cum canticis.*	And with songs.
שכב	וּבְשָׁכְבְּךָ	*Et cubando te.*	And when thou liest down.
שכר	וּבַשֵּׁכָר	*Et propter siceram.*	And with strong drink.
בשל	וּבַשֵּׁל	*Et coque.*	And seethe, boil thou.
—	וּבַשֵּׁל	*Et coquendo.*	And in seething. [seethe.
—	וּבִשְּׁלוּ	*Et coxerunt,coquent*	And they have sodden, shall.
שלה	וּבְשַׁלְוָה	*Et in tranquillitate.*	And by peace.
שלם	וּבְשָׁלוֹם	*Et in pace.*	And with peace.
שלח	וּבְשַׁלֵּחַ	*Et mittendo.*	And in sending.
שלה	וּבְשִׁלְיָתָהּ	*Et in parvulum ejus*	And towards her young one.
שלם	וּבַשְּׂלָמוֹת	*Et cum vestibus.*	And with raiment.
—	וּבְשַׁלְמֵינוּ	*Et cum pacificis victimis nostris.*	And with our peace offerings.
שלש	וּבְשָׁלֹשׁ	*Et in tribus.* [*mentis.*	And in three. [ments.
—	וּבְשָׁלִשִׁים	*Et in trifidis instru-*	And on three-stringed instru-
—	וּבִשְׁלֹשֶׁת	*Et contra tres.*	And against three.
בשל	וּבִשַּׁלְתָּ	*Et coques.*	And thou shalt seethe.
שם	וּבְשֵׁם	*Et in nomine.*	And in the name.
—	וּבִשְׁמוֹ	*Et in nomine ejus.*	And in his name.
שמן	וּבִשְׁמוֹנָה	*Et in octavo.*	And in the eighth.

ROOTS.	DERIVATIVES.	VERSIO.	SIGNIFICATION.
שמח	וּבְשִׂמְחָתוֹ	*Et cum lætitia ejus.*	And with his joy.
שם	וּבִשְׁמִי	*Et in nomine meo.*	And in my name.
בשם	וּבְשָׂמִים	*Et aromata.*	And sweet spices.
שם	וּבִשְׁמְךָ	*Et in nomine tuo.*	And in thy name.
שמם	וּבְשִׁמָּמוֹן	*Et cum desolatione.*	And with desolation.
שם	וּבִשְׁמֹת	*Et cum nominibus.*	And with the names.
שנה	וּבְשָׁנָה וּבִשְׁנַת	*Et in anno.*	And in the year.
——	וּבִשְׁנֵי	*Et cum duobus.*	And with two. [let.
——	וּבִשְׁנִי	*Et cum dibapho.*	And with the twice-dipt, scar-
——	וּבִשְׁנַיִם	*Et in duobus.*	And in the two.
שער	וּבִשְׂעָרָה	*Et in turbine.*	And in the storm, tempest.
——	וּבִשְׁעָרֶיךָ	*Et in portis tuis.*	And upon thy gates.
שפט	וּבִשְׁפָטִים	*Et cum judiciis.*	And with judgments.
שפל	וּבַשְּׁפֵלָה	*Et in valle, planitie.*	And in a valley, a plain.
——	וּבַשִּׁפְלָה	*Et in humili loco.*	And in a low place.
——	וּבְשִׁפְלוּת	*Et propter pigritiam*	And through idleness.
שפה	וּבְשִׂפְתֵיו	*Et per labia eorum.*	And with their lips.
שקץ	וּבְשִׁקּוּצֵיהֶם	*Et in abominationibus eorum.*	And in their abominations.
שק	וּבַשַּׂקִּים	*Et cum saccis.*	And with sacks.
שקר	וּבַשֶּׁקֶר	*Et in falsitate.*	And in, with falsehood.
בשר	וּבָשָׂר וּבְשַׂר	*Et caro.*	And flesh.
——	וּבְשָׂרוֹ	*Et caro ejus.*	And his flesh.
——	וּבְשָׂרִי	*Et caro mea.*	And my flesh.
שרד	וּבַשְּׂרִידִים	*Et inter residuos.*	And among them that remain
שור	וּבְשָׁרִים	*Et cum canticis.*	And with songs.
בשר	וּבְשָׂרְךָ	*Et caro tua.*	And thy flesh.
——	וּבְשַׂרְכֶם	*Et caro vestra.*	And your flesh.
——	וּבְשָׂרָם	*Et caro eorum.*	And the flesh of them.
——	וּבִשַּׂרְתָּ	*Et nunciabis.*	And thou shalt bear tidings.
שש	וּבַשֵּׁשׁ	*Et in bysso.*	And in fine linen.
ששה	וּבְשִׁשִּׁים	*Et cum sexaginta.*	And with threescore.
בוש	וּבֹשֶׁת	*Et pudor.*	And the shame.
——	וָבֹשְׁתְּ	*Et pudore afficieris.*	And thou shalt be confounded
——	וּבָשְׁתִּי	*Et pudor meus.*	And my shame.
שנה	וּבִשְׁתֵּי־־תַיִם .	*Et in, cum duobus.*	And in the two, with two.
——	וּבִשְׁתַּיִם עֶשְׂרֵה	*Et in duodecimo.*	And in the twelfth.

ROOTS.	DERIVATIVES.	VERSIO.	SIGNIFICATION.
בנה	וּבַת	*Et filia.*	And a daughter.
בית	וּבָת	*Et pernoctavit.*	And he passed the night.
בוא	וּבִתְבוּאַת	*Et in proventibus.*	And in the revenues, produce.
בון	וּבִתְבוּנָה	*Et in intelligentia.*	And in, by understanding.
—	וּבִתְבוּנוֹת	*Et per intelligentias*	And by the skilfulness.
—	וּבִתְבוּנָתוֹ	*Et intelligentiâ ejus.*	And by his understanding.
—	וּבִתְבוּנָתְךָ	*Et intelligentiâ tuâ.*	And with thy understanding.
בנה	וּבִתָּהּ	*Et filia ejus.*	And her daughter.
תהה	וּבְתֹהוּ	*Et in deserto.*	And in a wilderness.
בנה	וּבִתּוֹ	*Et filia ejus.*	And his daughter.
ידה	וּבְתוֹדוֹת	*Et cum laude.*	And with praise.
תוך	וּבְתוֹךְ	*Et in, in medio.*	And in, in the midst.
תוך	וּבְתוֹכָם	*Et in medio eorum.*	And in the midst of them.
בתל	וּבְתוּלָה	*Et virgo.*	And the maid, virgin.
תלע	וּבְתוֹלַעַת	*Et in coccino.*	And in scarlet or crimson.
בתל	וּבְתוּלֹתָיו	*Et virgines ejus.*	And his virgins.
ירה	וּבַתּוֹרָה	*Et in lege.*	And in the law.
—	וּבְתוֹרָתוֹ־־תָךְ׳	*Et in lege ejus.*	And in his law.
חבל	וּבְתַחְבֻּלוֹת	*Et per consilia prudentia.*	And with good advice.
חנן	וּבְתַחֲנוּנִים	*Et cum deprecationibus.*	And with supplications.
בית	וּבָתֵּי	*Et domus.*	And the houses.
—	וּבָתֵּיהֶם	*Et domus eorum.*	And their houses.
—	וּבָתֵּיהֶן	*Et domus earum.*	And their houses.
—	וּבֵיתֶךָ־תְךָ־תֵךְ	*Et domus tua.*	And thy house, household.
—	וּבָתֵּיכוֹן־־כֶם	*Et domus vestræ.*	And your houses.
—	וּבָתִּים	*Et domus.*	And houses.
—	וּבָתֵּינוּ	*Et domus nostræ.*	And our houses.
בנה	וּבִתֶּךָ	*Et filia tua.*	And thy daughter.
—	וּבְתֹכָחוֹת	*Et cum increpationibus.*	And with rebukes.
תמה	וּבְתִמְהוֹן	*Et in stupore.*	And in astonishment.
תמם	וּבְתָמִים	*Et in integritate.*	And sincerely, in uprightness.
מרק	וּבְתַמְרוּקֵי	*Et in purgationibus.*	And in the purifications.
תנר	וּבְתַנּוּרֶיךָ	*Et in furnos tuos.*	And into thine ovens.
תפף	וּבְתֻפִּים	*Et cum tympanis.*	And with timbrels.
בתק	וּבִתְּקוּךְ	*Et confodient te.*	And they will thrust thee through.

ROOTS.	DERIVATIVES.	VERSIO.	SIGNIFICATION.
קום	וּבְתְקוֹמְמֶיךָ	*Et in insurgentes in te.*	And with those that rise up against thee.
רבה	וּבְתַרְבִּית	*Et cum fœnore.*	And with usury.
רוע	וּבִתְרוּעָה	*Et cum clangore.*	And with shouting.
ירה	וּבְתֹרָתֶךָ	*Et in lege tua.*	And in thy law.
בתר	וּבְתְרָךְ וּבְ״	*Et post te.*	And after thee.
נתן	וּבְתִתְּךָ	*Et dando te.*	And when thou givest.
	וג		
גאה	וְגָאוֹן	*Et superbia, fastus.*	And pride, arrogancy.
—	וּגְאוֹנוֹ	*Et excellentia ejus.*	And his excellency, majesty.
—	וְגֵאוּת	*Et fastus.*	And the haughtiness.
—	וְגַאֲוָתוֹ	*Et superbia ejus.*	And his pride.
גאל	וְגָאַל	*Et redimet.*	And he shall redeem.
—	וּגְאָלוֹ	*Et redemit illum.*	And he ransomed him.
—	וְגֹאֲלוֹ	*Et redemptor ejus.*	And his redeemer.
—	וְגֹאֲלִי	*Et redemptor meus.*	And my redeemer.
—	וְגֹאֲלָיו	*Et redemptores, vindices, propinqui ejus*	And his redeemers, avengers, relatives.
—	וְגֹאֲלֵךְ	*Et redemptor tuus.*	And thy redeemer.
—	וּגְאָלֵנִי	*Et libera me.*	And deliver thou me.
—	וְגָאַלְתִּי	*Et redimam.*	And I will redeem.
—	וּגְאַלְתִּיךְ	*Et redimam te* [*ejus*	And I will redeem thee.
גבא	וּגְבָאָיו	*Et fossæ, paludes*	And his ditches, marshes.
גבה	וְגָבַהּ	*Et altus erit.*	And he shall be high.
—	וְגֹבַהּ	*Et sublimitate.*	And excellency.
—	וּגְבַהּ	*Et altus.*	And high.
—	וְגֹבַהּ	*Et altitudo.*	And height.
—	וּגְבֹהִים	*Et elati.*	And the high, lofty.
גבב	וְגַבֵּהֶם	*Et dorsum eorum.*	And their back.
גבה	וְגָבוֹהַּ	*Et superbus.*	And the proud. [dary.
גבל	וּגְבוּל־־בֻל	*Et terminus.*	And the border, coast, boun-
—	וּגְבוּלָהּ	*Et terminus ejus.*	And his border.
גבר	וְגִבּוֹר	*Et fortis, potens.*	And valiant, mighty.
—	וּגְבוּרָה	*Et robur, potentia.*	And strength, might, power.
—	וְגִבּוֹרֵי	*Et fortes, potentes.*	And the valiant, mighty.
—	וְגִבּוֹרֵיהֶם	*Et potentes eorum.*	And their mighty ones.

ROOTS.	DERIVATIVES.	VERSIO.	SIGNIFICATION.
גבר	וּגְבוּרְתָּא	*Et potentia.*	And might.
—	וּגְבוּרָתוֹ	*Et potentiæ ejus.*	And his might.
—	וּגְבוּרֹתֶיךָ	*Et potentiæ tuæ.*	And thy mighty acts.
—	וּגְבוּרָתְךָ	*Et robur tuum.*	And thy strength.
—	וּגְבוּרָתֶךָ	*Et potentia tua.*	And thy might.
—	וּגְבוּרָתָם	*Et potentia eorum.*	And their force, power.
גבב	וְגַבֵּיהֶם וְגַבֹּתָם	*Et canthi eorum.*	And their naves, fellies, rings.
—	וְגַבֵּיהֶן	*Et canthi earum.*	And their naves, fellies, rings.
גבש	וְגָבִישׁ	*Et unio, margarita.*	And an union, or large pearl.
גבע	וְגִבְעָה	*Et collis.*	And a hill.
—	וּגְבָעוֹת	*Et colles.*	And the hills.
גבר	וְגָבַר	*Et prævaluit.*	And he prevailed.
—	וְגֶבֶר	*Et vir.*	And a man.
—	וְגֻבְרַיָּא	*Et viri.*	And men.
—	וְגִבֹּרֶיהָ	*Et fontes ejus.*	And her valiant men.
—	וְגִבֹּרָיו	*Et potentes ejus.*	And his mighty men.
—	וְגִבַּרְתִּי	*Et corroborabo.*	And I will strengthen.
—	וְגִבַּרְתִּים	*Et corroborabo eos.*	And I will strengthen them.
גדד	וּגְדוּדֵי	*Et turmæ, agmina.*	And the bands, troops.
גדל	וְגָדוֹל וּגְדָול	*Et magnus, crescens*	And great, growing.
—	וּגְדוֹלָה־דֹלָה	*Et magna.*	And great.
—	וּגְדוּלָּה	*Et magnificentia.*	And dignity.
גדף	וּגְדוּפָה	*Et convitium.*	And a taunt.
גרה	וּגְדִי	*Et hædus.*	And a kid.
גדל	וְגָדֵל	*Et magnus.*	And great.
—	וּגְדֻלּוֹתֶיךָ	*Et magnitudo tua.*	And thy greatness.
—	וּגְדֹלָיו	*Et magnates ejus.*	And his nobles.
—	וְגָדַלְתִּי	*Et magnus fui.*	And I was great.
גדע	וְגִדַּעְתִּי	*Et abscindam.*	And I will cut off.
גדף	וְגִדֻּפֵי	*Et convitia.*	And the revilings.
—	וְגִדַּפְתָּ	*Et blasphemasti.*	And thou hast blasphemed.
גדר	וְגֶדֶר	*Et maceria, paries.*	And the fence, wall.
—	וְגָדֵר	*Et sepes, maceria.*	And a mound, wall.
—	וּגְדֵרָה	*Et sepes, paries.*	And a hedge, wall.
—	וְגִדְרוֹת־־רֹ׳ וּגְדֵ׳	*Et sepia.*	And inclosures, folds.
—	וְגָדַרְתִּי	*Et sepiam.*	And I have hedged, inclosed.
גאה	וְגֵוָה	*Et superbia.*	And pride.

ROOTS.	DERIVATIVES.	VERSIO.	SIGNIFICATION.
גזל	וְגוֹזָל	*Et pipio.*	And a young pigeon.
גוי	וְגוֹי	*Et gens.*	And a nation.
—	וְגוֹיֵךְ	*Et gens tua, gentes* [*tuæ.*	And thy nation, nations.
—	וְגוֹיִם	*Et gentes.*	And nations.
גוה	וּגְוִיָּתוֹ	*Et corpus ejus.*	And his body.
גוע	וְגֹוֵעַ	*Et expirans.*	And expiring, ready to die.
גור	וְגוּרוּ	*Et timete.*	And fear ye.
—	וְגוּרִי	*Et peregrinare.*	And sojourn thou.
גרל	וְגוֹרָל	*Et sors.*	And the lot.
גרר	וּגְרוֹנֵךְ	*Et guttur tuum.*	And thy throat.
גזל	וְגָזוּל	*Et raptus, direptus.*	And seized, carried off, spoiled
גזז	וָגֹזִּי	*Et tonde.*	And poll thou, cut off.
—	וְגָזִית	*Et lapis cæsus.*	And hewn stone.
גזל	וְגָזֵל	*Et rapina.*	And rapine, violence.
—	וּגְזֵלָה	*Et raptum.*	And a thing taken by violence
—	וְגָזְלוּ־־ןָ"	*Et rapuerunt.*	And they robbed.
גזר	וְגָזְרַיָּא	*Et divini.*	And the soothsayers, diviners.
—	וּגְזֵרַת	*Et decretum.*	And the decree.
גוח	וָגֹחִי	*Et ingemisce.*	And labour thou to bring forth
גחל	וְגַחֲלֵי	*Et prunæ, carbones.*	And the coals.
גיא	וְגֵיא	*Et vallis.*	And the valley.
—	וְגֵיאוֹתֶיךָ	*Et valles tuæ.*	And thy vallies.
גיד	וְגִיד	*Et nervus.*	And a sinew.
—	וְגִידִים	*Et nervi.*	And sinews.
גול	וְגִיל וָגִיל	*Et exultatio.*	And rejoicing.
—	וְגִילוּ	*Et exultate.*	And be ye glad.
—	וְגִילִי	*Et exulta.*	And be thou joyful.
גוש	וְגִישׁ	*Et gleba.*	And a clod of earth.
גלא	וְגָלֵא וְגָלֵה	*Et revelans.*	And he that revealeth.
גלל	וְגַלְגַּל	*Et rota.*	And a wheel.
—	וְגַלְגַּלָּיו	*Et rotæ eorum.*	And their wheels.
—	וְגִלְגַּלְתִּיךָ	*Et devolvam te.*	And I will roll thee down.
גלה	וּגְלֵה	*Et migra.*	And remove, depart thou.
—	וְגֹלֶה	*Et revelans.*	And opening, revealing.
—	וְגִלָּה	*Et deteget.*	And he shall uncover.
גלל	וְגֻלָּהּ	*Et lecythus ejus.*	And her bowl. [tivity.
גלה	וְגָלוּ	*Et demigrabunt.*	And they shall go into cap-

ROOTS.	DERIVATIVES.	VERSIO.	SIGNIFICATION.
גלה	וְגָלוּי	*Et discoopertus.*	And being opened.
—	וְגָלוּתִי	*Et captivitas mea.*	And my captivity.
גלח	וְגִלַּח	*Et radet, tondet.*	And he shall shave.
—	וְגִלְּחָה	*Et radet.*	And she shall shave.
—	וְגִלְּחוּ	*Et totondit eum.*	And he polled him.
גלל	וְגַלֶּיךָ	*Et fluctus tui.*	And thy billows.
גלה	וְגָלִיתָ	*Et demigrabis.*	And thou shalt remove.
—	וְגִלִּית	*Et deteges.*	And thou shalt uncover.
—	וְגִלֵּיתִי	*Et detegam.*	And I will uncover.
—	וְגִלֵּיתִי	*Et revelabo.*	And I will reveal.
גלל	וְגַלֹּתִי	*Et devolvam.*	And I will roll.
—	וְגֹלֵל	*Et devolvens.*	And he that rolleth.
—	וְגָלְלוּ	*Et devolverunt.*	And they rolled.
גלמד	וְגַלְמוּדָה	*Et solitaria.*	And solitary, desolate.
גלה	וְגָלַת	*Et captivitas.*	And the captivity.
גלל	וְגֻלַּת	*Et lenticula.*	And the bowl.
גלה	וְגִלְּתָה	*Et deteget.*	And she shall disclose.
גול	וְגַלְתִּי	*Et exultabo.*	And I will rejoice.
גם	וְגַם	*Et etiam, insuper.*	And also, besides, moreover.
גמא	וְגֹמֶא	*Et juncus.*	And a rush, bulrush.
גמל	וּגְמוּל	*Et retributio.*	And the recompence.
—	וּגְמֻלוֹ	*Et beneficium ejus.*	And his benefit, kindness.
—	וּגְמַלֵּיהֶם	*Et cameli eorum.*	And their camels
—	וּגְמַלִּים	*Et cameli.*	And camels.
גנב	וְגַנָּב	*Et fur.*	And a thief.
—	וְגָנֹב	*Et furari.*	And to steal, in stealing.
—	וְגֹנֵב	*Et furans.*	And he that stealeth.
—	וּגְנֻבַ	*Et furtim ablatus.*	And stolen.
—	וּגְנֻבְתִי	*Et furtim ablata.*	And stolen.
—	וְגָנַבְתִּי	*Et furabor.*	And I shall steal.
גנן	וְגַנּוֹתִי	*Et protegam.*	And I will defend.
גנז	וְגִנְזָכָיו	*Et thesauri ejus.*	And his treasuries.
נגע	וְגַע	*Et tange.*	And touch thou.
געה	וְגָעוֹ	*Et mugiendo.*	And when lowing.
געל	וְגָעֲלָה	*Et abominabitur.*	And she shall abhor.
גער	וְגָעַר	*Et increpabit.*	And he shall rebuke.
—	וְגַעֲרָתוֹ	*Et objurgatio ejus.*	And his rebuke.

ROOTS.	DERIVATIVES.	VERSIO.	SIGNIFICATION.
גער	וְגָעַרְתִּי	*Et objurgabo.*	And I will rebuke.
גפף	וְגַפִּין	*Et alæ.*	And wings.
גפן	וְגֶפֶן ךָ	*Et vitis.*	And the vine.
גפר	וְגָפְרִית	*Et sulphur.*	And brimstone.
גור	וְגָר	*Et habitabit.*	And he shall dwell.
——	וְגֵר	*Et peregrinus, adve-* [*na.*	And a stranger.
גרה	וְגֵרָה	*Et rumen, ruminatio*	And the cud, rumination.
גרש	וּגְרוּשָׁה	*Et repudiata.*	And divorced.
גור	וְגָרִים	*Et peregrini.*	And strangers.
——	וְגֵרְךָ	*Et peregrinus tuus.*	And thy stranger.
גרן	וְגָרְנְךָ	*Et area tua.*	And thy floor, barn-floor.
גרש	וְגֵרְשָׁה	*Et expellet.*	And she shall drive out.
——	וְגֵרַשְׁתִּי	*Et ejiciam.*	And I will drive out.
——	וְגֵרַשְׁתִּיו	*Et expellam eum.*	And I will drive him out.
——	וְגֵרַשְׁתָּמוֹ	*Et expelles eos.*	And thou shalt drive them out
נגש	וּגְשׁוּ	*Et accedite.*	And draw ye near.
גשם	וְגֶשֶׁם	*Et pluvia, imber.*	And the rain, shower.

וד

ROOTS.	DERIVATIVES.	VERSIO.	SIGNIFICATION.
דאב	וְדַאֲבוֹן	*Et mæror.*	And sorrow.
דאג	וְדָאַג	*Et solicitus, metuens*	And solicitous, afraid.
דור	וְדָאְרֵי	*Et habitatores.*	And the inhabitants.
דבב	וָדֹב וְדֹב	*Et ursus, ursa.*	And a bear.
דבר	וּדְבִיר	*Et oraculum.*	And the oracle.
דבק	וְדָבַק	*Et adhæsit, adhære-* [*bit.*	And he clave, shall cleave.
——	וְדָבְקוּ	*Et adhærebunt.*	And they shall cleave.
——	וּדְבַקְתֶּם	*Et adhærebitis.*	And ye shall cleave.
דבר	וְדֹבֵר	*Et loquens.*	And speaking.
——	וְדֶבֶר ךָ	*Et pestis.*	And the pestilence.
——	וְדַבֵּר	*Et loquendo.*	And in speaking.
——	וְדִבֶּר	*Et locutus est, loque-* [*tur.*	And he spoke, will speak.
——	וְדָבָר	*Et verbum, res.*	And a word, thing, business.
——	וּדְבַר	*Et sermo, res, causa*	And the word, matter, cause.
——	וְדַבֵּר	*Et loquere, loqui.*	And speak thou, to speak.
——	וְדַבְּרוּ	*Et loquimini.*	And speak ye.
——	וְדִבְּרוּ	*Et loquentur.*	And they shall speak.
——	וְדִבְרֵי	*Et verba, res, facta.*	And the words, things, acts.

ROOTS.	DERIVATIVES.	VERSIO.	SIGNIFICATION.
דבר	וּדְבָרַי	*Et verba mea.*	And my words.
—	וּדְבָרָיו	*Et verba ejus.*	And his words.
—	וּדְבָרֶיךָ	*Et verba tua.*	And thy words.
—	וּדְבָרִים	*Et verba, res.*	And words, matters.
—	וְדִבַּרְתָּ־־תְּ	*Et loqueris.* [*quar.*	And thou shalt speak.
—	וְדִבַּרְתִּי	*Et locutus sum, lo-*	And I have talked, will talk.
—	וְדִבַּרְתֶּם	*Et loquemini.*	And ye will speak.
דבש	וּדְבַשׁ־־בָשׁ	*Et mel.*	And honey.
דבב	וְדִבַּת	*Et calumnia.*	And a slander.
—	וְדִבָּתְךָ	*Et infamia tua.*	And thine infamy.
דוג	וּדְגֵי	*Et pisces.*	And the fishes.
דגל	וְדִגְלוֹ	*Et vexillum ejus.*	And his banner.
דגן	וְדָגָן	*Et frumentum.*	And corn.
—	וּדְגַן	*Et frumentum.*	And the corn.
דגר	וְדָגְרָה	*Et colliget, fovebit.*	And he shall gather, cherish.
דהב	וּדְהַב	*Et aurum.*	And gold.
—	וְדַהֲבָא־־בָה	*Et aurum.*	And the gold.
דוד	וְדוֹדִי	*Et dilectus meus.*	And my beloved.
דום	וְדוּמָם	*Et silens, expectans.*	And silent, quietly waiting.
—	וְדוֹמַמְתִּי	*Et silere feci.*	And I have quieted.
דור	וָדוֹר־־רְ״	*Et generatio.*	And a generation.
דרך	וְדוֹרֵךְ	*Et calcans.*	And he that treadeth.
דוש	וָדוֹשִׁי	*Et tritura.* [*sica.*	And thresh thou.
דחה	וְדַחֲוָן	*Et instrumenta mu-*	And instruments of music.
דחף	וּדְחוּפִים	*Et impulsi.*	And pressed on, hastened.
דחל	וְדָחֲלִין	*Et metuentes.*	And fearing.
דחן	וְדֹחַן	*Et milium.*	And millet.
דחק	וְדֹחֲקֵיהֶם	*Et vexantes eos.*	And those that vex them.
די	וְדֵי	*Et sufficiens.*	And enough.
—	וְדִי	*Et qui, quæ, quod.*	And who, which, what.
דוג	וְדִיגוּם	*Et piscabuntur eos.*	And they shall fish them.
דון	וְדַיָּן	*Et judex.* [*judicium*	And a judge. [judgment.
—	וְדִין	*Et discepta, judica,*	And plead, judge thou, the
—	וְדִין וְדִינָא	*Et judicium.*	And judgment.
—	וְדִינִי	*Et causa mea.*	And my cause. [cates.
—	וְדַיָּנִין	*Et judices, causidici.*	And judges, pleaders, advo-

ROOTS.	DERIVATIVES.	VERSIO.	SIGNIFICATION.
דשן	וְדִישֹׁן	*Et pyrargus, vel strepsiceros.*	And the pygarg, or animal with white buttocks, the lidmee.
דכה	וְדַךְ	*Et attritus, afflictus.*	And bruised, afflicted [*himself.*
—	וּדְכֶּה	*Et pressit, affliget se.*	And he depressed, will afflict
דכר	וְדִכְרִין	*Et arietes.*	And rams.
דלל	וְדַל וָדָל	*Et attenuatus.*	And exhausted, poor.
—	וָדָל	*Et pauper.*	And poor.
דלה	וְדָלִיּוֹתָיו	*Et rami ejus.*	And his branches.
דלל	וְדַלִּים	*Et pauperes, egeni.*	And the poor, needy.
דלף	וְדֶלֶף	*Et stilla, stillicidium.*	And a dropping.
דלק	וְדָלְקוּ	*Et accendent.*	And they shall kindle.
דלל	וְדַלַּת	*Et cincinnus.*	And the curling hair.
דלת	וּדְלָתוֹת	*Et portæ, valvæ.*	And gates, folding doors.
—	וְדַלְתוֹתֵיהֶם	*Et fores eorum.*	And their doors.
—	וְדַלְתוֹתָיו	*Et fores ejus.*	And his doors.
—	וְדַלְתֵי	*Et fores.*	And the doors.
—	וּדְלָתַיִם--תָיִם	*Et januæ, fores.*	And gates, doors.
דם	וְדָם וְדַם וָדָם	*Et sanguis.*	And blood.
דמה	וּדְמֵה	*Et similis esto.*	And be thou like.
דם	וְדָמוֹ	*Et sanguis ejus.*	And his blood.
דמם	וְדֹמּוּ	*Et tacete, quiescite.*	And be ye silent, still.
דמה	וּדְמוּת	*Et similitudo.* [*stine.*	And the likeness. [thou.
דמם	וְדֹמִּי	*Et tace, quiesce, ab-*	And be silent, be still, forbear
דם	וְדָמִי	*Et sanguis meus.*	And my blood.
—	וּדְמֵי	*Et sanguines.*	And the blood.
—	וְדָמָיו	*Et sanguines ejus.*	And his blood.
—	וְדָמִים	*Et sanguines.*	And blood.
דמה	וְדָמִיתִי	*Et excidam.*	And I will cut off, destroy.
דם	וְדָמָם	*Et sanguines eorum.*	And their blood.
דמע	וְדָמֹעַ	*Et lachrymando.*	And in weeping.
—	וְדִמְעֲךָ	*Et lachryma tua, liquor tuus.*	And thy liquor, which drops or oozes from the press, as oil.
—	וְדִמְעָתָהּ	*Et lachrymæ ejus.*	And her tears.
דן	וּדְנָה	*Et hæc.*	And this.
ידע	וְדַע וָדַע	*Et scito, cognosce.*	And know, mark, observe thou
—	וּדְעוּ	*Et scitote, agnoscite*	And know, acknowledge ye.
—	וּדְעִי	*Et scito, agnosce.*	And know, acknowledge thou

ROOTS.	DERIVATIVES.	VERSIO.	SIGNIFICATION.
ידע	וְדַעַת	*Et scientia, scire.*	And knowledge, to know.
—	וְדַעַת וָדַ'	*Et scientia, cognitio.*	And the knowledge.
—	וְדַעְתֵּךְ	*Et scientia tua.*	And thy knowledge.
—	וְדַעְתָּם	*Et scientia eorum.*	And their knowledge.
דפק	וּדְפָקוּם	*Et propellent eos.*	And they will overdrive them.
דקק	וְדַקּוֹת־־קֹּת	*Et tenues.*	And thin, lean. [through.
דקר	וּדְקָרֻהוּ	*Et perfodient eum.*	And they shall thrust him
—	וּדְקָרֵנִי	*Et transfige me.*	And thrust thou me through.
—	וּדְקָרֻנִי	*Et transfigent me.*	And they will thrust me thro'.
דר	וְדַר	*Et lapis parius.*	And white marble.
דור	וְדֹר וָדָר	*Et generatio.*	And a, the generation.
דרדר	וְדַרְדַּר	*Et tribulus, carduus.*	And thistle.
דרם	וְדָרוֹם	*Et auster [agrestis.*	And the south.
דרר	וּדְרוֹר	*Et turtur, columba*	And the turtle, wild pigeon.
דרך	וְדָרַךְ	*Et calcabit.*	And he will tread.
—	וְדֹרֵךְ	*Et calcans.*	And treading.
—	וְדֶרֶךְ דָ'	*Et via. [derunt.*	And a way.
—	וְדָרְכוּ	*Et calcarunt, teten-*	And they have trodden, bent.
—	וְדַרְכּוֹ	*Et via ejus.*	And his way.
—	וְדֹרְכֵי	*Et tendentes.*	And bending, stretching.
—	וּדְרָכָיו	*Et viæ ejus.*	And his ways.
—	וּדְרָכֶיךָ	*Et viæ tuæ.*	And thy ways.
דרע	וּדְרָעוֹהִי	*Et brachia ejus.*	And his arms.
דרש	וְדֹרֵשׁ	*Et quærens, quærere*	And seeking, to seek.
—	וְדִרְשׁוּ	*Et quærite.*	And seek ye.
—	וְדָרְשׁוּ	*Et quærent.*	And they shall seek.
—	וּדְרָשׁוּהוּ	*Et quæsiverunt eum*	And they sought him.
—	וְדֹרְשֵׁי	*Et quærentes.*	And they that seek. [seek.
—	וְדָרַשְׁתָּ	*Et quæsiisti, quæres*	And thou hast sought, wilt
—	וְדָרַשְׁתִּי	*Et petam, requiram*	And I will seek, require.
דשן	וְדֶשֶׁן	*Et pinguedo. [atus.*	And fatness.
—	וְדָשֵׁן	*Et pinguis, impingu-*	And fat, grown fat. [ashes.
—	וְדִשְּׁנוּ	*Et cinerem tollent.*	And they shall take away the
דוש	וְדַשְׁתִּי	*Et calcabo, triturabo*	And I will trample, thresh.
דת	וְדָת	*Et lex.*	And a law.
—	וְדָתָא	*Et lex.*	And the law.
—	וְדָתוֹ	*Et lex, edictum ejus.*	And his law, decree.

ROOTS.	DERIVATIVES.	VERSIO.	SIGNIFICATION.
דת	וְדָתֵיהֶם	*Et leges eorum.*	And their laws.
	וה		
אבד	וְהַאֲבַדְתָּ	*Et perdes.*	And thou shalt destroy.
—	וְהַאֲבַדְתִּי	*Et perdam.*	And I will destroy.
—	וְהַאֲבַדְתִּיךָ־ךְ	*Et disperdam te.*	And I will cause thee to perish
—	וְהַאֲבַדְתָּם	*Et disperdes eos.*	And thou shalt destroy them.
אבה	וְהָאָבוֹת	*Et patres.*	And the fathers.
אבד	וְהֶאֱבִיד	*Et disperdet.*	And he shall destroy.
אבה	וְהָאֶבְיוֹנִים	*Et egeni.*	And the needy.
אבן	וְהָאֶבֶן	*Et lapis.*	And the stone.
—	וְהָאֲבָנִים	*Et lapides.*	And the stones.
אדם	וְהָאֲדָמָה	*Et terra.*	And the earth.
אדן	וְהָאֲדָנִים	*Et bases.*	And the sockets.
אהל	וְהָאֹהֶל	*Et tentorium.*	And the tent.
אלם	וְהָאוּלָם	*Et porticus.*	And the porch.
אפן	וְהָאוֹפַנִּים	*Et rotæ.*	And the wheels.
אור	וְהָאוֹר	*Et lux.*	And the light. [in wait.
ארב	וְהָאוֹרֵב־אֹרֵב	*Et insidians.*	And the ambush, he that lies
אזן	וְהַאֲזִין	*Et auscultavit.*	And he gave ear.
—	וְהַאֲזִינוּ	*Et auscultaverunt.*	And they gave ear.
—	וְהַאֲזִינִי	*Et auscultate.* [lent.	And give ear, attend ye [away.
זנח	וְהֶאֶזְנִיחוּ	*Et abjicient, depel-*	And they shall cast off, turn
אזן	וְהַאֲזַנְתָּ	*Et auscultabis.*	And thou wilt give ear.
אחד	וְהָאֶחָד	*Et unus, alter.*	And the one, the other.
אחז	וְהֵאָחֲזוּ	*Et possessores estote.*	And take ye possession.
אחר	וְהָאַחֲרוֹן	*Et posterius.*	And the last.
—	וְהָאַחֲרוֹנִים־רֹנ"	*Et posteriores, ultimi*	And the latter, last.
אחשד	וְהָאֲחַשְׁדַּרְפְּנִים	*Et satrapæ, proreges*	And the lieutenants, viceroys.
אחד	וְהָאַחַת	*Et una, altera.*	And the one, the other.
אור	וְהֵאִיר	*Et illuminabit.*	And he will give light.
איש	וְהָאִישׁ	*Et vir.*	And the man.
אכל	וְהַאֲכִילֻהוּ־־כִלֻ"	*Et cibate illum.*	And feed ye him.
—	וְהָאֹכֵל	*Et comedens.*	And he that eateth.
—	וְהַאֲכַלְתִּי	*Et cibabo.*	And I will feed.
—	וְהַאֲכַלְתִּיךָ	*Et cibabo te.*	And I will feed thee.
—	וְהַאֲכַלְתִּים	*Et edere faciam eos.*	And I will cause them to eat.

ROOTS.	DERIVATIVES.	VERSIO.	SIGNIFICATION.
אלה	וְהָאֵל	*Et Deus.*	And God.
—	וְהָאֱלֹהִים	*Et Deus.*	And God.
—	וְהָאַלְיָה	*Et cauda.*	And the rump.
אלל	וְהָאֱלִילִים	*Et idola.*	And the idols.
אלם	וְהָאַלְמָנָה	*Et vidua.*	And the widow.
אלף	וְהָאֲלָפִים	*Et boves.*	And the oxen.
אמם	וְהָאֵם	*Et mater.*	And the mother.
—	וְהָאַמָּה	*Et cubitus.*	And a cubit.
אמן	וְהָאֱמוּנָה	*Et fides, veritas.*	And faithfalness, truth.
—	וְהֶאֱמִינוּ	*Et credent.*	And they will believe.
אמר	וְהָאָמִיר	*Et ramus summus.*	And an uppermost branch.
אמן	וְהֶאֱמִן	*Et credidit.*	And he believed.
—	וְהָאֹמְנִים	*Et educatores.*	And those who bring up.
אמץ	וְהָאֲמֻצִּים	*Et validi, subrufi.*	And the strong, bay-coloured.
אמן	וְהָאֱמֶת	*Et veritas.*	And the truth.
אנה	וְהָאֳנִיָּה	*Et navis.*	And the ship.
אנף	וְהָאֲנָפָה	*Et ardea, vel falco, vel species aquilæ.*	And the heron, or hawk, or a species of eagle.
אנק	וְהָאֲנָקָה	*Et stellio,* dictus a *luctuoso stridore.*	And a kind of lizard or newt, *called from its* doleful cry.
אנש	וְהָאֲנָשִׁים	*Et viri.*	And the men.
אסף	וְהֵאָסֵף	*Et colligeris.*	And thou shalt be gathered.
—	וְהָאסַפְסֻף	*Et colluvies, turba promiscua.*	And the rabble, mixt multitude.
אפה	וְהָאֹפֶה	*Et pistor.*	And the baker.
אור	וְהָאֵר	*Et lucere fac.*	And cause thou to shine.
ארה	וְהָאֲרִיאֵל	*Et ariel, altare.*	And ariel, the altar.
ארג	וְהָאַרְגָּמָן	*Et purpura.*	And the purple.
ארה	וְהָאַרְיֵה	*Et leo.*	And the lion.
ארך	וְהַאֲרַכְתָּ	*Et prolongabis.*	And thou shalt prolong.
—	וְהַאֲרַכְתִּי	*Et prolongabo.*	And I will lengthen.
—	וְהַאֲרַכְתֶּם	*Et prolongabitis.*	And ye shall prolong.
ארץ	וְהָאָרֶץ	*Et terra.*	And the earth.
אש	וְהָאֵשׁ	*Et ignis.*	And the fire.
אשד	וְהָאֲשֵׁדוֹת	*Et decursus, radices*	And the springs, bottoms.
איש	וְהָאִשָּׁה	*Et mulier.*	And the woman.
אשם	וְהָאָשָׁם	*Et oblatio pro delicto*	And the trespass-offering.

ROOTS.	DERIVATIVES.	VERSIO.	SIGNIFICATION.
אשר	וְהָאֲשֵׁרָה	*Et lucus.*	And the grove.
—	וְהָאֲשֵׁרִים	*Et luci.*	And the groves.
אתן	וְהָאֲתוֹנוֹת־־תֹנ׳	*Et asinæ.*	And the asses.
נתק	וְהָאַתִּיקִים	*Et porticus.*	And the galleries.
אית	וְהָאֵתָנִים	*Et validi.*	And the strong.
אות	וְהָאֹתֹת	*Et signa.*	And the signs, tokens.
בוא	וְהַבָּא	*Et veniens.*	And he that cometh.
—	וְהָבֵא	*Et adduc.*	And bring thou.
—	וַהֲבֵאוֹתָם	*Et introduces eos.*	And thou shalt bring in them.
—	וְהַבָּאִים	*Et venientes.*	And they that come.
—	וְהֵבֵאתָ	*Et adduces.*	And thou shalt bring.
—	וַהֲבֵאתָהּ	*Et adduces eam.*	And thou shalt bring her.
—	וַהֲבֵאתוֹ	*Et adduces eum.*	And thou shalt bring him.
—	וַהֲבֵאתִי־־אוֹתִי	*Et adducam.*	And I will bring.
	וַהֲבֵאתִיו־־בִי	*Et adducam eum.*	And I will bring him.
—	וַהֲבֵאתִים־בִיאוֹ׳	*Et adducam eos.*	And I will bring them.
—	וַהֲבֵאתֶם	*Et adducetis.*	And ye shall bring.
בגד	וְהַבֶּגֶד	*Et vestimentum,*	And the garment.
בדל	וְהִבְדִּילָה	*Et separabit.*	And she shall separate.
—	וְהִבְדִּילוֹ	*Et separabit eum.*	And he shall separate him.
—	וְהִבָּדְלוּ	*Et separate vos.*	And separate yourselves.
—	וְהִבְדַּלְתָּ	*Et separabis.*	And thou shalt separate.
—	וְהִבְדַּלְתֶּם	*Et discernetis.*	And ye shall make a difference
בהם	וְהַבְּהֵמָה	*Et jumentum, pecus.*	And the beasts, the cattle.
בוא	וַהֲבִוּאֹתִים	*Et adducam eos.*	And I will bring them.
בזז	וְהָבוֹז	*Et diripiendo.*	And in spoiling.
בטח	וְהַבּוֹטֵחַ	*Et confidens.*	And he that trusteth.
בנה	וְהַבּוֹנִים	*Et ædificantes.*	And the builders.
בור	וְהַבּוֹר	*Et fovea, cisterna.*	And the pit, cistern.
בחר	וְהַבַּחוּרִים	*Et juvenes.*	And the young men.
נבט	וְהַבֵּט	*Et intuere, respice.*	And look thou, have respect.
בטח	וְהַבֹּטְחִים	*Et confidentes.*	And they that trust.
נבט	וְהִבַּטְתָּ	*Et videbis.*	And thou shalt see.
בוא	וְהֵבִיא	*Et adduxit, afferet.*	And he brought, shall bring.
—	וֶהֱבִיאָהּ	*Et adducet eam.*	And he shall bring her.
—	וְהֵבִיאָה	*Et afferet.*	And she shall bring.
—	וְהָבִיאָה	*Et affer.*	And bring thou.

ROOTS.	DERIVATIVES.	VERSIO.	SIGNIFICATION.
בוא	וְהֵבִיאוּ	*Et adducent.*	And they shall bring.
—	וְהָבִיאוּ	*Et adducite.*	And bring ye.
—	וֶהֱבִיאוּם	*Et adducent eos.*	And they shall bring them.
—	וַהֲבִיאוֹתִיהוּ	*Et adducam eum.*	And I will bring him.
—	וַהֲבִיאוֹתִיךָ־תִךְ	*Et adducam te.*	And I will bring thee.
—	וֶהֱבִיאֲךָ	*Et adducet te.*	And he will bring thee.
—	וֶהֱבִיאָם	*Et adducent eos.*	And they will bring them.
—	וְהֵבֵאתָ	*Et introduces.*	And thou wilt bring.
—	וְהֵבֵאתִי	*Et adduxi, adducam*	And I have brought, will bring
—	וַהֲבֵאתֶם	*Et adducetis.*	And ye will bring.
נבט	וְהַבִּיט	*Et aspiciendo.*	And when beholding.
—	וְהַבֵּט	*Et aspexit, aspiciet.*	And he looked, shall look.
—	וְהַבִּיטָה	*Et intuere, respice.*	And behold, consider thou.
—	וְהִבִּיטוּ	*Et aspexerunt.*	And they looked.
—	וְהִבִּיטוּ	*Et aspicient.*	And they shall look.
בֹש	וְהֹבִישׁוּ	*Et pudore afficierunt*	And they shall put to shame.
יבש	וְהֹבִישׁוּ	*Et exsiccabuntur.*	And they shall be dried up.
בנה	וְהַבַּיִת־־בֵּ׳	*Et domus, templum.*	And the house, temple.
בכר	וְהַבְּכֹרָה	*Et primogenitura.*	And the birth-right.
הבל	וְהֶבֶל	*Et vanitas.*	And vanity.
—	וַהֲבָלִים	*Et vanitates.*	And vanities.
במה	וְהַבָּמוֹת	*Et excelsa.*	And the high *places.*
בון	וְהָבֵן	*Et intellige.*	And understand, consider thou
בנה	וְהַבֵּן	*Et filius.*	And the son.
—	וְהַבִּנְיָה־־יָן	*Et ædificium.*	And the building.
—	וְהַבָּנִים	*Et filii.*	And the sons, children.
בער	וְהִבְעַרְתִּי	*Et accendam.*	And I will burn.
בצר	וְהַבְּצֻרוֹת	*Et munitæ.*	And the fenced.
בקר	וְהַבֹּקֶר	*Et diluculum, mane.*	And the morning, in the morning.
—	וְהַבָּקָר	*Et boves.*	And the oxen.
ברד	וְהַבָּרָד	*Et grando.*	And the hail.
—	וְהַבְּרֻדִּים	*Et grandinati, varii.*	And the grisled, speckled.
ברש	וְהַבְּרוֹשִׁים	*Et abietes.*	And the fir-trees.
ברזל	וְהַבַּרְזֶל	*Et ferrum.*	And the iron.
ברא	וְהַבְּרִיאֹת	*Et pingues.*	And the fat.
ברח	וְהַבְּרִיחַ	*Et vectis.*	And the bar.
ברת	וְהַבְּרִית	*Et fœdus.*	And the covenant.

ROOTS.	DERIVATIVES.	VERSIO.	SIGNIFICATION.
בשם	וְהַבְּשָׂמִים	*Et aromata.*	And the spices.
בשר	וְהַבָּשָׂר	*Et caro.*	And the flesh.
בוש	וְהַבֹּשֶׁת	*Et pudor.*	And the shame.
בת	וְהַבַּת	*Et bathus*, mod.	And the bath, *measure.*
גבה	וְהַגְּבֹהַ	*Et excelsa.*	And the high.
—	וְהַגֹּבַהּ	*Et altitudo.*	And the height.
—	וְהַגְּבֹהָה	*Et altissima.*	And very high.
—	וְהַגְּבֹהִים	*Et excelsi, superbi.*	And the high, haughty.
גבל	וְהַגְּבוּל	*Et terminus.*	And the border.
גבר	וְהַגְּבוּרָה	*Et potentia.*	And the power.
—	וְהַגִּבּוֹרִים־־בֹּרִ״	*Et potentes.*	And the mighty.
—	וְהִגְבִּיר	*Et confirmabit.*	And he shall confirm.
—	וְהַגְּבִירָה	*Et regina.*	And the queen.
גבל	וְהִגְבַּלְתָּ	*Et terminum pones.*	And thou shalt set bounds.
גבע	וְהַגְּבָעוֹת	*Et colles.*	And the hills.
נגד	וְהַגֵּד־־גֵּד	*Et annuncia.*	And tell, declare thou.
—	וְהֻגַּד	*Et nunciatus est.*	And he or it has been told.
גדל	וְהַגָּדוֹל	*Et magnus, major.*	And the great, greater, elder.
—	וְהַגְּדוֹלָה	*Et magna, major.*	And the great, greater, elder.
—	וְהִגְדִּיל	*Et magnus evasit, sese extulit.*	And he became great, exalted himself.
נגד	וְהִגַּדְתָּ	*Et nunciabis.*	And thou shalt tell.
—	וְהִגַּדְתִּי	*Et annunciabo.*	And I will tell.
—	וְהִגַּדְתֶּם	*Et annunciabitis.*	And you shall tell.
הגה	וָהֶגֶה	*Et gemitus.*	And the mourning.
—	וְהֶגֶה	*Et murmur, loquela.*	And the muttering, speech.
—	וְהֹגוֹ	*Et meditari.*	And to meditate.
גוי	וְהַגּוֹי	*Et gens.*	And the nation.
—	וְהַגּוֹיִם	*Et gentes.*	And the nations.
הגה	וְהָגוּת	*Et meditatio.*	And the meditation.
גזם	וְהַגָּזָם	*Et eruca.* [*rata.*	And the palmer worm [place.
גזר	וְהַגִּזְרָה	*Et structura sepa-*	And the separate structure, or
גיא	וְהַגַּי וְהַגַּיְא	*Et vallis.* [*abit*	And the valley.
נגד	וְהִגִּיד	*Et nunciavit, nunci-*	And he hath told, will tell.
—	וְהִגִּידָה	*Et nunciavit.*	And she told.
—	וְהַגִּידוּ	*Et annunciate.*	And tell, declare ye.
—	וְהִגִּידוּ	*Et annunciabunt.*	And they shall tell.

ROOTS.	DERIVATIVES.	VERSIO.	SIGNIFICATION.
הגה	וְהֶגְיוֹן	*Et meditatio.*	And the meditation.
—	וְהֶגְיוֹנָם	*Et sermo, cogitatio.*	And their speech, thought.
נגע	וְהִגִּיעוּ	*Et advenient.*	And they shall reach, come to
נגש	וְהִגִּישָׁהּ	*Et afferet eam.*	And he shall bring her near.
—	וְהִגִּישׁוֹ	*Et afferet eum.*	And he shall bring him.
—	וְהַגִּישׁוּ	*Et afferte.*	And bring ye hither.
הגה	וְהָגִיתָ	*Et meditaberis.*	And thou shalt meditate.
—	וְהָגִיתִי	*Et meditabor.*	And I will meditate.
גלה	וְהִגְלָה	*Et deportavit.* [tella	And he carried away [*chapiters*
גלל	וְהַגֻּלּוֹת	*Et globi* super capi-	And the round tops *on the*
גלה	וְהִגְלֵיתִי	*Et migrare faciam.*	And I will cause to go away.
—	וְהִגְלָם	*Et deportabit eos.*	And he shall carry them away
גמל	וְהַגְּמַלִּים	*Et cameli.*	And the camels.
נגע	וְהִגַּעְתִּיהוּ	*Et dejiciam eum.*	And I will bring him down.
—	וְהִגַּעְתֶּם	*Et percutietis.*	And ye shall strike.
גפן	וְהַגְּפָנִים	*Et vites.*	And the vines.
גור	וְהַגֵּר	*Et peregrinus.*	And the stranger.
גרז	וְהַגַּרְזֶן	*Et securis.*	And the axe.
גור	וְהַגָּרִים	*Et peregrini.*	And the strangers.
—	וְהַגָּרִים	*Et peregrinantes.*	And the strangers.
גרל	וְהַגֹּרָלוֹת	*Et sortes.*	And the lots.
נגר	וְהַגִּרֵם	*Et fluere fac eos.*	And make thou them to flow.
—	וְהִגַּרְתִּי	*Et dejiciam.*	And I will cast down.
דבק	וְהִדְבַּקְתִּי	*Et adhærere faciam.*	And I will cause to stick.
דבר	וְהַדָּבָר--דָּבָר	*Et verbum, causa.*	And the word, cause.
—	וְהַדֶּבֶר--דֶּבֶר	*Et pestis.*	And the pestilence.
—	וְהַדָּבְרֵי	*Et consiliarii.*	And the counsellors.
—	וְהַדְּבָרִים	*Et verba, res.*	And the words, things.
—	וְהַדֹּבְרִים	*Et loquentes.*	And they that speak.
דוג	וְהַדָּגָה	*Et piscis.*	And the fish.
דגן	וְהַדָּגָן	*Et frumentum.*	And the corn.
דוד	וְהַדּוּד	*Et canistrum* [*trua*	And the basket. [ous.
דוה	וְהַדָּוָה	*Et languida, mens-*	And she that is faint, menstru-
דכף	וְהַדּוּכִיפַת	*Et upupa.*	And the upupa, or houp.
הדר	וַהֲדוּרִים	*Et tortuosi* loci.	And the crooked *places.*
נדח	וְהִדַּחְתִּי	*Et expellam.*	And I will drive out.
—	וְהִדַּחְתִּיו	*Et expellam eum.*	And I will drive him out.

ROOTS.	DERIVATIVES.	VERSIO.	SIGNIFICATION.
דיה	וְהַדַּיָּה	*Et vultur.*	And the vulture.
נדח	וְהִדִּיחַ	*Et impellet.*	And he shall drive.
הדך	וַהֲדֹךְ	*Et contere.*	And tread down, crush thou.
דלל	וְהַדַּל	*Et tenuis, pauper.*	And the mean, poor.
דלת	וְהַדֶּלֶת	*Et ostium, janua.*	And the door, gate.
דם	וְהַדָּם	*Et sanguis.*	And the blood.
הדס	וַהֲדַס	*Et myrtus.*	And the myrtle.
הדף	וַהֲדַפְתִּיךָ	*Et expellam te.*	And I will drive thee.
דקק	וְהֵדַק	*Et comminuit.*	And he beat to pieces, to dust
—	וַהֲדִקּוֹת	*Et conteres.*	And thou shalt beat in pieces.
—	וְהֵדֵקֶת	*Et comminuit.*	And she brake in pieces.
הדר	וְהָדָר	*Et honor.*	And honour.
—	וַהֲדַר וְהַדְרָא	*Et decor, gloria.*	And the beauty, glory.
דרך	וְהִדְרִיךְ	*Et incedere faciet.*	And he will cause to walk.
הדר	וַהֲדָרְךָ־־רֵךְ	*Et majestas tua.*	And thy majesty.
—	וְהַדְּרֵת	*Et glorificavi.*	And I glorified. [ence.
—	וְהָדַרְתָּ	*Et revereberis.*	And thou shalt honour, rever-
דשן	וְהַדֶּשֶׁן	*Et cinis.*	And the ashes.
דת	וְהַדָּת	*Et decretum.*	And the decree.
הוד	וְהַהוֹד	*Et majestas.*	And the majesty.
הכל	וְהַהֵיכָל	*Et templum.* [*tus.*	And the temple. [noise.
המן	וְהֶהָמוֹן	*Et multitudo, tumul-*	And the multitude, tumult,
הרר	וְהָהָר	*Et mons.*	And the mount.
—	וֶהָהָרִים	*Et montes.*	And the mountains.
הוא	וְהוּא וָהוּא	*Et ipse.*	And he.
—	וְהִוא	*Et illa.*	And she, it.
בוא	וְהוּבָא	*Et adducetur.*	And he shall be brought.
אבד	וְהוּבַד	*Et perditus est.*	And he was destroyed.
הבן	וְהָובְנִים	*Et ebena.*	And ebony.
יבש	וְהוֹבַשְׁתִּי	*Et exsiccabo.*	And I will make dry.
הוד	וְהוֹד	*Et gloria.* [*lebrate.*	And glory. [ye.
ידה	וְהוֹדוּ	*Et confitebuntur, ce-*	And they shall confess, praise
—	וְהוֹדוֹת	*Et celebrare, laudes.*	And to praise, the praises.
הוד	וְהוֹדִי	*Et decor meus* [*tende*	And my beauty. [thou to me.
ידע	וְהוֹדִיעֵנִי	*Et mihi ostendes, os-*	And thou shalt shew. shew
—	וְהוֹדַע	*Et notum fecit.*	And he made known.
—	וְהוֹדַעְנָא	*Et notum fecimus.*	And we have made known.

ROOTS.	DERIVATIVES.	VERSIO.	SIGNIFICATION.
ידע	וְהוֹדַעְתָּ	*Et ostendes.*	And thou shalt shew. [to her.
—	וְהוֹדַעְתָּהּ	*Et ostendes ei.*	And thou shalt make known
—	וְהוֹדַעְתִּי	*Et notum faciam.*	And I shall make known.
—	וְהוֹדַעְתָּם	*Et indicabis illos.*	And thou shalt inform them.
—	וְהוֹדַעְתֶּם	*Et notum facietis.*	And ye shall let know.
הוה	וַהֲווֹ	*Et fuerunt.*	And they were, became.
יחל	וְהוֹחַלְתִּי	*Et expectavi.*	And I waited.
הוי	וְהוֹי	*Et væ.*	And ah, alas, woe.
יכח	וְהוֹכֵחַ	*Et disceptare.*	And to plead, reason, argue.
—	וְהוֹכִחַ	*Et increpavit.*	And he reproved. [rected.
—	וְהוּכַח	*Et corripietur.*	And he will be rebuked, cor-
—	וְהוֹכִיחַ	*Et increpabit.*	And he shall reprove.
כון	וְהוּכַן־הִ״	*Et præparabitur.*	And he shall be prepared.
ילד	וְהוֹלֵיד	*Et pariendo.*	And in bringing forth.
—	וְהוֹלִיד	*Et genuit.* [eam.	And he begat. [forth.
—	וְהוֹלִידָהּ	*Et germinare feci*	And he has made her to bring
—	וְהוֹלִידוּ	*Et gignite.*	And beget ye.
ילד	וְהוֹלִיכוֹ	*Et deducet eum.*	And he will lead him.
—	וְהוֹלֵךְ	*Et ite.* [adducam.	And go ye. [bring.
—	וְהוֹלַכְתִּי	*Et ambulare faciam,*	And I will cause to walk, will
הלל	וְהוֹלֵלוֹת	*Et insaniæ.*	And extravagancies, madness.
מות	וְהוּמָת	*Et interfectus erit.*	And he shall be put to death.
הון	וְהוֹן	*Et opes, substantia.*	And the wealth, substance.
—	וְהוֹן	*Et divitiæ.*	And riches.
יסף	וְהוֹסַפְתִּי	*Et adjeci, addam.*	And I have added, will add.
עד	וְהוּעַד	*Et contestatum est.*	And it hath been testified.
יעל	וְהוֹעֵיל	*Et proficiendo.*	And in profiting.
יצא	וְהוֹצֵא	*Et educ.*	And bring thou forth.
—	וְהוֹצִא	*Et produxit.*	And he brought forth.
—	וְהוֹצֵאתָ	*Et educes.*	And thou shalt bring forth.
—	וְהוֹצֵאתְ	*Et afferto.*	And bring thou.
—	וְהוֹצֵאת	*Et afferes.*	And thou shalt bring. [forth.
—	וְהוֹצֵאתוֹ	*Et eduxisti eum.*	And thou broughtest him
—	וְהוֹצֵאתִי	*Et educam.*	And I will bring forth.
—	וְהוֹצֵאתִים	*Et educam eos.*	And I will bring them out.
—	וְהוֹצֵאתֶם	*Et educetis.*	And ye shall bring out.
—	וְהוֹצֵאתָנִי	*Et educ me.*	And bring thou me out.

ROOTS.	DERIVATIVES.	VERSIO.	SIGNIFICATION.
יצא	וְהוֹצִיא	*Et producet.*	And he shall bring forth.
—	וְהוֹצִיאֻהוּ	*Et educite eum.*	And bring ye him out. [forth.
—	וְהוֹצִיאוּ	*Et educent, educite.*	And bring ye, they shall bring
—	וְהוֹצִיאַנִי	*Et eduxit me.*	And he brought me forth.
—	וְהוֹצִיאֵנִי	*Et effer me.*	And carry thou me out.
יצת	וְהַצִּיתֻהָ	*Et incendite eam.*	And set ye her on fire.
יקע	וְהוֹקַע	*Et suspende.*	And do thou hang up.
—	וְהוֹקַעֲנוּם	*Et suspendemus eos.*	And we will hang them up.
ירד	וְהוּרַד	*Et dejicietur.*	And he shall be cast down.
—	וְהוֹרִדֵהוּ	*Et dejice eum.*	And cast thou him down.
—	וְהוֹרִדוּ	*Et dejicient.*	And they shall cast down.
—	וְהוֹרַדְתָּ וְהוֹ״	*Et deduces.*	And thou shalt bring down.
—	וְהוֹרַדְתִּי	*Et demisi, demittam.*	And I sent, will send down.
—	וְהוֹרַדְתִּיךְ	*Et deducam te.*	And I will bring thee down.
—	וְהוֹרַדְתִּים	*Et deducam eos.*	And I will bring them down.
—	וְהוֹרַדְתֶּם	*Et deducetis.*	And ye will bring down.
—	וְהוֹרִיד	*Et dejiciet.* [cite.	And he will cast down. [down
—	וְהוֹרִידוּ	*Et deducent, dedu-*	And they will bring, bring ye
—	וְהוֹרִידֵמוֹ	*Et dejice illos.*	And bring thou them down.
ירש	וְהוֹרֵשׁ־רֵשׁ	*Et expellendo.*	And in casting out.
—	וְהוֹרִישׁ	*Et expellet.*	And he shall cast out.
ירה	וְהוֹרֵיתִי	*Et docebo.*	And I will teach.
—	וְהוֹרֵיתִיךְ	*Et docebo te.*	And I will teach thee.
ירש	וְהוֹרַשְׁתִּים	*Et expellam eos.*	And I will cast out them.
—	וְהוֹרַשְׁתָּם	*Et expelles eos.*	And thou shalt cast out them.
—	וְהוֹרַשְׁתֶּם	*Et in hæreditatem transmittetis.*	And ye shall leave for an inheritance.
ישב	וְהוֹשַׁבְתִּי	*Et habitare faciam.*	And I will cause to dwell.
—	וְהוֹשַׁבְתִּיךְ	*Et collocabo te.* [eos	And I will place thee.
—	וְהוֹשַׁבְתִּים	*Et habitare faciam*	And I will make them to dwell
—	וְהוֹשַׁבְתֶּם	*Et collocabimini.*	And ye shall be placed.
—	וְהוֹשִׁיבוּ	*Et collocate.*	And place ye.
ישע	וְהוֹשִׁיעַ	*Et servabit.*	And he will save.
—	וְהוֹשִׁיעָה	*Et serva.*	And save thou.
—	וְהוֹשִׁיעָם	*Et servavi eos.*	And he saved them.
—	וְהוֹשִׁיעֵנוּ	*Et serva nos.*	And save thou us.
—	וְהוֹשִׁיעֵנִי	*Et serva me.*	And save thou me.

ROOTS.	DERIVATIVES.	VERSIO.	SIGNIFICATION.
ישע	וְהוֹשֵׁעַ	*Et servavit, servan-*	And he saved, in saving.
—	וְהִוָּשְׁעוּ	*Et servamini.* [*do.*	And be ye saved.
—	וְהוֹשִׁעֵנִי	*Et serva me.*	And save thou me.
—	וְהוֹשַׁעְתָּ	*Et servabis.*	And thou wilt save.
—	וְהוֹשַׁעְתִּי	*Et servavi, servabo.*	And I have saved, will save.
—	וְהוֹשַׁעְתִּיךְ	*Et servabo te.*	And I will save thee.
—	וְהוֹשַׁעְתִּים	*Et servabo eos.*	And I will save them.
הוה	וַהֲוַת	*Et fuit.*	And he was.
—	וְהַוַּת	*Et pravitas.*	And the wickedness.
יתב	וְהוֹתֵב	*Et collocavit.* [*te.*	And he set, placed.
יתר	וְהוֹתִירְךָ־תְךָ	*Et abundare faciet*	And he will make thee abound
—	וְהוֹתֵר	*Et relinquere.*	And to leave.
—	וְהוֹתַרְתִּי	*Et relinquam.*	And I will leave.
זוב	וְהַזָּב	*Et fluens.* [*tima.*	And flowing.
זבח	וְהַזֶּבַח	*Et sacrificium, vic-*	And the sacrifice, victim.
—	וְהַזְּבָחִים	*Et sacrificia.*	And the sacrifices.
נזה	וְהִזָּה	*Et sparget.*	And he shall sprinkle.
זהב	וְהַזָּהָב	*Et aurum.*	And the gold.
זהר	וְהִזְהִיר	*Et admonuit.*	And he warned.
—	וְהִזְהִירֹה	*Et admonuit eum.*	And he warned him.
—	וְהִזְהַרְתָּ	*Et admonebis.*	And thou shalt warn.
—	וְהִזְהַרְתָּה	*Et admonebis.*	And thou shalt warn.
—	וְהִזְהַרְתֶּם	*Et admonebitis.*	And ye shall warn.
זור	וְהַזּוּרֶה	*Et compressa.*	And she that is pressed, crushed
נזר	וְהִזִּיר	*Et separabit.*	And he shall separate.
נזה	וְהִזֵּיתָ	*Et sparges.*	And thou shalt sprinkle.
זכך	וַהֲזִכּוֹתִי	*Et purificabo.*	And I will purify. [of me.
זכר	וְהִזְכַּרְתַּנִי	*Et memorabis me.*	And thou shalt make mention
זנה	וְהִזְנוּ	*Et scortari facient.*	And they will cause to commit fornication.
זון	וְהַזֹּנוֹת	*Et arma.*	And the arms.
זקן	וְהַזְּקֵנִים	*Et senes, seniores*[*us*	And the old men, the elders.
זור	וְהַזָּר	*Et alienus, extrane-*	And the strange, foreign.
זרע	וְהַזְּרֹעַ	*Et brachium.*	And the arm.
נזר	וְהִזַּרְתֶּם	*Et separabitis.* [*tas.*	And ye will separate.
חגג	וְהֶחָג	*Et festum, solemni-*	And the feast, festival.
חדל	וְהֶחָדֵל	*Et desinens.*	And he that ceases.

ROOTS.	DERIVATIVES.	VERSIO.	SIGNIFICATION.
חדש	וְהַחֹדֶשׁ	*Et mensis.*	And the month.
חוט	וְהַחוּט	*Et filum.*	And the thread.
חטא	וְהַחוֹטֶא	*Et peccator.*	And the sinner.
חנה	וְהַחוֹנִם־־חֹנִים	*Et castrametantes.*	And those that encamp, pitch.
חסה	וְהַחוֹסֶה	*Et sperans.*	And he that hopes, trusts.
חזה	וְהַחֹזִים	*Et videntes.* [nebit.	And they that see.
חזק	וְהֶחֱזִיק	*Et prehendet, obti-*	And he will take, obtain.
——	וְהֶחֱזִיקָה	*Et apprehendet.*	And she will take, seize.
——	וְהֶחֱזִיקוּ	*Et apprehendent.*	And they will take hold.
——	וְהַחֲזִיקִי	*Et apprehende.*	And take thou hold.
——	וְהַחֲזָקָה	*Et potens, valida.*	And the mighty, strong.
——	וְהֶחֱזַקְתָּ	*Et confirmabis.*	And thou shalt strengthen.
——	וְהַחֲזַקְתִּי	*Et confirmabo.*	And I will strengthen.
——	וְהֶחֱזַקְתִּי	*Et apprehendi.* [to.	And I have seized, taken.
חטא	וְהַחַטָּאת	*Et victima pro delic-*	And the sin-offering.
חנט	וְהַחִטָּה	*Et triticum.*	And the wheat.
חטא	וְהֶחֱטִיאָם	*Et peccare fecit eos.*	And he made them to sin.
חנט	וְהַחִטִּים	*Et tritica.*	And the wheats.
חיה	וְהַחַי	*Et vivens.* [vando.	And the living.
——	וְהַחֲיֵה	*Et in vita conser-*	And in preserving in life.
——	וְהַחַיּוֹת	*Et animalia* [bis me	And the animals. [life.
——	וְהַחֲיֵינִי	*Et in vita conserva-*	And thou wilt preserve me in
חיל	וְהַחַיִל	*Et exercitus.*	And the army.
חיק	וְהַחֵיק	*Et sinus.*	And the bosom.
חיה	וְהַחֲיִיתֶם	*Et vivum servabitis.*	And ye will save alive.
חכם	וְהַחָכְמָה	*Et sapientia.*	And the wisdom.
——	וְהַחֲכָמִים	*Et sapientes.*	And the wise.
חלב	וְהַחֲלָבִים	*Et adipes.*	And the fat.
חלל	וְהַחַלּוֹנִים־לֹּנוֹת	*Et fenestræ.* [tus.	And the windows.
חלץ	וְהֶחָלוּץ	*Et expeditus, arma-*	And ready, armed.
חלף	וְהַחֲלִיפוּ	*Et mutate.*	And change ye.
——	וְהֶחֱלִף	*Et mutavit.*	And he changed.
יחם	וְהַחֵמָה	*Et furor.*	And the fury, rage.
חמר	וְהַחֲמוֹר	*Et asinus.*	And the ass.
חמט	וְהַחֹמֶט	*Et lacertæ species.*	And a species of lizard.
חמש	וְהַחֲמִישִׁי	*Et quintus.* [ria.	And the fifth. [sun.
חמן	וְהַחַמָּנִים וְהַ׳	*Et simulachra sola-*	And images dedicated to the

ROOTS.	DERIVATIVES.	VERSIO.	SIGNIFICATION.
חמר	וְהַחֹמֶר	*Et lutum.*	And the clay.
חנה	וְהַחֲנִית	*Et lancea, hasta.*	And the javelin, spear.
חסד	והַחֶסֶד	*Et misericordia.*	And the mercy.
חסה	וְהֶחָסוּת	*Et fiducia.*	And the trust, confidence.
חסד	וְהַחֲסִידָה	*Et ciconia.*	And the stork.
חסל	וְהֶחָסִיל	*Et bruchus.*	And a kind of locust or cater-[pillar.
חצה	וְהַחֲצִי	*Et dimidium.*	And the half.
—	וְהֶחֶצְיוֹ	*Et dimidium ejus.*	And the half of him or it.
חצר	וְהַחֲצֹצְרוֹת	*Et tubæ.*	And the trumpets.
—	וְהֶחָצֵר	*Et atrium.*	And the court.
חקק	וְהַחֻקִּים	*Et statuta.*	And the ordinances, statutes.
חרב	וְהֶחֶרֶב	*Et gladius.*	And the sword.
—	וְהֶחֳרָבוֹת	*Et vastitates.*	And the wastes.
—	וְהַחֲרַבְתִּי	*Et exsiccabo.*	And I will dry up.
חרד	וְהַחֲרֵדִים	*Et trementes.*	And they that tremble.
—	וְהַחֲרַדְתִּי	*Et terrebo.*	And I will make afraid.
חרט	וְהַחֲרִיטִים	*Et acus.*	And the bodkins, crisping pins
חרר	וְהַחֹרִים	*Et nobiles, magnates*	And the nobles, grandees.
חרם	וְהֶחֱרִים	*Et exterminabit.*	And he will exterminate.
—	וְהַחֲרִימוּהָ	*Et exterminate.*	And destroy ye utterly.
חרש	וְהֶחֱרִישׁ	*Et tacebit.*	And he shall be silent.
—	וְהֶחֱרִישׁוּ	*Et tacuerunt.*	And they kept silence.
חרם	וְהַחֲרֵם	*Et extermina.*	And exterminate thou.
—	וְהַחֲרַמְתָּה	*Et funditus excides.*	And thou shalt utterly destroy
—	וְהַחֲרַמְתִּי	*Et funditus excidam*	And I will utterly destroy.
—	וְהַחֲרַמְתִּים	*Et exterminabo eos.*	And I will exterminate them.
—	וְהַחֲרַמְתֶּם	*Et funditus excidetis*	And ye shall utterly destroy.
חרש	וְהֶחָרָשׁ	*Et faber, artifex.*	And the workman, artificer.
—	וְהֶחֱרִשׁ	*Et tacuit.*	And he kept silence.
—	וְהֶחֱרַשְׁתִּי	*Et tacui.*	And I kept silence.
חשך	וְהַחֹשֶׁךְ	*Et obscuritas, tene-[bræ.*	And the darkness.
—	וְהַחֲשַׁכְתִּי	*Et obtenebrabo.*	And I will darken.
חתל	וְהָחְתֵּל	*Et fascia involven-[do.*	And in swaddling, binding in [a swathe.
חתת	וְהַחִתֹּתִי	*Et terrebo.*	And I will make afraid.
יטב	וְהֵטַבְנוּ	*Et benefaciemus.*	And we will do good.
טוב	וְהֵטַבֹתִי	*Et benefaciam.*	And I will do good.
טהר	וְהַטָּהוֹר	*Et mundus, purus.*	And the clean, pure.

ROOTS.	DERIVATIVES.	VERSIO.	SIGNIFICATION.
טהר	וְהִטַּהֲרוּ	*Et mundamini.*	And be ye purified.
—	וְהִטֶּהָרוּ	*Et mundabunt se.*	And they will cleanse themselves.
נטה	וְהַטּוּ	*Et inclinate.*	And incline ye.
טוב	וְהַטּוֹב	*Et bonum.*	And the good.
טור	וְהַטּוּר	*Et ordo.*	And the row.
נטה	וְהַטִּי	*Et inclina.*	And incline thou.
טול	וַהֲטִילֻנִי	*Et ejicite me.*	And cast ye me forth.
נטף	וְהִטִּיפוּ	*Et stillabunt.*	And they shall drop.
טלא	וְהַטְּלֻאִים	*Et maculosi.*	And the patched, or variegated.
—	וְהַטְּלֻאֹת	*Et maculosæ.*	And the patched, or spotted.
טול	וְהֵטַלְתִּי	*Et ejiciam.*	And I will cast out.
טמן	וְהִטָּמֵן	*Et absconde te.*	And hide thyself.
טפף	וְהַטָּף־־טַּף	*Et parvuli.*	And the little ones.
נטף	וְהַטֵּף	*Et stilla.*	And the drop.
הוי	וָהִי	*Et væ.*	And wo.
הוא	וְהִיא ךּ״	*Et ipsa.*	And she, it.
—	וְהִיא ךּ״	*Et ipse.*	And he, it.
יבל	וְהֵיבֵל	*Et attulit.*	And he brought.
יד	וְהַיָּד	*Et manus.*	And the hand.
—	וְהַיָּדַיִם	*Et manus.*	And the hands.
היה	וְהָיָה־־יָן	*Et erit.*	And it shall be.
—	וֶהְיֵה	*Et esto.*	And be thou.
—	וְהָיָה־־יוּ	*Et erunt.*	And they shall be.
—	וְיִהְיוּ	*Et sint.*	And let them be.
—	וִהְיוּ	*Et estote.*	And be ye.
יום	וְהַיּוֹם	*Et dies.*	And the day.
יצא	וְהַיּוֹצֵא	*Et egrediens.*	And he that goeth out.
—	וְהַיּוֹצֵאת	*Et exiens.*	And she that goeth forth.
ישב	וְהַיּוֹשְׁבִים	*Et habitantes.*	And they that dwell.
יטב	וְהֵיטִב	*Et benefaciet.*	And he shall do well.
—	וְהֵיטִבְךָ	*Et benefaciet tibi.*	And he will do thee good.
—	וְהֵיטִיבוּ	*Et benefacite.*	And do ye good, make good.
יין	וְהַיַּיִן	*Et vinum.*	And the wine.
היה	וְהָיִינוּ	*Et erimus.*	And we will be.
—	וְהָיִיתָ־ת־תְ־תָה	*Et eris.*	And thou shalt be.
—	וְהָיִיתִי	*Et ero.*	And I will be.
—	וִהְיִיתֶם	*Et eritis.*	And ye shall be.

ROOTS.	DERIVATIVES.	VERSIO.	SIGNIFICATION.
היך	וְהֵיךְ	*Et quomodo.*	And how.
הכל	וְהֵיכַל־־כָל	*Et templum.*	And the temple.
ילד	וְהַיֹּלְדָהּ	*Et genitor ejus.*	And he that begat her.
——	וְהַיַּלְדָּה	*Et puella.*	And the damsel.
——	וְהַיְלָדִים	*Et nati.*	And the children.
ילל	וְהֵילִילוּ	*Et ejulabunt, ejulate*	And they shall howl, howl ye.
——	וְהֵילִל	*Et ejulabit.*	And he shall howl.
——	וְהֵילֵל	*Et ejula.*	And howl thou.
ים	וְהַיָּם	*Et mare.*	And the sea.
יום	וְהַיָּמִים	*Et dies.*	And the days.
משש	וַהֲיִמִשֵׁנִי	*Et palpare fac me.*	And cause thou me to feel.
ינק	וְהֵינִקֵהוּ	*Et lacta eum.*	And nurse, suckle thou him.
יעץ	וְהַיֹּעֲצִים	*Et consulentes.*	And they that counsel.
יצא	וְהַיֹּצֵא	*Et egrediens.*	And he that goeth out.
——	וְהַיֹּצֵאת	*Et egrediens.*	And she that goeth out.
צהר	וְהַיִּצְהָר	*Et oleum.*	And the oil.
ירד	וְהַיֹּרְדִים	*Et descendentes.*	And those that come down.
ירח	וְהַיָּרֵחַ	*Et luna.*	And the moon.
ישב	וְהַיֹּשֵׁב	*Et sedens.*	And he that sitteth.
——	וְהַיֹּשְׁבִים	*Et habitantes.*	And they that dwell.
ישר	וְהַיָּשָׁר	*Et rectum.*	And the right.
——	וְהַיְשָׁרָה	*Et rectitudo.*	And uprightness.
היה	וְהָיִתָ־־תָה	*Et eris.*	And thou shalt be.
——	וְהָיְתָ־־תָה	*Et erit.*	And she shall be.
יתד	וְהַיָּתֵד	*Et clavus.*	And the nail, pin.
יתם	וְהַיָּתוֹם	*Et pupillus.*	And the fatherless.
הוה	וְהַיָּתִי	*Et calamitas mea.*	And my calamity.
אתה	וְהֵיתִיו	*Et adduxerunt.*	And they brought.
——	וְהֵיתָיִת	*Et allatus est.*	And he was brought.
היה	וִהְיִתֶם	*Et eritis.*	And ye shall be.
נכה	וְהַךְ	*Et percute.*	And smite thou.
כבד	וְהַכְבֵּד	*Et aggravavit.*	And he hardened.
——	וְהִכְבַּדְתִּים	*Et honorabo eos.*	And I will glorify them.
——	וְהַכָּבוֹד	*Et honor.*	And the honour.
נכה	וְהִכָּה	*Et percutiet.*	And he shall smite.
——	וְהֻכָּה	*Et percussus est.*	And he was smitten.
——	וְהִכָּהוּ	*Et percutiet eum.*	And he will smite him.

ROOTS.	DERIVATIVES.	VERSIO.	SIGNIFICATION.
כהן	וְהַכֹּהֵן	*Et sacerdos.*	And the priest.
—	וְהַכֹּהֲנִים	*Et sacerdotes.*	And the priests.
נכה	וְהַכּוּ	*Et percutite.*	And smite ye.
—	וְהִכּוּ	*Et percusserunt.*	And they smote.
ככב	וְהַכּוֹכָבִים	*Et stellæ.*	And the stars.
כון	וְהָכִונוּ־־כִינוּ	*Et parate.* [*me.*	And prepare ye.
נכה	וְהִכּוּנִי	*Et percutient, cædent*	And they will smite, slay me.
—	וְהַכּוֹת	*Et percutiendo.*	And in smiting.
כוח	וְהַכֹּחַ	*Et lacerti species validissima.*	And a species of lizard remarkable for its strength.
כחד	וְהִכְחַדְתִּיו	*Et excidam eas.*	And I will cut them off.
יכח	וְהֹכַחְתִּיו	*Et castigabo eum.*	And I will chastise him.
כון	וְהָכִין	*Et præparare.*	And to make ready.
—	וְהֵכִינוּ	*Et parabunt.*	And they shall prepare.
—	וַהֲכִינוֹתָ	*Et præparasti.*	And thou hast prepared. [lish.
—	וַהֲכִינוֹתִי־־נֹתִי	*Et paravi, stabiliam*	And I have prepared, will estab-
—	וַהֲכִינֹתָה	*Et parabis.*	And thou shalt prepare.
נכה	וְהִכִּיתָ־תָה	*Et percuties.*	And thou shalt smite.
—	וְהִכֵּיתִי	*Et percutiam.*	And I will smite.
—	וְהִכִּיתָם	*Et percuties eos.*	And thou shalt smite them.
—	וְהִכִּיתֶם	*Et percutietis.* [*te.*	And ye shall smite.
—	וְהִכְּךָ	*Et percutiet, cædet*	And he shall smite, slay thee.
כלל	וְהַכֹּל	*Et omnis, omnes.*	And all.
כלב	וְהַכְּלָבִים	*Et canes.* [*ta.*	And the dogs.
כלה	וְהַכֵּלִים	*Et vasa, instrumen-*	And the vessels, instruments.
—	וְהַכְּלָיוֹת	*Et renes.*	And the kidneys.
כלם	וְהִכָּלֵם	*Et erubescere* [*sunt*	And to blush, to be ashamed.
—	וְהָכְלְמוּ	*Et pudore affecti*	And they were confounded.
—	וְהִכָּלְמוּ	*Et pudore afficimini.*	And be ye confounded.
נכה	וְהִכָּם	*Et percutiet eos.*	And he shall slay them.
כון	וְהָכֵן	*Et præpara.* [*me.*	And make thou ready.
נכה	וְהִכָּנִי־כַּ״	*Et percutiet, cædet*	And he will smite, kill me.[low
כנע	וְהִכְנַעְתִּי	*Et depressi.*	And I have humbled, brought
כנף	וְהַכָּנָף	*Et ala.*	And the wing.
כסל	וְהַכְּסִיל	*Et stultus.*	And the fool.
כסם	וְהַכֻּסֶּמֶת	*Et zea, spelta.*	And the spelt, *a kind of wheat.*
כסף	וְהַכֶּסֶף	*Et argentum.*	And the silver.

ROOTS.	DERIVATIVES.	VERSIO.	SIGNIFICATION.
בעס	וְהִכְעַסְתִּי	*Et irritabo.*	And I will vex.
כפף	וְהַכַּפּוֹת	*Et cochlearia.*	And the spoons.
כפר	וְהַכְּפִיר	*Et catulus leonis.*	And the young lion.
כרב	וְהַכְּרֻבִים	*Et cherubim.*	And the cherubim.
כרז	וְהִכְרִיזוּ	*Et proclamarunt.*	And they made proclamation.
כרת	וְהִכְרִיתָה	*Et excidet.*	And they shall cut off, destroy.
—	וְהִכְרִיתוּ	*Et excident.*	And they shall cut off.
כרע	וְהַכְּרָעַיִם	*Et crura.*	And the legs.
כרת	וְהִכְרַתִּי	*Et excidam.*	And I will cut off.
—	וְהִכְרַתִּיו	*Et excidam eum.*	And I will cut him off.
—	וְהִכְרַתִּיךָ	*Et excidam te.*	And I will cut thee off.
כשב	וְהַכְּשָׂבִים	*Et agni.*	And the lambs.
נכה	וְהִכִּתִיו	*Et percutiam eum.*	And I will smite, kill him.
—	וְהִכִּתִיךָ	*Et percutiam te.*	And I will smite thee.
כתר	וְהַכֹּתָרוֹת	*Et capitula.*	And the chapiters.
הלא	וָהָלְאָה	*Et ultra, postea.*	And beyond, afterwards.
לבן	וְהַלְּבוֹנָה	*Et thus.*	And the frankincense.
לבש	וְהִלְבִּישׁוּ--בְּשׁוּ	*Et induerunt, induent.*	And they clothed, will clothe.
לבן	וְהַלְּבָנִים	*Et albi.*	And the white.
לבש	וְהַלְבֵּשׁ	*Et induere.*	And to clothe.
—	וְהִלְבִּשׁוּ	*Et induerunt.*	And they have clothed.
—	וְהִלְבַּשְׁתָּ	*Et indues.*	And thou shalt clothe.
—	וְהִלְבַּשְׁתִּיו	*Et induam eum.*	And I will clothe him.
—	וְהִלְבַּשְׁתָּם	*Et indues eos.*	And thou shalt clothe them.
לא	וַהֲלוֹא	*Et annon?*	And not?
לוה	וְהִלְוִיתָ	*Et mutuabis.*	And thou shalt lend.
לחה	וְהַלְּחָיַיִם	*Et maxillæ.*	And the cheeks.
לחם	וְהִלָּחֶם--חֵם	*Et pugna.*	And fight thou.
—	וְהִלָּחֲמוּ	*Et pugnate.*	And fight ye.
לחש	וְהַלְּחָשִׁים	*Et inaures.*	And the ear-rings.
לוח	וְהַלֻּחֹת	*Et tabulæ.*	And the tables.
לטא	וְהַלְּטָאָה	*Et chamæleon, species lacertæ.*	And the cameleon, *a species of lizard.*
ליל	וְהַלַּיְלָה	*Et nox.*	And the night.
הלך	וַהֲלָךְ	*Et reditus, vectigal.*	And income, revenue, custom
—	וְהָלַךְ	*Et ibit, abibit.*	And he will go, go away.
—	וְהָלֹךְ	*Et ire, ambulare.*	And to go, walk.

ROOTS.	DERIVATIVES.	VERSIO.	SIGNIFICATION.
הלך	וְהַלֵּךְ	*Et ambula.*	And walk thou.
—	וְהָלַךְ	*Et ivit, ibit.*	And he went, will go.
—	וְהָלְכָה	*Et abiit, ibit.*	And she went away, will go.
—	וְהָלְכוּ	*Et ierunt, ibunt.*	And they went, will go.
—	וְהֹלְכֵי־־כִים	*Et ambulantes.*	And they that walk.
—	וְהָלַכְנוּ	*Et abibimus.*	And we will go away.
—	וְהָלַכְתָּ־־לַכְתְּ	*Et ibis, venies.*	And thou shalt go, come.
—	וְהָלַכְתִּי־־לִי	*Et ibo, ambulabo.*	And I will go, walk.
ילד	וְהֹלַכְתִּיהָ	*Et ducam eam.*	And I will bring her.
הלך	וַהֲלַכְתֶּם	*Et ibitis.*	And ye shall go.
הלל	וְהַלֵּל	*Et lauda, laudare.*	And praise thou, to praise.
—	וְהִלְלוּ	*Et laudabunt.*	And they shall praise.
—	וְהִלַּלְתֶּם	*Et laudabitis.*	And ye shall praise.
הלם	וַהֲלֹם	*Et contundere.*	And to beat down.
—	וְהָלְמָה	*Et percussit.*	And she smote.
לשך	וְהַלִּשְׁכָּה	*Et cubiculum.*	And the chamber.
—	וְהַלְּשָׁכוֹת	*Et cubicula.*	And the chambers.
לשן	וְהַלְּשֹׁנוֹת	*Et linguæ.*	And the tongues.
	וְהֵם־־ן״־־ם	*Et ipsi.*	And they.
מאה	וְהַמֵּאוֹת	*Et centum, centuriæ.*	And the hundred, hundreds.
אסף	וְהַמְאַסֵּף	*Et colligens.*	And the reward.
ארב	וְהַמַּאֲרָב	*Et insidiæ.*	And the ambushment.
מאה	וְהַמָּאתַיִם	*Et ducenti.*	And the two hundred.
נבל	וְהַמַּבּוּל	*Et diluvium.*	And the flood.
בוא	וְהַמֵּבִי־־יא	*Et afferens.*	And he that bringeth.
בון	וְהַמְּבִינִים	*Et intelligentes.*	And those that understand.
בקש	וְהַמְבַקְשִׁים	*Et quærentes.*	And they that seek.
גדל	וְהַמִּגְדָּל	*Et turris.*	And the tower.
נגף	וְהַמַּגֵּפָה	*Et plaga.*	And the stroke, plague
מדן	וְהַמְּדִינוֹת	*Et provinciæ.*	And the provinces.
ידע	וְהַמַּדָּע	*Et scientia.*	And knowledge.
הוא	וְהֵמָּה	*Et ipsi, ipsæ.*	And they, those.
הגה	וְהַמַּהְגִּים	*Et mussitantes.*	And they that mutter.
הלל	וְהַמְהַלְלִים	*Et laudantes.* [*pent.*	And praising.
המה	וְהָמוּ	*Et fremuerunt, stre-*	And they roared, will rage.
מכר	וְהַמּוֹכֵר	*Et vendens.*	And he that sells.
המן	וַהֲמוֹן	*Et tumultus, clamor.*	And the tumult, clamour.

ROOTS.	DERIVATIVES.	VERSIO.	SIGNIFICATION.
המן	וַהֲמוֹנָהּ	*Et multitudo ejus.*	And her multitude.
—	וַהֲמוֹנוֹ	*Et multitudo ejus.*	And his multitude.
מנך	וְהַמּוּנְכָא--נוּ	*Et torques.*	And a chain.
יעד	וְהַמּוֹעֵד	*Et tempus statutum.*	And the appointed time.
יפת	וְהַמּוֹפֵת	*Et portentum.*	And the wonder, prodigy.
—	וְהַמּוֹפְתִים--פִּ״	*Et portenta.*	And the wonders, prodigies.
מרג	וְהַמּוֹרִגִּים--מֹ״	*Et tribulæ.*	And the threshing instruments
מות	וְהַמָּוֶת	*Et mors.*	And the death.
זבח	וְהַמִּזְבֵּחַ	*Et ara, altare.*	And the altar.
—	וְהַמִּזְבְּחוֹת	*Et aræ.*	And the altars.
זוז	וְהַמְּזוּזָה	*Et postis.*	And the post.
—	וְהַמְּזוּזוֹת	*Et postes.*	And the posts.
זלג	וְהַמִּזְלֵג	*Et fuscina.*	And the flesh-hook.
—	וְהַמִּזְלָגוֹת	*Et fuscinæ.*	And the flesh-hooks.
זמר	וְהַמְזַמְּרוֹת	*Et emunctoria.*	And the snuffers.
זרק	וְהַמִּזְרָקוֹת	*Et pelves.*	And the basons.
חלל	וְהַמְּחֹלוֹת	*Et chori.*	And the dances.
חנה	וְהַמַּחֲנֶה	*Et castra, exercitus.*	And the camp, host, army.
חתה	וְהַמַּחְתּוֹת	*Et acerræ, trullæ.*	And the censers, fire-pans.
נטה	וְהַמַּטֶּה	*Et virga.*	And the staff, rod. [selves.
טהר	וְהַמִּטַּהֲרִים	*Et purificantes se.*	And they that purify them-
נטה	וְהַמַּטִּים	*Et divertentes.*	And those that turn aside.
טפח	וְהַמִּטְפָּחוֹת	*Et pepla.* [am.	And the veils or mantles.
מטר	וְהִמְטַרְתִּי	*Et pluere feci, faci-*	And I caused, will cause to rain
מים	וְהַמַּיִם	*Et aquæ.*	And the waters.
מות	וְהֵמִית	*Et interfecit, occidet*	And he hath killed, will kill.
—	וְהָמִיתוּ	*Et interficite.*	And slay ye.
—	וָאֲמִיתֵהוּ	*Et interfeci eum.*	And I slew him.
—	וֶהֱמִיתֶךָ	*Et interficiet te.*	And he shall slay thee.
מכך	וְהֻמַּכּוּ	*Et depressi sunt.*	And they were brought low.
כון	וְהַמְּכֹנוֹת	*Et bases.*	And the bases. [cealeth.
כסה	וְהַמְכַסֶּה	*Et operiens, celans.*	And he that covereth, con-
כשל	וְהַמַּכְשֵׁלָה	*Et ruina.*	And the ruin.
—	וְהַמַּכְשֵׁלוֹת	*Et offendicula.*	And the stumbling blocks.
כתב	וְהַמִּכְתָּב	*Et scriptum.*	And the writing.
מלא	וְהַמָּלֵא	*Et plenus.*	And he that is full.
—	וְהַמְלֵאוֹת	*Et plenæ.*	And they that are full.

ROOTS.	DERIVATIVES.	VERSIO.	SIGNIFICATION.
לאך	וְהַמַּלְאָךְ	*Et nuncius, angelus.*	And the messenger, angel.
—	וְהַמְּלָאכָה	*Et opus.*	And the work.
מלח	וְהָמְלֵחַ	*Et saliendo.*	And in salting.
—	וְהַמְּלָחִים	*Et corrupti.*	And the rotten.
לחם	וְהַמִּלְחָמָה	*Et bellum, prælium.*	And the war, battle.
מלט	וְהִמְלִיט	*Et eripiet.*	And he will deliver.
—	וְהִמְלִיטָה	*Et peperit.*	And she was delivered.
מלך	וְהַמֶּלֶךְ	*Et rex.*	And the king.
—	וְהַמַּלְכָּה	*Et regina.*	And the queen.
—	וְהַמְּלָכִים	*Et reges.*	And the kings.
—	וְהִמְלַכְתָּ	*Et regnare facies.*	And thou wilt make to reign.
—	וְהִמְלַכְתָּנִי	*Et regnare fecisti me*	And thou hast made me reign.
לקח	וְהַמֶּלְקָחַיִם	*Et forcipes.*	And the tongs. [them.
המם	וְהָמָּם	*Et conteret eos.*	And he shall crush, destroy
—	וְהָמַם	*Et conteret.*	And he shall crush.
מלא	וְהַמְמַלְאִים	*Et implentes.*	And they that fill.
מלך	וְהַמַּמְלָכָה	*Et regnum.*	And the kingdom.
מעט	וְהַמַּמְעִיט	*Et minuens, minimum colligens.*	And he that gathereth least.
מן	וְהַמָּן	*Et manna.*	And the manna.
נהג	וְהַמִּנְהָג	*Et ductus.* [*fertum.*	And the driving. [ing.
מנח	וְהַמִּנְחָה	*Et munus, oblatio,*	And the oblation, meat offer-
נור	וְהַמְּנֹרָה	*Et candelabrum.*	And the candlestick.
סגר	וְהַמַּסְגֵּר	*Et faber.*	And the smith. [ing.
סכך	וְהַמָּסָךְ	*Et operimentum.*	And the veil, covering, hang-
נסך	וְהַמַּסֵּכָה	*Et idolum fusile.*	And the molten image.
—	וְהַמַּסֵּכוֹת	*Et idola fusilia.*	And the molten images.
עבר	וְהַמַּעְבָּרוֹת	*Et vada, transitus.*	And the fords, passages.
עטף	וְהַמַּעֲטָפוֹת	*Et operimenta.*	And the mantles.
מעט	וְהִמְעַטְתִּים	*Et minuam eos.*	And I will diminish them [ber
—	וְהִמְעִיטָה	*Et imminuet.*	And she will make few in num-
ענג	וְהַמְּעֻנָּגָה	*Et delicata.*	And delicate.
מער	וְהַמְּעָרָה	*Et spelunca.*	And the cave.
עשר	וְהַמַּעֲשֵׂר	*Et decimæ.*	And the tithes.
מצד	וְהַמְּצָדוֹת	*Et munitiones.*	And the strong holds.
צוה	וְהַמִּצְוָה	*Et præceptum.*	And the commandment.
צוק	וְהַמְּצִיקִים	*Et prementes.*	And they that press, distress.

ROOTS.	DERIVATIVES.	VERSIO.	SIGNIFICATION.
קום	וְהַמְּקֹמוֹת	*Et loca.*	And the places.
מרר	וְהָמֵר	*Et amarè plangere.*	And to be in bitterness.
מרג	וְהַמֹּרִגִּים	*Et tribulæ.*	And the threshing instruments
מרק	וְהַמָּרָק	*Et jus.*	And the broth.
נשא	וְהַמַּשְׂאֵת	*Et incendium.*	And the flame, fire.
שור	וְהַמְשׁוֹרְרִים	*Et cantores.*	And the singers.
שחת	וְהַמַּשְׁחִית	*Et vastator.* [eos.	And the spoiler, destroyer.
משל	וְהִמְשִׁילָם	*Et dominari faciet*	And he shall cause them to rule
שכל	וְהַמַּשְׂכִּילִים	*Et intelligentes.*	And they that are wise.
שלח	וְהַמְשַׁלֵּחַ	*Et emittens.*	And he that lets go, sends forth
שמן	וְהַמִּשְׁנִים	*Et secundarii.*	And those of the second degree
שפח	וְהַמִּשְׁפָּחָה	*Et familia.*	And the family.
שפט	וְהַמִּשְׁפָּטִים	*Et judicia.*	And the judgments.
שור	וְהַמְשֹׁרְרִים	*Et cantores.*	And the singers.
שרת	וְהַמְשָׁרְתִים	*Et ministrantes.*	And they that minister.
שכר	וְהַמִּשְׂתַּכֵּר	*Et mercede locans se*	And he that earneth wages.
מות	וְהָמֵת	*Et interficiendo.*	And in killing.
—	וְהַמֵּת	*Et mortuus.*	And the dead.
—	וַהֲמִתָּה	*Et interficies.*	And thou shalt slay.
—	וַהֲמִתִּי	*Et interficiam.*	And I will kill.
המם	וְהַמֹּתִי	*Et perdam.*	And I will destroy.
מות	וַהֲמִתִּיהָ	*Et interficiam eum.*	And I will slay her.
—	וְהַמֵּתִים	*Et mortui.*	And the dead.
—	וַהֲמִתֶּם־־תֶּן	*Et interficietis.*	And ye shall kill.
—	וֶהֱמִתָנִי	*Et interficiet me.*	And he will kill me.
נשא	וְהַמִּתְנַשֵּׂא	*Et elevatus.*	And exalted.
הן	וְהֵן	*Et en, ecce, si, sive.*	And lo, behold, if, whether.
אנק	וְהַנֶּאֱנָקִים	*Et clamantes.*	And they that cry.
נאף	וְהַנֹּאֶפֶת	*Et adultera.*	And the adulteress.
נבא	וְהִנָּבֵא	*Et vaticinare.*	And prophesy thou.
—	וְהִנַּבֵּאתִי	*Et vaticinatus sum.*	And I prophesied.
—	וְהַנְּבוּאָה	*Et vaticinium.*	And the prophecy.
—	וְהַנָּבִיא	*Et propheta.*	And the prophet.
—	וְהַנְּבִיאִים	*Et prophetæ.*	And the prophets.
נגב	וְהַנֶּגֶב	*Et auster.*	And the south.
גלה	וְהַנִּגְלֹת	*Et revelatæ.*	And those revealed.
נגע	וְהַנֶּגַע	*Et plaga.*	And the plague.

ROOTS.	DERIVATIVES.	VERSIO.	SIGNIFICATION.
נגע	וְהַנֹּגֵעַ	*Et tangens.*	And he that toucheth.
נגש	וְהַנֹּגְשִׂים	*Et exactores.*	And the task-masters.
נדח	וְהַנִּדָּחָה	*Et expulsa.*	And she that was driven out.
—	וְהַנִּדָּחִים	*Et expulsi.*	And the outcasts.
הן	וְהֵנָּה	*Et huc, illuc.*	And hither, thither.
—	וְהִנֵּה וְהִנֵּה	*Et ecce.*	And behold.
—	וְהִנֵּהוּ	*Et ecce ipse.*	And behold he.
הלא	וְהַנַּהֲלָאָה	*Et procul rejecta.*	And she that was cast far off.
נהר	וְהַנָּהָר	*Et flumen.*	And the river.
הרס	וְהַנֶּהֱרָסוֹת	*Et dirutæ.*	And ruined *cities*.
הן	וְהִנּוֹ	*Et ecce ille.*	And behold he.
ילד	וְהַנּוֹלָד	*Et natus.*	And he that was born.
ירא	וְהַנּוֹרָא	*Et formidabilis.*	And the dreadful.
נשא	וְהַנּוֹשֵׂא	*Et ferens.*	And he that beareth.
יתר	וְהַנּוֹתָר־־בּ׳	*Et reliquus.*	And he that remaineth.
—	וְהַנּוֹתָרִים	*Et relicti.*	And those that were left behind
—	וְהַנּוֹתֶרֶת	*Et reliquum.*	And the remnant.
ינח	וְהַנַּח	*Et pone, repone.*	And lay thou, lay up.
נוח	וַהֲנָחָה	*Et requies.*	And a release.
נחל	וְהַנַּחַל	*Et torrens, vallis.*	And the brook, valley.
—	וְהִנְחַלְתִּי	*Et possidere faciam.*	And I will cause to possess.
—	וְהִנְחַלְתֶּם	*Et possidere facietis*	And ye shall cause to inherit.
נחם	וְהִנָּחֵם	*Et pœniteat te.*	And repent thou.
—	וְהִנֶּחָמְתִּי	*Et consolabor.*	And I will be comforted.
נחש	וְהַנָּחָשׁ	*Et serpens.*	And the serpent.
—	וְהַנְּחֹשֶׁת	*Et æs.*	And the brass.
ינח	וְהִנַּחְתָּ	*Et depones.*	And thou shalt lay up.
—	וְהִנַּחְתּוֹ	*Et pones eum.*	And thou shalt set him.
נוח	וַהֲנִחֹתִי	*Et quiescere faciam*	And I will give rest.
ינח	וְהִנַּחְתִּי	*Et relinquam.*	And I will leave.
—	וְהִנַּחְתִּיו	*Et relinquam eum.*	And I will leave him.
—	וְהִנַּחְתָּם	*Et repones eos.*	And thou shalt lay them up.
—	וְהִנַּחְתֶּם	*Et relinquetis.*	And ye shall leave.
נטף	וְהַנְּטִיפוֹת	*Et torques.* [*dabit.*	And the collars. [rest.
נוח	וְהֵנִיחַ	*Et requiem dedit,*	And he hath given, will give
ינח	וְהִנִּיחַ	*Et reponet.*	And he will lay up.
—	וְהֻנִּיחָה	*Et collocabitur.*	And she shall be set.

ROOTS.	DERIVATIVES.	VERSIO.	SIGNIFICATION.
ינח	וְהִנִּיחוֹ	*Et ponet eum.*	And he will set him.
—	וְהִנִּיחוּ	*Et reponent.*	And they will lay up.
—	וְהִנִּיחוּךָ	*Et demittent te.*	And they will let thee go.
נוח	וַהֲנִיחוֹתִי־־חֹתִי	*Et quiescere feci, faciam.* [*eos.*	And I have given, will give rest.
ינח	וְהִנִּיחָם	*Et ponet, relinquet*	And he will set, leave them.
נוף	וְהֵנִיף	*Et agitabit, offeret.*	And he will wave, offer.
הן	וְהִנְּךָ	*Et ecce tu.*	And behold thou.
כחד	וְהַנִּכְחֶדֶת	*Et excisa.*	And she that is cut off.
הן	וְהִנְּכֶם	*Et ecce vos.*	And behold ye.
נכר	וְהַנָּכְרִי	*Et alienigena.*	And the stranger.
הן	וְהִנָּם	*Et ecce ipsi.*	And behold I.
מהר	וְהַנִּמְהָר	*Et festinus, præceps.*	And the hasty, headlong.
מלט	וְהַנִּמְלָט	*Et effugiens.*	And he that escapeth.
מצא	וְהַנִּמְצָא	*Et inventus.*	And he that is found.
הן	וְהִנְנִי	*Et ecce ego.*	And behold I.
נסך	וְהַנֶּסֶךְ	*Et libamen.*	And the drink-offering.
סתר	וְהַנִּסְתָּרִים	*Et absconditi.*	And the hidden.
נוע	וַהֲנִעוֹתִי	*Et movere faciam.*	And I will cause to move.
נעם	וְהַנְּעִמִים	*Et jucundi.*	And the sweet.
נער	וְהַנַּעַר	*Et puer, juvenis.*	And the boy, lad, young man.
—	וְהַנַּעֲרָ־־רָה	*Et puella.*	And the maid, damsel.
נפל	וְהַנֹּפְלִים	*Et cadentes.*	And they that fall.
נפש	וְהַנֶּפֶשׁ	*Et anima.*	And the soul.
נוף	וַהֲנֵפֹתָ	*Et agitabis.*	And thou shalt shake, wave.
נצר	וְהַנָּצוּר	*Et servatus.*	And he that is kept.
נצח	וְהַנֵּצַח	*Et victoria.*	And the victory.
נצל	וְהִנָּצֵל	*Et erue te.*	And deliver thyself.
קלה	וְהַנִּקְלֶה	*Et spretus.*	And despised.
נקם	וְהִנָּקֵם	*Et ulciscere.*	And avenge thou.
נור	וְהַנֵּרוֹת־־רֹת	*Et lucernæ.*	And the lamps, lights.
נשא	וְהַנֹּשֵׂא	*Et portans.*	And he that beareth.
—	וְהִנָּשְׂאוּ	*Et attollite vos.*	And lift up yourselves.
—	וְהַנִּשָּׂאִים	*Et elevati.*	And they that are lifted up.
—	וְהַנֹּשְׂאִים	*Et portantes.*	And they that bear, carry.
—	וְהַנְּשִׂאִם־שִׂיאֵי	*Et principes.* [*tus.*	And the princes, rulers.
שאר	וְהַנִּשְׁאָר	*Et remanens, relic-*	And he that remains, is left.

ROOTS.	DERIVATIVES.	VERSIO.	SIGNIFICATION.
שאר	וְהַנִּשְׁאָרוֹת	*Et relictæ.*	And they that are left.
—	וְהַנִּשְׁאָרִים	*Et relicti.*	And they that remain.
שבע	וְהַנִּשְׁבָּע	*Et jurans.*	And he that sweareth.
—	וְהַנִּשְׁבָּעִים	*Et jurantes.*	And they that swear.
שבר	וְהַנִּשְׁבֶּרֶת	*Et fracta.*	And she that is broken.
נשה	וְהַנֹּשֶׁה	*Et creditor.*	And the creditor.
נשא	וְהַנָּשִׂיא	*Et princeps.*	And the prince.
אנש	וְהַנָּשִׁים	*Et mulieres.*	And the women.
שמם	וְהַנְּשַׁמּוֹת	*Et desolatæ.*	And the desolate.
נשק	וְהַנָּשֶׁק	*Et armamentarium.*	And the armoury.
סבב	וְהֵסֵב	*Et convertit.*	And he turned.
—	וַהֲסִבֹּתִי	*Et avertam.*	And I will turn.
נסג	וְהִסַּג	*Et aversus est.*	And he is turned away.
סגר	וְהִסְגִּיר	*Et includet.*	And he will shut up.
—	וְהִסְגִּירוֹ	*Et includet eum.*	And he will shut him up.
סגן	וְהַסְּגָנִים	*Et principes.*	And the rulers.
סגר	וְהִסְגַּרְתִּי	*Et includam.*	And I will shut up.
סדן	וְהַסְּדִינִים	*Et sindones.*	And the fine linen.
סוס	וְהַסּוּס	*Et equus.*	And the horse.
—	וְהַסּוּסִים	*Et equi.*	And the horses.
סחר	וְהַסֹּחֲרִים	*Et negotiatores.*	And merchants.
נסך	וְהִסִּיךְ־־סֵךְ	*Et amovebit.*	And he will remove.
סור	וְהָסִיר־־רָה	*Et amovete.*	And remove ye.
—	וְהֵסִירוּ־־סָרוּ	*Et amovebunt.*	And they shall remove.
—	וְהָסִירוֹ	*Et amovebis.*	And thou shalt remove.
—	וַהֲסִירֹתָ	*Et auferam.*	And I will take away.
—	וַהֲסִירֹתִי־־סָר	*Et libare.*	And to pour out.
נסך	וְהִסְּכוּ	*Et libaverunt.*	And they poured out.
סכל	וְהַסָּכָל	*Et stultus.*	And the fool.
—	וְהַסִּכְלוּת	*Et stultitia.*	And the folly.
סלח	וְהַסְּלִחוֹת	*Et condonationes.*	And the forgivenesses.
סנה	וְהַסְּנֶה	*Et rubus.*	And the bush.
ספף	וְהַסִּפּוֹת	*Et pelves.*	And the bowls.
נסק	וְהִסַּק	*Et eductus est.*	And he was brought out.
סור	וְהָסֵר	*Et amove.* [*larii.*	And remove thou. [lains.
סרס	וְהַסָּרִיסִים	*Et eunuchi, cubicu-*	And the eunuchs, chamber-
סתר	וְהִסְתַּרְתִּי	*Et abscondam.*	And I will hide.

ROOTS.	DERIVATIVES.	VERSIO.	SIGNIFICATION.
עבד	וְהָעֹבֵד	*Et ministrans.*	And he that serves.
—	וְהַעֲבַדְתִּיךָ	*Et servire faciam te*	And I will cause thee to serve
עבט	וְהַעֲבֵט	*Et mutuum dando.*	And in lending.
—	וְהַעֲבַטְתָּ	*Et mutuum dabis.*	And thou shalt lend.
עבב	וְהָעֳבִים	*Et trabes* [*transtulit*	And thick planks. [removed.
עבר	וְהֶעֱבִיר	*Et transire fecit,*	And he caused to pass over,
—	וְהֶעֱבִירוּ	*Et traducent.*	And they will cause to pass.
—	וְהֶעֱבִירַנִי	*Et traduxit me.*	And he caused me to pass.
—	וְהַעֲבֵר	*Et aufer.*	And remove thou.
—	וְהַעֲבַרְתָּ	*Et transferes.*	And thou shalt remove.
—	וְהַעֲבַרְתִּי	*Et transire faciam.*	And I will cause to pass.
—	וְהַעֲבַרְתֶּם	*Et transferetis.*	And ye shall carry over.
עגל	וְהָעֲגָלָה	*Et plaustrum.*	And the cart, waggon.
עד	וְהָעֵד	*Et contestare, contestando.*	And charge thou, in protesting. [quity.
עוה	וְהֶעֱוִינוּ	*Et inique egimus.*	And we have committed ini-
עלה	וְהָעֹלֶה--עֹלֶה	*Et ascendens.*	And he that goeth up.
עף	וְהָעוֹף	*Et volatile, avis.*	And the fowl, bird.
עור	וְהָעִוְרִים וְהַ'	*Et cæci.*	And the blind.
עזז	וְהָעָזְנִיָּה	*Et haliæetus.*	And the sea-eagle.
עזר	וְהָעֲזָרָה	*Et atrium.*	And the court.
עטלף	וְהָעֲטַלֵּף	*Et vespertilio.*	And the bat.
עטר	וְהָעֲטָרֹת	*Et coronæ.*	And the crowns.
עד	וְהָעִדוּ	*Et testificabimini.*	And ye shall testify.
עיר	וְהָעִיר	*Et civitas.*	And the city.
—	וְהָעֲיָרִים	*Et pulli.*	And the foles.
עכבר	וְהָעַכְבָּר	*Et mus agrestis.*	And the field-mouse.
עלה	וְהַעַל	*Et educito.*	And bring thou out, up.
—	וְהָעֹלָה	*Et holocaustum.*	And the burnt-offering.
—	וְהֶעָלֶה	*Et folium.*	And the leaf.
—	וְהֶעֱלָה	*Et ascendere faciet, offeret, obtulit.*	And he will cause to ascend, will offer, hath offered.
—	וְהַעֲלֵהוּ	*Et offer illum.*	And offer thou him.
—	וְהֶעֱלוּ	*Et adducent, offerent*	And they will bring, offer.
—	וְהֶעֱלוּךָ	*Et educent te.*	And they will bring thee out.
—	וְהַעֲלוֹת	*Et afferre, pistilla.*	And to offer, pestles.
—	וְהָעֹלוֹת	*Et holocausta.*	And the burnt-offerings.

ROOTS.	DERIVATIVES.	VERSIO.	SIGNIFICATION.
עלה	וְהַעֲלִי	*Et ascendere fac.*	And bring thou up.
—	וְהָעֲלֶיהָ	*Et quod super eam.*	And that which *is* upon her.
—	וְהָעֲלִיּוֹת	*Et cœnacula.*	And the chambers.
—	וְהַעֲלִיתָ	*Et ascendes.*	And thou shalt go up.
—	וְהַעֲלִיתָ	*Et educes, offeres.*	And thou shalt bring up, offer
—	וְהַעֲלִיתִי	*Et educam.*	And I will bring up.
—	וְהַעֲלִיתִיהוּ	*Et offeram eum.*	And I will offer him.
—	וְהַעֲלִיתִיךָ	*Et educam te.*	And I will bring thee out.
—	וְהַעֲלִיתִים	*Et educam eos[ferte*	And I will bring them out.
—	וְהַעֲלִיתֶם	*Et transferetis, of-*	And ye shall remove, offer ye.
—	וְהַעַלְתָּה	*Et afferet.*	And she shall bring.
—	וְהַעֲלִתֶם	*Et educetis.*	And ye shall bring up.
עמם	וְהָעָם	*Et populus.*	And the people.
עמד	וְהֶעֱמִדָהּ	*Et sistet eam.*	And he shall place her.
—	וְהֶעֱמַדְנוּ	*Et constituimus.*	And we have appointed.
—	וְהַעֲמַדְתָּ	*Et pones, constitues.*	And thou wilt place, settle.
—	וְהַעֲמַדְתִּיהוּ	*Et stabiliam eum.*	And I will establish him.
—	וְהָעַמּוּדִים	*Et columnæ.*	And the pillars.
—	וְהַעֲמִיד	*Et constituere.*	And to appoint.
—	וְהֶעֱמִיד	*Et constituit, ponet.*	And he hath set up, will place.
—	וְהַעֲמִידָהּ	*Et statue id.*	And place thou it.
—	וְהֶעֱמִידוֹ	*Et sistet eum.*	And he will place him.
עמק	וְהָעֲמָקִים	*Et valles.*	And the vallies.
ענג	וְהָעָנֹג	*Et delicatus.*	And the delicate.
—	וְהָעֲנֻגָּה	*Et delicata.*	And the delicate.
ענן	וְהֶעָנָן	*Et nubes.*	And the cloud.
עפר	וְהֶעָפָר	*Et pulvis.*	And the dust.
עצץ	וְהָעֵצִים	*Et arbores, ligna.*	And the trees, wood.
עצם	וְהָעֲצָמוֹת	*Et ossa.*	And the bones.
ערב	וְהָעֶרֶב וְהָעֶרֶב	*Et vespere.*	And in the evening.
—	וְהָעֲרָבָה	*Et planities.*	And the plain.
—	וְהָעֹרְבִים	*Et corvi.*	And the ravens.
ערך	וְהֶעֱרִיךְ	*Et taxabit.*	And he will tax.
—	וְהֶעֱרִיכוֹ	*Et taxabit eum.*	And he will tax him.
עיר	וְהֶעָרִים	*Et civitates. [pare-*	And the cities. [ed.
ערל	וְהֵעָרֵל	*Et præputiatus ap-*	And appear thou uncircumcis-
ערף	וְהָעֲרָפֶל	*Et caligo.*	And the thick darkness.

ROOTS.	DERIVATIVES.	VERSIO.	SIGNIFICATION.
עשר	וְהָעֹשֶׁר	*Et opulentia, divitiæ.*	And the wealth, riches.
עתת	וְהָעֵת	*Et tempus.*	And the time.
—	וְהָעִתִּים	*Et tempora.*	And the times.
עתר	וְהַעְתִּירוּ	*Et orate.*	And pray, intreat ye.
—	וְהֵעָתֵר	*Et exorari.*	And to be intreated.
—	וְהַעְתַּרְתִּי	*Et orabo.*	And I will intreat.
—	וְהַעְתַּרְתֶּם	*Et multiplicastis.*	And ye have multiplied.
פדה	וְהָפְדֵּה	*Et redimendo.[eam.*	And in redeeming. [her.
—	וְהֶפְדָּהּ	*Et redimere faciet*	And he shall cause to redeem
—	וְהַפֹּדְךָ	*Et redimens te.*	And he that redeemeth thee.
פשע	וְהַפּוֹשְׁעִים	*Et deficientes.*	And they that fail, faint.
פחה	וְהַפַּחוֹת	*Et duces, principes.*	And the captains, governors.
נפח	וְהִפַּחְתֶּם	*Et flatu repulistis.*	And ye have snuffed at.
נפל	וְהִפִּיל	*Et jecit, dejiciet.*	And he has cast, will cast down
—	וְהִפִּילְךָ	*Et dejiciet eum.*	And he will cast him down.
—	וְהִפִּילוּ	*Et jacient.*	And they will cast.
יפע	וְהוֹפִיעַ	*Et splendere fecit.*	And he caused to shine.
פוץ	וְהֵפִיץ	*Et disperget.*	And he will scatter.
—	וַהֲפִיצוֹתִי	*Et dispergam.*	And I will scatter.
—	וַהֲפִיצוֹתִים	*Et dispergam eos.*	And I will scatter them.
—	וְהֱפִיצְךָ	*Et disperget te.*	And he will scatter thee.[turn
הפך	וְהָפַךְ	*Et vertit, evertet.*	And he hath turned, will over-
—	וְהֹפֵךְ	*Et vertens.*	And turning.
—	וְהָפַכְתִּי	*Et vertam, evertam*	And I will turn, overturn.
—	וַהֲפַכְתֶּם	*Et vertistis.*	And ye have turned.
פלא	וְהַפֶּלֶא	*Et mirabilis.*	And the wonderful.
—	וְהִפְלָא	*Et mirifice aget.*	And he will do wonderfully.
פלה	וְהִפְלָה	*Et seliget, distinguet*	And he will select, distinguish
—	וְהִפְלֵיתִי	*Et distinguam.*	And I will distinguish.
נפל	וְהִפַּלְתִּי	*Et dejiciam.*	And I will cast down.
—	וְהִפַּלְתִּיו	*Et dejiciam eum.*	And I will cast him down.
—	וְהִפַּלְתִּים	*Et dejiciam eos.*	And I will cast them down.
פסח	וְהַפִּסְחִים	*Et claudi.*	And the lame.
פסל	וְהַפְּסִילִים--סלי	*Et sculptilia.*	And the carved images.
פוץ	וֶהֱפִיצוּהוּ	*Et dispergent eum.*	And they will scatter him.
—	וַהֲפִצֹתִי	*Et dispergam.*	And I will scatter.
פקד	וְהִפְקַדְתִּי	*Et præficiam.*	And I will appoint, set over.

ROOTS.	DERIVATIVES.	VERSIO.	SIGNIFICATION.
—	וְהִפְקִיד	*Et præfecit.*	And he hath appointed.
—	וְהַפְקִידוּ	*Et præficite.*	And appoint ye.
פור	וְהָפֵר	*Et irritum fac.*	And make thou void.
—	וְהֵפַר	*Et irritum faciet.*	And he will make void.
פרד	וְהַפֶּרֶד	*Et mulus.*	And the mule.
פרח	וְהַפֶּרַח	*Et flos.*	And the flower.
—	וְהִפְרַחְתִּי	*Et florere feci.*	And I have made to flourish.
פרה	וְהִפְרֵיתִי־רִתִי	*Et fœcundabo.*	And I will make fruitful.
פרס	וְהַפֶּרֶס	*Et ossifraga.*	And the ossifrage.
פרש	וְהַפָּרָשִׁים	*Et equites.*	And the horsemen.
פור	וְהֵפֵרֹתָה	*Et irritum facies.*	And thou wilt make void.
פשט	וְהַפְשֵׁט	*Et detrahe.*	And strip thou.
—	וְהִפְשִׁיט	*Et detrahet.*	And he will strip off.
—	וְהִפְשִׁיטוּ	*Et detrahent.*	And they will strip.
—	וְהִפְשִׁיטוּךְ	*Et nudabunt te.*	And they will strip thee.
פשע	וְהַפֶּשַׁע	*Et prævaricatio.*	And the transgression.
פשת	וְהַפִּשְׁתָּה	*Et linum.*	And the linen.
פות	וְהַפֹּתוֹת	*Et cardines.*	And the hinges.
פתח	וְהַפֶּתַח	*Et ostium.*	And the door.
פתל	וְהַפְּתִילִים	*Et torques, armillæ.*	And the collars, bracelets.
פתה	וְהִפְתִּיתָ	*Et pellicies.*	And thou shalt deceive.
צאן	וְהַצֹּאן	*Et grex, pecus.*	And the flock, cattle.
יצא	וְהֹצֵאתִי	*Et educam.*	And I will bring out.
צב	וְהַצָּב	*Et testudo, vel* lacerti species, *crocodilus terrestris.*	And the tortoise, or *a species of lizard,* the land crocodile
יצב	וְהֻצַּב	*Et regina,* vel *statio.*	And the queen, *or* bulwark.
יצג	וְהִצַּגְתִּיהָ	*Et statuam eam.*	And I will set her.
—	וְהִצַּגְתִּיו	*Et sistam eum.*	And I will set him.
צדק	וְהִצְדִּיקוּ	*Et justificabunt.*	And they will justify.
—	וְהִצְדַּקְתִּיו	*Et justificabo eum.*	And I will pronounce him just
יצג	וְהַצִּיגוּ	*Et constituite.*	And establish ye.
—	וְהִצִּיגַנִי	*Et constituit me.*	And he hath set, made me.
נצל	וְהִצִּיל	*Et eripiet,* } *evadet.*	And he will deliver, escape.
—	וְהַצִּילוּ	*Et eripite.*	And deliver ye.
—	וְהִצִּילוּ	*Et eripuerunt.*	And they delivered.
—	וְהִצִּילָם	*Et eripiet eos.*	And he will deliver them.

ROOTS.	DERIVATIVES.	VERSIO.	SIGNIFICATION.
נצל	וְהַצִּילֵנוּ־־נִי	*Et eripe me.*	And deliver thou me.
צוק	וַהֲצִיקוֹתִי	*Et angustabo.*	And I will straiten, distress.
יצת	וְהִצִּיתוּ	*Et accendent.*	And they will kindle.
נצל	וְהַצֵּל	*Et eripiendo.*	And in delivering.
—	וְהַצָּלָה	*Et liberatio.*	And the deliverance.
צלח	וְהַצְלַח	*Et prosperare.*	And prosper thou, be prosper-[ous.
—	וְהִצְלַחְתָּ	*Et prosperabis.*	And thou shalt prosper.
—	וְהִצְלִיחַ	*Et prosperavit, secundabit.*	And he hath prospered, will make prosperous.
—	וְהַצְלִיחָה	*Et secunda.*	And prosper thou, send pros-[perity.
—	וְהִצְלִיחָה	*Et prosperabit.*	And she will prosper.
—	וְהַצְלִיחוּ	*Et prosperabitis.*	And ye shall prosper.
צלע	וְהַצְּלָעוֹת	*Et tabulata.*	And the boards, cielings.
נצל	וְהִצַּלְתָּ	*Et eripuisti.*	And thou hast delivered.
—	וְהִצַּלְתִּי	*Et eripui, liberabo.*	And I have delivered, will res-[cue.
—	וְהִצַּלְתִּיךָ	*Et eripiam te.*	And I will deliver thee.
—	וְהִצַּלְתִּים	*Et eripiam eos.*	And I will deliver them.
—	וְהִצַּלְתֶּם	*Et eripuistis.*	And ye have delivered.
צמד	וְהַצְּמִידִים	*Et armillæ.*	And the bracelets.
צמח	וְהִצְמִיחָה	*Et germinare fecit.*	And he made to grow.
צנף	וְהַצְּנִיפוֹת	*Et diademata.*	And the turbans, diadems.
צנע	וְהַצְנֵעַ	*Et humiliter agere.*	And to be humble.
צעד	וְהַצְּעָדוֹת	*Et armillæ*, vel *ornamenta crurum.*	And the bracelets, *or* ornaments worn on the legs.
צער	וְהַצָּעִיר	*Et natu minimus.*	And the youngest.
—	וְהַצְּעִירָה	*Et natu minor.*	And the younger.
צפה	וְהַצֹּפֶה	*Et speculator.*	And the watchman.
צפן	וְהַצָּפוֹנָה	*Et ad aquilonem.*	And towards the north.
צפר	וְהַצָּפִיר	*Et hircus.*	And the he-goat.
צפע	וְהַצְּפִעוֹת	*Et fœtus.*	And the issue.
צפת	וְהַצֹּפֶת	*Et capitellum.*	And the chapiter.
צור	וְהֵצַר	*Et obsidebit.*	And he shall besiege.
צרע	וְהַצָּרוּעַ	*Et leprosus.*	And the leper.
צור	וְהַצֻּרִים	*Et rupes.*	And the rocks.
צרע	וְהַצָּרַעַת	*Et lepra.*	And the leprosy.
צור	וַהֲצֵרֹתִי	*Et angam.*	And I will straiten, distress.
יצת	וְהִצַּתִּי	*Et accendam.*	And I will kindle.

ROOTS.	DERIVATIVES.	VERSIO.	SIGNIFICATION.
קאת	וְהַקָּאַת	*Et pelicanus.*	And the pelican.
קוא	וַהֲקֵאתוֹ	*Et evomes eum.*	And thou shalt vomit him up.
קבב	וְהַקֵּבָה	*Et ventriculus.*	And the maw.
קדש	וְהִקְדִּישׁוּ	*Et sanctificabunt.*	And they shall sanctify.
קדר	וְהִקְדַּרְתִּי	*Et atratum reddam*	And I will make dark.
קדש	וְהַקֹּדֶשׁ	*Et sanctuarium.*	And the sanctuary.
—	וְהַקֳּדָשִׁים־־קֳ׳׳	*Et res consecratæ.*	And the dedicated things.
—	וְהִקְדִּשֵׁם	*Et præpara eos.*	And prepare thou them.
—	וְהִקְדַּשְׁנוּ	*Et sanctificavimus.*	And we have sanctified.
—	וְהִקְדַּשְׁתִּי	*Et sanctificavi.*	And I have sanctified.
קהל	וְהַקָּהָל	*Et cœtus.*	And the assembly.
—	וְהִקְהֵל	*Et congrega.*	And gather thou together.
—	וְהִקְהַלְתָּ	*Et congregabis.*	And thou shalt gather.
קול	וְהַקּוֹל	*Et vox.*	And the voice.
קסם	וְהַקּוֹסְמִים־קֹסְ׳׳	*Et divinatores.*	And the diviners, soothsayers.
קטר	וְהַקְטֵיר	*Et adolendo.*	And in burning. [cense.
—	וְהִקְטִיר	*Et adolebit.*	And he shall burn, burn in-
—	וְהִקְטִירוֹ	*Et adolebit eum.*	And he shall burn him or it.
—	וְהִקְטִירוּ	*Et adolebunt.*	And they shall burn.
—	וְהִקְטִירָם	*Et adolebit eos.*	And he shall burn them.
קטן	וְהַקָּטֹן	*Et natu minor.*	And the younger.
—	וְהַקְּטַנִּים	*Et parvuli, minimi.*	And the small, the least.
קטר	וְהַקְּטֹרֶת	*Et suffimentum.*	And the incense.
—	וְהִקְטַרְתָּ	*Et adolebis.*	And thou shalt burn.
קום	וַהֲקֵים	*Et stabilivit.*	And he hath established.
—	וַהֲקִים	*Et eriget.*	And she will lift up.
—	וְהֵקִימוּ	*Et statuerunt.*	And they have set.
—	וַהֲקִימוּ	*Et erexerunt.*	And they have set up.
—	וַהֲקִימוֹתִי־מֹתִי	*Et excitabo.*	And I will raise up.
—	וַהֲקִימֵנִי	*Et suscita me.*	And raise thou me up.
יקף	וְהִקִּיפוּ	*Et circumdabunt.*	And they shall compass.
—	וְהַקִּיפוּהָ	*Et circuite eam.*	And go ye round about her.
קוץ	וְהַקַּיִץ	*Et æstas, æstivus.*	And the summer, summer *fruit*
—	וְהֵקִיץ	*Et evigilabit.*	And he will awake.
—	וְהָקִיצָה	*Et evigila.*	And awake thou.
—	וַהֲקִיצוֹתָ	*Et evigilabis.*	And thou wilt awake.
קיר	וְהַקִּיר	*Et paries.*	And the wall.

ROOTS.	DERIVATIVES.	VERSIO.	SIGNIFICATION.
קלל	וְהָקֵל	*Et leva.*	And lighten thou.
קול	וְהַקֹּל	*Et sonus, vox.*	And the sound, voice.
קלל	וְהַקְּלָלָה	*Et maledictio.*	And the curse.
קול	וְהַקֹּלֹת	*Et tonitrua.*	And the thunders.
קום	וְהָקֵם	*Et erige.*	And raise thou up.
—	וַהֲקֵמֹנוּ	*Et stabiliemus.*	And we will establish.
—	וַהֲקֵמֹתָ	*Et statues, eriges.*	And thou shalt set, raise up.
—	וַהֲקֵמֹתוֹ	*Et eriges eum.*	And thou shalt raise him up.
—	וַהֲקִמֹתִי	*Et stabiliam.*	And I will establish.
יקף	וְהִקַּפְתֶּם	*Et circumdabitis.*	And ye shall encompass.
קרב	וְהַקָּרֹב־־רוֹב	*Et propinquus.*	And he that is near.
—	וְהַקֶּרֶב	*Et intestinum.*	And the inwards.
—	וְהַקְרֵב	*Et offer.*	And offer thou.
—	וְהַקְרִבוּ	*Et obtulerunt.*	And they offered.
—	וְהַקְּרֹבוֹת	*Et propinquæ.*	And they that are near.
—	וְהִקְרַבְתָּ	*Et adduces, offeres.*	And thou shalt bring, offer.
—	וְהִקְרַבְתִּיו	*Et adducam eum.*	And I will bring him.
—	וְהִקְרַבְתָּם	*Et offeres eos.*	And thou shalt offer them.
—	וְהִקְרַבְתֶּם	*Et offeretis.*	And ye shall offer.
—	וְהִקְרִיב־־בָה	*Et adducet, offeret.*	And he shall bring, offer.
—	וְהִקְרִיבָהּ	*Et offeret, offeret eam.*	And she shall offer, he shall offer her.
—	וְהִקְרִיבוֹ	*Et offeret eum.*	And he shall offer him.
—	וְהִקְרִיבוּ	*Et offerent.*	And they shall offer.
קרח	וְהִקְרִיחוּ	*Et calvabunt.*	And they shall make bald.
קרה	וְהִקְרִיתֶם	*Et constituetis.*	And ye shall appoint.
קרן	וְהַקֶּרֶן	*Et cornu.*	And the horn.
—	וְהַקְּרָנַיִם	*Et cornua.*	And the horns.
קשה	וְהַקְּשָׂוֹת	*Et opercula.*	And the covers.
קשב	וְהִקְשִׁיב	*Et attendit.*	And he attended.
—	וְהַקְשִׁיבָה	*Et attende.*	And attend thou.
—	וְהַקְשִׁיבוּ	*Et attendite.*	And attend ye.
קשר	וְהַקִּשֻּׁרִים	*Et redimicula.*	And the head-bands or fillets.
—	וְהַקְּשֻׁרִים	*Et firmi, vegeti.*	And the strong, lively.
קשת	וְהַקְּשָׁתוֹת	*Et arcus.*	And the bows.
הרר	וְהַר	*Et mons.*	And a mount, mountain.
ראה	וְהָרָאָה	*Et milvus.*	And the kite or glede.

ROOTS.	DERIVATIVES.	VERSIO.	SIGNIFICATION.
ראה	וְהָרְאָה	*Et videbit.*	And he shall see.
—	וְהֶרְאָה	*Et ostendet.*	And he shall shew.
—	וְהַרְאֵיתִי	*Et ostendam.*	And I will shew.
—	וְהִרְאַנִי	*Et ostendet mihi.*	And he will shew to me.
ראש	וְהָרֹאשׁ	*Et agmen.*	And the company, band, troop,
—	וְהָרָאשִׁים	*Et agmina.* [care	And the companies, bands.
רבה	וְהַרְבֵּה	*Et multus, multipli*	And much, to multiply.
—	וְהַרְבָּה	*Et multiplicando.*	And in multiplying.
—	וְהִרְבָּה	*Et multiplicavit.*	And he multiplied.
רבב	וְהָרַבִּים	*Et multi.*	And the many.
רבע	וְהָרְבִיעִי	*Et quartus.*	And the fourth.
רבה	וְהִרְבִּיתָ	*Et augebis.*	And thou shalt increase.
—	וְהִרְבֵּיתִי	*Et multiplicabo.*	And I will multiply.
—	וְהִרְבִּיתְךָ	*Et multiplicabo te.*	And I will multiply thee.
—	וְהִרְבְּךָ־־בְּךָ	*Et augebit te.*	And he will increase thee.
—	וְהִרְבֵּתִים	*Et augebo eos.*	And I will increase them.
הרג	וְהָרַג	*Et occidit, interfecit*	And he slew, killed.
—	וְהֶרֶג	*Et occisio, cædes.*	And slaughter.
—	וְהָרְגוּ	*Et occident.*	And they will slay.
—	וְהִרְגוּ	*Et occidite.*	And slay ye.
—	וַהֲרָגוּם	*Et occiderunt eos.*	And they slew them.
—	וַהֲרָגוּנִי־גֻנִי	*Et occident me.*	And they will kill me.
רגז	וְהִרְגִּיז	*Et concutiet.*	And he will shake.
רגל	וְהָרַגְלָיִם	*Et pedes.*	And the feet.
הרג	וַהֲרַגְנֻהוּ	*Et occidemus eum.*	And he will kill him.
—	וַהֲרַגְנוּם	*Et occidemus eos.*	And we will kill them.
—	וַהֲרָגָנִי	*Et interficiet me.*	And he will kill me.
—	וְהָרַגְתָּ	*Et occides.*	And thou wilt slay.
—	וְהָרַגְתִּי	*Et occidam.*	And I will slay.
—	וַהֲרָגָתַם	*Et occidet eos.*	And it shall slay them.
רדד	וְהָרְדִידִים	*Et vela.*	And the veils.
הרה	וְהָרָת	*Et concepit.*	And she conceived.
—	וְהַרְהֹרִין	*Et cogitationes.*	And the thoughts.
הרג	וְהָרוֹג	*Et occidere.*	And to kill, slay.
רוח	וְהָרוּחַ	*Et spiritus, ventus.*	And the spirit, wind.
רחב	וְהָרֹחַב	*Et latitudo.*	And the breadth.
—	וְהָרְחָבָה	*Et lata.*	And the broad.

ROOTS.	DERIVATIVES.	VERSIO.	SIGNIFICATION.
רחב	וְהִרְחַבְתִּי	*Et dilatabo.*	And I will enlarge.
חרק	וְהָרְחוֹקִים־־חֹקִ׳	*Et longinqui.*	And they that are far off.
—	וְהָרְחֹקוֹת	*Et longinquæ.*	And they that are far off.
הרה	וְהָרִיּוֹתָיו	*Et prægnantes ejus.*	And his pregnant women.
ריח	וַהֲרִיחוֹ	*Et faciet odorari eum*	And he shall make him smell.
רום	וְהָרֵים	*Et attolle.*	And lift thou up.
—	וְהֵרִים	*Et attollet.*	And he shall lift up.
—	וְהָרִימוּ	*Et tollite.*	And take ye.
רוע	וְהָרִיעוּ	*Et clangite.*	And shout ye.
—	וַהֲרֵיעֹתֶם	*Et clangetis.*	And ye shall shout.
ריק	וְהֵרִיקוּ	*Et evaginabunt.*	And they will draw out.
—	וַהֲרִיקוֹתִי	*Et evaginabo.*	And I will draw out.
הרה	וְהָרִית	*Et concipies.* [*te*	And thou shalt conceive.
רכב	וְהִרְכַּבְתִּיךָ	*Et equitare faciam*	And I will cause thee to ride.
—	וְהִרְכַּבְתֶּם	*Et equitare facietis.*	And ye will cause to ride [ride
—	וְהִרְכִּיבֻהוּ	*Et facient ut equitet*	And they will cause him to
רכל	וְהָרֹכְלִים	*Et aromatarii.*	And the spice merchants.
רכס	וְהָרְכָסִים	*Et prærupti* loci.	And the rough, rugged *places*.
רכש	וְהָרְכֻשׁ	*Et substantia.*	And the substance, the goods.
רמן	וְהָרִמּוֹן	*Et malum punicum.*	And the pomegranate.
—	וְהָרִמּוֹנִים	*Et mala punica.*	And the pomegranates.
רמח	וְהָרְמָחִים	*Et hastæ.*	And the spears.
רום	וַהֲרֵמֹתָ	*Et auferes.*	And thou shalt take away.
—	וַהֲרֵמֹתֶם	*Et extolletis.*	And ye shall lift up.
רנן	וְהַרְנִינוּ	*Et cantate, exultate*	And sing, exult ye.
הרה	וְהֵרֹנֵךְ	*Et conceptus tuus.*	And thy conception.
הרס	וְהָרְסָהּ	*Et destrue illam.*	And destroy thou her.
—	וְהָרְסוּ	*Et evertent.*	And they will overturn.
—	וְהָרַסְתָּ	*Et dirues.*	And thou wilt throw down.
—	וְהָרַסְתִּי	*Et destruam.*	And I will destroy.
—	וַהֲרִסֹתָיו	*Et ruinæ ejus.*	And his ruins.
רוע	וְהָרָע־־רַע	*Et malum.*	And the evil.
—	וְהָרֵעַ	*Et male facere.*	And to do evil.
—	וְהֵרַע	*Et male faciet.*	And he will do evil.
רעב	וְהָרָעָב	*Et fames.*	And the famine.
רוע	וְהֵרֵעוּ	*Et clanxerunt.*	And they shouted.
—	וְהָרָעוֹת־־עֹת	*Et malæ, mala.*	And the wicked.

ROOTS.	DERIVATIVES.	VERSIO.	SIGNIFICATION.
רעה	וְהָרֹעִים	*Et pastores.*	And the shepherds.
רעל	וְהָרְעָלוֹת	*Et bracteolæ.*	And the spangles, *ornaments.*
רעש	וְהִרְעַשְׁתִּי	*Et tremere faciam.*	And I will cause to shake.
רוע	וַהֲרֵעֹתֶם	*Et clangetis.*	And ye shall shout.
רוץ	וְהָרֵץ	*Et currere fac.*	And cause thou to run.
רצף	וְהָרִצְפָּה	*Et pavimentum.*	And the pavement.
רצה	וְהִרְצָת	*Et acquiescet.*	And she will be pleased with.
ריק	וְהָרֵק	*Et exsere.*	And draw thou out.
רקח	וְהַרְקַח	*Et condi.*	And season thou.
ריק	וַהֲרִקֹתִי	*Et exseram.* [*agent.*	And I will draw out [wickedly
רשע	וְהִרְשִׁיעוּ	*Et damnabunt, impie*	And they shall condemn, will do
——	וְהָרָשָׁע	*Et improbus, impius*	And the wicked.
——	וְהָרְשָׁעִים	*Et impii.*	And the wicked, ungodly.
——	וְהִרְשַׁעְנוּ	*Et impie egimus* [*um*	And we have done wickedly.
הרה	וְהָרוֹתֵיהֶם	*Et prægnantes cor-*	And their pregnant women.
שאר	וְהִשְׁאִיר	*Et relinquet.*	And he will leave.
——	וְהִשְׁאַרְתִּי	*Et reliqui, relinquam*	And I have left, will leave.
שוב	וְהָשֵׁב	*Et restituendo, reduc, redde.*	And in restoring, bring back, return thou.
——	וֶהֱשִׁבוּם	*Et retulerunt eos.*	And they brought them again
——	וַהֲשִׁבוֹתִים-בֹתִי	*Et reducam eos.*	And I will bring them again.
שבט	וְהַשֵּׁבֶט	*Et tribus.*	And the tribe.
שבס	וְהַשְּׁבִיסִים	*Et reticula.*	And the cauls.
שבע	וְהִשְׁבִּיעַ	*Et adjuravit.*	And he charged with an oath.
——	וְהִשְׂבִּיעַ	*Et satiabit.*	And he will satisfy.
שבע	וְהַשְּׁבִיעִת	*Et septima.* [*ciet.*	And the seventh. [to cease.
שבת	וְהִשְׁבִּית	*Et cessare fecit, fa-*	And he hath caused, will cause
——	וְהִשְׁבִּיתוּ	*Et cessare facient.*	And they will cause to cease.
שבך	וְהַשְּׂבָכוֹת	*Et reticula.*	And the net works.
שוב	וַהֲשִׁבֵנִי	*Et refer mihi.*	And bring thou back to me.
——	וֶהֱשִׁבֵנִי	*Et reducet mihi.*	And he shall bring back to me.
שבע	וְהַשָּׂבָע	*Et saturitas.*	And the plenty.
——	וְהִשָּׁבֵעַ	*Et jurare.*	And to swear.
——	וְהַשְּׁבֻעָה	*Et adjuratio.*	And the oath, adjuration.
——	וְהַשִּׁבְעִים	*Et septuaginta.*	And the seventy.
——	וְהִשְׂבַּעְתִּי	*Et satiabo.*	And I will satisfy.
שבר	וְהַשֶּׁבֶר	*Et clades.*	And the destruction.

ROOTS.	DERIVATIVES.	VERSIO.	SIGNIFICATION.
שבר	וְהַשֶּׁבֶר	*Et contritio.*	And the bruising, crushing.
שבת	וְהַשַּׁבָּת	*Et sabbatum.*	And the sabbath.
שוב	וַהֲשֵׁבֹתָ	*Et reddidisti.*	And thou returnedst.
—	וַהֲשֵׁבֹתוֹ	*Et reddes eum* [*tam*	And thou wilt restore him.
—	וַהֲשִׁבֹתִי	*Et reducam, conver-*	And I will bring again, will turn
שבת	וְהִשְׁבַּתִּי	*Et cessare faciam.*	And I will cause to cease.
שוב	וַהֲשִׁבֹתִיךְ־־שִׁי	*Et reducam te.*	And I will bring thee back.
שבת	וְהִשְׁבַּתִּיךְ	*Et cessare faciam te*	And I will cause thee to cease
—	וְהִשְׁבַּתִּים	*Et reducam eos.* [*eos*	And I will bring them again.
ישב	וְהֹשְׁבוֹתִים	*Et habitare faciam*	And I will cause them to dwell
שוב	וַהֲשֵׁבֹתָם־שִׁבוֹ	*Et reduces eos.*	And thou wilt bring them back
שבת	וְהִשְׁבַּתֶּם	*Et cessare facietis.*	And ye will cause to cease.
—	וְהִשְׁבַּתְנוּ	*Et cessare faciemus.*	And we shall cause to cease.
שגל	וְהַשֵּׁגָל	*Et regina.*	And the queen.
נשג	וְהִשִּׂגָנוּ	*Et assequetur nos.*	And he will overtake us.
—	וְהִשַּׂגְתָּם	*Et assequeris eos.*	And thou shalt overtake us.
שהר	וְהַשַּׂהֲרֹנִים	*Et lunulæ.*	And the little moons.
שדד	וְהַשּׁוֹדֵד	*Et vastator.*	And the spoiler.
שער	וְהַשּׁוֹעֲרִים־שֹׁעֲ׳	*Et janitores.*	And the porters.
שור	וְהַשּׁוֹר	*Et bos.*	And the ox. [destroy.
שחת	וְהִשְׁחִית	*Et disperdidit, perdet*	And he hath destroyed, will
—	וְהַשְׁחִיתָהּ	*Et disperde eam.*	And destroy thou her.
—	וְהִשְׁחִיתוּ	*Et corruperunt.*	And they have corrupted.
שחר	וְהַשַּׁחֲרוּת	*Et juventus.*	And youth.
שחת	וְהִשְׁחַתִּי	*Et disperdam.*	And I will destroy.
—	וְהִשְׁחַתֶּם	*Et corrumpetis.*	And ye will corrupt.
נשא	וְהִשִּׂיאוּ	*Et ferre facient.*	And they will cause to bear.
שוב	וְהֵשִׁיב	*Et reddidit, reducet.*	And he restored, will restore.
שוב	וַהֲשִׁיבֵהוּ	*Et reduc eum.*	And bring thou him back.
—	וַהֲשִׁיבֻהוּ	*Et reducite eum.*	And bring ye him again.
ישב	וְהֹשִׁיבוּ	*Et habitare facite, fecerunt.* [*dent.*	And cause ye, they have caused to dwell. [restore.
שוב	וְהֵשִׁיבוּ	*Et reduxerunt, red-*	And they brought back, will
—	וְהָשִׁיבוּ.	*Et convertite.*	And turn ye.
—	וֶהֱשִׁיבוּם	*Et reduxerunt eos.*	And they brought them back.
—	וַהֲשִׁיבוֹתִי־־בֹתִ׳	*Et convertam.*	And I will turn.
—	וֶהֱשִׁיבְךָ־־וְהִ׳	*Et reducet te.*	And he will bring thee again.

ROOTS.	DERIVATIVES.	VERSIO.	SIGNIFICATION.
שוב	וַהֲשִׁיבֹנִי	*Et reducam.*	And I will bring back.
—	וַהֲשִׁיבֹתִים	*Et reducam eos.*	And I will bring them back.
—	וַהֲשֵׁבֹתֶם	*Et reducetis.*	And ye will bring back.
נשג	וְהִשִּׂיג	*Et assequetur.*	And he shall overtake.
—	וְהִשִּׂיגָה	*Et assequetur.*	And she shall overtake.
—	וְהִשִּׂיגוֹ	*Et assequetur eum.*	And he shall overtake him.
—	וְהִשִּׂיגוּךָ-גֻךְ	*Et assequentur te.*	And they shall overtake thee.
נשק	וְהִשִּׂיקוּ	*Et comburent.*	And they shall burn.
שוק	וְהֵשִׁיקוּ	*Et redundabunt.*	And they shall overflow.
שור	וְהַשִּׁיר	*Et canticum.*	And the song.
שכב	וְהַשֹּׁכֵב	*Et cubans.*	And he that lieth.
—	וְהָשְׁכַּב	*Et prostratus est.*	And he has been laid.
—	וְהָשְׁכְּבָה	*Et prosternere.* [*eos.*	And be thou laid.
—	וְהִשְׁכַּבְתִּים	*Et cubare faciam*	And I will make thee lie down
שכח	וְהִשְׁכִּחוּ	*Et invenerunt.*	And they have found.
שכל	וְהַשְׂכֵּיל	*Et intelligentia.*	And understanding.
—	וְהִשְׂכִּיל	*Et prudenter aget.*	And he will act wisely.
שכם	וְהִשְׁכִּים	*Et mane surrexit.*	And he rose early.
שכל	וְהַשְׂכֵּל	*Et intelligentia.*	And understanding.
שכם	וְהַשְׁכֵּם	*Et mane surgendo.*	And in rising early.
—	וְהִשְׁכַּמְתֶּם	*Et mane surgetis.*	And ye shall rise early.
שכן	וְהִשְׁכַּנְתִּי	*Et habitare faciam.*	And I will cause to dwell.
שכר	וְהִשְׁכַּרְתִּי	*Et inebriabo.*	And I will make drunk.
—	וְהִשְׁכַּרְתִּים	*Et inebriabo eos.*	And I will make them drunk.
שכך	וַהֲשִׁכֹּתִי	*Et desinere faciam.*	And I will make to cease.
שלג	וְהַשֶּׁלֶג	*Et nix.*	And the snow.
שלם	וְהַשָּׁלוֹם	*Et pax.*	And the peace.
שלח	וְהַשֻּׁלְחָן	*Et mensa.*	And the table.
—	וְהִשְׁלַחְתִּי	*Et mittam.*	And I will send.
שלט	וְהִשְׁלִטֹה	*Et præfecit eum.*	And he hath made him ruler.
—	וְהִשְׁלִטְךָ	*Et præfecit te.* [*ei.*	And he hath made thee ruler.
—	וְהִשְׁלִיטוֹ	*Et potestatem dedit*	And he hath given him power
שלך	וְהִשְׁלִיךְ	*Et projecit, abjiciet.*	And he hath cast, will cast off
—	וְהִשְׁלִיכוּ	*Et projicient.*	And they shall cast.
—	וְהַשְׁלִיכִי	*Et projice.*	And cast thou.
שלש	וְהַשְּׁלִישִׁי-לִשִׁי	*Et tertius.*	And the third.
—	וְהַשְּׁלִישִׁית-לִשִׁי	*Et tertia pars.*	And the third *part.*

ROOTS.	DERIVATIVES.	VERSIO.	SIGNIFICATION.
שלך	וְהַשְׁלֵךְ	*Et jace, projicere.*	And cast thou, to cast.
—	וְהָשְׁלַךְ	*Et conjectus est.*	And he was cast down.
—	וְהָשְׁלְכוּ	*Et abjecti sunt.*	And they were cast off.
—	וְהִשְׁלַכְתָּ	*Et projicies.*	And thou shalt cast.
—	וְהִשְׁלַכְתּוֹ	*Et ejicies eum.*	And thou shalt cast him out.
—	וְהִשְׁלַכְתִּי	*Et projiciam.*	And I will cast.
—	וְהִשְׁלַכְתֶּנָּה	*Et projicietis.*	And ye shall cast.
שלם	וְהַשְׁלָמָה	*Et perfecit eam.*	And he finished her or it.
—	וְהַשְּׁלָמִים	*Et sacrificia pacifica*	And the peace offerings.
שלש	וְהַשְּׁלֹשִׁים	*Et triginta.*	And the thirty.
שמד	וְהִשְׁמַדְתִּי	*Et disperdam.*	And I will destroy.
—	וְהִשְׁמַדְתִּיו	*Et disperdam eum.*	And I will destroy him.
שמם	וְהָשַׁמּוּ	*Et obstupescite.*	And be ye astonished.
—	וַהֲשִׁמּוֹתִי־מֹתִי	*Et vastabo.*	And I will desolate, destroy.
שום	וַהֲשִׂמוֹתִיהוּ	*Et ponam eum.*	And I will place him.
שמד	וְהִשְׁמִידְךָ	*Et disperdet te.*	And he will destroy thee.
שם	וְהַשָּׁמַיִם	*Et cœlum, cœli.*	And the heaven, heavens.
שמע	וְהִשְׁמִיעַ	*Et audiri faciet.*	And he will make to be heard.
—	וְהַשְׁמִיעוּ	*Et audiri facite.*	And publish ye.
—	וְהִשְׁמִיעוּ	*Et audiri facient.*	And they will proclaim.
—	וְהַשְׁמִיעוּהָ	*Et audire facite eam*	And cause ye her to hear.
שמן	וְהַשֶּׁמֶן	*Et oleum.*	And the oil.
—	וְהַשְּׁמֵנָה	*Et pinguis.*	And the fat.
שמע	וְהַשְּׁמֻעָה	*Et fama.* [*ciam.*	And the report. [to be heard.
—	וְהִשְׁמַעְתִּי	*Et audiri feci, fa-*	And I have caused, will cause
שמש	וְהַשֶּׁמֶשׁ	*Et sol.*	And the sun.
שום	וַהֲשִׂמֹתִיו	*Et ponam eum.*	And I will place him.
שנא	וְהַשְּׂנוּאָה	*Et exosa.*	And the hated.
שנה	וְהַשֵּׁנִית	*Et secundus* locus.	And the second place, again.
שער	וְהַשָּׂעִיר	*Et hircus.* [*escite.*	And the he-goat.
שען	וְהִשָּׁעֲנוּ	*Et innitimini, requi-*	And lean, stay, rest ye.
שער	וְהַשַּׁעַר	*Et porta, janua.*	And the gate.
—	וְהַשְּׂעֹרָה	*Et hordeum.*	And the barley
—	וְהַשְּׂעֹרִים	*Et hordea.*	And the barley.
שפט	וְהַשֹּׁפֵט	*Et judicans.*	And he that judgeth, the judge
—	וְהַשֹּׁפְטִים	*Et judices.*	And the judges.
שפל	וְהַשְׁפִּיל	*Et deprimet.*	And he will lay low.

ROOTS.	DERIVATIVES.	VERSIO.	SIGNIFICATION.
שפל	וְהַשְׁפִּילֵהוּ	*Et deprime eum.*	And bring thou him low.
—	וְהַשְּׁפֵלָה	*Et vallis, planities,*	And the valley, plain.
שפה	וְהַשְּׁפַתַּיִם	*Et labia*, al. *uncini*, al. *lapides focarii.*	And the lips, *or* hooks, *or* fire stones.
שקה	וְהִשְׁקָה	*Et irrigabit.*	And he will water.
—	וְהִשְׁקָהּ	*Et bibere faciet eum.*	And he will cause him to drink
—	וְהִשְׁקוּ	*Et adaquabunt.*	And they shall water.
—	וְהַשְׁקוֹת	*Et potum dare.*	And to give drink.
שקט	וְהַשְׁקֵט	*Et quiesce.*	And rest thou.
שקה	וְהִשְׁקִינוּ	*Et adaquabimus.*	And we will water.
—	וְהִשְׁקִיתָ	*Et irrigabis.*	And thou shalt water.
—	וְהִשְׁקִיתָה	*Et bibere facies.*	And thou shalt cause to drink
—	וְהִשְׁקֵיתִי	*Et irrigabo.*	And I will water,
—	וְהִשְׁקִיתִים	*Et bibere faciam eos*	And I will make them drink.
שקל	וְהַשֶּׁקֶל	*Et siclus.*	And the shekel.
שקם	וְהַשִּׁקְמִים	*Et sycomori.*	And the sycamore-trees.
שקץ	וְהַשֶּׁקֶץ	*Et abominatio.*	And the abomination.
שקה	וְהִשְׁקִתִים	*Et bibendum dabo eis*	And I will give them to drink
שור	וְהַשָּׁרוֹת	*Et cantatrices.*	And the singing-women.
שיר	וְהַשֵּׁרוֹת	*Et armillæ.*	And the bracelets.
שרד	וְהַשְּׂרִידִים	*Et reliqui.*	And the persons left.
שור	וְהַשָּׂרִים	*Et duces, principes.*	And the captains, chiefs.
שרה	וְהַשִּׁרְיֹנִים	*Et loricæ.*	And the coats of mail.
שרף	וְהַשֹּׂרֵף	*Et comburens.*	And he that burneth.
שש	וְהַשִּׁשִּׁי	*Et sextus.*	And the sixth.
שחה	וְהִשְׁתַּחֲוָה	*Et incurvabit se.*	And he will bow down himself
—	וְהִשְׁתַּחֲווּ	*Et incurvabunt se, incurvate vos.*	And they will bow down themselves, bow down yourselves
שחה	וְהִשְׁתַּחֲוִי	*Et incurva te.*	And bow down thyself.
—	וְהִשְׁתַּחֲוִיתָ	*Et incurvabis te.*	And thou shalt bow down thyself.
—	וְהִשְׁתַּחֲוֵיתִי	*Et incurvabo me.*	And I will bow down myself.
—	וְהִשְׁתַּחֲוִיתֶם	*Et incurvabitis vos.*	And ye shall bow yourselves.
שתה	וְהַשְּׁתִיָּה	*Et potus.*	And the drinking.
שכח	וְהִשְׁתַּכַּח	*Et inventus est.*	And he was found.
—	וְהִשְׁתְּכַחַת	*Et inventa est.*	And she was found.
שנה	וְהִשְׁתַּנִּית	*Et vestes muta.*	And change thy garments.
תא	וְהַתָּא	*Et conclave.*	And the chamber.

ROOTS.	DERIVATIVES.	VERSIO.	SIGNIFICATION.
תאה	וְהִתְאַוִּיתֶם	*Et describetis.*	And ye shall mark out.
תאן	וְהַתְּאֵנָה	*Et ficus.*	And the fig-tree.
אשש	וְהִתְאֹשָׁשׁוּ	*Et confirmate vos.*	And strengthen yourselves.
בון	וְהִתְבּוֹנֵן	*Et animadverte.*	And consider thou.
—	וְהִתְבּוֹננוּ	*Et intelligite.*	And understand ye.
—	וְהִתְבּוֹנַנְתָּ	*Et animadvertes.*	And thou shalt consider.
תבן	וְהַתֶּבֶן	*Et stramen, palea.*	And the straw, stubble.
ברך	וְהִתְבָּרֵךְ	*Et benedicet sibi.*	And he will bless himself.
—	וְהִתְבָּרֲכוּ־־רְ׳	*Et benedicentur.*	And they shall be blessed.
גדל	וְהִתְגַּדִּלְתִּי	*Et magnificabo te.*	And I will magnify thee.
גלח	וְהִתְגַּלָּח	*Et radet se.*	And he shall be shaven.
געש	וְהִתְגַּעֲשׁוּ	*Et commovebuntur.*	And they shall be moved.
גרה	וְהִתְגָּר	*Et contende.*	And contend thou.
הלל	וְהִתְהוֹלָלוּ־הֹלָ׳	*Et insanient.*	And they will rage, be mad.
הלך	וְהִתְהַלֵּךְ	*Et ambulabit.*	And he shall walk.
—	וְהִתְהַלְּכוּ	*Et ambulate.*	And walk ye.
—	וְהִתְהַלַּכְתִּי	*Et ambulabo.*	And I will walk.
הלל	וְהִתְהֹלְלוּ	*Et insanient.*	And they shall rage.
ידה	וְהַתּוֹדָה	*Et chorus.*	And the choir.
—	וְהִתְוַדָּה	*Et confitebitur.*	And he shall confess.
—	וְהִתְוַדּוּ	*Et confitebuntur.*	And they shall confess.
תוה	וְהִתְוִיתָ	*Et determinabis.*	And thou shalt limit.
תקע	וְהַתּוֹקֵעַ	*Et clangens.*	And he that shouteth.
ירה	וְהַתּוֹרָה	*Et lex.*	And the law.
—	וְהַתּוֹרֹת	*Et leges.*	And the laws.
חול	וְהִתְחוֹלֵל	*Et expecta.*	And wait thou.
חזק	וְהִתְחַזַּקְתֶּם	*Et confirmate vos.*	And strengthen yourselves.
חלה	וְהִתְחָל	*Et ægrotum te fac.*	And make thyself sick.
חלק	וְהִתְחַלְּקוּ	*Et divident.*	And they shall divide.
חנן	וְהַתְּחִנָּה	*Et deprecatio.*	And the supplication. [tion.
—	וְהִתְחַנְּנוּ	*Et deprecabuntur.*	And they will make supplica-
חתן	וְהִתְחַתְּנוּ	*Et affinitatem con-*	And make ye marriages.
		trahite. [*trahetis.*	[ages.
—	וְהִתְחַתַּנְתֶּם	*Et affinitatem con-*	And ye shall contract marri-
יחש	וְהִתְיַחְשָׂם	*Et recensendo eos.*	And in reckoning them by genealogies.
תוך	וְהַתִּיכוֹנָה	*Et media.*	And the middle.

ROOTS.	DERIVATIVES.	VERSIO.	SIGNIFICATION.
יצב	וְהִתְיַצֵּב	*Et consiste.*	And stand thou fast.
—	וְהִתְיַצְּבוּ	*Et stabunt, state.*	And they shall stand, stand ye
ירש	וְהַתִּירוֹשׁ	*Et vinum, mustum.*	And the wine, new wine.
נתך	וְהִתַּכְתִּי	*Et fundam.*	And I will pour.
תמה	וְהִתַּמְּהוּ	*Et obstupescite.*	And be ye astonished.
מהמה	וְהִתְמַהְמָהוּ	*Et morati sunt.*	And they tarried, lingered.
תמם	וַהֲתִמּוֹתִי	*Et consumam.*	And I will consume.
מכר	וְהִתְמַכַּרְתֶּם	*Et venundabimini.*	And ye shall be sold.
תמר	וְהַתִּמֹּרִים	*Et palmæ.*	And the palm-trees.
נבא	וְהִתְנַבִּי	*Et vaticinatus est.*	And he prophesied.
—	וְהִתְנַבִּיתָ	*Et vaticinaberis.*	And thou shalt prophesy.
נדד	וְהִתְנוֹדְדָה	*Et agitabit se.*	And she shall shake herself.
נחל	וְהִתְנַחֲלוּם	*Et possidebunt eos.*	And they shall possess them.
—	וְהִתְנַחַלְתֶּם	*Et vosmet possessores reddetis.*	And ye shall make yourselves the possessors.
(נשם)	וְהַתִּנְשֶׁמֶת	*Et noctua*, al. *cygnus*, al. *anser.*	And the owl, *or* swan, *or* goose.
עתה	וְהִתְעוּ	*Et errare fecerunt.*	And they have caused to err.
עור	וְהִתְעֹרַרְתִּי־רַע	*Et excitavi me.*	And I have lifted up myself.
עוה	וְהִתְעַוְּתוּ	*Et incurvabunt se.*	And they will bow themselves
תעב	וְהִתְעִיבוּ	*Et turpiter egerunt.*	And they have acted basely.
עלל	וְהִתְעַלְּלוּ	*Et illudent.*	And they will mock.
עלם	וְהִתְעַלַּמְתָּ	*Et abscondes te.*	And thou shalt hide thyself.
עמר	וְהִתְעַמֵּר	*Et premet, opprimet*	And he shall press, oppress.
ענג	וְהִתְעַנַּג	*Et delecta te.*	And delight thyself. [selves.
—	וְהִתְעַנְּגוּ	*Et delectabunt se.*	And they shall delight them-
—	וְהִתְעַנַּגְתֶּם	*Et delectabitis vos.*	And ye shall delight yourselves
ענה	וְהִתְעַנִּי	*Et subjice te.*	And submit thyself.
ערב	וְהִתְעָרְבוּ	*Et commiscuerunt se*	And they mingled themselves.
פאר	וְהַתִּפְאֶרֶת	*Et decor, gloria.*	And the beauty, glory.
פלל	וְהִתְפַּלֵּל	*Et orabit, ora.*	And he shall pray, pray thou.
—	וְהִתְפַּלְלוּ	*Et orabunt, orate.*	And they shall pray, pray ye.
—	וְהִתְפַּלַּלְתֶּם	*Et orabitis.*	And ye shall pray.
פלש	וְהִתְפַּלְּשׁוּ	*Et volvite vos.*	And roll yourselves.
—	וְהִתְפַּלְּשִׁי	*Et volve te.*	And roll thyself. [themselves.
פרד	וְהִתְפָּרְדוּ	*Et separarunt se.*	And they have separated
קדש	וְהִתְקַדְּשׁוּ	*Et sanctificate vos.*	And sanctify yourselves.

ROOTS.	DERIVATIVES.	VERSIO.	SIGNIFICATION.
קדש	וְהִתְקַדִּשְׁתִּי	*Et sanctificabo me.*	And I will sanctify myself.
—	וְהִתְקַדִּשְׁתֶּם	*Et sanctificabitis vos*	And ye shall sanctify yourselves.
קצף	וְהִתְקַצַּף	*Et irascetur.*	And he will be angry.
רום	וְהַתְּרוּמָה	*Et oblatio elevata.*	And the heave offering.
שוט	וְהִתְשׁוֹטַטְנָה	*Et cursitate.*	And run ye to and fro.
	וו		
וו			
וו	וָוֵי	*Et uncini.*	And the hooks.
—	וָוֵיהֶם	*Et uncini eorum.*	And their hooks.
—	וָוִים	*Et uncini.*	And hooks.
	וז		
זה	וְזֹאת	*Et ista, hæc.*	And she, that, this.
זבח	וָזֶבַח־־זֶ״ וְזֶ׳	*Et victima.*	And the victim, sacrifice.
—	וְזָבַח	*Et immolabit.*	And he shall sacrifice.
—	וְזֹבֵחַ	*Et immolans.*	And he that sacrificeth.
—	וְזָבְחוּ	*Et sacrificabunt.*	And they shall sacrifice.
—	וְזִבְחֵיהֶם	*Et victimæ eorum.*	And their sacrifices.
—	וּזְבָחֶיךָ	*Et sacrificia tua.*	And thy sacrifices.
—	וְזִבְחֵיכֶם	*Et victimæ vestræ.*	And your sacrifices.
—	וּזְבָחִים	*Et sacrificia.*	And the sacrifices.
—	וְזָבַחְנוּ	*Et immolabimus.*	And we will sacrifice.
—	וְזָבַחְתָּ	*Et immolabis.*	And thou shalt sacrifice.
—	וּזְבַחְתֶּם	*Et immolabitis.*	And ye shall sacrifice.
זה	וְזֶה	*Et ille, hic, alius.*	And he, this, another.
זהב	וְזָהָב וּזְהַב	*Et aurum.*	And gold, the gold.
—	וּזְהָבִי	*Et aurum meum.*	And my gold.
—	וּזְהָבְךָ	*Et aurum tuum.*	And thy gold.
—	וּזְהָבָם	*Et aurum eorum.*	And their gold.
זהר	וּזְהִירִין	*Et cauti.*	And cautious.
זהם	וְזִהֲמַתּוּ	*Et nauseare fecit eum.*	And he hath made him nauseate.
זלל	וְזוֹלֵל	*Et comessator.*	And a glutton.
זקף	וְזוֹקֵף	*Et erigens.*	And raising up.
זיו	וְזִיוֵהּ	*Et splendor ejus.*	And his brightness.
—	וְזִיוֹהִי	*Et splendores ejus.*	And his brightness of countenance.
—	וְזִיוִי	*Et splendor meus.*	And my splendour.

ROOTS.	DERIVATIVES.	VERSIO.	SIGNIFICATION.
זיו	וְזִיוַי	Et splendores mei.	And my brightness of face.
—	וְזִינָיִךְ	Et splendores tui.	And thy brightness of face.
זין	וְזִין	Et animal.	And the animal.
זית	וְזֵיתֵיכֶם	Et oliveta vestra.	And your olive-yards.
—	וְזֵיתִים	Et olivæ.	And olive-trees.
זכך	וְזַךְ	Et purus.	And pure.
—	וּזְכוֹכִית	Et gemma nitidissima.	And the purest gem.
זכר	וּזְכֹר	Et recordare.	And remember thou.
—	וְזָכְרוּ	Et recordabuntur.	And they shall remember.
—	וְזִכָּרוֹן	Et monimentum.	And a memorial.
—	וְזִכְרְךָ	Et memoria tui.	And the remembrance of thee
—	וְזִכְרָם	Et memoria ipsorum	And the remembrance of them
—	וְזָכַרְתָּ וְזָכַרְתְּ	Et recordaberis.	And thou shalt remember.
—	וְזָכַרְתִּי	Et recordabor.	And I will remember.
—	וּזְכַרְתֶּם	Et recordabimini.	And ye shall remember
—	וּזְכַרְתַּנִי	Et memorabis me.	And thou shalt make mention [of me
זמן	וְזִמְנָא־־נִין	Et tempus.	And the time.
—	וְזִמְנָא	Et tempora.	And the seasons, times.
זמר	וְזֶמֶר	Et rupicapra.	And the wild goat.
—	וְזַמְּרוּ	Et canite.	And sing ye.
—	וּזְמֹרֵיהֶם	Et palmites eorum.	And their vine-branches.
—	וְזִמְרַת־־רָת	Et cantio, canticum.	And the melody, song.
—	וּזְמֹרַת	Et palmes.	And the vine-branch.
זמה	וְזִמָּתֵךְ	Et scelus tuum.	And thy wickedness.
זנב	וְזָנָב	Et cauda.	And the tail.
—	וְזִנַּבְתֶּם	Et caudam præcidetis.	And ye shall cut off the tail.
זנה	וְזָנָה	Et scortabitur.	And he will go a whoring.
—	וְזָנוּ	Et scortabuntur.	And they will go a whoring.
זון	וּזְנִים	Et species.	And species, sorts.
זנה	וְזָנְתָה	Et scortabitur.	And she will go a whoring.
זעם	וְזָעַם	Et irascetur.	And he will be angry.
—	וָזַעַם	Et furor.	And indignation.
זעף	וְזָעֵף	Et indignabundus.	And indignant.
זעק	וְזָעֲקָה	Et clamavit.	And she cried.
—	וּזְעָקָה	Et clamor.	And the cry.
—	וְזָעֲקוּ	Et clamabunt.	And they will cry.
—	וְזַעֲקוּ וּזְעָקִי	Et clamate.	And cry ye.

ROOTS.	DERIVATIVES.	VERSIO.	SIGNIFICATION.
זעק	וּזְעַקְתֶּם	*Et clamabitis.*	And ye shall cry.
—	וְזַעֲקָתָם	*Et clamor eorum.*	And their cry.
זקף	וּזְקִיף	*Et erigetur.*	And he shall be set up.
זקן	וְזָקֵן	*Et senex.*	And the old man.
—	וּזְקֵנוֹת	*Et anus.*	And old women.
—	וּזְקֵנַי	*Et senes mei.*	And my elders.
—	וּזְקָנִי	*Et barba mea.*	And my beard.
—	וְזִקְנֵי	*Et senes.*	And the elders.
—	וּזְקֵנָיו	*Et senes ejus.*	And his elders.
—	וְזִקְנֵיכֶם	*Et senes vestri.*	And your old men.
—	וּזְקֵנִים	*Et senes.*	And the elders.
זקק	וְזִקַּק	*Et defæcabit.*	And he shall purge.
זור	וְזָר ־ר׳	*Et alienus, alienigena.*	And strange, a stranger.
זרה	וְזֵרוּהָ	*Et ventilabunt eam.*	And they shall fan her.
זרע	וּזְרוֹעַ	*Et brachium.*	And the arm.
—	וּזְרוֹעֲךָ־־רֹעֲ״	*Et brachium tuum.*	And thy arm.
—	וּזְרוֹעָם	*Et brachium eorum.*	And their arm.
זרח	וְזָרַח	*Et ortus est, orietur.*	And he rose, will rise.
—	וְזָרְחָה	*Et orietur.*	And she shall rise.
זור	וְזָרִים	*Et alieni.*	And strangers.
זרה	וְזֵרִיתִי	*Et dispergam.*	And I will scatter.
—	וְזֵרִיתִיךְ	*Et dispergam te.*	And I will scatter thee.
—	וְזֵרִיתִים־־תִם	*Et dispergam eos.*	And I will scatter them.
זרם	וְזֶרֶם	*Et inundatio.*	And an inundation.
זרה	וְזֵרָם	*Et disperget eos.*	And he will scatter them.
זרם	וְזִרְמַת	*Et fluxus.*	And the issue.
זרע	וָזֶרַע	*Et semen.*	And seed.
—	וְזֶרַע	*Et semen.*	And the seed.
—	וְזֹרֵעַ	*Et seminans.*	And he that sows.
—	וְזַרְעוֹ	*Et semen ejus.*	And his seed.
—	וּזְרֹעוֹ	*Et semen, brachium ejus*	And his seed, his arm.
—	וּזְרֹעוֹת	*Et brachia.*	And the arms.
—	וְזֹרְעֵי	*Et seminantes.*	And they that sow.
—	וּזְרֹעַי	*Et brachia mea.*	And my arms.
—	וְזַרְעֵיכֶם	*Et semina vestra.*	And your seed.
—	וּזְרֹעִים	*Et brachia.*	And the arms.
—	וְזַרְעֲךָ־עֶךָ־עֶךָ	*Et semen tuum.*	And thy seed.

ROOTS.	DERIVATIVES.	VERSIO.	SIGNIFICATION.
זרע	וְזַרְעָם	*Et semen eorum.*	And their seed.
—	וְזָרַעְתִּי	*Et seram.*	And I will sow.
—	וּזְרַעְתִּיהָ	*Et seram eam.*	And I will sow her.
—	וּזְרֹעֹתָיו	*Et brachia ejus.*	And his arms.
—	וּזְרַעְתֶּם	*Et seretis.*	And ye shall sow.
זרק	וְזָרַק	*Et sparget.*	And he shall sprinkle.
—	וּזְרֹק	*Et sparge.*	And sprinkle thou.
—	וְזָרְקוּ	*Et spargent.*	And they shall sprinkle.
—	וּזְרָקוֹ	*Et sparget eum.*	And he shall sprinkle him.
—	וְזָרַקְתָּ	*Et sparges.*	And thou shalt sprinkle.
—	וְזָרַקְתִּי	*Et spargam.*	And I will sprinkle.
זרת	וְזֶרֶת יָד׳	*Et palmus.*	And a span.
	וח		
חבר	וְחַבּוּרָה	*Et livor.*	And bruises, stripes.
חבל	וַחֲבָל	*Et corruptio.*	And corruption.
—	וְחִבֵּל	*Et disperdet.*	And he shall destroy.
—	וְחֶבֶל	*Et exitium.*	And destruction.
—	וְחֻבַּל	*Et perdetur.*	And he shall be destroyed.
—	וְחַבְּלוּהִי	*Et disperdite eam.*	And destroy ye her.
—	וְחֹבְלַיִךְ	*Et naucleri tui.*	And thy pilots.
—	וַחֲבָלִים	*Et funes, dolores.*	And cords, bands, sorrows.
חבר	וְחֹבֵר	*Et incantans.*	And charming.
—	וְחֻבַּר	*Et conjungetur.*	And he shall be joined.
חבר	וְחַבְרוֹהִי	*Et socii ejus.*	And his companions.
—	וְחַבְרֵי	*Et socii.*	And the companions.
—	וְחִבַּרְתָּ	*Et conjunges.*	And thou shalt couple.
חבש	וְחָבַשְׁתָּ	*Et alligabis.* [*tas.*	And thou shalt bind on.
חגג	וְחַג	*Et festum, solemni-*	And the feast, festival.
—	וְחֹגְגִים	*Et saltantes.*	And dancing.
חגר	וַחֲגוֹר	*Et cingulum* [*gulum*	And a girdle.
—	וַחֲגֹרָה	*Et accingite vos, cin-*	And gird yourselves, a girdle.
—	וְחָגְרוּ	*Et accingent se.*	And they shall gird themselves
—	וַחֲגֹרוּ	*Et accingite vos.*	And gird yourselves.
—	וְחָגַרְתָּ	*Et cinges.*	And thou shalt gird.
חגג	וְחַגֹּתֶם	*Et celebrabitis.* [*res.*	And ye shall celebrate.
חדד	וְחַדּוּ	*Et erunt acuti, acrio-*	And they will be sharp, fiercer

ROOTS.	DERIVATIVES.	VERSIO.	SIGNIFICATION.
חדה	וְחֶדְוָה	*Et lætitia.*	And gladness.
חדל	וַחֲדַל	*Et derelictus*	And forsaken.
—	וְחָדַל	*Et desinit.*	And he will cease.
—	וְחָדַלְתָּ	*Et cessabis.*	And thou shalt cease.
חדר	וַחֲדָרֵי	*Et penetralia.*	And the inner chambers.
—	וַחֲדָרָיו	*Et cubicula ejus.*	And his chambers.
חדש	וְחִדְּשׁוּ	*Et instaurabunt.*	And they shall repair.
—	וַחֲדָשׁוֹת	*Et novæ.*	And new.
חוג	וְחוּג	*Et ambitus.*	And the circuit.
חוח	וָחוֹחַ	*Et spina.*	And a thorn, bramble.
חוט	וְחוּט	*Et filum.*	And a thread.
חטא	וְחוֹטֵא	*Et peccans, peccator*	And sinning, the sinner.
—	וְחוֹטֶא	*Et peccator.*	And a sinner.
חמם	וְחוּם	*Et fuscus.*	And brown.
—	וְחוֹמָה־־מַת	*Et murus.*	And the wall.
חמץ	וְחוֹמֵץ	*Et opprimens.*	And he that oppresseth.
חוס	וְחוּסָה	*Et parce.*	And spare thou.
חוץ	וָחוּצָה	*Et extrinsecus.*	And without.
—	וְחוּצוֹת־־חֹ״	*Et plateæ.*	And the streets.
חור	וָחוּר	*Et candidus.*	And white.
חשך	וְחוֹשֵׂךְ־־חשֵׂ״	*Et cohibens.*	And he that restraineth.
חזה	וַחֲזֶה	*Et pectus.*	And the breast.
—	וְחֶזְוֵהּ	*Et aspectus ejus.*	And his look.
—	וְחֶזְוֵי	*Et visiones.*	And the visions.
—	וַחֲזוֹתֵהּ	*Et aspectus ejus.*	And the sight of him.
—	וְחָזוּתְכֶם	*Et pactum vestrum.*	And your agreement.
—	וַחֲזִיתֶם	*Et vidistis.*	And ye have seen.
חזק	וַחֲזַק	*Et confirma te.*	And strengthen thyself.
—	וַחֲזַק	*Et fortis esto.*	And be thou strong.
—	וְחָזָק	*Et fortis.*	And stronger.
—	וְחָזֵק	*Et invalescens.*	And growing stronger.
—	וְחַזְּקֵהוּ	*Et confirma eum.*	And strengthen thou him.
—	וְחָזְקוּ	*Et confirmabuntur.*	And they shall be strengthened
—	וְחִזְּקוּ	*Et confirmarunt.*	And they strengthened.
—	וְחִזְקִי	*Et valida.*	And strong.
—	וְחַזְּקֵנִי	*Et confirma me.*	And strengthen thou me. [self.
—	וְחִזַּקְתָּ	*Et confirmabis te.*	And thou shalt strengthen thy-

ROOTS.	DERIVATIVES.	VERSIO.	SIGNIFICATION.
חזק	וְחִזַּקְתִּי	*Et confirmabo.*	And I will strengthen, confirm
—	וַחֲזַקְתֶּם	*Et confirmabimini.*	And ye shall be strengthened.
חטא	וְחִטֵּא	*Et mundabit.* [to.	And he shall cleanse.
—	וַחֲטָאָה	*Et victima pro delic-*	And the sin offering.
—	וְחַטְאָה	*Et peccatum.*	And sin.
—	וְחָטְאָה	*Et peccabit.*	And she shall or will sin.
—	וְחִטְּאוֹ	*Et mundabit eum.*	And he shall cleanse him.
—	וְחִטְּאוּ	*Et mundabunt.*	And they shall cleanse.
—	וְחַטְּאוֹת־טאר	*Et peccata.*	And the sins.
—	וְחַטֹּאותֵיכֶם	*Et peccata vestra.*	And your sins.
—	וְחַטֹּאותֵינוּ	*Et peccata nostra.*	And our sins.
—	וַחֲטָאֵי	*Et peccata.*	And the sins.
—	וְחֹטְאִי	*Et peccans in me.*	And he that sinneth against me
—	וְחַטָּאֶיהָ	*Et peccatores ejus.*	And her sinners.
—	וְחַטָּאִים	*Et peccatores.*	And sinners.
—	וַחֲטָאֲךָ	*Et peccatum tuum.*	And thy sin.
—	וְחָטָאת	*Et peccavit.*	And she hath sinned.
—	וְחַטַּאת	*Et peccatum.*	And the sin.
—	וְחִטֵּאתָ	*Et purgabis.*	And thou shalt cleanse.
—	וְחַטָּאתוֹ	*Et peccatum ejus.*	And his sin.
—	וְחָטָאתִי	*Et peccavi.*	And I have sinned.
—	וְחַטָּאתִי	*Et peccatum meum.*	And my sin.
—	וְחַטֹּאתֶיךָ	*Et peccatum tuum.*	And thy sin.
—	וְחַטֹּאתֵינוּ	*Et crimen nostrum.*	And our sin.
—	וְחַטָּאתְךָ	*Et peccatum tuum.*	And thy sin.
—	וְחַטָּאתָם	*Et peccatum eorum, victima pro peccato eorum.*	And their sin, their sin offering
—	וַחֲטָאתֶם	*Et peccabitis.*	And ye will sin.
חטב	וְחֹטְבֵי	*Et cædentes.*	And hewing, cutting down.
חטא	וַחֲטָאֶיךָ	*Et peccata tua.*	And thy sins.
חנט	וְחִטִּים	*Et tritica.*	And the wheats.
חטף	וַחֲטַפְתֶּם	*Et rapietis.*	And ye shall seize, catch.
חיה	וְחָי־חָי	*Et vixit, vivet.*	And he lived, shall live.
—	וְחַי־חָי	*Et vivet.*	And he shall live.
חוב	וְחִיַּבְתֶּם	*Et condemnabitis.*	And ye will condemn.
חוד	וְחִידֹתָם	*Et ænigmata eorum*	And their dark sayings.

ROOTS.	DERIVATIVES.	VERSIO.	SIGNIFICATION.
חיה	וְחָיָה ך״	*Et vivet.*	And he shall live.
—	וְחַיָּה	*Et animal, bestia.*	And an animal, wild beast.
—	וֶחְיֵה	*Et vive.*	And live thou.
—	וְחָיוּ	*Et vivent.*	And they shall live.
—	וִחְיוּ	*Et vivetis, vivete.*	And ye shall live, live ye.
—	וְחַיַּי	*Et vita mea.*	And my life.
—	וְחַיִּים	*Et vitæ.*	And lives.
—	וְחָיִיתָ	*Et vives.*	And thou shalt live.
—	וִחְיִיתֶם	*Et vivetis.*	And ye shall live.
חיל	וְחָיִל	*Et robur, exercitus.*	And the strength, army.
—	וְחַיִל	*Et robur, exercitus.*	And the strength, army.
—	וְחֵיל	*Et exercitus.* [*ejus.*	And the army.
—	וְחֵילוֹ	*Et exercitus, copia*	And his army,substance,wealth
—	וַחֲיָלִים	*Et vires.*	And strength.
—	וְחֵילֵךְ	*Et exercitus tuus.*	And thy army.
—	וְחֵילָם	*Et facultas eorum.*	And their wealth [proportion.
חנן	וְחִין	*Et gratia, decor.*	And the gracefulness, comely
חוק	וְחֵיק	*Et sinus.* [*terva.*	And the bosom.
חיה	וְחַיַּת	*Et vita, bestia, ca-*	And the life, beast, troop.
—	וְחָיְתָה	*Et vivet.*	And she shall live.
—	וְחָיִיתָה	*Et vives.*	And thou shalt live.
—	וְחַיָּתוֹ	*Et vita, bestia ejus.*	And his life, beast.
—	וְחַיְתוֹ	*Et bestia.* [*eorum.*	And the beast.
—	וְחַיָּתָם	*Et vita, animalia*	And their life, animals[mouth
חכך	וְחֵךְ	*Et palatum.*	And the mouth, roof of the
חכם	וְחַכִּימַיָּא	*Et sapientes.*	And the wise men.
חכה	וְחִכִּינוּ	*Et expectabimus.*	And we will wait.
—	וְחִכֵּיתִי	*Et expectabo.*	And I will wait.
חכך	וְחִכֵּךְ	*Et palatum tuum.*	And the roof of thy mouth.
חכם	וַחֲכָם	*Et sape.*	And be thou wise.
—	וְחֲכַם	*Et sapiens.*	And the wise man.
—	וְחָכָם	*Et sapiens.*	And a wise man.
—	וְחָכְמָה	*Et sapientia.*	And wisdom.
—	וַחֲכָמוּ	*Et sapite.*	And be ye wise.
—	וְחַכְמֵי	*Et sapientes.*	And the wise men.
—	וַחֲכָמֶיהָ	*Et sapientes ejus.*	And her wise men.
—	וַחֲכָמִים	*Et sapientes.*	And wise men.

ROOTS.	DERIVATIVES.	VERSIO.	SIGNIFICATION.
חכם	וְחָכְמַת	*Et sapientia.*	And the wisdom.
—	וְחָכְמָתוֹ	*Et sapientia ejus.*	And his wisdom.
חיל	וְחֵל	*Et fossa, murus.*	And the trench, wall.
חלא	וְחֶלְאָתָהּ	*Et spuma ejus.*	And her scum.
חלב	וְחָלָב וְחָלָב	*Et lac.*	And milk, the milk.
—	וְחֵלֶב	*Et adeps.*	And fat.
—	וְחֶלְבְּנָה	*Et galbanum.*	And galbanum.
חלד	וְחֶלְדִּי	*Et tempus meum.*	And my time.
חול	וְחָלָה	*Et manebit.*	And she shall remain.
חלה	וְחֹלֶה	*Et ægrotus.*	And sick.
חול	וְחָלוּ	*Et dolebunt.*	And they shall be in pain.
חלה	וְחִלּוּ	*Et deprecabuntur.*	And they shall intreat.
חלל	וְחַלּוֹנָיו	*Et fenestræ ejus.*	And his windows.
—	וְחַלּוֹנוֹת־־נִים	*Et fenestræ.*	And the windows.
חול	וְחַלְחָלָה	*Et dolor.*	And pain.
חלה	וְחֳלִי	*Et morbus.*	And a disease.
—	וַחֲלִי	*Et ornamentum.*	And an ornament.
—	וְחָלְיוֹ	*Et morbus ejus.*	And his sickness.
חלל	וְחָלִיל	*Et tibia.*	And a pipe.
חלה	וָחֳלָיִם	*Et morbi.*	And diseases.
—	וְחֶלְיָתָהּ	*Et ornamentum ejus*	And her ornament.
—	וְחָלִיתִי	*Et ægrotabo.*	And I shall be sick.
חלל	וַחֲלָלָה	*Et profana.* [*luent.*	And profane.
—	וְחִלְּלוּ־־לִ״	*Et profanabunt, pol-*	And they will profane, defile.
—	וְחִלְּלוּהָ	*Et polluent eam.*	And they will defile her.
—	וְחִלְּלוּהָ	*Et polluent eum.*	And they will defile him.
—	וְחַלְלֵיהֶם	*Et occisi eorum.*	And their slain.
—	וְחִלַּלְתֶּם	*Et profanabitis.*	And ye will profane.
חלם	וְחֶלְמָא	*Et somnium.*	And a dream.
—	וַחֲלֹמוֹת	*Et somnia.*	And the dreams.
חלף	וְחָלַף־־לִ״	*Et transibit.*	And he shall pass over.
—	וְחָלְפָה	*Et pertransibit.*	And she shall pass through.
—	וְחָלַפְתָּ	*Et transibis.*	And thou shalt pass over.
חלץ	וְחָלְצָה	*Et detrahet.*	And she shall draw off.
—	וְחִלְּצוּ	*Et eruent.*	And they will take out.
—	וְחַלְּצֵנִי	*Et eripe me.*	And deliver thou me.
חלק	וְחָלָק	*Et blandus, mollis.*	And soft, smooth.

ROOTS.	DERIVATIVES.	VERSIO.	SIGNIFICATION.
חלק	וְחֻלַּק	*Et dividetur.*	And he shall be divided.
—	וְחֵלֶק וְחֶלְקָה	*Et pars.*	And the part, portion.
—	וְחֶלְקִי	*Et pars mea.*	And my portion.
—	וַחֲלַקְלַקּוֹת	*Et lubricitates.*	And slipperiness.
—	וַחֲלֻקַּת	*Et divisio.*	And the division.
—	וְחִלַּקְתָּם	*Et divides eos.*	And thou shalt divide them.
—	וְחִלַּקְתֶּם	*Et dividetis.*	And ye shall divide.
חלל	וְחַלַּת	*Et placenta.*	And a cake.
—	וְחַלּוֹת	*Et placentæ.*	And cakes.
חמם	וְחֹם	*Et æstus.*	And heat
—	וְחַם	*Et incaluit.*	And he became hot.
יהם	וַחֲמָא	*Et furor.*	And wrath.
חמא	וְחֶמְאָה	*Et butyrum.*	And butter.
חמד	וְחָמְדוּ	*Et concupierunt.*	And they have desired.
יחם	וְחֵמָה	*Et indignatio.*	And indignation.
חמד	וַחֲמוּדֵיהֶם	*Et desideria eorum.*	And their delectable things.
חמר	וַחֲמוֹר	*Et asinus.*	And the ass.
—	וַחֲמוֹרִים־־מֹרִי	*Et asini.*	And asses.
חמש	וַחֲמִישִׁתוֹ	*Et quinta* pars *ejus.*	And the fifth *part* of it.
חמל	וְחָמַלְתִּי	*Et parcam.* [*ria.*	And I will spare. [sun.
חמן	וְחַמָּנִים	*Et simulachra sola-*	And images dedicated to the
חמס	וַחֲמַס	*Et violentia.*	And the violence.
—	וְחָמָס	*Et violentia.*	And violence.
חמץ	וְחֹמֶץ	*Et acetum.*	And vinegar.
חמר	וַחֲמֹרוֹ	*Et asinus.*	And the ass.
—	וַחֲמֹרֵיהֶם	*Et asini eorum.*	And their asses.
—	וַחֲמֹרְךָ־־רְךָ	*Et asinus tuus.*	And thy ass.
חמש	וַחֲמֵשׁ	*Et quinque.*	And the five.
—	וְחָמֵשׁ	*Et quinque.* [*capiet.*	And five.
—	וְחִמֵּשׁ	*Et quintam partem*	And he shall take the fifth part
—	וַחֲמִשָּׁה	*Et quinque.* [*sius.*	And five.
—	וַחֲמִשָּׁיו	*Et quinquaginta ip-*	And his fifty.
—	וַחֲמִשִּׁים	*Et quinquaginta.*	And fifty.
—	וַחֲמֻשִׁים	*Et armati.*	And armed.
—	וַחֲמֵשֶׁת	*Et quinque.* [*sius.*	And five.
—	וַחֲמִשִׁתָיו	*Et quintæ partes ip-*	And the fifth parts of it.
יחם	וַחֲמַת	*Et ira.*	And the anger.

ROOTS.	DERIVATIVES.	VERSIO.	SIGNIFICATION.
חמה	וְחֵמֶת	*Et uter, lagena.*	And the bottle.
יחם	וַחֲמָתוֹ	*Et ira ejus.*	And his anger.
—	וַחֲמָתִי	*Et ira mea.*	And my anger.
—	וַחֲמָתְךָ	*Et furor tuus.*	And thy wrath.
חנן	וְחֵן	*Et gratia.*	And grace.
חנה	וַחֲנֵה	*Et castrametare.*	And encamp thou.
—	וְחָנוּ	*Et castra ponent.*	And they will encamp.
חנן	וְחַנּוּן	*Et propitius.* [vi-	And gracious.
—	וְחַנּוֹתִי	*Et gratiam implora-*	And I sought grace, favour.
חנה	וַחֲנִית	*Et lancea, hasta.*	And a spear, javelin.
—	וַחֲנִיתוֹ	*Et lancea ejus.*	And his spear.
—	וַחֲנִיתוֹתֵיהֶם־ת׳	*Et lanceæ eorum.*	And their spears.
—	וְחָנִיתִי	*Et castrametabor.*	And I will encamp.
חנן	וְחָנֵּנִי	*Et miserere mei.*	And be thou merciful to me.
חנף	וְחַנְפֵי	*Et hypocritæ.*	And the hypocrites.
חנן	וְחַנֹּתִי	*Et propitius ero.*	And I will be gracious.
חסל	וְחָסִיל	*Et bruchus.*	And a species of locust.
חסד	וְחֶסֶד־וָחֶ׳־וְחֶ׳	*Et benignitas.*	And goodness, kindness.
—	וְחַסְדּוֹ	*Et benignitas ejus.*	And his goodness.
—	וְחַסְדִּי	*Et benignitas mea.*	And my goodness.
—	וַחֲסָדָיו	*Et benignitates ejus.*	And his kindness.
—	וַחֲסָדֶיךָ	*Et benignitates tuæ.*	And thy kindnesses.
—	וְחַסְדְּכֶם	*Et benignitas vestra*	And your goodness.
חסה	וְחָסָה	*Et sperabit.*	And he will hope, trust.
—	וְחֹסֶה	*Et sperans.*	And hoping.
—	וְחָסוּ	*Et sperabunt.*	And they will hope.
חסר	וְחָסוֹר	*Et decrescendo.*	And in decreasing.
חסד	וְחָסִיד	*Et benignus.*	And good, kind, gracious.
—	וַחֲסִידֶיהָ	*Et benigni ejus.*	And her good ones.
—	וַחֲסִידֶיךָ	*Et benigni tui.*	And thy good ones.
חסם	וְחֹסֶמֶת	*Et obturans.*	And stopping.
חסן	וְחָסֹן	*Et robustus.*	And strong.
חסף	וְחַסְפָּא	*Et lutum.*	And clay.
חסר	וַחֲסַר	*Et deficiens.*	And deficient.
—	וְחֹסֶר וְחֶסְרוֹן	*Et defectus.*	And the deficiency.
חפה	וְחָפוּ	*Et operuerunt.*	And they covered.
—	וְחָפוּי	*Et opertus.*	And covered.

ROOTS.	DERIVATIVES.	VERSIO.	SIGNIFICATION.
חפץ	וְחֵפֶץ	*Et voluntas.*	And the pleasure.
חפר	וְחָפְרָה	*Et erubuit.*	And she was ashamed.
—	וְחָפְרָה	*Et erubescet.*	And she shall be ashamed.
—	וְחָפְרוּ	*Et erubescent.*	And they will be ashamed.
—	וְחָפַרְתָּ	*Et fodies.*	And thou shalt dig.
—	וְחָפַרְתָּה	*Et fodies.*	And thou shalt dig.
חפש	וְחִפְּשׂוּ	*Et scrutabuntur.*	And they shall search.
—	וְחִפַּשְׂתִּי	*Et scrutabor.*	And I will search.
עץ	וְחֵץ	*Et arbor.*	And the tree.
חצץ	וְחֵץ	*Et sagitta.*	And an arrow.
חצה	וְחָצוּ	*Et divident.*	And they shall divide.
—	וַחֲצוֹת	*Et medium.*	And the middle.
—	וָחֵצִי	*Et dimidium.*	And a half.
—	וַחֲצִי	*Et dimidius, medius.*	And half, the middle.
—	וְחֶצְיוֹ	*Et dimidium ejus.*	And the half of him.
חצץ	וְחִצָּיו	*Et sagittæ ejus.*	And his arrows.
—	וְחִצֶּיךָ	*Et sagittæ tuæ.*	And thy arrows.
חצה	וְחֶצְיָם	*Et dimidium eorum.*	And their arrows.
חצץ	וְחִצִּים	*Et sagittæ.*	And arrows.
חצה	וְחָצִיתָ	*Et divides.*	And thou shalt divide.
חצן	וְחִצְנוֹ	*Et sinus ejus.*	And his bosom.
חצר	וַחֲצֹצְרוֹת	*Et tubæ.*	And the trumpets.
—	וְחָצֵר	*Et atrium.*	And a, the court.
—	וַחֲצֵרוֹתָי	*Et atria mea.*	And my courts.
—	וַחֲצֵרֶיהָ	*Et pagi ejus.*	And her villages, towns.
—	וְחַצְרֵיהֶם	*Et pagi eorum.*	And their villages.
—	וְחַצְרֵיהֶן	*Et pagi earum.*	And their villages.
חקק	וְחֹק וְחָק	*Et statutum.*	And a, the statute.
—	וְחַקּוֹתָ	*Et describes.*	And thou shalt pourtray.
—	וְחֻקּוֹתַי־ק״ וְחֻקַּי	*Et statuta mea,*	And my statutes.
—	וְחֻקָּיו	*Et statuta ejus.*	And his statutes.
—	וְחֻקֶּיךָ	*Et statuta tua.*	And thy statutes.
—	וְחֻקִּים	*Et statuta.*	And statutes.
חקר	וְחֵקֶר	*Et exploratio.*	And investigation, search.
—	וְחִקֵּר	*Et exploravit.*	And he examined.
—	וַחֲקָרוֹ	*Et explorabit eum.*	And he will examine him.
—	וְחָקַרְתָּ	*Et explorabis.*	And thou shalt investigate.

ROOTS.	DERIVATIVES.	VERSIO.	SIGNIFICATION.
חקק	וְחֻקֹּתָיו	*Et statuta ejus.*	And his statutes.
חרב	וְחֶרֶב	*Et gladius.*	And a sword.
—	וֶחָרָבָה	*Et siccum.*	And the dry land.
—	וְחָרְבָּה	*Et desertum.*	And a desert.
—	וְחַרְבּוֹ	*Et gladius ejus.*	And his sword.
—	וְחָרְבוּ	*Et siccabuntur.*	And they shall be dried up.
—	וְחָרָבוֹת	*Et loca deserta.*	And desert places.
—	וְחָרְבוֹתֶיהָ	*Et deserta ejus.*	And her deserts.
—	וְחַרְבִּי	*Et gladius meus.*	And my sword.
חרד	וְחָרַד	*Et trepidabit.*	And he shall tremble.
—	וְחָרֵד	*Et tremens.*	And trembling.
—	וְחָרְדוּ	*Et trepidabunt.*	And they shall be afraid.
חרה	וְחָרָה	*Et exardescet.*	And he shall kindle, be wroth.
—	וַחֲרוֹן	*Et furor.*	And wrath, rage, fury.
חרץ	וְחָרוּץ	*Et aurum, ruina.*	And gold, ruin.
חרם	וְחֵרֶם	*Et exitium.*	And destruction.
—	וַחֲרָמִים	*Et retia, plagæ.*	And nets, toils.
חרמש	וְחֶרְמֵשׁ	*Et falx.*	And a sickle.
חרף	וָחֹרֶף	*Et hyems.*	And winter.
—	וְחֶרְפָּה וְחֶרְפַּת	*Et opprobrium.*	And a, the reproach.
—	וְחֶרְפּוֹת	*Et opprobria.*	And reproaches.
—	וְחֶרְפָּתוֹ	*Et opprobrium ejus.*	And his reproach.
חרק	וְחֹרֵק	*Et frendens.*	And gnashing.
חרש	וְחָרָשׁ	*Et faber.*	And a smith, artificer.
—	וְחֵרֵשׁ	*Et surdus.*	And deaf.
—	וְחֹרֶשׁ	*Et virgultum.*	And a bough.
—	וְחָרָשֵׁי	*Et fabri.*	And workmen.
—	וְחָרָשִׁים	*Et artifices.*	And artificers.
—	וְחֵרְשִׁים	*Et surdi.*	And the deaf.
חוש	וְחָשׁ	*Et festinabit.*	And he shall hasten.
חשב	וְחָשַׁב	*Et excogitabit.*	And he will devise.
—	וְחֵשֶׁב	*Et politura.*	And the skilful workmanship.
—	וְחִשַּׁב	*Et supputabit.* [*fex.*	And he shall reckon. [man.
—	וְחֹשֵׁב	*Et excogitans, arti-*	And devising, the skilful work-
—	וְחֶשְׁבּוֹן	*Et excogitatio, ratio*	And the device, reason.
—	וְחֹשְׁבֵי	*Et excogitantes.*	And they that devise.
—	וְחָשַׁבְתָּ	*Et excogitabis.*	And thou wilt devise.

ROOTS.	DERIVATIVES.	VERSIO.	SIGNIFICATION.
חשף	וַחֲשׂוּפַי	*Et retecti.*	And uncovered.
חשק	וַחֲשׁוּקֵיהֶם	*Et canthi eorum.*	And their fellies.
חשך	וְחֹשֶׁךְ וַחֲשֵׁכָה	*Et tenebræ.*	And darkness.
—	וְחָשְׁכָה	*Et obtenebrescet.*	And she shall become dark.
—	וְחָשְׁכוּ	*Et obtenebrescent.*	And they shall become dark.
חשל	וְחָשֵׁל	*Et conterens.*	And crushing.
חשק	וְחִשַּׁק	*Et cinxit.*	And he bound.
—	וַחֲשֻׁקֵיהֶם וְחִשּׁ׳	*Et canthi eorum.*	And their fellies.
—	וְחָשַׁקְתָּ	*Et devincies te.*	And thou shalt attach thyself.
חשר	וְחִשֻּׁרֵיהֶם	*Et radii eorum.*	And their spokes.
חשש	וַחֲשַׁשׁ	*Et gluma.*	And the chaff.
חתת	וְחָתָּה	*Et perterrita est.*	And she was terrified.
—	וְחָתּוּ וְחַתּוּ	*Et conterentur.*	And they shall be crushed.
—	וָחֹתּוּ	*Et conteremini.*	And ye shall be broken.
חתם	וְחָתוֹם	*Et obsignare.*	And to seal.
חתת	וְחִתְחַתִּים	*Et terrores.*	And terrors.
—	וְחִתְּכֶם	*Et terror vestrûm.*	And the dread of you.
חתם	וַחֲתֹם	*Et obsigna.*	And seal thou.
—	וְחִתְמָהּ	*Et obsignavit eam.*	And he sealed her.
—	וְחִתְמוּ	*Et obsignate.*	And seal ye.
—	וַחֲתֻמִים	*Et obsignati.*	And sealed.
חתן	וַחֲתַן	*Et gener.*	And the son-in-law.
חתת	וְחִתַּתַּנִי	*Et contrivisti me.*	And thou hast broken, scared [me.
	וט		
טאט	וְטֵאטֵאתִיהָ	*Et everram eam.*	And I will sweep it.
טוב	וְטֹבוֹת־־בֹת	*Et bonæ, optimæ.*	And the good, best.
טבח	וְטֶבַח	*Et mactatio.*	And a, the slaughter.
—	וּטְבֹחַ	*Et macta.*	And slay thou.
—	וּטְבָחוֹ	*Et mactabit eum.*	And he shall kill him.
טוב	וְטֹבִים וְטו״	*Et boni, meliores.*	And the good, better.
טבל	וְטָבַל	*Et immerget, tinget.*	And he shall plunge, dip, dye.
—	וְטֹבֵל	*Et immergens.*	And dipping.
—	וְטָבַלְתָּ	*Et immerges.*	And thou shalt dip.
—	וּטְבַלְתֶּם	*Et immergetis.*	And ye shall dip.
טבע	וְטַבַּעַת	*Et annulus.*	And a ring.
טוב	וְטֹבָתָם וְטו״	*Et bonum eorum.*	And their good, prosperity.

ROOTS.	DERIVATIVES.	VERSIO.	SIGNIFICATION.
טהר	וטהורים	*Et mundi, puri.*	And the clean, pure.
—	וְטָהֵר	*Et mundabitur.*	And he shall be cleansed.
—	וְטִהַר	*Et mundabit, mundum pronunciabit.*	And he shall cleanse, pronounce clean.
—	וּטְהָר	*Et mundus esto.*	And be thou clean.
—	וּטָהֹר	*Et mundus, purus.*	And clean, pure.
—	וְטָהֲרָה־הֵרָה	*Et mundabitur.*	And she shall be cleansed.
—	וּטְהֹרָה	*Et munda, pura.*	And clean, pure.
—	וְטִהֲרוֹ	*Et mundabit se, mundum declarabit eum*	And he shall cleanse himself, shall pronounce him clean.
—	וְטִהֲרוּ	*Et mundabunt.*	And they shall cleanse, purify.
—	וְטִהַרְתָּ	*Et mundabis.*	And thou shalt cleanse.
—	וְטָהַרְתִּי	*Et mundabor.*	And I shall be cleansed.
—	וְטִהַרְתִּי	*Et mundabo.*	And I will cleanse.
—	וְטִהַרְתִּים	*Et mundavi eos.*	And I have cleansed them.
—	וּטְהַרְתֶּם	*Et mundabimini.*	And ye shall be cleansed.
טוב	וָטוֹב וְטוֹב	*Et bonus, decorus, jucundus, bene.*	And good, goodly, pleasant, well.
—	וְטוֹבָה	*Et bona.*	And good.
—	וְטוֹבָהּ	*Et bonum ejus.*	And her good, goodness.
—	וְטוֹבֵי	*Et boni, læti.*	And the good, glad.
—	וְטוֹבַת	*Et bona, formosa.*	And the good, beautiful.
טור	וְטוּר	*Et ordo.*	And a row.
טח	וְטָח	*Et oblinet.*	And he shall plaister.
טחן	וְטָחֲנוּ	*Et moluerunt.*	And they ground.
—	וְטַחֲנִי	*Et mole.*	And grind thou.
טיט	וָטִיט	*Et lutum.*	And clay.
טלל	וְטַל	*Et ros.*	And the dew.
טלא	וּטְלֻאִים	*Et maculosi.*	And spotted.
טלה	וְטָלֶה	*Et agnus.*	And the lamb.
טלא	וְטָלוּא	*Et maculosus.*	And the spotted.
טמא	וְטָמֵא	*Et immundus erit.*	And he shall be unclean.
—	וְטִמֵּא	*Et polluet, immundum pronunciabit.*	And he will defile, shall pronounce unclean.
—	וְטָמְאָה	*Et immunda erit.*	And she shall be unclean.
—	וְטָמְאוּ	*Et immundi erunt.*	And they shall be unclean.
—	וְטִמְּאוּ	*Et polluerunt.*	And they have defiled.

ROOTS.	DERIVATIVES.	VERSIO.	SIGNIFICATION.
טמא	וְטִמְּאוֹ	*Et immundum pronunciabit eum.*	And he shall pronounce him unclean.
—	וּטְמֵאִים	*Et immundi.*	And the unclean.
—	וְטֻמְאָתוֹ	*Et immunditiес ejus.*	And his uncleanness.
—	וְטִמֵּאתֶם	*Et polluetis.*	And ye will defile.
טמן	וְטָמְנֵהוּ	*Et absconde illum.*	And hide thou him.
—	וּטְמְנֵתֶם	*Et absconde illos.*	And hide thou them.
טעם	וְטַעַם	*Et prudentia.*	And prudence.
—	וּטְעֵם	*Et consilium.*	And the counsel.
—	וְטַעְמוֹ	*Et sapor ejus.* [*li.*	And his taste.
טפף	וְטָף־וְטַף	*Et parvulus, parvu-*	And the little one, little ones.
—	וְטָפוֹף	*Et incedere more parvulorum.*	And to walk in a childish manner.
טפח	וְטֹפַח	*Et palmus.*	And a span, hand-breadth.
טפף	וְטַפְּכֶם	*Et parvuli vestri.*	And your little ones.
—	וְטַפָּם	*Et parvuli eorum.*	And their little ones.
—	וְטַפֵּנוּ	*Et parvuli nostri.*	And our little ones.
טפסר	וְטִפְסְרַיִךְ	*Et duces tui.*	And thy leaders, captains.
טפר	וְטִפְרוֹהִי ־רַיהּ	*Et ungues ejus.*	And his nails.
טרם	וְטֶרֶם	*Et nondum.* [*bit.*	And not yet. [pieces.
טרף	וְטָרַף	*Et rapiet, dilacera-*	And he shall plunder, tear in
—	וְטֶרֶף	*Et præda.*	And the prey. [pieces.
—	וּטְרֵפָה	*Et discerptum.*	And that which is torn in

וי

ROOTS.	DERIVATIVES.	VERSIO.	SIGNIFICATION.
אבד	וִיאַבֵּד	*Et perdet.*	And he will destroy.
—	וַיֹּאבְדוּ	*Et perierunt.*	And they have perished.
—	וְיֹאבֵדוּ־בְדוּ	*Et peribunt.*	And they shall perish.
—	וַיְאַבְּדוּם	*Et perdiderunt eos.*	And they destroyed them.
—	וַיְאַבְּדֵם	*Et disperdidit eos.*	And he hath destroyed them.
אבל	וַיְאַבֶּל	*Et lugere fecit.*	And he caused to mourn.
אבק	וַיֵּאָבֵק	*Et luctatus est.*	And he wrestled.
אדר	וְיַאְדִּיר	*Et magnificabit.*	And he will magnify.
אהב	וַיֶּאֱהַב־אֱהַב	*Et dilexit.*	And he loved.
—	וַיֶּאֱהָבֶהָ	*Et dilexit eam.*	And he loved her.
—	וַיֶּאֱהָבֵהוּ־בֵוּ	*Et dilexit eum.*	And he loved him.
—	וְיֶאֱהָבְךָ וְיֶא״	*Et diliget te.*	And he will love thee.

ROOTS.	DERIVATIVES.	VERSIO.	SIGNIFICATION.
אהל	וַיֶּאֱהַל	*Et tentorium teten-*	And he pitched *his* tent.
אחז	וַיֹּאחֶז	*Et apprehendit.* [*dit.*	And he took hold.
—	וַיֶּאֱחֹז	*Et apprehendit.*	And he took hold.
—	וַיֹּאחֵז	*Et apprehendet* [*sunt*	And he will take hold.
—	וַיֵּאָחֲזוּ	*Et possessores facti*	And they became possessors.
—	וַיֹּאחֲזוּ	*Et apprehenderunt.*	And they took hold.
—	וַיֹּאחֲזוּהוּ	*Et prehenderunt eum*	And they took hold of him.
אוץ	וַיָּאִיצוּ	*Et urserunt.*	And they urged, hastened.
אכל	וַיַּאֲכִילֵהוּ	*Et cibavit eum.*	And he fed him.
—	וַיֵּאָכֵל	*Et consumptus est.*	And he is consumed.
—	וַיֹּאכַל	*Et edit, consumpsit.*	And he ate, consumed.
—	וַיֹּאכֵל	*Et comedet.*	And he will eat.
—	וַיֹּאכְלוּ־כָלוּ	*Et comederunt.*	And they ate.
—	וַיֹּאכֵלוּ־כֵלוּ	*Et comedent.*	And they will eat.
—	וַיֹּאכְלוּהָ	*Et comedent eam.*	And they will devour her.
—	וַיַּאֲכִלוּם	*Et cibarunt eos.*	And they fed them.
—	וַיַּאֲכִלְךָ	*Et cibavit te.*	And he fed thee.
—	וַיֹּאכְלֵם	*Et consumpsit eos*	And he cousumed them.
—	וַיַּאֲכִלֵנִי	*Et cibavit me.*	And he fed me. [swear.
אלה	וַיֹּאֶל	*Et adjuravit.*	And he adjured, made to
יאל	וַיֹּאֶל	*Et voluit.*	And he wished.
—	וְיֹאֶל	*Et volet.*	And he will wish.
אמן	וַיַּאֲמִינוּ	*Et crediderunt.*	And they believed.
—	וַיַּאֲמֵן	*Et credidit.*	And he believed.
—	וְיֵאָמֵן	*Et confirmabitur.*	And he will be confirmed.
—	וְיֵאָמְנוּ	*Et confirmabuntur.*	And they will be confirmed.
אמץ	וַיְאַמֵּץ	*Et roboravit.*	And he strengthened.
—	וַיְאַמֵּץ וַיְאַמֶּץ	*Et induravit.*	And he hardened.
—	וַיְאַמְּצֵהוּ	*Et roborarunt eum.*	And they strengthened him.
—	וַיֶּאֶמְצוּ	*Et prævaluerunt.*	And they prevailed. [ened.
—	וַיְאַמְּצוּ	*Et confirmarunt.*	And they confirmed, strength-
אמר	וָאֹמַר	*Et dixi.*	And I said.
—	וַיֵּאָמֵר	*Et dictum est.*	And it was said.
—	וַיֹּאמֶר־מַר־מֶרוּ	*Et dixit.*	And he said.
—	וַיֹּאמְרוּ־מְרוּ	*Et dixerunt.*	And they said.
—	וְיֹאמַר	*Et dicet.*	And he will say.
—	וְיֹאמַר	*Et dicet.*	And he shall say.

ROOTS.	DERIVATIVES.	VERSIO.	SIGNIFICATION.
אמר	וְיֹאמְרוּ	*Et dicent.*	And they shall say.
אנח	וַיֵּאָנְחוּ	*Et suspirarunt.*	And they sighed.
אנש	וַיֵּאָנַשׁ	*Et morbo desperato laboravit.*	And he was extremely sick.
אסף	וַיֵּאָסֵף	*Et recepit se.*	And he betook himself.
—	וַיֵּאָסֶף	*Et aggregatus est.*	And he was gathered.
יסף	וַיֹּאסֶף	*Et addidit.*	And he added.
אסף	וַיֶּאֱסֹף	*Et collegit.*	And he gathered.
—	וַיַּאַסְפָהּ	*Et collegit eam.*	And he fetched her.
—	וַיַּאַסְפֵהוּ־וּ	*Et collegit eum.*	And he took him.
—	וַיַּאַסְפוּ	*Et collegerunt.*	And they gathered.
—	וַיֵּאָסְפוּ	*Et congregati sunt.*	And they were assembled.
—	וְיֵאָסְפוּ	*Et congregabuntur.*	And they shall be assembled.
—	וַיַּאַסְפֵם	*Et collegit eos.*	And he gathered them.
אסר	וַיֶּאְסֹר־אֱסֹר	*Et vinxit, instruxit.*	And he bound, set in array.
—	וַיַּאַסְרֵהוּ	*Et vinxit eum.*	And he bound him.
—	וַיַּאַסְרֻהוּ־רוּהוּ	*Et ligarunt eum.*	And they bound him.
—	וַיַּאַסְרוּם	*Et ligarunt eos.*	And they tied them.
אפד	וַיֶּאְפֹּד	*Et cinxit.*	And he bound, girded.
אפה	וַיֹּאפוּ	*Et coxerunt.*	And they baked.
אצל	וַיָּאצֶל	*Et partitus est.*	And he distributed.
אור	וַיָּאֶר	*Et illuminavit.*	And he gave light.
—	וַיֹּאר	*Et illuxit.*	And he shined.
ארב	וַיֶּאֱרֹב	*Et insidiatus est.*	And he lay in wait.
—	וַיֶּאֶרְבוּ	*Et insidiati sunt.*	And they lay in wait. [ed.
ארך	וַיַּאֲרִיכוּ	*Et produxerunt.*	And they drew out, lengthen-
אשם	וַיֶּאְשַׁם־אָשֵׁם	*Et deliquit* [*tati sunt*	And he transgressed. [waste.
—	וַיֶּאְשְׁמוּ	*Et deliquerunt, vas-*	And they offended, were laid
—	וְיֶאְשְׁמוּ	*Et desolabuntur.*	And they shall be laid waste.
אשר	וַיְאַשְּׁרוּהָ	*Et eam beatam prædicarunt, prædicabunt.*	And they have called, shall call her blessed.
אתה	וַיֵּאת	*Et venit, veniet.*	And he came, shall come.
—	וַיֵּאתוּ	*Et acquieverunt.*	And they consented.
—	וַיֶּאֱתָיוּן	*Et evenit mihi.*	And it hath befallen me.
—	וַיֶּאֱתָיֻנִי	*Et venerunt.* [*civit.*	And they came.
בוא	וַיָּבֵא	*Et attulit, deduxit,*	And he brought, led, called for

ROOTS.	DERIVATIVES.	VERSIO.	SIGNIFICATION.
בוא	וַיָּבֹא־־בֹּו־־בוֹא	*Et ivit, venit, in-gressus est.* [*trabit*	And he went, came, entered.
—	וְיָבֹא־־בוֹא	*Et ibit, veniet, in-*	And he will go, come, enter.
—	וַיְבִאֶהָ	*Et adduxit eam.*	And he brought her.
—	וַיְבִאֵהוּ	*Et adduxit eum.*	And he brought him.
—	וַיְבִאֻהוּ	*Et adduxerunt eum.*	And they brought him.
—	וַיָּבֹאוּ־־בָּיאוּ	*Et intrarunt, addux-erunt.* [*attulerunt*	And they entered, brought.
—	וַיָּבֹאוּ	*Et ierunt, venerunt,*	And they went, came, brought
—	וְיָבֹאוּ־־בֹו״	*Et venient.*	And they will come.
—	וַיְבִאוּם־־בִי״	*Et attulerunt eos.*	And they brought them.
—	וַיְבִאֵם־־בִי״	*Et adduxit eos.*	And he brought them.
—	וַיְבִאֵנוּ	*Et adduxit nos.*	And he brought us.
—	וַיְבִאֵנִי־־בִי״	*Et adduxit me.*	And he brought me.
—	וִיבֹאֻנִי	*Et venient mihi.*	And they shall come to me.
באש	וַיִּבְאַשׁ	*Et fœtuit.*	And he stank.
בגד	וַיִּבְגְּדוּ	*Et perfide egerunt.*	And they acted treacherously.
בדל	וַיַּבְדִּילוּ	*Et separarunt.*	And they separated.
—	וַיַּבְדִּילֵם	*Et separavit eos.*	And he separated them.
—	וַיַּבְדֵּל	*Et divisit.*	And he divided.
—	וַיִּבָּדֵל	*Et separatus est.*	And he was separated.
—	וַיִּבָּדְלוּ	*Et separati sunt.*	And they were separated.
בהל	וַיַּבְהִילוּהוּ	*Et festinarunt eum.*	And they hastened him.
—	וַיִּבָּהֵל	*Et territus est.*	And he was terrified.
—	וַיִּבָּהֵל	*Et festinavit.*	And he hastened.
—	וַיִּבְהֲלוּ	*Et festinarunt.*	And they hastened.
—	וְיִבָּהֲלוּ	*Et turbabuntur.*	And they will be disturbed.
—	וַיַּבְהִלוּהוּ	*Et festinarunt eum.*	And they hastened him.
—	וִיבַהֶלְךָ	*Et turbavit te.*	And he troubled thee.
יבל	וַיָּבוֹל	*Et pabulum dedit.*	And he gave provender.
בוש	וְיֵבוֹשׁ	*Et erubescet.*	And he shall be ashamed.
יבש	וְיֵבוֹשׁ	*Et aruit, arescet.*	And he hath dried, will dry up
בזה	וַיִּבֶז	*Et contempsit.*	And he despised.
—	וַיִּבְזֵהוּ	*Et sprevit eum.*	And he despised him.
—	וַיִּבְזֻהוּ	*Et spreverunt eum.*	And they despised him.
בזז	וַיָּבֹזּוּ	*Et diripuerunt.*	And they plundered.
בזה	וַיִּבְזוּ	*Et contempserunt.*	And they despised.

ROOTS.	DERIVATIVES.	VERSIO.	SIGNIFICATION.
בזז	וְיָבֹזוּ	*Et diripient.*	And they will spoil.
בחן	וְיִבָּחֲנוּ	*Et probabuntur.*	And they shall be proved, tried
בחר	וַיִּבְחַר	*Et elegit.*	And he chose.
—	וְיִבְחֲרוּ	*Et eligent.*	And they will choose.
—	וַיִּבְחָרְךָ	*Et elegit te.*	And he chose thee.
נבט	וַיַּבֵּט	*Et aspexit.*	And he looked.
בטא	וַיְבַטֵּא	*Et temere pronunci- [avit.*	And he spoke rashly.
בטח	וַיַּבְטַח	*Et confidere fecit.*	And he caused to trust.
—	וַיִּבְטַח	*Et confidit.*	And he trusted.
—	וַיִּבְטְחוּ	*Et confiderunt.*	And they trusted.
—	וְיִבְטְחוּ	*Et sperabunt.*	And they will hope.
בוא	וַיָּבֵיא־־בִ״	*Et adduxit.*	And he brought.
—	וַיְבִאֶהָ	*Et adduxit eam.*	And he brought her.
—	וַיְבִיאֵהוּ	*Et adduxit eum.*	And he brought him.
—	וַיְבִיאֻהוּ	*Et adduxerunt eum.*	And they brought him.
בון	וַיְבִינֵהוּ	*Et intellexerunt.*	And they understood.
—	וַיְבִינוּ	*Et instruxit eum.*	And he instructed him.
בכה	וַיֵּבְךְּ	*Et flevit.*	And he wept.
—	וַיִּבְכּוּ	*Et fleverunt.*	And they wept.
יבל	וִיבָלָהּ	*Et proventus ejus.*	And her increase, produce.
בלע	וַיִּבְלַע	*Et deglutivit.*	And he swallowed.
יבם	וְיַבֵּם	*Et ex affinitatis jure uxorem ducito.*	And marry thou in right of affinity.
—	וְיִבְּמָהּ	*Et ex affinitatis jure eam ducet.*	And he shall marry her in right of affinity.
בון	וַיָּבֶן	*Et intellexit, intelligere fecit.*	And he understood, caused to understand.
בנה	וַיִּבֶן	*Et ædificavit.*	And he hath built.
בון	וְיָבֵן	*Et intelliget.*	And he will understand.
בנה	וְיִבֶן	*Et ædificabit.*	And he will build.
—	וַיִּבְנֶה	*Et ædificavit.*	And she hath built.
—	וְיִבְנֶה	*Et ædificabit.*	And she will build.
—	וַיִּבְנֵהוּ	*Et ædificavit eum.*	And he hath built him.
—	וַיִּבְנוּ	*Et ædificarunt.*	And they have built.
בעט	וַיִּבְעַט	*Et calcitravit.*	And he kicked, spurned.
בער	וַיִּבְעַר־־עֶר	*Et accendit.*	And he kindled, burned.
—	וַיִּבְעַר	*Et accensus est.*	And he was burned.

ROOTS.	DERIVATIVES.	VERSIO.	SIGNIFICATION.
בצע	וַיְבַצְּעֵנִי	*Et abscindet me.*	And he will cut me off.
בצר	וַיִּבְצְרוּ	*Et vindemiarunt.*	And they gathered grapes.
בקע	וַיִּבְקַע־יִּבָּקַע״	*Et fidit.*	And he cleft, divided.
——	וַיִּבָּקְעוּ	*Et divisi sunt.*	And they were divided.
——	וַיְבַקְּעוּ	*Et fiderunt.*	And they cleft, divided.
——	וַיִּבְקְעוּ	*Et perruperunt.*	And they broke through.
——	וַיִּבְקָעוּהָ	*Et irruperunt in eam*	And they broke into her.
בקק	וַיְבֹקְקוּ	*Et evacuabunt.*	And they shall empty.
בקש	וַיְבַקֵּשׁ	*Et quæsiit, petiit.*	And he sought, asked, inquired
——	וַיְבֻקַּשׁ	*Et quæsitus est.*	And he was sought.
——	וַיְבַקְשֵׁהוּ	*Et quæsivit eum.*	And he sought him.
——	וַיְבַקְשֻׁהוּ	*Et quæsierunt eum.*	And they sought him.
——	וַיְבַקְשׁוּ	*Et quæsiverunt.*	And they sought.
——	וִיבַקְשׁוּ	*Et quærent.*	And they shall seek.
ברא	וַיִּבְרָא	*Et creavit.*	And he created.
ברח	וַיִּבְרַח	*Et fugit.*	And he fled.
——	וַיִּבְרְחוּ	*Et fugerunt.*	And they fled.
——	וַיַּבְרִיחוּ	*Et fugaverunt.*	And they put to flight.
ברך	וַיַּבְרֵךְ	*Et genua flectere fecit*	And he caused to kneel down
——	וַיְבָרֶךְ	*Et benedixit.*	And he blessed.
——	וִיבָרֵךְ	*Et benedicet.*	And he will bless.
——	וַיְבָרְכֵהוּ־־רָ״	*Et benedixit ei.*	And he blessed him.
——	וַיְבָרֲכוּ־־רְכוּ	*Et benedixerunt.*	And they blessed.
——	וִיבָרְכוּ	*Et benedicet.*	And they will bless.
——	וִיבָרֶכְךָ	*Et benedicet tibi.*	And he will bless thee.
——	וַיְבָרְכֵם־־רֲכֵם	*Et benedixit eis.*	And he blessed them.
——	וִיבָרְכֵנוּ	*Et benedicet nobis.*	And he will bless us.
——	וַיְבָרְכֵנִי	*Et benedixit mihi.*	And he blessed me.
יבש	וַיִּבַשׁ וְיָבֵשׁ	*Et aruit, arescet.*	And he hath dried, will dry up.
——	וַיְבַּשֵׁהוּ	*Et exsiccavit eum.*	And he dried up him. [ered.
——	וַיִּבָשׁוּ	*Et aruerunt.*	And they have dried up, with-
בוש	וַיֵּבֹשׁוּ	*Et erubuerunt.* [cent	And they were ashamed. [up.
יבש	וְיָבֵשׁוּ	*Et aruerunt ares-*	And they have dried, will dry
——	וְיִבָשׁוּ	*Et arescent.*	And they shall become dry.
בוש	וַיֵּבֹשׁוּ	*Et pudefacti sunt.*	And they were made ashamed
יבש	וִיבֵשִׁים	*Et sicci.*	And dry.
בשל	וַיְבַשְּׁלוּ	*Et coxerunt.*	And they roasted, baked.

ROOTS.	DERIVATIVES.	VERSIO.	SIGNIFICATION.
יבש	וְיַבֶּשֶׁת	*Et aridæ.*	And dry.
בתר	וַיְבַתֵּר	*Et divisit.*	And he divided.
גאה	וְיִגְאֶה	*Et crescet.*	And he shall increase.
גאל	וַיִּגָּאֲלוּ	*Et polluti sunt.*	And they were polluted.
—	וַיִּגְאָלֵם	*Et eripuit eos.* [*etur*	And he delivered them. [up.
גבה	וַיִּגְבַּהּ	*Et altus erat, effer-*	And he was high, will be lifted
—	וְיִגְבְּהוּ	*Et elevabuntur.*	And they shall be exalted.
—	וַיְגַבְּיהֶהָ	*Et exaltavit eam.*	And he exalted her.
יגב	וִיגֵבִים	*Et agri.*	And the fields.
גבר	וַיִּגְבְּרוּ	*Et prævaluerunt.*	And they prevailed.
נגד	וַיַּגֶּד־־גֶּד	*Et indicavit.*	And he shewed.
—	וְיַגֵּד	*Et indicabit.*	And he will shew.
—	וַיֻּגַּד	*Et nunciatum est*	And it was told.
—	וְיַגִּדָה	*Et indicabit eam.*	And he shall declare her or it.
—	וַיַּגִּדוּ	*Et indicarunt.*	And they told.
גדל	וַיַּגְדִּילוּ	*Et magnificarunt.*	And they magnified.
נגד	וְיַגֶּדְךָ	*Et narrabit tibi.*	And he will tell thee.
גדל	וַיִּגְדַּל־־דָּל	*Et crevit.*	And he grew.
—	וַיְגַדֵּל	*Et magnificavit.*	And he magnified.
—	וְיִגְדַּל	*Et magnificabitur.*	And he shall be magnified.
—	וְיַגְדֵּל	*Et magnificabit.*	And he will magnify.
—	וַיְגַדְּלֵהוּ	*Et magnificavit eum*	And he magnified him.
—	וַיִּגְדְּלוּ	*Et creverunt.*	And they grew.
גדע	וַיְגַדַּע	*Et succidit.*	And he cut down.
—	וַיְגַדְּעוּ	*Et succiderunt.*	And they cut down.
יגה	וַיַּגֶּה	*Et mærore affecit.*	And he grieved, afflicted.
גהר	וַיִּגְהַר	*Et incurvavit se.*	And he bowed himself down.
יגה	וְיָגוֹן	*Et tristitia.*	And sorrow.
גוע	וַיִּגְוַע	*Et expiravit.*	And he died.
—	וְיִגְוְעוּ	*Et expirabunt.*	And they shall die.
גזז	וַיָּגָז	*Et abripuit,totondit.*	And he took away, sheared.
גזל	וַיִּגְזֹל	*Et rapuit.*	And he took by violence.
—	וַיִּגְזְלוּ	*Et diripuerunt.*	And they spoiled.
גזר	וַיִּגְזֹר	*Et scidit.*	And he cut.
—	וַיִּגְזְרוּ	*Et exciderunt.*	And they cut down.
נגד	וְיַגִּידֶהָ	*Et indicabit eam.*	And he will declare her or it.
—	וַיַּגִּדוּ	*Et nunciarunt.*	And they told, declared.

ROOTS.	DERIVATIVES.	VERSIO.	SIGNIFICATION.
נגד	וַיַּגִּידוּ	*Et nunciabunt.*	And they will tell, declare.
גול	וְיָגִיל	*Et exultabit.*	And he will rejoice.
נגע	וְיַגִּיעַ	*Et perveniet.*	And he shall reach, arrive.
—	וַיַּגִּיעוּ	*Et advenerunt.*	And they came.
יגע	וִיגִיעֲכֶם	*Et labor vester.*	And your labour.
—	וִיגִיעָם	*Et labor eorum.*	And their labour.
נגש	וַיַּגִּשׁוּ	*Et adduxerunt.*	And they brought.
גלל	וַיָּגֶל	*Et devolvit.*	And he rolled.
גול	וַיָּגֶל	*Et exultavit.*	And he rejoiced.
גלה	וַיֶּגֶל	*Et deportavit.* [*est.*	And he carried away. [away.
—	וַיְגַל	*Et retexit, abductus*	And he discovered, was carried
—	וַיְגַל	*Et retexit, amovit.*	And he discovered, removed.
גלל	וְיִגַּל	*Et devolvetur.*	And he shall be rolled down.
גלה	וִיגַל	*Et reteget.*	And he will discover.
—	וַיַּגְלֶהָ	*Et transtulit eam.*	And he removed her. [selves.
—	וַיִּגָּלוּ	*Et revelarunt se.*	And they discovered them-
—	וַיַּגְלוּם	*Et deportarunt eos.*	And they carried them away.
גלח	וַיְגַלַּח	*Et totondit.*	And he shaved.
—	וַיְגַלְּחֵם	*Et rasit eos.*	And he shaved them.
גלה	וַיַּגְלֵם	*Et deportavit eos.*	And he transported them.
גלם	וַיִּגְלֹם	*Et convolvit.*	And he rolled together.
גמל	וַיִּגָּמַל	*Et ablactatus est.*	And he was weaned.
—	וַיִּגְמֹל	*Et edidit.*	And he yielded, produced.
גנב	וַיִּגְנֹב-וַיְגַנֵּב	*Et furatus est.*	And he stole.
נגע	וַיִּגַּע וַיַּגַּע	*Et tetigit, advenit.*	And he touched, came.
—	וְיִגַּע	*Et attinget.*	And he shall touch.
יגע	וְיָגֵעַ	*Et fatigatus.*	And wearied.
—	וְיִגְעוּ וְיִגָעוּ	*Et laborabunt.*	And they shall labour.
גער	וַיִּגְעַר	*Et increpuit.*	And he rebuked.
—	וְיִגְעַר	*Et increpabit.*	And he will chide.
נגף	וַיִּגֹּף	*Et percussit.*	And he smote.
—	וַיִּגְּפֵהוּ	*Et percussit eum.*	And he struck him.
נגר	וַיִּגַּר	*Et effudit.* [*timuit.*	And he poured out.
גור	וַיָּגָר	*Et peregrinatus est,*	And he sojourned, feared.
גרס	וַיְגָרֶס	*Et confregit.*	And he broke in pieces.
גרש	וַיְגָרֶשׁ	*Et expulit, ejecit.*	And he drove out, cast out.
—	וַיְגָרְשֵׁהוּ	*Et expulit eum.*	And he expelled him.

ROOTS.	DERIVATIVES.	VERSIO.	SIGNIFICATION.
גרש	וַיְגָרְשׁוּ וַיְגָ׳	*Et expulerunt.*	And they cast out.
—	וַיְגָרְשׁוּם	*Et ejecerunt eos.*	And they cast out them.
נגש	וַיַּגֵּשׁ־וַיַּגֶּשׁ	*Et adduxit.*	And he brought.
—	וַיַּגֵּשׁ	*Et obtulit.*	And he presented.
—	וַיִּגַּשׁ	*Et accessit.*	And he came near.
—	וַיַּגִּשׁוּ	*Et adduxerunt.*	And they brought.
—	וַיִּגְּשׁוּ־וַיִּגְּשׁוּ	*Et accesserunt.*	And they came near.
יד	וְיָד־וְיַד וִידוֹ	*Et manus.*	And the hand.
נדח	וַיַּדַּא וַיַּדַּח	*Et avertit.*	And he turned away.
דאה	וַיֵּדֶא	*Et volavit.*	And he did fly.
—	וְיִדְאֶה	*Et volabit.* [*ti sunt.*	And she will fly.
דבק	וַיַּדְבִּיקוּ	*Et persecuti, assecu-*	And they pursued, overtook.
—	וַיַּדְבֵּק	*Et assecutus est.*	And he overtook.
—	וַיִּדְבַּק	*Et adhæsit.*	And he clave.
—	וַיִּדְבְּקוּ	*Et persecuti sunt.*	And they pursued.
דבר	וַיְדַבֵּר	*Et locutus est.*	And he spoke.
—	וַיַּדְבֵּר	*Et subjecit*	And he subdued.
—	וַיְדַבְּרוּ־בְּרוּ־בֵּר	*Et locuti sunt.*	And they spoke.
—	וִידַבְּרוּ	*Et loquentur.*	And they will speak.
—	וַיְדַבְּרֵם	*Et nunciavit eos.*	And he rehearsed them.
דגה	וְיִדְגּוּ	*Et multiplicabuntur.*	And they shall be multiplied.
נדד	וְיֻדַּד	*Et fugabitur.*	And he shall be chased away.
ידה	וַיַּדּוּ	*Et projecerunt.*	And they cast forth.
יד	וְיָדוֹ	*Et manus ejus.*	And his hand
ידע	וִידוּעַ	*Et notus.*	And known.
יד	וְיָדוֹת־דֹת	*Et fulcra.*	And stays, props.
—	וִידוֹת	*Et axes.*	And axles.
דחל	וִידַחֲלֻנַּנִי	*Et terruit me.*	And he affrighted me.
יד	וְיָדִי	*Et manus mea.*	And my hand.
—	וְיָדַי	*Et manus meæ.*	And my hands.
—	וִידֵי וִידֵי	*Et manus.*	And the hands.
—	וְיָדֶיהָ	*Et manus ejus.*	And her hands.
—	וִידֵיהֶם	*Et manus eorum.*	And their hands.
—	וְיָדָיו וְיָדָיו	*Et manus ejus.*	And his hands.
נדח	וַיַּדִּיחוּ	*Et impulerunt.*	And they drave.
יד	וְיָדֶיךָ וְיָדְךָ	*Et manus tuæ.*	And thy hands.
—	וְיָדַיִם	*Et manus.*	And the hands.

ROOTS.	DERIVATIVES.	VERSIO.	SIGNIFICATION.
דכא	וִידַכֵּא	*Et confringet.*	And he will break in pieces.
—	וַיְדַכְּאוּ־כָּאוּ	*Et contererentur.*	And they shall be crushed.
—	וִידַכְּאֵנִי	*Et conteret me.*	And he will crush me.
דמם	וְיִדֹּם	*Et silebit.* [*tus est.*	And he will be silent.
—	וַיִּדֹּם	*Et conticuit, mora-*	And he held his peace, stood
—	וְיִדְּמוּ	*Et tacebunt.*	And they shall be silent.
יד	וְיָדֵנוּ	*Et manus nostra.*	And our hand.
ידע	וַיֵּדַע	*Et cognovit.*	And he knew.
—	וַיּוֹדַע	*Et ostendit.*	And he shewed.
—	וְיֵדַע וְיֵדָע	*Et noscet.*	And he will know.
—	וְיָדֹעַ	*Et cognoscere.*	And to know.
—	וְיוֹדַע	*Et indicabit.*	And he will make known.
—	וְיֹדֵעַ	*Et sciens, peritus.*	And knowing, skilful.
—	וַיֵּדְעוּ	*Et cognoverunt.*	And they knew.
—	וְיֵדְעוּ וְיֵדְעוּ	*Et cognoscent.*	And they will know.
—	וְיֹדְעָו	*Et scientes eum.*	And knowing him.
—	וְיֹדְעַי	*Et noti mei.*	And my acquaintance.
—	וְיֹדְעֵי	*Et scientes.*	And knowing.
—	וְיֹדְעֵם	*Et noscet eos.*	And he shall know them.
—	וִידֻעִים	*Et noti.*	And known.
—	וְיֵדָעֵם	*Et noscet eos.*	And he shall know them.
—	וְנֵדְעָה	*Et intelligemus.*	And we shall understand.
—	וְיִדְּעֹנִי	*Et divinus.*	And a diviner, wizard.
—	וְיִדְּעֹנִים	*Et divinatores.*	And diviners.
—	וְיָדַעְתָּ וְיָדַעַתְּ	*Et cognosces.*	And thou shalt know.
—	וְיָדַעְתִּי	*Et sciam, novi.*	And I shall know, did know.
—	וִידַעְתֶּם־תֶּן	*Et cognoscetis.*	And ye shall know.
דקק	וַיָּדֶק	*Et comminuit.*	And he beat to pieces.
דקר	וַיִּדְקֹר	*Et transfixit.*	And he pierced through.
—	וַיִּדְקְרֵהוּ	*Et perfodit eum.*	And he stabbed him.
נדר	וַיִּדַּר	*Et vovit.*	And he vowed.
—	וַיִּדְּרוּ	*Et voverunt.*	And they vowed.
דרך	וַיַּדְרִיכֵם	*Et deduxit eos.*	And he led them.
—	וַיַּדְרְכוּ	*Et tetenderunt.*	And they bent.
—	וַיִּדְרְכוּ	*Et conculcarunt.*	And they trod.
דרש	וַיִּדְרֹשׁ	*Et percunctatus est.*	And he inquired.
—	וְיִדְרֹשׁ	*Et requiret.*	And he will require.

ROOTS.	DERIVATIVES.	VERSIO.	SIGNIFICATION.
דרש	וַיִּדְרְשֵׁהוּ	*Et quæsivit eum.*	And he sought him.
—	וַיִּדְרְשׁוּ	*Et quæsierunt.*	And they sought.
יהב	וִיהַבוּ	*Et tradiderunt.*	And they yielded, delivered.
הבל	וַיֶּהְבָּלוּ	*Et inanes facti sunt.*	And they became vain.
הוה	וַיהוָֹה	*Et Dominus.*	And the Lord.
היה	וַיְהִי וַיֶּהִי	*Et fuit.*	And he was.
—	וִיהִי	*Et erit.*	And he will be.
יהב	וִיהִיבוּ	*Et traditi sunt.*	And they were delivered.
—	וִיהִיבַת	*Et data est.*	And she, it was given.
היה	וַיִּהְיוּ	*Et fuerunt.*	And they were.
—	וְיִהָיוּ וִיהְיוּ	*Et erunt.*	And they will be.
הוך	וִיהָךְ וִיהַךְ	*Et adveniet.*	And he shall come.
הלך	וַיַּהֲלֹךְ	*Et abibit.*	And he will go away.
—	וַיְהַלֵּךְ	*Et incedit.*	And he walked.
הלל	וַיְהַלְלֶהָ	*Et laudavit eam.*	And he praised her.
—	וַיְהַלְלוּ וַיְהַלֲלוּ	*Et laudaverunt.*	And they praised, commended
—	וַיְהַלְלוּהָ	*Et laudarunt eam.*	And they praised her.
—	וִיהַלְלוּהָ	*Et laudabunt eam.*	And they shall praise her.
הלם	וַיַּהֲלֹם	*Et adamas.*	And a diamond.
המם	וַיָּהָם	*Et conturbavit.*	And he discomfited.
המה	וַיֶּהֱמוּ	*Et perstrepuerunt.*	And they roared.
—	וַיָּהֹמֵם וַיְהֻמֵּם	*Et contrivit eos.*	And he crushed them.
הסה	וַיַּהַס	*Et silere fecit.* [tit.	And he made silent.
הפך	וַיַּהֲפֹךְ וַיַּהֲפֹךְ	*Et mutavit, subver-*	And he changed, overturned
—	וַיֵּהָפֵךְ	*Et conversus est.*	And he was turned.
—	וַיַּהַפְכֵהוּ	*Et evertit eum.*	And he overthrew him.
—	וַיַּהַפְכוּ וַיֵּהָפְכוּ	*Et conversi sunt.*	And they were turned.
—	וַיַּהַפְכוּ	*Et subvertent.*	And they will overthrow.
הרג	וַיַּהֲרֹג	*Et occidit.*	And he slew.
—	וַיַּהַרְגֵהוּ	*Et occidit eum.*	And he slew him.
—	וַיַּהַרְגֻהוּ	*Et occiderunt eum.*	And they slew him.
—	וַיַּהַרְגוּ	*Et occiderunt.*	And they slew.
—	וַיַּהַרְגוּם	*Et occiderunt eos.*	And they slew them.
—	וַיַּהַרְגֵם	*Et occidit eos.*	And he slew them.
הרס	וַיֶּהֶרְסֶהָ	*Et evertit eam.*	And he overturned her.
התל	וַיְהַתֵּל	*Et illusit.*	And he mocked.
יאל	וַיּוֹאֶל	*Et voluit.*	And he wished, desired.

ROOTS.	DERIVATIVES.	VERSIO.	SIGNIFICATION.
ידה	וְיוֹדוּ	*Et laudabunt.*	And they will praise.
—	וְיוֹדֻךָ	*Et laudabunt te.*	And they will praise thee.
ידע	וַיּוֹדַע	*Et notum fecit.*	And he made known.
יכח	וַיּוֹכַח	*Et increpavit.*	And he rebuked.
—	וְיוֹכַח	*Et corripiet.*	And he will reprove.
—	וְיוֹכִיחוּ	*Et dijudicabunt.*	And they shall judge.
—	וְיוֹכִיחֵנִי	*Et corripiet me.*	And he shall reprove me.
ילד	וַיִּוָּלֶד	*Et natus est.*	And he was born.
—	וַיּוֹלֶד	*Et genuit.*	And he begat.
—	וַיִּוָּלְדוּ	*Et nati sunt.*	And they were born.
ילך	וַיּוֹלִיכֻהוּ	*Et adduxerunt eum.*	And they brought him.
—	וַיּוֹלִיכֵם	*Et deduxit eos.*	And he led them.
—	וַיּוֹלֶךְ	*Et deduxit.*	And he led.
—	וַיּוֹלִכֵנִי	*Et duxit me.*	And he brought me.
יום	וְיוֹם וְיוֹם	*Et dies.*	And a, the day.
—	וְיוֹמָם	*Et dies.*	And days.
ינק	וְיוֹנֵק	*Et sugens.*	And sucking.
—	וְיוֹנְקֵי	*Et sugentes.*	And they that suck.
—	וְיוֹנַקְתּוֹ	*Et ramus ejus.*	And his branch.
יסף	וְיוֹסִיף וְיוֹסֵף	*Et addet, perget.*	And he will add, go on.
—	וַיּוֹסִיפוּ־־ספוּ וַיֹּ׳	*Et addiderunt.*	And they added.
—	וְיוֹסִיפוּ וְיֹסִפוּ	*Et addent.*	And they will add.
—	וַיּוֹסֶף וַיֹּסֶף	*Et addidit.*	And he added.
יעד	וַיִּוָּעֲדוּ	*Et convenerunt.*	And they met. [sel.
יעץ	וַיִּוָּעַץ	*Et consilium iniit.*	And he consulted, took coun-
—	וְיוֹעֵץ	*Et consiliarius.*	And a counsellor.
—	וַיִּוָּעֲצוּ	*Et consilium iniêre.*	And they took counsel.
—	וְיוֹעֲצָיו	*Et consiliarii ejus.*	And his counsellors.
יצא	וַיּוֹצֵא וַיֹּצֵא	*Et eduxit.*	And he brought forth, out of.
—	וַיּוֹצִאֶהָ	*Et eduxit eam.*	And he brought her out.
—	וַיּוֹצִאֲךָ וַיֹּצִ׳	*Et eduxit te.*	And he brought thee out.
—	וַיּוֹצִיאֻהוּ וַיֹּצִ׳	*Et eduxerunt eum.*	And they brought him out.
—	וְיוֹצִיאוּ וְיֹצִ׳	*Et educent.*	And they will bring out.
—	וַיּוֹצִיאוּ וַיֹּצִ׳	*Et eduxerunt.*	And they brought out, forth.
—	וַיּוֹצִיאֵם	*Et eduxit eos.*	And he brought us forth.
—	וַיּוֹצִיאֵנִי	*Et eduxit me.*	And he brought me forth.
יצר	וְיוֹצְרוֹ וְיֹצְ׳	*Et formator ejus.*	And his maker.

ROOTS.	DERIVATIVES.	VERSIO.	SIGNIFICATION.
ירה	וַיּוֹר	*Et jaculatus est.*	And he shot. [down.
ירד	וַיּוֹרֶד וַיֹּרֶד	*Et deduxit, dejecit.*	And he brought down, cast
—	וַיּוֹרִדֵהוּ וַיֹּר׳	*Et deduxit eum.*	And he brought him down.
—	וַיֹּרִדוּ	*Et demiserunt.*	And they brought down.
—	וַיֹּרִדֵם	*Et deduxit eos.*	And he brought them down.
ירה	וְיוֹרֶה	*Et docebit.* [lis.	And he will teach. [rain.
—	וְיוֹרֶה	*Et pluvia* autumna-	And the *autumnal or former*
—	וַיּוֹרֵהוּ	*Et ostendit ei.*	And he shewed to him.
ירד	וַיּוֹרִדוּ	*Et demiserunt eum.*	And they sent him down.
ירה	וְיוֹרֵנוּ	*Et docebit nos.*	And he shall teach us.
ירש	וַיּוֹרֶשׁ וַיֹּרֶשׁ	*Et expulit.*	And he drove out.
ישב	וַיּוּשַׁב	*Et reductus est.*	And he was brought again.
—	וַיּוֹשֶׁב--שֶׁב	*Et habitare fecit.*	And he caused to dwell.
—	וְיוֹשֵׁב	*Et incola.*	And an inhabitant.
—	וְיוֹשְׁבֵי וְישְׁ׳	*Et habitatores.*	And the inhabitants.
—	וְיוֹשְׁבִים וְישְׁ״	*Et sedentes.*	And they that sit. [out.
ישט	וַיּוֹשֶׁט	*Et extendit.*	And he held out, stretched
ישב	וַיּוֹשִׁיבוּ	*Et collocarunt.*	And they placed.
—	וַיּוֹשִׁיבֵנִי	*Et collocavit me.*	And he placed me.
ישע	וַיּוֹשִׁיעוּם	*Et servarunt eos.*	And they delivered them.
—	וְיוֹשִׁיעֶךָ	*Et servabit te.*	And he shall save thee.
—	וְיוֹשִׁיעֻךָ	*Et servabunt te.*	And they shall save thee.
—	וַיּוֹשִׁיעֵם	*Et servavit eos.*	And he saved them.
—	וְיוֹשִׁיעֵם	*Et servabit eos.*	And he will save them.
—	וְיוֹשִׁיעֵנוּ	*Et servabit nos.*	And he will save us.
—	וְיוֹשִׁיעֵנִי	*Et servabit me.*	And he will save me.
—	וַיּוֹשַׁע־יֹשַׁע	*Et servavit.*	And he saved, delivered.
—	וַיּוֹשִׁעוּם	*Et servarunt eos.*	And they saved them.
—	וְיוֹשִׁעוּם	*Et servabunt eos.*	And they will save them.
—	וַיּוֹשִׁעָן	*Et servavit eas.*	And he saved them.
יתר	וַיִּוָּתֵר	*Et remansit.*	And he remained, was left.
—	וַיּוֹתֵר	*Et reservavit.*	And he reserved.
—	וַיִּוָּתְרוּ	*Et remanserunt.*	And they remained, were left.
—	וַיּוֹתִרוּ	*Et reliquerunt.*	And they left.
נזה	וַיֵּז	*Et aspersit.*	And he sprinkled.
—	וַיִּז	*Et aspersus est.*	And he was sprinkled.
—	וְיִז	*Et aspergetur.*	And he shall be sprinkled.

ROOTS.	DERIVATIVES.	VERSIO.	SIGNIFICATION.
זוב	וַיָּזֻבוּ־־זוּבוּ	*Et effluxerunt.*	And they gushed out, flowed.
זבח.	וַיִּזְבַּח וַיִּזְבַּח	*Et immolavit.*	And he sacrificed.
—	וַיִּזְבָּחֵהוּ	*Et mactavit eum.*	And he slew him.
—	וַיִּזְבְּחוּ	*Et immolaverunt.*	And they sacrificed.
—	וְיִזְבְּחוּ	*Et sacrificabunt.*	And they shall sacrifice.
נזד	וַיָּזֶד	*Et coxit.*	And he boiled.
זור	וַיְזוֹרֵר	*Et sternutavit.*	And he sneezed.
זכר.	וַיִּזְכֹּר	*Et recordatus est.*	And he remembered.
—	וְיִזְכֹּר	*Et recordabitur.*	And he shall remember.
—	וַיִּזְכְּרֶהָ	*Et meminit illius.*	And he remembered her.
—	וַיִּזְכְּרוּ	*Et recordati sunt.*	And they remembered,
זמר	וִיזַמְּרוּ	*Et canent.*	And they shall sing. [nication.
זנה	וַיֶּזֶן	*Et scortari fecit.*	And he caused to commit for-
זנב	וַיְזַנֵּב	*Et extremos præcidit*	And he smote the hindmost.
זנה	וַיִּזְנוּ	*Et scortati sunt.*	And they went a whoring.
זעף	וַיִּזְעַף	*Et indignatus est.*	And he was wroth.
זעק	וַיַּזְעֵק	*Et convocavit.*	And he called together.
—	וַיִּזָּעֵק	*Et congregatus est.*	And he was gathered.
—	וַיִּזְעַק	*Et clamavit.*	And he cried out.
—	וַיִּזְעֲקוּ־־צְ״־־זָעֲ״	*Et clamarunt.*	And they cried, called aloud.
—	וְיִזְעֲקוּ	*Et clamabunt.*	And they will cry.
—	וַיִּזְעֲקוּךָ	*Et invocaverunt te.*	And they called upon thee.
זקן	וַיִּזְקַן	*Et senuit.*	And he grew old.
ער	וַיָּזַר	*Et compressit.*	And he pressed together.
זרה	וַיִּזֶר	*Et dispersit.*	And he scattered.
—	וַיִּזָּרוּ	*Et dispersi sunt.*	And they were dispersed.
זרח	וַיִּזְרַח	*Et ortus est.*	And he rose.
זרע	וַיִּזְרַע	*Et sevit.*	And he sowed.
—	וַיִּזְרָעֶהָ	*Et sevit eam.*	And he sowed her or it.
—	וַיִּזְרְעוּ	*Et seminaverunt.*	And they sowed.
זרק	וַיִּזְרֹק	*Et sparsit.*	And he sprinkled.
—	וַיִּזְרְקֵהוּ	*Et sparsit eum.*	And he sprinkled him.
—	וַיִּזְרְקוּ	*Et sparserunt.*	And they sprinkled.
חבא	וַיֵּחָבְאוּ	*Et absconderunt se.*	And they hid themselves.
—	וַיַּחְבִּיאֵם	*Et abscondit eos.*	And he hid them.
חבק	וַיְחַבֶּק־־בֵּק	*Et amplexus est* [*est*	And he embraced.
—	וַיְחַבְּקֵהוּ	*Et illum amplexus*	And he embraced him.

ROOTS.	DERIVATIVES.	VERSIO.	SIGNIFICATION.
חבר	וַיְחַבֵּר	*Et conjunxit.*	And he coupled.
—	וַיְחַבְּרֵהוּ	*Et associavit se.*	And he joined himself.
חבש	וַיַּחֲבֹשׁ־חֲב״	*Et stravit.*	And he saddled.
—	וַיְחַבֵּשׁ	*Et obligabit.*	And he will bind up.
—	וַיַּחַבְשׁוּ־חֲבְ״	*Et straverunt.*	And they saddled.
—	וַיְחַבְּשֵׁנוּ	*Et obligabit nos.*	And he will bind us up.
חגג	וַיָּחֹגּוּ	*Et festum agent.*	And they shall celebrate a festival.
חגר	וַיַּחְגֹּר	*Et cinxit, accinxit se*	And he girded, girded himself
—	וַיַּחְגְּרוּ	*Et accinxerunt se.*	And they girded themselves.
חדה	וַיִּחַדְּ	*Et lætatus est.*	And he rejoiced.
יחד	וַיַּחַד	*Et pariter.*	And likewise.
—	וַיַּחְדָּו	*Et simul.*	And together.
חדל	וַיֶּחְדַּל	*Et desiit.*	And he left off.
—	וַיֶּחְדַּל	*Et cessabit.*	And he will cease.
—	וַיֶּחְדְּלוּ	*Et desierunt.*	And they ceased.
חדש	וַיְחַדֵּשׁ	*Et renovavit.*	And he renewed.
חזה	וַיֶּחֱזוּ	*Et viderunt.*	And they saw.
חזק	וַיַּחֲזִיקוּ־זִקוּ	*Et apprehenderunt.*	And they took hold, held.
—	וַיַּחֲזֶק־זֵק	*Et prehendit*	And he laid hold.
—	וַיְחַזֵּק	*Et confirmavit, induravit.*	And he strengthened, hardened.
—	וְיֶחֱזַק	*Et fortis erit.*	And he shall be strong.
—	וַיֶּחֱזַק־חֱ״־חֱזָ״	*Et invaluit, prævaluit.*	And he grew strong, prevailed
—	וַיְחַזְּקֵהוּ	*Et confirmavit eum.*	And he strengthened him.
—	וַיְחַזְּקוּ	*Et confirmarunt.*	And they strengthened.
—	וַיְחַזְּקוּם	*Et confirmarunt eos*	And they strengthened them.
—	וַיְחַזְּקֵם	*Et confirmavit eos.*	And he encouraged them.
—	וַיְחַזְּקֵנִי	*Et confirmavit me.*	And he strengthened me.
חטא	וְחִטֵּא	*Et purgabit*	And he shall cleanse.
—	וַיְחַטְּאֵהוּ	*Et obtulit eum pro* [peccato	And he offered him *for sin.*
—	וַיְחַטְּאוּ	*Et expiaverunt.*	And they expiated.
—	וַיַּחֲטִיא	*Et peccare fecit.*	And he caused to sin.
חיה	וַיְחִי־יְ״	*Et vixit, revixit.*	And he lived, revived.
—	וִיחִי־יִ״	*Et vivet.*	And he shall live.
יחד	וְיָחִיד	*Et unicus.*	And only.
חיה	וַיְחַיֶּהָ	*Et in vita servavit, eam.*	And he kept her alive.
—	וִיחַיֵּהוּ	*Et vivum servabit eum.*	And he will keep him alive.

ROOTS.	DERIVATIVES.	VERSIO.	SIGNIFICATION.
חיה	וַיְחִיוּ	*Et vixerunt.*	And they lived.
—	וִיחִיוּ	*Et vivent.*	And they shall live.
יחל	וְיָחִיל	*Et expectabit.*	And he will wait.
—	וַיָּחִילוּ	*Et expectaverunt.*	And they waited.
חכם	וַיֶּחְכַּם	*Et sapiens fuit.*	And he was wise.
—	וְיֶחְכָּם	*Et sapiens erit.*	And he will be wise.
חלה	וַיָּחַל	*Et ægrotavit.*	And he was sick.
חלל	וַיָּחֶל	*Et vulneratus est.*	And he was wounded.
יחל	וַיָּחֶל	*Et expectavit.*	And he waited, expected.
חלה	וַיְחַל	*Et oravit.*	And he prayed.
—	וַיֶּחֱלֶא	*Et ægrotavit.*	And he was sick.
חול	וַיָּחִילוּ	*Et doluerunt.*	And they were in pain.
יחל	וִיחַלוּ	*Et expectabunt, sperare fecerunt.*	And they will wait, have made to hope.
—	וִיחַלוּ־וְיֵ״	*Et expectabunt.*	And they will wait, expect.
—	וַיָּחֵלּוּ	*Et cœperunt.*	And they began.
חלט	וַיַּחְלְטוּ	*Et verbum rapuerunt.*	And they caught the word.
חלל	וַיְחַלְּלוּ	*Et polluerunt.*	And they defiled.
חלם	וַיַּחֲלֹם	*Et somniavit.*	And he dreamed.
—	וַיַּחַלְמוּ	*Et somniaverunt.*	And they dreamed.
חלף	וַיַּחֲלֵף	*Et mutavit.*	And he changed.
—	וְיַחֲלֹף	*Et præteribunt.*	And he shall pass by.
—	וְיַחֲלֹפוּ	*Et mutabuntur.*	And they shall be changed.
חלץ	וַיְחַלְּצֵם	*Et liberavit eos.*	And he delivered them.
חלק	וַיֵּחָלֵק	*Et divisit se.*	And he divided himself.
—	וַיְחַלֵּק־לֵק	*Et divisit, mutavit.*	And he divided, changed.
—	וַיְחַלְּקוּ־יְחַלְּ׳	*Et partiti sunt.*	And they divided.
—	וַיַּחְלְקוּם	*Et diviserunt eos.*	And they divided them.
—	וַיְחַלְּקֵם	*Et divisit eos.*	And he divided them.
חלש	וַיַּחֲלשׁ	*Et fregit.*	And he broke, discomfited.
—	וַיֶּחֱלָשׁ	*Et debilitatus est.*	And he was weakened.
חמם	וַיָּחָם	*Et incaluit.*	And he grew warm.
—	וַיֶּחֱמוּ	*Et incaluerunt*	And they grew hot.
חמר	וַיַּחְמוֹר	*Et asinus.*	And an ass.
חמל	וַיַּחְמֹל	*Et pepercit.*	And he spared.
יחם	וַיֵּחַמְנָה	*Et incaluerunt.*	And they grew hot.
חמס	וַיַּחְמֹס	*Et abripuit.*	And he took away.

ROOTS.	DERIVATIVES.	VERSIO.	SIGNIFICATION.
חנן	וַיָּחָן	*Et propitius fuit.*	And he was gracious.
חנה	וַיִּחַן	*Et castrametatus est*	And he encamped.
—	וַיַּחֲנוּ־כֵן	*Et castrametati sunt*	And they encamped.
—	וַיַּחֲנוּ	*Et castra ponent.*	And they will encamp.
חנט	וַיַּחַנְטוּ	*Et condiverunt.*	And they embalmed.
חנן	וִיחֻנֶּךָּ	*Et miserebitur tui.*	And he will have pity on thee
חנך	וַיַּחְנְכוּ	*Et dedicarunt.* [*tri.*	And they dedicated.
חנן	וִיחָנֵּנוּ	*Et miserebitur nos-*	And he will have mercy on us
—	וַיְחָנֶּנּוּ	*Et miserebor ejus.*	And I will be merciful to him
חנק	וַיֵּחָנַק	*Et strangulavit se.*	And he strangled himself.
חסן	וַיַּחְסְנוּן	*Et possidebunt.*	And they will possess.
חסר	וַיַּחְסְרוּ	*Et defecerunt.*	And they failed, abated.
חפה	וַיְחַף	*Et obtexit.*	And he overlaid.
יחף	וְיָחֵף	*Et discalceatus.*	And unshod, bare-footed.
חפה	וַיְחַפְּאוּ	*Et operuerunt.*	And they covered, concealed.
—	וַיְחַפֵּהוּ	*Et texit eum.*	And he covered him.
חפר	וְיַחְפִּיר	*Et pudore afficiet.*	And he will put to shame.
—	וַיַּחְפֹּר	*Et fodit.*	And he dug.
—	וַיַּחְפְּרֵהוּ	*Et effodit eum.*	And he digged it.
—	וַיַּחְפְּרֻהוּ	*Et effodient eum.*	And they will dig for him,or it
—	וַיַּחְפְּרוּ	*Et foderunt.*	And they digged.
—	וַיֶּחְפָּרוּ	*Et erubuerunt.*	And they were ashamed.
—	וַיַּחְפְּרוּ	*Et foderunt, explorabunt, pudore afficientur.*	And they digged, shall search out, shall be put to shame.
חפש	וַיְחַפֵּשׂ	*Et investigavit.*	And he examined.
חצה	וַיַּחַץ	*Et divisit.*	And he divided.
חצב	וַיַּחְצֹב	*Et fodit.*	And he digged.
חצה	וַיֵּחָצוּ	*Et divisi sunt.*	And they were divided.
—	וַיֶּחֱצֵם	*Et divisit eos.*	And he divided them.
חקק	וְיֻחָקוּ	*Et insculpentur.*	And they shall be engraven.
חקר	וְיֵחָקְרוּ	*Et pervestigabuntur*	And they shall be searched out
חרר	וַיֵּחַר	*Et combustus est.*	And he was burned.
חרה	וַיִּחַר	*Et exarsit.*	And he was inflamed, angry.
—	וַיַּחַר	*Et accendit.*	And he kindled.
—	וְיִחַר	*Et excandescet.*	And he will be displeased.
חרב	וַיֶּחֱרַב	*Et exsiccatus est.*	And he was dried up.

ROOTS.	DERIVATIVES.	VERSIO.	SIGNIFICATION.
חרב	וְיֶחֱרַב	*Et exsiccabitur.*	And he will be dried up.
חרג	וְיַחְרְגוּ	*Et contremiscent.*	And they shall be afraid.
חרד	וַיֶּחֱרַד	*Et tremuit, pavit.*	And he trembled, was afraid.
—	וַיֶּחֶרְדוּ	*Et trepidarunt.*	And they trembled.
—	וְיֶחֶרְדוּ	*Et trepidabunt.*	And they shall tremble.
חרם	וַיַּחֲרִמֶהָ	*Et disperdidit eam.*	And he destroyed her.
—	וַיַּחֲרִימוּ	*Et destruxerunt.*	And they destroyed. [them.
—	וַיַּחֲרִמֵם	*Et exciderunt eos.*	And they cut off, destroyed
חרש	וַיַּחֲרִישׁוּ־־רְשׁוּ	*Et siluerunt.*	And they held their peace.
חרם	וַיַּחֲרֵם	*Et devovit, delevit.*	And he devoted, destroyed.
חרף	וַיְחָרֵף	*Et conviciatus est.*	And he reproached.
חרק	וַיַּחַרְקוּ	*Et frenduerunt.*	And they gnashed.
חשב	וַיַּחְשְׁבֶהָ	*Et imputavit illud, cogitavit eam.*	And he imputed or counted it, he thought her.
—	וַיַּחְשְׁבֵנִי	*Et reputavit me.*	And he counted me.
חשה	וַיֶּחֱשׁוּ	*Et siluerunt.*	And they were silent.
חשך	וַיַּחְשִׁךְ	*Et tenebrescere fecit*	And he made it dark.
חשף	וַיֶּחֱשֹׂף	*Et nudavit.*	And he uncovered, made bare
חתת	וַיֵּחַתּוּ	*Et consternati sunt.*	And they were dismayed.
חתם	וַיַּחְתֹּם	*Et obsignavit.*	And he sealed.
חתר	וַיַּחְתְּרוּ	*Et remigarunt.*	And they rowed.
נטה	וַיֵּט־־יַּט־יַּט	*Et tetendit, extendit*	And he stretched, pitched.
—	וְיֵט	*Et extendet.* [*erit.*	And he will stretch out.
יטב	וְיִטַב	*Et bene, jucundum*	And it shall be well, pleasant.
טבל	וַיִּטְבֹּל	*Et immersit, intinxit*	And he dipped, dyed.
—	וַיִּטְבְּלוּ	*Et immerserunt, intinxerunt.*	And they dipped, dyed.
טבע	וַיִּטְבַּע	*Et demersus est.*	And he was sunk.
נטה	וַיַּטֵּהוּ	*Et divertit eum.*	And he turned him aside.
טהר	וַיִּטְהָר	*Et mundatus est.*	And he was cleansed.
—	וַיְטַהֵר	*Et mundavit.*	And he cleansed, purified.
—	וַיְטַהֲרוּ־וַיְט׳	*Et mundaverunt.*	And they purified.
נטה	וַיַּטּוּ	*Et perverterunt.*	And they perverted.
—	וַיִּטּוּ	*Et declinarunt.*	And they turned aside.
טחן	וַיִּטְחַן	*Et moluit.*	And he ground.
יטב	וִיטִבְךָ	*Et exhilarabit te.*	And he shall cheer thee.
טול	וַיָּטֶל	*Et projecit.*	And he cast forth.

ROOTS.	DERIVATIVES.	VERSIO.	SIGNIFICATION.
טול	וַיְטִלֻהוּ	*Et ejecerunt eum.*	And they cast him out.
—	וַיָּטִלוּ	*Et ejecerunt.*	And they cast.
טלל	וַיְטַלְלֵנוּ	*Et texit eum.*	And he covered him.
טמא	וַיְטַמֵּא	*Et polluit.*	And he defiled.
—	וַיְטַמְּאֵהוּ	*Et polluit eum.*	And he defiled him.
—	וַיְטַמְּאוּ	*Et polluerunt.*	And they defiled.
—	וַיִּטַּמְאוּ	*Et polluti sunt.*	And they were defiled.
טמן	וַיִּטְמֹן	*Et abscondit.*	And he hid.
—	וַיִּטְמְנֵהוּ	*Et abscondit eum.*	And he hid him.
—	וַיִּטְמְנוּ	*Et absconderunt.*	And they hid.
נטע	וַיִּטַּע	*Et plantavit.*	And he planted.
—	וְיִטַּע	*Et plantabit.*	And he shall plant.
—	וַיִּטָּעֵהוּ	*Et plantavit eum.*	And he planted him.
—	וַיִּטְּעוּ	*Et plantaverunt.*	And they planted.
טרף	וַיִּטְרֹף	*Et discerpsit.*	And he tore.
נטש	וַיִּטֹּשׁ	*Et demisit, deseruit.*	And he let fall, forsook.
—	וַיִּטְּשֵׁהוּ	*Et deseruerunt eum.*	And they forsook him.
יבש	וַיִּיבָשׁ וַיִּיבַשׁ	*Et aruit, exaruit.*	And he dried up, withered.
יגע	וְיִיגְעוּ--גָ׳	*Et laborabunt.*	And they shall labour.
יחל	וַיְיָחֶל--רּס״	*Et expectavit.*	And he waited.
אחר	וַיֵּאחֶר	*Et moratus est.*	And he delayed.
יטב	וַיֵּיטֶב	*Et benefecit.* [*fuit.*	And he did well.
—	וַיִּיטַב	*Et placuit, bonum*	And it pleased, was good.
—	וְיִיטַב	*Et bene erit.*	And it shall be well.
—	וַיִּיטְבוּ	*Et placuerunt.*	And they pleased.
יין	וְיֵין וָיַיִן וְיַיִן	*Et vinum.*	And wine.
יפה	וַיִּיף	*Et pulcher fuit.*	And he was fair.
יצר	וַיִּיצֶר	*Et formavit.*	And he formed.
יקץ	וַיִּיקַץ--קֶץ	*Et evigilabit.*	And he awoke.
יקר	וַיִּיקַר	*Et pretiosus fuit.*	And he was precious.
—	וְיִיקַר	*Et pretiosus erit.*	And he shall be precious.
ירא	וַיִּירָא	*Et timuit.*	And he feared, was afraid.
—	וַיִּירָאוּ וַיִּירְאוּ	*Et timuerunt.* [*bunt*	And they feared.
—	וְיִירָאוּ--רְ״	*Et timuerunt, time-*	And they feared, will fear.
—	וַיִּירָאֵנִי	*Et timuit me.*	And he feared me.
ירש	וַיִּירַשׁ	*Et possedit.*	And he possessed.
—	וַיּוֹרֶשׁ	*Et expulit.*	And he expelled.

ROOTS	DERIVATIVES.	VERSIO.	SIGNIFICATION.
ירשׁ	וְיִירַשׁ	*Et possidebit.*	And he shall possess.
—	וַיִּירְשׁוּ	*Et possederunt.*	And they possessed.
—	וְיִירְשׁוּ	*Et possidebunt.*	And they shall possess.
—	וַיִּירָשׁם	*Et expulerunt eos.*	And they expelled them.
שׂום	וַיִּישַׂם	*Et positus est.*	And he was placed.
—	וַיִּישַׂם	*Et oppositus est.*	And he, it was set before.
—	וַיִּישַׁן־־שָׁן	*Et dormivit.*	And he slept.
ישׁר	וַיִּישַׁר	*Et rectum fuit.*	And it was right.
—	וַיְיַשְּׁרֵם	*Et direxit eos.*	And he directed them.
נכה	וַיַּךְ־־יַ״	*Et percussit.*	And he smote, slew.
—	וְיַךְ	*Et percutiet.*	And he shall smite.
כבד	וַיְכַבֵּד־־יַכְבֵּד	*Et induravit.*	And he hardened.
—	וִיכַבְּדוּ	*Et honorabunt.*	And they shall glorify.
כבה	וַיְכַבּוּ	*Et extinxerunt.*	And they have put out.
כבשׁ	וַיְכַבְּשׁוּם	*Et subegerunt eos.*	And they subjected them.
כבס	וַיְכַבְּסוּ	*Et abluerunt.*	And they washed.
נכה	וַיַּכֶּהָ	*Et percussit eam.*	And he smote her.
—	וַיַּכֶּה	*Et percussit.*	And he smote.
—	וַיַּכֵּהוּ	*Et percussit eum.*	And he smote him.
—	וַיַּכֻּהוּ	*Et percusserunt eum*	And they smote him.
כהן	וַיְכַהֵן	*Et sacerdotio funct- tus est.*	And he executed the priest's office.
		[ti sunt.	[ly office.
—	וַיְכַהֲנוּ	*Et sacerdotio func-*	And they discharged the priest-
נכה	וַיַּכּוּ	*Et percusserunt.*	And they smote.
—	וַיַּכֻּו	*Et percussit eum.*	And he smote him.
—	וַיֻּכּוּ	*Et percussi sunt.*	And they were smitten.
—	וְיַכּוּ	*Et percutient.*	And they shall smite.
—	וַיַּכּוּהָ	*Et percusserunt eam*	And they smote her.
—	וַיַּכּוּם	*Et percusserunt eos.*	And they smote them.
כון	וְיִכּוֹן	*Et stabilietur.*	And he shall be established.
—	וַיְכוֹנְנֶהָ	*Et paravit eam.*	And he prepared her.
—	וַיְכוֹנֶנּוּ	*Et formavit nos.*	And he formed us.
—	וַיְכוֹנְנוּ	*Et paraverunt.*	And they prepared. [selves.
—	וִיכוֹנְנוּ	*Et parabunt se.*	And they shall prepare them-
—	וַיְכוֹנְנוּנִי	*Et disposuerunt me*	And they have fashioned me.
כזב	וִיכַזֵּב	*Et mentietur.*	And he will lie.
כחד	וַיְכַחֵד	*Et excidit.*	And he cut off.

ROOTS.	DERIVATIVES.	VERSIO.	SIGNIFICATION.
כחש	וְיִכָּחֲשׁוּ	*Et mendaces deprehendentur.*	And they shall be found liars.
כון	וַיָּכִינוּ	*Et paraverunt.*	And they made ready.
נכר	וַיַּכִּירָהּ	*Et cognovit eam.*	And he knew her.
כלה	וַיְכַל	*Et absolvit, desiit, consumpsit.*	And he finished, left off, consumed.
יכל	וַיֻּכַל	*Et prevaluit.*	And he prevailed.
כלא	וַיִּכָּלֵא	*Et cohibitus est.*	And he was restrained.
—	וַיִּכָּלְאוּ	*Et cohibiti sunt.*	And they were stayed.
יכל	וַיּוּכְלָה	*Et prevaluit.*	And she prevailed.
כלה	וַיְכַלֵּהוּ	*Et perfecit. [eum.*	And he finished him or it.
—	וַיְכַלֻּהוּ	*Et consumpserunt*	And they consumed him.
—	וַיְכַלּוּ	*Et absolverunt.*	And they made an end.
—	וַיִּכְלוּ	*Et consumpti sunt.*	And they were consumed.
—	וַיִּכְלוּ	*Et perfecti sunt.*	And they were finished.
יכל	וַיּוּכְלוּ	*Et prevaluerunt.*	And they prevailed.
כלה	וַיִּכְלוּ	*Et absolventur.*	And they shall be ended.
כול	וַיְכַלְכֵּל	*Et aluit.*	And he nourished.
—	וַיְכַלְכְּלֵם	*Et pavit eos.*	And he fed them.
כלם	וַיִּכָּלְמוּ	*Et pudore afficientur*	And they shall be put to shame.
יכל	וְיָכָלְתָּ	*Et poteris.*	And thou shalt be able.
נכה	וַיַּכֵּם	*Et percussit eos.*	And he smote them.
—	וַיַּכּוּם	*Et percusserunt eos.*	And they smote them.
כון	וַיָּכֶן וַיָּכֶן	*Et paravit.*	And he prepared.
—	וְיִכֹּנוּ	*Et stabilientur.*	And they shall be established.
כנע	וַיַּכְנִיעֵם	*Et subjecit eos.*	And he subdued them.
כון	וַיְכֹנְנֶךָ	*Et confirmavit te.*	And he established thee.
כנע	וַיַּכְנַע	*Et depressit.*	And he brought down.
—	וַיִּכָּנַע	*Et depressit se, depressus est.*	And he humbled himself, he was brought under.
—	וַיִּכָּנְעוּ	*Et depresserunt se, depressi sunt.*	And they humbled themselves, they were brought under.
—	וַיִּכָּנְעוּ	*Et subjecti sunt.*	And they were subdued [selves
—	וְיִכָּנְעוּ	*Et deprimені se.*	And they shall humble them-
כסה	וַיְכַס	*Et operuit.*	And he covered.
—	וַיְכַסֵּהוּ	*Et operuit eum.*	And he covered him.
—	וַיְכַסֻּהוּ	*Et texerunt eum.*	And they covered him.

ROOTS.	DERIVATIVES.	VERSIO.	SIGNIFICATION.
כסה	וַיְכַסּוּ	*Et operuerunt.*	And they covered.
—	וַיְכֻסּוּ	*Et operti sunt.*	And they were covered.
כסל	וַיִּכְסְלוּ	*Et stulte agent.*	And they will act foolishly.
כעס	וַיַּכְעִיסוּ	*Et provocarunt.*	And they provoked.
—	וַיַּכְעִיסֻהוּ	*Et provocarunt eum*	And they provoked him.
—	וַיַּכְעֵס	*Et irritavit.*	And he made angry.
—	וַיִּכְעַס	*Et iratus est.*	And he was angry.
—	וַיַּכְעִסוּ	*Et irritaverunt.*	And they provoked.
כפר	וַיְכַפֵּר	*Et expiavit.*	And he made atonement.
נכר	וַיַּכֵּר	*Et cognovit.*	And he knew.
כרה	וַיִּכְרֶה	*Et paravit.*	And he prepared.
נכר	וַיַּכִּרֵהוּ	*Et cognovit eum.*	And he knew him.
כרה	וַיִּכְרוּ	*Et foderunt.*	And they digged.
נכר	וַיַּכִּרֵם	*Et cognovit eos.*	And he knew them.
כרע	וַיִּכְרַע	*Et procubuit.*	And he fell down, bowed down
—	וַיִּכְרְעוּ	*Et procubuerunt.*	And they bowed down.
כרת	וַיִּכְרֹת	*Et excidit* [sc. fœdus	And he cut off. [*covenant.*
—	וַיִּכְרֹת־־רָת	*Et succidit, pepigit*	And he cut down, made *a*
—	וַיַּכְרֵת	*Et excidit.*	And he will cut off.
—	וַיִּכְרְתֻהוּ	*Et exciderunt eum.*	And they cut him off.
—	וַיִּכְרְתוּ	*Et exciderunt.*	And they cut off.
—	וְיִכְרְתוּ	*Et excident.*	And they will cut off.
כשל	וַיַּכְשִׁילֻהוּ	*Et impingere fece-*	And they made him stumble.
		runt eum [*runt eos*	[stumble.
—	וַיַּכְשִׁלוּם	*Et impingere fece-*	And they caused them to
כתב	וַיִּכָּתֵב	*Et scriptus est.* [*sit*	And he, it was written.
—	וַיִּכְתֹּב־־תָּב	*Et scripsit, descrip-*	And he wrote, described.
—	וְיִכָּתֵב	*Et scribetur.*	And it shall be written.
—	וַיִּכְתְּבוּ	*Et scripserunt.*	And they wrote.
—	וְיִכְתְּבוּ	*Et scribent.* [*eam.*	And they shall write.
—	וַיִּכְתְּבוּהָ	*Et descripserunt*	And they described her.
—	וְיִכָּתְבוּן	*Et scribentur.*	And they shall be written.
—	וַיִּכְתְּבֵם	*Et scripsit eos.*	And he wrote them.
כתת	וַיַּכְּתוּ	*Et contriverunt.*	And they crushed.
—	וַיַּכְּתוּם	*Et contriverunt eos.*	And they crushed them.
לאה	וַיִּלְאוּ	*Et defessi sunt.*	And they were wearied.
—	וַיַּלְאוּךָ	*Et fatigarunt te.*	And they wearied thee.

ROOTS.	DERIVATIVES.	VERSIO.	SIGNIFICATION.
לבש	וַיַּלְבֵּשׁ	*Et induit.*	And he clothed, arrayed. [self
—	וַיִּלְבַּשׁ	*Et induit se.*	And he put on, clothed him-
—	וַיַּלְבִּשֻׁהוּ	*Et induerunt eum.*	And they clothed him.
—	וַיִּלְבְּשׁוּ	*Et induerunt,*	And they put on.
—	וַיַּלְבִּשׁוּם	*Et induerunt eos.*	And they arrayed them.
—	וַיַּלְבִּשֵׁם	*Et induit eos.*	And he clothed them.
—	וַיַּלְבִּשֵׁנִי	*Et induit me.*	And he clothed me.
ילד	וַיֹּלֶד	*Et peperit.*	And he brought forth.
—	וְלָלֶד	*Et parere.*	And to bring forth.
—	וְיֶלֶד	*Et puer.*	And a boy, child.
—	וְיָלְדָה	*Et peperit.*	And she bare, brought forth.
—	וְיָלְדוּ־יָלֵ״־וַיֵּלֵ״	*Et pepererunt.*	And they bare.
—	וְיַלְדוֹת	*Et puellæ.*	And girls.
—	וְיַלְדֵי	*Et nati.*	And the children.
—	וִילָדֶיהָ	*Et nati ejus.*	And her children.
—	וְיַלְדֵיהֶם	*Et nati eorum.*	And their children.
—	וְיַלְדֵיהֶן	*Et nati earum.*	And their children.
—	וִילָדִים	*Et nati.*	And children.
—	וְיָלַדְתְּ וְיָלַ״	*Et paries.*	And thou shalt bring forth.
—	וְיֹלֶדֶת	*Et parturiens.*	And bearing, bringing forth.
לוה	וְיִלָּווּ	*Et adhærebunt*[*runt*	And they shall cleave to.
לון	וַיַּלִּונוּ	*Et murmurare fece-*	And they caused to murmur.
לחם	וַיִּלָּחֶם	*Et pugnavit.*	And he fought.
—	וַיִּלָּחֲמוּ	*Et pugnarunt.*	And they fought.
—	וַיִּלָּחֲמוּנִי	*Et oppugnarunt me.*	And they fought against me.
לחץ	וַיִּלְחֲצוּ	*Et oppresserunt.*	And they oppressed.
—	וַיִּלְחָצוּם	*Et oppresserunt eos.*	And they oppressed them.
לוט	וַיָּלֶט	*Et involvit.*	And he rolled, wrapped.
ילד	וְיִלִּיד	*Et natus.*	And he that is born.
לון	וַיָּלִינוּ	*Et pernoctarunt, murmurarunt.*	And they tarried all night, they murmured.
—	וַיִּלֹּנוּ	*Et murmurarunt.*	And they murmured.
ילך	וַיֵּלַךְ	*Et abiit.*	And he departed.
—	וַיּוֹלֶךְ וַיֹּלַךְ	*Et adduxit.*	And he brought.
—	וְיֵלֵךְ	*Et ibit.* [*secutus est.*	And he will go. [followed.
—	וַיֵּלֶךְ	*Et ivit, abiit, venit,*	And he went, departed, came,
לכד	וַיִּלָּכֵד	*Et captus est.*	And he was taken.

ROOTS.	DERIVATIVES.	VERSIO.	SIGNIFICATION.
לכד	וַיִּלְכֹּד־־כָּד	*Et cepit.*	And he took.
—	וַיִּלְכְּדָהּ	*Et cepit eam.*	And he took her.
—	וַיִּלְכְּדֻהָ	*Et ceperunt eam.*	And they took her.
—	וַיִּלְכְּדֻהוּ	*Et ceperunt eum.*	And they took him.
—	וַיִּלָּכֵדוּ	*Et capti sunt.*	And they were taken.
—	וַיִּלְכְּדוּ	*Et ceperunt.*	And they took, caught.
—	וְיִלָּכְדוּ	*Et capientur.*	And they shall be taken.
—	וַיִּלְכְּדוּהָ	*Et ceperunt eam.*	And they took her.
ילך	וַיֵּלְכוּ	*Et abierunt.*	And they departed.
—	וְיֵלְכוּ	*Et ibunt.*	And they will go.
—	וַיֵּלְכוּ וַיֵּלֵכוּ	*Et iverunt, abierunt venerunt, secuti sunt, fluxerunt.*	And they went, departed, came, followed, flowed.
—	וַיּוֹלִכוּ	*Et adduxerunt.*	And they brought.
ילל	וִילָלָה וִילְלַת	*Et ejulatus.*	And a howling.
למד	וַיִּלְמַד	*Et didicit.*	And he learned.
—	וִילַמֵּד	*Et docebit.*	And he will teach.
—	וַיְלַמְּדָהּ	*Et docuit eam.*	And he taught her.
—	וַיְלַמְּדֵהוּ	*Et docuit eum.*	And he taught him.
—	וַיְלַמְּדוּ	*Et docuerunt.*	And they taught.
—	וַיִּלְמְדוּ	*Et didicerunt.*	And they learned.
לון	וַיָּלֶן	*Et pernoctavit, murmuravit.*	And he passed the night, he murmured.
—	וַיָּלִנוּ	*Et pernoctarunt.*	And they passed the night.
—	וַיִּלֹּנוּ	*Et murmurarunt.*	And they murmured.
לעג	וַיִּלְעַג	*Et subsannavit.*	And he mocked.
—	וַיַּלְעִגוּ	*Et subsannarunt.*	And they laughed to scorn.
לפת	וַיִּלָּפֵת	*Et inclinavit se.*	And he turned himself.
—	וַיִּלְפֹּת	*Et apprehendit.*	And he took hold of.
ילק	וְיֶלֶק	*Et bruchus.*	And the canker-worm.
לקק	וַיָּלֹקּוּ	*Et linxerunt.*	And they licked.
לקט	וַיְלַקֵּט	*Et collegit.*	And he gathered up.
—	וַיִּלְקְטוּ	*Et collegerunt.*	And they gathered.
ים	וְיָם	*Et mare.*	And the sea.
מאן	וַיְמָאֵן	*Et renuit.*	And he refused.
—	וַיְמָאֲנוּ	*Et renuerunt.*	And they refused.
מאס	וַיִּמָּאֵס	*Et liquefactus est.*	And he was melted.

ROOTS.	DERIVATIVES.	VERSIO.	SIGNIFICATION.
מאס	וַיִּמְאַס	*Et abhorruit, rejecit*	And he abhorred, rejected.
—	וַיִּמְאֲסוּ	*Et spreverunt, rejecerunt.*	And they despised, rejected.
—	וַיִּמְאָסְךָ	*Et rejecit te.*	And he rejected thee.
—	וַיִּמְאָסֵם	*Et rejecit eos.*	And he rejected them.
מדד	וַיָּמָד	*Et mensus est.*	And he measured.
—	וַיָּמָד־־מֹדֶד	*Et mensus est.*	And he measured.
—	וַיְמַדֵּם	*Et mensus est eos.*	And he measured them.
—	וַיָּמֹדּוּ	*Et mensi sunt.*	And they measured.
ים	וָיָמָּה וָיָמָּה	*Et ad mare, ad occidentem.*	And to the sea, to the west.
מהר	וַיְמַהֵר	*Et festinavit.*	And he hastened.
—	וַיְמַהֲרוּ	*Et festinarunt.*	And they hastened.
—	וִימַהֲרוּ	*Et festinabunt.*	And they will hasten.
מות	וַיָּמוּתוּ	*Et mortui sunt.*	And they died.
מחה	וַיִּמַּח	*Et deletus est.*	And he was destroyed.
—	וַיִּמָּחוּ	*Et deleti sunt.*	And they were destroyed.
מטר	וַיַּמְטֵר	*Et pluit.*	And he rained.
—	וְיַמְטֵר	*Et pluet.*	And he shall rain.
יום	וְיָמַי	*Et dies mei.*	And my days.
—	וִימֵי	*Et dies.*	And the days.
—	וְיָמֶיהָ	*Et dies ejus.*	And her days.
ימן	וְיָמִין	*Et auster.*	And the south.
—	וִימִינָהּ	*Et dextera ejus.*	And her right hand.
—	וִימִינוֹ	*Et dextera ejus.*	And his right hand.
—	וִימִינִי	*Et dextera mea.*	And my right hand.
—	וִימִינְךָ־־נֶךָ	*Et dextera tua.*	And thy right hand.
—	וִימִינָם	*Et dextera eorum.*	And their right hand.
מור	וַיָּמִירוּ	*Et mutarunt.*	And they changed.
מות	וַיְמִיתֵהוּ	*Et occidit eum.*	And he slew him.
—	וַיְמִיתֻהוּ	*Et occiderunt eum.*	And they slew him.
—	וַיָּמִיתוּ	*Et occiderunt.*	And they slew.
—	וַיְמִיתוּהָ	*Et occiderunt eam.*	And they slew her.
—	וַיְמִיתֵם	*Et occidit eos.*	And he slew them.
מכך	וַיָּמֹכּוּ	*Et depressi sunt.*	And they were brought down.
מכר	וַיִּמְכֹּר	*Et vendidit.*	And he sold.
—	וַיִּמְכְּרוּ	*Et vendiderunt.*	And they sold.

ROOTS.	DERIVATIVES.	VERSIO.	SIGNIFICATION.
מכר	וַיִּמְכְּרֵם	Et vendidit eos.	And he sold them.
מל	וַיָּמָל	Et circumcidit.	And he circumcised.
נמל	וַיִּמַּל	Et succisus est. [est.	And he was cut down.
מלא	וַיִּמְלָא	Et implevit, repletus	And he fulfilled, he was filled.
——	וַיְמַלֵּא וַיְ	Et complevit.	And he filled, fulfilled.
——	וְיִמָּלֵא	Et implebitur.	And he shall be fulfilled.
——	וַיְמַלְאוּ	Et compleverunt.	And they filled.
——	וַיִּמָּלְאוּ	Et completi sunt.	And they were fulfilled.
——	וְיִמָּלְאוּ	Et implebuntur.	And they shall be filled.
——	וַיְמַלְאוּם	Et impleverunt eos.	And they filled them.
מול	וַיִּמֹּלוּ	Et circumcisi sunt.	And they were circumcised.
מלט	וַיִּמָּלֵט	Et evasit.	And he escaped.
——	וִימַלֵּט	Et eripiet.	And he will deliver.
——	וַיִּמָּלְטוּ	Et evaserunt.	And they escaped.
——	וַיְמַלְּטוּ	Et eripuerunt [eam	And they delivered.
מלך	וַיַּמְלִיכָהּ	Et reginam fecit	And he made her queen.
——	וַיַּמְלִיכֻהוּ	Et regem constitu- erunt eum [erunt	And they made him king.
——	וַיַּמְלִיכוּ	Et regem constitu-	And they made king.
——	וַיַּמְלֵךְ	Et regem constituit.	And he made king.
——	וַיִּמָּלֵךְ	Et consilium cepit.	And he took counsel.
——	וַיִּמְלָךְ־לוֹ	Et regnavit. [eum.	And he reigned.
——	וַיַּמְלִכֻהוּ	Et regem constituit	And he made him king.
——	וַיַּמְלִכוּ	Et regem constitu- erunt.	And they made king.
——	וַיִּמְלְכוּ	Et regnarunt.	And they reigned.
מנה	וַיִּמֶן	Et constituit.	And he appointed.
——	וַיִּמְנוּ	Et numerarunt.	And they numbered.
מנע	וְיִמָּנַע	Et cohibebitur.	And he shall be withholden.
——	וַיִּמָּנְעוּ	Et cohibiti sunt.	And they have been withholden.
——	וְיִמְנָעֶהָ	Et continebit eam.	And he will retain her or it.
מסס	וַיִּמַּס	Et liquefactus est.	And he was melted.
——	וַיִּמַּסּוּ	Et dissoluti sunt.	And they were dissolved.
מסה	וְיִמְסְם	Et liquefaciet eos.	And he will melt them.
מסר	וַיִּמָּסְרוּ	Et traditi sunt.	And they were delivered.
מעט	וַיִּמְעֲטוּ	Et imminuti sunt.	And they are diminished.
מעל	וַיִּמְעַל	Et deliquit.	And he transgressed.

ROOTS.	DERIVATIVES.	VERSIO.	SIGNIFICATION.
מעל	וַיִּמְעֲלוּ	*Et deliquerunt.*	And they transgressed.
מצה	וַיִּמֶץ	*Et expressit.*	And he wrung, strained.
מצא	וַיִּמָּצֵא	*Et inventus est.*	And he was found.
—	וַיִּמְצָא	*Et invenit.*	And he found.
—	וַיִּמְצָאֶהָ	*Et invenit eam.*	And he found her.
—	וַיִּמְצָאֵהוּ	*Et invenit eum.*	And he found him.
—	וַיִּמְצָאֻהוּ	*Et invenerunt eum.*	And they found him.
—	וַיַּמְצִאוּ	*Et obtulerunt.*	And they presented.
—	וַיִּמָּצְאוּ	*Et inventi sunt.*	And they were found.
—	וַיִּמְצְאוּ	*Et invenerunt.*	And they found.
—	וְיִמְצְאוּ	*Et invenient.*	And they shall find.
—	וַיִּמְצָאֵם	*Et invenit eos.*	And he found them.
מרד	וַיִּמְרֹד־־רָד	*Et rebellavit.*	And he rebelled.
—	וַיִּמְרְדוּ	*Et rebellarunt.*	And they rebelled.
מרה	וַיַּמְרוּ	*Et exacerbarunt, rebellarunt.*	And they provoked, rebelled.
מרח	וְיִמְרְחוּ	*Et emplastrum imponent*	And they shall lay on a plaister.
מרר	וַיְמָרֲרֻהוּ	*Et exacerbarunt eum.*	And they provoked him.
—	וַיְמָרֲרוּ	*Et amarum reddiderunt.*	And they made bitter.
משש	וְיָמֵשׁ	*Et palpabit.*	And he will feel.
—	וַיְמֻשֵּׁהוּ	*Et palpavit eum.*	And he felt him.
משח	וַיִּמְשַׁח	*Et unxit.*	And he anointed.
—	וַיִּמְשָׁחֻהוּ	*Et unxerunt eum.*	And they anointed him.
—	וַיִּמְשְׁחוּ	*Et unxerunt.*	And they anointed.
—	וַיִּמְשָׁחֲךָ	*Et unxit te.*	And he anointed thee.
—	וַיִּמְשָׁחֵם	*Et unxit eos.*	And he anointed them.
משך	וַיִּמְשֹׁךְ	*Et protraxit.*	And he drew along.
—	וַיִּמְשְׁכוּ	*Et extraxerunt.*	And they drew out.
משל	וַיִּמְשְׁלוּ	*Et dominati sunt.*	And they ruled.
משש	וַיְמַשֵּׁשׁ	*Et contrectavit.*	And he searched, groped, felt.
מות	וַיָּמָת־מֹת	*Et mortuus est.*	And he died.
—	וַיָּמֶת	*Et occidit.*	And he slew.
—	וְיָמֹת	*Et morietur.*	And he will die.
—	וַיְמִתֵהוּ	*Et occidit eum.*	And he slew him.
—	וַיְמִתֻהוּ	*Et occiderunt eum.*	And they slew him.
—	וַיָּמֻתוּ	*Et mortui sunt.*	And they died.

ROOTS.	DERIVATIVES.	VERSIO.	SIGNIFICATION.
מתח	וַיִּמְתָּחֵם	*Et expandit eos.*	And he spread them abroad.
מות	וַיְמִתֵם	*Et occidit eos.*	And he slew them.
מתק	וַיִּמְתְּקוּ	*Et dulcuerunt.*	And they became sweet.
מות	וַיְמִתְתֵהוּ	*Et occiderunt eum.*	And they slew him.
נאם	וַיִּנְאֲמוּ	*Et dixerunt.*	And they said.
נאף	וַיִּנְאָפוּ וַיִּנְאֲפוּ	*Et adulteri sunt.*	And they committed adultery
נאץ	וַיְנַאֵץ וַיִּנְאָץ	*Et sprevit.*	And he despised.
נרץ	וְיָנֵאץ	*Et florebit.*	And he shall flourish.
נבא	וַיִּנָּבֵא	*Et vaticinatus est.*	And he prophesied.
—	וַיִּנָּבְאוּ	*Et vaticinati sunt.*	And they prophesied.
נבל	וַיְנַבֵּל	*Et despexit.*	And he disregarded.
נגע	וַיְנַגַּע	*Et plagis affecit.*	And he smote, plagued.
—	וַיִּנָּגְעוּ	*Et percussi sunt.*	And they were beaten.
נגף	וַיִּנָּגֶף	*Et percussus est.*	And he was smitten.
—	וַיִּנָּגְפוּ וַיִּנָּגֵפוּ	*Et percussi sunt.*	And they were smitten.
נוד	וַיָּנֻדוּ	*Et condoluerunt.*	And they bemoaned.
נהג	וַיְנַהֵג	*Et adduxit.*	And he brought.
—	וַיִּנְהַג	*Et duxit, adduxit.*	And he led, carried away.
—	וַיְנַהֲגֵהוּ	*Et abduxit eum.*	And he carried him away.
—	וַיִּנְהֲגוּ	*Et abduxerunt.*	And they carried away.
—	וְיִנְהֲגוּ	*Et abducent.*	And they will lead away.
—	וַיְנַהֲגֵם	*Et duxit eos.*	And he guided them.
נהה	וַיִּנָּהוּ	*Et lamentati sunt.*	And they lamented.
נהל	וַיְנַהֲלוּם	*Et deduxerunt eos.*	And they led them.
—	וַיְנַהֲלֵם	*Et deduxit eos.*	And he led them.
נהם	וְיִנְהֹם	*Et rugiet.*	And he shall roar.
נוח	וַיָּנוּחוּ	*Et quieverunt.*	And they rested.
נוס	וַיָּנוּסוּ	*Et fugerunt.*	And they fled.
—	וְיָנוּסוּ	*Et fugient.*	And they will flee.
נוע	וְיָנוּעוּ	*Et vaccillabunt.*	And they will stagger.
נזר	וְיִנָּזֵר	*Et separabit se.*	And he shall separate himself.
—	וַיִּנָּזְרוּ	*Et separarunt se.*	And they separated themselves
—	וְיִנָּזְרוּ	*Et separabunt se.*	And they shall separate themselves.
נוח	וַיָּנַח	*Et quievit, requiem dedit.*	And he rested, gave rest.
ינח	וַיַּנַּח	*Et posuit, reposuit, collocavit, reliquit*	And he laid, laid up, placed, left.

ROOTS.	DERIVATIVES.	VERSIO.	SIGNIFICATION.
ינח	וַיַּנִּחֵהוּ	*Et posuit eum.*	And he laid him, put him.
—	וַיַּנִּחֻהוּ	*Et posuerunt eum.*	And they put him.
—	וַיַּנִּחוּם־־נִּי"	*Et deposuerunt eos.*	And they laid them down.
נחל	וַיִּנְחֲלוּ	*Et possederunt.*	And they possessed.
נחה	וַיַּנְחֵם	*Et duxit eos.*	And he brought them.
נחם	וַיִּנָּחֶם־־יִנָּ־־חֶם	*Et consolatus est.*	And he comforted.
—	וְיִנָּחֵם	*Et pœnitebit ei.*	And he will repent.
—	וַיִּנָּחֲמוּ־־יִנָּ"	*Et pœnituit illis, consolati sunt.*	And they repented, comforted
נחש	וַיְנַחֲשׁוּ	*Et augurati sunt.*	And they used auguries.
נטל	וַיְנַטְּלֵם	*Et sustulit eos.*	And he bare, carried them.
נטש	וַיִּנָּטְשׁוּ	*Et expanderunt se.*	And they spread themselves.
נוא	וַיָּנִיאוּ	*Et fregerunt.*	And they broke.
נוד	וְיָנִיד	*Et movebit, agitabit.*	And he will move, shake.
ינח	וַיַּנִּיחֵהוּ	*Et posuit eum.*	And he laid him.
—	וַיַּנִּיחֻהוּ	*Et posuerunt eum.*	And they put him.
—	וְיַנִּיחֻהוּ	*Et ponent eum.*	And they will set him.
—	וַיַּנִּיחוּ	*Et collocarunt, reposuerunt.*	And they placed, laid up.
—	וְיַנִּיחוּ	*Et ponent.* [*tibi.*	And they will lay.
נוח	וְיָנִיחֶךָ	*Et requiem afferet*	And he will give thee rest.
ינח	וַיַּנִּיחֵם	*Et collocavit eos.*	And he placed them.
נוח	וַיְנִיחֵנִי	*Et me quiescere fecit, collocavit.*	And he made me rest, set me down.
נוף	וַיְנִיפֵהוּ	*Et agitavit eum.*	And he waved him or it.
נכר	וַיְנַכְּרוּ	*Et alienaverunt.*	And they estranged.
נוס	וַיָּנָס־נָס	*Et fugit.*	And he fled.
—	וַיָּנֻסוּ־נִסּוּ	*Et fugerunt.*	And they fled.
—	וְיָנֻסוּ	*Et fugient.*	And they shall flee.
נסה	וַיְנַסּוּ	*Et tentaverunt.*	And they tempted.
נסך	וַיְנַסֵּךְ	*Et effudit.* [*eos.*	And he poured out.
נסה	וַיְנַסֵּם	*Et tentavit, probavit*	And he tried, proved them.
נוע	וַיָּנַע	*Et commotus est.*	And he was moved, shaken.
—	וַיָּנִעוּ	*Et moverunt, agitarunt.*	And they moved, wagged.
—	וַיָּנֻעוּ	*Et commoti sunt.*	And they were moved, shaken
נעל	וַיַּנְעִלוּם	*Et calcearunt eos.*	And they shod them.

ROOTS.	DERIVATIVES.	VERSIO.	SIGNIFICATION.
נוע	וַיְנִעֵם	*Et vagari fecit eos.*	And he made them wander.
נער	וַיְנַעֵר	*Et excussit.*	And he shook off.
—	וְיִנָּעֲרוּ	*Et excutientur.*	And they shall be shaken off.
נוף	וַיָּנֶף	*Et agitavit.*	And he waved.
נפש	וַיִּנָּפֵשׁ־וַיִּנָּפַשׁ	*Et recreatus est.*	And he was refreshed.
—	וְיִנָּפֵשׁ	*Et recreabitur.*	And he shall be refreshed.
נצה	וַיִּנָּצוּ	*Et rixati sunt.*	And they strove, contended.
נצל	וַיְנַצְּלוּ	*Et spoliarunt.*	And they spoiled.
ינק	וַיְנִקֵהוּ	*Et lactavit eum.*	And she suckled him.
—	וְיֹנְקִים	*Et sugentes.*	And those that suck.
נקם	וַיִּנָּקְמוּ	*Et ulti sunt.*	And they took vengeance.
נקר	וַיְנַקְּרוּ	*Et effoderunt.* [runt	And they dug out.
נקש	וַיְנַקְשׁוּ	*Et laqueos tetende-*	And they laid snares.
ינק	וְיָנַקְתְּ	*Et suges.*	And thou shalt suck.
—	וִינַקְתֶּם	*Et sugetis.*	And ye shall suck.
נשא	וַיִּנַּשֵּׂא	*Et exaltatus est.*	And he was exalted.
—	וַיְנַשְּׂאֵהוּ	*Et extulit eum.*	And he advanced him.
—	וַיְנַשְּׂאֵם	*Et portavit eos.*	And he carried them. [bittern
נשף	וְיַנְשׁוּף	*Et ibis, ulula,* vel *bubo*	And the ibis, the owl, or the
נשך	וַיְנַשְּׁכוּ	*Et momorderunt.*	And they bit.
נשל	וַיְנַשֵּׁל	*Et ejecit.*	And he cast out.
נשק	וַיְנַשֵּׁק־שֶּׁק	*Et osculatus est.*	And he kissed.
נתח	וַיְנַתַּח	*Et dissecuit.*	And he cut in pieces.
—	וַיְנַתְּחֶהָ	*Et dissecuit eam.*	And he cut her in pieces.
—	וַיְנַתְּחֵהוּ	*Et dissecuit eum.*	And he cut him in pieces.
—	וִינַתְּחֻהוּ	*Et dissecabunt eum.*	And they shall cut him in pieces.
נתן	וְיִנָּתֵן	*Et dabitur.*	And it shall be given.
—	וַיִּנָּתְנוּ	*Et traditi sunt*	And they were delivered,
—	וְיִנָּתְנוּ	*Et tradentur.*	And they shall be delivered.
נתץ	וַיְנַתֵּץ	*Et diruit.*	And he brake down.
—	וַיְנַתְּצוּ	*Et diruerunt.*	And they brake down.
נתק	וַיְנַתֵּק	*Et rupit.*	And he brake.
—	וַיִּנָּתְקוּ	*Et avulsi sunt.*	And they were broken off.
—	וַיְנַתְּקֵם	*Et rupit eos.*	And he brake them.
סבב	וַיָּסָב	*Et circumivit.*	And he encompassed.

ROOTS.	DERIVATIVES.	VERSIO.	SIGNIFICATION.
סבב	וַיַּסֵּב	*Et circuivit, circumduxit, vertit, transtulit, mutavit.*	And he compassed, led about, turned, removed, changed.
—	וַיִּסֹּב	*Et circuivit, conversus, reversus est.*	And he went about, turned, returned.
—	וַיַּסֵּבּוּ	*Et circumduxerunt, verterunt, averterunt.*	And he carried about, turned, turned away.
—	וַיָּסֹבּוּ	*Et circuierunt, circumduxerunt.*	And they compassed, carried about.
—	וַיְסֻבּוּ	*Et circumdederunt.*	And they compassed.
—	וַיְסִבֵּנִי	*Et circumduxit me.*	And he led me about.
סבר	וְיִסְבֹּר	*Et putabit.*	And he will think.
סגד	וַיִּסְגֹּד	*Et procubuit.*	And he fell prostrate.
—	וְיִסְגֹּד	*Et adorabit.*	And he shall worship.
סוג	וַיִּסֹּגוּ	*Et aversi sunt.*	And they were turned back.
—	וְיִסֹּגוּ	*Et revertentur.*	And they will turn back.
סגר	וְיַסְגִּיר־־יִסְגֹּר	*Et claudet.*	And he will shut.
—	וַיַּסְגֵּר	*Et tradidit.*	And he delivered.
—	וַיִּסְגֹּר	*Et clausit.*	And he shut.
—	וַיִּסָּגְרוּ	*Et clausi sunt.*	And they were shut.
—	וַיִּסְגְּרוּ	*Et clauserunt.*	And they shut.
יסד	וְיֹסֵד	*Et fundans.*	And laying the foundation.
—	וְיִסְּדוּ	*Et fundarunt.*	And they laid the foundation.
—	וִיסֹדֶיהָ	*Et fundamenta ejus.*	And her foundations.
—	וִיסַדְתִּיךְ	*Et fundabo te.*	And I will lay thy foundation.
סבב	וִיסוֹבְבוּ	*Et circumibunt.*	And they shall go round about
יסד	וִיסוֹד	*Et fundamentum.*	And the foundation.
סור	וְיָסוּר	*Et discedet.*	And he will depart.
—	וַיָּסוּרוּ	*Et diverterunt.*	And they turned.
נסח	וְיִסָּחֲךָ	*Et evellet te.*	And he shall pluck thee up.
סחר	וְיִסְחֲרוּ	*Et negotiabuntur.*	And they will trade.
נסך	וַיַּסִּיכוּ	*Et libarunt.*	And they poured out.
יסף	וַיֹּסִיפוּ	*Et addiderunt.*	And they added.
סור	וַיְסִירֵהוּ	*Et amovit eum.*	And he removed him.
—	וַיָּסִירוּ	*Et amoverunt.*	And they removed.
—	וְיָסִירוּ	*Et amovebunt.*	And they shall remove.

ROOTS.	DERIVATIVES.	VERSIO.	SIGNIFICATION.
סות	וַיְסִיתֵהוּ	*Et persuasit ei.*	And he persuaded him.
—	וַיְסִיתֵם	*Et excitavit eos.*	And he excited, moved them.
סוך	וַיָּסֶךְ	*Et unxit.*	And he anointed.
סכך	וַיָּסֶךְ	*Et obtexit, inclusit.*	And he covered, shut in.
נסך	וַיַּסֵּךְ	*Et libavit.*	And he poured.
סכך	וַיָּסֹכּוּ	*Et texerunt.*	And they covered.
סוך	וַיְסֻכוּם	*Et unxerunt eos.*	And they anointed them.
סכר	וַיִּסָּכְרוּ	*Et clausi sunt.*	And they were shut, stopped.
סלל	וַיָּסֹלּוּ	*Et aggerarunt.*	And they raised up.
סלף	וַיְסַלֵּף	*Et pervertit.*	And he perverted.
—	וִיסַלֵּף	*Et evertit.*	And he overthrew.
סמך	וַיִּסָּמֵךְ	*Et innixus est.*	And he was supported.
—	וַיִּסְמֹךְ	*Et imposuit.*	And he supported, laid upon.
—	וַיִּסָּמְכוּ	*Et innixi sunt.*	And they rested.
—	וַיִּסְמְכוּ	*Et imposuerunt.*	And they laid upon.
נסע	וַיַּסַּע	*Et proficisci fecit, transtulit.*	And he made to go forth, transported, removed.
—	וַיִּסַּע	*Et profectus est.*	And he journeyed.
—	וַיַּסִּעוּ	*Et adduxerunt.*	And they brought.
—	וַיִּסְעוּ־־סָעוּ	*Et profecti sunt.*	And they went, journeyed.
—	וְיִסָּעוּ	*Et ibunt.*	And they will go.
—	וַיִּסָּעֵם	*Et profectus est cum [eis.*	And he went away with them
סער	וַיִּסָּעֵר	*Et turbatus est.*	And he was troubled, disturbed
יסף	וְיָסַף־־סָפָה	*Et addet.*	And he, she will add.
ספד	וַיִּסְפְּדוּ	*Et planxerunt.*	And they lamented.
ספן	וַיִּסְפֹּן	*Et texit.*	And he covered.
ספק	וַיִּסְפֹּק	*Et complosit.*	And he smote.
ספר	וַיְסַפֵּר־־פֵּר	*Et narravit.*	And he told.
—	וַיִּסְפֹּר	*Et numeravit.*	And he numbered.
—	וַיְסַפְּרָהּ	*Et enarravit eam.*	And he declared her or it.
—	וַיְסַפְּרוּ	*Et narraverunt.*	And they told.
—	וַיִּסָּפְרוּ	*Et numerati sunt.*	And they were numbered.
—	וִיסַפְּרוּ	*Et narrabunt.*	And they will tell.
—	וַיְסַפְּרוּם ·	*Et narrarunt eos.*	And they told them.
—	וַיִּסְפְּרֵם	*Et numeravit eos.*	And he numbered them.
יסף	וְיָסַפְתָּ	*Et addes.*	And thou shalt add.
—	וְיָסַפְתִּי	*Et addam.*	And I will add.

ROOTS.	DERIVATIVES.	VERSIO.	SIGNIFICATION.
סקל	וַיִּסְקֹל	*Et lapidavit.*	And he stoned. [of it.
—	וַיְסַקְּלֵהוּ	*Et elapidavit eum.*	And he gathered the stones out
—	וַיִּסְקְלֻהוּ	*Et lapidarunt eum.*	And they stoned him.
—	וַיִּסְקְלוּ	*Et lapidarunt.*	And they stoned.
סור	וַיָּסַר	*Et amovit.*	And he removed.
—	וְיָסֵר	*Et amovebit.*	And he will remove.
—	וַיְסִרֶהָ	*Et amovit eam.*	And he removed her.
—	וַיְסִרֵהוּ	*Et amovit eum.*	And he removed him.
—	וַיָּסֻרוּ	*Et diverterunt.*	And they turned aside.
יסר	וְיִסְּרוּ	*Et castigabunt.*	And they shall chastise.
—	וְיִסְרוֹ	*Et erudiet eum.*	And he will instruct him.
סור	וַיְסִרֵם	*Et amovit eos.*	And he removed them.
יסר	וַיְסְּרֵנִי	*Et erudivit me.*	And he instructed me.
—	וְיִסַּרְתִּי	*Et castigabo.*	And I will chastise.
—	וְיִסַּרְתִּיךָ	*Et castigabo te.*	And I will correct, chastise thee.
סות	וַיָּסֶת	*Et excitavit.*	And he exerted, stirred up.
סבל	וְיִסְתַּבֵּל	*Et onerabit se.*	And he shall burden himself.
סתם	וַיִּסְתְּמוּ	*Et obturarunt.*	And they stopped.
—	וַיְסַתְּמוּם	*Et obturarunt eos.*	And they stopped them.
סתר	וַיִּסָּתֵר	*Et abscondit se.*	And he hid himself.
—	וַיַּסְתֵּר	*Et abscondit.*	And he hid.
—	וְיִסָּתֵר	*Et abscondet se.*	And he will hide himself.
—	וְיַסְתֵּר	*Et abscondet.*	And he will hide.
—	וַיִּסָּתְרוּ	*Et absconderunt.*	And they hid.
—	וַיַּסְתִּרֵם	*Et abscondit eos.*	And he hid them.
עבד	וַיַּעֲבֵד	*Et servire fecit.*	And he made to serve.
—	וַיַּעֲבֹד	*Et servivit, coluit.*	And he served.
—	וַיַּעַבְדֻהוּ	*Et servierunt ei.*	And they served him.
—	וַיַּעֲבִדוּ	*Et servire fecerunt.*	And they made to serve.
—	וְיַעַבְדוּ--עָבְדוּ	*Et colent.* [erunt.	And they shall serve.
—	וַיַּעַבְדוּ	*Et coluerunt, servi-*	And they served.
—	וַיַּעַבְדוּם	*Et servierunt eis.*	And they served them.
—	וַיַּעַבְדֵם	*Et colunt eos.*	And he served them.
—	וְיַעַבְדֵנִי	*Et colet me.*	And he shall serve me.
—	וְיַעַבְדֻנִי	*Et colent me.*	And they shall serve me.
עבר	וַיַּעֲבוֹר--בֹר	*Et transiit, præteriit*	And he passed over, passed.
—	וַיַּעֲבִירֻהוּ	*Et transtulerunt eum*	And they brought him over.

ROOTS.	DERIVATIVES.	VERSIO.	SIGNIFICATION.
עבר	וַיַּעֲבִירוּ־־בִרוּ	*Et transire fecerunt*	And they conducted.
—	וְיַֽעֲבִירוּ	*Et transire fecerunt*	And they caused to pass.
—	וְיַעֲבִירוּ	*Et transire facient.*	And they will cause to pass.
—	וַיַּעֲבִירֵם	*Et trajecit eos.*	And he sent, brought them over
—	וַיַּעֲבֶר־־בֵר	*Et transire facient, transmisit.*	And he made to pass over, sent over.
—	וַיַּעֲבֵר	*Et transmisit.*	And he sent over.
—	וְיַעֲבֹר	*Et transibit.*	And he shall pass over.
—	וַיַּעֲבִרֵהוּ	*Et trajecit eum.*	And he brought him over.
—	וַיַּעַבְרוּ	*Et transierunt.*	And they passed over.
—	וַיַּעֲבִרוּ	*Et transire fecerunt*	And they caused to pass.
—	וְיַעֲבֹרוּ	*Et transibunt.*	And they will pass over.
—	וַיַּעֲבִרוּם	*Et transtulerunt eos*	And they carried them over.
—	וַיַּעֲבִרֵם	*Et trajecit eos.*	And he brought them over.
—	וַיַּעֲבִרֵנִי	*Et traduxit me.*	And he brought me through.
עבה	וַיַּעַבְּתוּהָ	*Et complicarunt eam*	And they wrapped her up.
עד	וַיָּעַד	*Et obtestatus est.*	And he protested.
—	וַיְעִדֻהוּ	*Et testati sunt contra eum.*	And they witnessed against him.
—	וִיעִדֻהוּ	*Et testabuntur con-* [*tra eum*	And they will bear witness [against him.
יעה	וְיָעָה	*Et everret.*	And he shall sweep away.
עזב	וַיַּעֲזָב־־זֹב	*Et reliquit.*	And he left.
—	וַיַּעַזְבֻהוּ	*Et dereliquerunt* [*eum.*	And they have forsaken him.
—	וַיַּעַזְבוּ	*Et reliquerunt.*	And they left.
—	וַיַּעַזְבֵנִי	*Et reliquit me.*	And he left me.
—	וַיַּעַזְבֻנִי	*Et dereliquerunt me*	And they have forsaken me.
עזק	וַיְעַזְּקֵהוּ	*Et sepivit eum.*	And he hedged, fenced him.
עזר	וַיַּעְזֹר	*Et auxilium tulit.*	And he succoured.
—	וַיַּעְזְרֵהוּ	*Et adjuvit eum.*	And he helped him.
—	וַיַּעְזְרֻהוּ	*Et adjuverunt eum.*	And they helped him.
—	וַיַּעְזְרוּ	*Et adjuverunt.*	And they helped.
—	וַיֵּעָזְרוּ	*Et adjuti sunt.*	And they were helped.
—	וְיַעְזְרוּנִי	*Et adjuvabunt me.*	And they will help me.
—	וְיַעְזְרֶךָּ	*Et adjuvabit te.*	And he will help thee.
—	וְיַעְזְרֻכֶם	*Et adjuvabunt vos.*	And they will help you.
—	וַיַּעְזְרֵם	*Et adjuvit eos.*	And he helped them.
עט	וַיָּעַט	*Et involavit.*	And he flew.

ROOTS.	DERIVATIVES.	VERSIO.	SIGNIFICATION.
עטה	וַיַּעַט	*Et involvit se.*	And he wrapped, clad himself.
—	וְיַעְטוּ	*Et operient se.*	And they will cover themselves
יעט	וְיָעֲטוּהִי	*Et consiliarii ejus.*	And his counsellors.
יעה	וְיָעָיו	*Et palæ, scopæ ejus.*	And his spades, shovels.
עור	וַיְעִירֵנִי	*Et evigilavit me.*	And he waked me.
עלה	וְיַעַל	*Et ascendet.* [*obtulit*	And he will go up. [offered.
—	וַיַּעַל	*Et ascendit, eduxit,*	And he went up, brought up,
—	וְיַעַל	*Et ascendet, offeret.*	And he will go up, offer up.
—	וַיַּעֲלֶה	*Et ascendit.*	And he came up.
—	וְיַעֲלֶה	*Et discedet.*	And he will go away.
—	וַיַּעֲלֵהוּ־־הָ	*Et obtulit, ascendere fecit eum.*	And he offered him, caused him to come up.
—	וַיַּעֲלֵהוּ־־לוּהוּ	*Et eduxerunt eum.*	And they brought him up.
—	וַיַּעֲלוּ וַיַּעַל	*Et ascenderunt, ascendere fecerunt, obtulerunt.*	And they went up, caused to go up, offered.
—	וַיֵּעָלוּ	*Et recesserunt.*	And they gat up, away.
—	וְיַעֲלוּ	*Et ascendent.*	And they will come up.
עלז	וַיַּעֲלֻז	*Et eduxerunt eum.*	And they brought him up.
עלל	וְיַעַלְלֵחוּ	*Et exultabit.*	And he shall rejoice.
עלה	וַיַּעֲלֵם	*Et eduxit eos.*	And he carried them up.
—	וַיַּעֲלֵנִי	*Et eduxit me.*	And he brought me up.
עלץ	וְיַעַלְצוּ	*Et exultabunt.*	And they shall be joyful.
עלה	וְיַעֲלַת	*Et rupicapra.*	And a wild goat.
עמד	וַיַּעֲמֵד־־מֵד	*Et stare fecit, statuit, constituit* [*desiit*	And he caused to stand, set, settled, appointed. [ceased.
—	וַיַּעֲמֹד־־מוֹד	*Et stetit, constitit,*	And he stood, stood still,
—	וְיַעֲמֹד	*Et stabit.*	And he shall stand.
—	וַיַּעֲמִדֵהוּ	*Et statuit eum.*	And he set him.
—	וַיַּעֲמִדוּ	*Et statuerunt.*	And they set, established.
—	וַיַּעַמְדוּ	*Et steterunt.*	And they stood, stood still.
—	וְיַעַמְדוּ	*Et stabunt.*	And they will stand.
—	וְיַעֲמִיד־־דוּ	*Et statuit.*	And he set up.
—	וַיַּעֲמִידֶהָ	*Et constituit eam.*	And he established her or it.
—	וַיַּעֲמִידוּ	*Et statuerunt.*	And they set, appointed.
—	וַיַּעֲמִידֵם	*Et constituit eos.*	And he made, established them
—	וַיַּעֲמִידֵנִי	*Et statuit me.*	And he set me.

ROOTS.	DERIVATIVES.	VERSIO.	SIGNIFICATION.
עמס	וַיַּעְמֵס	*Et oneravit.*	And he loaded.
ענה	וַיַּעַן	*Et respondit.*	And he answered.
—	וַיַּעֲנֶה	*Et respondit.*	And she answered.
—	וַיְעַנֶּהָ	*Et subegit eam.*	And he humbled her.
—	וַיַּעֲנֵהוּ	*Et respondit ei.*	And he answered him.
—	וַיַּעֲנוּ	*Et responderunt.*	And they answered.
—	וַיְעַנּוּנוּ	*Et afflixerunt nos.*	And they afflicted us.
—	וַיְעַנְּךָ	*Et humiliavit te.*	And he humbled thee.
—	וַיַּעֲנֵם	*Et respondit eis.*	And he answered them.
—	וַיְעַנֵּם	*Et afflixit eos.*	And he afflicted them.
—	וַיְעַנֵּם	*Et affliget eos.*	And he will afflict them.
—	וַיַּעֲנֵנִי	*Et respondit mihi.*	And he answered me.
—	וַיְעַנֵּנִי	*Et afflixit me.*	And he afflicted me.
ענש	וַיַּעֲנֹשׁ	*Et mulctavit.*	And he amerced, fined.
עוף	וַיָּעַף--עָף	*Et volavit.*	And he flew.
—	וַיָּעַף	*Et fessus est.*	And he was weary.
יעף	וַיִּעַף	*Et defetiscetur.*	And he shall faint.
—	וְיָעֲפוּ וְיִעֲפוּ	*Et defetiscentur* [*se*	And they shall faint.
עפל	וַיַּעְפִּלוּ	*Et superbe gessêre*	And they acted proudly.
יעץ	וְיֹעֲצַי	*Et consiliarii.*	And counsellors.
—	וְיֹעֲצָיו	*Et consiliarii ejus.*	And his counsellors.
—	וְיֹעֲצַיִךְ	*Et consiliarii tui.*	And thy counsellors.
עצם	וַיְעַצֵּם	*Et obturavit.*	And he shut, closed.
—	וַיַּעַצְמֵהוּ	*Et roboravit eum.*	And he strengthened him.
—	וַיַּעַצְמוּ	*Et roborati sunt.*	And they were strengthened.
עצר	וַיַּעַצְרֵהוּ	*Et inclusit eum.*	And he shut him up.
עקב	וַיַּעְקְבֵנִי	*Et supplantavit me.*	And he hath supplanted me.
עקד	וַיַּעֲקֹד	*Et ligavit.*	And he bound.
עקר	וַיְעַקֵּר	*Et subnervavit.*	And he houghed, cut the
		[*ostendit.*	nerves or sinews. [verse.
עקש	וַיַּעְקְשֵׁנִי	*Et perversum me*	And he shall prove me per-
עור	וַיָּעַר	*Et excitavit.*	And he stirred up.
—	וְיָעֵר	*Et excitabit.*	And he shall stir up.
ערה	וַיְעָרוּ	*Et evacuarunt.*	And they emptied.
ערך	וַיַּעֲרֹךְ	*Et disposuit.*	And he set in order, in array.
—	וְיַעַרְכֶהָ	*Et disponet eam.*	And he shall set her in order.
—	וַיַּעַרְכוּ	*Et instruxerunt.*	And they put in array.

ROOTS.	DERIVATIVES.	VERSIO.	SIGNIFICATION.
עטה	וַיַּעַשׂ	*Et irruit.*	And he fell upon.
עשה	וַיַּעַשׂ וַיַּ׳	*Et fecit.*	And he made.
—	וְיַעַשׂ	*Et faciet.*	And he will do.
—	וַיַּעֲשֶׂהָ	*Et fecit, paravit eam*	And he did, dressed it.
—	וַיַּעֲשֶׂה	*Et fecit.*	And he did.
—	וְיֵעָשֶׂה	*Et fiet.*	And it shall be done.
—	וַיַּעֲשֵׂהוּ	*Et fecit eum.*	And he made him.
—	וְיַעֲשֵׂהוּ	*Et faciet eum.*	And he will make him.
—	וַיַּעֲשׂוּ	*Et fecerunt.*	And they made, did.
—	וְיַעֲשׂוּ	*Et facient.*	And they shall do.
—	וַיַּעֲשׂוּנִי	*Et fecerunt me.*	And they have made me.
עשר	וַיַּעֲשִׁירוּ	*Et ditati sunt.*	And they were enriched.
עשה	וְיַעֲשֵׂם	*Et transiget eos.*	And he shall spend, pass them
עשן	וְיֶעֶשְׁנוּ	*Et fumabunt.*	And they shall smoke.
עתק	וַיַּעְתֵּק	*Et transtulit.*	And he removed.
—	וְיֶעְתַּק	*Et transferetur.*	And he shall be removed.
עתר	וַיֶּעְתַּר	*Et supplex oravit.*	And he intreated.
—	וַיֵּעָתֵר־תֶר	*Et exoratus est* [cit	And he was intreated.
פוג	וַיָּפָג	*Et singultavit, defe-*	And he gasped, fainted.
פגע	וַיִּפְגַּע	*Et incidit, irruit.*	And he lighted, fell upon.
—	וַיִּפְגְּעוּ	*Et occurrerunt.*	And they met.
פגש	וַיִּפְגְּשֵׁהוּ	*Et occurrit ei.*	And he met him.
—	וַיִּפְגְּשׁוּם	*Et occurrerunt eis.*	And they met them.
פדה	וַיִּפְדּוּ	*Et redemerunt.*	And they delivered, rescued.
—	וַיִּפְדְּךָ	*Et redemit te.*	And he redeemed thee.
יפה	וִיפֵה	*Et pulcher.*	And beautiful.
נפל	וַיִּפּוֹל	*Et cecidit, corruit.*	And he fell, is fallen.
פזז	וַיָּפֹזּוּ	*Et roborati sunt.*	And they were made strong.
נפח	וַיִּפַּח	*Et inflavit.*	And he breathed into.
פוח	וְיָפֵחַ	*Et loquetur.*	And he will speak.
—	וְיָפֵחַ וְיָפִיחַ	*Et efflabit.*	And he will breathe out, utter
—	וִיפֵחַ	*Et efflans.*	And breathing out.
פטר	וַיִּפְטַר	*Et subduxit se.*	And he withdrew himself.
נפל	וַיַּפִּילוּ־פִּלוּ	*Et jecerunt.* [sorte.	And they cast. [lot.
—	וַיַּפִּלֵם	*Et cadere fecit eos*	And he caused them to fall by
פוץ	וַיְפִיצֵם	*Et dispersit eos.*	And he scattered them.
נפל	וַיַּפֵּל	*Et dejecit.*	And he cast down.

ROOTS.	DERIVATIVES.	VERSIO.	SIGNIFICATION.
נפל	וַיִּפֹּל וַיִּפֹּל	*Et cecidit.*	And he fell.
—	וְיִפֹּל	*Et cadet.*	And he shall fall.
פלא	וַיִּפָּלֵא	*Et mirus fuit* [*erunt*	And he was marvellous.
נפל	וַיִּפְּלוּ	*Et ceciderunt, corru-*	And they fell, came to ruin.
פלח	וַיְפַלַּח	*Et dissecuit.*	And he cut asunder.
פלט	וַיְפַלְּטֵם	*Et liberavit eos.*	And he delivered them.
—	וְיַפְלִיט	*Et liberabit.*	And he shall deliver.
פלל	וַיְפַלֵּל	*Et judicavit.*	And he executed judgment.
פנה	וַיֶּפֶן	*Et vertit.*	And he turned.
—	וַיִּפֶן	*Et vertit se, respexit*	And he turned himself, looked
—	וַיִּפְנוּ	*Et verterunt se, re-spexerunt.*	And they turned themselves, looked.
פסח	וַיִּפְסַח	*Et claudus factus est*	And he became lame.
—	וַיְפַסְּחוּ	*Et saltarunt.*	And they leaped.
פסל	וַיִּפְסֹל	*Et dolavit.*	And he hewed.
—	וַיִּפְסְלוּ	*Et dolarunt.* [*sit se.*	And they hewed. [himself.
פוץ	וַיָּפֶץ	*Et dispersit, disper-*	And he scattered, scattered
—	וַיָּפֻצוּ	*Et dispersi sunt.*	And they were scattered.
—	וְיָפֻצוּ	*Et dispergentur.*	And they shall be scattered.
פצל	וַיְפַצֵּל	*Et decorticavit.*	And he peeled.
פוץ	וַיְפַצְפְּצֵנִי	*Et dispersit, confre-git me.*	And he dispersed me, broke me in pieces.
פצר	וַיִּפְצַר	*Et ursit, institit.*	And he urged, pressed.
—	וַיִּפְצְרוּ	*Et instilerunt.*	And they pressed, urged. [out.
פוק	וַיָּפֶק	*Et elicuit, eliciet.*	And he drew out, shall draw
פקד	וַיַּפְקֵד	*Et præfecit.*	And he set over, appointed.
—	וַיִּפָּקֵד	*Et vacavit.*	And he was empty.
—	וַיִּפְקֹד	*Et præfecit, visitavit, numeravit.*	And he appointed, visited, numbered.
—	וְיַפְקֵד	*Et præficiet.*	And he shall appoint.
—	וְיִפְקֹד	*Et visitabit.*	And he shall visit.
—	וַיַּפְקִדֵהוּ	*Et præfecit eum.*	And he made him overseer.
—	וַיַּפְקִדוּ	*Et deposuerunt.*	And they committed, entrusted
—	וַיִּפָּקְדוּ	*Et desiderati sunt, constituti sunt.*	And they were found wanting, they were appointed.
—	וַיִּפְקְדוּ	*Et recensuerunt.*	And they reckoned, numbered
—	וַיִּפְקְדֵם	*Et præfecit eos.*	And he appointed them.

ROOTS.	DERIVATIVES.	VERSIO.	SIGNIFICATION.
פקח	וַיִּפְקַח	*Et aperuit.*	And he opened. [them.
פקד	וַיִּפְקְדֵם	*Et recensuit eos.*	And he reckoned, numbered
פרה	וַיֶּפֶר	*Et crescere fecit.*	And he increased.
פור	וַיָּפֶר	*Et irritum fecit.*	And he made void.
פרד	וַיִּפָּרְדוּ	*Et diviserunt.*	And they parted.
—	וַיִּפָּרְדוּ	*Et separati sunt.*	And they were separated.
פור	וַיָּפֵרוּ	*Et irritum fecerunt*	And they broke, made void.
פרה	וַיִּפְרוּ	*Et creverunt.*	And they grew. [forth.
—	וְיִפְרוּ	*Et edent, proferent.*	And they shall produce, bring
פרח	וְיִפְרְחוּ	*Et florebunt.*	And they shall flourish.
פרה	וְיַפְרְךָ	*Et fœcundabit te.*	And he shall make thee fruitful
פור	וַיְפַרְפְּרֵנִי	*Et confregit me.*	And he broke me in pieces.
פרץ	וַיִּפְרָץ	*Et ursit, institit.*	And he urged, pressed.
—	וַיִּפְרֹץ	*Et diruit, dispersit.*	And he brake down, dispersed
—	וַיִּפְרְצוּ	*Et coegerunt.*	And they compelled.
פרק	וַיִּפְרְקֵנוּ	*Et redemit nos.*	And he redeemed us.
פרש	וַיִּפְרֹשׂ	*Et expandit.*	And he spread them abroad.
—	וְיִפְרֹשׂ	*Et expandet.*	And he will spread out.
—	וַיִּפְרְשֵׂהוּ	*Et expandit eum.*	And he did spread him.
—	וַיִּפְרְשׂוּ	*Et expanderunt.*	And they have spread.
פשח	וַיְפַשְּׁחֵנִי	*Et discerpsit me.*	And he pulled me in pieces.
פשט	וַיַּפְשֵׁט	*Et exuit.*	And he stripped.
—	וַיִּפְשֹׁט	*Et exuit se.*	And he stripped himself.
—	וַיִּפְשְׁטוּ־־שׁי	*Et exuerunt, irruerunt, grassati sunt*	And they stripped, rushed upon, attacked.
—	וַיִּפְשְׁטוּ	*Et eruperunt, irruerunt.*	And they broke forth, sallied out, fell upon.
—	וַיַּפְשִׁיטֻהוּ	*Et exuerunt eum.*	And they stripped him.
פשע	וַיִּפְשַׁע	*Et defecit, rebellavit*	And he revolted, rebelled.
—	וַיִּפְשְׁעוּ	*Et rebellarunt.*	And they rebelled.
פתה	וַיִּפְתְּ	*Et pellectus est.*	And he was deceived.
יפה	וְיָפַת	*Et pulchra.*	And fair, beautiful.
—	וִיפַת	*Et pulchræ.*	And fair.
פתה	וַיְפַתּוּהוּ	*Et pellexerunt eum.*	And they allured, deceived him
פתח	וַיִּפְתַּח	*Et aperuit.*	And he opened. [girded.
—	וַיְפַתַּח	*Et sculpsit, solvit.*	And he engraved, loosed, un-
—	וְיִפְתַּח	*Et aperiet.*	And he shall open.

ROOTS.	DERIVATIVES.	VERSIO.	SIGNIFICATION.
פתח	וַיִּפָּתַח	*Et apertus est.*	And he was opened.
—	וַיְפַתְּחֵהוּ	*Et solvit eum.*	And he loosed him.
—	וַיִּפְתְּחוּ־תְּחוּ	*Et aperuerunt.*	And they opened.
פתר	וַיִּפְתָּר	*Et interpretatus est.*	And he interpreted.
יצא	וַיֵּצֵא	*Et egressus est.*	And he went out, came forth.
—	וַיּוֹצֵא וַיֹּצֵא	*Et eduxit.*	And he brought forth.
—	וְיֵצֵא וְיָצָא	*Et egredietur.*	And he will go forth, come out
—	וְיֹצֵא	*Et egrediens.*	And he that cometh forth.
—	וְיָצְאָה	*Et egredietur, exivit*	And she will go out, came out.
—	וַיּוֹצִאֻהוּ	*Et eduxerunt eum.*	And they brought him out.
—	וַיֹּצְאוּ וַיֵּצְאוּ	*Et egressi sunt.*	And they went out.
—	וַיּוֹצִאוּ	*Et eduxerunt.*	And they brought out.
—	וְיֵצְאוּ וְיָצְאוּ	*Et egredientur.*	And they shall go forth.
—	וְיָצְאוּ	*Et exibunt.*	And they will go out.
—	וְיָצָאנוּ	*Et egrediemur.*	And we will go forth.
—	וְיָצָאתָ־צָאת	*Et egredieris.*	And thou shalt go forth.
—	וְיָצָאתִי	*Et egressus sum.*	And I went out.
—	ויצאתֶם	*Et egrediemini.*	And ye shall go forth.
יצב	וַיַּצֵּב	*Et statuit, erexit.*	And he set up, erected.
—	וַיַּצֶּב	*Et stare fecit.*	And he made to stand.
—	וְיַצֵּב	*Et constituet*[*tarunt*	And he will establish.
צבא	וַיִּצְבְּאוּ	*Et pugnarunt, mili-*	And they fought, warred.
יצב	וַיַּצְּבוּ	*Et statuerunt.*	And they did set up.
צבט	וַיִּצְבָּט	*Et porrexit.* [*geret.*	And he stretched out. [up.
צבר	וַיִּצְבֹּר	*Et congregavit, con-*	And he gathered, shall heap
—	וַיִּצְבְּרוּ	*Et collegerunt.*	And they gathered.
—	וְיִצְבְּרוּ	*Et colligent.*	And they shall gather.
יצג	וַיַּצֵּג	*Et statuit, posuit.*	And he set, put.
—	וַיַּצִּגוּ־צִּיגוּ	*Et statuerunt.*	And they did set.
—	וַיַּצִּגֵם	*Et stitit eos.*	And he presented them.
צדק	וְיִצְדְּקוּ	*Et justificabuntur.*	And they shall be justified.
צהר	וְיִצְהָר	*Et oleum.*	And the oil.
—	וְיִצְהָרְךָ־רֶךָ	*Et oleum tuum.*	And thy oil.
צוה	וַיְצַו־וֶּה־וֶּהוּ	*Et præcepit.*	And he commanded.
—	וַיְצַוּוּ	*Et præceperunt.*	And they commanded. [him.
—	וַיְצַוֵּהוּ	*Et præcepit ei.*	And he charged, commanded
—	ויצוְּךָ	*Et præcepit tibi.*	And he commanded thee.

ROOTS.	DERIVATIVES.	VERSIO.	SIGNIFICATION.
צום	וַיָּצוֹם־צָם	*Et jejunavit.*	And he fasted.
צוה	וַיְצַוֵּם	*Et præcepit eis.*	And he commanded them.
צום	וַיָּצוּמוּ־צֹמוּ	*Et jejunarunt.*	And they fasted.
צוה	וַיְצַוֵּנוּ	*Et præcepit nobis.*	And he commanded us.
יצק	וְיָצוּק	*Et firmus, durus.*	And firm, hard.
צחק	וַיִּצְחַק וַיִּצְחָק	*Et risit.* [*runt.*	And he laughed. [ambassadors
צור	וַיִּצְטַיְּרוּ	*Et legatos se finxe-*	And they feigned themselves
יצא	וַיְצִיאֵנוּ	*Et eduxit nos.*	And he brought us out.
יצב	וְיַצִּיב	*Et verus.*	And true, certain.
—	וְיַצִּיבָא	*Et veritas.*	And the truth.
—	וַיַּצִּיבֵנִי	*Et statuit.*	And he set me.
נצל	וַיַּצִּילֶהָ	*Et eripuit eam.*	And he delivered her.
—	וַיַּצִּילוּהָ	*Et eripuerunt eam.*	And they delivered her.
—	וַיַּצִּילֵנוּ	*Et eripuit nos.*	And he delivered us.
ציץ	וַיָּצִיצוּ	*Et floruerunt.*	And they flourished.
—	וְיָצִיצוּ	*Et florebunt.*	And they shall flourish.
יצת	וַיַּצִּיתוּ	*Et accenderunt.*	And they set on fire.
נצל	וַיַּצֵּל	*Et eripuit.*	And he delivered.
—	וְיַצֵּל	*Et eripiet.*	And he will deliver.
—	וַיַּצִּלֵהוּ	*Et eripuit eum.*	And he delivered him.
צלח	וַיִּצְלַח	*Et prosperatus est.*	And he prospered.
—	וַיַּצְלִיחוּ	*Et prosperati sunt.*	And they prospered.
—	וְיַצְלִיחוּ	*Et prosperabuntur.*	And they shall prosper.
נצל	וַיַּצִּלֵם	*Et eripuit eos.*	And he delivered them.
—	וַיַּצִּלֵנִי	*Et eripuit me.*	And he delivered me.
—	וְיַצִּלֵנִי	*Et liberabit me.*	And he will deliver me.
צמא	וַיִּצְמָא	*Et sitivit.*	And he thirsted.
—	וַיִּצְמְאוּ	*Et sitiverunt.*	And they thirsted.
צמד	וַיִּצָּמֶד	*Et adjunxit se.*	And he joined himself.
—	וַיִּצָּמְדוּ	*Et adjunxerunt se.*	And they joined themselves.
צמח	וַיַּצְמַח	*Et germinare fecit.*	And he made to spring up, grow
—	וַיִּצְמַח	*Et germinavit.*	And he or it grew. [ther.
צעק	וַיַּצְעֵק	*Et convocavit.*	And he called, gathered toge-
—	וַיִּצָּעֵק	*Et convocatus est.*	And he was called together.
—	וַיִּצְעַק	*Et clamavit.*	And he cried, called upon.
—	וַיִּצָּעֲקוּ	*Et convocati sunt.*	And they were called together
—	וַיִּצְעֲקוּ	*Et clamarunt.*	And they cried, called.

ROOTS.	DERIVATIVES.	VERSIO.	SIGNIFICATION.
צער	וְיִצְעֲרוּ	*Et diminuentur, deprimentur.*	And they will be diminished, brought low.
צוף	וַיָּצֶף	*Et natare fecit.*	And he caused to swim.
צפה	וַיְצַף	*Et texit, obduxit.*	And he covered, overlaid.
——	וַיְצַפֵּהוּ	*Et obduxit eum.*	And he overlaid him or it.
——	וַיְצַפּוּ	*Et obduxerunt.*	And they overlaid.
——	וַיְצַפֵּם	*Et obduxit eos.*	And he overlaid them.
צפר	וְיִצְפֹּר	*Et mane discedet.*	And he shall depart early.
ציץ	וַיָּצֵץ	*Et floruit.*	And he flourished, bloomed.
יצק	וַיִּצֶק	*Et effluxit.*	And he or it flowed, ran out.
——	וַיִּצֹק	*Et fudit, conflavit.*	And he poured, cast, melted.
——	וְיָצַק	*Et fundet.*	And he will pour.
——	וַיַּצִּקוּ	*Et statuerunt.*	And they sat down.
——	וַיִּצְקוּ	*Et fuderunt.*	And they poured.
——	וְיִצְקוּ	*Et fundite.*	And pour ye.
——	וַיַּצִּקֻם	*Et deposuerunt eos.*	And they laid them down.
——	וְיָצַקְתָּ־קְתְּ	*Et fundes, effundes.*	And thou shalt pour, pour out
צור	וַיָּצַר	*Et formavit, conflavit, obsedit, ligavit*	And he fashioned, cast, besieged, bound.
——	וַיָּצֶר	*Et anxit.*	And he distressed.
יצר	וַיִּיצֶר	*Et formavit.*	And he formed. [imagination
——	וְיֵצֶר	*Et figmentum.*	And the thing formed, the
——	וְיֹצֵר	*Et formans.*	And he that formeth.
——	וְיֹצְרָהּ	*Et formator ejus.*	And her former.
צור	וַיָּצֵרוּ	*Et anxerunt.*	And they straitened, distressed
——	וַיָּצֻרוּ	*Et obsiderunt.*	And they besieged.
יצר	וִיצֻרַי	*Et membra mea.*	And my members.
——	וְיֹצֶרְךָ	*Et formans te.*	And he that formed thee.
צרף	וְיִצָּרְפוּ	*Et expurgabuntur.*	And they shall be tried, refined
יצר	וִיצַרְתִּיהָ	*Et formavi eam.*	And I have formed her.
יצת	וַיַּצֵּת	*Et accendit.*	And he kindled.
קוא	וַיָּקֵא	*Et evomuit.*	And he vomited out.
——	וַיְקִאֶנּוּ	*Et evomet eum.*	And he shall vomit it up again
יקב	וָיֶקֶב	*Et torcular.*	And the wine-press.
נקב	וַיִּקֹּב	*Et perforavit.*	And he bored.
קבל	וַיְקַבְּלוּ	*Et acceperunt.*	And they took, received.
——	וִיקַבְּלוּן	*Et suscipient.*	And they shall take.

ROOTS.	DERIVATIVES.	VERSIO.	SIGNIFICATION.
קבל	וַיְקַבְּלֵם	*Et accepit eos.*	And he received them.
קבץ	וַיִּקְבֹּץ	*Et collegit.*	And he gathered, assembled.
—	וַיִּקָּבְצוּ	*Et congregati sunt.*	And they were assembled.
—	וַיִּקְבְּצוּ	*Et collegerunt.*	And they gathered. [together.
—	וְיִקָּבְצוּ	*Et congregabuntur.*	And they will be gathered
—	וְיִקְבְּצוּ	*Et colligent.*	And they shall gather together
—	וַיְקַבְּצֵם	*Et congregavit eos.*	And he assembled them.
קבר	וַיִּקָּבֵר	*Et sepultus est.*	And he was buried.
—	וַיִּקְבֹּר	*Et sepelivit.*	And he buried.
—	וַיִּקְבְּרֻהוּ	*Et sepelierunt eum.*	And they buried him.
—	וַיִּקְבְּרוּ	*Et sepelierunt.*	And they buried.
קדד	וַיִּקֹּד	*Et inclinavit se.*	And he bowed himself down.
—	וַיִּקְּדוּ	*Et inclinarunt se.*	And they bowed down.
קדש	וַיִּקָּדֵשׁ	*Et sanctificatus est.*	And he was sanctified.
—	וַיְקַדֵּשׁ	*Et sanctificavit.*	And he sanctified.
—	וַיְקַדְּשֵׁהוּ	*Et sanctificavit eum*	And he sanctified him.
—	וַיְקַדְּשׁוּ וַיְקַד״	*Et sanctificarunt.*	And they sanctified.
—	וַיִּקְדְּשׁוּ	*Et sanctificati sunt.*	And they were sanctified.
—	וַיְקַדְּשֵׁם	*Et sanctificavit eos.*	And he sanctified them.
קהל	וְיַקְהִיל	*Et congregabit.*	And he will gather together.
—	וַיַּקְהֵל	*Et congregavit.*	And he gathered together.
—	וַיִּקָּהֵל	*Et congregatus est.*	And he was gathered.
—	וַיַּקְהִלוּ	*Et congregarunt.*	And they gathered. [gether.
—	וַיִּקָּהֲלוּ	*Et congregati sunt.*	And they were gathered to-
קוה	וַיְקַו	*Et expectavit.*	And he waited, looked for.
קום	וְיָקוּם	*Et surget.*	And he will rise.
—	וַיָּקוּמוּ	*Et surrexerunt.*	And they rose.
קון	וַיְקוֹנֵן	*Et lamentatus est.*	And he lamented.
לקח	וַיִּקַּח־־קַּח	*Et cepit.*	And he took.
—	וְיִקַּח	*Et capiet.*	And he will take.
—	וַיִּקָּחֶהָ	*Et cepit eam.*	And he took her.
—	וְיִקָּחֶהָ	*Et capiet eam.*	And he shall take her.
—	וַיִּקָּחֵהוּ	*Et cepit eum.*	And he took him.
—	וַיִּקָּחֻהוּ	*Et ceperunt eum.*	And they took him.
—	וַיִּקְחוּ	*Et ceperunt.*	And they took.
—	וְיִקְחוּ	*Et capient.*	And they shall take.
—	וַיִּקָּחוּם	*Et ceperunt eos.*	And they took them.

ROOTS.	DERIVATIVES.	VERSIO.	SIGNIFICATION.
לקח	וַיִּקָּחֵם	*Et cepit eos.*	And he took them.
—	וַיִּקָּחֵנִי	*Et cepit me.*	And he took me.
קטר	וַיְקַטְּירוּ--טְּרוּ	*Et adoleverunt.*	And they burned incense.
—	וַיְקַטֵּר--יַקְטֵּר	*Et adolevit.*	And he burned incense.
—	וַיְקַטֵּר	*Et adolebit.*	And he shall burn incense.
קום	וַיְקִימֶהָ	*Et erexit eam.*	And they set it up.
—	וַיְקִימוּ	*Et erexerunt.*	And they raised, set up.
—	וַיְקִימֵנִי	*Et erexit me.*	And they set me up.
יקע	וַיֹּקִיעֻם	*Et suspenderunt eos.*	And they hanged them up.
יקר	וַיִּקִירָא	*Et inclytus.*	And noble, famous.
קהל	וַיִּקָּלְהוּ	*Et congregati sunt.*	And they were gathered together.
קלל	וַיְקַלֵּל	*Et maledixit.*	And he cursed.
—	וַיְקַלֵּל	*Et maledicet.*	And he will curse.
—	וַיְקַלְלוּ	*Et maledixerunt.*	And they cursed.
—	וַיְקַלְלֵם	*Et maledixit eis.*	And he cursed them.
קלע	וַיְקַלַּע	*Et funda jecit.*	And he slang, threw with a sling
קום	וַיָּקָם	*Et surrexit.*	And he rose.
—	וַיָּקֹם	*Et surget.*	And he shall rise.
—	וַיָּקֶם	*Et erexit, excitavit, præstitit, statuit.*	And he reared up, raised up, performed, established.
—	וַיָּקֻמוּ	*Et surrexerunt.*	And they rose.
—	וַיָּקֻמוּ	*Et surgent.*	And they will rise.
קנה	וַיִּקֶן	*Et emit.*	And he bought.
קנא	וַיְקַנֵּא	*Et invidit.*	And he envied.
—	וַיְקַנְאֻהוּ	*Et inviderunt ei.*	And they envied him.
—	וַיְקַנְּאוּ	*Et inviderunt.*	And they envied.
קנה	וַיִּקְנֵהוּ	*Et emit eum.*	And he bought him.
קון	וַיְקֹנֵן	*Et lamentatus est.*	And he lamented.
קסם	וַיִּקְסְמוּ	*Et divinarunt.*	And they used divination.
יקף	וַיַּקֵּף	*Et circumdedit.*	And he encompassed.
—	וַיַּקִּפוּ	*Et circumdederunt.*	And they compassed about.
קוץ	וַיָּקָץ	*Et tæduit eum, fastidivit.*	And he was weary of, disgusted with, abhorred.
יקץ	וַיִּקַץ	*Et evigilavit.*	And he awoke.
—	וַיִּקַץ	*Et evigilabit.*	And he shall awake.
קצב	וַיִּקְצָב	*Et succidit.*	And he cut down.
יקץ	וַיִּקְצוּ	*Et evigilabunt.*	And they shall awake.

ROOTS.	DERIVATIVES.	VERSIO.	SIGNIFICATION.
קוץ	וַיָּקֻצוּ	*Et tædio, fastidio affecti sunt.*	And they were wearied, grieved, disgusted.
קצף	וַיַּקְצִיפוּ	*Et irritaverunt.*	And they provoked, angered.
—	וַיִּקְצֹף	*Et iratus est.*	And he was wroth.
—	וַיִּקְצְפוּ	*Et irati sunt.*	And they were wroth.
קצץ	וַיְקַצֵּץ	*Et abscidit.*	And he cut off.
—	וַיְקַצְּצוּ	*Et absciderunt.*	And they cut off.
קרה	וַיִּקֶר	*Et contigit.*	And it happened.
—	וַיִּקֶר	*Et occurrit.*	And he met.
יקר	וַיֵּקַר	*Et pretiosus erit.*	And he shall be precious.
—	וִיקָר	*Et honor.*	And honour.
קרה	וַיִּקָּרֵא	*Et contigit.*	And it came to pass.
קרא	וַיִּקָּרֵא	*Et vocatus.*	And called.
—	וַיִּקְרָא	*Et vocavit, accersivit, clamavit, promulgavit, legit.*	And he called, invited, cried, proclaimed, read.
—	וַיִּקָּרֵא	*Et vocabitur.*	And he shall be called.
יקר	וִיקָרָא	*Et gloria.*	And glory.
קרא	וַיִּקְרָאֶהָ	*Et vocavit, legit eam*	And he called her, read it.
—	וַיִּקְרָאֵהוּ	*Et legit eum.*	And he read him or it.
—	וַיִּקָּרְאוּ	*Et vocati sunt.*	And they were called.
—	וַיִּקְרְאוּ	*Et proclamarunt.*	And they proclaimed.
—	וַיִּקְרְאוּ	*Et vocarunt, accersiverunt, clamarunt, promulgarunt, legerunt.*	And they called, invited, cried, published, proclaimed, read
—	וַיִּקְרְאוּ	*Et clamabunt.*	And they will cry.
—	וַיִּקְרָאֵם	*Et legit eos.*	And he read them.
קרב	וַיַּקְרֵב	*Et adduxit, obtulit.*	And he brought offered.
—	וַיִּקְרַב	*Et accessit.*	And he drew near.
—	וַיַּקְרִבוּ־רִיבוּ	*Et adduxerunt, obtulerunt*	And they brought, offered.
—	וַיִּקְרְבוּ	*Et accesserunt.*	And they drew near.
יקר	וִיקָרָה	*Et gloria.*	And glory.
קרם	וַיִּקְרַם	*Et texit.*	And he covered.
קרע	וַיִּקָּרַע	*Et scissus est.*	And he was rent.
—	וַיִּקְרַע	*Et laceravit.*	And he tore, rent.
—	וַיִּקְרָעֶהָ	*Et discidit eam.*	And he rent her or it.

ROOTS.	DERIVATIVES.	VERSIO.	SIGNIFICATION.
קרע	וַיִּקְרְעוּ	*Et lacerarunt.*	And they rent.
—	וַיִּקְרָעֵם	*Et laceravit eos.*	And he rent them.
קשה	וַיֶּקֶשׁ	*Et obduravit.* [*fuit.*	And he stiffened, hardened.
—	וַיִּקֶשׁ	*Et durior, sævior*	And he was harder, fiercer.
קשב	וַיַּקְשֵׁב	*Et auscultavit.*	And he hearkened.
קשה	וַיַּקְשׁוּ	*Et obdurarunt.*	And they hardened.
קשר	וַיִּקְשָׁר וַיִּקְשֹׁר	*Et conspiravit.*	And he conspired.
—	וַיִּקְשְׁרוּ	*Et conspirarunt* [*tii*	And they conspired.
ראה	וַיַּרְא	*Et vidit, animadver-*	And he saw, looked, regarded
ירא	וַיִּרָא	*Et timuit.*	And he was afraid.
ראה	וַיַּרְא־־אֶה	*Et vidit.* [*est.*	And he saw.
—	וַיֵּרָא	*Et apparuit, visus*	And he appeared, was seen.
ירא	וְיִרֵא	*Et timebit.*	And he will be afraid.
ראה	וְיֵרָא	*Et apparebit.*	And he shall appear.
—	וְיִרְא	*Et videbit.*	And he shall see.
ירא	וְיָרֵא	*Et timens.*	And he that feareth.
ראה	וַיִּרְאֶהָ	*Et vidit eam.*	And he saw her.
ירא	וְיִרְאָה	*Et timor, terror.*	And fear, terror.
ראה	וְיִרְאֶה	*Et videbit.*	And he will see.
—	וַיַּרְאֵהוּ	*Et ostendit illi.*	And he shewed to him.
—	וַיִּרְאֵהוּ	*Et vidit illum.*	And he saw him.
—	וַיִּרְאֻהוּ	*Et viderunt eum.*	And they saw him.
—	וַיֵּרָאוּ	*Et apparuerunt.*	And they appeared.
—	וַיִּרְאוּ	*Et vidēre, ostendēre*	And they saw, shewed.
ירה	וַיֹּרְאוּ	*Et jaculati sunt.*	And they shot, hurled.
ירא	וַיִּרְאוּ	*Et timuerunt.*	And they feared.
—	וְיִרְאוּ־־און	*Et timebunt.*	And they shall be afraid.
—	וְיִרְאוּ־־וְיָרְאוּ	*Et timebunt.*	And they will fear.
ראה	וְיִרְאוּ	*Et videbunt.*	And they shall see.
—	וְיֵרָאוּ	*Et videbuntur.*	And they shall be seen.
—	וַיַּרְאוּם	*Et ostenderunt eis.*	And they shewed to them.
—	וַיַּרְאֵם	*Et ostendit eis.*	And he shewed to them.
—	וַיִּרְאֵם	*Et vidit eos.*	And he saw them.
—	וַיַּרְאֵנִי	*Et ostendit mihi.*	And he shewed to me.
—	וַיִּרְאֵנִי	*Et vidit me.*	And he saw me.
ירא	וְיָרֵאתָ	*Et timebis.*	And thou shalt fear.
—	וְיִרְאַת	*Et timor.*	And fear.

ROOTS.	DERIVATIVES.	VERSIO.	SIGNIFICATION.
ירא	וְיִרְאָתְךָ	*Et timor tui.*	And the fear of thee.
ריב	וַיָּרֶב	*Et contendit* [*ausit.*	And he contended, strove.
רבה	וַיֶּרֶב	*Et multiplicavit,*	And he multiplied, increased.
—	וַיִּרֶב	*Et multiplicatus est.*	And he was multiplied.
ריב	וְיָרֵב	*Et rixabitur.*	And he will contend.
רבה	וְיַרֵב	*Et multiplicabit.*	And he will multiply.
—	וַיִּרְבּוּ	*Et multiplicati sunt.*	And they were multiplied.
—	וְיִרְבּוּ	*Et multiplicabuntur*	And they shall be multiplied.
—	וְיַרְבֶּךָ	*Et multiplicabit te.*	And he will multiply thee.
רגז	וַיִּרְגַּז	*Et commotus est.*	And he was much moved.
—	וַיִּרְגְּזוּ	*Et commoti sunt.*	Andthey were moved, trembled
רגל	וַיְרַגֵּל	*Et calumniatus est.*	And he slandered.
—	וַיְרַגְּלוּ	*Et explorarunt.*	And they searched.
רגם	וַיִּרְגְּמֻהוּ	*Et lapidarunt eum.*	And they stoned him.
—	וַיִּרְגְּמוּ	*Et lapidarunt.*	And they stoned.
רגן	וַיֵּרָגְנוּ	*Et murmurarunt.*	And they murmured.
ירד	וַיָּרֶד	*Et obduxit.*	And he spread, overlaid.
—	וַיֵּרֶד וַיֵּרַד	*Et descendit.*	And he went down, came down
—	וְיֵרֵד וְיֵרַד	*Et descendet.*	And he will come down.
רדה	וְיֵרְדְּ	*Et dominabitur.*	And he shall have dominion.
—	וַיִּרְדֵּהוּ	*Et deduxit eum.*	And he brought him down.
ירד	וַיֹּרִדֻהוּ	*Et deduxerunt eum.*	And they brought him down.
—	וַיֵּרְדוּ	*Et descenderunt.*	And they went down.
רדה	וַיִּרְדּוּ	*Et dominati sunt, dominabuntur.*	And they had dominion, shall have dominion.
ירד	וְיֵרְדוּ	*Et descendent.*	And they will go down.
רדה	וְיִרְדּוּ	*Et dominabuntur.*	And they shall have dominion
ירד	וְיֹרְדִים	*Et descendentes.*	And descending.
רדם	וַיֵּרָדַם	*Et soporatus fuit.*	And he was fast asleep.
רדה	וַיִּרְדֶּנָּה	*Et domuit eum.*	And it prevailed over him.
ירד	וְיָרַדְנוּ	*Et descendemus.*	And we will go down.
רדף	וַיִּרְדֹּף	*Et persecutus est.*	And he followed, pursued.
—	וַיִּרְדְּפֵהוּ	*Et secutus est eum.*	And he pursued him.
—	וַיִּרְדְּפוּ	*Et persecuti sunt.*	And they pursued, chased.
—	וַיִּרְדְּפוּם	*Et persecuti sunt eos*	And they chased them.
—	וַיִּרְדְּפֵם	*Et persecutus est eos*	And he pursued, chased them.
ירד	וְיָרַדְתָּ־־תִּי	*Et descendes.*	And thou shalt go down.

ROOTS.	DERIVATIVES.	VERSIO.	SIGNIFICATION.
ירד	וְיֹרֶדֶת	*Et descendens.*	And she that cometh down.
—	וְיָרַדְתִּי	*Et descendam.*	And I will go down.
ירה	וַיֹּרוּ	*Et jaculati sunt.*	And they shot, hurled.
רוח	וְיִרְוַח	*Et respiratio erit.*	And there will be breathing, respite, refreshment.
רום	וְיָרוּם	*Et extolletur.*	And he shall be exalted.
רמם	וַיֵּרוֹמּוּ	*Et elati sunt.*	And they were lifted up.
רום	וירוֹמְמוּהוּ	*Et extollent eum.*	And they shall exalt him.
—	וירוֹמִמְךָ	*Et extollet te.*	And he will exalt thee.
רוץ	וַיָּרוּצוּ	*Et cucurrerunt.*	And they ran.
ריח	וַיָּרַח	*Et odoratus est.*	And he smelled.
ירח	וְיָרֵחַ	*Et luna..*	And the moon.
רחב	וַיַּרְחִיבוּ	*Et dilatarunt.*	And they enlarged.
ירח	וִירֵחֵךְ	*Et luna tua.*	And thy moon.
רחם	וִירַחֲמֵהוּ	*Et miserebitur ejus.*	And he will have mercy upon him.
—	וַיְרַחֲמֵם	*Et misertus est eorum.*	And he had compassion on them.
רחץ	וַיִּרְחַץ	*Et lavit, abluit se.*	And he washed, bathed himself.
—	וַיִּרְחֲצוּ	*Et laverunt.*	And they washed.
ריב	וַיָּרִיבוּ	*Et contenderunt.*	And they contended.
—	וַיְרִיבוּן	*Et objurgarunt.*	And they did chide.
ירד	וַיֹּרִידוּ	*Et deduxerunt.*	And they brought down.
—	ויוֹרִידוּם	*Et deduxerunt eos.*	And they took them down.
רום	וַיְרִימֶהָ	*Et erexit eam.*	And they set her up.
רוע	וַיָּרִיעוּ־רֵעַ	*Et clanxerunt.*	And they shouted.
ירע	וִירִיעוֹת	*Et cortinæ.*	And the curtains.
רוץ	וַיָּרִיצוּ	*Et celeriter distribuerunt.*	And they speedily distributed.
ירה	וְיָרִיתִי	*Et jaculabor.*	And I will shout.
רכב	וַיַּרְכֵּב	*Et equitare fecit.*	And he made to ride.
—	וַיִּרְכַּב	*Et equitavit.*	And he rode.
—	וַיַּרְכִּבֻהוּ־כִּי	*Et vexerunt, equitare fecerunt eum.*	And they carried him, made him ride.
—	וַיַּרְכִּבוּ־כִּי	*Et vexerunt, equitare fecerunt.*	And they carried, caused to ride.
—	וַיִּרְכְּבוּ	*Et equitarunt.*	And they rode.
—	וַיַּרְכִּבֵם	*Et equitare fecit eos*	And he made them ride.
—	וַיַּרְכִּיבֻהוּ	*Et equitare fecit eum*	And he made him ride.

ROOTS.	DERIVATIVES.	VERSIO.	SIGNIFICATION.
רכס	וַיִּרְכְּסוּ	Et strinxerunt.	And they bound, tied fast.
—	וְיִרְכְּסוּ	Et stringent.	And they shall bind.
ירך	וַיַּרְכָתָהּ	Et femur ejus.	And his thigh.
—	וְיַרְכָּתוֹ	Et latus ejus.	And his side, coast, border
רום	וַיָּרָם	Et elatus est.	And he was exalted.
—	וַיָּרֶם	Et sustulit, extulit.	And he took up, exalted.
רמם	וַיָּרֻם	Et vermiculatus est.	And he or it bred worms.
רום	וְיָרֻם וְיָרֹם	Et extolletur. [eos.	And he shall be exalted.
ירה	וַיֹּרֵם	Et jaculatus est in	And he shot at them.
—	וְיֹרֵם	Et docebit eos.	And he will teach them.
רום	וְיָרֵם	Et tollet, extollet.	And he shall take up, exalt.
רמם	וַיֵּרֹמּוּ	Et elati sunt.	And they were lifted up.
רמס	וְיִרְמֹס	Et conculcabit.	And he shall tread down.
—	וַיִּרְמְסֵהוּ	Et conculcavit eum.	And he trampled on him.
—	וַיִּרְמְסֻהוּ	Et conculcarunt eum	And they trod upon him.
—	וַיִּרְמְסוּ	Et conculcarunt.	And they trod, trampled.
—	וַיִּרְמְסֶנָּה	Et conculcavit eam.	And they trampled on her.
רנן	וַיָּרֹנּוּ	Et læti acclamarunt	And they shouted for joy.
ירה	וַיֹּרֵנִי	Et docuit me.	And he taught me.
רנן	וִירַנְּנוּ	Et læti acclamabunt	And they shall shout for joy.
רוע	וַיָּרַע	Et male fecit, clanxit	And he did evil, shouted.
ירע	וַיֵּרַע	Et displicuit, piguit.	And it displeased, grieved [ger
רעב	וַיַּרְעִבֶךָ	Et esurire fecit te.	And he suffered thee to hun-
רוע	וַיָּרֵעוּ	Et malefecerunt.	And they vexed, ill-treated.
—	וַיָּרִיעוּ	Et clanxerunt.	And they shouted.
רעה	וַיִּרְעוּ	Et paverunt.	And they fed.
רעם	וַיַּרְעֵם	Et tonuit.	And he thundered.
רעה	וַיִּרְעֵם וַיִּרְעֵם	Et pavit eos.	And he fed them.
רעץ	וַיִּרְעֲצוּ	Et confregerunt.	And they broke to pieces.
רעש	וַיִּרְעֲשׁוּ	Et contremuerunt.	And they shook, trembled.
—	וְיִרְעֲשׁוּ	Et contremiscent.	And they will shake, tremble.
רפה	וַיֶּרֶף	Et remisit.	And he let go.
רפא	וַיְרַפֵּא	Et instauravit.	And he repaired.
—	וַיִּרְפָּא	Et sanavit.	And he healed.
—	וַיִּרְפְּאוּ	Et sanarunt.	And they healed.
—	וְיֵרָפְאוּ	Et sanabuntur.	And they shall be healed.
—	וְיִרְפָּאֵם	Et sanabit eos.	And he will heal them.

ROOTS.	DERIVATIVES.	VERSIO.	SIGNIFICATION.
רפא	וְיִרְפָּאֵנוּ	*Et sanabit nos.*	And he will heal us.
—	וַיֵּרָפוּ	*Et sanati sunt.*	And they were healed [feebled
רפה	וַיִּרְפּוּ	*Et remissi sunt.*	And they were loosened, en-
רוץ	וַיָּרָץ וַיָּרֹץ	*Et cucurrit. [eum,*	And he ran [vourable to him.
רצה	וְיִרְצֵהוּ	*Et acceptum habebit*	And he will accept or be fa-
רוץ	וַיְרִצֻהוּ	*Et celeriter addux-erunt eum.*	And they brought him quickly
—	וַיָּרֻצוּ	*Et cucurrerunt.*	And they ran.
רצץ	וַיְרַצֵּץ	*Et contrivit.*	And he oppressed, crushed.
—	וַיְרֹצְצוּ	*Et contriverunt.*	And they crushed.
ריק	וַיָּרֶק	*Et evaginare fecit, armavit.*	And he caused to draw *the sword,* he armed.
ירק	וְיֶרֶק	*Et viriditas.*	And verdure, green.
—	וְיָרְקָה	*Et spuet.*	And she shall spit.
—	וְיֵרָקוֹן	*Et rubigo.*	And mildew.
רקד	וַיַּרְקִידֵם	*Et exilire faciet eos.*	And he will make them leap.
רקע	וַיְרַקְּעוּ	*Et expanderunt, procuderunt.*	And they spread out, beat out.
—	וַיְרַקְּעוּם	*Et expanderunt eos.*	And they spread out.
ירש	וְיִירַשׁ וְיָרַשׁ	*Et possidebit.*	And he shall possess.
—	וַיִּרְשׁוּ	*Et possederunt.*	And they possessed.
—	וְיָרְשׁוּ וְיִרְ׳	*Et possidebunt.*	And they shall possess.
—	וַיִּרָשׁוּהָ	*Et possederunt eam.*	And they possessed her.
—	וִירֵשׁוּהָ	*Et possidebunt eam.*	And they shall possess her.
—	וִירֵשׁוּךָ	*Et possidebunt te.*	And they shall possess thee.
רשע	וַיַּרְשִׁיעוּ	*Et condemnarunt.*	And they condemned.
ירש	וַיֹּרִשֵׁם	*Et expulit eos.*	And he cast them out.
—	וְיָרַשְׁנוּ	*Et possidebimus.*	And we shall possess.
—	וִירַשְׁנוּהָ	*Et possidebimus eam*	And we shall possess her.
—	וְיָרַשְׁתָּ	*Et possidebis.*	And thou shalt possess.
—	וִירִשְׁתָּהּ	*Et possidebis eam.*	And thou shalt possess her.
—	וִירִשְׁתָּם	*Et possidebitis eos.*	And ye shall possess them.
—	וִירִשְׁתֶּם	*Et possedistis, possidebitis.*	And ye have possessed, shall possess.
ישה	וְיֵשׁ	*Et fuit.*	And he was.
—	וְיֵשׁ	*Et est [tavit, levavit.*	And he is. [lifted up.
נשא	וַיִּשָּׂא	*Et sumpsit, tulit, por-*	And he took, brought, carried,

ROOTS.	DERIVATIVES.	VERSIO.	SIGNIFICATION.
שאב	וַיִּשְׁאֲבוּ	*Et hauserunt.*	And they drew.
נשא	וַיִּשָּׂאֶהָ	*Et tulit eam.*	And he took her.
—	וַיִּשָּׂאֵהוּ	*Et sumpsit eum.*	And he took him.
—	וַיִּשָּׂאֻהוּ	*Et tulerunt eum.*	And they bare, brought him.
—	וַיִּשְׂאוּ	*Et sumpserunt, tulerunt, portarunt.*	And they took, brought, carried.
—	וַיִּשָּׂאוּם	*Et duxerunt eos.*	And they brought them.
שאל	וַיִּשְׁאַל	*Et interrogavit, quæsiit, petiit.*	And he asked, inquired, requested, demanded.
—	וַיִּשְׁאָלֵהוּ	*Et interrogavit eum*	And he inquired of him.
—	וַיִּשְׁאֲלוּ	*Et interrogarunt.*	And they asked, inquired.
—	וַיִּשְׁאָלוּ	*Et mutuabuntur.*	And they will borrow.
—	וַיַּשְׁאִלוּם	*Et commodarunt eis*	And they lent them.
נשא	וַיִּשָּׂאֵם	*Et abstulit eos.*	And he took them away.
—	וַיִּשָּׂאֻם	*Et tulerunt eos.*	And they carried them.
שאר	וַיִּשָּׁאֵר	*Et remansit.*	And he remained.
—	וַיִּשָּׁאֲרוּ	*Et remanserunt.*	And they remained.
שוב	וַיָּשָׁב־שָׁב־יָשׁוּב	*Et reversus est.*	And he returned.
—	וַיָּשֶׁב	*Et reddidit, reduxit, recuperavit, retulit, reddet, reducet*	And he restored, brought back, recovered, requited, will render, shall bring back.
נשב	וַיַּשֵּׁב	*Et difflavit, abegit.*	And he blew away, drove away
ישב	וַיֵּשֶׁב־־יֵשֶׁב	*Et sedit, habitavit, mansit.*	And he sat, sat down, dwelt, remained.
שום	וְיָשֵׂב	*Et ponet.* [*duxit.*	And he will put, set.
שבה	וַיִּשְׁבְּ	*Et captivum cepit,*	And he took, carried captive.
ישב	וְיֹשֵׁב	*Et permanens.*	And he that abideth.
—	וַיֹּשֶׁב	*Et collocavit, habitare fecit.*	And he placed, caused to dwell
—	וְיָשַׁב	*Et manebit, habitabit*	And he shall tarry, abide, dwell
שוב	וְיָשֹׁב	*Et convertet.* [*tetur.*	And he shall turn. [away.
—	וְיָשֹׁב	*Et revertetur, aver-*	And he shall return, be turned
—	וַיְשִׁבֶהָ	*Et retulit eam* [*bitur*	And he restored her [inhabited
ישב	וְיָשְׁבָה	*Et manebit, inhabita-*	And she shall remain, shall be
שוב	וַיְשִׁבֻהוּ־־שִׁי׳	*Et retulerunt eum.*	And they carried it back again
ישב	וַיֵּשְׁבוּ־־שְׁבוּ	*Et sederunt, manserunt, habitarunt.*	And they sat down, tarried, abode, dwelt.

ROOTS.	DERIVATIVES.	VERSIO.	SIGNIFICATION.
שוב	וַיָּשִׁבוּ־־שִׁי"	*Et retulerunt, responderunt.*	And they carried back, answered.
—	וַיָּשֻׁבוּ־־שׁוּבוּ	*Et reversi sunt* [*runt*	And they returned.
שבה	וַיִּשְׁבּוּ	*Et captivos abduxe-*	And they carried away captive
ישב	וַיֵּשְׁבוּ	*Et habitarunt.*	And they dwelt.
—	וְיָשְׁבוּ	*Et habitabunt.*	And they shall dwell. [swer.
שוב	וְיָשִׁבוּ־־שִׁי"	*Et referent.*	And they will bring again, an-
—	וְיָשֻׁבוּ	*Et revertentur.*	And they will return.
ישב	וְיֵשְׁבוּ	*Et habitabunt.*	And they shall dwell.
—	וְיֹשִׁבוּ	*Et collocabunt.*	And they will place.
שוב	וַיְשִׁבוּם־־שִׁי"	*Et reduxerunt eos.*	And they brought them again
ישב	וְיֹשְׁבֶיהָ	*Et habitatores ejus.*	And her inhabitants.
—	וְיֹשְׁבֵיהֶם	*Et habitatores eorum.* [*rum.*	And their inhabitants.
—	וְיֹשְׁבֵיהֶן	*Et habitatores ea-*	And their inhabitants.
—	וְיָשַׁבְנוּ	*Et habitabimus.*	And we will dwell.
שוב	וַיְשִׁבֵנִי	*Et reduxit me.*	And he brought me again.
שבע	וַיִּשָּׁבַע	*Et juravit.* [*fecit.*	And he sware.
—	וַיַּשְׁבַּע	*Et juravit, jurare*	And he sware, made to swear.
—	וַיִּשְׂבַּע	*Et satiatus est.*	And he was satisfied, sufficed.
—	וְיִשְׂבָּע	*Et saturabitur.*	And he shall be satisfied.
—	וַיִּשָּׁבְעוּ וַיִּשָּׁבְעוּ	*Et jurarunt.*	And they sware.
—	וַיִּשְׂבָּעוּ־בְּ׳	*Et saturati sunt.*	And they were satisfied.
—	וְיִשְׂבָּעוּ	*Et saturabuntur.*	And they shall be satisfied.
—	וַיַּשְׁבִּעֵנִי	*Et adjuravit me.*	And he made me swear.
שבר	וַיְשַׁבֵּר	*Et confregit.*	And he brake down.
—	וַיִּשָּׁבֵר	*Et confractus est.*	And he was broken.
—	וַיִּשְׁבֹּר	*Et vendidit.*	And he sold.
—	וַיְשַׁבְּרֵהוּ	*Et confregit eum.*	And he brake him.
—	וַיִּשָּׁבְרוּ	*Et confracti sunt.*	And they were broken.
—	וַיְשַׁבְּרוּ וַיְשַׁבְּרוּ	*Et confregerunt.*	And they brake.
—	וְיִשָּׁבֵרוּ	*Et confringentur.*	And they shall be broken.
שבת	וַיַּשְׁבֵּת	*Et cessare fecit.*	And he caused to cease.
—	וַיִּשְׁבֹּת	*Et desiit, quievit.*	And he ceased, rested.
—	וְיִשְׁבֹּת	*Et cessabit.*	And he shall cease.
ישב	וַיָּשַׁבְתָּ־שַׁבְתְּ־תָּה	*Et sedisti, manebis, habitabis.*	And thou satest, shalt remain, shalt dwell.

ROOTS.	DERIVATIVES.	VERSIO.	SIGNIFICATION.
שבת	וַיִּשְׁבְּתוּ	*Et cessarunt.*	And they ceased.
ישב	וְיָשַׁבְתִּי	*Et sedi, mansi.*	And I sat, abode.
—	וִישַׁבְתֶּם	*Et habitabitis.*	And ye shall dwell.
נשג	וַיַּשֵּׂג	*Et assecutus est.*	And he overtook.
—	וְיַשֵּׂג	*Et assequetur.*	And he will overtake.
שגב	וַיְשַׂגֵּב	*Et extulit, extollet.*	And he exalted, will exalt.
נשג	וַיַּשִּׂגוּ־שִׂי	*Et assecuti sunt.*	And they overtook.
—	וַיַּשִּׂגֵם	*Et assecutus est eos.*	And he overtook them.
שדד	וִישַׂדֵּד	*Et occabit, confrin- [get.*	And he will harrow, break up.
ישע	וִישׁוּעָה	*Et salus.*	And safety, salvation.
—	וִישׁוּעָתָהּ	*Et salus ejus.*	And her salvation.
—	וִישׁוּעָתִי	*Et salus mea.*	And my salvation.
שחח	וַיִּשַּׁח	*Et deprimetur.*	And he shall be brought down.
—	וַיָּשֹׁחוּ	*Et depressi sunt.*	And they were brought low.
—	וְיָשֹׁחוּ	*Et deprimentur.*	And they shall be brought low.
שחט	וַיִּשְׁחָט־חַט	*Et mactavit, jugula- [vit.*	And he sacrificed, slew.
—	וַיִּשְׁחָטֵהוּ	*Et jugulavit eum.*	And he killed him, or it.
—	וַיִּשְׁחֲטוּ	*Et jugularunt.*	And they slew.
—	וַיִּשְׁחָטוּהוּ	*Et jugularunt eum.*	And they slew him, or it.
—	וַיִּשְׁחָטוּם	*Et jugularunt eos.*	And they slew them.
—	וַיִּשְׁחָטֵם	*Et jugulavit eos.*	And he slew them.
שחת	וַיַּשְׁחִיתוּ	*Et perdiderunt.*	And they destroyed.
שחח	וְיֶשְׁחֲךָ	*Et depressio tua.*	And thy casting down.
שחק	וְיִשְׂחָק	*Et ridebit.*	And he will laugh.
—	וִישַׂחֵק	*Et ludet.*	And he shall make sport.
—	וִישַׂחֲקוּ	*Et ludent.*	And they will play.
שחת	וַיַּשְׁחֵת	*Et perdidit.*	And he destroyed.
—	וַיַּשְׁחִתוּ	*Et perdiderunt.*	And they destroyed.
שוט	וַיָּשֹׁטוּ	*Et discurrerunt.*	And they ran about.
שטח	וַיִּשְׁטְחוּ	*Et expanderunt.*	And they spread.
שטם	וַיִּשְׂטֹם	*Et odit.*	And he hated.
—	וַיִּשְׂטְמֻהוּ	*Et oderunt eum.*	And they hated him.
—	וַיִּשְׂטְמֵנִי	*Et odit me.*	And he hath hated me.
שטף	וַיִּשְׁטֹף	*Et immersit.*	And he plunged, washed.
—	וְיִשְׁטְפוּ	*Et inundabunt.*	And they shall overflow.
שוב	וַיְשִׁיבֶהָ	*Et restituit eam.*	And he restored her.
—	וַיְשִׁיבֵהוּ	*Et reduxit eum.*	And he brought him back.

ROOTS.	DERIVATIVES.	VERSIO.	SIGNIFICATION.
ישב	וַיֹּשִׁיבוּם	Et habitare fecerunt	And they made them dwell.
שוב	וַיְשִׁיבֵם	Et reduxit eos. [eos.	And he brought them back.
ישב	וְיֹשִׁיבֵם	Et collocabit eos.	And he will place them.
—	וַיֹּשִׁיבֵם	Et collocarunt eos.	And they placed them.
שום	וַיְשִׂימֶהָ־שִׂמֶהָ	Et statuit eam.	And he made it.
—	וַיְשִׂימֵהוּ־שִׂמֵ״	Et constituit eum.	And he made, appointed him.
	וַיְשִׂימֻהוּ	Et constituerunt eum	And they made him.
—	וַיָּשִׂימוּ־שִׂמוּ	Et posuerunt, collocarunt, constituerun.	And they put, laid, placed, set, madė, appointed.
—			
—	וְיָשִׂימוּ	Et ponent.	And they will put, lay, set.
—	וַיְשִׂימְךָ	Et constituit te.	And he made, appointed thee.
—	וַיְשִׂימֵנִי	Et constituit me.	And he hath made me.
ישע	וְיוֹשִׁיעֵנוּ	Et servabit nos.	And he will save us.
שור	וְיָשִׁירוּ	Et cantabunt.	And they shall sing.
שוש	וְיָשִׂישׂ	Et lætabitur.	And he shall rejoice.
—	וְיָשִׂישׂוּ	Et gaudebunt.	And they shall rejoice.
ישש	וִישִׁישִׁים	Et senes, decrepiti.	And the very old, decrepid.
שות	וִישִׁיתֵהוּ	Et constituet eum.	And he will appoint him.
—	וַיָּשִׁיתוּ	Et constituerunt.	And they made.
שכב	וַיִּשְׁכַּב־כָּב	Et cubavit, dormivit.	And he lay down, slept.
—	וַיַּשְׁכִּבֵהוּ	Et deposuit eum.	And he laid him.
—	וַיִּשְׁכְּבוּ	Et cubarunt.	And they lay.
שכך	וַיָּשֹׁכּוּ	Et sedati sunt.	And they subsided.
שכן	וַיִּשְׁכּוֹן־כֹּן	Et habitavit.	And he dwelt, abode.
שכח	וַיִּשְׁכַּח	Et oblitus est.	And he forgot.
—	וְיִשְׁכַּח	Et obliviscetur.	And he will forget.
—	וַיִּשְׁכָּחֵהוּ	Et oblitus est ejus.	And he forgat him.
—	וַיִּשְׁכְּחוּ	Et obliti sunt.	And they forgot.
שכב	וַיַּשְׁכִּיבֻהוּ	Et deposuerunt eum.	And they laid him.
שכל	וְיַשְׂכִּילוּ	Et intelligent.	And they will understand.
שכם	וַיַּשְׁכִּימוּ־כִּמוּ	Et mane surrexêre.	And they rose early.
שכן	וַיַּשְׁכִּינוּ	Et collocarunt.	And they placed.
שכם	וַיַּשְׁכֵּם	Et mane surrexit.	And he rose early.
שכן	וַיַּשְׁכֵּן	Et habitarefecit.	And he made to dwell.
—	וְיִשְׁכֹּן	Et habitabit.	And he shall dwell.
—	וַיִּשְׁכְּנוּ	Et habitarunt.	And they dwelt.

ROOTS.	DERIVATIVES.	VERSIO.	SIGNIFICATION.
שכן	וַיִּשְׁכְּנוּ	*Et habitabunt.*	And they shall dwell.
שכר	וַיִּשְׁכָּר	*Et inebriatus est.*	And he was drunken.
—	וַיִּשְׂכֹּר	*Et mercede conduxit*	And he hired.
—	וַיְשַׁכְּרֵהוּ	*Et inebriavit eum.*	And he made him drunk.
—	וַיִּשְׁכְּרוּ	*Et saturati, exhila-*	And they were satisfied, were
		rati sunt. [*erunt.*	enlivened, merry.
—	וַיִּשְׂכְּרוּ	*Et mercede condux-*	And they hired.
—	וַיִּשְׂכְּרֵנִי	*Et mercede conduxit*	And he hath hired me.
שלח	וַיְשַׁלַּח	*Et misit.* [*me.*	And he sent.
—	וַיִּשְׁלַח	*Et emisit, dimisit.*	And he sent forth, sent away.
—	וְיִשְׁלַח וְשִׁלַּח	*Et mittet.*	And he shall send.
—	וַיְשַׁלְּחֶהָ	*Et dimisit eam.*	And he sent her away.
—	וַיְשַׁלְּחֵהוּ	*Et dimisit eum.*	And he sent him away.
—	וַיִּשְׁלָחֵהוּ	*Et misit eum.*	And he sent him.
—	וַיִּשְׁלְחוּ	*Et miserunt* [*serunt*	And they sent.
—	וַיְשַׁלְּחוּ	*Et emiserunt, dimi-*	And they sent forth, sent away.
—	וַיְשַׁלְּחוּ-לִ״	*Et emittent.*	And they shall send forth.
—	וַיְשַׁלְּחוּהָ	*Et dimiserunt eam.*	And they let her go.
—	וַיְשַׁלְּחוּם	*Et dimiserunt eos.*	And they let them go.
—	וַיִּשְׁלָחֲךָ	*Et misit te.* [*eos.*	And he sent thee. [them down.
—	וַיְשַׁלְּחֵם	*Et dimisit, demisit*	And he sent them away, let
—	וַיְשַׁלְּחֵם	*Et emittet eos.*	And he will send them out.
—	וַיְשַׁלְּחֵנוּ	*Et misit nos.*	And he hath sent us.
—	וַיִּשְׁלָחֵנִי	*Et misit me.*	And he hath sent me.
שלט	וְיִשְׁלַט	*Et dominabitur.*	And he shall have rule.
שלך	וַיַּשְׁלִיכֵהוּ-לְבֵ״	*Et dejecit eum.*	And he cast him down.
—	וַיַּשְׁלִיכוּ-לְכוּ	*Et projecerunt.*	And they cast, cast forth.
—	וַיַּשְׁלִיכוּם-כֻם	*Et dejecerunt eos.*	And they cast them down.
שלם	וַיַּשְׁלִימוּ-לְמוּ	*Et pacem fecerunt.*	And they made peace.
שלך	וְיַשְׁלֵךְ	*Et abjiciet.* [*jecit.*	And he shall cast off. [down.
—	וַיַּשְׁלֵךְ	*Et jecit, abjecit, de-*	And he cast, cast away, cast
—	וַיַּשְׁלִכֵם	*Et ejecit eos.*	And he cast them out.
שלם	וַיְשַׁלֵּם	*Et pacem fecit.*	And he made peace. [pered.
—	וַיִּשְׁלָם	*Et pacem habuit.*	And he hath had peace, pros-
שלף	וַיִּשְׁלֹף	*Et detraxit.*	And he drew it off.
—	וַיִּשְׁלְפָהּ	*Et extraxit eum.*	And he drew him out.
שלש	וַיְשַׁלֵּשׁוּ	*Et tertio fecerunt.*	And they did it the third time.

ROOTS.	DERIVATIVES.	VERSIO.	SIGNIFICATION.
שׂום	וַיָּשֶׂם	*Et posuit, statuit.*	And he put, appointed, made.
—	וְיָשֵׂם	*Et ponet, constituet.*	And he will put, set, make.
שׁמד	וַיַּשְׁמֵד	*Et disperdidit.*	And he destroyed.
שׂמח	וַיְשַׂמַּח	*Et lætificavit.*	And he caused to rejoice.
—	וַיִּשְׂמַח	*Et lætatus est.*	And he rejoiced, was glad.
—	וְיִשְׂמַח	*Et lætabitur.*	And he shall rejoice.
—	וַיִּשְׂמְחוּ־מ׳	*Et lætati sunt.*	And they rejoiced, were glad.
—	וְיִשְׂמְחוּ־מ׳	*Et lætabuntur.*	And they shall rejoice.
שׁמט	וַיִּשְׁמְטוּהָ	*Et dejecerunt eam.*	And they threw her down.
שׁמד	וַיַּשְׁמִידוּם	*Et perdiderunt eos.*	And they destroyed them.
—	וַיַּשְׁמִדֵם	*Et disperdidit eos.*	And he destroyed them.
שׁמן	וַיַּשְׁמִינוּ	*Et saginati sunt.*	And they became fat.
שׁמע	וַיַּשְׁמִיעוּ	*Et audiri fecerunt.*	And they caused to be heard.
—	וְיַשְׁמִיעוּ	*Et audiri facient.*	And they will make to be heard.
שׁמם	וַיְשִׁמֵּם	*Et vastavit eos.*	And he destroyed them.
שׂום	וַיְשִׂמֵם	*Et posuit eos.*	And he put them.
שׁמן	וַיִּשְׁמַן	*Et saginatus est.*	And he became fat.
שׁמע	וַיְשַׁמַּע	*Et audiri fecit, congregavit.*	And he caused to be heard, assembled.
—	וַיִּשָּׁמַע	*Et exauditus est.*	And he was heard.
—	וְיִשְׁמַע	*Et audiet.* [*vit.*	And he will hear.
—	וַיִּשְׁמַע־מע	*Et audivit, ausculta-*	And he heard, hearkened.
—	וַיִּשְׁמְעוּ	*Et audiverunt.*	And they heard.
—	וַיִּשָּׁמְעוּ	*Et auditi sunt.*	And they were heard.
—	וְיִשְׁמְעוּ־מ׳	*Et audient.*	And they will hear.
—	וְיִשְׁמָעֲךָ	*Et audiet te.*	And he will hear thee.
—	וְיַשְׁמִעֵנוּ	*Et audire faciet nos.*	And he shall make us hear.
שׁמר	וַיִּשְׁמֹר	*Et custodivit.*	And he kept, preserved.
—	וְיִשְׁמֹר	*Et observabit.*	And he will observe, keep.
—	וַיִּשְׁמְרוּ	*Et custodiverunt.*	And they kept, observed.
—	וְיִשְׁמְרוּ	*Et observabunt.*	And they shall keep, observe.
—	וְיִשְׁמְרֶךָ	*Et custodiet te.*	And he shall keep thee.
—	וַיִּשְׁמְרֵנוּ	*Et custodivit nos.*	And he hath preserved us.
ישׁן	וְיָשָׁן	*Et vetus.*	And old.
שׂנא	וַיִּשְׂנָאֶהָ	*Et odit eam.*	And he hated her.
—	וַיִּשְׂנְאוּ	*Et oderunt.* [*lit eam.*	And they hated.
שׁנה	וַיְשַׁנֶּהָ	*Et mutavit, transtu-*	And he changed, removed her.

ROOTS.	DERIVATIVES.	VERSIO.	SIGNIFICATION.
שנה	וִישַׁנֶּה	*Et mutabit, perver-*	And he will alter, pervert.
—	וַיְשַׁנּוֹ	*Et mutavit se.* [*tet.*	And he changed himself.
ישן	וְיָשְׁנוּ	*Et dormient.*	And they will sleep.
שנה	וַיִּשְׁנוּ	*Et iterarunt.*	And they repeated, did it again
שנס	וַיְשַׁנֵּס	*Et accinxit.*	And he girded up.
שסס	וַיָּשֹׁסּוּ	*Et diripuerunt.*[*cuit*	And they spoiled.
שסע	וַיְשַׁסַּע	*Et confregit, compes-*	And he broke off, restrained.
—	וַיְשַׁסְּעֵהוּ	*Et discidit ipsum.*	And he rent him.
שסף	וַיְשַׁסֵּף	*Et dissecuit.*	And he cut in pieces [regarded
שעה	וַיִּשַׁע	*Et respexit.*	And he respected, favourably
ישע	וְיֹשַׁע	*Et servabit.*	And he shall save.
—	וְיִשְׁעִי	*Et salus mea.*	And my salvation.
—	וְיֶשְׁעֲךָ	*Et salus tua.*	And thy salvation.
—	וְיֹשַׁעֲכֶם	*Et servabit vos.*	And he shall save you.
שען	וְיִשָּׁעֵן	*Et innitetur.*	And he will stay, rest upon.
שער	וִישָׂעֲרֵהוּ	*Et turbine abripiet eum.*	And he shall take him away, as with a whirlwind.
ישפ	וְיָשְׁפֵה	*Et jaspis.*	And a jasper.
שפט	וַיִּשְׁפֹּט	*Et judicavit.*	And he judged.
—	וְיִשְׁפֹּט	*Et judicabit.*	And he will judge. [me.
—	וְיִשְׁפְּטֵנִי	*Et vindicabit me.*	And he will vindicate, deliver
שפך	וַיִּשָּׁפֵךְ	*Et effusus est.*	And he was poured out.
—	וַיִּשְׁפֹּךְ	*Et effudit.*	And he poured, shed.
—	וְיִשְׁפֹּךְ	*Et effundet.*	And he shall pour out.
—	וַיִּשְׁפְּכוּ	*Et effuderunt.*	And they poured out, shed.
—	וַיִּשְׁפְּכֵם	*Et effudit eos.*	And he poured them out.
שפל	וַיִּשְׁפַּל	*Et depressus est, deprimetur.*	And he hath been humbled, shall be brought down.
שקה	וַיַּשְׁקְ	*Et bibere fecit.*	And he caused to drink.
נשק	וַיִּשַּׁק	*Et osculatus est.*	And he kissed.
שקד	וַיִּשְׁקֹד	*Et vigilavit.* [*eum.*	And he hath watched.
שקה	וַיַּשְׁקֻהוּ	*Et bibere fecerunt*	And they made him drink.
נשק	וַיִּשָּׁקֵהוּ	*Et osculatus est eum.*	And he kissed him.
—	וַיִּשְּׁקוּ	*Et osculati sunt* [*eos*	And they kissed.
שקה	וַיַּשְׁקוּם	*Et bibere fecerunt*	And they gave them to drink.
שקף	וַיַּשְׁקִיפוּ וַיַּשְׁקִפוּ	*Et prospexerunt.*	And they looked, looked out.
שקל	וַיִּשְׁקֹל	*Et appendit.*	And he weighed.

ROOTS.	DERIVATIVES.	VERSIO.	SIGNIFICATION.
שקל	וַיִּשְׁקְלוּ	*Et appenderunt.*	And they weighed.
שקה	וַיַּשְׁקֵנוּ	*Et potum dedit nobis.*	And he gave us drink.
שקף	וַיַּשְׁקֵף	*Et prospexit.*	And he looked, looked out.
ישר	וְיֹשֶׁר	*Et rectitudo.*	And uprightness. [ness.
——	וְיָשָׁר	*Et rectus, rectum.*	And right, upright, upright-
נשר	וַיָּשַׂר	*Et serravit. [sit.*	And he cut, sawed.
שור	וַיָּשַׂר	*Et principatum ges-*	And he reigned, had power.
ישר	וַיִּשַׁר	*Et rectus fuit.*	And he was right.
——	וִישָׁרִים	*Et recti.*	And the upright. [right way.
——	וַיִּשַּׁרְנָה	*Et recte ierunt.*	And they went the straight or
שרף	וַיִּשְׂרֹף	*Et combussit.*	And he burnt.
——	וַיִּשְׂרְפֶהָ	*Et combussit eam.*	And he burnt her or it.
——	וַיִּשָּׂרְפוּ	*Et combusti sunt.*	And they were burnt.
——	וַיִּשְׂרְפוּ	*Et incenderunt [eam*	And they burnt.
——	וַיִּשְׂרְפוּהָ	*Et combusserunt*	And they burnt her.
——	וַיִּשְׂרְפֵם	*Et combussit eos.*	And he burnt them.
שרץ	וַיִּשְׁרְצוּ	*Et produxerunt.*	And they brought forth.
שרק	וְיִשְׁרֹק	*Et sibilabit.*	And he shall hiss.
שרת	וַיְשָׁרֶת	*Et ministravit.*	And he served.
——	וַיְשָׁרְתֵהוּ	*Et ministravit ei.*	And he ministered to him.
——	וִישָׁרְתוּךָ	*Et ministrabunt tibi.*	And they shall minister to thee.
ישש	וְיָשֵׁשׁ	*Et decrepitus.*	And very old, decrepid.
שות	וַיָּשֶׁת	*Et posuit.*	And he put, set.
שתה	וַיֵּשְׁתְּ וַיִּשְׁתֶּה	*Et bibit.*	And he drank.
——	וְיֵשְׁתְּ	*Et bibet.*	And he shall drink.
——	וַיִּשְׁתּוּ	*Et biberunt.*	And they drank.
——	וְיִשְׁתּוּ	*Et bibent.*	And they shall drink.
שמם	וַיִּשְׁתּוֹמֵם	*Et obstupuit.*	And he was astonished.
שתה	וַיִּשְׁתּוּן	*Et biberunt.*	And they drank. [shipped.
שחה	וַיִּשְׁתַּחוּ-תָּחוּ	*Et prostravit se.*	And he bowed himself, wor-
——	וְיִשְׁתַּחוּ	*Et incurvabit se.*	And he shall bow down.
——	וַיִּשְׁתַּחֲוּ-וּ	*Et incurvarunt se.*	And they bowed themselves.
——	וְיִשְׁתַּחֲוּ-וּ	*Et incurvabunt se.*	And they shall bow down.
——	וַיִּשְׁתַּחֲוֶה	*Et incurvavit se.*	And he bowed himself down.
שכח	וְיִשְׁתַּכְּחוּ	*Et obliviosi traden-*	And they shall be forgotten.
שמע	וְיִשְׁתַּמְּעוּן	*Et audient. [tur.*	And they shall hear.
שמר	וְיִשְׁתַּמֵּר	*Et observabitur.*	And he or it shall be kept.

ROOTS.	DERIVATIVES.	VERSIO.	SIGNIFICATION.
שער	וְיִשְׂתָּעֵר	*Et instar turbinis veniet.*	And he shall come like a whirlwind.
שתק	וְיִשְׁתֹּק	*Et sedabitur.*	And he shall be quieted, calmed.
סתר	וַיִּשָּׁתְרוּ	*Et absconditi sunt.*	And they were hidden.
אתה	וַיֵּתֵא	*Et venit.*	And he came.
אבך	וַיִּתְאַבְּכוּ	*Et extulerunt se.*	And they lifted up themselves.
אבל	וַיִּתְאַבֵּל	*Et luxit.*	And he mourned.
—	וַיִּתְאַבְּלוּ־בָּלוּ	*Et luxerunt.*	And they mourned.
אוה	וַיִּתְאָו וַיִּתְאַוֶּה	*Et desideravit.*	And he desired.
—	וְיִתְאָו	*Et concupiscet.*	And he will desire.
—	וַיִּתְאַוּוּ	*Et desiderarunt.*	And they desired.
אמץ	וַיִּתְאַמְּצוּ	*Et confirmarunt.*	And they strengthened.
אנף	וַיִּתְאַנַּף	*Et iratus est.*	And he was angry.
אפק	וַיִּתְאַפַּק	*Et continuit se.*	And he restrained himself.
בון	וְיִתְבּוֹנְנוּ	*Et intelligent.*	And they shall understand.
ברך	וְיִתְבָּרְכוּ	*Et benedicentur.*	And they shall be blessed.
גדד	וַיִּתְגֹּדְדוּ	*Et inciderunt se.*	And they cut themselves.
גדל	וְיִתְגַּדֵּל	*Et magnificabit se.*	And he shall magnify himself.
גלה	וַיִּתְגַּל	*Et retexit se.*	And he uncovered himself.
גנב	וַיִּתְגַּנֵּב	*Et furatus est se.*	And he stole, went by stealth.
געש	וַיִּתְגָּעֲשׁוּ	*Et commoti sunt.*	And they were shaken.
גרה	וְיִתְגָּרֶה	*Et miscebitur, bellum movebit.*	And he shall be stirred up, shall wage war.
יתד	וְיָתֵד	*Et paxillus.*	And a pole.
—	וִיתֵדֹתֶיהָ	*Et paxilli ejus.*	And her stakes, pins.
—	וִיתֵדֹתַיִךְ	*Et paxilli tui.*	And thy stakes, pins.
—	וִיתֵדֹתָם	*Et paxilli eorum.*	And their stakes, pins.
הלך	וַיִּתְהַלֵּךְ	*Et ivit, ambulavit.*	And he went, walked.
—	וַיִּתְהַלְּכוּ	*Et profecti sunt.*	And they went.
—	וְיִתְהַלָּכוּ	*Et ibunt.*	And they shall go.
הלל	וַיִּתְהֹלֵל	*Et insanum se finxit*	And he feigned himself mad.
—	וְיִתְהַלְלוּ	*Et gloriabuntur.*	And they shall glory.
תוה	וַיְתָו	*Et signavit.*	And he made marks.
ידה	וַיִּתְוַדּוּ	*Et confessi sunt.*	And they confessed.
יתם	וְיָתוֹם	*Et pupillus.*	And fatherless.
—	וִיתוֹמִים	*Et pupilli.*	And the fatherless.
חבא	וַיִּתְחַבֵּא	*Et abscondit se.*	And he hid himself.

ROOTS.	DERIVATIVES.	VERSIO.	SIGNIFICATION.
חבא	וַיִּתְחַבְּאוּ	*Et absconderunt se.*	And they hid themselves.
חזק	וַיִּתְחַזֵּק וַיִּתְחַזֵּק	*Et confirmavit se.*	And he strengthened himself.
חטא	וַיִּתְחַטְּאוּ	*Et purificarunt se.*	And they purified themselves.
חלה	וַיִּתְחָל	*Et ægrotum se finxit*	And he feigned himself sick.
חנן	וַיִּתְחַנֵּן וַיִּתְחַנָּן	*Et deprecatus est.*	And he besought. [himself.
חפש	וַיִּתְחַפֵּשׂ	*Et mutavit se.*	And he changed, disguised
חרש	וַיִּתְחָרְשׁוּ	*Et tacuerunt [traxit*	And they were silent.
חתן	וַיִּתְחַתֵּן	*Et affinitatem con-*	And he made affinity.
יהב	וַיִּתְיַהֲבוּן	*Et tradentur.*	And they shall be given.
נתך	וַיִּתִּיכוּ	*Et effuderunt.*	And they poured out.
ילד	וַיִּתְיַלְדוּ	*Et genus suum pro-*	And they declared their pedi-
		fessi sunt. [runt.	gree.
יעץ	וַיִּתְיָעֲצוּ	*Et consilium inie-*	And they took counsel.
יצב	וַיִּתְיַצֵּב	*Et stetit. [runt se.*	And he stood. [themselves.
——	וַיִּתְיַצְּבוּ	*Et steterunt, stite-*	And they stood, presented
——	וַיִּתְיַצְּבוּ	*Et stabunt.*	And they will stand.
נתר	וַיַּתִּירֵהוּ	*Et solvit eum. [runt*	And he loosed him. [descry.
תור	וַיָּתִירוּ	*Et explorare fece-*	And they caused to explore,
נתך	וַיִּתְּכוּ	*Et effusi sunt.*	And they were poured out.
כסה	וַיִּתְכַּס	*Et operuit se.*	And he covered himself [selves
——	וַיִּסְכַּסּוּ	*Et operient se.*	And they shall cover them-
לבן	וַיִּתְלַבְּנוּ	*Et dealbabuntur.*	And they shall be made white
תלה	וַיִּתָּלוּ	*Et suspensi sunt.*	And they were hanged.
——	וַיִּתְלוּ	*Et suspenderunt.*	And they hanged.
——	וְיִתְלוּ	*Et suspendent.*	And they will hang.
לון	וַיִּתְלוֹנָן־ל״ו	*Et pernoctavit.*	And he tarried all night.
תלה	וַיִּתְלֵם	*Et suspendit eos.*	And he hanged them.
לקט	וַיִּתְלַקְּטוּ	*Et collegerunt se.*	And they gathered, assembled
			themselves.
תמם	וַיִּתֹּם	*Et consumptus est.*	And he, it was consumed.
——	וַיִּתֵּם	*Et perficiet.*	And he shall perfect, count all
מדד	וַיִּתְמֹדֵד	*Et sese extendit.*	And he stretched himself.
תמה	וַיִּתְמְהוּ	*Et mirati sunt.*	And they wondered.
——	וְיִתְמְהוּ	*Et obstupescent.*	And they shall be amazed.
מהמה	וַיִּתְמַהְמָהּ	*Et cunctatus est.*	And he lingered.
תמם	וַיִּתַּמּוּ	*Et completi sunt.*	And they were ended.
תמך	וַיִּתְמֹךְ	*Et sustentavit.*	And he upheld.

ROOTS.	DERIVATIVES.	VERSIO.	SIGNIFICATION.
מכר	וַיִּתְמַכְּרוּ	*Et vendiderunt se.*	And they sold themselves.
מרר	וַיִּתְמַרְמַר	*Et exacerbatus est.*	And he was exasperated.
—	וְיִתְמַרְמַר	*Et exacerbabitur.*	And he shall be exasperated.
נתן	וַיִּתֵּן־תֶּן	*Et dedit, tradidit, posuit, commisit.*	And he gave, bestowed, delivered, put, committed.
—	וַיֻּתַּן	*Et datus est.*	And he was given.
—	וְיִתֵּן־תֶּן	*Et dabit, tradet.*	And he shall give, deliver.
נבא	וַיִּתְנַבֵּא	*Et vaticinatus est.*	And he prophesied.
—	וַיִּתְנַבְּאוּ	*Et vaticinati sunt.*	And they prophesied.
נדב	וַיִּתְנַדְּבוּ	*Et sponte obtulerunt*	And they offered freely.
נתן	וַיִּתְּנָהּ	*Et dedit eam.*	And he gave her, it.
—	וְיִתְּנֻהֽ־הוּ	*Et tradent eum.*	And they shall deliver him.
—	וַיִּתְּנֵהוּ	*Et tradidit eum.*	And he delivered him.
—	וַיִּתְּנוּ	*Et dederunt.*	And they gave, delivered.
—	וְיִתְּנוּ	*Et dabunt, tradent.*	And they shall give, deliver.
—	וַיִּתְּנוּהוּ	*Et tradiderunt eum.*	And they delivered him.
—	וַיִּתְּנוּם־נֻם	*Et posuerunt eos.*	And they put them.
נחם	וְיִתְנֶחָם	*Et pœnitebit eum.*	And he shall repent.
נתן	וַיִּתֶּנְךָ	*Et dedit te.*	And he gave thee.
נכל	וַיִּתְנַכְּלוּ	*Et machinati sunt.*	And they plotted, conspired.
נכר	וַיִּתְנַכֵּר	*Et alienum se gessit*	And he made himself strange.
נתן	וַיִּתְּנֵם	*Et dedit, tradidit eos*	And he gave, delivered them.
—	וַיִּתְּנֵנוּ	*Et tradidit nos.*	And he gave us.
נצל	וַיִּתְנַצְּלוּ	*Et se spoliarunt.*	And they stripped themselves.
תעה	וַיַּתַע	*Et errare fecit.*	And he made to err.
תעב	וַיַּתְעֵב	*Et turpiter egit.*	And he acted abominably.
—	וַיְתָעֵב	*Et abominatus est.*	And he abhorred.
עבר	וַיִּתְעַבֵּר־בָּר	*Et iratus est.*	And he was angry.
עדן	וַיִּתְעַדְּנוּ	*Et oblectarunt se.*	And they delighted themselves
תעה	וַיַּתְעוּ	*Et errare fecerunt.*	And they caused to err.
—	וַיַּתְעוּם	*Et seduxerunt eos.*	And they caused them to err.
עלל	וַיִּתְעַלְּלוּ	*Et illuserunt.*	And they abused.
עלף	וַיִּתְעַלָּף	*Et defecit.*	And he fainted.
תעה	וַיַּתְעֵם	*Et errare fecit eos.*	And he caused them to err.
עצב	וַיִּתְעַצֵּב	*Et doluit.*	And he was grieved.
—	וַיִּתְעַצְּבוּ	*Et doluerunt.*	And they were grieved.
ערב	וַיִּתְעָרְבוּ	*Et miscuerunt se.*	And they mingled themselves.

ROOTS.	DERIVATIVES.	VERSIO.	SIGNIFICATION.
פלל	וַיִּתְפַּלֵּל	*Et oravit.*	And he prayed.
——	וְיִתְפַּלֵּל	*Et orabit.*	And he shall pray.
——	וְיִתְפַּלְלוּ	*Et orabunt.*	And they shall pray.
פוץ	וַיִּתְפַּצְּצוּ	*Et dissipati sunt.*	And they were scattered.
פקד	וַיִּתְפָּקֵד	*Et recensitus est.*	And he was reckoned.
——	וַיִּתְפָּקְדוּ	*Et numerati sunt.*	And they were numbered.
תפר	וַיִּתְפְּרוּ	*Et consuerunt.*	And they sewed.
פרק	וַיִּתְפָּרְקוּ	*Et disruperunt.*	And they brake off.
תפש	וַיִּתְפֹּשׂ	*Et cepit, prehendit.*	And he took, took hold of.
——	וַיִּתְפְּשֶׂהָ	*Et cepit eam.*	And he took her or it.
——	וַיִּתְפְּשׂוּ	*Et prehenderunt.*	And they took.
——	וַיִּתְפְּשׂוּם	*Et prehenderunt eos*	And they took them.
פשט	וַיִּתְפַּשֵּׁט	*Et exuit se.*	And he stripped himself.
תפש	וַיִּתְפְּשֵׂם	*Et prehendit eos.*	And he took them.
נתץ	וַיִּתֹּץ	*Et diruit.*	And he beat down. [it.
——	וַיִּתְּצֻהוּ	*Et diruerunt illum.*	And they brake down him or
——	וַיִּתְּצוּ	*Et diruerunt.*	And they brake down.
קבץ	וַיִּתְקַבְּצוּ	*Et congregarunt se.*	And they gathered themselves
קדש	וַיִּתְקַדְּשׁוּ	*Et sanctificarunt se*	And they sanctified themselves
קלס	וַיִּתְקַלְּסוּ	*Et illuserunt.*	And they mocked.
תקע	וַיִּתְקַע	*Et clanxit.*	And he shouted.
——	וַיִּתְקָעֶהָ	*Et infixit eam.*	And he fixed, thrust her or it.
——	וַיִּתְקָעֵהוּ	*Et conjecit eum.*	And he cast him.
——	וַיִּתְקְעוּ	*Et clanxerunt.*	And they shouted.
——	וַיִּתְקָעֵם	*Et infixit eos.*	And he thrust them.
קשר	וַיִּתְקַשֵּׁר	*Et conspiravit.*	And he conspired.
נתר	וַיַּתֵּר	*Et solvit.*	And he loosed, freed.
——	וְיִתַּר	*Et subsiliet.* [*lentia.*	And he will leap, spring. [cy.
——	וְיֶתֶר	*Et residuum, excel-*	And the residue, the excellen-
——	וְיֹתֵר	*Et amplius.* [*cem.*	And more, further.
ראה	וַיִּתְרָאוּ	*Et viderunt se invi-*	And they saw one another.
תור	וַיָּתֻרוּ	*Et explorarunt.*	And they searched.
——	וְיָתֻרוּ	*Et explorabunt.*	And they shall search.
יתר	וְיִתְרוֹ	*Et reliquum illius.*	And the remainder of it.
רום	וְיִתְרוֹמֵם	*Et extollet se.*	And he shall exalt himself.
יתר	וְיִתְרוֹן	*Et emolumentum, præstantia.*	And the profit, excellence.

ROOTS.	DERIVATIVES.	VERSIO.	SIGNIFICATION.
יתר	וְיִתְרָם	*Et residuum eorum.*	And the remnant of them.
רצץ	וַיִּתְרֹצְצוּ	*Et collidebant se.*	And they bruised each other.
יתר	וְיֹתֶרֶת	*Et reticulum.*	And the caul.
נתש	וַיִּתְּשֵׁם	*Et extirpavit eos.*	And he rooted them out.
	וכ		
אבה	וּכְאָב	*Et sicut pater.*	And as a father.
כאב	וּכְאֵב	*Et dolor.*	And grief.
—	וּכְאֵבִי	*Et dolor meus.*	And my grief.
אור	וּכְאוֹר	*Et sicut lux.*	And as the light.
אחד	וּכְאַחַד	*Et sicut unus.* [*tri.*	And as one.
אחה	וְכַאֲחֵיכֶם	*Et sicut fratres ves-*	And as your brethren.
אחר	וְכָאַחֲרֹנָה	*Et sicut posterius.*	And as the latter.
איל	וְכָאַיָּל	*Et sicut cervus.*	And as the hart.
אין	וּכְאֵין	*Et veluti absque.*	And as without.
אלה	וְכָאֵלֶּה	*Et sicut istæ.*	And like those.
—	וְכָאַלּוֹן	*Et sicut quercus.*	And as an oak.
אלם	וּכְאִלֵּם	*Et sicut mutus.*	And as a dumb man.
אמם	וּכְאִמּוֹ	*Et sicut mater ejus.*	And like his mother.
—	וּכְאַמָּתַיִם	*Et quasi duo cubiti.*	And as it were two cubits.
אסף	וְכֶאֱסֹף	*Et sicut colligitur.*	And as it is gathered.
אפס	וּכְאֶפֶס	*Et sicut nihilum.*	And as a thing of nought.
ארח	וּכְאֹרַח	*Et juxta viam.*	And according to the way.
—	וּכְאֹרֵחַ	*Et sicut viator.*	And as a wayfaring man.
ארה	וְכָאֲרִי	*Et sicut leo* [*delicto.*	And as a lion.
אשם	וְכָאָשָׁם	*Et sicut victima pro*	And as the tresspass-offering.
אשר	וְכַאֲשֶׁר	*Et quemadmodum, quando, cum.*	And as, when.
בוא	וּכְבֹא־־בוֹא	*Et sicut venire, occidere.*	And at the coming, setting.
בגד	וּכְבֶגֶד	*Et sicut vestis.*	And as a garment.
כבד	וְכָבֵד וְכָבֵד	*Et gravis.*	And heavy.
—	וְכֹבֶד	*Et gravitas.*	And heaviness, a load.
—	וּכְבַד	*Et gravis.*	And heavy, slow *in speech.*
—	וּכְבוֹד־־בוֹד	*Et gloria.*	And glory,
—	וְכִבְדֵי	*Et graves.*	And the heavy, slow *in speech.*
—	וְכִבַּדְנוּךָ	*Et honorabimus te.*	And we shall honour thee.

ROOTS.	DERIVATIVES.	VERSIO.	SIGNIFICATION.
כבד	וְכִבַּדְתּוֹ	*Et honorabis eum.*	And thou shalt honour him.
כבה	וְכִבּוּ	*Et subigent.*	And they shall subdue.
כבד	וְכָבוֹד	*Et gloria, honor.*	And glory, honour.
——	וּכְבוֹדוֹ	*Et gloria ejus.*	And his glory.
——	וּכְבוֹדִי	*Et gloria mea.*	And my glory.
——	וּכְבוֹדֶךָ	*Et gloria tua.*	And thy glory.
כבר	וּכְבִיר	*Et pulvinar.*	And a pillow *of goat's hair.*
בית	וּכְבֵית	*Et sicut domus.*	And like the house.
כבס	וְכִבֶּס	*Et lavabit.*	And he shall wash.
——	וְכֻבַּס	*Et lavabitur.*	And he shall be washed.
——	וְכִבְּסוּ	*Et lavabunt.*	And they shall wash.
——	וְכִבַּסְתֶּם	*Et lavabitis.*	And ye shall wash.
ברר	וּכְבֹרִית	*Et instar smegmatis*	And like soap.
כבש	וְכֶבֶשׂ ךְ	*Et agnus.*	And a lamb.
——	וְכִבְשָׂה	*Et agna.*	And an ewe-lamb.
——	וְכִבְשֻׁהָ	*Et subjicite eam.*	And subdue ye her or it.
——	וְכָבְשׁוּ	*Et subjicient.*	And they shall subdue.
——	וּכְבָשִׂים	*Et agni.*	And lambs.
בשר	וּכְבָשָׂר	*Et sicut caro.* [*tuas.*	And as flesh.
גבר	וְכִגְבוּרֹתֶיךָ	*Et juxta potentias*	And according to thy might.
גבן	וְכַגְּבִינָה־בְּנָה	*Et sicut caseus.*	And like cheese.
גבר	וּכְגֶבֶר	*Et sicut vir.*	And like a man.
גלל	וּכְגַלְגַּל	*Et sicut rota.*	And like a rolling thing.
גנן	וּכְגַנָּה	*Et sicut hortus.*	And like a garden.
דבר	וּכְדַבְּרוֹ	*Et juxta loqui eum.*	And as he spoke.
כדד	וְכַדָּהּ	*Et hydria ejus.*	And her pitcher.
די	וּכְדֵי	*Et quum.* [*tiam.*	And when. [ciency.
——	וּכְדֵי	*Et juxta sufficien-*	And according to the suffi-
כדד	וְכַדִּים	*Et hydriæ.*	And pitchers. [cle.
כדכד	וְכַדְכֹּד	*Et pyropus.*	And a sparkling gem, carbun-
דם	וְכִדְמֵי	*Et juxta sanguinem*	And by the blood.
דן	וְכִדְנָה	*Et juxta hoc, sic.*	And according to this, thus.
דרך	וּכְדֶרֶךְ	*Et quasi iter.*	And as it were a journey.
כה	וְכֹה וְכֹה	*Et sic, hic.*	And so, here.
	וְכָהֶם	*Et sicut illi.* [*tur.*	And like them. [priest's office.
כהן	וְכִהֵן	*Et sacerdotio funge-*	And he shall minister in the
——	וְכֹהֵן	*Et sacerdos.*	And the priest.

ROOTS.	DERIVATIVES.	VERSIO.	SIGNIFICATION.
	וְכָהֵנָּה	*Et sicut illa.* [*gentur*	And like them. [priest's office.
כהן	וְכִהֲנוּ	*Et sacerdotio fun-*	And they shall minister in the
—	וְכַהֲנוֹהִי	*Et sacerdotes ejus.*	And his priests.
—	וְכַהֲנַיָּא	*Et sacerdotes.*	And the priests.
—	וְכֹהֲנֶיהָ	*Et sacerdotes ejus.*	And her priests.
—	וְכֹהֲנֵיהֶם	*Et sacerdotes eorum*	And their priests.
—	וְכֹהֲנָיו	*Et sacerdotes ejus.*	And his priests.
—	וְכֹהֲנִים	*Et sacerdotes* [*sent.*	And priests.
צור	וּכְהָצֵר	*Et cum angustiæ es-*	And when there were afflictions
רום	וּכְהָרִים	*Et attollendo.*	And in lifting.
שחת	וּכְהַשְׁחִית	*Et disperdendo.*	And in destroying.
כהה	וְכָהֲתָה	*Et defecit.*	And he failed.
ידה	וּכְהִתְוַדֹּתוֹ	*Et in confiteri eum.*	And as he confessed.
פלל	וּכְהִתְפַּלֵּל	*Et orando.*	And in praying.
כאב	וְכוֹאֵב	*Et dolens.*	And sorrowful.
כבע	וְכוֹבַע־־בַע	*Et galea.*	And a helmet.
—	וְכוֹבָעִים	*Et galeæ.*	And helmets.
כוא	וְכַוִּין	*Et fenestræ.*	And windows.
ככב	וכוֹכָבִים־־כֹבֵי	*Et stellæ.*	And the stars.
כמז	וְכוּמָז	*Et cingulus,* ornamentum muliebre	And a girdle, *a female ornament.* [establish.
כון	וְכוֹנֵן	*Et para te, stabiliet*	And prepare thyself, he shall
כוס	וְכוֹס	*Et poculum.*	And the cup.
—	וְכוֹסִי	*Et poculum meum.*	And my cup.
כור	וְכוּר	*Et fornax.*	And the furnace.
זה	וְכָזֹאת	*Et sic.*	And so, thus.
—	וְכָזֶה	*Et sic, sic ille.* [*rum*	And thus, thus he.
זמן	וְכִזְמַנָּם	*Et juxta tempus eo-*	And according to their time.
כוח	וְכֹחַ	*Et robur, vires.*	And strength, power.
חול	וְכַחוֹל וכ"	*Et sicut arena.*	And as the sand.
חמה	וּכְחוֹמָה	*Et sicut murus.*	And as a wall.
חוץ	וְכַחוּץ	*Et sicut platea.* [*se.*	And as the street. [ed himself.
חזק	וּכְחֶזְקָתוֹ	*Et cum confirmasset*	And when he had strengthen-
חכה	וּכְחַכֵּי	*Et sicut expectant.*	And as they wait.
חלק	וּכְחֵלֶק	*Et ita portio.*	And so the portion.
חמר	וְכַחֹמֶר	*Et sicut lutum.*	And as clay.
יחם	וְכַחֲמָתִי	*Et juxta iram meam*	And according to my wrath.

ROOTS.	DERIVATIVES.	VERSIO.	SIGNIFICATION.
כחש	וְכַחֵשׁ	*Et mentiri.*	And to lie, deceive.
—	וְכִחֵשׁ־־חֵשׁ	*Et mentitus est.*	And he lied.
—	וְכִחַשְׁתִּי	*Et abnegabo.*	And I shall deny.
טלל	וְכַטַּל וּכְטַל	*Et sicut ros.*	And as the dew.
כי	וְכִי	*Et quia, cum.*	And because, when.
כיד	וְכִידוֹן־־דֹן	*Et hasta.*	And a spear, lance.
יום	וּכְיוֹם	*Et juxta diem.*	And according to the day.
ינה	וּכְיוֹנָה	*Et sicut columba.*	And like a dove.
—	וְכַיּוֹנִים	*Et sicut columbæ.*	And as doves.
כלף	וְכֵילַפּוֹת	*Et mallei.*	And hammers.
כים	וְכִימָה	*Et pleiades.*	And the pleiades, the seven [stars.
יום	וְכִימֵי	*Et sicut dies.*	And as the days.
—	וּכְיָמֶיךָ	*Et sicut dies tui.*	And as thy days.
ירא	וּכְיִרְאָתְךָ	*Et ut timor tuus.*	And as thy fear.
כיר	וְכִירַיִם	*Et ollæ.*	And pots, pans.
ירק	וּכְיֶרֶק	*Et sicut viridis.*	And as the green.
ישר	וְכַיָּשָׁר	*Et sicut rectus.*	And as right.
כד	וְכָכָה	*Et sic.*	And thus.
כוח	וּכְכֹחִי	*Et sic robur meum.*	And so my strength.
כלל	וּכְכָל־־כֹּל	*Et sicut omnes, tota.*	And as all, whole.
—	וְכַכַּלָּה	*Et sicut sponsa.*	And as a bride.
כלה	וּכְכַלּוֹת	*Et finiendo.*	And in making an end.
—	וּכְכַלּוֹתָם	*Et juxta absolvere*	And when *they had* finished.
כסף	וְכַכֶּסֶף	*Et sicut argentum.*	And as silver.
כפר	וְכַכְּפִיר־־כְּכְ׳	*Et sicut leo juvenis.*	And as a young lion.
ככר	וְכִכַּר	*Et frustum, talentum*	And a morsel, a talent.
כלל	וְכָל	*Et omnis, quisque.*	And all, every one.
—	וְכֹל	*Et omnis, quisquis.*	And all, whosoever.
—	וּכֹּל	*Et universi.*	And all.
כול	וְכָל	*Et complexus est.*	And he comprehended.
לבא	וּכְלָבִיא	*Et instar leænæ.*	And like a lioness.
לבב	וּכִלְבָבְךָ	*Et juxta cor tuum.*	And according to thy heart.
כלה	וְכָלָה	*Et explebitur, deficiet, consummatio*	And he shall be completed, shall fail, cease, a full end.
כלל	וְכַלָּה	*Et sponsa.*	And the bride.
כלה	וְכִלָּה וְכַלֵּה	*Et finivit, consumet.*	And he ended, shall consume.
להב	וּכְלֶהָבָה	*Et sicut flamma.*	And as the flame.

ROOTS.	DERIVATIVES.	VERSIO.	SIGNIFICATION.
כלל	וְכֻלּוֹ	*Et totus, totus ipse.*	And whole, all, he all over.
כלה	וְכָלוֹת	*Et deficientes.*	And failing.
כלל	וְכַלּוֹתֵיכֶם	*Et sponsæ vestræ.*	And your spouses. [a churl.
כלה	וְכֵלַי	*Et avarus, tenax.*	And covetous, close-fisted,
—	וּכְלִי	*Et vas.*	And the vessel.
—	וּכְלֵי	*Et vasa, instrumenta*	And the vessels, instruments.
—	וְכֵלָיו	*Et vasa, arma, instrumenta ejus.*	And his vessels, arms, instruments.
—	וְכִלָּיוֹן	*Et consumptio.*	And a failing, consumption.
—	וּכְלָיוֹת	*Et renes.*	And the reins, kidneys.
—	וְכִלְיוֹתַי	*Et renes mei.*	And my reins.
כלל	וְכָלִיל	*Et tota victima.*	And whole victim, sacrifice.
—	וּכְלִיל	*Et perfectus.*	And perfect.
ליל	וְכַלָּיְלָה	*Et veluti nocte.*	And as by night.
כלה	וְכֵלִים	*Et vasa.*	And vessels.
—	וְכִלִּיתָ	*Et consummabis.*	And thou shalt accomplish.
—	וְכִלֵּיתִי	*Et consummabo.*	And I will accomplish.
—	וְכִלִּיתִיךָ	*Et consumam.*	And I will consume thee.
—	וְכִלִּיתֶם	*Et consumemini.*	And ye shall be consumed.
כלל	וְכָלְכְּלוּ	*Et omnes adfuerunt.*	And they were all present.
כול	וְכִלְכְּלוּ	*Et aluerunt.*	And they nourished, fed.
—	וְכִלְכְּלָם	*Et aluit eos.*	And he nourished, fed them.
—	וְכִלְכַּלְתִּי	*Et alam.*	And I will nourish, feed.
כלל	וְכֻלְּכֶם	*Et vos omnes.*	And all ye.
—	וְכֻלָּם	*Et omnes hi, ipsi.*	And all these, all those. [nour.
כלם	וּכְלִמָּה	*Et pudor, ignominia*	And shame, confusion, disho-
—	וּכְלִמּוּת	*Et ignominia.*	And disgrace.
—	וּכְלִמָּתִי	*Et ignominia mea.*	And my dishonour.
כלל	וְכֻלָּנוּ	*Et omnes nos.*	And all we.
לפד	וּכְלַפִּיד	*Et sicut fax.*	And like a torch.
לשן	וְכִלְשׁוֹן	*Et juxta linguam.*	And according to the language.
—	וְכִלְשׁוֹנָם	*Et secundum linguam eorum.*	And according to their language.
כלה	וְכִלְּתָה	*Et consumet.*	And he shall consume.
כלל	וְכַלָּתוֹ	*Et nurus ejus.*	And his daughter-in-law.
כלה	וְכִלָּתוֹ	*Et consumet eum.*	And he shall consume him.
כלל	וְכַלֹּתֶיהָ	*Et nurus ejus.*	And her daughter-in-law.

ROOTS.	DERIVATIVES.	VERSIO.	SIGNIFICATION.
מה	וְכַמָּה	*Et quantus.*	And what, how much.
—	וְכַמֹהוּ	*Et sicut ipse.*	And as he.
כמו	וּכְמוֹ	*Et cum, instar.*	And when, like.
מוץ	וּכְמוֹץ־מֹץ	*Et sicut gluma.*	And like chaff.
יצא	וּכְמוֹצָא	*Et sicut scaturigo.*	And like a spring.
מות	וּכְמוֹתוֹ	*Et moriendo eum.*	And when he died.
טמן	וְכַמַּטְמֹנִים	*Et sicut thesauri.*	And as hidden treasures.
מטר	וְכַמָּטָר	*Et sicut pluvia.*	And as rain.
מים	וְכַמַּיִם	*Et sicut aqua.*	And as water.
מלא	וּכְמְלֹאָה	*Et sicut plenitudo.*	And as the fulness.
כמן	וְכַמֹּן	*Et cyminum.* [*tum.*	And the cummin.
מנח	וְכַמִּנְחָה	*Et sicut oblatio, fer-*	And as the meat-offering.
סתר	וּכְמַסְתֵּר	*Et veluti abscondens*	And as it were hiding.
עלל	וּכְמַעֲלָלֵינוּ	*Et juxta actiones nostras.*	And according to our actions, doings.
עשה	וּכְמַעֲשֵׂה	*Et secundum opus.*	And according to the work.
צבא	וּכְמִצְבְּיֵהּ	*Et juxta velle suum.*	And according to his will.
צוה	וְכַמִּצְוָה	*Et juxta præceptum*	And according to a commandment. [mandment.
—	וּכְמִצְוַת	*Et juxta mandatum.*	And according to the com-
קרב	וּכְמִקְרְבֵהּ	*Et accedendo eum.*	And as he approached. [ance.
ראה	וּכְמַרְאֵה	*Et juxta visionem.*	And according to the appear-
כמר	וּכְמָרָיו	*Et sacrificuli ejus.*	And his priests.
סמר	וּכְמַשְׂמְרוֹת	*Et sicut clavi.*	And as nails. [of it.
שפט	וּכְמִשְׁפָּטוֹ	*Et juxta ritum ejus.*	And according to the manner
—	וּכְמִשְׁפָּטֵי	*Et secundum judicia*	And according to the judgments.
—	וּכְמִשְׁפְּטֵיהֶן	*Et secundum ordines earum* [*rum.*	And according to their fashions. [ments.
—	וּכְמִשְׁפָּטָם	*Et juxta judicia eo-*	And according to their judg-
כון	וְכֵן	*Et sic, similiter.*	And so, in like manner.
נבל	וּכְנֹבֶלֶת	*Et sicut decidens.*	And as fading, failing.
כנן	וְכַנָּה	*Et planta, surculus.*	And the plant, scion, branch.
נהר	וְכַנְּהָרוֹת	*Et tanquam flumina*	And like the rivers.
כון	וְכַנּוֹ	*Et basis ejus.*	And his base.
נוח	וּכְנוֹחַ	*Et juxta quiescere.*	And when there was rest.
כנר	וְכִנּוֹר	*Et cithara.*	And a harp.

ROOTS.	DERIVATIVES.	VERSIO.	SIGNIFICATION.
כנה	וּכְנָוָתֵהּ	*Et socii ejus.*	And his companions.
—	וּכְנָוָתְהוֹן	*Et socii eorum.*	And their companions.
נחל	וּכְנַחַל	*Et sicut torrens.*	And like a stream.
כנם	וּכְנֵמָא	*Et hujusmodi.*	And thus, of this manner.
כון	וְכֹנַנְתִּי	*Et stabiliam.*	And I will establish.
נסס	וְכַנֵּס	*Et sicut vexillum.*	And as an ensign.
נסך	וּכְנִסְכָּהּ	*Et juxta libamen ejus.*	And according to her drink offering.
—	וּכְנִסְכּוֹ	*Et sicut libamen ejus*	And as his drink offering.
כנס	וְכִנַּסְתִּי	*Et congregabo.*	And I will gather.
—	וְכִנַּסְתִּים	*Et congregabo eos.*	And I will gather them.
כנף	וּכְנַף	*Et ala.*	And the wing.
—	וְכַנְפֵי	*Et alæ.*	And the wings.
—	וְכַנְפֵיהֶם	*Et alæ eorum.*	And their wings.
נפש	וּכְנֶפֶשׁ	*Et sic anima.*	And so the soul.
כנר	וְכִנֹּרוֹת	*Et citharæ.*	And harps.
כסא	וְכִסֵּא	*Et sella, solium.*	And a stool, the throne.
—	וְכִסְאוֹ	*Et thronus ejus.*[sos	And his throne.
סבא	וּכְסָבְאָם	*Et juxta inebriari ip-*	And while they are drunken.
כסה	וְכִסָּה	*Et teget.*	And he shall cover.
—	וְכֹסֶה	*Et tegens.*	And covering.
—	וְכִסָּהוּ	*Et teget eum.*	And he shall cover him.
—	וְכִסּוּ	*Et operient.*	And they shall cover.
—	וְכִסּוּךְ	*Et teget te.*	And he shall cover thee.
סוף	וְכַסּוּפָה	*Et sicut turbo.*	And like a whirlwind.
כוס	וְכֹסוֹת	*Et pocula.*	And cups.
כסל	וּכְסִיל	*Et stultus, Orion.*	And a, the fool, foolish, Orion
—	וּכְסִילֵיהֶם	*Et sidera vel constellationes eorum.*	And their stars or constellations.
—	וּכְסִילִים	*Et stulti.*	And fools.
כסה	וְכִסִּינוּ	*Et celabimus.*	And we will cover, conceal.
—	וְכִסִּיתָ	*Et teges.*	And thou shalt cover.
—	וְכִסִּיתוֹ	*Et teges eum.*	And thou shalt cover him.
—	וְכִסֵּיתִי	*Et operiam.*	And I will cover.
סכך	וּכְסֻכָּה	*Et sicut tugurium.*	And as a booth.
כסם	וְכֻסְּמִים	*Et speltæ.*	And spelt.
—	וְכֻסֶּמֶת	*Et spelta.*	And spelt, *a kind of wheat.*

ROOTS.	DERIVATIVES.	VERSIO.	SIGNIFICATION.
כסף	וְכֶסֶף וְכָ״	*Et argentum.* [*nia.*	And the silver.
—	וְכֶסֶף וְכַסְפָּא	*Et argentum, pecu-*	And the silver, the money.
כסה	וְכִסְּתָה	*Et teget.*	And she shall cover.
עבה	וּכְעָב	*Et sicut nubes.*	And as a cloud.
עבת	וְכַעֲבוֹת	*Et veluti funis.*	And as a rope.
יעד	וְכַעֲדָתוֹ	*Et sicut cœtus ejus.*	And as his company.
עכס	וּכְעֶכֶס	*Et sicut compes.*	And as the stocks.
עלה	וְכֶעָלֶה־־לֶה	*Et sicut folium* [*tuas*	And as a leaf.
עלל	וְכַעֲלִילוֹתֶיךָ	*Et juxta actiones*	And according to thy doings.
—	וְכַעֲלִילוֹתֵיכֶם	*Et juxta actiones vestras.* [*earum.*	And according to your doings.
—	וְכַעֲלִילוֹתָם	*Et juxta actiones*	And according to their doings.
עמד	וּכְעָמְדוֹ	*Et cum stabit ipse.*	And when he shall stand up.
עמר	וּכְעָמִיר	*Et sicut manipulus.*	And as the handful.
עמם	וּכְעַמְּךָ	*Et sicut populus tuus*	And as thy people.
כען	וּכְעַן	*Et nunc.*	And now.
ענן	וְכֶעָנָן	*Et veluti nubes.*	And as a cloud.
ענת	וּכְעֶנֶת	*Et juxta tempus.*	And at such a time.
כעס	וְכַעַס וְכַעַס	*Et iracundia.*	And wrath.
—	וְכָעַס־־עַס	*Et irascetur, ira.*	And he will be angry, wrath.
—	וְכַעְסִי	*Et indignatio mea.*	And my indignation.
עסס	וְכֶעָסִיס	*Et tanquam mustum*	And as sweet, new wine.
כעס	וְכִעֲסַתָּה	*Et provocavit eam.*	And she provoked her.
עצם	וּכְעֶצֶם	*Et sicut ipsa substantia.* [*fuit.*	And as the very substance.
—	וּכְעָצְמוֹ	*Et cum robustus*	And when he was strong.
עשן	וְכֶעָשָׁן וּכְעָשָׁן	*Et sicut fumus.*	And as smoke.
עתת	וּכְעֵת וְכָעֵת	*Et juxta tempus.*	And at the time.
ענת	וּכְעֶת	*Et juxta tempus.*	And at the time.
כפף	וְכַף	*Et manus.*	And a hand.
כפר	וּכְפוֹר	*Et crater, pelvis.*	And a bowl, bason.
—	וּכְפוֹרֵי	*Et crateres.*	And the bowls, basons.
כפף	וְכַפּוֹת	*Et palmæ, cochlearia, acerræ.*	And the palms, spoons, censers.
פטש	וּכְפַטִּישׁ	*Et sicut malleus.*	And like a hammer,
כפף	וְכַפֶּיהָ	*Et manus ejus.*	And her hand.
—	וְכַפָּיו	*Et manus ejus.*	And his hand.

ROOTS.	DERIVATIVES.	VERSIO.	SIGNIFICATION.
כפה	וְכֵפִים	*Et rupes.*	And the rocks.
כפס	וְכָפִים	*Et tignum.*	And the beam.
כפר	וּכְפִיר	*Et leo juvenis [tui.*	And a young lion.
—	וּכְפִירַיִךְ	*Et leones juvenes*	And thy young lions.
כפל	וְכָפַלְתָּ	*Et duplicabis.*	And thou shalt double.
כפר	וְכַפֵּר	*Et expia.*	And make thou an atonement
—	וְכִפֶּר	*Et expiabit, propitius erit.*	And he shall make an atonement, he will be merciful.
—	וְכֻפַּר	*Et expiabitur.*	And it shall be expiated.
—	וּכְפֹר	*Et pruina.*	And the hoar frost.
—	וְכִפְּרוּ	*Et expiabunt.*	And they shall expiate.
פרץ	וְכִפְרוֹץ וְכִפְרֹץ	*Et cum crumperet.*	And when he came abroad.
פרזל	וּכְפַרְזְלָא	*Et sicut ferrum.*	And as iron.
פרה	וְכִפְרִי	*Et juxta fructum.*	And according to the fruit.
פרש	וּכְפָרָשִׁים	*Et sicut equites.*	And as horsemen.
כפר	וְכָפַרְתָּ	*Et oblines, pice obduces.*	And thou shalt daub, cover with pitch.
—	וְכִפַּרְתָּהוּ	*Et expiabis eum.*	And thou shalt purge him.
—	וְכִפַּרְתֶּם	*Et expiabitis.*	And ye shall expiate.
פשע	וּכְפִשְׁעֵיהֶם	*Et secundum prævaricationes eorum.*	And according to their transgressions.
כפה	וְכִפָּתוֹ	*Et ramus ejus [eum*	And his branch.
פתח	וּכְפִתְחוֹ	*Et juxta aperire*	And when he opened.
—	וּכְפִתְחֵי	*Et secundum ostia.*	And according to the doors.
—	וּכְפִתְחֵיהֶן	*Et juxta ostia eorum*	And according to their doors.
כפף	וְכַפֹּתָיו	*Et cochlearia ejus.*	And his spoons.
כפתר	וְכַפְתֹּר	*Et globulus, sphærula*	And a round or globular knob
צאן	וּכְצֹאן	*Et sicut pecus. [*	And as a sheep, flock.
צבא	וְכִצְבָאִים	*Et sicut capreæ.*	And as the roes.
צמר	וְכַצֶּמֶר	*Et sicut lana.*	And as wool.
צפר	וּכְצִפּוֹר	*Et sicut avis.*	And as a bird. [pent.
צפע	וּכְצִפְעֹנִי	*Et regulus.*	And a basilisk, poisonous ser-
צפר	וְכַצִּפֳּרִים	*Et sicut aves.*	And as the birds.
קנא	וּכְקִנְאָתְךָ	*Et juxta zelum tuum*	And according to thy jealousy
ראה	וְכִרְאוֹת	*Et videndo.*	And in seeing.
—	וְכִרְאוֹתָם	*Et juxta videre eos.*	And when they saw.
ראש	וּכְרֹאשׁ	*Et velut fastigium.*	And as the top.

ROOTS.	DERIVATIVES.	VERSIO.	SIGNIFICATION.
רבב	וּכְרֹב	*Et secundum multitudinem.*	And according to the multitude.
—	וְכִרְבִיבִים	*Et sicut imbres.*	And as the showers.
כרבל	וְכַרְבְּלָתְהוֹן	*Et tiaræ eorum.*	And their turbans.
כרב	וּכְרוּב	*Et cherub.*	And the cherub.
—	וּכְרוּבִים	*Et cherubim.*	And the cherubim.
כרז	וְכָרוֹזָא	*Et præco.*	And the herald.
כרת	וְכָרוֹת	*Et ferire, pangere.*	And to strike, covenant.
—	וְכָרוֹת וּכְרוֹת	*Et excisus.*	And cut off.
רחל	וּכְרָחֵל	*Et sicut ovis.*	And as a sheep.
רחם	וּכְרַחֲמֶיךָ	*Et juxta misericordias tuas.*	And according to thy mercies
כרכם	וְכַרְכֹּם	*Et crocus.*	And saffron.
כרם	וְכֶרֶם וְכָרֶם	*Et vinea.*	And the vineyard, vintage.
—	וְכַרְמֵיכֶם	*Et vineæ vestræ.*	And your vineyards.
—	וְכֹרְמֵיכֶם	*Et vinitores vestri.*	And your vine-dressers.
כרמל	וְכַרְמִיל	*Et coccinum.*	And crimson or scarlet.
כרם	וּכְרָמִים	*Et vineæ.*	And the vineyards.
—	וְכֹרְמִים	*Et vinitores.*	And vine-dressers.
—	וּכְרָמֵינוּ	*Et vineæ nostræ.*	And our vineyards.
—	וְכַרְמְךָ	*Et vinea tua.*	And thy vineyard.
כרמל	וְכַרְמֶל	*Et spica tenera, arvum.*	And green ears, the cultivated field.
רוע	וּכְרֹעַ	*Et juxta nequitiam.*	And according to the wickedness.
כרע	וּכְרָעָיו	*Et crura ejus.*	And his legs.
רקב	וְכָרָקָב וּכְרָקָב	*Et sicut putredo.*	And as rottenness.
כרת	וְכָרַתָּ	*Et succides.*	And thou shalt cut down.
—	וְכָרַת	*Et excidet.*	And he shall cut off.
—	וְכָרְתוּ	*Et succident.*	And they shall cut down.
—	וּכְרֻתוֹת	*Et abscissæ.*	And cut off.
—	וְכָרַתִּי	*Et feriam, pangam.*	And I will strike, make, covenant.
כשב	וְכֶשֶׂב	*Et agnus.*	And a lamb.
שדד	וּכְשֹׁד	*Et sicut vastatio.*	And as a destruction.
שוב	וּכְשׁוּב	*Et revertendo.*	And in returning.
שוק	וּכְשׁוֹק	*Et sicut armus.*	And as the shoulder.
שחק	וּכְשַׁחַק	*Et sicut pulvis.*	And as dust.
שכב	וּכְשֹׁכֵב	*Et sicut cubans.*	And as he that lieth down.

ROOTS.	DERIVATIVES.	VERSIO.	SIGNIFICATION.
שכר	וּכְשָׂכִיר	*Et sicut mercenarius*	And as an hireling.
כשל	וְכָשַׁל	*Et corruet.* [*dent.*	And he shall fall.
—	וְכָשְׁלוּ	*Et impingent, ca-*	And they shall stumble, fall.
—	וְכָשַׁלְתָּ	*Et corrues.*	And thou shalt fall.
שמן	וְכַשֶּׁמֶן־־שֶּׁ	*Et sicut oleum.*	And like oil.
שמע	וְכִשְׁמֹעַ	*Et audiendo.*	And upon hearing.
—	וּכְשָׁמְעוֹ	*Et cum audisset.*	And when he had heard.
—	וּכְשָׁמְעִי	*Et cum audissem.*	And when I had heard.
שנה	וּכְשָׁנִים	*Et sicut anni.* [*est.*	And like the years.
כשף	וְכִשֵּׁף	*Et divinatione usus*	And he used witchcraft.
—	וּכְשָׁפֶיהָ	*Et incantationes ejus*	And her witchcrafts.
כשר	וְכָשֵׁר	*Et rectus.*	And right.
שרש	וְכַשֹּׁרֶשׁ	*Et sicut radix.*	And as a root.
תאן	וְכַתְּאֵנִים	*Et sicut ficus.*	And like figs.
כתב	וְכָתַב	*Et scribet.*	And he shall write.
—	וּכְתַב־־תָבָא	*Et scriptura.*	And the writing.
—	וּכְתֹב	*Et scribe.*	And write thou.
—	וְכִתְבוּ	*Et describite.*	And describe ye.
בוא	וְכִתְבוּאַת	*Et sicut proventus.*	And as the produce, increase.
כתב	וְכֹתְבִים	*Et scribentes.*	And writing.
—	וְכֹתְבֹן	*Et scribentes.*	And writing.
—	וְכָתַבְתָּ	*Et scribes.*	And thou shalt write.
—	וּכְתֹבֶת	*Et scriptura.*	And the writing.
—	וְכָתַבְתִּי	*Et scribam.*	And I will write.
—	וּכְתַבְתָּם	*Et scribes ea.*	And thou shalt write them.
—	וְכָתוֹב	*Et scribere.*	And to write.
—	וְכָתוּב	*Et scriptura.*	And the writing.
תעב	וּכְתוֹעֲבוֹתֵיהֶן	*Et secundum abominationes earum.*	And according to their abominations.
ירה	וְכַתּוֹרָה	*Et juxta legem.*	And according to the law.
כתת	וְכָתוּת	*Et contusus.*	And crushed.
—	וְכַתּוֹתִי	*Et contundam.*	And I will beat down.
תמם	וּכְתֻמִּי	*Et juxta integritatem meam.*	And according to my integrity
כתן	וְכָתְנוֹת־־נֹת	*Et tunicæ.*	And coats.
—	וּכְתֹנֶת	*Et tunica.*	And a coat.
כתף	וְכָתֵף	*Et humerus.*	And the shoulder.

ROOTS.	DERIVATIVES.	VERSIO.	SIGNIFICATION.
כתף	וְכִתְפוֹת	*Et latera.*	And the sides.
תקע	וּבְתִקְעַ	*Et cum clangit.*	And when he bloweth.
כתר	וְכֹתָרֹת	*Et capitella.*	And the chapiters.
—	וְכֹתֶרֶת	*Et capitellum.*	And the chapiter.
כתת	וְכִתַּת	*Et confregit.*	And he brake in pieces.
—	וְכִתְּתוּ	*Et contundent.*	And they shall beat. [stroyed
—	וְכֻתְּתוּ	*Et contritæ sunt.*	And they were crushed, de-
	ול		
לא	וְלֹא וְלָא־לֹא־לוֹא	*Et non, nunquam.*	And not, never.
לו	וְלֻא	*Et si, nisi.*	And if, unless.
אבד	וּלְאַבֵּד	*Et ad perdendum.*	And to destroy.
—	וּלְאַבְּדָם	*Et ad perdendum eos*	And to destroy them.
אבה	וְלַאֲבוֹתֵיהֶם־ב׳	*Et patribus eorum.*	And to their fathers.
—	וְלַאֲבוֹתֵיכֶם־ב׳	*Et patribus vestris.*	And to your fathers.
—	וּלְאָבִיו	*Et patri ejus, propter patrem ejus.*	And to his father, for his father.
—	וּלְאֶבְיוֹנְךָ	*Et egeno tuo.*	And to thy needy.
אבל	וְלַאֲבֵלָיו	*Et lugentibus ejus.*	And to his mourners.
אבן	וְלָאֶבֶן ול׳	*Et in lapidem.*	And for, to a stone.
—	וּלְאַבְנֵי	*Et ad lapides.*	And to stones.
אבה	וְלַאֲבֹתֶיךָ	*Et patribus tuis.*	And to thy fathers.
—	וְלַאֲבֹתֵינוּ	*Et patribus nostris.*	And to our fathers.
אדן	וְלָאָדוֹן	*Et domino.*	And to a lord.
אדב	וְלַאֲדִיב	*Et ad cruciandum.*	And to vex, torment.
אדם	וּלְאָדָם	*Et homini.*	And to a man.
אהב	וּלְאַהֲבָה	*Et ad diligendum.*	And to love.
אמם	וּלְאוּמִּי	*Et gens mea.*	And O my nation. [country.
זרח	וְלָאֶזְרָח	*Et indigenæ.* [um.	And for the native of the
אחד	וּלְאַחַד־אֶחָד	*Et ad unum, alter-*	And to one, the other.
אחה	וּלְאָחוֹת	*Et sorori.*	And to a sister.
—	וְלְאַחוֹתֵיכֶם	*Et sororibus vestris.*	And to your sisters.
אחז	וְלֶאֱחֹז	*Et ad prehendendum*	And to lay hold.
—	וְלַאֲחֻזַּת	*Et ad possessionem.*	And to the possession.
אחה	וְלַאֲחֵיהֶם	*Et fratribus eorum.*	And to their brethren.
—	וּלְאָחִיו	*Et fratri ejus.*	And for, to his brother.
—	וּלְאֶחָיו	*Et fratribus ejus.*	And to his brethren.

ROOTS.	DERIVATIVES.	VERSIO.	SIGNIFICATION.
אחה	וּלְאָחִיךָ	*Et fratri tuo.*	And to thy brother.
אחר	וְלַאֲחֵרִים	*Et aliis.*	And for, to others.
אחה	וְלַאֲחֹתוֹ ולא׳	*Et sorori ejus.*	And to his sister.
אלם	וְלְאֵילָמָו־־אֵלָ׳	*Et vestibula ejus.*	And his porches.
אין	וּלְאֵין	*Et cui non.*	And to whom not.
איש	וּלְאִישׁ ול״	*Et viro, unicuique.*	And to a man, every one.
——	וּלְאִישָׁהּ	*Et viro ejus.*	And to her husband.
אכל	וְלֶאֱכֹל	*Et ad comedendum*	And to eat.
——	וּלְאָכְלְכֶם	*Et pro cibo vestro.*	And for your food.
אלה	וּלְאֵלֶּה	*Et his, istis.*	And for these, to those.
——	וְלֶאֱלֹהַּ־לֶאֱלָהָא	*Et deo.*	And to a god, the god.
——	וּלְאלֹהֵי	*Et diis.*	And to the gods.
——	וְלֵאלֹהֵיהֶם	*Et diis eorum.*	And to their gods.
אלל	וְלֶאֱלִילֶיהָ	*Et idolis ejus.*	And to her idols.
אלם	וּלְאֻלָם	*Et porticui.*	And for the porch.
——	וְלָאַלְמָנָה	*Et ad viduas.*	And to the widows.
אלף	וּלְאַלְפֵיכֶם	*Et per millia vestra*	And by your thousands.
——	וְלַאֲלָפִים	*Et per millia.*	And by thousands.
אמם	וּלְאֵם	*Et matri.*	And for a mother.
——	וּלְאֹם	*Et populus.*	And a people.
——	וּלְאִמָּהּ	*Et matri ejus.*	And to her mother.
——	וּלְאִמּוֹ	*Et matri ejus.*	And to, for his mother.
——	וּלְאִמִּי	*Et matri meæ.*	And to my mother.
——	וּלְאֻמִּים	*Et populi, gentes.*	And ye people, the nations.
אמר	וְלֵאמֹר	*Et dicendum.*	And to say, speak.
——	וּלְאִמְרַת	*Et verbo.*	And to, for the word.
אמה	וְלַאֲמָתְךָ	*Et ancillæ tuæ.*	And to, for thy maid servant.
אנש	וּלְאַנְשֵׁיהֶם	*Et viris eorum.*	And to their men.
——	וְלַאֲנָשִׁים	*Et hominibus.*	And to the men.
אסר	וְלַאֲסוּרִים	*Et vinctus.*	And to them that are bound.
——	וְלֶאֱסוּרִין	*Et ad vincula.*	And to bonds, chains.
אסף	וְלַאֲסֻפִּים	*Et ad cœtus.*	And to the assemblies.
אסר	וּלְאִסָּר	*Et in obligatione.*	And in the bond.
אפה	וּלְאֹפוֹת	*Et in pistrices.*	And for bakers. [sures.
אצר	וּלְאֹצָרוֹת	*Et in thesauros.*	And towards, over the trea-
——	וּלְאֹצָרוֹת	*Et de thesauris.*	And of the treasuries.
ארץ	וְלָאָרֶץ	*Et terræ.*	And to the land.

ROOTS.	DERIVATIVES.	VERSIO.	SIGNIFICATION.
ארץ	וּלְאַרְצִי	*Et ad terram meam*	And to my country.
—	וּלְאַרְצְךָ	*Et terræ tuæ.*	And to thy land.
—	וּלְאַרְצָם	*Et terræ eorum.*	And to their land.
איש	וְלָאִשָּׁה וּלְ׳	*Et mulieri. [delicto.*	And for, to a woman.
אשם	וְלָאָשָׁם	*Et de victima pro*	And for the trespass offering.
אשף	וְלָאַשָּׁפִים	*Et astrologos.*	And the astrologers.
אשר	וְלַאֲשֶׁר	*Et ei qui, eis qui.*	And to him who, to them who
—	וְלָאֲשֵׁרָה	*Et luco.*	And for the grove.
איש	וּלְאִשְׁתּוֹ	*Et uxori ejus.*	And to his wife.
את	וְלָאִתִּים	*Et pro ligonibus.*	And for the coulters.
אתן	וְלָאֲתֹנוֹת	*Et quoad asinos.*	And as for the asses.
לבב	וְלֵב וְ־־לֶב	*Et cor.*	And the heart.
בוא	וְלַבָּא	*Et ingredienti.*	And to him who entereth.
לבב	וּלְבַב	*Et cor.*	And the heart.
—	וּלְבָבָהּ	*Et cor ejus.*	And her heart.
—	וּלְבָבוֹ	*Et cor ejus.*	And his heart.
—	וּלְבָבִי	*Et cor meum.*	And my heart.
—	וּלְבָבְךָ	*Et cor tuum.*	And thy heart.
בגד	וּלְבִגְדֵי	*Et ad vestes.*	And for the garments.
בדד	וּלְבַד	*Et præter.*	And beside.
בהל	וּלְבַהֲלָם	*Et ad turbandum eos*	And to trouble them.
בהם	וְלַבְּהֵמָה	*Et de bestia, in pecus*	And of beast, for, on the cattle
—	וּלְבֶהֱמַת	*Et pecudi.*	And for the cattle.
—	וּלְבְהֶמְתְּךָ	*Et pecudi tuæ.*	And for thy cattle.
בהר	וְלַבַּהֶרֶת	*Et de vitiligine.*	And for a freckled spot.
לבב	וְלִבּוֹ	*Et cor ejus.*	And his heart.
בוא	וְלָבוֹא	*Et ad ingrediendum*	And to enter.
לבן	וּלְבוֹנָה	*Et thus.*	And frankincense.
ברר	וְלָבוּר	*Et ad explorandum.*	And to explore.
לבש	וּלְבוּשֵׁיהוֹן	*Et in vestibus eorum*	And in their garments.
בזז	וְלָבַז	*Et in prædam.*	And for spoil.
—	וְלָבֹז	*Et ad diripiendum.*	And to take away.
לבב	וְלִבִּי	*Et cor meum.*	And my heart.
בית	וְלַבַּיִת־־בַּיִת	*Et domui, templo.*	And to, for the house, temple.
—	וּלְבֵית	*Et domui.*	And to, for the house.
—	וּלְבֵיתוֹ	*Et ad domum ejus.*	And to his house.
—	וּלְבֵיתְךָ	*Et domui tuæ.*	And to thy house.

ROOTS.	DERIVATIVES.	VERSIO.	SIGNIFICATION.
לבב	וְלִבְךָ	*Et cor tuum.*	And thy heart.
בכר	וְלַבִּכּוּרִים	*Et primitiis.*	And for the first fruits.
בכה	וְלִבְכּוֹתָהּ	*Et ad flendam eam.*	And to weep for her.
בלת	וּלְבִלְתִּי	*Et ut non.*	And that not.
לבב	וְלִבָּם	*Et cor eorum.*	And their heart.
בנה	וּלְבֵן־־בֵּן	*Et filio.*	And to, for a son.
לבן	וְלָבָן	*Et albus.*	And white.
—	וְלִבְנֶה	*Et populus.*	And the poplar.
—	וּלְבֹנָה	*Et thus.*	And frankincense.
בנה	וְלִבְנוֹ	*Et filio ejus.*	And to his son.
—	וְלִבְנוֹת	*Et ad ædificandum.*	And to build.
—	וְלִבְנוֹתֶיהָ	*Et in filiabus ejus.*	And in her daughters.
—	וְלִבְנוֹתָיו	*Et filiabus ejus.*	And to his daughters.
—	וְלִבְנֵי	*Et filiis.*	And to, for the sons.
—	וְלִבְנִי	*Et filio meo.*	And for my son.
—	וְלְבָנַי	*Et filiis meis.*	And for my children.
—	וְלִבְנֵיהֶם	*Et filiis eorum.*	And to, for, with their sons.
—	וּלְבָנָיו	*Et filiis ejus.*	And to his sons.
—	וּלְבָנֶיךָ	*Et filiis tuis.*	And to, for thy sons.
—	וְלַבֹּנִים	*Et ad ædificatores.*	And to the builders.
לבן	וּלְבָנִים	*Et albi.*	And white.
—	וּלְבֵנִים	*Et lateres.*	And the bricks.
בנה	וּלְבָנֵינוּ	*Et filiis nostris.*	And to our children.
—	וְלִבְנְךָ וּלְבִנְךָ	*Et filio tuo.*	And to thy son.
—	וְלִבְנֹתָי־־תַי	*Et filiabus meis.*	And to my daughters.
—	וְלִבְנֹתֶיךָ	*Et filiabus tuis.*	And to thy daughters.
בקר	וְלַבָּקָר	*Et bovem.*	And to the cattle.
—	וְלַבֹּקֶר	*Et mane.*	And to, in the morning.
—	וּלְבַקֵּר	*Et ad inquirendum.*	And to inquire.
בקש	וּלְבַקֵּשׁ	*Et ad quærendum.*	And to seek, request.
ברזל	וְלַבַּרְזֶל	*Et ferro.*	And in iron.
ברך	וּלְבָרֵךְ	*Et ad benedicendum*	And to bless.
—	וּלְבָרְכוֹ	*Et ad benedicendum ei.*	And to bless him.
ברר	וּלְבָרֵר	*Et ad purgandum.*	And to purge.
לבש	וְלָבַשׁ	*Et induet.*	And he shall put on.
—	וְלָבְשׁוּ	*Et indue.*	And put thou on.

ROOTS.	DERIVATIVES.	VERSIO.	SIGNIFICATION.
לבש	וְלָבְשׁוּ	*Et induent.*	And they shall put on.
—	וְלִבְּשָׁם	*Et induet eos.*	And he shall put them on.
בשם	וְלִבְשָׂמִים	*Et aromatibus.*	And for spices.
בוש	וּלְבֹשֶׁת	*Et ad pudorem.*	And *o the shame, confusion.
בנה	וּלְבַת	*Et propter filiam.*	And for a daughter.
—	וּלְבִתּוֹ	*Et filiæ ejus.*	And for his daughter.
לג	וְלֹג	*Et logus,* modius.	And a log, *a measure.*
גיא	וְלַגֵּאָיוֹת־־יאוֹת	*Et vallibus.*	And to the vallies.
גבב	וּלְגֹב	*Et in foveam.*	And into the pit.
גבר	וְלִגְבוּרָה	*Et in robur.*	And for strength.
—	וְלַגְּבִירָה	*Et reginæ.*	And to the queen.
גבע	וְלַגְּבָעוֹת	*Et collibus.*	And to the hills.
גבר	וּלְגֻבְרִין	*Et viris.*	And to the men.
גדל	וּלְגַדְּלָם	*Et adnutriendum eos*	And to nourish them.
—	וּלְגָדְלָתוֹ	*Et magnitudini ejus.*	And for his greatness [hedges.
גדר	וְלַגֹּדְרִים	*Et sepientibus.*	And to builders of walls or
גזל	וְלִגְזֹל	*Et rapiendum.*	And to take away.
גמל	וְלִגְמַלֵּיהֶם	*Et camelis eorum.*	And for their camels.
גור	וְלַגֵּר	*Et peregrino.*	And to the stranger.
נגש	וְלָגֶשֶׁת	*Et ad accedendum.*	And to approach, come near.
ילד	וְלָד־וָלָד	*Et proles, natus.*	And a child.
דבר	וְלִדְבוֹרָה	*Et api. [lum.*	And for the bee. [the oracle.
—	וְלִדְבִיר	*Et ad adytum, oracu-*	And to the most holy place,
דבק	וּלְדָבְקָה	*Et ad adhærendum.*	And to cleave.
דבר	וּלְדָבֶר	*Et de peste.*	And of the pestilence.
—	וּלְדַבֵּר	*Et ad loquendum.*	And to speak.
—	וּלְדְבָרוֹ	*Et in verbo ejus.*	And in his word.
ידע	וְלָדַעַת	*Et ad cognoscendum*	And to know.
	וְלָהּ־וְלָהּ־וְלָהּ	*Et illi.*	And to him.
אבד	וּלְהַאֲבִיד	*Et ad disperdendum.*	And to destroy.
להב	וְלַהַב־וְלֶהָבָה	*Et flamma.*	And the flame.
בדל	וּלְהַבְדִּיל	*Et ad dividendum, discernendum.*	And to divide, to make a difference.
בוא	וּלְהָבִיא	*Et ad ducendum. [te.*	And to bring.
—	וְלַהֲבִיאֲךָ	*Et ad introducendum*	And to bring thee in.
להב	וְלַהֶבֶת	*Et cuspis. [meditatio*	And the head or point [tation.
להג	וְלַהַג	*Et lectio, doctrina,*	And reading, learning, medi-

ROOTS.	DERIVATIVES.	VERSIO.	SIGNIFICATION.
גדל	וּלְהַגְדִּיל	*Et ad magnificandum.*	And to magnify.
נגד	וּלְהַגִּיד	*Et ad indicandum.*	And to declare.
גלה	וּלְהַגְלוֹת	*Et ad deportandum.*	And to carry away.
גור	וּלְהַגֵּרִים	*Et peregrinis.*	And to the strangers.
ידה	וּלְהֹדוֹת־יְהוָה	*Et ad celebrandum.*	And to praise, celebrate.
הדם	וְלַהֲדֹם	*Et scabello.*	And for the footstool.
אבד	וּלְהוֹבָדָה	*Et ad perdendum.*	And to destroy.
ירה	וּלְהוֹרֹת	*Et ad docendum.*	And that ye may teach.
ישע	וּלְהוֹשִׁיעַ	*Et ad servandum.*	And to save.
זכר	וּלְהַזְכִּיר	*Et ad memorandum.*	And to record, make mention
חיה	וּלְהַחֲיוֹת	*Et ad vivum servandum.*	And to save alive.
חרם	וּלְהַחֲרִים	*Et ad occidendum.*	And to kill, slay.
להט	וְלִהַט	*Et incendet.*	And he shall burn.
יבל	וּלְהֵיבָלָה	*Et ad ferendum.*	And to carry.
היה	וְלִהְיוֹת	*Et ut essent.*	And that they should be.
יטב	וּלְהֵיטִיב	*Et ad benefaciendum*	And to do good.
היה	וְלִהְיֹתְךָ	*Et ut sis tu.*	And that thou mayest be.
נכה	וּלְהַכּוֹת	*Et ad percutiendum.*	And to smite.
כחד	וּלְהַכְחִיד	*Et ad excidendum.*	And to cut off.
כון	וּלְהָכִין	*Et ad parandum.*	And to prepare.
כרת	וּלְהַכְרִית	*Et ad excidendum.*	And to cut off.
כשל	וּלְהַכְשִׁיל	*Et ad impingere faciendum-*	And to cause to stumble, cast down.
לחם	וְלַהַלֶּחֶם	*Et panis.*	And the bread.
—	וּלְהִלָּחֵם	*Et ad pugnandum.*	And to fight.
הלל	וּלְהַלֵּל	*Et ad laudandum.*	And to praise.
	וְלָהֶם	*Et illis, sibiipsis.*	And to them, to themselves.
מות	וּלְהָמִית	*Et ad occidendum.*	And to slay, kill.
—	וְלַהֲמִיתוֹ	*Et ad occidendum [eum.*	And to slay him.
	וְלָהֵנָּה	*Et eis.*	And to, for them.
סור	וּלְהָסִיר	*Et ad amovendum.*	And to remove.
נסך	וּלְהַסֵּךְ	*Et ad libandum.*	And to pour out.
עלה	וּלְהַעֲלֹתוֹ	*Et ad educendum eum [instaurandum*	And to bring him up from.
עמד	וּלְהַעֲמִיד	*Et ad stabiliendum,*	And to establish, repair.

ROOTS.	DERIVATIVES.	VERSIO.	SIGNIFICATION.
נפל	וּלְהַפִּיל	*Et ad dejiciendum.*	And to cast down.
הפך	וְלַהֲפֹךְ	*Et ad evertendum.*	And to overturn.
—	וּלְהָפְכָהּ	*Et ad evertendum eam.*	And to overthrow it.
צדק	וּלְהַצְדִּיק	*Et justificando.*	And by justifying.
יצב	וּלְהַצִּיב	*Et ad statuendum, acuendum.*	And to fix, set, sharpen.
נצל	וּלְהַצִּיל	*Et ad eripiendum.*	And to deliver.
—	וּלְהַצִּילְךָ	*Et ad liberandum te.*	And to deliver thee.
צמח	וּלְהַצְמִיחָהּ	*Et ad germinare faciendum.*	And to cause to spring forth.
קום	וּלְהָקִים	*Et ad erigendum.*	And to raise up, set up.
קרדם	וּלְהַקַּרְדֻּמִּים	*Et securibus.*	And for the axes.
רבה	וּלְהַרְבּוֹת	*Et ad multiplicandum.*	And to multiply.
הרס	וְלַהֲרוֹס־רֹס	*Et ad diruendum.*	And to throw down.
רוע	וּלְהָרֵעַ	*Et ad malefaciendum*	And to bring evil, to afflict.
שחת	וּלְהַשְׁחִית	*Et ad perdendum.*	And to destroy.
שוב	וּלְהָשִׁיב	*Et ad restituendum.*	And to restore.
שכל	וּלְהַשְׂכִּיל	*Et ad intelligendum.*	And to understand.
שמד	וּלְהַשְׁמִיד	*Et ad perdendum.*	And to destroy.
שמל	וּלְהַשְׂמִיל	*Et ad sinistram petendam.*	And to go to the left.
שחה	וּלְהִשְׁתַּחֲוֹת	*Et ad incurvandum [se.*	And to bow down, worship.
חתן	וּלְהִתְחַתֵּן	*Et ad affinitatem contrahendam.*	And to contract affinity.
יחש	וּלְהִתְיַחֵשׂ	*Et ad recensendum.*	And to reckon by genealogy.
נפל	וּלְהִתְנַפֵּל	*Et ad cadendum.*	And to fall.
ענה	וּלְהִתְעַנּוֹת	*Et ad affligendum.*	And to afflict.
	וְלוֹ	*Et ei.*	And to, for him.
לו	וְלוּ	*Et utinam.*	And O that, I wish that.
לוז	וְלוּז	*Et amygdalus.*	And the walnut-tree.
זבח	וְלַזֹּבֵחַ	*Et sacrificanti.*	And to him that sacrificeth.
—	וְלִזְבֹּחַ	*Et ad immolandum.*	And to sacrifice.
—	וּלְזֶבַח־וּלְךָ	*Et pro sacrificio.*	And for a sacrifice.
זהב	וּלְזָהָב	*Et auri, auro.*	And of, for gold.
—	וְלִזְהָבִי	*Et auro meo.*	And for my gold.
לוז	וּלְזוּת	*Et pravitas.*	And wickedness.

ROOTS.	DERIVATIVES.	VERSIO.	SIGNIFICATION.
זכר	וּלְזִכָּרוֹן	*Et in monumentum.*	And for a memorial.
—	וּלְזֹכְרֵי	*Et recordantibus.*	And to those that remember.
—	וּלְזִכְרְךָ	*Et ad memoriam tui*	And to the remembrance of thee.
זמר	וּלְזַמֵּר	*Et psallere.*	And to sing praises.
זעק	וְלִזְעֹק	*Et ad clamandum.*	And to cry.
זקן	וּלְזִקְנֵי	*Et ad seniores.*	And to the elders.
זרה	וּלְזָרוֹת	*Et ad spargendum.*	And to scatter.
—	וּלְזָרוֹתָם	*Et ad spargendum eos.*	And to scatter them.
זרע	וּלְזַרְעוֹ	*Et semini ejus.*	And to his seed.
—	וּלְזַרְעֲךָ־עֶךָ	*Et semini tuo.*	And to thy seed.
—	וּלְזַרְעָם	*Et semini eorum.*	And to their seed.
זרק	וְלִזְרֹק	*Et ad spargendum.*	And to sprinkle.
חגג	וְלָחֹג	*Et ad celebrandum.*	And to celebrate.
חגר	וְלַחֲגֹר	*Et ad accingendum.*	And to gird up.
חדש	וּלְחֳדָשִׁים	*Et noviluniis.*	And for the new moons.
חטא	וְלַחוֹטֶא	*Et peccatori.*	And to the sinner.
חמה	וּלְחוֹמַת	*Et muro.*	And for the wall.
חוץ	וְלַחוּץ וְלַחוּצָה	*Et extrinsecus.*	And without, outside.
חזה	וְלַחֹזִים	*Et videntibus.*	And to the seers.
חזק	וּלְחַזֵּק	*Et ad confirmandum*	And to strengthen.
חטא	וְלַחַטָּאוֹת	*Et in victimas pro peccato.*	And for the sin-offerings.
—	וּלְחַטֹּאתֵיכֶם	*Et peccatis vestris.*	And to your sins.
—	וְלַחַטָּאת	*Et de victima pro peccato.*	And of the sin-offering.
—	וּלְחַטָּאתִי	*Et in peccatum meum.*	And after my sin.
—	וּלְחַטָּאתָם	*Et peccato eorum.*	And to their sin.
—	וּלְחַטָּאתֵנוּ	*Et peccato nostro.*	And to our sin.
חיה	וּלְחַי	*Et viventem.*	And him that liveth.
—	וְלַחַיָּה וּלְחַיַּת	*Et bestiæ.*	And to the beast.
—	וּלְחַיּוֹת	*Et ad vivum servandum.*	And to save alive.
—	וּלְהַחֲיוֹתָם	*Et ad vivos servandum eos.*	And to save them alive.
—	וּלְחָיַי	*Et genæ meæ.*	And my cheeks.
חיל	וּלְחֵילוֹ	*Et exercitui ejus.*	And to his army.
חוץ	וְלַחִיצוֹן	*Et extrinsecus.*	And without.
חכם	וּלְחָכְמָה	*Et in sapientia.*	And for, in wisdom.

ROOTS.	DERIVATIVES.	VERSIO.	SIGNIFICATION.
חלה	וּלְחַלּוֹת	*Et ad deprecandum.*	And to pray, beseech.
חלל	וּלְחַלֵּל	*Et ad profanandum.*	And to profane.
לחם	וְלֶחֶם־וְלֶ׳	*Et panis, victus.*	And bread, victuals.
חמה	וּלְחֹמוֹת	*Et muris.*	And to the walls.
לחם	וְלַחְמִי	*Et panis meus.*	And my bread.
—	וּלְחֻמֵי	*Et devorati.*	And devoured.
—	וְלַחְמְךָ	*Et panis tuus.*	And thy bread.
—	וּלְחֻמָם	*Et caro eorum.*	And their flesh.
לחן	וּלְחֵנָתֵהּ	*Et concubinæ ejus.*	And his concubines.
—	וּלְחֵנָתָךְ	*Et concubinæ tuæ.*	And thy concubines.
חסה	וְלַחְסוֹת	*Et ad confidendum.*	And to trust.
חצב	וּלְחֹצְבֵי	*Et ad cæsores.*	And to hewers.
לחץ	וְלָחֲצוּ	*Et prement.*	And they will oppress, afflict.
חצה	וְלַחֲצִי	*Et dimidio.*	And for, to half.
—	וּלְחֶצְיוֹ	*Et dimidio ejus.*	And to the half of him or it.
לחץ	וְלַחֲצֵנוּ	*Et oppressio nostra.*	And our oppression.
חצר	וְלַחֲצַר וְלֶחָצֵר	*Et atrii, in atrio.*	And of, in the court. [fast.
לחץ	וּלְחַצְתֶּם	*Et premetis.* [eam.	And ye shall press, detain, hold
חקר	וּלְחָקְרָהּ	*Et ad quærendum*	And to search it.
חרב	וּלְחָרְבוֹת	*Et in vastitates.*	And into desolations.
חרר	וְלַחֹרִים	*Et proceribus.*	And to the nobles.
חרף	וּלְחֶרְפָּה	*Et in opprobrium.*	And for a reproach.
חרש	וְלַחֲרֹשׁ	*Et ad arandum.*	And to plough.
—	וְלֶחָרָשִׁים	*Et fabris.*	And to the artificers.
חשב	וְלַחְשֹׁב	*Et ad excogitandum*	And to devise.
—	וּלְחֹשְׁבֵי	*Et cogitantibus.*	And for them that think upon
חשף	וְלַחְשׂוֹף	*Et ad hauriendum.*	And to draw.
חשך	וְלַחשֶׁךְ	*Et tenebræ.*	And the darkness.
חשן	וְלַחֹשֶׁן	*Et pectorali.*	And for the breast-plate.
חתם	וְלַחְתֹּם	*Et ad obsignandum.*	And to seal up.
תמם	וּלְהָתֵם	*Et ad finiendum.*	And to make an end of.
לוט	וָלֹט	*Et ladanum,* gummi odoriferum.	And ledum or ladanum, *a sweet-scented gum.*
טבח	וּלְטַבָּחוֹת	*Et in coquas.*	And for cooks.
טהר	וְלַטָּהוֹר	*Et mundo.*	And to the clean.
טוב	וְלְטוֹב	*Et bonum.*	And good.
טטף	וּלְטוֹטָפֹת	*Et in frontalia.*	And for frontlets.

ROOTS.	DERIVATIVES.	VERSIO.	SIGNIFICATION.
טמא	וְלַטָּמֵא	*Et immundo.*	And to the unclean.
טפף	וּלְטַפֵּנוּ	*Et parvulis nostris.*	And for our little ones.
	וְלִי	*Et me, mihi.*	And me, to me.
יגב	וּלְיֹגְבִים	*Et in agricolas*	And for husbandmen.
הוה	וְלַיהוָה וְלֵיהוִֹה	*Et Domini, Domino*	And of, to the Lord.
יום	וּלְיוֹם	*Et in die.*	And in the day.
יעץ	וּלְיוֹעֲצֵי-וּלְי׳	*Et consiliariis.*	And to the counsellors.
יצא	וְלַיוֹצֵא	*Et exeunti.*	And to him that goeth out.
ישב	וּלְיוֹשְׁבָיו	*Et habitatoribus ejus*	And to the inhabitants thereof.
לוה	וְלֹיוֹת	*Et additamenta.*	And additions.
ליל	וָלַיְלָה וָלַי׳ וְלַ״	*Et nox.*	And night.
——	וְלֵילוֹת	*Et noctes.*	And nights.
יום	וּלְיָמִים	*Et dierum.*	And of the days.
לון	וְלִין	*Et pernocta.*	And tarry thou all night.
——	וְלִינוּ	*Et pernoctate.*	And pass ye the night.
יסד	וּלְיַסֵּד	*Et ad fundandum.*	And to lay the foundation.
יקר	וְלִיקָר־־קַ׳	*Et ad gloriam.*	And for the glory.
ירא	וּלְיִרְאָה	*Et ad timendum.*	And to fear.
ירח	וְלַיָּרֵחַ	*Et lunæ.*	And to the moon.
ירד	וּלְיַרְכְּתֵי	*Et ad latera.*	And at the sides.
ליש	וָלַיִשׁ	*Et leo.*	And the lion.
ישב	וּלְיֹשְׁבֵי	*Et habitatoribus.*	And to the inhabitants.
ישר	וּלְיִשְׁרֵי	*Et rectis.*	And to, for the upright.
——	וְלַיְשָׁרִים	*Et rectis.*	And to the upright.
יתר	וּלְיֶתֶר	*Et residuo.*	And to the rest.
ילד	וָלֵךְ וּלֵךְ וְלֶךְ	*Et ito, veni.*	And go, come thou.
	וְלָךְ וָלָךְ וּלְךָ	*Et tibi.*	And for thee.
כבד	וּלְכָבוֹד	*Et in gloria.*	And in glory.
——	וְלִכְבוֹדִי	*Et in gloriam meam*	And for my glory.
כבש	וְלַכְּבָשִׂים	*Et agnis.*	And for, to the lambs.
לכד	וְלָכַד	*Et capiet.*	And he shall take.
——	וְלָכְדָהּ	*Et cape eam.*	And take thou her.
——	וּלְכָדָהּ	*Et cepit, capiet eam*	And he took, will take her.
——	וּלְכָדָהָ־־דוּהָ	*Et capient eam.*	And they shall take her.
——	וְלִכְדוּ	*Et occupate.*	And take, seize ye.
ילד	וּלְכָה	*Et veni.*	And come thou
	וּלְכָה	*Et tibi.*	And to thee.

ROOTS.	DERIVATIVES.	VERSIO.	SIGNIFICATION.
כהן	וְלַכֹּהֵן	*Et sacerdoti.*	And to the priest.
—	וְלַכֹּהֲנִים	*Et sacerdotibus*[*tros*	And to, for the priests.
—	וּלְכֹהֲנֵינוּ	*Et in sacerdotes nos-*	And on our priests.
ילך	וְלֵכוּ וּלְכוּ	*Et ite, venite.*	And go, come ye.
לכד	וְלָכוֹד	*Et capiendo.*	And in taking.
ילך	וּלְכִי	*Et ito, veni.*	And go, come thou. [churl.
כלה	וּלְכִילַי	*Et avaro, tenaci.*	And to the covetous, the
כלל	וּלְכָל וּלְכֹל	*Et in, de, ex omni.*	And in, of, from all.
כול	וּלְכַלְכֵּל	*Et ad alendum.* [*eos*	And to nourish.
—	וּלְכַלֹּתָם	*Et ad consumendum*	And to consume them.
	וְלָכֶם וּלְכֹם	*Et vobis.*	And to, for you.
כון	וְלָכֵן	*Et proptérea.*	And therefore.
כנס	וְלִכְנוֹס	*Et ad colligendum.*	And to collect, gather.
כסא	וּלְכִסְאוֹ	*Et solio ejus.*	And upon his throne.
כסף	וְלַכֶּסֶף	*Et ad argentum.*	And to the silver.
—	וּלְכַסְפִּי	*Et pro argento meo.*	And for my silver.
כפר	וְלִכְפּוֹרֵי	*Et in pelves.*	And for the basons.
כפן	וּלְכָפָן	*Et in fame.*	And in famine.
כפר	וּלְכַפֵּר	*Et ad expiandum.*	And to make atonement.
כתם	וְלַכֶּתֶם	*Et ad aurum.*	And to the gold.
כתף	וְלַכָּתֵף	*Et ad latus.*	And on the side.
לא	וּללֹא	*Et absque.*	And without.
לבן	וְלַלְבֵּן	*Et ad dealbandum.*	And to make white.
לחם	וְלַלֶּחֶם וּלְלֶ׳	*Et in pane.*	And in bread.
ילך	וְלָלֶכֶת	*Et ad incedendum.*	And to walk.
למד	וּלְלַמֵּד	*Et ad docendum.*	And to teach.
—	וּלְלַמְּדָם	*Et ad docendum eos.*	And to teach them.
לעג	וּלְלַעַג	*Et ad subsannationem.*	And in derision.
לקט	וְלִלְקֹט	*Et ad colligendum.*	And to gather, glean.
מאן	וּלְמָאנַיָּא	*Et vasa.*	And the vessels.
בית	וּלְמִבֵּית	*Et intus.* [*rum.*	And within.
מגד	וּלְמִגְדָּנוֹת	*Et rerum pretiosa-*	And of precious things.
גנן	וּלְמָגִנִּים	*Et in scuta.*	And for shields.
גרש	וּלְמִגְרָשׁ	*Et in suburbium.*	And for suburbs.
למד	וְלַמֵּד	*Et docendo.*	And in teaching.
—	וְלַמְּדָהּ	*Et doce illam.*	And teach thou her.

ROOTS.	DERIVATIVES.	VERSIO.	SIGNIFICATION.
למד	וְלָמְדוּ	*Et discent.*	And they shall learn.
—	וְלַמֵּדְנָה	*Et docete.*	And teach ye.
—	וְלַמְּדֵנִי	*Et doce me.*	And teach thou me.
—	וְלִמַּדְתֶּם	*Et docebitis.*	And ye shall teach.
—	וּלְמַדְתֶּם	*Et discetis.*	And ye shall learn.
מה	וְלָמָּה וְלָמֶה	*Et cur, quare.*	And why, wherefore.
למד	וּלְמוּדֵי	*Et periti.*	And the skilful.
יכח	וְלַמּוֹכִיחַ	*Et corripienti.*	And for him that reproveth.
—	וְלַמּוֹכִיחִים	*Et increpantibus.*	And to them that rebuke.
ילד	וּלְמוֹלַדְתֶּךָ־־תֵּךְ	*Et ad cognationem tuam.* [*nostra.*	And to thy kindred.
—	וּלְמוֹלַדְתֵּנוּ	*Et de cognatione*	And of our kindred.
יעד	וְלַמּוֹעֲדוֹת־־דִים	*Et statis temporibus.*	And at the stated seasons.
—	וּלְמוֹעֲדֵי	*Et solennitatibus.*	And on the solemn feasts.
—	וּלְמוֹעֲדִים	*Et in stata tempora.*	And for seasons.
יפת	וּלְמוֹפֵת	*Et in portentum.*	And for a wonder.
—	וּלְמוֹפְתִים	*Et in portenta.*	And for wonders.
יקש	וּלְמוֹקֵשׁ	*Et in laqueum.*	And for a snare.
מות	וְלַמָּוֶת	*Et ad mortem.*	And unto death.
זבח	וְלַמִּזְבֵּחַ וּלְמִזְבַּח	*Et altari.*	And for the altar.
מזח	וּלְמֵזַח	*Et pro zona, cingulo*	And for a girdle.
מזל	וְלַמַּזָּלוֹת	*Et planetis, signis, sideribus.*	And to the planets, signs, stars.
זרח	וְלַמִּזְרָח	*Et ad orientem.*	And toward the east.
חבר	וְלַמְחַבְּרוֹת	*Et ad juncturas.*	And to the joinings.
חבת	וְלַמַּחֲבַת	*Et in sartagine.*	And in the pan.
חלק	וּלְמַחְלְקוֹת	*Et ad classes.*	And for the courses.
חסה	וּלְמַחְסֶה	*Et in refugium.*	And for a refuge.
חתת	וְלִמְחִתָּה	*Et in terrorem.*	And for terror.
נטה	וּלְמַטָּה־־מַטָּה	*Et infra.*	And under.
—	וּלְמַטֵּה	*Et de tribu.*	And of the tribe.
מי	וּלְמִי	*Et cui, erga quem.*	And to whom, toward whom.
יום	וּלְמִיָּמִים	*Et a diebus.*	And from the days.
כסה	וְלִמְכַסֶּה	*Et in tegumentum.*	And for covering, cloathing.
כשל	וּלְמִכְשׁוֹל	*Et in offendiculum.*	And for an offence.
כשף	וְלַמְכַשְּׁפִים	*Et divinos.*	And the diviners, sorcerers.
מלא	וּלְמַלֵּא	*Et ad consecrandum*	And to consecrate.

ROOTS.	DERIVATIVES.	VERSIO.	SIGNIFICATION.
מלא	וְלְמַלְּאָם	*Et ad implendum eos*	And to fill them.
—	וְלַמִּלּוּאִים	*Et de consecrationi-*	And of the consecrations.
מלך	וְלַמֶּלֶךְ	*Et regi.* [*bus.*	And to the king.
—	וּלְמַלְכָּה	*Et regi ejus.*	And to her king.
—	וּלְמַלְכֵי	*Et reges.*	And the kings.
למד	וְלִמְלַמְּדַי	*Et docentibus me.*	And to those who teach me.
מלך	וּלְמַמְלְכוֹת	*Et de regnis.*	And concerning the kingdoms
מן	וּלְמַן	*Et cuicunque.*	And to whomsoever.
—	וּלְמִן וּלְמִנֵּי	*Et a.*	And from. [comforters.
נחם	וְלִמְנַחֲמִים	*Et ad consolantes.*	And for those who comfort,
מנח	וּלְמִנְחֹתֵיכֶם	*Et oblationibus, fer-tris vestris.*	And for your oblations, meat offerings.
נור	וְלַמְּנֹרוֹת	*Et pro candelabris.*	And for the candlesticks.
נסע	וּלְמַסַּע	*Et ad profectionem.*	And for the journeying.
ספד	וּלְמִסְפֵּד	*Et ad planctum.*	And to mourning.
סתר	וּלְמִסְתּוֹר	*Et in latibulum.*	And for a covert.
יעד	וּלְמֹעֲדִים וְלַמּ׳	*Et in statuta tempo-ra, solennitatibus.*	And for stated times, for sea-sons, on the solemn feasts.
עזז	וּלְמָעוֹז	*Et in robur.*	And for strength, to strengthen
מעט	וְלַמְעַט	*Et minori.*	And to less.
עלה	וּלְמַעְלָה־־מ׳	*Et supra.*	And above. [of.
מען	וּלְמַעַן	*Et propter.*	And for the sake, on account
ערב	וְלַמַּעֲרָב	*Et ad occidentem.*	And toward the west.
עשר	וְלַמַּעַשְׂרוֹת	*Et ad decimas.*	And for the tithes.
קוה	וּלְמִקְוֵה	*Et collectio.*	And the gathering.
קום	וְלַמָּקוֹם	*Et ad locum.*	And to the place.
קנה	וּלְמִקְנֵהוּ	*Et pecori ejus.*	And for his cattle.
קצה	וּלְמִקְצֵה	*Et ab extremo.*	And from an or the extremity
—	וּלְמִקְצָת	*Et ad finem.*	And at the end.
רבך	וְלַמֻּרְבֶּכֶת	*Et in frixum.* [*nem.*	And for that which is fried.
רמס	וּלְמִרְמָס	*Et in conculcatio-*	And for treading.
נשא	וּלְמַשָּׂא	*Et in onus.*	And for a burden.
משח	וְלִמְשֹׁחַ	*Et ad ungendum.*	And to anoint.
משל	וְלִמְשֹׁל	*Et ad dominandum.*	And to rule, have dominion.
—	וּלְמָשָׁל	*Et in proverbium.*	And for a proverb.
—	וְלִמְשָׁלִים	*Et in parabolas.*	And for parables, proverbs.
שנא	וְלִמְשַׂנְאַי	*Et odio habentibus.*	And to them that hate me.

ROOTS.	DERIVATIVES.	VERSIO.	SIGNIFICATION.
שסס	וְלִמְשִׁסָּה	*Et in prædam.*	And for a prey.
שפח	וּלְמִשְׁפָּחָה	*Et familiæ.*	And to a family.
—	וּלְמִשְׁפְּחוֹת	*Et familiis.*	And to the families.
—	וּלְמִשְׁפַּחְתּוֹ	*Et ad familiam ejus*	And to his family.
שפט	וּלְמִשְׁפָּט	*Et in jus.*	And for an ordinance, statute.
—	וּלְמִשְׁפָּטִים	*Et ad jura, judicia.*	And to statutes, judgments.
שור	וְלַמְשֹׁרְרִים	*Et canentibus.*	And to the singers.
לון	וָלָן	*Et pernoctavit.*	And he passed the night.
נבא	וְלִנְבִיאַי	*Et prophetis meis.*	And to my prophets.
—	וְלִנְבִיאֵינוּ	*Et prophetis nostris*	And for, on our prophets.
נגה	וּלְנֹגַהּ	*Et in splendorem.*	And for brightness.
נגד	וּלְנָגִיד	*Et in ducem.*	And for a leader.
נדה	וּלְנִדָּה	*Et pro immunditie.*	And for uncleanness.
נדר	וּלְנֶדֶר	*Et in votum.*	And for a vow.
לון	וְלָנָה	*Et pernoctabit, commorabitur*	And she will pass the night, will remain.
	וְלָנוּ	*Et nobis.*	And to us.
לון	וְלַנּוּ	*Et pernoctabimus.*	And we will lodge all night,
נחם	וּלְנַחֲמוֹ	*Et ad consolandum eum.*	And to comfort him.
נחש	וְלִנְחֹשֶׁת	*Et æris.*	And of brass.
נטע	וְלִנְטוֹעַ	*Et ad plantandum.*	And to plant.
נין	וּלְנִינִי	*Et erga filium meum*	And towards my son.
נכד	וּלְנֶכְדִּי	*Et erga nepotem meum.*	And towards my son's son.
נסך	וְלִנְסֹךְ	*Et ad fundendum.*	And to pour out.
—	וּלְנִסְכֵּיכֶם	*Et pro libaminibus vestris.*	And for your drink-offerings.
נער	וְלַנַּעַר	*Et puero.*	And for the lad.
—	וְלַנַּעֲרָ	*Et ad puellam.*	And to the damsel.
נפל	וְלִנְפֹּל	*Et ad dejiciendum.*	And to cast down.
נקב	וְלַנְּקֵבָה	*Et fæminæ.*	And of the woman.
שבר	וְלַנִּשְׁבֶּרֶת	*Et confractam.*	And her that is broken.
נשא	וְלַנָּשִׂיא	*Et principi.*	And for the prince.
אנש	וּלְנְשֵׁיכֶם	*Et uxoribus vestris.*	And for your wives.
נתץ	וְלִנְתוֹץ	*Et ad diruendum.*	And to break or pull down.
נתק	וְלַנָּתֶק	*Et de porrigine.*	And of the scall, morbid baldness.
סגן	וְלַסְּגָנִים	*Et ad principes.*	And to the rulers.
סלת	וּלְסֹלֶת	*Et pro simila.*	And for the fine flower.
סעד	וּלְסַעֲדָהּ	*Et ad sustentandum eam.*	And to support her.

ROOTS.	DERIVATIVES.	VERSIO.	SIGNIFICATION.
ספח	וְלַסַּפַּחַת	*Et scabiei.*	And for a scab.
ספר	וּלְסַפֵּר	*Et ad narrandum.*	And to tell.
סרן	וּלְסַרְנֵיכֶם	*Et in principibus vestris.*	And on your princes, chiefs.
עבד	וְלַעֲבֹד	*Et ad serviendum, operandum.*	And to serve, work, effect.
—	וּלְעָבְדוֹ	*Et ad serviendum ei.*	And to serve him.
—	וְלַעֲבָדָיו	*Et ad servos ejus.*	And to his servants.
—	וְלַעֲבָדֶיךָ	*Et pro servis tuis, contra servos tuos*	And for thy servants, against thy servants.
—	וּלְעַבְדְּךָ	*Et servo tuo.*	And to or for thy servant.
—	וְלַעֲבֹדַת	*Et ad ministerium.*	And in the service.
—	וְלַעֲבֹדָתוֹ	*Et ad laborem ejus.*	And to his labour.
עגל	וְלַעֲגָלִים	*Et vitulis.*	And to or for the calves.
עוד	וּלְעֵד	*Et in testimonium.*	And for a witness, testimony.
—	וּלְעֵדְוֹתֶיךָ	*Et ad testimonia tua*	And to thy testimonies.
עדר	וְלַעֲדֹר	*Et ad instruendum.*	And to array, set in order.
לוע	וְלָעוּ	*Et deglutient.*	And they will swallow down.
עלה	וּלְעוֹלָה-עֹלָה	*Et in holocaustum.*	And for a burnt offering.
עלם	וּלְעוֹלָם	*Et in seculum, æternum.*	And for ever.
עלה	וּלְעוֹלַת	*Et ad holocaustum.*	And for the burnt offering.
עוף	וּלְעוֹף	*Et ad volucrem.*	And to the fowl.
עות	וּלְעַוֵּת	*Et ad pervertendum*	And to pervert.
עטלף	וְלָעֲטַלֵּפִים	*Et vespertilionibus.*	And to the bats.
עין	וּלְעֵינֵי	*Et in oculis.*	And in the eyes, sight, presence.
עלא	וּלְעִלָּיָא	*Et ad altissimum.*	And to the Most High.
עמם	וְלָעָם וּלְעַם	*Et populo.*	And to or for the people.
עמד	וְלַעֲמֹד	*Et ad standum.*	And to stand.
—	וּלְעַמּוּד	*Et in columnam.*	And for a pillar.
עמם	וּלְעַמְּךָ	*Et pro populo tuo.*	And for thy people.
לען	וְלַעֲנָה	*Et absinthium.*	And wormwood.
ענה	וְלַעֲנָיִּים	*Et humilibus.*	And to the lowly, humble.
עפר	וְלֶעָפָר	*Et in pulverem.*	And into the dust.
עצב	וְלַעֲצַבֶּיהָ	*Et simulachris ejus.*	And to her idols.
ערב	וְלָעֶרֶב-עָרֶב	*Et vespere.*	And in the evening.
עיר	וּלְעָרֵי	*Et ad civitates.*	And to the cities.
—	וְלֶעָרִים	*Et civitatibus.*	And to the cities.

ROOTS.	DERIVATIVES.	VERSIO.	SIGNIFICATION.
עשה	וְלַעֲשׂוֹת	*Et ad faciendum.*	And to do, make, perform.
עתת	וּלְעֵת	*Et ad tempus.*	And for the time.
עתד	וְלָעַתּוּדִים	*Et hircos.*	And the he-goats.
עתת	וּלְעִתִּים	*Et ad tempora.*	And for the times.
פאה	וְלִפְאַת	*Et ad latus.*	And for, at the side.
פי	וּלְפִי	*Et secundum, juxta.*	And according to.
לפד	וּלַפִּיד	*Et lampas, fax.*	And a lamp, torch.
—	וְלַפִּידִים	*Et lampades, faces.*	And lamps, torches.
פנה	וְלִפְנֵי	*Et ante, coram.*	And before, in the presence of
—	וְלִפְנֵיהֶם	*Et coram illis.*	And before them.
—	וּלְפָנָיו	*Et coram eo.*	And before him.
—	וּלְפָנֶיךָ	*Et coram te.*	And in thy presence.
פסל	וְלַפְּסִלִים	*Et sculptilibus.*	And to graven images.
פעל	וּלְפֹעֲלִי	*Et opifici meo.*	And to my maker.
פקד	וְלִפְקֹד	*Et ad puniendum.*	And to punish.
פרש	וּלְפָרָשִׁים	*Et propter equites, cum equitibus.*	And for, with horsemen.
פשע	וְלַפֹּשְׁעִים	*Et prævaricatoribus*	And to or for the transgressors.
פתה	וּלְפֹתֶה	*Et cum blandiente.*	And with him that flattereth.
פתח	וּלְפַתֵּחַ	*Et ad sculpendum.*	And to engrave.
לוץ	וְלֵץ	*Et derisor.*	And a scorner.
יצא	וְלָצֵאת	*Et ad egrediendum.*	And to go out.
צוה	וּלְצַוּוֹת	*Et ad mandandum.*	And to command.
צור	וּלְצוּר	*Et in rupem.*	And for a rock.
לוץ	וְלֵצִים	*Et derisores.*	And the scorners.
צלם	וּלְצֶלֶם	*Et ad statuam.*	And to the image, statue.
צלע	וּלְצֶלַע	*Et ad latus.*	And at the side.
צמא	וְלִצְמָאִי	*Et in siti mea.*	And in my thirst.
צמר	וְלַצֶּמֶר	*Et ex lana.*	And of wool.
צנה	וְלִצְנִינִם־נִנִים	*Et instar spinarum.*	And like thorns.
צפר	וְלִצְפִירַת	*Et in cidarim.*	And for a diadem, turban.
רע	וּלְצָרַעַת	*Et lepræ.*	And to or for the leprosy.
לוץ	וְלַצְתָּ	*Et deridebis.*	And thou wilt scorn.
קבל	וּלְקֳבֵל	*Et coram. [eum.*	And before, in presence of.
קבר	וּלְקָבְרוֹ	*Et ad sepeliendum*	And to bury him.
קדש	וְלִקְדוֹשׁ	*Et ad sanctum.*	And to the holy one.
קדם	וְלַקָּדִים	*Et versus orientem.*	And toward the east.

ROOTS.	DERIVATIVES.	VERSIO.	SIGNIFICATION.
קדש	וְלִקְדֹישַׁי	*Et sanctos.*	And the saints.
קדד	וּלְקָדְקֹד	*Et in vertice.*	And on the crown of the head.
קדש	וְלַקֹּדֶשׁ	*Et sanctuario.*	And to or for the sanctuary.
—	וּלְקַדֵּשׁ	*Et sanctificando.*	And in sanctifying.
—	וְלַקֳּדָשִׁים־־קָ׳	*Et ad res sanctas.*	And to the holy things.
לקח	וְלָקַח־־קְחָה	*Et sumpsit, capiet.*	And he took, shall take [neth
—	וְלֹקֵחַ	*Et alliciens.*	And he that attracteth, win-
—	וְלֻקַּח	*Et sumetur.*	And he shall be taken.
—	וּקְחַ	*Et sume.*	And take thou.
—	וּלְקָחָהּ	*Et ducet eam.*	And he shall take her.
—	וְלָקְחוּ	*Et auferent.*	And they shall take away.
—	וְלָקְחוּ	*Et sument, abducent*	And they shall take, take away
—	וּלְקָחוּם	*Et afferent eos.*	And they will bring them.
—	וְלָקַחְנוּ	*Et capiemus.*	And we will take.
—	וְלָקַחְתָּ־־חַתְּ	*Et sumes, recipies.*	And thou shalt take, receive.
—	וְלָקַחַת	*Et ad recipiendum.*	And to receive.
—	וְלָקַחְתִּי	*Et sumam, auferam*	And I will take, take away.
—	וּלְקַחְתִּיךָ	*Et adducam te.*	And I will bring thee.
—	וּלְקַחְתִּים	*Et capiam eos.*	And I will take them.
—	וּלְקַחְתֶּם	*Et sumetis, ducetis.*	And ye shall take, bring.
לקט	וְלָקֶט	*Et in pera.*	And in a scrip.
—	וְלִקְּטָה	*Et colliget.*	And she shall glean.
—	וְלָקְטוּ	*Et colligent.*	And they shall gather.
קטר	וְלִקְטֹרֶת	*Et ad suffitum.*	And for incense.
קול	וּלְקֹלִי	*Et ad vocem meam.*	And to my voice.
קלל	וְלִקְלָלָה	*Et ad maledictionem*	And for a curse.
קלס	וּלְקֶלֶס	*Et in irrisionem.*	And for a derision.
קנה	וְלִקְנוֹת	*Et ad emendum.*	And to buy. [session.
—	וּלְקִנְיָנָם	*Et possessioni eorum*	And for their substance, pos-
קסם	וְלִקֹסְמִים	*Et divinos.*	And the diviners.
קצץ	וּלְקֵץ	*Et ad finem.*	And at the end.
קצן	וּלְקָצִין	*Et in ducem.*	And for a captain.
קצר	וְלִקְצֹר	*Et ad metendum.*	And to reap.
קצה	וְלִקְצָת	*Et ad finem.*	And at the end.
קרא	וְלִקְרַאת	*Et obviam.*	And to meet.
קרב	וּלְקָרְבָּן	*Et in oblationem.*	And for the offering.
—	וְלַקָּרוֹב	*Et propinquo.*	And to him that is near.

ROOTS.	DERIVATIVES.	VERSIO.	SIGNIFICATION.
קרה	וּלְקָרוֹת	*Et ad contignandum*	And to lay the beams.
קרח	וְלַקֶּרַח	*Et ad gelu.*	And to the frost.
—	וּלְקָרְחָה	*Et ad calvitium.*	And to baldness.
קרן	וּלְקַרְנוֹת	*Et in cornibus.*	And on the horns.
ראה	וְלִרְאוֹת	*Et ad videndum.*	And to see.
ראש	וּלְרָאשָׁיו	*Et principibus ejus.*	And for his chiefs.
רגל	וּלְרַגֵּל	*Et ad explorandum.*	And to spy out.
—	וּלְרֶגֶל	*Et ad pedem.*	And according to the foot.
—	וּלְרַגְּלָהּ	*Et ad explorandum [eam.*	And to spy it out.
רזן	וּלְרוֹזְנִים	*Et dominatoribus.*	And for rulers.
רוח	וּלְרוּחַ	*Et sicut ventus, pro spiritu.*	And as wind, for a spirit.
רחב	וּלְרָחְבָּהּ	*Et in latitudine ejus*	And in the breadth of it.
רחם	וּלְרַחֲמִים	*Et in misericordia.*	And in mercy.
ריב	וְלָרִיב	*Et ad litem.*	And for controversy.
רכב	וּלְרִכְבּוֹ	*Et curribus ejus.*	And to his chariots.
—	ולרכבו	*Et ad equitem ejus.*	And to his horseman, rider.
רכש	וְלָרֶכֶשׁ	*Et pro mulis [eorum*	And for mules.
—	וְלִרְכֻשָׁם	*Et pro facultatibus*	And for their goods.
רוע	וּלְרָעָה	*Et de malo.*	And of evil.
רוץ	וְלָרָצִים	*Et ad cursores.*	And to the runners.
רקק	וּלְרְקִיקֵי	*Et in lagana.*	And for the cakes.
רוש	וְלָרָשׁ	*Et ad pauperem.*	And to the poor.
רשע	וְלָרָשָׁע	*Et impio.*	And to the wicked.
—	וּלְרִשְׁעֵי	*Et impiis.*	And to the wicked.
—	וְלָרְשָׁעִים	*Et impiis.*	And to the wicked.
שאר	וְלִשְׁאֵרִית	*Et in reliquum.*	And upon the remainder.
נשא	לָשֵׂאת	*Et ad ferendum.*	And to bear, take.
—	וְלַשְׂאֵת	*Et de tumore.*	And of a rising, swelling.
שבט	וּלְשֵׁבֶט	*Et ad tribum.*	And to the tribe.
שוב	וּלְשָׁבֵי	*Et ad seniores.*	And to the elders.
—	וּלְשָׁבֵי	*Et ad revertentes.*	And to them that turn.
שבת	וְלַשְׁבִּית	*Et ad delendum.*	And to abolish.
שבע	וְלִשְׁבֻעָה	*Et cum juramento.*	And with an oath.
שאה	וּלְשׁוֹאָה	*Et in vastatione.*	And in the desolation.
שוב	וְלָשׁוּב	*Et reverti.*	And to turn, return.
שום	וְלָשׂוּם	*Et ad constituendum*	And to appoint.

ROOTS.	DERIVATIVES.	VERSIO.	SIGNIFICATION.
לשן	וְלָשׁוֹן וְלְ״	*Et lingua.*	And a, the tongue.
——	וּלְשׁוֹנוֹ	*Et lingua ejus.*	And his tongue.
——	וּלְשׁוֹנִי	*Et lingua mea.*	And my tongue.
——	וּלְשׁוֹנְךָ	*Et lingua tua.*	And thy tongue.
——	וּלְשׁוֹנָם	*Et lingua eorum.*	And their tongue.
——	וּלְשׁוֹנֵנוּ	*Et lingua nostra.*	And our tongue.
שוט	וּלְשֹׁטֵט	*Et in flagellum.*	And for a scourge.
שטר	וְלַשֵּׁטֶר	*Et ad latus.*	And on a side, one side.
——	וּלְשֹׁטְרָיו	*Et præfectos ejus.*	And his overseers.
שום	וּלְשִׂימוֹ	*Et ad ponendum eum*	And to put him.
שית	וְלַשָּׁיִת	*Et in sentes.*	And for thorns.
שכב	וְלִשְׁכַּב	*Et ad concumbendum*	And to lie with.
לשך	וּלְשָׁכָּה	*Et cubiculum.*	And the chamber. [vant.
שכר	וְלִשְׂכִירְךָ	*Et mercenario tuo.*	And to or for thy hired ser-
שכן	וְלִשְׁכֵנַי	*Et inter vicinos meos*	And among my neighbours.
שכר	וְלַשֵּׁכָר ;	*Et pro sicera.*	And for strong drink.
שלם	וְלַשָּׁלוֹם	*Et de pace.*	And of the peace.
——	וּלְשָׁלוֹם	*Et cum pace.*	And with peace.
——	וְלִשְׁלוֹמִים	*Et ad paces.*	And for peace.
שלח	וּלְשַׁלַּח	*Et ad mittendum.*	And to send.
שלם	וּלְשַׁלְמֵיכֶם	*Et pro sacrificiis pa-*	And for your peace offerings.
		cificis vestris. [*fica*	
——	וְלִשְׁלָמִים	*Et in sacrificia paci-*	And for peace offerings. [forks
שלש	וְלִשְׁלֹשׁ	*Et pro tridentibus.*	And for the three pronged
——	וְלַשָּׁלִשִׁים	*Et tribunis, ducibus.*	And to the captains, leaders.
שם	וּלְשֵׁם	*Et in nomen, nomine*	And for a name, in name.
שמם	וּלְשַׁמָּה	*Et in stuporem.*	And for an astonishment.
שמח	וְלִשְׂמוֹחַ־־מֹחַ	*Et ad lætandum.*	And to rejoice.
שמר	וְלִשְׁמוֹר־־מֹר	*Et ad servandum.*	And to keep, observe.
שמח	וּלְשִׂמְחָה	*Et ad lætitiam.*	And to joy, mirth, gladness.
——	וּלְשִׂמְחַת	*Et in lætitiam.*	And for rejoicing.
שם	וּלְשִׁמְךָ	*Et nomini tuo.*	And to thy name.
שמן	וּלְשֶׁמֶן	*Et ad oleum.*	And for oil.
שמע	וְלִשְׁמֹעַ	*Et ad auscultandum*	And to hearken.
שמר	וּלְשָׁמְרָהּ	*Et ad custodiendum*	And to keep her.
——	וּלְשֹׁמְרֵי	*Et servantibus.* [*eam*	And to those that keep.
שמש	וְלַשֶּׁמֶשׁ	*Et soli.*	And to the sun.

ROOTS.	DERIVATIVES.	VERSIO.	SIGNIFICATION.
לשן	וְלָשׁוֹן	*Et lingua.*	And tongue, language.
שנא	וְלִשְׂנֹא	*Et odio habendo.*	And in hating.
—	וּלְשֹׂנְאַי	*Et odio habentes.*	And they that hate.
לשן	וְלִשָּׁנַיָּא	*Et linguæ.*	And tongues, languages.
שנה	וְלִשְׁנַיִם	*Et duobus.* [*cutum.*	And to the two.
שנן	וְלִשְׁנִינָה	*Et in dicterium a-*	And for a by-word.
שער	וְלַשְּׂעִירִים	*Et pro dæmonibus hirsutis.*	And for the hairy deities, *worshipped in Egypt.*
—	וְלַשַּׁעַר	*Et ad portam.*	And at the gate.
שפח	וְלִשְׁפָחוֹת	*Et in ancillas.*	And for handmaids.
—	וְלִשְׁפְחָתְךָ	*Et ancillæ tuæ.*	And of thy handmaid.
שפט	וּלְשֹׁפְטָיו	*Et judices ejus.*	And his judges.
—	וּלְשֹׁפְטִים וְלַשֹּׁ'	*Et judicibus.*	And to the judges.
שפך	וְלִשְׁפֹּךְ	*Et ad effundendum.*	And to pour out.
שור	וּלְשַׂר	*Et in principem.*	And for a chief, prince.
—	וּלְשָׂרֵי	*Et ducibus.*	And to the captains.
—	וְלַשָּׂרִים וּלְשָׂ'	*Et ad principes.*	And to the princes.
שרק	וְלַשֹּׂרֵקָה	*Et ad vitem selectam*	And to the choice vine.
—	וְלִשְׁרֵקָה	*Et in sibilum.*	And for a hissing.
שרת	וּלְשָׁרֵת	*Et ad ministrandum*	And to minister.
—	וּלְשָׁרְתוֹ	*Et ad ministrandum*	And to minister unto him.
שתה	וְלִשְׁתּוֹת	*Et ad bibendum.* [*ei.*	And to drink.
בנה	וּלְתַבְנִית	*Et in formam, exem-*	And for the form, pattern.
הלל	וְלִתְהִלָּה	*Et in laudem.* [*plar.*	And for praise.
תור	וְלָתוּר	*Et ad explorandum.*	And to search out.
ירה	וּלְתוֹרָתוֹ	*Et in legem ejus.*	And for his law.
ישב	וְלַתּוֹשָׁב	*Et incolis.*	And to the inhabitants.
—	וּלְתוֹשָׁבְךָ	*Et advenæ tuo.*	And for thy stranger.
ימן	וּלְתֵימָן	*Et austro.*	And to the south.
עוד	וְלִתְעוּדָה	*Et ad testimonium.*	And to the testimony.
פאר	וּלְתִפְאֶרֶת--אֶ'	*Et in decorem, splendorem, gloriam.*	And for beauty, splendour, glory.
תקף	וּלְתַקְּפָה	*Et ad roborandum.*	And to strengthen, make firm
שוב	וְלִתְשׁוּבַת	*Et ad reversionem.*	And at the return.
נתן	וְלָתֵת--תֵּת	*Et ad dandum, tradendum, constituendum.*	And to give, bestow, deliver up, appoint, set up.

ROOTS.	DERIVATIVES.	VERSIO.	SIGNIFICATION.
נתן	וְלְתִתְּךָ	*Et ad ponendum te.*	And to place thee.
——	וְלְתִתֵּנוּ	*Et ad dandum nobis.*	And to give to us.
	ומ		
אבל	וּמֵאֵבֶל	*Et a luctu.*	And from mourning.
אדם	וּמֵאֲדָמָה	*Et e terra.*	And out of the earth.
מאה	וּמֵאָה	*Et centum.*	And a hundred.
אהב	וּמְאַהֲבַיִךְ	*Et amatores tui.*	And thy lovers.
מאם	וּמְאוּמָה	*Et quicquam.[puere*	And any thing.
מאס	וּמָאוֹס	*Et contemnere, res-*	And to despise, reject.
אז	וּמֵאָז	*Et postquam.*	And after that.
אזן	וּמֹאזְנֵי	*Et bilances.*	And the balances.
אחר	וּמֵאָחוֹר	*Et a tergo.*	And behind.
אחז	וּמֵאֲחֻזַּת	*Et de possessione.*	And from the possession.
אחר	וּמֵאַחֲרַי	*Et a post me.*	And from after me.
איב	וּמֵאֹיְבַי	*Et ab inimicis meis.*	And from my enemies.
אי	וּמֵאִיֵּי	*Et ab insulis.*	And from the islands.
אין	וּמֵאַיִן	*Et unde.*	And whence.
——	וּמֵאֵין	*Et absque.*	And without.
איש	וּמֵאִישָׁהּ	*Et a marito ejus.*	And from her husband.
אכל	וּמַאֲכָל־־כל	*Et cibus.*	And food, meat.
——	וּמַאֲכָלוֹ	*Et cibus ejus.*	And his food.
——	וּמַאֲכָלוֹת	*Et cultri.*	And knives.
——	וּמַאֲכָלְךָ	*Et cibus tuus.*	And thy meat.
אלה	וּמֵאָלָה	*Et præ execratione.*	And for cursing.
אל	וּמֵאֵלֶּה	*Et ab illis, istis.*	And from them, those.
אלה	וּמֵאֱלֹהַי	*Et a Deo meo.*	And from my God.
——	וּמֵאֱלֹהִים	*Et a Deo.*	And from God
אמר	וּמַאֲמַר	*Et edictum.*	And the edict, decree.
——	וּמֵאֹמֶר	*Et verbum.*	And the word.
מאן	וּמָאנַיָּא	*Et vasa.*	And the vessels
אנש	וּמֵאַנְשֵׁי	*Et a viris.*	And from the men.
אסף	וּמְאַסִּפְכֶם	*Et colligens, claudens vos.*	And he that gathereth you in, bringeth up your rear.
מאס	וּמְאַסְתִּי	*Et abjiciam.*	And I will cast off.
אפל	וּמֵאֹפֶל	*Et ex caligine.[ejus.*	And out of obscurity, darkness
אצל	וּמֵאֲצִילֶיהָ	*Et ab optimatibus*	And from her nobles.

ROOTS.	DERIVATIVES.	VERSIO.	SIGNIFICATION.
ארד	וּמַאֲרִיךְ	*Et prolongans.*	And he that prolongeth.
ארץ	וּמֵאֶרֶץ	*Et e terra.*	And out of, from the land,
—	וּמֵאַרְצוֹ	*Et e terra ejus.*	And out of his land. [country
—	וּמֵאֲרָצוֹת	*Et ex terris.*	And out of the lands.
אשר	וּמֵאֲשֶׁר	*Et de quibus.*	And of whom.
—	וּמְאֻשָּׁרָיו	*Et beati prædicati ab eo, qui dirigun-tur ab eo.* [ma.	And they that are called blessed by him, they that are led by him.
מאה	וּמְאַת	*Et centum, centesi-*	And a hundred, the hundredth.
את	וּמֵאֵת	*Et a, pro.*	And from, for.
אות	וּמֵאֹתוֹת	*Et a signis.*	And from the signs.
מאה	וּמָאתַיִם־־תָּ֫יִם	*Et ducenti.*	And two hundred.
בוך	וּמְבוּכָה	*Et perplexitas.*	And perplexity. [ling.
בוס	וּמְבוּסָה	*Et conculcatio.*	And the treading down, tramp-
בוק	וּמְבוּקָה	*Et vacua, inanis.*	And void, empty.
בחר	וּמְבַּחוּרֵיכֶם	*Et ex juvenibus ves-*	And of your young men.
—	וּמִבְחַר	*Et delectus.* [tris.	And the choice.
בטן	וּמִבֶּטֶן	*Et ab utero.*	And from the womb.
בוא	וּמְבִיאֵי	*Et adducentes.*	And they that bring.
—	וּמְבִיאֶיהָ	*Et adducentes eam.*	And they that bring her.
—	וּמְבִיאִים	*Et afferentes.*	And bringing.
בון	וּמֵבִין	*Et intelligens.*	And understanding.
בין	וּמִבֵּין	*Et inter.* [rili.	And between, among. [ning.
בון	וּמְבִינֵי	*Et intelligentes, pe-*	And the understanding, cun-
בית	וּמִבֵּית	*Et ex domo.*	And from, out of the house.
בהל	וּמְבַהֲלִים	*Et conturbantes.*	And they that trouble, disturb
בל	וּמִבְּלִי	*Et absque.*	And without.
—	וּמִבַּלְעָדַי	*Et præter me.*	And beside me.
בלק	וּמְבֻלָּקָה	*Et vastata.*	And she that is laid waste.
בנה	וּמִבֶּן	*Et a filio.*	And from the son.
—	וּמִבָּנוֹת	*Et quam filiæ.*	And than daughters
—	וּמִבְּנֵי	*Et ex filiis.*	And of, from the sons.
—	וּמִבָּנֶיךָ	*Et ex filiis tuis.*	And of thy sons.
בצר	וּמִבְצָר	*Et munitio.*	And the fortress.
בקע	וּמְבֻקָּעִים	*Et scissi, fissi.*	And rent.
בקר	וּמִבְּקָרוֹ	*Et ex bove ejus.*	And of his herd.
בקש	וּמְבַקֵּשׁ	*Et quærens.*	And he that seeketh.

ROOTS.	DERIVATIVES.	VERSIO.	SIGNIFICATION.
בקש	וּמְבַקְשֵׁי	*Et quærentes.*	And they that seek.
ברך	וּמְבֹרָךְ	*Et benedictus.*	And blessed.
—	וּמְבָרֲכֶךָ	*Et benedicentes tibi.*	And they that bless thee.
—	וּמִבִּרְכָתְךָ	*Et ex benedictione tua.*	And from thy blessing.
בשל	וּמְבַשְּׁלוֹת	*Et loci parati ad coquendum.*	And boiling places.
בשר	וּמִבְּשָׂרִי	*Et de carne mea.*	And of my flesh.
—	וּמִבְּשָׂרְךָ	*Et a carne tua.*	And from thy flesh.
בית	וּמִבָּתֶּיךָ	*Et ex domibus tuis.*	And from thy houses.
גבע	וּמִגְּבָעוֹת	*Et a collibus.*	And from the hills.
גדל	וּמִגְדָּל־־דַּל	*Et turris.*	And a, the tower.
—	וּמִגְדָּלִים	*Et turres.*	And towers.
—	וּמִגְדְּלֹתַיִךְ	*Et turres tuæ.*	And thy towers.
מגד	וּמִגְדָּנוֹת־־נֹת	*Et res pretiosæ.*	And precious things.
גדף	וּמְגַדֵּף	*Et blasphemans.*	And blaspheming.
—	וּמִגִּדֻּפֹתָם	*Et ob convicia eorum*	And on account of their revilings.
גור	וּמְגוּרֹתָם	*Et timores eorum.*	And their fears.
גזז	וּמִגֵּז	*Et de vellere.*	And of the fleece.
נגד	וּמַגִּיד	*Et nuncians, nuncius*	And declaring, a messenger.
נגש	וּמַגִּישׁ	*Et offerentem.*	And him that offereth.
גנן	וּמָגֵן	*Et clypeus.*	And the shield.
—	וּמָגִנִּי	*Et clypeus meus.*	And my shield.
—	וּמָגִנִּים	*Et clypei.*	And shields.
—	וּמָגִנָּם	*Et clypeus eorum.*	And their shield.
—	וּמָגִנֵּנוּ	*Et clypeus noster.*	And our shield.
גער	וּמִגְּעָר	*Et ab increpando.*	And from rebuking.
גרל	וּמִגּוֹרָל	*Et de sorte.*	And from the lot.
גרן	וּמִגָּרְנְךָ	*Et ex area tua.*	And out of thy floor.
גרש	וּמִגְרָשׁ	*Et suburbium.*	And suburbs.
—	וּמִגְרְשֵׁי	*Et suburbia.*	And the suburbs.
—	וּמִגְרָשֶׁיהָ	*Et suburbia ejus.*	And her suburbs.
—	וּמִגְרְשֵׁיהֶם	*Et suburbia eorum.*	And their suburbs.
—	וּמִגְרְשֵׁיהֶן	*Et suburbia earum.*	And their suburbs.
גור	וּמִגָּרַת	*Et ab hospita.*	And from the female stranger
דבר	וּמְדַבֵּר	*Et loquens.*	And speaking.
—	וּמִדֶּבֶר	*Et a peste.*	And from the pestilence.
—	וּמִדַּבֵּר	*Et loquendo.*	And in speaking.

ROOTS.	DERIVATIVES.	VERSIO.	SIGNIFICATION.
דבר	וּמִדִּבְרֵיהֶם	*Et a verbis eorum.*	And from their words.
—	וּמִדְּבָרֶיךָ	*Et ad verbum tuum.*	And at thy word.
—	וּמִדְבָּרֵךְ	*Et eloquium tuum.*	And thy speech.
מדד	וּמָדַד־־מַדַּד	*Et mensus est.*	And he measured.
—	וּמָדְדוּ	*Et metientur.*	And they shall measure.
—	וּמְדָדוֹ	*Et mensus est illum.*	And he measured him or it.
—	וּמִדָּה	*Et mensura.*	And measure.
דון	וּמָדוֹן	*Et contentio.*	And contention.
—	וּמִדְוָנִים	*Et lites.*	And contentions.
נדח	וּמַדּוּחִים	*Et expulsiones.*	And expulsions, banishments.
מדע	וּמַדּוּעַ	*Et cur, quare ?*	And why, why then ?
די	וּמִדֵּי	*Et de.* [tes.	And from.
דאב	וּמְדִיבֹת	*Et mœrore afficien-*	And making sorrowful.
מדד	וּמַדָּיו	*Et vestes ejus.*	And his garments.
מדן	וּמְדִינָה	*Et provincia.*	And the province.
—	וּמְדִינָן־־דִּנָן	*Et provinciæ.*	And provinces.
דלל	וּמִדַּלּוֹת	*Et de pauperibus.*	And of the poor.
—	וּמִדַּלַּת	*Et de paupere.*	And of the poor.
אדם	וּמִדַּם	*Et de sanguine.*	And of the blood.
ידע	וּמַדַּע־־דַּע	*Et scientia.*	And knowledge.
דקק	וּמְדַקָּה	*Et comminuens*	And beating to pieces.
דקר	וּמְדֻקָּרִים	*Et confossi.*	And they that are thrust thro'
דרך	וּמִדַּרְכּוֹ	*Et a via ejus.*	And from his way.
—	וּמִדַּרְכְּכֶם	*Et a via eorum.*	And from their way.
מדד	וּמִדַּת	*Et mensura.*	And the measure.
—	וּמַדֹּתִי	*Et metiar.*	And I shall measure.
—	וּמַדֹּתֶם	*Et metiemini.*	And ye shall measure. [why.
מה	וּמָה וּמַה וּמֶה	*Et quæ, quæquæ, cur*	And that which, whatsoever,
גור	וּמֵהַגֵּר	*Et ab advena.*	And from the stranger.
גשם	וּמֵהַגְּשָׁמִים	*Et propter pluvias.*	And on account of the rains.
הדר	וּמֵהָדָר	*Et propter gloriam.*	And for the glory.
—	וּמְהַדֵּר	*Et honorans.*	And honouring.
הום	וּמְהוּמָה	*Et tumultus, turbatio*	And the tumult, trouble.
אמן	וּמְהֵימַן	*Et fidelis.* [dus.	And faithful.
הלל	וּמְהֻלָּל	*Et laudatus, laudan-*	And praised, to be praised.
—	וּמְהַלְלִים	*Et laudantes.* [bera	And praising.
הלם	וּמַהֲלֻמוֹת	*Et contusiones, ver-*	And strokes, bruises, stripes.

ROOTS.	DERIVATIVES.	VERSIO.	SIGNIFICATION.
	וּמֵהֶם	*Et ab eis.* [*eorum.*	And from them.
המן	וּמֵהֲמוֹנָם	*Et propter tumultum*	And for their tumult, noise.
נזק	וּמְהַנְזֶקֶת	*Et nocens.*	And hurting.
עזר	וּמֵהָעֲזָרָה	*Et ab atrio.*	And from the court.
קום	וּמְהָקִים	*Et erigens, statuens.*	And raising up, setting up.
מהר	וּמַהֵר	*Et festinus.*	And hasty.
—	וּמְהֹר	*Et festinans.*	And hastening.
הרה	וּמֵהֵרָיוֹן	*Et a conceptu.*	And from the conception.
הרר	וּמֵהֲרָרֶיהָ	*Et de montibus ejus.*	And from his mountains, hills
מהר	וּמִהַרְתֶּם	*Et festinabitis.*	And ye shall haste.
הלך	וּמֵהִתְהַלֵּךְ	*Et a perambulando.*	And from walking up and down
תוך	וּמֵהַתִּיכוֹנוֹת-כֹ׳	*Et ex mediis.*	And from the middle.
בוא	וּמוֹבָאָיו	*Et introitus ejus.*	And his entrance.
ידה	וּמוֹדֶא--ה	*Et gratias agens.*	And giving thanks.
ידע	וּמוֹדִיעִים	*Et notum facientes.*	And making known.
—	וּמוֹדָע	*Et cognatam.*	And a kinswoman.
יכח	וּמוֹכִיחַ	*Et corripiens.*	And he that rebuketh.
מכר	וּמוֹכְרִים	*Et vendentes.*	And selling, sellers.
מול	וּמוּל	*Et e regione.*	And over against.
ילד	וּמוֹלְדוֹתַיִךְ-מֹלְ׳	*Et natales tui.*	And thy nativity.
—	וּמוֹלַדְתְּךָ	*Et progenies tua.*	And thy issue, offspring.
מום	וּמוּם	*Et macula, vitium.*	And a spot, blemish.
יסד	וּמוֹסְדֵי	*Et fundamenta.* [*tio.*	And the foundations.
יסר	וּמוּסָר--סַר	*Et eruditio, castiga-*	And instruction, correction.
—	וּמוֹסְרוֹתֵיהֶם	*Et vincula eorum.*	And their bonds.
—	וּמוֹסְרוֹתַיִךְ־תַיִךְ	*Et vincula tua.* [*træ*	And thy bonds.
יעד	וּמוֹעֲדֵיכֶם	*Et solennitates ves-*	And your solemn feasts.
יפת	וּמוֹפֵת	*Et portentum.*	And a wonder.
—	וּמוֹפְתָיו	*Et portenta ejus.*	And his wonders.
—	וּמוֹפְתִים--מֹפְ׳	*Et portenta.*	And wonders.
יצא	וּמוֹצָא	*Et egressus.*	And the going forth.
מצא	וּמוֹצֵא--צֵא	*Et inveniens.*	And finding.
יצא	וּמוֹצָאָיו	*Et exitus ejus.*	And his goings out.
—	וּמוֹצְאֹתָיו	*Et exortus ejus.*	And his goings forth.
—	וּמוֹצִיא	*Et educens.*	And he that bringeth forth.
—	וּמוֹצִיאִי	*Et educens me.*	And he that bringeth me out.
—	וּמוֹצִיאִים	*Et educentes.*	And they that bring out.

ROOTS.	DERIVATIVES.	VERSIO.	SIGNIFICATION.
יקש	וּמוֹקֵשׁ	*Et laqueus.*	And a snare.
ירא	וּמוֹרַאֲכֶם	*Et timor vestrum.*	And the fear of you.
מרה	וּמוֹרָה	*Et novacula.*	And a rasor.
ירה	וּמוֹרֶה וּמֹרֶה	*Et docens, doctor.*	And teaching, a teacher.
מרה	וּמוֹרֶה	*Et rebellans.*	And rebelling, rebellious.
מרט	וּמוֹרָט	*Et depilatus.*	And peeled.
ישב	וּמוֹשָׁב	*Et habitatio, sessio.*	And the dwelling, sitting.
ישע	וּמוֹשִׁיעַ	*Et servans, servator*	And saving, a saviour.
משל	וּמוֹשֵׁל	*Et dominans.*	And ruling.
מות	וָמֶוֶת	*Et mors.*	And death.
יתר	וּמוֹתַר	*Et præstantia.*	And the excellence, pre-eminence.
מות	וּמוֹתְתֵנִי וּמ׳	*Et interfice me.*	And slay thou me.
זבח	וּמִזְבֵּחַ	*Et altare.*	And the altar.
—	וּמְזַבְּחוֹת	*Et immolantes.*	And they that sacrifice.
נזה	וּמַזֶּה	*Et spargens.*	And he that sprinkleth.
זה	וּמִזֶּה	*Et inde, illinc.*	And thence.
זהב	וּמִזָּהָב	*Et præ auro.*	And in comparison of gold.
זוז	וּמְזוּזָתָם	*Et postis eorum.*	And their post.
זון	וּמָזוֹן	*Et alimentum.*	And food, meat.
מזח	וּמְזִיחַ	*Et cingulum.*	And a girdle.
זלג	וּמִזְלְגֹתָיו	*Et fuscinæ ejus.*	And his flesh-hooks.
זמם	וּמְזִמָּה	*Et prudentia.*	And discretion.
—	וּמְזִמּוֹת	*Et cogitationes.*	And thoughts, devices.
זמר	וּמַזְמְרוֹתֵיכֶם	*Et falces vestræ.*	And your pruning-hooks.
זקן	וּמִזְּקֵנִי	*Et ex senibus.*	And of the ancients, aged.
זרח	וּמִזְרָחָה	*Et versus orientem.*	And toward the east.
זרע	וּמִזֶּרַע	*Et de semine.*	And of the seed.
—	וּמִזַּרְעוֹ	*Et de semine ejus.*	And of his seed.
—	וּמִזַּרְעֲךָ	*Et de semine tuo.*	And of thy seed.
זרק	וּמִזְרְקֹתָיו	*Et crateres ejus.*	And his basons.
מוח	וּמֹחַ	*Et medulla.*	And marrow.
חבש	וּמְחַבֵּשׁ	*Et alligans.*	And binding up.
חדר	וּמֵחֲדָרִים	*Et in conclavibus.*	And in the chambers.
חדש	וּמֵחֹדֶשׁ	*Et de mense.*	And from month.
מחה	וּמָחָה	*Et delebit, absterget*	And he shall blot, wipe away
חלל	וּמָחוֹל	*Et chorus.*	And dance.
חנן	וּמְחוֹנֵן	*Et miserescens.*	And pitying, shewing mercy.

ROOTS.	DERIVATIVES.	VERSIO.	SIGNIFICATION.
חוץ	וּמִחוּץ	*Et extrinsecus.*	And without.
—	וּמְחוּצָה	*Et extra.*	And without.
—	וּמֵחוּצוֹת	*Et ex plateis.*	And from the streets.
חזה	וּמֶחֱזָה	*Et aspectus, fenestra*	And sight, window.
—	וּמֶחֶזְיוֹנוֹת	*Et per visiones.*	And through visions.
חזק	וּמַחֲזִיק	*Et tenens.*	And holding.
—	וּמַחֲזִיקָהּ	*Et confirmans eam.*	And strengthening her.
—	וּמַחֲזִיקִים	*Et prehendentes.*	And taking hold.
חטא	וּמֵחַטָּאתִי	*Et a peccato meo.*	And from my sin.
—	וּמֵחַטָּאתָם	*Et a peccato eorum.*	And from their sin.
חי	וּמְחִי	*Et balista vel aries* [*ejus.*	And his missile or battering [engine.
חיה	וּמְחַיֶּה	*Et vivificans.*	And making alive.
חיק	וּמֵחֵיק	*Et ex sinu.*	And from the bosom.
מחר	וּמְחִיר	*Et pretium.*	And the price.
חיה	וּמֵחַיַּת	*Et ex bestia*	And from the beast.
—	וּמִחְיַת	*Et vivus, vivax.*	And quick *flesh.*
מחה	וּמָחִיתִי	*Et delebo.*	And I will blot out, destroy.
חיה	וּמִחְיָתְךָ	*Et victus tuus.*	And thy victuals.
חלב	וּמֵחֶלְבֵּהֶן	*Et de adipibus earum*	And of their fat.
חלל	וּמְחַלְלִים	*Et profanantes.*	And they that profane.
חלק	וּמַחֲלֻקְתּוֹ	*Et classis ejus.*	And his class, course.
חלל	וּמְחֹלֹת	*Et chori.*	And dances.
חמד	וּמַחֲמַדַּי	*Et desiderabilia mea*	And my desirable things.
חמל	וּמַחְמַל	*Et clementia.*	And mercy, pity.
חמס	וּמֵחָמָס	*Et a violentia.*	And from violence.
יחם	וּמֵחֲמַת	*Et de furore.*	And of the wrath.
חנה	וּמַחֲנֶה	*Et castra, exercitus*	And the camp, host, army.
—	וּמַחֲנֵיהֶם	*Et exercitus eorum.*	And their hosts.
חנק	וּמַחֲנָק	*Et strangulatio.*	And strangling.
חסר	וּמְחַסֵּר	*Et destituens.*	And depriving, disappointing.
—	וּמַחְסֹרֶיךָ	*Et egestates tuæ.*	And thy wants.
—	וּמַחְסֹרְךָ	*Et egestates tuæ.*	And thy want.
חפר	וּמַחְפִּיר	*Et probro afficiens.*	And bringing reproach.
מחץ	וּמָחַץ	*Et transfodiet.* [*dum*	And he shall thrust through.
—	וּמַחַץ	*Et vulnus profun-*	And the deep wound.
—	וּמָחֲצָה	*Et transfixit.*	And he pierced.
חצה	וּמֵחֲצִי	*Et ex dimidio.*	And out of the half.

ROOTS.	DERIVATIVES.	VERSIO.	SIGNIFICATION.
חצה	וּמֶחֱצִיתָהּ	*Et dimidium ejus.*	And the half of her or it.
חקק	וּמְחֹקֵק	*Et legislator, judex.*	And a lawgiver, judge.
מחר	וּמָחָר	*Et cras.*	And to-morrow.
חרץ	וּמֵחָרוּץ	*Et præ auro.*	And than gold.
חרב	וּמַחֲרִיבַיִךְ	*Et vastantes te.*	And those that make thee [waste.
חשב	וּמַחְשְׁבוֹתַי	*Et cogitationes meæ.*	And my thoughts.
—	וּמַחְשְׁבוֹתָיו	*Et cogitationes ejus.*	And his thoughts.
—	וּמַחְשְׁבֹתֵיהֶם	*Et cogitationes suæ.*	And their thoughts.
—	וּמַחְשְׁבֹתֶיךָ	*Et cogitationes tuæ.*	And thy thoughts.
חשך	וּמֵחֹשֶׁךְ	*Et ex tenebris.*	And out of darkness.
מחא	וּמָחַת	*Et percussit.*	And he smote.
מחה	וּמָחֲתָה	*Et abstersit.*	And she wiped.
חתת	וּמְחִתָּה	*Et terror.*	And the terror.
חתה	וּמַחְתֹּתֶיהָ	*Et trullæ ejus.*	And her fire-pans.
—	וּמַחְתֹּתָיו	*Et trullæ ejus.*	And his fire-pans.
יטב	וּמֵטִב	*Et benefaciens.*	And doing well, doing good.
מוט	וּמָטָה	*Et nutabit.*	And he shall slide.
נטה	וּמַטֶּה וּמַטֵּה	*Et virga, tribus.*	And the rod, tribe.
—	וּמַטֵּהוּ	*Et virga ejus.*	And his rod.
טהר	וּמְטַהֵר	*Et purgans.*	And purifying.
מוט	וּמֹטוֹת	*Et juga.*	And yokes.
נטה	וּמַטֵּי	*Et divertentes.*	And they that turn aside.
יטב	וּמֵטִיב	*Et benefaciens.*	And doing good.
נטה	וּמָטִים	*Et divertentes.*	And they that turn aside.
—	וּמַטְּךָ	*Et virga tua.*	And thy rod, staff.
טלל	וּמִטַּל	*Et per rorem.*	And by the dew.
טלא	וּמְטֻלָּאוֹת	*Et maculosæ.* [diti.	And spotted.
טמן	וּמַטְמֹנֵי	*Et thesauri abscon-*	And hidden treasures.
טעם	וּמִטַּעַם	*Et ex mandato.*	And according to the com-
מטר	וּמָטָר וּמְטַר	*Et pluvia.*	And rain. [mandment.
מטא	וּמָטַת	*Et pertigit.*	And she reached.
מי	וָמִי וּמִי	*Et qui, quæ.*	And who, what.
מים	וּמֵי	*Et aquæ.*	And waters.
יגע	וּמִיגִיעוֹ	*Et e labore ejus.*	And from his labour.
יד	וּמִיַּד	*Et ex manu.*	And out of the hand.
—	וּמִיָּדְךָ	*Et de manu tua.*	And from thy hand.
ידע	וּמְיֻדָּעַי	*Et noti mei.*	And my friends.

ROOTS.	DERIVATIVES.	VERSIO.	SIGNIFICATION.
ידע	וּמְיֻדָּעִי	*Et notus meus.*	And my acquaintance.
—	וּמְיֻדָּעָיו	*Et noti ejus.*	And his friends.
הוה	וּמֵיְהוָה	*Et a Domino.*	And from the Lord.
יום	וּמִיּוֹם	*Et à die.*	And from the day.
יטב	וּמֵיטַב	*Et optimum.*	And the best.
יין	וּמִיַּיִן	*Et de vino.*	And of the wine.
מים	וְמַיִם וָמַ׳ וּמַ׳	*Et aqua, aquæ.*	And water, waters.
ים	וּמִיָּם	*Et ab occidente.*	And from the west.
מים	וּמֵימַי	*Et aquæ meæ.*	And my waters.
—	וּמֵימֵיהֶם	*Et aquæ eorum.*	And their waters.
—	וּמֵימֶיךָ	*Et aquæ tuæ.*	And thy waters.
יסד	וּמְיֻסָּד	*Et fundatus.* [*sura.*	And founded.
מרץ	וּמִיץ	*Et exprimens, pres-*	And squeezing out, a wringing
יצא	וּמִיֹּצְאָו	*Et egressi, prognati*	And they that came forth, the offspring.
יקב	וּמִיִּקְבֶךָ	*Et ex torculari tuo.*	And out of thy wine-press.
ישר	וּמֵישָׁרִים	*Et rectitudines.*	And uprightness.
יתר	וּמִיֶּתֶר	*Et de residuo.*	And of the rest.
—	וּמֵיתְרֵיהֶם	*Et funes eorum.*	And their cords.
מוך	וּמָךְ	*Et deprimetur.*	And he shall be brought low.
כאב	וּמַכְאֹבוֹ	*Et dolor ejus.*	And his sorrow.
—	וּמַכְאֹבֵינוּ	*Et dolor noster.*	And our sorrow.
—	וּמַכְאוֹבִי	*Et dolor meus.*	And my sorrow.
כבד	וּמְכַבְּדוֹ	*Et honorans eum.*	And he that honoureth him.
—	וּמַכְבִּיד	*Et onerans.*	And burdening.
נכה	וּמַכָּה	*Et plaga.*	And a wound.
—	וּמַכֵּה	*Et percutiens.*	And he that smiteth.
כון	וּמָכוֹן	*Et locus paratus.*	And a prepared place.
נכה	וּמַכּוֹת	*Et plagæ.* [*vestris.*	And wounds.
כוח	וּמִכֹּחֲכֶם	*Et ex facultatibus*	And of your substance.
כחש	וּמִכַּחַשׁ	*Et propter menda-cium.* [*nibus.*	And for lying.
כלל	וּמִכָּל־־כֹּל	*Et ex, de omni, om-*	And from, of all.
כלה	וּמִכְּלֵי	*Et ex vasis.*	And of the vessels.
כלל	וּמִכֻּלָּם	*Et a cunctis ipsis.*	And from them all.
כנס	וּמִכְנְסֵי	*Et femoralia.*	And breeches, drawers.
כסה	וּמְכַסֶּה	*Et operimentum.*	And the covering.

ROOTS.	DERIVATIVES.	VERSIO.	SIGNIFICATION.
כוס	וּמִכֹּסוֹ	*Et ex calice ejus.*	And from his cup.
כסה	וּמְכַסַּיִךְ	*Et operientes te.*	And those that cover thee.
כסס	וּמִכְסָם	*Et census eorum.*	And their tribute.
כסף	וּמִכַּסְפִּי	*Et de argento meo.*	And of my silver.
כפף	וּמִכַּף	*Et ex manu.*	And out of the hand.
מכר	וּמָכַר	*Et vendidit.*	And he sold.
——	וּמָכֹר	*Et vendendo.*	And in selling.
כרה	וּמִכְרֵה	*Et fossa, fodina.*	And a pit, quarry, mine.
מכר	וּמָכְרוּ	*Et vendent.*	And they shall sell.
——	וּמְכָרוֹ	*Et vendet eum.*	And he shall sell him.
——	וּמְכָרוּם	*Et vendent eos.*	And they will sell them.
——	וּמֹכְרֵי	*Et vendentes.*	And those that sell.
——	וּמֹכְרֵיהֶן	*Et vendentes eas.*	And those that sell them.
כרכר	וּמְכַרְכֵּר	*Et saltans.*	And dancing.
מכר	וּמָכַרְתִּי	*Et vendam.*	And I will sell.
כשל	וּמִכְשׁוֹל	*Et offendiculum.*	And the stumbling block.
כשף	וּמְכַשֵּׁף	*Et divinus.*	And a diviner, sorcerer.
כתב	וּמְכַתְּבִים	*Et scribentes.*	And they that write.
נכה	וּמַכָּתִי	*Et plaga mea.*	And my wound.
מול	וּמָל	*Et circumcidet.*	And he will circumcise.
מלא	וּמָלֵא	*Et plenus.*	And full.
——	וּמַלֵּא	*Et imple.*	And fill thou.
——	וּמְלֹא	*Et plenitudo.*	And the fulness.
——	וּמִלֵּא	*Et implevit, consecravit.*	And he filled, consecrated.
——	וּמָלְאָה	*Et implebitur.*	And she shall be filled.
——	וּמְלֹאָהּ־־לוֹ׳	*Et plenitudo ejus.*	And her fulness.
——	וּמָלְאוּ	*Et impleverunt, implebunt, implebuntur.*	And they filled, will fill, shall be filled.
——	וּמִלְאוּ	*Et implete.*	And fill ye.
——	וּמְלֹאוֹ־־לוֹ״	*Et plenitudo ejus.*	And his fulness.
——	וּמִלְאוּ	*Et replete.*	And fill ye.
——	וּמִלְּאוּ	*Et implebunt.*	And they shall fill, consecrate
——	וּמִלְאוּהָ	*Et impleverunt eam*	And they filled her.
לאך	וּמַלְאַךְ־־אָךְ	*Et angelus, nuncius.*	And the angel, messenger.
——	וּמְלָאכָה	*Et opus.*	And business.
——	וּמַלְאָכָיו	*Et legati ejus.*	And his ambassadors.
——	וּמַלְאָכִים	*Et nuncii.*	And messengers.

ROOTS.	DERIVATIVES.	VERSIO.	SIGNIFICATION.
מלא	וּמִלֵּאת	*Et implevit.* [*crabis.*	And he filled.
—	וּמִלֵּאתָ	*Et implebis, conse-*	And thou shalt fill, consecrate
—	וּמִלֵּאתִי	*Et implebo, complebo*	And I will fill, fulfil, complete
—	וּמִלֵּאתֶם	*Et implevistis.*	And ye have filled.
בדד	וּמִלְּבַד	*Et præter.*	And beside.
לבש	וּמַלְבּוּשֵׁיהֶם־־בֵ׳	*Et vestes eorum.*	And their garments.
—	וּמַלְבּוּשֶׁךָ	*Et vestes tuæ.*	And thy garments.
לבב	וּמִלִּבָּם	*Et ex corde eorum.*	And out of their heart.
מלל	וּמִלָּה	*Et sermo, verbum.*	And a word.
מלא	וּמִלֻּאִים	*Et impletiones.*	And the fillings.
לוה	וּמַלְוֶה	*Et commodans.*	And lending.
מלח	וְמֶלַח וּמְלַח	*Et sal.*	And salt.
—	וּמַלָּחֵיהֶם	*Et nauiæ eorum.*	And their mariners.
לחם	וּמִלְחָמָה	*Et bellum, prælium.*	And war, battle.
—	וּמִלְחָמוֹת־־חֹ׳	*Et bella.*	And wars.
מלט	וּמִלֵּט	*Et liberavit.*	And he delivered.
—	וּמַלְּטוּ	*Et eripite.*	And deliver ye.
—	וּמַלְּטוּנִי	*Et liberate me.*	And deliver ye me.
—	וּמַלְּטִי	*Et libera.*	And deliver thou.
מלל	וּמִלִּים וּמִלִּין	*Et sermones, verba.*	And speeches, words.
לוץ	וּמְלִיצָה	*Et interpretatio.*	And the interpretation.
—	וּמְלִיצֶיךָ	*Et interpretes tui.*	And thy interpreters.
מלך	וָמֶלֶךְ ו׳ וּמַלְכָּא	*Et rex.*	And a king.
—	וּמָלַךְ	*Et regnabit.*	And he shall reign.
לכד	וּמִלְכַּדְתּוֹ	*Et decipula ejus.*	And his snare, trap.
מלך	וּמַלְכוּ־־כוּתָא	*Et regnum.*	And a, the kingdom.
—	וּמַלְכוּתָהּ־־תֵהּ	*Et regnum ejus.*	And his kingdom.
—	וּמַלְכוּתוֹ	*Et regnum ejus.*	And his kingdom.
—	וּמַלְכוּתֶךָ	*Et regnum tuum.*	And thy kingdom.
—	וּמַלְכֵי	*Et reges.*	And the kings.
—	וּמַלְכֵיהֶם	*Et reges eorum.*	And their kings.
—	וּמְלָכִים וּמַלְכִין	*Et reges.*	And kings.
—	וּמָלַכְתָּ	*Et regnabis.*	And thou shalt reign.
—	וּמַלְכַּת	*Et regina.*	And the queen.
עלה	וּמִלְמַעְלָה	*Et supra.*	And above.
לעג	וּמַלְעִגִים	*Et subsannantes.*	And mocking. [count of.
פנה	וּמִלִּפְנֵי	*Et a facie, propter.*	And from the face, on ac-

ROOTS.	DERIVATIVES.	VERSIO.	SIGNIFICATION.
פנה	וּמִלְּפָנִים	*Et antea.*	And in time past, before.
מלק	וּמָלַק	*Et contorquebit, extorquebit, ungue secabit.*	And he shall twist off, wring off, pinch off with the nail.
לקח	וּמַלְקוֹחַ	*Et præda.*	And the prey.
לקש	וּמַלְקוֹשׁ	*Et pluvia serotina.*	And the latter rain.
לקח	וּמַלְקָחֶיהָ	*Et forcipes ejus.*	And his tongs.
מלל	וּמִלַּת וּמִלְּתָא	*Et verbum, res.*	And the word, matter, thing.
מול	וּמַלְתָּ	*Et circumcides.*	And thou shalt circumcise.
מלל	וּמִלָּתוֹ	*Et verbum ejus.*	And his word.
מול	וּמַלְתֶּם	*Et circumcidetis* [re	And ye shall circumcise.
מגד	וּמִמֶּגֶד	*Et de pretioso mune-*	And for the precious gift.
דבר	וּמִמִּדְבָּר	*Et a deserto.*	And from the desert.
מהר	וּמְמַהֵר	*Et festinans.*	And hastening.
ילד	וּמִמּוֹלַדְתְּךָ	*Et e cognatione tua.*	And from thy kindred.
יעץ	וּמִמּוֹעֲצֹתֵיהֶם	*Et consiliis eorum.*	And with their counsels, devi- [ces.
זרח	וּמִמִּזְרָח	*Et ab ortu.*	And from the rising.
מזר	וּמִמְּזָרִים	*Et a septentrione.*	And out of the north.
חצה	וּמִמַּחֲצִית--צַת	*Et de dimidio.*	And from the half.
מחר	וּמִמָּחֳרָת	*Et in crastino.*	And on the morrow.
חתת	וּמִמְּחִתָּה	*Et a terrore.*	And from terror.
נטה	וּמִמַּטֵּה	*Et ex tribu.*	And out of the tribe.
מטר	וּמִמָּטָר	*Et a pluvia.*	And from rain.
מים	וּמִמֵּי	*Et ex aquis.*	And out of the water.
נכה	וּמִמַּכּוֹתַיִךְ	*Et e plagis tuis.*	And from thy wounds.
מלך	וּמַמְלָכָה	*Et regnum.*	And the kingdom.
——	וּמַמְלְכוֹת	*Et regna.*	And the kingdoms.
——	וּמַמְלַכְתִּי	*Et regnum meum.*	And my kingdom.
——	וּמַמְלַכְתְּךָ	*Et regnum tuum.*	And thy kingdom.
——	וּמִמַּמְלָכָה	*Et a regno.*	And from the kingdom.
מן	וּמִמֶּנָּה	*Et ab ea.*	And from her.
——	וּמִמֶּנּוּ	*Et ab eo.*	And from him.
יסד	וּמִמַּסַּד	*Et a fundamento.*	And from the foundation.
ען	וּמִמְּעוֹן	*Et de habitaculo.*	And from the habitation.
עלה	וּמִמַּעַל וּמֵעַל	*Et sursum.*	And above.
עמד	וּמִמַּעֲמָדְךָ	*Et a statione tua.*	And from thy station.
עמק	וּמִמַּעֲמַקֵּי	*Et e profundis.*	And out of the depths.

ROOTS.	DERIVATIVES.	VERSIO.	SIGNIFICATION.
ערב	וּמִמַּעֲרָב־בָה	*Et ab occidente.*	And from the west.
פרס	וּמִמַּפְרִיסֵי־־רְסִי	*Et de findentibus.*	And of them that divide.
צוק	וּמִמְּצֻקוֹתֵיהֶם	*Et ex angustiis eorum.*	And out of their straits, distresses.
קדש	וּמִמִּקְדָּשִׁי	*Et ex sanctuario* [*meo.*	And out of my sanctuary.
קום	וּמִמָּקוֹם	*Et ex loco.*	And out of, from the place.
קנה	וּמִמִּקְנֵה	*Et de pecore.*	And of the cattle.
מרר	וּמֶמֶר	*Et amaritudo.*	And bitterness.
ראה	וּמִמַּרְאֵה	*Et ab aspectu.*	And from the sight, appear-[ance.
שכן	וּמִמִּשְׁכָּן	*Et e tentorio.*	And from the tabernacle.
משל	וּמֶמְשַׁלְתְּךָ	*Et dominium tuum.*	And thy dominion.
שפח	וּמִמִּשְׁפְּחוֹת	*Et de familiis.*	And of the families.
——	וּמִמִּשְׁפַּחְתָּם	*Et ex familia eorum*	And from their family.
שפט	וּמִמִּשְׁפָּט	*Et a judicio.*	And from judgment.
——	וּמִמִּשְׁפָּטֶיךָ	*Et a judiciis tuis.*	And from thy judgments.
מתן	וּמִמָּתְנָיו	*Et a lumbis ejus.*	And from his loins.
מן	וּמַן	*Et quisquis.*	And whosoever.
——	וּמִן	*Et ab, de, ex, prop-*[*ter.*	And from, of, out of, because [of.
נאף	וּמְנָאָפֶת	*Et adultera.*	And an adulteress.
נבא	וּמִנָּבִיא	*Et a propheta.*	And from the prophet.
נגב	וּמִנֶּגֶב	*Et ab austro.*	And from the south.
ידע	וּמַנְדַּע־דְּעָא	*Et scientia.*	And knowledge.
——	וּמַנְדְּעִי	*Et intelligentia mea.*	And my understanding.
מן	וּמִנָּהּ	*Et ab ea.*	And from her.
——	וּמִנֵּה	*Et ex eo.*	And from him.
——	וּמִנְּהֵון	*Et ex illis.*	And out of them.
נהר	וּמִנָּהָר	*Et a flumine.*	And from the river.
נוח	וּמְנוּחָה	*Et requies.*	And rest.
נוס	וּמָנוֹס	*Et fuga, refugium.*	And flight, refuge.
——	וּמְנוּסִי	*Et refugium meum.*	And my refuge.
נור	וּמְנוֹרָה וּמְנוֹרַת	*Et candelabrum.*	And the candlestick.
מנח	וּמִנְחָה	*Et oblatio, fertum.*	And the oblation, meat-offer-[ing.
נחל	וּמִנַּחֲלַת	*Et de hæreditate.*	And from the inheritance.
נחש	וּמְנַחֵשׁ	*Et augurans, divinans.*	And one who useth auguries, a diviner.
מנח	וּמִנְחַת	*Et oblatio, fertum.*	And the oblation, meat-offer-[ing.
——	וּמִנְחָתָהּ	*Et fertum ejus.*	And her meat-offering.

ROOTS.	DERIVATIVES.	VERSIO.	SIGNIFICATION.
—	וּמִנְחָתוֹ	*Et oblatio ejus.*	And his meat-offering.
—	וּמִנְחֹתֵיכֶם	*Et oblationes vestræ.*	And your meat-offerings.
—	וּמִנְחָתָם־תְהוֹן	*Et oblationes eorum.*	And their meat-offerings.
מנא	וּמַנִּי	*Et constituit.*	And he appointed, set.
מן	וּמִנִּי	*Et a me.*	And from me.
מנה	וּמָנִיתִי	*Et numerabo.*	And I will number.
מן	וּמַנְךָ	*Et manna tuum.*	And thy manna.
נכס	וּמִנִּכְסֵי	*Et de facultatibus.*	And of the goods.
נעל	וּמַנְעָלָיו	*Et seræ ejus.*	And his locks, bolts.
נער	וּמִנְּעָרַי	*Et e servis meis.*	And of my servants. [dents.
נצח	וּמְנַצְּחִים	*Et præfecti.* [vernis	And overseers, superinten-
נקק	וּמִנְּקִיקֵי	*Et ex fissuris, ca-*	And out of the holes, caverns.
נקה	וּמְנַקִּיֹּתָיו	*Et scopulæ ejus.*	And his bowls.
מנה	וּמְנָת	*Et portio.*	And the portion.
סבב	וּמִסְּבִי	*Et in circuitibus.*	And in the places round about
—	וּמִסְּבִיבוֹת	*Et ex circuitibus.*	And from the places about.
סגר	וּמִסְגֶּרֶת	*Et claustra.*	And the borders, inclosures.
—	וּמְסֻגֶּרֶת	*Et occlusa est.*	And she was shut up.
—	וּמִסְגְּרֹתֶיהָ	*Et claustra ejus.*	And her borders.
—	וּמִסְגְּרֹתֵיהֶם	*Et limbi eorum.*	And their borders.
סחר	וּמִסְחַר	*Et negotiatio.*	And the traffick. [ing.
סכך	וּמָסָךְ	*Et operimentum.*	And the veil, covering, hang-
—	וּמַסֵּכָה	*Et idolum fusile.*	And the molten image.
—	וּמַסֵּכוֹת	*Et idola fusilia.*	And the molten images.
סכן	וּמִסְכְּנוֹת	*Et horrea, thesauri.*	And store-houses, treasuries.
סל	וּמִסַּל	*Et ex canistro.*	And out of the basket.
סלל	וּמְסִלֹּתַי	*Et semitæ meæ.*	And my ways.
ספד	וּמִסְפֵּד	*Et planctus.*	And mourning.
ספא	וּמִסְפּוֹא	*Et pabulum.*	And provender.
ספר	וּמִסְפָּר־פַּר	*Et numerus.*	And the number.
יסר	וּמֹסֵרוֹת	*Et vincula.*	And bonds.
סרף	וּמְסָרְפוֹ	*Et comburens eum,* al. *ungens eum.*	And he that burneth him, *al.* he that anointeth him.
סתר	וּמִסְתְּרָתָא	*Et res absconditæ.*	And secret things.
עבד	וּמֵעֲבֹדָה	*Et præ servitute.*	And for bondage.
—	וּמֵעֲבָדֶיךָ	*Et a servis tuis.*	And from thy servants.
עבר	וּמֵעֵבֶר	*Et trans.*	And on the other side.

ROOTS.	DERIVATIVES.	VERSIO.	SIGNIFICATION.
ענל	וּמַעְגְּלֶיךָ	*Et semitæ, orbitæ tuæ.*	And thy paths, tracks.
עזז	וּמָעוֹז	*Et robur.*	And the strength.
מעך	וּמָעוּךְ	*Et pressus.*	And pressed, bruised.
מעל	וּמָעוֹל	*Et prævaricando.*	And in transgressing.
עלם	וּמֵעוֹלָם	*Et a seculo, ab ævo.*	And from of old, from everlasting
עוה	וּמֵעֲוֹנִי	*Et ab iniquitate mea*	And from my iniquity.
ענן	וּמְעוֹנְנִים	*Et harioli.*	And diviners, soothsayers.
עון	וּמְעוֹנָתוֹ	*Et habitatio ejus.*	And his dwelling place.
—	וּמְעוֹנֹתָיו־עֹנ׳	*Et habitacula ejus.*	And his dens.
עוה	וּמֵעֲוֹנֹתֵיהֶם	*Et propter iniquitates eorum.*	And because of their iniquities
עוף	וּמֵעוֹף	*Et a volucri.*	And from the fowl.
עזז	וּמֵעַז	*Et ex forti.*	And out of the strong.
—	וּמָעֻזִּי	*Et robur, præsidium meum.*	And my strength, fortress.
מעט	וּמְעָט	*Et parum.*	And a little.
מעה	וּמֵעַי	*Et viscera mea.*	And my bowels.
—	וּמֵעֵיהֶם	*Et viscera eorum.*	And their bowels.
—	וּמֵעֶיךָ	*Et viscera tua.*	And thy bowels.
מעל	וּמְעִיל	*Et pallium.*	And a robe.
—	וּמְעִילִי	*Et pallium meum.*	And my robe, mantle.
עין	וּמַעְיָן	*Et fons.*	And a fountain.
עלה	וָמַעְלָה וָמַ׳	*Et supra, sursum.*	And above, upwards.
—	וּמַעֲלָה	*Et adducens.*	And bringing.
מעל	וּמָעֲלָה	*Et prævaricabitur.*	And she will transgress.
—	וּמַעֲלוֹ	*Et prævaricatio ejus*	And his trespass.
עלל	וּמֵעֻלּוֹ	*Et de jugo ejus.*	And from his yoke.
עלה	וּמַעֲלוֹת	*Et gradus, quæ oriuntur.*	And the steps, the things which arise.
—	וּמֵעָלָיו	*Et ab eo.*	And from him.
עלל	וּמַעַלְלֵיכֶם־לְלֵ׳	*Et opera vestra.*	And your works, doings.
עלם	וּמַעֲלִים	*Et occultans.*	And he that hideth.
עלל	וּמַעַלְלֵיהֶם	*Et opera eorum.*	And their works.
עלל	וּמַעֲלָלָיו	*Et actiones tuæ.*	And thy actions, doings.
—	וּמַעֲלָלֶיךָ	*Et opera vestra.*	And your works.
עלה	וּמַעֲלֹתֵהוּ	*Et gradus ejus.*	And his steps, stairs.
עמם	וּמֵעָם	*Et de populo.*	And from a people.
—	וּמֵעִם	*Et a.*	And from.

ROOTS.	DERIVATIVES.	VERSIO.	SIGNIFICATION.
עמד	וּמֵעֲמַד	*Et statio.*	And the standing, attendance.
עמם	וּמֵעַמּוֹ	*Et a populo ejus.*	And from his people.
—	וּמֵעַמִּי	*Et a populo meo.*	And from my people.
—	וּמֵעַמִּים	*Et ex populis.*	And of the people, nations.
—	וּמֵעַמֶּךָ	*Et a populo tuo.*	And from thy people.
ענה	וּמְעֻנֶּה	*Et afflictus.*	And afflicted.
עפר	וּמֵעָפָר	*Et e pulvere.*	And out of the dust.
עוץ	וּמֵעֵץ	*Et ex arbore.*	And of, from the tree.
עצב	וּמֵעִצְּבוֹן	*Et de dolore.*	And concerning the sorrow.
עקש	וּמְעַקֵּשׁ	*Et pervertens.*	And he that perverteth.
—	וּמַעֲקַשִּׁים	*Et perversitates.*	And perverse, crooked things.
ערב	וּמַעֲרָבַיִךְ	*Et commercium tuum*	And thy commerce.
ערה	וּמְעָרָה	*Et spelunca.*	And the den.
ערך	וּמַעֲרֶכֶת	*Et dispositio, ordinatio.*	And the arrangement, setting in order.
עשה	וּמַעֲשֶׂה	*Et opus.*	And the work.
—	וּמַעֲשֵׂהוּ	*Et opus ejus.*	And his work.
—	וּמַעֲשֵׂיהֶם	*Et opus eorum.*	And their work.
עשר	וּמַעֲשִׁיר	*Et ditans.*	And he that maketh rich.
—	וּמַעְשַׂר	*Et decima.*	And the tithe.
עתת	וּמֵעֵת	*Et a tempore.*	And from the time.
פאה	וּמִפְּאַת	*Et a latere, ad latus.*	And from the side, on the side.
פה	וּמִפּוֹ	*Et inde.*	And thence, on that side.
פזז	וּמִפָּז	*Et præ auro.*	And in comparison of gold.
פה	וּמִפִּי	*Et ex ore meo.*	And out of my mouth.
נפל	וּמַפִּיל	*Et proferens.*	And presenting.
—	וּמַפַּל	*Et quisquiliæ.*	And the refuse.
פלא	וּמַפְלִא	*Et mirifice agens.*	And doing wonderfully.
פלט	וּמְפַלְטִי	*Et liberator meus.*	And my deliverer.
פנה	וּמִפָּנַי	*Et ex facie mea.*	And from my face.
—	וּמִפְּנֵי	*Et a conspectu.*	And from the presence.
—	וּמִפְּנֵיהֶם	*Et a facie eorum.*	And from their face.
פנה	וּמִפָּנֶיךָ	*Et a facie tua.*	And from thy face.
פוץ	וּמְפִצִים	*Et dispergentes.*	And those who scatter.
פקד	וּמִפִּקּוּדֶיךָ	*Et a præceptis tuis.*	And from thy precepts.
פרד	וּמְפֹרָד	*Et dissipatus.*	And dispersed.
פרה	וּמִפְּרִי	*Et de fructu.*	And of the fruit.

ROOTS.	DERIVATIVES.	VERSIO.	SIGNIFICATION.
פרס	וּמַפְרִיס	*Et findens.*	And he that divideth.
פשע	וּמִפִּשְׁעֵיהֶם	*Et propter prævaricationes eorum.*	And because of their transgressions.
פתח	וּמִפְתַּח	*Et apertio.*	And the opening.
—	וּמִפֶּתַח	*Et ex ostio.*	And out of the door. [foolish.
פתה	וּמִפֶּתִי	*Et de fatuo.*	And concerning the simple,
יפת	וּמֹפְתִים	*Et portenta.*	And wonders.
מצא	וּמָצָא	*Et inveniet, sufficiet, inventus est.*	And he will find, will suffice, was found.
—	וּמְצָא	*Et inveni.*	And find thou.
—	וּמָצְאָה	*Et invenit, inveniet.*	And she hath found, will find.
—	וּמְצָאָהּ	*Et inveniet eam.*	And he shall find her.
—	וּמְצָאֻהוּ	*Et accident ei.*	And they shall befal him.
—	וּמָצְאוּ	*Et invenient.*	And they shall find.
—	וּמִצְאוּ וּמְצֶאןָ	*Et invenite.* [*ent tibi*	And find ye. [to thee.
—	וּמְצָאוּךָ	*Et occurrent, eveni-*	And they shall meet, happen
יצא	וּמֹצָאֵי	*Et exortus, exitus.*	And the springs, goings forth.
מצא	וּמְצָאָנוּ	*Et inveniet nos.*	And he will come upon us.
צאן	וּמִצֹּאנְךָ	*Et de grege tuo.*	And of thy flock.
מצא	וּמָצָאתָ	*Et invenisti, invenies*	And thou hast found, wilt find
—	וּמְצָאתָהּ	*Et invenisti eum.*	And thou hast found her.
יצא	וּמוֹצָאתוֹ	*Et ab exitu ejus.*	And from his goings out.
מצא	וּמְצָאתֶם	*Et invenietis.*	And ye shall find.
יצב	וּמַצָּב	*Et statio, præsidium*	And the station, garrison.
—	וּמַצֵּבָה	*Et statua, cippus.* [*dia.*	And the statue, image, monumental pillar.
—	וּמַצְּבוֹת־צְ׳	*Et stationes, præsi-*	And the stations, garrisons.
—	וּמַצֵּבוֹתֶיךָ	*Et statuæ tuæ.*	And thy statues.
צבע	וּמִצְבָּעוֹת	*Et tiaræ.*	And diadems, turbans.
יצב	וּמַצֵּבֹתָם	*Et statuæ eorum.*	And their statues.
צדק	וּמַצְדִּיקֵי	*Et justificantes.*	And they that justify.
צוד	וּמְצֻדָתָהּ	*Et arx, munitio.*	And a fortress.
צוד	וּמְצֻדָתִי־צוּ׳	*Et munitio mea.*	And my fortress.
נצה	וּמַצָּה	*Et jurgium, rixa.*	And debate, strife, contention
צהל	וּמִצְהֲלוֹתַיִךְ	*Et hinnitus tui.*	And thy neighings.
צהר	וּמִצָּהֳרַיִם	*Et præ meridie.*	And than the noon-day.
צוד	וּמְצוּדָה	*Et arx.*	And the strong hold.

ROOTS.	DERIVATIVES.	VERSIO.	SIGNIFICATION.
צוד	וּמְצוּדוֹ	*Et rete ejus*	And his net. [commands.
צוה	וּמְצַוֶּה	*Et præcipiens.*	And he that instructs, charges,
—	וּמִצְוֹות־צְוֹת	*Et præcepta.*	And commandments. [tion.
צוק	וּמָצוֹק וּמְצוּקָה	*Et angustia, afflictio*	And anguish, distress, afflic-
צור	וּמִצּוּר	*Et e rupe.*	And out of the rock.
מצץ	וּמַצּוֹת	*Et azyma.*	And unleavened *cakes.*
צוה	וּמִצְוֹתַי	*Et præcepta mea.*	And my commandments.
—	וּמִצְוֹתָיו	*Et præcepta ejus.*	And his commandments.
—	וּמִצְוֹתֶיךָ	*Et præcepta tua.*	And thy commandments.
מצח	וּמֵצַח	*Et frons.*	And the forehead.
—	וּמִצְחֲךָ	*Et frons tua.*	And thy brow.
—	וּמִצְחַת	*Et ocrea.*	And greaves.
מצה	וּמָצִית	*Et exsuges.*	And thou shalt suck out.
נצל	וּמַצִּל	*Et eripiens.*	And he that rescueth.
צלא	וּמְצַלֵּא	*Et orans.*	And he that prayeth.
צלח	וּמַצְלַח	*Et prosperans.*	And he that prospereth.
—	וּמַצְלְחִין	*Et prosperantes.*	And they that prosper.
צלא	וּמְצַלַּיִן	*Et orantes.*	And they that pray.
צלל	וּמְצִלְתַּיִם־תַּיִם	*Et cymbala.*	And cymbals.
צפן	וּמִצָּפוֹן	*Et ab aquilone.* [rans	And from the north. [tereth.
צפצף	וּמְצַפְצֵף	*Et garriens, susur-*	And he that chattereth, mut-
צור	וּמְצָרֵי	*Et angustiæ.*	And the distresses.
צרע	וּמְצֹרָע	*Et leprosus.*	And a leper.
צרר	וּמְצֹרָרִים	*Et colligati.*	And bound up.
נקב	וּמַקָּבוֹת	*Et mallei.*	And hammers.
קבץ	וּמְקַבְּצָיו	*Et colligentes eum.*	And they that gather him or it.
קדם	וּמִקֶּדֶם	*Et diu ante.*	And long before, from ancient
קדש	וּמִקְדַּשׁ־דָּשׁ	*Et sanctuarium.*	And the sanctuary. [times.
—	וּמִקְדָּשִׁי	*Et sanctuarium me-*	And my sanctuary.
—	וּמִקְדְּשֵׁי	*Et sanctuaria.* [um.	And the sanctuaries.
—	וּמְקַדְּשִׁים	*Et sanctificantes.*	And they that sanctify.
קוה	וּמִקְוֵא־וֵה	*Et netum, expecta-tio, spes.*	And linen yarn, expectation, hope.
—	וּמִקְוֵה	*Et alveus, fossa.*	And a channel, ditch.
קום	וּמָקוֹם וּמְקוֹם	*Et locus.*	And the place.
קור	וּמָקוֹר	*Et fons, scaturigo.*	And the fountain, spring.
לקח	וּמַקַּח	*Et acceptio.*	And accepting, taking.

ROOTS.	DERIVATIVES.	VERSIO.	SIGNIFICATION.
קטר	וּמַקְטִיר	Et adolens.	And he that burneth incense.
——	וּמַקְטִרִים־מְקַטֵּ֯	Et adolentes.	And they that burn incense.
קום	וּמֵקִים	Et statuens.	And he that setteth up.
מקל	וּמַקְלוֹ	Et baculus ejus.	And his staff.
קלל	וּמַקֶּלְכֶם	Et baculus vester.	And your staff.
——	וּמְקַלֵּל	Et maledicens.	And he that curseth. [him.
——	וּמְקַלְלָיו	Et maledicti ab eo.	And they that are cursed by
——	וּמְקַלֶּלְךָ	Et maledicenti tibi.	And to him that curseth thee.
קום	וּמִקָּמַי	Et ab insurgentibus in me.	And from them that rise up against me.
קנה	וּמִקְנֶה	Et pecus, possessio.	And cattle, possession.
——	וּמִקְנֶה	Et pecus, grex.	And cattle, a flock.
——	וּמִקְנֵהוּ	Et pecus ejus.	And his cattle.
——	וּמִקְנַי	Et pecudes meæ.	And my flocks, herds.
——	וּמִקְנִי	Et pecus meum.	And my cattle.
——	וּמִקְנֵיהֶם	Et pecudes eorum.	And their flocks, herds.
——	וּמִקְנֵיכֶם־נָכֶם	Et pecudes vestræ.	And your flocks, herds.
——	וּמִקְנַת	Et acquisitio.	And the purchase.
קסם	וּמִקְסָם	Et divinatio.	And divination.
קצה	וּמִקְצֵה וּמִקְצָת	Et pars, ab extremitate, ad finem.	And part, some from the extremity, at the end.
קצע	וּמִקְצֹעוֹתָיו	Et anguli ejus.	And his corners.
קצה	וּמִקְצָתָם	Et ad finem eorum.	And at the end of them.
קרה	וּמִקְרֵה־	Et eventus.	And the event, what befalleth
קרן	וּמִקַּרְנֵי	Et a cornibus.	And from the horns.
קשה	וּמַקְשֶׁה	Et obdurans.	And he that hardeneth.
יקש	וּמִקְשׁוֹת	Et a laqueis.	And from the snares.
מרר	וָמָר	Et amarus.	And bitter.
מרא	וּמָרֵא	Et dominus.	And a lord.
ראה	וּמַרְאֶהָ	Et aspectus ejus.	And the sight of her or it.
——	וּמַרְאֵה־אָה	Et facies, aspectus,	And the face, appearance, vi-
——	וּמַרְאֵהוּ	Et vultus ejus. [visio	And his countenance. [sion.
——	וּמַרְאוֹת	Et visiones.	And the visions.
——	וּמַרְאֵיהֶם	Et aspectus eorum.	And their appearance.
——	וּמַרְאֵיהֶן	Et species earum.	And their appearance.
——	וּמַרְאַיִךְ	Et facies tua.	And thy face, countenance.
ראש	וּמֵרֹאשׁ	Et de capite.	And from the head.

ROOTS.	DERIVATIVES.	VERSIO.	SIGNIFICATION.
ראש	וּמֵרָאשֵׁי	*Et de principibus.*	And of the chiefs.
—	וּמֵרֵאשִׁית	*Et e primitiis.*	And from the first fruits.
רבב	וּמֵרֹב	*Et præ multitudine. post multitudinem*	And by reason of the multitude, after a multitude.
רבה	וּמַרְבִּים	*Et multiplicantes.*	And they that multiply.
רגז	וּמֵרָגְזָךְ	*Et a timore tuo.*	And from thy fear.
רגל	וּמַרְגְּלֹתָיו	*Et pedes ejus.*	And his feet.
מרד	וּמֶרֶד	*Et rebellio.*	And rebellion.
—	וּמָרָדְנוּ	*Et rebellavimus.*	And we have rebelled. [eth.
רדף	וּמְרַדֵּף	*Et sequens, sectans.*	And he that followeth, pursu-
—	וּמֵרֹדְפָי	*Et a persequentibus me.*	And from them that persecute me.
מרר	וּמָרָה	*Et amara. [mea.*	And bitter.
מרד	וּמְרוּדִי	*Et depressio, afflictio*	And my humiliation, affliction
—	וּמְרוּדֶיהָ	*Et afflictiones ejus.*	And her afflictions.
רוה	וּמַרְוֶה	*Et irrigans.*	And he that watereth.
רוח	וּמֵרוּחַ	*Et per spiritum.*	And by the breath.
רום	וּמְרוֹמָם	*Et exaltatus.*	And he that is exalted.
—	וּמְרוֹמֵם	*Et extollens.*	And he that extolleth.
רחק	וּמֵרָחוֹק	*Et e longinquo.*	And from afar off.
מרר	וּמָרִי	*Et amari. [ginatum*	And the bitter.
מרא	וּמְרִיא	*Et pecus pingue, sa-*	And fat cattle, the fatling.
ירד	וּמוֹרִיד	*Et subjiciens.*	And he that bringeth down.
רום	וּמֵרִים	*Et extollens.*	And he that lifteth up.
מרה	וּמָרִינוּ	*Et rebellavimus.*	And we have rebelled.
—	וּמְרִיתֶם	*Et rebellabitis.*	And ye will rebel.
רכך	וּמֵרֹךְ	*Et præ mollitie.*	And for softness, tenderness.
רכב	וּמֶרְכָּבָה	*Et currus.*	And the chariot.
—	וּמַרְכְּבוֹת	*Et currus.*	And the chariots.
רמה	וּמִרְמָה	*Et dolus.*	And deceit, guile.
—	וּמִרְמוֹת	*Et doli.*	And deceits.
רוע	וּמֵרַע	*Et maleficus.*	And an evil doer.
—	וּמֵרָע	*Et a malo.*	And from the evil.
רעב	וּמֵרָעֵב	*Et a famelico.*	And from the hungry.
רעה	וּמִרְעֶה	*Et pascuum.*	And a pasture, feeding-place.
רפא	וּמַרְפֵּא	*Et medela, sanatio, sanitas.*	And cure, healing, health.

ROOTS.	DERIVATIVES.	VERSIO.	SIGNIFICATION.
רפש	וּמִרְפָּשׂ	*Et turbatus.*	And troubled or made foul.
מרק	וּמֹרַק	*Et abstergetur.*	And he shall be scoured, [cleansed.
מרר	וּמְרֹרִים	*Et amaræ* herbæ.	And bitter *herbs.*
רשע	וּמַרְשִׁיעַ	*Et condemnans.*	And he that condemneth.
—	וּמַרְשִׁיעֵי	*Et impie agentes.*	And they that do wickedly.
מרש	וּמָשׁ	*Et discedet.*	And he will depart, remove.
נשה	וּמַשָּׁא	*Et exactio.*	And the exaction.
—	וּמַשֹּׂא	*Et honoratio.*	And the respect.
נשא	וּמַשָּׂא	*Et onus, prophetia.*	And the burden, the prophecy
שאה	וּמְשֹׁאָה-שׁוֹ״	*Et vastitas.*	And desolation, waste.
נשא	וּמַשַּׂאֲכֶם	*Et onus vestrum.*	And your burden.
שאר	וּמִשְׁאַרְתֶּךָ	*Et mactra tua.*	And thy kneading-trough.
נשא	וּמַשְׂאַת	*Et onus.*	And the burden.
—	וּמַשְׂאַת	*Et munus.*	And a reward.
שאה	וּמִשֹּׁאת	*Et a vastatione.*	And from the desolation.
נשא	וּמִשְּׂאֵתוֹ	*Et præ excellentia ejus.*	And by reason of his highness, excellence.
שוב	וּמִשָּׁב	*Et a redeunte.*	And from him that returneth.
ישב	וּמִשְּׁבוֹתָם	*Et habitationes eorum*	And from their habitations.
שבח	וּמְשַׁבֵּחַ	*Et laudans.*	And praising.
שבע	וּמַשְׂבִּיעַ	*Et saturans.*	And satisfying.
שבר	וּמְשַׁבֵּר	*Et confringens.*	And breaking in pieces.
—	וּמִשֶּׁבֶר	*Et propter confractionem.*	And because of the breaking.
שבת	וּמִשַּׁבְּתוֹתַי	*Et a sabbatis meis.*	And from my sabbaths.
שוב	וּמְשֻׁבוֹתַיִךְ	*Et aversiones tuæ.*	And thy backslidings.
שגה	וּמַשְׁגֶּה	*Et errare faciens.*	And causing to err, deceiving
שדה	וּמִשָּׂדֶה	*Et de agro.*	And of the field.
—	וּמִשָּׂדוֹת	*Et ex agris.*	And out of the fields.
—	וּמִשַּׁדְמֹת	*Et ex agris.*	And out of the fields.
משח	וּמָשׁוֹחַ	*Et illitus, pictus.*	And besmeared, painted.
—	וּמָשׁוּחַ	*Et unctus.*	And anointed.
שוש	וּמָשׂוֹשׂ	*Et gaudium.*	And joy.
משח	וּמָשַׁח	*Et unget.*	And he shall anoint.
—	וּמֶשַׁח	*Et oleum.*	And oil.
שחת	וּמַשְׁחִית	*Et perdens.*	And he that destroyeth.
שחק	וּמְשַׂחֵק	*Et ludens.*	And playing.

ROOTS.	DERIVATIVES.	VERSIO.	SIGNIFICATION.
שחר	וּמְשַׁחֲרַי	*Et quærentes me*	And they that seek me early.
משח	וּמָשַׁחְתָּ	*Et unges.* [*mane.*	And thou shalt anoint.
—	וּמִשְׁחַת	*Et unctio.*	And the anointing.
—	וּמָשַׁחְתּוֹ	*Et unges eum.*	And thou shalt anoint him.
משה	וָמֶשִׁי	*Et sericum.*	And silk, *or rather* muslin.
שור	וּמִשִּׁירִי	*Et cum cantico meo.*	And with my song.
משך	וּמָשַׁךְ	*Et traxit, extendit.*	And he drew, stretched out.
—	וּמֶשֶׁךְ	*Et tractio, attractio.*	And the drawing, attraction.
שכל	וּמַשְׂכִּלֵי	*Et intelligentes.*	And they that understand.
—	וּמַשְׂכִּילִים־כָּלִים	*Et sapientes, periti.*	And the wise, skilful. [barren.
—	וּמְשַׁכֵּלָה	*Et abortiens, sterilis*	And she that miscarrieth, the
—	וּמְשַׁכֶּלֶת	*Et orbans.*	And bereaving.
שכן	וּמִשְׁכַּן	*Et tentorium.*	And the tabernacle.
—	וּמִשְׁכְּנוֹתָיו	*Et tentoria, habitationes ejus.*	And his tabernacles, dwelling-places.
משך	וּמָשַׁכְתָּ	*Et trahes.*	And thou shalt draw.
—	וּמָשַׁכְתִּי	*Et traham, alliciam*	And I will draw, allure.
משל	וּמָשַׁל וּמָשָׁל	*Et dominabitur, parabola.* [*re.*	And he shall have dominion, a parable, proverb.
—	וּמְשֹׁל	*Et parabolice loque-*	And speak thou a parable.
—	וּמֹשֵׁל	*Et dominans.*	And he that ruleth, the go-
שלג	וּמִשֶּׁלֶג	*Et præ nive.*	And than snow. [vernor.
משל	וּמֶמְשַׁלְתּוֹ	*Et dominium ejus.*	And his dominion.
—	וּמֹשְׁלוֹ	*Et dominator ejus.*	And his governor. [forth.
שלח	וּמְשַׁלֵּחַ	*Et mittens, projici-*	And he that sendeth, casteth
—	וּמִשְׁלֹחַ	*Et missio.* [*ens*	And sending.
שלל	וּמִשָּׁלָל וּמִשְּׁלַל	*Et de præda.*	And of the spoil.
שלם	וּמְשַׁלֵּם	*Et rependens.*	And he that repayeth.
—	וּמְשַׁלְּמֵי	*Et reddentes.*	And they that render.
משל	וּמָשַׁלְתָּ	*Et dominaberis.*	And thou shalt reign.
שם	וּמִשָּׁם	*Et illinc, inde, ex iis*	And thence, from them.
שמל	וּמִשְּׂמֹאלוֹ	*Et a sinistra ejus.*	And on his left hand. [hand.
—	וּמַשְׂמְאִלִים	*Et sinistra utentes.*	And they that use the left
—	וּמִשְּׂמֹאלָם	*Et a sinistra eorum.*	And on their left.
שמם	וּמְשַׁמָּה	*Et desolatio, stupor.*	And desolation, astonishment.
שמע	וּמַשְׁמִיעַ	*Et prædicans.*	And publishing.
שמן	וּמִשְׁמַן	*Et pinguedo.*	And the fatness.

ROOTS.	DERIVATIVES.	VERSIO.	SIGNIFICATION.
שמן	וּמִשֶּׁמֶן	*Et ex oleo.*	And of the oil.
—	וּמִשַּׁמְנָהּ	*Et ex oleo ejus.*	And of her oil.
—	וּמִשְׁמַנֵּי	*Et pinguedines* [*eum*	And the fatness.
שמר	וּמִשְׁמְרוֹ	*Et ad custodiendum*	And to keep him.
—	וּמִשְׁמֶרֶת	*Et custodia, cura.*	And the custody, charge, care
—	וּמִשְׁמַרְתָּם	*Et custodia eorum.*	And their charge.
שנא	וּמִשֹּׂנְאַי וּמִשֹּׂנְ׳	*Et ab odio habentibus me.*	And from them that hate me.
—	וּמְשַׂנְאָיו	*Et odio habentes eum*	And they that hate him.
—	וּמְשַׂנְאֶיךָ	*Et odio habentes te.*	And they that hate thee.
—	וּמְשַׂנְאֵינוּ	*Et odio habentes nos*	And they that hate us.
—	וּמִשִּׂנְאָתוֹ	*Et propter odium*	And because of his hatred.
שנה	וּמִשְׁנֶה	*Et duplex.* [*ejus.*	And double.
—	וּמִשְׁנֵהוּ	*Et secundus ejus.*	And his second.
שן	וּמִשִּׁנָּיו	*Et e dentibus ejus.*	And out of his teeth.
שע	וּמִשְׁעֵנָה	*Et fulcimentum.*	And the stay, support.
—	וּמִשְׁעַנְתֶּךָ	*Et baculus tuus.*	And thy staff.
שער	וּמִשַּׁעַר	*Et a porta.*	And from the gate.
שפח	וּמִשְׁפָּחָה--חַת	*Et familia.*	And the family.
—	וּמִשְׁפְּחוֹת-פְּחֹ׳	*Et familiæ.*	And families.
—	וּמִשְׁפַּחְתִּי	*Et familia mea.*	And my family.
שפט	וּמִשְׁפָּט--פַּט	*Et judicium, jus, consuetudo.*	And the judgment, right, cause, custom.
—	וּמִשְׁפָּטַי	*Et judicia mea.*	And my judgments.
—	וּמִשְׁפָּטִי	*Et judicium meum.*	And my judgment.
—	וּמִשְׁפְּטֵי	*Et judicia.*	And the judgments.
—	וּמִשְׁפָּטָיו	*Et judicia ejus.*	And his judgments.
—	וּמִשְׁפָּטֶיךָ	*Et judicia tua.*	And thy judgments.
—	וּמִשְׁפָּטִים	*Et judicia.*	And judgments.
—	וּמִשְׁפָּטֶךָ	*Et judicium tuum.*	And thy judgment.
שקה	וּמַשְׁקֶה	*Et potus.*	And the drink.
—	וּמַשְׁקָיו	*Et pincernæ ejus.*	And his cup-bearers.
שקל	וּמִשְׁקָל--קַל	*Et pondus.*	And the weight.
—	וּמִשְׁקָלָהּ	*Et pondus ejus.*	And her weight.
שקע	וּמִשְׁקַע	*Et sedimentum.*	And the dregs, bottom.
שקר	וּמְשַׂקְּרוֹת	*Et nictantes, lascive innuentes.*	And winking, looking wantonly.

ROOTS.	DERIVATIVES.	VERSIO.	SIGNIFICATION.
שרא	וּמְשָׁרֵא	*Et solvens.*	And dissolving.
ישר	וּמֵישָׁרִים	*Et rectitudines.*	And uprightness, equity.
שור	וּמְשֹׁרְרוֹת	*Et cantatrices.*	And singing women.
שרת	וּמְשָׁרְתוֹ	*Et minister ejus.*	And his servant.
—	וּמְשָׁרְתִים	*Et ministrantes.*	And they that minister.
שתה	וּמִשְׁתֶּה	*Et potus, convivium*	And drink, feasting.
שחה	וּמִשְׁתַּחֲוֶה	*Et prosternens se.*	And prostrating himself.
—	וּמִשְׁתַּחֲוִים	*Et incurvantes se.*	And bowing themselves down.
מוש	וּמַשְׁתִּי	*Et amovebo.* [*rietur*	And I will remove.
מות	וָמֵת ו׳	*Et mortuus est, mo-*	And he died, shall die.
—	וָמֻת ו׳	*Et morere.*	And die thou.
תבל	וּמִתֵּבֵל	*Et ex orbe.*	And out of the world.
גדד	וּמִתְגּוֹדְדִים	*Et incidentes se.*	And cutting themselves.
מתג	וּמִתְגִי	*Et frænum meum.*	And my bridle.
מות	וָמַתָּה	*Et morieris.*	And thou shalt die.
—	וָמֵתָה	*Et morietur.*	And he shall die.
תהם	וּמִתְּהוֹם	*Et ex abysso.*	And from the deep.
—	וּמִתְּהוֹמוֹת	*Et ex abyssis.*	And from the depths.
מות	וָמֵתוּ ו׳	*Et morientur.*	And they shall die.
ידה	וּמִתְוַדֶּה	*Et confitens.*	And confessing.
—	וּמִתְוַדִּים	*Et confitentes.*	And making confession. [or it.
תוך	וּמִתּוֹכָהּ	*Et e medio ejus.*	And out of the midst of her
מתק	וּמָתוֹק	*Et dulcis.*	And sweet.
—	וּמְתוּקִים	*Et dulciores.*	And sweeter.
ירה	וּמִתּוֹרָתְךָ	*Et ex lege tua.*	And out of thy law.
חנן	וּמִתְחַנֵּן	*Et deprecans.*	And making supplication.
תחת	וּמִתַּחַת־־תָּהּ	*Et infra, subter.*	And beneath, underneath.
—	וּמִתַּחְתָּיו	*Et e loco ejus.*	And out of his place.
מות	וָמַתִּי	*Et moriar.*	And I shall die.
מתי	וּמָתַי	*Et quando?*	And when?
ימן	וּמִתֵּימָן	*Et ab austro.*	And from the south.
כנש	וּמִתְכַּנְּשִׁין	*Et convenientes.*	And they that meet, assemble.
לתע	וּמְתַלְּעוֹת	*Et molares.*	And the cheek, teeth.
נתן	וּמַתָּן	*Et donum.*	And a gift.
נבא	וּמִתְנַבֵּא	*Et vaticinans.*	And he that prophesieth.
מות	וָמָתְנוּ ־־מֵ״	*Et moriemur.*	And we shall die.
נתן	וּמַתָּנוֹת וּמַתְּנָן.	*Et dona.*	And gifts.

ROOTS.	DERIVATIVES.	VERSIO.	SIGNIFICATION.
מתן	וּמָתְנֵי	*Et lumbi.*	And the loins.
—	וּמָתְנֵיהֶם	*Et lumbi eorum.*	And their loins.
—	וּמָתְנָיו	*Et lumbi ejus.*	And his loins.
נפל	וּמִתְנַפֵּל	*Et prosternens se.*	And prostrating himself.
נקם	וּמִתְנַקֵּם	*Et ultor.*	And the avenger.
ערה	וּמִתְעָרֶה	*Et diffundens se.*	And pouring out, spreading himself.
תעתע	וּמִתַּעְתְּעִים	*Et errare facientes.*	And causing to err.
פלל	וּמִתְפַּלֵּל	*Et orans.*	And he that prayeth.
—	וּמִתְפַּלְלִים	*Et orantes.*	And they that pray.
מתק	וּמֶתֶק	*Et dulcedo.*	And the sweetness.
קום	וּמִתְקוֹמְמַי	*Et insurgens in me.*	And he that riseth up against me.
תרגם	וּמְתֻרְגָּם	*Et expositus.*	And expounded, interpreted.
מות	וּמֹתְתֵנִי	*Et interfice me.*	And slay thou me.
	ונ		
נאד	וְנֹאד	*Et uter.*	And a bottle *made of skin.*
—	וְנֹאדוֹת	*Et utres.*	And bottles.
נאה	וְנָאוָה	*Et decora.*	And comely.
אחז	וְנֹאחֲזוּ	*Et possessores fient.*	And they shall become possessors.
אכל	וְנֶאֱכַל	*Et consumetur.*	And he shall be consumed.
—	וְנֹאכְלָה־־כֵ״	*Et comedemus.*	And we shall eat.
—	וְנֹאכְלָהוּ	*Et comedimus eum.*	And we did eat him.
—	וְנֹאכְלֶנּוּ	*Et comedemus.*	And we shall eat.
יאל	וְנֹאָלוּ	*Et stulti fient.*	And they shall become fools.
אלח	וְנֶאֱלָח	*Et fœtidus factus est*	And he became filthy, fetid.
אלם	וְנֶאֱלַמְתָּ	*Et mutus eris.*	And thou shalt be dumb.
—	וְנֶאֱלַמְתִּי	*Et obmutui.*	And I became dumb.
נאם	וּנְאֻם	*Et dixit.*	And he said.
אמן	וְנֶאֱמָן־־מַן	*Et fidus, fidelis.*	And sure, faithful.
—	וְנֶאֱמַן	*Et firmus erit.*	And he shall be established.
—	וְנֶאֱמָנוֹת־־נִים	*Et permanentes.*	And those that continue long.
אמר	וַנֹּאמֶר	*Et diximus.*	And we have said.
—	וְנֹאמַר	*Et dicemus.*	And we will say.
אסף	וְנֶאֱסַף	*Et tolletur.*	And he shall be taken away.
—	וְנֶאֶסְפָה	*Et tolletur.*	And she shall be taken away
—	וְנֶאֶסְפוּ	*Et congregarunt se*	And they gathered themselves together.

ROOTS.	DERIVATIVES.	VERSIO.	SIGNIFICATION.
אסף	וְנֶאֶסְפוּ	*Et congregarunt, congregabunt se.*	And they gathered, will gather themselves together.
—	וְנֶאֱסַפְתָּ	*Et aggregaberis.*	And thou shalt be gathered.
—	וְנֶאֶסְפְתֶּם	*Et congregabitis vos* [*mittere.*	And ye shall assemble yourselves.
נאף	וְנָאֹף	*Et adulterium com-*	And to commit adultery.
—	וְנַאֲפוּפֶיהָ	*Et adulteria ejus.*	And her adulteries.
נאץ	וּנְאָצָה	*Et contumelia.*	And blasphemy.
—	וְנִאֲצוּנִי	*Et irritabunt me.*	And they will provoke me.
נאק	וְנָאַק	*Et gemet.*	And he will groan.
שאר	וָאֶשָּׁאֵר	*Et relictus sum.*	And I was left.
בוא	וַנָּבֹא	*Et venimus.*	And we came.
—	וְנָבֹאָה	*Et veniemus.*	And we will come.
נבא	וְנִבְּאוּ	*Et vaticinabuntur.*	And they shall prophesy.
—	וְנִבֵּאתָ	*Et vaticinaberis.*	And thou shalt prophesy.
—	וְנִבֵּאתִי	*Et vaticinatus sum.*	And I prophesied.
בהל	וְנִבְהֲלוּ־הֲ״	*Et terrebuntur.*	And they shall be terrified.
—	וְנִבְהַלְתִּי	*Et conturbatus sum.*	And I was troubled.
בוא	וַנָּבוֹא	*Et venimus.*	And we came.
—	וְנָבוֹא	*Et ingrediemur.*	And we will enter.
—	וְנָבוֹאָה	*Et inibimus.* [*gens*	And we will enter. [ing.
בון	וְנָבוֹן וּנְ׳	*Et prudens, intelli-*	And the prudent, understand-
בזה	וּנְבִזְבָּה	*Et honorarium.*	And an honourable gift.
—	וּנְבִזְבְּיָתָךְ־־ב״	*Et honoraria tua.*	And thy honourable rewards.
בזז	וְנָבֹזָּה	*Et diripiemus.*	And we will spoil.
בזה	וְנִבְזֶה	*Et contemptus.*	And despised.
בזז	וְנָבֹזּוּ	*Et diripientur.*	And they shall be spoiled.
בחר	וְנִבְחַר	*Et eligetur.*	And he shall be chosen.
נבט	וְנִבַּט	*Et intuebitur.*	And he shall look.
בוא	וְנָבִיא	*Et afferemus.*	And we will bring.
נבא	וְנָבִיא	*Et propheta.*	And a prophet.
—	וּנְבִיאֵי	*Et prophetæ.*	And prophets.
—	וּנְבִיאֶיהָ	*Et prophetæ ejus.*	And her prophets.
—	וּנְבִיאֵיהֶם	*Et prophetæ eorum.*	And their prophets.
בוא	וּנְבִיאֵם	*Et adducemus eos.*	And we will bring them.
נבל	וְנֵבֶל	*Et nablium, psalte-*	And the lute, psaltery.
—	וְנָבֵל	*Et decidimus* [*rium.*	And we have faded, fallen.

ROOTS.	DERIVATIVES.	VERSIO.	SIGNIFICATION.
נבל	וְנָבָל	*Et stultus.*	And a fool.
—	וְנֵבֶל	*Et uter.*	And a bottle.
בלל	וְנָבְלָה	*Et confundemus.*	And we will confound.
נבל	וּנְבָלָה	*Et stultitia, flagitium*	And folly, villany. [carrion.
—	וּנְבֵלָה	*Et morticinus.*	And that which dieth of itself,
—	וְנִבְלֵי	*Et utres.*	And the bottles.
—	וְנִבְלֵיהֶם	*Et utres eorum.*	And their bottles.
—	וּנְבָלִים	*Et nablia, psalteria.*	And lutes, psalteries.
—	וְנִבְלָתוֹ	*Et cadaver ejus.*	And his dead body.
—	וְנִבַּלְתִּיךְ	*Et vilem reputabo, contumeliose tractabo te.*	And I will count thee vile, will treat thee disgracefully
בנה	וַנִּבְנֶה	*Et ædificavimus.*	And we have built.
—	וְנִבְנֶה	*Et ædificabimus.*	And we will build.
—	וְנִבְנוּ	*Et ædificabuntur.*	And they shall be built.
בון	וּנְבֹנִים	*Et intelligentes.*	And the understanding.
בנה	וְנִבְנֵית	*Et ædificaberis.*	And thou shalt be built.
—	וְנִבְנְתָה	*Et ædificabitur.*	And she shall be built.
בער	וּנְבַעֲרָה	*Et auferemus.*	And we will take away.
בקק	וְנָבְקָה	*Et evacuabitur.*	And she shall be emptied.
בקע	וְנַבְקִיעֶנָּה	*Et perrumpemus eam.*	And let us break through, make a breach in her or it.
—	וְנִבְקַע	*Et diffindetur.*	And he shall be rent.
בקש	וּנְבַקְשָׁה	*Et quæsivimus.*	And we sought.
—	וּנְבַקְשֶׁנָּה	*Et quæremus eum.*	And we will seek him.
ברא	וְנִבְרָאוּ	*Et creati sunt.*	And they were created.
ברח	וְנִבְרְחָה	*Et fugiemus.*	And we will flee.
ברך	וְנִבְרְכוּ	*Et benedicentur.*	And they shall be blessed.
בשל	וַנְּבַשֵּׁל	*Et coximus.*	And we boiled.
גאל	וְנִגְאָל	*Et redimet eum.*	And he shall redeem him.
—	וְנִגְאָלָה	*Et polluta.*	And polluted.
נגב	וְנֶגְבָּה ןּ"	*Et ad austrum.*	And toward the south.
נגד	וַנַּגֵּד	*Et indicavimus.*	And we told.
—	וְנֶגֶד	*Et coram, e regione.*	And before, over against.
—	וְנֶגְדָּם	*Et e regione eorum.*	And over against them.
גדע	וְנִגְדְּעָה	*Et succidetur.*	And she shall be cut down.
—	וְנִגְדְּעוּ	*Et exscindentur.*	And they shall be cut off.

ROOTS.	DERIVATIVES.	VERSIO.	SIGNIFICATION.
נגה	וְנֹגַהּ	*Et splendor.*	And the brightness.
גזל	וְנִגְזְלָה	*Et auferetur.*	And she shall be taken away.
נגד	וְנָגִיד	*Et dux.*	And a leader.
—	וְנַגִּידָה	*Et nunciabimus.*	And we will tell.
—	וְנַגִּידֶנּוּ	*Et nunciabimus eum*	And we will report it.
נגן	וּנְגִינוֹת	*Et cantica.*	And the songs.
—	וּנְגִינֹתַי	*Et cantica mea.*	And my songs.
גלה	וְנִגְלָה	*Et discooperuit se, revelabitur.*	And he discovered himself, he shall be revealed.
גלל	וְנָגֹלּוּ	*Et convolventur.*	And they shall be rolled to- [gether.
גלה	וְנִגְלֵינוּ	*Et revelabimus nos.*	And we will discover ourselves
נגן	וְנִגֵּן	*Et pulsavit, pulsabit.*	And he played, shall play.
נגע	וְנָגַע	*Et tanget.*	And he will touch.
—	וְנֶגַע	*Et plaga.*	And a wound, plague.
—	וְנֹגֵעַ	*Et tangens.*	And he that toucheth.
—	וּנְגֹעַ	*Et tangere.*	And to touch.
—	וְנָגְעָה	*Et pertiget.*	And she will reach.
נגף	וְנָגַף	*Et percutiet.*	And he will smite.
—	וְנָגְפוּ	*Et percutient.*	And they will smite.
—	וְנִגַּפְתֶּם	*Et cædemini.*	And ye shall be slain.
גרע	וְנִגְרַע	*Et minuetur.*	And he shall be abated, dimi- [nished.
—	וְנִגְרְעָה	*Et adimetur.*	And she shall be taken away.
גרש	וְנִגְרְשָׁה	*Et expelletur.*	And she shall be cast out.
נגש	וְנִגַּשׁ	*Et accedet.*	And he shall come near.
—	וְנִגַּשׂ	*Et opprimetur.*	And he shall be oppressed.
—	וְנִגְּשָׁה	*Et accedet.*	And she shall come near.
—	וְנִגְּשׁוּ	*Et accedent.*	And they shall come near.
—	וְנֹגְשַׂיִךְ	*Et exactores tui.*	And thy exactors.
נוד	וָנָד	*Et profugus, vagus.*	And a fugitive, vagabond.
דבך	וְנִדְבָּךְ	*Et ordo.*	And a row.
נדב	וְנִדְבֹתֶיךָ	*Et* victimæ *sponta- neæ tuæ.*	And thy free-will *offerings.*
—	וְנִדְבֹתֵיכֶם	*Et* victimæ *sponta- neæ vestræ.*	And your free-will *offerings.*
דוש	וְנָדוֹשׁ	*Et conculcabitur.*	And he shall be trodden down.
נדח	וְנִדְּחָה	*Et dispelletur.*	And she shall be driven away
—	וְנִדַּחְתָּ	*Et impelleris.*	And thou shalt be driven.
—	וְנִדַּחְתֶּם	*Et expellemini.*	And ye shall be driven out.

ROOTS.	DERIVATIVES.	VERSIO.	SIGNIFICATION.
נדב	וְנָדִיב	*Et liberalis.*	And the liberal.
—	וּנְדִיבִים	*Et munifici.*	And the munificent.
דכה	וְנִדְכֶּה	*Et contritus.*	And contrite.
—	וְנִדְכֵּיתִי	*Et fractus sum.*	And I have been broken.
דמם	וְנִדְּמָה	*Et silebimus.*	And we will be silent.
דמה	וְנִדְמָה	*Et assimilatus sum.*	And I am made like.
דמם	וְנִדְמוּ	*Et succisi sunt.*	And they are cut down.
ידע	וְנֵדְעָה־־ד׳	*Et cognoscemus.*	And we shall know.
—	וַנֵּדָעֵם	*Et cognovimus eos.*	And we knew them.
—	וְנֵדָעֵנוּ	*Et cognoscemus eum*	And we shall know him.
נדר	וְנֶדֶר	*Et votum.*	And a vow.
—	וְנֹדֵר	*Et vovens.*	And vowing.
—	וְנָדְרוּ	*Et vovebunt.*	And they shall vow.
—	וּנְדָרֶיהָ	*Et vota ejus.*	And her vows.
—	וּנְדָרֶיךָ	*Et vota tua.*	And thy vows.
—	וְנִדְרֵיכֶם	*Et vota vestra.*	And your vows.
דרש	וְנִדְרְשָׁה	*Et quaeremus.*	And we shall seek, inquire.
נהה	וְנָהָה	*Et lamentabitur.*	And he shall lament.
נהר	וּנְהוֹרָא	*Et lux.*	And the light.
נהה	וָנֶהִי	*Et planctus.*	And wailing.
היה	וַנְּהִי־־נִּהְיֶה	*Et eramus, fuimus.*	And we were, we have been.
נהר	וְנָהִירוּ־־נ׳	*Et lux.*	And light.
היה	וְנִהְיְתָה	*Et facta est, fiet.*	And she became, will become.
נהם	וְנָהַמְתָּ	*Et rugies.*	And thou shalt roar.
—	וּנְהַמְתֶּם	*Et gemetis.*	And ye shall groan, mourn.
הפך	וְנֶהְפּוֹךְ וְנֶהְפָּךְ	*Et convertetur.*	And he shall be turned.
—	וְנֶהֶפְכוּ	*Et conversi sunt, convertentur.*	And they are turned, shall be turned.
—	וְנֶהְפַּכְתְּ	*Et converteris.*	And thou shalt be turned.
נהר	וְנָהָר וּנְהַר	*Et fluvius.*	And a river.
הרג	וְנַהַרְגֵהוּ	*Et occidemus eum.*	And we will slay him.
נהר	וְנָהֲרוּ	*Et confluxerunt, illuminati sunt.*	And they flowed together, were enlightened.
—	וְנָהֲרוּ	*Et confluent.*	And they shall flow together.
—	וּנְהָרוֹת	*Et flumina.*	And the rivers.
—	וְנַהֲרוֹתָם	*Et flumina eorum.*	And their rivers.
הרס	וְנֶהֶרְסוּ	*Et diruentur.*	And they shall be thrown down

ROOTS.	DERIVATIVES.	VERSIO.	SIGNIFICATION.
נהר	וְנָהַרְתְּ	Et conflues, illumi-naberis.	And thou shalt flow together, shalt be enlightened.
—	וּנְהָרֹתַיִךְ	Et flumina tua.	And thy rivers.
יאש	וְנוֹאָשׁ	Et desperabit.	And he shall despair. [away.
נדד	וְנוֹדֵד־דֵד	Et vagans, fugiens.	And he that wandereth, fleeth
ידע	וְנוֹדִיעָה	Et ostendemus.	And we will shew.
—	וְנוֹדַע־דַע	Et cognitus est, cog-noscetur.	And he was known, shall be known.
—	וְנוֹדְעָה	Et cognoscetur.	And she shall be known.
—	וְנוֹדַעְתִּי	Et cognoscar.	And I will be known.
נוה	וּנְוֵה	Et habitatio.	And the habitation.
נזל	וְנוֹזְלֵיהֶם	Et flumina eorum.	And their streams, floods.
—	וְנוֹזְלִים וְנֹזְ׳	Et flumina.	And streams.
נוח	וְנוֹחַ	Et quiescere.	And to rest.
נטה	וְנוֹטֵיהֶם	Et extendens eos.	And stretching them.
נטר	וְנוֹטֵר	Et servans.	And reserving.
יכח	וְנִוָּכְחָה	Et disceptabimus.	And we will reason together.
יכל	וְנוּכְלָה	Et prævalebimus.	And we shall prevail.
יסף	וְנוֹסַף־סָף	Et addetur.	And he will be added.
—	וְנוֹסְפָה	Et addetur.	And she will be added.
יסר	וְנִוַּסְּרוּ	Et erudientur.	And they shall be taught.
נוע	וְנוֹעַ	Et vagando.	And in wandering.
יעד	וְנִוָּעֲדָה	Et conveniemus.	And we will meet together.
—	וְנוֹעֲדוּ	Et convenient. [mus	And they shall meet.
יעץ	וְנִוָּעֲצָה	Et consilium inibi-	And we will take counsel.
יקש	וְנוֹקְשׁוּ	Et irretientur.	And they will be insnared.
ירא	וְנוֹרָא	Et terribilis.	And terrible.
—	וְנוֹרָאוֹת וְנֹרָ׳	Et terribiles.	And terrible.
ישב	וְנוֹשְׁבוּ	Et habitabuntur.	And they shall be inhabited.
ישן	וְנוֹשַׁנְתֶּם	Et longe manebitis, consenescetis.	And ye shall remain long, shall grow old.
ישע	וְנוֹשָׁע	Et servatus.	And saved.
—	וְנִוָּשֵׁעַ־עָה	Et servabimur.	And we shall be saved.
—	וְנוֹשַׁעְתֶּם	Et servabimini.	And ye shall be saved.
נוה	וּנְוַת	Et habitans.	And she that dwelleth.
נתן	וְנוֹתֵן	Et largiens.	And giving.
יתר	וְנוֹתְרָה	Et relinquetur.	And she shall be left.

ROOTS.	DERIVATIVES.	VERSIO.	SIGNIFICATION.
זבח	וְנִזְבְּחָה	*Et sacrificabimus.*	And we will sacrifice.
זכר	וְנִזְכַּרְתֶּם	*Et memorabimini.*	And ye shall be remembered.
נזם	וְנֶזֶם	*Et inauris.*	And the ear-ring.
——	וְנִזְמֵי	*Et inaures.*	And the ear-rings.
זמר	וְנְזַמְּרָה	*Et psallemus.*	And we will sing praises.
זעק	וְנִזְעַק	*Et clamabimus.*	And we will cry.
זרע	וְנִזְרְעָה	*Et seretur, concipiet*	And she shall be sown, shall conceive.
——	וְנִזְרַעְתֶּם	*Et seremini.*	And ye shall be sown.
חבא	וְנֶחְבָּאוּ	*Et absconderunt se.*	And they hid themselves.
——	וְנַחְבֵּאתָ	*Et abscondes te.*	And thou shalt hide thyself.
——	וְנֶחְבָּה	*Et abscondere se.*	And to hide himself.
——	וְנַחְבֵּתֶם	*Et abscondetis vos.*	And ye shall hide yourselves.
חדש	וּנְחַדֵּשׁ	*Et renovabimus.*	And we will renew.
נחה	וְנָחָה	*Et quiescet.*	And he shall rest.
——	וְנָחוּ	*Et quiescent.*	And they shall rest.
חזה	וְנֶחֱזֶה	*Et videbimus.*	And we shall see.
חטא	וַנֶּחֱטָא	*Et peccavimus.*	And we have sinned.
חיה	וּנְחַיֶּה	*Et vivemus.*	And we shall live.
——	וְנְחַיֶּה	*Et vivum servabimus*	And we shall save alive.
נחה	וְנַחֲךָ	*Et ducet te.*	And he shall lead, guide thee.
נחל	וְנָחַל וְנַחַל	*Et torrens.*	And a brook, river.
——	וְנָחַל	*Et possidebit.*	And he shall possess, inherit.
——	וְנַחֲלָה־לַת	*Et hæreditas, possessio.*	And an inheritance, possession
——	וְנָחֲלוּ	*Et possidebunt.*	And they shall possess, inherit
חלל	וְנִחֲלוּ	*Et polluentur.*	And they shall be defiled.
נחל	וְנַחֲלֵי	*Et torrentes.*	And the brooks, streams.
——	וּנְחָלִים	*Et flumina, valles.*	And the rivers, vallies.
חלה	וְנֶחֱלֵיתִי	*Et ægrotavi.*	And I was sick.
חלם	וַנַּחַלְמָה	*Et somniavimus.*	And we dreamed.
נחל	וְנָחַלְתָּ	*Et possidebis.*	And thou shalt possess, inherit
חלל	וְנִחַלְתְּ	*Et polluta es.*	And thou hast been defiled.
נחל	וְנַחֲלָתוֹ	*Et hæreditas ejus.*	And his inheritance.
——	וְנַחֲלָתִי	*Et hæreditas mea.*	And my inheritance
——	וְנַחֲלָתְךָ־תֶךָ	*Et hæreditas tua.*	And thy inheritance.
——	וְנַחֲלָתָם	*Et hæreditas eorum.*	And their inheritance.
——	וּנְחַלְתֶּם	*Et possidebitis.*	And ye shall possess, inherit.
——	וּנְחַלְתָּנוּ	*Et possidebis nos.*	And thou shalt possess us.

ROOTS.	DERIVATIVES.	VERSIO.	SIGNIFICATION.
נחם	וְנִחָם וְנִחַם	*Et pœnitens, pœnitebit eum, consolabitur, solatium capiet.*	And he that repenteth, he will repent, will comfort, will be comforted.
חמד	וְנֶחְמָד	*Et desiderabilis* [*lum*	And desirable.
—	וְנֶחְמְדֵהוּ	*Et desiderabimus il-*	And we shall desire him.
נחם	וְנִחֲמוּ	*Et consolabuntur.*	And they shall comfort.
—	וְנִחַמְתִּי	*Et resipiscam.*	And I shall repent.
—	וְנִחַמְתִּים	*Et consolabor eos.*	And I will comfort them.
—	וְנִחַמְתֶּם	*Et consolationem capietis.*	And ye shall be comforted.
—	וְנִחַמְתָּנִי	*Et consolatus es me.*	And thou hast comforted me.
חנה	וַנַּחֲנֶה	*Et castra posuimus*	And we pitched tents.
אני	וְנַחְנוּ	*Et nos.*	And we.
חנה	וְנַחֲנוּ	*Et castra ponemus.*	And we will encamp.
נחה	וּנְחֵנִי	*Et duc me.*	And lead thou me.
חקר	ונחקְרָה	*Et pervestigabimus.*	And we will examine.
חרם	וַנַּחֲרֵם	*Et disperdidimus.*	And we destroyed.
חרץ	וְנֶחֱרָצָה	*Et decisa.*	And determined.
נחש	וְנָחָשׁ	*Et serpens.*	And the serpent.
—	וְנִחֵשׁ	*Et auguratus est.*	And he used auguries.
—	וּנְחֹשֶׁת	*Et æs.*	And brass.
חשב	וְנֶחְשַׁב	*Et reputabitur.*	And he shall be reckoned.
—	וְנַחְשְׁבָה	*Et excogitabimus.*	And we will devise.
נחש	וּנְחשֶׁת	*Et æs.*	And brass.
נוח	נָחַת וְנַחַת	*Et requies.*	And rest. [terror.
חתת	וְנַחַת	*Et descensus, terror*	And the lighting down, the
—	וְנִחַת	*Et fractus est.*	And he was broken.
—	וְנִחֲתָה	*Et frangetur.*	And she shall be broken.
חתם	וְנֶחְתּוֹם וְנֶחְתָּם	*Et obsignatus est.*	And he was sealed. [out.
נטה	וְנָטָה	*Et tetendit, extendet*	And he pitched, shall stretch
—	וּנְטֵה	*Et extende.*	And do thou stretch out.
נטל	וּנְטִילַת	*Et elevata est.*	And she was lifted up.
נטה	וְנָטִיתִי	*Et extendam.*	And I will stretch out.
נטל	וְנֵטֶל	*Et onus, pondus.*	And the load, weight.
טמא	וְנִטְמָאָה	*Et polluetur.*	And she will be defiled.
—	וְנִטְמֵתֶם	*Et polluemini.*	And ye will be defiled.

ROOTS.	DERIVATIVES.	VERSIO.	SIGNIFICATION.
נטע	וְנָטְעוּ	*Et plantabunt.*	And they shall plant.
—	וְנִטְעוּ	*Et plantate.* [bo.	And plant ye.
—	וְנָטַעְתִּי	*Et plantavi, planta-*	And I have planted, will plant
—	וּנְטַעְתִּיהוּ־עְתִּיו	*Et plantabo eum.*	And I will plant him.
—	וּנְטַעְתִּים	*Et plantabo eos.*	And I will plant them.
—	וּנְטַעְתֶּם	*Et plantabitis.*	And ye shall plant.
נשש	וְנִטֹּשׁ	*Et deseremus.*	And we will forsake.
—	וּנְטַשְׁתָּה	*Et relinques eum.*	And thou shalt leave him.
—	וְנָטַשְׁתִּי	*Et deseram.*	And I will forsake.
—	וּנְטַשְׁתִּיךָ	*Et relinquam te.*	And I will leave thee.
נוב	וְנִיבוֹ	*Et fructus ejus.*	And his fruit.
נוד	וְנִיד	*Et motus.*	And the moving.
	וַנְיָה	*Vania.*	Vaniah, N. M.
נוח	וְנִיחֹחֵין	*Et odores grati.*	And agreeable odours.
נין	וְנִין	*Et filius.*	And a son.
ירא	וַנִּירָא	*Et timuimus.* [eos.	And we feared.
ירה	וַנִּירָם	*Et jaculati sumus in*	And we have shot at them.
נכה	וַנַּךְ	*Et percussimus.*	And we smote. [rited.
כאה	וְנִכְאָה	*Et frangetur.*	And he shall be broken, dispi-
—	וְנִכְאֵה	*Et fractus.*	And broken.
כבד	וְנִכְבָּד	*Et honorabilis.*	And honourable.
—	וְנִכְבַּדֵּיהֶם	*Et honorabiles, nobi-les eorum.*	And their honourable men, nobles.
—	וְנִכְבָּדִים	*Et honorabiles.*	And honourable. [rified.
—	וְנִכְבַּדְתִּי	*Et honorabor.*	And I will be honoured, glo-
כבש	וְנִכְבְּשָׁה	*Et domita est, subi-getur.*	And she is subdued, shall be subdued.
נכד	וְנֶכֶד	*Et nepos.*	And a son's son.
נכה	וְנַכֶּה	*Et percutiemus.*	And we will smite.
—	וְנִכָּה	*Et percutietur.*	And he shall be smitten.
—	וְנִכֶּה	*Et percussus.*	And smitten.
—	וַנַּכֵּהוּ וְנַ׳	*Et percussimus eum.*	And we smote him.
כזב	וְנִכְזַבְתָּ	*Et mendax invenieri-*	And thou shalt be found a liar
נכח	וּנְכֹחָה	*Et rectum, æquitas.*	And right. equity.
—	וְנַכְחִידֵם	*Et excindemus eos.*	And we will cut them off.
יכח	וּנְכֹחִים	*Et recti, correcti.*	And right, corrected.
—	וְנֹכָחַת	*Et correpta est.*	And she was reproved.

ROOTS.	DERIVATIVES.	VERSIO.	SIGNIFICATION.
כלם	וְנִכְלַמְתְּ	*Et erubesces.*	And thou shalt be ashamed.
—	וְנִכְלַמְתִּי	*Et pudefiam.*	And I shall be confounded.
נכה	וַנַּכֵּם	*Et percussimus eos.*	And we smote them.
נכס	וּנְכָסִים	*Et opes.*	And wealth.
כפר	וְנִכַּפֵּר	*Et abolebitur.*	And he shall be disannulled.
נכר	וְנֵכָר	*Et alienus.*	And strange, foreign.
—	וְנָכְרִי	*Et alienus, alienigena.*	And strange, a stranger.
—	וְנָכְרִים	*Et extranei.*	And foreigners.
כרת	וְנַכְרִיתֶנָּה	*Et exscindemus eam*	And we will cut her off.
כרע	וְנִכְרָעָה	*Et procumbemus.*	And we will bow down.
כרת	וְנִכְרַתָּ	*Et exscinderis.*	And thou shalt be cut off.
—	וְנִכְרַת־־רְתָה	*Et excisus est, exscindetur.*	And he or she was cut off, shall be cut off.
—	וְנִכְרְתוּ	*Et exscindentur.*	And they shall be cut off.
—	וְנַכְרִתֶנּוּ	*Et exscindemus eum*	And we will cut him off.
כשל	וְנִכְשַׁל	*Et impinget.*	And he will stumble.
—	וְנִכְשְׁלוּ וְנִכְשָׁלוּ	*Et impingent, cadent*	And they will stumble, will fall
—	וְנִכְשָׁלִים	*Et collapsi.*	And they that stumbled.
כתב	וְנִכְתָּב	*Et scriptus est.*	And he was written.
לאה	וְנִלְאָה	*Et defessa.*	And fatigued, weary.
—	וְנִלְאוּ	*Et fatigabuntur.*	And they will be tired.
—	וְנִלְאֵיתִי	*Et defessus sum.*	And I was weary.
לוה	וְנִלְוָה	*Et adjungetur.*	And he shall be joined.
—	וְנִלְווּ	*Et adjungentur.*	And they shall be joined.
לוז	וְנָלוֹז וּנְ״	*Et perversus.*	And perverse.
—	וּנְלוֹזִים	*Et perversi.*	And the perverse, froward.
לחם	וְנִלְחַם	*Et pugnabit.*	And he will fight.
—	וְנִלָּחֲמָה	*Et pugnabimus.*	And we will fight.
—	וְנִלְחֲמוּ	*Et pugnabunt.*	And they will fight.
—	וְנִלְחַמְנוּ	*Et pugnabimus.*	And we will fight.
—	וְנִלְחַמְתָּ	*Et pugnabis.*	And thou shalt fight.
—	וְנִלְחַמְתִּי	*Et pugnabo.*	And I will fight.
—	וְנִלְחַמְתֶּם	*Et pugnabitis.*	And ye shall fight.
לון	וְנָלִין	*Et pernoctabimus.*	And we will pass the night.
ילד	וַנֵּלֶךְ	*Et ivimus, venimus.*	And we went, came.
—	וְנֵלֵךְ	*Et ibimus.*	And we will go.
לכד	וַנִּלְכֹּד	*Et cepimus.*	And we took.

ROOTS.	DERIVATIVES.	VERSIO.	SIGNIFICATION.
לכד	וְנִלְכְּדָה	*Et capietur.*	And she shall be taken.
—	וְנִלְכְּדוּ	*Et capti sunt.*	And they were taken.
—	וְנִלְכְּדוּ	*Et capientur.*	And they shall be taken.
ילך	וְנֵלְכָה וְנֵלְכָה	*Et ibimus, veniemus.*	And we will go, come.
מחה	וְנִמְחוּ	*Et delebuntur.*	And they shall be abolished.
מות	וּנְמִיתֵם	*Et occidemus eos.*	And we will kill them.
מכר	וְנִמְכַּר	*Et vendetur.*	And he shall be sold.
—	וְנִמְכְּרוּ	*Et vendentur.*	And they shall be sold.
—	וְנִמְכְּרֶנּוּ	*Et vendemus eum.*	And we will sell him.
מלט	וְנִמְלַט--לָט	*Et eripietur.*	And he shall be delivered.
—	וְנִמְלָטָה	*Et evasit.*	And she escaped.
—	וְנִמְלָטוּ	*Et erepti sunt.*	And they were delivered.
—	וְנִמְלַטְתִּי	*Et evadam.*	And I shall escape.
מלך	וְנַמְלִיךְ	*Et regnare faciemus*	And we will cause to reign.
נמל	וּנְמַלְתֶּם	*Et circumcidetis.*	And ye shall circumcise.
מסס	וְנָמַס	*Et liquefactus est, liquescet.* [*fiet.*	And he melted, shall melt away. [away.
—	וְנָמֵס	*Et dissolutus, lique-*	And dissolved, he will melt
—	וְנָמַסּוּ	*Et liquefient.*	And they shall be melted.
מצא	וְנִמְצָא	*Et inventus est, invenietur.*	And he was found, shall be found.
—	וְנִמְצְאוּ	*Et invenientur.*	And they shall be found.
—	וְנִמְצֵאתִי	*Et inveniar.*	And I will be found. [out.
מצה	וְנִמְצָה	*Et exprimetur.*	And he shall be pressed, wrung
מקק	וְנָמַקּוּ	*Et contabescent.*	And they shall waste away.
—	וּנְמַקֹּתֶם	*Et contabescetis.*	And ye shall pine away.
נמר	וְנָמֵר	*Et pardus.*	And a leopard.
משל	וְנִמְשַׁלְתִּי	*Et assimilatus sum.*	And I am become like.
מות	וּנְמִתֵהוּ	*Et occidemus eum.*	And we will slay him.
נוס	וְנָס	*Et fugiet.*	And he will flee.
סבב	וַנָּסָב	*Et circuivimus.*	And we compassed.
—	וְנָסַב	*Et circumdedit, circumibit.*	And he compassed, will compass.
—	וְנָסֵב	*Et circumducemus.*	And we will bring about.
סבא	וְנִסְבְּאָה	*Et potabimus.*	And we will drink.
סבב	וְנָסֵבָּה	*Et circumducemus.*	And we will bring about.
—	וְנָסַבָּה	*Et circumivit.*	And she went round.

ROOTS.	DERIVATIVES.	VERSIO.	SIGNIFICATION.
סבב	וְנָסַבּוּ	*Et circumdabunt, convertentur.*	And they will surround, shall be turned.
סגר	וְנִסְגְּרָה	*Et claudemus.*	And we will shut.
נוס	וְנָסוּ	*Et fugient.*	And they will flee.
—	וְנֻסוּ	*Et fugite.*	And flee ye.
נסג	וְנָסוֹג	*Et discedere.*	And to depart.
נסע	וְנָסוֹעַ	*Et progrediendo.*	And in going forward.
סור	וְנָסוּרָה	*Et divertemus.*	And we will turn aside.
נסח	וּנְסַחְתֶּם	*Et evellemini.*	And ye shall be plucked up.
נסך	וְנֶסֶךְ וְנֶ״ וְנֶ״	*Et libamen.*	And the drink-offering.
—	וְנִסְכָּהּ	*Et libamen ejus.*	And her drink-offering.
—	וְנִסְכֵּהֶם	*Et libamina eorum.*	And their drink-offerings.
—	וְנִסְכּוֹ־־כֹה	*Et libamen ejus [um*	And his drink-offering.
—	וְנִסְכִּי	*Et idolum fusile me-*	And my molten image.
—	וּנְסָכֶיהָ	*Et libamina ejus.*	And her drink-offerings.
—	וְנִסְכֵּיהוֹן־־הֶם	*Et libamina eorum.*	And their drink-offerings.
—	וּנְסָכִים	*Et libamina.*	And drink-offerings.
סלח	וְנִסְלַח	*Et condonabitur.*	And he shall be forgiven.
נוס	וְנָסְנוּ	*Et fugiemus.*	And we will flee.
נסה	וְנַסֵּנִי	*Et proba me.*	And prove thou me.
נסע	וַנִּסַּע	*Et profecti sumus.*	And we went.
—	וְנָסַע	*Et profectus est, proficiscetur.*	And he journeyed, will go forward.
—	וַנִּסְעָה	*Et profecti sumus.*	And we journeyed.
—	וְנָסְעוּ וְנָסָעוּ	*Et profecti sunt, proficiscentur.*	And they went forward, will journey.
ספה	וְנִסְפָּה	*Et occidetur.*	And he shall be slain.
ספח	וְנִסְפְּחוּ	*Et adhærebunt.*	And they shall cleave.
ספר	וַנְּסַפֵּר	*Et narravimus.*	And we told.
—	וּנְסַפְּרָה	*Et enarrabimus.*	And we will declare.
נוס	וְנַסְתָּה	*Et fugies.*	And thou shalt flee.
—	וְנַסְתֶּם	*Et fugietis.*	And ye shall flee.
סתר	וְנִסְתְּרָה	*Et latebit.*	And she shall hide herself.
—	וְנִסְתַּרְתָּ	*Et abscondes te.*	And thou shalt hide thyself.
—	וְנִסְתַּרְתִּי	*Et abscondam me.*	And I will hide myself.
עבד	וַנַּעֲבֹד	*Et coluimus.*	And we have served.
—	וְנַעַבְדָה	*Et serviemus.*	And we will serve.

ROOTS.	DERIVATIVES.	VERSIO.	SIGNIFICATION.
עבד	וְנַעַבְדֶךָּ	*Et serviemus tibi.*	And we will serve thee.
—	וְנָעַבְדֵם	*Et colemus eos.*	And we will serve them.
—	וְנֶעֱבַדְתֶּם	*Et colemini.*	And ye shall be cultivated.
עבר	וַנַּעֲבֹר	*Et transivimus.*	And we passed over.
—	וְנַעְבְּרָה־עֲבִ׳	*Et transibimus.*	And we will go over.
יעד	וְנֹעַדְתִּי	*Et conveniam.*	And I will meet.
נוע	וְנָעוּ	*Et movebuntur, vagabuntur.*	And they shall be moved, shall wander.
עוה	וְנַעֲוֵה	*Et perversus.*	And he that is perverse.
עזב	וְנֶעֱזָב	*Et derelicta.*	And left, forsaken.
עזר	וְנֶעֱזַרְתִּי	*Et adjutus sum.*	And I was helped.
נעם	וְנָעִים וְנָעִים	*Et suavis, jucundus.*	And sweet, pleasant.
עלה	וַנַּעַל	*Et ascendimus.*	And we went up.
נעל	וְנָעַל־־עַל	*Et obseravit.*	And he bolted, locked.
—	וּנְעֹל	*Et claude, obsera.*	And shut, bolt, lock thou.
עלה	וְנַעֲלֶה	*Et ascendemus.*	And we will go up.
—	וְנַעֲלָה	*Et elatus est.*	And he was lifted up.
נעל	וּנְעָלוֹת	*Et calcei.*	And shoes.
—	וּנְעָלֶיךָ	*Et calcei tui.*	And thy shoes.
—	וְנַעֲלֵיכֶם	*Et calcei vestri.*	And your shoes.
—	וּנְעָלֵינוּ	*Et calcei nostri.*	And our shoes.
—	וְנַעַלְךָ	*Et calceus tuus.*	And thy shoe.
עלם	וְנֶעְלַם	*Et abscondetur.*	And he shall be hidden.
—	וְנֶעֶלְמָה	*Et occulta est.*	And she is hidden.
עמד	וַנַּעֲמִיד	*Et constituimus.*	And we have set, appointed.
ענש	וְנֶעֶנְשׁוּ	*Et mulctabuntur, punientur.*	And they shall be amerced, fined, punished.
עוף	וַנָּעֻפָה	*Et avolavimus.*	And we flew away.
עקש	וְנֶעְקָשׁ	*Et perversus.*	And perverse.
נער	וְנַעַר וְנַעַר	*Et puer.*	And the boy, lad, child.
—	וְנִעֵר	*Et excussit.*	And he shook.
—	וְנֹעֵר	*Et excutiens.*	And shaking.
—	וְנַעֲרָה	*Et puella.*	And a maid, damsel.
—	וְנַעֲרוֹ	*Et puer, servus ejus*	And his lad, servant.
—	וּנְעָרַי־רִים	*Et pueri mei.*	And my servants, children.
—	וְנַעֲרֹתַי	*Et puellæ meæ.*	And my maidens.
—	וְנַעֲרֹתֶיהָ	*Et puellæ ejus.*	And her maids, damsels.

ROOTS.	DERIVATIVES.	VERSIO.	SIGNIFICATION.
עשה	וַנַּעַשׂ־עֲשֶׂה	*Et fecimus.*	And we have done.
—	וְנַעֲשָׂה	*Et parabitur.*	And he shall be prepared.
—	וְנַעֲשֶׂה	*Et faciemus.*	And we will do.
—	וְנַעֲשִׂים	*Et acti.*	And done, kept.
—	וְנַעֲשֶׂנָּה	*Et faciemus eum.*	And we will do it.
עתר	וַנֵּעָתוֹר	*Et exoratus est.*	And he was intreated.
—	וְנֶעְתַּר	*Et exorabitur* [*lentæ*	And he shall be intreated.
—	וְנַעְתָּרוֹת	*Et extortæ, fraudu-*	And extorted, deceitful.
נפץ	וְנָפוֹץ	*Et collidere, commi-nuere.*	And to dash, break in pieces.
נפח	וְנָפַחְתִּי	*Et efflavi, sufflabo.*	And I blew, will blow.
נפל	וְנַפִּילָה	*Et projiciemus.*	And we will cast.
—	וְנָפַל	*Et cecidit, cadet.*	And he fell, will fall.
—	וְנֹפֵל	*Et cadens.*	And falling.
פלא	וְנִפְלָאוֹת	*Et mirabilia.*	And wonders.
—	וְנִפְלְאוֹתָיו־א"	*Et mirabilia ejus.*	And his wonders.
נפל	וְנָפְלָה	*Et cadet.*	And she will fall.
—	וְנִפְּלָה	*Et cademus.*	And we shall fall.
—	וְנָפְלוּ וּנְפָלוּ	*Et ceciderunt.*	And they fell.
—	וְנָפְלוּ	*Et cadent.*	And they will fall.
—	וְנִפְלוּ	*Et cadite* [*tinguemur*	And fall ye. [distinguished.
פלה	וְנִפְלִינוּ	*Et separabimur, dis-*	And we shall be separated,
נפל	וְנִפַּל	*Et cadet.*	And he shall fall.
—	וְנָפַלְתָּ־־תָּה	*Et cades.*	And thou wilt fall.
—	וְנָפַלְתִּי	*Et cadam.*	And I shall fall.
—	וּנְפַלְתֶּם	*Et cadetis.*	And ye shall fall. [turned.
פנה	וַנֵּפֶן	*Et vertimus nos.*	And we turned ourselves, re
נפץ	וְנִפֵּץ	*Et allidet.*	And he shall dash.
פוץ	וְנָפֹצוּ	*Et dispergentur.*	And they shall be scattered.
נפץ	וּנְפֻצוֹת	*Et dispersi* [*minuam*	And the dispersed. [pieces.
—	וְנִפַּצְתִּי	*Et dispergam, com-*	And I will scatter, break in
—	וְנִפַּצְתִּים	*Et dispergam, colli-*	And I scatter, will dash them.
נפק	וְנָפֵק	*Et exiens.* [*dam eos.*	And coming forth. [ing.
פקד	וְנִפְקַדְתָּ	*Et desideraberis.*	And thou shalt be found want-
פקח	וְנִפְקְחוּ	*Et aperientur.*	And they shall be opened.
נפק	וְנִפְקְתָא	*Et sumptus.*	And the expences.
פרש	וַנִּפְרֹשׂ	*Et extendimus.*	And we stretched out.

ROOTS.	DERIVATIVES.	VERSIO.	SIGNIFICATION.
נפש	וְנֶפֶשׁ	*Et anima.*	And the soul.
—	וְנַפְשׁוֹ	*Et anima ejus.*	And his soul.
—	וְנַפְשׁוֹת וּנְפָ״	*Et animæ.*	And the souls.
—	וְנַפְשִׁי	*Et anima mea.* [*tra.*	And my soul.
—	וְנַפְשְׁכֶם	*Et anima, mens ves-*	And your soul, mind.
—	וְנַפְשָׁם	*Et anima eorum.*	And their soul.
—	וְנַפְשֵׁנוּ	*Et anima nostra.*	And our soul. [comb.
נוף	וְנֹפֶת	*Et stillatio, favus.*	And the dropping, the honey-
פתח	וְנִפְתְּחָה	*Et aperuimus, exponemus.*	And we opened, will set forth.
יצא	וְנֵצֵא	*Et egrediemur.*	And we will go out.
יצב	וְנִצְּבוּ	*Et stabunt.*	And they will stand.
—	וְנִצַּבְתָּ	*Et stabis.* [*ficabitur.*	And thou shalt stand. [ed.
צדק	וְנִצְדַּק	*Et absolvetur, justi-*	And he shall be justified, clear-
נצה	וְנֹצָה	*Et pluma.*	And feathers.
צום	וְנָצוּמָה	*Et jejunavimus.*	And we have fasted.
נצב	וּנְצִיב	*Et præfectus, præsi-*	And the officer, the garrison.
נצר	וּנְצִירֵי	*Et servati.* [*dium.*	And the preserved.
נצל	וְנִצַּלְתֶּם	*Et spoliabitis.*	And ye shall spoil.
צעק	וַנִּצְעַק	*Et clamavimus.*	And we cried.
נצץ	וְנֹצְצִים	*Et scintillantes.*	And sparkling.
נצר	וְנֵצֶר	*Et surculus.*	And a branch.
—	וְנֹצֵר	*Et custodiens.*	And he that keepeth.
צרב	וְנִצְרְבוּ	*Et comburentur.*	And they shall be burned.
נצר	וּנְצֻרוֹת	*Et reservatæ.*	And reserved.
—	וּנְצֻרַת	*Et servata.* [*tabitur*	And preserved. [desolate.
יצת	וְנִצְּתָה	*Et accendetur, vas-*	And he shall be kindled, made
נקב	וְנֹקֵב	*Et execrans.*	And blaspheming.
—	וּנְקָבָהּ	*Et perforabit eam.*	And he shall pierce her or it.
—	וּנְקֵבָה	*Et fœmina.*	And a female.
—	וּנְקָבֶיךָ	*Et fistulæ tuæ.* [*tur.*	And thy pipes. [sembled.
קבץ	וְנִקְבְּצוּ	*Et cum congregabun-*	And when they shall be as-
—	וְנִקְבְּצוּ	*Et congregabuntur.*	And they shall be assembled.
נקד	וְנָקֹד	*Et punctis respersæ.*	And speckled with points.
—	וְנִקֻּדִים	*Et placentæ.*	And cakes.
קדש	וְנִקְדַּשׁ	*Et sanctificabitur.*	And he shall be sanctified.
—	וְנִקְדַּשְׁתִּי	*Et sanctificabor.*	And I shall be sanctified.

ROOTS.	DERIVATIVES.	VERSIO.	SIGNIFICATION.
נקה	וְנַקֵּה	*Et absolvere, impunitum dimittere.*	And to acquit, leave unpunished.
—	וְנִקָּה	*Et innocens erit.*	And he shall be guiltless.
קוה	וּנְקַוֶּה	*Et expectabimus.*	And we will wait. [together.
—	וְנִקְווּ	*Et congregabuntur.*	And they shall be gathered
קום	וְנָקוּמָה	*Et surgemus.*	And we will rise.
לקח	וַנִּקַּח	*Et cepimus.*	And we took.
—	וְנִקְחָה	*Et sumemus. [tur.*	And we will take.
קוט	וְנָקֹטּוּ	*Et fastidio habebun-*	And they shall be loathed.
—	וּנְקֹטֹתֶם	*Et tædebit vos.*	And ye shall loathe yourselves
נקה	וְנָקִי	*Et innocens.*	And the innocent.
קוץ	וּנְקִיצֶנָּה	*Et vexabimus eam.*	And we will vex her or it.
נקה	וְנִקִּיתָ	*Et innocens eris.*	And thou shalt be innocent.
—	וְנִקֵּיתִי	*Et innocens ero.*	And I shall be innocent, clear.
קלל	וְנָקַל	*Et levis, vilis fuit.*	And he was light, worthless.
קלה	וְנִקְלָה	*Et vilis fiet, spernetur. [tus.*	And he will become vile, shall be contemned.
—	וְנִקְלֶה	*Et vilipensus, spre-*	And lightly esteemed, despised.
קלל	וּנְקַלֹּתִי	*Et vilior fiam.*	And I will become more vile.
נקם	וְנָקָם	*Et vindicta.*	And vengeance.
—	וְנֹקֵם	*Et ulciscens.*	And he that avengeth.
—	וְנִקְמוּ	*Et ulti sunt.*	And they revenged.
—	וּנְקָמַנִי	*Et vindicabit me.*	And he will avenge me.
—	וְנִקַּמְתִּי	*Et ulciscar.*	And I will avenge.
קנה	וְנִקְנָה	*Et emetur.*	And he shall be bought.
נקף	וְנִקַּף	*Et excidet.*	And he shall cut down.
קרא	וְנִקְרָא־רָאָה	*Et vocabitur.*	And he shall be called.
קרב	וַנַּקְרֵב	*Et obtulimus.*	And we have presented.
—	וְנִקְרַב	*Et adducetur.*	And he shall be brought.
—	וְנִקְרְבָה	*Et accedemus.*	And we will draw near.
—	וְנִקְרַבְתֶּם	*Et adducemini.*	And ye shall be brought. [tied
נקה	וְנִקָּתָה	*Et mundabitur.*	And she shall be cleared, emp-
—	וְנִקְּתָה	*Et innocens erit.*	And she shall be innocent.
נור	וְנֵר	*Et lucerna.*	And the lamp, candle.
ראה	וְנִרְאֶ־אֶה	*Et videbimus.*	And we shall see.
—	וַנִּרְאֶה	*Et vidimus.*	And we saw.
—	וְנִרְאָה	*Et videtur.*	And he shall be seen.

ROOTS.	DERIVATIVES.	VERSIO.	SIGNIFICATION.
ראה	וְנִרְאֵהוּ	*Et videbimus eum.*	And we shall see him.
—	וְנִרְאֲתָה	*Et videbitur.*	And she will be seen.
רגן	וְנִרְגָּן	*Et susurro.*	And a whisperer, talebearer.
ירד	וַנֵּרֶד	*Et venimus.*	And we came.
נור	וְנֵרוֹ	*Et lucerna ejus.*	And his lamp, candle.
רום	וּנְרוֹמְמָה	*Et exaltabimus.*	And we will exalt.
רנן	וּנְרַנְּנָה	*Et cantabimus.*	And we will sing.
רפא	וְנִרְפָּא	*Et sanata est.*	And she was healed.
—	וְנִרְפְּאוּ	*Et sanabuntur.*	And they shall be healed.
רצץ	וְנָרֹץ	*Et confringetur.*	And he will be broken.
רצה	וְנִרְצָה	*Et accipietur.*	And he will be accepted.
נור	וְנֵרֹתֶיהָ	*Et lucerna ejus.*	And her lamp, candle.
—	וְנֵרֹתֵיהֶם	*Et lucernæ eorum.*	And their lamps.
נשא	וְנָשָׂא	*Et sumpsit, tulit, feret, educet.*	And he took, bare, will bear, bring forth.
—	וְנִשָּׂא	*Et elevatus, elatus est, extolletur.*	And extolled, high, he was lifted up, shall be exalted.
—	וְנֹשֵׂא	*Et ferens.*	And bearing.
—	וְנִשָּׂא	*Et abstulit.* [*ratus.*	And he carried away.
—	וּנְשֻׂא	*Et acceptus, hono-*	And accepted, honoured.
—	וְנָשְׂאוּ	*Et abstulerunt.*	And they carried away.
—	וְנָשְׂאוּ	*Et tollent, ferent.*	And they will take up, bear.
—	וְנִשְּׂאוּ	*Et sublevarunt.*	And they helped.
—	וּנְשָׂאוֹ	*Et tollet eum.*	And he shall take him up.
—	וּנְשָׂאוּם	*Et sumpserunt eos.*	And they took them.
—	וְנֹשְׂאִים	*Et accipientes.*	And accepting.
—	וּנְשָׂאֲךָ	*Et extulit te.*	And he lifted thee up.
שאל	וְנִשְׁאֲלָה	*Et interrogabimus.*	And we will inquire.
נשא	וְנָשְׂאֵם	*Et extolle eos.*	And lift thou them up.
שאר	וְנִשְׁאַר	*Et relinquetur.*	And he shall be left.
—	וְנִשְׁאֲרוּ	*Et superfuerunt.*	And they remained.
—	וְנִשְׁאַרְתֶּם	*Et remanebitis.*	And ye shall remain.
נשא	וְנָשָׂאתָ	*Et tolles, feres.*	And thou shalt take up, carry.
—	וְנָשָׂאתִי	*Et parcam.*	And I will spare.
—	וּנְשָׂאתֶם	*Et adducetis.*	And ye shall bring.
—	וּנְשָׂאתַנִי	*Et portabis me.*	And thou shalt carry me.
שוב	וַנָּשָׁב	*Et reversi sumus.*	And we returned.

ROOTS.	DERIVATIVES.	VERSIO.	SIGNIFICATION.
ישב	וַנֵּשֶׁב	*Et habitavimus.*	And we dwelt.
—	וַנֵּשֶׁב	*Et duximus.*	And we have taken.
שוב	וְנָשֻׁבָה	*Et revertemur.*	And we will return.
שבר	וְנַשְׁבִּירָה	*Et vendemus.*	And we will sell.
שבע	וַנִּשְׂבָּע	*Et saturati sumus.*	And we were satisfied.
—	וְנִשְׁבַּע	*Et juravit.*	And he sware.
—	וְנִשְׁבָּעוֹת	*Et jurantes.*	And they that swear.
—	וְנִשְׁבַּעְתָּ	*Et jurabis.*	And thou shalt swear.
שבר	וְנִשְׁבַּר	*Et confringetur.*	And he shall be broken.
—	וְנִשְׁבְּרָה	*Et ememus.*	And we will buy.
—	וְנִשְׁבְּרוּ וְנִשְׁבָּרוּ	*Et confringentur.*	And they shall be broken.
שבת	וְנִשְׁבַּת	*Et cessabit.*	And he shall cease.
—	וְנִשְׁבְּתוּ	*Et desinent.*	And they shall cease.
שגב	וְנִשְׂגַּב-גָּב	*Et exaltabitur.*	And he shall be exalted.
נשא	וְנָשׂוּ	*Et ferent.*	And they shall bear, carry.
—	וְנָשׂוּא	*Et acceptus, honoratus.*	And accepted, honoured.
שוב	וַנָּשׁוּב	*Et reversi sumus.*	And we have returned.
—	וְנָשׁוּב	*Et revertemur.*	And we will return.
—	וְנָשׁוּבָ-בָה	*Et convertemur, revertemur.*	And we shall be turned, will return.
שחת	וְנַשְׁחִיתָה	*Et disperdemus.*	And we will destroy.
—	וְנִשְׁחָת	*Et corruptus est.*	And he was marred.
אנש	וּנְשֵׁי	*Et uxores.*	And the wives.
נשא	וְנָשִׂיא וּנְשִׂיא	*Et princeps.*	And the chief, prince.
—	וּנְשִׂיאֵי	*Et principes.*	And the chiefs, princes.
שוב	וְנָשִׁיב	*Et respondebimus.*	And we will answer.
אנש	וּנְשֵׁיהוֹן-שֵׁיהֶם	*Et uxores eorum.*	And their wives.
—	וְנָשָׁיו	*Et uxores ejus.*	And his wives.
—	וְנָשֶׁיךָ	*Et uxores tuæ.*	And thy wives.
—	וּנְשֵׁיכֶם	*Et uxores vestræ.*	And your wives.
נשה	וַנַּשִּׁים	*Et vastavimus.*	And we have laid waste.
שום	וְנָשִׂים	*Et ponemus.*	And we will put, set.
אנש	וְנָשִׁים	*Et uxores, mulieres.*	And wives, women.
שום	וְנָשִׂימָה	*Et ponemus.*	And we will put, set.
אנש	וְנָשֵׁינוּ	*Et uxores nostræ.*	And our wives.
נשה	וְנָשִׁיתִי	*Et obliviscar.*	And I shall forget.
שכב	וְנִשְׁכְּבָה	*Et cubabimus.*	And we will lie.

ROOTS.	DERIVATIVES.	VERSIO.	SIGNIFICATION.
נשך	וְנָשְׁכוּ	*Et mordebunt.*	And they shall bite.
—	וּנְשָׁכוֹ	*Et mordebit eum.*	And he shall bite him.
שכח	וְנִשְׁכַּח	*Et oblivioni tradetur*	And he shall be forgotten.
—	וְנִשְׁכַּחַת	*Et oblivioni tradetur*	And she shall be forgotten.
נשך	וּנְשָׁכָם	*Et mordebit eos.*	And he shall bite them. [out.
נשל	וְנָשַׁל	*Et ejecit, ejiciet.*	And he has cast out, will cast
שלח	וְנִשְׁלוֹחַ	*Et missus est.*	And he was sent.
—	וְנִשְׁלְחָה	*Et mittemus.*	And we will send.
—	וַנְּשַׁלֵּחֲךָ	*Et dimisimus te.*	And we sent thee away.
שלך	וְנַשְׁלִיכָה	*Et abjiciemus.*	And we will cast off.
—	וְנַשְׁלִכֵהוּ	*Et projiciemus eum.*	And we will cast him.
שלם	וּנְשַׁלְּמָה	*Et reddemus.*	And we will render.
שמד	וְנִשְׁמַד	*Et disperdetur.*	And he shall be destroyed.
—	וְנִשְׁמְדוּ	*Et disperdentur.*	And they shall be destroyed.
—	וְנִשְׁמַדְתִּי	*Et disperdar.*	And I shall be destroyed.
נשם	וּנְשָׁמָה	*Et halitus.*	And breath. [late.
שמם	וּנְשַׁמָּה	*Et desolabitur.*	And she shall be made deso-
—	וְנָשַׁמּוּ	*Et vastabuntur, desolabuntur, obstupescent.*	And they shall be laid waste, desolated, astonished.
נשם	וְנִשְׁמוֹת	*Et animæ.*	And the souls.
שמח	וְנִשְׂמְחָה	*Et lætabimur.*	And we will rejoice.
שמד	וְנַשְׁמִידָה	*Et disperdemus.*	And we will destroy.
שמע	וַנִּשְׁמַע	*Et audivimus, obtemperavimus.*	And we have heard, obeyed.
—	וְנִשְׁמָע	*Et audiemus.*	And we will hear.
—	וְנִשְׁמַע	*Et audietur.*	And he shall be heard.
—	וְנִשְׁמְעָה־מַּעָה	*Et audiemus.*	And we will hear.
—	וְנִשְׁמָעֶנָּה	*Et audiemus illam.*	And we will hear her.
שמר	וְנִשְׁמַר	*Et cavebit.*	And he will take heed.
—	וְנִשְׁמַרְתָּ	*Et cavebis.*	And thou shalt take heed.
—	וְנִשְׁמַרְתֶּם	*Et cavebitis vobis.*	And take heed unto yourselves
נשם	וְנִשְׁמַת	*Et halitus, spiritus.*	And the breath, spirit.
—	וְנִשְׁמָתוֹ	*Et halitus ejus.*	And his breath. [dered.
שסס	וְנָשַׁסּוּ	*Et diripientur.*	And they will be robbed, plun-
שען	וְנִשְׁעַן	*Et innitetur.*	And he will lean.
שפט	וְנִשְׁפַּטְתִּי	*Et judicabo.*	And I will judge.
שפך	וְנִשְׁפַּךְ	*Et effundetur.*	And he shall be poured out.

ROOTS.	DERIVATIVES.	VERSIO.	SIGNIFICATION.
נשק	וְנָשַׁק	*Et osculatus est.*	And he kissed.
—	וְנֵשֶׁק	*Et arma.*	And arms.
—	וְנָשְׁקָה	*Et osculata est.*	And she kissed.
שקע	וְנִשְׁקְעָה	*Et submergetur.*	And she will sink, be drowned.
שקף	וְנִשְׁקְפָה	*Et respexit.*	And she looked.
שרף	וְנִשְׂרְפָה	*Et comburemus.*	And we will burn.
שתה	וְנִשְׁתֶּה	*Et bibemus.*	And we will drink.
נשת	וְנִשְּׁתוּ	*Et deficient.*	And they will fail.
שחה	וְנִשְׁתַּחֲוֶה	*Et adorabimus.*	And we will worship.
שעה	וְנִשְׁתָּעָה	*Et narrabimus.*	And we will tell, declare.
נתן	וְנָתוֹן	*Et dare, tradere, adjicere, constituere.*	And to give, deliver, apply, make, appoint.
נתק	וְנָתוּק	*Et avulsus, disruptus*	And pulled, broken, torn off.
נתח	וְנִתַּח	*Et concidet.* [*nos.*	And he shall cut up. [selves.
חזק	וְנִתְחַזֵּק	*Et confirmabimus*	And we will strengthen our-
—	וְנִתְחַזְּקָה	*Et viriliter agemus.*	And we will act manfully, va-
נתב	וּנְתִיבוֹתֶיהָ	*Et semitæ ejus.*	And her paths. [liantly.
נתך	וְנִתְּכָה	*Et fundetur.*	And she shall be fused, melted
—	וְנִתַּכְתֶּם	*Et fundemini.*	And ye shall be poured, melted.
נתן	וְנָתַן	*Et dedit, edidit, posuit, dabit, tradet,*	And he gave, cast, put; will give, deliver, put.
—	וְנִתַּן וְנָתֹן	*Et dabitur.* [*ponet.*	And he shall be given.
—	וְנֹתֵן	*Et dans.*	And giving.
—	וַנִּתְּנָהּ	*Et dedimus eam.*	And we gave her.
—	וְנָתְנָה	*Et edet.*	And she will yield.
—	וְנִתְּנָה	*Et dabitur.*	And she shall be given.
—	וּנְתָנָהּ	*Et dedit, tradet eam*	And he gave, will deliver her.
—	וְנָתַנּוּ	*Et dabimus.*	And we will give.
—	וְנָתְנוּ	*Et donarunt, injecerunt; dabunt, tradent, ponent.*	And they gave, cast; will give, deliver, put.
—	וּנְתָנוֹ	*Et tradet eum.*	And he will deliver him.
—	וּנְתַנּוּךָ	*Et trademus te.*	And we will deliver thee.
—	וּנְתָנְךָ	*Et ponet te.*	And he will set thee.
—	וּנְתָנָם	*Et dabit, tradet eos.*	And he will give, deliver them
עור	וַנִּתְעוֹדֵד	*Et ereximus nos.*	And we have raised ourselves
פלל	וַנִּתְפַּלֵּל	*Et oravimus.*	And we prayed. [up.

ROOTS.	DERIVATIVES.	VERSIO.	SIGNIFICATION.
תפש	וְנִתְפַּשׂ	*Et capietur.*	And he shall be taken.
—	וְנִתְפְּשֵׂם	*Et capiemus eos.*	And we shall catch them.
נתץ	וְנָתַץ	*Et diruit, diruet.*	And he broke,shall break down
—	וְנִתְּצוּ	*Et diruent.*	And they shall break down.
—	וְנִתַּצְתֶּם	*Et diruetis.*	And ye shall overthrow.
נתק	וּנְתַקְּנוּהוּ	*Et abstrahemus eum*	And we will draw him off.
נתש	וְנָתַשׁ	*Et extirpabit.*	And he will root up.
—	וְנָתַשְׁתִּי	*Et evellam.*	And I will pluck up.
—	וּנְתַשְׁתִּים	*Et extirpabo eos.*	And I will root them out.
נתן	וְנָתַתָּ וְנָתַתָּה	*Et dabis, trades, pones, constitues.*	And thou shalt give, deliver, put, appoint.
—	וְנָתַתִּי	*Et ponam, statuam.*	And I will put, set.
—	וְנָתַתִּי	*Et dabo, afferam, ponam, constituam, reddam, emittam.*	And I will give, bring, put, make, appoint, recompense, pay, cast, send forth.
—	וּנְתַתִּיהָ	*Et dedi, dabo eam.*	And I have given, will give her
—	וּנְתַתִּיהוּ	*Et tradam eum, constituisti eum.*	And I will deliver him, thou hast set him up.
—	וּנְתַתִּיו	*Et dabo eum.*	And I will give him or it.
—	וּנְתַתִּיךָ־־ךְ	*Et constitui te, dabo, ponam te.* [eos.	And I have set, appointed thee, will give, put, make thee.
—	וּנְתַתִּים	*Et tradam, ponam*	And I will deliver, place them
—	וּנְתַתֶּם	*Et trademini.*	And ye shall be delivered.
—	וּנְתַתֶּם	*Et dabis, pones eos.*	And ye shall give, put, lay.
—	וּנְתַתֶּם	*Et dabitis, ponetis.*	And thou shalt give, put them
	וס		
סבא	וְסֹבֵא	*Et ebriosus* [*cumibit.*	And a drunkard. [pass
סבב	וְסָבַב	*Et circumdedit, cir-*	And he surrounded, will com-
—	וְסָבְבוּ	*Et circumibunt.*	And they will go about.
—	וְסֹבּוּ	*Et circuite.*	And compass ye.
—	וְסַבּוֹתִי	*Et circumivi.*	And I went about.
—	וְסָבִיב	*Et circa.*	And about, round about.
—	וּסְבִיב	*Et circuitus.*	And the circuit.
—	וּסְבִיבוֹת	*Et circuitus.*	And the circuits.
—	וּסְבִיבוֹתֶיהָ	*Et circuitus ejus.*	And her circuits.
—	וּסְבִיבָיו	*Et circuitus ejus.*	And his circuits, around him.

ROOTS.	DERIVATIVES.	VERSIO.	SIGNIFICATION.
סבל	וְסֻבֳּלוֹ	*Et onus ejus.*	And his burden.
סבב	וְסַבֹּתֶם	*Et circuibitis.*	And ye shall compass.
סגר	וְסְגוֹר־נֵר	*Et claude.* [um.	And shut thou. [property.
סגל	וּסְגֻלַּת	*Et peculium, propri-*	And the peculiar treasure, or
סגן	וּסְגָנֶיהָ	*Et principes ejus.*	And her rulers.
—	וּסְגָנִים	*Et principes.*	And rulers.
סגר	וְסָגַר	*Et claudet.*	And he will shut.
—	וְסָגַר	*Et occlusit.*	And he hath shut up.
—	וְסֻגְּרוּ	*Et claudentur.*	And they shall be shut.
—	וְסָגַרְתָּ	*Et claudes.*	And thou shalt shut.
סבב	וְסוֹבֵב	*Et vertens se.*	And turning about.
סוד	וְסוֹד	*Et arcanum.*	And a secret.
סוך	וְסוֹךְ	*Et ungendo.*	And in anointing.
סמך	וְסוֹמֵךְ	*Et sustentans.*	And upholding.
סמף	וְסוּמְפֹּנְיָה וְסִי״	*Et* musicum aliquod instrumentum.	And *some musical instrument.*
סוס	וְסוּס וְסוּס	*Et equus.*	And a horse.
—	וְסוּס	*Et hirundo.*	And the swallow.
—	וְסוּסֵי	*Et equi.*	And horses.
—	וְסוּסֵיהֶם	*Et equi eorum.*	And their horses.
סוף	וְסוּף	*Et juncetum, alga.*	And the flags, sea-weed.
ספר	וְסוֹפֵר	*Et scriba.*	And a scribe.
סוף	וְסוּפָתָה	*Et turbo.*	And a whirlwind. [thou.
סור	וְסוֹר וְסוּר	*Et divertere, discede*	And to turn aside, depart
—	וְסוּרָה	*Et discedens.*	And departing.
סחב	וְסָחַבְנוּ	*Et trahemus.* [ram.	And we will draw. [away.
סחה	וְסָחֵיתִי	*Et abradam, ever-*	And I will scrape off, sweep
סחר	וְסַחַר	*Et merx, negotiatio.*	And merchandise, traffick.
—	וְסֹחֵרָה	*Et parma.*	And a buckler.
—	וּסְחָרוּהָ	*Et negotiamini in ea*	And trade ye in her.
—	וְסֹחֲרֵי	*Et mercatores.*	And the merchants.
—	וְסֹחָרֶת	*Et onyx, vel marmor variegatum.*	And alabaster, or variegated marble.
סכך	וְסֻכָּה	*Et tentorium.*	And the tabernacle.
—	וְסֹכְכִים	*Et tegentes.*	And covering.
סכל	וְסִכְלוּת	*Et stultitia.* [miscebo	And folly. [gle, embroil.
סכך	וְסִכְסַכְתִּי	*Et instigabo, com-*	And I will stir up, will min-

ROOTS.	DERIVATIVES.	VERSIO.	SIGNIFICATION.
שכר	וְסֹכְרִים	*Et mercede condu-*	And they that hire.
סכר	וְסִכַּרְתִּי	*Et tradam.* [*centes.*	And I will deliver up.
סוך	וָסַכְתָּ	*Et unges.*	And thou shalt anoint.
סכך	וְסַכֹּתָ	*Et proteges.*	And thou wilt protect, defend.
סלל	וְסַל	*Et canistrum.*	And a basket.
—	וְסַלּוֹנִים	*Et spinæ.*	And thorns, briars.
סלח	וְסַלָּח	*Et condonans.*	And forgiving. [forgive.
—	וְסָלַחְתָּ־־לִי	*Et condonabis.*	And thou shalt pardon, wilt
—	וְסָלַחְתִּי	*Et condonabo.*	And I will pardon.
סלע	וְסַלְעוֹ	*Et rupes ejus.*	And his rock.
סלף	וְסֶלֶף	*Et perversitas.*	And perverseness.
סלת	וְסֹלֶת	*Et simila.*	And the fine flour.
סמך	וְסָמַךְ	*Et fulciet, innitetur.*	And he will support, lean.
—	וְסָמְכוּ	*Et nitentur.*	And they will lean, rest.
—	וְסָמַכְתָּ	*Et impones.*	And thou shalt lay.
סוס	וְסוּסִים	*Et equi.*	And horses.
סעד	וְסָעַד	*Et sustentabit.*	And he will uphold.
—	וּסְעָדָה	*Et refice te.*	And refresh thyself.
—	וְסַעֲדוּ	*Et reficite.*	And refresh, comfort ye.
נסע	וּסְעוּ	*Et proficiscimini.*	And take ye your journey.
סער	וְסַעַר	*Et turbo.*	And a whirlwind. [tuous.
—	וְסֹעֵר	*Et turbatus, agitatus*	And troubled, tossed, tempes-
—	וּסְעָרָה	*Et turbo, procella.*	And a whirlwind, storm, tem-
ספף	וְסַף	*Et limen.*	And the threshold. [pest.
ספד	וְסָפְדָה	*Et planget.*	And she shall mourn.
—	וְסָפְדוּ	*Et plangent.*	And they shall mourn.
—	וְסִפְדוּ	*Et plangite.* [*mentur*	And mourn ye. [sumed.
סוף	וְסָפוּ	*Et deficient, consu-*	And they shall fail, be con-
—	וְסֹפוֹ	*Et finis ejus.*	And his end.
ספד	וְסָפוֹד	*Et plangere.* [*latus.*	And to mourn, lament.
ספן	וְסָפוּן וְסָפֻן	*Et tectus, contabu-*	And covered, floored, cieled.
ספף	וְסִפּוֹת	*Et crateres.*	And the bowls.
ספר	וְסַפִּיר	*Et sapphirus.*	And a sapphire. [low.
ספק	וְסָפַק	*Et volutabit se.*	And he will roll himself, wal-
ספר	וְסָפַר־־פְרָה	*Et numerabit.*	And he, she will number.
—	וְסֵפֶר	*Et liber.*	And a book.
—	וּסְפֹר	*Et numera.*	And number, tell thou.

ROOTS.	DERIVATIVES.	VERSIO.	SIGNIFICATION.
ספר	וּסְפָרִים וְסִפְרִין	*Et epistolæ, libri.*	And letters, books.
—	וְסָפַרְתָּ	*Et numerabis.*	And thou shalt number.
—	וּסְפַרְתֶּם	*Et numerabitis.*	And ye shall number.
סקל	וְסִקְלֻהוּ	*Et lapidate eum.*	And stone ye him.
—	וּסְקָלוּהָ	*Et lapidabunt eam.*	And they shall stone her.
—	וּסְקָלֻנִי	*Et lapidabunt me.*	And they will stone me.
—	וּסְקַלְתּוֹ	*Et lapidabis eum.*	And thou shalt stone him.
—	וּסְקַלְתָּם	*Et lapidabis eos.*	And thou shalt stone them.
—	וּסְקַלְתֶּם	*Et lapidabitis.*	And ye shall stone.
סור	וְסָר־־רָה	*Et discessit, discedet, discedens, defectio.*	And he, she departed, will depart, departing, a revolt.
סרבל	וְסַרְבָּלֵיהוֹן	*Et vestes eorum.*	And their garments.
—	וְסָרוּ	*Et discedent.*	And they will depart.
סרח	וְסֶרַח	*Et superfluitas.*	And the overplus [selves out.
—	וּסְרֻחִים	*Et sese extendentes.*	And they that stretch them-
סרס	וְסָרִיסֵי וְסָרִסִים	*Et eunuchi.*	And the eunuchs.
—	וְסָרִיסֶיהָ	*Et eunuchi, cubicu- larii ejus [larii ejus*	And her eunuchs, chamber- lains.
—	וְסָרִיסָיו	*Et eunuchi, cubicu-*	And his eunuchs, officers.
סרן	וְסַרְנֵי	*Et principes; tabu- læ.*	And the lords, princes; the plates, tablets.
סרר	וְסֹרֶרֶת	*Et contumax.[ciens.*	And the stubborn, rebellious.
סור	וְסָרַת	*Et discedens, defi-*	And departing, deficient.
—	וְסַרְתֶּם	*Et discedetis.*	And ye shall depart.
סתר	וְסֵתֶר	*Et latibulum.*	And the covert.
	וע		
עבה	וְעָב	*Et trabs.*	And the beam, plank.
עבד	וְעָבַד	*Et ministrabit.*	And he shall minister, serve.
—	וְעֶבֶד	*Et servus.*	And a servant.
—	וַעֲבֹדָה	*Et ministerium[um.*	And work, service. [servants.
—	וַעֲבֻדָּה	*Et familia, famulili-*	And a household, company of
—	וַעֲבָדָהּ	*Et colet eam.*	And he shall cultivate, till it.
—	וַעֲבָדֻהוּ	*Et servient ei.*	And they shall serve him.
—	וְעָבְדֵהוּ	*Et cole eum.*	And serve thou him.
—	וְעִבְדֻהוּ	*Et colite eum.*	And serve ye him.
—	וַעֲבָדָו־־דָיו	*Et servi ejus.*	And his servants.

ROOTS.	DERIVATIVES.	VERSIO.	SIGNIFICATION.
עבד	וַעֲבָדוֹ	*Et serviet ei.*	And he shall serve him.
—	וַעֲבָדוּ	*Etobservarunt*[*cient*	And they kept, observed.
—	וְעָבְדוּ־־בְדוּ	*Et ministrabunt, fa-*	And they shall serve, do.
—	וְעַבְדּוֹ	*Et servus ejus.* [*ni.*	And his servant.
—	וְעִבְדוּ	*Et servite, operami-*	And serve, work ye.
—	וַעֲבָדוּךָ	*Et servient tibi.*	And they shall serve thee.
—	וַעֲבָדוּם	*Et servient eis.*	And they shall serve them.
—	וַעֲבָדַי	*Et servi mei.*	And my servants.
—	וְעַבְדֵי	*Et servi.*	And the servants.
—	וְעַבְדִּי	*Et servus meus.*	And my servant.
—	וַעֲבָדֶיהָ	*Et servi ejus.*	And her servants.
—	וְעַבְדֵיהֶם	*Et opera eorum.*	And their works.
—	וַעֲבָדֶיךָ	*Et servi tui.*	And thy servants.
—	וְעַבְדֵיכֶם	*Et servi vestri.*	And your servants.
—	וַעֲבָדִים־־דִם	*Et servi.*	And the servants.
—	וְעֹבְדִים	*Et servientes.*	And they that serve.
—	וַעֲבָדְךָ	*Et serviet tibi.*	And he shall serve thee.
—	וְעַבְדְּךָ	*Et servus tuus.*	And thy servant.
—	וַעֲבֹדַת	*Et opus, ministerium*	And the work, service.
—	וְעָבַדְתָּ־־בְ׳	*Et servies, coles, ob-*	And thou shalt serve, dress,
		servabis.	cultivate, keep, observe.
—	וְעָבַדְתִּי	*Et serviam.*	And I will serve.
—	וַעֲבַדְתֶּם	*Et servies eis.*	And thou wilt serve them.
—	וַעֲבַדְתֶּם	*Et servietis,*	And ye will serve.
—	וַעֲבַדְתַּנִי	*Et servies mihi.*	And thou shalt serve me.
—	וַעֲבוֹדָה־־דַת	*Et ministerium.*	And the service.
—	וַעֲבִידְתָּא	*Et opus.*	And the work.
עבה	וְעָבְיוֹ	*Et crassitudo ejus.*	And his thickness.
עבר	וַעֲבֹר	*Et transi.* [*sibit.*	And pass thou over.
—	וְעָבַר־־בַר	*Et transivit, tran-*	And he passed, will pass over.
—	וְעֹבֵר	*Et transiens.*	And passing over.
—	וְעָבְרָה	*Et transivit.*	And she went over.
—	וְעֶבְרָה	*Et furor.*	And wrath.
—	וְעָבְרוּ	*Et transibunt.*	And they will go over.
—	וְעִבְרוּ	*Et transite.*	And go ye over.
—	וְעָבַרְנוּ	*Et transibimus.*	And we will go over.
—	וְעִבַּרְתָּ	*Et transire facies.*	And thou shalt cause to pass.

ROOTS.	DERIVATIVES.	VERSIO.	SIGNIFICATION.
עבר	וְעֶבְרָתוֹ	*Et furor ejus.*	And his wrath.
—	וְעָבַרְתִּי	*Et transibo.*	And I will pass over.
—	וַעֲבַרְתֶּם	*Et transferetis.*	And ye shall carry over.
—	וְעֶבְרָתָם	*Et furor eorum.*	And their wrath.
ענב	וְעֻגָב	*Et organum.*	And the organ.
—	וְעֻגָּבִי	*Et organum meum.*	And my organ.
ענר	וְעָגוּר	*Et grus.*	And a crane.
ענל	וַעֲגִילִים	*Et inaures.*	And ear-rings.
—	וְעֵגֶל	*Et vitulus.*	And a calf.
—	וַעֲגָלִים	*Et vituli.*	And calves.
עוג	וְעֻגַּת	*Et placenta.*	And the cake.
עוד	וָעֵד ו׳	*Et testis.*	And a witness.
עד	וָעֶד	*Et perpetuus, in perpetuum.*	And perpetual, for ever.
—	וְעַד	*Et usque ad, donec.*	And even to, until.
יעד	וַעֲדָה	*Et cœtus.*	And the assembly.
עוד	וְעֵדָה	*Et testimonium.*	And the testimony.
—	וְעֵדוֹתָיו־דו״־ד״	*Et testimonia ejus.*	And his testimonies.
—	וְעֵדֵיהֶם	*Et testes eorum.*	And their witnesses.
עד	וְעָדֶיךָ	*Et usque ad te.*	And even to thee.
—	וְעָדֵיכֶם	*Et ad vos.*	And to you.
עדה	וְעָדִית	*Et ornasti te.*	And thou hast adorned thyself
עדן	וְעִדָּן	*Et tempus.*	And time.
עד	וְעָדֶנּוּ־־עוֹ״	*Et adhuc ipse.*	And still he.
עדן	וְעִדָּנִין	*Et tempora.*	And times.
עדר	וְעֶדְרוֹ	*Et grex ejus.*	And his flock.
—	וְעֶדְרֵיהֶם	*Et greges eorum.*	And their flocks.
—	וַעֲדָרִים	*Et greges.*	And the flocks.
עדש	וַעֲדָשִׁים	*Et lentes.*	And lentiles.
יעד	וַעֲדַת	*Et cœtus.*	And the assembly, congregation.
—	וַעֲדָתוֹ	*Et cœtus ejus.*	And his assembly.
עוד	וְעֵדֹתַי	*Et testimonia mea.*	And my testimonies.
—	וְעֵדֹתֶיךָ	*Et testimonia tua.*	And thy testimonies.
ענב	וְעוּגָב	*Et organum.*	And the organ.
עוד	וְעוֹד	*Et adhuc, præterea, iterum, quamvis.*	And still, yet, besides, again, although.
—	וְעוֹדִי	*Et adhuc ego.*	And still I.
—	וְעוֹדְךָ	*Et adhuc tu.*	And yet thou.

ROOTS.	DERIVATIVES.	VERSIO.	SIGNIFICATION.
עוה	וְעָוָה	*Et pervertet.*	And he will pervert.
עזז	וָעֹז	*Et robur.*	And strength.
עוה	וְעָוִינוּ	*Et perperam egimus*	And we have done wickedly.
—	וַעֲוֹנֹתֶיךָ	*Et iniquitates tuæ.*	And thy iniquities.
עול	וְעַוְלָה	*Et iniquitas.*	And iniquity.
עלל	וְעוֹלֵל	*Et fac.*	And do thou.
עול	וְעוֹלָתָה־־עֹ'	*Et iniquitas.*	And iniquity.
עלה	וְעֹלֹתֶיךָ	*Et holocausta tua.*	And thy burnt-offerings.
—	וְעֹלָתֶךָ	*Et holocaustum tuum.*	And thy burnt-offering.
עוה	וַעֲוֹנוֹת־־נֹת	*Et iniquitates.*	And the iniquities.
—	וַעֲוֹנִי	*Et iniquitas mea.*	And my iniquity.
ענן	וְעוֹנֵן	*Et auguratus est, conjecit ex nubibus.*	And he used auguries, divined by the clouds.
עוה	וַעֲוֹנֵנוּ	*Et iniquitates nostræ.*	And our iniquities.
—	וַעֲוֹנֹתֵינוּ	*Et iniquitates nostrum.*	And our iniquities.
—	וַעֲוֹנֹתָם	*Et iniquitates eorum.*	And their iniquities.
עוף	וְעוֹף ר'	*Et volucer, avis.*	And a fowl, bird.
עפר	וְעוֹפֶרֶת־־עֹפֶ'	*Et plumbum.*	And lead.
עור	וְעִוֵּר	*Et cæcus.*	And blind.
—	וְעוּרָה	*Et evigila.*	And awake thou.
—	וְעוֹרִי	*Et cutis mea.*	And my skin.
—	וְעוֹרָם	*Et cutis eorum.*	And their skin.
—	וְעוֹרֵר	*Et excitabit.*	And he shall stir up.
—	וְעוֹרַרְתִּי	*Et excitavi.*	And I have raised up.
עז	וָעֵז ר'	*Et capra.*	And a she-goat.
עזז	וָעֹז ר'	*Et robur.*	And strength.
עזב	וַעֲזֹב	*Et relinque.*	And leave thou.
—	וְעָזַב	*Et relinquet.*	And he shall leave.
—	וְעֹזֵב	*Et deserens.*	And forsaking.
—	וְעָזְבוּ	*Et relinquet.*	And they will leave.
—	וַעֲזָבוּךָ	*Et relinquent te.*	And they shall leave thee.
—	וְעִזְבוֹנַיִךְ	*Et nundinæ tuæ.*	And thy fairs.
—	וְעֹזְבֵי	*Et deserentes.*	And they that forsake.
—	וַעֲזָבַנִי	*Et deseret me.*	And he will forsake me.
—	וַעֲזַבְתִּים	*Et derelinquam eos*	And I will forsake them.

ROOTS.	DERIVATIVES.	VERSIO.	SIGNIFICATION.
עזב	וַעֲזַבְתֶּם	*Et derelinquetis.*	And ye will leave, forsake.
עזז	וְעֻזּוֹ וֶעֱזוּזוֹ	*Et robur ejus.*	And his strength.
עזב	וְעָזוֹב	*Et deserere.*	And to forsake.
—	וְעָזוּב	*Et derelictus.*	And left, forsaken.
עזז	וֶעֱזוּז	*Et robur, potentia.*	And the strength, power.
—	וְעִזּוּז	*Et robustus.*	And strong.
עז	וְעֻזֶּךָ	*Et robur ejus.*	And his strength.
—	וְעִזִּים	*Et capræ tuæ.*	And thy she-goats.
עזר	וְעֵזֶר	*Et caprini* pili [*trum*	And goats' hair.
—	וְעָזְרֵנוּ	*Et auxilium nos-*	And our help.
—	וְעָזְרֵנִי	*Et auxiliare nobis.*	And help thou us.
—	וַעֲזַרְתֶּם	*Et adjuvabitis.*	And ye shall help.
עטה	וְעָטָה	*Et induet.*	And he shall clothe.
—	וְעָטוּ	*Et tegent.*	And they shall cover.
—	וְעֹטְךָ	*Et amiciens te.*	And he that clotheth thee.
עטר	וַעֲטֶרֶת	*Et corona.*	And a crown.
עין	וְעַיִן־־עֵין	*Et oculus.*	And an eye.
—	וְעֵינָיו־־נָיו	*Et oculi ejus.* [*lius.*	And his eyes.
—	וְעֵינוֹ	*Et color, species il-*	And his colour, appearance.
—	וְעֵינַי	*Et oculi mei.*	And my eyes.
—	וְעֵינֵי	*Et oculi.*	And the eyes.
—	וְעֵינִי	*Et oculus meus.*	And my eye.
—	וְעֵינֵיהוּ	*Et oculi ejus.*	And his eyes.
—	וְעֵינֵיהֶם	*Et oculi eorum.*	And their eyes.
—	וְעֵינֶיךָ־־נֶיךָ	*Et oculi tui.*	And thy eyes.
—	וְעֵינֵיכֶם־־נֵכֶם	*Et oculi vestri.*	And your eyes.
—	וְעֵינַיִם־־עֵינַיִן	*Et oculi.*	And the eyes.
—	וְעֵינֵינוּ	*Et oculi nostri.*	And our eyes.
עיף	וְעָיֵף	*Et defessus.*	And weary.
עיר	וְעִיר וָ״	*Et civitas.*	And a city.
—	וְעַיִר	*Et pullus.*	And a fole, colt.
—	וַעֲיָרִם	*Et pulli.*	And foles.
ערם	וְעֵירֹם	*Et nudus.*	And naked.
עיש	וְעַיִשׁ	*Et Arcturus.*	And Arcturus.
עכבר	וְעַכְבְּרֵי	*Et mures.*	And the mice.
עכר	וְעֹכֵר	*Et turbans.*	And he that troubleth.
—	וַעֲכַרְתֶּם	*Et conturbabitis.*	And ye will trouble.

ROOTS.	DERIVATIVES.	VERSIO.	SIGNIFICATION.
עלה	וְעַל	*Et super, juxta, cum contra, de, per.*	And upon, above, near, according to, with, against, from, of, by, through.
—	וְעַל אדוֹתֶיךָ	*Et propter te.*	And for thee, on thy account.
—	וְעַל אֲשֶׁר	*Et quia.*	And because.
—	וְעַל דְּבַר	*Et propter.*	And because of, on account of
—	וְעַל יָדוֹ	*Et post eum.*	And after him.
—	וְעַל מָה	*Et quare.*	And wherefore.
—	וְעַל פְּנֵי	*Et e regione.*	And over against.
—	וְעֵלָּא	*Et supra.*	And above.
—	וַעֲלֵה	*Et ascende.*	And go thou up.
—	וְעָלָה	*Et ascendit, ascendet*	And he went up, will go up.
—	וְעֹלָה־־לַת	*Et holocaustum.*	And a burnt-offering.
—	וְעָלֵהוּ	*Et folium ejus.*	And his leaf.
—	וַעֲלוּ	*Et ascendite.*	And go ye up.
—	וְעָלוּ	*Et ascenderunt, ascendent.*	And they went up, will go up.
—	וְעֻלּוֹ	*Et jugum ejus.*	And his yoke.
—	וְעֹלוֹת־־לֹת	*Et holocausta.*	And burnt offerings.
עלז	וְעָלֵז	*Et exultans.*	And he that rejoiceth.
—	וְעִלְזוּ	*Et exultate.*	And rejoice ye.
—	וְעִלְזִי	*Et exulta.*	And rejoice thou.
עלט	וַעֲלָטָה	*Et caligo.*	And the dark.
עלה	וַעֲלֵי	*Et folia, super.*	And leaves, upon.
—	וְעָלַי	*Et super, ad me.*	And upon, to me.
—	וְעָלֶיהָ	*Et super, propter.*	And upon, because of her.
—	וַעֲלֵיהֶם	*Et super, apud, prætereos. [juxta eum*	And over, with, beside them.
—	וְעָלָיו־לָיו	*Et super, præter,*	And upon, by, next to him.
—	וְעֶלְיוֹן	*Et excelsus.*	And high.
—	וַעֲלִיּוֹת	*Et cœnacula.*	And the upper chambers.
—	וַעֲלִיּוֹתָיו־־יֹּתָיו	*Et cœnacula ejus.*	And his upper chambers.
—	וְעָלֶיךָ	*Et super, in te.*	And upon, towards thee.
—	וְעָלֵימוֹ	*Et super, in eos.*	And upon, towards them.
—	וְעָלִינוּ	*Et ascendemus.*	And we will go up. [go up.
—	וְעָלִיתָ	*Et ascende, ascendes*	And go thou up, thou shalt
—	וַעֲלִיָּתוֹ	*Et ascensus ejus.*	And his ascent.

ROOTS	DERIVATIVES.	VERSIO.	SIGNIFICATION.
עלה	וְעָלִיתִי	*Et ascendam.*	And I will go up.
—	וַעֲלִיתֶם	*Et ascendetis.*	And ye shall go up.
עלל	וְעֹלְלֵיהֶם	*Et parvuli eorum.*	And their children.
—	וְעֹלַלְתִּי	*Et illusi.*	And I have abused.
עלם	וַעֲלָמוֹת	*Et puellæ, virgines.*	And damsels, virgins.
עלה	וְעָלְתָה	*Et ascendet.*	And she will go up.
—	וְעָלָתוֹ	*Et ascensus ejus.*	And his ascent.
עמם	וְעָם וָעָם וְעָם	*Et populus.*	And people.
עם	וְעִם	*Et cum.*	And with.
עמד	וַעֲמֹד	*Et sta.*	And stand thou.
—	וְעָמַד וְעָמַד	*Et stetit, stabit.*	And he stood, shall stand.
—	וְעָמֹד	*Et stare.*	And to stand.
—	וְעֹמֵד	*Et stans.*	And standing.
—	וְעָמְדָה	*Et stabit.*	And she shall stand.
—	וְעַמֻּדָיו־דָיו־מוֹ	*Et columnæ ejus.*	And his pillars.
—	וְעָמְדוּ	*Et steterunt, stabunt*	And they stood, will stand.
—	וְעִמְדוּ	*Et assistite.*	And stand ye.
—	וְעַמֻּדֵי־מוֹ	*Et columnæ.*	And the pillars.
עם	וְעִמָּדִי	*Et mecum.*	And with me.
עמד	וְעַמֻּדֵיהֶם	*Et columnæ eorum.*	And their pillars.
—	וְעַמֻּדִים	*Et columnæ.*	And the pillars.
—	וְעָמַדְנוּ	*Et consistemus.*	And we will stand still.
—	וְעָמַדְתָּ	*Et stabis.*	And thou shalt stand.
—	וְעָמַדְתִּי	*Et stabo.*	And I will stand.
—	וַעֲמַדְתֶּם	*Et stabitis.*	And ye shall stand.
עמם	וְעָמָּה	*Et populus.*	And a people.
—	וְעַמָּהּ	*Et populus ejus.*	And her people.
עם	וְעִמְּהוֹן־מָּהֶם	*Et cum eis.*	And with them.
עמם	וְעַמּוֹ	*Et populus ejus.*	And his people.
עם	וְעִמּוֹ	*Et cum eo.*	And with him.
עמד	וְעַמּוּד	*Et columna.*	And the pillar.
—	וְעַמּוּדֶיהָ	*Et columnæ ejus.*	And her pillars.
עמם	וְעַמֵּי וְעַמִּים	*Et populi.*	And the people, nations.
—	וְעַמִּי	*Et populus meus.*	And my people.
—	וְעַמְּךָ־מְּךָ־מֶּךָ	*Et populus tuus.*	And thy people.
עם	וְעִמְּךָ	*Et tecum.*	And with thee.
—	וְעִמָּכֶם	*Et vobiscum.*	And with you.

ROOTS.	DERIVATIVES.	VERSIO.	SIGNIFICATION.
עמל	וְעָמָל	*Et labor.*	And the labour.
—	וְעָמָל	*Et molestia, vexatio*	And the trouble, vexation.
—	וַעֲמָלוֹ	*Et labor ejus.*	And his labour.
—	וַעֲמָלִי	*Et labor meus.*	And my labour.
עמם	וַעֲמָמִים	*Et populi.*	And the people, nations.
עם	וְעִמָּנוּ	*Et nobiscum.*	And with us.
עמס	וְעֹמְסִים	*Et onerantes.*	And loading, burdening.
עמק	וְעָמֹק	*Et profundus, pro-*	And deep, deeper.
—	וְעֵמֶק	*Et vallis.* [*fundior.*	And the valley.
—	וַעֲמָקִים	*Et valles.*	And the vallies.
ענב	וַעֲנָבִים	*Et uvæ.*	And the grapes.
ענג	וְהָעֲנֻגָּה	*Et delicata.* [*mabit*	And delicate.
ענה	וְעָנָה	*Et testatus est, cla-*	And he testified, will cry.
—	וְעֹנֶה	*Et respondens, dis-* *cipulus.* [*debunt.*	And he that answereth, a scholar. [answer.
—	וְעָנוּ	*Et loquentur, respon-*	And they shall speak, shall
—	וְעַנּוּ	*Et affligite, humiliate*	And afflict, humble ye.
—	וְעִנּוּ	*Et affligent.* [*etudo.*	And they shall afflict.
—	וַעֲנָוָה	*Et humilitas, mansu-*	And humility, meekness.
—	וַעֲנָוִים	*Et humiles, mansueti*	And the humble, lowly, meek.
—	וְעַנְוְתְךָ	*Et mansuetudo tua.*	And thy gentleness.
—	וְעָנִי	*Et pauper, afflictus.*	And the poor, afflicted.
—	וַעֲנִיָּו	*Et afflicti ejus.*	And his afflicted.
—	וַעֲנִיֶּיךָ	*Et pauperes tui.*	And thy poor.
—	וַעֲנִיִּים	*Et pauperes, egeni.*	And the poor, needy.
—	וְעִנְיַן	*Et occupatio, nego-*	And occupation, business.
—	וְעָנִית	*Et loqueris.* [*tium.*	And thou shalt speak.
—	וַעֲנִיתָם	*Et respondebis eis.*	And thou wilt answer them.
—	וְעִנִּיתֶם	*Et affligetis.*	And ye shall afflict.
ענן	וַעֲנַן וְעָנָן	*Et nubes.*	And the cloud.
ענה	וַעֲנֵנִי־נִי	*Et exaudi me.*	And hear thou me.
—	וְעָנָנִי	*Et exaudivit me.*	And he heard me.
—	וְעֹנְנִים	*Et divini.*	And soothsayers, diviners.
ענן	וַעֲנָנְךָ	*Et nubes tua.*	And thy cloud.
ענף	וַעֲנַף וְעָנָף	*Et ramus.*	And a branch.
—	וַעֲנֵפָה	*Et ramosa.*	And full of branches.
—	וַעֲנָפֶיהָ	*Et rami ejus*	And her boughs.

ROOTS.	DERIVATIVES.	VERSIO.	SIGNIFICATION.
ענק	וַעֲנָקִים	*Et torques.*	And a chain.
ענש	וְעָנְשׁוּ	*Et mulctabunt.*	And they shall amerce, fine.
ענה	וְעָנְתָה	*Et respondebit, testabitur.*	And she shall answer, shall testify.
עון	וְעֹנָתָהּ	*Et cohabitatio ejus, officium matrimonii*	And her cohabitation, duty of marriage.
ענה	וַעַנְוְתְךָ	*Et mansuetudo tua.*	And thy gentleness.
—	וְעִנִּתִךְ	*Et afflixi te.*	And I have afflicted thee.
עסס	וְעַסּוֹתֶם	*Et conculcabitis.*	And ye shall tread under foot
עוף	וְעָפוּ	*Et volabunt.*	And they shall fly.
עפא	וְעָפְיֵהּ	*Et ramus, frons ejus*	And his branch, leaf.
עוף	וְעַפְעַפָּיו	*Et palpebræ ejus.*	And his eyelids.
—	וְעַפְעַפֶּיךָ	*Et palpebræ tuæ.*	And thy eyelids.
—	וְעַפְעַפֵּינוּ	*Et palpebræ nostræ.*	And our eyelids.
עפר	וַעֲפַר וְעָפָר	*Et pulvis [pulveravit*	And the dust. [with dust.
—	וְעִפַּר	*Et pulverem sparsit,*	And he scattered dust, covered
—	וַעֲפָרָהּ	*Et pulvis ejus.*	And her dust.
—	וְעַפְרוֹת	*Et pulveres.*	And dust.
—	וַעֲפָרֶךָ	*Et pulvis tuus.*	And thy dust.
—	וַעֲפָרָם	*Et pulvis eorum.*	And their dust.
עוץ	וָעֵץ וְעֵץ	*Et arbor, lignum.*	And the tree, wood.
עצב	וְעִצְּבוּ	*Et dolore affecerunt.*	And they vexed, grieved.
—	וַעֲצָבֶיךָ	*Et labores tui.*	And thy labours.
יעץ	וְעֵצָה	*Et consilium.*	And counsel.
עצב	וַעֲצוּבַת	*Et dolens.*	And grieving, distressed.
עצם	וְעָצוּם	*Et validus, potens.*	And strong, mighty.
—	וַעֲצוּמִים--צֻמִ״	*Et robusti, potentes.*	And the strong, mighty.
עצר	וְעָצוּר	*Et clausus, cohibitus*	And shut up, restrained.
עוץ	וַעֲצֵי וְעֵצִים	*Et arbores, ligna.*	And the trees, wood, timber.
—	וְעֵצַיִךְ	*Et ligna tua.*	And thy timber.
עצל	וְעָצֵל	*Et piger. [valuit.*	And the slothful. [prevail.
עצם	וְעָצַם	*Et validus erit, præ-*	And he shall be strong, shall
—	וְעֶצֶם	*Et os.*	And a bone.
—	וְעֹצֵם	*Et obstipans.*	And shutting.
—	וְעֹצֶם	*Et robur.*	And strength.
—	וַעֲצָמוֹת	*Et ossa.*	And bones.
—	וְעַצְמוֹתַי	*Et ossa mea.*	And my bones.

ROOTS.	DERIVATIVES.	VERSIO.	SIGNIFICATION.
עצם	וְעַצְמוֹתֵיכֶם	*Et ossa vestra.*	And your bones.
—	וַעֲצָמַי	*Et ossa mea.*	And my bones.
—	וְעַצְמִי	*Et os meum.*	And my bone.
—	וְעַצְמֹתֵיהֶם	*Et ossa eorum.*	And their bones.
—	וְעַצְמֹתֶיךָ	*Et ossa tua.*	And thy bones.
עצר	וַעֲצֹר	*Et cohibere.*	And to withhold.
—	וְעָצַר	*Et claudet.*	And he will shut up.
—	וְעֶצֶר	*Et cohibitio.*	And restraint.
—	וַעֲצָרָה	*Et solennitas.*	And the solemn assembly.
—	וְעָצַרְתִּי	*Et claudam.*	And I shall shut.
יעץ	וַעֲצַת	*Et consilium.*	And the counsel.
—	וַעֲצָתוֹ	*Et consilium ejus.*	And his counsel.
עקב	וְעִקְּבוֹתֶיךָ	*Et vestigia tua.*	And thy footsteps.
עקרב	וְעַקְרָב	*Et scorpio.*	And the scorpion.
עקר	וַעֲקָרָה	*Et sterilis.*	And the barren women.
עקש	וְעִקֵּשׁ	*Et perversum.*	And perverse.
ערב	וָעֶרֶב	*Et vespera.*	And evening.
—	וְעֹרֵב	*Et corvus.*	And the raven.
—	וַעֲרָבָה	*Et solitudo.*	And a desert, wilderness.
—	וְעָרְבָה	*Et suavis, grata erit*	And she will be sweet, pleasant
—	וְעַרְבֵי	*Et salices.* [*emptæ.*	And willows.
—	וְעֹרְבֵי	*Et negotiantes, prox-*	And traders, brokers, agents.
—	וְעַרְבָתָהּ	*Et solitudo ejus.*	And her desert.
ער	וְעֹרָה	*Et nudamini.*	And be ye made bare.
ערם	וְעָרֹם־רוֹם וְעֵרֹם	*Et nudus.*	And naked.
—	וְעָרוּם	*Et callidus, astutus.*	And the cunning, crafty.
—	וַעֲרוּמִים	*Et callidi.*	And the cunning.
ערה	וְעֶרְוַת	*Et nudatio, probrum*	And the exposure, dishonour.
—	וְעֶרְוַת	*Et nuditas.*	And the nakedness.
עיר	וְעָרֵי וְעָרִים	*Et civitates.*	And the cities.
—	וְעָרֶיהָ	*Et civitates ejus.*	And her cities.
ערה	וְעֶרְיָה	*Et discooperta.*	And uncovered.
עיר	וְעָרֵיהֶם	*Et civitates eorum.*	And their cities.
—	וְעָרָיו	*Et civitates ejus.*	And his cities.
—	וְעָרֶיךָ	*Et civitates tuæ.*	And thy cities.
—	וְעָרֵיכֶם	*Et civitates vestræ.*	And your cities. [ble.
ערץ	וְעָרִיצִים	*Et fortes, terribiles.*	And the strong, mighty, terri-

ROOTS.	DERIVATIVES.	VERSIO.	SIGNIFICATION.
ערד	וְעָרַךְ	*Et ordinabit.* [tium	And he will set in order.
—	וְעֵרֶךְ	*Et apparatus ves-*	And a suit *of clothes.*
—	וְעָרְכוּ	*Et disponent, instru-*	And they will dispose, array.
—	וְעָרַכְתָּ	*Et ordinabis.* [*ent.*	And thou shalt set in order.
ערל	וְעָרֵל וְעָרֶל	*Et incircumcisus.*	And uncircumcised.
—	וַעֲרֵלִי	*Et præputiati.*	And the uncircumcised.
—	וַעֲרַלְתֶּם	*Et præputiatum habebitis.*	And ye shall count as uncircumcised.
ערם	וְעַרְמוֹן	*Et platanus.*	And the plane-tree.
—	וְעַרְמֹנִים	*Et platani.*	And the plane-trees. [neck.
ערף	וְעָרְפוּ	*Et decollabunt.*	And they shall strike off the
—	וְעָרְפְּכֶם	*Et cervix vestra.*	And your neck.
ערפל	וַעֲרָפֶל	*Et caligo.*	And darkness.
ערף	וְעָרְפָּם	*Et cervix eorum.*	And their neck.
—	וַעֲרַפְתּוֹ	*Et cervicem ejus franges.*	And thou shalt break his neck
עקר	וְעֹרְקַי	*Et rosiones meæ.*	And my gnawings.
עור	וְעֹרֹת	*Et pelles.*	And skins.
עשב	וְעֵשֶׂב	*Et herba.*	And the herb, grass.
—	וְעִשְׂבָּא	*Et herba.*	And grass.
עשה	וַעֲשֵׂה	*Et fac.*	And do, make thou.
—	וְעָשָׂה	*Et fecit, egit, paravit, executus est.*	And he made, did, prepared, executed, performed.
—	וְעָשֹׂה	*Et facere.*	And to do, make, perform.
—	וְעֹשָׂהּ	*Et faciens eam.*	And he that maketh her or it.
—	וְעֹשֵׂה וְעֹשֶׂה	*Et faciens, operans.*	And making, doing, working.
—	וְעָשָׂהוּ	*Et faciet eum.*	And he will make him.
—	וַעֲשׂוּ	*Et facite.*	And do, make ye.
—	וְעָשׂוּ וְעָ׳	*Et feccrunt, agent.*	And they have made, will do.
—	וְעָשׂוּי	*Et factus.*	And made.
—	וַעֲשׂוּיָה	*Et facta.*	And made.
עשק	וַעֲשׁוּקִים	*Et oppressi.*	And the oppressed.
עשה	וְעֹשׂוֹת	*Et facientes.*	And they that make, do.
—	וַעֲשִׂי	*Et fac.* [*tes.*	And make, do thou.
—	וְעֹשֵׂי וְעֹשִׂים	*Et facientes, paran-*	And they that do, preparing.
—	וְעָשִׂינוּ	*Et faciemus.*	And we will do.
עשר	וְעָשִׁיר	*Et dives.*	And the rich.

ROOTS.	DERIVATIVES.	VERSIO.	SIGNIFICATION.
עשר	וַעֲשִׁירִים	*Et divites.*	And the rich.
—	וַעֲשִׂירִית־־רִת	*Et decima* pars.	And a tenth part.
עשה	וְעָשִׂיתָ	*Et facies.*	And thou shalt do.
—	וְעָשִׂיתִי־־תִ	*Et feci, faciam.*	And I did, made, will do.
—	וַעֲשִׂיתִיהוּ	*Et parabo eum.*	And I will prepare it.
—	וַעֲשִׂיתִיו	*Et faciam eum.*	And I will perform it.
—	וַעֲשִׂיתָם	*Et facies eos.*	And thou shalt do them.
—	וַעֲשִׂיתֶם	*Et facietis.*	And ye shall do.
—	וַעֲשִׂיתִם	*Et faciam eos.*	And I will make them.
עשן	וְעָשָׁן	*Et fumus.*	And smoke.
עשק	וְעֹשֵׁק	*Et opprimens.*	And he that oppresseth.
—	וְעָשְׁקוּ	*Et oppresserunt.*	And they have oppressed.
עשר	וְעֶשֶׂר וְעֶ׳	*Et decem.*	And ten.
—	וְעֹשֶׁר וְעֹשֶׁר	*Et divitiæ.*	And riches.
—	וַעֲשָׂרָה־־שֶׂרֶת	*Et decem.*	And ten.
—	וְעִשָּׂרוֹן־־רֹן	*Et decima* pars.	And a tenth *part.*
—	וְעֶשְׂרִים־־רִין	*Et viginti, vicesimus*	And twenty, the twentieth.
עשה	וְעָשָׂת	*Et proferet.*	And she shall bring forth[pare
—	וְעָשְׂתָה	*Et faciet, parabit.*	And she shall make, do, pre-
עשתר	וַעֲשְׁתְּרוֹת־־לֹת	*Et greges.*	And flocks.
עתת	וְעַתָּ־־תָּה	*Et nunc.*	And now.
—	וְעֵת	*Et tempus.*	And a time.
עתד	וַעֲתְּדָהּ	*Et para eam.*	And prepare thou her or it.
—	וַעֲתּוּדִים	*Et hirci.*	And he-goats.
—	וַעֲתִידֹתֵיהֶם	*Et thesauri eorum.*	And their treasures.
עתק	וְעַתִּיק	*Et antiquus.* [*dantia*	And the ancient.
עתר	וַעֲתַר	*Et densitas, abun-*	And thickness, abundance.
	ופ		
פה	וּפֹא	*Et hic.*	And here.
פאר	וּפְאֵרֵכֶם	*Et tiaræ vestræ.*	And your bonnets, turbans.
פאה	וּפְאַת	*Et angulus, latus.*	And the corner, side.
פגע	וָפֶגַע	*Et casus, occasio*[*et*	And chance, occasion.
—	וּפָגַע	*Et pervenit, perveni-*	And he reached, will reach.
—	וּפְגַע	*Et irrue.*	And do thou fall upon.
—	וּפְגָעוֹ	*Et occurret ei.*	And he will meet him.
—	וּפִגְעוּ	*Et orate.*	And pray, intreat ye.

ROOTS.	DERIVATIVES.	VERSIO.	SIGNIFICATION.
פגע	וּפָגַעְתָּ	*Et occurres.*	And thou shalt meet.
פגר	וּפִגְרֵי וּפְגָרִים	*Et cadavera.*	And the carcases, dead bodies.
—	וּפִגְרֵיהֶם	*Et cadavera eorum.*	And their carcases.
—	וּפִגְרֵיכֶם	*Et cadavera vestra.*	And your carcases.
פגש	וּפָגְשׁוּ	*Et occurrent.*	And they shall meet.
פדה	וּפָדָה	*Et redimet.*	And he shall redeem.
—	וּפְדוּיָו	*Et redempti ejus.*	And his redeemed.
—	וּפְדוּיֵי	*Et redempti.*	And the ransomed, redeemed
—	וּפְדֵנוּ	*Et redime nos.*	And redeem thou us.
—	וּפְדִתִיךָ	*Et liberabo te.*	And I will deliver thee.
פה	וּפֶה וּפְנִי	*Et os.*	And the mouth.
—	וּפֹה	*Et hic.*	And here.
פול	וּפוֹל	*Et faba.*	And a bean.
פוח	וָפָח	*Et laqueus.*	And the snare.
פחד	וָפַחַד וּפ׳	*Et pavor.*	And a, the fear.
—	וּפָחַד	*Et pavebit.*	And he shall fear.
—	וּפָחֲדוּ	*Et expavescent.*	And they shall fear.
—	וּפַחְדּוֹ	*Et pavor ejus.*	And his fear.
—	וּפָחַדְתָּ	*Et pavebis.*	And thou shalt fear.
פחה	וּפַחֲוֹות	*Et duces, principes.*	And the captains, governors.
—	וּפַחוֹת־־חֲוָתָא	*Et duces.*	And the leaders, governors.
פחז	וּפֹחֲזִים	*Et leves.*	And the light, inconstant.
נפח	וּפְחִי	*Et effla.*	And breathe thou.
פוח	וּפַחִים	*Et laquei.*	And snares.
פחת	וָפַחַת	*Et fovea.*	And a, the pit.
פטר	וּפְטוּרֵי־־טָרֵי	*Et apertiones.* [*nitus*	And openings. [born.
—	וּפֶטֶר	*Et apertio, primoge-*	And the opening, the first-
פה	וּפִי	*Et os, os meum.*	And the mouth, my mouth.
פיד	וּפִיד	*Et calamitas.*	And the calamity.
פה	וּפִיהָ	*Et os ejus.*	And her mouth.
—	וּפִיהוּ	*Et os ejus.*	And his mouth.
—	וּפִיהֶם	*Et os eorum.*	And their mouth.
—	וּפִיו	*Et os ejus.*	And his mouth.
פלגש	וּפִילַגְשֵׁהוּ	*Et concubina ejus.*	And his concubine.
—	וּפִילַגְשׁוֹ	*Et concubina ejus.*	And his concubine.
—	וּפִילַגְשִׁי	*Et concubina mea.*	And my concubine.
—	וּפִילַגְשָׁיו	*Et concubinæ ejus.*	And his concubines.

ROOTS.	DERIVATIVES.	VERSIO.	SIGNIFICATION.
פלגש	וּפִילַגְשִׁים	*Et concubinæ.*	And concubines.
פוק	וּפִיק וּפָק	*Et vacillatio.*	And a tottering.
פלא	וָפֶלֶא	*Et mirabile.*	And a wonder.
פלג	וּפְלַג	*Et dimidium.* [*tri.*	And the half.
פלח	וּפָלְחֵי	*Et servientes, minis-*	And they that serve, ministers
פלט	וּפִלְטוּ	*Et evadent.* [*gi.*	And they shall escape.
—	וּפְלֵטִים	*Et evadentes, profu-*	And they that escape.
—	וּפָלִיט	*Et profugus.*	And one who escapeth.
—	וּפְלֵיטָה--טַת	*Et residuum.*	And the remainder.
—	וּפְלִיטֵי	*Et profugi.*	And the fugitives.
פלל	וּפִלְלוֹ	*Et judicabit eum.*	And he shall judge him.
פום	וּפֶם	*Et os.*	And the mouth.
פון	וּפֶן	*Et ne forte.*	And lest perhaps. [look.
פנה	וּפָנָה	*Et vertet se, aspiciet*	And he will turn himself, will
—	וּפַנֵּה	*Et parabit.*	And he shall prepare.
—	וּפִנּוּ	*Et purgabunt.*	And they will clear.
—	וּפָנַי	*Et facies mea.*	And my face.
—	וּפְנֵי	*Et facies, vultus.*	And the face, countenance.
—	וּפָנֶיהָ	*Et facies ejus.*	And her face.
—	וּפְנֵיהֶם	*Et facies eorum.*	And their face.
—	וּפָנָיו	*Et facies ejus.*	And his face
—	וּפָנֶיךָ	*Et facies tua.*	And thy face.
—	וּפָנִים	*Et facies.* [*cies*	And faces. [regard.
—	וּפָנִיתָ	*Et vertes te, respi-*	And thou shalt turn, shalt
—	וּפָנִיתִי	*Et verti me, aspexi, vertam me, respi-*	And I turned, looked, will turn, will have respect.
פסח	וּפָסַח	*Et transibit.* [*ciam.*	And he will pass over.
—	וּפִסֵּחַ	*Et claudus.*	And the lame.
—	וּפָסַחְתִּי	*Et transibo.*	And I will pass over.
—	וָפְסִי	*Vophsi.*	Vophsi, N. M.
פסל	וּפְסִילֵי	*Et sculptilia.*	And the graven images.
—	וּפְסִילֵיהֶם	*Et sculptilia eorum.*	And their graven images.
—	וּפֶסֶל	*Et sculptile.*	And the graven image.
—	וּפִסְלִי	*Et sculptile meum.*	And my graven image.
פעל	וּפָעַל	*Et operabitur.*	And he will work.
—	וּפֹעַל	*Et opus.*	And the work.
—	וּפֹעֵל	*Et operans.*	And he that worketh.

ROOTS.	DERIVATIVES.	VERSIO.	SIGNIFICATION.
פעל	וּפָעֳלוֹ	*Et opus ejus*, merces *operis ejus.*	And his work, *the reward* of his work.
—	וּפֹעֲלֵי	*Et operantes.*	And they that work.
—	וּפָעָלְךָ	*Et opus tuum.*	And thy work.
—	וּפָעָלְכֶם	*Et opus vestrum.*	And your work.
—	וּפְעֻלָּתוֹ	*Et opus ejus.*	And his work.
—	וּפְעֻלָּתִי	*Et opus meum.*	And my work.
פעם	וּפַעֲמֹנֵי	*Et tintinnabula.*	And the bells.
פער	וּפָֽעֲרָה	*Et aperuit.*	And he opened.
פצה	וּפֹצֶה	*Et aperiens.*	And opening,
פצע	וּפָצֹעַ	*Et vulnerando.*	And in wounding.
פצה	וּפָצְתָה	*Et aperiet.*	And she will open.
פקד	וּפְקֹד	*Et visita.*	And visit thou.
—	וּפָקְדוּ	*Et præficient.*	And they shall appoint, set over
—	וּפִקְדוּ	*Et recensete.*	And number ye. [of them
—	וּפְקֻדֵיהֶם	*Et numerati eorum.*	And those that were numbered
—	וּפְקֻדָיו	*Et numerati ejus.*	And those that were numbered
—	וּפָקְדֵנִי	*Et visita me.*	And visit thou me. [of him
—	וּפָֽקַדְתָּ	*Et visitabis.*	And thou shalt visit. [charge.
—	וּפְקֻדַּת	*Et visitatio, custodia*	And the visitation, custody,
—	וּפָֽקַדְתִּי	*Et visitabo, puniam.*	And I will visit, punish.
—	וּפְקֻדָּתְךָ	*Et visitatio, cura tua*	And thy visitation, charge.
—	וּפְקַדְתֶּם	*Et præficietis.*	And ye shall appoint. [up.
—	וּפְקֻדָּתָם	*Et depositum eorum*	And that which they have laid
—	וּפְקוּדֵי	*Et numerati.*	And those that were numbered
—	וּפָקִיד וּפְקִיד	*Et præfectus.*	And the superintendent, over-
פקע	וּפְקָעִים	*Et cucurbitæ.*	And knops, gourds. [seer.
פר	וּפַר	*Et juvencus.*	And a, the bullock.
פרא	וּפְרָאִים	*Et onagri.*	And the wild asses.
פרד	וָפֶרֶד	*Et mulus.*	And the mule.
—	וּפְרָדִים	*Et muli.*	And mules.
פרדס	וּפַרְדֵּסִים	*Et horti, pomaria.*	And gardens, orchards.
פר	וּפָרָה	*Et vacca.*	And the cow.
פרה	וּפָרוּ	*Et fœcundi erunt.*	And they shall be fruitful.
פרח	וָפָרַח־־פֶּ״ וְ״	*Et flos.* [*bit*	And the flower. [flourish.
—	וּפָרַח	*Et germinabit, flore-*	And he shall spring up, bud,
—	וּפְרָחֶיהָ	*Et flores ejus.*	And his, her flowers.

ROOTS.	DERIVATIVES.	VERSIO.	SIGNIFICATION.
פרח	וּפִרְחָם	*Et flos eorum.*	And their flower, blossom.
פרט	וּפֶרֶט	*Et uva* seorsum decidens, relicta tempore vindemiæ.	And a grape *falling from the cluster, or left in the time of the vintage.*
פרה	וּפְרִי	*Et fructus.*	And the fruit.
—	וּפִרְיוֹ	*Et fructus ejus.*	And his fruit.
—	וּפֶרְיְכֶם	*Et fructus vester.*	And your fruit.
פר	וּפָרִים	*Et juvenci.*	And the bullocks.
פרה	וּפָרִינוּ	*Et fœcundi erimus.*	And we shall be fruitful.
פרץ	וּפְרִיץ	*Et rapax.*	And ravenous, rapacious.
פרה	וּפְרִיתֶם	*Et crescetis.*	And ye shall increase.
פרס	וּפַרְסָה	*Et ungula.*	And the hoof.
—	וּפַרְסוֹת	*Et ungulæ.*	And the hoofs.
—	וּפַרְסֵיהֶן	*Et ungulæ earum.*	And their hoofs.
—	וּפַרְסִין	*Et dividentes.*	And dividing.
—	וּפַרְסֹתַיִךְ	*Et ungulæ tuæ.*	And thy hoofs.
פרע	וּפָרַע	*Et deteget.*	And he shall uncover.
—	וּפֶרַע	*Et coma, cæsaries.*	And the hair.
פרץ	וּפָרַץ	*Et diruet.*	And he shall break down.
—	וּפֹרֵץ	*Et rumpens.*	And he that breaketh.
—	וּפְרָצִים	*Et rupturæ.*	And the breaches.
—	וּפָרַצְתָּ	*Et prorumpes, crescès.*	And thou shalt break forth, increase.
פרק	וּפְרַק	*Et jusculum.*	And the broth.
—	וּפֵרַקְתָּ	*Et franges.*	And thou shalt break.
פרש	וּפָרַשׂ	*Et expandet.*	And he shall spread forth.
—	וּפָרְשׂוּ	*Et expandent, discident.*	And they shall spread abroad, shall cut asunder
-	וּפִרְשׁוֹ	*Et fimus ejus.*	And his dung.
—	וּפֹרְשֵׂי	*Et expandentes.*	And they that spread forth.
—	וּפָרָשָׁיו	*Et equites ejus.*	And his horsemen.
—	וּפָרָשִׁים	*Et equites.*	And horsemen.
—	וּפָרָשַׁת	*Et declaratio.*	And the declaration.
—	וּפֵרַשְׂתָּ	*Et extendes.*	And thou shall stretch out.
—	וּפֵרַשְׂתִּי	*Et expandam.*	And I will spread out.
פרש	וּפָשׁוּ	*Et sese diffundent.*	And they shall spread themselves.
פשט	וּפָשַׁט	*Et exuet.*	And he shall put off.
—	וּפָשַׁטְתָּ	*Et irrues.*	And thou shalt fall upon.

ROOTS.	DERIVATIVES.	VERSIO.	SIGNIFICATION.
פשע	וְפֶשַׁע־פֶּ״	*Et prævaricatio.*	And transgression.
—	וּפֹשֵׁעַ	*Et prævaricator.*	And a transgressor.
—	וּפִשְׁעוּ	*Et prævaricamini.*	And transgress ye.
—	וּפְשָׁעַי	*Et prævaricationes meæ.*	And my transgressions.
—	וּפִשְׁעֵיהֶם	*Et prævaricationes* [*eorum.*	And their transgressions.
—	וּפֹשְׁעִים	*Et prævaricantes.*	And the transgressors.
פשר	וּפֵשֶׁר	*Et interpretatio.*	And the interpretation.
—	וּפִשְׁרָא־־רֵה	*Et interpretatio.*	And the interpretation.
—	וּפִשְׁרֵא־־רֵהּ	*Et interpretatio ejus*	And the interpretation of it.
פשת	וּפִשְׁתָּה	*Et linum.*	And the flax.
—	וּפִשְׁתִּי	*Et linum meum.*	And my flax.
—	וּפִשְׁתִּים	*Et lina.*	And flax, linen.
פוש	וּפִשְׁתֶּם	*Et crescetis.*	And ye shall grow up.
פתא	וּפִתְאֹם	*Et subito.*	And suddenly.
פתה	וּפֹתֶה	*Et fatuus.*	And foolish, silly.
פתח	וּפָתַח	*Et aperiet.*	And he shall open.
—	וּפֶתַח	*Et ostium, porta.*	And the door, gate.
—	וּפִתַּח	*Et insculpsit.*	And he engraved.
—	וּפָתְחָה	*Et aperiet.*	And she will open.
—	וּפִתְחָהּ	*Et ostium ejus.*	And her door.
—	וּפִתְּחוּ	*Et aperientur.*	And they shall be opened.
—	וּפִתְחֵיהֶם	*Et ostia eorum.*	And their doors.
—	וּפָתַחְתָּ	*Et aperies.*	And thou shalt open. [loose.
—	וּפִתַּחְתָּ	*Et insculpes, solves.*	And thou shalt engrave, shalt
פתה	וּפֶתִי וּפְתָיִים	*Et simplex, simplices*	And the simple.
פתל	וּפְתִיל	*Et filum.* [*fascia tua*	And a thread. [bracelet.
—	וּפְתִילְךָ	*Et sudarium tuum;*	And thy handkerchief; thy
—	וּפְתַלְתֹּל	*Et contortus.*	And twisted, crooked.
פתן	וָפֶתֶן	*Et aspis.*	And the asp.
פתר	וּפֹתֵר	*Et interpretans.*	And he that interpreteth.
	וצ		
יצא	וְצֵא וָצֵאָה	*Et egredere.*	And go thou forth.
—	וּצְאוּ	*Et egredimini.*	And go ye out.
צאן	וְצֹאן וָצֹאן	*Et grex, oves.*	And a flock, sheep.
—	וְצֹאנִי	*Et grex meus.*	And my flock.

ROOTS.	DERIVATIVES.	VERSIO.	SIGNIFICATION.
צאן	וְצֹאנֵינוּ	*Et greges nostri.*	And our flocks.
—	וְצֹאנְךָ־־נֶךָ	*Et greges tui.*	And thy flocks.
—	וְצֹאנְכֶם	*Et greges vestri.*	And your flocks.
—	וְצֹאנָם	*Et greges eorum.*	And their flocks.
יצא	וְצֶאֱצָאַי	*Et prognati mei.*	And my offspring.
—	וְצֶאֱצָאֵי	*Et prognati.*	And the offspring, descendants
—	וְצֶאֱצָאֶיהָ	*Et prognati ejus.*	And her offspring.
—	וְצֶאֱצָאֵיהֶם	*Et prognati eorum.*	And their offspring.
—	וְצֶאֱצָאָיו	*Et prognati ejus.*	And his offspring.
—	וְצֶאֱצָאֶיךָ	*Et prognati tui.*	And thy offspring.
—	וְצֵאתְךָ	*Et egredi tuum.*	And thy going out.
צבא	וְצָבָא וּצְבָא	*Et exercitus.*	And the host, army.
—	וּצְבָאוֹ	*Et exercitus ejus.*	And his host.
צבה	וּצְבִי	*Et decus, gloria.*	And the beauty, glory.
צבא	וּצְבִי	*Et caprea mas, vel antelaphus.*	And the roe-buck, or antelope
צבה	וְצָבְתָה	*Et intumescet.*	And she shall swell.
צוד	וְצָדוּם	*Et venabuntur eos.*	And they shall hunt them.
צדק	וְצַדִּיק	*Et justus.*	And just, the righteous.
—	וְצַדִּיקִים־דִּקִ׳	*Et justi.*	And the just, righteous.
—	וְצֶדֶק ־ֶ֫ר וּצְדָקָה	*Et justitia.*	And justice, righteousness.
—	וְצִדְקַת	*Et justitia.*	And the righteousness.
—	וְצִדְקָתוֹ	*Et justitia ejus.*	And his righteousness.
—	וְצָדַקְתִּי	*Et justus ero.*	And I shall be righteous.
—	וְצִדְקָתִי	*Et justitia mea.*	And my righteousness.
—	וְצִדְקָתְךָ	*Et justitia tua.*	And thy righteousness.
—	וְצִדְקָתָם	*Et justitia eorum.*	And their righteousness.
צהל	וְצַהֲלוּ	*Et exultate.*	And exult ye.
—	וְצַהֲלִי	*Et exulta.*	And exult thou.
צהר	וְצָהֳרַיִם	*Et meridies.*	And noon.
צוה	וְצַו	*Et præcipe.*	And charge, command thou.
צוד	וְצוּדָה	*Et venare. [bit.*	And hunt thou. [command.
צוה	וְצִוָּה	*Et præcepit, manda-*	And he hath commanded, shall
—	וְצַוּוּ	*Et mandate.*	And command ye.
צוח	וְצִוְחַת	*Et clamor.*	And the cry.
—	וְצִוְחָתֵךְ	*Et clamor tuus.*	And thy cry.
צוה	וְצִוִּיתָ	*Et mandabis.*	And thou shalt command.

ROOTS.	DERIVATIVES.	VERSIO.	SIGNIFICATION.
צוה	וְצִוִּיתָה	*Et præcipies.*	And thou shalt charge.
—	וְצִוִּיתִי	*Et præcipiam.*	And I will command.
—	וְצִוְּךָ	*Et præcipiet tibi.*	And he shall command thee.
צום	וְצוֹם	*Et jejunium.*	And fasting, the fast.
—	וְצוּמוּ	*Et jejunate.*	And fast ye.
צוק	וְצוּקָה	*Et angustia.*	And anguish, distress.
צור	וְצוּר	*Et rupes.*	And the rock.
ציה	וְצִי	*Et navis.*	And a ship.
צוד	וְצֵידָה	*Et viaticum.*	And provision.
ציה	וְצִיָּה	*Et siccum.*	And the dry place.
—	וְצִים	*Et naves.*	And the ships.
ציץ	וְצִיץ	*Et flos.*	And a flower.
ציר	וְצִיר	*Et legatus.*	And an ambassador.
—	וְצִירָם	*Et forma eorum.*	And their form, beauty.
צלח	וְצָלְחָה	*Et transibit.*	And he will pass over.
—	וְצָלְחוּ	*Et transiverunt.*	And they went over.
צלם	וְצֶלֶם	*Et imago, forma, aspectus.*	And the image, form, appearance.
צלל	וְצַלְמָוֶת	*Et umbra mortis.*	And the shadow of death.
צלם	וְצַלְמֵי	*Et imagines.*	And images.
צלע	וְצַלְעוֹת	*Et tabulata.*	And the cielings.
צמא	וְצָמָא	*Et sitis.*	And thirst.
—	וְצָמֵא	*Et sitiens.*	And thirsting.
—	וְצִמָּאוֹן	*Et terra siticulosa.*	And thirsty land.
צמד	וְצֶמֶד	*Et par.*	And a couple.
—	וְצִמְדּוֹ	*Et par boum ejus.*	And his yoke of oxen.
צמח	וְצֶמַח	*Et germen.*	And a bud, branch.
—	וְצָמְחוּ	*Et germinabunt.*	And they shall bud, spring forth.
צמד	וְצָמִיד	*Et armilla.*	And a bracelet.
צמק	וְצִמֻּקִים	*Et uvæ passæ.*	And bunches of grapes.
צמר	וְצֶמֶר	*Et lana.*	And wool.
צמא	וְצָמֵת	*Et sities.*	And thou shalt thirst.
צנן	וְצִנָּה	*Et scutum.*	And a shield.
צנף	וְצָנוֹף וְצָנִיף	*Et cidaris, diadema.*	And a turban, mitre, diadem.
צעה	וְצֵעֲהוּ	*Et vagari facient eum.*	And they shall cause him to wander.
צעק	וְצַעֲקִי וּצְעָקִי	*Et clama.*	And cry thou.
—	וְצַעֲקַת	*Et clamor.*	And the cry.

ROOTS.	DERIVATIVES.	VERSIO.	SIGNIFICATION.
צפה	וְצִפָּה	*Et texit, obduxit.*	And he covered, overlaid.
—	וְצֹפוּ	*Et speculans.*	And watching.
—	וְצִפּוּי	*Et obductio.*	And the overlaying.
צפן	וְצָפוֹן־־נָה־־פ״	*Et aquilo.*	And the north.
—	וְצָפוּן	*Et reconditus.*	And laid up.
צפר	וְצִפּוֹר	*Et avis.*	And a fowl, bird.
צפח	וְצַפַּחַת	*Et lecythus, ampulla*	And the cruse, vial, jug.
צפה	וְצַפִּי	*Et speculare.*	And watch, spy thou.
צפן	וּצְפִינְךָ	*Et absconditus tuus.*	And thy hidden.
צפר	וּצְפִיר	*Et hircus.*	And the he-goat.
—	וּצְפִירֵי	*Et hirci.*	And the he-goats.
צפה	וְצִפִּיתָ	*Et teges, obduces.*	And thou shalt cover, overlay.
צפן	וּצְפֹן	*Et recondet.*	And he shall lay up.
צפרדע	וּצְפַרְדֵּעַ	*Et rana.*	And the frog.
צפר	וְצִפֲּרַיָּא־־פֳּרִים	*Et aves.*	And the birds, fowls.
צור	וְצָרָה	*Et angustia.*	And trouble.
—	וְצָרוֹת	*Et angustiæ.*	And troubles.
צרה	וְצֳרִי וּצְרִי	*Et balsamum.*	And balm.
צור	וְצָרַי	*Et hostes mei.*	And my enemies
—	וְצָרֵיהֶם	*Et hostes eorum.*	And their enemies.
צרע	וְצָרַעַת	*Et lepra.* [*ber.*	And the leprosy. [smith.
צרף	וְצֹרֵף	*Et conflans, aurifa-*	And the founder, smith, gold-
—	וּצְרַפְתִּים	*Et probabo, conflabo*	And I will prove, melt, refine
צרר	וְצָרְרוּ	*Et affligent.* [*eos.*	And they will afflict. [them.
—	וְצֹרְרֵי	*Et hostes.* [*obsidebis.*	And the adversaries. [besiege.
צור	וְצַרְתָּ	*Et vincies, anges,*	And thou shalt bind, straiten,
—	וְצַרְתִּי	*Et obsidebo.*	And I will besiege.
—	וְצָרֹתֵיכֶם	*Et angustiæ vestræ.*	And your troubles, tribulations

וק

ROOTS.	DERIVATIVES.	VERSIO.	SIGNIFICATION.
קום	וְקָאם	*Et surget.*	And he shall arise.
—	וְקָאמִין	*Et stantes.*	And they that stand.
קבל	וְקַבֵּל	*Et accipe.*	And receive thou.
—	וְקִבֵּל	*Et suscepit.*	And he undertook.
—	וְקִבְּלְ	*Et susceperunt.*	And they took.
—	וְקִבְּלוּ	*Et susceperunt.*	And they took.
קבב	וְקָבְנוֹ	*Et execrare eum.*	And curse thou him.

ROOTS.	DERIVATIVES.	VERSIO.	SIGNIFICATION.
קבע	וְקָבַע	*Et spoliabit.*	And he will spoil.
קבץ	וְקֹבֵץ	*Et colligens.*	And he that gathereth.
—	וְקִבְצוּ	*Et colligite.*	And gather ye.
—	וְקִבֶּצְךָ	*Et colliget te.*	And he will gather thee.
—	וְקַבְּצֵנוּ	*Et congrega nos.*	And gather, assemble thou us.
—	וְקִבַּצְתִּי	*Et congregabo.*	And I will gather, assemble.
—	וְקִבַּצְתִּים	*Et colligam eos.*	And I will gather them.
קבר	וּקְבֹר	*Et sepeli.*	And bury thou.
—	וְקָבְרוּ	*Et sepelient.*	And they shall bury.
—	וְקִבְרוּהָ	*Et sepelite eam.*	And bury ye her.
—	וּקְבָרוּם	*Et sepelient eos.*	And they shall bury them.
—	וּקְבַרְתּוֹ	*Et sepelies eum.*	And thou shalt bury him.
—	וּקְבַרְתֶּם	*Et sepelietis.*	And ye shall bury.
—	וּקְבַרְתַּנִי	*Et sepelies me.*	And thou shalt bury me.
קבב	וְקַבֹּתוֹ	*Et maledices ei.*	And thou shalt curse him.
קדד	וְקִדָּה	*Et casia.*	And cassia.
קדש	וְקָדוֹשׁ וּקְדוֹשׁ	*Et sanctus.*	And holy, the holy one.
—	וּקְדוֹשׁוֹ	*Et sanctus ejus.*	And his holy one.
קדם	וְקָדִימָה	*Et ad orientem.*	And toward the east.
קדש	וְקַדִּישׁ	*Et sanctus.*	And a holy one.
קדם	וָקֶדֶם	*Et ante.*	And before.
—	וָקֵדְמָה	*Et ad orientem.*	And toward the east.
—	וּקְדָמוֹהִי	*Et coram eo.*	And before him.
—	וְקַדְמֹנִיּוֹת	*Et res antiquæ.*[*res.*	And the things of old.
—	וְקַדְמֹנִים	*Et priores, antiquio-*	And the former, more ancient.
קדד	וְקָדְקֹד	*Et vertex.*	And the crown of the head.
קדר	וְקָדַר	*Et obscurabitur.*	And he shall be darkened.
—	וְקָדְרוּ	*Et atrati reddentur.*	And they shall be made black.
—	וּקְדֹרִים	*Et pullati, mœrentes*	And clad in dark apparel,
קדש	וְקֹדֶשׁ	*Et sanctuarium.*	And the sanctuary [mourning.
—	וְקָדַשׁ	*Et sanctificabitur.*	And he shall be hallowed.
—	וְקִדֵּשׁ	*Et sanctificabit.*	And he shall hallow. [things.
—	וְקָדְשֵׁי־שֵׁי	*Et res sacræ.*	And the holy, consecrated
—	וְקַדְּשׁוּ	*Et sanctificate.*	And sanctify ye.
—	וְקִדְּשׁוֹ	*Et sanctificabit eum.*	And he shall sanctify him.
—	וְקִדְּשׁוּ	*Et pararunt.* [*ejus.*	And they prepared.
—	וְקָדָשָׁיו	*Et res consecratæ*	And his consecrated things.

ROOTS.	DERIVATIVES.	VERSIO.	SIGNIFICATION.
קדש	וְקִדַּשְׁתָּ	*Et sanctificabis, consecrabis.*	And thou shalt sanctify, hallow, consecrate.
—	וְקִדַּשְׁתּוֹ	*Et sanctificabis illum*	And thou shalt sanctify him.
—	וְקִדַּשְׁתִּי	*Et sanctificabo.*	And I will sanctify.
—	וְקִדַּשְׁתָּם	*Et sanctificabis eos.*	And thou shalt sanctify them.
—	וְקִדַּשְׁתֶּם	*Et sanctificabitis.*	And ye shall sanctify.
קהל	וְקָהָל וְקְהַל	*Et cœtus, congregatio*	And the assembly, congregation
קוה	וְקָו וְקָוה	*Et linea, filum.*	And a line, the thread.
קבע	וְקוֹבַע	*Et galea.*	And a helmet.
קוה	וְקַוֵּה	*Et expecta.*	And wait thou.
—	וְקֹוֵי	*Et expectantes.* [bo.	And they that wait.
—	וְקִוִּיתִי	*Et expectabo, sperabo.*	And I will wait, hope for.
—	וְקִוִּיתֶם	*Et expectabitis.*	And ye shall expect.
קול	וְקוֹל וְקֹל	*Et vox, sonitus, strepitus, mugitus.*	And the voice, sound, noise, lowing.
—	וְקוֹלָהּ	*Et vox ejus.*	And her voice.
—	וְקוֹלוֹ	*Et vox ejus.*	And his voice.
—	וְקוֹלִי	*Et vox mea.*	And my voice.
קום	וְקוּם וְקוּמָה	*Et surge.*	And arise thou.
—	וְקוֹמָה וְקֹ־מַת	*Et altitudo.*	And the height.
—	וְקוּמוּ	*Et surgite.*	And arise ye.
—	וְקוּמִי	*Et surgere meum.*	And my uprising.
קון	וְקוֹנְנוּ	*Et lamentabuntur.*	And they shall lament,
—	וְקוֹנְנוּהָ	*Et deplorabunt eam.*	And they shall lament her.
קוף	וְקוֹפִים	*Et simiæ.*	And apes, monkeys.
קוץ	וְקוֹץ	*Et spina.*	And a thorn.
קור	וְקוּרֵי	*Et telæ.*	And the webs.
קשש	וָקוֹשׁוּ	*Et congregate.*	And gather ye together.
לקח	וְקַח	*Et cape, accipe.*	And take, receive thou.
—	וּקְחוּ	*Et sumite, afferte.*	And take, bring ye.
—	וּקְחִי	*Et cape.*	And take thou.
—	וּקְחֻהוּ	*Et afferte eum.*	And bring ye him.
קטב	וְקֶטֶב	*Et lues, exitium.*	And destruction.
קטן	וּקְטַנָּה	*Et minor.*	And less.
—	וּקְטַנִּים	*Et parvi.*	And the small.
קטף	וְקָטַפְתָּ	*Et decerpes.*	And thou shalt pluck, crop off
קטר	וְקַטֵּר	*Et adolere.*	And to burn incense.

ROOTS.	DERIVATIVES.	VERSIO.	SIGNIFICATION.
קטר	וְקִטְּרֵי	*Et ligamina, vincula*	And the ligaments, bonds.
—	וְקִטְרִין	*Et nodi.*	And knots, difficulties.
—	וּקְטֹרֶת	*Et suffitus.*	And incense, perfume.
—	וּקְטָרְתִּי	*Et suffitus meus.*	And my incense.
קוא	וְקִיוּ	*Et evomite.*	And vomit, spue ye.
קטר	וְקִיטוֹר	*Et vapor.*	And vapour.
קום	וְקַיָּם	*Et stabilis.*	And stedfast.
—	וּקְיָם	*Et statutum.*	And a statute.
—	וְקִימָתָם	*Et surrectio eorum.*	And their rising up.
קוץ	וְקַיִץ וָקַיִץ	*Et æstas,* fructus *æstivus.* [*ignominia.*	And summer, summer *fruit.* [disgrace.
קוא	וְקִיקָלוֹן	*Et vomitus fœdus,*	And foul spuing, ignominy,
קיר	וְקִיר	*Et paries.*	And the wall.
—	וְקִירוֹתֶיהָ	*Et parietes ejus.*	And her walls.
—	וְקִירוֹתָיר־־ר״	*Et parietes ejus.*	And his walls.
קלל	וְקַל	*Et levis, velox.*	And light, swift.
—	וְקַלּוּ	*Et celeriores erunt.*	And they will be swifter.
קלט	וְקָלוּט	*Et contractus, mutilatus.*	And contracted, mutilated.
קלה	וְקָלוּי	*Et hordeum tostum.*	And parched barley.
—	וְקָלוֹן וְקָלִי	*Et ignominia.*	And ignominy, dishonour.
קלל	וִקַלֵּל	*Et maledicet.*	And he will curse.
—	וּקְלָלָה	*Et maledictio.*	And a curse.
קלס	וְקֶלֶס	*Et derisio.*	And derision.
—	וְקַלָּסָה	*Et illusio.*	And mocking.
קלע	וְקָלַע	*Et insculpsit.*	And he carved, figured.
—	וְקַלְעוֹ	*Et funda ejus.*	And his sling.
—	וְקַלְעֵי	*Et vela.* [*stabit.*	And the curtains. [stand.
קום	וְקָם וָקָם	*Et surrexit, surget,*	And he rose, shall rise, shall
—	וְקָמָה	*Et stabilitur.*	And she shall be established.
—	וְקָמוּ וָקָמוּ	*Et surgent, stabilientur.*	And they shall arise, shall be established.
קמח	וְקֶמַח	*Et farina.*	And meal.
קמץ	וְקָמַץ	*Et capiet, colliget.*	And he shall take, gather.
קום	וְקַמְתָּ	*Et surges.*	And thou shalt arise.
—	וְקַמְתִּי	*Et insurgam.*	And I will rise up.
קנא	וְקִנֵּא	*Et zelotypus erit.*	And he will be jealous.

ROOTS.	DERIVATIVES.	VERSIO.	SIGNIFICATION.
קנא	וְקִנְאָה	*Et zelotypia.*	And jealousy.
—	וְקִנְאָתוֹ	*Et zelus ejus.*	And his jealousy.
—	וְקִנֵּאתִי	*Et zelotypus ero.*	And I will be jealous.
קנה	וְקָנָהּ	*Et calamus ejus.*	And her reed, branch.
—	וְקָנֶה וּקְנֵה	*Et canna, calamus.*	And the cane, reed, calamus.
—	וּקְנוֹת	*Et acquirere.*	And to purchase.
—	וְקִנְיָן	*Et acquisitio, possessio.*	And a purchase, possession.
—	וְקִנְיָנָם	*Et possessio eorum.*	And their possession.
—	וְקָנִיתָ	*Et eme.*	And buy thou.
קנם	וְקִנְּמוֹן־־נֶּמֶן	*Et cinnamomum.*	And cinnamon.
קנה	וּקְנֹתָם	*Et calami, rami eorum.*	And their reeds, branches.
קסם	וְקֹסֵם	*Et divinus.*	And a soothsayer, diviner.
—	וְקֶסֶם	*Et divinatio.*	And divination.
—	וְקֹסְמֵיכֶם	*Et divini vestri.*	And your diviners.
—	וְקֹסְמִים	*Et divinantes, divini*	And divining, diviners.
—	וּקְסָמִים	*Et pretia divinationis*	And the rewards of divination
קסת	וְקֶסֶת	*Et atramentarium.*	And an ink-horn.
קפד	וְקִפּוֹד	*Et ericius.*	And the hedge-hog.
קוף	וְקֹפִים	*Et simiæ.*	And apes, monkeys.
קוץ	וְקָץ	*Et æstivabit.*	And he shall pass the summer
קצב	וְקֶצֶב	*Et cæsura.*	And the cutting off.
קצץ	וְקִצּוֹ	*Et finis ejus.*	And his end.
קוץ	וְקֹצִים	*Et spinæ.*	And thorns.
קצן	וּקְצִינֵי	*Et duces.*	And leaders.
קצר	וְקָצִיר וּקְצִיר	*Et messis.*	And harvest.
קצף	וָקֶצֶף וְקֶצֶף	*Et ira.*	And wrath.
—	וְקָצַף	*Et iratus est.*	And he was wroth.
—	וְקִצְפְּךָ	*Et ira tua.*	And thy wrath.
קצץ	וְקִצֵּץ	*Et abscidit.*	And he cut off.
—	וְקַצְּצוּ	*Et amputate.*	And cut ye off.
קצר	וּקְצַר	*Et brevis.*	And short.
—	וְקִצְרוּ	*Et metite.*	And reap ye.
—	וּקְצַרְתֶּם	*Et metetis.*	And ye shall reap.
קצץ	וְקַצֹּתָה	*Et abscindes.*	And thou shalt cut off.
קרר	וְקֹר	*Et frigus.*	And cold.
קרא	וְקָרָא	*Et vocavit, clamavit, vocabit, leget.*	And he called, cried, shall call, will read.

ROOTS.	DERIVATIVES.	VERSIO.	SIGNIFICATION.
קרא	וְקָרָא	*Et vocabitur.* [*dica.*	And he shall be called. [thou.
—	וּקְרָא	*Et voca, clama, præ-*	And call, cry, proclaim, preach
קרה	וּקְרָאָהוּ וְקָרָהוּ	*Et accidet ei.*	And it shall befal him.
קרא	וְקָרְאוּ	*Et vocarunt, vocabunt, clamabunt.*	And they called, shall call, cry, proclaim.
—	וְקִרְאוּ	*Et vocate, clamate.*	And call, cry ye.
—	וּקְרָאוּ	*Et legite.*	And read ye.
—	וּקְרָאֶנָּה	*Et lege eam.*	And read thou it.
—	וּקְרָאֵנִי	*Et invoca me.*	And call thou upon me.
—	וְקָרָאת־רָאתָ	*Et accidet, vocabis, clamabis, leges.*	And it will befal, thou shalt call, cry, proclaim, read.
—	וְקָרָאתִי	*Et vocabo.* [*mabitis.*	And I will call.
—	וּקְרָאתֶם	*Et vocabitis, procla-*	And ye shall call, proclaim.
קרב	וְקָרֵב	*Et adduc.*	And bring thou.
—	וְקָרֵב	*Et appropinquans.*	And approaching.
—	וְקֶרֶב	*Et intimum.*	And the inward part.
—	וּקְרָב	*Et bellum, prælium.*	And war, battle.
—	וְקָרְבָה	*Et accedet.*	And she will draw near.
—	וְקָרְבוּ	*Et accedent.*	And they shall approach.
—	וְקִרְבּוֹ	*Et intestina ejus.*	And his inwards.
—	וְקִרְבִּי	*Et intestinum meum*	And my inward parts.
—	וּקְרֹבַי	*Et propinqui mei.*	And my kinsmen.
—	וְקָרְבָּנוֹ	*Et oblatio ejus.*	And his offering.
—	וְקָרַבְתָּ	*Et accedes.*	And thou shalt draw near.
—	וְקָרַבְתִּי	*Et accedam.*	And I will come near.
קרא	וּקְרוּאִים	*Et vocati.*	And called.
קרב	וְקָרוֹב	*Et propinquus.*	And near.
קרח	וְקֶרַח	*Et frigus.*	And cold.
קרה	וְקִרְיְתָא	*Et civitas.*	And a city.
קרם	וְקָרַמְתִּי	*Et tegam, obducam.*	And I will cover, spread over
קרן	וְקֶרֶן־קַרְנָא	*Et cornu.*	And the horn.
—	וְקַרְנֵי־נַיָּא־יִן	*Et cornua.*	And horns, the horns.
קרע	וְקָרַע	*Et findet.*	And he shall rend.
—	וְקִרְעוּ	*Et findite.*	And rend ye.
—	וּקְרֻעֵי	*Et fissi.*	And rent.
—	וּקְרָעִים	*Et lacerati.*	And torn.
—	וְקָרַעְתִּי	*Et lacerabo.*	And I will tear.

ROOTS.	DERIVATIVES.	VERSIO.	SIGNIFICATION.
קיר	וְקַרְקַר	*Et diruam, destruam*	And I will break down, destroy
קשה	וְקָשָׁה	*Et dura fuit.*	And she was hard.
—	וּקְשׂוֹתָיו	*Et opercula ejus.*	And his covers.
—	וּקְשֵׁי	*Et duri.*	And hard.
קשש	וְקַשְׂקֶשֶׂת	*Et squama.*	And a scale, scales.
קשר	וְקִשְׁרוֹ	*Et conspiratio ejus.*	And his conspiracy.
—	וּקְשַׁרְתָּם	*Et ligabis eos.*	And thou shalt bind them.
—	וּקְשַׁרְתֶּם	*Et ligabitis.*	And ye shall bind.
קשש	וְקֹשְׁשׁוּ	*Et colligent.*	And they shall gather.
קשת	וְקֶשֶׁת	*Et arcus.*	And the bow.
—	וּקְשָׁתוֹת	*Et arcus.*	And the bows.
—	וְקַשְׁתוֹתָם	*Et arcus eorum.*	And their bows.
—	וְקַשְׁתִּי	*Et arcus meus.*	And my bow.
—	וְקַשְׁתְּךָ	*Et arcus tuus.*	And thy bow.
—	וְקַשְּׁתֹתֵיהֶם	*Et arcus eorum.*	And their bows.
	ור		
ראה	וְרָאָה	*Et vidit, videbit, aspiciet, animadver-* [*tet.*	And he saw, shall see, look, consider.
—	וְרָאֹה	*Et videndo.*	And in seeing.
—	וְרֹאֶה	*Et animadvertens.*	And observing.
—	וּרְאֵה וּרְאִי	*Et vidi, videbo.*	And look, behold thou.
—	וְרָאָהוּ	*Et aspiciet eum.*	And he shall look on him.
—	וְרָאוּ	*Et viderunt, videbunt*	And they saw, shall see.
—	וּרְאוּ	*Et videte.*	And see ye.
—	וּרְאֶינָה	*Et vide, aspice.*	And behold ye.
—	וְרָאִיתָ־־תָה	*Et aspicite.*	And thou shalt see.
—	וְרָאִיתִי	*Et videbis.*	And I saw, shall see.
—	וּרְאִיתִיהָ	*Et videbo illam.*	And I shall see her.
—	וּרְאִיתִיו	*Et vidi eum.*	And I saw him.
—	וּרְאִיתֶם־־תֶן	*Et videbitis, aspicie-* [*tis.*	And ye shall see, look.
—	וּרְאִיתַנִי	*Et vidisti me.*	And thou hast seen me.
—	וְרָאֲךָ	*Et videbit te.*	And he shall see thee.
רום	וְרָאֲמָה	*Et exaltata est.*	And she was exalted
ראם	וְרָאמוֹת־־מֹת	*Et corallia.*	And coral.
ראש	וְרֹאשׁ	*Et caput, vertex, agmen, primus, virus*	And the head, top, company, first, venom, poison.

ROOTS.	DERIVATIVES.	VERSIO.	SIGNIFICATION.
ראש	וָרֹאשׁ	*Et cicuta, fel.* [*ejus.*	And the hemlock, gall.
—	וְרֹאשׁוֹ	*Et caput, fastigium*	And his head, top.
—	וְרָאשֵׁי	*Et capita, duces.*	And the heads, chiefs.
—	וְרֵאשִׁית	*Et principium, primitiæ.*	And the beginning, first fruits
—	וְרֹאשָׁם	*Et caput eorum.*	And their head.
—	וְרִאשֹׁנוֹת	*Et primæ, priores.*	And the first, former.
ראה	וְרָאֲתָה	*Et vidit* [*numerosus.*	And she saw.
רבב	וָרָב־־רַ״ וָרָ׳	*Et multus, magnus,*	And much, great, numerous.
—	וְרַב־־רֹב־־רוֹב	*Et multus, major, multiplicabitur, multitudo.*	And much, greater, elder, he shall be multiplied, a multitude. [troversy.
ריב	וְרִיב	*Et lis, causa.*	And the cause, strife, con-
רבב	וְרֹב	*Et multitudo.*	And the multitude.
—	וּרְבָבָה וְרִבּוֹ	*Et myrias.*	And ten thousand.
—	וְרַבָּה	*Et multiplicabitur, magna, frequens.*	And she shall be multiplied, great, frequent.
—	וּרְבֵה	*Et multiplicare.*	And to multiply.
ריב	וָרֹבוּ	*Et litigarunt.*	And they strove, contended.
רבב	וְרָבוּ	*Et multiplicabuntur.*	And they shall be multiplied.
—	וְרַבּוּ	*Et multiplicati sunt, multiplicabuntur.*	And they have been multiplied, shall be multiplied.
—	וּרְבוּ	*Et multiplicamini, magnitudo, majes-*	And be ye multiplied, greatness, majesty.
ריב	וְרִבּוֹת	*Et contentiones* [*tas.*	And the contentions.
רבב	וְרַבּוֹת	*Et multæ.* [*jestas.*	And many.
רבה	וּרְבוּתָא	*Et magnitudo, ma-*	And greatness, majesty.
—	וּרְבוּתָךְ	*Et magnitudo tua.*	And thy greatness.
רבב	וְרַבֵּי	*Et magnates.*	And the lords, princes.
רבד	וְרָבִיד	*Et torques.*	And a chain.
רבב	וְרַבִּים	*Et multi.*	And many.
רבע	וּרְבִיעִית־־עִת	*Et quarta.*	And a fourth.
רבה	וְרָבִיתָ	*Et multiplicaberis.*	And thou shalt be multiplied.
—	וְרִבִּיתִי	*Et alui, educavi.*	And I nourished.
—	וּרְבִיתֶם	*Et multiplicabimini.*	And ye shall be increased,
רבע	וְרֹבַע	*Et quarta.*	And a fourth.
—	וְרִבְעִי	*Et accubitus meus.*	And my lying down.

ROOTS.	DERIVATIVES.	VERSIO.	SIGNIFICATION.
רבץ	וְרָבְצָה	*Et cubabit.*	And she shall lie.
—	וְרָבְצוּ	*Et recumbent.*	And they shall lie down.
—	וְרָבַצְתָּ	*Et recumbes.*	And thou shalt lie down.
רבב	וְרַבְרְבָנוֹהִי	*Et magnates ejus.*	And his lords, princes.
—	וְרַבְרְבָנַי	*Et magnates mei.*	And my lords, princes.
—	וְרַבְרְבָנָיךְ	*Et magnates tui.*	And thy lords, princes.
—	וְרַבַּת	*Et multa, abundans.*	And much, abundant.
רגב	וּרְגָבִים	*Et glebæ.*	And the clods.
רגז	וְרָגַז	*Et irascetur.*	And he will be angry.
—	וְרֹגֶז	*Et furor.*	And rage.
—	וְרָגְזוּ	*Et timebunt, trement*	And they will fear, tremble.
רגל	וְרֶגֶל	*Et pes.*	And a foot.
—	וְרַגְּלוּ	*Et explorate.*	And search, examine ye.
—	וְרַגְלַי	*Et pedes mei.*	And my feet.
—	וְרַגְלֵי־־לַיִם	*Et pedes.*	And the feet.
—	וְרַגְלֵיהֶם	*Et pedes eorum.*	And their feet.
—	וְרַגְלָיו	*Et pedes ejus.*	And his feet.
—	וְרַגְלֶיךָ	*Et pedes tui.*	And thy feet.
—	וְרַגְלְךָ	*Et pes tuus.*	And thy foot.
רגם	וּרְגָמֻהוּ	*Et lapidabunt eum.*	And they shall stone him.
—	וְרָגְמוּ	*Et lapidabunt.*	And they shall stone. [denly.
רגע	וְרֶגַע	*Et momentum, subito*	And a moment, instant, sud-
ירד	וְרֵד	*Et descende.*	And go down, descend thou.
—	וּרְדוּ	*Et descendite.*	And go ye down.
רדה	וְרָדוּ	*Et dominabuntur.*	And they shall rule, reign.
—	וּרְדוּ	*Et dominamini.*	And have ye dominion.
רדף	וְרָדַף	*Et persequetur.*	And he shall pursue, chase.
—	וּרְדֹף	*Et persequere.*	And pursue thou. [chased.
—	וְרֻדַּף	*Et insectabitur.*	And he shall be pursued,
—	וּרֹדֵף	*Et sequens, perse-*	And he that followeth, pur-
—	וְרִדְּפָה	*Et sequetur. [quens*	And she shall follow. [sueth.
—	וְרָדְפֵהוּ	*Et sequere illum.*	And follow thou him.
—	וְרָדְפוּ	*Et persequentur.*	And they shall pursue, chase.
—	וּרְדָפוּךְ	*Et persequentur te.*	And they shall pursue thee.
—	וְרֹדְפִים	*Et persequentes.*	And pursuing.
—	וְרָדַפְתִּי	*Et persequar.*	And I will persecute.
—	וּרְדַפְתֶּם	*Et persequimini.*	And pursue, persecute ye.

ROOTS.	DERIVATIVES.	VERSIO.	SIGNIFICATION.
רהב	וּרְהַב	*Et corrobora.*	And strengthen thou.
—	וְרָהְבָּם	*Et robur eorum.*	And their strength.
רגן	וְרוֹגְנִים	*Et murmurantes.*	And they that murmur.
ראה	וְרֵוָהּ	*Et species, forma ejus.*	And his form.
רזן	וְרוֹזְנִים־־רֹזְ"	*Et dominatores.*	And the rulers, princes.
רוח	וְרָוַח	*Et respiravit, relax-*	And he breathed, was refreshed
—	וְרֶוַח	*Et spatium.[atus est*	And a space.
—	וְרוּחַ	*Et halitus, ventus, flatus, spiritus.*	And the breath, wind, blast, spirit.
—	וְרוּחָהּ וְרוּחוֹ	*Et spiritus ejus.*	And his spirit.
—	וְרוּחִי	*Et spiritus meus.*	And my spirit.
—	וְרוּחֲךָ	*Et spiritus tuus.*	And thy spirit.
רוה	וְרִוֵּיתִי	*Et satiabo.*	And I will satiate.
רום	וְרוּמָהּ	*Et altitudo ejus.*	And his height.
—	וְרוֹמַם	*Et exaltatus est.*	And he was exalted.
—	וְרוֹמַמְתִּי	*Et extuli.*	And I have raised up.
רעה	וְרוֹעֶה	*Et pastor.*	And a shepherd. [soaked.
רוה	וְרָוְתָה	*Et irrigabitur.*	And she shall be watered,
רחב	וְרָחַב	*Et dilatabitur.*	And he shall be enlarged.
—	וְרֹחַב	*Et latitudo.*	And the breadth.
—	וּרְחַב	*Et latus, superbus.*	And wide, proud.
—	וְרָחֲבָה	*Et dilatata est.*	And she was enlarged.
—	וְרָחְבָּה	*Et latitudo ejus.*	And her breadth.
—	וּרְחָבָה	*Et ampla,lata,latior*	And large, broad, broader.
—	וְרָחְבּוֹ	*Et latitudo ejus.*	And his breadth.
—	וּרְחֹבוֹת	*Et plateæ.*	And the streets.
רחם	וְרַחוּם	*Et misericors.*	And merciful.
רחק	וְרָחוֹק־־חֹק	*Et longinquus.*	And he that is far off.
—	וּרְחוֹקִים	*Et longinqui.*	And they that are far off.
רחם	וְרֶחֶם	*Et uterus.*	And the womb.
—	וְרִחַם	*Et miserebitur.*	And he will have mercy.
—	וְרַחְמָהּ	*Et uterus ejus* [rum	And her womb. [them.
—	וְרִחֲמוּם	*Et miserebuntur eo-*	And they shall have mercy on
—	וְרַחֲמֵי	*Et misericordiæ.*	And the mercies.
—	וְרַחֲמָיו	*Et misericordiæ ejus*	And his mercies.
—	וְרַחֲמֶיךָ	*Et misericordiæ tuæ*	And thy mercies.

ROOTS.	DERIVATIVES.	VERSIO.	SIGNIFICATION.
רחם	וְרַחֲמִים־־ין	*Et misericordiæ.*	And mercies, compassions.
—	וְרִחַמְךָ־־חַמְךָ	*Et miserebitur tui.*	And he will have mercy on
—	וְרִחַמְתִּי	*Et miserebor.*	And I will shew mercy. [thee.
—	וְרִחַמְתִּים	*Et miserebor eorum*	And I will have mercy on them
רחץ	וּרְחַץ	*Et lava.*	And wash thou. [shall bathe.
—	וְרָחַץ	*Et lavabit se, abluet.*	And he shall wash himself,
—	וְרַחֲצוּ	*Et lavate. [se.*	And wash ye. [themselves.
—	וְרָחֲצוּ	*Et lavabunt, abluent*	And they shall wash, shall bathe
—	וְרָחַצְתָּ־־צְתְּ	*Et lavabis te.*	And thou shalt wash thyself.
רחק	וְרִחַק	*Et procul amovebit.*	And he shall remove far away
—	וְרָחֲקוּ	*Et procul aberunt.*	And they shall be far away.
רטט	וְרֶטֶט	*Et horror, tremor.*	And the horror, trembling, fear. [versy.
רוב	וְרִיב	*Et causa, lis.*	And the cause, strife, contro-
—	וְרִיבָה	*Et contende, litiga.*	And contend, strive, plead thou
—	וְרִיבְכֶם	*Et lites vestræ.*	And your strifes.
ריח	וְרֵיחַ	*Et odor.*	And the smell.
—	וְרֵיחוֹ	*Et odor ejus.*	And his scent.
ריק	וָרִיק	*Et frustrà.*	And in vain, to no purpose.
—	וְרֵיקָה־־קָם	*Et vacua, vacuus.*	And empty.
רכך	וְרַךְ וְרַךְ	*Et mollis.*	And soft, tender.
רכב	וְרֶכֶב וָר׳ וְר׳	*Et currus.*	And a chariot.
—	וְרֹכֵב	*Et equitans.*	And he that rideth.
—	וְרֹכְבוֹ	*Et ascensor ejus.*	And his rider.
—	וְרֹכְבֶיהָ	*Et sessores ejus.*	And those that sit or ride in.
—	וְרֹכְבֵיהֶם	*Et ascensores eorum*	And their riders.
רכש	וּרְכוּשׁ	*Et substantia.*	And the substance.
—	וּרְכֻשׁוֹ	*Et facultates ejus.*	And his goods.
רום	וָרָם	*Et altus, procerior.*	And lofty, taller.
—	וָרָם	*Et elatio, arrogantia*	And haughtiness, arrogance.
—	וָרָם	*Et elatus est, exal-*	And he was extolled, shall be
רמם	וְרִמָּה	*Et vermis. [tabitur.*	And a worm. [exalted.
רמה	וְרֹמֵה	*Et jaciens, projiciens*	And he that throweth, casteth
—	וּרְמוּ	*Et conjecerunt.*	And they cast.
רמן	וְרִמּוֹן־מֹן	*Et malum punicum.*	And a pomegranate.
—	וְרִמּוֹנִים־מֹנ״	*Et mala punica.*	And pomegranates.
רמח	וְרֹמַח	*Et hasta.*	And a spear.

ROOTS.	DERIVATIVES.	VERSIO.	SIGNIFICATION.
רמח	וּרְמָחִים	*Et hastæ.*	And the spears.
רום	וְרָמֵי	*Et excelsi.*	And the high.
רמה	וּרְמִיָּה	*Et remissa.*	And the slack, slothful.
—	וּרְמָיו	*Et projecerunt.*	And they cast.
רמס	וְרָמַס	*Et calcavit.*	And he trod upon.
—	וְרִמְסִי	*Et calca.*	And tread thou.
—	וָרֶמֶשׂ ךְ	*Et reptile.*	And the creeping thing.
רום	וְרָמָתֵךְ	*Et excelsum tuum.*	And thy high place.
רנן	וָרֹנִּי	*Et canta, clama.*	And sing, shout thou.
—	וְרַנֵּן	*Et cantare.*	And to sing.
—	וְרַנְּנוּ)	*Et cantate, exultate*	And sing, rejoice ye.
—	וִירַנְּנוּ	*Et cantabunt.*	And they shall sing.
רסן	וָרֶסֶן וְרֶסֶן	*Et frænum.*	And a, the bridle.
רוע	וָרָע וְרַע	*Et malum.*	And evil.
רעה	וָרֵעַ וְרֵעַ	*Et socius, amicus.*	And a companion, friend.
רעב	וְרָעָב	*Et fames.*	And famine.
—	וְרָעֵב	*Et famelicus.*	And hungry.
—	וְרָעֵבוּ	*Et esurierunt.*	And they hungered.
—	וּרְעֵבִים	*Et famelici.*	And the hungry.
רעד	וָרַעַד וּרְעָדָה	*Et tremor.*	And trembling.
רוע	וְרָעָה	*Et malus, malitia, malum, calamitas.*	And evil, wicked, wickedness, mischief, calamity.
רעה	וְרָעָה	*Et pascet.*	And he shall feed.
—	וְרֵעָה	*Et amicus.*	And a friend.
—	וְרֹעֶה	*Et pascens, pastor.*	And he that feedeth, a shepherd.
—	וּרְעֵה וּרְעִי	*Et pasce.*	And feed thou.
—	וְרֵעֵהוּ	*Et amici ejus.*	And his friends.
—	וְרָעוּ	*Et pascent, depascent.*	And they shall feed, eat up.
רעע	וְרָעוּ	*Et confringent.*	And they shall break to pieces
רעה	וְרֵעוֹ	*Et amicus ejus.*	And his friend.
—	וְרָעוּם	*Et pascent eos.*	And they shall feed them.
רוע	וְרָעוֹת	*Et malæ, malitiæ.*	And evil, wickedness.
רעה	וּרְעוּת	*Et voluntas.*	And will, pleasure.
—	וְרֵעוֹתֶיהָ	*Et amicæ ejus.*	And her friends.
—	וְרֵעַי וְרֵעִיתָי	*Et amici mei,*	And my friends.
—	וְרֵעַי	*Et sodales mei.*	And my companions.
—	וְרֹעֵיהֶם	*Et pastores eorum.*	And their shepherds.

ROOTS.	DERIVATIVES.	VERSIO.	SIGNIFICATION.
רעה	וְרַעְיוֹן	*Et solicitudo, vexatio*	And anxiety, vexation.
—	וְרַעְיוֹנֵי	*Et cogitationes.*	And the thoughts.
—	וְרֵעֶיךָ	*Et socii tui.*	And thy fellows.
רוע	וְרָעִים	*Et mali.*	And evil, wicked.
רעה	וְרֹעִים	*Et pastores.*	And the shepherds.
—	וְרַעְיֹנֹהִי	*Et cogitationes ejus.*	And his thoughts.
—	וּרְעִיתִים	*Et pascam eos.*	And I will feed them.
רעם	וְרַעַם	*Et tonitru.*	And thunder.
רעה	וּרְעֵם	*Et pasce eos.*	And feed thou them.
רען	וְרַעֲנָן	*Et virens.*	And green.
—	וְרַעֲנַנִּים	*Et virentes.*	And green.
רעש	וְרַעַשׁ	*Et commotio.*	And a commotion.
—	וְרָעֲשׁוּ	*Et trement.*	And they shall tremble.
רוע	וְרָעַת	*Et malum.*	And the evil.
—	וְרָעָתוֹ	*Et calamitas ejus.*	And his calamity.
רפא	וְרָפָא	*Et sanabit.*	And he shall heal.
—	וְרַפֹּא	*Et medendo.*	And in healing.
—	וּרְפָאָם	*Et sanabit eos.*	And he shall heal them.
—	וּרְפָאתִיו	*Et sanabo eum.*	And I will heal him.
—	וּרְפָאתִים	*Et curabo eos.*	And I will cure them.
רפה	וּרְפֵה	*Et debilis.*	And weak.
—	וְרָפוּ	*Et remisse se gerent*	And they shall faint, fail.
רפא	וְרָפוֹא	*Et sanare.*	And to heal.
רצה	וְרָצָאתִי	*Et acceptos habebo.*	And I will accept.
רוץ	וְרָצוּ	*Et current.*	And they shall run.
רצה	וְרָצוּי	*Et acceptus.*	And accepted.
—	וּרְצוֹן	*Et benevolentia.*	And the good will.
—	וּרְצוֹנוֹ	*Et benevolentia, delectatio ejus.*	And his good will, favour, delight.
רצץ	וְרָצוּץ	*Et contritus.*	And crushed.
רצח	וְרָצַח	*Et occidet.*	And he will kill.
—	וְרָצֹחַ	*Et interficere.*	And to kill.
—	וּרְצָחוֹ	*Et occidet eum.*	And he will slay him.
רצה	וּרְצִיתָם	*Et gratificaberis eis.*	And thou shalt please them.
רצע	וְרָצַע	*Et perforabit, transfiget.*	And he shall bore, pierce through.
רצף	וְרִצְפַּת	*Et pavimentum.*	And the pavement.

ROOTS.	DERIVATIVES.	VERSIO.	SIGNIFICATION.
ריק	וָרֵק	*Et vacuus.*	And empty.
רקק	וָרֹק	*Et sputum, saliva.*	And the spitting, spittle.
רק	וְרַק	*Et tantum.*	And only.
רקב	וּרְקַב	*Et putredo.*	And rottenness.
רקק	וְרַקּוֹת	*Et tenues.*	And the thin, lean.
—	וּרְקִיק וּרְקִיק	*Et laganum.*	And the wafer or thin cake.
—	וּרְקִיקֵי	*Et lagana* [*tor.*	And the wafers.
רקם	וְרֹקֵם	*Et phrygio, acupic-*	And an embroiderer.
—	וְרִקְמָה	*Et varii colores, opus phrygionicum.*	And the various colours, the embroidered work. [abroad
רקע	וּרְקַע	*Et excude, expande.*	And do thou beat out, spread
—	וְרַקְּעֶךָ	*Et excudere te.*	And thou beatest out.
רוש	וָרָשׁ וְרָשׁ	*Et pauper, egenus.*	And the poor, needy.
ירש	וּרְשׁוּ	*Et possidete.*	And possess ye.
רשע	וְרָשָׁע	*Et impius.*	And the wicked.
—	וְרִשְׁעָה—עַת	*Et improbitas.*	And the wickedness.
—	וּרְשָׁעִים	*Et impii.*	And the wicked, ungodly.
—	וְרָשָׁעְנוּ	*Et impie egimus.*	And we have done wickedly.
רשת	וְרֶשֶׁת	*Et rete.*	And a net.
—	וְרִשְׁתּוֹ	*Et rete illius.*	And his net.
רתק	וּרְתֻקוֹת	*Et catenæ.*	And chains.

וש

ROOTS.	DERIVATIVES.	VERSIO.	SIGNIFICATION.
נשא	וְשָׂא	*Et leva, condona.*	And lift up, forgive thou.
שאב	וְשֹׁאֲבֵי	*Et haurientes.*	And drawers.
—	וּשְׁאַבְתֶּם	*Et haurietis.*	And ye shall draw.
שאג	וְשְׁאַג	*Rugiet.*	He shall roar.
—	וְשֹׁאֵג	*Et rugiens.*	And roaring.
נשא	וּשְׂאוּ	*Et attollite.*	And lift ye up.
שאל	וְשָׁאוֹל	*Et interrogando.*	And in inquiring.
שאה	וּשְׁאוֹן	*Et strepitus.*	And the noise, tumult.
—	וּשְׁאוֹנָהּ	*Et strepitus ejus.*	And her noise, pomp.
נשא	וּשְׂאִי	*Et tolle.*	And take up.
שאת	וּשְׁאִיָּה	*Et vastitas.*	And the desolation.
שאל	וְשָׁאַל	*Et petet, mutuabitur*	And he will ask, borrow.
—	וְשֹׁאֵל	*Et consulens.*	And he that consulteth.
—	וְשָׁאֲלָה	*Et mutuabitur.*	And she shall borrow.

ROOTS.	DERIVATIVES.	VERSIO.	SIGNIFICATION.
שאל	וְשָׁאֲלוּ	*Et interrogabunt.*	And they will inquire.
—	וְשַׁאֲלוּ	*Et interrogate.*	And ask, inquire ye.
—	וְשָׁאֲלוּ	*Et petent.*	And they will ask, beg.
—	וְשַׁאֲלִי	*Et pete.*	And ask thou.
—	וּשְׁאֵלְךָ־־אֵלֶךָ	*Et interrogabit te.*	And he will ask thee.
—	וְשָׁאַלְתָּ	*Et petiisti, interrogabis.*	And thou hast asked, shalt inquire.
—	וּשְׁאֶלְתֶּם	*Et interrogabitis.*	And ye shall inquire.
שאן	וְשַׁאֲנַן	*Et requiescet.*	And he shall rest.
—	וְשַׁאֲנַנְךָ	*Et strepitus tuus.*	And thy noise, tumult.
שאף	וְשָׁאַף	*Et absorbebit.*	And he will swallow up.
—	וְשָׁאֹף	*Et absorbere.* [um.	And to swallow up. [nant.
שאר	וּשְׁאָר־אַר־אָרָא	*Et reliquus, residu-*	And the rest, residue, rem-
—	וּשְׁאֵרִי	*Et caro mea.*	And my flesh.
—	וּשְׁאֵרִית	*Et residuum.*	And the remnant, residue.
—	וּשְׁאֵרִיתוֹ	*Et residuum ejus.*	And the residue of it.
—	וּשְׁאֵרִיתֵךְ	*Et residuum tui.*	And the remnant of thee.
—	וּשְׁאֵרִיתָם	*Et residuum eorum.*	And the residue of them.
—	וּשְׁאֵרֵךְ	*Et corpus tuum.*	And thy body.
—	וּשְׁאֵרָם	*Et caro eorum.*	And their flesh.
נשא	וּשְׂאֵתוֹ	*Et elatio ejus.*	And his exaltation, dignity.
שוב	וְשָׁב וְשָׁב	*Et rediit, revertetur, revertens.*	And he returned, will return, returning.
ישב	וְשֵׁב וְשֵׁב	*Et mane, habita.*	And abide, remain, dwell thou
שוב	וְשַׁבְבְתִּי	*Et reducam.*	And I will bring back.
—	וְשַׁבְבְתִּיךְ וְשׁוֹ"	*Et reducam te.*	And I will bring thee back.
—	וְשָׁבָה	*Et redibit.*	And she shall return.
—	וְשֻׁבָה	*Et revertere.*	And return thou.
שבה	וּשֲׁבֵה	*Et captivum duc.*	And do thou lead captive.
שוב	וְשָׁבוּ וְשָׁבוּ	*Et reversi sunt, revertentur.*	And they have returned, will return.
ישב	וְשֵׁבוּ וּשְׁבוּ	*Et manete, habitate, habitabitis.* [eos.	And remain, dwell ye, ye shall dwell. [away captives.
שבה	וְשָׁבוּם	*Et captivos abducent*	And they shall carry them
שבע	וְשָׂבוֹעַ	*Et saturari.*	And to be satisfied.
—	וּשְׁבוּעָתוֹ	*Et juramentum ejus*	And his oath.
שבח	וְשַׁבֵּחַ	*Et laudans.*	And praising.

ROOTS.	DERIVATIVES.	VERSIO.	SIGNIFICATION.
שבח	וְשִׁבְּחוּ	*Et laudarunt.*	And they praised.
—	וְשִׁבַּחְתִּי	*Et laudavi.* [*tribus.*	And I praised.
שבט	וְשֵׁבֶט	*Et virga, sceptrum,*	And a rod, sceptre, tribe.
—	וְשִׁבְטֵי	*Et tribus.*	And the tribes.
שוב	וְשָׂבֵי	*Et senes.*	And the old, elders.
—	וְשֻׁבוּ	*Et redite.*	And return ye.
ישב	וְשְׁבִי	*Et sede.*	And sit thou.
שוב	וְשָׁבֶיהָ	*Et conversi ejus.*	And her converts.
שבה	וְשִׁבְיָה ושבית	*Et captivitas.*	And captivity.
—	וּשְׁבִיכֶם	*Et captivi vestri.*	And your captives.
שבל	וּשְׁבִילֶיךָ	*Et semita tua.*	And thy path.
שבה	וְשָׁבִיתָ	*Et captivum capies.*	And thou wilt take captive.
שבך	וּשְׂבָכָה	*Et reticulum, can-*	And the net-work, lattice.
שבל	וְשִׁבֹּלֶת	*Et fluctus.* [*cellum.*	And the wave, floods.
שבה	וְשָׁבָם	*Et captivos abducet*	And he will carry them away
שבע	וְשָׁבֵעַ	*Et septimus.* [*eos.*	And the seventh. [captives.
—	וְשֶׁבַע וש" וש"	*Et septem.*	And seven. [tisfied.
—	וְשָׂבֵעַ-בֵעַ ושבע	*Et satur, saturabitur*	And full, he will be filled, sa-
—	וְשָׂבְעָה	*Et saturabitur.*	And she shall be satiated.
—	וְשִׁבְעָה-עַת	*Et septem, septies.*	And seven, seven times. [fied
—	וְשָׂבֵעוּ	*Et saturabuntur.*	And they will be filled, satis-
—	וְשָׁבֻעִים	*Et hebdomadæ.*	And weeks.
—	וְשִׁבְעִים	*Et septuaginta.*	And seventy. [fied.
—	וְשָׂבָעְתָּ	*Et saturaberis.*	And thou shalt be filled, satis-
—	וּשְׁבֻעַת	*Et juramentum.*	And the oath.
—	וְשָׂבַעְתִּי	*Et satiatus sum.*	And I am full, satisfied.
—	וּשְׂבַעְתֶּם	*Et saturabimini*[*ges*	And ye shall be satisfied.
שבץ	וְשִׁבַּצְתָּ	*Et stringes, acupin-*	And thou shalt set, embroider
שבר	וְשֶׁבֶר וְשׁ'	*Et confractio, clades*	And the crashing, destruction
—	וְשַׁבֵּר	*Et confringendo.*	And in breaking in pieces.
—	וְשִׁבַּר	*Et fregit, confrin-get.*	And he brake, will break in pieces.
—	וּשְׁבָרָהּ	*Et franget eam.*	And he will break her or it.
—	וְשִׁבְרוּ	*Et emite.*	And buy ye.
—	וְשִׁבַּרְתָּ	*Et franges.*	And thou shalt break.
—	וְשִׁבַּרְתִּי	*Et frangam.*	And I will break.
—	וְשִׁבַּרְתֶּם	*Et confringetis.*	And ye shall break.

ROOTS.	DERIVATIVES.	VERSIO.	SIGNIFICATION.
שׁוב	וְשָׁבַת	*Et revertetur.*	And he shall return.
שׁבת	וְשַׁבָּת	*Et sabbatum.*	And the sabbath.
שׁוב	וְשַׁבְתָּ	*Et reverteris.*	And thou shalt return.
שׁבת	וְשַׁבַּתָּהּ	*Et sabbatum ejus.*	And her sabbath.
—	וְשָׁבְתָה	*Et quiescet.*	And she shall rest. [headed.
שׁוב	וְשַׁבְתִּי	*Et incanui.*	And I have become grey-
—	וְשַׁבְתִּי	*Et reversus sum, revertar, reducam.*	And I returned, will return, will bring again.
ישׁב	וְשִׁבְתְּךָ	*Et sessio, habitatio*	And thy sitting, abode.
שׁוב	וְשַׁבְתֶּם	*Et revertemini* [*tua*	And ye shall return.
שׁדד	וָשֹׁד וְשֹׁד	*Et direptio, præda,*	And the robbery, spoil, deso-
שׁד	וְשֹׁד	*Et mamma* [*vastitas*	And the breast. [lation.
שׁדד	וְשָׁדְדוּ	*Et vastabunt, vastate*	And they shall spoil, spoil ye.
שׂדה	וְשָׂדֶה וּשְׂדֵה	*Et ager.*	And the field.
שׁדף	וּשְׁדוּפֹת	*Et adustæ.*	And parched, blasted.
שׂדה	וְשָׂדוֹת וּשְׂדֵי	*Et agri.* [*sica.*	And the fields.
שׁדד	וְשִׁדּוֹת	*Et instrumenta mu-*	And musical instruments.
שׁד	וְשָׁדַי	*Et ubera mea.*	And my breasts.
שׁדד	וְשַׁדַּי	*Et omnipotens.*	And the almighty.
שׁד	וְשָׁדַיִךְ	*Et ubera tua.*	And thy breasts.
—	וְשָׁדַיִם	*Et ubera, mammæ.*	And breasts.
שׁדד	וְשָׁדֵּם	*Vastabit eos.*	He shall destroy them.
שׁדם	וּשְׁדֵמָה	*Et uredo.*	And blasting
—	וּשְׁדֵמוֹת	*Et agri.*	And the fields.
שׁדף	וּשְׁדֵפָה	*Et adusta.*	And parched, blasted.
סדר	וּשְׂדֵרֹת	*Et ordines.*	And the rows, ranges.
שׂוד	וְשַׂדְתָּ	*Et oblines.*	And thou shalt plaister.
שׂדה	וּשְׂדֹתֶיהָ	*Et agri ejus.*	And her fields.
—	וּשְׂדֹתֵינוּ	*Et agri nostri.*	And our lands.
שׂה	וָשֶׂה וְשֵׂה וְשֶׂה	*Et ovis, agna, pecus*	And a sheep, a lamb, cattle.
שׂהד	וְשָׂהֲדִי־־הָיֵ	*Et testis meus.*	And my witness.
שׁהם	וְשֹׁהַם	*Et onyx.*	And the onyx.
שׁוא	וְשָׁוְא	*Et vanitas.*	And vanity.
שׁוב	וָשׁוּב	*Et reverti.*	And to return.
—	וָשׁוּב וְשׁוּ" וְשׁוּב	*Et revertere.*	And return thou.
—	וָשׁוּבוּ ךְ"	*Et revertemini.*	And ye shall return.
שׁוח	וְשׁוּחָה	*Et fovea.*	And a pit.

ROOTS.	DERIVATIVES.	VERSIO.	SIGNIFICATION.
שול	וְשׁוּלָיו	*Et fimbriæ ejus.*	And his skirts, train.
שום	וְשׂוּם	*Et ponere.*	And to put.
שמר	וְשׁוֹמְרֵי וְשֹׁ׳	*Et custodientes.*	And keeping.
שנא	וְשׂוֹנֵא	*Et odio habens.*	And hating.
שוע	וְשׁוֹעַ	*Et clamor.*	And the shout.
שער	וְשׁוֹעֲרִים	*Et janitores.*	And porters.
שוע	וְשַׁוְעָתִי	*Et clamor meus.*	And my cry.
שור	וְשׁוֹר וְשׁוֹר	*Et bos.*	And an ox, bullock.
—	וְשׁוּר	*Et intuere.*	And behold thou.
—	וְשׁוֹרוֹ	*Et bos ejus.*	And his bullock.
—	וְשׁוּרֵךְ־יָא־יָה	*Et muri.*	And walls.
—	וְשׁוֹרְךָ	*Et bos tuus.*	And thy ox.
שתה	וְשׁוֹתִים וְשֹׁתִים	*Et bibentes.*	And drinking.
שזב	וְשֵׁיזִיב	*Et eripuit.*	And he delivered.
שחח	וְשַׁח	*Et deprimetur, depressus, humilis.*	And he shall be brought down, brought low, humble.
שחד	וְשֹׁחַד	*Et donum, munus.*	And a gift, reward.
שחט	וְשָׁחַט	*Et jugulabit.*	And he shall kill.
—	וְשָׁחֹט	*Et jugulando.*	And in killing.
—	וְשַׁחֲטָה	*Et jugulare.*	And to slaughter.
—	וְשָׁחֲטוּ	*Et jugulabunt.*	And they shall kill.
—	וְשַׁחֲטוּ	*Et jugulate.*	And kill ye.
—	וּשְׁחָטוֹ	*Et occidet eum.*	And he shall kill him.
—	וְשָׁחַטְתָּ	*Et mactabis.*	And thou shalt kill.
—	וּשְׁחַטְתֶּם	*Et mactabitis.* [tela.	And ye shall kill.
שחת	וּשְׁחִיתָה	*Et corrupta, corrup-*	And corrupt, fault, corrupting
חכם	וְשֶׁחָכַמְתִּי	*Et in quo sapiens fui, sapienter egi.*	And wherein I have been wise, acted wisely.
שחל	וּשְׁחֵלֶת	*Et onyx aromaticus.*	And the babylonian onyx.
שחק	וְשָׂחַק	*Et ridebit.*	And he shall laugh.
—	וּשְׁחָקִים	*Et nubes, cœli.*	And the clouds, heavens.
—	וְשָׁחַקְתָּ	*Et contundes.*	And thou shalt beat.
—	וְשִׂחַקְתִּי	*Et ludam.* [runt.	And I will play.
שחר	וְשִׁחֲרוּ	*Et diluculo quæsive-*	And they inquired early.
—	וְשִׁחֲרִתַּנִי	*Et quæres me mane.*	And thou shalt seek me in the morning.
שחת	וְשִׁחַתָּ	*Et perdes.*	And thou wilt lose, destroy.

ROOTS.	DERIVATIVES.	VERSIO.	SIGNIFICATION.
שחת	וְשִׁחֵת	*Et corrupit, depravavit, perdidit.*	And he corrupted, spoiled, threw away, wasted.
—	וְשִׁחֲתָהּ	*Et corrumpet eam.*	And he will corrupt it.
—	וְשַׁחֲתוּ	*Et disperdite.*	And destroy ye.
—	וְשִׁחֲתוּ	*Et disperdent.*	And they shall destroy.
—	וְשִׁחַתֶּם	*Et disperdetis.*	And ye shall destroy.
שטח	וְשָׁטְחוּם	*Et expandent eos.*	And they shall spread them.
שטה	וְשָׂטֵי	*Et declinantes.*	And those that turn aside.
שטף	וְשָׁטַף	*Et inundabit.*	And he shall overflow.
—	וְשֶׁטֶף	*Et inundatio.*	And a flood, inundation.
—	וְשֻׁטַּף	*Et immergetur.*	And he shall be plunged.
שטר	וְשֹׁטְרֵיהֶם	*Et præfecti eorum.*	And their officers.
—	וְשֹׁטְרָיו	*Et præfecti ejus.*	And his officers.
—	וְשֹׁטְרֵיכֶם	*Et præfecti vestri.*	And your officers.
—	וְשֹׁטְרִים	*Et præfecti.*	And the officers.
שוב	וְשֵׂיבָה	*Et canities.*	And old age, grey hairs.
שום	וְשִׂים	*Et pone.*	And put, lay thou.
—	וְשִׂימוּ	*Et ponite.*	And put, lay ye.
שצא	וְשֵׁיצִיא	*Et perfecta est.*	And she was perfected, finished
שית	וְשַׁיִת וָשַׁיִת	*Et sentis.*	And a thorn.
שות	וְשִׁית	*Et pone.*	And put, lay thou.
שכב	וְשָׁכַב	*Et jacuit, cubabit.*	And he lay, shall lie.
—	וְשָׁכְבָה	*Et cubabit.*	And she shall lie.
—	וְשָׁכַבְתָּ־תְּי	*Et jacebis.*	And thou shalt lie.
—	וְשָׁכַבְתִּי	*Et occumbam.*	And I will lie.
—	וּשְׁכַבְתֶּם	*Et occumbetis.*	And ye shall lie down.
שכח	וְשָׁכַח	*Et obliviscetur.*	And he will forget.
—	וְשִׁכְחִי	*Et obliviscere.*	And forget thou.
—	וְשָׁכַחְתָּ	*Et obliviscaris.*	And thou shalt forget.
שכר	וְשָׂכִיר	*Et mercenarius.*	And a hired servant.
שכל	וְשֵׂכֶל	*Et intellectus.*	And understanding.
—	וְשַׁכֻּלָה	*Et orbata, sterilis.*	And bereaved, barren.
—	וְשִׁכְּלָה	*Et orbabit.*	And she shall bereave.
—	וְשִׂכְלוּת	*Et stultitia.*	And folly.
—	וְשִׁכְּלֻךְ	*Et orbabunt te.*	And they shall bereave thee.
שכלל	וְשַׁכְלְלֵהּ	*Et perfecit eam.*	And he finished it.
—	וְשַׁכְלִלוּ	*Et perfecerunt.*	And they finished, completed.

ROOTS.	DERIVATIVES.	VERSIO.	SIGNIFICATION.
שכל	וְשִׁכְּלָתָּה	*Et orbabit eam.*	And he shall bereave her.
—	וְשִׁכַּלְתִּים	*Et orbabo eos.*	And I will bereave them.
—	וְשִׂכְלְתָנוּ	*Et intelligentia.*	And understanding.
שכן	וְשָׁכַן	*Et habitabit.*	And he shall dwell, inhabit.
—	וּשְׁכֹן	*Et habita.*	And dwell thou.
—	וְשָׁכְנוּ	*Et habitabunt.*	And they shall dwell.
—	וְשִׁכְנוּ	*Et habitate.*	And dwell ye.
—	וּשְׁכֵנוֹ	*Et vicinus ejus.*	And his neighbour.
—	וְשֹׁכְנֵי	*Et habitantes.*	And the inhabitants.
—	וּשְׁכֵנֶיהָ	*Et vicini ejus.* [*rum*	And her neighbours.
—	וְשֹׁכְנֵיהֶם	*Et habitatores eo-*	And their inhabitants.
—	וּשְׁכֵנָיו	*Et vicini ejus.*	And his neighbours.
—	וְשָׁכַנְתָּ	*Et habitabis.*	And thou shalt dwell.
—	וְשָׁכַנְתִּי	*Et habitabo.*	And I will dwell.
—	וְשִׁכַּנְתִּי	*Et collocabo.*	And I will place.
שכר	וְשָׂכָר וּשְׂכַר	*Et merces.*	And wages.
—	וְשֵׁכָר	*Et sicera.*	And strong drink.
—	וְשֹׂכֵר	*Et mercedem dans.*	And he that rewardeth.
—	וְשִׁכְרוּ	*Et inebriamini.*	And drink ye abundantly.
—	וּשְׁכֻרַת	*Et ebria.*	And drunk.
סכך	וְשַׂכֹּתִי	*Et tegam.*	And I will cover.
שלה	וְשַׁלְוָה	*Et tranquillitas.*	And quietness, peace.
—	וּשְׁלֵוָה	*Et tranquilla.*	And quiet, peaceable.
שלח	וְשַׁלּוֹחַ	*Et mittendo.*	And in sending.
שלה	וְשַׁלְוֵי	*Et felices.*	And happy.
שלם	וְשָׁלוֹם	*Et pax.*	And peace.
שלש	וְשָׁלוֹשׁ--לֹשׁ	*Et tres.*	And three.
שלה	וְשַׁלְוַת	*Et tranquillitas.*	And the peace, quietness.
שלח	וְשָׁלַח	*Et misit.*	And he sent.
—	וְשַׁלַּח	*Et mittere.*	And to send. [away.
—	וְשִׁלַּח	*Et dimisit, dimittet.*	And he sent away, will send
—	וְשֹׁלֵחַ	*Et mittens.*	And sending.
—	וּשְׁלַח	*Et mitte.*	And send thou.
—	וְשִׁלְּחָה	*Et emittet.*	And she will send forth.
—	וְשִׁלְּחָהּ	*Et dimittet eam.*	And he shall send her away.
—	וְשִׁלְּחוּ	*Et miserunt, mittent*	And they sent, shall send.
—	וְשִׁלְּחוֹ	*Et dimittet eum.*	And he shall send him away.

ROOTS.	DERIVATIVES.	VERSIO.	SIGNIFICATION.
שלח	וְשִׁלְחוּ	*Et mittite.*	And send ye.
—	וְשֻׁלְחָן	*Et mensa.*	And the table.
—	וְשִׁלַּחְתָּהּ	*Et dimittes eam.*	And thou shalt let her go.
—	וְשִׁלַּחְתּוֹ	*Et dimittes eum.*	And thou shalt let him go.
—	וְשָׁלַחְתִּי־־שִׁלַּ׳	*Et mittam, dimittam.*	And I will send, will let go.
—	וְשִׁלַּחְתִּיךָ	*Et dimittam te.*	And I will send thee away.
—	וְשִׁלַּחְתָּם	*Et mittes eos.* [*tis.*	And thou shalt send them.
—	וְשִׁלַּחְתֶּם־־וְשִׁלַּ׳	*Et mittetis, dimitte-*	And ye shall send, send away.
—	וְשִׁלַּחְתַּנִי	*Et dimittes me.*	And thou shalt let me go.
שלט	וְשָׁלְטָן־־נָא	*Et dominatio.*	And dominion.
—	וְשָׁלְטָנֵהּ	*Et dominatio ejus.*	And his dominion.
—	וְשָׁלְטָנָךְ	*Et dominatio tua.*	And thy dominion.
שלה	וְשָׁלֵיו	*Et tranquillus.*	And quiet.
שלט	וְשַׁלִּיט	*Et dominator.*	And a ruler.
—	וְשַׁלִּיטִין	*Et dominatores.*	And the rulers.
שלש	וּשְׁלִישִׁת	*Et tertia* pars.	And a third *part.*
שלל	וְשָׁלָל וּשְׁלַל	*Et spolium, præda.*	And the spoil, prey.
—	וְשָׁלַל	*Et spoliabit.*	And he shall spoil.
—	וְשָׁלְלוּ	*Et prædabuntur.*	And they shall spoil.
—	וּשְׁלָלָם	*Et spolium eorum.*	And their spoil.
שלם	וְשַׁלֵּם	*Et repende.* [*floum.*	And pay thou.
—	וְשֶׁלֶם	*Et sacrificium paci-*	And the peace-offering.
—	וְשִׁלַּם	*Et perfecit, reddet, pacem faciet.*	And he finished, shall restore, shall make peace.
—	וְשִׁלֵּם	*Et retributio.*	And a recompense.
—	וּשְׁלָם	*Et pacem habe.*	And be thou at peace.
—	וְשָׁלְמוּ	*Et absolventur.*	And they shall be ended.
—	וְשַׁלְּמוּ	*Et rependite.*	And pay ye.
—	וְשִׁלְּמוּ	*Et reddent, perficient*	And they shall pay, perform.
—	וּשְׂלָמוֹת	*Et vestes.*	And garments.
—	וְשַׁלְּמִי	*Et redde.* [*fica.*	And pay thou.
—	וּשְׁלָמִים	*Et sacrificia paci-*	And peace-offerings.
—	וְשִׁלֻּמַת	*Et retributio.* [*dam.*	And the reward. [restore.
—	וְשִׁלַּמְתִּי	*Et rependam, red-*	And I will recompense, render,
שלש	וּשְׁלֹשׁ	*Et tres.*	And three.
—	וּשְׁלִשׁ־שָׁה־שֶׁת	*Et tertius.* [*ejus.*	And the third.
—	וְשָׁלִשָׁיו	*Et tribuni, duces*	And his captains, leaders.

ROOTS.	DERIVATIVES.	VERSIO.	SIGNIFICATION.
שלש	וּשְׁלִשִׁים	*Et tertii, tertiani.*	And the third, belonging to [the third.
—	וּשְׁלשִׁים	*Et triginta.*	And thirty.
—	וְשָׁלִשִׁם	*Et tribuni, duces.*	And the captains, leaders.
—	וְשִׁלַּשְׁתָּ	*Et in tres partes divides.*	And thou shalt divide into three parts.
שם	וְשֵׁם ךָ	*Et nomen.*	And the name.
שום	וְשָׂם	*Et posuit, constituit, ponet, dabit, dis-* [*posuit.*	And he laid, made, will put, give, order.
שם	וְשָׁם	*Et ubi, ibi.*	And where, there.
שמל	וּשְׂמֹאול--אל	*Et sinistra.*	And the left, left hand.
—	וּשְׂמֹאלוֹ	*Et sinistra ejus.*	And his left hand.
שום	וְשָׂמָהּ	*Et ponet eam.*	And he will put her.
שם	וְשָׁמָּה	*Et ibi.*	And there.
—	וּשְׁמָהּ	*Et nomen ejus.*	And her name.
שום	וְשָׂמוֹ	*Et ponet eum.*	And he will put him.
—	וְשָׂמוּ	*Et ponent, constitu-* [*ent.*	And they will put, appoint.
—	וְשִׂמוּ	*Et ponite.*	And put, lay ye.
שם	וּשְׁמוֹ	*Et nomen ejus.*	And his name.
שמן	וּשְׁמוֹנָה--מ׳ ־נֶ׳	*Et octo.*	And eight.
—	וּשְׁמוֹנִים־־מֹנ׳	*Et octaginta.*	And eighty.
—	וּשְׁמוֹנַת--מֹנ׳	*Et octo.*	And eight.
שמע	וּשְׁמוּעָה	*Et fama, rumor.*	And the fame, rumour, tidings
שם	וּשְׁמוֹתָן	*Et nomina earum.*	And their names.
שמח	וְשָׂמַח--מֵחַ	*Et lætabitur.*	And he shall rejoice.
—	וְשַׂמַּח	*Et lætifica.*	And make thou glad.
—	וְשִׂמַּח	*Et exhilarabit.*	And he shall cheer.
—	וּשְׂמַח	*Et lætare.*	And be glad.
—	וְשָׂמֵחָה	*Et læta est.*	And she rejoiced.
—	וְשִׂמְחָה--חַת	*Et lætitia.*	And joy, gladness.
—	וְשָׂמֵחוּ--מְ׳	*Et lætabuntur.*	And they shall rejoice.
—	וְשִׂמְחוּ	*Et lætamini.*	And rejoice ye.
—	וּשְׂמָחִי וְשִׂמְ׳	*Et lætare.*	And rejoice thou.
—	וּשְׂמֵחִים	*Et lætantes.*	And rejoicing.
—	וְשָׂמַחְתָּ	*Et lætaberis.*	And thou shalt rejoice.
—	וְשִׂמַּחְתִּים	*Et lætificabo eos.*	And I will make them joyful.
—	וּשְׂמַחְתֶּם	*Et lætabimini.*	And ye shall rejoice.
שמט	וְשָׁמַטְתָּה	*Et dimittes, remittes*	And thou shalt let go, relax.

ROOTS.	DERIVATIVES.	VERSIO.	SIGNIFICATION.
שם	וּשְׁמֵי וְשָׁמַיִם־מַ׳	*Et cœlum, cœli.*	And heaven, the heavens.
—	וּשְׁמִי	*Et nomen meum.*	And my name.
שמר	וּשְׁמִירוֹ	*Et sentes ejus.*	And his thorns, briars.
שם	וְשִׁמְךָ	*Et nomen tuum.*	And thy name.
—	וְשִׁמְכֶם	*Et nomen vestrum.*	And your name.
שמל	וְשִׂמְלָה	*Et vestis.*	And a garment.
—	וּשְׂמָלֹת	*Et vestes.*	And garments,
—	וְשַׂלְמֹתֵינוּ	*Et vestes nostræ.*	And our garments.
שמם	וְשֹׁמֵמָה	*Et desolata.*	And desolate.
—	וּשְׁמָמָה	*Et desolatio.*	And a desolation.
—	וְשָׁמְמוּ	*Et vastabuntur, obstupescent.*	And they shall be made desolate, shall be astonished.
—	וְשֹׁמְמוֹתַיִךְ	*Et desolatæ tuæ.*	And thy desolate *places*.
שמן	וְשֶׁמֶן וְשֶׁ׳	*Et oleum, unctio.*	And the oil, the anointing.
—	וְשָׁמֵן	*Et pinguis.*	And fat.
—	וְשַׁמְנִי	*Et oleum meum.*	And my oil.
שמע	וְשָׁמַע	*Et audivit, audiet.*	And he heard, shall hear.
—	וְשֹׁמֵעַ	*Et audiens.*	And he that heareth.
—	וּשְׁמַע וּשְׁ־מַע	*Et ausculta, audi.*	And hearken, hear thou.
—	וְשָׁמְעָה	*Et audiet.*	And she shall hear.
—	וּשְׁמֻעָה	*Et fama, rumor.*	And the report,rumour,tidings
—	וְשָׁמְעוֹ	*Et fama ejus.* [*dient.*	And his fame.
—	וְשָׁמְעוּ	*Et auscultabunt, au-*	And they shall hearken, hear.
—	וְשִׁמְעוּ וּשְׁמָעוּ	*Et audite, obedite.*	And hear, obey ye.
—	וּשְׁמֻעוֹת	*Et rumores.*	And the tidings.
—	וְשֹׁמְעִים	*Et audientes.*	And they that hear.
—	וְשָׁמָעְנוּ	*Et audiemus.*	And we will hear.
—	וְשָׁמַעְתָּ־מְ׳	*Et auscultabis, audies, obtemperabis.*	And thou shalt hearken, hear, obey, be obedient.
—	וְשָׁמַעַתְ	*Et audivi.*	And I have heard.
—	וְשָׁמַעְתִּי	*Et audiam.*	And I will hear.
—	וּשְׁמַעְתִּיו	*Et audiam eum.*	And I will hear him.
—	וּשְׁמַעְתֶּם	*Et obtemperabitis.*	And ye shall obey.
שמר	וְשָׁמַר	*Et servabit, obser-*	And he shall keep, observe.
—	וְשֹׁמֵר	*Et custodiens.* [*vabit*	And he that keepeth.
—	וּשְׁמֹר	*Et serva.*	And keep thou.
—	וּשְׁמֻרָה	*Et servata.*	And kept, preserved.

ROOTS.	DERIVATIVES.	VERSIO.	SIGNIFICATION.
שמר	וְשָׁמְרוּ	*Et servabunt.*	And they shall keep.
—	וְשָׁמְרוּ	*Et custodiverunt, custodient.*	And they kept, shall keep.
—	וְשִׁמְרוּ	*Et observate.*	And observe, keep ye.
—	וְיִשְׁמְרוֹ	*Et servabit eum.*	And he shall keep him.
—	וְיִשְׁמְרֵנִי	*Et custodiet me.*	And he will keep me.
—	וְשָׁמַרְתָּ	*Et observabis.*	And thou shalt keep, observe.
—	וּשְׁמַרְתִּיךָ	*Et custodiam te.*	And I will keep thee.
—	וּשְׁמַרְתֶּם	*Et observabitis.*	And ye shall observe, keep.
—	וּשְׁמַרְתָּנִי	*Et observabis me.*	And thou wilt observe me.
שמש	וְשָׁמֶשׁ	*Et sol.*	And the sun.
שום	וְשַׂמְתָּ	*Et posuisti, pones, statues, collocabis*	And thou hast put, shalt put, set, place.
—	וְשֻׂמַת	*Et positus est.*	And he was put.
—	וְשַׂמְתּוֹ	*Et pones eum.*	And thou shalt put him.
—	וְשַׂמְתִּי	*Et pones.*	And thou shalt put.
—	וְשַׂמְתִּי וְשַׂ"	*Et ponam, statuam, constituam, sanciam.*	And I will put, lay, set, appoint, settle, ordain.
—	וְשַׂמְתִּיהָ	*Et ponam eam.*	And I will put, make her.
—	וְשַׂמְתִּיךְ־תִּיךָ	*Et ponam te.*	And I will set, make thee.
—	וְשַׂמְתִּים	*Et ponam eos.*	And I will put, make them.
—	וְשַׂמְתֶּם	*Et collocabitis, reponetis.* [eos.	And ye shall set, place, lay up
—	וְשַׂמְתָּם	*Et pones, constitues*	And thou shalt put, make them
שן	וְשֵׁן וְשֶׁן	*Et dens, scopulus.*	And the tooth, rock, crag.
שנה	וְשִׁנָּא וְשִׁנָּה	*Et mutavit.*	And he changed.
שנא	וְשִׂנְאָה־אַת	*Et odium.*	And hatred.
—	וּשְׂנֵאָהּ	*Et oderit eam.*	And he will hate her.
—	וְשֹׂנְאַי	*Et odio habentes.*	And they that hate.
—	וּשְׂנֵאֲךָ	*Et odio habebit te.*	And he will hate thee.
—	וְשָׂנֵאתִי	*Et odi.*	And I hated.
שנה	וְשָׁנָה	*Et annus.*	And the year.
—	וְשֹׁנֶה	*Et iterans.*	And he that repeateth.
שנא	וּשְׂנוּאָה	*Et exosa.*	And hated.
שנה	וּשְׁנוֹת וְשָׁנִים	*Et anni.*	And years.
—	וּשְׁנוֹתַי	*Et anni mei*	And my years.
—	וּשְׁנוֹתֶיךָ־נֹתֶ'	*Et anni tui.*	And thy years.

ROOTS.	DERIVATIVES.	VERSIO.	SIGNIFICATION.
שנה	וּשְׁנוֹתָם	*Et anni eorum.*	And their years.
שן	וְשִׁנֵּי וְשִׁנָּיִן	*Et dentes.*	And the teeth.
שנה	וּשְׁנֵי	*Et anni, duo.*	And years, two.
—	וּשְׁנִי	*Et bis tinctus, coccus*	And the twice dyed, the scarlet
	וַשְׁנִי	*Vasni.* [*eorum.*	Vashni. N. M.
—	וּשְׁנֵיהֶם	*Et ambo ipsi, anni*	And they both, their years.
—	וּשְׁנַיִם־נַיִם־נֵים	*Et duo, duæ.*	And the two.
—	וּשְׁנִיִּם	*Et secundi.* [*eos.*	And the second [culcate them.
שנן	וְשִׁנַּנְתָּם	*Et sæpe inculcabis*	And thou shalt frequently in-
שנה	וּשְׁנַת	*Et annus.*	And the year.
ישן	וּשְׁנָתוֹ וְשְׁנָתָהּ	*Et somnus ejus.*	And his sleep.
—	וּשְׁנָתִי	*Et somnus meus.*	And my sleep.
שסה	וְשָׁסוּי	*Et direptus.*	And spoiled.
שסע	וְשֶׁסַע	*Et fissura.*	And the cleft, division.
—	וְשֹׁסַע	*Et findet.*	And he shall cleave.
—	וְשֹׁסַע־סַעַת	*Et findens.*	And cleaving.
שוע	וְשִׁוְּעוּ	*Et clamaverunt.*	And they cried.
שער	וּשְׂעוֹרִים	*Et hordea.*	And barley.
—	וְשָׂעִיר וּשְׂעִיר	*Et hircus, hædus.*	And the goat, kid.
—	וּשְׂעִירֵי־רִים	*Et hirci, hædi.*	And the goats, kids.
—	וָשַׁעַר וְשַׁעַר	*Et porta, janua.*	And a gate.
—	וְשֵׂעָר וְשֵׂעָר	*Et pilus.*	And the hair.
—	וּשְׂעַר־עָרָה	*Et pilus.*	And the hair.
—	וּשְׂעָרָהּ	*Et pilus ejus.*	And her hair.
—	וּשְׂעֹרָה	*Et hordeum.*	And barley.
—	וְשַׂעֲרוּ	*Et horrescite.*	And be ye horribly afraid.
—	וְשַׁעֲרוּרָה	*Et horror.*	And horror.
—	וְשַׁעֲרֵי וּשְׁעָרִים	*Et portæ, januæ.*	And gates.
—	וּשְׁעָרֶיהָ	*Et portæ ejus.*	And her gates.
—	וּשְׁעָרֶיךָ	*Et portæ tuæ.*	And thy gates.
—	וּשְׁעָרִים	*Et portæ.*	And the gates.
—	וּשְׂעָרֵךְ	*Et pilus tuus.*	And thy hair.
שעשע	וְשִׁעֲשַׁע	*Et ludet.*	And he shall play.
שעה	וְשַׁעֲשֻׁעַי	*Et deliciæ meæ.*	And my delights.
שפה	וְשָׂפָה	*Et labium, sermo.*	And the lip, speech.
שפט	וּשְׁפוּטִים	*Et judicia.*	And judgments.
שפה	וּשְׁפוֹת	*Et casei.*	And cheeses.

ROOTS.	DERIVATIVES.	VERSIO.	SIGNIFICATION.
שפח	וְשִׂפַּח	*Et scabie afficiet.*	And he will smite with a scab.
—	וְשִׁפְחָה	*Et ancilla.*	And a handmaid, female ser-
—	וּשְׁפָחוֹת־־חֹת	*Et ancillæ.* [bit.	And handmaids. [vant.
שפט	וְשָׁפַט	*Et judicavit, judica-*	And he judged, shall judge.
—	וְשֹׁפֵט	*Et judex.*	And a judge.
—	וּשְׁפָטֻהוּ	*Judicabunt eum.*	They will judge him.
—	וְשָׁפְטוּ	*Et judicabunt.*	And they shall judge.
—	וּשְׁפָטוּךְ	*Et judicabunt te.*	And they shall judge thee.
—	וּשְׁפָטוּם	*Et judicabunt eos.*	And they shall judge them.
—	וְשֹׁפְטֶיהָ	*Et judices ejus.*	And her judges.
—	וְשֹׁפְטָיו	*Et judices ejus.*	And his judges.
—	וְשֹׁפְטֶיךָ	*Et judices tui.*	And thy judges.
—	וְשֹׁפְטִים	*Et judices.*	And judges.
—	וּשְׁפָטָנוּ	*Et judicabit nos.*	And he will judge us.
—	וְשָׁפַטְתָּ	*Et judicabis.*	And thou shalt judge.
—	וְשָׁפַטְתִּי	*Et judicabo.*	And I will judge.
—	וּשְׁפַטְתִּיךְ	*Et judicabo te.*	And I will judge thee.
—	וּשְׁפַטְתֶּם	*Et judicabitis.*	And ye shall judge.
שפה	וְשֻׁפּוּ	*Et eminebunt.*	And they shall jut or stick out
שפך	וְשָׁפַךְ	*Et effundet.*	And he shall pour out.
—	וְשֻׁפַּךְ	*Et effundetur.*	And he shall be poured out.
—	וְשָׁפְכוּ	*Et effundent.*	And they shall pour out.
—	וְשִׁפְכוּ	*Et effundite.*	And pour ye out, spread abroad
—	וְשָׁפַכְתָּ	*Et effundes.*	And thou shalt pour out.
—	וְשֹׁפְכֹת	*Et effundentes.*	And they that shed.
—	וְשָׁפַכְתִּי	*Et effundam.*	And I will pour out.
שפל	וְשָׁפָל וּשְׁפַל	*Et humilis.*	And low, lowly, humble.
—	וְשָׁפֵל	*Et deprimetur.*	And he shall be brought low.
—	וּשְׁפָלָה	*Et inferior.*	And lower.
—	וּשְׁפָלִים	*Et humiles.*	And humble. [down.
—	וְשָׁפַלְתְּ	*Et deprimeris.* [ejus	And thou shalt be brought
—	וּשְׁפֵלָתָהּ	*Et planities, vallis*	And her plain, valley.
ספן	וּשְׂפֻנֵי	*Et thesauri.*	And treasures.
שפע	וְשִׁפְעַת	*Et abundantia.*	And abundance.
שפה	וּשְׂפָתוֹ	*Et labium ejus.*	And his lip.
—	וּשְׂפָתוֹת	*Et labia.*	And lips.
—	וְשִׂפְתֵי	*Et labia.*	And the lips.

ROOTS.	DERIVATIVES.	VERSIO.	SIGNIFICATION.
שפה	וּשְׂפָתָיו	*Et labia ejus.*	And his lips.
—	וּשְׂפָתֶיךָ	*Et labia tua.*	And thy lips.
שקק	וְשַׂק	*Et saccus.*	And sackcloth.
שקד	וּשְׁקֵדִים	*Et amygdalæ.*	And almond-trees.
נשק	וּשְׁקָה	*Et osculare.*	And kiss thou.
שקה	וְשִׁקּוּי	*Et irrigatio.*	And watering.
—	וְשִׁקּוּיִ	*Et potus meus.*	And my drink.
—	וְשִׁקּוּיָי	*Et potationes meæ.*	And my drinkings.
שקט	וָשֶׁקֶט	*Et quies.*	And quietness.
—	וְשָׁקַט	*Et quiescet.*	And he shall rest.
—	וְשֹׁקֵט	*Et quiescens.*	And being at rest.
—	וְשָׁקְטָה	*Et quievit.*	And she was still.
—	וְשָׁקֶטֶת־־קֶטֶת	*Et quieta.*	And quiet.
—	וְשָׁקַטְתִּי	*Et quiescam.*	And I will be quiet.
שקל	וְשָׁקַל	*Et ponderavit.*	And he weighed.
שקם	וְשִׁקְמוֹתָם	*Et sycomori.*	And the sycamore-trees.
שקע	וְנִשְׁקְעָה	*Et submergetur.*	And he shall be drowned.
שקף	וּשְׁקֻפִים	*Et fenestræ.*	And windows.
שקץ	וְשֶׁקֶץ	*Et abominatio.* [lius	And the abomination.
—	וְשִׁקּוּצָיו	*Et abominationes il-*	And his abominations.
שקר	וָשֶׁקֶר	*Et mendacium.*	And falsehood.
שור	וְשָׁר	*Et canens.*	And he that singeth. [prince.
—	וְשַׂר וְשָׂר	*Et dux, princeps.*	And the captain, general,
—	וְשָׁרוֹת	*Et cantatrices.*	And the singing women.
—	וְשָׂרוֹתֵיהֶם	*Et reginæ eorum.*	And their queens.
שרט	וְשֶׂרֶט	*Et incisio.*	And a cutting.
שור	וְשָׂרֵי־רִים	*Et principes.*	And princes.
שרד	וְשָׂרִיד	*Et residuus.*	And he that remaineth.
שור	וְשָׂרֶיהָ	*Et principes ejus.*	And her princes.
שרה	וְשִׁרְיָה	*Et lorica.*	And a coat of mail.
שור	וְשָׂרֵיהֶם	*Et principes eorum.*	And their princes.
—	וְשָׂרָיו	*Et principes ejus.*	And his princes.
שרא	וְשֵׁרָיו	*Et cœperunt.*	And they began.
שרה	וְשִׁרְיוֹן	*Et lorica.*	And the coat of mail.
שור	וְשָׂרַיִךְ	*Et principes tui.*	And thy princes.
—	וְשָׂרֵיכֶם	*Et principes vestri.*	And your princes.
—	וְשָׁרִים	*Et cantores.*	And the singers.

ROOTS.	DERIVATIVES.	VERSIO.	SIGNIFICATION.
שור	וְשָׂרֵינוּ	*Et principes nostri.*	And our princes.
שרה	וְשִׁרְיֹנוֹת	*Et loricæ.*	And coats of mail.
שרף	וְשָׂרָף	*Et serpens ignitus.*	And a fiery serpent.
—	וְשָׂרַף	*Et comburet.*	And he shall burn.
—	וּשְׂרָפָה	*Et comburet eam.*	And he shall burn her.
—	וּשְׂרָפֻהָ־פוּהָ	*Et succendent eam.*	And they shall burn her.
—	וְשָׂרְפוּ	*Et comburent.*	And they shall burn.
—	וּשְׂרָפוּ	*Et comburent eum.*	And they shall burn him.
—	וּשְׂרָפָם	*Et comburet eos.*	And he shall burn them.
—	וְשָׂרַפְתָּ	*Et combures.*	And thou shalt burn. [dantly.
שרץ	וְשָׁרַץ	*Et abunde progignet.*	And he shall bring forth abun-
—	וְשָׁרְצוּ	*Et abunde progig-*	And they shall breed abun-
שרק	וְשָׁרַק וְשָׁרַק	*Et sibilavit.* [*nent.*	And he shall hiss. [dantly.
—	וּשְׁרֵקָה	*Et sibilus.*	And a hiss, hissing.
שרש	וְשֹׁרֶשׁ	*Et radix.*	And the root.
—	וְשָׁרָשַׁי	*Et radices.*	And the roots.
—	וְשָׁרָשָׁיו	*Et radices ejus.*	And his roots.
—	וְשֵׁרֶשְׁךָ	*Et eradicabit te.*	And he will root thee out.
—	וְשַׁרְשְׁרֹת	*Et catenæ.*	And chains.
שרת	וְשֵׁרֵת	*Et ministrabit.*	And he shall minister.
—	וְשֵׁרְתוּ	*Et ministrabunt* [*sus*	And they shall minister.
שש	וְשֵׁשׁ וְשֵׁשׁ	*Et sex, marmor, bys-*	And six, marble, fine linen.
שוש	וְשָׂשׂ	*Et lætabitur.*	And he shall rejoice.
ששה	וְשִׁשֵּׁאתִיךָ	*Et ad sextam partem*	And I will leave but a sixth
שש	וְשִׁשָּׁה וְשֵׁשֶׁת	*Et sex.* [*redigam te.*	And six. [part of thee.
שוש	וְשָׂשׂוֹן־־שֹׂן	*Et gaudium.*	And joy.
שש	וְשִׁשִּׁים	*Et sexaginta*[*dabitis*	And sixty. [part.
ששה	וְשִׁשִּׁיתֶם	*Et sextam partem*	And ye shall give the sixth
שוש	וְשַׂשְׂתִּי	*Et gaudebo.*	And I shall rejoice.
שתה	וְשָׁתָה	*Et bibit, bibet.*	And he drank, will drink.
שות	וְשַׁתִּהָ וְשַׁתִּיהָ	*Et ponam eam.*	And I will set her.
שתה	וּשְׁתֵה	*Et bibe.*	And drink thou.
—	וְשָׁתוֹ	*Et bibere.*	And to drink.
—	וְשָׁתוּ	*Et bibent.*	And they shall drink.
—	וּשְׁתוּ	*Et bibite.*	And drink ye.
—	וְשָׁתוֹת	*Et bibendo.*	And in drinking.
	וַשְׁתִּי	*Vasti.*	Vashti, N. W.

ROOTS.	DERIVATIVES.	VERSIO.	SIGNIFICATION.
שות	וְשַׁתִּי	*Et ponam.*	And I will put.
שנה	וּשְׁתֵּי	*Et duo, duæ.*	And two.
שתה	וְשֹׁתִים	*Et bibentes.[dus, bis.*	And they that drink.
שנה	וּשְׁתָּיִם־תֵּי־תַּיִם	*Et duo, duæ, secun-*	And two, the second, twice.
שתה	וְשָׁתִית	*Et bibes.*	And thou shalt drink.
—	וְשָׁתִיתִי	*Et bibi, bibam.*	And I have drunk, will drink.
—	וּשְׁתִיתֶם	*Et bibetis.*	And ye shall drink.
שתל	וְשָׁתַלְתִּי	*Et plantabo.*	And I will plant.
	ות		
אבד	וַתְּאַבֵּד	*Et perdidit, perdidisti.*	And she hath destroyed, thou hast destroyed.
—	וְתֹאבְדוּ	*Et peribitis.*	And ye shall perish.
—	וַתֹּאבַדְנָה	*Et amissæ sunt.*	And they were lost.
אהב	וַתֶּאֱהַב	*Et dilexit.*	And she loved.
תא	וְתָאָו	*Et thalami ejus.*	And his chambers.
תאה	וּתְאוֹ	*Et oryges.*	And the buffalos.
אוה	וְתַאֲוַת	*Et desiderium.*	And the desire.
—	וְתַאֲוָתָם	*Et desiderium eorum*	And their desire.
אזר	וַתְּאַזְּרֵנִי	*Et accinxisti me.*	And thou hast girded me.
אחז	וַתֹּאחֶז	*Et tenuit.*	And she held.
—	וְתֹאחֵז	*Et prehendet.*	And she will take hold.
—	וְתֹאחֲזֵנִי	*Et tenebit me.*	And she will hold me.
תא	וְתָאֵי	*Et thalami.*	And the chambers.
אכל	וַתֹּאכַל	*Et comedisti, comedit, consumpsit, consumet.*	And thou hast eaten, she ate, consumed, devoured, shall consume. [vour.
—	וְתֹאכַל	*Et consumet.*	And she shall consume, de-
—	וְתֵאָכֵל	*Et devorabit.*	And she shall devour.
—	וְתֹאכְלֵם	*Et consumet eos.*	And she shall devour them.
—	וַתֹּאכַלְנָה	*Et voraverunt.*	And they devoured.
אלץ	וַתְּאַלְצֵהוּ	*Et ursit eum.*	And she urged him.
אמן	וְתַאֲמִינוּ	*Et credetis.*	And ye shall believe.
—	וְתֵאָמֵנוּ	*Et confirmabimini.*	And ye shall be established.
אמץ	וַתְּאַמֵּץ	*Et confirmavit.*	And she strengthened.
אמר	וַתֹּאמַר־מָר	*Et dixit, dixisti.*	And she said, thou saidst.
—	וַתֹּאמְרוּ	*Et dixistis.*	And ye said.

ROOTS.	DERIVATIVES.	VERSIO.	SIGNIFICATION.
אמר	וַתֹּאמְרִי	*Et dixisti.*	And thou hast said.
—	וַתֹּאמַ֫רְןָ־נָה	*Et dixerunt.*	And they said.
תאן	וּתְאֵנָה	*Et ficus.*	And the fig-tree.
—	וּתְאֵנֵיכֶם	*Et ficus vestræ.*	And your fig-trees.
—	וּתְאֵנִים	*Et ficus.*	And the fig-trees.
—	וּתְאֵנָתָהּ	*Et ficus ejus.*	And her fig-tree.
—	וּתְאֵנָתִי	*Et ficus mea.*	And my fig-tree.
—	וּתְאֵנָתֶךָ	*Et ficus tua.*	And thy fig-tree.
—	וּתְאֵנָתָם	*Et ficus eorum.*	And their fig-tree.
אסר	וַתַּאַסְרֵהוּ	*Et ligavit eum.*	And she bound him.
תאר	וְתָאַר	*Et descriptus est, describetur.*	And he was or shall be described, marked out.
—	וְתֹאֲרוֹ	*Et forma ejus.*	And his form. [lengthened.
ארך	וַתֶּאֱרַכְנָה	*Et prolongatæ sunt.*	And they were prolonged.
אשר	וּתְאַשּׁוּר	*Et buxus.* [vit me.	And the box-tree.
—	וַתְּאַשְּׁרֻנִי	*Et beatum prædica-*	And she called me blessed.
בוא	וַתָּבֵא	*Et attulit.* [buit.	And she brought. [down.
—	וַתָּבֹא־בוֹא	*Et ivit, venit, occu-*	And she went, came, set, went
—	וְתָבֹא	*Et veniet.*	And she will come.
—	וַתְּבִאֵהוּ	*Et adduxit eum.*	And she brought him.
—	וַתָּבֹאוּ	*Et venistis, ingressi*	And ye came, entered.
—	וַתָּבֹאִי	*Et ingressa es.*[estis	And thou hast entered.
—	וְתָבֹאנָה	*Et evenient*[sæ sunt	And they will come to pass.
—	וַתְּבֹאנָה־בוֹא	*Et venerunt, ingres-*	And they came, entered.
—	וַתְּבִאֵנִי	*Et adduxit me.*	And she brought me.
באש	וַתִּבְאַשׁ	*Et fœtuit.*	And she stank.
בוא	וַתָּבֹאתִי	*Et venisti.*	And thou camest.
בהל	וַתִּבָּהֵל	*Et turbatus es.*	And thou hast been troubled.
בוא	וְתָבוֹאָה	*Et eveniet.*	And she will happen.
—	וַתְּבוֹאֵהוּ	*Et invadet ei.*	And she will come upon him.
—	וּתְבוֹאֶינָה	*Et venerunt, venient*	And they came, will come.
—	וְתָבוֹאנָה	*Et venerunt, venient*	And they came, will come.
—	וּתְבוּאַת	*Et proventus.*	And the produce, fruit.
—	וּתְבוּאָתָהּ	*Et proventus ejus.*	And her produce, increase.
—	וּתְבוּאָתִי	*Et proventus meus.*	And my revenue.
בין	וּתְבוּנָה	*Et intelligentia.*	And understanding.
בזה	וַתִּבֶז	*Et sprevit.*	And she despised.

ROOTS.	DERIVATIVES.	VERSIO.	SIGNIFICATION.
בוז	וְתָבֻז	*Et contemnet.*	And she will despise.
בחר	וַתִּבְחַר	*Et elegit.*	And she hath chosen.
—	וְתִבְחַר	*Et eliges.* [*isti.*	And thou wilt choose.
נבט	וַתַּבֵּט	*Et respexit, respex-*	And she looked, thou lookedst
בטח	וַתִּבְטַח	*Et confidisti.*	And thou hast trusted.
—	וַתִּבְטְחוּ	*Et confidistis.*	And ye have trusted.
—	וַתִּבְטְחִי	*Et confidisti.*	And thou hast trusted.
בוא	וַתְּבִיאֵהוּ	*Et adduxit eum.*	And she brought him.
—	וַתְּבִיאֵם	*Et adduxisti eos.*	And thou broughtest them.
—	וַתְּבִיאֵנִי	*Et adduxit me.*	And she brought me.
בון	וְתָבִינוּ	*Et intelligetis.*	And ye shall understand [wept
בכה	וַתֵּבְךְּ־תִּבְכֶּה	*Et flevit, flevisti.*	And she hath wept, thou hast
—	וַתִּבְכּוּ	*Et flevistis.*	And ye have wept.
—	וַתִּבְכֶּינָה	*Et fleverunt.*	And they wept.
תבל	וְתֵבֵל	*Et orbis.*	And the world.
בלע	וַתִּבְלַע	*Et absorbuit.*	And she swallowed up.
—	וַתִּבְלָעֵם	*Et absorbuit eos.*	And she swallowed them up.
—	וַתִּבְלַעְ־נָה	*Et degluliverunt.*	And they devoured.
—	וַתְּבַלְּעֵנִי	*Et absorbebis me.*	And thou wilt swallow me up.
בון	וַתָּבֶן	*Et intellexit.*	And she understood.
בנה	וַתִּבֶן	*Et ædificavit.*	And she built.
תבן	וְתֶבֶן	*Et stramen, palea.*	And straw, stubble.
בנה	וַתִּבְנִי	*Et ædificasti.*	And thou hast built.
—	וְתַבְנִית	*Et forma, exemplar*	And a form, pattern.
בער	וַתִּבְעַר	*Et exarsit, irata est*	And she burned, was angry.
בצע	וַתְּבַצְּעִי	*Et concupisti, lucrata es.*	And thou hast coveted, gained
בקע	וַתִּבָּקַע	*Et fissa, divisa, perrupta, dirupta est.*	And she was cleft, divided, rent through, broken up.
—	וַתְּבַקַּעְנָה	*Et discerpserunt.*	And they tore.
בקש	וּתְבֻקְשִׁי	*Et requireris.*	And thou shalt be sought for.
ברח	וַתִּבְרַח	*Et fugit.*	And she fled. [food.
ברה	וְתַבְרֵנִי	*Et pastu reficiet me.*	And she shall refresh me with
בשל	וַתְּבַשֵּׁל	*Et coxit.*	And she baked.
גבה	וַתִּגְבַּה	*Et elata est.*	And she was exalted.
—	וַתִּגְבְּהֶינָה	*Et extulerunt se, superbiverunt.*	And they exalted themselves, were proud, haughty.

ROOTS.	DERIVATIVES.	VERSIO.	SIGNIFICATION.
נגד	וַתַּגֵּד־־גֵּד	*Et nunciavit, indica-*	And she told, shewed.
גדל	וַתַּגְדִּילוּ	*Et gloriati estis* [*vit.*	And ye have boasted.
—	וַתַּגְדֵּל	*Et magnificasti.*	And thou hast magnified.
—	וַתִּגְדַּל	*Et crevit, magna e-*	And she grew, became great.
		vasit.	
—	וַתִּגְדְּלִי	*Et magna evasisti.*	And thou hast become great.
גדר	וַתִּגְדְּרוּ	*Et sepivistis.*	And ye have fenced, hedged up
גזר	וְתִגְזַר	*Et decernes.*	And thou shalt decree. [forth.
גוח	וַתָּגַח	*Et erupisti, exiisti.*	And thou brakest, camest
נגד	וְתַגִּיד	*Et nunciabis.*	And thou shalt tell.
נגש	וַתַּגִּישׁוּן	*Et adduxistis.* [*vit.*	And ye have brought near.
גלה	וַתְּגַל	*Et detexit, revela-*	And she uncovered, discovered
גול	וְתָגֵל	*Et exultabit.*	And she shall rejoice.
גלה	וַתִּגָּלֶה	*Et detecta est.*	And she was discovered.
גלח	וַתְּגַלַּח	*Et abradere fecit.*	And she caused to shave off.
גול	וַתָּגֵלְנָה	*Et exultaverunt.*	And they rejoiced.
גמל	וַתִּגְמֹל	*Et ablactavit.*	And she weaned.
—	וַתִּגְמְלֵהוּ	*Et ablactavit eum.*	And she weaned him.
גנב	וַתִּגְנֹב	*Et furatus es, fura-*	And thou hast stolen away, she
נגע	וַתַּגַּע	*Et abjecit.* [*ta est.*	And she cast off. [stole.
—	וַתִּגַּע	*Et tetigit.*	And she touched.
געש	וַתִּגְעַשׁ	*Et mota est.*	And she was moved.
—	וַתִּגָּעַשׁ	*Et commota est.*	And she was shaken.
גור	וַתָּגָר	*Et peregrinata est.*	And she sojourned.
נגר	וַתַּגֵּר	*Et effudisti.*	And thou hast poured out, shed
גרע	וְתִגְרַע	*Et diminues, sub-*	And thou shalt diminish, with-
		trahes.	draw.
גרש	וַתְּגָרֶשׁ	*Et expulisti.*	And thou hast driven out.
—	וַתְּגָרְשׁוּנִי	*Et expulistis me.*	And ye have expelled me.
נגש	וַתַּגֵּשׁ	*Et adduxit.*	And she brought.
—	וַתִּגַּשׁ	*Et accessit.*	And she came near.
—	וַתִּגַּשְׁןָ	*Et accesserunt.*	And they came near.
דבק	וַתִּדְבַּק	*Et adhæsit.*	And she clave to.
דבר	וַתְּדַבֵּר	*Et locutus es, locuta*	And thou spakest, she spoke,
		est, perdidit.	she destroyed.
—	וּתְדַבֵּר	*Et loqueris.*	And thou shalt speak.
—	וּתְדַבֵּר	*Et loquetur.*	And she shall speak.

ROOTS.	DERIVATIVES.	VERSIO.	SIGNIFICATION.
דבר	וַתְּדַבֵּרְנָה	Et locutæ sunt, locu-	And they spoke, ye have spoken
נדד	וַתִּדַּד	Et discessit [tæ estis	And she departed.
דוש	וּתְדוּשָׁהּ־־נָּהּ	Et calcabit eam.	And she shall tread it down.
נדח	וַתַּדִּחוּם	Et expulistis eos.	And ye have driven them away
דכא	וּתְדַכְּאוּנַנִי	Et confringetis me.	And ye shall break me in pieces
דלח	וַתִּדְלַח	Et turbasti.	And thou troubledst.
דלה	וַתִּדְלֶנָה	Et hauserunt.	And they drew.
ידע	וַתֵּדַע	Et novisti.	And thou hast known. [stand.
—	וְתֵדַע	Et scies, intelliges.	And thou shalt know, under-
—	וַתֵּדָעֵהוּ	Et cognovisti eum.	And thou hast known him.
דקק	וְתָדֹק	Et comminues.	And thou shalt beat in pieces.
—	וַתַּדְקֶנָּה־־קֶנָּה	Et comminuet eam.	And she shall beat her to pieces
נדר	וַתִּדֹּר	Et vovit.	And she vowed.
תהה	וָתֹהוּ	Et vanitas, inanitas	And vanity, emptiness.
היה	וַתְּהִי	Et fuisti, fuit.	And thou hast been, thou wast,
—	וּתְהִי	Et erit.	And she shall be. [she was.
—	וַתִּהְיוּ	Et fuistis.	And ye have been.
—	וַתִּהְיֶיןָ־־נָה	Et fuerunt.	And they were, have been.
—	וְתִהְיֶינָה	Et eritis, erunt.	And ye shall be, they shall be
הין	וַתָּהִינוּ	Et voluistis, parati	And ye were willing, ready,
הלל	וּתְהִלָּה	Et laus. [estis.	And praise. [prepared.
—	וּתְהִלּוֹת	Et laudes.	And the praises.
הלך	וַתֵּהֲלַךְ	Et ambulavit.	And she walked.
—	וְתַהֲלְכוֹת	Et agmina euntium.	And troops of persons going.
הלל	וּתְהַלְלֶךָּ	Et laudabit te.	And she shall praise thee.
—	וּתְהִלָּתוֹ	Et laus ejus.	And his praise.
—	וּתְהִלָּתִי	Et laus mea.	And my praise.
הום	וַתֵּהֹם	Et commota est, per-strepuit. [nuisti.	And she was moved, made a great noise. [a great noise.
המה	וַתֶּהֱמִי	Et fremuisti, perso-	And thou hast raged, made
המם	וּתְהֻמֵּם	Et conteres eos.	And thou shalt crush them.
תהם	וּתְהֹמֹת	Et abyssi.	And the depths, abysses.
הפך	וַתֵּהָפֵךְ	Et vertit se.	And she turned.
הרה	וַתַּהַר	Et concepit.	And she conceived.
הרג	וַתַּהַרְגוּ	Et occidistis.	And ye have slain.
הרה	וַתַּהֲרֶיןָ	Et conceperunt.	And they conceived.
שכח	וּתְהַשְׁכַּח	Et invenies.	And thou shalt find.

ROOTS.	DERIVATIVES.	VERSIO.	SIGNIFICATION.
ידה	וְתוֹדָה	*Et laus.*	And praise.
—	וְתוֹדוֹת	*Et sacrificia laudis.*	And sacrifices of praise.
יחל	וְתוֹחֶלֶת	*Et spes.*	And hope.
—	וְתוֹחַלְתִּי	*Et spes mea.*	And my hope.
תוך	וְתוֹךְ	*Et inter, e medio.*	And among, from the midst.
—	וְתוֹכוֹ	*Et medium ejus.*	And his midst.
יכח	וְתוֹכֵחָה־־כַחַת	*Et increpatio.*	And reproof, rebuke.
—	וְתוֹכַחְתִּי	*Et castigatio mea.*	And my chastisement.
—	וְתוֹכִיחוּ	*Et disceptabitis.*	And ye shall plead.
תכך	וְתוּכִּיִּים	*Et pavones.* [*luisti*	And peacocks. [prevailed.
יכל	וַתּוּכָל	*Et potuisti, præva-*	And thou couldst, thou hast
ילל	וְתוֹלְלֵינוּ	*Et ejulatus nostri.*	And our howlings.
תלע	וְתוֹלַעַת	*Et coccus.*	And the scarlet.
תמך	וְתוֹמֵךְ	*Et tenens.*	And he that holdeth.
מות	וַתּוּמַת	*Et occisa est.*	And she was slain.
יסף	וַתּוֹסֶף	*Et addidit.*	And she added.
תעב	וְתוֹעֵבָה־־עֲבַת	*Et abominatio.*	And an abomination.
—	וְתוֹעֲבוֹתֵיהֶם־ב׳	*Et abominationes eorum.* [*ejus.*	And their abominations.
—	וְתוֹעֲבוֹתָיו־בֹתָ״	*Et abominationes*	And his abominations.
—	וְתוֹעֲבוֹתַיִךְ־בֹתַ׳	*Et abominationes tuæ.* [*rum.*	And thy abominations.
—	וְתוֹעֲבוֹתָם	*Et abominationes eo-*	And their abominations.
יעף	וְתוֹעָפוֹת	*Et altitudines, vires*	And the heights, strength.
יצא	וַתּוֹצֵא	*Et produxit.*	And she brought forth.
—	וַתּוֹצִיאֵנוּ	*Et eduxisti nos.*	And thou broughtest us out.
תקע	וְתוֹקֵעַ	*Et clangens.*	And shouting, blowing.
תור	וְתוֹר־־תֹּר	*Et turtur.*	And the turtle.
ירד	וַתּוֹרֶד־־תֹּרֶד	*Et demisit.*	And she let down.
—	וַתּוֹרִדֵם	*Et demisit eos.*	And she let them down.
ירה	וְתוֹרָה־־רַת	*Et lex.*	And the law.
—	וְתוֹרוֹת	*Et leges.* [*me.*	And the laws. [sess.
ירש	וְתוֹרִישֵׁנִי	*Et possidere facies*	And thou wilt make me to pos-
ירה	וְתוֹרֵךְ	*Et docebit te.*	And she shall teach thee.
—	וְתוֹרֹתַי	*Et leges meæ.*	And my laws.
—	וְתוֹרָתִי	*Et lex mea.*	And my law.
—	וְתוֹרֹתָיו	*Et leges ejus.*	And his laws.

ROOTS.	DERIVATIVES.	VERSIO.	SIGNIFICATION.
ירה	וְתוֹרָתְךָ	*Et lex tua.*	And thy law.
ישב	וַתּוֹשֶׁב	*Et collocasti.* [*nus.*	And thou hast placed.
—	וְתוֹשָׁב	*Et advena, inquili-*	And a stranger, sojourner.
—	וְתוֹשָׁבִים	*Et advenæ.*	And the strangers.
ישה	וְתוּשִׁיָּה	*Et substantia, essentia, scientia, sapi-*	And substance, reality, essence, knowledge, wisdom.
ישע	וְתוֹשִׁיעַ	*Et servabis.* [*entia.*	And thou wilt save.
—	וְתוֹשִׁיעֵנִי	*Et servabit me.*	And she shall save me.
—	וַתּוֹשַׁע	*Et servavit.*	And she saved.
זבח	וַתִּזְבָּחֵהוּ	*Et jugulavit eum.*	And she killed him.
—	וַתִּזְבָּחִים	*Et immolasti eos.*	And thou hast sacrificed them
זוד	וַתָּזִדוּ	*Et superbe egistis.*	And ye acted proudly.
זכר	וְתִזְכְּרֵנִי	*Et recordaberis mei.*	And thou shalt remember me
זנה	וַתִּזֶן־־זָנָה	*Et scortata est.*	And she committed fornication
—	וַתַּזְנֶה	*Et scortari fecisti.*	And thou hast caused to commit fornication.
—	וְתַזְנוּתַיִךְ־־נֻתִ״	*Et scortationes tuæ.*	And thy whoredoms.
זנח	וַתִּזְנַח	*Et abjecisti.*	And thou hast cast off.
זנה	וַתִּזְנִי	*Et scortata es.* [*eis.*	And thou hast committed fornication [nication with them
—	וַתִּזְנִים	*Et scortata es cum*	And thou hast committed for-
—	וַתִּזְנֶינָה	*Et scortatæ sunt.*	And they committed fornica-
זעק	וַתִּזְעַק	*Et clamavit.*	And she cried out. [tion.
אזר	וַתְּזָרֵנִי	*Et accinxisti me.*	And thou hast girded me.
חבא	וַתַּחְבָּא	*Et abscondit.*	And she hath hidden.
חבט	וַתַּחְבֹּט	*Et excussit.*	And she shook out.
חבק	וּתְחַבֵּק	*Et amplecteris.*	And thou wilt embrace.
חבש	וַתַּחֲבֹשׁ	*Et ligavit, stravit.*	And she saddled.
חגר	וַתַּחְגְּרוּ	*Et accinxistis.*	And ye girded.
חדל	וַתֶּחְדַּל	*Et desiit.*	And she ceased.
חדש	וּתְחַדֵּשׁ	*Et renovabis.*	And thou wilt renew.
חול	וַתְּחוֹלֵל	*Et formasti.*	And thou hast formed.
—	וּתְחוֹלֵל	*Et expecta.*	And wait thou.
אחז	וַתֹּחֶז	*Et apprehendit.*	And she took, held.
חזה	וְתַחַז	*Et videbit.* [*git.*	And she shall see. [strained.
חזק	וַתַּחֲזֵק וַתֶּחֱזַק	*Et apprehendit coe-*	And she caught hold, con-
—	וַתֶּחֱזַק	*Et ursit.*	And she urged.

ROOTS.	DERIVATIVES.	VERSIO.	SIGNIFICATION.
חטא	וַתַּחֲטִא	*Et peccare fecisti.*	And thou hast made to sin.
—	וַתֶּחֱטָא	*Et peccasti.*	And thou hast sinned.
חיה	וַתְּחִי	*Et revixit.*	And she revived.
—	וּתְחִי	*Et vivet.*	And she shall live.
—	וַתְּחַיֶּין	*Et vivos servavistis, vivos servarunt.*	And ye saved alive, they saved alive.
חול	וְתָחִיל וַתָּחֹל	*Et dolebit.*	And she shall be sorrowful.
—	וַתָּחֶל	*Et contremuit.*	And she trembled.
חלל	וַתָּחֶל	*Et cœpit.*	And she began.
חלם	וְתַחֲלִימֵנִי	*Et sanabis me.*	And thou wilt recover me.
חלל	וַתְּחִלֶּינָה	*Et inceperunt.*	And they began.
—	וַתְּחַלְּלוּ	*Et polluistis.*	And ye have polluted.
—	וַתְּחַלְלֶיהָ	*Et polluisti eam.*	And thou hast polluted her.
—	וַתְּחַלֶּלְנָה	*Et polluistis.*	And ye have polluted.
חלף	וַתַּחֲלֵף	*Et mutasti.*	And thou hast changed.
חלק	וַתֶּחֱלְקֵם	*Et divisisti eos.*	And thou hast divided them.
חמל	וַתַּחְמֹל	*Et miserta est.*	And she had compassion.
חמר	וַתַּחְמְרָה	*Et oblevit eam.*	And he daubed it.
חנן	וְתַחֲנוּנִים	*Et deprecationes.*	And supplications.
חנף	וַתַּחֲנִיפִי	*Et polluisti.*	And thou hast polluted.
—	וַתַּחֲנֹף	*Et polluit.*	And she defiled.
—	וַתֶּחֱנַף	*Et polluta est.*	And she was polluted.
חוס	וַתָּחָס	*Et pepercit.*	And she spared.
חסר	וַתְּחַסְּרֵהוּ	*Et minuisti eum.*	And thou hast made him less.
חפר	וְתַחְפְּרוּ	*Et pudebit vos.*	And ye shall be ashamed.
חצה	וְתֵחָץ	*Et dividetur.*	And she shall be divided.
חוש	וַתָּחַשׁ	*Et festinavit.*	And she made haste.
חשב	וַתֵּחָשֵׁב	*Et reputata est.*	And she was counted.
—	וַתַּחְשְׁבֵהוּ	*Et æstimasti eum.*	And thou hast esteemed, taken account of him.
—	וְתַחְשְׁבֵנִי	*Et reputabis me.*	And thou wilt account me.
חשך	וַתֶּחְשַׁךְ	*Et obscurata est.*	And she was darkened.
תחת	וְתַחַת	*Et sub, pro.*	And under, for, instead of.
נחת	וְתַחֵת	*Et repones.*	And thou shalt lay up.
תחת	וְתַחְתַּי	*Et intra me.*	And within myself.
—	וְתַחְתֶּיהָ	*Et sub illa.*	And under her.
חתם	וַתַּחְתֹּם	*Et obsignavit.*	And she sealed.

ROOTS.	DERIVATIVES.	VERSIO.	SIGNIFICATION.
נטה	וַתֵּט	*Et declinavit.*	And she declined, turned aside
טבע	וַתִּטְבַּע	*Et infixa est.*	And she was fixed.
נטה	וַתִּטֵּהוּ	*Et tetendit eum.*	And she spread it.
טהר	וַתְּטַהֲרֵם	*Et mundavit eos.*	And she cleansed them.
טמא	וַתִּטְמָא	*Et polluta est.*	And she was polluted.
—	וַתְּטַמְּאוּ	*Et polluistis.*	And ye defiled.
טמן	וַתִּטְמְנֵם	*Et abscondit eos.*	And he hid them.
נטע	וַתִּטָּעֶהָ	*Et plantasti eam.*	And thou hast planted her.
—	וַתִּטָּעֵם	*Et plantasti eos.*	And thou hast planted them.
—	וַתִּטָּעֵמוֹ	*Et plantabis eos.*	And thou shalt plant them.
טפל	וַתִּטְפֹּל	*Et consuisti.* [*dit se.*	And thou sewedst up. [self.
נטש	וַתִּטֹּשׁ	*Et explicavit, diffu-*	And she unfolded, spread her-
יבב	וַתְּיַבֵּב	*Et vociferata est.*	And she cried aloud.
יבש	וַתִּיבַשׁ	*Et exaruit.*	And she dried up, withered.
יטב	וַתֵּיטֶב	*Et ornavit.*	And she adorned.
—	וַתִּיטַב	*Et placuit.*	And it pleased.
—	וְתִיטַב	*Et placebit.*	And it shall please,
ימן	וְתֵימָנָה	*Et ad austrum.*	And toward the south.
ינק	וַתֵּינֶק	*Et lactavit.*	And she suckled.
—	וַתֵּינִק	*Et lactabit.*	And she shall suckle, nurse.
יפה	וַתִּיפִי	*Et pulchra fuisti.*	And thou wast beautiful.
יקד	וַתִּיקַד	*Et exarsit.*	And she burned.
ירא	וְתִירָא	*Et timebit.*	And she shall fear.
—	וַתִּירְאוּ	*Et timuistis.*	And ye feared.
—	וְתִירְאוּ	*Et timebitis.*	And ye shall fear. [fear.
—	וַתִּירְאִי	*Et timuisti, timebis.*	And thou hast feared, shalt
—	וַתִּירֶאןָ	*Et timuère.* [*novum.*	And they feared.
ירש	וְתִירוֹשׁ־־רֹשׁ	*Et mustum, vinum*	And wine, new wine.
—	וְתִירוֹשִׁי	*Et mustum meum.*	And my wine.
—	וְתִירוֹשָׁם	*Et mustum eorum.*	And their wine.
—	וַתִּירָשׁוּ	*Et possedistis.*	And ye have possessed.
—	וְתִירשְׁךָ	*Et mustum tuum.*	And thy wine.
תיש	וּתְיָשִׁים	*Et hirci.*	And he-goats.
ישן	וַתְּיַשְּׁנֵהוּ	*Et dormire fecit eum*	And she made him sleep.
ישר	וַתִּישַׁר	*Et recta fuit, placuit*	And she was right, pleased.
תוך	וָתֹךְ	*Et fraus.*	And fraud.
נכה	וַתַּךְ	*Et percussit.*	And she smote.

ROOTS.	DERIVATIVES.	VERSIO.	SIGNIFICATION.
כבד	וַתְּכַבֵּד	*Et honorasti.* [*fuit.*	And thou hast honoured.
—	וַתִּכְבַּד	*Et prævaluit, gravis*	And she prevailed, was heavy
—	וַתִּכָּבְדִי	*Et glorificata es.*	And thou hast been made glorious. [rify me.
—	וּתְכַבְּדֵנִי	*Et honorabis me.*	And thou shalt honour, glo-
כבש	וַתִּכְבְּשׁוּ	*Et subegistis.*	And ye have subjected.
כהה	וַתֵּכַהּ	*Et caligavit.*	And she was dim, dark.
—	וַתִּכְהֶיןָ	*Et caligarunt.*	And they were dim, dark.
כון	וַתִּכּוֹן	*Et parata, stabilita est.*	And she was prepared, established.
—	וַתְּכוֹנֵן	*Et confirmasti.*	And thou hast confirmed.
—	וְתִכּוֹנֵן	*Et præparabitur.*	And she shall be prepared.
—	וּתְכוֹנֵן	*Et stabilies.*	And thou shalt establish.
—	וּתְכוּנָתוֹ	*Et dispositio ejus.*	And his arrangement.
כחד	וַתִּכָּחֵד	*Et excisus es.* [*est.*	And thou hast been cut off.
כחש	וַתְּכַחֵשׁ	*Et negavit, mentita*	And she denied, lied.
תכך	וְתֻכִּיִּים	*Et pavones.*	And peacocks.
כלה	וַתֵּכֶל	*Et desiit.*	And she ceased.
—	וַתֵּכֶל	*Et absoluta est.*	And she was finished.
—	וּתְכַל	*Et cessare facies.*	And thou shalt cause to cease
כלם	וַתַּכְלִימֵנוּ	*Et ignominia affecisti nos.*	And thou hast put us to shame
כלה	וַתִּכְלֶינָה	*Et absolutæ sunt.*	And they were ended.
תכל	וּתְכֵלֶת	*Et hyacinthus.* [*est.*	And blue or violet. [blished.
כון	וַתִּכֹּן	*Et parata, stabilita*	And she was prepared, esta-
תכן	וְתֹכֵן	*Et perpendens.* [*ra, modus.*	And he that weigheth, pondereth. [tale.
—	וְתֹכֶן	*Et numerus, mensu-*	And the number, measure,
כנע	וַתַּכְנַע וַתִּכָּנַע	*Et depressisti, abjecisti te, depressus est.*	And thou hast brought down, thou hast humbled thyself, he hath been brought low.
כסה	וַתְּכַס	*Et operuisti, operuit, texit se.*	And thou hast covered, she covered, covered herself.
—	וּתְכַסֶּהָ	*Et operiet eam.*	And she shall cover her.
—	וַתְּכַסֵּהוּ	*Et operuit eum.*	And she covered him.
—	וַתְּכַסֵּים	*Et texisti eos.*	And thou hast covered them.
—	וַתְּכַסֵּנוּ	*Et operuit nos.*	And she hath covered us.

ROOTS.	DERIVATIVES.	VERSIO.	SIGNIFICATION.
כסה	וַתְּכַסֵּנִי	*Et operuit me.*	And she hath covered me.
כפל	וְתִכָּפֵל	*Et duplicabitur.*	And she shall be doubled.
כרה	וְתִכְרוּ	*Et fodietis.*	And ye shall dig.
כרך	וְתַכְרִיךְ	*Et pallium.*	And a robe, garment.
כרע	וַתִּכְרַע	*Et incurvavit se.*	And she bowed herself.
כרת	וַתִּכְרֹת	*Et pepigisti* fœdus.	And thou hast made *a covenant.*
—	וַתִּכְרֹת	*Et abscidit.*	And she cut off.
—	וַתִּכְרְתוּ	*Et pepigistis.*	And ye have made.
כתב	וַתִּכְתֹּב	*Et scripsit.*	And she wrote.
לאה	וַתֵּלֶא	*Et ægre tulisti, defatigata es.*	And thou hast been grieved at, been wearied.
—	וּתְלָאָה	*Et molestia, lassitudo*	And trouble, weariness.
לבב	וַתְּלַבֵּב	*Et placentas fecit.*	And she made cakes.
—	וּתְלַבֵּב	*Et placentas faciet.*	And she shall make cakes.
לבש	וַתִּלְבַּשׁ	*Et induit.*	And she put on.
—	וַתִּלְבַּשׁ	*Et induit se.*	And she clothed herself.
ילד	וַתֵּלֶד	*Et peperit.*	And she bare.
—	וְתֵלֵד	*Et pariet.*	And she shall bear.
—	וַתֵּלַדְןָ־נָה	*Et pepererunt.*	And they bare.
—	וְתֵלַדְנָה	*Et parient.*	And they shall bear.
להה	וַתֵּלַהּ	*Et turbata est, insanivit.*	And she was in confusion, outrageous.
תלה	וְתָלָה	*Et suspendet.*	And she shall hang.
להט	וַתְּלַהֵט	*Et inflammavit.*	And she set on fire.
—	וְתִלַהֵט	*Et succendet.*	And she shall burn up.
—	וַתְּלַהֲטֵהוּ	*Et accendit eum.*	And she set him on fire.
תלה	וְתָלוּ	*Et suspendent.*	And they shall hang.
תלל	וְתָלוּל	*Et eminens, aggestus.*	And high, eminent, heaped up
לוש	וַתָּלָוש וַתָּלָשׁ	*Et depsuit.*	And she kneaded.
לחץ	וַתִּלָּחֵץ־לָחַץ	*Et compressit.*	And she crushed.
תלה	וְתָלִיתָ	*Et suspendes.*	And thou shalt hang.
ילד	וַתֵּלֶךְ	*Et ivisti, ambulasti, ivit, abiit.*	And thou hast gone, walked, she went, departed.
לכד	וַתִּלָּכֵד	*Et capta est.*	And she was taken.
ילד	וַתֵּלְכוּ	*Et abiistis.*	And ye have gone away.
—	וַתֵּלְכִי	*Et venisti.*	And thou hast come.
—	וַתֵּלַכְנָה	*Et iverunt.*	And they went.
לעג	וַתִּלְעַג	*Et subsannasti.*	And thou mockedst.

ROOTS.	DERIVATIVES.	VERSIO.	SIGNIFICATION.
תלע	וְתֹלַעַת	*Et coccus.*	And the scarlet.
לקח	וַתִּלָּקַח	*Et capta est.*	And she was taken.
לקט	וַתְּלַקֵּט	*Et collegit.*	And she gleaned.
תלת	וּתְלָת	*Et tertia.*	And the third.
—	וְתַלְתַּא־־תַּי	*Et tertius.*	And the third.
—	וּתְלָתָה	*Et tres.*	And three.
תמם	וְתַם	*Et absumetur.*	And she shall be consumed.
—	וְתֹם	*Et integritas.*	And the uprightness.
מאן	וַתְּמָאֵן	*Et renuisti, renuit.*	And thou hast refused, she refused.
—	וַתְּמָאֲנוּ	*Et renuistis.*	And ye have refused.
מאס	וַתִּמְאָס	*Et abominatus es.*	And thou hast abhorred.
מוג	וּתְמֹגְגֵנִי	*Et dissolves me.*	And thou wilt dissolve me.
תמה	וּתְמָהוּ	*Et admiramini.*	And wonder ye.
—	וְתִמְהוֹהִי	*Et mirabilia ejus.*	And his wonders.
—	וְתִימְהַיָּא־־הַיִן	*Et mirabilia.*	And wonders.
מהר	וַתְּמַהֵר	*Et festinavit.*	And she hasted.
—	וּתְמַהֵרְנָה	*Et festinabunt.*	And they shall make haste.
תמם	וְתַמּוּ	*Et consumentur.*	And they shall be consumed.
מוג	וַתָּמוֹג	*Et liquefiet.*	And she shall melt.
—	וַתְּמוּגֵנוּ	*Et dissolvisti nos.*	And thou hast dissolved us.
מון	וּתְמוּנָה	*Et imago, similitudo*	And an image, likeness.
מור	וּתְמוּרָתָהּ	*Et mutatio, commutatio ejus*	And her change, exchange.
—	וּתְמוּרָתוֹ	*Et mutatio, commutatio ejus*	And his change, exchange.
תמד	וְתָמִיד	*Et jugiter.*	And continually.
תמם	וּתְמִימִים	*Et integri.*	And the upright, perfect.
מכר	וַתִּמְכּוֹר	*Et vendidit.*	And she sold.
תמך	וְתֹמְכֶיהָ	*Et tenentes eam.*	And they that hold her.
מלא	וַתְּמַלֵּא	*Et implevit.*	And she filled.
—	וַתִּמָּלֵא	*Et repleta est.*	And she was filled.
—	וַתִּמָּלְאִי	*Et repleta es.*	And thou wast replenished.
—	וַתְּמַלֶּאנָה	*Et impleverunt.*	And they filled.
מלט	וַתְּמַלֵּט	*Et ova edidit.*	And she laid eggs.
מלך	וַתַּמְלִיכוּ	*Et regem constituistis.*	And ye have made king.
מון	וּתְמֻנַת	*Et similitudo.*	And the likeness.
מסה	וַתֶּמֶס	*Et liquescere fecisti.*	And thou hast caused to melt away.
מעל	וַתִּמְעֹל	*Et prævaricata est.*	And she transgressed.

ROOTS.	DERIVATIVES.	VERSIO.	SIGNIFICATION.
מצא	וַתִּמָּצֵא	*Et inventa est.*	And she was found.
—	וַתִּמְצָא	*Et invenit.*	And she found.
מור	וַתֶּמֶר	*Et mutavit.*	And she changed.
תמר	וְתִמֹּרָה	*Et palma.*	And a palm-tree.
מרה	וַתַּמְרוּ	*Et rebellastis.*	And ye rebelled.
תמר	וְתִמֹרָו	*Et palmæ ejus.*	And his palm-trees.
—	וְתִמְרוֹת	*Et columnæ.*	And pillars.
—	וְתִמֹּרוֹת־רֹ־רִים	*Et palmæ.*	And palm-trees.
משך	וַתִּמְשֹׁךְ	*Et distulisti.*	And thou hast deferred.
משל	וְתַמְשִׁלֻנִי	*Et comparabitis me.*	And ye will compare me.
מות	וַתָּמֹת וַתָּמָת	*Et mortua est.*	And she died, is dead.
—	וְתָמֹת	*Et morietur.*	And she will die.
נתן	וְתֵן	*Et da.*	And give thou.
נאף	וַתִּנְאַף	*Et adulterata est.*	And she committed adultery.
ידע	וְתִנְדַּע	*Et nosces.*	And thou shalt know.
נהג	וַתְּנַהֵג	*Et adduxisti.*	And thou hast brought.
נתן	וּתְנֵהוּ	*Et da eum.*	And give thou him.
נהל	וּתְנַהֲלֵנִי	*Et deduces me.*	And thou shalt lead, guide me
נתן	וּתְנוּ	*Et date, ponite.*	And give, put ye.
בוא	וּתְנוּבַת	*Et fructus, proventus.*	And the fruit, increase, produce.
נוח	וְתָנוּחַ	*Et quiesces.*	And thou shalt rest.
נום	וּתְנוּמָה	*Et dormitatio.*	And slumber, drowsiness.
תנר	וְתַנּוּר	*Et fornax.*	And a furnace.
נוח	וַתָּנַח	*Et requievit.*	And she rested.
ינח	וַתַּנַּח	*Et reposuit.*	And she laid up.
נחם	וּתְנַחֲמֵנִי	*Et consolaberis me.*	And thou wilt comfort me.
נחת	וַתִּנְחַת	*Et descendit.*	And she came down.
תנה	וְתַנִּים	*Et dracones.*	And the dragons.
—	וְתַנִּין	*Et draco.*	And the dragon.
נוע	וַתְּנִיעֵנִי	*Et movit me.*	And she moved me.
ינק	וַתְּנִיקֵהוּ	*Et lactavit eum.*	And she suckled him.
נתן	וּתְנֵם	*Et da eos.*	And give thou them.
נוס	וַתָּנָס	*Et fugit.*	And she fled.
נצל	וַתִּנָּצֵל	*Et erepta est.*	And she was delivered.
נשא	וְתִנַּשֵּׂא	*Et efferet se.*	And he will exalt himself.
נתן	וַתִּנָּתֵן־־תֶן	*Et data est.*	And she was given.
—	וְתִנָּתֵן־־תֶן	*Et tradetur.*	And she will be given up.

ROOTS.	DERIVATIVES.	VERSIO.	SIGNIFICATION.
סבב	וַתִּסֹּב	*Et vertit se.*	And she turned herself about.
—	וְתִסֹּב	*Et circumibis.*	And thou shalt go about.
נסג	וְתַסֵּג	*Et assequeris.*	And thou shalt overtake.
סגד	וְתִסְגְּדוּן	*Et procumbetis, adorabitis.*	And ye shall bow down, shall worship.
סגר	וַתִּסָּגֵר	*Et exclusa est.*	And she was shut out.
—	וַתִּסְגֹּר	*Et clausit.*	And she shut.
סות	וַתְּסִיתֵהוּ	*Et incitavit eum.*	And she moved him.
—	וַתְּסִיתֵנִי	*Et incitasti me.*	And thou hast moved me.
סכך	וְתָסֵךְ	*Et proteges.*	And thou wilt protect.
יסף	וַתֹּסֶף	*Et addidit.*	And she added.
סוף	וְתָסֵף	*Et consumet.*	And she will consume.
ספד	וַתִּסְפֹּד	*Et planxit.*	And she mourned.
ספר	וַתְּסַפֵּר	*Et narravit.*	And she told.
סור	וַתָּסַר	*Et amovit.*	And she removed.
—	וְתָסַר	*Et auferet.*	And she shall take away.
סתר	וַתַּסְתִּירֵהוּ	*Et abscondit eum.*	And she hid him.
תעב	וְתַעֵב	*Et abominando.*	And in abhorring.
עבד	וַתַּעַבְדוּ	*Et coluistis.* [me.	And ye served.
תעב	וְתִעֲבוּנִי	*Et abominabuntur*	And they shall abhor me.
עבר	וְתַעֲבִיר	*Et auferes.*	And thou shalt remove.
—	וַתַּעֲבֹר	*Et transivit.*	And she went over.
—	וַתַּעַבְרוּ	*Et transivistis.* [lius	And ye went over.
תעב	וְתֹעֲבֹתָיו	*Et abominationes il-*	And his abominations.
עגב	וַתַּעְגַּב וַתֶּעְגָּב	*Et adamavit.*	And she loved exceedingly.
—	וַתַּעְגְּבָ־־בָה	*Et adamavit.*	And she loved exceedingly.
עוד	וַתָּעַד	*Et testatus es.*	And thou testifiedst.
עדה	וַתַּעַד	*Et ornavit se.*	And she adorned herself.
—	וַתַּעְדִּי	*Et ornasti te.*	And thou hast adorned thyself.
עזז	וַתָּעָז	*Et prævaluit.*	And she prevailed.
עזב	וְתַעֲזֹב	*Et derelinques.*	And thou wilt leave, forsake.
—	וַתַּעַזְבִי	*Et reliquisti.*	And thou hast left.
—	וַתַּעַזְבֵם	*Et dereliquisti eos.*	And thou hast forsaken them.
עטה	וַתַּעַט	*Et declinasti, involasti.* [hibuit mihi.	And thou hast turned aside to, didst fly upon.
עוד	וַתְּעִידֵנִי	*Et testimonium per-*	And she gave testimony to me.
עלה	וַתַּעַל וַתַּעֲלֶה	*Et ascendit.*	And she came up.

ROOTS.	DERIVATIVES.	VERSIO.	SIGNIFICATION.
עלה	וַתַּעַל	*Et ascendit, invaluit, eduxit, eduxisti.*	And she went up, increased, brought up, thou brought-
—	וְתַעַל	*Et ascendet.*	And she will go up. [est up.
—	וַתַּעֲלֵהוּ	*Et eduxit eum.*	And she brought him up.
—	וַתַּעֲלוּ וַתַּעֲלוּ	*Et ascendistis.*	And ye went up.
עלל	וְתַעֲלוּלִים	*Et infantes, pueriles*	And babes, childish.
עלז	וְתַעֲלֹזְנָה	*Et exultabunt.*	And they shall rejoice.
עלה	וַתַּעֲלִי	*Et ascendisti.*	And thou hast gone up.
—	וַתַּעֲלֶינָה	*Et ascenderunt.*	And they came up.
עלם	וְתַעֲלֻמָה	*Et abscondita.*	And she that is hidden.
עלה	וַתַּעֲלֶנָה	*Et ascenderunt.*	And they went up.
עמד	וַתַּעֲמֹד	*Et stetit, desiit.*	And she stood, stopped, ceased
—	וְתַעֲמֹד	*Et stabis.*	And thou shalt stand.
—	וַתַּעַמְדוּן	*Et stetistis.*	And ye stood.
—	וַתַּעֲמֹדְנָה	*Et steterunt.*	And they stood.
—	וַתַּעֲמִדֵנִי	*Et statuit me.*	And she set me.
—	וַתַּעֲמוֹד	*Et mansit.*	And she continued, remained.
ענה	וַתַּעַן	*Et respondit.*	And she answered.
ענג	וְתַעֲנֻגוֹת	*Et deliciæ.*	And the delights.
ענה	וַתַּעֲנוּ	*Et respondistis.*	And ye answered.
—	וַתְּעַנֶּהָ	*Et afflixit eam.*	And she afflicted her.
—	וַתַּעֲנֶינָה	*Et responderunt.*	And they answered.
—	וּתְעַנֵּנוּ	*Et affliges nos.*	And thou wilt afflict us.
—	וַתַּעֲנֵנִי	*Et exaudisti me, respondisti mihi.*	And thou heardst me, thou answeredst me.
עצם	וְתַעֲצֻמוֹת	*Et vires.*	And strength. [ped.
עצר	וַתֵּעָצַר	*Et cohibebitur.*	And she shall be stayed, stop-
—	וַתֵּעָצַר	*Et cohibita est.*	And she was stayed, stopped.
ערה	וַתְּעַר	*Et evacuavit.*	And she emptied.
ערך	וַתַּעֲרֹךְ	*Et disposuit, instruxit.* [*duxit.*	And she put in order, set in array. [made, brought forth
עשה	וַתַּעַשׂ וַתַּעֲשֶׂה	*Et fecisti, fecit, pro-*	And thou hast done, she did,
—	וְתֵעָשׂ	*Et fiet.*	And it shall be done, perform-
—	וַתַּעֲשׂוּ	*Et fecistis.*	And ye did, have made. [ed.
—	וַתַּעֲשִׂי	*Et fecisti.*	And thou madest, hast done.
עשה	וַתַּעֲשֶׂינָה	*Et fecerunt.*	And they did, performed.
תפף	וְתֹף	*Et tympanum.*	And a timbrel.

ROOTS.	DERIVATIVES.	VERSIO.	SIGNIFICATION.
פאר	וְתִפְאֶרֶת	*Et decor, gloria.*	And the beauty, glory.
—	וְתִפְאַרְתּוֹ	*Et gloria ejus.*	And his glory.
—	וְתִפְאַרְתְּךָ	*Et gloria tua.*	And thy glory.
—	וְתִפְאַרְתֵּנוּ	*Et gloria nostra.*	And our glory.
פגש	וַתִּפְגֹּשׁ	*Et occurrit.*	And she met.
אפה	וַתֹּפֵהוּ	*Et coxit eum.*	And she baked it.
תפח	וְתַפּוּחַ	*Et malus.* [*træ.*	And the apple-tree.
פוץ	וּתְפוֹצוֹתֵיכֶם	*Et dispersiones ves-*	And your dispersions.
—	וּתְפוּצֶין	*Et dispergentur.*	And they shall be scattered.
—	וַתְּפוּצֶינָה	*Et dispersæ sunt.*	And they were scattered.
פזר	וַתְּפַזְּרִי	*Et sparsisti.*	And thou hast scattered.
פחד	וַתִּפְחַד	*Et expavisti.*	And thou hast feared.
פוץ	וּתְפִיצֵם	*Et disperges eos.*	And thou shalt scatter them.
נפל	וַתַּפֵּל	*Et dejecit.*	And she cast down.
תפל	וְתָפֵל	*Et insulsans.*	And foolish.
נפל	וַתִּפֹּל	*Et cecidit.*	And she fell.
—	וְתִפֹּל	*Et cadet.*	And she shall fall.
פלל	וּתְפִלָּה	*Et oratio.*	And prayer.
פלט	וַתְּפַלְּטֵמוֹ	*Et liberasti eum.*	And thou deliveredst him.
—	וַתְּפַלְּטֵנִי	*Et liberasti me.*	And thou deliveredst me.
—	וּתְפַלְּטֵנִי	*Et liberabis me.*	And thou wilt deliver me.
פלל	וּתְפִלַּת	*Et oratio.*	And prayer.
—	וּתְפִלָּתוֹ	*Et oratio ejus.*	And his prayer.
—	וּתְפִלָּתִי	*Et oratio mea.*	And my prayer.
פנה	וַתֵּפֶן	*Et vertit se.*	And she turned.
יפע	וַתֹּפַע	*Et splendebit.*	And she will shine.
פעם	וַתִּפָּעֶם	*Et turbata est.*	And she was troubled.
פיק	וְתָפֵק	*Et expromes.*	And thou shalt draw out.
פקד	וַתִּפְקֹד	*Et visitasti.*	And thou hast visited. [brance.
—	וַתִּפְקְדִי	*Et recordata es.*	And thou calledst to remem-
—	וַתִּפְקְדֶנּוּ	*Et visitasti eum.*	And thou hast visited him.
פקח	וַתִּפָּקַחְנָה	*Et aperti sunt.* [*est.*	And they were opened.
פור	וַתֻּפַר	*Et irritum factum*	And it came to nought.
—	וְתָפֵר	*Et deficiet.*	And she shall fail.
—	וְתֻפַר	*Et irritum fiet.*	And it will come to nought.
פרח	וְתִפְרַח	*Et florebit.*	And she shall blossom, flourish
פרע	וַתִּפְרְעוּ	*Et rejecistis.*	And ye have rejected.

ROOTS.	DERIVATIVES.	VERSIO.	SIGNIFICATION.
פרץ	וַתִּפְרָץ	*Et irrupit.*	And she broke in.
פרש	וַתִּפְרֹשׂ	*Et expandit.*	And she spread.
תפש	וְתָפַשׂ	*Et cepit.*	And he took.
—	וְתֹפֵשׂ	*Et tenens, tractans.*	And he that handleth.
—	וּתְפָשָׂהּ	*Et apprehendet eam*	And he shall lay hold on her.
—	וְתָפְשׂוּ	*Et prehendent.*	And they will take hold.
—	וְתִפְשׂוּהוּ	*Et prehendite.*	And take ye him.
—	וְתֹפְשֵׂי	*Et tractantes.*	And they that handle.
פשק	וַתְּפַשְּׂקִי	*Et divaricasti.*	And thou hast opened wide.
תפש	וְתָפַשְׂתִּי	*Et capiam.*	And I will take.
תפת	וְתֹפֶת	*Et tympanum.*	And a timbrel.
פתח	וַתִּפְתַּח	*Et aperuit.*	And she opened.
יצא	וַתֵּצֵא	*Et egressa est.*	And she went out, came out.
—	וְתֹצֵא	*Et eduxisti.*	And thou broughtest out.
—	וְתֵצֵא	*Et egredictur.*	And she will come out.
—	וַתֵּצֶאןָ־נָה	*Et egressæ sunt.*	And they came out.
צבר	וַתִּצְבֹּר	*Et coacervavit.*	And she heaped up.
צדק	וַתְּצַדְּקִי	*Et justificasti.*	And thou hast justified.
צהל	וְתִצְהֲלוּ	*Et exultabitis.* [*ei.*	And ye will exult. [ment.
צוה	וַתְּצַוֵּהוּ	*Et mandatum dedit*	And she gave him a command-
צחק	וַתִּצְחַק	*Et risit.*	And she laughed.
יצב	וַתַּצִּיבֵנִי	*Et statuisti.*	And thou hast set me.
נצל	וַתַּצִּילֵם	*Et liberasti eos.*	And thou deliveredst them.
צלח	וַתִּצְלַח	*Et invasit.*	And she came upon.
—	וַתִּצְלְחִי	*Et prosperata es.*	And thou hast prospered.
צנח	וַתִּצְנַח	*Et descendit, infixit.*	And she came down upon, fastened.
צעד	וְתִצְעָדֵהוּ	*Et deducet eum.*	And she shall lead him.
צעק	וַתִּצְעֲקוּ	*Et clamastis.*	And ye cried.
צפן	וַתִּצְפְּנֵהוּ־נוּ	*Et abscondit eum.*	And she hid him.
יצק	וַתִּצֹּק	*Et effudit.*	And she poured out.
יצר	וַתֵּצֶר	*Et angustiata est, angustia fuit.*	And she was straitened, there was distress.
נצר	וְתִצְּרֶךָּ	*Et custodiet te.*	And she shall keep thee.
יצת	וַתִּצַּת	*Et incendet.*	And she shall kindle.
קוא	וַתָּקֵא	*Et evomuit.*	And she vomited.
קבץ	וַתִּקָּבְצוּ	*Et collegistis.*	And ye gathered together.

ROOTS.	DERIVATIVES.	VERSIO.	SIGNIFICATION.
קבר	וַתִּקָּבֵר	*Et sepulta est.*	And she was buried.
—	וַתִּקְבְּרוּ	*Et sepelistis.*	And ye buried.
קדד	וַתִּקֹּד	*Et incurvavit se.*	And she bowed.
קדם	וְתַקְדִּים	*Et præveniet.*	And she shall prevent.
קהל	וַתִּקָּהֵל	*Et congregata est.*	And she was gathered together
קוה	וְתִקְוָה־וַת	*Et spes, expectatio.*	And hope, expectation.
תקע	וְתָקוֹעַ	*Et clangendo.*	And in blowing, shouting.
יקף	וּתְקוּפָתוֹ	*Et circuitus, revolutio ejus.*	And his circuit, revolution.
קוה	וְתִקְוָתִי	*Et spes mea.*	And my hope.
—	וְתִקְוָתְךָ	*Et spes tua.*	And thy hope.
—	וְתִקְוָתָם	*Et spes eorum.*	And their hope.
לקח	וְתִקַּח	*Et cepisti, sumpsit.*	And thou hast taken, she took
—	וַתֻּקַּח	*Et capta est.*	And she was taken.
—	וְתִקַּח	*Et accipiet.*	And she shall receive.
—	וַתִּקָּחֵהוּ	*Et comparavit, abstulit eum.*	And she bought, took him away.
—	וַתִּקְחִי	*Et sumpsisti.*	And thou hast taken.
—	וַתִּקָּחֶיהָ	*Et sumpsit eam.*	And she took, fetched her.
—	וַתִּקָּחֵם	*Et abstulit eos.*	And she took them away.
—	וַתִּקָּחֵנִי	*Et cepit me.*	And she took me.
קטן	וַתִּקְטַן	*Et parva fuit, parum fuit.*	And she was little, it was a small thing.
תקף	וְתַקִּיפָא	*Et robustus, fortis.*	And strong, mighty.
קלל	וַתֵּקַל	*Et vilis habita est.*	And she was despised.
קום	וַתָּקָם	*Et surrexit.*	And she arose.
—	וַתָּקֶם	*Et confirmasti.*	And thou hast confirmed.
קמט	וַתִּקְמְטֵנִי	*Et corrugasti me.*	And thou hast filled me with [wrinkles.
קנא	וַתְּקַנֵּא	*Et invidit.*	And she envied.
יקע	וַתֵּקַע	*Et luxata, divulsa est.*	And she was out of joint, was alienated from.
תקע	וְתָקַע	*Et clanget.*	And he shall blow, shout.
—	וְתָקֹעַ	*Et clangens.* [*gent.*	And blowing, sounding.
—	וְתָקְעוּ	*Et clanxerunt, clan-*	And they blew, shall blow.
—	וְתִקְעוּ	*Clangite.*	Blow ye.
—	וְתָקַעְתִּי	*Et clangam.*	And I will blow.
—	וּתְקַעְתִּיו	*Et figam eum.*	And I will fix, fasten him.

ROOTS.	DERIVATIVES.	VERSIO.	SIGNIFICATION.
תקע	וּתְקַעְתֶּם	*Et clangetis.*	And ye shall blow.
תקף	וּתְקַף	*Et invaluit.*	And he was strong.
—	וְתָקְפָּא	*Et robur.*	And strength.
—	וּתְקֵפְתְּ	*Et invaluisti.*	And thou hast become strong
קצר	וַתִּקְצַר	*Et angustata est.*	And she was straitened.
קרא	וַתַּקְרֵא	*Et evenire fecisti.*	And thou hast caused to happen.
—	וַתִּקְרָא	*Et vocavit, clamavit*	And she called, cried.
—	וַתִּקְרֶאןָ־נָה	*Et vocaverunt, acciderunt.*	And they called, happened.
קרב	וַתִּקְרַב	*Et appropinquavit.*	And she drew near.
—	וְתִקְרַב	*Et appropinquabit.*	And she shall draw nigh.
—	וּתְקָרֵב	*Et adduces, offeres.*	And thou shalt bring, shalt offer.
—	וַתִּקְרְבוּ־רַבְנָה	*Et accesserunt.*	And they came near.
—	וַתִּקְרְבוּן	*Et accessistis.*	And ye came near.
—	וַתַּקְרִיבִי	*Et accedere fecisti.*	And thou hast caused to draw near.
קרע	וַתִּקְרַע	*Et lacerasti, lacerata vit.* [sa est.	And thou hast rent, she hath rent.
קשה	וַתְּקַשׁ	*Et difficultatem passa*	And she experienced difficulty
קשר	וַתִּקָּשֵׁר	*Et ligata est.*	And she was bound.
—	וַתִּקְשֹׁר	*Et ligavit.*	And she bound.
—	וּקְשַׁרְתָּם	*Et alligabis eos.*	And thou shalt bind them.
—	וְתִקְשְׁרֵנוּ	*Et ligabis eum.*	And thou shalt bind him.
ראה	וַתֵּרֶא־רֶאה	*Et vidisti, vidit.*	And thou sawest, she saw.
—	וְתֵרֶא	*Et videbit.*	And she shall see.
—	וְתֵרָאֶה	*Et apparebit.*	And she shall appear.
—	וַתִּרְאֵהוּ	*Et vidit ipsum.*	And she saw him.
—	וַתִּרְאוּ	*Et vidistis.*	And ye saw.
—	וַתִּרְאֶינָה	*Et viderunt.*	And they have seen.
—	וַתִּרְאֶנָה	*Et viderunt.*	And they saw.
—	וַתִּרְאֵנִי	*Et vidit me.*	And she saw me.
רבה	וַתֵּרֶב	*Et major fuit, superavit.*	And she was greater, exceeded, excelled.
—	וְתֵרֶב	*Et augebitur.*	And she shall be increased.
—	וַתִּרְבֶּה	*Et multiplicavit.*	And she multiplied.
—	וְתִרְבֶּה	*Et augebitur.*	And she shall be increased.
—	וַתַּרְבִּי	*Et multiplicasti, auxisti.*	And thou hast multiplied, increased.

ROOTS.	DERIVATIVES.	VERSIO.	SIGNIFICATION.
רבה	וַתִּרְבִּי	*Et multiplicata es.*	And thou hast been multiplied
—	וַתִּרְבִּי	*Et multiplicabis.*	And thou shalt multiply.
—	וַתִּרְבֶּינָה	*Et multiplicatæ sunt*	And they were multiplied.
—	וְתַרְבִּית	*Et augmen, fœnus.*	And increase, usury.
רבץ	וַתִּרְבַּץ	*Et succubuit.*	And she lay down.
רגז	וַתִּרְגַּז	*Et commota est, contremuit.*	And she shook, quaked, trembled.
—	וַתִּרְגְּזִי	*Et provocasti me.*	And thou hast provoked me.
רגן	וַתֵּרָגְנוּ	*Et murmurastis.*	And ye murmured.
ירד	וַתֵּרֶד	*Et descendit.*	And she came down.
—	וַתֹּרֶד	*Et demisit.*	And she let down.
—	וְתֵרֵד	*Et descendet.*	And she shall go down.
—	וְתֵרֵד	*Et descendes.*	And thou shalt go down.
רדם	וְתַרְדֵּמָה	*Et sopor.*	And a deep sleep.
ירד	וְתֵרַדְנָה	*Et descendent.*	And they shall go down.
רדף	וַתִּרְדְּפֵנוּ	*Et persecutus es nos*	And thou hast persecuted us.
רום	וּתְרוּמָה	*Et oblatio elevata.*	And a heave-offering.
—	וּתְרוֹמְמֶךָּ	*Et exaltabit te.*	And she shall exalt, promote [thee.
—	וַתְּרוֹמֵם	*Et extulit.*	And she lifted up.
—	וּתְרוּמַת	*Et oblatio elevata.*	And the heave-offering.
—	וּתְרוּמֹתֵינוּ	*Et oblationes elevatæ nostræ.*	And our heave-offerings.
רוע	וּתְרוּעָה־־עַת	*Et clangor.*	And the shout.
רחק	וַתִּרְחַק	*Et procul discessit.*	And she removed far off.
ירה	וְתוֹרְךָ	*Et docebit te.*	And she will teach thee.
רכב	וַתִּרְכַּב	*Et insedit.*	And she rode.
—	וַתִּרְכַּבְנָה	*Et insederunt.*	And they rode.
רום	וַתָּרָם	*Et elevata est.*	And she was lifted up.
—	וַתָּרֶם	*Et extulisti.*	And thou hast lifted up.
רמה	וְתַרְמוּת	*Et dolus.*	And deceit.
רמס	וַתִּרְמֹס	*Et conculcavit.*	And she trod down.
—	וַתִּרְמְסֵם	*Et conculcavit eos.*	And she trampled upon them.
רום	וּתְרֻמַת	*Et oblatio elevata.*	And a heave-offering.
רנן	וְתָרֹן	*Et cantabit.*	And she will sing.
רוע	וַתָּרַע	*Et malefecisti.*	And thou hast done evil.
רעע	וְתֵרֹעַ	*Et confringet.*	And she will break in pieces.
רעב	וַתִּרְעַב	*Et esuriit.*	And she was hungry, famished

ROOTS.	DERIVATIVES.	VERSIO.	SIGNIFICATION.
רעד	וַתִּרְעַד	*Et tremuit.*	And she trembled.
רוע	וְתָרֵעוּ	*Et male facietis.*	And ye will do evil.
רעה	וַתִּרְעֶינָה	*Et pascebant.*	And they fed.
רעש	וַתִּרְעַשׁ	*Et contremuit.*	And she shook, trembled.
——	וְתִרְעַשׁ	*Et contremiscet.*	And she shall tremble.
רפא	וַתִּרְפָּאֵנִי	*Et sanasti me.*	And thou hast healed me.
תרף	וּתְרָפִים	*Et imagines.*	And images, idols.
רפס	וַתִּרְפֹּס	*Et conculcasti, turbasti.* [*basti.*	And thou hast trodden, disturbed. [turbed.
רפש	וַתִּרְפֹּשׂ	*Et conculcasti, tur-*	And thou hast trodden, dis-
רוץ	וַתָּרָץ	*Et cucurrit.*	And she ran.
רצץ	וַתָּרָץ	*Et fregit.*	And she broke. [satisfied.
רצה	וַתִּרֶץ	*Et acquievisti.*	And thou hast been pleased,
רצץ	וְתָרֹץ	*Et conteretur.*	And she shall be broken.
רצה	וְתִרֶץ	*Et acquiescet.*	And she shall be pleased with.
——	וַתִּרְצֵנִי	*Et complacuisti mihi*	And thou hast been pleased
רשם	וְתִרְשֹׁם	*Et consignabis.*	And thou wilt sign. [with me.
נשא	וַתִּשָּׂא	*Et extulisti, sumpsit, sustulit, adepta est, exarsit.*	And thou hast lifted up, she took, took up, obtained, burned.
——	וְתִשָּׂא	*Et attolles.*	And thou wilt lift up.
שאב	וַתִּשְׁאָב־־אַב	*Et hausit.*	And she drew.
נשא	וַתִּשָּׂאֵהוּ	*Et sustulit eum.*	And she took him up.
שאל	וַתִּשְׁאַל	*Et petiisti.*	And thou hast asked.
נשא	וַתִּשֶּׂאנָה	*Et sustulerunt.*	And they took up, lifted up.
——	וַתִּשָּׂאֵנִי	*Et sustulit me.*	And she took me up.
שאר	וַתִּשָּׁאֵר	*Et relicta est.*	And she was left.
שוב	וַתָּשָׁב	*Et reversus es, rediit, conversa est.*	And thou camest back, she came back, was turned.
ישב	וַתֵּשֶׁב	*Et sedit, mansit, habitavit.* [*vertetur.*	And she sat, remained, dwelt. [shall return.
שוב	וְתָשֹׁב	*Et reverteris, re-*	And thou wilt return, she
——	וַתָּשֻׁבוּ	*Et reversi estis.*	And ye returned.
——	וַתָּשִׁבוּ	*Et reduxistis* [*tastis.*	And ye brought back.
ישב	וַתֵּשְׁבוּ	*Et mansistis, habi-*	And ye remained, dwelt.
שוב	וַתָּשֹׁבְנָה	*Et reversae sunt.*	And they returned.
שבע	וַתִּשְׂבַּע	*Et satiata est.*	And she was satisfied.

ROOTS.	DERIVATIVES.	VERSIO.	SIGNIFICATION.
שבר	וַתִּשָּׁבֵר	*Et confracta est.*	And she was broken, destroyed
——	וְתִשָּׁבֵר	*Et confringetur.*	And she shall be broken.
——	וַתִּשָּׁבַרְנָה	*Et confractæ sunt.*	And they were broken.
שוב	וּתְשֻׁבָתוֹ	*Et reditus ejus.*	And his return.
——	וּתְשׁוּבֹתֵיכֶם	*Et responsa vestra.*	And your answers.
שוה	וְתַשְׁווּ	*Et æquabitis.*	And ye will make equal.
ישע	וּתְשׁוּעָה־־עַת	*Et salus.*	And salvation.
——	וּתְשׁוּעָתִי	*Et salus mea.*	And my salvation.
——	וּתְשׁוּעָתְךָ	*Et salus tua.*	And thy salvation.
שור	וּתְשׁוּרָה	*Et munus.*	And a present, gift.
שחד	וַתִּשְׁחֳדִי	*Et munerasti, mercede conduxisti.*	And thou rewardest, hiredst.
שחט	וַתִּשְׁחֲטִי	*Et jugulasti.*	And thou hast slain.
שחת	וַתַּשְׁחִיתֵם	*Et disperdidit eos.*	And she destroyed them.
שחק	וַתִּשְׂחַק	*Et ridebit.*	And she will laugh.
שחת	וַתַּשְׁחֵת	*Et corrupit.*	And she corrupted.
——	וַתִּשָּׁחֵת	*Et corrupta est.*	And she was corrupted.
——	וַתַּשְׁחִתִי	*Et corrupta es.*	And thou wast corrupted.
שטח	וַתִּשְׁטַח	*Et expandit.*	And she spread abroad.
ישב	וַתֹּשִׁיבוּ	*Et duxistis.*	And ye have taken.
שחה	וְתִשְׁתַּח	*Et incurvabit se.*	And she will bow down.
שום	וַתְּשִׂימוּן	*Et statuistis.*	And ye have sat.
——	וַתָּשִׂימִי	*Et posuisti.*	And thou hast laid.
שכב	וַתִּשְׁכַּב־־כָּב	*Et cubavit.*	And she lay.
——	וְתִשְׁכַּב	*Et jacebis.*	And thou shalt lie.
——	וַתַּשְׁכִּבֵהוּ־כִּיב׳	*Et deposuit eum* [*est*	And she laid him or it [forgat
שכח	וַתִּשְׁכַּח	*Et oblitus es, oblita*	And thou hast forgotten, she
שכל	וְתַשְׂכִּל	*Et intelliges.*	And thou shalt understand.
שלח	וַתְּשַׁלַּח	*Et misisti, misit.*	And thou didst send, she sent.
——	וַתְּשַׁלַּח	*Et misit.* [*eum.*	And she sent. [him away.
——	וַתְּשַׁלְּחֵהוּ	*Et dimisisti, dimittes*	And thou hast sent, wilt send
——	וַתְּשַׁלְּחוּנִי	*Et dimisistis me.*	And ye have sent me away.
——	וַתְּשַׁלְּחִי	*Et misisti, dimisisti.*	And thou hast sent, sent away.
——	וַתְּשַׁלְּחֵם	*Et ejecisti eos, dimisit eos.*	And thou hast cast them out, she sent them away.
שלך	וְתַשְׁלִיךְ	*Et projicies.*	And thou wilt cast.
——	וְתַשְׁלִיכֵהוּ	*Et dejiciet eum.*	And she shall cast him down.

ROOTS.	DERIVATIVES.	VERSIO.	SIGNIFICATION.
שלך	וַתַּשְׁלִיכִי	*Et abjecisti.*	And thou hast cast off.
—	וַתַּשְׁלִיכֵנִי	*Et dejecisti me.*	And thou hast cast me down.
—	וַתַּשְׁלֵךְ	*Et projecisti, dejecit*	And thou hast cast, she cast
—	וְתַשְׁלֵךְ	*Et dejiciet.*	And she will cast down. [down
—	וַתֻּשְׁלְכִי	*Et projecta es. [est.*	And thou wast cast.
שלם	וַתִּשְׁלַם	*Et absoluta, perfecta*	And she was ended, finished.
שום	וַתָּשֶׂם	*Et posuit, constituit.*	And she put, laid, set.
ישם	וַתֵּשַׁם	*Et desolata est.*	And she was made desolate
שום	וְתָשֵׂם	*Et pones.*	And thou wilt put.
שמח	וַתִּשְׂמַח	*Et lætatus es.*	And thou rejoicedst.
—	וַתִּשְׂמַח	*Et lætata est.*	And she rejoiced.
שמד	וַתַּשְׁמִידֵם	*Et disperdidisti eos.*	And thou hast destroyed them
—	וְתַשְׁמִידֵם	*Et disperdes eos.*	And thou wilt destroy them.
שום	וַתְּשִׂמֵם	*Et posuit eos.*	And she put them.
שמע	וַתִּשָּׁמַע	*Et audita est.*	And she was heard.
—	וַתִּשְׁמַע	*Et audivit.*	And she heard. [hear.
—	וְתִשְׁמַע	*Et audies, audiet.*	And thou wilt hear, she will
—	וַתִּשְׁמְעוּ	*Et obtemperastis.*	And ye obeyed.
—	וְתִשְׁמַעְנָה	*Et audient.*	And they shall hear.
שמר	וַתִּשְׁמֹר	*Et observasti.*	And thou hast kept.
—	וְתִשְׁמֹר	*Et observabis.*	And thou shalt observe.
—	וַתִּשְׁמְרוּ	*Et observastis.*	And ye have kept.
—	וְתִשְׁמְרֶךָּ	*Et custodiet te.*	And she shall keep thee.
שנא	וַתִּשְׂנָא	*Et odisti.*	And thou hatedst.
—	וַתִּשֶּׂנָה	*Et sustulerunt.*	And they took up.
—	וְתִשֶּׂנָה	*Et tollent.*	And they shall take up.
תשע	וְתֵשַׁע וְתִשַׁע	*Et novem, nonus.*	And nine, the ninth.
—	ותשע וְתִשְׁעָה	*Et novem.*	And nine.
—	וְתִשְׁעִים	*Et nonaginta.*	And ninety.
שעת	וַתִּשָּׁעֲנוּ	*Et innixi estis.*	And ye stayed, leaned.
שפל	וַתַּשְׁפִּילִי	*Et humiliasti te.*	And thou hast abased thyself.
שפך	וַתִּשְׁפְּכִי	*Et effudisti.*	And thou pouredst out.
שקה	וַתַּשְׁקְ	*Et bibere fecit.*	And she caused to drink.
נשק	וַתִּשַּׁק	*Et osculata est.*	And she kissed.
שקה	וַתַּשְׁקֵהוּ	*Et potum dedit ei.*	And she gave him drink.
—	וַתַּשְׁקוּ	*Et bibendum dedistis*	And ye gave to drink.
שקט	וַתִּשְׁקֹט	*Et quievit.*	And she rested, was quiet.

ROOTS.	DERIVATIVES.	VERSIO.	SIGNIFICATION.
שקה	וַתַּשְׁקֶין	*Et bibere fecerunt.*	And they made to drink.
—	וַתַּשְׁקֵמוֹ	*Et bibendum dedisti eis.*	And thou gavest them to drink.
שקע	וַתִּשְׁקַע	*Et submersa est, subsedit.*	And she sank, subsided.
שקף	וַתַּשְׁקֵף	*Et prospexit.*	And she looked out.
שקק	וַתְּשֹׁקְקֶהָ	*Et irrigasti eam.*	And thou wateredst her.
שור	וַתָּשַׁר	*Et cecinit.*	And she sang.
—	וַתָּשֻׁרִי	*Et progressa es.*	And thou wentest.
שרף	וְתִשָּׂרֵף	*Et comburetur.*	And she shall be burnt.
שרש	וַתַּשְׁרֵשׁ	*Et radicare fecisti.*	And thou hast caused to take root.
שרת	וַתְּשָׁרְתֵהוּ	*Et ministravit ei.*	And she ministered to him.
שות	וַתָּשֶׁת	*Et posuisti.*	And thou hast set, laid.
שתה	וַתֵּשְׁתְּ	*Et bibisti.*	And thou hast drunk.
שות	וַתְּשִׁתֵהוּ	*Et posuit eum.*	And she laid him.
שחה	וַתִּשְׁתַּחוּ־תַּחוּ	*Et incurvavit se.*	And she bowed herself.
—	וַתִּשְׁתַּחֲוֶין	*Et incurvaverunt se*	And they bowed themselves.
בון	וַתִּתְבּוֹנָן	*Et animadvertisti.*	And thou regardedst.
הלך	וַתִּתְהַלַּכְנָה	*Et obambularunt.*	And they walked to and fro.
חול	וַתִּתְחַלְחַל	*Et doluit.*	And she was grieved.
חנן	וַתִּתְחַנֵּן	*Et precata est.*	And she besought.
נתך	וַתִּתַּךְ	*Et effusa est, effundetur.*	And she was poured out, shall be poured out.
כסה	וַתִּתְכַּס	*Et operuit se.*	And she covered herself.
תמם	וַתִּתֹּם	*Et absoluta, perfecta est.*	And she was ended, finished.
נתן	וַתִּתֵּן־תֵּן	*Et dedisti, donavit, tradidit, collocavit*	And thou gavest, she gave, delivered, placed.
—	וַתִּתְּנָהּ	*Et dedit eam.*	And she gave her.
—	וַתִּתְּנֵהוּ	*Et tradidit eum.*	And she delivered him.
—	וַתִּתְּנֵים	*Et dedisti eos.*	And thou gavest them.
—	וַתִּתְּנֵם	*Et tradidisti eos.*	And thou deliveredst them.
תעה	וַתֵּתַע	*Et erravit.*	And she wandered.
תעב	וַתְּתַעֲבִי	*Et abominata est.*	And thou hast abhorred.
עטף	וַתִּתְעַטֵּף	*Et obruta est, defecit.*	And she is overwhelmed, hath failed.
—	וְתִתְעַטֵּף	*Et obruetur, deficiet*	And she will be overwhelmed, will fail.
עלף	וַתִּתְעַלָּף	*Et involvit se.*	And she wrapped herself.
ענג	וְתִתְעַנַּג	*Et delectabitur.*	And she will be delighted.

ROOTS.	DERIVATIVES.	VERSIO.	SIGNIFICATION.
ערה	וְתִתְעָרִי	*Et nudabis te.*	And thou shalt make thyself [naked.
פלל	וַתִּתְפַּלֵּל	*Et oravit.*	And she prayed.
פעם	וַתִּתְפָּעֶם	*Et turbata est.*	And she was troubled.
תפש	וַתִּתָּפֵשׂ	*Et capta est.*	And she was taken.
—	וַתִּתְפְּשֵׂהוּ	*Et prehendit eum.*	And she caught him.
יצב	וַתֵּתַצַּב	*Et stetit.*	And she stood.
נתץ	וַתִּתְּצוּ	*Et diruistis.*	And ye have broken down.
תקע	וַתִּתְקַע	*Et fixisti, infixit.*	And thou hast fastened, she fastened, drove in.
יתר	וַתֹּתַר־־תֵּר	*Et reliquum habuit.*	And she had remaining, she [reserved
נתש	וַתִּתַּשׁ	*Et evulsa est.*	And she was plucked up.

זא

ROOTS.	DERIVATIVES.	VERSIO.	SIGNIFICATION.
	זְאֵב	*Zeeb.*	Zeeb, N. M.
זאב	זְאֵב	*Lupus.*	A wolf.
—	זְאֵבֵי	*Lupi.*	Wolves.
זוע	זָאֲעִין	*Trementes.*	Trembling.
זה	זֹאת	*Hæc.*	This.

זב

ROOTS.	DERIVATIVES.	VERSIO.	SIGNIFICATION.
זבב זוב	זָב	*Fluens, fluxu laborans.*	Flowing, having an issue.
	זָבָד	*Zabad.*	Zabad, N. M.
זָבַד		*Dotavit, donavit.*	He endowed, gave a dowry.
—	זֶבֶד	*Dos.*	A dowry.
	זַבְדִּי	*Zabdi.*	Zabdi, N. M.
	זַבְדִּיאֵל	*Zabdiel.*	Zabdiel, N. M.
	זְבַדְיָה־יָהוּ	*Zebadia.*	Zebadiah, N. M.
זבד	זְבָדַנִי	*Dotavit me.*	He hath endowed me.
זבב	זָבָה	*Fluens.*	Flowing.
זוב	זוֹבָהּ	*Fluxus ejus.*	His issue.
—	זְבוּב	*Musca.*	A fly.
—	זְבוּבֵי	*Muscæ.*	Flies.
	זָבוּד	*Zabud.*	Zabud, N. M.
	זְבִידָּה	*Zebuda.*	Zebudah, N. M.

ROOTS	DERIVATIVES.	VERSIO.	SIGNIFICATION.
	זְבוּלוּן־לֻן	*Zebulon.*	Zebulon, N. M.
	זְבוּלֹנִי	*Zebulonita.*	Zebulonite, N. F.
זָבַח		*Jugulavit, immolavit, mactavit, sacrificavit; sacrificium.*	He killed, slew, immolated, offered, sacrificed; a, the sacrifice.
—	זְבַח	*Immola.*	Sacrifice, offer thou.
—	זֶבַח	*Sacrificium, victima.*	A, the sacrifice, victim.
—	זְבֹחַ	*Immolare.*	To sacrifice.
	זֶבַח	*Zebach.*	Zebah, N. M.
—	זִבַּח	*Immolavit.*	He sacrificed.
—	זֹבֵחַ	*Immolans.*	Sacrificing, he that sacrificeth
—	זָבְחוּ זִבְּחוּ	*Immolaverunt.*	They sacrificed.
—	זִבְחוֹ	*Sacrificium ejus.*	His sacrifice.
—	זִבְחוּ	*Sacrificate.*	Sacrifice ye.
—	זִבְחֵי	*Sacrificia.*	The sacrifices.
—	זִבְחִי	*Sacrificium meum.*	My sacrifice.
—	זֹבְחֵי	*Immolantes.*	They that sacrifice.
—	זִבְחֵיהֶם	*Sacrificia eorum.*	Their sacrifices.
—	זְבָחֶיךָ	*Sacrificia tua.*	Thy sacrifices.
—	זִבְחֵיכֶם	*Sacrificia vestra.*	Your sacrifices.
—	זְבָחִים	*Sacrificia.*	The sacrifices.
—	זֹבְחִים	*Immolantes.*	They that sacrifice.
—	זְבָחֵימוֹ	*Sacrificia ejus.*	His sacrifices.
—	זִבְחֲכֶם	*Sacrificia vestra.*	Your sacrifices.
—	זָבַחְתִּי	*Immolavi.*	I sacrificed.
	זַבַּי	*Zabai.*	Zabbai, N. M.
	זְבִינָא	*Zebina.*	Zebina, N. M.
	זְבֻל	*Zebul.*	Zebul, N. M.
זָבַל		*Habitavit, cohabitavit.*	He dwelt, lived, cohabited.
—	זְבֻל־לָה	*Habitatio.*	A habitation.
	זְבֻלוּן	*Zebulon.*	Zebulon, N. M.
זָבַן		*Emit.*	He bought.
—	זָבְנִין	*Ementes.*	Buying, gaining.
זוב	זָבַת	*Fluens.*	Flowing.
	זג		
זוג	זָג	*Cortex.*	The rind, bark, peel.

ROOTS.	DERIVATIVES.	VERSIO.	SIGNIFICATION.
	זד		
זוד	זֵד	*Superbus.*	Proud.
זָדָה		*Superbe egit.*	She acted proudly.
—	זָדוּ	*Superbe egerunt.*	They acted proudly.
—	זָדוֹן	*Superbia, superbus.*	Pride, proud.
—	זְדוֹן	*Superbia.*	Pride.
—	זֵדִים	*Superbi.*	Proud.
—	זְדֹנְךָ	*Superbia tua.*	Thy pride.
	זה		
זה			
זה	זֶה	*Ipse, hic, hi; jam.*	He, that, this, these; now.
—	זֹה	*Hæc, hoc.*	This.
זהב			
—	זְהַב זָהָב	*Aurum.*	Gold.
—	זְהָבוֹ	*Aurum ejus.*	His gold.
—	זְהָבְךָ	*Aurum tuum.*	Thy gold.
—	זְהָבָם	*Aurum eorum.*	Their gold.
זָהַם		*Nauseare fecit.*	He made to nauseate.
	זַהַם	*Zaham.*	Zaham, N. M.
זָהַר		*Splenduit, fulsit, monuit.*	He shone, gave light, instructed, warned.
—	זֹהַר	*Splendor.*	Brightness.
	זו		
	זִו	*Zif.*	Ziv, N. Mth.
זה	זוֹ	*Ipsa, quæ,*	That, which.
—	זוּ	*Hic, hæc, ipse, qui, quæ.*	This, that, he, who, which.
זוב		*Fluxit, effluxit, liquefactus est.*	He flowed, issued forth, pined away.
—	זוֹב	*Fluxus.*	The flow, issue.
—	זוֹבָהּ	*Fluxus ejus.*	Her issue.
—	זוֹבוֹ	*Fluxus ejus.*	His issue.
—	זוֹבֵחַ	*Immolans.*	Sacrificing.
זוד		*Tumuit, efferbuit, superbivit, superbe egit.*	He swelled, boiled over, was proud, acted proudly.
זוה			

ROOTS.	DERIVATIVES.	VERSIO.	SIGNIFICATION.
זוח			
	זוֹחֵת	*Zocheth.*	Zocheth, N. M.
זול		*Prodegit, abjecit ut vile, sprevit.*	He lavished, cast away as vile, despised.
זלל	זוֹלֵל	*Comessator.*	A glutton.
זול	זוֹלֵלָה	*Vilis.*	Vile, worthless.
זלל	זוֹלְלִים	*Commessatores.*	Gluttons, revellers.
זלת	זוּלַת	*Præter.*	Beside, except.
—	זוּלָתָהּ	*Præter eam.*	Beside, except her.
—	זוּלָתִי	*Præter me.*	Beside me.
—	זוּלָתְךָ־־תֶ״	*Præter te.*	Beside thee.
זון		*Cibavit, aluit.*	He fed, nourished.
—	זוֹנָה	*Caupona.*	A woman who keeps a public house.
זנה	זוֹנֶה זֹנֶה	*Scortans.*	She that commits whoredom.
—	זוֹנָה זֹנָה	*Meretrix.*	A, the harlot.
—	זוּנָּה	*Scortatio acta est.*	Whoredom has been committed.
—	זוֹנוֹת זֹנוֹת	*Meretrices.*	Whores.
זוע		*Movit se, nutavit, vacillavit, agitatus est.*	He moved himself, shook, wavered, was agitated.
—	זְוָעָה	*Agitatio, commotio.*	An agitation, the commotion.
זור		*Compressit, constrinxit, sternutavit, alienavit se, alienus factus est.*	He compressed, bound up, sneezed, estranged himself, was treated as a stranger.
זרח	זוֹרֵחַ	*Oriens.*	Rising.
זרע	זוֹרֵעַ	*Seminans.*	He that soweth, the sower.
	זז		
	זָזָא	*Zaza.*	Zaza, N. M.
	זח		
זחח			
זָחַל		*Recessit, latitavit, repsit, pavit.*	He withdrew, skulked, crept, dreaded.
—	זֹחֲלֵי	*Serpentes.*	Serpents.
	זֹחֶלֶת	*Zocheleth.*	Zocheleth, N. P.
זחל	זָחַלְתִּי	*Pavi.*	I dreaded, was afraid.

ROOTS.	DERIVATIVES.	VERSIO.	SIGNIFICATION.
	זי		
זיו			
—	זִיוֹהִי	*Splendor ejus.*	His brightness *of countenance.*
זיז			
	זִיזָא	*Ziza.*	Ziza, N. M.
זין			
	זִינָא	*Zina.*	Zina, N. M.
	זִיעַ	*Zia.*	Zia, N. M.
	זִיף זִיפָה	*Ziph, Zipha.*	Ziph, Zipha, N. M. P.
זיק			
—	זִיקוֹת	*Scintillæ, flammæ.*	Sparks, flames.
זית			
—	זַיִת זָיִת זֵית	*Oliva.*	A, the olive, olive-tree.
—	זֵיתֵיהֶם	*Oliveta eorum.*	Their olive-yards.
—	זֵיתִים	*Olivæ.*	Olives, olive-trees.
—	זֵיתְךָ־־תֶךָ	*Oliva.*	Thy olive, olive-tree.
	זֵיתָן	*Zethan.*	Zethan, N. M.
	זכ		
זכך	זַךְ זָךְ	*Purus, mundus.*	Pure, clean.
זָכָה		*Mundavit, purificavit.*	He cleansed, purified.
—	זַכָּה	*Pura, munda.*	Pure, clean.
—	זָכוּ	*Innocentia.*	Innocence.
זכך	זַכּוּ	*Puri fuerunt.*	They were pure.
זכר	זָכוֹר	*Recordatus est.*	He remembered.
—	זָכוֹר	*Recordare, recordari, recordando.*	Remember thou, to remember, in remembering.
	זַכּוּר	*Zacchur.*	Zacchur, N. M.
זכר	זָכוֹר	*Memento.*	Remember thou.
—	זְכוּרָהּ	*Mas ejus.*	The male thereof.
—	זְכוּרְךָ	*Mas tuus.*	Thy male, males.
	זַכַּי	*Zaccai.*	Zacchai, N. M.
זכה	זִכִּיתִי	*Mundavi.*	I have cleansed.
זָכַךְ		*Limpidus, mundus, purus fuit; purum habuit, purificavit*	He was clear, transparent, clean, pure; he accounted pure, purified.

ROOTS.	DERIVATIVES.	VERSIO.	SIGNIFICATION.
	זָכֶר	*Zacher.*	Zacher, N. M.
זָכַר		*Viguit, præsertim acri odore, adolevit, recordatus est, meminit, celebravit.*	He was vigorous, especially in a potent scent, burned, remembered, mentioned, celebrated.
—	זְכֹר זָכְרָה	*Memento.*	Remember thou.
—	זֵכֶר	*Memoria.*	The memory, remembrance.
—	זָכֹר	*Recordando.*	In remembering.
—	זְכֹר	*Recordare.*	Remember thou.
—	זָכְרָה	*Recordata est.*	She hath remembered.
—	זָכְרוּ	*Recordati sunt.*	They remembered.
—	זִכְרוּ	*Mementote.*	Remember ye.
—	זִכְרוֹ	*Memoria ejus.*	His remembrance, memorial.
—	זִכְרוּ	*Recordamini.*	Remember ye.
—	זִכָּרוֹן זִכְ־־רֹן	*Monimentum.*	A memorial.
—	זִכְרוֹנְךָ	*Monimentum tuum.*	Thy memorial.
	זִכְרִי	*Zichri.*	Zichri, N. M.
זכר	זִכְרִי	*Memoria mea, monimentum meum.*	My remembrance, memorial.
	זְכַרְיָה־־הוּ	*Zecharias.*	Zechariah, N. M.
זכר	זִכְרְךָ־־רֶךָ	*Memoria tua.*	Thy remembrance.
—	זִכְרָם	*Memoria eorum.*	The memory of them.
—	זָכַרְנוּ	*Recordati sumus.*	We remembered.
—	זְכָרָנוּ	*Recordatus est nostri.*	He hath remembered us.
—	זָכְרֵנִי	*Recordare mei.*	Remember thou me.
—	זִכְרֹנֵיכֶם	*Memoriæ vestræ.*	Your remembrances.
—	זָכַרְתְּ־־תִּי	*Recordata es.*	Thou hast remembered.
—	זָכַרְתִּי־־כְ״	*Recordatus sum.*	I remembered.
—	זְכַרְתִּיךָ	*Recordatus sum tui.*	I have remembered thee.
—	זְכַרְתָּם	*Recordatus es eorum*	Thou rememberedst them.
—	זָכַרְתַּנִי	*Recordare mei.*	Remember thou me.
	זל		
זלב			
זלזל			
זלל	זְלוּת	*Vilitas.*	The vileness.
זלל			

ROOTS.	DERIVATIVES.	VERSIO.	SIGNIFICATION.
זלעף		[*adurens.*	[horrible tempest.
—	זַלְעָפָה	*Ventus procellosus*	A stormy scorching wind,
—	זַלְעֲפוֹת זַלְעָ"	*Venti procellosi adurentes, terrores.*	Stormy scorching winds, terrors.
	זִלְפָּה	*Zilpa.*	Zilpah, N. W.
זלת			
	זמ		
	זִמָּה	*Zima.*	Zimmah, N. M.
זמם	זִמָּה	*Scelus, nefas.*	The wickedness, mischief.
זמר	זְמוֹרָה	*Palmes.*	A branch.
זמם	זַמּוֹתָ	*Excogitasti.*	Thou hast devised.
—	זִמּוֹת	*Cogitationes.*	The thoughts, purposes.
—	זִמּוֹתַי	*Cogitationes meæ.*	My thoughts, purposes.
	זַמְזֻמִּים	*Zamzumæi.*	Zamzummims, N. N.
זמר	זְמִיר	*Palmes.*	A branch.
	זְמִירָה	*Zemira.*	Zemirah, N. M.
זמר	זְמִירוֹת	*Cantica.*	Songs.
זָמַם		*Excogitavit, destinavit aliquod in animo vel bonum vel malum.*	He devised, determined on any thing in his mind, either good or evil.
—	זֹמֵם	*Excogitans.*	Devising, plotting.
—	זָמְמָה	*Excogitavit.*	She devised, considered.
—	זָמָמוּ	*Excogitarunt.*	They devised.
—	זְמָמוֹ	*Cogitatio ejus.*	His device.
—	זַמֹּתִי	*Destinavi.* [*paravit.*	I purposed.
זִמֵּן		*Constituit tempus,*	He appointed a time, prepared
—	זְמָן זִמַן זִמְנָא	*Tempus.*	Time, season.
—	זִמְנִין	*Tempora.*	Times, seasons.
זָמַר		*Secuit, præcidit, putavit, cecinit.*	He cut asunder, cut off, pruned, sang.
—	זְמָרָא	*Musica.*	Music.
—	זַמְּרָה	*Canere.*	To sing.
—	זִמְרָה	*Cantio, canticum.*	Melody, song.
—	זַמְּרוּ־מְ"	*Canite.*	Sing ye.
—	זְמִרוֹת	*Cantiones, cantica.*	Melodies, songs.

ROOTS.	DERIVATIVES.	VERSIO.	SIGNIFICATION.
	זִמְרִי	*Zimri.*	Zimri, N. M.
זמר	זִמְרַיָּא	*Cantores.*	Singers.
	זִמְרָן	*Zimran.*	Zimran, N. M.
זמר	זְמֹרֹת	*Cantica.*	Songs.
זמם	זִמָּת	*Scelus.* [*lium meum.*	Wickedness. [purpose.
—	זַמֹּתִי	*Excogitavi; consi-*	I have thought, devised; my
—	זִמָּתֵךְ	*Scelus tuum.*	Thy wickedness.
—	זִמַּתְכֵנָה	*Scelus vestrum.*	Your wickedness.
	זנ		
זון	זַן	*Species, genus.*	A sort, kind.
זָנַב		*Caudam amputavit, extremos præcidit*	He cut off the tail, smote the hindmost.
—	זָנָב	*Cauda.*	A, the tail.
—	זְנָבוֹ	*Cauda ejus.*	His tail.
—	זְנָבוֹת	*Caudæ.* [*tituit se.*	Tails. [tituted herself.
זָנָה		*Scortatus est, pros-*	He went a whoring, she pros-
—	זָנָה	*Scortati sunt.*	They went a whoring.
—	זְנֹה	*Scortando.*	In whoring. [dom.
—	זָנוּ	*Scortati sunt.*	They have committed whore-
	זָנוֹחַ	*Zanoach.*	Zanoah, N. M. P.
זנה	זְנוּנֵי	*Scortationes.*	Whoredoms.
—	זְנוּנֶיהָ	*Scortationes ejus.*	Her whoredoms.
—	זְנוּנַיִךְ	*Scortationes tuæ.*	Thy whoredoms.
—	זְנוּנִים	*Scortationes.*	Whoredoms.
—	זְנוּת	*Scortatio.*	Whoredom.
—	זֹנוֹת	*Meretrices.*	Harlots, whores.
—	זְנוּתָהּ	*Scortatio ejus.*	Her whoredom.
—	זְנוּתֵיכֶם	*Scortationes vestræ.*	Your whoredoms.
—	זְנוּתֵךְ	*Scortatio tua.*	Thy whoredom.
—	זְנוּתָם	*Scortatio eorum.*	Their whoredom.
זָנַח		*Rejecit, abjecit, procul amovit.*	He rejected, cast off, removed to a distance.
—	זָנַחְתָּ	*Abjecisti.*	Thou hast cast off.
—	זְנַחְתִּים	*Rejeci eos.*	I have rejected them.
—	זְנַחְתָּנוּ	*Abjecisti nos.*	Thou hast cast us off.
—	זְנַחְתָּנִי	*Abjecisti me.*	Thou hast cast me off.

ROOTS.	DERIVATIVES.	VERSIO.	SIGNIFICATION.
זון	זְנֵי	*Species, genera.*	Sorts, kinds.
זנה	זֹנִים	*Scortantes.*	Committing whoredom.
—	זָנִית זָנִיתְ	*Scortatus es.*	Thou hast gone a whoring.
זִנֵּק		*Exiliit impetu agili.*	He sprang out, leaped suddenly.
זנה	זָנְתָה	*Scortata es.*	Thou hast played the harlot.
	זע		
זוע	זָע	*Movit se.*	He moved himself.
זעם	זְעוּם	*Detestatus.*	He that is abhorred.
—	זְעוּמָה	*Detestata.*	She that is abhorred, abominable.
	זַעֲוָן	*Zaavan.*	Zaavan, N. M.
זער	זְעֵיר זְעִירָה	*Parum, paululum.*	A little, little.
זָעַךְ		*Excidit, breviavit.*	He cut off, shortened.
זָעַם		*Spumavit, iratus est, deseævit; detestatus, execratus est: furor.*	He foamed, was angry, raged, detested, execrated: indignation.
—	זַעַם	*Ira, furor.*	Wrath, indignation.
—	זֹעֵם	*Iratus.*	Angry.
—	זָעֲמָה	*Detestare, execrare.*	Detest, execrate, curse thou.
—	זַעְמוֹ	*Furor ejus.*	His wrath, indignation.
—	זַעְמִי	*Indignatio mea.*	My indignation.
—	זַעְמֶךָ־זַעְמְךָ	*Indignatio tua.*	Thy indignation.
—	זָעַמְתָּה	*Iratus es.*	Thou hast been angry.
זָעַף		*Æstuavit, turbatus, indignatus est.*	He was agitated, disturbed, angry.
—	זַעַף	*Ira, indignatio.*	Wrath, the indignation.
—	זֹעֲפִים	*Æstuantes, turbati, macilenti.*	Agitated, disturbed, lean, thin
זָעַק		*Clamavit, vociferatus est, convocavit*	He called, cried out, shouted, called together.
—	זְעַק	*Clama.*	Call, cry thou.
—	זָעַק	*Clamavit.*	He cried.
—	זַעֲקָה	*Clamor.*	A, the cry.
—	זָעֲקוּ	*Clamarunt.*	They cried.
—	זַעֲקִי	*Clama.*	Call, cry thou.

ROOTS.	DERIVATIVES.	VERSIO.	SIGNIFICATION.
זעק	זַעֲקָךְ	*Clamare tuum.*	Thy cry.
—	זַעֲקַת	*Clamor.*	The cry.
—	זַעֲקָתִי	*Clamavi.*	I cried.
—	זַעֲקָתָם	*Clamor eorum.*	Their cry.
זער			
	זפ		
	זִפִים	*Ziphæi.*	Ziphites, N. M.
	זִפְרֹנָה	*Ziphrona.*	Ziphron, N. M.
זפת			
	זק		
זיק	זִקִּים	*Scintillæ, flammæ.*	Sparks, flames.
זקן	זְקֵינֵינוּ	*Seniores nostri.*	Our elders.
זָקֵן		*Senex fuit, senuit.*	He was old, grew old.
—	זָקָן	*Barba.*	A beard.
—	זָקֵן	*Senex.*	Old.
—	זְקַן	*Senex ; barba.*	Old ; a beard.
—	זָקְנָה	*Senuit.*	She has grown old.
—	זִקְנָה	*Senectus.*	Old age.
—	זְקָנוֹ	*Barba ejus.*	His beard.
—	זִקְנֵי זְקֵנִים	*Senes, seniores.*	The old, elders, ancients.
—	זְקֵנֶיהָ	*Seniores ejus.*	Her elders.
—	זְקֵנָיו	*Seniores ejus.*	His elders.
—	זְקֵנֶיךָ	*Seniores tui.*	Thy elders.
—	זִקְנֵיכֶם	*Seniores vestri.*	Your elders.
—	זְקֻנִים	*Senectus.*	Old age.
—	זְקָנְךָ	*Barba tua.*	Thy beard.
—	זְקַנְכֶם	*Barba vestra.*	Your beard.
—	זְקָנָם	*Barba eorum.*	Their beard.
—	זָקַנְתְּ־תָּה	*Senuisti.*	Thou hast grown old.
—	זִקְנַת	*Senectus.*	Old age.
—	זִקְנָתָהּ	*Senectus ejus.*	Her old age.
—	זִקְנָתוֹ	*Senectus ejus.*	His old age.
—	זָקַנְתִּי	*Senui.*	I am old.
זָקַף		*Elevavit, erexit.*	He raised up, set upright.
—	זֹקֵף	*Elevans, erigens.*	Raising up, setting upright.

ROOTS.	DERIVATIVES.	VERSIO.	SIGNIFICATION.
	זר		
זור	זָר	*Alienus, alius.*	A stranger, another.
זרה	זֵר	*Corona.*	A crown.
זָרַב		*Diffluxit, effluxit.*	He dissolved, evaporated.
	זְרֻבָּבֶל	*Zerubbabel.*	Zerubbabel, N. M.
	זֶרֶד זֶרֶד	*Zered.*	Zered.
זָרָה		*Sparsit, dispersit, disjecit, ventilavit, investigavit, cinxit, alienatus est.*	He scattered, dispersed, cast away, sifted, examined, encompassed, was estranged.
זור	זָרָה	*Alienus fuit; aliena*	He was a stranger, a strange [woman.
זרה	זְרֵה	*Disperge.*	Disperse, scatter thou.
—	זֹרֶה	*Ventilans.*	Sifting, winnowing.
זור	זָרוּ זֹרוּ	*Alienati sunt.*	They were estranged.
זרה	זֵרוּ	*Sparserunt.*	They scattered.
זרע	זֵרוּעַ	*Satus.*	A, the sowing.
—	זְרוֹעַ זְרֹעַ	*Brachium.*	The, an arm.
—	זְרוּעָה	*Sata.*	Sown.
—	זְרוֹעוֹ זְרֹעוֹ	*Brachium ejus.*	His arm.
—	זְרוֹעוֹת זְרֹ׳	*Brachia.*	Arms.
—	זְרוֹעִי־־רֹעִי	*Brachium meum.*	My arm.
—	זֵרוּעֶיהָ	*Semina ejus.*	Her seeds.
—	זְרוֹעֲךָ־עֶךָ זְרֹעֲךָ	*Brachium tuum.*	Thy arm.
—	זְרוֹעֹתַי זְרֹ׳	*Brachia mea.*	My arms.
—	זְרוֹעֹתֶיהָ	*Brachia ejus.*	Her arms.
—	זְרוֹעֹתָיו זְרֹ׳	*Brachia ejus.*	His arms.
—	זְרוֹעֹתֵיכֶם זְרֹ׳	*Brachia vestra.*	Your arms.
—	זְרוֹעֹתָם	*Brachia eorum.*	Their arms.
זור	זָרוֹת	*Alienæ.*	Strange women.
זרף	זַרְזִיף	*Irrigatio, stillatio.*	Watering, dropping.
זור	זַרְזִיר	*Compressus, constrinctus.*	Compressed, bound up.
זָרַח		*Ortus est, diffudit se.*	He rose, diffused himself.
	זֶרַח זֶרַח	*Zarach, Zerach.*	Zarah, Zerah, N. M.
זרח	זָרְחָה	*Orta est.*	She is risen.
	זַרְחִי	*Zarchitæ.*	Zarhites, N. F.

ROOTS.	DERIVATIVES.	VERSIO.	SIGNIFICATION.
	זַרְחְיָה	*Zerachias.*	Zerahiah, N. M.
זרח	זַרְחֵךְ	*Ortus tuus.*	Thy rising.
זור	זָרַיִךְ	*Alieni tui.*	Thy strangers.
—	זָרִים	*Alieni, extranei.*	Strangers.
זרה	זָרִים	*Ventilatores.*	Winnowers, fanners.
—	זֵרִיתָ	*Cinxisti.*	Thou hast encompassed.
—	זֵרִיתָנוּ	*Dispersisti nos.*	Thou hast scattered us.
זָרַם		*Exundavit, inundavit.*	He overflowed, overwhelmed.
—	זֶרֶם זֶרֶם	*Inundatio.*	An inundation.
—	זֹרְמוּ	*Exundarunt.*	They overflowed.
—	זְרַמְתָּם	*Inundasti eos.*	Thou hast overwhelmed them
—	זִרְמָתָם	*Fluxus eorum.*	Their issue.
זָרַע		*Deprompsit, seminavit, sevit; concepit, peperit: semen*	He drew forth, sowed, planted; she conceived, brought forth; seed.
—	זֵרַע	*Satus.*	Sown.
—	זֶרַע	*Semen.*	Seed.
—	זֵרַע	*Semina.*	Seeds.
—	זֹרֵעַ	*Seminans.*	Sowing.
—	זַרְעָהּ	*Semen ejus.*	Her seed.
—	זָרְעוּ	*Seminarunt.*	They have sown.
—	זַרְעוֹ	*Semen ejus.*	His seed.
—	זִרְעוּ	*Seminate.*	Sow ye.
—	זֹרָעוּ	*Sati sunt.*	They have been sown.
—	זְרֹעוֹתָיו	*Brachia ejus.*	His arms.
—	זַרְעִי	*Semen meum.*	My seed.
—	זְרֹעֵי	*Brachia.*	Arms.
—	זְרֹעִי	*Brachium meum.*	My arm.
—	זֹרְעֵי	*Seminantes.*	They that sow.
—	זְרֹעָיו	*Brachia ejus.*	His arms.
—	זַרְעֲךָ־עֶךָ־עֶךָ	*Semen tuum.*	Thy seed.
—	זַרְעֲכֶם	*Semen vestrum.*	Your seed.
—	זַרְעָם	*Semen eorum.*	Their seed.
—	זְרֹעָם	*Brachium eorum.*	Their arm.
—	זֵרְעֹנִים	*Legumina.*	Pulse.
—	זְרֹעֹת	*Brachia.*	Arms.
—	זְרַעְתֶּם	*Seminastis.*	Ye have sown.

ROOTS.	DERIVATIVES.	VERSIO.	SIGNIFICATION.
זרף			
זָרַק		*Sparsit, aspersit.*	He sprinkled, besprinkled.
—	זֹרַק	*Aspersus est.*	He was besprinkled.
—	זָרְקָה	*Sparsit se.*	She hath sprinkled, scattered herself.
—	זֹרְקִים	*Spargentes.*	Sprinkling.
	זֶרֶשׁ	*Zeres.*	Zeresh, N. M.
זרת			
—	זֶרֶת	*Palmus.*	A span.
	זת		
	זַתּוּא	*Zattu.*	Zattu, N. M.
	זֵתָם	*Zetam.*	Zetham, N. M.
	זֵתַר	*Zetar.*	Zethar, N. M.

ROOTS.	DERIVATIVES.	VERSIO.	SIGNIFICATION.
	חב		
חָבָא } חָבָה }		*Operuit, abscondit, occultavit, latuit.*	He covered, hid, concealed, lay hid.
חבא	חֻבְּאוּ	*Absconderunt se.*	They hid themselves.
	חֹבָב	*Chobab.*	Hobab, N. M.
חָבַב		*Sinu gessit, dilexit.*	He carried in his bosom, loved
—	חֹבֵב	*Diligens.*	Loving.
חבל	חֲבוּלָה	*Corruptio, perditio.*	Corruption, destruction, ruin.
	חָבוֹר	*Chabor.*	Habor, N. P. R.
חבר	חָבוּר	*Socius.*	A companion.
—	חַבּוּרָה	*Livor.*	Bruises, stripes.
—	חַבּוּרוֹתַי	*Livores mei.*	My stripes.
חבש	חָבוּשׁ	*Alligatus.*	Bound.
—	חֲבוֹשׁ	*Alliga, cinge.*	Bind, gird thou.
—	חֲבוּשִׁים	*Alligati, instrati.*	Bound, saddled.
חָבַט		*Excussit, decussit, trituravit.*	He shook out, shook off, threshed.
—	חֹבֵט	*Triturans.*	Threshing.
חבא	חֲבִי	*Absconde te.*	Hide thyself.
	חֲבָיָה חֳבַיָּה	*Chabaias.*	Habaiah, N. M.
חבה	חֶבְיוֹן	*Absconsio.*	The hiding.

ROOTS.	DERIVATIVES.	VERSIO.	SIGNIFICATION.
חָבַל		*Torsit, illigavit, astrinxit, oppigneravit, corrupit, perdidit, parturi-*	He twisted, bound, straitened, pledged, bound to a creditor, corrupted, destroyed; she brought forth.
—	חָבֹל	*Pignerando.* [*vit.*	In pledging.
—	חֲבָל	*Corruptio.* [*nus.*	Corruption.
—	חֲבֹל	*Corrumpendo; pig-*	In corrupting; the pledge.
—	חֵבֶל	*Dolor.*	Pain, throe, pang.
—	חֶבֶל	*Regio, ora, portio, funis, cœtus.*	The region, coast, part, lot, cord, company.
—	חֹבֵל	*Malus* navis.	A mast.
—	חֹבֵל	*Pignerans.*	Pledging, receiving in pledge.
—	חֲבָלָא	*Corruptio, perditio.*	Corruption, destruction.
—	חִבְּלָה	*Corrupta est.*	She has been corrupted.
—	חִבְּלָה	*Parturiit.*	She brought forth.
—	חַבְלֵהוּ	*Pignerare eum, accipe pignus ab eo.*	Pledge thou him, take a pledge from him.
—	חַבְלוֹ	*Funis ejus.*	His cord, rope.
—	חִבְּלוּנִי	*Perdiderunt me.*	They have destroyed me.
—	חֶבְלֵי תֵּ'	*Funes, dolores.*	Ropes, bands, sorrows.
—	חֹבְלֵי	*Naucleri.*	Pilots.
—	חֶבְלֵיהֶם	*Dolores eorum.*	Their sorrows.
—	חֲבָלָיו	*Funes ejus.*	His cords.
—	חֲבָלָיִךְ	*Funes tui.*	Thy cords.
—	חֹבְלָיִךְ	*Naucleri tui.* [*lores.*	Thy pilots.
—	חֲבָלִים	*Funes, portiones, do-*	Cords, ropes, portions, sorrows.
—	חֲבֻלִים	*In pignus dati.*	Given in pledge.
—	חֹבְלִים	*Chobelim.*	Chobelim, *the name of a staff.*
חבל	חִבַּלְנוּ	*Corrupimus.*	We have corrupted.
—	חֲבֹלָתוֹ	*Pignus ejus.*	His pledge.
—	חִבְּלָתְךָ	*Peperit te.*	She brought thee forth.
חצל	חֲבַצֶּלֶת	*Rosa.*	The rose.
	חֲבַצִּנְיָה	*Chabazinias.* [*us est.*	Habaziniah, N. M.
חָבַק		*Complicuit, amplex-*	He folded, embraced.
—	חִבֵּק	*Complicans.* [*us.*	A folding.
—	חֹבֵק	*Complexus, amplex-*	He that foldeth.
—	חִבְּקוּ	*Amplexi sunt.*	They embraced.

ROOTS.	DERIVATIVES.	VERSIO.	SIGNIFICATION.
	חֲבַקּוּק	*Chabaccuc.*	Habakkuk, N. M.
חבק	חֹבֶקֶת	*Amplectens.*	Embracing.
חָבַר		*Nexuit, junxit, associavit, incantavit.*	He coupled, joined, associated, enchanted.
—	חֶבֶר	*Incantans; societas.*	Charming, enchanting; the company.
—	חֶבֶר	*Societas.*	The company.
—	חָבֵר	*Socius.*	A companion.
—	חִבֵּר	*Nexuit, junxit.*	He coupled, joined.
—	חֻבַּר	*Junctus, nexus est.*	He was joined, coupled.
	חֶבֶר ח״	*Cheber.*	Heber, N. M.
חבר	חַבַרְבֻּרֹתָיו	*Livor ejus.*	His stripes.
—	חָבְרוּ	*Conjuncti sunt.*	They were joined together.
—	חֲבֵרָו־־רָיו	*Socii ejus.*	His companions.
—	חֲבֵרוֹ	*Socius ejus.*	His companion.
—	חֲבֵרוֹהִי	*Socii ejus.*	His companions.
	חֶבְרוֹן	*Chebron.*	Hebron, N. M. P.
חבר	חַבּוּרוֹת	*Livores.*	Stripes, bruises.
—	חֹבְרוֹת	*Junctæ.*	Coupled.
—	חֲבָרַיִךְ	*Incantationes tuæ.*	Thy enchantments.
—	חֲבֵרֶיךָ	*Socii tui.*	Thy companions.
—	חַבָּרִים	*Socii.*	The companions.
—	חֲבָרִים	*Incantationes.*	Enchantments.
—	חֲבֵרִים	*Socii.*	The companions.
	חֶבְרֹנִי	*Chebronitæ.*	Hebronites, N. F.
חבר	חֹבְרֹת	*Junctæ.*	Joined, coupled.
—	חַבְרָתָהּ	*Sociæ ejus.*	His companions.
—	חֲבֶרְתְּךָ	*Socia tua.*	Thy companion.
חָבַשׁ		*Ligavit, cinxit, instravit.*	He bound, girded, saddled.
—	חֲבשׁ	*Ligare.*	To bind.
—	חָבַשׁ	*Ligavit.*	He hath bound.
—	חֹבֵשׁ	*Ligans.*	He that bindeth up.
—	חֻבָּשָׁה	*Ligata est.*	She hath been bound.
—	חִבְשׁוּ	*Insternite.*	Saddle ye.
—	חֻבָּשׁוּ	*Ligati sunt.*	They have been bound.
—	חֲבֻשִׁים	*Ligati, strati.*	Bound, saddled.
—	חֲבַשְׁתֶּם	*Ligastis.*	Ye have bound up.

ROOTS.	DERIVATIVES.	VERSIO.	SIGNIFICATION.
	חג		
חוג	חָג	*Circuivit, circumdedit.* [*sacrificium.*	He encompassed. [nity, sacrifice.
חגג	חָג חַג	*Festum, solemnitas,*	A, the feast, festival, solem-
חגב			
—	חָגָב	*Locusta.*	The locust.
	חָגָב	*Chagab.*	Hagab, N. M.
	חֲגָבָא־־בָה	*Chagaba.*	Hagabah, N. M.
חָגַג		*Tripudiavit, gyravit, festum celebravit.*	He danced, reeled round, celebrated a festival.
—	חַגָּהּ	*Festum ejus.*	Her feast.
חגר	חָגוּר	*Accinctus.*	Girded.
—	חֲגוֹר	*Accinge; cingulum.*	Gird thou up; a girdle.
—	חֲגוֹרָה־־נֹ״	*Cingulum.*	A girdle.
—	חֲגוֹרֵי־־חֲגֻרֵ״	*Accincti.*	Girded.
—	חֲגוּרִים	*Accincti.*	Girded.
	חַגַּי־־גִּי	*Chaggai.*	Haggai, N. M.
חגג	חַגִּי	*Celebra.*	Celebrate, keep thou.
—	חָגִּי	*Festum meum.*	My feast.
	חַגִּיָּה	*Chagias.*	Haggiah, N. M.
חגג	חַגַּיִךְ	*Festa tua.*	Thy feasts.
—	חַגֵּיכֶם	*Festa vestra.*	Your festivals.
—	חַגִּים	*Festa, sacrificia.*	Feasts, sacrifices.
	חַגִּית	*Chaghit.*	Haggith, N. W.
	חָגְלָה	*Chogla.*	Hoglah, N. W.
חגג	חַגֵּנוּ	*Festum nostrum.*	Our feast.
חָגַר		*Cinxit, accinxit.*	He bound, girded round.
—	חֲגֹר	*Accinge.*	Gird thou up.
—	חֹגֵר	*Accinctus.*	Girded.
—	חָגְרָה	*Accinxit.*	She hath girded.
—	חָגְרוּ	*Accinxerunt se.*	They have girded themselves.
—	חֲגֹרוֹ	*Cingulum ejus.*	His girdle.
—	חִגְרוּ	*Accingite*	Gird ye.
—	חִגְרִי	*Accinge.*	Gird thou.
—	חֲגֹרְנָה	*Accingite vos.*	Gird up yourselves.
—	חֲגֹרֶת	*Accincta.*	Girded.

ROOTS.	DERIVATIVES.	VERSIO.	SIGNIFICATION.
חגר	חֲגֹרֹת	*Cingula.*	Girdles.
	חד		
חד			
—	חַד	*Unus, alter, quidam.*	One, another, some one.
שבע	חַד שִׁבְעָה	*Septuplum.*	Seven times, seven-fold.
חד	חֲדָא חֲדָה	*Una.*	One.
	חֲדַד	*Chadad.*	Hadid, N. M.
חָדַד		*Exacuit, acutus fuit*	He sharpened, was sharp.
חָדָה		*Lætatus est, exhila-*	He rejoiced, gladdened.
חדד	חַדָּה	*Acuta.* [*ravit.*	Sharp.
—	חַדּוּדֵי	*Acumina.*	Sharp points.
חדי	חֲדוֹהִי	*Pectus ejus.*	His breast.
	חַדּוֹן חַדֹּן	*Chaddon.*	Haddon, N. M.
חדה	חֶדְוַת	*Lætitia.*	Joy, gladness.
חדי			
	חָדִיד	*Chadid.*	Hadid, N. P.
חָדַל		*Cessavit, desiit, destitit, abstinuit.*	He ceased, left off, desisted, refrained, forbore.
—	חָדֵל	*Cessans, transiens,*	Ceasing, transient, fleeting,
—	חֶדֶל	*Mundus.* [*caducus.*	The world. [frail.
—	חֲדַל חֲדָל	*Desine, desiste.*	Leave off, forbear thou.
—	חָדְלוּ	*Cessarunt.*	They ceased.
—	חִדְלוּ חִדְלוּ	*Desinite.*	Cease ye.
—	חָדֵלוּ	*Desierunt.*	They left off.
	חַדְלָי	*Chadlai.*	Hadlai, N. M.
חדל	חָדַלְנוּ	*Desivimus.*	We left off.
חדק			
—	חֵדֶק	*Spina.*	A thorn.
	חִדֶּקֶל חִדָּ֑	*Chidechel.*	Hiddekel, N. R.
	חֲדַר	*Chadar.*	Hadar, N. M.
חָדַר		*Intravit, penetravit.*	He entered, penetrated.
—	חֶדֶר	*Cubiculum.*	A chamber.
—	חַדְרֵי חֲדָרִים	*Cubicula.*	The chambers.
—	חֲדָרָיו	*Penetralia.*	His chambers.
	חַדְרָךְ	*Chadrach.* [*ravit.*	Hadrach, N. P.
חִדֵּשׁ		*Renovavit, restau-*	He renewed, restored.

ROOTS.	DERIVATIVES.	VERSIO.	SIGNIFICATION.
חדשׁ	חָדָשׁ	*Novus, recens.*	New, fresh.
—	חַדֵּשׁ	*Renova.*	Renew thou.
—	חֹדֶשׁ	*Mensis, novilunium.*	A month, new-moon.
	חֹדֶשׁ	*Chodes.*	Hodesh, N. W.
חדשׁ	חָדְשָׁהּ	*Novilunia ejus.*	Her new-moons.
—	חֲדָשָׁה	*Nova.*	New.
	חֲדָשָׁה	*Chadasa.*	Hadashah, N. P.
חדשׁ	חָדְשׁוֹ	*Mensis ejus.*	His month.
—	חֲדָשׁוֹת	*Novæ res.*	New things.
—	חָדְשֵׁי	*Menses.*	The months.
	חָדְשִׁי	*Chodsi.*	Hodshi, N. P.
חדשׁ	חֳדָשָׁיו	*Menses ejus.*	His months.
—	חָדְשֵׁיכֶם	*Menses vestri, novilunia vestra.*	Your months, your new-moons.
—	חֲדָשִׁים	*Novi.*	New.
—	חֳדָשִׁים	*Menses.*	Months.
חדת			
—	חֲדַת	*Novus.*	New.
חוד	חַדְתָּ	*Ænigmatice locutus es, proposuisti.*	Thou hast spoken parabolically, hast proposed, put forth.
	חו		
חוב		*Debitorem reddidit, reum effecit, condemnavit.*	He rendered a debtor, made guilty, condemned.
—	חוֹב	*Debitor.*	A debtor.
	חֹבָה	*Choba.*	Hobah, N. P.
חבר	חוֹבֵר	*Incantans.*	Charming, enchanting.
—	חוֹבְרוֹת	*Junctæ.*	Joined, coupled.
חוג		*Circuivit, circumdedit.*	He encompassed, encircled.
—	חוּג	*Ambitus, circuitus.*	A compass, the circle.
חגג	חוֹגֵג	*Festum celebrans.*	Keeping holy-day.
חוד		*Ænigmatice locutus est, ænigma proposuit.*	He spoke parabolically, proposed a riddle.
—	חוּדָה	*Propone.*	Propose thou.
חָוָה		*Indicavit, nunciavit.*	He shewed, declared.
	חַוָּה	*Chava.*	Eve, N. W.

ROOTS.	DERIVATIVES.	VERSIO.	SIGNIFICATION.
חזה	חוֹזֶה	*Videns.*	He that sees, the seer.
	חוֹזָי	*Chozai.*	Hozai, N. M.
חוח			
——	חוֹחַ	*Spina.*	A thorn, thistle.
חוט		*Consuit, conjunxit.*	He sewed together, joined.
——	חוּט	*Filum.*	A thread.
חטא	חוֹטֵא	*Peccator.*	A sinner.
	חִוִּי	*Chivi.*	Hivi, Hivite, N. M. N. P.
	חֲוִילָה	*Chavila.*	Havilah, N. M. P.
חכה	חוֹכֵי	*Expectantes.*	They that wait.
	חוּל	*Chul.*	Hul, N. M.
חול		*Doluit, parturivit, trepidavit, expectavit, mansit, genuit, formavit.*	He—she—was in pain, travailed, trembled, expected, waited, remained, begat, formed.
——	חוֹל	*Arena.*	The sand.
——	חוּל	*Dolendo.*	In having pain.
——	חוּלָה	*Dolor.*	Pain, sorrow.
חלה	חוֹלֶה	*Ægrotus.*	Sick.
חול	חוּלִי	*Dole, trepida.*	Be in pain, tremble thou.
——	חוֹלַלְתָּ	*Formatus es.* [*sum.*	Thou wast formed.
——	חוֹלָלְתִּי	*Formatus, formata,*	I was formed.
חלם	חוֹלֵם	*Somnians.*	Dreaming.
חלק	חוֹלֵק	*Dividens.*	Dividing.
חלש	חוֹלֵשׁ	*Debilitans.*	Weakening.
חלה	חוֹלַת	*Ægrota.*	Sick.
חום			
——	חוּם	*Fuscus.*	Brown.
חמה	חוֹמָה	*Murus, murata.*	A wall, walled.
——	חוֹמוֹת	*Muri.*	Walls.
——	חוֹמוֹתַיִךְ־־חוֹמֹ׳	*Muri tui.*	Thy walls.
——	חוֹמַת	*Murus.*	A, the wall.
——	חוֹמֹת	*Muri.*	The walls.
——	חוֹמָתָהּ	*Murus ejus.*	Her wall.
——	חוֹמֹתֶיהָ	*Muri ejus.*	Her walls.
חנן	חוֹנֵן	*Miserescens, gratiam faciens.*	Having mercy, shewing favour

ROOTS.	DERIVATIVES.	VERSIO.	SIGNIFICATION.
חוס		*Pepercit.*	He spared, pitied.
—	חוּסָה	*Parce.*	Spare thou.
חסה	חוֹסֵי	*Sperantes.*	They that hope.
—	חוֹסִים	*Confidentes.*	They that trust.
חפף	חוֹף	*Littus.*	The shore.
	חוּפָם	*Chupham.*	Hupham, N. M.
	חוּפָמִי	*Chuphamitæ.*	Huphamites, N. F.
חוץ		*Cinxit.*	He bound, girded.
—	חוּץ	*Platea, extra, plus.*	The street, without, more.
—	חוּצָה	*Extra, extrinsecus.*	Without, out of, abroad.
—	חוּצוֹת	*Plateæ.*	The streets.
—	חוּצוֹתֶיהָ	*Plateæ ejus.*	Her streets.
—	חוּצוֹתָיִךְ	*Plateæ tuæ.*	Thy streets.
—	חוּצוֹתָם	*Plateæ eorum.*	Their streets.
חיק	חֵוקֶךָ	*Sinus tuus.*	Thy bosom.
	חוּקֹק	*Chucoc.*	Hukok, Hukkok, N. P.
חקר	חוֹקֵר	*Scrutans.*	Searching.
חָוַר		*Albus fuit, palluit.*	He was white, grew pale.
—	חִוָּר	*Albus.*	White.
—	חוּר	*Candidus.*	White.
	חוּר	*Chur.*	Hur, N. M.
	חוֹרֵב חֹרֵב	*Choreb.*	Horeb, N. P.
	חוֹרוֹן	*Choron.*	Horon, N. P.
חור	חוֹרֵי	*Reticula.*	Net-works, lattices.
—	חוֹרֵי	*Foramina.*	Holes.
	חוֹרִי	*Chori.*	Hori, N. M.
	חוּרַי	*Churai.*	Hurai, N. M.
חור	חוֹרִים	*Nobiles, magnates.*	Nobles, grandees.
	חוּרָם	*Churam.*	Huram, Hiram, N. M.
	חַוְרָן	*Chauran.*	Hauran, N. P.
חרף	חוֹרְפֶיךָ	*Exprobrantes te.*	They that reproach thee.
חרש	חוֹרֵשׁ	*Arans, arator.* [*vit.*	Ploughing, a ploughman.
חוש		*Festinavit, accelera-*	He made haste, hastened.
חשב	חוֹשֵׁב	*Faber.*	A smith, artificer.
חוש	חוּשָׁה	*Festina.*	Hasten thou.
	חוּשָׁה	*Chushah.*	Hushah, N. M.
	חוּשַׁי	*Chushai.*	Hushai, N. M.

ROOTS.	DERIVATIVES.	VERSIO.	SIGNIFICATION.
חוש	חוּשִׁי	*Festinare me.*	That I make haste.
	חוּשִׁים	*Chusim.*	Hushim, N. M. W.
חשך	חוֹשֵׂךְ	*Cohibens.*	He that withholdeth, spareth.
	חוּשָׁם	*Chusam.*	Husham, N. M.
	חַוֹּת יָאִיר	*Chavot-jair.*	Havoth-jair, N. P.
חיה	חַוֹּתֵיהֶם	*Oppida eorum.*	Their towns.
	חוֹתָם	*Chotam.*	Hotham, N. M.
חתם	חוֹתָם חֹתָם	*Sigillum.*	The signet.
—	חוֹתֵם	*Obsignans,occludens*	Signing, sealing, shutting up.
	חז		
חזה	חֲזָא חֲזָה	*Vidit.*	He saw.
	חֲזָאֵל חֲזָה אֵל	*Chazael.*	Hazael, N. M.
חָזָה		*Vidit, aspexit.*	He saw, looked, beheld.
—	חָזֵה חֹזֶה	*Videns.*	Seeing.
—	חֲזֵה	*Vide; pectus.*	See thou; the breast.
—	חֹזֶה	*Videns.*	Seeing, the seer.
	חֲזוֹ	*Chazo.*	Hazo, N. M.
חזה	חֲזוּ	*Viderunt.*	They saw.
—	חֲזוּ	*Videte.*	See ye.
—	חֶזְוֵי	*Visiones.*	The visions.
—	חָזוֹן חֲזוֹן	*Visio.*	A, the vision.
—	חָזוּת	*Visio, species; conspicuus.*	A, the vision, appearance, form; conspicuous,notable.
	חֲזִיאֵל	*Chaziel.*	Haziel, N. M.
	חֲזָיָה	*Chazaia.*	Hazaiah, N. M.
	חֶזְיוֹן	*Chezion.*	Hezion, N. M.
חזה	חֶזְיוֹן חִזָּיוֹן	*Visio.*	A vision.
—	חֲזִיזִים	*Fulgetra.*	Lightnings.
—	חֹזִים	*Videntes.*	Seeing.
—	חָזַיִן	*Aspicientes.*	Beholding.
—	חֶזְינוֹת	*Visiones.*	Visions.
חזר	חֲזִיר	*Aper, sus.*	The boar, swine.
	חֵזִיר	*Chezir.*	Hezir, N. M.
חזה	חָזִיתָ חֲזַיְתָ-תָה	*Vidisti.*	Thou sawest.
—	חָזִית	*Vidisti.*	Thou sawest.
—	חֲזֵית חָזִית	*Vidi.*	I saw.

ROOTS.	DERIVATIVES.	VERSIO.	SIGNIFICATION.
חזה	חֲזִיתוּן	*Vidistis.*	Ye saw.
—	חֲזִיתִי	*Vidi.*	I have seen.
—	חֲזִיתָךְ	*Vidi te.*	I have seen thee.
—	חֲזִיתֶם	*Vidistis.*	Ye have seen.
חָזַק		*Fortis fuit, invaluit, prævaluit, roboravit, confirmavit, instauravit, induravit, apprehendit, tenuit.*	He was strong, became strong, prevailed, strengthened, confirmed, repaired, hardened, laid hold, held fast.
—	חֲזַק חֲזַק	*Fortis esto.*	Be thou strong, courageous.
—	חַזֵּק	*Robora; roborare.*	Strengthen thou; to strengthen.
—	חִזַּק	*Instauravit.*	He repaired.
—	חֹזֶק	*Robur.*	Strength.
—	חָזְקָה	*Fortis fuit.*	She was strong.
—	חָזְקָה	*Confirmata est.*	She was confirmed.
—	חֲזָקָה	*Fortis.*	Strong, mighty.
—	חָזְקוּ	*Invaluerunt.*	They became strong.
—	חֲזָקוֹ	*Róboravit eum.*	He strengthened him.
—	חַזְּקוּ	*Confirmate.*	Strengthen ye.
—	חִזְקוּ	*Fortes estote.*	Be ye strong, courageous.
—	חִזְּקוּ	*Confirmarunt, roboraruni.*	They strengthened, hardened.
—	חַזְּקִי	*Confirmato.*	Confirm thou.
—	חַזְּקִי	*Robora.*	Strengthen thou.
—	חִזְקֵי	*Fortes, duri.*	Strong, hard.
—	חִזְקִי	*Robur meum.*	My strength.
	חִזְקִי	*Chezechi.*	Hezeki, N. M.
	חִזְקִיָּה־יָהוּ	*Chezechias.*	Hezekiah, N. M.
חזק	חֲזָקִים	*Fortes, robusti.*	Strong.
—	חִזַּקְתִּי	*Roboravi.*	Strengthened.
—	חִזַּקְתֶּם	*Confirmastis.*	Ye have confirmed, strengthened.
—	חֲזַקְתַּנִי	*Fortior fuisti me.*	Thou hast been stronger than I
—	חִזַּקְתַּנִי	*Confirmasti me.*	Thou hast strengthened me.
חזר			

חח

ROOTS.	DERIVATIVES.	VERSIO.	SIGNIFICATION.
חוח	חָח	*Fibula, armilla.*	A clasp, bracelet.

ROOTS.	DERIVATIVES.	VERSIO.	SIGNIFICATION.
חוה	חָחִי	*Hamus meus.*	My hook.
—	חַחִיים־־חִים	*Hami.*	The hooks.
	חט		
חָטָא		*Aberravit, deliquit, peccavit, expiavit, purgavit, pœnam peccati luit.*	He missed, wandered from, transgressed, sinned, expiated, cleansed, suffered the punishment of sin.
—	חֲטֹא	*Peccare.*	To sin.
—	חֵטְא	*Peccatum.*	Sin.
—	חֹטֶא	*Peccans, peccator.*	Sinning, a sinner.
—	חֹטֵא	*Peccans.*	Sinning.
—	חָטְאָה חָטְ׳	*Peccavit.*	Sho hath sinned.
—	חֲטָאָה חַטָ״	*Peccatum.*	Sin.
—	חָטְאוּ חָטְאוּ	*Peccaverunt.*	They have sinned.
—	חֲטָאָיו	*Peccata ejus.*	His sins.
—	חֶטְאוֹ	*Peccatum ejus.*	His sin.
—	חִטְּאוּ	*Purgarunt.*	They cleansed.
—	חַטָּאוֹת	*Peccata; victimæ pro peccatis.*	Sins, sin-offerings.
—	חַטֹּאות	*Peccata.*	Sins.
—	חַטֹּאותַי	*Peccata mea.*	My sins.
—	חַטֹּאותֶיךָ	*Peccata tua.*	Thy sins.
—	חַטֹּאותֵיכֶם חַטֹ׳	*Peccata vestra.*	Your sins.
—	חַטֹּאותָם חַטֹ׳	*Peccata eorum.*	Their sins.
—	חֲטָאַי־־אַי	*Peccata mea.*	My sins.
—	חַטָּאֵי	*Peccatores.*	Sinners.
—	חֲטָאֵי־־אִים	*Peccata.*	Sins.
—	חֲטָאֵיכֶם	*Peccata vestra.*	Your sins.
—	חַטָּאִים חֹטְאִים	*Peccatores, rei.*	Sinners, offenders.
—	חֶטְאָם	*Peccatum eorum.*	Their sin.
—	חָטָאנוּ	*Peccavimus.*	We have sinned.
—	חָטָאתָ	*Peccavisti.*	Thou hast sinned.
—	חַטָּאת חַטַּאת	*Peccatum, victima pro peccato, purgatio, expiatio.*	Sin, a sacrifice for sin, a purification, expiation.

ROOTS.	DERIVATIVES.	VERSIO.	SIGNIFICATION.
חטא	חַטֹּאת	*Peccata, victimæ pro peccato.*	Sins, sin-offerings.
—	חַטָּאתוֹ	*Peccatum ejus, victima pro peccatò*	His sin, his sin-offering.
—	חֲטֹאתוֹ	*Peccare eum.* [*ejus.*	That he sinneth.
—	חָטָאתִי	*Peccavi.*	I have sinned.
—	חַטָּאתִי	*Peccatum meum.*	My sin.
—	חַטֹּאתֶיהָ	*Peccata ejus.*	Her sins.
—	חַטֹּאתֵיהֶם	*Peccata eorum.*	Their sins.
—	חַטֹּאתָיו־־תָו	*Peccata ejus.*	His sins.
—	חַטֹּאתֶיךָ־־תֶיךָ	*Peccata tua.*	Thy sins.
—	חַטֹּאתֵינוּ	*Peccata nostra.*	Our sins.
—	חַטָּאתְךָ	*Peccatum tuum; victima pro peccato tuo.*	Thy sin; thy sin-offering.
—	חַטַּאתְכֶם	*Peccatum vestrum.*	Your sin.
—	חַטָּאתָם	*Peccatum eorum; victima pro peccato eorum.*	Their sin; their sin-offering.
—	חַטֹּאתָם	*Peccata eorum.*	Their sins.
—	חֲטָאתֶם	*Peccastis.*	Ye have sinned.
—	חַטָּאתֵנוּ	*Peccatum nostrum.*	Our sin.
— -	חַטֹּאתֵנוּ	*Peccata nostra.*	Our sins.
חָטַב		*Cecidit, succidit.*	He hewed, felled, cut down.
—	חֲטֻבוֹת	*Cælaturæ.*	Carved works.
—	חֹטְבֵי	*Cædentes.*	Hewing, hewers.
חנט	חִטָּה	*Triticum.*	Wheat.
	חַטּוּשׁ	*Chatus.*	Hatush, N. M.
	חֲטִיטָא	*Chatita.*	Hatita, N. M.
	חַטִּיל	*Chatil.*	Hattil, N. M.
חנט	חִטִּים	*Tritica.*	Wheats.
—	חִטִּין	*Triticum.*	Wheat.
	חֲטִיפָא	*Chatipha.* [*vel.*	Hatipha, N. M.
חָטַם		*Cohibuit, prolongavit.*	He refrained, delayed.
חָטַף		*Rapuit, diripuit.*	He seized, spoiled.
חטר			
—	חֹטֶר	*Virga, surculus.*	A rod, shoot.

ROOTS.	DERIVATIVES.	VERSIO.	SIGNIFICATION.
	חי		
חיה	חָי חַי	*Vixit; vivens; vivus*	He lived; living; alive.
—	חֵי	*Vivit, vivat; vita.*	He lives, let him live; life.
—	חַיָּא	*Vivens.*	Living.
—	חִיאֵל	*Chiel.* [*um fecit.*	Hiel, N. M. [guilty.
חָיַב		*Debitorem fecit, re-*	He made debtor, he made
חוד	חִידָה	*Ænigma.*	A riddle.
—	חִידוֹת	*Ænigmata.*	Dark sayings.
—	חִידָתִי	*Ænigma meum.*	My dark saying.
—	חִידָתְךָ	*Ænigma tuum.*	Thy riddle.
חָיָה		*Vixit, convaluit, re-* *vixit, vivum ser-* *vavit, vitam resti-*	He lived, recovered health, revived, kept alive, restored life.
—	חָיוֹה--וֹן	*Vivendo.* [*tuit.*	In living.
—	חַיָּה	*Vivens; vita; animal*	Living; life; an animal.
—	חִיָּה	*In vita servavit.*	He hath kept alive.
—	חָיוּ	*Vixerunt.*	They lived.
—	חַיָּו	*Vita ejus.*	His life.
—	חִיּוּ	*In vita conservarunt*	They preserved alive.
—	חֵיוָא--וָה--וַת	*Animal.*	An animal.
—	חֵיוָן	*Bestiæ, animalia.*	Beasts, animals.
—	חָיוֹת	*Vegetæ.*	Lively.
—	חַיּוֹת	*Feræ, animalia.*	Beasts, animals.
—	חַיּוּת	*Vita.*	Health.
—	חֵיוָתָא--ךְ	*Bestiæ, animalia.*	The beasts, animals.
—	חֲיוֹתָם	*Convalescere eos.*	That they recover health.
—	חַיַּי--יַּי	*Vita mea.*	My life.
—	חַיֵּי	*Vita.*	Life.
—	חֲיֵי חֱיֵי	*Vive.*	Live thou.
—	חַיַּיא	*Viventes.*	Living.
—	חַיֶּיהָ	*Vita ejus.*	Her life.
—	חַיֵּיהוּ	*Vitam restitue illi.*	Revive thou him.
—	חַיֵּיהֶם	*Vita eorum.*	Their life.
—	חַיָּיו	*Vita ejus.*	His life.
—	חַיֶּיךָ--יִךְ	*Vita tua.*	Thy life.
—	חַיָּיכִי	*Vita mea.*	My life.

ROOTS.	DERIVATIVES.	VERSIO.	SIGNIFICATION.
חיה	חַיֵּיכֶם	*Vita vestra.*	Your life.
—	חַיִּים	*Vitæ; vivi; viventes*	Lives; alive; living.
—	חַיֵּינוּ	*Vita nostra.*	Our life.
—	חִיִּיתָנִי־־תַ״	*Vivum servasti me.*	Thou hast kept me alive.
חיל			
—	חָיִל־־חַ״ חֵיל	*Robur, fortitudo; opes; virtus; agmen, exercitus, propugnaculum.*	Strength, valour; wealth; virtue; a host, army, fortress.
חול	חִיל	*Dolor.*	Pain, sorrow.
חיל	חֵילָהּ	*Robur ejus.* [*tus ejus*	Her strength.
—	חֵילוֹ	*Robur, opes, exerci-*	His strength, substance, army
חול	חִילוּ	*Contremiscite.*	Tremble ye.
חיל	חֵילִי	*Robur meum, exercitus meus.*	My strength, my army.
—	חֵילֵיהֶם	*Divitiæ eorum.*	Their riches.
—	חֲיָלִים	*Vires, copiæ.*	Strength, forces, armies.
—	חֵילֶךָ־־לֵךְ־־לְךָ	*Vires, opes, divitiæ, copiæ tuæ.*	Thy power, strength, substance, riches, army.
	חֵילָם	*Chelam.*	Helam, N. P.
חיל	חֵילָם	*Robur, substantia, facultates, opes eorum.*	Their strength, substance, goods, riches.
	חִילֵן	*Chilen.*	Hilen, N. P.
חיה	חַיֵּנִי	*Vivifica me.*	Quicken thou me.
חיץ			
—	חַיִץ	*Paries.*	A wall.
חוץ	חִיצוֹנָה	*Exterior.*	Outer.
חיק			
—	חֵיק	*Sinus.*	The bosom.
—	חֵיקָהּ	*Sinus ejus.*	Her bosom.
—	חֵיקוֹ	*Sinus ejus.*	His bosom.
—	חֵיקִי	*Sinus meus.*	My bosom.
—	חֵיקֶךָ	*Sinus tuus.*	Thy bosom.
—	חֵיקָם	*Sinus eorum.*	Their bosom.
	חִירָה	*Chiras.*	Hirah, N. M.
	חִירוֹם־־רָם	*Chiram.*	Hiram, N. M.

ROOTS.	DERIVATIVES.	VERSIO.	SIGNIFICATION.
חוש	חִישׁ	*Cito.*	Soon.
—	חִישָׁה	*Festina.*	Hasten thou.
חיה	חַיַּת	*Vivens, animal.*	A living creature, animal.
—	חַיָּתוֹ	*Vita ejus.*	His life.
—	חַיְתוֹ	*Fera, bestia.*	A beast.
—	חַיָּתִי	*Vita mea.*	My life.
—	חַיָּתְךָ	*Cœtus tuus.*	Thy company.
—	חַיָּתָם	*Vita, animal eorum.*	Their life, animal.
—	חִיְּתָנִי	*Vivificavit me.*	He hath quickened me.
	חכ		
חך חָכָה		*Expectavit, præstolatus est.*	He expected, waited, tarried.
—	חַכָּה	*Hamus.*	A hook.
—	חַכֵּה	*Expecta.*	Wait thou.
חך	חִכָּהּ	*Palatum ejus.*	Her palate, roof of her mouth
חכה	חִכָּה	*Præstolatus est.*	He waited.
—	חַכּוּ	*Expectate.*	Wait ye.
—	חִכּוּ	*Præstolati sunt.*	They waited.
חך	חִכּוֹ	*Palatum ejus.*	The roof of his mouth.
—	חִכִּי	*Palatum meum.*	The roof of my mouth.
	חֲכִילָה	*Chachila.*	Hachilah, N. P.
חכם	חַכִּימֵי־מַיָּא־מִין	*Sapientes.*	The sages, wise men.
חך	חִכֵּךְ־־כֵּךְ	*Palatum tuum.*	The roof of thy mouth.
חכל			
	חֲכַלְיָה	*Chachalias.*	Hachaliah, N. M.
חכל	חַכְלִלוּת	*Rubor.*	Redness.
—	חַכְלִילִי	*Rubicundus admodum.*	Very ruddy.
חָכַם		*Sapiens fuit, sapienter egit, sapientem fecit.*	He was wise, acted wisely, made wise.
—	חָכָם חֲכַם	*Peritus, sapiens, sapientior.*	Skilful, cunning, wise, wiser.
—	חָכְמָה	*Sapiens fuit.*	She was wise.
—	חָכְמָה	*Sapientia.*	Wisdom.
—	חַכְמַת	*Sapiens* fœmina.	A wise *woman.*
—	חָכְמוּ	*Sapientes fuerunt.*	They were wise.
	חַכְמוֹנִי	*Chachmoni.*	Hachmoni, N. M.

ROOTS.	DERIVATIVES.	VERSIO.	SIGNIFICATION.
חכם	חָכְמוֹת	*Sapientiæ.*	Wisdom, wisdoms.
—	חֲכָמוֹת	*Sapientes.*	Wise.
—	חַכְמֵי	*Sapientes, periti.*	Wise, skilful.
—	חֲכָמֶיהָ	*Sapientes ejus.*	Her wise men.
—	חֲכָמָיו	*Sapientes ejus.*	His wise men.
—	חֲכָמַיִךְ־מֶיךָ	*Sapientes tui.*	Thy wise men.
—	חֲכָמִים	*Sapientes.*	Wise men.
—	חָכַמְתָּ	*Sapiens fuisti.*	Thou hast been wise.
—	חָכְמַת חַ׳	*Sapientia.*	Wisdom.
—	חָכְמְתָא	*Sapientia.*	Wisdom.
—	חָכְמָתוֹ	*Sapientia ejus.*	His wisdom.
—	חָכַמְתִּי	*Sapiens fui.*	I have been wise.
—	חָכְמָתִי	*Sapientia mea.*	My wisdom.
—	חָכְמָתֶךָ־תְךָ־תֵךְ	*Sapientia tua.*	Thy wisdom.
—	חָכְמַתְכֶם	*Sapientia vestra.*	Your wisdom.
—	חָכְמָתָם	*Sapientia eorum.*	Their wisdom.
חכה	חִכְּתָה	*Expectavit.*	She expected, waited.
	חל		
חלה	חַל	*Deprecare.*	Intreat thou.
חיל	חֵל	*Propugnaculum.*	A fortress.
חלל	חֹל	*Profanus, communis*	Profane, common.
חלא			
	חֶלְאָה	*Chela.* [ris.	Helah, N. W.
חלה	חֲלָאִים	*Ornamentum* mulie-	A *female* ornament.
	חֲלָאם	*Chelam.*	Helam, N. P.
חלא	חֶלְאָתָהּ	*Spuma ejus.*	Her scum.
חלב			
—	חָלָב חֲלֵב	*Lac.*	Milk.
—	חֵלֶב	*Adeps; opimum.*	Fat; the best.
	חֵלֶב	*Cheleb.*	Heleb, N. M.
חלב	חֶלְבָּהּ	*Adeps ejus.*	Her fat.
	חֶלְבָּה	*Chelba.*	Helbah, N. P.
חלב	חֶלְבְּהֶן	*Adeps earum.* [ejus.	Their fat.
—	חֶלְבּוֹ	*Adeps ejus; opimum*	His fat; the best thereof.
	חֶלְבּוֹן	*Chelbon.*	Helbon, N. P.
חלב	חֲלָבִי	*Lac meum.*	My milk.

ROOTS.	DERIVATIVES.	VERSIO.	SIGNIFICATION.
חלב	חֲלָבֵי	*Adipes.*	The fat.
—	חֲלָבְךָ	*Lac tuum.*	Thy milk.
—	חֶלְבָּם	*Adeps eorum.*	Their fat.
—	חֶלְבָּמוֹ	*Adeps eorum.*	Their fat.
חלד			
—	חֶלֶד	*Mundus, ævum.*	The world, age.
	חֵלֶד	*Cheled.*	Heled, N. M.
	חֻלְדָּה	*Chulda.*	Huldah, N. W.
	חֶלְדַּי	*Cheldai.*	Heldai, N. M.
חָלָה		*Ægrotavit, languit, doluit, debilitatus est, ægrum fecit, oravit, deprecatus est.*	He was sick, he languished, grieved, grew weak, made sick, prayed, intreated.
חלל	חַלָּה	*Placenta.*	A cake.
חול	חָלָה	*Doluit, parturivit.*	She was in pain, travailed.
חלה	חָלָה	*Ægrotavit, oravit.*	He was sick, prayed, besought
—	חֹלָה	*Ægrotus, dolens.*	Sick, being in pain.
חול	חָלוּ	*Doluerunt.*	They were in pain, grieved.
חלה	חָלוּ	*Debilitatæ sunt.*	They were weakened.
—	חַלּוּ	*Deprecamini.*	Beseech ye.
חלם	חֲלוֹם	*Somnium, somniando*	A dream, in dreaming.
חלל	חַלּוֹן	*Fenestra.*	A window.
	חֹלוֹן חֹלֹן	*Cholon.*	Holon, N. P.
חלל	חַלּוֹנֵי־־נַי	*Fenestræ.*	Windows.
חלף	חֲלוֹף	*Transitus, mutatio.*	A passage, change.
חלץ	חָלוּץ חֲ־	*Expeditus, detractus*	Loosed, drawn off.
—	חֲלוּצֵי־־צִים	*Expediti.*	Prepared.
חליש	חֲלוּשָׁה	*Debilitas, clades.*	Weakness, defeat, overthrow.
חלל	חַלּוֹת־־לֹת	*Placentæ.*	Cakes.
חלה	חֲלוֹתִי	*Morbus meus.*	My disease.
	חֲלַח	*Chalach.*	Helah, N. R.
	חַלְחוּל	*Chalchul.*	Halhul, N. P.
חול	חַלְחָלָה	*Dolor.*	Pain.
חָלַט		*Diligenter observavit, verbum rapuit, festinavit, præcidit.*	He observed diligently, caught the word, hastened, cut off.

ROOTS.	DERIVATIVES.	VERSIO.	SIGNIFICATION.
	חָלִי	*Chali.*	Hali, N. P.
חלה	חֳלִי חֹ׳	*Morbus.*	Sickness.
—	חָלְיוֹ	*Morbus ejus.*	His sickness.
חלל	חָלִילָה־־לָלָה	*Absit.*	Far be it.
חלה	חִלִּינוּ	*Deprecati sumus.*	We have instructed.
—	חֳלָיֵנוּ	*Morbi, dolores nostri*	Our sicknesses, griefs.
חלף	חֲלִיפוֹת־לִפ־פֹת	*Mutationes, vices.*	Changes, courses.
—	חֲלִיפָתִי	*Mutatio mea.*	My change.
חלץ	חֲלִיצוֹתָם	*Vestes mutatoriæ, exuviæ eorum.*	Their changeable suits of apparel, their spoil.
חלה	חָלִית	*Ægrotasti.*	Thou wast sick.
—	חֻלֵּיתָ	*Debilitatus est.*	Thou hast been weakened.
—	חָלִיתִי	*Ægrotavi.*	I was sick.
—	חִלִּיתִי	*Precatus sum.*	I made supplication.
חלך			
—	חֲלְכָּאִים	*Pauperes.*	The poor.
—	חֲלֵכָה	*Pauper.*	Poor.
חָלַל		*Perforatus, confossus, vulneratus, occisus est; polluit, profanavit, violavit; fistulavit, saltavit, cœpit.*	He was bored through, stabbed, wounded, slain; he polluted, profaned, violated; he piped, danced, began.
—	חַלֵּל	*Polluere.*	To profane.
—	חֻלָּל	*Occisus est.*	He was slain.
—	חִלֵּל	*Profanavit, polluit.*	He profaned, polluted.
חול	חֹלֵל	*Parturire fecit.*	He made to bring forth.
חלל	חֹלְלָה	*Formavit.*	She hath formed.
—	חִלְלֻהוּ	*Profanarunt illum.*	They profaned him.
—	חִלְלוֹ	*Profanavit eum.*	He hath profaned him.
—	חִלְלוּ־־לֻ׳	*Profanarunt.*	They have profaned.
—	חַלְלֵי	*Vulnerati, occisi.*	The wounded, slain.
—	חֲלָלֶיהָ	*Occisi ejus.*	Her slain.
—	חַלְלֵיהֶם	*Occisi eorum.*	Their slain.
—	חֲלָלָיו	*Occisi ejus.*	His slain.
—	חֲלָלַיִךְ־־לַיִךְ	*Occisi tui.*	Thy slain.
—	חַלְלֵיכֶם	*Occisi vestri.*	Your slain.

ROOTS.	DERIVATIVES.	VERSIO.	SIGNIFICATION.
חלל	חֲלָלִים	*Vulnerati, occisi.*	Wounded, slain.
—	חֲלָלֵינוּ	*Occisi nostri.*	Our slain.
—	חַלְּלָם	*Polluere eos.*	That they defile.
—	חִלַּלְתְּ	*Profanasti.*	Thou hast profaned.
—	חִלַּלְתָּ	*Polluisti.*	Thou hast defiled.
—	חִלַּלְתִּי	*Pollui.*	I have polluted.
—	חִלַּלְתֶּם	*Profanastis.*	Ye have profaned.
	חֵלֶם	*Chelem.*	Helem, N. M.
חָלַם		*Somniavit, dormivit, revaluit, sanavit.*	He dreamed, slept, recovered his health, cured.
—	חֲלֹם חֶלְמָא־מָה	*Somnium.*	A dream.
—	חֹלֵם	*Somnians.*	Dreaming.
—	חֲלֹמוֹ	*Somnium ejus.*	His dream.
—	חֲלֹמוֹת	*Somnia.*	Dreams.
—	חֲלֹמוֹת חֶלְמִין	*Somnia.*	Dreams.
—	חֶלְמִי	*Somnium meum.*	My dream.
חלמש	חַלָּמִישׁ	*Silex.*	The flint.
חלם	חֶלְמָךְ	*Somnium tuum.*	Thy dream.
—	חָלַמְנוּ־־לִי	*Somniavimus.*	We have dreamed.
חלמש			
חלם	חָלַמְתָּ	*Somniasti.*	Thou hast dreamed.
—	חָלַמְתִּי־־לִי	*Somniavi.*	I have dreamed.
—	חֲלֹמֹתָיו	*Somnia ejus.*	His dreams.
—	חֲלֹמֹתֵיכֶם	*Somnia vestra.*	Your dreams.
—	חֲלֹמֹתֵינוּ	*Somnia nostra.*	Our dreams.
	חֵלֹן	*Chelon.*	Helon, N. M. P.
	חֹלֹן	*Cholon.*	Holon, N. P.
חול	חַלְנוּ	*Doluimus.*	We have been in pain.
חָלַף		*Transivit, præterivit, mutavit, re-*	He passed by, through, over, changed, renewed.
	חֵלֶף	*Cheleph.* [*novavit.*	Heleph, N. P.
חלף	חֵלֶף	*Pro, vice.* [*runt.*	For, instead of.
—	חָלְפוּ	*Transierunt, muta-*	They passed away, changed.
חָלַץ		*Detraxit, eruit, exuit, subtraxit, eripuit, liberavit, ex-*	He drew off, drew out of, put off, withdrew, rescued, delivered, loosed, prepared.
	חֶלֶץ חֵי חַי״	*Chalets.* [*pedivit.*	Helez, N. M.

ROOTS.	DERIVATIVES.	VERSIO.	SIGNIFICATION.
חלץ	חָלַץ	*Detraxit.*	He hath drawn off, taken away.
—	חַלְּצָה	*Libera.*	Deliver thou.
—	חָלְצוּ	*Eruerunt.*	They drew out of.
—	חֲלֻצֵי	*Expediti.*	Prepared.
—	חֲלָצָיו־צוֹ	*Lumbi ejus.*	His loins.
—	חֲלָצֶיךָ	*Lumbi tui.*	Thy loins.
—	חֲלָצַיִם	*Lumbi.*	The loins.
—	חַלְּצֵנִי	*Libera me.*	Deliver thou me.
—	חִלַּצְתָּ	*Eripuisti.*	Thou hast delivered.
—	חֲלִצָתוֹ	*Vestis ejus.*	His garment.
	חֵלֶק	*Cheleck.*	Helek, N. M.
חָלַק		*Divisit, partitus est, mollivit, lenivit,*	He divided, distributed, softened, smoothed, flattered.
—	חֵלֶק	*Portio.* [*blanditus est*	A portion.
—	חָלָק	*Lenis, blandiens.*	Smooth, flattering.
—	חַלֵּק	*Divide.*	Divide thou.
—	חֵלֶק	*Pars, portio.*	A part, portion.
—	חֻלַּק	*Divisus est.*	He hath been divided.
—	חֶלְקָהּ	*Pars ejus.*	Her part.
—	חֶלְקָה	*Ager, pars.*	A field, ground, piece.
—	חָלְקוּ	*Diviserunt.*	They divided.
—	חֶלְקוֹ	*Pars ejus.*	His part.
—	חִלְּקוּ	*Partiti sunt.*	They have parted.
—	חַלְּקוּ	*Dividite.*	Divide ye.
—	חֲלַקּוֹת	*Blanditiæ.*	Flatteries.
—	חַלְּקֵי	*Læves.*	Smooth.
	חֶלְקִי	*Chelechitæ.*	Helekites, N. F.
	חֶלְקַי	*Chleckai.*	Helkai, N. M.
חלק	חֶלְקִי	*Pars, hæreditas mea*	My part, portion, inheritance
	חִלְקִיָּה־־יָּהוּ	*Chilkiah.*	Hilkiah, N. M.
חלק	חֶלְקֵיהֶם	*Partes eorum.*	Their parts, portions.
—	חֲלָקִים	*Partes.*	Portions.
—	חֶלְקְךָ־קֵךְ־קֶךָ	*Pars tua.*	Thy portion.
—	חֶלְקָם	*Pars eorum.*	Their portion.
—	חִלְּקָם	*Divisit eos.*	He divided them.
	חֶלְקַת חֶלְקַת	*Chelkath.*	Helcath, N. P. [smoothness.
חלק	חֶלְקַת	*Pars, ager; lævitas.*	A part, piece, portion, field,

ROOTS.	DERIVATIVES.	VERSIO.	SIGNIFICATION.
חלק	חִלְּקָהּ	*Divisit eam.*	He divided her.
—	חֶלְקִי	*Pars mea.*	My portion.
—	חֶלְקָם	*Pars eorum.*	Their portion.
חָלַשׁ		*Debilitavit, fregit, infirmus fuit.*	He weakened, broke, was weak or infirm.
חלל	חַלֹּת	*Placenta.*	A cake.
חול	חַלְתִּי	*Parturivi.*	I travailed.
	חם		
	חָם	*Cham.*	Ham, N. M. P.
חמם	חָם	*Calidus.*	Hot, warm.
—	חַם	*Incaluit.* [*calidus.*	He grew hot. [warm.
—	חֹם	*Incalescere; calor;*	To grow warm, or hot; heat;
חמא			
יחם	חֵמָא	*Furor.*	Wrath.
חמא	חֶמְאָה־־אַת	*Butyrum.* [*givit.*	Butter.
חָמַד		*Desideravit, concu-*	He coveted, eagerly desired.
—	חֶמֶד	*Desiderium; deside-rabilis.* [*rabilis.*	Desire; desirable.
—	חֶמְדָּה	*Desiderium; deside-*	Desire; desirable.
—	חָמְדוּ	*Desiderarunt.*	They desired.
—	חֲמֻדוֹת	*Desideria.*	Desires.
	חֶמְדָּן	*Chemdan.*	Hemdan, N. M.
חמד	חֶמְדַּת	*Desiderium.* [*pivi.*	Desire.
—	חִמַּדְתִּי	*Desideravi, concu-*	I coveted, eagerly desired.
—	חֶמְדָּתִי	*Desiderium meum.*	My desire.
—	חֶמְדָּתֶךָ	*Desiderium tuum.*	Thy desire.
—	חֶמְדָּתָם	*Desiderium eorum.*	Their desire.
—	חֲמַדְתֶּם	*Desiderastis.*	Ye have desired.
חמה			
חמם	חַמָּה	*Sol.*	The sun.
יחם	חֵמָה	*Furor.*	Wrath, fury.
חמה	חוֹמָה	*Murus.*	A wall.
	חַמּוּאֵל	*Chamuel.*	Hamuel, N. M.
חמד	חֲמוּדוֹ	*Desiderium ejus.*	His desire.
—	חֲמֻדוֹת־־דֹת	*Desideria; res desi-*	Desires; desirable things.
	חֲמוּטַל	*Chamutal.* [*derabiles*	Hamutal, N. W.

ROOTS.	DERIVATIVES.	VERSIO.	SIGNIFICATION.
	חֲמוּל	*Chamul.*	Hamul, N. M.
	חַמּוֹן	*Chamon.*	Hammon, N. P.
חמץ	חָמוּץ	*Exacerbatus.*	Grieved, exasperated.
—	חָמוּץ	*Aspersus, tinctus.*	Sprinkled, dyed.
חמק	חַמּוּקֵי	*Periscelides.*	Drawers *worn by women.*
	חֲמוֹר	*Chamor.*	Hamor, N. M.
חמר	חֲמוֹר	*Asinus; acervus.*	An ass; a heap.
—	חֲמוֹרֵיכֶם	*Asini vestri.*	Your asses.
—	חֲמוֹרִים חֲמֹ׳	*Asini.*	Asses.
יחם	חֵמוֹת	*Furores.*	Rage, fury.
חמה	חֹמוֹת	*Muri.*	Walls.
—	חֲמוֹתָהּ	*Socer ejus.*	Her father in law.
חמם	חַמּוֹתִי	*Incalui.*	I have become warm.
חמה	חֹמוֹתֶיהָ	*Muri ejus.*	Her walls.
—	חֹמוֹתַיִךְ	*Muri tui.*	Thy walls.
—	חֲמוֹתֵךְ	*Socrus tua.*	Thy mother in law.
חמט			
	חֻמְטָה	*Chumta.*	Humtah, N. M.
חמה	חֲמִיהָ	*Socrus ejus.*	Her mother in law.
—	חָמִיךְ	*Socer tuus.*	Thy father in law.
חמם	חַמִּים	*Calidi.*	Warm.
חמץ	חָמִיץ	*Subacidus.*	Somewhat sour.
חמש	חֲמִישִׁי	*Quintus.* [*quinto.*	The fifth. [fifth time.
—	חֲמִישִׁית חֲמִשׁ׳	*Quinta; pars quinta;*	The fifth; the fifth *part*; the
—	חֲמִשִׁתוֹ	*Quinta* pars *ejus.*	The fifth part of it.
חָמַל		*Pepercit, misertus est, clementia usus*	He spared, pitied, had compassion.
—	חָמַל	*Pepercit.* [*est.*	He spared.
—	חָמַלְתָּ	*Misertus es.*	Thou hast pitied.
—	חֲמַלְתֶּם	*Clementia usi estis.*	Ye have had compassion.
חָמַם		*Incaluit, calefecit.*	He grew hot, warmed.
חמן			
—	חַמָּנֵיכֶם	*Simulachra solaria vestra.* [*attulit.*	Your images *dedicated* to the sun. [violence.
חָמַס		*Rapuit, abripuit, vim*	He seized, took away, used
—	חָמָס	*Vis, iniquitas, injuria; injurius.*	Violence, injustice, injury, damage; injurious.

ROOTS.	DERIVATIVES.	VERSIO.	SIGNIFICATION.
חמס	חָמָס	*Violentia.*	Violence.
—	חֹמֵס	*Injuriam faciens.*	Doing injury.
—	חָמְסוּ	*Vim attulerunt.*	They violated, used violence.
—	חֲמָסוֹ	*Injuria ejus.*	His violent dealing.
—	חֲמָסִי	*Injuria mea.*	My wrong.
—	חֲמָסִים	*Injuriæ.*	Injuries, acts of violence.
חָמֵץ		*Fermentatus, contristatus, exacerbatus est.*	He was leavened, grieved, enraged.
—	חֹמֶץ	*Acetum.*	Vinegar.
—	חֻמְצָתוֹ	*Fermentari eam.*	That it is leavened.
חָמַק		*Abiit, subduxit se, circuivit.*	He departed, withdrew himself, compassed about.
חָמַר		*Rubuit, ferbuit, lutulentus fuit; bituminavit.*	He was red, troubled, muddy; he covered with pitch or slime.
—	חֶמֶר חַמְרָא	*Vinum.*	Wine.
—	חָמֶר	*Merus, rubens.*	Pure, red.
—	חֲמֹר	*Asinus.*	An ass.
—	חֹמֶר	*Lutum.*	Clay.
—	חָמֹר	*Rubens.*	Red.
—	חֹמֶר	*Lutum; acervus.*	Clay; a heap.
—	חֹמֶר	*Chomer.*	Homer, N. M.
חמר	חֲמֹרוֹ	*Asinus ejus.*	His ass.
—	חֲמֹרֵיהֶם	*Asini eorum.*	Their asses.
—	חֲמָרִים ־רִם	*Acervi.*	Heaps.
—	חֲמֹרֵינוּ	*Asini nostri.*	Our asses.
—	חֲמֹרְךָ	*Asinus tuus.*	Thy ass.
—	חֲמַרְמְרָה חָ׳	*Lutulentæ fuerunt.*	They have been foul, muddy.
—	חֳמַרְמָרוּ ־מְרוּ	*Ferbuerunt.*	They have been troubled.
	חַמְרָן	*Chamran.*	Hamran, N. M.
חמר	חֲמֹרָתַיִם	*Duo acervi.*	Two heaps.
חָמֵשׁ		*Quintum tulit, expedivit, instruxit.*	He took the fifth, prepared, armed, arrayed.
—	חָמֵשׁ חֲמֵשׁ	*Quinque.*	Five.
—	חֲמִשָּׁה ־מֵשֶׁת	*Quinque.*	Five.
—	חֲמִשֵּׁיהֶם	*Quinquaginta illorum.*	Their fifties.
—	חֲמִשָּׁיו	*Quinquaginta ejus.*	His fifty.
—	חֲמִשֶּׁיךָ	*Quinquaginta tui.*	Thy fifty.

ROOTS.	DERIVATIVES.	VERSIO.	SIGNIFICATION.
חמש	חֲמִשִּׁים	*Quinquaginta.*	Fifty.
—	חֲמֻשִׁים	*Expediti.*	Prepared.
—	חֲמִשִׁיתוֹ־שִׁתוֹ	*Quinta pars ejus.*	The fifth part of it.
	חֲמָת	*Chamat.*	Hamath, N. P.
חמת			
יחם	חֵמֹת	*Furores.* [*uter.*	Fury, rage. [*of leather.*
—	חֵמָת	*Furor; venenum;*	Fury; poison; a bottle *made*
—	חֲמָתוֹ	*Furor ejus.*	His fury.
חמה	חֲמָתִי	*Furor meus.*	My fury.
	חֲמָתִי	*Chamati.*	Hamathite, N. M.
חמה	חוֹמֹתַיִךְ	*Muri tui.*	Thy walls.
יחם	חֲמָתֶךָ	*Furor tuus.*	Thy fury.
—	חֲמָתְךָ	*Furor, uter tuus.*	Thy fury, bottle.
—	חֲמָתָם	*Venenum eorum.*	Their poison.

חן

ROOTS.	DERIVATIVES.	VERSIO.	SIGNIFICATION.
	חֵן	*Chen.*	Hen, N. M.
חנן	חֵן	*Gratia, favor.*	Grace, favour.
	חֵנָדָד	*Chenadad.*	Henadad, N. M.
	חַנָּה	*Chana.*	Hannah, N. W.
חָנָה		*Castrametatus est, consedit, mansit.*	He encamped, settled, remained.
—	חֹנֶה חוֹנֶה	*Castra ponens.*	Encamping.
—	חָנוּ	*Castrametati sunt.*	They encamped.
—	חֲנוּ	*Castra ponite, ma-*	Encamp, abide ye.
חנן	חִנּוֹ	*Gratia ejus.* [*nete.*	His favour.
	חֲנוֹךְ	*Chanoch.*	Enoch, Hanoch, N. M. P.
	חָנוּן	*Chanun.*	Hanun, N. M.
חנן	חָנוֹן	*Gratiam faciendo.*	In shewing favour.
—	חַנּוּן	*Propitius.*	Gracious.
—	חָנֵּנוּ	*Propitius esto nobis.*	Be gracious to us.
חנף	חֲנוֹף	*Polluendo.*	In polluting.
חנן	חַנּוֹת	*Propitius esse.*	To be gracious.
חנה	חֲנוֹת	*Castrametari.*	To encamp.
חָנַט		*Aromatibus condivit, pollinxit, pro-*	He preserved by spices, embalmed, shot forth.
—	חָנְטָה	*Protrusit.* [*trusit.*	He shot forth.

ROOTS.	DERIVATIVES.	VERSIO.	SIGNIFICATION.
חנט	חִנְטִין	*Tritica.*	Wheats.
	חַנִּיאֵל	*Chaniel.*	Haniel, N. M.
חנך	חֲנִיכָיו	*Instituti, edocti ejus.*	His trained, disciplined.
חנה	חֹנִים	*Castra ponentes.*	Encamping.
חנן	חֲנִינָה	*Gratia.*	Favour.
—	חָנֵּינוּ	*Gratiam fac nobis.*	Be thou favourable to us.
חנה	חֲנִית	*Lancea, hasta.*	A javelin, spear.
—	חֲנִיתוֹ	*Hasta ejus.*	His spear.
—	חֲנִיתֶךָ	*Hasta tua.* [*dicavit.*	Thy spear. [plined, dedicated.
חָנַךְ		*Instituit, edocuit, de-*	He instructed, trained, disci-
—	חֲנֹךְ	*Institue, instrue.* [*te.*	Instruct, train thou. [thee.
חנה	חֹנָךְ	*Castra ponens contra*	He that encampeth against
חנך	חֲנֻכָּה	*Dedicatio.*	The dedication.
—	חֲנָכוֹ	*Dedicavit eam.*	He dedicated her or it.
	חֲנֹכִי	*Chanochitæ.*	Hanochites, N. F.
חנך	חֲנֻכַּת	*Dedicatio.*	The dedication.
חנן	חִנָּם	*Gratis.*	Freely, for nothing.
	חֲנַמְאֵל	*Chanameel.*	Hanameel, N. M.
חנמל			
	חָנָן	*Chanan.*	Hanan, N. M.
חָנַן		*Misertus est, largitus est, gratiam fecit, propitius fuit, oravit, deprecatus*	He pitied, had mercy, freely gave, shewed favour, was gracious, prayed, intreated.
—	חֹנֵן	*Miserescens.* [*est.*	Pitying, shewing mercy.
	חֲנַנְאֵל	*Chananel.*	Hananeel, N. M.
חנן	חָנָנוּ	*Gratiam fecerunt.*	They shewed favour.
—	חָנֵּנוּ	*Miserere nostri.*	Do thou have mercy upon us.
	חֲנָנִי	*Chanani.*	Hanani, N. M.
חנן	חַנָּנִי	*Gratiam fecit mihi.*	He hath shewn favour to me.
—	חָנֵּנִי	*Miserere mei; largire mihi.*	Be thou merciful unto me; grant thou unto me.
—	חָנֻּנִי	*Miseremini mei.*	Do ye have pity upon me.
	חֲנַנְיָה־יָהוּ	*Chananias.*	Hananiah, N. M.
חנן	חַנְנֵנִי חָנְ"	*Miserere mei.*	Be thou merciful to me.
	חָנֵס	*Chanes.* [*simulavit.*	Hanes, N. P. [hypocritically.
חָנֵף		*Polluit, profanavit,*	He defiled, profaned, acted

ROOTS.	DERIVATIVES.	VERSIO.	SIGNIFICATION.
חנף	חָנֵף חֹנֶף	*Simulator.*	A hypocrite.
—	חָנְפָה	*Polluta est.*	She hath been defiled.
—	חֲנֻפָּה	*Simulatio.* [*mularunt*	Hypocrisy. [hypocritically.
—	חָנֵפוּ	*Profani fuerunt, si-*	They have been profane, acted
—	חֲנֵפִים	*Simulatores.* [*cavit.*	Hypocrites.
חנק		*Strangulavit, suffo-*	He strangled, suffocated.
חנה	חֲנֹתֵנוּ	*Castrametari nos.*	That we encamp.
	חס		
חָסַד		*Probro affecit; benignum, misericordem se exhibuit*	He put to shame; shewed himself kind, merciful.
—	חֶסֶד חָסֶד	*Benignitas, misericordia; probrum.*	Kindness, mercy; a disgrace, shame.
—	חַסְדּוֹ	*Misericordia ejus.*	His mercy.
—	חֲסָדַי	*Benignitates meæ.*	My kindnesses.
—	חַסְדֵי	*Misericordiæ.*	Mercies.
—	חַסְדִּי־דּוֹ	*Misericordia mea.*	My mercy.
	חֲסַדְיָה	*Chasadias.*	Hasadiah, N. M.
חסד	חֲסָדָיו־דוֹ	*Misericordiæ ejus.*	His mercies.
—	חֲסָדֶיךָ	*Benignitates tuæ.*	Thy loving-kindnesses.
—	חַסְדְּךָ־דֶּךָ	*Misericordia tua.*	Thy mercy.
—	חֲסָדֶךָ־חַסְדֶּךָ	*Benignitas tua.*	Thy kindness.
—	חַסְדָּם	*Misericordia eorum.*	Their mercy.
חוס	חָסָה	*Pepercit.*	He pitied, spared.
	חֹסָה	*Chosas.* [*dit, confugit*	Hosah, N. M. P. [for refuge.
חָסָה		*Speravit, fidit, confi-*	He hoped, relied, trusted, fled
—	חָסוּ	*Sperarunt, confide-*	They hoped, trusted.
—	חֲסוּ	*Confidite.* [*runt.*	Trust ye.
—	חֹסֵי	*Sperantes.*	They that hope.
חסד	חָסִיד	*Benignus, misericors, sanctus.*	Kind, merciful, holy.
—	חֲסִידָה	*Ciconia.*	A stork.
—	חֲסִידָי	*Sancti mei.*	My saints.
—	חֲסִידָיו־דָו	*Sancti ejus.*	His saints.
—	חֲסִידֶיךָ	*Sancti tui.*	Thy saints.
—	חֲסִידְךָ	*Sanctus tuus.*	Thy holy one.

ROOTS.	DERIVATIVES.	VERSIO.	SIGNIFICATION.
חסד	חֲסִידִים	*Sancti.*	Saints.
—	חֲסִידֶךָ	*Sanctus tuus.*	Thy holy one.
חסה	חָסִיָה	*Speravit.*	He hath hoped, trusted.
—	חָסָיוּ	*Confiderunt.*	They trusted.
חסל	חָסִיל	*Bruchus.*	A kind of locust or caterpillar
חסן	חֲסִין	*Robustus.*	Strong.
חסר	חַסִּיר	*Deficiens.*	Deficient, wanting.
חסה	חָסִיתִי	*Speravi.*	I have hoped.
חָסַל		*Consumpsit, perdidit*	He consumed, destroyed.
חָסַם		*Obturavit, capistravit.*	He stopped, muzzled.
חָסַן		*Robustus fuit, repositus est, possedit.*	He was strong, was laid up, possessed.
—	חֹסֶן	*Robur; opes.*	Strength; riches.
—	חִסְנָא	*Potentia.*	Power.
—	חִסְנִי	*Potentia mea.*	My power.
חסף			
—	חֲסַף חַסְפָּא	*Lutum.*	Clay.
חָסַר		*Defuit, defecit, decrevit, caruit, indiguit, destituit.*	He was deficient, he failed, decreased, wanted, needed, forsook.
—	חָסֵר	*Defecit, caruit; indigens.*	He failed, wanted; he that needeth.
—	חֲסַר	*Deficiens, carens.*	Failing, wanting, needing.
—	חֶסֶר	*Defectus, inopia.*	Deficiency, want, poverty.
	חַסְרָה	*Chasras.*	Hazrah, N. M.
חסר	חָסֵרוּ	*Eguerunt.*	They lacked.
—	חָסַרְנוּ	*Caruimus.*	We have wanted.
—	חָסַרְתָּ	*Indiguisti.*	Thou hast lacked.
חסה	חַסְתָּ	*Pepercisti.*	Thou hast spared, pitied.
	חפ		
חפף	חַף	*Tectus, protectus, purus.*	Covered, protected, pure.
חָפָא		*Obtexit.*	He covered.
	חֻפָּה	*Chupas.*	Huppah, N. M.
חָפָה		*Operuit, obtexit.*	He covered, overlaid.
—	חִפָּה	*Obtexit.*	He overlaid.

ROOTS.	DERIVATIVES.	VERSIO.	SIGNIFICATION.
חפף	חֻפָּה	*Protectio.*	A protection, defence.
חפה	חָפוּ	*Operuerunt.*	They covered.
—	חָפוּי	*Opertus.*	Being covered.
חָפַז		*Festinavit, trepidavit, commotus est.*	He hastened, trembled, was troubled, hurried.
	חֻפִּים	*Chuppim.*	Huppim, N. M.
חפן			
	חָפְנִי	*Chophni.*	Hophni, N. M.
חפן	חָפְנֵי	*Manus.*	The hands.
—	חָפְנָיו	*Manus ejus.*	His hands.
—	חָפְנֶיךָ	*Manus tuæ.*	Thy hands.
—	חָפְנֵיכֶם	*Manus vestræ.*	Your hands.
—	חָפְנַיִם	*Pugilli.*	The fists, handfuls.
חָפַף		*Obtexit, protexit, obumbravit.*	He covered, protected, overshadowed.
—	חֹפֵף	*Tegens.*	He that covereth.
חָפֵץ		*Voluit, complacuit, adamavit, delectatus est.*	He willed, desired, pleased, loved much, was delighted.
—	חֵפֶץ	*Voluntas, desiderium*	Will, pleasure, purpose, desire
—	חָפְצָה	*Delectata est.*	She hath been delighted.
—	חֲפֵצָה	*Volens.*	Willing.
—	חֶפְצָהּ	*Desiderium ejus.*	Her desire.
—	חֶפְצוֹ	*Voluntas, delectatio*	His will, pleasure, delight.
—	חֲפֵצֵי	*Volentes.* [*ejus.*	They that wish, desire, will.
—	חֶפְצִי	*Voluntas mea.*	My will, pleasure.
	חֶפְצִי בָהּ	*Chaphtsiba.*	Hephzi-bah, N. W.
חפץ	חֶפְצֵיהֶם	*Desideria eorum.*	Their desires.
—	חֲפָצֶיךָ	*Desideria tua*[*menta*	Thy desires. [sure.
—	חֲפָצִים	*Desideria, oblecta-*	Desires, things that give plea-
—	חֲפֵצִים	*Desiderantes.*	They that desire.
—	חֶפְצְךָ חֶפְצֵ״	*Voluntas tua.*	Thy will, desire, pleasure.
—	חֶפְצָם	*Voluntas eorum.*	Their desire.
—	חָפַצְנוּ	*Voluimus.* [*tibi.*	We have desired. [ed.
—	חָפַצְתָּ	*Voluisti, complacuit*	Thou hast desired, been pleas-
—	חָפַצְתִּי	*Volui, delectatus sum*	I have desired, been delighted
חפץ	חֲפַצְתֶּם	*Voluistis.*	Ye have desired.

ROOTS.	DERIVATIVES.	VERSIO.	SIGNIFICATION.
חָפַר		*Fodit,exploravit,pudore affecit, eru-*	He sank, dug, searched, put to shame, was ashamed.
	חֵפֶר	*Chepher.* [*buit.*	Hepher, N. M.
חפר	חֹפֵר	*Fodiens.*	He that diggeth.
—	חָפְרָה	*Erubuit.* [*runt.*	She was ashamed. [ed.
—	חָפְרוּ־פִּ״	*Foderunt, erubue-*	They have digged,been asham-
—	חֲפָרוּהָ	*Foderunt eam.*	They digged it.
	חֶפְרִי	*Chepheritæ.*	Hepherites, N. F.
	חֲפָרַיִם	*Chapharaim.*	Hapharaim, N. P.
	חָפְרַע	*Chophra.*	Hophra, N. M.
חפר	חָפַרְתִּי	*Fodi.* [*sus est.*	I have digged.
חֻפַּשׁ		*Liberatus,manumis-*	He was freed, set at liberty.
חָפַשׂ		*Investigavit, quæsivit, mutavit.*	He examined, sought, changed.
—	חֵפֶשׂ	*Investigatio.*	An examination, search.
—	חֹפֵשׂ	*Investigans.*	Examining.
—	חֹפֶשׁ	*Libertas.*	Liberty.
—	חֻפָּשָׁה	*Manumissa est.*	She hath been set at liberty.
—	חֻפְשָׁה	*Libertas ejus.*	Her freedom.
—	חִפְשׂוּ	*Investigate.*	Search, examine ye.
—	חָפְשִׁי	*Liber.*	Free.
—	חָפְשִׁים	*Liberi.*	Free.
	חצ		
חצץ	חֵץ	*Sagitta.* [*sit, fodit.*	An arrow.
חָצַב		*Cecidit,dolavit,sculp-*	He cut, hewed, engraved, dug
—	חָצֵב	*Cecidit.*	He hewed.
—	חֹצֵב	*Cædens.*	Cutting, hewing.
—	חָצְבָה	*Excidit.*	She hath hewed out.
—	חֹצְבִי	*Excidens.*	He that heweth out.
—	חֹצְבִים	*Cædentes.*	Hewing, hewers.
—	חָצַבְתָּ	*Cædisti, fodisti.*	Thou hast cut, hewed, digged
—	חָצַבְתִּי	*Cecidi.*	I have hewed.
—	חֲצַבְתֶּם	*Excisi estis.*	Ye have been hewn.
חָצָה		*Divisit, distribuit, bi-*	He divided, distributed, part-
חוץ	חֻצָה	*Foras.* [*partitus est.*	Without. [ed in two.
—	חִצּוֹ	*Sagitta ejus.*	His arrow.

ROOTS.	DERIVATIVES.	VERSIO.	SIGNIFICATION.
חצב	חֲצוּבִים	*Fossi.*	Digged.
חצר	חֲצוֹצְרוֹת	*Tubæ.*	Trumpets.
	חָצוֹר--צֹר	*Chatsor.*	Hazor, N. P.
חצה	חֲצוֹת	*Medius.*	Middle.
חוץ	חֻצוֹת	*Plateæ.*	The streets.
	חֻצוֹת	*Chutsot.* [*dia.*	Huzot, N. P.
חצה	חֲצִי	*Medium, pars dimi-*	The middle, the half.
חצץ	חִצַּי	*Sagittæ meæ.*	My arrows.
—	חִצֵּי	*Sagittæ.*	Arrows.
—	חִצִּי	*Sagitta mea.*	My arrow.
חצה	חֶצְיָהּ	*Dimidium ejus.*	The half of her.
—	חֶצְיוֹ	*Medium ejus.*	The midst of him.
חצץ	חִצָּיו-ו	*Sagittæ ejus.*	His arrows.
—	חִצֶּיךָ	*Sagittæ tuæ.*	Thy arrows.
חצה	חֶצְיָם	*Dimidium eorum.*	The half of them.
חצץ	חִצִּים	*Sagittæ.*	Arrows.
חצה	חֶצְיֵנוּ	*Dimidium nostri.*	Half of us.
חצר	חָצִיר	*Gramen; atrium.*	Grass; a court.
—	חֲצִיר	*Gramen.*	The grass.
חצץ	חִצָּם	*Sagitta eorum.*	Their arrow.
חצן			
—	חָצְנִי	*Sinus meus.*	My bosom.
חָצַף		*Ursit, acceleravit.*	He urged, hastened.
חָצַץ		*Excidit, succidit, dispertivit, jaculatus est.* [*ens.*	He cut off, cut down, divided, distributed, shot, darted.
—	חוֹצֵץ	*Excidens, disperti-*	Cutting off, distributing.
—	חָצָץ	*Lapillus, scrupus.*	Gravel, stone.
—	חֻצָּצוּ	*Excisi sunt.*	They have been cut off.
—	חֲצָצֶיךָ	*Sagittæ tuæ.*	Thy arrows.
	חַצְצוֹן תָּמָר	*Chatsatson-tamar.*	Hazezon-tamar, N. P.
חִצְצֵר		*Clanxit, buccinavit.*	He blew or sounded a trumpet
חצר	חֲצֹצְרָה	*Tuba.*	A trumpet.
—	חֲצֹצְרוֹת	*Tubæ.*	Trumpets.
חצר			
—	חָצֵר חֲצַר	*Atrium.*	A court.
	חֲצַר אַדָּר	*Chatsar-adar.*	Hazar-adder, N. P.

ROOTS.	DERIVATIVES.	VERSIO.	SIGNIFICATION.
	חֲצַר גַּדָּה	*Chatsar-gadas.*	Hazar-gaddah, N. P.
	חֲצַר סוּסָה	*Chatsar-susas.*	Hazar-susah, N. P.
	חֲצַר סוּסִים	*Chatsar-susim.*	Hazar susim, N. P.
	חֲצַר עֵינוֹן	*Chatsar-enon.*	Hazar-enon, N. P.
	חֲצַר שׁוּעָל	*Chatsar-sual.*	Hazar-shual, N. P.
חצר	חֲצֵרָה	*In atrium.*	Into the court.
	חֶצְרוֹ	*Chetsro.*	Hezro, N. M.
	חֶצְרוֹן־־רֹן	*Chetsron.*	Hezron, N. M. P.
	חֶצְרוֹנִי	*Chetsronitæ.*	Hezronites, N. F.
	חֲצֵרוֹת־־רֹת	*Chatserot.*	Hazeroth, N. P.
חצר	חֲצֵרוֹת חַצְ׳	*Atria, villæ.*	Courts, villages.
	חֶצְרַי	*Chetsrai.*	Hezrai, N. M.
חצר	חֲצֵרָי	*Atria mea.*	My courts.
—	חַצְרֵי	*Villæ.*	Villages.
—	חֲצֵרֶיהָ	*Villæ ejus.*	Her villages.
—	חַצְרֵיהֶם	*Villæ eorum.*	Their villages.
—	חֲצֵרֶיךָ	*Atria tua.*	Thy courts.
	חֲצֵרִים	*Chatserim.*	Hazerim, N. P.
חצר	חֲצֵרִים	*Villæ.*	Villages.
	חֲצַרְמָוֶת	*Chatzarmavet.*	Hazarmaveth, N. M.
חצר	חֲצֵרֹתָיו	*Atria ejus.*	His courts.
	חק		
חקק	חָק חֹק	*Decretum, statutum, institutum, pars statuta, certus finis, mensura.*	A decree, statute, ordinance, custom, appointed portion, fixed limit, measure.
חיק	חֵק	*Sinus.*	The bosom.
חָקָה		*Sculpsit, expressit.*	He cut, carved, imprinted.
—	חֻקֶּהָ	*Describe eam.*	Describe, mark her.
—	חֻקָּה	*Statutum.*	An ordinance.
—	חֻקּוֹ	*Decretum ejus.*	His decree.
	חֲקוּפָא	*Chachupha.*	Hakupha, N. M.
חקק	חֻקּוֹת־־קֹּת	*Instituta, decreta.*	Customs, ordinances, decrees.
—	חֻקּוֹתַי־־קֹּתַי	*Instituta mea.*	My ordinances.
—	חֻקַּי־־קָּי	*Statuta mea.*	My statutes.
—	חֻקֵּי־־קִּים	*Statuta.*	The statutes.

ROOTS.	DERIVATIVES.	VERSIO.	SIGNIFICATION.
חקק	חֻקִּי	*Statutum meum.*	My appointed.
—	חֻקָּיו־קָו	*Statuta ejus.*	His statutes.
—	חֻקֶּיךָ	*Statuta tua.*	Thy statutes.
—	חָקְךָ חֻקֶּךָ	*Demensum tuum.*	Thy allotted portion.
—	חָקְכֶם	*Demensum vestrum.*	Your allotted portion.
—	חֻקָּם	*Demensum eorum.*	Their allotted portion.
חָקַק		*Sculpsit, depinxit, descripsit, constituit, decrevit.*	He engraved, pourtrayed, described, appointed, decreed.
	חֻקֹּקָה	*Chuchocas.*	Hukkok, N. P.
חקק	חִקְקֵי	*Decreta.*	Decrees.
—	חֹקְקֵי	*Sculpens.*	He that engraveth.
—	חֲקֻקִּים	*Depicti.*	Pourtrayed.
חָקַר		*Quæsivit, scrutatus est, pervestigavit.*	He sought, inquired, carefully examined.
—	חֲקֹר	*Scrutari.*	To search.
—	חֵקֶר	*Scrutatio.*	A searching.
—	חֹקֵר	*Scrutans.*	Searching, inquiry.
—	חֲקָרָהּ	*Pervestigavit eam.*	He carefully examined her.
—	חִקְרוּ	*Scrutamini.*	Search ye.
—	חִקְרֵי	*Scrutationes.*	Searchings.
—	חֲקַרְנוּהָ	*Pervestigavimus illam.*	We have thoroughly searched it.
—	חָקְרֵנִי	*Scrutare me.*	Search thou me.
—	חֲקַרְתַּנִי	*Pervestigasti me.*	Thou hast searched me.
חקק	חֻקַּת	*Statutum.*	A statute, ordinance.
—	חֻקֹּתָיו	*Statuta ejus.*	His statutes.
—	חַקֹּתִיךְ	*Descripsi te.*	I have graven thee.
	חר		
חור	חֻר חֹר	*Foramen.*	A hole.
—	חֹרָאיהֶם	*Stercora eorum.*	Their dung.
חָרֵב		*Exsiccavit, vastavit, desolavit, diruit, gladio occidit.*	He dried up, laid waste, desolated, destroyed, slew with the sword.
—	חֶרֶב חֶ׳	*Gladius.*	A sword.
—	חָרֵב	*Vastatus, desolatus.*	Laid waste, desolated.
—	חָרֹב	*Vastando.*	In laying waste.

ROOTS.	DERIVATIVES.	VERSIO.	SIGNIFICATION.
חרב	חֲרֹב	*Vasta, gladio occide.*	Lay thou waste, slay with the sword.
—	חֹרֶב חָרְבָה	*Vastitas, desolatio.*	Waste, desolation.
—	חָרָבָה	*Siccitas.*	Dryness, drought.
—	חֲרֵבָה	*Vastata.*	Laid waste.
—	חָרְבוּ	*Exsiccatæ sunt.*	They have been dried up.
—	חַרְבּוֹ	*Gladius ejus.*	His sword.
—	חִרְבוּ	*Desolamini; occidite*	Be ye desolate; slay ye.
—	חֹרָבוּ	*Exsiccati sunt.*	They have been dried up.
—	חַרְבוֹנָא־־נָה	*Charbonas.*	Harbona, N. M.
חרב	חַרְבוֹת חֲרָ׳	*Gladii.*	Swords.
—	חֳרָבוֹת חָרְבוֹת	*Vastitates.*	Wastes.
—	חַרְבוֹתָם־תֵיהֶם	*Gladii eorum.*	Their swords.
—	חָרָבִי	*Exsicca.*	Dry thou up.
—	חַרְבִּי	*Gladius meus.*	My sword.
—	חַרְבְּךָ־־בֶּ״	*Gladius tuus.*	Thy sword.
—	חַרְבְּכֶם	*Gladius vester.*	Your sword.
—	חַרְבָּם	*Gladius eorum.*	Their sword.
—	חָרְבֹתֶיהָ	*Vastitates ejus.*	Her wastes.
—	חָרְבֹתָיו	*Vastitates ejus.*	His waste places.
—	חָרְבֹתַיִךְ	*Vastitates tuæ.*	Thy desolations.
חָרַג		*Contremuit.*	He feared, was affrighted.
חָרַד		*Pavit, tremuit, trepidavit; terruit.*	He feared, trembled, was affrighted; he terrified.
—	חָרֵד	*Pavens.*	Fearing.
	חֲרֹד	*Charod,* nom. fontis.	Harod, *the name of a well.*
חרד	חָרְדָה	*Trepidavit.*	She was affrighted.
—	חֲרָדָה חֶרְדַּת	*Pavor, terror, tremor.*	Fear, trembling.
	חֲרָדָה	*Charadas.*	Haradah, N. M.
חרד	חָרְדוּ	*Tremuerunt.*	They trembled.
—	חִרְדוּ	*Trepidate.*	Tremble ye.
—	חֲרָדוֹת	*Terrores.*	Terrors.
	חֲרֹדִי	*Charodita.*	Harodite, N. F.
חרד	חָרַדְתְּ	*Pavisti.*	Thou hast been afraid.
חָרָה		*Excanduit, iratus est, exarsit, combustus est, commovit se, accendit.*	He grew warm, was angry, was kindled, was burned, fretted himself, inflamed.

ROOTS.	DERIVATIVES.	VERSIO.	SIGNIFICATION.
חרה	חָרֹה	*Irascendo.*	In being angry.
	חַרְהֲיָה־־הֲיָה	*Charhaias.*	Harhaiah, N. M.
חרה	חָרוּ	*Combusti sunt.*	They have been burned.
חרל	חָרוּל	*Spina, carduus.*	A thorn, thistle.
	חֲרוּמַף	*Charumaph.*	Harumaph, N. M.
חרה	חָרוֹן חֲ״ חֲרִי	*Iracundia.*	Wrath.
—	חֲרוֹנִי	*Iracundia mea.*	My wrath.
—	חֲרוֹנֶךָ	*Iracundia tua.*	Thy wrath.
	חֹרוֹנַיִם חֹר״	*Choronaim.*	Horonaim, N. P.
	חֲרוּפִי	*Charuphita.*	Haruphite, N. F.
	חָרוּץ	*Charuts.*	Haruz, N. M.
חרץ	חָרוּץ	*Statutus; sedulus; mutilus; tribula; [aurum.*	Decreed; diligent; maimed; a threshing flail; gold.
—	חֲרוּצִים	*Statuti.*	Determined.
—	חֲרוּצִים־־רֻצִ״	*Seduli; statuti.*	Diligent; determined.
חרש	חֲרוּשָׁה	*Insculpta.*	Engraven.
חרת	חָרוּת	*Exarata.*	Engraven.
חרז			
	חַרְחוּר	*Charchur.*	Harhur, N. M.
	חַרְחַס	*Charchas.*	Harhas, N. M.
חרט			
—	חֲרִטִים	*Sacculi.*	Bags.
חרטם			
—	חַרְטֹם	*Divinus.*	A diviner, magician.
—	חַרְטֻמֵּי־מַיָּא־מִין	*Divini.*	Diviners, magicians.
חור	חֹרֵי	*Foramina; magnates*	Holes; the nobles.
	חֹרִי	*Chori.*	Hori, N. M.
חור	חֹרִי	*Candidus* panis.	White *bread.*
—	חֹרֶיהָ	*Magnates ejus.*	Her nobles.
—	חֹרֵיהֶם	*Stercus eorum.*	Their dung.
—	חֹרָיו	*Foramina ejus.*	His holes.
—	חֲרֵיוֹנִים	*Stercus columbarum*	Doves' dung.
	חֹרִים	*Chorim.*	Horims, N. N.
	חָרִים־־רִם	*Charim.*	Harim, N. M.
	חָרִיף־־רִף	*Chariph.*	Hariph, N. M.
חרץ	חֲרִיצֵי	*Casei.*	Cheeses.
חרש	חָרִישׁ	*Aratio.*	Earing, ploughing.

ROOTS.	DERIVATIVES.	VERSIO.	SIGNIFICATION.
חרשׁ	חֲרִישׁוֹ	*Aratio ejus.*	His ploughing.
—	חֲרִישִׁית	*Silens, tenuis, placida, surda, exsurdans, vehemens.*	Silent, gentle, placid, deaf, deafening, vehement.
חָרַךְ		*Adussit, torruit, adustus est.*	He burned, roasted, was burned.
חרל			
—	חֲרֻלִּים	*Urticæ.*	Nettles.
חָרַם		*Vovit, devovit, internecioni devovit anathematizavit, occidit, disperdidit.*	He consecrated, devoted, doomed to destruction, pronounced accursed, slew, destroyed.
—	חֵרֶם	*Anathema, res devota; rete.*	A curse, devoted thing, net.
—	חָרֻם	*Scissum habens nasum vel aurem, simus.*	One who has the bridge of his nose or his lip cut, flat-nosed.
	חֹרֵם	*Chorem.*	Horem, N. P.
	חָרְמָה	*Chormas.*	Horma, N. P.
חרם	חֶרְמוֹ	*Rete ejus.*	His net.
	חֶרְמוֹן	*Chermon.*	Hermon, N. P.
	חֶרְמוֹנִים	*Chermonim.*	Hermonites, N. F. or P.
חרם	חֶרְמִי	*Anathema meum, quem devovi.*	My curse, *he* whom I have devoted.
—	חֲרָמִים	*Retia, plagæ.*	Nets, toils.
חרמשׁ			
—	חֶרְמֵשׁ	*Falx.*	A sickle.
	חָרָן	*Charan.*	Haran, N. M. P.
	חֹרֹנִי	*Choronita.*	Horonite, N. N. or F.
חרה	חֲרֹנְךָ	*Iracundia tua.*	Thy wrath.
	חַרְנֶפֶר	*Charnepher.*	Harnepher, N. M.
	חֶרֶס	*Cheres.*	Heres, N. P.
חרס			
חָרַף		*Exprobravit, conviciatus est, contempsit, hyemavit.*	He upbraided, reproached, contemned, defied, despised, wintered.
	חָרֵף	*Chareph.* [*tempsit.*	Hareph, N. M. [defied.

ROOTS.	DERIVATIVES.	VERSIO.	SIGNIFICATION.
חרף	חֶרְפָּה	*Probrum.*	Reproach, disgrace.
—	חֵרְפוּ	*Probris affecerunt.*	They have reproached.
—	חֵרְפוּךָ	*Probris affecerunt te*	They have reproached thee.
—	חֵרְפוּנִי	*Exprobrarunt me.*	They have reproached me.
—	חָרְפִּי	*Juventus mea.*	My youth.
—	חֹרְפִי	*Exprobrans me.*	He that reproacheth me.
—	חֵרַפְתָּ	*Probris affecisti.*	Thou hast reproached.
—	חֶרְפַּת	*Opprobrium.*	A, the reproach.
—	חֶרְפָּתוֹ	*Opprobrium ejus.*	His reproach.
—	חֵרַפְתִּי	*Probro affeci, contempsi.*	I have reproached, contemned, defied.
	חֶרְפָּתִי	*Opprobrium meum.*	My reproach, shame.
—	חֶרְפָּתֵךְ־תְךָ	*Opprobrium tuum.*	Thy reproach, shame.
—	חֶרְפָּתָם	*Opprobrium eorum.*	Their reproach.
—	חֵרַפְתֶּם	*Exprobrastis.*	Ye have upbraided.
—	חֶרְפָּתֵנוּ	*Opprobrium nostrum*	Our reproach.
חָרַץ		*Movit, movit se, excidit, statuit, decrevit.*	He moved, moved himself, cut off, decided, determined
—	חַרְצֻבּוֹת	*Vincula.*	Bands, chains.
—	חַרְצָהּ	*Lumbi ejus.*	His loins.
—	חָרַצְתָּ	*Statuisti.*	Thou hast decided.
חָרַק		*Frenduit.*	He gnashed.
—	חָרֹק	*Frendere.*	To gnash.
חָרַר		*Exarsit, combustus est, exaruit, accendit.*	He burned, was burned, dried up, kindled.
—	חֲרֵרִים	*Loca adusta.*	Parched places.
חָרַשׁ		*Aravit, molitus est, sculpsit, siluit, obsurduit, tacite paravit.*	He ploughed, wrought, carved, engraved, was silent, became deaf, silently prepared
—	חֶרֶשׂ חָרָשׁ	*Testa.*	An earthen vessel, potsherd.
—	חָרָשׁ	*Faber, artifex.*	A workman, artificer.
—	חֵרֵשׁ	*Surdus.*	Deaf.
—	חֶרֶשׁ	*Tacite, clam.*	Silently, secretly
—	חֹרֵשׁ	*Arans; faber.*	Ploughing; an artificer.
	חַרְשָׁא	*Charsa.*	Harsa, N. P.
—	חֹרְשָׁה	*In sylvam.*	Into the wood.
—	חָרְשׁוּ	*Araverunt.*	They have ploughed.

ROOTS.	DERIVATIVES.	VERSIO.	SIGNIFICATION.
חרש	חֹרְשׁוֹת	*Arantes.*	They that plough.
—	חָרָשֵׁי חָרָשִׁים חָרָ״	*Fabri, artifices.*	The workmen, artificers.
—	חַרְשֵׂי	*Testæ.*	Potsherds.
—	חֹרְשֵׁי	*Molientes.*	They that devise.
—	חֲרָשֶׂיהָ	*Testæ ejus.*	Her potsherds.
—	חֵרְשִׁים	*Surdi.*	Deaf.
—	חֹרְשִׁים	*Arantes.*	They that plough.
	חֲרֹשֶׁת	*Charoset.*	Harosheth.
חרש	חֲרַשְׁתֶּם	*Aravistis.*	Ye have ploughed.
	חָרֶת	*Charet.*	Hareth, N. P.
חָרַת		*Exaravit, exsculpsit*	He engraved, carved.
	חש		
חוש	חָשׁ	*Festinavit, acceleravit; festinans.*	He hastened, made haste; making haste.
חָשַׁב		*Cogitavit, putavit, imputavit, reputavit, excogitavit, computavit, habitus est.*	He thought, considered, imputed, reputed, devised, computed, was accounted.
—	חֵשֶׁב	*Politura.*	The skilful workmanship.
—	חֹשֵׁב	*Cogitans, excogitans*	He that thinketh, deviseth.
	חַשְׁבַּדָּנָה	*Chasbadanas.*	Hashbadana, N. M.
	חֲשֻׁבָה	*Chasubas.*	Hashuba, N. M.
חשב	חֲשָׁבָהּ	*Cogitavit eam.*	He thought it.
—	חָשְׁבָה	*Cogitavit.*	She thought.
—	חָשְׁבוּ חָשָׁבוּ	*Excogitarunt.*	They thought, devised, purposed.
	חֶשְׁבּוֹן	*Chesbon.*	Heshbon, N. P.
חשב	חֶשְׁבּוֹן	*Supputatio.*	The account, computation.
—	חֹשְׁבֵי חֹשְׁבִים	*Excogitantes.*	They that think, devise.
	חֲשַׁבְיָה־הוּ	*Chasabias.*	Hashabiah, N. M.
	חֲשַׁבְנָה	*Chasabnas.*	Hashabnah, N. M.
חשב	חֲשַׁבְנֻהוּ	*Reputavimus eum.*	We reputed, esteemed him.
—	חִשְּׁבֹנוֹת	*Excogitationes, machinæ*	Devices, inventions, engines.
	חֲשַׁבְנְיָה	*Chasabnias.*	Hashabniah, N. M.
חשב	חָשַׁבְתָּ־־תָּה	*Cogitasti.*	Thou hast thought.
—	חָשַׁבְתִּי חִשַּׁ׳	*Cogitavi, reputavi.*	I thought, considered.
—	חֲשַׁבְתֶּם	*Cogitastis.*	Ye have thought.

ROOTS	DERIVATIVES.	VERSIO.	SIGNIFICATION.
חָשָׁה		*Siluit, quievit, abstinuit, silentium*	He was silent, still, forbore, made silence.
	חָשׁוּב	*Chasub.* [*imposuit.*	Hashub, N. M.
חשך	חֲשׂוֹךְ	*Cohibe.*	Withhold thou, keep back.
	חֲשׂוּפָא	*Chasupha.*	Hasupha, N. M.
חשף	חֲשׂוּפָה	*Nudata.*	Made naked.
חָשַׁח		*Sategit, opus habuit.*	He was concerned, had need.
—	חַשְׁחוּת	*Necessaria.*	Necessary.
—	חַשְׁחִין	*Opus habentes.*	They that have need of.
—	חַשְׁחָן	*Necessariæ.*	Necessary.
חשב	חֲשִׁיבִין	*Reputati.*	Reputed, considered.
	חֻשִׁים חֻשִׁם	*Chusim.*	Hushim, N. M.
חוש	חָשִׁים	*Festinantes*[*retinuit*	Making haste[back, retained.
חָשַׂךְ		*Cohibuit, subduxit,*	He withheld, withdrew, kept
—	חָשַׂךְ	*Cohibuit.*	He withheld, hindered.
חָשַׁךְ		*Obscurus fuit, obscuratus est, caligavit.*	He was dark, was darkened, he made dark.
—	חֲשׂךְ	*Cohibe.* [*gavit.*	Withhold thou.
—	חֹשֶׁךְ	*Caligo, obscuritas.*	Darkness, obscurity.
—	חֲשֵׁכָה	*Tenebræ.*	Darkness.
—	חָשְׂכוּ	*Prohibuerunt.*	They have hindered.
—	חָשְׂכוּ	*Cohibuerunt.*	They have restrained.
—	חָשְׁכִּי	*Caligo mea.*	My darkness.
—	חֲשֵׁכִים	*Tenebræ.*	Darkness.
—	חֲשֻׁכִּים	*Obscuri.*	Obscure, mean.
—	חָשַׂכְתָּ	*Cohibuisti.*	Thou hast withheld.
—	חֶשְׁכַּת	*Caligo.*	The darkness.
—	חָשַׂכְתִּי	*Retinui.*	I have retained, reserved.
חֲשַׁל		*Debilitavit, contrivit*	He weakened, wore out.
	חָשֻׁם	*Chasum.*	Hashum, N. M.
	חֻשָׁם	*Chusam.*	Husham, N. M.
	חֶשְׁמוֹן	*Chesmon.*	Heshmon, N. P.
חשמל			
—	חַשְׁמַל	***Electrum,*** **metallum ex auro et argento vel ære conflatum.**	**Electrum,** ***a metal composed of gold and silver or brass.***

ROOTS.	DERIVATIVES.	VERSIO.	SIGNIFICATION.
חשמן			
	חַשְׁמֹנָה	*Chasmonas.*	Hashmonah, N. P.
חשמן	חַשְׁמַנִּים	*Magnates, principes*	Nobles, princes.
חשן			
—	חֹשֶׁן	*Pectorale.*	A, the breast-plate. [out.
חָשַׂף		*Nudavit, exhausit.*	He made naked or bare, drew
—	חָשֹׂף	*Nudando.*	In making bare.
	חֲשׂוּפָא	*Chasupha.*	Hasupha, N. M.
חשף	חֲשָׂפָהּ	*Nudavit eam.*	He made it bare.
—	חֲשִׂפֵי	*Greges.*	Flocks.
—	חֶשְׂפִּי	*Nuda.*	Make thou bare.
—	חָשַׂפְתִּי	*Nudavi.*	I have made bare.
חָשַׁק		*Conjunxit, connexuit, devinxit se, adhæsit, dilexit, desi-*	He joined together, connected, attached himself, clave to, loved, desired.
—	חֵשֶׁק	*Desiderium [deravit*	Desire.
—	חָשְׁקָה	*Dilexit, desideravit, devinxit se.*	She hath loved, desired, longed for, attached herself.
—	חִשְׁקִי	*Desiderium meum.*	My desire.
—	חָשַׁקְתָּ	*Amasti.*	Thou hast loved.
חשר			
—	חַשְׁרַת	*Colligatio.*	A binding together.
חשש			
—	חֲשַׁשׁ	*Gluma.*	Chaff.
	חֻשָׁתִי	*Chusatita.*	Hushathite, N. F. or P.
חוש	חַשְׁתִּי	*Festinavi.*	I have made haste.
	חת		
חתת	חַת	*Terror.*	Terror, fear.
—	חַת	*Fractus est.*	He hath been broken.
	חֵת	*Chet.*	Heth, N. M.
חָתָה		*Cepit.*	He took.
חתת	חַתָּה	*Contrita est.*	She hath been crushed.
חתה	חֹתֶה	*Capiens.*	Taking.
חתת	חַתּוּ	*Contriti, territi sunt*	They were crushed, terrified.
חתל	חִתּוּל	*Fascia.*	A swathe, roller.
חתם	חָתוּם	*Obsignatus.*	Sealed.

ROOTS.	DERIVATIVES.	VERSIO.	SIGNIFICATION.
חתם	חֲתוֹם	*Obsigna.*	Seal thou.
	חִתִּי	*Chitæi.*	Hittites, N. N.
חתת	חַתִּים	*Fracti, territi.*	Broken, terrified.
	חִתִּים	*Chitim, Chitæi.*	Chittim, Hittites, N. N. or P.
חתת	חִתִּית	*Terror.*	Terror.
	חִתִּית	*Chitæa.*	A Hittite *woman.*
	חִתִּיּוֹת	*Chitææ.*	Hittite *women.*
חתת	חִתִּיתוֹ	*Terror meus.*	My terror.
—	חִתִּיתָם	*Terror eorum.*	Their terror.
חָתַךְ		*Decidit, constituit.*	He decided, determined.
חָתַל		*Fasciavit, fasciis in-*	He swaddled, wrapped in a
	חֶתְלֹן	*Chetlon.* [*volvit.*	Hethlon, N. P. [swathe.
חתל	חֻתָּלְתְּ	*Fascia involuta es.*	Thou hast been swaddled.
—	חֲתֻלָּתוֹ	*Fascia ejus.*	His swathe, swaddling band.
חָתַם		*Obsignavit, occlusit, abscondit.*	He signed, sealed, shut up, hid
—	חָתֻם	*Absconditus.*	Hidden.
—	חִתְּמוּ	*Obsignarunt.*	They signed, sealed.
—	חֹתָמְךָ	*Sigillum tuum.* [*it.*	Thy seal.
חתן		*Affinitatem contrax-*	He contracted affinity.
—	חָתָן חֲתַן	*Sponsus, gener.*	The bridegroom, son in law.
—	חֹתֵן	*Socer.*	A father in law.
—	חֲתָנוֹ	*Gener ejus.*	His son in law.
—	חֹתְנוֹ	*Socer ejus.*	His father in law.
—	חֲתָנָיו	*Generi ejus.*	His sons in law.
—	חֹתֶנְךָ	*Socer tuus.*	Thy father in law.
—	חֲתֻנָּתוֹ	*Desponsatio tua.*	Thy espousal.
—	חֹתַנְתּוֹ	*Socrus ejus.*	His mother in law.
חָתַף		*Rapuit, diripuit.*	He took away, spoiled.
חָתַר		*Fodit, perfodit, re-*	He digged, digged through,
—	חֲתָר	*Fode.* [*migavit.*	Dig thou. [rowed.
—	חָתַרְתִּי	*Fodi.*	I digged.
	חֲתַת	*Chatat.*	Hathath, N. M.
חָתַת		*Fractus, contritus, territus, consternatus est; fregit, terruit.*	He was broken, crushed, terrified, dismayed; he broke, terrified.

ROOTS.	DERIVATIVES.	VERSIO.	SIGNIFICATION.
חתת	חִתַּת חֲתַת	*Terror.*	The terror.
—	חֻתְּתָה	*Fracta, contrita est.*	She was broken, crushed.

טא

ROOTS.	DERIVATIVES.	VERSIO.	SIGNIFICATION.
טָאֵב		*Bonus, lætus fuit.*	He was good, joyful, glad.
—	טְאֵב	*Lætus fuit.*	He was glad.
טָאַט		*Scopavit, everrit.*	He swept, brushed, made clean

טב

ROOTS.	DERIVATIVES.	VERSIO.	SIGNIFICATION.
טוב	טָב	*Bonus, præstans.*	Good, excellent.
	טָבְאֵל	*Tabeal.*	Tabeal, N. M.
	טָבְאֵל	*Tabeel.* [*erunt.*	Tabeel, N. M. [pleasant.
טוב	טֹבוּ	*Pulchri, jucundi fu-*	They were goodly, beautiful,
טבח	טָבוּחַ	*Mactatus.*	Slain.
טבל	טְבוּלִים	*Intincti.*	Dyed.
טבר	טַבּוּר	*Umbilicus.* [*cundæ.*	The navel, middle.
טוב	טֹבוֹת	*Bonæ, pulchræ, ju-*	Good, goodly, pleasant.
	טֶבַח	*Tebach.* [*immolavit.*	Tebah, N. M.
טָבַח		*Jugulavit, mactavit,*	He butchered, slew, sacrificed.
—	טֶבַח	*Clades, mactatio.*	A slaughter.
—	טְבֹחַ	*Jugulare.*	To slaughter.
—	טָבְחָה	*Jugulavit.*	She hath killed.
—	טִבְחָה	*Laniena.* [*ejus.*	The slaughter.
—	טִבְחָהּ	*Laniena, animal*	Her slaughter, animal, beast.
—	טַבָּחַיָּא־־תִּים	*Stipatores.*	The guards.
	טִבְחַת	*Tibchat.*	Tibhath, N. P.
טבח	טָבַחְתָּ	*Jugulasti.*	Thou hast killed.
—	טָבַחְתִּי	*Mactavi.*	I have killed.
—	טִבְחָתִי	*Laniena mea.*	My slaughter.
טוב	טֹבִים	*Boni, pulchri.*	Good, goodly.
טָבַל		*Immersit, intinxit.*	He plunged, dipped, dyed.
	טְבַלְיָהוּ	*Tebalias.*	Tebaliah, N. M.
טָבַע		*Demersus, submersus, infixus est.*	He sank, was overwhelmed, fixed, settled.
—	טֻבְּעוּ	*Demersi sunt.*	They sank.

ROOTS.	DERIVATIVES.	VERSIO.	SIGNIFICATION.
טבע	טֻבְּעוּ	*Submersi sunt.*	They were overwhelmed.
	טַבָּעוֹת	*Tabaot.*	Tabbaoth, N. M.
טבע	טַבָּעוֹת־עֹת טַבְּ׳	*Annuli.*	Rings.
—	טַבַּעַת	*Annulus.*	A ring.
—	טַבַּעְתּוֹ	*Annulus ejus.*	His ring.
—	טָבַעְתִּי	*Demersus sum.*	I sank.
—	טַבְּעֹתֵיהֶם־תָם	*Annuli eorum.*	Their rings.
טרב			
	טַבְרִמֹּן	*Tabrimon.*	Tabrimon, N. M.
	טַבַּת	*Tabat.*	Tabbath, N. M.
טוב	טֹבַת	*Bona, pulchra.*	Good, fair.
	טֵבֵת	*Tebet.*	Tebeth, N. Mth.
טוב	טֹבֹת	*Pulchræ.*	Fair, beautiful.
	טה		
טהר	טָהוֹר טְהוֹר	*Purus, mundus.*	Pure, clean.
—	טְהוֹרָה טְהֹרָה	*Pura, munda.*	Pure, clean.
—	טְהוֹרִים־הֹרוֹת	*Puri, mundi.*	Pure, clean.
טָהֵר		*Mundus fuit, purgatus est; mundavit, purificavit, mundum declaravit.*	He was pure, was cleansed; he cleansed, purified, pronounced clean.
—	טַהֵר	*Mundare.*	To cleanse.
—	טֹהַר	*Mundities.*	Purity, pureness.
—	טָהֲרָה	*Purgata est.*	She was cleansed.
—	טָהֳרָה	*Purgatio.*	The purifying.
—	טָהֳרָהּ	*Purificatio ejus.*	Her purification.
—	טַהֲרִי	*Mundare me.*	That I cleanse.
—	טִהַרְנוּ	*Mundavimus.*	We have cleansed.
—	טַהֲרֵנִי	*Munda me.*	Cleanse thou me.
—	טָהַרְתְּ	*Mundata es.*	Thou wast cleansed.
—	טָהֳרַת	*Purificatio.*	The purification.
—	טָהֳרָתוֹ	*Purificatio ejus.*	His purification.
—	טָהַרְתִּי	*Mundus fui.*	I have been pure.
—	טִהַרְתִּיךְ	*Purgavi te.*	I have purged thee.

ROOTS.	DERIVATIVES.	VERSIO.	SIGNIFICATION.
	טו		
	טוב	*Tob.*	Tob, N. P.
טוב		*Bonus, pulcher, jucundus fuit; benefecit.*	He was good, goodly, beautiful, pleasant; he did good.
	טוב אֲדוֹנִיָּה	*Tob-adonias.*	Tob-adonijah, N. M.
טוב	טוב עין	*Bonus oculo, benignus, liberalis*[*num*	Good in the eye, kind, liberal, bountiful.
—	טוב	*Bonus, pulcher; bonum*	Good, fair; a good, goodness.
—	טוב טוֹבָה	*Bonum, pulchritudo; bonus, pulcher; melior, pulchrior; bene, melius.*	Goodness, beauty; good, goodly, fair; better, fairer; well, better.
—	טוֹבָהּ	*Bonitas ejus.*	Her goodness.
—	טוּבוֹ	*Bonitas ejus.*	His goodness.
—	טובות	*Bonæ, pulchræ.*	Good, goodly, fair.
—	טוּבִי	*Bonitas mea.*	My goodness.
	טוֹבִיָּה--הוּ	*Tobias.*	Tobiah, N. M.
טוב	טובים	*Boni, meliores.*	Good, better.
—	טוּבְךָ	*Bonitas tua.*	Thy goodness.
—	טוֹבָם	*Optimus eorum.*	The best of them.
—	טוּבָם	*Bonitas eorum.*	Their goodness.
—	טוֹבַת	*Bona, pulchra.*	Good, fair.
—	טוֹבָתִי	*Bonitas mea.*	My goodness.
—	טוֹבֹתָיו	*Bona ejus.*	His good *deeds*.
—	טוֹבָתֶךָ	*Bonitas tua.*	Thy goodness.
טָוָה		*Nevit.*	He spun.
—	טָווּ	*Neverunt.*	They spun.
טוח		*Linivit, oblevit, obduxit.*	He daubed, plaistered, overlaid.
טחן	טוֹחֵן	*Molens.*	Grinding.
טול		*Jecit, ejecit, projecit, dejecit.*	He cast, cast out, cast forth, cast down.
טור			
—	טוּר	*Ordo.*	A row.
טרד	טוֹרֵד טֹרֵד	*Continuans.*	Continuing, continual.
טור	טוּרֵי טוּרִים	*Ordines.*	The rows.
טוש		*Volavit.*	He flew.

ROOTS.	DERIVATIVES.	VERSIO.	SIGNIFICATION.
טות			
	טְוָת	*Jejunus.*	Fasting.
	טח		
טוח	טָח	*Oblevit.*	He plaistered.
טָחָה		*Jecit, propulit.*	He cast, shot, thrust forward.
—	טָחוּ	*Liniverunt.*	They daubed.
טחן	טְחוֹן	*Molendo.*	In grinding.
—	טְחוֹן	*Molere.*	To grind.
—	טָחֵי	*Linentes.*	They that daub.
—	טָחִים	*Oblinentes.*	They that plaister.
טָחַן		*Moluit, contudit, comminuit.*	He ground, beat to pieces, reduced to powder.
טחר			
—	טְחֹרֵי	*Mariscæ.*	Emerods.
—	טְחֹרֵיהֶם	*Mariscæ eorum.*	Their emerods.
—	טְחְתֶּם	*Linistis.*	Ye have daubed.
	טט		
טטף			
	טי		
טיט			
—	טִיט	*Lutum.*	Clay.
טין			
—	טִינָא	*Lutum.*	Clay.
טיר			
טור	טִירוֹתֵיהֶם	*Arces, palatia eorum*	Their castles, palaces.
—	טִירַת	*Arx, palatium.*	The castle, palace.
—	טִירָתָם־רֹתָם	*Palatium, arces.*	Their palace, castles.
	טל		
טלל	טַל טָל	*Ros.*	Dew.
טָלָא		*Maculosus fuit.*	He was spotted, speckled.
טלא	טְלֻאוֹת	*Maculosæ.*	Spotted, speckled.
—	טְלָאִים	*Agni.*	Lambs.
טלה			

ROOTS.	DERIVATIVES.	VERSIO.	SIGNIFICATION.
טלה	טְלֵה	*Agnus.*	A lamb. [pulsion.
טלל	טַלְטֵלָה	*Dejectio, ejectio.*	Casting down, casting out, ex-
—	טַלְּךָ	*Ros tuus.*	Thy dew.
טָלַל		*Texit, obumbravit.*	He covered, overshadowed.
	טֶלֶם	*Telem.*	Telem, N. M. P.
טלל	טַלָּם	*Ros eorum.*	Their dew.
	טַלְמוֹן־מֹן	*Talmon.*	Talmon, N. M.
	טמ		
טָמֵא		*Immundus fuit, pollutus est; polluit, pollutum declara-*	He was unclean, polluted; he defiled, pronounced unclean
—	טַמֵּא	*Polluere.* [*vit.*	To defile.
—	טָמֵא	*Immundus, pollutus.*	Unclean, defiled.
—	טִמֵּא	*Polluit.*	He hath defiled.
—	טְמֵאָה טְמֵ׳	*Immunda, polluta.*	Unclean, polluted.
—	טֻמְאָה	*Immundities, res im-*	Uncleanness, an unclean thing
—	טַמְּאוּ	*Polluite.* [*munda.*	Defile ye.
—	טִמְּאוּ	*Polluerunt.*	They have defiled.
—	טִמְּאוּהָ	*Polluerunt eam.*	They have polluted her.
—	טֻמְאוֹתֵיכֶם	*Impuritates vestræ.*	Your uncleannesses.
—	טְמֵאִים	*Immundi, polluti.*	Unclean, defiled.
—	טָמֵאת	*Polluta es.*	Thou hast been defiled.
—	טְמֵאַת	*Polluta.*	Polluted.
—	טִמֵּאת	*Polluisti.*	Thou hast defiled.
—	טֻמְאָתָהּ	*Immundities ejus.*	Her uncleanness.
—	טֻמְאָתוֹ	*Immundities ejus.*	His uncleanness.
—	טֻמְאָתֵךְ	*Immundities tua.*	Thy uncleanness.
—	טִמֵּאתֶם	*Polluistis.*	Ye have defiled.
—	טֻמְאֹתָם	*Immundities eorum.*	Their uncleanness.
טמן	טָמוּן טְמוּנָה	*Absconditus.*	Hidden.
—	טְמוּנֵי טְמֻנִים	*Absconditi.*	Hidden.
טָמַן		*Abscondit, recondit.*	He hid, concealed, covered up
—	טָמְנוּ־מָ׳	*Absconderunt.*	They have hidden.
טמן	טָמְנֵם	*Absconde eos.*	Hide thou them.
—	טָמַנְתִּי	*Abscondi.*	I have hidden.
—	טְמַנְתִּיו	*Abscondi eum.*	I have hidden him or it.

ROOTS	DERIVATIVES.	VERSIO.	SIGNIFICATION.
	טנ		
טנא			
—	טַנְאֲךָ	*Canistrum tuum.*	Thy basket.
טָנַף		*Inquinavit.*	He defiled.
	טע		
טָעָה		*Erravit, errare fe-*	He erred, caused to err.
טָעַם		*Gustavit, cibavit. [cit*	He tasted, fed.
—	טַעַם	*Gustus, judicium, intelligentia, man-*	Taste, judgment, discretion, understanding, command.
—	טְעֹם	*Gustando. [datum.*	In tasting.
—	טְעֵם	*Mandatum, decretum, ratio.*	A command, decree, reason, regard.
—	טַעֲמָא—עְ׳	*Ratio, causa.*	The account, matter, cause.
—	טָעֲמָה	*Gustavit.*	She tasted, perceived.
—	טַעֲמוּ	*Gustate.*	Taste ye.
—	טַעְמוֹ	*Gustus ejus.*	His taste.
—	טַעְמֵךְ	*Gustus tuus, judi-*	Thy taste, judgment.
—	טָעַמְתִּי	*Gustavi. [cium tuum*	I have tasted.
טָעַן		*Pupugit, stimulavit, transfixit, confos-*	He pricked, goaded, stabbed, pierced, was thrust through
—	טַעֲנוּ	*Stimulate. [sus est.*	Goad, urge ye.
	טפ		
טפף	טַף	*Parvulus.*	A little child.
טָפַח		*Palmis gestavit, expandit, metitus est*	He carried, spread out, measured with the hands.
—	טֶפַח טְ׳	*Palmus.*	A span, hand-breadth.
—	טִפְּחָה	*Palmis metita est.*	She hath spanned.
—	טְפָחוֹת	*Palmi.*	Spans.
—	טְפָחִים	*Palmi.*	Spans, of a span long.
—	טִפַּחְתִּי	*Palmis gestavi.*	I have carried in my hands.
טפף	טַפְּכֶם	*Parvuli vestri.*	Your little ones.
טָפַל		*Consuit.*	He sewed together.
—	טָפְלוּ	*Consuerunt.*	They have sewed together.
—	טֹפְלֵי	*Consarcinatores.*	Patchers.

ROOTS.	DERIVATIVES.	VERSIO.	SIGNIFICATION.
טפף	טַפָּם	*Parvuli eorum.*	Their little ones.
—	טַפֵּנוּ	*Parvuli nostri.*	Our little ones.
טפסר			
—	טִפְסָר	*Dux, princeps.*	A captain, prince.
טָפַף		*More parvulorum incessit.*	He walked in a childish manner.
טפר			
טָפַשׁ		*Obesatus est.*	He was made fat.
	טָפַת	*Taphat.*	Taphath, N. W.
	טר		
טָרַד		*Continuavit, propulit, ejecit.*	He continued, thrust forth, cast out.
—	טֹרְדִין	*Ejicientes.*	They that cast out.
טרח			
טָרַח		*Laboravit, fatigavit.*	He laboured, wearied.
—	טָרְחֲכֶם	*Opera, fatigatio vestra.*	Your labour, weariness.
טרד	טְרִיד	*Ejectus est.*	He was cast out.
טרה	טְרִיָּה	*Recens.*	Fresh, new.
טור	טִרִים	*Ordines.*	Rows.
טרם			
—	טֶרֶם	*Antequam, nondum.*	Before, not yet.
טָרַף		*Rapuit, laceravit, discerpsit, folium.*	He seized, rent, tore in pieces, plucked off; a leaf.
—	טָרָף	*Laceravit; discerptus; folium.*	He tore; plucked off; a leaf
—	טֶרֶף	*Præda.*	The prey.
—	טְרֹף	*Lacerando.*	In rending.
—	טָרֶף	*Præda.*	Prey.
—	טֹרָף־־רַ״	*Discerptus est.*	He hath been torn in pieces.
—	טֹרֵף	*Discerpens.*	Tearing in pieces.
—	טְרֵפָה	*Discerpta; præda.*	Torn; prey.
—	טַרְפּוֹ	*Præda ejus.*	His prey.
—	טַרְפֵּי	*Folia.*	Leaves.
—	טֹרְפֵי	*Rapientes.*	Ravening.
—	טַרְפֵּךְ	*Præda tua.*	Thy prey.
	טַרְפְּלָיֵא	*Tarpelæi.*	Tarpelites, N. N.

ROOTS.	DERIVATIVES.	VERSIO.	SIGNIFICATION.
	יא		
יָאַב		*Desideravit, concu-*	He desired, longed for.
אבד	יְאַבֵּד־־בֵּד	*Perdet.* [*pivit.*	He shall destroy.
—	יֹאבַד־־בֵד	*Peribit.*	He shall perish.
—	יֹאבְדוּ יֹאבֵדוּ	*Peribunt.*	They shall perish.
—	יֹאבֵדוּ־־בֵ״	*Peribunt.*	They shall perish. [*sent.*
אבה	יֹאבֶה	*Volet, acquiescet.*	He will be willing, will con-
—	יֹאבוּ	*Volent.*	They will be willing.
אבר	יַאֲבֶר	*Volabit.* [*pivi.*	He will fly.
יאב	יָאַבְתִּי	*Desideravi, concu-*	I have desired, longed.
אדם	יַאְדִּימוּ	*Rubebunt.*	They will be red. [becoming.
יָאָה		*Convenit, decuit.*	It was convenient, suitable,
אהב	יֶאֱהַב יֶאֱהָב	*Diliget.*	He will love.
—	יֶאֱהָבֵנִי	*Diliget me.*	He will love me.
אהל	יַאְהִיל	*Figet tentorium.*	He shall pitch *his* tent.
יאר	יְאֹור	*Rivus, flumen.*	A brook, river.
—	יְאֹרֵי	*Rivi.*	Brooks.
אזן	יַאֲזִין	*Auscultabit.*	He shall hearken.
—	יַאֲזִינוּ	*Auscultabunt.*	They shall hearken.
	יַאֲזַנְיָה־־הוּ	*Jaazanias.*	Jaazaniah, N. M.
אזר	יַאַזְרֵנִי	*Accinget me.*	*He shall* gird me.
אחז	יֹאחֵז	*Capiet.*	He shall take.
—	יֹאחֲזוּךָ	*Apprehendent te.*	They shall take hold of thee.
—	יֹאחֵזוּן	*Prehendent.*	They shall seize.
—	יֹאחֲזוּנִי	*Prehendent me.*	They will seize me.
—	יֹאחֲזֵמוֹ	*Apprehendet eos.*	He shall take hold of them.
אחר	יְאַחֵר	*Tardabit.*	He will delay.
אטם	יַאְטֵם	*Obturabit.*	He will stop.
	יָאִיר	*Jair.* [*ciet.*	Jair, N. M.
אור	יָאִיר	*Lucebit, lucere fa-*	He will shine, cause to shine.
—	יָאִירוּ	*Lucebunt.*	They shall shine.
	יָאִירִי	*Jairitæ.*	Jairites, N. F.
אכל	יֵאָכֵל	*Comedetur.*	He shall be eaten.
—	יֹאכַל יֹאכַל־־כֵל	*Comedet, consumet.*	He shall eat, consume.
—	יֹאכְלֻהוּ	*Comedent eum.*	They shall eat it.

ROOTS.	DERIVATIVES.	VERSIO.	SIGNIFICATION.
אכל	יְאֻכְּלוּ־־כְּלוּ	*Absumentur.*	They shall be consumed, devoured
—	יֹאכְלוּ־־כְלוּ	*Comedent.*	They shall eat, eat up
—	יֹאכְלוּהָ	*Comedent eam.*	They shall eat it.
—	יֹאכְלוּם	*Comedent eos.*	They shall eat them.
—	יֹאכְלוּן־־כֻ״	*Comedent.*	They shall eat.
—	יֹאכְלֵם	*Comedet eos.*	He shall eat them up.
—	יֹאכְלֵמוֹ	*Devorabit eum.*	He shall devour him.
—	יֹאכְלֶנָּה	*Comedet eam.*	He shall eat her or it.
—	יַאֲכִלֵנוּ	*Comedere faciet nos.*	He shall cause us to eat.
—	יֹאכְלֶנּוּ	*Comedet eum.*	He shall eat him or it.
יָאַל		*Voluit, acquievit, incepit, stulte egit, stultus factus est.*	He wished, willed, consented, began, acted foolishly, became a fool.
אלף	יַאַלֵּף	*Docebit.*	He shall teach.
אמן	יַאֲמִין־־מִן	*Credet, confidet.*	He will believe, trust.
—	יַאֲמִינוּ	*Credent.*	They will believe.
—	יֵאָמֵן־־מֶן	*Confirmabitur.*	He shall be established.
אמץ	יְאַמֵּץ	*Firmabit.*	He shall strengthen.
—	יֶאֱמָץ	*Robustior erit.*	He shall be stronger.
אמר	יֵאָמֵר־־מֶר־־מֵר	*Dicetur.*	He or it shall be said.
—	יֹאמַר יֹא״	*Dicet.*	He will speak, say.
—	יֹאמְרוּ־־מֻ״	*Dicent.*	They will speak.
אנה	יְאַנֶּה	*Occidet.*	It shall happen.
אנח	יֵאָנַח	*Mærebit.*	He will mourn.
אנף	יֶאֱנַף	*Irascetur.*	He will be angry.
אנק	יֶאֱנֹק	*Gemet.*	He will groan.
אסף	יֵאָסֵף	*Colligetur, retrahet se.*	He will be gathered, will withdraw himself.
—	יֶאֱסֹף	*Colliget.*	He will gather.
—	יֵאָסְפוּ־־סֻ״	*Congregabuntur.*	They shall be assembled.
—	יֵאָסֵפוּן	*Congregabunt se.*	They shall assemble themselves.
—	יַאַסְפְךָ	*Colliget te.*	He shall gather thee.
—	יַאַסְפֵנִי	*Colliget me.*	He will gather me.
אסר	יֵאָסֵר	*Vincietur.*	He shall be bound.
—	יֶאְסֹר	*Instruet.*	He shall set in array.
—	יַאַסְרוּנִי־־רֻנִי	*Ligabunt me.*	They will bind me.
אפה	יֹאפוּ	*Coquent.*	They shall bake.
אצר	יֵאָצֵר	*Recondetur.*	He shall be laid up.

ROOTS.	DERIVATIVES.	VERSIO.	SIGNIFICATION.
אור	יָאֵר	*Lucere faciet.*	He shall cause to shine.
יאר			
—	יְאֹר	*Fluvius.*	A river.
ארב	יֶאֱרֹב	*Insidiabitur.*	He will lie in wait.
—	יֶאֶרְבוּ	*Insidiabuntur.*	They will lie in wait.
ארג	יֶאֶרְגוּ	*Texent.*	They will weave.
יאר	יְאֹרֵי	*Flumina, rivi.*	Rivers, brooks.
—	יְאֹרִי	*Fluvius meus.*	My river.
—	יְאֹרֵיהֶם	*Fluvii eorum.*	Their rivers.
—	יְאֹרָיו	*Flumina ejus.*	His rivers.
ארך	יַאֲרִיךְ	*Prolongabit.*	He shall prolong.
יאר	יְאֹרֶיךָ	*Fluvii tui.*	Thy rivers.
ארך	יַאֲרִיכוּ־רִכוּ	*Prolongabunt.*	They shall prolong.
—	יַאֲרִיכֻן־רִכֻן	*Prolongabuntur.*	They shall be lengthened.
יאר	יְאֹרִים	*Flumina.*	Rivers.
—	יְאֹרְךָ	*Fluvius tuus.*	Thy river.
ארך	יַאַרְכוּ	*Prolongabuntur.*	They shall be prolonged.
יָאַשׁ		*Renunciavit, destitit, desperavit.*	He renounced, left off, despaired.
	יֹאָשׁ יוֹאָשׁ	*Joas.*	Joash, N. M.
	יֹאשִׁיָּה־הוּ	*Josias.*	Josiah, N. M.
אשם	יֶאְשַׁם	*Delinquet, reus erit.*	He will offend, be guilty.
—	יֶאְשְׁמוּ־שָׁמוּ	*Delinquent, desolabuntur.*	They will transgress, shall be desolate.
אשר	יְאֻשַּׁר	*Benedicetur*	He shall be blessed.
—	יְאַשְּׁרֻהוּ	*Eum beatum prædicabunt*	They shall call him blessed.
יָאַת		*Acquievit, consensit; convenit, decet.*	He acquiesced, consented; it is suitable, becometh.
—	יָאֲתָה	*Convenit, decet.*	It is suitable, becometh.
אתה	יֶאֱתֶה	*Venit.*	He shall come.
יאת	יֵאֹתוּ	*Acquiescent.*	They will agree, consent,
אתה	יֶאֱתָיוּ	*Venient.*	They shall come.
	יְאָתְרַי	*Jeaterai.*	Jeaterai, N. M.
	יב		
בוא	יָבֹא־בוֹא	*Veniet, vadet, ingredietur, occumbet.*	He shall come, go, enter, set, go down.
—	יָבָא	*Adducet.*	He shall bring.

ROOTS.	DERIVATIVES.	VERSIO.	SIGNIFICATION.
בוא	יָּבָא	*Et venit.*	And he came.
—	יְבִאֵהוּ־אֲהוּ	*Adducet eum.*	He shall bring him.
—	יְבִאוּ יָבֹאוּ	*Adducent eum.*	They shall bring him.
—	יְבֹאוּן	*Venient, trabunt, ingredientur. [ibunt*	They shall come, go, enter.
—	יְבֹאוּנִי	*Ingredientur.*	They shall enter.
—	יְבִאוּנִי	*Adducent me.*	They shall bring me.
—	יְבֹאוּנִי	*Evenient mihi.*	They shall come, happen to me
באש	יַבְאִישׁ	*Fœtere faciet.*	He will cause to stink.
בוא	יְבֹאֶנּוּ	*Eveniet ei.*	It shall happen to him.
יָבַב		*Clamavit, ululavit.*	He cried out, yelled.
בגד	יִבְגֹּד	*Perfide aget.*	He will deal treacherously.
—	יִבְגְּדוּ	*Perfide agent.*	They shall deal treacherously.
בדל	יַבְדִּיל	*Dividet.*	He shall divide, sever.
—	יַבְדִּילוּ	*Separabunt.*	They shall separate.
—	יַבְדִּילַנִי	*Separabit me.*	He shall separate me.
—	יִבָּדֵל	*Separabitur.*	He shall be separated.
בהל	יְבַהֲלֻהוּ	*Turbabunt eum.*	They shall trouble him.
—	יְבַהֲלוּךָ	*Turbabunt te.*	They shall trouble thee.
—	יִבָּהֵלוּן	*Turbabuntur.*	They shall be troubled.
—	יְבַהֲלוּנֵּהּ־לְנֵּהּ	*Turbabunt eum.*	They shall trouble him.
—	יְבַהֶלְךָ	*Turbabit te.*	He shall trouble thee.
—	יְבַהֲלֵמוֹ	*Turbabit eos.*	He shall trouble them.
—	יְבַהֲלֻנְנִי	*Turbabunt me.*	They will trouble me.
בוא	יָבוֹאוּ	*Venient.*	They will come.
—	יְבוֹאֵנוּ	*Eveniet nobis.*	It will happen to us.
—	יְבוֹאֶנּוּ	*Eveniet ei.*	It will befal him.
בוז	יָבוּז	*Spernet.*	He will despise.
—	יָבוּזוּ־־בָזוּ	*Spernent.*	They will despise.
נבל	יִבּוֹל	*Decidet, emarcescet.*	He shall fall off, fade, wither.
יבל	יְבוּל	*Proventus.*	Increase, produce.
—	יְבוּלָהּ	*Proventus ejus.*	Her increase.
—	יְבוּלָם	*Proventus eorum.*	Their increase.
בון	יְבוֹנְנֵהוּ	*Docebit eum.*	He shall teach him.
בוס	יָבוּס	*Conculcabit.*	He shall tread down.
	יְבוּס	*Jebus.*	Jebus, N. P.
	יְבוּסִי	*Jebusi.*	Jebusite, Jebusites, N. M. N.
יבש	יָבוֹשׁ	*Arescendo.*	In drying up, withering.

ROOTS.	DERIVATIVES.	VERSIO.	SIGNIFICATION.
בוש	יֵבוֹשׁ	*Erubescet.*	He shall be ashamed.
—	יֵבוֹשׁוּ	*Pudore afficientur.*	They shall be put to shame.
בזז	יָבֹזּוּ	*Diripientur.*	They shall rob.
—	יְבָזּוּם	*Diripient eos.*	They will spoil them.
בזר	יְבַזּוֹר	*Disperget.*	He shall scatter.
בחן	יִבָּחֵן	*Probabitur.*	He shall be tried.
—	יִבְחָן	*Probabit, explorabit.*	He shall try, prove.
—	יִבְחָנוּ	*Probabunt.*	They shall try.
	יִבְחָר	*Ibchar.*	Ibhar, N. M.
בחר	יִבְחַר־חָר	*Eliget.*	He shall choose.
—	יְבֻחַר	*Jungetur.*	He shall be joined.
בטא	יְבַטֵּא	*Effutiet.*	He will utter rashly.
בטח	יַבְטַח	*Confidere faciet.*	He will cause to trust.
—	יִבְטַח־טְ	*Confidet.*	He will trust.
בוא	יָבִיא	*Adducet.*	He will bring.
—	יְבִיאֶהָ־אֶנָּה	*Adducet eam.*	He will bring her.
—	יָבִיאוּ	*Adducent.*	They shall or will bring.
—	יְבִיאוּם	*Adducent eos.*	They shall bring them.
—	יְבִיאוּן	*Adducent.*	They will bring.
—	יְבִיאוּנִי	*Adducent me.*	They shall bring me.
—	יְבִיאֲךָ	*Adducet te.*	He shall bring thee.
—	יְבִיאֵם	*Adducet eos.*	He shall bring them.
—	יְבִיאֶנּוּ	*Adducet eum.*	He shall bring him.
נבט	יַבִּיט	*Intuebitur, respiciet*	He shall look, see, regard.
—	יַבִּיטוּ	*Videbunt, respicient*	They shall see, regard.
	יָבִין	*Jabin.* [*vertet.*	Jabin, N. M. [consider.
בון	יָבִין	*Intelliget, animad-*	He shall understand, perceive,
—	יָבִינוּ	*Intelligent, animad-vertent, docebunt.*	They shall understand, consider, teach, instruct.
נבע	יַבִּיעַ	*Eloquetur, emittere*	He shall utter, cause to send
—	יַבִּיעוּ	*Eloquentur.* [*faciet.*	They shall utter. [forth.
—	יַבִּיעוּן	*Eloquentur, emittent*	They shall utter, send forth.
	יָבֵישׁ יָבֵשׁ	*Jabes.*	Jabesh, N. M. P.
בכה	יִבְכּוּ־כְּיוּן	*Flebunt, plorabunt.*	They shall weep, lament.
בכר	יְבַכֵּר	*Maturabit.*	He shall bring to maturity.
—	יְבֻכַּר	*Primogenitus con-*	He shall be made the first born
	יָבָל	*Jabal.* [*stituetur.*	Jabal, N. M.

ROOTS.	DERIVATIVES.	VERSIO.	SIGNIFICATION.
יָבַל		*Adduxit, deduxit.*	He brought, led along.
בלא	יְבַלֶּא	*Conteret, consumet*	He shall wear out, consume.
בלה	יִבְלֶה	*Veterascet.*	He shall grow old.
—	יִבְלוּ יִבְלוּ	*Veterascent.*	They shall grow old.
נבל	יִבֹּלוּ	*Consumentur.*	They shall be consumed, spent
יבל	יֹבִלוּהָ	*Adducent eam* [*cent*	They shall bring her.
נבל	יִבּוֹלוּן	*Decident, emarces-*	They shall fade, fall off, wither
יבל	יִבְלֵי	*Rivi, aquæductus.*	Rivers, streams, watercourses.
—	יֹבִלֵנִי	*Deducet me.*	He shall lead me.
בלע	יְבַלַּע יִבְלַע	*Deglutiet.*	He shall swallow down.
—	יְבֻלַּע־־לָע	*Absorbebitur.*	He shall be swallowed up.
—	יִבְלָעֻהוּ	*Absorbebunt eum.*	They shall swallow him up.
—	יְבַלְּעֵם	*Absorbebunt eos.*	They shall swallow them up.
	יִבְלְעָם	*Ibleam.*	Ibleam, N. P.
בלע	יְבַלְּעֶנָּה	*Absorbebit eam.*	He shall swallow her up.
—	יְבַלְּעֶנּוּ	*Deglutiet eum.*	He will swallow it down.
נבל	יַבֶּלֶת	*Verruca, struma, papula, tuberculum formicarum, vel defluxus pilorum.*	A wart, wen, red pimple, pustule from the bite of pismires, or a falling off of the hair.
יִבֵּם		*Ex affinitatis jure uxorem duxit.*	He married in right of affinity
—	יְבָמָהּ	*Levir ejus.*	Her husband's brother.
—	יַבְּמִי	*Leviri officium fungi erga me.*	To perform the duty of a husband's brother to me.
—	יְבָמִי	*Levir meus.*	My husband's brother.
—	יְבִמְתּוֹ	*Glos ejus.*	His brother's wife.
—	יְבִמְתֵּךְ	*Glos tua.*	Thy sister in law.
	יַבְנְאֵל	*Jabneel.*	Jabneel, N. P.
	יַבְנֶה	*Jabne.*	Jabneh, N. P.
בנה	יִבָּנֶה	*Ædificabitur.*	He shall be built.
—	יִבְנֶה	*Ædificabit.*	He shall build.
—	יִבְנֵהוּ־־נֶנּוּ	*Ædificabit eum.*	He shall build him,
—	יִבְנוּ־־נוּן	*Ædificabunt.*	They shall build.
	יִבְנִיָּה	*Ibnias.*	Ibnijah, N. M.
בנה	יִבְנֵם	*Ædificabit eos.*	He shall build them.

ROOTS.	DERIVATIVES.	VERSIO.	SIGNIFICATION.
בעא	יִבְעֶא	*Petet.*	He shall ask.
—	יִבְעָיוּן	*Quærent.*	They will seek.
בעל	יִבְעַל	*Uxorem ducet.*	He will marry a wife.
—	יִבְעָלוּךְ	*Ducent te.*	They shall marry them.
בער	יַבְעֶר	*Depascet.*	He will eat up.
—	יִבָּעֵר	*Auferetur.*	He shall be taken away.
—	יִבְעַר יִבְעַר	*Ardebit, succenditur*	He will burn, will be kindled,
—	יַבְעֲרוּ	*Accendent.*	They shall burn. [burned.
—	יִבְעֲרוּ	*Desipient.*	They will be foolish.
בעת	יְבַעֲתֻהוּ	*Terrebunt eum.*	They shall terrify him.
—	יְבַעֲתוּנִי־־תֻנִי	*Terrebunt me.*	They will terrify me.
בצע	יְבַצַּע	*Perficiet.*	He will perform, finish.
—	יִבְצַע	*Lucrabitur.*	He will gain.
—	יִבָּצֵעוּ	*Sauciabuntur.*	They shall be wounded.
—	יְבַצְּעֵנִי	*Abscindet me.*	He shall cut me off.
בצר	יִבָּצֵר	*Cohibebitur.*	He will be restrained.
—	יִבְצֹר	*Eripiet.*	He shall take away.
	יַבֹּק	*Jabboc.*	Jabbok, N. R.
בקע	יִבָּקַע	*Erumpet.*	He shall break forth.
—	יִבָּקֵעַ	*Perrumpetur.*	He shall be broken.
—	יְבַקַּע	*Fidet.* [tur.	He will cleave.
—	יִבָּקֵעוּ	*Findentur, dividen-*	They shall be cleft, divided.
בקר	יְבַקֵּר־־קֵּר	*Perquiret.*	He shall search diligently.
בקש	יְבַקֵּשׁ־־קֶּשׁ	*Quæret, requiret.*	He shall seek, require.
—	יְבֻקַּשׁ	*Quæretur.*	He shall be sought.
—	יְבַקְשׁוּ יְבַקְ׳	*Quærent.*	They shall seek.
ברא	יִבְרָא	*Creabit.*	He will create.
—	יִבָּרֵאוּן	*Creabuntur.*	They will be created.
ברח	יִבְרַח	*Fugiet.*	He shall or will flee.
—	יִבְרְחוּ	*Fugient.*	They shall flee.
—	יַבְרִיחַ	*Fugabit.*	He will cause to flee.
—	יַבְרִיחֶנּוּ	*Fugabit eum.*	He will make him flee.
ברך	יְבָרֵךְ	*Benedicet.*	He shall bless.
—	יְבֹרַךְ־־רַךְ	*Benedicetur.*	He shall be blessed.
—	יְבָרְכוּ	*Benedicent.*	They shall bless.
—	יְבָרְכוּכָה	*Benedicent tibi.*	They shall bless thee.
	יְבֶרֶכְיָהוּ	*Jeberechias.*	Jeberechiah, N. M.

ROOTS.	DERIVATIVES.	VERSIO.	SIGNIFICATION.
ברך	יְבָרֶכְךָ יְבָרֶכְךָ	*Benedicet tibi.*	He shall bless thee.
—	יְבָרְכֶנְהוּ	*Benedicet ei.*	He shall bless him.
—	יְבָרְכֵנוּ	*Benedicet nobis.*	He shall bless us.
יָבֵשׁ		*Aruit, exaruit; siccavit, exsiccavit.*	He became dry, withered; he made dry, dried up.
—	יָבֹשׁ	*Siccando, arescendo.*	In drying, withering.
—	יִבָשׁ	*Arescet.*	He will wither.
—	יַבָּשָׁה יְבֵשָׁה	*Arida* terra.	The dry *ground.*
—	יָבְשָׁה	*Aruit.*	She became dry.
—	יָבֵשׁוּ יָבְשׁוּ	*Exaruerunt.*	They have withered.
בוש	יֵבֹשׁוּ	*Pudore afficientur.*	They will be put to shame.
יבש	יִבָשׁוּ	*Exarescent.*	They will be dried up.
—	יְבֵשׁוֹת	*Arida* terra.	The dry *land.*
בשל	יְבַשְּׁלוּ	*Coquent.*	They shall boil.
	יִבְשָׂם	*Ibsam.*	Jibsam, N. M.
בשר	יְבַשֵּׂרוּ	*Nunciabunt.*	They shall declare.
יבש	יְבֹשֶׁת	*Siccare.*	To dry.
—	יַבֶּשְׁתָּא	*Arida* terra.	Dry ground, the earth.
	יג		
גאל	יִגָּאֵל	*Redimetur.*	He shall be redeemed.
	יִגְאָל	*Igal.*	Igeal, N. M.
גאל	יִגְאָל	*Redimet.*	He shall redeem.
—	יִגְאַל	*Vindicabit.*	He shall claim, restore, avenge
—	יִגְאָלֵהוּ	*Polluet eum.*	He will pollute, defile him.
—	יִגְאָלֵךְ	*Redimet te.*	He shall redeem thee.
—	יִגְאָלֶנָּה	*Redimet eam.*	He shall redeem her.
—	יִגְאָלֶנּוּ	*Redimet eum.*	He shall redeem him.
יגב			
גבה	יִגְבַּהּ	*Efferetur.*	He will be lifted up.
	יָגְבְּהָה	*Jogbeha.*	Jogbehah, N. P.
גבה	יִגְבְּהוּ	*Efferentur.*	They will be lifted up.
גבל	יִגְבּוֹל	*Terminabit.*	He will bound, limit.
גבה	יַגְבִּיהַּ	*Efferet se.*	He will lift up *himself.*
—	יַגְבִּיהוּ	*Exaltabunt.*	They will exalt.
גבר	יִגְבַּר	*Roboravit.*	He shall strengthen.
—	יִגְבַּר	*Prævalebit.*	He shall prevail.

ROOTS.	DERIVATIVES.	VERSIO.	SIGNIFICATION.
גדד	יָגֹד	*Vastabit.*	He shall lay waste.
נגד	יַגִּדוּ	*Nunciabunt.*	They shall declare.
גדל	יַגְדִּיל	*Magnificabit.*	He shall magnify.
—	יְגַדֵּל	*Enutriet, educabit.*	He will nourish, bring up.
—	יִגְדַּל יִגְדָּל	*Crescet, magnus erit, magnificabitur.*	He shall grow, be great, be magnified.
—	יְגַדְּלוּ	*Educabunt.*	They shall bring up.
—	יִגְדְּלוּ	*Crescent.*	They shall grow, grow up.
	יִגְדַּלְיָהוּ	*Igdalias.* [*flixit.*	Igdaliah, N. M.
יָגָה		*Mærore affecit, af-*	He grieved, afflicted.
נגה	יַגִּהַּ	*Splendebit.*	He shall shine.
נהה	יִגְהֶה	*Sanabit.* [*ent.*	He will heal.
גדד	יָגוֹדוּ	*Turmatim convent-*	They will assemble in troops.
—	יְגוּדֶנּוּ	*Vastabit eum.*	He shall lay him waste.
גול	יָגוּל יָגִיל	*Lætabitur.*	He shall rejoice.
יגה	יָגוֹן	*Mæror.*	Grief.
גוע	יִגְוַע יִגְוָע	*Expirabit, obibit.*	He shall expire, die.
—	יִגְוְעוּ־עוּן	*Expirabunt.*	They shall expire, die.
	יָגוּר	*Jagur.*	Jagur, N. P.
יגר	יָגוֹר	*Metuens.*	Fearing.
גור	יָגוּר	*Commorabitur, peregrinabitur.*	He shall sojourn, dwell, abide
—	יָגוּרוּ	*Convenient, commorabuntur, metu-*	They shall assemble, dwell, be afraid.
—	יְגוֹרֵם	*Terrebit eos.* [*ent.*	He shall make them afraid.
גזל	יִגְזֹל	*Diripiet.*	He will spoil.
—	יִגְזְלוּ	*Rapient.*	They will take away.
נגח	יִגַּח יִגָּח	*Cornu petet, feriet.*	He shall perish, gore.
נגד	יַגֵּד יַגִּיד	*Nunciabit, indicabit.*	He shall tell, declare, shew.
—	יַגִּידוּ	*Indicabunt, annunciabunt* [*luminabit*	They shall shew, tell, declare. [enlighten.
נגה	יַגִּיהַּ	*Splendere faciet, il-*	He will cause to shine, will
גוח	יָגִיחַ	*Educet, erumpet.*	He shall bring forth, break
גול	יָגִיל	*Lætabitur.*	He shall rejoice. [forth.
—	יָגִילוּ יְגִילוּן	*Lætabuntur.*	They shall rejoice.
נגע	יַגִּיעַ	*Tanget.*	He shall touch.
יגע	יְגִיעַ	*Labor.*	Labour.

ROOTS.	DERIVATIVES.	VERSIO.	SIGNIFICATION.
יגע	יְגִיעָהּ	*Labor ejus.*	Her labour.
נגע	יַגִּיעוּ	*Tangent, pertingent.*	They shall touch, reach.
יגע	יְגִיעוֹ	*Labor ejus.*	His labour.
—	יְגִיעַי	*Labores mei.*	My labours.
—	יְגִיעִי	*Defessi.*	Weary.
—	יְגִיעֲךָ־עֶךָ־עֵךְ	*Labor tuus.*	Thy labour.
נגע	יַגִּיעֶנָּה	*Admovebit eam.*	He shall bring her.
נוף	יְנִיפוּ	*Claudent.*	They shall shut.
נגר	יַגִּירֻהוּ	*Diffluere facient eum*	They shall cause him to flow [abroad.
נגש	יַגִּישׁוּ	*Accedent.*	They shall come near.
נול	יָגֵל	*Exultabit.*	He shall exult, rejoice.
גלה	יִגֶל	*Migrabit.*	He shall depart.
—	יִגָּלֶה	*Revelabitur.*	He shall be revealed.
—	יְגַלֶּה	*Revelabit.*	She shall reveal, discover.
—	יִגְלֶה	*Revelabit, migrabit.*	She shall reveal, depart.
—	יִגָּלוּ	*Retegentur.*	They shall be discovered.
—	יְגַלּוּ	*Revelabunt.*	They shall reveal.
—	יִגְלוּ	*Migrabunt.*	They shall depart.
גלח	יְגַלַּח־־לֵּחַ	*Radet, tondebit.*	He shall shave.
—	יְגַלְּחוּ	*Radent, tondebunt.*	They shall shave.
—	יְגַלְּחֶנּוּ	*Radet illum.*	He shall shave him.
	יָגְלִי	*Jogli.*	Jogli, N. M.
גמא	יְגַמֶּא	*Absorbebit.*	He will swallow.
גמל	יִגָּמֵל	*Ablectabitur.*	He shall be weaned.
—	יִגְמְלֵנִי	*Retribuet mihi.*	He will reward me.
גמר	יִגְמֹר	*Deficiet, desinet.*	He will fail, cease.
—	יִגְמֹר	*Perficiet.*	He will perfect.
גנן	יָגֵן	*Proteget.*	He will protect, defend.
גנב	יִגָּנֵב	*Furtim auferetur.*	He shall be stolen.
—	יִגְנֹב־נוֹב	*Furabitur.*	He will steal. [away.
—	יְגֻנַּב	*Furtim abducetur.*	He shall be privately conveyed
—	יִגְנְבוּ	*Furabuntur.*	They will steal.
יָגַע		*Laboravit, fatigavit, defessus est.*	He laboured, wearied, was fatigued.
—	יְגַע	Fructus *laboris.*	*The fruit or reward of* labour
—	יָגֵעַ	*Fessus.*	Weary.
נגע	יִגַּע	*Tanget.*	He will touch.

ROOTS.	DERIVATIVES.	VERSIO.	SIGNIFICATION.
יגע	יָגְעָה	*Defessa est.*	She was wearied.
נעה	יִגְעֶה	*Mugiet.*	He will low.
יגע	יִגְעוּ	*Laborabunt.* [*gent.*	They shall labour.
נגע	יִגְּעוּ	*Attingent, pertin-*	They will touch, reach to.
יגע	יְגֵעִים	*Laboriosi.*	Full of labour.
נעל	יִגְעַל	*Fastidiet, respuet.*	He will loathe, reject.
יגע	יָגַעְנוּ	*Laboravimus.*	We have laboured.
נער	יִגְעַר	*Increpabit.*	He will rebuke.
נעש	יִגָּעֲשׁוּ	*Commovebuntur.*	They shall be moved, agitated
יגע	יָגַעְתָּ יָגַעַתְּ	*Laborasti.*	Thou hast laboured.
—	יְגִעַת	*Fatigatio.*	A weariness. [wearied.
—	יָגַעְתִּי	*Laboravi, defessus.*	I have laboured, have been
נגף	יִגֹּף	*Percutiet.*	He will smite.
—	יִגְּפֶנּוּ	*Percutiet eum.*	He will strike him.
יָגֹר		*Metuit, formidabit.*	He feared, dreaded.
גרר	יִגָּר	*Ruminabit,*	He will chew the cud.
	יְגַר שָׂהֲדוּתָא	*Jegar-sahaduta,* nomen cumuli.	Jegar-sahadutha, *the name of a heap of stones.*
גרה	יְגָרֶה	*Excitabit.*	He will stir up.
גור	יְגֹרְהוּ	*Colliget eum.* [*cum.*	He will gather him.
—	יָגֻרְךָ	*Commorabitur te-*	He shall abide with thee.
גרם	יְגָרֵם	*Ossa confringet.*	He shall break the bones.
גרע	יִגָּרַע יִגָּרֵעַ	*Minuet, subtrahet.*	He shall diminish, withdraw.
—	יִגָּרַע יִגָּרֵעַ	*Minuetur, subtrahe-*	He shall be diminished, with-
—	יִגְרַע	*Subtrahet.* [*tur.*	He shall withdraw. [drawn.
גרש	יְגָרֵשׁ	*Expellet.*	He shall thrust out.
—	יְגֹרָשׁוּ	*Expellentur.*	They shall be driven out.
—	יְגָרְשׁוּהָ	*Expellent eam.*	They shall drive her out.
—	יְגָרְשֵׁם	*Expellet eos.*	He shall drive them out.
יגר	יָגֹרְתָּ	*Metuisti.*	Thou wast afraid.
—	יָגֹרְתִּי	*Metui.*	I was afraid.
נגש	יִגָּשׁ	*Appropinquabunt.*	He shall approach.
—	יַגֵּשׁ	*Accedere faciet.*	He will make to approach.
—	יִגַּשׁ	*Accedet.*	He shall come near.
—	יִגֹּשׂ	*Exiget.*	He shall exact.
—	יִגְּשׁוּ	*Accedent.*	They shall draw near.
—	יִגְּשׁוּ יִגָּשׁוּ	*Appropinquabunt.*	They shall approach.

ROOTS.	DERIVATIVES.	VERSIO.	SIGNIFICATION.
	יד		
יד			
יד	יָד	*Manus ; vis.*	A, the hand; strength, power
—	יַד	*Manus, potestas, ditio, latus, ora.*	A hand, power, authority, dominion, side, coast, border.
—	יַד יְדָא	*Manus.*	A, the hand.
דאג	יִדְאָג	*Solicitus erit.*	He will be solicitous, anxious.
דאה	יִדְאֶה	*Volabit.*	He will fly.
	יִדְאֲלָה	*Idala.* [*gietur eum.*	Idala, N. P.
נדב	יִדְּבֶנּוּ	*Sponte offeret, lar-*	He will willingly offer, give it.
דבק	יַדְבֵּק	*Adhærere faciet.*	He will make to cleave.
—	יִדְבַּק	*Adhærebit.*	He will cleave to.
—	יִדְבָּקוּ יִדְבְּקוּ	*Adhærebunt.*	They will adhere to. [destroy
דבר	יַדְבֵּר	*Subjiciet, perdet.*	He will subdue, overthrow,
—	יְדַבֵּר יְדַבֵּר	*Loquetur.*	He will speak.
—	יְדַבְּרוּ יְדַבְּרוּ	*Loquentur.*	They will speak.
	יִדְבָּשׁ	*Idbas.*	Idbash, N. M.
יָדַד		*Dilexit.*	He loved.
נדד	יִדּוֹדוּן	*Fugient.*	They shall flee.
ידד	יְדִדוּת	*Dilectio.*	Love.
יָדָה		*Projecit, ejecit, confessus est, gratias egit, laudavit, cele-*	He cast forth, cast out, confessed, gave thanks, praised, celebrated.
יד	יָדָהּ יָדָהּ	*Manus ejus.* [*bravit.*	Her hand.
—	יָדוֹ	*Manus ejus.*	His hand.
	יַדַּי	*Jadai.*	Jadau.
ידד	יַדּוּ	*Jecerunt.*	They have cast.
ידה	יְדוּ	*Projicite.*	Cast forth, shoot ye.
	יִדּוֹ	*Ido.*	Iddo, N. M.
נדד	יִדּוֹד	*Fugiet.*	He will flee.
	יָדוֹן	*Jadon.*	Jadon, N. M.
דון	יָדוֹן	*Disceptabit.*	He shall contend, strive.
ידע	יָדוֹעַ	*Scire.*	To know.
	יַדּוּעַ	*Jadua.*	Jadduah, N. M.
דוש	יְדוּשֶׁנּוּ	*Triturabit eum.*	He will thresh him.
יד	יָדוֹת	*Partes.*	Parts.

ROOTS.	DERIVATIVES.	VERSIO.	SIGNIFICATION.
	יְדוּתוּן	*Jedutun.*	Jeduthun, N. M.
יד	יְדוֹתָם	*Axes eorum.*	Their axle-trees.
נדח	יַדַּח	*Dispellet, expellet.*	He shall drive away, expel.
דחה	יִדָּחֶה	*Expelletur.*	He shall be driven away.
—	יִדַּחוּ	*Impellentur.*	They shall be driven forward.
דחק	יִדְחָקוּן	*Prement, vexabunt.*	They shall press, oppress, harass.
	יַדַּי	*Jadai.*	Jadau, N. M.
יד	יָדַי יָדַי יְדָי	*Manus meæ.*	My hands.
—	יָדִי	*Manus mea.*	My hand.
—	יְדֵי	*Manus, oræ, termini, mandata.*	Hands, coasts, borders, commands, orders.
ידד	יְדִיד	*Dilectus.*	Beloved.
	יְדִידָה	*Jedida.*	Jedidah, N. W.
ידד	יְדִידוֹת-דֹת	*Dilectæ.*	Beloved.
	יְדִידְיָה	*Jedidias.*	Jedidiah, N. M.
ידד	יְדִידֶיךָ	*Dilecti tui.*	Thy beloved ones.
—	יְדִידֹת	*Amores.*	Loves.
	יְדָיָה	*Jedias.*	Jedaiah, N. M.
יד	יָדֶיהָ	*Manus ejus.*	Her hands.
—	יְדֵיהוּ יָדָיו יָדָו	*Manus ejus.*	His hands.
—	יְדֵיהֶם־־הֶן	*Manus eorum, earum*	Their hands.
דוח	יָדִיחַ	*Abluet.*	He will wash, purify.
—	יָדִיחוּ	*Abluent.*	They will wash, cleanse.
יד	יָדֶיךָ יָדַיִךְ יְדֵיךְ	*Manus tuæ.*	Thy hands.
—	יְדֵיכֶם	*Manus vestræ.*	Your hands.
—	יָדַיִם יָדַיִם	*Manus, loca, spatia.*	Hands, places, spaces.
דון	יָדִין	*Judicabit.*	He will judge.
יד	יָדֵינוּ	*Manus nostræ.*	Our hands.
ידע	יְדִיעַ	*Notus.*	Known.
	יְדִיעֲאֵל	*Jediael.*	Jediael, N. M.
ידע	יְדִיעוּ	*Ostendent, docent.*	They shall shew, discover, teach.
יד	יֶדְךָ־־דְךָ־־דֵךְ	*Manus tua.*	Thy hand.
—	יֶדְךָ יָדְךָ יְדֶכָה	*Manus tua.*	Thy hand.
דכא	יִדְכָּא	*Confringetur.*	He shall be broken in pieces.
—	יְדַכְּאוּ	*Confringent.*	They shall break in pieces.
—	יְדַכְּאוּם	*Conterent eos.*	They shall crush them.
יד	יֶדְכֶם יְדֵ"	*Manus vestra.*	Your hand.

ROOTS.	DERIVATIVES.	VERSIO.	SIGNIFICATION.
דלל	יֵדַל	*Diminuetur.*	He shall be diminished.
דלג	יְדַלֵּג	*Saliet.*	He shall leap.
דלק	יַדְלִיקֵם	*Accendet eos.*	He shall inflame them.
דלה	יְדַלֶּנָּה	*Hauriet eam.*	He shall draw her out.
	יִדְלָף	*Idlaph.*	Jidlaph, N. M.
דלף	יִדְלֹף	*Stillabit, diffluet.*	He shall drop, fall asunder.
דלק	יִדְלַק	*Persequetur.*	He will persecute.
יד	יָדָם	*Manus eorum.*	Their hand.
דמם	יִדֹּם	*Conticescet.*	He shall keep silence.
דמה	יְדַמֶּה	*Cogitabit.*	He will think.
—	יִדְמֶה	*Assimilabitur.*	He will be likened.
דמם	יִדְּמוּ	*Conticescent.*	They shall keep silence.
—	יִדַּמּוּ	*Excidentur.*	They shall be cut off.
—	יִדְּמוּ	*Tacebunt.*	They will be silent.
יד	יָדֵנוּ	*Manus nostra.*	Our hand.
	יָדָע	*Jada.*	Jada, N. M.
יָדַע		*Sensit, percepit, scivit, cognovit, intellexit, discrevit, expertus est, docuit, ostendit, in-*	He felt, perceived, knew, understood, distinguished, experienced, taught, shewed, instructed.
—	יְדֹעַ	*Sciendo.* [*struxit.*	In knowing.
—	יֵדַע־־דַע	*Sciet.*	He shall know.
—	יְדַע	*Cognovit.*	He knew.
—	יֹדֵעַ	*Sciens.*	Knowing, he that knoweth.
—	יָדְעָה	*Scivit.*	She knew.
—	יְדָעָהּ	*Cognovit eam.*	He knew her.
—	יְדָעֻהוּ	*Cognoverunt eum.*	They knew him.
—	יָדְעוּ־־דֻ״	*Cognoverunt.*	They knew.
—	יְדָעוֹ	*Cognovit eum.*	He knew him.
—	יֵדְעוּ־־עוּן	*Cognoscent.*	They shall know.
—	יְדָעוּךָ	*Cognoverunt te.*	They knew thee.
—	יְדָעוּם	*Cognoverunt eos.*	They knew them.
—	יְדָעוּן	*Cognoverunt.*	They knew.
—	יְדָעוּנִי	*Cognoverunt.*	They have known me.
—	יֹדְעֵי ״	*Scientes.*	They that know.
	יְדַעְיָה	*Jedaias.*	Jedaiah, N. M.

ROOTS.	DERIVATIVES.	VERSIO.	SIGNIFICATION.
ידע	יֹדְעָיו	*Cognoscentes eum.*	They that know him.
—	יֹדְעִים יָדְעִין	*Scientes.*	They that know. [quenched
דעך	יִדְעַךְ־־עַךְ	*Extinguetur.*	He shall be extinguished.
ידע	יָדַעְנוּ־־דַ׳	*Scivimus.*	We have known.
—	יֵדָעֵנוּ	*Cognoscet nos.*	He will know us.
—	יֵדָעֶנּוּ	*Cognoscet eum.*	He will know him.
—	יֹדְעֵנוּ	*Cognoscens nos.*	He that knoweth us.
—	יְדַעֲנוּךָ	*Cognovimus te.*	We have known thee.
—	יְדַעֲנוּם	*Cognovimus eas.*	We have known them.
—	יִדְּעֹנִי	*Ariolus.*	A wizard.
—	יָדַעְתָּ־־דַ״־־תָּה	*Scivisti.*	Thou hast known.
—	יָדַעַתְּ־־דַ׳	*Scivisti.*	Thou hast known.
—	יַדַעְתְּ	*Cognovisti.*	Thou knewest.
—	יִדַּעְתָּ	*Ostendisti.*	Thou hast shown, made known
—	יָדֵעַתְ	*Scivi.*	I have known.
—	יֹדַעַת	*Sciens.*	He that knoweth.
—	יִדַּעְתָּה	*Ostendisti.*	Thou hast discovered.
—	יְדַעְתּוֹ	*Cognosces eum.*	Thou wilt know him.
—	יָדַעְתִּי־־דַ״	*Scivi.*	I have known.
—	יְדַעְתִּיהָ	*Cognovi eam.*	I have known her.
—	יְדַעְתִּיו	*Cognovi eum.*	I have known him.
—	יְדַעְתִּיךָ	*Cognovi te.*	I knew thee.
—	יְדַעְתִּים	*Cognovi eos.*	I have known them.
—	יְדַעְתִּין	*Cognovi eas.*	I knew them.
—	יְדַעְתָּם	*Cognosti eos.*	Thou knewest them.
—	יְדַעְתֶּם־־ן	*Cognovistis.*	Ye knew, have known.
—	יְדַעְתָּנִי	*Cognosti me.*	Thou hast known me.
נדף	יִדְּפֶנּוּ	*Depellet, dispellet eum.*	He shall thrust him down, drive him away.
דקק	יְדִקֶנּוּ	*Comminuet eum.*	He shall beat him to pieces.
דקר	יְדֻקַּר	*Perfodietur.*	He shall be thrust through.
נדר	יִדֹּר	*Vovebit.*	He shall vow.
דור	יְדֻרוּן	*Habitabunt.*	They shall dwell.
דרש	יִדְרוֹשׁ־־רשׁ	*Quærent.*	They shall seek.
דרך	יַדְרֵךְ	*Deducet.*	He will lead, guide.
—	יִדְרֹךְ	*Calcabit, tendet.*	He shall tread, stretch, bend.
—	יִדְרְכוּ	*Calcabunt.*	They will tread.

ROOTS.	DERIVATIVES.	VERSIO.	SIGNIFICATION.
דרך	יִדְרְכוּן	*Tendent.*	They will bend.
—	יַדְרִכֵנִי	*Incedere faciet me.*	He will make me to walk.
דרש	יִדְרְשֵׁהוּ	*Requiret eum.*	He will inquire after, regard
—	יִדְרְשׁוּ־־שׁוּן	*Quærent.*	They shall seek. [him or it.
—	יִדְרְשׁוּהוּ	*Quærent eum.*	They shall seek him.
—	יִדְרְשֶׁנּוּ	*Requiret eum.*	He will require him or it.
דשן	יְדֻשָּׁן	*Pinguis fiet.*	He shall be made fat.
—	יְדַשְּׁנֶה	*In cinerem rediget.*	He will reduce to ashes.
יד	יְדֹת	*Cardines.*	Tenons.
—	יְדֹתֶיהָ	*Latera ejus.*	Her sides.
—	יְדֹתָיו	*Cardines ejus.*	His tenons.
	יה		
הוה	יָהּ	*Jah, Dominus.*	Jah, the Lord.
יָהַב		*Dedit, concessit, tribuit, tradidit, reddidit.*	He gave, granted, ascribed, delivered, rendered, yielded
—	יָהֵב	*Dans.*	Giving.
—	יְהַב־־יִב	*Datus est.*	He was given.
—	יָהֲבִין	*Dantes.*	They that give.
—	יְהָבְךָ	*Onus tuum.*	Thy burden.
—	יְהַבְתְּ	*Dedisti.*	Thou gavest.
הגה	יֶהְגֶּה	*Loquetur, meditabitur; gemet, rugiet.* [*buntur.*	He will speak, study, meditate; groan, mourn, roar.
—	יֶהְגּוּ	*Loquentur, medita-*	They will speak, meditate.
יָהַד		*Factus est Judæus, Judaismum amplexus est.*	He became a Jew, embraced Judaism.
	יְהֻד־־הוּד	*Jehud.*	Jehud, N. P.
	יְהֻדִיָּא	*Jehudia.*	Jehudijah, N. W.
הדף	יֶהְדֹּף	*Trudet, pellet.*	He will thrust, drive away.
—	יֶהְדָּפֻהוּ	*Pellent eum.*	They shall drive him.
—	יֶהְדֳּפֵם	*Pellet eos.*	He will drive them.
—	יֶהְדָּפֶנּוּ	*Pellet eum.*	He will thrust him.
	יֵהוּא	*Jehu.*	Jehu, N. M.
	יְהוֹאָחָז	*Jehoachaz.*	Jehoahaz, N. M.
	יְהוֹאָשׁ	*Jehoas.*	Jehoash, N. M.
אבד	יְהוֹבְדוּן	*Perdent.*	They will destroy.

ROOTS.	DERIVATIVES.	VERSIO.	SIGNIFICATION.
	יְהוּדָה	*Jehudas.*	Judah, N. M. F. P.
ידה	יְהוֹדֶה	*Laudabit.*	He shall praise.
—	יְהוֹדוּךָ	*Laudabunt te.*	They shall praise thee.
	יְהוּדִי	*Jehuda.*	A Jew, N. N.
	יְהוּדָיֵא	*Jehudæ.*	Jews, N. N.
	יְהוּדִים	*Jehudæi.*	Jews, N. N.
	יְהוּדִית	*Judith.*	Judith, N. W.
ידה	יְהוּדִית	*Judaicè.*	In the Jews' language.
ידע	יְהוֹדַע	*Notum faciet.*	He will make known.
—	יְהוֹדְעוּן	*Notum facient.*	They will make known.
—	יְהוֹדְעִנַּנִי	*Ostendet mihi.*	He will shew to me.
—	יְהוֹדְעֻנַּנִי	*Ostendent mihi.*	They shall make known to me
הוה	יְהוָֹה	*Jehova, Dominus.*	Jehovah, the Lord.
—	יֱהוִֹה	*Deus.*	God.
	יְהוֹזָבָד	*Jehozabad.*	Jehozabad, N. M.
	יְהוֹחָנָן	*Jehochanan.*	Jehohanan, N. M.
	יְהוֹיָדָע	*Jehoiada.*	Jehoiada, N. M.
	יְהוֹיָכִין	*Jehoiachin.*	Jehoiachin, N. M.
	יְהוֹיָקִים	*Jehoiakim.*	Jehoiakim, N. M.
	יְהוֹיָרִיב	*Jehoiarib.*	Jehoiarib, N. M.
	יְהוּכַל	*Jehucal.*	Jehucal, N. M.
הלל	יְהוֹלֵל	*Insanire faciet.*	He will make mad.
	יְהוֹנָדָב	*Jehonadab.*	Jehonadab, N. M.
	יְהוֹנָתָן	*Jehonatan.*	Jonathan, N. M.
	יְהוֹסֵף	*Jehoseph.*	Joseph, N. M.
	יְהוֹעַדָּה	*Jehoada.*	Jehoadah, N. M.
	יְהוֹעַדִּין־דָּן	*Jehoadan.*	Jehoadan, N. W.
	יְהוֹצָדָק	*Jehotsadac.*	Jehozadak, N. M.
	יְהוֹרָם	*Jehoram.*	Jehoram, N. M.
	יְהוֹשֶׁבַע	*Jehoseba.*	Jehoshebah, N. W.
	יְהוֹשַׁבְעַת	*Jehosabat.*	Jehoshabeath, N. W.
	יְהוֹשׁוּעַ־שֻׁעַ	*Jehosua.*	Joshua, N. M.
ישע	יְהוֹשִׁיעַ	*Liberabit.*	He will deliver.
	יְהוֹשָׁפָט	*Jehosaphat.*	Jehoshaphat.
חוה	יְהַחֲוֶה	*Indicabit.*	He will shew.
היה	יְהִי	*Erit.*	He shall or will be.
יהב	יְהִיבַת	*Data est, dabitur.*	She was given, shall be given.

ROOTS.	DERIVATIVES.	VERSIO.	SIGNIFICATION.
היה	יִהְיֶה	*Et erit.*	And he will be.
—	יִהְיֶה--יְהִי	*Erit.*	He will be.
—	יִהְיוּ--יוּ	*Erunt.*	They shall or will be.
ילל	יְהֵילִילוּ	*Ejulabunt.*	They will howl.
יהר	יָהִיר	*Arrogans, superbus*	Haughty, proud.
הוך	יְהָךְ	*Vadet, veniet.*	He will go, come.
הלל	יָהֵל	*Splendebit.*	He shall shine.
אהל	יַהֵל	*Tentorium tendet.*	He shall stretch, pitch his tent.
הלל	יָהֵלּוּ	*Splendebunt.*	They shall shine.
הלך	יְהַלֵּךְ	*Ambulabit.*	He shall walk.
—	יַהֲלֹךְ	*Ibit, incedet.*	He shall go, walk.
—	יַהַלְכוּ	*Ibunt, ambulabunt.*	They shall go, walk.
—	יְהַלֵּכוּ--כוּן	*Ambulabunt, vadent*	They shall walk, go.
הלל	יְהַלֵּל	*Laudabit.*	He shall praise.
—	יְהֻלָּל	*Laudabitur.*	He shall be praised.
	יְהַלֶּלְאֵל	*Jehalelel.*	Jehaleleel, N. M.
הלל	יְהַלְלוּ	*Laudabunt.*	They shall praise.
—	יְהַלְלוּהוּ	*Laudabunt eum.*	They shall praise him.
—	יְהַלְלוּךָ	*Laudabunt te.*	They shall praise thee.
—	יְהַלֶלְךָ--לְלֶךָ	*Laudabit te.*	He shall praise thee.
הלם	יַהַלְמוּן	*Contundent.*	They shall beat down.
—	יֶהֶלְמֵנִי	*Percutiet me.*	He shall smite me.
המה	יֶהֱמֶה	*Fremet.* [*bunt.*	He shall roar. [a noise.
—	יֶהֱמוּ--מָיוּ	*Frement, persona-*	They shall roar, sound, make
עדה	יְהַעְדּוּן	*Auferent.*	They shall take away.
הפך	יַהֲפֹךְ	*Vertet.*	He shall turn.
—	יֵהָפֵךְ	*Convertetur.*	He shall be converted, turned
	יַהַץ	*Jahats.*	Jahats, N. P.
	יַהְצָה	*Jatsa.*	Jatsa, N. P.
קום	יְהָקִים	*Statuet, constituet.*	He shall set up, appoint.
יהר			
הרג	יַהֲרֹג--רָג	*Occidet.*	He will slay.
—	יֵהָרֵג	*Occidetur.*	He shall be slain.
—	יַהַרְגוּ	*Occident.*	They shall slay.
—	יַהַרְגֻן	*Occident.*	They shall slay.
—	יַהַרְגֵנִי	*Occidet me.*	He shall slay me.
—	יַהַרְגֻנִי	*Occident me.*	They will kill me.

ROOTS.	DERIVATIVES.	VERSIO.	SIGNIFICATION.
הרס	יֶהֱרוֹס	*Diruet.*	He will break down.
—	יֵהָרֵס	*Diruetur.*	He shall be thrown down.
—	יַהַרְסוּ	*Diruent.*	They will break down.
—	יֶהֶרְסוּ	*Perrumpent.*	They will break through.
—	יֵהָרְסוּן	*Destruentur.*	They shall be destroyed.
—	יֶהֶרְסְךָ	*Destruet te.*	He shall destroy thee.
—	יֶהֶרְסֵם	*Destruet eos.*	He shall destroy them.
—	יֶהֶרְסֶנָּה	*Evertet eam.*	He will overthrow her.
שנא	יְהַשְׁנֵא	*Mutabit.*	He will change, alter.
שפל	יְהַשְׁפֵּל	*Deprimet.*	He will bring down, subdue.
תוב	יְהַתְבוּן	*Restituent.*	They shall restore.
התל	יְהָתֵלּוּ	*Illudent, fallent.*	They will mock, deceive.
	יו		
	יוֹאָב	*Joab.*	Joab, N. M.
	יוֹאָח	*Joach.*	Joah, N. M.
	יוֹאָחָז	*Joachaz.*	Joahaz, N. M.
	יוֹאֵל	*Joel.*	Joel, N. M.
ארר	יוּאָר	*Maledicetur.*	He shall be cursed.
	יוֹאָשׁ	*Joas.*	Joash, N. M.
	יוֹב	*Job.*	Job, N. M.
בוא	יוּבָא	*Adducetur.*	He shall be brought.
—	יוּבָאוּ	*Adducentur.*	They shall be brought.
	יוֹבָב	*Jobab.*	Jobab, N. M.
יבל	יוֹבִילוּ	*Adducent.*	They shall bring.
	יוּבָל	*Jubal.*	Jubal, N. M.
יבל	יוּבַל--בַל	*Adducetur.*	He shall be brought.
—	יוֹבֵל	*Jubilæus.*	The jubilee.
—	יוּבְלוּ	*Adducentur.*	They shall be brought.
—	יוֹבִלוּן	*Adducent.*	They shall bring.
—	יוֹבְלִים	*Cornua arietina.*	Rams' horns.
—	יוֹבִלֵנִי	*Deducet me.*	He will lead, bring me.
ידה	יוֹדֶה	*Gratias aget.*	He shall give thanks.
—	יוֹדוּ	*Laudabunt.*	They shall praise.
—	יוֹדוּךָ	*Celebrabunt te.*	They shall celebrate, praise [thee.
ידע	יוֹדִיעַ	*Ostendet.*	He will shew.
—	יוֹדִיעוּ	*Docebunt.*	They will teach.

ROOTS.	DERIVATIVES.	VERSIO.	SIGNIFICATION.
ידע	יוֹדִיעֶנּוּ	*Docebit eum.*	He shall teach him.
ידה	יוֹדֶךָּ	*Laudabit te.*	He shall praise thee.
ידע	יִוָּדַע־־דֵעַ	*Cognoscetur.*	He shall be known.
—	יוֹדֵעַ	*Sciens, cognoscens.*	He that knoweth.
—	יוֹדְעוֹ	*Cognoscens eum* [tes	He that knoweth him.
—	יוֹדְעֵי־־עִים	*Scientes, cognoscen-*	They that know.
—	יוֹדְעֶיךָ	*Cognoscentes te.*	They that know thee. [them.
—	יוֹדִעֵם	*Ostendent eis.*	He shall shew, discover to
—	יוֹדַעְתִּי	*Instruxi.*	I have instructed.
דקק	יוּדַק	*Comminuetur.*	He shall be beaten to pieces.
דוש	יוּדַשׁ	*Triturabitur.*	He shall be threshed.
	יוֹזָבָד	*Jozabad.*	Jozabad, N. M.
	יוֹזָכָר	*Jozacar.*	Jozachar, N. M.
	יוֹחָא	*Jocha.*	Joha, N. M.
	יוֹחָנָן	*Jochanan.*	Johanan, N. M.
	יוּטָּה	*Juta.*	Juttah, N. P.
טול	יוּטַל־־טָל	*Dejicietur.*	He shall be cast down.
	יוֹיָדָע	*Joiada.*	Joiada, N. M.
	יוֹיָקִים	*Joiakim.*	Joiakim, N. M.
	יוֹיָרִיב	*Joiarib.*	Joiarib, N. M.
	יוֹכֶבֶד	*Jochebed.*	Jochebed, N. W.
יכח	יוֹכַח	*Arguet.*	He shall reprove.
—	יוֹכִיחַ	*Increpabit, corripiet*	He shall rebuke, correct.
—	יֹכִיחֶךָ	*Arguet te.*	He will reprove thee.
—	יוֹכִיחֶנּוּ	*Corripiet.*	He shall correct him.
	יוּכַל	*Jucal.*	Jucal, N. M.
יכל	יוּכַל־כַל	*Poterit.*	He will be able.
—	יָכְלוּ	*Potuerunt.*	They were able.
אכל	יוּכְלוּ יו״	*Comedent.* [bunt.	They will set.
יכל	יוּכְלוּ־־כְלוּ־־לוּן	*Poterunt, prævale-*	They will be able, will prevail
ילד	יִוָּלֵד	*Nascetur.*	He shall be born.
—	יִוָּלֵד	*Parietur.*	He shall be brought forth.
—	יוּלַּד־־לַד י״	*Natus est.*	He was born.
—	יוֹלֵדָה	*Parturiens.*	She that travaileth.
—	יִוָּלְדוּ־־ל״	*Nascentur.*	They shall be born.
—	יוֹלַדְתֶּךָ	*Genetrix tua.*	Thy mother.
—	יוֹלַדְתְּכֶם	*Genetrix vestra.*	She that bare you.

ROOTS.	DERIVATIVES.	VERSIO.	SIGNIFICATION.
ילד	יוֹלִיד	*Gignet.*	He shall beget.
ילד	יוֹלִיךְ־־לִךְ	*Ducet, deducet.*	He shall carry, lead.
——	יוֹלִיכֶם	*Deducet eos.*	He shall lead them.
יום			
——	יוֹם	*Dies.*	A day.
——	יוֹמוֹ	*Dies ejus.*	His day.
——	יוֹמָיָא־־מִין	*Dies.*	Days.
——	יוֹמַיִם־־מַ״ יְמֵי	*Biduum.*	Two days.
——	יוֹמְךָ	*Dies tui.*	Thy day.
——	יוֹמָם	*Dies eorum, quoti-*	Their days, daily, by day.
——	יוֹמָת	*Dies.* [*die, interdiu.*	Days.
מות	יוּמַת־־מַ׳	*Occidetur.*	He shall be slain.
——	יְוּמַת יָמֹת	*Occidetur.*	He shall be slain.
——	יוּמְתוּ־־מְ״	*Interficientur.*	They shall be put to death.
יון			
	יָוָן	*Javan.*	Javan, N. M. P.
	יוֹנָדָב	*Jonadab.*	Jonadab, N. M.
	יוֹנָה	*Jonas.*	Jonah, N. M.
ינה	יוֹנָה	*Columba.*	A dove.
——	יוֹנֶה	*Opprimet.*	He will oppress.
——	יוֹנוּ	*Opprimerit.*	They shall oppress.
	יְוָנִים	*Javanitæ.*	*Grecians*, N. N.
ינה	יוֹנִים	*Columbæ.*	Doves.
ינק	יוֹנֵק	*Sugens.*	He that sucketh.
——	יוֹנְקוֹתֶיהָ	*Rami ejus.*	Her branches.
——	יוֹנְקוֹתָיו יֹנְ׳	*Rami ejus.*	His branches.
——	יוֹנַקְתּוֹ	*Ramus ejus.*	His branch.
ינה	יוֹנַת	*Columba.*	A dove.
——	יוֹנָתִי	*Columba mea.*	My dove.
	יוֹנָתָן	*Jonatan.*	Jonathan, N. M. [about.
סבב	יוּסַב	*Circumagetur.* [*bit.*	He shall be driven, carried
יסף	יוֹסִיף יֹסִיף יוֹסֵף	*Addet, perget, auge-*	He shall add, proceed, increase
——	יוֹסִיפוּ יֹסִ׳	*Addens, pergens.*	Adding, proceeding.
	יוֹסִפְיָה	*Josiphias.*	Josiphiah, N. M.
יסף	יוֹסַף	*Addidit.*	He added.
	יוֹסֵף	*Joseph.*	Joseph, N. M.
יסף	יוֹסֵף	*Addet.*	He shall add.

ROOTS.	DERIVATIVES.	VERSIO.	SIGNIFICATION.
יסף	יוֹסִפוּ־־פוּן	*Addent.*	They shall add.
	יוֹסִפְיָה	*Josiphias.*	Josiphiah, N. M.
יסר	יִוָּסֵר	*Corripietur.*	He shall be corrected.
סור	יוּסַר	*Auferetur.*	He shall be taken away.
	יוֹעֵאלָה	*Joelas.*	Joelah, N. M.
	יוֹעֵד	*Joed.*	Joed, N. M.
יעד	יוֹעִדֵנִי	*Condicet me.*	He shall appoint me.
	יוֹעֶזֶר	*Joezer.* [*mihi.*	Joezer, N. M.
יעד	יוֹעִדֵנִי	*Tempus constituet*	He shall set me a time.
יעל	יוֹעִיל	*Proderit.*	He will profit.
—	יוֹעִילוּ	*Proderunt.*	They will profit.
—	יוֹעִילוּךָ	*Proderunt tibi.*	They shall profit thee.
—	יוֹעָלוּ	*Profuerunt.*	They profited.
עמם	יוּעַם	*Obscurabitur.*	He will be darkened.
יעץ	יוֹעֵץ	*Consiliarius.*	A counsellor.
—	יִוָּעֲצוּ	*Consilium capient.*	They shall take counsel.
—	יוֹעֲצִים	*Consiliarii.*	Counsellors.
—	יוֹעֲצֶךָ	*Consiliarius tuus.*	Thy counsellor.
—	יוֹעֲצָתוֹ	*Consiliarii ejus.*	His counsellors.
	יוֹעָשׁ	*Joas.*	Joash, N. M.
יצא	יוֹצֵא יֹצֵא	*Egrediens, prodiens.*	Going out, going forth.
—	יוֹצְאוֹת יֹצְ׳	*Egredientes.*	They that go out.
—	יוֹצְאֵי יֹצְ׳	*Egredientes.*	They that go out.
—	יוֹצְאִים יֹצְ׳	*Prodeuntes.*	They that go forth.
—	יוֹצֵאת יֹצֵ׳	*Egrediens.*	She that goeth out.
	יוֹצָדָק	*Jotsadac.*	Jozadak, N. M.
יצא	יוֹצִיא	*Educet.*	He shall bring out.
—	יוֹצִיאוּ יֹצִ׳	*Educent.*	They shall bring.
—	יוֹצִיאוּם	*Educent eos.*	They shall bring them out.
—	יוֹצִיאֵם	*Educet eos.*	He shall bring them out.
—	יוֹצִיאֵנוּ	*Educet me.*	He shall bring me out.
יצק	יוּצַק	*Fundetur.*	He will be poured.
יצר	יוּצַר	*Formabitur.*	He will be formed.
—	יוֹצֵר יֹצֵ׳	*Formans, fingens.*	He that formeth, fashioneth.
—	יוֹצְרִים	*Figuli.*	Potters.
יקש	יוֹקְשִׁים	*Aucupes.*	Fowlers.
—	יוּקָשִׁים	*Irretiti.*	Ensnared.

ROOTS.	DERIVATIVES	VERSIO.	SIGNIFICATION.
ירא	יוֹרֶא	*Pluvia autumnalis.*	The former or autumnal rain.
ירד	יוֹרֵד יֹרֵד	*Descendens.*	Going down.
—	יוֹרִדוּךָ	*Deprimunt te.*	They shall bring thee down.
—	יוֹרְדוֹת יֹר׳	*Descendentes.*	Coming down.
—	יוֹרְדֵי יֹרְדִים	*Descendentes.*	They that go down.
	יוֹרָה	*Joras.*	Jorah, N. M.
ירה	יוֹרֶה	*Jaculabitur; docebit; pluvia autumnalis.*	He shall shoot; shall teach; the autumnal rain.
—	יוֹרוּ	*Jaculabuntur; docebunt.*	They shall shoot; shall teach.
—	יוֹרוּךָ	*Docebunt te.*	They shall teach thee.
	יוֹרַי	*Jorai*	Jorai, N. M.
ירד	יוֹרִידוּ	*Demittent.*	They shall bring down.
—	יוֹרִידֵנִי	*Deprimet me.*	He shall bring me down.
ירש	יוֹרִישׁ	*Expellet.*	He shall drive out.
—	יוֹרִישְׁךָ	*Possidere faciet te.*	He shall cause thee to possess
ירם	יוֹרָם	*Separabitur.*	He shall be separated.
	יוֹרָם	*Joram.*	Joram, N. M.
ירה	יוֹרֶנּוּ	*Docebit eum.*	He shall teach him.
ירש	יִוָּרֵשׁ	*Pauper fiet.*	He shall become poor.
—	יוֹרֵשׁ	*Expellens; possessor; hæres.*	Driving out; a possessor; an heir.
—	יוֹרִשֶׁנָּה	*Expellet eam.*	He shall drive her out.
—	יוֹרִשֶׁנּוּ יֹר׳	*Expellet eum.*	He shall drive him out.
	יוּשַׁב חֶסֶד	*Jushab-chesed.*	Jushab-hesed.
ישב	יוֹשֵׁב יֹשֵׁב	*Sedens, considens, manens, habitans.*	Sitting, sitting down, abiding, remaining, dwelling.
—	יוֹשְׁבֵי יֹשְׁ׳	*Habitantes.*	They that dwell, inhabitants.
—	יוֹשְׁבֶיהָ יֹשְׁ׳	*Habitatores ejus.*	Her inhabitants.
	יוֹשִׁבְיָה	*Josibias.*	Josibiah, N. M.
ישב	יוֹשְׁבָיו יֹשְׁ׳	*Habitatores ejus.*	His inhabitants.
—	יוֹשְׁבִים יֹשְׁ׳	*Habitantes, manentes.*	They that dwell, remain.
—	יוֹשֶׁבֶת	*Habitans.*	She that dwelleth.
—	יוֹשֶׁבֶת יֹשְׁ׳	*Sedens, habitans.*	Sitting, dwelling, an inhabitant
שדד	יוּשַׁד	*Vastabitur.*	He shall be laid waste.
	יוֹשָׁה	*Josa.*	Josha, N. M.
	יוֹשַׁוְיָה	*Josavias.*	Joshaviah, N. M.

ROOTS.	DERIVATIVES.	VERSIO.	SIGNIFICATION.
ישב	יוֹשִׁיבוּ	*Habitare facient.*	They shall cause to inhabit.
ישט	יוֹשִׁיט	*Extendet, porriget.*	He shall extend, hold out.
ישע	יוֹשִׁיעַ	*Servabit.* [*bunt.*	He shall save.
—	יוֹשִׁיעוּ	*Servabunt, libera-*	They shall save, deliver.
—	יוֹשִׁיעוּךָ	*Liberabunt te.*	He shall deliver thee.
—	יוֹשִׁיעֵם	*Servabit eos.*	He shall save them.
—	יוֹשִׁיעֵנוּ	*Servabit nos.*	He will save us.
—	יוֹשִׁיעֶנּוּ	*Servabit eum.*	He will save him.
—	יוֹשִׁיעֵנִי	*Servabit me.*	He will save me.
	יוֹשָׁפָט	*Josaphat.*	Joshaphat, N. M.
ישע	יִוָּשֵׁעַ	*Servabitur.*	He shall be saved.
—	יוֹשַׁע	*Servabit.*	He shall save.
—	יוֹשִׁעֲךָ	*Servabit te.*	He shall save thee.
שור	יוּשַׁר	*Cantabitur.*	He shall be sung.
שות	יוּשַׁת	*Imponetur.*	He shall be laid.
יתר	יוֹתִיר	*Relinquet.*	He shall leave.
	יוֹתָם	*Jotam.*	Jotham, N. M.
יתר	יִוָּתֵר	*Remanebit.*	He shall remain.
—	יִוָּתֶר	*Relinquetur.*	He shall be left.
—	יוֹתֵר	*Relinquet.*	He shall leave.
—	יִוָּתְרוּ	*Manebunt.*	They shall remain.
	יז		
זוב	יָזֻבוּ	*Liquefient, contabes-*	They will melt, pine away.
זבח	יִזְבַּח	*Immolabit.* [*cent.*	He will sacrifice.
—	יַזְבְּחוּ יִזְבְּחוּ	*Immolabunt.*	They will sacrifice.
זבל	יִזְבְּלֵנִי	*Habitabit mecum.*	He shall dwell with me.
זוד	יָזֵד	*Superbe aget.*	He will act proudly.
נזה	יַזֶּה יִזֶּה	*Asperget.*	He shall sprinkle.
זהר	יַזְהִירוּ יַזְהִרוּ	*Splendebunt.*	They shall shine.
זוב	יָזוּב	*Fluet.*	He shall flow. [place.
זחח	יִזַּח	*Dimovebitur.*	He shall be moved out of his
	יְזִיאֵל	*Jeziel.*	Jeziel, N. M.
זוד	יָזִיד	*Superbe aget.*	He will act proudly.
—	יְזִידוּן	*Superbe agent.*	They will act proudly.
	יִזִּיָּה	*Jezias.*	Jeziah, N. M.
	יָזִיז	*Jaziz.*	Jaziz, N. M.

ROOTS.	DERIVATIVES.	VERSIO.	SIGNIFICATION.
נזר	יַזִּיר	*Separabit se.*	He shall separate himself.
זכה	יְזַכֶּה	*Purificabit.*	He shall cleanse.
——	יִזְכֶּה	*Mundus erit.*	He shall be clean.
זכר	יִזְכּוֹר	*Recordabitur.*	He will remember.
——	יַזְכִּיר	*Memorabit.*	He will mention.
——	יַזְכִּירוּ	*Memorabunt.*	They shall mention. [tioned.
——	יִזָּכֵר	*Memorabitur.*	He will be remembered, men-
——	יִזְכָּר יִזְכֹּר	*Recordabitur.*	He will remember. [mentioned
——	יִזָּכְרוּ	*Memorabuntur.*	They shall be remembered,
——	יִזְכְּרוּ	*Recordabuntur.*	They shall remember.
——	יִזְכְּרוּךָ	*Recordabuntur tui.*	They shall remember thee.
——	יִזְכְּרוּנִי	*Recordabuntur mei.*	They shall remember me.
נזל	יִזַּל	*Fluet, fluere faciet.*	He shall flow, cause to flow.
——	יִזְּלוּ	*Fluent, fluere faci-*	They shall flow, cause to flow
	יִזְלִיאָה	*Izlias.* [*ent.*	Jezliah, N. M.
יָזַם		*Cogitavit.*	He thought.
——	יָזְמוּ	*Cogitaverunt.*	They have thought.
זמר	יִזָּמֵר	*Putabitur.*	He shall be pruned.
——	יְזַמְּרוּ	*Canent.*	They shall sing.
——	יְזַמֶּרְךָ	*Canet tibi.*	He shall sing to thee.
יָזַן		*Armavit, cinxit.*	He armed, girded.
זנה	יִזְנֶה	*Scortabuntur.*	They will go a whoring.
זנח	יִזְנַח	*Rejiciet.*	He will cast off.
	יְזַנְיָה	*Jezanias.*	Jaazaniah, N. M.
זנח	יַזְנִיחֲךָ	*Rejiciet te.*	He will cast thee off.
זנק	יְזַנֵּק	*Exiliet.*	He shall leap.
יזע			
זעק	יַזְעִיקוּ	*Clamare facient.*	They will make to cry.
זעם	יִזְעָמוּהוּ	*Detestabuntur eum.*	They shall detest, abhor him.
זעף	יִזְעַף	*Turbabitur, indigna-*	He will be disturbed, angry.
זעק	יִזְעַק	*Clamabit.* [*bitur.*	He will cry out.
——	יִזְעֲקוּ יִזְעָקוּ	*Clamabunt.*	They shall cry.
זקק	יָזֹקּוּ	*Stillabunt, fundent.*	They shall drop, pour.
זקן	יַזְקִין	*Consenescet.*	He shall grow old.
זרב	יְזֹרְבוּ	*Diffluent, effluent.*	They shall dissolve, evaporate.
זרה	יְזֹרֶה	*Spargetur.*	He shall be scattered.
——	יְזָרוּ	*Dispergent.*	They shall disperse.

ROOTS.	DERIVATIVES.	VERSIO.	SIGNIFICATION.
זרח	יִזְרַח־רָח	*Orietur.*	He shall arise.
	יִזְרָח	*Izrachita.*	Izrahite, N. F.
	יִזְרַחְיָה	*Izrachias.*	Izrahiah, N. M.
זרע	יִזָּרַע	*Seretur, generabitur*	He shall be sown, propagated.
—	יִזָּרֵעַ	*Seminabitur.*	He shall be sown.
—	יִזְרַע	*Seminabit.*	He shall sow.
	יִזְרְעֶאל־עֶאל	*Izreel.*	Jezreel, N. M. P.
	יִזְרְעֵלִי־לִית	*Izreelita.*	Jezreelite, Jezreelitess.
זרע	יִזְרְעוּ	*Seminabunt.*	They shall sow.
זרק	יִזְרֹק	*Asperget.*	He shall sprinkle.
	יִזָּתָא	*Jezata.*	Jezatha, N. M.
	יח		
חבא	יֵחָבְאוּ	*Abscondent se.*	They will hide themselves.
	יְחֻבָּה	*Jechubas.*	Jehubbah, N. M.
חבש	יַחֲבוֹשׁ	*Ligabit.*	He will bind.
חבט	יַחְבֹּט	*Excutiet.*	He shall shake off.
—	יֵחָבֵט	*Decutietur.* [detur.	He shall be shaken off. [ed.
חבל	יֵחָבֵל	*Corrumpetur, per-*	He will be corrupted, destroy-
—	יַחְבֹּל	*Pignerabitur.*	He shall take in pledge.
—	יְחַבֵּל	*Parturiet.*	He shall travail with.
—	יַחְבְּלוּ יַחְבֹלוּ	*In pignus accipient.*	They shall take as a pledge.
חגר	יַחְגֹּר	*Accinget se.*	He shall gird *himself.*
—	יַחְגְּרָה	*Accinget eum.*	He shall gird her.
—	יַחְגְּרוּ	*Accingent se.*	They shall gird *themselves.*
יָחַד		*Conjunxit, univit.*	He connected, united.
—	יַחַד יָחַד	*Simul, pariter.*	Together, at once, alike.
חדד	יָחַד יַחַד	*Exacuet.*	He will sharpen.
יחד	יַחַד יַחְדָּ	*Simul, pariter.*	Together, alike.
חדה	יִחַדְּ	*Lætabitur.*	He shall rejoice.
יחד	יַחְדָּו	*Simul, pariter.*	Together, alike.
	יַחְדּוֹ	*Jachdo.*	Jahdo, N. M.
	יַחְדַּי	*Jachdai.*	Jahdai, N. M.
	יַחְדִּיאֵל	*Jachdiel.*	Jahdiel, N. M.
	יֶחְדְּיָהוּ	*Jechdeias.*	Jehdeiah, N. M.
יחד	יַחְדָּיו יַחְדָּ	*Simul.*	Together, at once.
חדל	יַחֲדָל	*Et desine.*	And cease thou.

ROOTS.	DERIVATIVES.	VERSIO.	SIGNIFICATION.
חדל	יֶחְדַּל יֶחְדָּל	*Desistet.*	He shall forbear.
—	יַחְדָּלוּ	*Desinent.*	They will forbear.
—	יֶחְדָּלוּן	*Cessabunt.*	They shall cease.
חגג	יָחוֹגּוּ	*Titubabunt.*	They shall reel.
חוה	יְחַוֶּה	*Indicabit.*	He will shew.
חול	יָחוּל	*Manebit.*	He shall remain.
—	יְחוֹלֵל	*Parturire faciet.*	He will make to travail.
—	יְחוֹלָלוּ	*Formabuntur.*	They will be formed.
חוה	יְחַוֶּנָּה	*Indicabit eam.*	He shall shew her.
—	יְחַוֵּנִּי	*Indicabit mihi.*	He shall shew to me.
חוס	יָחוֹס	*Parcet.*	He shall spare.
חקק	יְחוֹקְקוּ	*Decernent.*	They will decree.
חור	יֶחֱוָרוּ	*Pallescet.*	He will grow pale.
חוש	יָחוּשׁ	*Festinabit.*	He will hasten.
חזה	יֶחֱזֶה	*Videbit.*	He will see.
—	יֶחֱזוּ	*Aspicient.*	They shall behold.
	יַחֲזִיאֵל	*Jachaziel.*	Jahaziel, N. M.
	יַחְזְיָה	*Jachazias.*	Jahaziah, N. M.
חזה	יֶחֱזָיוּן	*Videbunt.*	They will see.
חזק	יַחֲזִיק	*Apprehendet.*	He shall take hold.
—	יַחֲזִיקוּ	*Apprehendent.*	They shall take hold.
—	יְחַזֵּק	*Prehendet, confirmabit*	He shall take hold of, confirm
—	יֶחֱזַק	*Constans erit.*	He shall be constant.
	יְחֶזְקֵאל	*Jechezkel.*	Ezekiel, N. M.
חזק	יַחֲזִקוּ	*Apprehendent, tenebunt.*	They shall seize, hold fast.
—	יְחַזְּקוּ	*Confirmabunt, instaurabunt.*	They shall strengthen, confirm, repair.
—	יֶחֶזְקוּ	*Roborabuntur.*	They shall be strengthened.
—	יֶחֶזְקוּ	*Fortes erunt.*	They shall be strong.
—	יְחַזְּקוּם	*Confirmabunt eos.*	They shall confirm them.
	יְחִזְקִיָּה־יָהוּ	*Jechizkias.*	Jehiskiah, N. M.
	יַחְזֵרָה	*Jachzeras.*	Jahzerah, N. M.
חטא	יַחֲטָא	*Aberrabit.*	He will miss.
—	יֶחֱטָא	*Peccabit.*	He shall or will sin.
—	יֶחֶטְאוּ	*Peccabunt.*	They shall or will sin.
חטב	יַחְטְבוּ	*Cædent.*	They shall cut down.
חטא	יַחֲטִיאוּ	*Peccare facient.*	They will cause to sin.

ROOTS.	DERIVATIVES.	VERSIO.	SIGNIFICATION.
חטף	יַחְטֹף	*Rapiet.*	He will seize.
חיה	יְחִי	*Vivet.*	He shall live.
	יְחִיאֵל	*Jechiel.*	Jehiel, N. M.
	יְחִיאֵלִי	*Jechieli.*	Jehieli, N. M.
יחד	יָחִיד	*Solus, unicus.*	Only.
—	יְחִידָה	*Unica.*	Only.
—	יְחִידִים	*Solitarii.*	Solitary.
—	יְחִידְךָ־־דָךְ	*Unicus tuus.*	Thy only.
—	יְחִידָתִי	*Unicus meus.*	My only.
	יְחִיָּה	*Jechijas.*	Jehiah, N. M.
חיה	יְחָיָה	*Et vivet.*	And he shall live.
—	יְחַיֶּה	*In vita servabit.*	He will preserve alive.
—	יְחְיֶה	*Vivet.*	He shall live.
—	יְחַיּוּ	*In vita servabunt.*	They will preserve alive.
—	יְחְיוּ	*Vivent.*	They shall live.
חוט	יַחִיטוּ	*Conjungent.* [*bis.*	They shall join.
חיה	יְחַיֵּינוּ	*Vitam restituit no-*	He will revive us.
חול	יָחִיל	*Dolebit, trepidare faciet, manebit.*	He will be in pain, will cause to shake, will remain.
—	יָחִילוּ	*Dolebunt, trepida-*	They shall be in pain, shall
—	יְחִילוּן	*Dolebunt.* [*bunt.*	They shall be in pain. [tremble
חיה	יְחַיֻּנוּ	*Vivos servabunt nos.*	They will save us alive.
חוש	יָחִישׁ	*Festinabit.*	He shall make haste.
—	יָחִישָׁה	*Accelerabit.*	He shall hasten.
חתת	יְחִיתַן	*Tenebit eas.*	He shall make them afraid.
חכה	יְחַכֶּה	*Expectabit.*	He will wait.
חכם	יְחַכֵּם	*Sapientem faciet.*	He will make wise.
—	יֶחְכָּם	*Sapiens erit.*	He shall be wise.
—	יֶחְכַּם	*Sapiens efficietur.*	He shall be made wise.
—	יֶחְכָּמוּ	*Sapientes erunt.*	They shall be wise.
—	יְחַכְּמֵנוּ	*Sapientes nos faciet.*	He shall make us wise.
יָחֵל		*Expectavit, moratus est, speravit.*	He expected, waited, delayed, hoped.
חלל	יָחֵל	*Incipiet.*	He will or shall begin.
יחל	יַחֵל	*Expecta, spera.*	Wait, expect, hope thou.
חלל	יַחֵל	*Violabit.*	He will violate, break.
—	יֵחָל	*Polluetur.*	He will be polluted.

ROOTS.	DERIVATIVES.	VERSIO.	SIGNIFICATION.
	יַחְלְאֵל	*Jachleel.*	Jahleel, N. M.
	יַחְלְאֵלִי	*Jachlealitæ.*	Jahlealites, N. F.
חול	יָחִלוּ	*Manebunt.*	They will remain.
חלה	יְחַלּוּ	*Deprecabuntur.*	They shall intreat.
חלף	יַחֲלִיף	*Renovabitur.*	He shall be renewed.
—	יַחֲלִיפוּ	*Renovabunt.*	They shall renew.
—	יַחֲלִיפֶנּוּ	*Mutabit eum.*	He shall alter it.
חלץ	יַחֲלִיץ	*Expediet.*	He will prepare.
חלק	יַחֲלִיקוּן	*Blandientur.*	They will flatter.
הלל	יְחַלֵּל	*Profanabit.*	He will profane.
—	יְחַלְּלֻהוּ	*Profanabunt eum.*	They shall profane it.
—	יְחַלְּלוּ	*Profanabunt.*	They shall profane.
—	יְחַלֵּלוּ	*Violabunt.*	They will violate, break.
—	יְחַלְּלֶנּוּ	*Profanabit eum.*	He shall profane it.
חלם	יַחֲלֹם	*Somniabit.*	He will dream.
—	יַחְלְמוּ	*Revalescent.*	They will recover their health
—	יַחֲלֹמוּן	*Somniabunt.*	They shall dream.
יחל	יִחַלְנוּ	*Speravimus.*	We have hoped. [change, alter
חלף	יַחֲלֹף	*Transibit: mutabit.*	He shall pass, pass away; shall
—	יַחֲלֹפוּן	*Præteribunt.*	They shall pass away.
חלץ	יְחַלֵּץ	*Eripiet.*	He shall deliver.
—	יֵחָלְצוּ	*Eripientur.*	They shall be delivered.
—	יֵחָלֵצוּן	*Liberabuntur.*	They shall be delivered.
—	יְחַלְּצֵנִי	*Liberabit me.*	He shall deliver me.
חלק	יְחַלֵּק	*Dividet, partietur.*	He shall divide, distribute.
—	יֵחָלֵק יֵחָלֶק	*Dividetur.*	He shall be divided.
—	יַחֲלֹק	*Dividet.*	He shall divide.
—	יַחֲלֹקוּ יְחַלְּקוּ	*Divident.*	They shall divide.
יחל	יִחַלְתִּי	*Expectavi, speravi.*	I have waited, hoped.
—	יִחַלְתָּנִי	*Sperare fecisti me.*	Thou hast caused me to hope.
יָחַם		*Caluit, incaluit, excanduit; concepit.*	He was warm, grew warm, was inflamed; she conceived
—	יַחַם	*Incalescere.*	To grow warm.
חמם	יָחֹם	*Calefaciet se.*	He shall warm *himself.*
—	יָחֹם־יֵחַ״	*Calefaciet.*	He will warm.
יחם	יָחַם	*Incaluit.*	He was warm.
חמד	יַחְמֹד	*Concupiscet.*	He shall desire.

ROOTS.	DERIVATIVES.	VERSIO.	SIGNIFICATION.
חמם	יֵחַמּוּ	*Incalescent.*	They will grow warm.
חמל	יַחְמוֹל־־מֹל	*Parcet, miserebitur.*	He will spare, have pity.
חמל	יַחְמַי	*Jachmai.*	Jahmai, N. M.
—	יַחְמְלוּ	*Parcent.*	They shall spare.
חמס	יַחְמֹס	*Rapiet, abripiet.*	He shall seize, take away.
חמץ	יֶחְמָץ	*Fermentabitur.*	He will be leavened.
חמר	יֶחְמְרוּ	*Turbabuntur, lutulenti erunt.*	They will be troubled, will be foul, muddy.
יחם	יֶחֱמַתְנִי	*Concepit me.*	She conceived me.
חנן	יָחֹן	*Gratiam faciet.*	He will shew favour. [favour
—	יֻחַן	*Gratus erit.*	He will be acceptable, find
חנה	יַחֲנוּ	*Castrametabuntur.*	They shall encamp.
חנף	יַחֲנִיף	*Polluet.*	He will defile.
חנן	יְחֻנְךָּ	*Miserebitur tui.*	He will have mercy upon thee
חנך	יַחְנְכֶנּוּ	*Dedicabit eum.*	He will dedicate it.
חנן	יְחֻנַּן	*Gratiam faciet.*	He will shew favour.
—	יֶחֱנַן	*Propitius erit.*	He will be gracious.
—	יְחָנֵּנוּ	*Miserebitur nostri.*	He will be merciful to us.
—	יִתְנְנוּ	*Gratiam facient.*	They will shew favour.
—	יְחָנֶּנּוּ	*Miserebitur illius.*	He will have mercy upon him
—	יְחָנֵּנִי	*Miserebitur mei.*	He will be merciful to me.
חוס	יָחֹס	*Parcet.*	He will spare.
חסד	יְחַסֶּדְךָ	*Probro afficiet te.*	He will put thee to shame.
חסה	יֶחֱסֶה	*Sperabit, confidet.*	He will hope, trust.
—	יֶחֱסוּ	*Confident.*	They will trust.
—	יֶחֱסָיוּן	*Confident.*	They will trust.
חסר	יַחְסִיר	*Deficere faciet.* [eum	He will cause to fail.
חסל	יַחְסְלֶנּוּ	*Consumet, disperdet*	He will consume, destroy him
חסן	יֵחָסֵן	*Reponetur.*	He shall be laid up.
חסר	יֶחְסַר	*Indigebit, deficiet.*	He shall need, shall fail.
—	יֶחְסַר	*Deerit, deficiet.*	He shall be wanting, shall fail
—	יַחְסְרוּ	*Indigebunt, deficient*	They shall need, want, fail.
—	יֶחְסָרוּן	*Deerunt.*	They shall be wanting.
יחף			
—	יָחֵף	*Discalceatus.*	Unshod, barefooted.
חפז	יַחְפּוֹז	*Festinabit* [vebuntur	He will hasten.
—	יַחְפְּזוּן	*Celerabunt, commo-*	They will hasten, be hurried.

ROOTS.	DERIVATIVES.	VERSIO.	SIGNIFICATION.
חפץ	יַחְפֹּץ	*Volet.*	He will be willing.
—	יֶחְפָּץ	*Delectabitur.*	He will be delighted.
—	יַחְפְּצוּ	*Delectabuntur.*	They will be delighted.
—	יֶחְפְּצוּ	*Volent.*	They will be willing, pleased.
—	יֶחְפָּצוּן	*Delectabuntur.*	They will be delighted.
חפר	יַחְפְּרוּ	*Effodient.*	They will dig.
—	יֶחְפָּרוּ	*Erubescent.* [*bitur.*	They will be ashamed. [out.
חפש	יְחֻפַּשׂ	*Quæretur, investiga-*	He will be sought, searched
—	יַחְפְּשׂוּ	*Investigabunt.*	They will search out.
	יַחְצְאֵל--צִיאֵ	*Jachiseel.*	Jahzeel, N. M.
	יַחְצְאֵלִי	*Jachiseelitæ.*	Jahzeelites, N. F.
חצב	יֵחָצְבוּן	*Sculpentur.*	They shall be engraven.
חצה	יֶחֱצֶה	*Dividet.*	He shall divide.
—	יֵחָצוּ	*Dividentur.*	They shall be divided.
—	יֶחֱצוּ	*Bipartientur.*	They shall part in two.
—	יֶחֱצוּהוּ	*Divident eum.*	They shall divide him.
—	יֶחֱצוּן	*Divident.*	They shall divide.
חקר	יַחְקֹר	*Pervestigabit.*	He shall search out.
—	יֵחָקֵר	*Pervestigabitur.*	He shall be searched.
—	יַחְקֹר	*Quæret.*	He shall seek.
—	יַחְקְרוּ	*Quærent.*	They shall seek.
—	יַחְקְרֶנּוּ	*Scrutabitur eum.*	He shall search him out.
יָחַר		*Tardavit, moratus est.*	He delayed, tarried. [be wrath.
חרה	יִחַר	*Irascetur, ira erit.*	He will be angry, there will
חרב	יֶחֱרַב	*Exsiccabitur.*	He shall be dried up.
—	יֶחֶרְבוּ	*Vastabuntur.*	They shall be laid waste.
—	יֶחֶרְבוּ	*Desolabuntur.*	They shall be desolated.
חרד	יֶחֱרַד	*Tremet.*	He shall tremble.
—	יֶחֶרְדוּ	*Pavebunt.*	They shall be afraid.
—	יֶחֶרְדוּ	*Trement.* [*cetur.*	They shall tremble.
חרה	יֶחֱרֶה	*Excandescet, iras-*	He will grow warm, be angry.
חרר	יֵחָרוּ	*Comburentur.*	They shall be burned.
חרש	יַחֲרוֹשׁ--רֹשׁ	*Arabit.*	He shall plough.
—	יַחֲרִישׁ יֶחֱרָשׁ	*Silebit.*	He shall keep silence.
—	יַחֲרִישׁוּ	*Silere facient.*	They shall make to be silent.
חרך	יַחֲרֹךְ	*Torrebit.*	He shall roast.

ROOTS.	DERIVATIVES.	VERSIO.	SIGNIFICATION.
חרם	יָחֳרָם	*Devovebitur.*	He shall be devoted, conse-
—	יַחֲרִם	*Devovebit.*	He shall devote. [crated.
—	יָחֳרָם	*Internecioni devove-*	He shall be doomed to de-
חרף	יְחָרֵף יְחָרֵף	*Probro afficiet* [*bitur*	He shall reproach. [struction.
—	יְחָרְפוּנִי	*Exprobrabit me.*	He will reproach me. [me
—	יְחָרְפֵנִי	*Conviciabitur me.*	He will reproach, blaspheme
חרץ	יֶחֱרַץ	*Movebit.*	He will move.
חרק	יַחֲרֹק	*Frendet.*	He shall gnash.
יָחַשׂ		*Recensuit per gene-alogiam, per fa-*	He reckoned by the genealogy, or family.
חשב	יַחְשֹׁב	*Imputabit.* [*miliam.*	He will impute.
—	יַחְשֹׁב	*Cogitabit, reputabit, imputabit, excogi-tabit.*	He will think, esteem, impute, devise.
—	יֵחָשֵׁב	*Reputabitur, habe-bitur; imputabi-*	He shall be esteemed, ac-counted; it shall be imputed
—	יְחַשֵּׁב	*Excogitabit.* [*tur.*	He shall devise. [counted.
—	יֵחָשְׁבוּ	*Reputabuntur.*	They shall be esteemed, ac-
—	יַחְשְׁבוּ	*Excogitabunt.*	They shall devise.
—	יַחְשְׁבוּ	*Reputabunt.*	They shall esteem, regard.
—	יַחְשְׁבוּ	*Computabunt, exco-gitabunt.*	They will reckon, devise.
—	יַחְשְׁבוּן	*Excogitabunt.*	They will devise.
—	יַחְשְׁבֵנִי	*Reputabit me.*	He will account me.
חשה	יֶחֱשׁוּ	*Tacebunt.*	They shall hold their peace.
חשך	יַחֲשִׁיךְ יַחְ׳	*Obscurabit.*	He shall obscure, darken, hide
—	יֶחְשַׁךְ	*Caligabit.*	He shall darken.
—	יַחְשֹׂךְ	*Cohibebit, subducet.*	He will restrain, keep back.
—	יֵחָשֵׂךְ־־שֶׂךְ	*Cohibebitur, subdu-cetur.*	He shall be restrained, with-held, withdrawn.
—	יֶחְשְׁכוּ	*Obscurabuntur.*	They shall be darkened.
	יַחַת ־ַ	*Jachat.*	Jahath, N. M.
חתת	יֵחָת־־חַת	*Terrebitur, frange-tur, conteretur.*	He shall be terrified, broken, crushed.
נחת	יֵחַת	*Descendet.* [*rentur.*	He shall come down. [crushed
חתת	יֵחַתּוּ	*Terrebuntur, conte-*	They shall be terrified, broken,
נחת	יֵחַתּוּ	*Descendent.*	They will go down.

ROOTS.	DERIVATIVES.	VERSIO.	SIGNIFICATION.
חתם	יַחְתּוֹם־־תֹּם	*Obsignabit.* [*ret te.*	He will seal. [take thee away.
חתה	יַחְתְּךָ	*Conteret te; aufe-*	He shall crush thee; he shall
חתת	יְחִתֵּנִי	*Terrebit me.*	He will terrify me.
חתף	יַחְתֹּף	*Rapiet.*	He will seize, take away
חתר	יַחְתְּרוּ	*Fodient.*	They shall dig.
	יט		
יָטַב		*Fuit, vel visus est, bonus, rectus, decorus, gratus, hilaris; bene fecit.*	He was, or seemed, good, right, graceful, agreeable, cheerful; he did good, did well.
—	יִיטַב	*Bonus, gratus erit.*	He will be good, agreeable.
	יָטְבָה	*Jotba.*	Jotbah, N. P.
	יֻטָּה	*Juta.*	Juttah, N. P.
נטה	יַטֶּה יַ־	*Extendet.* [*gabitur.*	He shall extend, prolong.
טהר	יִטְהָר־־הַ־	*Mundus erit, pur-*	He shall be pure, cleansed.
נטה	יַטּוּ	*Declinabunt, divertent, porrigent, demittent.*	They will decline, turn aside, stretch forth, let down.
נטל	יִטּוֹל	*Levabit, projiciet.*	He will take up, cast.
נטר	יִטּוֹר	*Servabit.*	He will keep.
	יְטוּר	*Jetur.*	Jetur, N. M. or N.
טוש	יָטוּשׁ	*Volabit.*	He will fly.
—	יִטּוֹשׁ	*Relinquet, deseret.*	He will leave, forsake.
נטף	יִטְּפוּ־־פוּן	*Stillabunt.*	They shall drop.
נטה	יַטְּךָ	*Divertet te.*	He will turn thee aside.
נטל	יֻטָּל	*Projicietur.*	He shall be cast down.
טמא	יִטַּמָּא	*Polluet se.*	He shall defile himself.
—	יִטְמָא	*Polluetur.*	He shall be defiled.
—	יִטַּמְּאוּ	*Polluent se.*	They shall defile themselves.
—	יְטַמְּאוּ	*Polluent.*	They shall defile.
—	יִטְמְאוּ	*Polluentur.* [*eum.*	They shall be defiled. [clean.
—	יְטַמְּאֶנּוּ	*Pollutum declarabit*	He shall pronounce him un-
נטה	יַטֶּנּוּ	*Vertet, inclinabit*	He shall turn, incline him.
נטע	יִטְּעוּ	*Plantabunt.* [*eum.*	They shall plant.
טעם	יִטְעַם	*Gustabit.*	He shall taste.
—	יִטְעֲמוּ	*Gustabunt.*	They shall taste.

ROOTS.	DERIVATIVES.	VERSIO.	SIGNIFICATION.
טעם	יַטְעִמוּן	*Gustare facient.*	They shall make to taste.
—	יַטְעִמוּנֶה	*Cibabunt eum.*	They shall feed him.
נטף	יַטִּפוּ	*Stillabunt.*	They shall drop.
טרח	יַטְרִיחַ	*Fatigabit.* [*tur.*	He will weary.
טרף	יִטָּרֵף	*Rapietur, discerpe-*	He will be seized, torn in pieces
—	יִטְרֹף־־רֹף	*Rapiet.*	He will seize, plunder.
נטש	יִטֹּשׁ	*Deseret, relinquet.*	He will forsake, leave.
—	יִטְּשֵׁנוּ	*Deseret nos.*	He will forsake us.
	יי		
יבש	יִיבַשׁ	*Exarescet.* [*ectur.*	He will become dry, wither.
יגע	יִיגַע	*Laborabit, defetis-*	He shall labour, shall be weary
—	יִיגְעוּ	*Defetiscentur.*	They shall be weary.
ידע	יֵידַע	*Sciet.*	He shall know.
יחל	יְיַחֵל	*Expectabit.* [*bunt.*	He shall wait.
—	יְיַחֲלוּ־־לוּן	*Expectabunt, spera-*	They shall wait, shall hope.
יטב	יִיטַב־־טַב	*Bonus videbitur.*	He shall seem good.
—	יִיטַב	*Bene, melius erit.*	It will be well, better.
—	יֵיטִיב	*Placebit, exhilarabit*	He will please, will make
—	יֵיטִיב יֵיטִיב	*Bonum faciet.*	He shall do good. [cheerful.
—	יֵיטִיבוּ	*Benefacient.*	They will do good.
ילל	יְיֵלִיל	*Ejulabit, ululabit.*	He shall shriek, howl.
—	יְיֵלִילוּ	*Ejulabunt, ululabunt*	They shall shriek, howl.
יין			
—	יַיִן יֵין יֵין יֵין	*Vinum.*	Wine.
—	יֵינָהּ	*Vinum ejus.*	Her wine.
—	יֵינִי	*Vinum meum.*	My wine.
—	יֵינֶךָ־־נֵךְ	*Vinum tuum.*	Thy wine.
—	יֵינָם	*Vinum eorum.*	Their wine.
ינק	יִינַק	*Suget.*	He shall suck.
—	יִינְקוּ	*Sugent.*	They shall suck.
יסד	יְיַסְּדֶנָּה	*Fundabit eam, fundamentum ejus ponet*	He shall found her, shall lay her foundation.
יסך	יִיסָךְ	*Ungetur.*	He shall be anointed.
יסר	יְיַסֵּר	*Erudiet, castigabit.*	He shall discipline, chasten.
יעד	יִיעָדֶנָּה	*Desponsabit eam.*	He shall betroth her.
—	יִיעַף	*Fatigabitur.*	He will be weary.

ROOTS.	DERIVATIVES.	VERSIO.	SIGNIFICATION.
יעף	יִעֲפוּ יָעֵ״	*Fatigabuntur.*	They will be weary.
יפה	יְיַפֵּהוּ	*Ornabit eum.*	He shall adorn him.
ירא	יִירָא	*Timebit.*	He shall fear.
—	יִירְאוּ־־ךָ״	*Timebunt.*	They shall fear.
—	יִירָאוּךָ	*Timebunt te.*	They shall fear thee.
ירה	יִיָּרֶה	*Confodietur.* [*bit.*	He shall be shot through.
ירש	יִירַשׁ־־רֶ׳	*Hæres erit, posside-*	He shall possess.
—	יְיָרֵשׁ	*Jure hæreditario possidebit.*	He shall possess by hereditary right.
—	יִירְשׁוּ־־רָ״	*Possidebunt.*	They shall possess, inherit.
—	יִירָשׁוּהָ	*Possidebunt eam.*	They shall possess it.
—	יִירָשׁוּם	*Possidebunt eos.*	They shall possess them.
—	יִירָשְׁךָ־־שֶׁךָּ	*Possidebit.*	He shall possess thee.
—	יִירָשֵׁם	*Possidebit eos.*	He shall possess them.
ישר	יְיַשְּׁרוּ	*Dirigent.*	They shall direct.
ישן	יִישַׁן	*Dormiet.*	He shall sleep.
ישר	יִישַׁר	*Rectus erit.*	He will be right.
—	יְיַשֵּׁר־־שֶּׁר	*Diriget.*	He shall direct.
	יכ		
יד׳	יַד	*Juxta.*	Near to.
נכה	יַךְ	*Percutiet.*	He will smite. [pain.
כאב	יִכְאַב־־אָב	*Dolebit.*	He will be sorrowful, be in
—	יַכְאִיב	*Dolore afficiet.*	He will make sorrowful.
כבד	יְכַבֵּד	*Honorabit.*	He will honour.
—	יִכְבַּד	*Gravis, gravior erit.*	He will be heavy, heavier.
—	יְכֻבַּד	*Honorabitur.*	He shall be honoured, glorified
—	יִכָּבֵד	*Honorabitur.*	He shall be glorified.
—	יְכַבְּדוּ	*Honorabunt.*	They shall honour.
—	יִכְבְּדוּ	*Honorabiles erunt.*	They shall be honourable.
—	יְכַבְּדוּךָ	*Honorabunt te.*	They shall honour thee.
—	יְכַבְּדָנְנִי	*Honorabit me.*	He shall glorify me. [out.
כבה	יִכְבֶּה	*Extinguetur.*	He shall be extinguished, put
כבש	יִכְבּוֹשׁ	*Subiget.*	He will subdue.
כבה	יְכַבֶּנָּה	*Extinguet eam.*	He shall quench it.
כבס	יְכַבֵּס	*Lavabit.* [*cabit*	He shall wash.
כבר	יַכְבִּר	*Abundabit, multipli-*	He will abound, multiply.

ROOTS.	DERIVATIVES.	VERSIO.	SIGNIFICATION.
נכה	יַכֶּה	*Percutiet.*	He will smite. [fail.
כהה	יִכְהֶה	*Caligabitur, deficiet.*	He shall be darkened, shall
נכה	יַכֻּהוּ	*Percutient eum.*	They shall smite him.
כהן	יְכַהֵן	*Ornabit se instar sa-*	He shall deck himself like a
נכה	יַכּוּ	*Percutient.* [*cerdotis*	They shall smite. [priest.
—	יַכּוּךָ	*Percutient te.*	They shall smite thee.
יכל	יָכוֹל--כֹּל	*Potuit, prævaluit; prævalendo.*	He was able, prevailed; in prevailing.
כון	יִכּוֹן	*Stabilietur.* [*entur.*	He shall be established.
—	יִכּוֹנוּ--כֹּנוּ	*Dirigentur, stabili-*	They shall be directed, esta-
—	יְכוֹנֵן	*Stabiliet.*	He shall establish. [blished.
—	יְכוֹנְנֶהָ	*Stabiliet eam.*	He shall establish her.
כזב	יְכַזֵּב	*Mentietur.*	He will lie.
—	יְכַזְּבוּ	*Mentientur, mendaces comperientur.*	They will lie, will be found liars.
—	יַכְזִיבֵנִי	*Mendacii arguet me.*	He will prove me a liar.
יָכַח		*Demonstravit, probavit, disceptavit, arguit, increpavit, corripuit, castiga-*	He demonstrated, proved, reasoned, argued, reproved, corrected; chastised.
כחד	יְכֻחַד	*Celabitur.* [*vit.*	He will be concealed.
—	יַכְחִידֶנָּה	*Abscondet eum.*	He will hide her or it.
כחש	יְכַחֶשׁ	*Deficiet, mentietur.*	He will fail, will lie.
—	יְכַחֲשׁוּ	*Mentientur.*	They will lie.
כול	יָכִיל	*Continebit.*	He will contain.
—	יְכִילוּ	*Capient, sustinebunt*	They will hold, sustain.
—	יְכִילֶנּוּ	*Sustinebit eum.*	He will sustain him.
	יָכִין	*Jachin.* [*get.*	Jachin, N. M. Col.
כון	יָכִין	*Parabit, aptabit, diri-*	He shall prepare, fit, direct.
בון	יָבִין	*Considerabit.*	He will consider.
נכר	יַכִּיר	*Noscet, agnoscet.*	He shall know, acknowledge.
—	יַכִּירוּם	*Agnoscent eos.*	They shall acknowledge them
—	יַכִּירֵנוּ	*Agnoscet nos.*	He will acknowledge us.
—	יַכִּירֶנּוּ	*Cognoscet eum.*	He shall know him.
נכה	יַכְּכָה--כֶּכָּ׳	*Percutiet te.*	He will smite thee.
יָכֹל		*Potuit, prævaluit.*	He could, was able, prevailed.
—	יָכֹל	*Potens.*	Being able.

ROOTS.	DERIVATIVES.	VERSIO.	SIGNIFICATIO N.
כלה	יְכַל	*Absumetur.*	He shall be consumed.
יכל	יְכַל	*Poterit.*	He will be able.
—	יָכְלָה	*Potuit.*	She could, was able.
כלה	יְכַלֶּה	*Consumet.*	He shall consume.
—	יִכְלֶה	*Deficiet, consumetur*	He shall fail, be consumed.
יכל	יָכְלוּ	*Potuerunt, præva-*	They were able, prevailed.
כול	יָכִלוּ	*Continebunt [luerunt*	They will hold, contain.
יכל	יָכְלוּ	*Potuerunt. [ment.*	They were able. [sume.
כלה	יְכַלּוּ	*Absolvent, consu-*	They shall finish, spend, con-
יכל	יָכְלוּ־כִי	*Poterunt, prævale-*	They shall be able, shall pre-
כלה	יִכְלוּ	*Absumentur. [bunt.*	They shall be consumed. [vail
	יְכָלְיָהוּ	*Jecolia.*	Jecoliah, N. W.
כלה	יִכְלְיוּן	*Deficient.*	They shall fail.
כלם	יַכְלִים	*Pudore afficiet.*	He shall make ashamed.
יכל	יְכָלִין	*Potentes. [alet.*	Being able. [feed.
כול	יְכַלְכֵּל	*Sustinebit, continebit,*	He will sustain, hold in, guide.
—	יְכַלְכְּלֻהוּ	*Continebunt eum.*	They will contain him.
—	יְכַלְכְּלוּךָ־לְךָ	*Continebunt te.*	He will sustain, nourish thee.
—	יְכַלְכְּלֶךָּ	*Sustentabit te.*	They will contain thee.
כלם	יִכָּלֵמוּ	*Pudore afficientur.*	They will be confounded.
יכל	יָכֹלְתָּ	*Potuisti.*	Thou couldst, wast able.
—	יְכֹלֶת	*Posse.*	To be able.
—	יָכֹלְתִּי	*Potui, prævalui.*	I was able, prevailed.
—	יְכָלְתִּיו	*Prævalui contra il-*	I have prevailed against him.
נכה	יַכֵּם	*Percutiet eos. [lum.*	He shall smite them.
כנה	יְכַנֶּה	*Cognominabit.*	He shall surname.
נכה	יַכֶּנּוּ	*Percutiet eum.*	He shall smite him.
	יְכָנְיָה־הוּ	*Jeconias.*	Jeconiah, N. M.
כנע	יַכְנִיעֵם	*Deprimet eos.*	He shall bring them down.
כנס	יְכַנֵּס	*Congregabit.*	He shall assemble. [humbled.
כנע	יִכָּנַע	*Abjiciet se.*	He shall abase himself, be
כנף	יִכָּנֵף	*Aufugiet, procul a- movebitur.*	He shall flee away, shall be re- moved far off.
כסה	יְכַסֶּה	*Teget, celabit.*	He shall cover, hide.
—	יְכֻסֶּה	*Tegetur.*	He shall be covered.
—	יְכַסּוּ	*Tegent.*	They shall cover.
—	יְכַסְיוּמוֹ	*Teget eos.*	He shall cover them.

ROOTS.	DERIVATIVES.	VERSIO.	SIGNIFICATIO N.
כסף	יִכְסוֹף	*Appetet.*	He will desire.
כסה	יְכַסְיֻמוּ	*Operient eos.*	They will cover them.
—	יְכַסֵּךְ יְכַסְּךָ	*Operiet te.*	He shall cover thee.
כסם	יִכְסְמוּ	*Tondebunt.*	They shall poll.
כסה	יְכַסֶּנָּה	*Operiet eam.*	He shall cover it.
—	יְכַסֶּנּוּ	*Operiet eum.*	He shall cover him.
כעס	יַכְעִיסֻהוּ	*Ad iram provocabunt eum.*	They will provoke him to anger.
כפה	יִכְפֶּה	*Sedabit, placabit,*	He will calm, pacify, turn away
כפר	יְכַפֵּר יְכַפֶּר	*Expiabit.* [*avertet.*	He shall make atonement.
—	יְכֻפַּר	*Expiabitur.*	He shall be purged, cleansed.
—	יְכַפְּרֶנָּה	*Placabit eam.*	He will pacify it.
כרה	יִכָּרֶה	*Fodietur.*	He shall be digged.
—	יִכְרֶה	*Fodiet.* [*tur.*	He shall dig. [banquet.
—	יִכְרוּ	*Concident, epulabun-*	They shall cut up, shall feast,
כרת	יַכְרִית־־רַת	*Excindet.*	He shall cut off.
כרסם	יְכַרְסְמֶנָּה	*Vastabit eam.*	He will lay it waste.
כרע	יִכְרַע	*Incurvabit se.*	He will bow down.
—	יִכְרְעוּ־־עוּן	*Incurvabunt se.*	They shall bow themselves.
כרת	יִכָּרֵת	*Excindetur, deficiet*	He shall be cut off, shall fail.
—	יִכָּרְתוּ יִכָּרֵ״־תוּן	*Excindentur.*	They shall be cut off.
—	יִכְרֹתוּ	*Pangent* fœdus.	They will make *a covenant.*
כשל	יַכְשׁוּלוּ	*Corruere facient.*	They will cause to fall.
—	יַכְשִׁילֻךָ	*Impingere facient te*	They will make thee stumble.
—	יִכָּשֵׁל	*Corruet.*	He shall fall.
—	יִכָּשְׁלוּ יִכָּשֵׁלוּ	*Impingent, corruent*	They will stumble, shall fall.
—	יִכָּשְׁלוּ	*Et impingent.*	And they shall stumble.
כשר	יִכְשַׁר	*Rectum erit.*	It will be right.
כתת	יֻכַּת	*Contundetur, confringetur.*	He will be beaten down, broken to pieces.
כתב	יִכָּתֵב	*Scribetur.*	It shall be written.
—	יִכְתֹּב	*Scribet, subscribet.*	He shall write, subscribe.
—	יִכָּתֵבוּ	*Scribentur*	They shall be written.
—	יִכְתְּבֵם	*Scribet eos.*	He shall write them.
כתת	יֻכָּתוּ יֻכַּתּוּ	*Contundentur, confringentur.*	They shall be beaten down, broken to pieces.

ROOTS.	DERIVATIVES.	VERSIO.	SIGNIFICATION.
כתר	יַכְתִּירוּ יַכְתְּרוּ	*Circumdabunt, coronabunt.*	They shall compass about, shall crown.
	יל		
לבב	יִלָּבֵב	*Cordatus erit.*	He shall be wise.
לבט	יִלָּבֵט	*Impinget, cadet.*	He shall stumble, fall.
לבן	יַלְבִּינוּ	*Albescent.*	They shall become white.
לבש	יִלְבַּשׁ־־בָּשׁ	*Induet se, vestietur.*	He shall clothe himself, be clothed.
—	יִלְבְּשׁוּ־־בָּשׁוּ	*Induent.*	They shall put on.
—	יַלְבִּשׁוּ	*Et vestientur.*	And they shall be clothed.
—	יַלְבִּשֵׁם	*Induet eos.*	He shall put them on.
יָלַד		*Genuit, generavit,* sicut mas; *peperit,* sicut fœm. *germinare fecit, natus est; censuit familiam suam.*	He begat, procreated; she bare, brought forth; he caused to bring forth, was born, reckoned his family.
—	יָלֻד	*Natus.*	Born, a child.
—	יֵלֵד	*Pariet.*	He shall bring forth.
—	יֶלֶד	*Natus, puer, adolescens.*	A child, boy, young man.
—	יֹלֵד	*Gignens, parturiens*	Begetting, travailing.
—	יָלְדָה יָלָדָה	*Peperit.*	She bare; brought forth.
—	יֻלְּדָה	*Nata est.*	She was born.
—	יָלְדוּ יָלָ׳ יֻלְ׳	*Genuerunt, pepererunt.*	They begat, bare, brought forth.
—	יְלָדוֹ	*Genuit eum.*	He hath begotten him.
—	יֻלְּדוּ יִוָּלְדוּ	*Nati sunt.*	They were born.
—	יֵלֵדוּן	*Parient.*	They shall bring forth.
—	יְלָדַי	*Nati mei.*	My children, sons.
—	יַלְדֵי	*Nati.*	The children.
—	יְלָדֵי	*Filii.*	Sons.
—	יְלָדֶיהָ	*Nati ejus.*	Her children.
—	יַלְדֵיהֶן	*Nati, pulli eorum.*	Their children, their young ones.
—	יְלָדָיו־־דָו	*Nati ejus.*	His children.
—	יֹלְדָיו	*Parentes ejus.*	His parents.
—	יְלָדִים	*Nati, pueri.*	Children, boys.
—	יְלָדֶךָ־־דְךָ	*Genuit te.*	He begat thee.
—	יָלַדְנוּ	*Peperimus.*	We have brought forth.

ROOTS.	DERIVATIVES.	VERSIO.	SIGNIFICATION.
• ילד	יָלַדְתְּ יָלַ־־תִּי	*Peperisti.*	Thou hast born, brought forth.
—	יֹלֶדֶת	*Pariens.*	She that beareth, bringeth forth.
—	יְלָדַתּוּ	*Peperit eum.*	She hath born him.
—	יָלַדְתִּי יָלַ	*Peperi.*	I bare, have born.
—	יֻלַּדְתִּי	*Natus sum.*	I was born.
—	יְלִדְתִּיהוּ	*Genui eum.*	I have begotten him.
—	יְלִדְתִּיךָ	*Genui te.*	I have begotten thee.
—	יְלָדַתְךָ יְלָדַ־	*Peperit te.*	She hath born thee.
—	יַלְדֻתֶךָ	*Juventus tua.*	Thy youth.
—	יֻלַּדְתֶּם	*Nati estis.*	Ye were born.
—	יְלָדַתְנִי	*Peperit me.*	She bare me.
—	יְלִדְתָּנִי	*Peperisti nos.*	Thou hast born us.
—	יְלִדְתַּנִי	*Peperisti me.*	Thou hast born me.
—	יִלּוֹד	*Natus.*	Born.
לוה	יִלָּוֶה	*Adjungetur.*	He will be joined to.
—	יַלְוְךָ	*Commodabit tibi.*	He shall lend to thee.
	יָלוֹן	*Jalon.*	Jalon, N. M.
לוה	יִלָּוֶנּוּ	*Adhærebit ei.*	He shall cleave to him.
לח	יָלֻזוּ	*Decedent.*	They shall depart.
לחך	יְלַחֲכוּ יְלַחֵכוּ	*Lambent, delingent.*	They shall lick, lick up.
לחם	יִלָּחֵם יִלָּחֶם	*Pugnabit.*	He shall fight.
לחץ	יִלְחָצֻנִי	*Opprimet me.*	He will oppress me.
לטש	יִלְטוֹשׁ	*Acuet.*	He will sharpen.
ילד	יִלִּיד	*Natus.*	He that is born.
—	יְלִידֵי	*Nati.*	They that are born.
לח	יַלִּיזוּ	*Decedent.*	They shall depart.
לון	יָלִין	*Pernoctabit, commorabitur.*	He will pass the night, will remain.
—	יָלִינוּ	*Pernoctabunt, commorabuntur, pernoctare facient.*	They will pass the night, remain, lodge, cause to stay all night.
לוץ	יָלִיץ	*Illudet, deridebit.*	He will mock, deride, scorn.
יָלַךְ		*Ambulavit, ivit, venit, abiit, duxit, adduxit, deduxit, abstulit.*	He walked, went, came, departed, carried, brought, led, carried away.
—	יֵלֵךְ יֵלֶךְ	*Ibit, ambulabit, abibit.*	He will go, walk, depart.
לכד	יִלָּכֵד יִלָּכֶד	*Capietur.*	He shall be taken.

ROOTS.	DERIVATIVES.	VERSIO.	SIGNIFICATION.
לכד	יִלָּכְדוּ־־כְדוּן	*Capientur.*	They shall be taken.
—	יִלְכְּדוּ יִלְכֹּדוּ	*Capient.*	They shall take, catch.
—	יִלְכְּדֶנָּה	*Capiet eam.*	He shall take her.
—	יִלְכְּדֶנּוּ	*Capiet eum.*	He shall catch him.
—	יִלְכְּדֻנוֹ	*Irretient eum.*	They shall entangle, ensnare [him.
ילך	יֵלְכוּ יֵלֵכוּ־־כוּן	*Ibunt, ambulabunt.*	They shall go, walk.
לכד	יִלְכּוֹד	*Capiet.*	He shall take.
יָלַל		*Ejulavit, ululavit.*	He cried out, shrieked, howled
—	יְלֵל יְלָלַת	*Ejulatus.*	Howling.
—	יְלָלָתָהּ	*Ejulatus ejus.*	Her howling.
למד	יְלַמֵּד	*Docebit.*	He shall teach.
—	יִלְמַד	*Discet.*	He shall learn.
—	יְלַמְּדוּ־־מֵּדוּן	*Docebunt.*	They shall teach.
—	יִלְמְדוּ־־דוּן	*Discent.*	They shall learn.
לוע	יָלַע	*Deglutiet.*	He will swallow down, devour.
לעג	יִלְעַג יִלְעָג	*Irridet, subsannabit*	He will mock, laugh to scorn.
—	יִלְעֲגוּ יַלְעִיגוּ	*Subsannabit.*	They will laugh to scorn.
ילף			
—	יַלֶּפֶת	*Impetigo.*	A ring-worm, a tetter.
לפת	יִלָּפְתוּ	*Inclinabunt.*	They will bow, turn.
ילק			
לקק	יָלֹק	*Linget, lambet.*	He will lick, lap.
ילק	יֶלֶק	*Bruchus,* species lo- [custæ.	A canker worm, *a species of* [*locust.*
לקק	יָלֹקּוּ	*Lingent.*	They will lick.
לקט	יְלַקְּטוּ־קְטוּן	*Colligent.*	They will gather.
לקש	יְלַקֵּשׁוּ	*Vindemiabunt.*	They will gather the vintage.
	ים		
ים			
—	יָם יַם יַמָּא	*Mare; occidens.*	The sea; the west, western.
מאן	יְמָאֵן	*Renuet.*	He will refuse.
—	יְמָאֲנוּ	*Renuent.*	They will refuse.
מאס	יִמְאָס	*Spernet; abhorrebit*	He will despise, abhor.
—	יִמְאַס	*Abjiciet.*	He will cast away.
מסס	יִמָּאֲסוּ	*Colliquescent.*	They shall melt away.
מאס	יִמְאָסוּן	*Abjicient.*	They shall cast away.
—	יִמְאָסֵם	*Rejiciet, abjiciet eos*	He will reject, cast them away

ROOTS.	DERIVATIVES.	VERSIO.	SIGNIFICATION.
מגר	יְמַגֵּר	*Perdet.*	He shall destroy.
מדד	יִמַּד	*Mensurabitur.*	He will be measured.
—	יִמַּדּוּ	*Mensurabuntur.*	They shall be measured.
ים	יָמָּה	*Ad mare; versus oc-*	To the sea; toward the west.
—	יַמָּהּ	*Mare ejus.* [*cidentem*	Her sea.
מהר	יְמַהֵר	*Festinabit, accelera-*	He will make haste, hasten.
—	יְמַהֲרוּ	*Festinabunt.* [*bit.*	They shall make haste.
—	יִמְהָרֶנָּה	*Dotabit eam.*	He shall endow her.
	יְמוּאֵל	*Jemuel.*	Jemuel, N. M.
מוט	יִמּוֹט	*Dimovebitur.*	He will be moved, removed.
—	יִמּוֹטוּ יִמּוֹטוּ	*Declinabunt, vacil-* *labunt, labentur.*	They will bend, totter, slip, slide.
מוך	יָמוּךְ	*Depauperabitur.*	He shall be impoverished.
מול	יִמּוֹל	*Circumcidetur.*	He shall be circumcised.
—	יְמוֹלֵל	*Excidetur.*	He shall be cut off.
מוש	יָמוּשׁ	*Discedet.*	He shall depart.
—	יָמוּשׁוּ יָמֻשׁוּ	*Discedent.*	They shall depart.
מות	יָמוּת יָמֻת	*Morietur.*	He shall die.
יום	יְמוֹת	*Dies.*	The days.
מות	יָמוּתוּ יְמוּתוּן	*Morientur.*	They will die. [stroyed.
מחה	יִמַּח	*Delebitur, abolebitur*	He shall be blotted out, de-
מחא	יְמַחֵא	*Percutiet.*	He will smite.
—	יִמְחֲאוּ	*Complodent* manus.	They shall clap *their hands.*
מחה	יִמְחֶה	*Terget, absterget.*	He will wipe, wipe off.
—	יִמָּחוּ	*Delebuntur.*	They shall be blotted out.
מחץ	יִמְחָץ־חֵץ	*Transfodiet, profun-* *dum infliget vul-*	He shall thrust through, in- flict a deep wound.
מטא	יִמְטֵא	*Pertinget.* [*nus.*	He will reach.
מטר	יַמְטֵר	*Pluet, pluere fecit.*	He shall rain, cause to rain.
יום	יָמַי יָמַי	*Dies mei.*	My days.
—	יְמֵי יָמִים	*Dies.*	The days.
—	יָמֶיהָ	*Dies ejus.*	Her days.
—	יְמֵיהֶם	*Dies eorum.*	Their days.
—	יָמָיו יָמָו	*Dies ejus.*	His days.
מוט	יָמִיטוּ	*Dimovebunt.*	They shall remove.
יום	יָמֶיךָ יָמֶיךָ	*Dies tui.*	Thy days.
—	יְמֵיכֶם	*Dies vestri.*	Your days.

ROOTS.	DERIVATIVES.	VERSIO.	SIGNIFICATION.
ים	יַמִּים	*Maria.*	Seas.
יום	יָמִימָה	*In dies.*	*From days* to days.
	יְמִימָה	*Jemima.*	Jemima, N. W.
	יָמִין	*Jamin.*	Jamin, N. M.
ימן	יָמִין יְמִין	*Dextera.*	The right hand.
יום	יָמֵינוּ	*Dies nostri.*	Our days.
ימן	יְמִינוֹ	*Dextera ejus.*	His right hand.
	יְמִינִי	*Jaminitæ.*	Jaminites, N. F.
	יְמִינִי	*Benjamita.*	Benjamite, N. F.
ימן	יְמִינִי	*Dextera mea.*	*My right* hand.
—	יְמִינְךָ--נֶךָ	*Dextera tua.*	Thy right hand.
—	יְמִינָם	*Dextera eorum.*	Their right hand.
מוק	יָמִיקוּ	*Contabescent.*	They shall waste away.
מור	יָמִיר	*Mutabit, commutabit*	He shall change, exchange.
—	יְמִירֶנּוּ	*Mutabit illum.*	He shall change him.
מוש	יָמִישׁ	*Discedet, amovebit.*	He shall depart, remove.
—	יְמִישׁוּן	*Palpabunt.*	They shall feel, grope.
מות	יָמִית	*Interficiet.*	He will slay.
—	יְמִיתֻנוּ	*Occident nos.* [*metur*	They will kill us. [low.
מכך	יָמֹךְ	*Attenuabitur, depri-*	He will be impaired, brought
מכר	יִמָּכֵר	*Vendetur.*	He shall be sold.
—	יִמְכֹּר--כֹּר	*Vendet.*	He shall sell.
—	יִמָּכְרוּ	*Vendentur.*	*They shall be sold.*
—	יִמְכְּרוּ	*Vendent.*	They shall sell.
נמל	יִמַּל	*Excindetur.*	He shall be cut off.
מלא	יִמָּלֵא	*Implebitur.*	He shall be filled.
—	יְמַלֵּא	*Implebit, complebit,*	He shall fill, fulfil, consecrate.
	יִמְלָא--לָה	*Imlas.* [*consecrabit.*	Imlah, N. M.
מלא	יִמָּלְאוּ--און	*Implebuntur.*	They shall be filled.
—	יִמְלְאוּ	*Implebunt.*	They shall fill. [plished.
—	יִמָּלְאוּ	*Complebuntur.*	They shall be fulfilled, accom-
—	יְמַלֵּה	*Implebit.*	He will fill.
נמל	יִמָּלוּ	*Succidentur.*	They shall be cut off.
מלך	יִמְלוֹךְ--לֹךְ--לֹךְ	*Regnabit.*	He shall reign.
מלט	יִמָּלֵט	*Evadet, eripietur.*	He shall escape, be delivered.
—	יְמַלֵּט	*Eripiet, liberabit.*	He will rescue, deliver.
—	יְמַלְּטֵהוּ	*Liberabit eum.*	He shall deliver him.

ROOTS.	DERIVATIVES.	VERSIO.	SIGNIFICATION.
מלט	יִמָּלְטוּ	*Evadent.*	They shall escape.
	יַמְלֵךְ	*Jamlec.*	Jamlech, N. M.
מלך	יִמְלְכוּ	*Regnabunt.*	They shall reign.
מלל	יְמַלֵּל	*Loquetur.*	He will speak, utter.
—	יְמַלֵּל	*Loquetur.*	He shall speak.
ימם			
יָמַן		*Dextera usus est, versus dexteram profectus est.*	He used the right hand, went towards the right.
	יִמְנָה	*Imnas.*	Imnah, N. M.
מנה	יִמָּנֶה	*Numerabitur.*	He shall be numbered. [bered
—	יִמָּנוּ	*Supputabuntur.*	They shall be reckoned, num-
	יִמְנָע	*Imna.*	Imna, N. M.
מנע	יִמְנַע	*Cohibebit, prohibebit.*	He will withhold, forbid.
—	יִמְנָעֵנִי	*Cohibebit me.* [bescet	He will withhold me.
מסס	יִמַּס יִמָּס	*Colliquescet, conta-*	He will melt, pine, waste away
	יַם־סוּף	*Jam-suph.*	The Red Sea, P. N.
מעט	יִמְעַט	*Minuetur.*	He shall be diminished.
—	יִמְעַט	*Parvus erit.*	He will be little.
—	יִמְעָטוּ	*Minuentur.*	They shall be diminished.
—	יַמְעִיט	*Minuet, minimum colliget.* [cabitur.	He shall diminish, shall gather least. [unfaithfully.
מעל	יִמְעַל	*Delinquet, prævari-*	He will fail, transgress, act
מצא	יִמָּצֵא	*Invenietur, deprehendetur, sufficiet.*	He shall be found, found out, will be sufficient.
—	יִמְצָא	*Inveniet, deprehendet, occurret, ac-*	He will find, find out, meet with, come to, befal.
—	יִמְצָאֵהוּ־אֶנָּה	*Inveniet eum.* [cidet.	He will find him.
—	יַמְצִאֵהוּ	*Accidere faciet eum.*	He will cause it to happen.
—	יִמְצָאֻהוּ	*Invenient eum.*	They shall find him.
—	יִמְצְאוּ־־צָאוּ	*Invenient.*	They shall find.
—	יִמָּצְאוּן	*Invenientur.*	They shall be found.
—	יִמְצָאוּנְהָ	*Invenient eam.*	They will find her.
—	יִמְצָאֲךָ־־אֶכָּה	*Inveniet te.*	He will find thee.
מצא	יַמְצִאֶנּוּ	*Invenire faciet eum.*	He shall cause him to find.
—	יִמְצָאֻנְנִי	*Invenient me.*	They will find me.
מצה	יִמָּצֶה	*Exprimetur.*	He shall be wrung out.

ROOTS.	DERIVATIVES.	VERSIO.	SIGNIFICATION.
מצה	יִמָּצוּ	*Exprimentur.* [*gent.*	They shall be wrung out. [out
—	יָמֹצּוּ	*Exprimenl, exsu-*	They shall wring out, suck
מקק	יִמַּקּוּ. יִמֹּקּוּ	*Contabescent.*	They shall pine away.
יָמַר		*Gloriatus est, extu-lit, mutavit, com-mutavit.*	He boasted, exalted, changed, altered, exchanged.
—	יָמֵר יָמַר	*Mutabit, commutabit*	He shall change, exchange.
מרר	יֵמַר	*Amarus erit.*	He shall be bitter.
מרה	יַמְרֶה	*Rebellavit.*	He will rebel.
	יִמְרָה	*Imrae.* [*tabunt.*	Imrah, N. M.
מרה	יַמְרוּ	*Exacerbabunt, irri-*	They will exasperate, provoke
—	יַמְרוּהוּ	*Irritabunt eum.*	They will provoke him.
אמר	יֹמְרוּךָ	*Obloquentur tibi.*	They will speak against thee.
מרט	יִמָּרֵט	*Depilabitur.*	He will be made bold.
מרץ	יַמְרִיצְךָ	*Confirmabit te.*	He will embolden thee.
משך	יִמְשׁוֹךְ	*Trahet.*	He shall draw.
משל	יִמְשׁוֹל	*Dominabitur.*	He shall rule.
משח	יִמְשַׁח	*Unget.*	He shall anoint.
—	יִמְשָׁחוּ	*Ungent se.*	They shall anoint themselves.
משך	יִמָּשֵׁכוּ	*Protrahentur, pro-longabuntur.*	They shall be protracted, pro-longed.
משל	יִמְשָׁל--שֹׁל	*Dominabitur, potes-tatem habebit, pa-rabolice loquetur.*	He shall rule, have dominion, speak in parables.
—	יִמְשְׁלוּ--שְׁלוּ	*Dominabuntur, pro-verbium dicent.*	They shall rule, reign, utter a proverb.
משה	יַמְשֵׁנִי	*Extrahet me.*	He shall draw me out.
משש	יְמֻשֵּׁנִי	*Palpabit me.*	He shall feel me.
משש	יְמַשֵּׁשׁ	*Palpabit.*	He will feel, grope.
—	יְמַשְׁשׁוּ	*Palpabunt.*	They will feel, grope.
מות	יָמֻתוּ יְמֻתוּן	*Morientur.*	They will die.
—	יְמִתֶנּוּ	*Interficiet eum.*	He will kill him.
מתק	יִמְתָּקוּ	*Dulces erunt.*	They will be sweet.
	ין		
נאף	יִנְאַף	*Adulterium commit-*	He will commit adultery.
נאץ	יְנָאֵץ	*Spernet.* [*tet.*	He will despise.

ROOTS.	DERIVATIVES.	VERSIO.	SIGNIFICATION.
נאץ	יִנְאַץ	*Respuet, conviciabi-*	He will reject, blaspheme.
—	יְנַאֲצוּן	*Contemnent.* [*tur.*	They will contemn, despise.
—	יְנַאֲצֻנִי	*Irritabunt me.*	They will provoke me.
נאק	יִנְאָקוּ	*Clamabunt, gement.*	They will cry out, groan.
נבא	יִנָּבֵא	*Vaticinabitur.*	He shall prophesy.
נגח	יְנַגַּח	*Cornu feriet.*	He shall push with the horn.
נגע	יִנָּגֵעוּ	*Percutientur, plagis afficientur.*	They shall be smitten, plagued.
נגף	יִנָּגֵף	*Percutietur.*	He shall be smitten.
נדד	יְנִדֻּהוּ	*Fugabunt eum.*	They shall chase him away.
ידע	יִנְדְּעוּן	*Cognoscent.* [*afflixit.*	They shall know.
יָגָה		*Pressit, oppressit,*	He pressed, oppressed, afflicted
נהג	יְנַהֵג ,יִנְהַג	*Ducet, deducet.*	He shall lead, guide.
—	יְנַהֵג	*Abducet.*	He shall lead away.
—	יְנַהֲגוּ	*Abducent.*	They shall lead away.
—	יְנַהֶגְךָ	*Deducet te.*	He shall lead thee.
—	יְנַהֲגֵם	*Deducet eos.*	He shall lead them.
—	יְנַהֲגֵנוּ	*Deducet nos.*	He will guide us.
נהל	יְנַהֵל	*Ducet leniter.*	He will gently lead.
—	יְנַהֲלֵם	*Ducet eos.*	He will lead them.
—	יְנַהֲלֵנִי	*Ducet me.*	He will lead me.
נהק	יִנְהֲקוּ	*Rudent.*	They will bray.
נהר	יִנְהֲרוּ	*Confluent.*	They shall flow together.
נוב	יָנוּב	*Crescet, proferet, loquetur.* [*ciet.*	He will grow, increase; will bring forth, speak.
—	יְנוֹבֵב	*Germinare, loqui fa-*	He will cause to bud, to speak
—	יְנוּבוּן	*Germinabunt, profe- rent.* [*bit.*	They shall bud, bring forth. [bemoan.
נוד	יָנוּד	*Movebitur, condole-*	He shall be shaken, will grieve,
נוה	יִנְוֶה	*Habitabit.*	He will dwell.
	יָנוֹחַ־־חָה	*Janoach, Janocha.*	Janoah, N. P.
נוח	יָנוּחַ	*Quiescet, considebit.*	He shall rest, be settled.
—	יָנוּחוּ	*Quiescent.*	They shall rest.
	יָנוּם	*Janum.*	Janum, N. P.
נום	יָנוּם	*Dormitabit.*	He will slumber.
נוס	יָנוּס	*Fugiet, aufugiet.*	He will flee, flee away.
—	יְנוּסוּן ,יָנוּסוּ	*Fugient.*	They will flee.

ROOTS.	DERIVATIVES.	VERSIO.	SIGNIFICATION.
נוע	יִנּוֹעַ	*Commovebitur.*	He shall be shaken.
—	יָנוּעוּ יְנוּעוּן	*Vagabuntur.*	They shall wander.
—	יִנּוֹעוּ	*Commovebuntur.*	They shall be shaken.
יָנַח		*Statuit, collocavit, reposuit, reliquit, permisit, sivit, di-*	He set, placed, laid up, left, permitted, suffered, let go.
נחה	יַנְחוּנִי	*Deducent me.* [*misit.*	They shall lead me.
נחל	יַנְחִיל יַנְחִל	*Possidendum dabit, in hæreditatem transmittet.* [*tibi.*	He shall give for a possession, shall leave for an inheritance. [possession.
—	יַנְחִילְךָ	*Possidendum dabit*	He shall give to thee for a
—	יִנְחַל	*Possidebit.*	He shall possess, inherit.
—	יִנְחָלוּ	*In hæreditatem acci-*	They shall receive for an in-
—	יִנְחֲלוּ	*Possidebunt.* [*pient.*	They shall possess. [heritance
—	יִנְחָלוּהָ	*Possidebunt eam.*	They shall possess it.
—	יִנְחָלוּם	*Possidebunt eos.*	They shall possess them.
—	יַנְחִלֶם	*Possidere eam faciet*	He shall cause to inherit it.
—	יַנְחִלֶנָּה	*Possidere faciet eos.*	He shall make them inherit.
נחה	יַנְחֵם	*Ducet eos.*	He will lead them.
נחם	יִנָּחֵם	*Pœnitebit.*	It will repent.
—	יְנַחֵם	*Consolabitur.*	He will comfort.
—	יְנַחֲמוּן	*Consolabuntur.*	They will comfort.
—	יְנַחֲמֵנוּ	*Consolabitur nos.*	He shall comfort us.
—	יְנַחֲמֻנִי	*Consolabuntur me.*	They shall comfort me.
נחה	יַנְחֶנּוּ	*Deducet, adducet illum.*	He will lead, bring him.
—	יַנְחֵנִי	*Deducet, adducet me.*	He will lead, bring me.
נחש	יְנַחֵשׁ	*Divinabit.*	He will divine.
—	יְנַחֲשׁוּ	*Attente observabunt*	They will attentively observe.
נטה	יִנָּטֶה	*Extendetur.*	He shall be stretched forth.
—	יִנָּטוּ	*Extendentur.*	They will be stretched out.
נוא	יָנִי	*Franget.*	He will break.
—	יָנִיא	*Irritum faciet.*	He will make void.
נוח	יָנִיחַ	*Recumbere faciet, quietem dabit.*	He will cause to lie down, will give rest.
ינח	יַנִּיחַ	*Relinquet.*	He will leave.
—	יַנִּיחוּ	*Reponent.*	Thou shalt lay up.

ROOTS.	DERIVATIVES.	VERSIO.	SIGNIFICATION.
נין	יִנּוֹן	*Propagabitur, sobolevit.*	He shall be propagated, continued in his offspring.
נוס	יָנִיסוּ	*Fugabunt.*	They shall put to flight.
נוע	יָנִיעַ	*Commovebit.*	He shall shake.
—	יָנִיעוּ יְנִיעוּן	*Commovebunt.*[*eum.*	They will shake.
נוף	יְנִיפֶנּוּ	*Elevabit, agitabit*	He shall lift, wave it.
ינק	יְנִיקוֹתָיו	*Rami ejus.*	His branches. [ger.
נכר	יִנָּכֵר	*Alienum se finget.*	He will feign himself a stran-
—	יְנַכְּרוּ	*Alienos se fingent.*	They will feign themselves different from what they
נוע	יָנֻעַ	*Commovebit.*	He will shake. [really are.
נעם	יִנְעָם	*Suavis, amœnus, jucundus erit.*	He will be sweet, pleasant, delightful.
נער	יְנַעֵר	*Excutiet.*	He will shake off, shake out.
נוף	יְנֹפֵף	*Agitabit.* [*nuet.*	He shall wave. [pieces.
נפץ	יְנַפְּצוּ	*Dispergent, commi-*	They shall disperse, break in
נצה	יִנָּצוּ	*Rixabuntur.* [*tur.*	They will contend, strive.
נצל	יִנָּצֵל	*Confugiet, liberabi-*	He shall escape, be delivered.
—	יִנָּצֵרוּ	*Eripientur.*	They shall be taken out.
—	יִנָּצְלוּ	*Liberabuntur.*	They shall be delivered.
—	יְנַצְּלוּ	*Liberabunt.*	They shall deliver.
נצר	יִנְצְרֻהוּ	*Conservabunt eum.*	They shall preserve him.
—	יִנְצֹרוּ	*Servabunt, observa-*	They shall preserve, keep.
יָנַק		*Suxit, lactavit.*[*bunt*	He sucked, suckled.
נקב	יִנְקֹב	*Perforabit.*	He shall bore, pierce.
נקה	יִנָּקֶה	*Innocens, impunitus*	He shall be innocent, unpu-
—	יְנַקֶּה	*erit.* [*solvet.*	nished. [quit, clear.
		Insontem habebit,ab-	He will hold guiltless, will ac-
נקם	יִנָּקֵם	*Vindicabitur.*	He shall be avenged.
נקף	יִנְקֹפוּ	*Concident.*	They shall cut up.
נקש	יְנַקֵּשׁ	*Illaqueabit.*	They will entangle.
נשא	יִנָּשֵׂא	*Efferetur.*	He will be exalted.
—	יִנָּשְׂאוּ	*Efferentur.*	They will be lifted up, exalted
—	יִנָּשֵׂאוּ	*Levabuntur.*	They will be lifted.
—	יִנַּשְּׂאוּ	*Attollent se.*	They will lift themselves.
—	יְנַשְּׂאוּהוּ	*Levabunt eum.*	They shall help him.
—	יִנָּשׂוּא	*Portabuntur.*	They shall be carried.

ROOTS.	DERIVATIVES.	VERSIO.	SIGNIFICATION.
נתן	יִנָּתֶן־־תַּן	*Dabitur, afferetur,*	He shall be given, brought,
—	יִנְתַּן	*Dabit.* [*tradetur.*	He will give. [delivered.
—	יִנְתְּנוּן	*Dabunt.* [*letur.*	They will give. [up.
נתק	יִנָּתֵק	*Disrumpetur, evel-*	He shall be broken off, rooted
—	יְנַתֵּק	*Disrumpet, evellet.*	He shall break asunder, pull up
—	יִנָּתֵקוּ	*Disrumpentur.*	They shall be broken asunder
נתש	יִנָּתֵשׁ	*Evelletur.*	He shall be plucked up.
—	יִנָּתְשׁוּ	*Evellentur, diruen-tur.*	They shall be plucked up, destroyed.
	יס		
סבב	יָסֹב	*Circumdabit.*	He shall compass, surround.
—	יִסֹּב	*Circumducetur, con-vertetur.*	He shall be carried about, turned.
—	יְסֹבְבֶנְהוּ	*Circumducet eum.*	He will lead him about.
—	יְסֹבְבֵנִי	*Circumdabit me.*	He will compass me about.
—	יְסֻבָּהוּ	*Circumdabunt eum.*	They will compass him about
—	יָסֹבּוּ	*Circuibunt.*	They will go round about.
—	יִסֹּבּוּ	*Convertentur.*	They will be turned.
סבך	יְסֻבָּכוּ	*Complicabuntur.*	They will be folded together.
סבל	יִסְבֹּל	*Portabit.*	He shall bear, carry.
—	יִסְבְּלֻהוּ	*Portabunt eum.*	They will carry him.
סבב	יְסֻבֶּנּוּ	*Circumdabit eum.*	He will compass him.
—	יְסֻבֵּנִי	*Circumdabit me.*	He shall compass me about.
נסג	יַסִּג	*Removebit.*	He shall remove.
שגא	יִשְׂגֵּא	*Multiplicabitur.*	He shall be multiplied.
סגד	יִסְגְּדוּ	*Procumbent.*	They shall bow down. [selves.
—	יִסְגְּדוּן	*Prosternent se.*	They shall prostrate them-
סוג	יִסֹּגוּ	*Avertentur.*	They shall be turned away.
סגד	יִסְגּוֹד	*Procumbet.*	He will fall down.
סגר	יַסְגִּירוּ	*Tradent.*	They will deliver up.
—	יַסְגִּירֶנּוּ	*Includet eum.*	He will shut him up.
—	יַסְגִּרֵנִי	*Tradet me.*	He will deliver me up.
—	יִסָּגֵר	*Claudetur.*	He shall be shut.
—	יִסְגֹּר	*Claudet.*	He will shut.
—	יַסְגִּרוּ	*Tradent.*	They will deliver up.
—	יִסָּגְרוּ	*Claudentur.*	They shall be shut.

ROOTS.	DERIVATIVES.	VERSIO.	SIGNIFICATION.
סגר	יַסְגִּרְךָ	*Tradet te.*	He will deliver thee.
—	יַסְגִּרֶנּוּ	*Includet eum.*	He shall shut him up.
יָסַד		*Fundavit, fundamentum posuit, constituit, firmavit, mandavit.*	He founded, laid the foundation, appointed, established, ordained.
—	יִסַּד	*Fundavit, constituit, mandavit.*	He founded, appointed, ordained.
—	יְסֹד	*Fundamentum.*	The foundation.
—	יֻסַּד־־סָּד	*Fundatus est, fundamentum posi-*	He was founded, the foundation was laid.
—	יָסְדָה	*Fundavit.* [*tum est.*	She founded.
—	יִסְּדָהּ יִסּ״	*Fundavit eam.*	He founded her.
—	יְסֹדוֹ	*Fundamentum ejus.*	His foundation.
—	יִסְּדוּ	*Fundaverunt.*	They founded.
—	יְסֹדוֹתֶיהָ	*Fundamenta ejus.*	Her foundations.
—	יָסַדְתָּ	*Fundasti.*	Thou hast founded.
—	יִסַּדְתָּ	*Constituisti.*	Thou hast appointed.
—	יְסַדְתּוֹ	*Fundasti eum.*	Thou hast founded him.
—	יְסֹדֹתֶיהָ	*Fundamenta ejus.*	Her foundations.
—	יְסַדְתָּם	*Fundasti eos.*	Thou hast founded them.
סבב	יִסּוֹב	*Circumducetur, convertetur.*	He shall be carried about, turned.
—	יְסוֹבְבֻהָ	*Circuibunt eum.*	They will go about it.
—	יְסוֹבְבֶנְהוּ	*Circumducet eum.*	He will lead him about.
יסד	יְסוֹד	*Fundamentum* [*rum.*	A foundation.
—	יְסוֹדָם	*Fundamentum illo-*	Their foundation.
—	יְסוּדָתוֹ	*Fundamentum ejus.*	His foundation.
סוף	יָסוּף	*Deficiet, desinet.*	He shall fail, cease.
סור	יָסוּר	*Discedet, divertet.*	He shall depart, will turn aside
—	יִסּוֹר	*Eruditio.*	Instruction, discipline.
—	יָסוּרוּ	*Discedent, deficient.*	They will depart, revolt.
—	יְסוּרַי	*Discedentes a me.*	They that depart from me.
סחב	יִסְחָבוּם	*Trahent, raptabunt*	They shall draw, drag them.
נסח	יִסַּח	*Evellet.* [*eos.*	He will pluck up.
—	יִסְּחוּ	*Extirpabuntur.*	They shall be rooted out.
סור	יָסִיר	*Auferet, divertet.*	He shall take away, turn aside

ROOTS.	DERIVATIVES.	VERSIO.	SIGNIFICATION.
סור	יְסִירוּ	*Auferent.*	They shall take away.
—	יְסִירֶנָּה	*Amovebit eam.*	He will remove her.
סות	יַסִּית	*Persuadebit, pelliciet*	He will persuade, entice.
—	יְסִיתְךָ	*Pelliciet, seducet te.*	He will entice, draw thee away
יָסַךְ		*Unxit.*	He anointed.
—	יָסֹךְ	*Teget.*	He will cover.
—	יִסַּךְ	*Tegetur.*	He shall be covered.
	יִסְכָּה	*Isca.*	Iscah, N. W.
סכך	יְסֻכֻּהוּ	*Tegent eum.*	They shall cover him.
—	יִסְּכוּ	*Libabunt.*	They shall pour out
סכן	יִסְכּוֹן־כָּן־כֹן	*Proderit.*	He will profit.
סכל	יְסַכֵּל	*Infatuabit.*	He will make foolish.
סכן	יִסָּכֶן	*Periclitabitur.* [cebit.	He will be in danger.
—	יְסַכְסֵךְ	*Instigabit, commis-*	He will stir up, embroil.
סכר	יִסָּכֵר	*Occludetur.*	He shall be shut up, stopped.
סלח	יִסְלַח	*Ignoscet, condonabit.*	He will pardon, forgive.
סלף	יְסַלֵּף	*Subvertet.*	He will overthrow.
סמך	יִסָּמֵךְ	*Innitetur.*	He will lean.
—	יִסְמְכוּ	*Imponent.*	They shall lay upon.
	יִסְמַכְיָהוּ	*Ismachias.*	Ismachias, N. M.
סמך	יִסְמְכֵנִי	*Sustentabit me.*	He will sustain me.
נסע	יַסִּע	*Progredi faciet.*	He will cause to go forward.
—	יִסַּע	*Discedet.*	He shall depart. [strengthen.
סעד	יִסְעָד	*Fulciet, reficiet.*	He will uphold, refresh,
—	יִסְעָדֶךָּ	*Fulciet te.*	He will hold thee up.
—	יִסְעָדֶנּוּ	*Sustentabit eum.*	He will support him.
—	יִסְעָדֵנִי	*Sustentabit me.*	He will support me.
נסע	יִסָּעוּ־סֻ	*Proficiscentur.*	They will journey.
סער	יְסֹעֵר	*Turbine abigetur.*	He will be driven away with the whirlwind. [a whirlwind
—	יִסְעֲרוּ	*Turbine irruent.*	They will rush forth as with
יָסַף		*Addidit, perrexit, iteravit, auxit.*	He added, proceeded, went forward, repeated, increased.
—	יֹסֵף	*Addet.*	He shall add.
ספד	יִסָּפְדוּ	*Plangentur.*	They shall be lamented.
—	יִסְפְּדוּ	*Plangent.*	They will lament.
יסף	יָסְפָה	*Addidit.*	She added.

ROOTS.	DERIVATIVES.	VERSIO.	SIGNIFICATION.
יסף	יָסְפוּ–סְ"	Addiderunt, perrexerunt. [tur.	They added, proceeded.
—	יָסְפוּ	Deficient, consumen-	They shall fail, be consumed.
—	וֹסְפוּ	Addent, pergent.	They will add, proceed.
ספק	יִסְפּוֹק	Complodet.	He shall clap.
ספר	יִסְפּוֹר–פֹּר	Numerabit.	He shall number. [ther.
ספח	יִסָּפְחוּ	Congregabuntur.	They shall be gathered toge-
יסף	יֹסְפִים	Addentes, pergentes.	Adding, proceeding.
—	יָסַפְנוּ	Addidimus.	We have added.
ספר	יְסַפֵּר	Enarrabit, numerabit. [sebitur.	He will declare, number. [ed, counted.
—	יְסֻפַּר–פֻּ"	Enarrabitur, recen-	He shall be declared, reckon-
—	יִסָּפֵר	Numerabitur.	He shall be numbered.
—	יִסָּפְרוּ	Numerabuntur.	They shall be numbered.
—	יְסַפְּרוּ–פֵּ"	Enarrabunt.	They shall declare.
—	יִסְפְּרוּ	Numerabunt.	They shall number.
יסף	יָסַפְתָּ	Addidisti.	Thou hast added.
סקל	יִסָּקֵל	Lapidabitur.	He shall be stoned.
—	יִסְקְלֻנוּ	Lapidabunt nos.	They will stone us.
יָסַר		Coercuit, corripuit, castigavit, erudi-vit, docuit.	He restrained, corrected, chastised, disciplined, taught.
סור	יָסֵר	Auferet. [vit, docuit.	He shall take away.
שור	יָשַׂר	Principatum gessit.	He held dominion.
סור	יָסֻר	Discedet, divertet.	He shall depart, turn aside.
יסר	יַסֵּר	Corripe, castiga.	Correct, chasten thou.
—	יַסֹּר	Castigando.	In chastening.
—	יִסַּר	Castigavit.	He hath chastised.
—	וֹסֵר	Corripiens. [buntur.	He that correcteth.
סור	יָסֻרוּ	Discedent, amove-	They shall depart, be removed.
יסר	יִסְּרוּנִי	Eruderunt me.	They have instructed me.
—	יַסְּרֵנִי	Corripe me.	Correct thou me.
—	יִסְּרַנִּי	Castigavit me. [ti.	He hath chastened me. [ed.
—	יִסַּרְתָּ	Corripuisti, erudivis-	Thou hast chastened, instruct-
—	יִסְּרָתּוּ	Erudivit eum.	He instructed him.
—	יִסַּרְתִּי	Erudivi.	I have disciplined, instructed.
—	יִסַּרְתַּנִי	Castigasti me.	Thou hast chastised me.
סתר	יַסְתִּיר	Abscondet.	He will hide.

ROOTS.	DERIVATIVES.	VERSIO.	SIGNIFICATION.
סתר	יַסְתִּירֵנִי	*Abscondet me.*	He shall hide me.
סתם	יִסְתְּמוּ	*Obturaverunt.*	They stopped.
סתר	יִסָּתֵר	*Abscondetur.*	He will be hidden.
—	יִסָּתֵרוּ	*Abscondentur.*	They will be hidden.
	יע		
עבד	יַעֲבֹד	*Serviet, laborabit.*	He shall serve, labour.
—	יֵעָבֵד	*Coletur.*	He shall be cultivated.
—	יַעַבְדוּ־עֲבֹדוּ	*Servient.*	They will serve.
—	יַעַבְדוּהוּ	*Servient ei.*	*They shall serve him.*
—	יַעַבְדוּךָ־־דוּךָ	*Servient tibi.*	They will serve thee.
—	יַעַבְדוּנִי	*Servient mihi.*	They shall serve me.
—	יַעַבְדֶנּוּ	*Serviet ei.*	He shall serve him.
—	יַעַבְדֻנִי	*Servient mihi.*	They shall serve me.
עבר	יַעֲבוּר	*Transferet.* [*dicitur.*	He shall remove, alienate.
—	יַעֲבוֹר יַעֲבָר	*Transibit, transgre-*	He shall pass over, transgress.
—	יַעֲבוֹר־בֹר	*Præteribit.*	He shall pass by, over.
עבט	יַעַבְטוּן	*Pervertent.*	They shall pervert, turn aside.
עבר	יַעֲבִירוּנִי	*Transferent me.*	They will convey me over.
	יַעְבֵּץ	*Jabets.*	Jabez, N. M. P.
עבר	יֵעָבֵר	*Transiri poterit.*	It can be passed over.
—	יַעַבְרוּ־עֲבֹרוּן	*Transibunt.*	They will pass over.
—	יַעַבְרוּם	*Præteribunt eos.*	*They will pass by* them.
—	יַעַבְרֶנְהוּ־רֶנּוּ	*Præteribit eum.*	He will pass by it.
—	יַעַבְרֻנְהוּ	*Transibit eum.*	He will pass over it.
יָעַד		*Condixit, constituit locum et tempus conveniendi, congregavit, convenit, desponsavit.*	He appointed, decreed, fixed a time and place for meeting, assembled, met, betrothed.
—	יְעָדָהּ	*Condixit eam, desponsavit eam.*	He appointed it, betrothed her. [away.
עדה	יֶעְדֶּה	*Transibit, auferetur*	He shall pass away, be taken
יעד	יְעָדוֹ	*Condixit ei.*	He appointed him.
	יְעְדִּי	*Jedo.*	Iddo, N. M.
עדר	יֵעָדֵר	*Sarrietur.*	He shall be harrowed or hoed

ROOTS.	DERIVATIVES.	VERSIO.	SIGNIFICATION.
עדר	יַעְדְּרוּ	*Deesse sinent.*	They shall suffer to be wanting.
יָעָה		*Vertit, subvertit, everrit.*	He turned, overturned, swept away.
—	יֵעָדֵרוּן	*Sarrientur.*	They shall be harrowed or hoed
	יְעוּאֵל	*Jehuel.*	Jeuel, N. M.
עד	יְעוֹדֵד	*Sublevabit.*	He will lift up, relieve.
עזז	יָעוֹז	*Prævalebit.*	He will prevail.
על	יְעַוֵּל	*Inique aget.*	He will do wickedly.
עלל	יְעוֹלְלוּ	*Racemabunt.*	They will glean after the vintage.
עף	יָעוּף יְעוֹפֵף	*Volabit, avolabit.*	He will fly, fly away.
	יְעוּץ	*Jehuts.*	Jeuz, N. M.
ער	יְעַוֵּר	*Excæcabit.*	He will blind.
—	יֵעוֹר	*Excitabitur, evigilabitur.*	He shall be stirred, raised up, awaked.
—	יְעוֹרוּ	*Suscitabunt.*	They shall raise up.
	יְעוּשׁ	*Jehus.*	Jeush, Jehush, N. M.
עות	יְעַוֵּת	*Pervertet; evertet.*	He will pervert, turn upside down.
יָעַז		*Fortis fuit, confirmatus est.*	He was strong, was strengthened.
עזז	יָעֹז	*Confirmabitur.*	He shall be strengthened.
עזב	יַעֲזֹב יַעֲזָב־זוֹב	*Relinquet, deseret.*	He will leave, forsake.
—	יַעַזְבוּ יַעַזְבוּ	*Deserent.*	They will forsake.
—	יֵעָזְבוּ	*Relinquentur.*	They shall be left.
—	יַעַזְבֶךָ	*Deseret te.*	He will forsake thee.
—	יַעַזְבֻךָ	*Deserent te.*	They shall forsake thee.
—	יַעַזְבֶנָּה	*Deseret eam.*	He shall forsake her.
—	יַעַזְבֵנוּ	*Relinquet nos.*	He shall leave us.
—	יַעַזְבֶנּוּ	*Relinquet eum.*	He will leave him.
	יַעֲזִיאֵל	*Jahaziel.*	Jaaziel, N. M.
	יַעֲזִיָּהוּ	*Jahazias.*	Jaaziah, N. M.
	יַעְזֵיר־זֵר	*Jahazer.*	Jaazer, N. P.
עזר	יַעֲזָר	*Adjuvabit.*	He will help.
עזר	יַעְזְרֶהָ	*Adjuvabit eam.*	He shall help her.
—	יַעְזְרוּ	*Adjuvabunt.*	They shall help.
—	יֵעָזְרוּ	*Adjuvabuntur.*	They shall be helped.
—	יַעְזְרֶךָ	*Adjuvabit te.*	He shall help thee.
—	יַעְזְרֵנִי	*Adjuvabit me.*	He shall help me.

ROOTS.	DERIVATIVES.	VERSIO.	SIGNIFICATION.
יָעַט		*Operuit, amicivit; consilium inivit.*	He covered, clothed; he took counsel.
עטה	יַעְטֶה	*Teget, induet, amiciet*	He shall cover, put on, clothe.
יעט	יַעֲטֹהִי	*Consiliarii ejus.*	His counsellors.
עטה	יַעֲטוּ	*Tegentur.*	They shall be covered.
עטף	יַעֲטוֹף יַעֲטֹף	*Operietur, obruetur, deficiet.*	He shall be covered, overwhelmed, shall fail.
יעט	יְעָטָנִי	*Operuit, amicivit me*	He hath covered, clothed me.
עטף	יַעֲטֶף—טֹף	*Operiet.*	He shall cover.
—	יַעַטְפוּ	*Operientur.*	They shall be covered.
	יְעִיאֵל יְעִי	*Jehiel.*	Jeiel, Jehiel, N. M.
עיב	יָעִיב	*Obnubilabit. [mihi.*	He will cover with a cloud.
יעד	יֹעִידֶנִי	*Tempus constituit*	He shall set me a time.
יעל	יֹעִילוּ	*Proderunt.*	They shall profit.
	יָעִיר	*Jahir.*	Jair, N. M.
עור	יָעִיר	*Excitabit, evigilabit.*	He will stir up, awake.
—	יְעִירֶנּוּ	*Excitabit eum.*	He will stir him up.
	יַעְכָּן	*Jacan.*	Jachan, N. M.
עכר	יַעְכָּרְךָ	*Perturbabit te.*	He will trouble thee.
יָעַל		*Profuit, utilitatem contulit aut accepit.*	He profited, contributed or received advantage.
עלה	יַעַל	*Ascendet.*	He shall go up.
	יָעֵל	*Jahel.*	Jael, N. W.
	יַעְלָא	*Jahala.*	Jaala, N. M.
עלה	יַעֲלֶה	*Ascendet.*	He shall go up.
	יַעֲלָה	*Jahalas.*	Jaalah, N. M.
עלה	יַעֲלֶה	*Ascendet, orietur, crescet; educet, offeret.*	He shall go up, rise, grow, increase; bring up, offer.
—	יַעֲלוּ	*Ascendet, accendentur, educent, offerent.*	They shall go up, be burnt, bring up, offer.
עלז	יַעֲלֹז	*Lætabitur.*	He shall rejoice.
—	יַעֲלֹזוּ	*Exultabunt.*	They shall triumph.
—	יַעַלְזוּ	*Lætabuntur.*	They shall rejoice.
יעל	יַעֲלֵי	*Rupicapræ.*	The wild goats.
עלם	יַעְלִימוּ	*Abscondent.*	They will hide.
	יַעְלָם יַעְ	*Jahalam.*	Jaalam, N. M.

ROOTS.	DERIVATIVES.	VERSIO.	SIGNIFICATION.
עלה	יַעֲלֵם	*Adducet eos.*	He will bring them.
—	יַעֲלֶנָּה	*Conscendet eam.*	He shall go up thereon.
עלס	יַעֲלֹס	*Gaudebit. [bunt.*	He shall rejoice. [low.
עלע	יַעַלְעוּ	*Lambent, absorbe-*	They will lick, suck up, swal-
עלץ	יַעֲלֹץ	*Lætabitur.*	He shall rejoice.
—	יַעֲלֹצוּ	*Exultabunt.*	They shall triumph.
עמד	יָעֳמַד	*Sistetur.*	He shall be presented.
—	יַעֲמֹד יַעֲמָד	*Stabit, consistet, manebit.*	He shall stand, stand still, abide, remain.
—	יַעַמְדוּ יַעַמְ׳	*Stabunt. manebunt.*	They shall stand, abide.
—	יַעַמְדוּ	*Et consistent.*	And they shall stand still.
—	יַעֲמֹדְנָה	*Stabunt.*	They shall stand.
—	יַעֲמוֹד	*Orietur, stabit.*	He shall arise, stand.
—	יַעֲמִיד	*Stabiliet.*	He will establish.
—	יַעֲמִידֵנִי	*Statuet me.*	He will set me.
עמל	יַעֲמֹל	*Laborabit.*	He will labour.
עמס	יַעֲמֹס	*Onerabit.*	He will load, burden.
יען			
—	יַעַן	*Quia, propter.*	Because, because of.
—	יַעַן אֲשֶׁר	*Quia, ut.*	Because, that.
ענה	יַעֲנֶה	*Exaudiet, respondebit, affliget, humiliabit se. [debitur.*	He will hear, answer, afflict, abase himself.
—	יֵעָנֶה	*Exaudietur, respon-*	He shall be heard, answered.
—	יְעַנֶּה	*Affliget.*	He will afflict.
—	יַעֲנֵהוּ	*Exaudiet eum.*	He will hear him.
—	יַעֲנוּ	*Exaudient, loquentur, respondebunt, testabuntur, affli-*	They will hear, speak, answer, testify, afflict themselves.
—	יְעַנּוּ	*Affligent. [gent se.*	They will afflict.
—	יַעֲנוּכָה	*Respondebunt tibi.*	They will answer thee.
—	יַעְנַי	*Janai. [debit tibi.*	Jaanai, N. M. [thee.
ענה	יַעַנְךָ	*Exaudiet te, respon-*	He will hear thee, will answer
—	יַעֲנֵם	*Exaudiet eos.*	He will hear them.
—	יַעֲנֶנָּה	*Respondebit ei.*	He will answer her.
—	יַעֲנֵנוּ	*Exaudiet nos.*	He shall hear us.
—	יַעֲנֶנּוּ	*Respondebit ei.*	He will answer him.

ROOTS.	DERIVATIVES.	VERSIO.	SIGNIFICATION.
עבה	יְעַנֶּנּוּ	*Affliget eum.*	He will afflict him.
—	יַעֲנֵנִי	*Respondebit mihi.*	He will answer me.
ענש	יֵעָנֵשׁ	*Mulctabitur, punie-*	He shall be fined, punished.
עור	יְעֹרְרוּ	*Excitabunt.* [*tur.*	They shall stir up, raise up.
יָעֵף		*Fatigatus, defessus*	He was wearied, was exhaust-
—	יָעֵף	*Defessus.* [*est.*	Weary. [ed, fainted.
—	יָעֻפוּ	*Volabunt.*	They will fly.
יָעַץ		*Consilium iniuit, cepit, dedit; consuluit, decrevit.*	He consulted, took counsel, gave advice, deliberated, determined.
—	יֹעֵץ	*Consultans, consilia-*	Consulting, a counsellor.
עצב	יֵעָצֵב	*Dolebit.* [*rius.*	He will be grieved.
—	יְעַצְּבוּ	*Torquebunt.*	They will wrest.
יעץ	יְעָצָהּ	*Decrevit eam.* [*ei.*	He hath determined it.
—	יְעָצֻהוּ	*Consilium dederunt*	They gave him counsel.
—	יָעָצוּ	*Consilium inierunt.*	They consulted.
—	יֹעֲצֵי	*Consiliarii.*	Counsellors.
עצב	יַעֲצִיבוּהוּ	*Dolore afficient eum*	They will grieve him.
יעץ	יְעָצָנִי	*Consilium dedit mihi.*	He hath given me counsel.
עצר	יַעְצֹר יַעֲצֹר	*Retinebit, cohibebit.*	He will retain, withhold.
—	יַעַצָרְכָה	*Detinebit te.*	He will detain, stop thee.
יעץ	יָעַצְתָּ	*Consilium iniisti.*	Thou hast consulted.
—	יָעַצְתִּי	*Consului, decrevi.*	*I have consulted*, determined.
עקב	יַעְקֹב	*Supplantabit.*	He will supplant.
	יַעֲקֹב־קוֹב	*Jaacob.*	Jacob, N. M.
עקב	יְעַקְּבֵם	*Tardabit eos.*	He will stay them.
	יַעֲקוֹבָה	*Jaacobas.*	Jaakobah, N. M.
	יַעֲקָן	*Jaacan.*	Jakan, N. M.
עקש	יַעְקְשׁוּ	*Pervertent.*	They will pervert.
יַעַר			
—	יַעַר יָעַר	*Silva.*	A, the wood.
ערב	יֶעֱרַב	*Suavis erit.*	He will be sweet.
—	יֶעֶרְבוּ	*Amœni erunt.*	They will be pleasant.
	יַעְרָה	*Jaras.*	Jarah, N. M.
יער	יַעְרָהּ	*Silva ejus.*	Her wood.
ערה	יֵעָרֶה	*Effundetur.*	He shall be poured out.
—	יְעָרֶה	*Deteget.*	He will discover.

CPSIA information can be obtained
at www.ICGtesting.com
Printed in the USA
LVHW021629070423
743786LV00002B/355